PHILOSOPHY OF LAW

Fourth Edition

EDITED BY

Joel Feinberg

AND

Hyman Gross

WADSWORTH PUBLISHING COMPANY

Belmont, California

A Division of Wadsworth, Inc.

Philosophy Editor: Kenneth King
Editorial Assistant: Cynthia Campbell
Production: Mary Douglas
Copy Editor: Sheryl Rose
Print Buyer: Martha Branch

Printed in the United States of America

2 3 4 5 6 7 8 9 10—95 94 93 92 91

Library of Congress Cataloging-in-Publication Data

Philosophy of Law   edited by Joel Feinberg and Hyman Gross.—4th
  ed.
        p.   cm.
  Includes bibliographical references.
  ISBN 0–534–15156–6 (hard cover)
    1. Law—Philosophy.   2. Law and ethics.   3. Law—United States.
  I. Feinberg, Joel, 1926–   . II. Gross, Hyman.
  K231.P47   1990
340′.1—dc20   90-43148
                                                                  CIP

CONTENTS

PART 4   Responsibility   485

There is currently a widespread and truly philosophical perplexity about law that is occasioned by the events of the day and by the legal proceedings to which they give rise. Increasing numbers of students have been attracted to courses in philosophy of law and social philosophy offered by philosophy departments, and law students, constantly challenged by the theoretical dimensions of law school subjects, are prompted more than ever to enroll in jurisprudence courses. These students often are disappointed by what seems to them an excessively abstract approach. Portentous terms such as "Law," "Morality," and "Justice" are manipulated like counters in an uncertain game, and hoary figures from the past are marched by, each with his distinctive dogmatic pronouncement and his own curious technical vocabulary. No wonder traditional jurisprudence often seems among the driest and most remote of academic subjects.

We have tried in this volume to relate the traditional themes of legal philosophy to the live concerns of modern society in a way that invigorates one and illuminates the other. The volume begins with essays by classic and contemporary figures on the essential nature of law and on the relation of law to morality or other sources of principle outside the legal system. No attempt is made to give contending doctrines equal time, or even to give them all a day in court. We have passed over much excellent material that might have been included, though this is sure to cause some displeasure in an area of jurisprudential concern that is so marked by doctrinal partisanship. Our endeavor is not to represent all important points of view, nor to represent any in a truly comprehensive way, but instead to offer a series of selections that raise sharply the most important issues. Many of these philosophical issues debated in the first part recur later in the book where authors take up specific problems about liberty, justice, responsibility, and punishment.

Opinions in fifteen court cases, together with two literary inventions and one newspaper story, serve to illuminate more abstract discussions and to test the adequacy of principles developed in them. These materials cover such problems as the law in conflict with itself during successive regimes in a single country, obscene public displays, compulsory medical treatment, the right to privacy, equality between the sexes, criminal insanity, and capital punishment. Our aim here is not to supplement the essays with further discussion but to make clear the concreteness and immediacy of matters of philosophical interest in a way that will stimulate their further discussion.

This fourth edition contains many new features. In Part One, Law, legal realism has a stronger representation than before in famous articles by Oliver Wendell Holmes, Jr., and Jerome Frank. Moreover, in the article by Andrew Altman, the realists are compared with the new Critical Legal Studies movement (its first appearance in this text) and with the legal philosophy of Ronald Dworkin. Dworkin's own influential essay, "Hard Cases," has been added, as well as his "The Law of the Slave-Catchers" (a review of Robert Cover's *Justice Accused*), which is criticized in the late J. L. Mackie's "The Third Theory of Law."

Part Two, Liberty, has been enriched by the addition of six new law cases or, as in Ronald Dworkin's "The Great Abortion Case," a discussion of a particular case. This section now includes *Rogers v. Okin,* a new case on paternalism and the right to die; *Bowers v. Hardwick,* illustrating "the legal enforcement of morality," and three new cases (one a civil case) involving freedom of expression: *Village of Skokie v. National Socialist Party of America, Texas v. Johnson* (the flag burning case), and *Hustler Magazine v. Falwell.* In addition, Part Two now contains two new articles on privacy, one by the leading political theorist, Alan Ryan, the other by Judge Richard A. Posner, and in the subsection on Rights, Judith Thomson's much discussed Lindley Lecture, "Self-Defense and Rights."

Once again, Part Three, Justice, has been revamped. We have added an entirely new subsection, "The Machinery of Justice," in which are discussed such concrete problems of legal justice as those raised by plea bargaining, the right to effective counsel, and dispute resolution. Part Three also contains a new selection in its subsection "Discrimination and Reverse Discrimination," "Equal Treatment and Compensatory Discrimination" by the distinguished philosopher Thomas Nagel.

Part Four, Responsibility, also contains a new subsection. Several of the most persistent conundrums of criminal responsibility are treated under the heading "Criminal Responsibility: Some Problems." The new subsection contains Lon L. Fuller's classic legal parable, "The Case of the Speluncean Explorers," as well as one of the cases that inspired it, *United State v. Holmes.* These cases, one actual and one fictitious, involve criminal defendants who have killed and cannibalized a human being in order, they claim, to avoid starvation themselves. The more recent case of *United States v. Oviedo* is an illustration of the riddle of "attempting the impossible." Edwin Curley's much discussed article, "Excusing Rape," concludes the subsection, adding its discussion of mistake to the other selections' analyses of such criminal defenses as necessity, duress, and self-defense. The subsection on "Mental Abnormality" now includes formal statements of the leading proposed insanity rules: *M'Naghten,* The Royal Commission nonrule and its supporting argument, the rule in *Durham v. United States* (the case itself is included), and the Model Penal Code two-prong rule. The student will no longer have to look up these rules in external sources.

Part Five, Punishment, also contains a new subsection, "Exactly What is Being Punished?" which deals with the ancient problem of explaining (or justifying) why attempted crimes deserve less punishment (if they do) than completed crimes. The articles by Richard Parker, Michael Davis, and David Lewis form a neat triad, each taking a different position on the problem. In addition, there are five other new articles in Part Five: H. L. A. Hart's classic "Prolegomenon to a Theory of Punishment," Michael S. Moore's "The Moral Worth of Retribution," Jean Hampton's "The Moral Education Theory of Punishment," Jeffrie G. Murphy's "Mercy and Legal Justice," and, in the subsection on "The Death Penalty," Hugo Bedau's "The Right to Life and the Right to Kill."

We have benefited from the advice of many professors who used the first, second, or third editions, and we especially wish to thank those who agreed to write formal reviews: Jerome Balmuth, Colgate University; Michael Martin, Boston University; Walter Sinnott-Armstrong, Dartmouth College; and Alan Wertheimer, University of Vermont.

We appreciate also the efficient assistance of Judith Garcia and Pamela Symes in the preparation of the manuscript.

Joel Feinberg
Hyman Gross

PART 1

Law

The question "What is law?" seems at first glance hardly to deserve a philosopher's attention. Ask a lawyer about the law: if he or she is unable to give an answer on the spot, such a professional knows where to look it up, or at least where to get the ingredients for a reliable opinion. Statutes, judicial opinions, administrative regulations, constitutional provisions are all official pronouncements of law. When these texts leave the matter ambiguous, a lawyer knows the appropriate techniques to resolve the ambiguity, and in aid of that consults scholarly works of interpretation and other sources of authoritative opinion. The question "What is law?" then seems simply a request for a general definition that covers all those, and only those, items of official pronouncement that lawyers finally treat as law. It is true that even the best dictionary may leave us unsatisfied, for something more informative than a mere guide for word use is wanted. Still, at first sight nothing in the question appears to need the fine grinding of the philosopher's mill, and we conclude that we are adequately acquainted with the notion of something as familiar as law, with only the details remaining to be filled in.

Our simple belief is shattered not only by philosophical reflection, but also by the common experience of those who use and are subject to the law. Professor H. L. A. Hart, whose work has dominated Anglo-American legal philosophy, has described this illusion of understanding with these words: "The same predicament was expressed by some famous words of St. Augustine about the notion of time. 'What then is time? If no one asks me I know: if I wish to explain it to one that asks I know not.' It is in this way that even skilled lawyers have felt that, though they know the law, there is much about law and its relations to other things that they cannot explain and do not fully understand. Like a man who can get from one point to another in a familiar town but cannot explain or show others how to do it, those who press for a definition need a map exhibiting clearly the relationships dimly felt to exist between the law they know and other things."[1]

What then are the further questions left unanswered by simple definitions, and what is their importance? In theories of law, three different interpretations have been given to the question "What is law?" These different versions are not always clearly distinguished, but an analogy may serve to clarify the difference.

Suppose the question were "What is a postage stamp?" One interpretation would call for a statement of *what counts as* a postage stamp, or, putting it another way, *what deserves to be called* a postage stamp. The answer would distinguish postage stamps from, and relate them to, revenue stamps, Christmas seals, postage meter imprints, postal privilege franks, and postage due stamps. A second way of viewing the question is as a request for information about *what is properly given effect* as a postage stamp. What counts as a postage stamp is not at issue, but it is recognized that a seriously torn or blemished stamp will not be treated as valid for postage, nor will a counterfeit stamp, one withdrawn from use, or a foreign stamp; and so *criteria of validity* are sought. Finally, a third way of interpreting the question stresses *the nature* of postage, requiring an explanation of the postal system of which stamps are a part, and a description of the role of stamps in this system. Turning to the far weightier question about law, we notice first that law is the ultimate social resource of civilized people when claims are in conflict. There are many other standards to which people may and often do turn in regulating their affairs, but, when these fail, standards bearing the authority of the state are the last resort. It is important, therefore, for the citizen as well as the judge weighing his or her claim to be able to tell exactly what is law. This insures that the force of law is not given to lawlike things of other sorts, such as standards of customary practice, moral precepts, by-laws and private regulations.

Once items that are properly called laws are distinguished from other lawlike pronouncements, how do we distinguish those that are valid from those that are not? Invalid licenses, arguments, coupons, and orders are not properly given effect, and neither are invalid laws (though it is important to note that in all these cases invalidity does not affect the *kind* of thing it is). What then in general supports the claim that a law may not be given effect? Suppose it is regularly disobeyed and unenforced? Suppose it is hideously unjust? Suppose it is the product of a political régime that is clearly illegitimate? Suppose there are no means for enforcing or changing the law? Here the issue is whether moral, social, or political standards of validity that are (in the first instance, at least) outside the law must be met if a law is to be valid.

A third range of questions concerns the nature of law, and particularly its relation to morality. At every turn lawyers, judges, legislators, and citizens grapple with moral questions: What is fair, who is to blame, what rights does one have, what is wrong with that action? To make sure the law reflects the lives we live as moral creatures, we need to understand the relation between our law and our morals. In addition, another aspect of the nature of law raises questions about its formal properties: Are laws rules or standards of some other sort? And, just what difference is there between what is included as an item of law and other expressions of the same form that are not part of law?

THE NATURE AND VALIDITY OF LAW

It is a truism that no question in legal philosophy is far removed from any other, and the reader will find that these closely related matters are not treated in isolation from one another. This is exemplified by the selection from the work of Thomas Aquinas, the first reading in this part. His unifying doctrine is one of natural law. Law, in this view, is universal because it springs from reason possessed by all people, and it is this natural law that shapes the positive law that we ordinarily speak of as "the law." Positive law stands in contrast both to natural law and to divine law, and the relations among the three in the ordering of human life are explained by Aquinas. In this connection the question of special importance is whether (and in what way) human law is derived from natural law. Positive law determined by natural law is for the common good, and it is binding upon the conscience of the human race because it is just. Aquinas's concept of law, then, is of an ideal to be found in laws. It is absent when unjust exercise of power produces laws in name only, and for the most part these need not be obeyed. Aquinas's views on law and morality may surprise those who think of objections to legislating morality as a modern movement. Only moral wrongs that are socially significant as harms to others properly concern the law, according to Aquinas. His idea of conscientious objection to unjust laws and his approval of a qualified civil disobedience will also seem surprising to those who think such views are of recent origin.

Several critical questions might usefully be kept in mind while reading this selection. Is there an adequate distinction drawn between what characterizes *good* law and what characterizes *any* law—whether good or bad? Is there sufficient appreciation of the difference in what appears to be just to equally rational persons whose interests or circumstances are different? Is reason really disinterested, so that everyone using reason will have the same view of what the law ought to be? Is it possible that a great many perfectly good laws make no appeal at all to conscience, but are recommended by sheer expediency? Is there an adequate criterion for determining the legitimacy of human laws, particularly when the political authority that promulgates them lacks the consent of those who are governed by such laws?

A word about form may help those who are reading Aquinas for the first time. The method is dialectical, with the issue posed in the form of a question at the start (there are fifteen such questions comprising this selection); objections making the matter problematic are then presented, many of these based on pronouncements of noted authorities. Next, Aquinas gives a general statement of his own position on the question; he begins always with a supporting statement from a church authority). Finally, there are the specific replies of Aquinas to each of the objections previously presented. The authorities cited are mostly religious, though "the Philosopher" (Aristotle) and "the jurists" (from the Code of Justinian) are secular.

The very brief excerpt from a work by Sir Ernest Barker, *Traditions of Civility,* concisely presents the "natural law" conception of law and contrasts it sharply with the view of those who reject natural law. The author also reminds us of the power of these jurisprudential ideas in political history, and particularly of their influence on the American Revolution. The contrast he presents continues to be reflected in the very different notions of constitutional principles found in the British and in the American legal systems.

John Austin's *The Province of Jurisprudence Determined* was published in England in 1832, and has long been regarded in the Anglo-American tradition as the leading work in opposition to natural law theory. It is an exceedingly careful work of great range and refinement. The portions reprinted here set forth only the essentials of Austin's views about the nature of law. Austin seeks to define positive law and this he does by distinguishing *laws properly so called* from other lawlike utterances and other things called laws. *Laws properly so called* turn out to be *commands* requiring conduct, and some, called positive law, issue from a sovereign to members of an *independent political society* over which sovereignty is exercised. *Commands* entail a purpose and a power to impose sanctions upon those who disobey; a *sovereign* is a determinate human superior (that is, one who can compel others to obey) who is not in a habit of obedience to such as superior and who also receives habitual obedience; and an *independent political society* is one in which the bulk of the society habitually obeys a sovereign.

Austin's theory of law has surely called forth more abundant and more eminent criticism than any other. The reader will likely wonder whether Austin's analysis is not too much influenced by his own legal system and form of government. Can, for example, the features of a federal system like that of the United States be comfortably accommodated in Austin's model? There are other troubling questions as well. Is the power-dependent notion of a command adequate, or would the authority-dependent notion of a rule prove more illuminating, since it allows subtler analysis of law in terms more complex than threats of force? Has Austin taken penal laws as the prototype for all laws, thereby distorting the features of other kinds of laws and exaggerating the role of sanctions in their operation? Are the rules that govern the validity of laws to be taken as commands by the sovereign to himself or herself; and, if so, does that account do justice to claims of invalidity that are advanced in modern legal systems? Austin's account of judge-made law is one of acquiescence by the sovereign to a minister's decision. That seems plausible enough with reference to the case being decided. But, looking at the way judicial opinions are used subsequently in legal arguments as a source of law, can they really be considered commands of the sovereign, "though not by its express declaration?" Does Austin's account of sovereignty distinguish *legitimate* exercise of political power through legislation from *effective* legislative exercise of political power, presumably only the former qualifying as law?

In the United States and the Scandinavian countries especially, the focus of jurisprudential interest has been on the courts. The authoritative interpretation of whatever sources of law a legal system provides is ultimately a job for judges. Of even greater importance, it is the judicial utterance about legal rights and duties that represents the state of the law at any time and tells those with contending views just what the law is. Saying that the law is whatever the courts say it is has a sobering effect and tends to undermine the comfortable belief that at any time the law is fixed and certain, waiting only to be brought out of the shadows by judges skilled in the arts of judicial revelation.

No single essay in Anglo-American jurisprudence has received more attention in representing this point of view than Oliver Wendel Holmes's "The Path of the Law," first published in 1897. His famous declaration that "The prophecies of what the courts will do in fact, and nothing more pretentious, are what I mean by the law" became the cornerstone of legal realism in America. How such prophecies are best made is a matter that occupies much of Holmes's attention in the selection that is included here. How courts ought to decide which prophecies to fulfill is a question that occupies a very large part of the agenda of contemporary jurisprudence.

The brief selection that follows next is from the writings of another distinguished American judge, Jerome Frank. Here one sees how the law appears to those who wish to use it and not simply make it the subject of a body of theory. A legal saga unfolds as the affairs of the Joneses and the Williamses are put in the hands of their lawyers, and the conception of law that emerges gives weight to Holmes's opening remarks, "When we study law we are not studying a mystery but a well known profession." Read together, these two selections concentrate our minds on the question that perhaps must precede all others in this branch of the philosophy of law: What, exactly, is its proper subject matter?

The work now generally regarded as the most important modern statement of the positivist position in the Anglo-American tradition is H. L. A. Hart's book *The Concept of Law*, published in 1961. It is not a narrow defense of a partisan tradition in legal theory, but undertakes a broad reexamination of the fundamental questions of jurisprudence, clarifying them and securing their importance. Perhaps more than any other book in the field this one deserves to be read in its entirety, and the excerpt presented here, while the core of Hart's notion of law, is nevertheless only part of an argument that is complex and interdependent in its parts.

In this selection the notion of law is presented as a union of two kinds of rules: one enjoining conduct, the other conferring powers. Such a conception must concern itself first with the question of why legal rules are binding, so Hart proceeds to examine the matter of legal obligation. He then discusses the need for the combination of two kinds of rules in a working legal system that serves the needs of a society that has advanced beyond its most primitive stages. Finally, the matter of legal validity is addressed and the idea of a rule of recognition is developed to provide a criterion for distinguishing false claims from true ones. There is a vast critical literature addressing these issues and many others to be found in *The Concept of Law*. No one interested in the subject can afford to ignore this work if he or she wishes to understand the great Anglo-American renaissance in jurisprudence that began with the publication of this book.

LAW AND MORALITY

Controversy about the nature and validity of law most often revolves around the question of what relationship morality has to law. Those who are spoken of as positivists tend to view a legal system as having its own criteria for valid laws, and so tend to regard moral judgments of laws as important in deciding what the law should be, yet not relevant in deciding what the law is. H. L. A. Hart's article entitled

"Positivism and the Separation of Law and Morals" was published three years before his book, and it is included here for the light it casts on many issues presented in some of the other selections.

Professor Lon L. Fuller, in his article "Positivism and Fidelity to Law—A Reply to Professor Hart," presents a view in opposition to Hart's on a number of important issues. Together the two articles have become a classic debate in the modern literature of legal philosophy on the role of moral considerations in rendering judgments about what the law is. The main points in controversy emerge with clarity and force. What is the relation between the law that is and the law that ought to be? Of what significance are attitudes toward the concept of law, particularly the attitude toward law as an ideal which can compel fidelity? Must definitions of law in some way reflect morally worthy ideals? Upon what social or political facts does the very existence of law depend, and in what way does this bind law to morality? Is there an indispensable minimum moral foundation for any legal system determined by certain universal features of the human condition and by principles of procedure that cannot be systematically ignored?

In the aftermath of World War II, these abstract questions acquired a new practical importance, as West German jurists struggled with the problem of dealing justly with moral outrages that had been committed by private citizens earlier under a morally bankrupt legal system. Gustav Radbruch had been a leading legal positivist before the war, but he converted to natural law theory as the only coherent way of dealing with the wrongs of the Nazi period. His own brief summary of his theory is included here.

THE OBLIGATION TO OBEY THE LAW

When there are laws that permit officials or citizens to do what is morally wrong, law and morality come into conflict. When the law requires choices that are morally wrong, or when it prohibits what is morally right, the conflict becomes a struggle rooted in the conscience of the community. At stake in this struggle is a presumed obligation to obey the law that normally influences law-abiding members of society to choose among different courses of conduct only those that are in accordance with the law. These occasions of moral crisis when law and morality are sharply at odds serve to remind us of questions that are always with us: What is the nature of our obligation to obey the law at any time, and what limits are there to this obligation? The answer calls for good and sufficient reasons for such an obligation to exist, and for further good and sufficient reasons for the suspension of such an obligation under certain special circumstances.

In A Theory of Justice, John Rawls sketches a theory of civil disobedience for "a nearly just society, one that is well-ordered for the most part but in which some serious violations of justice nevertheless do occur." He first makes clear what he means by civil disobedience, distinguishing it from conscientious refusal and from acts hostile to the constituted public order. It is nonviolent but unlawful, a form of conscientious public protest that is meant to bring about "a change in the law or policies of the government." Professor Rawls's underlying concern is with the duties and obligations of the good citizen in what we think of as a modern liberal democratic society, and civil disobedience turns out to be justifiable as an altogether expedient way of appealing in an urgent and dramatic fashion to the conscience of the majority when some serious injustice weighs upon the conscience of others in the community.

Rawls introduces a number of conditions that must be met, among them the infringement of "the principle of equal liberty," or "blatant violations of . . . the principle of fair equality of opportunity." The first of these grounds for justifiable civil disobedience comprehends laws and acts of government that violate "liberty of conscience and freedom of thought, liberty of the person, and equal political rights"—what Rawls conceives as "the liberties of equal citizenship" in chapter IV of his book. The second restriction makes reference to a fundamental principle of justice that requires positions of responsibility and authority to be equally accessible to all members of society. But Rawls does not view purported transgressions of "the difference principle" as grounds for civil disobedience, since it is normally too uncertain whether particular laws and policies tend to promote or to alleviate inequalities in the distribution of property and other benefits of life.

The warrant for civil disobedience that Professor Rawls presents seems well-suited to ease the discomforts of the law-abiding citizen whose deep convictions are offended by unjust measures and who wishes to protest with the special drama that accompanies violation of law. But there are questions for advocates of this view. Why must civil disobedience be an act of conscience? Why must it be a political act? Suppose a member of the community perceives some serious injustice but accepts it with an air of resignation as only one among many countervailing injustices that, on balance, leave the world quite imperfect but sufficiently tolerable. Why should he not be free to join in acts of civil disobedience with his politically militant friends out of sociability or simply because he finds the activity a rather exciting diversion from what is normally a rather dull existence? Why should his motives or state of mind matter, so long as he behaves in an appropriately restrained way in circumstances that make it likely that the conscience of the majority will be moved against the prevailing injustice by what he and others are doing?

Another problem in Rawls's account: it would seem that civil disobedience is justifiable as a matter of expediency in a nearly just society. But prevailing attitudes among the majority may well be unsympathetic to unlawful conduct engaged in for the purpose of drawing attention to what is said to be the exceedingly unjust character of some unrelated law. Law and order may be the formula insisted on by most people in the community, with attempts to change the law limited to lawful means only. Civil disobedience would then seem to have very little chance of success, and its uselessness would then count heavily against it when it is to be justified as a measure of expediency. In such a social atmosphere civil disobedience may be a less practical remedy for the good citizen to adopt. Do we really wish to conclude, however, that it is a less justifiable measure of opposition to injustice?

Finally, we might well want to know more about those occasions when civil disobedience is justifiable, and particularly when it is "that in one's sincere and considered opinion the conditions of free cooperation are being violated." It seems a good bet that rarely, if ever, can we count on those who contemplate civil disobedience to examine carefully their opinions in the light of fundamental principles of social justice. But if there is not such an examination, and hence quite understandably the majority view the unlawful acts only as a dramatic expression of dissenting views, does civil disobedience then play a role that can be justified along the lines Rawls suggests?

In "Civil Disobedience in the Modern World," Joel Feinberg begins his discussion of the topic with a careful examination of Rawls's account, first drawing careful distinctions among various forms of lawbreaking that differ from civil disobedience but might sometimes be confused with it. Feinberg distinguishes the narrower view of Rawls, which allows only disobedience as moral protest to pass muster as civil disobedience, from a broader notion that admits conscientious evasion and conscientious refusal as well. The crucial elements in Rawls's theory are then analyzed with some very interesting results.

The main part of Feinberg's article addresses the long-standing problem of whether there is a moral *prima facie* obligation to obey the law (most often answered in the affirmative), why such an obligation should exist, and under what conditions such an obligation ceases to exist. Feinberg argues that there is no general moral *prima facie* obligation to obey valid law, "even in a democracy with a just constitution." In defending that position, Feinberg investigates moral *prima facie* obligations more generally and considers how they bear on this question. In the end one might wish to consider whether or not the prevailing attitude of most law-abiding citizens toward the law ought to be modified in view of the arguments presented here.

LAW AND THE JUDICIAL DECISION

Several selections that have already been discussed draw attention to the fact that courts are most often the legal institution of greatest interest to those who want to know what law is. Within the legal system, whenever there is a question about what the law is, it is judges who give the official answer. In the course of deciding what the law is, judges' words becomes sources of law for the future since what they say is later interpreted and applied by other judges in other cases. In reaching his or her decision, a judge turns to sources of law such as legislation and decisions in previous cases. But judicial decision is hardly ever an enterprise in which rules of law dictate a decision to which the judge merely attaches authority by his or her pronouncement of it. Reasoned argument that requires judicial choice among competing grounds of decision is the essence of the judicial process. This suggests a considerable latitude of discretion enjoyed by judges, as well as characteristic modes of reasoning to be followed in reaching a proper judicial decision. The discretion is limited by the provisions of legislation and other clear statements of the law; and the judge's discretion is not as great as that of the legislator who (except for the constitutional limitations upon him or her that judges announce) is untrammeled by prior judicial decision. But when the judge exercises discretion, it is to decide what the law is and to give it effect, not simply to decide what the law will be. This is great power, and it must be exercised in a responsible way. Legislators who abuse their power are subject to retribution through the political process, but judges are kept insulated from political retaliation. It is especially important, therefore, that judicial decisions be defensible under the standards and according to the modes of reasoning that are deemed fitting in the legal system.

In the selection titled "Problems of Legal Reasoning," Professor H. L. A. Hart canvasses the main issues of judicial reasoning that have become embroiled in jurisprudential controversy. One such issue is the character of judicial logic and the role it plays in the process of reaching a decision. The character, origin, and function of rules in the process of decision is another matter that has generated controversy. Still another concerns the role of precedent: When does it "bind" subsequent decision; how can clear cases be distinguished from hard cases; what makes clear cases clear; to what extent does precedent allow for judicial discretion? The question of acceptable modes of interpreting legislation presents yet another difficulty in giving account of judicial reasoning. In reading Professor Hart's illuminating exposition, it is a good idea to bear in mind the threefold distinction regarding theories of judicial reasoning which he presents. The account of judicial reasoning that is relevant here is not an account of the usual processes or habits of thought by which judges reach their decisions. Nor is it an account of how judges should ideally reach their decisions. Rather it is an account of how decisions are justified, and of the standards judges are bound to respect (and normally do) in justifying their decisions. It would seem that much needless cynicism, which understandably results from discovery of irrational influences in actual procedures of decision, could be avoided by observing this distinction, as could needless disappointed expectations by those who look in vain for logical rigor. The right sort of theory of judicial reasoning provides sound principles to guide the exercise of judicial authority as well as critical tools to expose bad decisions and thus nullify their effect on the law.

The judicial decision is currently the most widely debated topic in the philosophy of law. The major problems are the extent to which judges do make law, the extent to which they should, and the proper way for them to decide novel questions of law. Those who have read the Hart-Fuller debate will already have some acquaintance with much of the terrain. The selection by Ronald Dworkin entitled "The Model of Rules" brings the main features sharply into focus. Initially Dworkin argues against the "realist" view (which he ironically styles "nominalist"), denying that the questions of what law *is* are answered by descriptions of what courts in fact *do* in exercising their power. He then subjects to critical analysis the theory of law presented by Professor Hart in *The Concept of Law*. The burden of his opposition to Hart as the exemplar of positivism claims that rules are only one variety of standard to be invoked by a judge in deciding legal issues. There are other standards, the most important of which are principles and policies, and those other standards are not extralegal, but are law as much as rules are. Furthermore, there is no master rule, no matter how complex, which determines their validity as law. The arguments are subtle, thorough, and complex, and they have set the stage for a continuing debate of this topic.

Professor Dworkin makes use of two cases—*Riggs v. Palmer* and *Henningsen v. Bloomfield Motors, Inc.*—to illustrate how standards other than rules function as law. The opinions in *Riggs* are included here to allow the reader to decide about the character of what the court provides as support for its decision. It is useful to distinguish the different kinds of standards as they appear in the opinions; to consider whether the judge is bound or has discretion in using them, and in what sense they are binding or discretionary; and also to consider the origins of whatever authority they have. Furthermore, it is worthwhile to consider how Dworkin might deal with the dissenting opinion in *Riggs,* and particularly to consider whether its arguments tend to undermine the model he is proposing.

In "Hard Cases" Ronald Dworkin takes a more positive position in developing a theory of law. In the portions of that essay reprinted here he again makes clear the role of principles and policies in a legal system, and defends the thesis that all cases, including the hard ones where the law is in doubt, should be decided on grounds of principle rather than policy. This can be viewed as a rights thesis which holds that judicial decisions enforce existing political rights. Those rights are all part of a general system of rules, principles, and policies that must be made to fit together consistently over time, and cannot simply emerge on an *ad hoc* basis to suit the interests of a good judicial decision in a particular case, the way a legislative enactment might be fashioned to compose conflicting interests and to promote the general welfare. This rights thesis is developed and then tested in the court of an imaginary judge called Hercules, whose immense powers of adjudication enable him to decide hard cases as they should be decided ideally. He therefore shows judges of more limited ability (as well as the rest of us) how the rights at issue ought to be dealt with in even the hardest cases when precedents seem to point clearly in opposite directions.

In the selection entitled "The Law of the Slave-Catchers" Ronald Dworkin discusses the extraordinary fact that eminent American judges in the mid-nineteenth century felt bound to uphold fugitive slave laws even though the procedures laid down by these laws were legally questionable, even though the laws were unpopular in the states in which enforcement was sought, and even though they ran counter to the moral convictions of the judges themselves. Dworkin's essay appeared originally as a review of a book on the subject by the legal historian Robert Cover, who argued that the judges conceived their proper judicial role as subordinate to the Congress and the Constitutional Convention, each of which, in its own way, had sanctioned slavery. Dworkin argues that such a conception of the judicial office represents a failure in jurisprudence that neglects the general principles of justice and fairness that the particular laws presuppose. In his investigation of what went wrong in the courts of Massachusetts at that time, Dworkin provides a particular clear statement of his own position regarding the proper exercise of judicial powers when the law is doubtful.

In his article entitled "The Third Theory of Law," John Mackie squarely confronts Dworkin's theory of judicial decision and the conception of law that proceeds from it. Little need be added to introduce this elegant and admirably economical critique. Mackie shows that it is not at all clear that Herculean judicial labor would produce the decision that Dworkin would expect, and concludes his discussion with some important observations about the likely effects of Dworkin's theory if it were adopted explicitly as a guide to adjudication in hard cases.

Andrew Altman's "Legal Realism, Critical Legal Studies, and Dworkin" represents a far more radical critique of Dworkin's position, and indeed is a critique of the entire mainstream of Anglo-American jurisprudence. The movement known as Critical Legal Studies (CLS), for which Altman is here the spokesman, does not share the assumption that judges are free to decide cases according to one or another theory of judicial decision. Judges are inevitably under the influence of ideological forces, though certainly they do not see themselves as acting under such constraints. Legal realism (some of whose themes appear in this volume in the selections by Holmes and Frank) serves in part as a foundation for CLS, particularly the realist view that the judge, rather than the law itself, is the primary source of legal authority governing a legal dispute. CLS goes beyond this and views every legal issue as entailing ideological conflicts that even Dworkin's Judge Hercules could not resolve in a neutral way.

NOTE

1. The Concept of Law (1961), pp. 13–14.

THOMAS AQUINAS

Concerning the Nature of Law*

WHETHER LAW IS SOMETHING PERTAINING TO REASON?

Objection I. It would seem that law is not something pertaining to reason. For the Apostle says (*Rom.* vii. *23*): *I see another law in my members,* etc. But nothing pertaining to reason is in the members, since the reason does not make use of a bodily organ. Therefore law is not something pertaining to reason.

Obj. 2. Further, in the reason there is nothing else but power, habit and act. But law is not the power itself of reason. In like manner, neither is it a habit of reason, because the habits of reason are the intellectual virtues, of which we have spoken above. Nor again is it an act of reason, because then law would cease when the act of reason ceases, for instance, while we are asleep. Therefore law is nothing pertaining to reason.

Obj. 3. Further, the law moves those who are subject to it to act rightly. But it belongs properly to the will to move to act, as is evident from what has been said above. Therefore law pertains, not to the reason, but to the will, according to the words of the Jurist: *Whatsoever pleaseth the sovereign has the force of law.*

On the contrary, It belongs to the law to command and to forbid. But it belongs to reason to command, as was stated above. Therefore law is something pertaining to reason.

I answer that, Law is a rule and measure of acts, whereby man is induced to act or is restrained from acting; for *lex* [*law*] is derived from *ligare* [*to bind*], because it binds one to act. Now the rule and measure of human acts is the reason, which is the first principle of human acts, as is evident from what has been stated above. For it belongs to the reason to direct to the end, which

is the first principle in all matters of action, according to the Philosopher. Now that which is the principle in any genus is the rule and measure of that genus: for instance, unity in the genus of numbers, and the first movement in the genus of movements. Consequently, it follows that law is something pertaining to reason.

Reply Obj. I. Since law is a kind of rule and measure, it may be in something in two ways. First, as in that which measures and rules; and since this is proper to reason, it follows that, in this way, law is in the reason alone.—Secondly, as in that which is measured and ruled. In this way, law is in all those things that are inclined to something because of some law; so that any inclination arising from a law may be called a law, not essentially, but by participation as it were. And thus the inclination of the members to concupiscence is called *the law of the members.*

Reply Obj. 2. Just as, in external action, we may consider the work and the work done, for instance, the work of building and the house built, so in the acts of reason, we may consider the act itself of reason, *i.e.,* to understand and to reason, and something produced by this act. With regard to the speculative reason, this is first of all the definition; secondly, the proposition; thirdly, the syllogism or argument. And since the practical reason also makes use of the syllogism in operable matters, as we have stated above and as the Philosopher teaches, hence we find in the practical reason something that holds the same position in regard to operations as, in the speculative reason, the proposition holds in regard to conclusions. Such universal propositions of the practical reason that are directed to operations have the nature of law. And these propositions are sometimes under our actual consideration, while sometimes they are retained in the reason by means of a habit.

Reply Obj. 3. Reason has its power of moving from the will, as was stated above; for it is due to the fact that one wills the end, that the reason issues its commands as regards things ordained to

*From *Summa Theologica, The Basic Writings of Saint Thomas Aquinas* ed. Anton C. Pegis (New York: Random House, Inc., 1945), Vol.II, pp. 742–53, 773–80, 784–85, 791–95. Copyright © 1945 Random House, Inc. Reprinted by permission of the publisher and The Very Rev. Prior Provincial O.P., St. Dominic's Priory, London. Footnotes appearing in the original of this edition are omitted.

the end. But in order that the volition of what is commanded may have the nature of law, it needs to be in accord with some rule of reason. And in this sense is to be understood the saying that the will of the sovereign has the force of law; or otherwise the sovereign's will would savor of lawlessness rather than of law.

WHETHER LAW IS ALWAYS DIRECTED TO THE COMMON GOOD?

Objection 1. It would seem that law is not always directed to the common good as to its end. For it belongs to law to command and to forbid. But commands are directed to certain individual goods. Therefore the end of law is not always the common good.

Obj. 2. Further, law directs man in his actions. But human actions are concerned with particular matters. Therefore law is directed to some particular good.

Obj. 3. Further, Isidore says: *If law is based on reason, whatever is based on reason will be a law.* But reason is the foundation not only of what is ordained to the common good, but also of that which is directed to private good. Therefore law is not directed only to the good of all, but also to the private good of an individual.

On the contrary, Isidore says that *laws are enacted for no private profit but for the common benefit of the citizens.*

I answer that, As we have stated above, law belongs to that which is a principle of human acts, because it is their rule and measure. Now as reason is a principle of human acts, so in reason itself there is something which is the principle in respect of all the rest. Hence to this principle chiefly and mainly law must needs be referred. Now the first principle in practical matters, which are the object of the practical reason, is the last end: and the last end of human life is happiness or beatitude, as we have stated above. Consequently, law must needs concern itself mainly with the order that is in beatitude. Moreover, since every part is ordained to the whole as the imperfect to the perfect, and since one man is a part of the perfect community, law must needs concern itself properly with the order directed to universal happiness. Therefore the Philospher, in the above definition of legal matters mentions both happiness and the body politic, since he says that we call these legal matters *just which are adapted to produce and preserve happiness and its parts for the body politic.* For the state is a perfect community, as he says in *Politics* i.

Now, in every genus, that which belongs to it chiefly is the principle of the others, and the others belong to that genus according to some order towards that thing. Thus fire, which is chief among hot things, is the cause of heat in mixed bodies, and these are said to be hot in so far as they have a share of fire. Consequently, since law is chiefly ordained to the common good, any other precept in regard to some individual work must needs be devoid of the nature of a law, save in so far as it regards the common good. Therefore every law is ordained to the common good.

Reply Obj. 1. A command denotes the application of a law to matters regulated by law. Now the order to the common good, at which law aims, is applicable to particular ends. And in this way commands are given even concerning particular matters.

Reply Obj. 2. Actions are indeed concerned with particular matters, but those particular matters are referable to the common good, not as to a common genus or species, but as to a common final cause, according as the common good is said to be the common end.

Reply Obj. 3. Just as nothing stands firm with regard to the speculative reason except that which is traced back to the first indemonstrable principles, so nothing stands firm with regard to the practical reason, unless it be directed to the last end which is the common good. Now whatever stands to reason in this sense has the nature of a law.

WHETHER THE REASON OF ANY MAN IS COMPETENT TO MAKE LAWS?

Objection 1. It would seem that the reason of any man is competent to make laws. For the Apostle says (Rom ii. 14) that *when the Gentiles, who have not the law, do by nature those things that are of the law, ... they are a law to themselves.* Now he says this of all in general. Therefore anyone can make a law for himself.

Obj. 2. Further, as the Philosopher says, *the intention of the lawgiver is to lead men to virtue.* But every man can lead another to virtue. Therefore the reason of any man is competent to make laws.

Obj. 3. Further, just as the sovereign of a state governs the state, so every father of a family governs his household. But the sovereign of a state can make laws for the state. Therefore every father of a family can make laws for his household.

On the contrary, Isidore says, and the *Decretals* repeat: *A law is an ordinance of the people, whereby something is sanctioned by the Elders together with the Commonalty.* Therefore not everyone can make laws.

I answer that, A law, properly speaking regards first and foremost the order to the common good. Now to order anything to the common good belongs either to the whole people, or to someone who is the viceregent of the whole people. Hence the making of a law belongs either to the whole people or to a public personage who has care of the whole people; for in all other matters the directing of anything to the end concerns him to whom the end belongs.

Reply Obj. 1. As we stated above, a law is in a person not only as in one that rules, but also, by participation, as in one that is ruled. In the latter way, each one is a law to himself, in so far as he shares the direction that he receives from one who rules him. Hence the same text goes on: *Who show the work of the law written in their hearts (Rom. ii.* 15).

Reply Obj. 2. A private person cannot lead another to virtue efficaciously; for he can only advise, and if his advice be not taken, it has not coercive power, such as the law should have, in order to prove an efficacious inducement to virtue, as the Philosopher says. But this coercive power is vested in the whole people or in some public personage, to whom it belongs to inflict penalties, as we shall state further on. Therefore the framing of laws belongs to him alone.

Reply Obj. 3. As one man is a part of the household, so a household is a part of the state; and the state is a perfect community, according to *Politics* i. Therefore, just as the good of one man is not the last end, but is ordained to the common good, so too the good of one household is ordained to the good of a single state, which is a perfect community. Consequently, he that governs a family can indeed make certain commands of ordinances, but not such as to have properly the nature of law.

WHETHER PROMULGATION IS ESSENTIAL TO LAW?

Objection 1. It would seem that promulgation is not essential to law. For the natural law, above all, has the character of law. But the natural law needs no promulgation. Therefore it is not essential to law that it be promulgated.

Obj. 2. Further, it belongs properly to law to bind one to do or not to do something. But the obligation of fulfilling a law touches not only those in whose presence it is promulgated, but also others. Therefore promulgation is not essential to law.

Obj. 3. Further, the binding force of law extends even to the future, since *laws are binding in matters of the future,* as the jurists say. But promulgation concerns those who are present. Therefore it is not essential to law.

On the contrary, It is laid down in the *Decretals* that *laws are established when they are promulgated.*

I answer that, As was stated above, a law is imposed on others as a rule and measure. Now a rule or measure is imposed by being applied to those who are to be ruled and measured by it. Therefore, in order that a law obtain the binding force which is proper to a law, it must needs be applied to the men who have to be ruled by it. But such application is made by its being made known to them by promulgation. Therefore promulgation is necessary for law to obtain its force.

Thus, from the four preceding articles, the definition of law may be gathered. Law is nothing else than an ordinance of reason for the common good, promulgated by him who has the care of the community.

Reply Obj. 1. The natural law is promulgated by the very fact that God instilled it into man's mind so as to be known by him naturally.

Reply Obj. 2. Those who are not present when a law is promulgated are bound to observe the law, in so far as it is made known or can be made known to them by others, after it has been promulgated.

Reply Obj. 3. The promulgation that takes place in the present extends to future time by reason of the durability of written characters, by which means it is continually promulgated. Hence Isidore says that *lex* [*law*] *is derived from legere* [*to read*] *because it is written.*

ON THE VARIOUS KINDS OF LAW

WHETHER THERE IS AN ETERNAL LAW?

Objection I. It would seem that there is no eternal law. For every law is imposed on someone. But there was not someone from eternity on whom a law could be imposed, since God alone was from eternity. Therefore no law is eternal.

Obj. 2. Further, promulgation is essential to law. But promulgation could not be from eternity, because there was no one to whom it could be promulgated from eternity. Therefore no law can be eternal.

Obj. 3. Further, law implies order to an end. But nothing ordained to an end is eternal, for the last end alone is eternal. Therefore no law is eternal.

On the contrary, Augustine says: *That law which is the supreme Reason cannot be understood to be otherwise than unchangeable and eternal.*

I answer that, As we have stated above, law is nothing else but a dictate of practical reason emanating from the ruler who governs a perfect community. Now it is evident, granted that the world is ruled by divine providence, as was stated in the First Part, that the whole community of the universe is governed by the divine reason. Therefore the very notion of the government of things in God, the ruler of the universe, has the nature of a law. And since the divine reason's conception of things is not subject to time, but is eternal, according to *Prov.* viii. 23, therefore it is that this kind of law must be called eternal.

Reply Obj. I. Those things that do not exist in themselves exist in God, inasmuch as they are known and preordained by Him, according to *Rom.* iv. 17: *Who calls those things that are not, as those that are.* Accordingly, the eternal concept of the divine law bears the character of an eternal law in so far as it is ordained by God to the government of things foreknown by Him.

Reply Obj. 2. Promulgation is made by word of mouth or in writing, and in both ways the eternal law is promulgated, because both the divine Word and the writing of the Book of Life are eternal. But the promulgation cannot be from eternity on the part of the creature that hears or reads.

Reply Obj. 3. Law implies order to the end actively, namely, in so far as it directs certain things to the end; but not passively,—that is to say, the law itself is not ordained to the end, except accidentally, in a governor whose end is extrinsic to him, and to which end his law must needs be ordained. But the end of the divine government is God Himself, and His law is not something other than Himself. Therefore the eternal law is not ordained to another end.

WHETHER THERE IS IN US A NATURAL LAW?

Objection I. It would seem that there is no natural law in us. For man is governed sufficiently by the eternal law, since Augustine says that *the eternal law is that by which it is right that all things should be most orderly.* But nature does not abound in superfluities as neither does she fail in necessaries. Therefore man has no natural law.

Obj. 2. Further, by the law man is directed, in his acts, to the end, as was stated above. But the directing of human acts to their end is not a function of nature, as is the case in irrational creatures, which act for an end solely by their natural appetite; whereas man acts for an end by his reason and will. Therefore man has no natural law.

Obj. 3. Further, the more a man is free, the less is he under the law. But man is freer than all the animals because of his free choice, with which he is endowed in distinction from all other animals. Since, therefore, other animals are not subject to a natural law, neither is man subject to a natural law.

On the contrary, The *Gloss* on *Rom* ii. 14 (*When the Gentiles, who have not the law, do by nature those things that are of the law*) comments as follows: *Although they have no written law, yet they have the natural law, whereby each one knows, and is conscious of, what is good and what is evil.*

I answer that, As we have stated above, law, being a rule and measure, can be in a person in two ways: in one way, as in him that rules and measures; in another way, as in that which is ruled and measured, since a thing is ruled and measured in so far as it partakes of the rule or measure. Therefore, since all things subject to divine providence are ruled and measured by the eternal law, as was stated above, it is evident that all things partake in some way in the eternal law, in so far as, namely, from its being imprinted on them, they derive their respective inclinations to their proper acts and ends. Now among all others, the rational creature is subject to divine providence in a more excellent way, in so far as it itself partakes of a share of providence, by being provident both for itself and for others. Therefore it has a share of the eternal reason, whereby it has a natural inclination to its proper act and end; and this participation of the eternal law in the rational creature is called the natural law. Hence the Psalmist, after saying (*Ps.* iv. 6): *Offer up the sacrifice of justice,* as though someone asked what the works of justice are, adds: *Many say, Who showeth us good things?* in answer to which question he says: *The light of Thy countenance, O Lord, is signed upon us.* He thus implies that the light of natural reason, whereby we discern what is good and what is evil, which is the function of the natural law, is nothing else than an imprint on us of the divine light. It is therefore evident that the natural law is nothing else than the rational creature's participation of the eternal law.

Reply Obj. I. This argument would hold if the natural law were something different from the eternal law; whereas it is nothing but a participation thereof, as we have stated above.

Reply Obj. 2. Every act of reason and will in us is based on that which is according to nature, as was stated above. For every act of reasoning is based on principles that are known naturally, and every act of appetite in respect of the means is derived from the natural appetite in respect of the last end. Accordingly, the first direction of our acts to their end must needs be through the natural law.

Reply Obj. 3. Even irrational animals partake in their own way of the eternal reason, just as the rational creature does. But because the rational creature partakes thereof in an intellectual and rational manner, therefore the participation of the eternal law in the rational creature is properly called a law, since a law is something pertaining to reason, as was stated above. Irrational creatures, however, do not partake thereof in a rational manner, and therefore there is no participation of the eternal law in them, except by way of likeness.

WHETHER THERE IS A HUMAN LAW?

Objection I. It would seem that there is not a human law. For the natural law is a participation of the eternal law, as was stated above. Now through the eternal law *all things are most orderly,* as Augustine states. Therefore the natural law suffices for the ordering of all human affairs. Consequently there is no need for a human law.

Obj. 2. Further, law has the character of a measure, as was stated above. But human reason is not a measure of things, but *vice versa,* as is stated in *Metaph.* x. Therefore no law can emanate from the human reason.

Obj. 3. Further, a measure should be most certain, as is stated in *Metaph.* x. But the dictates of the human reason in matters of conduct are uncertain, according to *Wis.* ix. 14: *The thoughts of mortal men are fearful, and our counsels uncertain.* Therefore no law can emanate from the human reason.

On the contrary, Augustine distinguishes two kinds of law, the one eternal, the other temporal, which he calls human.

I answer that, As we have stated above, a law is a dictate of the practical reason. Now it is to be observed that the same procedure takes place in the practical and in the speculative reason, for each proceeds from principles to conclusions, as was stated above. Accordingly, we conclude that, just as in the speculative reason, from naturally known indemonstrable principles we draw the conclusions of the various sciences, the knowledge of which is not imparted to us by nature, but acquired by the efforts of reason, so too it is that from the precepts of the natural law, as from common and indemonstrable principles, the human reason needs to proceed to the more particular determination of certain matters. These particular determinations, devised by human reason, are called human laws, provided that the other essential conditions of law be observed, as was stated above. Therefore Tully says in his *Rhetoric* that *justice has its source in nature; thence certain things came into custom by reason of their utility; afterwards these things which emanated from nature, and were approved by custom, were sanctioned by fear and reverence for the law.*

Reply Obj. I. The human reason cannot have a full participation of the dictate of the divine reason, but according to its own mode, and imperfectly. Consequently, just as on the part of the speculative reason, by a natural participation of divine wisdom, there is in us the knowledge of certain common principles, but not a proper knowledge of each single truth, such as that contained in the divine wisdom, so, too, on the part of the practical reason, man has a natural participation of the eternal law, according to certain common principles, but not as regards the particular determinations of individual cases, which are, however, contained in the eternal law. Hence the need for human reason to proceed further to sanction them by law.

Reply Obj. 2. Human reason is not, of itself, the rule of things. But the principles impressed on it by nature are the general rules and measures of all things relating to human conduct, of which the natural reason is the rule and measure, although it is not the measure of things that are from nature.

Reply Obj. 3. The practical reason is concerned with operable matters, which are singular and contingent, but not with necessary things, with which the speculative reason is concerned. Therefore human laws cannot have that inerrancy that belongs to the demonstrated conclusions of the sciences. Nor is it necessary for every measure to be altogether unerring and certain, but according as it is possible in its own particular genus.

WHETHER THERE WAS ANY NEED FOR A DIVINE LAW?

Objection I. It would seem that there was no need for a divine law. For, as was stated above, the natural law is a participation in us of the eternal law. But the eternal law is the divine law, as was stated above. Therefore there is no need for a divine law in addition to the natural law and to human laws derived therefrom.

Obj. 2. Further, it is written (*Ecclus.* xv. 14) that *God left man in the hand of his own counsel.* Now counsel is an act of reason, as was stated above. Therefore man was left to the direction of his reason. But a dictate of human reason is a human law, as was stated above. Therefore there is no need for man to be governed also by divine law.

Obj. 3. Further, human nature is more self-sufficing than irrational creatures. But irrational creatures have no divine law besides the natural inclination impressed on them. Much less, therefore, should the rational creature have a divine law in addition to the natural law.

On the contrary, David prayed God to set His law before him, saying (*Ps.* cxviii. 33): *Set before me for a law the way of Thy justifications, O Lord.*

I answer that, Besides the natural and the human law it was necessary for the directing of human conduct to have a divine law. And this for four reasons. First, because it is by law that man is directed how to perform his proper acts in view of his last end. Now if man were ordained to no other end than that which is proportionate to his natural ability, there would be no need for man to have any further direction, on the part of his reason, in addition to the natural law and humanly devised law which is derived from it. But since man is ordained to an end of eternal happiness which exceeds man's natural ability, as we have stated above, therefore it was necessary that, in addition to the natural and the human law, man should be directed to his end by a law given by God.

Secondly, because, by reason of the uncertainty of human judgment, especially on contingent and particular matters, different people form different judgments on human acts; whence also different and contrary laws result. In order, therefore, that man may know without any doubt what he ought to do and what he ought to avoid, it was necessary for man to be directed in his proper acts by a law given by God, for it is certain that such a law cannot err.

Thirdly, because man can make laws in those matters of which he is competent to judge. But man is not competent to judge of interior movements, that are hidden, but only of exterior acts which are observable; and yet for the perfection of virtue it is necessary for man to conduct himself rightly in both kinds of acts. Consequently, human law could not sufficiently curb and direct interior acts, and it was necessary for this purpose that a divine law should supervene.

Fourthly, because, as Augustine says, human law cannot punish or forbid all evil deeds, since, while aiming at doing away with all evils, it would do away with many good things, and would hinder the advance of the common good, which is necessary for human living. In order, therefore, that no evil might remain unforbidden and unpunished, it was necessary for the divine law to supervene, whereby all sins are forbidden.

And these four causes are touched upon in *Ps.* cxviii. 8, where it is said: *The law of the Lord is unspotted, i.e.,* allowing no foulness of sin; *converting souls,* because it directs not only exterior, but also interior, acts; *the testimony of the Lord is faithful,* because of the certainty of what is true and right; *giving wisdom to little ones,* by directing man to an end supernatural and divine.

Reply Obj. I. By the natural law the eternal law is participated proportionately to the capacity of human nature. But to his supernatural end man needs to be directed in a yet higher way. Hence the additional law given by God, whereby man shares more perfectly in the eternal law.

Reply Obj. 2. Counsel is a kind of inquiry, and hence must proceed from some principles. Nor is it enough for it to proceed from principles imparted by nature, which are the precepts of the natural law, for the reasons given above; but there is need for certain additional principles, namely, the precepts of the divine law.

Reply Obj. 3. Irrational creatures are not ordained to an end higher than that which is proportionate to their natural powers. Consequently the comparison fails . . .

THE NATURAL LAW

WHETHER THE NATURAL LAW CONTAINS SEVERAL PRECEPTS, OR ONLY ONE?

Objection I. It would seem that the natural law contains not several precepts, but only one. For law is a kind of precept, as was stated above. If therefore there were many precepts of the natural law, it would follow that there are also many natural laws.

Obj. 2. Further, the natural law is consequent upon human nature. But human nature, as a whole, is one, though, as to its parts, it is manifold. Therefore, either there is but one precept of the law of nature because of the unity of nature as a whole, or there are many by reason of the number of parts of human nature. The result would be that even things relating to the inclination of the concupiscible power would belong to the natural law.

Obj. 3. Further, law is something pertaining to reason, as was stated above. Now reason is but one in man. Therefore there is only one precept of the natural law.

On the contrary, The precepts of the natural law in man stand in relation to operable matters as first principles do to matters of demonstration. But there are several first indemonstrable principles. Therefore there are also several precepts of the natural law.

I answer that, As was stated above, the precepts of the natural law are to the practical reason what the first principles of demonstrations are to the speculative reason, because both are self-evident principles. Now a thing is said to be self-evident in two ways: first, in itself; secondly, in relation to us. Any proposition is said to be self-evident in itself, if its predicate is contained in the notion of the subject; even though it may happen that to one who does not know the definition of the subject, such a proposition is not self-evident. For instance, this proposition, *Man is a rational being,* is, in its very nature, self-evident, since he who says *man,* says *a rational being*; and yet to one who does not know what a man is, this proposition is not self-evident. Hence it is that, as Boethius says, certain axioms or propositions are universally self-evident to all; and such are the propositions whose terms are known to all, as, *Every whole is greater than its part,* and, *Things equal to one and the same are equal to one another.* But some propositions are self-evident only to the wise, who understand the meaning of the terms of such propositions. Thus to one who understands that an angel is not a body, it is self-evident that an angel is not circumscriptively in a place. But this is not evident to the unlearned, for they cannot grasp it.

Now a certain order is to be found in those things that are apprehended by men. For that which first falls under apprehension is *being,* the understanding of which is included in all things whatsoever a man apprehends. Therefore the first indemonstrable principle is that *the same thing cannot be affirmed and denied at the same time,* which is based on the notion of *being* and *not-being*: and on this principle all others are based, as is stated in *Metaph.* iv. Now as *being* is the first thing that falls under the apprehension absolutely, so *good* is the first thing that falls under apprehension of the practical reason, which is directed to action (since every agent acts for an end, which has the nature of good). Consequently, the first principle in the practical reason is one founded on the nature of good, viz., that *good is that which all things seek after.* Hence this is the first precept of law, that *good is to be done and promoted, and evil is to be avoided.* All other precepts of the natural law are based upon this; so that all the things which the practical reason naturally apprehends as man's good belong to the precepts of the natural law under the form of things to be done or avoided.

Since, however, good has the nature of an end, and evil, the nature of the contrary, hence it is that all those things to which man has a natural inclination are naturally apprehended by reason as being good, and consequently as objects of pursuit, and their contraries as evil, and objects of avoidance. Therefore, the order of the precepts of the natural law is according to the order of natural inclinations. For there is in man, first of all, an inclination to good in accordance with the nature which he has in common with all substances, inasmuch, namely, as every substance seeks the preservation of its own being, according to its nature; and by reason of this inclination, whatever is a means of preserving human life and of warding off its obstacles, belongs to the natural law. Secondly, there is in man an inclination to things that pertain to him more specially, according to that nature which he has in common with other animals; and in virtue of this inclination, those things are said to belong to the natural law *which nature has taught to all animals,* such as sexual intercourse, the education of offspring and so forth. Thirdly, there is in man an inclination to good according to the nature of his reason, which nature is proper to him. Thus man has a natural inclination to know the truth about God, and to live in society; and in this respect, whatever pertains to this inclination belongs to the natural law: *e.g.,* to shun ignorance, to avoid offending those among whom one has to live, and other such things regarding the above inclination.

Reply Obj. I. All these precepts of the law of nature have the character of one natural law, inasmuch as they flow from one first precept.

Reply Obj. 2. All the inclinations of any parts whatsoever of human nature, *e.g.,* of the concupiscible and irascible parts, in so far as they are ruled by reason, belong to the natural law, and are reduced to one first precept, as was stated above. And thus the precepts of the natural law are many in themselves, but they are based on one common foundation.

Reply Obj. 3. Although reason is one in itself, yet it directs all things regarding man; so that whatever can be ruled by reason is contained under the law of reason.

WHETHER ALL THE ACTS OF THE VIRTUES ARE PRESCRIBED BY THE NATURAL LAW?

Objection I. It would seem that not all the acts of the virtues are prescribed by the natural law. For, as was stated above, it is of the nature of law that it be ordained to the common good. But some acts of the virtues are ordained to the private good of the individual, as is evident especially in regard to acts of temperance. Therefore, not all the acts of the virtues are the subject of natural laws.

Obj. 2. Further, every sin is opposed to some virtuous act. If therefore all the acts of the virtues are prescribed by the natural law, it seems to follow that all sins are against nature; whereas this applies to certain special sins.

Obj. 3. Further, those things which are according to nature are common to all. But the acts of the virtues are not common to all, since a thing is virtuous in one, and vicious in another. Therefore, not all the acts of the virtues are prescribed by the natural law.

On the contrary, Damascene says that *virtues are natural.* Therefore virtuous acts also are subject to the natural law.

I answer that, We may speak of virtuous acts in two ways: first, in so far as they are virtuous; secondly, as such and such acts considered in their proper species. If, then, we are speaking of the acts of the virtues in so far as they are virtuous, thus all virtuous acts belong to the natural law. For it has been stated that to the natural law belongs everything to which man is inclined according to his nature. Now each thing is inclined naturally to an operation that is suitable to it according to its form: *e.g.,* fire is inclined to give heat. Therefore, since the rational soul is the proper form of man, there is in every man a natural inclination to act according to reason; and this is to act according to virtue. Consequently, considered thus, all the acts of the virtues are prescribed by the natural law, since each one's reason naturally dictates to him to act virtuously. But if we speak of virtuous acts, considered in themselves, *i.e.,* in their proper species, thus not all virtuous acts are prescribed by the natural law. For many things are done virtuously, to which nature does not primarily incline, but which, through the inquiry of reason, have been found by men to be conducive to well-living.

Reply Obj. I. Temperance is about the natural concupiscences of food, drink and sexual matters, which are indeed ordained to the common good of nature, just as other matters of law are ordained to the moral common good.

Reply Obj. 2. By human nature we may mean either that which is proper to man, and in this sense all sins, as being against reason, are also against nature, as Damascene states; or we may mean that nature which is common to man and other animals, and in this sense, certain special sins are said to be against nature: *e.g.,* contrary to sexual intercourse, which is natural to all animals, is unisexual lust, which has received the special name of the unnatural crime.

Reply Obj. 3. This argument considers acts in themselves. For it is owing to the various conditions of men that certain acts are virtuous for some, as being proportioned and becoming to them, while they are vicious for others, as not being proportioned to them.

WHETHER THE NATURAL LAW IS THE SAME IN ALL MEN?

Objection 1. It would seem that the natural law is not the same in all. For it is stated in the *Decretals* that *the natural law is that which is contained in the Law and the Gospel.* But this is not common to all men, because, as it is written (*Rom.* x. 16), *all do not obey the Gospel.* Therefore the natural law is not the same in all men.

Obj. 2. Further, *Things which are according to the law are said to be just,* as is stated in *Ethics* v. But it is stated in the same book that nothing is so just for all as not to be subject to change in regard to some men. Therefore even the natural law is not the same in all men.

Obj. 3. Further, as was stated above, to the natural law belongs everything to which a man is inclined according to his nature. Now different men are naturally inclined to different things,—

some to the desire of pleasures, other to the desire of honors, and other men to other things. Therefore, there is not one natural law for all.

On the contrary, Isidore says: *The natural law is common to all nations.*

I answer that, As we have stated above, to the natural law belong those things to which a man is inclined naturally; and among these it is proper to man to be inclined to act according to reason. Now it belongs to the reason to proceed from what is common to what is proper, as is stated in *Physics i.* The speculative reason, however, is differently situated, in this matter, from the practical reason. For, since the speculative reason is concerned chiefly with necessary things, which cannot be otherwise than they are, its proper conclusions, like the universal principles, contain the truth without fail. The practical reason, on the other hand, is concerned with contingent matters, which is the domain of human actions; and, consequently, although there is necessity in the common principles, the more we descend towards the particular, the more frequently we encounter defects. Accordingly, then, in speculative matters truth is the same in all men, both as to principles and as to conclusions; although the truth is not known to all as regards the conclusions, but only as regards the principles which are called *common notions.* But in matters of action, truth or practical rectitude is not the same for all as to what is particular, but only as to the common principles; and where there is the same rectitude in relation to particulars, it is not equally known to all.

It is therefore evident that, as regards the common principles whether of speculative or of practical reason, truth or rectitude is the same for all, and is equally known by all. But as to the proper conclusions of the speculative reason, the truth is the same for all, but it is not equally known to all. Thus, it is true for all that the three angles of a triangle are together equal to two right angles, although it is not known to all. But as to the proper conclusions of the practical reason, neither is the truth or rectitude the same for all, nor where it is the same, is it equally known by all. Thus, it is right and true for all to act according to reason, and from this principle it follows, as a proper conclusion, that goods entrusted to another should be restored to their owner. Now this is true for the majority of cases. But it may happen in a particular case that it would be injurious, and therefore unreasonable, to restore goods held in trust; for instance, if they are claimed for the purpose of fighting against one's country. And this principle will be found to fail the more, according as we descend further towards the particular, for example, if one were to say that goods held in trust should be restored with such and such a guarantee, or in such and such a way; because the greater the number of conditions added, the greater the number of ways in which the principle may fail, so that it be not right to restore or not to restore.

Consequently, we must say that the natural law, as to the first common principles, is the same for all, both as to rectitude and as to knowledge. But as to certain more particular aspects, which are conclusions, as it were, of those common principles, it is the same for all in the majority of cases, both as to rectitude and as to knowledge; and yet in some few cases, it may fail, both as to rectitude, by reason of certain obstacles (just as natures subject to generation and corruption fail in some few cases because of some obstacle), and as to knowledge, since in some the reason is perverted by passion, or evil habit, or an evil disposition of nature. Thus at one time theft, although it is expressly contrary to the natural law, was not considered wrong among the Germans, as Julius Caesar relates.

Reply Obj. 1. The meaning of the sentence quoted is not that whatever is contained in the Law and the Gospel belongs to the natural law, since they contain many things that are above nature; but that whatever belongs to the natural law is fully contained in them. Therefore Gratian, after saying that *the natural law is what is contained in the Law and the Gospel,* adds at once, by way of example, *by which everyone is commanded to do to others as he would be done by.*

Reply Obj. 2. The saying of the Philosopher is to be understood of things that are naturally just, not as common principles, but as conclusions drawn from them, having rectitude in the majority of cases, but failing in a few.

Reply Obj. 3. Just as in man reason rules and commands the other powers, so all the natural inclinations belonging to the other powers must needs be directed according to reason. Therefore it is universally right for all men that all their inclinations should be directed according to reason.

WHETHER THE NATURAL LAW CAN BE CHANGED?

Objection I. It would seem that the natural law can be changed. For on *Ecclus.* xvii. 9 (*He gave them instructions, and the law of life*) the *Gloss* says: *He wished the law of the letter to be written, in order to correct the law of nature.* But that which is corrected is changed. Therefore the natural law can be changed.

Obj. 2. Further, the slaying of the innocent, adultery and theft are against the natural law. But we find these things changed by God: as when God commanded Abraham to slay his innocent son (*Gen.* xxii. 2); and when He ordered the Jews to borrow and purloin the vessels of the Egyptians (*Exod.* xii. 35); and when He commanded Osee to take to himself *a wife of fornications* (*Osee* i. 2). Therefore the natural law can be changed.

Obj. 3. Further, Isidore says that *the possession of all things in common, and universal freedom, are matters of natural law.* But these things are seen to be changed by human laws. Therefore it seems that the natural law is subject to change.

On the contrary, It is said in the *Decretals: The natural law dates from the creation of the rational creature. It does not vary according to time, but remains unchangeable.*

I answer that, A change in the natural law may be understood in two ways. First, by way of addition. In this sense, nothing hinders the natural law from being changed, since many things for the benefit of human life have been added over and above the natural law, both by the divine law and by human laws.

Secondly, a change in the natural law may be understood by way of subtraction, so that what previously was according to the natural law, ceases to be so. In this sense, the natural law is altogether unchangeable in its first principles. But in its secondary principles, which, as we have said, are certain detailed proximate conclusions drawn from the first principles, the natural law is not changed so that what it prescribes be not right in most cases. But it may be changed in some particular cases of rare occurrence, through some special causes hindering the observance of such precepts, as was stated above.

Reply Obj. I. The written law is said to be given for the correction of the natural law, either because it supplies what was wanting to the natural law, or because the natural law was so perverted in the hearts of some men, as to certain matters, that they esteemed those things good which are naturally evil; which perversion stood in need of correction.

Reply Obj. 2. All men alike, both guilty and innocent, die the death of nature; which death of nature is inflicted by the power of God because of original sin, according to *I Kings* ii. 6: *The Lord killeth and maketh alive.* Consequently, by the command of God, death can be inflicted on any man, guilty or innocent, without any injustice whatever.—In like manner, adultery is intercourse with another's wife; who is allotted to him by the law emanating from God. Consequently intercourse with any woman, by the command of God, is neither adultery nor fornication.— The same applies to theft, which is the taking of another's property. For whatever is taken by the command of God, to Whom all things belong, is not taken against the will of its owner, whereas it is in this that theft consists.—Nor is it only in human things that whatever is commanded by God is right; but also in natural things, whatever is done by God is, in some way, natural, as was stated in the First Part.

Reply Obj. 3. A thing is said to belong to the natural law in two ways. First, because nature inclines thereto: *e.g.,* that one should not do harm to another. Secondly, because nature did not bring with it the contrary. Thus, we might say that for man to be naked is of the natural law, because nature did not give him clothes, but art invented them. In this sense, *the possession of all things in common and universal freedom* are said to be of the natural law, because, namely, the distinction of possessions and slavery were not brought in by nature, but devised by human reason for the benefit of human life. Accordingly, the law of nature was not changed in this respect, except by addition . . .

HUMAN LAW

WHETHER EVERY HUMAN LAW IS DERIVED FROM THE NATURAL LAW?

Objection I. It would seem that not every human law is derived from the natural law. For the Philosopher says that *the legal just is that which originally was a matter of indifference.* But those things which arise from the natural law are not matters of indifference. Therefore the enactments of human laws are not all derived from the natural law.

Obj. 2. Further, positive law is divided against natural law, as is stated by Isidore and the Philosopher. But those things which flow as conclusions from the common principles of the natural law belong to the natural law, as was stated above. Therefore that which is established by human law is not derived from the natural law.

Obj. 3. Further, the law of nature is the same for all, since the Philosopher says that *the natural just is that which is equally valid everywhere.* If therefore human laws were derived from the natural law, it would follow that they too are the same for all; which is clearly false.

Obj. 4. Further, it is possible to give a reason for things which are derived from the natural law. But *it is not possible to give the reason for all the legal enactments of the lawgivers,* as the Jurist says. Therefore not all human laws are derived from the natural law.

On the contrary, Tully says: *Things which emanated from nature, and were approved by custom, were sanctioned by fear and reverence for the laws.*

I answer that, As Augustine says, *that which is not just seems to be no law at all.* Hence the force of a law depends on the extent of its justice. Now in human affairs a thing is said to be just from being right, according to the rule of reason. But the first rule of reason is the law of nature, as is clear from what has been stated above. Consequently, every human law has just so much of the nature of law as it is derived from the law of nature. But if in any point it departs from the law of nature, it is no longer a law but a perversion of law.

But it must be noted that something may be derived from the natural law in two ways: first, as a conclusion from principles; secondly, by way of a determination of certain common notions. The first way is like to that by which, in the sciences, demonstrated conclusions are drawn from the principles; while the second is likened to that whereby, in the arts, common forms are determined to some particular. Thus, the craftsman needs to determine the common form of a house to the shape of this or that particular house. Some things are therefore derived from the common principles of the natural law by way of conclusions: *e.g.,* that *one must not kill* may be derived as a conclusion from the principle that *one should do harm to no man;* while some are derived therefrom by way of determination: *e.g.,* the law of nature has it that the evil-doer should be punished, but that he be punished in this or that way is a determination of the law of nature.

Accordingly, both modes of derivation are found in the human law. But those things which are derived in the first way are contained in human law, not as emanating therefrom exclusively, but as having some force from the natural law also. But those things which are derived in the second way have no other force than that of human law.

Reply Obj. I. The Philosopher is speaking of those enactments which are by way of determination or specification of the precepts of the natural law.

Reply Obj. 2. This argument holds for those things that are derived from the natural law by way of conclusion.

Reply Obj. 3. The common principles of the natural law cannot be applied to all men in the same way because of the great variety of human affairs; and hence arises the diversity of positive laws among various people.

Reply Obj. 4. These words of the Jurist are to be understood as referring to the decisions of rulers in determining particular points of the natural law; and to these determinations the judgment of expert and prudent men is related as to its principles, in so far, namely, as they see at once what is the best thing to decide. Hence the Philosopher says that, in such matters, *we ought to pay as much attention to the undemonstrated sayings and opinions of persons who surpass us in experience, age and prudence, as to their demonstrations* . . .

WHETHER IT BELONGS TO HUMAN LAW TO REPRESS ALL VICES?

Objection 1. It would seem that it belongs to human law to repress all vices. For Isidore says that *laws were made in order that, in fear thereof, man's audacity might be held in check.* But it would not be held in check sufficiently unless all evils were repressed by law. Therefore human law should repress all evils.

Obj. 2. Further, the intention of the lawgiver is to make the citizens virtuous. But a man cannot be virtuous unless he forbear from all kinds of vice. Therefore it belongs to human law to repress all vices.

Obj. 3. Further, human law is derived from the natural law, as was stated above. But all vices are contrary to the law of nature. Therefore human law should repress all vices.

On the contrary, We read in *DeLibero Arbitrio,* i: *It seems to me that the law which is written for the governing of the people rightly permits these things, and that divine providence punishes them. But divine providence punishes nothing but vices. Therefore human law rightly allows some vices, by not repressing them.*

I answer that, As we stated above, law is framed as a rule or measure of human acts. Now a measure should be homogeneous with that which it measures, as is stated in *Metaph.* x, since different things are measured by different measures. Therefore laws imposed on men should also be in keeping with their condition, for, as Isidore says, law should be *possible both according to nature, and according to the customs of the country.* Now the ability or facility of action is due to an interior habit or disposition, since the same thing is not possible to one who has not a virtuous habit, as is possible to one who has. Thus the same thing is not possible to a child as to a full-grown man, and for which reason the law for children is not the same as for adults, since many things are permitted to children, which in an adult are punished by law or at any rate are open to blame. In like manner, many things are permissible to men not perfect in virtue, which would be intolerable in a virtuous man.

Now human law is framed for the multitude of human beings, the majority of whom are not perfect in virtue. Therefore human laws do not forbid all vices, from which the virtuous abstain, but only the more grievous vices, from which it is possible for the majority to abstain; and chiefly those that are injurious to others, without the prohibition of which human society could not be maintained. Thus human law prohibits murder, theft and the like.

Reply Obj. 1. Audacity seems to refer to the assailing of others. Consequently, it belongs to those sins chiefly whereby one's neighbor is injured. These sins are forbidden by human law, as was stated.

Reply Obj. 2. The purpose of human law is to lead men to virtue, not suddenly, but gradually. Therefore it does not lay upon the multitude of imperfect men the burdens of those who are already virtuous, to wit, that they should abstain from all evil. Otherwise these imperfect ones, being unable to bear such precepts, would break out into yet greater evils. As it is written (*Prov.* xxx. 33): *He that violently bloweth his nose, bringeth out blood;* again (*Matt.* ix. 17): if *new wine, that is,* precepts of a perfect life, is *put into old bottles,* that is, into imperfect men, *the bottles break, and the wine runneth out,* that is, the precepts are despised, and those men, from contempt, break out into evils worse still.

Reply Obj. 3. The natural law is a participation in us of the eternal law, while human law falls short of the eternal law. For Augustine says: *The law which is framed for the government of states allows and leaves unpunished many things that are punished by divine providence. Nor, if this law does not attempt to do everything, is this a reason why it should be blamed for what it does.* Therefore, human law likewise does not prohibit . . . everything that is forbidden by the natural law.

WHETHER HUMAN LAW BINDS A MAN IN CONSCIENCE?

Objection 1. It would seem that human law does not bind a man in conscience. For an inferior power cannot impose its law on the judgment of a higher power. But the power of man, which frames human law, is beneath the divine power. Therefore human law cannot impose its precept on a divine judgment, such as is the judgment of conscience.

Obj. 2. Further, the judgment of conscience depends chiefly on the commandments of God. But sometimes God's commandments are made void by human laws, according to *Matt.* xv. 6: *You have made void the commandment of God for your tradition.* Therefore human law does not bind a man in conscience.

Obj. 3. Further, human laws often bring loss of character and injury on man, according to *Isa.* x. 1, 2: *Woe to them that make wicked laws, and when they write, write injustice; to oppress the poor in judgment, and do violence to the cause of the humble of My people.* But it is lawful for anyone to avoid oppression and violence. Therefore human laws do not bind man in conscience.

On the contrary, It is written (*I Pet.* ii. 19): *This is thanksworthy, if for conscience . . . a man endure sorrows, suffering wrongfullly.*

I answer that, Laws framed by man are either just or unjust. If they be just, they have the power of binding in conscience from the eternal law whence they are derived, according to *Prov.* viii. 15: *By Me kings reign, and lawgivers decree just things.* Now laws are said to be just, both from the end (when, namely, they are ordained to the common good), from their author (that is to say, when the law that is made does not exceed the power of the lawgiver), and from their form (when, namely, burdens are laid on the subjects according to an equality of proportion and with a view to the common good). For, since one man is a part of the community, each man, in all that he is and has, belongs to the community; just as a part, in all that it is belongs to the whole. So, too, nature inflicts a loss on the part in order to save the whole; so that for this reason such laws as these, which impose proportionate burdens, are just and binding in conscience, and are legal laws.

On the other hand, laws may be unjust in two ways: first, by being contrary to human good, through being opposed to the things mentioned above:—either in respect of the ends, as when as authority imposes on his subjects burdensome laws, conducive, not to the common good, but rather to his own cupidity or vainglory; or in respect of the author, as when a man makes a law that goes beyond the power committed to him; or in respect of the form, as when burdens are imposed unequally on the community, although with a view to the common good. Such are acts of violence rather than laws, because, as Augustine says, *a law that is not just seems to be no law at all.* Therefore, such laws do not bind in conscience, except perhaps in order to avoid scandal or disturbance, for which cause a man should even yield his right, according to *Matt.* v. 40, 41: *If a man . . . take away thy coat, let go thy cloak also unto him; and whosoever will force thee one mile, go with him other two.*

Secondly, laws may be unjust through being opposed to the divine good. Such are the laws of tyrants inducing to idolatry, or to anything else contrary to the divine law. Laws of this kind must in no way be observed, because, as is stated in *Acts* v. 29, *we ought to obey God rather than men.*

Reply Obj. 1. As the Apostle says (*Rom.* xiii. 1, 2), all human power is from God . . . *therefore he that resisteth the power,* in matters that are within its scope, *resisteth the ordinance of God;* so that he becomes guilty in conscience.

Reply Obj. 2. This argument is true of laws that are contrary to the commandments of God, which is beyond the scope of [human] power. Therefore in such matters human law should not be obeyed.

Reply Obj. 3. This argument is true of a law that inflicts an unjust burden on its subjects. Furthermore, the power that man holds from God does not extend to this. Hence neither in such matters is man bound to obey the law, provided he avoid giving scandal or inflicting a more grievous injury. . . .

ERNEST BARKER

Natural Law and English Positivism*

There were two ways in which the theory of natural law affected American thought and action. The first way was that of destruction. It served as a charge of powder which blasted the connection with Great Britain and cleared the way for the Declaration of Independence. The second way was that of construction. It served as a foundation for the building of new constitutions in the independent colonies from 1776 onwards, and for the addition to those constitutions (or rather to some of them) of an entrance-hall or façade called a declaration of rights. The idea of nature can be revolutionary; but it can also promote and support evolution. It worked in both ways in the American colonies. First it made revolution; and then, when that was done, it fostered evolution. In order to understand its accomplishment, we must pause to consider its principles and to examine its potentialities.

We may begin by noting (for it is a fact of crucial importance) that the English thinkers and lawyers of the eighteenth century have little regard for natural law and natural rights. Indeed, it may be said that natural law is generally repugnant to the genius of English legal thought, generally busied with a "common law" which, however common, is still peculiar, and anyhow is sufficiently actual, sufficiently practical, sufficiently definite, to suit the English temper. To Burke any speech of natural law and natural rights is metaphysics, and not politics. To Blackstone—though he is inconsistent, writing in one way when he theorises on the nature of laws in general, and in another when he comments on the laws of England—the law of nature is not a concern of English courts, and may therefore be treated, for their purposes, as nonexistent. To Bentham, when he wrote the *Fragment on Government* in 1776, the law of nature was "nothing but a

phrase": its natural tendency was "to impel a man, by the force of conscience, to rise up in arms against any law whatever that he happens not to like"; and a far better clue—indeed "the only clue to guide a man through these straits"—was the principle of utility.

The general view of the English thinkers of the period may be resumed in two propositions. In the first place, law is a body of rules which is recognised and enforced in courts of law; and it is simply that body of rules. Since the courts of law recognise and enforce both the judge-made law of tradition and the statute law enacted by parliament, law is these two things, and only these two things. Since, again, the judge-made law of tradition may be regarded as an *opus perfectum* (so, at any rate, Blackstone seems to think), and since law now grows only or mainly by the addition of the statutes enacted by parliament—since, in a word, it is parliament only which now gives new rules to the judges, either by amending the law of the past, both judge-made and parliament-made, or by enacting fresh law *de novo*—parliament must be acknowledged as "the sovereign legislative", maker and author supreme of all law, an uncontrollable authority acting by its own motion, "as essential to the body politic" (so a member of parliament declared) "as the Deity to religion." Such is the gist and sweep of the first of the two propositions. The second proposition is similar, and may be said to be consequential. It is a proposition affirming that constitutional law is not in any way different in kind from the rest of the law, but is merely a part of the general law. It is simply that part of the general law which, as Paley says, "regulates the form of the legislative." Being part of the general law, it is subject, like all other law, to the control of the sovereign legislature—which thus regulates itself and determines its own form. You cannot therefore distinguish between constitutional law and ordinary law, or say that the one is made and amended by one process and the other by another. In origin, and in kind, the two are simply

*From *Traditions of Civility* by Sir Ernest Barker (London: Cambridge University Press, 1948), pp. 310–12. Reprinted by permission of the publisher.

identical; and they are under the same control. You cannot say that a law is unconstitutional; if it is a law—that is to say, if it is made by parliament—it is necessarily constitutional. In a word, the legal is also the constitutional: "the terms *constitutional* and *unconstitutional*," as Paley writes, "mean the legal and illegal."

In the light of these two propositions we may now turn to natural law, and note how it differs from English law in regard to both. The origin of the idea of natural law may be ascribed to an old and indefeasible movement of the human mind (we may trace it already in the *Antigone* of Sophocles) which impels it towards the notion of an eternal and immutable justice; a justice which human authority expresses, or ought to express— but does not make; a justice which human authority may fail to express—and must pay the penalty for failing to express by the diminution, or even the forfeiture, of its power to command. This justice is conceived as being the higher or ultimate law, proceeding from the nature of the universe from the Being of God and the reason of man. It follows that law—in the sense of the law of the last resort—is somehow above lawmaking. It follows that lawmakers, after all, are somehow under and subject to law.

JOHN AUSTIN

A Positivist Conception of Law*

LECTURE I

The matter of jurisprudence is positive law: law, simply and strictly so called: or law set by political superiors to political inferiors. But positive law (or law, simply and strictly so called) is often confounded with objects to which it is related by *resemblance,* and with objects to which it is related in the way of *analogy:* with objects which are *also* signified, *properly* and *improperly,* by the large and vague expression *law.* To obviate the difficulties springing from that confusion, I begin my projected Course with determining the province of jurisprudence, or with distinguishing the matter of jurisprudence from those various related objects: trying to define the subject of which I intend to treat, before I endeavour to analyse its numerous and complicated parts.

A law, in the most general and comprehensive acceptation in which the term, in its literal meaning, is employed, may be said to be a rule laid down for the guidance of an intelligent being by an intelligent being having power over him. Under this definition are concluded, and without impropriety, several species. It is necessary to define accurately the line of demarcation which separates these species from one another, as much mistiness and intricacy has been infused into the science of jurisprudence by their being confounded or not clearly distinguished. In the comprehensive sense above indicated, or in the largest meaning which it has, without extension by metaphor or analogy, the term *law* embraces the following objects:—Laws set by God to his human creatures, and laws set by men to men.

The whole or a portion of the laws set by God to men is frequently styled the law of nature, or natural law: being, in truth, the only natural law of which it is possible to speak without a metaphor, or without a blending of objects which ought to be distinguished broadly. But, rejecting the appellation Law of Nature as ambiguous and

misleading, I name those laws or rules, as considered collectively or in a mass, the *Divine law,* or the *law of God.*

Laws set by men to men are of two leading or principal classes: classes which are often blended, although they differ extremely; and which, for that reason, should be severed precisely, and opposed distinctly and conspicuously.

Of the laws or rules set by men to men, some are established by *political* superiors, sovereign and subject: by persons exercising supreme and subordinate *government,* in independent nations, or independent political societies. The aggregate of the rules thus established, or some aggregate forming a portion of that aggregate, is the appropriate matter of jurisprudence, general or particular. To the aggregate of the rules thus established, or to some aggregate forming a portion of that aggregate, the term *law,* as used simply and strictly, is exclusively applied. But, as contradistinguished to *natural* law, or to the law of *nature* (meaning, by those expressions, the law of God), the aggregate of the rules, established by political superiors, is frequently styled *positive* law, or law existing *by position.* As contradistinguished to the rules which I style *positive morality,* and on which I shall touch immediately, the aggregate of the rules, established by political superiors, may also be marked commodiously with the name of *positive law.* For the sake, then, of getting a name brief and distinctive at once, and agreeable to frequent usage, I style that aggregate of rules, or any portion of that aggregate, *positive law:* though rules, which are *not* established by political superiors, are also *positive,* or exist *by position,* if they be rules or laws, in the proper signification of the term.

Though *some* of the laws or rules, which are set by men to men, are established by political superiors, *others* are *not* established by political superiors, or are *not* established by political superiors, in that capacity or character.

Closely analogous to human laws of this second class, are a set of objects frequently but *im-*

*From *The Province of Jurisprudence Determined,* Selections from Lectures I and VI. First published in 1832.

properly termed *laws,* being rules set and enforced by *mere opinion,* that is, by the opinions or sentiments held or felt by an indeterminate body of men in regard to human conduct. Instances of such a use of the term *law* are the expressions—'The law of honour'; 'The law set by fashion'; and rules of this species constitute much of what is usually termed 'International law.'

The aggregate of human laws properly so called belonging to the second of the classes above mentioned, with the aggregate of objects *improperly* but by *close analogy* termed laws, I place together in a common class, and denote them by the term *positive morality.* The name *(morality* severs them from *positive law,* while the epithet *positive* disjoins them from the *law of God.)* And to the end of obviating confusion, it is necessary or expedient that they *should* be disjoined from the latter by that distinguishing epithet. For the name *morality* (or *morals*), when standing unqualified or alone, denotes indifferently either of the following objects: namely, positive morality *as it is,* or without regard to its merits; and positive morality *as it would be,* if it conformed to the law of God, and were, therefore, deserving of *approbation.*

Besides the various sorts of rules which are included in the literal acceptation of the term law, and those which are by a close and striking analogy, though improperly, termed laws, there are numerous applications of the term law, which rest upon a slender analogy and are merely metaphorical or figurative. Such is the case when we talk of *laws* observed by the lower animals; of *laws* regulating the growth or decay of vegetables; of *laws* determining the movements of inanimate bodies or masses. For where *intelligence* is not, or where it is too bounded to take the name of *reason,* and, therefore, is too bounded to conceive the purpose of a law, there is not the *will* which law can work on, or which duty can incite or restrain. Yet through these misapplications of a *name,* flagrant as the metaphor is, has the field of jurisprudence and morals been deluged with muddy speculation.

Having suggested the *purpose* of my attempt to determine the province of jurisprudence: to distinguish positive law, the appropriate matter of jurisprudence, from the various objects to which it is related by resemblance, and to which it is related, nearly or remotely, by a strong or slender analogy: I shall now state the essentials of *a law* or *rule* (taken with the largest signification which

can be given to the term *properly*).

Every *law or rule* (taken with the largest signification which can be given to the term *properly*) is a *command.* Or, rather, laws or rules, properly so called, are a *species* of commands.

Now, since the term *command* comprises the term *law,* the first is the simpler as well as the larger of the two. But, simple as it is, it admits of explanation. And, since it is the *key* to the sciences of jurisprudence and morals, its meaning should be analysed with precision.

Accordingly, I shall endeavour, in the first instance, to analyse the meaning of *'command':* an analysis which I fear, will task the patience of my hearers, but which they will bear with cheerfulness, or, at least, with resignation, if they consider the difficulty of performing it. The elements of a science are precisely the parts of it which are explained least easily. Terms that are the largest, and, therefore, the simplest of a series, are without equivalent expressions into which we can resolve them *concisely.* And when we endeavour to *define* them, or to translate them into terms which we suppose are better understood, we are forced upon awkward and tedious circumlocutions.

If you express or intimate a wish that I shall do or forbear from some act, and if you will visit me with an evil in case I comply not with your wish, the *expression* or *intimation* of your wish is a *command.* A command is distinguished from other significations of desire, not by the style in which the desire is signified, but by the power and the purpose of the party commanding to inflict an evil or pain in case the desire be disregarded. If you cannot or will not harm me in case I comply not with your wish, the expression of your wish is not a command, although you utter your wish in imperative phrase. If you are able and willing to harm me in case I comply not with your wish, the expression of your wish amounts to a command, although you are prompted by a spirit of courtesy to utter it in the shape of a request. *'Preces* erant, sed *quibus contradici non posset.'* Such is the language of Tacitus, when speaking of a petition by the soldiery to a son and lieutenant of Vespasian.

A command, then, is a signification of desire. But a command is distinguished from other significations of desire by this peculiarity: that the party to whom it is directed is liable to evil from the other, in case he comply not with the desire. Being liable to evil from you if I comply not with a wish which you signify, I am *bound* or *obliged* by your command, or I lie under a *duty to obey it*. If, in spite of that evil in prospect, I comply not with the wish which you signify, I am said to disobey your command, or to violate the duty which it imposes.

Command and duty are, therefore, correlative terms: the meaning denoted by each being implied or supposed by the other. Or (changing the expression) wherever a duty lies, a command has been signified; and whenever a command is signified, a duty is imposed.

Concisely expressed, the meaning of the correlative expressions is this: He who will inflict an evil in case his desire be disregarded, utters a command by expressing or intimating his desire. He who is liable to the evil in case he disregard the desire, is bound or obliged by the command.

The evil which will probably be incurred in case a command be disobeyed or (to use an equivalent expression) in case a duty be broken, is frequently called a *sanction,* or an *enforcement of obedience.* Or (varying the phrase) the command or the duty is said to be *sanctioned* or *enforced* by the chance of incurring the evil.

Considered as thus abstracted from the command and the duty which it enforces, the evil to be incurred by disobedience is frequently styled a *punishment.* But, as punishments, strictly so called, are only a *class* of sanctions, the term is too narrow to express the meaning adequately.

I observe that Dr. Paley, in his analysis of the term *obligation,* lays much stress upon the *violence* of the motive to compliance. In so far as I can gather a meaning from his loose and inconsistent statement, his meaning appears to be this: that unless the motive to compliance be *violent* or *intense,* the expression or intimation of a wish is not a *command,* nor does the party to whom it is directed lie under a *duty* to regard it.

If he means, by a *violent* motive, a motive operating with certainty, his proposition is manifestly false. The greater the evil to be incurred in case the wish be disregarded, and the greater the chance of incurring it on that same event, the greater, no doubt, is the *chance* that the wish will *not* be disregarded. But no conceivable motive will *certainly* determine to compliance, or no conceivable motive will render obedience inevitable. If Paley's proposition be true, in the sense which I have now ascribed to it, commands and duties are simply impossible. Or, reducing his proposition to absurdity by a consequence as manifestly false, commands and duties are possible, but are never disobeyed or broken.

If he means by a *violent* motive, an evil which inspires fear, his meaning is simply this: that the party bound by a command is bound by the prospect of an evil. For that which is not feared is not apprehended as an evil: or (changing the shape of the expression) is not an evil in prospect.

The truth is, that the magnitude of the eventual evil, and the magnitude of the chance of incurring it, are foreign to the matter in question. The greater the eventual evil, and the greater the chance of incurring it, the greater is the efficacy of the command, and the greater is the strength of the obligation: Or (substituting expressions exactly equivalent), the greater is the *chance* that the command will be obeyed, and that the duty will not be broken. But where there is the smallest chance of incurring the smallest evil, the expression of a wish amounts to a command, and, therefore, imposes a duty. The sanction, if you will, is feeble or insufficient; but still there *is* a sanction, and, therefore, a duty and a command.

By some celebrated writers (by Locke, Bentham, and, I think, Paley), the term *sanction,* or *enforcement of obedience,* is applied to conditional good as well as to conditional evil: to reward as to punishment. But, with all my habitual veneration for the names of Locke and Bentham, I think that this extension of the term is pregnant with confusion and perplexity.

Rewards are, indisputably, *motives* to comply with the wishes of others. But to talk of commands and duties as *sanctioned* or *enforced* by rewards, or to talk of rewards as *obliging* or *constraining* to obedience, is surely a wide departure from the established meaning of the terms.

If *you* expressed a desire that *I* should render a service, and if you proffered a reward as the motive or inducement to render it, *you* would scarcely be said to *command* the service, nor should *I,* in ordinary language, be *obliged* to render it. In ordinary language, *you* would *promise* me a reward, on condition of my rendering the service, whilst *I* might be *incited* or *persuaded* to render it by the hope of obtaining the reward.

Again: If a law hold out a *reward* as an inducement to do some act, an eventual *right* is conferred, and not an *obligation* imposed, upon those who shall act accordingly. The *imperative* part of the law being addressed or directed to the party whom it requires to *render* the reward.

In short, I am determined or inclined to comply with the wish of another, by the fear of disadvantage or evil. I am also determined or inclined to comply with the wish of another, by the hope of advantage or good. But it is only by the chance of incurring *evil*, that I am *bound* or *obliged* to compliance. It is only by conditional *evil*, that duties are *sanctioned* or *enforced*. It is the power and the purpose of inflicting eventual *evil*, and *not* the power and the purpose of imparting eventual *good*, which gives to the expression of a wish the name of a *command*.

If we put *reward* into the import of the term *sanction*, we must engage in a toilsome struggle with the current of ordinary speech; and shall often slide unconsciously, notwithstanding our efforts to the contrary, into the narrower and customary meaning.

It appears, then, from what has been premised, that the ideas or notions comprehended by the term *command* are the following. 1. A wish or desire conceived by a rational being, that another rational being shall do or forbear. 2. An evil to proceed from the former, and to be incurred by the latter, in case the latter comply not with the wish. 3. An expression or intimation of the wish by words or other signs.

It also appears from what has been premised, that *command, duty,* and *sanction* are inseparably connected terms: that each embraces the same ideas as the others, though each denotes those ideas in a peculiar order or series.

'A wish conceived by one, and expressed or intimated to another, with an evil to be inflicted and incurred in case the wish be disregarded,' are signified directly and indirectly by each of the three expressions. Each is the name of the same complex notion.

But when I am talking *directly* of the expression or intimation of the wish, I employ the term *command:* The expression or intimation of the wish being presented *prominently* to my hearer; whilst the evil to be incurred, with the chance of incurring it, are kept (if I may so express myself) in the background of my picture.

When I am talking *directly* of the chance of incurring the evil, or (changing the expression) of the liability or obnoxiousness to the evil, I employ the term *duty*, or the term *obligation:* The liability or obnoxiousness to the evil being put foremost, and the rest of the complex notion being signified implicitly.

When I am talking *immediately* of the evil itself, I employ the term *sanction*, or a term of the like import: The evil to be incurred being signified directly; whilst the obnoxiousness to that evil, with the expression or intimation of the wish, are

indicated indirectly or obliquely.

To those who are familiar with the language of logicians (language unrivalled for brevity, distinctness, and precision), I can express my meaning accurately in a breath:—Each of the three terms *signifies* the same notion; but each *denotes* a different part of that notion, and *connotes* the residue.

Commands are of two species. Some are *laws* or *rules*. The others have not acquired an appropriate name, nor does language afford an expression which will mark them briefly and precisely. I must, therefore, note them as well as I can by the ambiguous and inexpressive name of '*occasional* or *particular* commands'.

The term *laws* or *rules* being not unfrequently applied to occasional or particular commands, it is hardly possible to describe a line of separation which shall consist in every respect with established forms of speech. But the distinction between laws and particular commands may, I think, be stated in the following manner.

By every command, the party to whom it is directed is obliged to do or to forbear.

Now where it obliges *generally* to acts or forbearances of a *class*, a command is a law or rule. But where it obliges to a *specific* act or forbearance, or to acts or forbearances which it determines *specifically* or *individually*, a command is occasional or particular. In other words, a class or description of acts is determined by a law or rule, and acts of that class or description are enjoined or forbidden generally. But where a command is occasional or particular, the act or acts, which the command enjoins or forbids, are assigned or determined by their specific or individual natures as well as by the class or description to which they belong.

The statement which I have given in abstract expressions I will now endeavour to illustrate by apt examples.

If you command your servant to go on a given errand, or *not* to leave your house on a given evening, or to rise at such an hour on such a morning, or to rise at that hour during the next week or month, the command is occasional or particular. For the act or acts enjoined or forbidden are specially determined or assigned.

But if you command him *simply* to rise at that hour, or to rise at that hour *always*, or to rise at that hour *till further orders*, it may be said, with propriety, that you lay down a *rule* for the guidance of your servant's conduct. For no specific act is assigned by the command, but the command obliges him generally to acts of a determined class.

If a regiment be ordered to attack or defend a post, or to quell a riot, or to march from their present quarters, the command is occasional or particular. But an order to exercise daily till further orders shall be given would be called a *general* order, and *might* be called a *rule*.

If Parliament prohibited simply the exportation of corn, either for a given period or indefinitely, it would establish a law or rule: a *kind* or *sort* of acts being determined by the command, and acts of that kind or sort being *generally* forbidden. But an order issued by Parliament to meet an impending scarcity, and stopping the exportation of corn *then shipped and in port,* would not be a law or rule, though issued by the sovereign legislature. The order regarding exclusively a specified quantity of corn, the negative acts or forbearances, enjoined by the command, would be determined specifically or individually by the determinate nature of their subject.

As issued by a sovereign legislature, and as wearing the form of a law, the order which I have now imagined would probably be *called* a law. And hence the difficulty of drawing a distinct boundary between laws and occasional commands.

Again: An act which is not an offence, according to the existing law, moves the sovereign to displeasure: and, though the authors of the act are legally innocent or unoffending, the sovereign commands that they shall be punished. As enjoining a specific punishment in that specific case, and as not enjoining generally acts or forbearances of a class, the order uttered by the sovereign is not a law or rule.

Whether such an order would be *called* a law, seems to depend upon circumstances which are purely immaterial: immaterial, that is, with reference to the present purpose, though material with reference to others. If made by a sovereign assembly deliberately, and with the forms of legislation, it would probably be called a law. If uttered by an absolute monarch, without deliberation or ceremony, it would scarcely be confounded with acts of legislation, and would be styled an arbitrary command. Yet, on either of these suppositions, its nature would be the same. It would not be a law or rule, but an occasional or particular command of the sovereign One or Number.

To conclude with an example which best illustrates the distinction, and which shows the importance of the distinction most conspicuously, *judicial commands* are commonly occasional or particular, although the commands which they are calculated to enforce are commonly laws or rules.

For instance, the lawgiver commands that thieves shall be hanged. A specific theft and a specified thief being given, the judge commands that the thief shall be hanged, agreeably to the command of the lawgiver.

Now the lawgiver determines a class or description of acts; prohibits acts of the class generally and indefinitely; and commands, with the like generality, that punishment shall follow transgression. The command of the lawgiver is, therefore, a law or rule. But the command of the judge is occasional or particular. For he orders a specific punishment, as the consequence of a specific offence.

According to the line of separation which I have now attempted to describe, a law and a particular command are distinguished thus:—Acts or forbearances of a *class* are enjoined *generally* by the former. Acts *determined specifically* are enjoined or forbidden by the latter.

A different line of separation has been drawn by Blackstone and others. According to Blackstone and others, a law and a particular command are distinguished in the following manner: —A law obliges *generally* the members of the given community, or a law obliges *generally* persons of a given class. A particular command obliges a *single* person, or persons whom it determines *individually.*

That laws and particular commands are not to be distinguished thus, will appear on a moment's reflection.

For, *first,* commands which oblige generally the members of the given community, or commands which oblige generally persons of given classes, are not always laws or rules.

Thus, in the case already supposed; that in which the sovereign commands that all corn actually shipped for exportation be stopped and detained; the command is obligatory upon the whole community, but as it obliges them only to a set of acts individually assigned, it is not a law. Again, suppose the sovereign to issue an order, enforced by penalties, for a general mourning, on occasion of a public calamity. Now, though it is addressed to the community at large, the order is scarcely a rule, in the usual acceptation of the term. For, though it obliges generally the members of the entire community, it obliges to acts which it assigns specifically, instead of obliging generally to acts or forbearances of a class. If the sovereign commanded that *black* should be the dress of his subjects, his command would amount to a law. But if he commanded them to wear it on a specified occasion, his command would be merely particular.

And, *secondly,* a command which obliges exclusively persons individually determined, may amount, notwithstanding, to a law or a rule.

For example, A father may set a *rule* to his child or children: a guardian, to his ward: a master, to his slave or servant. And certain of God's *laws* were as binding on the first man, as they are binding at this hour on the millions who have sprung from his loins.

Most, indeed, of the laws which are established by political superiors, or most of the laws which are simply and strictly so called, oblige generally the members of the political community, or oblige generally persons of a class. To frame a system of duties for every individual of the community, were simply impossible: and if it were possible, it were utterly useless. Most of the laws established by political superiors are, therefore, *general* in a twofold manner: as enjoining or forbidding generally acts of kinds or sorts; and as binding the whole community, or, at least, whole classes of its members.

But if we suppose that Parliament creates and grants an office, and that Parliament binds the grantee to services of a given description, we suppose a law established by political superiors, and yet exclusively binding a specified or determinate person.

Laws established by political superiors, and exclusively binding specified or determinate persons, are styled, in the language of the Roman jurists, *privilegia.* Though that, indeed, is a name which will hardly denote them distinctly: for, like most of the leading terms in actual systems of law, it is not the name of a definite class of objects, but a heap of heterogeneous objects.[1]

It appears, from what has been premised, that a law, properly so called, may be defined in the following manner.

A law is a command which obliges a person or persons.

But, as contradistinguished or opposed to an occasional or particular command, a law is a command which obliges a person or persons, and obliges *generally* to acts or forbearances of a class.

In language more popular but less distinct and precise, a law is a command which obliges a person or persons to a *course* of conduct.

Laws and other commands are said to proceed from *superiors,* and to bind or oblige *inferiors.* I will, therefore, analyse the meaning of those correlative expressions; and will try to strip them of a certain mystery, by which that simple meaning appears to be obscured.

Superiority is often synonymous with *precedence* or *excellence.* We talk of superiors in rank; of superiors in wealth; of superiors in virtue: comparing certain persons with certain other persons; and meaning that the former precede or excel the latter in rank, in wealth, or in virtue.

But, taken with the meaning wherein I here understand it, the term *superiority* signifies *might:* the power of affecting others with evil or pain, and of forcing them, through fear of that evil, to fashion their conduct to one's wishes.

For example, God is emphatically the *superior* of Man. For his power of affecting us with pain, and of forcing us to comply with his will, is unbounded and resistless.

To a limited extent, the sovereign One or Number is the superior of the subject or citizen: the master, of the slave or servant: the father, of the child.

In short, whoever can *oblige* another to comply with his wishes, is the *superior* of that other, so far as the ability reaches: The party who is obnoxious to the impending evil, being, to that same extent, the *inferior.*

The might or superiority of God, is simple or absolute. But in all or most cases of human superiority, the relation of superior and inferior, and the relation of inferior and superior, are reciprocal. Or (changing the expression) the party who is the superior as viewed from one aspect, is the inferior as viewed from another.

For example, To an indefinite, though limited extent, the monarch is the superior of the governed: his power being commonly sufficient to enforce compliance with his will. But the governed, collectively or in mass, are also the superior of the monarch: who is checked in the abuse of his might by his fear of exciting their anger; and of rousing to active resistance the might which slumbers in the multitude.

A member of a sovereign assembly is the superior of the judge: the judge being bound by the law which proceeds from that sovereign body. But, in his character of citizen or subject, he is the inferior of the judge: the judge being the minister of the law, and armed with the power of enforcing it.

It appears, then, that the term *superiority* (like the terms *duty* and *sanction*) is implied by the term *command*. For superiority is the power of enforcing compliance with a wish: and the expression or intimation of a wish, with the power and the purpose of enforcing it, are the constituent elements of a command.

('That *laws* emanate from *superiors*' is, therefore, an identical proposition.) For the meaning which it affects to impart is contained in its subject.

If I mark the peculiar source of a given law, or if I mark the peculiar source of laws of a given class, it is possible that I am saying something which may instruct the hearer. But to affirm of laws universally 'that they flow from *superiors*', or to affirm of laws universally 'that *inferiors* are bound to obey them,' is the merest tautology and trifling.

Like most of the leading terms in the sciences of jurisprudence and morals, the term *laws* is extremely ambiguous. Taken with the largest signification which can be given to the term properly, *laws* are a species of *commands*. But the term is improperly applied to various objects which have nothing of the imperative character: to objects which are *not* commands; and which, therefore, are *not* laws, properly so called.

Accordingly, the proposition 'that laws are commands' must be taken with limitations. Or, rather, we must distinguish the various meanings of the term *laws;* and must restrict the proposition to that class of objects which is embraced by the largest signification that can be given to the term properly.

I have already indicated, and shall hereafter more fully describe, the objects improperly termed laws, which are *not* within the province of jurisprudence (being either rules enforced by opinion and closely analogous to laws properly so called, or being laws so called by a metaphorical application of the term merely). There are other objects improperly termed laws (not being commands) which yet may properly be included within the province of jurisprudence. These I shall endeavour to particularise:—

1. Acts on the part of legislatures to *explain* positive law, can scarcely be called laws, in the proper signification of the term. Working no change in the actual duties of the governed, but simply declaring what those duties *are,* they properly are acts of *interpretation* by legislative authority. Or, to borrow an expression from the writers on the Roman Law, they are acts of *authentic* interpretation.

But, this notwithstanding, they are frequently styled laws; *declaratory* laws, or declaratory statutes. They must, therefore, be noted as forming an exception to the proposition 'that laws are a species of commands.'

It often, indeed, happens (as I shall show in the proper place), that laws declaratory in name are imperative in effect: Legislative, like judicial interpretation, being frequently deceptive; and establishing new law, under guise of expounding the old.

2. Laws to repeal laws, and to release from existing duties, must also be excepted from the proposition 'that laws are a species of commands.' In so far as they release from duties imposed by existing laws, they are not commands, but revocations of commands. They authorize or permit the parties, to whom the repeal extends, to do or to forbear from acts which they were commanded to forbear from or to do. And, considered with regard to *this,* their immediate or direct purpose, they are often named *permissive laws,* or, more briefly and more properly, *permissions.*

Remotely and indirectly, indeed, permissive laws are often or always imperative. For the parties released from duties are restored to liberties or rights: and duties answering those rights are, therefore, created or revived.

But this is a matter which I shall examine with exactness, when I analyse the expressions 'legal right', 'permission by the sovereign or state', and 'civil or political liberty'.

3. Imperfect laws, or laws of imperfect obligation, must also be excepted from the proposition 'that laws are a species of commands'.

An imperfect law (with the sense wherein the term is used by the Roman jurists) is a law which wants a sanction, and which, therefore, is not binding. A law declaring that certain acts are crimes, but annexing no punishment to the commission of acts of the class, is the simplest and most obvious example.

Though the author of an imperfect law signifies a desire, he manifests no purpose of enforcing compliance with the desire. But where there is not a purpose of enforcing compliance with the desire, the expression of a desire is not a command. Consequently, an imperfect law is not so properly a law, as counsel, or exhortation, addressed by a superior to inferiors.

Examples of imperfect laws are cited by the Roman jurists. But with us in England, laws professedly imperative are always (I believe) perfect or obligatory. Where the English legislature affects to command, the English tribunals not unreasonably presume that the legislature exacts obedience. And, if no specific sanction be annexed to a given law, a sanction is supplied by the courts of justice, agreeably to a general maxim which obtains in cases of the kind.

The imperfect laws, of which I am now speaking, are laws which are imperfect, in the sense of *the Roman jurists:* that is to say, laws which speak the desires of political superiors, but which their authors (by oversight or design) have not provided with sanctions. Many of the writers on *morals,* and on the so called *law of nature,* have annexed a different meaning to the term *imperfect.* Speaking of imperfect obligations, they commonly mean duties which are *not legal:* duties imposed by commands of God, or duties imposed by positive morality, as contradistinguished to duties imposed by positive law. An imperfect obligation, in the sense of the Roman jurists, is exactly equivalent to no obligation at all. For the term *imperfect* denotes simply, that the law wants the sanction appropriate to laws of the kind. An imperfect obligation, in the other meaning of the expression, is a religious or a moral obligation. The term *imperfect* does not denote that the law imposing the duty wants the appropriate sanction. It denotes that the law imposing the duty is *not* a law established by a political superior: that it wants that *perfect,* or that surer or more cogent sanction, which is imparted by the sovereign or state.

I believe that I have now reviewed all the classes of objects, to which the term *laws* is improperly applied. The laws (improperly so called) which I have here lastly enumerated, are (I think) the only laws which are not commands, and which yet may be properly included within the province of jurisprudence. But though these, with the so called laws set by opinion and the objects metaphorically termed laws, are the only laws which *really* are not commands, there are certain laws (properly so called) which may *seem* not imperative. Accordingly, I will subjoin a few remarks upon laws of this dubious character.

1. There are laws, it may be said, which *merely* create *rights:* And, seeing that every command imposes a *duty,* laws of this nature are not imperative.

But, as I have intimated already, and shall show completely hereafter, there are no laws *merely* creating *rights.* There are laws, it is true, which *merely* create *duties:* duties not correlating with correlating rights, and which, therefore may be styled *absolute.* But every law, really conferring a right, imposes expressly or tacitly a *relative* duty, or a duty correlating with the right. If it specify the remedy to be given, in case the right shall be infringed, it imposes the relative duty expressly. If the remedy to be given be not specified, it refers tacitly to pre-existing law, and clothes the right which it purports to create with a remedy provided by that law. Every law, really conferring a right, is, therefore, imperative: as imperative, as if its only purpose were the creation of a duty, or as if the relative duty, which it inevitably imposes, were merely absolute.

The meanings of the term *right,* are various and perplexed; taken with its proper meaning, it comprises ideas which are numerous and complicated; and the searching and extensive analysis, which the term, therefore, requires, would occupy more room than could be given to it in the present lecture. It is not, however, necessary, that the analysis should be performed here. I purpose, in my earlier lectures, to determine the province of jurisprudence; or to distinguish the laws established by political superiors, from the various laws, proper and improper, with which they are frequently confounded. And this I may accomplish exactly enough, without a nice inquiry into the import of the term *right.*

2. According to an opinion which I must notice *incidentally* here, though the subject to which it relates will be treated *directly* hereafter, *customary laws* must be excepted from the proposition 'that laws are a species of command.'

By many of the admirers of customary laws (and, especially, of their German admirers), they are thought to oblige legally (independently of the sovereign or state), *because* the citizens or subjects have observed or kept them. Agreeably to this opinion, they are not the *creatures* of the sovereign or state, although the sovereign or state may abolish them at pleasure. Agreeably to this opinion, they are positive law (or law, strictly so called), inasmuch as they are enforced by the courts of justice: But, that notwithstanding, they exist as *positive law* by the spontaneous adoption of the governed, and not by position or establishment on the part of political superiors. Consequently, customary laws, considered as positive law, are not commands. And, consequently, customary laws, considered as positive law, are not laws or rules properly so called.

An opinion less mysterious, but somewhat allied to this, is not uncommonly held by the adverse party: by the party which is strongly opposed to customary law; and to all law made judicially, or in the way of judicial legislation. According to the latter opinion, all judge-made law, or all judge-made law established by *subject* judges, is purely the creature of the judges by whom it is established immediately. To impute it to the sovereign legislature, or to suppose that it speaks the will of the sovereign legislature, is one of the foolish or knavish *fictions* with which lawyers, in every age and nation, have perplexed and darkened the simplest and clearest truths.

I think it will appear, on a moment's reflection, that each of these opinions is groundless: that customary law is *imperative,* in the proper signification of the term; and that all judge-made law is the creature of the sovereign or state.

At its origin, a custom is a rule of conduct which the governed observe spontaneously, or not in pursuance of a law set by a political superior. The custom is transmuted into positive law, when it is adopted as such by the courts of justice, and when the judicial decisions fashioned upon it are enforced by the power of the state. But before it is adopted by the courts, and clothed with the legal sanction, it is merely a rule of positive morality: a rule generally observed by the citizens or subjects; but deriving the only force, which it can be said to possess, from the general disapprobation falling on those who transgress it.

Now when judges transmute a custom into a legal rule (or make a legal rule not suggested by a custom), the legal rule which they establish is established by the sovereign legislature. A subordinate or subject judge is merely a minister. The portion of the sovereign power which lies at his disposition is merely delegated. The rules which he makes derive their legal force from authority given by the state: an authority which the state may confer expressly, but which it commonly imparts in the way of acquiescence. For, since the state may reverse the rules which he makes, and yet permits him to enforce them by the power of the political community, its sovereign will 'that his rules shall obtain as law' is clearly evinced by its conduct, though not by its express declaration.

The admirers of customary law love to trick out their idol with mysterious and imposing attributes. But to those who can see the difference between positive law and morality, there is nothing of mystery about it. Considered as rules of positive morality, customary laws arise from the consent of the governed, and not from the position or establishment of political superiors. But, considered as moral rules turned into positive laws, customary laws are established by the state: established by the state directly, when the customs are promulgated in its statutes; established by the state circuitously, when the customs are adopted by its tribunals.

The opinion of the party which abhors judge-made laws, springs from their inadequate conception of the nature of commands.

Like other significations of desire, a command is express or tacit. If the desire be signified by *words* (written or spoken), the command is express. If the desire be signified by conduct (or by any signs of desire which are *not* words), the command is tacit.

Now when customs are turned into legal rules by decisions of subject judges, the legal rules which emerge from the customs are *tacit* commands of the sovereign legislature. The state, which is able to abolish, permits its ministers to enforce them: and it, therefore, signifies its pleasure, by that its voluntary acquiescence, 'that they shall serve as a law to the governed.'

My present purpose is merely this: to prove that the positive law styled *customary* (and all positive law made judicially) is established by the state directly or circuitously, and, therefore, is *imperative.* I am far from disputing, that law made judicially (or in the way of improper legislation) and law made by statute (or in the properly legislative manner) are distinguished by weighty differences. I shall inquire, in future lectures, what those differences are; and why subject judges, who are properly ministers of the law, have commonly shared with the sovereign in the business of making it.

I assume, then, that the only laws which are not imperative, and which belong to the subject-matter of jurisprudence, are the following:—1. Declaratory laws, or laws explaining the import of existing positive law. 2. Laws abrogating or repealing existing positive law. 3. Imperfect laws, or laws of imperfect obligation (with the sense wherein the expression is used by the Roman jurists).

But the space occupied in the science by these improper laws is comparatively narrow and insignificant. Accordingly, although I shall take them into account so often as I refer to them directly, I shall throw them out of account on other occasions. Or (changing the expression) I shall limit the term *law* to laws which are imperative, unless I extend it expressly to laws which are not.

3 non-imp laws

LECTURE VI

. . . The superiority which is styled sovereignty, and the independent political society which sovereignty implies, is distinguished from other superiority, and from other society, by the following marks or characters:—1. The *bulk* of the given society are in a *habit* of obedience or submission to a *determinate* and *common* superior: let that common superior be a certain individual person or a certain body or aggregate of individual persons. 2. That certain individual, or that certain body of individuals, is *not* in a habit of obedience to a determinate human superior. Laws (improperly so called) which opinion sets or imposes, may permanently affect the conduct of that certain individual or body. To express or tacit commands of other determinate parties, that certain individual or body may yield occasional submission. But there is no determinate person, or determinate aggregate of persons, to whose commands, express or tacit, that certain individual or body renders habitual obedience.

Or the notions of sovereignty and independent political society may be expressed concisely thus. —If a *determinate* human superior, *not* in a habit of obedience to a like superior, receive *habitual* obedience from the *bulk* of a given society, that determinate superior is sovereign in that society, and the society (including the superior) is a society political and independent.

To that determinate superior, the other members of the society are *subject:* or on that determinate superior, to other members of the society are *dependent.* The position of its other members towards that determinate superior, is *a state of subjection,* or *a state of dependence.* The mutual relation which subsists between that superior and them, may be styled *the relation of sovereign and subject,* or *the relation of sovereignty and subjection.*

Hence it follows, that it is only through an ellipsis, or an abridged form of expression, that the *society* is styled *independent.* The party truly independent (independent, that is to say, of a determinate human superior), is not the society, but the sovereign portion of the society: that certain member of the society, or that certain body of its members, to whose commands, expressed or intimated, the generality or bulk of its members render habitual obedience. Upon that certain person, or certain body of persons, the other members of the society are *dependent:* or to that certain person, or certain body of persons, the other

members of the society are *subject.* By 'an independent political society,' or 'an independent and sovereign nation,' we mean a political society consisting of a sovereign and subjects, as opposed to a political society which is merely subordinate: that is to say, which is merely a limb or member of another political society, and which therefore consists entirely of persons in a state of subjection.

In order that a given society may form a society political and independent, the two distinguishing marks which I have mentioned above must unite. The *generality* of the given society must be in the *habit* of obedience to a *determinate* and *common* superior: whilst that determinate persons, or determinate body of persons must *not* be habitually obedient to a determinate person or body. It is the union of that positive, with this negative mark, which renders that given society (including that certain superior) a society political and independent.

To show that the union of those marks renders a given society a society political and independent, I call your attention to the following positions and examples.

1. In order that a given society may form a society political, the generality or bulk of its members must be in a *habit* of obedience to a determinate and common superior.

In case the generality of its members obey a determinate superior, but the obedience be rare or transient and not habitual or permanent, the relation of sovereignty and subjection is not created thereby between that certain superior and the members of that given society. In other words, that determinate superior and the members of that given society do not become thereby an independent political society. Whether that given society be political and independent or not, it is not an independent political society whereof that certain superior is the sovereign portion.

For example: In 1815 the allied armies occupied France; and so long as the allied armies occupied France, the commands of the allied sovereigns were obeyed by the French government, and, through the French government, by the French people generally. But since the commands and the obedience were comparatively rare and transient, they were not sufficient to constitute the relation of sovereignty and subjection between the allied sovereigns and the members of the invaded nation. In spite of those commands, and in spite of that obedience, the French government was sovereign or independent. Or in spite of those commands, and in spite of that obedience, the French government and its subjects were an independent political society whereof the allied sovereigns were not the sovereign portion.

Now if the French nation, before the obedience to those sovereigns, had been an independent society in a state of nature or anarchy, it would not have been changed by the obedience into a society political. And it would not have been changed by the obedience into a society political, because the obedience was not habitual. For, inasmuch as the obedience was not habitual, it was not changed by the obedience from a society political and independent, into a society political but subordinate. —A given society, therefore, is not a society political, unless the generality of its members be in a *habit* of obedience to a determinate and common superior.

Again: A feeble state holds its independence precariously, or at the will of the powerful states to whose aggressions it is obnoxious. And since it is obnoxious to their aggressions, it and the bulk of its subjects render obedience to commands which they occasionally express or intimate. Such, for instance, is the position of the Saxon government and its subjects in respect of the conspiring sovereigns who form the Holy Alliance. But since the commands and the obedience are comparatively few and rare, they are not sufficient to constitute the relation of sovereignty and subjection between the powerful states and the feeble state with its subjects. In spite of those commands, and in spite of that obedience, the feeble state is sovereign or independent. Or in spite of those commands, and in spite of that obedience, the feeble state and its subjects are an independent political society whereof the powerful states are not the sovereign portion. Although the powerful states are permanently *superior,* and although the feeble state is permanently *inferior,* there is neither a *habit* of command on the part of the former, nor a *habit* of obedience on the part of the latter. Although the latter is unable to defend and maintain its independence, the latter is independent of the former in fact or practice.

From the example now adduced, as from the example adduced before, we may draw the following inference: that a given society is not a society political, unless the generality of its members be in a *habit* of obedience to a determinate and common superior.—By the obedience to the powerful states, the feeble state and its subjects are not changed from an independent, into a sub-

ordinate political society. And they are not changed by the obedience into a subordinate political society, because the obedience is not habitual. Consequently, if they were a natural society (setting that obedience aside), they would not be changed by that obedience into a society political.

2. In order that a given society may form a society political, habitual obedience must be rendered, by the *generality* or *bulk* of its members, to a determinate and *common* superior. In other words, habitual obedience must be rendered, by the *generality* or *bulk* of its members, to *one and the same* determinate person, or determinate body of persons.

Unless habitual obedience be rendered by the *bulk* of its members, and be rendered by the bulk of its members to *one and the same* superior, the given society is either in a state of nature, or is split into two or more independent political societies.

For example: In case a given society be torn by intestine war, and in case the conflicting parties be nearly balanced, the given society is in one of the two positions which I have now supposed.— As there is no common superior to which the bulk of its members render habitual obedience, it is not a political society single or undivided.—If the bulk of each of the parties be in a habit of obedience to its head, the given society is broken into two or more societies, which, perhaps, may be styled independent political societies.—If the bulk of each of the parties be not in that habit of obedience, the given society is simply or absolutely in a state of nature or anarchy. It is either resolved or broken into its individual elements, or into numerous societies of an extremely limited size: of a size so extremely limited, that they could hardly be styled societies independent and *political.* For, as I shall show hereafter, a given independent society would hardly be styled *political,* in case it fell short of a *number* which cannot be fixed with precision, but which may be called considerable, or not extremely minute.

3. In order that a given society may form a society political, the generality or bulk of its members must habitually obey a superior *determinate* as well as common.

On this position I shall not insist here. For I have shown sufficiently in my fifth lecture, that no indeterminate party can command expressly or tacitly, or can receive obedience or submission: that no indeterminate body is capable of corporate conduct, or is capable, as a body, of positive or negative deportment.

4. It appears from what has preceded, that, in order that a given society may form a society political, the bulk of its members must be in a habit of obedience to a certain and common superior. But, in order that the given society may form a society political and independent, that certain superior must *not* be habitually obedient to a determinate human superior.

The given society may form a society political and independent, although that certain superior be habitually affected by laws which opinion sets or imposes. The given society may form a society political and independent, although that certain superior render occasional submission to commands of determinate parties. But the society is not independent, although it may be political, in case that certain superior habitually obey the commands of a certain person or body.

Let us suppose, for example, that a viceroy obeys habitually the author of his delegated powers. And, to render the example complete, let us suppose that the viceroy receives habitual obedience from the generality or bulk of the persons who inhabit his province.—Now though he commands habitually within the limits of his province, and receives habitual obedience from the generality or bulk of its inhabitants, the viceroy is not sovereign within the limits of his province, nor are he and its inhabitants an independent political society. The viceroy, and (through the viceroy) the generality or bulk of its inhabitants, are habitually obedient or submissive to the sovereign of a larger society. He and the inhabitants of his province are therefore in a state of subjection to the sovereign of that larger society. He and the inhabitants of his province are a society political but subordinate, or form a political society which is merely a limb of another.

NOTE

1. Where a *privilegium* merely imposes a duty, it exclusively obliges a determinate person or persons. But where a *privilegium* confers a right, and the right conferred *avails against the world at large,* the law is *privilegium* as viewed from a certain aspect, but is also *a general law* as viewed from another aspect. In respect of the right conferred, the law exclusively regards a determinate person, and, therefore, is *privilegium.* In respect of the duty imposed, and corresponding to the right conferred, the law regards generally the members of the entire community.

This I shall explain particularly at a subsequent point of my Course, when I consider the peculiar nature of so-called *privilegia,* or of so-called *private laws.*

O. W. HOLMES, JR.

The Path of the Law*

When we study law we are not studying a mystery but a well known profession. We are studying what we shall want in order to appear before judges, or to advise people in such a way as to keep them out of court. The reason why it is a profession, why people will pay lawyers to argue for them or to advise them is that in societies like ours the command of the public force is intrusted to the judges in certain cases, and the whole power of the state will be put forth, if necessary, to carry out their judgments and decrees. People want to know under what circumstances and how far they will run the risk of coming against what is so much stronger than themselves, and hence it becomes a business to find out when this danger is to be feared. The object of our study, then, is prediction, the prediction of the incidence of the public force through the instrumentality of the courts.

The means of the study are a body of reports, of treatises, and of statutes, in this country and in England, extending back for six hundred years, and now increasing annually by hundreds. In these sibylline leaves are gathered the scattered prophecies of the past upon the cases in which the axe will fall. These are what properly have been called the oracles of the law. Far the most important and pretty nearly the whole meaning of every new effort of legal thought is to make these prophecies more precise, and to generalize them into a thoroughly connected system. The process is one, from a lawyer's statement of a case, eliminating as it does all the dramatic elements with which his client's story has clothed it, and retaining only the facts of legal import, up to the final analyses and abstract universals of theoretic jurisprudence. The reason why a lawyer does not mention that his client wore a white hat when he made a contract, while Mrs. Quickly would be sure to dwell upon it along with the parcel gilt goblet and the sea-coal fire, is that he forsees that the public force will act in the same way whatever his client had upon his head. It is to make the prophecies easier to be remembered and to be understood that the teachings of the decisions of the past are put into general propositions and gathered into text-books, or that statutes are passed in a general form. The primary rights and duties with which jurisprudence busies itself again are nothing but prophecies. One of the many evil effects of the confusion between legal and moral ideas, about which I shall have something to say in a moment, is that theory is apt to get the cart before the horse, and to consider the right or the duty as something existing apart from and independent of the consequences of its breach, to which certain sanctions are added afterward. But, as I shall try to show, a legal duty so called is nothing but a prediction that if a man does or omits certain things he will be made to suffer in this or that way by judgment of the court;—and so of a legal right.

The number of our predictions when generalized and reduced to a system is not unmanageably large. They present themselves as a finite body of dogma which may be mastered within a reasonable time. It is a great mistake to be frightened by the ever increasing number of reports. The reports of a given jurisdiction in the course of a generation take up pretty much the whole body of the law, and restate it from the present point of view. We could reconstruct the corpus from them if all that went before were burned. The use of the earlier reports is mainly historical, a use about which I shall have something to say before I have finished.

I wish, if I can, to lay down some first principles for the study of this body of dogma or systematized prediction which we call the law, for men who want to use it as the instrument of their business to enable them to prophesy in their turn, and, as bearing upon the study, I wish to point out an ideal which as yet our law has not attained.

The first thing for a business-like understanding of the matter is to understand its limits, and therefore I think it desirable at once to

*Oliver Wendell Holmes, "The Path of the Law," *Harvard Law Review*, Vol. 10 (1897), pp. 457–68.

point out and dispel a confusion between morality and law, which sometimes rises to the height of conscious theory, and more often and indeed constantly is making trouble in detail without reaching the point of consciousness. You can see very plainly that a bad man has as much reason as a good one for wishing to avoid an encounter with the public force, and therefore you can see the practical importance of the distinction between morality and law. A man who cares nothing for an ethical rule which is believed and practised by his neighbors is likely nevertheless to care a good deal to avoid being made to pay money, and will want to keep out of jail if he can.

I take it for granted that no hearer of mine will misinterpret what I have to say as the language of cynicism. The law is the witness and external deposit of our moral life. Its history is the history of the moral development of the race. The practice of it, in spite of popular jests, tends to make good citizens and good men. When I emphasize the difference between law and morals I do so with reference to a single end, that of learning and understanding the law. For that purpose you must definitely master its specific marks, and it is for that that I ask you for the moment to imagine yourselves indifferent to other and greater things.

I do not say that there is not a wider point of view from which the distinction between law and morals becomes of secondary or no importance, as all mathematical distinctions vanish in presence of the infinite. But I do say that that distinction is of the first importance for the object which we are here to consider,—a right study and mastery of the law as a business with well understood limits, a body of dogma enclosed within definite lines. I have just shown the practical reason for saying so. If you want to know the law and nothing else, you must look at it as a bad man, who cares only for the material consequences which such knowledge enables him to predict, not as a good one, who finds his reasons for conduct, whether inside the law or outside of it, in the vaguer sanctions of conscience. The theoretical importance of the distinction is no less, if you would reason on your subject aright. The law is full of phraseology drawn from morals, and by the mere force of language continually invites us to pass from one domain to the other without perceiving it, as we are sure to do unless we have the boundary constantly before our minds. The law talks about rights, and duties, and malice,

and intent, and negligence, and so forth, and nothing is easier, or, I may say, more common in legal reasoning, than to take these words in their moral sense, at some stage of the argument, and so to drop into fallacy. For instance, when we speak of the rights of man in a moral sense, we mean to mark the limits of interference with individual freedom which we think are prescribed by conscience, or by our ideal, however reached. Yet it is certain that many laws have been enforced in the past, and it is likley that some are enforced now, which are condemned by the most enlightened opinion of the time, or which at all events pass the limit of interference as many consciences would draw it. Manifestly, therefore, nothing but confusion of thought can result from assuming that the rights of man in a moral sense are equally rights in the sense of the Constitution and the law. No doubt simple and extreme cases can be put of imaginable laws which the statute-making power would not dare to enact, even in the absence of written constitutional prohibitions, because the community would rise in rebellion and fight; and this gives some plausibility to the proposition that the law, if not a part of morality, is limited by it. But this limit of power is not coextensive with any system of morals. For the most part it falls far within the lines of any such system, and in some cases may extend beyond them, for reasons drawn from the habits of a particular people at a particular time. I once heard the late Professor Agassiz say that a German population would rise if you added two cents to the price of a glass of beer. A statute in such a case would be empty words, not because it was wrong, but because it could not be enforced. No one will deny that wrong statutes can be and are enforced, and we should not all agree as to which were the wrong ones.

The confusion with which I am dealing besets confessedly legal conceptions. Take the fundamental question, What constitutes the law? You will find some text writers telling you that it is something different from what is decided by the courts of Massachusetts or England, that it is a system of reason, that it is a deduction from principles of ethics or admitted axioms or what not, which may or may not coincide with the decisions. But if we take the view of our friend the bad man we shall find that he does not care two straws for the axioms or deductions, but that he does want to know what the Massachusetts or English courts are likely to do in fact. I am much of his mind. The prophecies of what the courts will do in fact, and nothing more pretentious, are what I mean by the law.

Take again a notion which as popularly understood is the widest conception which the law contains;—the notion of legal duty, to which already I have referred. We fill the word with all the content which we draw from morals. But what does it mean to a bad man? Mainly, and in the first place, a prophecy that if he does certain things he will be subjected to disagreeable consequences by way of imprisonment or compulsory payment of money. But from his point of view, what is the difference between being fined and being taxed a certain sum for doing a certain thing? That his point of view is the test of legal principles is shown by the many discussions which have arisen in the courts on the very question whether a given statutory liability is a penalty or a tax. On the answer to this question depends the decision whether conduct is legally wrong or right, and also whether a man is under compulsion or free. Leaving the criminal law on one side, what is the difference between the liability under the mill acts or statutes authorizing a taking by eminent domain and the liability for what we call a wrongful conversion of property where restoration is out of the question? In both cases the party taking another man's property has to pay its fair value as assessed by a jury, and no more. What significance is there in calling one taking right and another wrong from the point of view of the law? It does not matter, so far as the given consequence, the compulsory payment, is concerned, whether the act to which it is attached is described in terms of praise or in terms of blame, or whether the law porports to prohibit it or allow it. If it matters at all, still speaking from the bad man's point of view, it must be because in one case and not in the other some further disadvantages, or at least some further consequences, are attached to the act by the law. The only other disadvantages thus attached to it which I ever have been able to think of are to be found in two somewhat insignificant legal doctrines, both of which might be abolished without much disturbance. One is, that a contract to do a prohibited act is unlawful, and the other, that, if one of two or more joint wrongdoers has to pay all the damages, he cannot recover contribution from his fellows. And that I believe is all. You see how the vague circumference of the notion of duty shrinks and at the same time grows more precise when we wash it with cynical acid and expel everything except the object of our study, the operations of the law.

Nowhere is the confusion between legal and moral ideas more manifest than in the law of contract. Among other things, here again the so called primary rights and duties are invested with a mystic significance beyond what can be assigned and explained. The duty to keep a contract at common law means a prediction that you must pay damages if you do not keep it,—and nothing else. If you commit a tort, you are liable to pay a compensatory sum. If you commit a contract, you are liable to pay a conpensatory sum unless the promised event comes to pass, and that is all the difference. But such a mode of looking at the matter stinks in the nostrils of those who think it advantageous to get as much ethics into the law as they can. It was good enough for Lord Coke, however, and here, as in many other cases, I am content to abide with him. In Bromage *v.* Genning,[1] a prohibition was sought in the King's Bench against a suit in the marches of Wales for the specific performance of a covenant to grant a lease, and Coke said that it would subvert the intention of the covenantor, since he intends it to be at his election either to lose the damages or to make the lease. Sergeant Harris for the plaintiff confessed that he moved the matter against his conscience, and a prohibition was granted. This goes further than we should go now, but it shows what I venture to say has been the common law point of view from the beginning, although Mr. Harriman, in his very able little book upon Contracts has been misled, as I humbly think, to a different conclusion.

I have spoken only of the common law, because there are some cases in which a logical justification can be found for speaking of civil liabilities as imposing duties in an intelligible sense. These are the relatively few in which equity will grant an injunction, and will enforce it by putting the defendant in prison or otherwise punishing him unless he complies with the order of the court. But I hardly think it advisable to shape general theory from the exception, and I think it would be better to cease troubling ourselves about primary rights and sanctions altogether, than to describe our prophecies concerning the liabilities commonly imposed by the law in those inappropriate terms.

I mentioned, as other examples of the use by the law of words drawn from morals, malice, intent, and negligence. It is enough to take malice as it is used in the law of civil liability for wrongs,—what we lawyers call the law of torts,—to show you that it means something different in law from what it means in morals, and also to show how the difference has been obscured by giving to principles which have little or nothing to do with each other the same name. Three hundred years ago a parson preached a sermon and told a story out of Fox's Book of Martyrs of a man who had assisted at the torture of one of the saints, and afterward died, suffering compensatory inward torment. It happened that Fox was wrong. The man was alive and chanced to hear the sermon, and thereupon he sued the parson. Chief Justice Wray instructed the jury that the defendant was not liable, because the story was told innocently, without malice. He took malice in the moral sense, as importing a malevolent motive. But nowadays no one doubts that a man may be liable, without any malevolent motive at all, for false statements manifestly calculated to inflict temporal damage. In stating the case in pleading, we still should call the defendant's conduct malicious; but, in my opinion at least, the word means nothing about motives, or even about the defendant's attitude toward the future, but only signifies that the tendency of his conduct under the known circumstances was very plainly to cause the plaintiff temporal harm.[2]

In the law of contract the use of moral phraseology has led to equal confusion, as I have shown in part already, but only in part. Morals deal with the actual internal state of the individual's mind, what he actually intends. From the time of the Romans down to now, this mode of dealing has affected the language of the law as to contract, and the language used has reacted upon the thought. We talk about a contract as a meeting of the minds of the parties, and thence it is inferred in various cases that there is no contract because their minds have not met; that is, because they have intended different things or because one party has not known of the assent of the other. Yet nothing is more certain than that parties may be bound by a contract to things which neither of them intended, and when one does not know of the other's assent. Suppose a contract is executed in due form and in writing to deliver a lecture, mentioning no time. One of the parties thinks that the promise will be construed to mean at once, within a week. The other thinks that it means when he is ready. The court says that it means within a reasonable time. The parties are bound by the contract as it is interpreted by the court, yet neither of them meant what the court declares that they have said. In my opinion no one will understand the true theory of contract or be able even to discuss some fundamental questions intelligently until he has understood that all contracts are formal, that the making of a contract depends not on the agreement of two minds in one intention, but on the agreement of two sets of external signs,—not on the parties' having *meant* the same thing but on their having *said* the same thing. Furthermore, as the signs may be addressed to one sense or another,—to sight or to hearing,—on the nature of the sign will depend the moment when the contract is made. If the sign is tangible, for instance, a letter, the contract is made when the letter of acceptance is delivered. If it is necessary that the minds of the parties meet, there will be no contract until the acceptance can be read,—none, for example, if the acceptance be snatched from the hand of the offerer by a third person.

This is not the time to work out a theory in detail, or to answer many obvious doubts and questions which are suggested by these general views. I know of none which are not easy to answer, but what I am trying to do now is only by a series of hints to throw some light on the narrow path of legal doctrine, and upon two pitfalls which, as it seems to me, lie perilously near to it. Of the first of these I have said enough. I hope that my illustrations have shown the danger, both to speculation and to practice, of confounding morality with law, and the trap which legal language lays for us on that side of our way. For my own part, I often doubt whether it would not be a gain if every word of moral significance could be banished from the law altogether, and other words adopted which should convey legal ideas uncolored by anything outside the law. We should lose the fossil records of a good deal of history and the majesty got from ethical associations, but by ridding ourselves of an unnecessary confusion we should gain very much in the clearness of our thought.

So much for the limits of the law. The next thing which I wish to consider is what are the forces which determine its content and its growth. You may assume, with Hobbes and

Bentham and Austin, that all law emanates from the sovereign, even when the first human beings to enunciate it are the judges, or you may think that law is the voice of the Zeitgeist, or what you like. It is all one to my present purpose. Even if every decision required the sanction of an emperor with despotic power and a whimsical turn of mind, we should be interested none the less, still with a view to prediction, in discovering some order, some rational explanation, and some principle of growth for the rules which he laid down. In every system there are such explanations and principles to be found. It is with regard to them that a second fallacy comes in, which I think it important to expose.

The fallacy to which I refer is the notion that the only force at work in the development of the law is logic. In the broadest sense, indeed, that notion would be true. The postulate on which we think about the universe is that there is a fixed quantitative relation between every phenomenon and its antecedents and consequents. If there is such a thing as a phenomenon without these fixed quantitative relations, it is a miracle. It is outside the law of cause and effect, and as such transcends our power of thought, or at least is something to or from which we cannot reason. The condition of our thinking about the universe is that it is capable of being thought about rationally, or, in other words, that every part of it is effect and cause in the same sense in which those parts are with which we are most familiar. So in the broadest sense it is true that the law is a logical development, like everything else. The danger of which I speak is not the admission that the principles governing other phenomena also govern the law, but the notion that a given system, ours, for instance, can be worked out like mathematics from some general axioms of conduct. This is the natural error of the schools, but it is not confined to them. I once heard a very eminent judge say that he never let a decision go until he was absolutely sure that it was right. So judicial dissent often is blamed, as if it meant simply that one side or the other were not doing their sums right, and, if they would take more trouble, agreement inevitably would come.

This mode of thinking is entirely natural. The training of lawyers is a training in logic. The processes of analogy, discrimination, and deduction are those in which they are most at home. The language of judicial decision is mainly the language of logic. And the logical method and form flatter that longing for certainty and for repose which is in every human mind. But certainty generally is illusion, and repose is not the destiny of man. Behind the logical form lies a judgment as to the relative worth and importance of competing legislative grounds, often an inarticulate and unconscious judgment, it is true, and yet the very root and nerve of the whole proceeding. You can give any conclusion a logical form. You always can imply a condition in a contract. But why do you imply it? It is because of some belief as to the practice of the community or of a class, or because of some opinion as to policy, or, in short, because of some attitude of yours upon a matter not capable of exact quantitative measurement, and therefore not capable of founding exact logical conclusions. Such matters really are battle grounds where the means do not exist for determinations that shall be good for all time, and where the decision can do no more than embody the preference of a given body in a given time and place. We do not realize how large a part of our law is open to reconsideration upon a slight change in the habit of the public mind. No concrete proposition is self-evident, no matter how ready we may be to accept it, not even Mr. Herbert Spencer's Every man has a right to do what he wills, provided he interferes not with a like right on the part of his neighbors.

Why is a false and injurious statement privileged, if it is made honestly in giving information about a servant? It is because it has been thought more important that information should be given freely, than that a man should be protected from what under other circumstances would be an actionable wrong. Why is a man at liberty to set up a business which he knows will ruin his neighbor? It is because the public good is supposed to be best subserved by free competition. Obviously such judgments of relative importance may vary in different times and places. Why does a judge instruct a jury that an employer is not liable to an employee for an injury received in the course of his employment unless he is negligent, and why do the jury generally find for the plaintiff if the case is allowed to go to them? It is because the traditional policy of our law is to confine liability to cases where a prudent man might have foreseen the injury, or at least the danger, while the inclination of a very large part of the community is to make certain classes of persons insure the safety of those with whom they deal.

Since the last words were written, I have seen the requirement of such insurance put forth as part of the programme of one of the best known labor organizations. There is a concealed, half conscious battle on the question of legislative policy, and if any one thinks that it can be settled deductively, or once for all, I only can say that I think he is theoretically wrong, and that I am certain that his conclusion will not be accepted in practice *semper ubique et ab omnibus*.

Indeed, I think that even now our theory upon this matter is open to reconsideration, although I am not prepared to say how I should decide if a reconsideration were proposed. Our law of torts comes from the old days of isolated, ungeneralized wrongs, assaults, slanders, and the like, where the damages might be taken to lie where they fell by legal judgment. But the torts with which our courts are kept busy to-day are mainly the incidents of certain well known businesses. They are injuries to person or property by railroads, factories, and the like. The liability for them is estimated, and sooner or later goes into the price paid by the public. The public really pays the damages, and the question of liability, if pressed far enough, is really the question how far it is desirable that the public should insure the safety of those whose work it uses. It might be said that in such cases the chance of a jury finding for the defendant is merely a chance, once in a while rather arbitrarily interrupting the regular course of recovery, most likely in the case of an unusually conscientious plaintiff, and therefore better done away with. On the other hand, the economic value even of a life to the community can be estimated, and no recovery, it may be said, ought to go beyond that amount. It is conceivable that some day in certain cases we may find ourselves imitating, on a higher plane, the tariff for life and limb which we see in the Leges Barbarorum.

I think that the judges themselves have failed adequately to recognize their duty of weighing considerations of social advantage. The duty is inevitable, and the result of the often proclaimed judicial aversion to deal with such considerations is simply to leave the very ground and foundation of judgments inarticulate, and often unconscious, as I have said. When socialism first began to be talked about, the comfortable classes of the community were a good deal frightened. I suspect that this fear has influenced judicial action both here and in England, yet it is certain that it is not a conscious factor in the decisions to which I refer. I think that something similar has led people who no longer hope to control the legislatures to look to the courts as expounders of the Constitutions, and that in some courts new principles have been discovered outside the bodies of those instruments, which may be generalized into acceptance of the economic doctrines which prevailed about fifty years ago, and a wholesale prohibition of what a tribunal of lawyers does not think about right. I cannot but believe that if the training of lawyers led them habitually to consider more definitely and explicitly the social advantage on which the rule they lay down must be justified, they sometimes would hesitate where now they are confident, and see that really they were taking sides upon debatable and often burning questions.

NOTES

1. I Roll. Rep. 368.

2. See Hanson *v.* Globe Newspaper Co., 159 Mass. 293, 302.

JEROME FRANK

Legal Realism*

We have talked much of the law. But what is "the law"? A complete definition would be impossible and even a working definition would exhaust the patience of the reader. But it may not be amiss to inquire what, in a rough sense, the law means to the average man of our times when he consults his lawyer.

The Jones family owned the Blue & Gray Taxi Company, a corporation incorporated in Kentucky. That company made a contract with the A. & B. Railroad Company, also a Kentucky corporation, by which it was agreed that the Blue & Gray Taxi Company was to have the exclusive privilege of soliciting taxicab business on and adjacent to the railroad company's depot.

A rival taxicab company, owned by the Williams family, the Purple Taxi Company, began to ignore this contract; it solicited business and parked its taxicabs in places assigned by the railroad company to the Blue & Gray Company and sought in other ways to deprive the Blue & Gray Company of the benefits conferred on it by the agreement with the railroad.

The Jones family were angered; their profits derived from the Blue & Gray stock, which they owned, were threatened. They consulted their lawyer, a Louisville practitioner, and this, we may conjecture, is about what he told them: "I'm afraid your contract is not legally valid. I've examined several decisions of the highest court of Kentucky and they pretty clearly indicate that you can't get away with that kind of an agreement in this state. The Kentucky court holds such a contract to be bad as creating an unlawful monopoly. But I'll think the matter over. You come back tomorrow and I'll try meanwhile to find some way out."

So, next day, the Joneses returned. And this time their lawyer said he thought he had discovered how to get the contract sustained: "You see, it's this way. In most courts, except those of Kentucky and of a few other states, an agreement like this is perfectly good, But, unfortunately, as things now stand, you'll have to go into the Kentucky courts.

"If we can manage to get our case tried in the federal court, there's a fair chance that we'll get a different result, because I think the federal court will follow the majority rule and not the Kentucky rule. I'm not sure of that, but it's worth trying.

"So this is what we'll do. We'll form a new Blue & Gray Company in Tennessee. And your Kentucky Blue & Gray Company will transfer all its assets to the new Tennessee Blue & Gray Company. Then we'll have the railroad company execute a new contract with the new Tennessee Blue & Gray Company, and at the same time cancel the old contract and, soon after, dissolve the old Kentucky Blue & Gray Company."

"But," interrupted one of the Joneses, "what good will all that monkey-business do?"

The lawyer smiled broadly. "Just this," he replied with pride in his cleverness: "The A. & B. Railroad Company is organized in Kentucky. So is the Purple Taxi which we want to get at. The federal court will treat these companies as if they were citizens of Kentucky. Now, a corporation which is a citizen of Kentucky can't bring this kind of suit in the federal court against other corporations which are also citizens of Kentucky. But if your company becomes a Tennessee corporation, it will be considered as if it were a citizen of Tennessee. Then your new Tennessee company can sue the other two in the federal court, because the suit will be held to be one between citizens of different states. And that kind of suit, based on what we lawyers call 'diversity of citizenship,' can be brought in the federal court by a corporation which organized in Tennessee against corporations which are citizens of another state, Kentucky.

*Jerome Frank, "Legal Realism," from *Law and the Modern Mind* (New York: Doubleday and Co. Anchor edition, 1963), 46–52. Originally published by Brentanos, Inc. in 1930. Copyright 1930, 1933, 1949 by Coward McCann, Inc. Copyright reviewed in 1958 by Florence K. Frank. Copyright © 1930 by Brentanos, Inc. Reprinted by arrangement with Barbara Kiastern and Peter Smith Publisher, Inc.

And the federal court, as I said, ought to sustain your contract."

"That sounds pretty slick," said one of the Joneses admiringly. "Are you sure it will work?"

"No," answered the lawyer. "You can't ever be absolutely sure about such a plan. I can't find any case completely holding our way on all these facts. But I'm satisfied that's the law and that that's the way the federal court ought to decide. I won't guarantee success. But I recommend trying out my suggestion."

His advice was followed. Shortly after the new Tennessee Blue & Gray Company was organized and had entered into the new contract, suit was brought by the Joneses' new Blue & Gray Corporation of Tennessee in the Federal District Court against the competing Purple Co. and the railroad company. In this suit, the Blue & Gray Taxi Company of Tennessee asked the court to prevent interference with the carrying out of its railroad contract.

As the Joneses' lawyer had hoped, the federal court held, against the protest of the Purple Company's lawyer, first, that such a suit could be brought in the federal court and, second, that the contract was valid. Accordingly the court enjoined the Purple Company from interfering with the depot business of the Joneses' Blue & Gray Company. The Joneses were elated, for now their profits seemed once more assured.

But not for long. The other side appealed the case to the Federal Circuit Court of Appeals. And the Joneses' lawyer was somewhat worried that that court might reverse the lower federal court. But it didn't, and the Joneses again were happy.

Still the Purple Company persisted. It took the case to the Supreme Court of the United States. That Court consists of nine judges. And the Joneses' lawyer couldn't be certain just how those judges would line up on all the questions involved. "Some new men on the bench, and you never can tell about Holmes and Brandeis. They're very erratic," was his comment.

When the United States Supreme Court gave its decision, it was found that six of the nine judges agreed with counsel for the Joneses. Three justices (Holmes, Brandeis, and Stone) were of the contrary opinion. But the majority governs in the United States Supreme Court, and the Joneses' prosperity was at last firmly established.

Now, what was "the law" for the Joneses, who owned the Blue & Gray Company, and the Williamses, who owned the Purple Company? The answer will depend on the date of the question. If asked before the new Tennessee Company acquired this contract, it might have been said that it was almost surely "the law" that the Joneses would lose; for any suit involving the validity of that contract could then have been brought only in the Kentucky state court and the prior decisions of that court seemed adverse to such an agreement.

After the suggestion of the Joneses' lawyer was carried out and the new Tennessee corporation owned the contract, "the law" was more doubtful. Many lawyers would have agreed with the Joneses' lawyer that there was a good chance that the Jones family would be victorious if suit were brought in the federal courts. But probably an equal number would have disagreed: they would have said that the formation of the new Tennessee company was a trick used to get out of the Kentucky courts and into the federal court, a trick of which the federal court would not approve. Or that, regardless of that question, the federal court would follow the well-settled Kentucky rule as to the invalidity of such contracts as creating unlawful monopolies (especially because the use of Kentucky real estate was involved) and that therefore the federal court would decide against the Joneses. "The law," at any time before the decision of the United States Supreme Court, was indeed unsettled. (That is, it was unsettled whether the Williamses had the energy, patience, and money to push an appeal. If not, then the decision of the lower federal court was the actual settled law for the Jones and Williams families.) No one could know what the court would decide. Would it follow the Kentucky cases? If so, the law was that no "rights" were conferred by the contract. Would it refuse to follow the Kentucky cases? If so, rights were conferred by the contract. To speak of settled law governing that controversy, or of the fixed legal rights of those parties, as antedating the decision of the Supreme Court, is mere verbiage. If two more judges on that bench had agreed with Justices Holmes, Brandeis, and Stone, the law and the rights of the parties would have been of a directly opposite kind.

After the decision, "the law" was fixed. There were no other courts to which an appeal could be directed. The judgment of the United States Supreme Court could not be disturbed and the legal "rights" of the Joneses and the Williamses were everlastingly established.

We may now venture a rough definition of law from the point of view of the average man: For any particular lay person, the law, with respect to any particular set of facts, is a decision of a court with respect to those facts so far as that decision affects that particular person. Until a court has passed on those facts no law on that subject is yet in existence. Prior to such a decision, the only law available is the opinion of lawyers as to the law relating to that person and to those facts. Such opinion is not actually law but only a guess as to what a court will decide. (The United States Supreme Court has wittily been called the "court of ultimate conjecture.")

Law, then, as to any given situation is either (a) actual law, that is, a specific past decision, as to that situation, or (b) probable law, that is, a guess as to a specific future decision.

Usually when a client consults his lawyer about "the law," his purpose is to ascertain not what the courts have actually decided in the past but what the courts will probably decide in the future. He asks, "Have I a right, as a stockholder of the American Taffy Company of Indiana, to look at the corporate books?" Or, "Do I have to pay an inheritance tax to the State of New York on bonds left me by my deceased wife, if our residence was in Ohio, but the bonds, at the time of her death, were in a safety-deposit box in New York?" Or, "Is there a right of 'peaceful' picketing in a strike in the State of California?" Or, "If Jones sells me his Chicago shoe business and agrees not to compete for ten years, will the agreement be binding?" The answers (although they may run "There is such a right," "The law is that the property is not taxable," "Such picketing is unlawful," "The agreement is not legally binding") are in fact prophecies or predictions of judicial action. It is from this point of view that the practice of law has been aptly termed an art of prediction. . . .

H. L. A. HART

A New Conception of Law*

LAW AS THE UNION OF PRIMARY AND SECONDARY RULES

A FRESH START

In the last three chapters we have seen that, at various crucial points, the simple model of law as the sovereign's coercive orders failed to reproduce some of the salient features of a legal system. To demonstrate this, we did not find it necessary to invoke (as earlier critics have done) international law or primitive law which some may regard as disputable or borderline examples of law; instead we pointed to certain familiar features of municipal law in a modern state, and showed that these were either distorted or altogether unrepresented in this over-simple theory.

The main ways in which the theory failed are instructive enough to merit a second summary. First, it became clear that though of all the varieties of law, a criminal statute, forbidding or enjoining certain actions under penalty, most resembles orders backed by threats given by one person to others, such a statute nonetheless differs from such orders in the important respect that it commonly applies to those who enact it and not merely to others. Secondly, there are other varieties of law, notably those conferring legal powers to adjudicate or legislate (public powers) or to create or vary legal relations (private powers) which cannot, without absurdity, be construed as orders backed by threats. Thirdly, there are legal rules which differ from orders in their mode of origin, because they are not brought into being by anything analogous to explicit prescription. Finally, the analysis of law in terms of the sovereign, habitually obeyed and necessarily exempt from all legal limitation, failed to account for the continuity of legislative authority characteristic of a modern legal system, and the sovereign, person or persons could not be identified with either the electorate or the legislature of a modern state.

It will be recalled that in thus criticizing the conception of law as the sovereign's coercive orders we considered also a number of ancillary devices which were brought in at the cost of corrupting the primitive simplicity of the theory to rescue it from its difficulties. But these too failed. One device, the notion of a *tacit* order, seemed to have no application to the complex actualities of a modern legal system, but only to very much simpler situations like that of a general who deliberately refrains from interfering with orders given by his subordinates. Other devices, such as that of treating power-conferring rules as mere fragments of rules imposing duties, or treating all rules as directed only to officials, distort the ways in which these are spoken of, thought of, and actually used in social life. This had no better claim to our assent than the theory that all the rules of a game are "really" directions to the umpire and the scorer. The device, designed to reconcile the self-binding character of legislation with the theory that a statute is an order given to *others*, was to distinguish the legislators acting in their official capacity, as *one* person ordering *others* who include themselves in their private capacities. This device, impeccable in itself, involved supplementing the theory with something it does not contain: this is the notion of a rule defining what must be done to legislate; for it is only in conforming with such a rule that legislators have an official capacity and a separate personality to be contrasted with themselves as private individuals.

The last three chapters are therefore the record of a failure and there is plainly need for a fresh start. Yet the failure is an instructive one, worth the detailed consideration we have given it, because at each point where the theory failed to fit the facts it was possible to see at least in outline why it was bound to fail and what is required for a better account. The root cause of failure is that the elements out of which the theory was constructed, viz. the ideas of orders, obedience, habits, and threats, do not include, and cannot by their combination yield, the idea of a rule, without which we cannot hope to elucidate even the most elementary forms of law. It is true that the idea of a rule is by no means a simple one: we have already seen in [a previous discussion] the need, if we are to do justice to

* ©Oxford University Press 1961. Reprinted from *The Concept of Law* by H. L. A. Hart (1961) by permission of Oxford University Press.

the complexity of a legal system, to discriminate between two different though related types. Under rules of the one type, which may well be considered (the basic or primary type, human beings are required to do or abstain from certain actions, whether they wish to or not. Rules of the other type are in a sense parasitic upon or secondary to the first; for they provide that human beings may by doing or saying certain things introduce new rules of the primary type, extinguish or modify old ones, or in various ways determine their incidence or control their operations. Rules of the first type impose duties; rules of the second type confer powers, public or private. Rules of the first type concern actions involving physical movement or changes; rules of the second type provide for operations which lead not merely to physical movement or change, but to the creation or variation of duties or obligations.

We have already given some preliminary analysis of what is involved in the assertion that rules of these two types exist among a given social group, and in this chapter we shall not only carry this analysis a little farther but we shall make the general claim that in the combination of these two types of rule there lies what Austin wrongly claimed to have found in the notion of coercive orders, namely, "the key to the science of jurisprudence." We shall not indeed claim that wherever the word "law" is "properly" used this combination of primary and secondary rules is to be found; for it is clear that the diverse range of cases of which the word "law" is used are not linked by any such simple uniformity, but by less direct relations—often of analogy of either form or content to a central case. What we shall attempt to show, in this and the succeeding chapters, is that most of the features of law which have proved most perplexing and have both provoked and eluded the search for definition can best be rendered clear, if these two types of rule and the interplay between them are understood. We accord this union of elements a central place because of their explanatory power in elucidating the concepts that constitute the framework of legal thought. The justification for the use of the word "law" for a range of apparently heterogeneous cases is a secondary matter which can be undertaken when the central elements have been grasped.

THE IDEA OF OBLIGATION

It will be recalled that the theory of law as coercive orders, notwithstanding its errors, started from the perfectly correct appreciation of the fact that where there is law, there human conduct is made in some sense non-optional or obligatory. In choosing this starting-point the theory was well inspired, and in building up a new account of law in terms of the interplay of primary and secondary rules we too shall start from the same idea. It is, however, here, at this crucial first step, that we have perhaps most to learn from the theory's errors.

Let us recall the gunman situation. A orders B to hand over his money and threatens to shoot him if he does not comply. According to the theory of coercive orders this situation illustrates the notion of obligation or duty in general. Legal obligation is to be found in this situation writ large; A must be the sovereign habitually obeyed and the orders must be general, prescribing courses of conduct not single actions. The plausibility of the claim that the gunman situation displays the meaning of obligation lies in the fact that it is certainly one in which we would say that B, if he obeyed, was "obliged" to hand over his money. It is, however, equally certain that we should misdescribe the situation if we said, on these facts, that B "had an obligation" or a "duty" to hand over the money. So from the start it is clear that we need something else for an understanding of the idea of obligation. There is a difference, yet to be explained, between the assertion that someone *was obliged* to do something and the assertion that he *had an obligation* to do it. The first is often a statement about the beliefs and motives with which an action is done: B was obliged to hand over his money may simply mean, as it does in the gunman case, that he believed that some harm or other unpleasant consequences would befall him if he did not hand it over and he handed it over to avoid those consequences. In such cases the prospect of what would happen to the agent if he disobeyed has rendered something he would otherwise have preferred to have done (keep the money) less eligible.

Two further elements slightly complicate the elucidation of the notion of being obliged to do something. It seems clear that we should not think of B as obliged to hand over the money if the threatened harm was, according to common judgments, trivial in comparison with the disadvantage or serious consequences, either for B or for others, of complying with the orders, as it would be, for example, if A merely threatened to pinch B. Nor perhaps should we say that B was obliged, if there were no reasonable grounds for thinking that A could or would probably implement his threat of relatively serious harm. Yet, though such references to common judgments of comparative harm and reasonable estimates of likelihood, are implicit in this notion, the statement that a person was obliged to obey someone is, in the main, a psychological one referring to the beliefs and motives with which an action was done. But the statement that someone *had an obligation* to do something is of a very different type and there are many signs of this difference. Thus not only is it the case that the facts about B's action and his beliefs and motives in the gunman case, though sufficient to warrant the statement that B was obliged to hand over his purse, are *not sufficient* to warrant the statement that he had an obligation to do this; it is also the case that facts of this sort, i.e. facts about beliefs and motives, are *not necessary* for the truth of a statement that a person had an obligation to do something. Thus the statement that a person had an obligation, e.g. to tell the truth or report for military service, remains true even if he believed (reasonably or unreasonably) that he would never be found out and had nothing to fear from disobedience. Moreover, whereas the statement that he had this obligation is quite independent of the question whether or not he in fact reported for service, the statement that someone was obliged to do something, normally carries the implication that he actually did it.

Some theorists, Austin among them, seeing perhaps the general irrelevance of the person's beliefs, fears, and motives to the question whether he had an obligation to do something, have defined this notion not in terms of these subjective facts, but in terms of the *chance* or *likelihood* that the person having the obligation will suffer a punishment or "evil" at the hands of others in the event of disobedience. This, in effect, treats statements of obligation not as psychological statements but as predictions or assessments of chances of incurring punishment or "evil." To many later theorists this has appeared as a revelation, bringing down to earth an elusive notion and restating it in the same clear, hard, empirical terms as are used in science. It has, indeed, been accepted sometimes as the only alternative to metaphysical conceptions of obligation or duty as invisible objects mysteriously existing "above" or "behind" the world of ordinary, observable facts. But there are many reasons for rejecting this interpretation of statements of obligation as predictions,

and it is not, in fact, the only alternative to obscure metaphysics.

The fundamental objection is that the predictive interpretation obscures the fact that, where rules exist, deviations from them are not merely grounds for a prediction that hostile reactions will follow or that a court will apply sanctions to those who break them, but are also a reason or justification for such reaction and for applying the sanctions. We have already drawn attention in [a previous discussion] to this neglect of the internal aspect of rules and we shall elaborate it later in this chapter.

There is, however, a second, simpler, objection to the predictive interpretation of obligation. If it were true that the statement that a person had an obligation meant that *he* was likely to suffer in the event of disobedience, it would be a contradiction to say that he had an obligation, e.g. to report for military service but that, owing to the fact that he had escaped from the jurisdiction, or had successfully bribed the police or the court, there was not the slightest chance of his being caught or made to suffer. In fact, there is no contradiction in saying this, and such statements are often made and understood.

It is, of course, true that in a normal legal system, where sanctions are exacted for a high proportion of offences, an offender usually runs a risk of punishment; so, usually the statement that a person has an obligation and the statement that he is likely to suffer for disobedience will both be true together. Indeed, the connexion between these two statements is somewhat stronger than this: at least in a municipal system it may well be true that, unless *in general* sanctions were likely to be exacted from offenders, there would be little or no point in making particular statements about a person's obligations. In this sense, such statements may be said to presuppose belief in the continued normal operation of the system of sanctions much as the statement "he is out" in cricket presupposes, though it does not assert, that players, umpire, and scorer will probably take the usual steps. Nonetheless, it is crucial for the understanding of the idea of obligation to see that in individual cases the statement that a person has an obligation under some rule and the prediction that he is likely to suffer for disobedience may diverge.

It is clear that obligation is not to be found in the gunman situation, though the simpler notion of being obliged to do something may well be defined in the elements present there. To understand the general idea of obligation as a necessary preliminary to understanding it in its legal form, we must turn to a different social situation which, unlike the gunman situation, includes the existence of social rules; for this situation contributes to the meaning of the statement that a person has an obligation in two ways. First, the existence of such rules, making certain types of behaviour a standard, is the normal, though unstated, background or proper context for such a statement; and, secondly, the distinctive function of such statement is to apply such a general rule to a particular person by calling attention to the fact that his case falls under it. We have already seen in [a previous discussion] that there is involved in the existence of any social rules a combination of regular conduct with a distinctive attitude to that conduct as a standard. We have also seen the main ways in which these differ from mere social habits, and how the varied normative vocabulary ("ought," "must," "should") is used to draw attention to the standard and to deviations from it, and to formulate the demands, criticisms, or acknowledgements which may be based on it. Of this class of normative words the words "obligation" and "duty" form an important sub-class, carrying with them certain implications not usually present in the others. Hence, though a grasp of the elements generally differentiating social rules from mere habits is certainly indispensable for understanding the notion of obligation or duty, it is not sufficient by itself.

The statement that someone has or is under an obligation does indeed imply the existence of a rule; yet it is not always the case that where rules exist the standard of behaviour required by them is conceived of in terms of obligation. "He ought to have" and "He had an obligation to" are not always interchangeable expressions, even though they are alike in carrying an implicit reference to existing standards of conduct or are used in drawing conclusions in particular cases from a general rule. Rules of etiquette or correct speech are certainly rules: they are more than convergent habits or regularities of behaviour; they are taught and efforts are made to maintain them; they are used in criticizing our own and other people's behaviour in the characteristic normative vocabulary. "You ought to take your hat off," "It is wrong to say 'you was.'" But to use in connexion with rules of this kind the words "obligation" or "duty" would be misleading and not merely stylistically odd. It

would misdescribe a social situation; for though the line separating rules of obligation from others is at points a vague one, yet the main rationale of the distinction is fairly clear.

Rules are conceived and spoken of as imposing obligations when the general demand for conformity is insistent and the social pressure brought to bear upon those who deviate or threaten to deviate is great. Such rules may be wholly customary in origin: there may be no centrally organized system of punishments for breach of the rules; the social pressure may take only the form of a general diffused hostile or critical reaction which may stop short of physical sanctions. It may be limited to verbal manifestations of disapproval or of appeals to the individuals' respect for the rule violated; it may depend heavily on the operation of feelings of shame, remorse, and guilt. When the pressure is of this last-mentioned kind we may be inclined to classify the rules as part of the morality of the social group and the obligation under the rules as moral obligation. Conversely, when physical sanctions are prominent or usual among the forms of pressure, even though these are neither closely defined nor administered by officials but are left to the community at large, we shall be inclined to classify the rules as a primitive or rudimentary form of law. We may, of course, find both these types of serious social pressure behind what is, in an obvious sense, the same rule of conduct; sometimes this may occur with no indication that one of them is peculiarly appropriate as primary and the other secondary, and then the question whether we are confronted with a rule of morality or rudimentary law may not be susceptible of an answer. But for the moment the possibility of drawing the line between law and morals need not detain us. What is important is that the insistence on importance or *seriousness* of social pressure behind the rules is the primary factor determining whether they are thought of as giving rise to obligations.

Two other characteristics of obligation go naturally together with this primary one. The rules supported by this serious pressure are thought important because they are believed to be necessary to the maintenance of social life or some highly prized feature of it. Characteristically, rules so obviously essential as those which restrict the free use of violence are thought of in terms of obligation. So too rules which require honesty or truth or require the keeping of promises, or specify what is to be done by one who

[handwritten margin note: primary factor d. if rule obliga]

performs a distinctive role or function in the social group are thought of in terms of either "obligation" or perhaps more often "duty." Secondly, it is generally recognized that the conduct required by these rules may, while benefiting others, conflict with what the person who owes the duty may wish to do. Hence obligations and duties are thought of as characteristically involving sacrifice or renunciation, and the standing possibility of conflict between obligation or duty and interest is, in all societies, among the truisms of both the lawyer and the moralist.

The figure of a *bond* binding the person obligated, which is buried in the word "obligation," and the similar notion of a debt latent in the word "duty" are explicable in terms of these three factors, which distinguish rules of obligation or duty from other rules. In this figure, which haunts much legal thought, the social pressure appears as a chain binding those who have obligations so that they are not free to do what they want. The other end of the chain is sometimes held by the group or their official representatives, who insist on performance or exact the penalty: sometimes it is entrusted by the group to a private individual who may choose whether or not to insist on performance or its equivalent in value to him. The first situation typifies the duties or obligations of criminal law and the second those of civil law where we think of private individuals having rights correlative to the obligations.

Natural and perhaps illuminating though these figures or metaphors are, we must not allow them to trap us into a misleading conception of obligation as essentially consisting in some feeling of pressure or compulsion experienced by those who have obligations. The fact that rules of obligation are generally supported by serious social pressure does not entail that to have an obligation under the rules is to experience feelings of compulsion or pressure. Hence there is no contradiction in saying of some hardened swindler, and it may often be true, that he had an obligation to pay the rent but felt no pressure to pay when he made off without doing so. To *feel* obliged and to have an obligation are different though frequently concomitant things. To identify them would be one way of misinterpreting, in terms of psychological feelings, the important internal aspect of rules to which we drew attention in [a previous discussion].

Indeed, the internal aspect of rules is some-thing to which we must again refer before we can dispose finally of the claims of the predictive theory. For an advocate of that theory may well ask why, if social pressure is so important a feature of rules of obligation, we are yet so concerned to stress the inadequacies of the predictive theory; for it gives this very feature a central place by defining obligation in terms of the likelihood that threatened punishment or hostile reaction will follow deviation from certain lines of conduct. The difference may seem slight between the analysis of a statement of obligation as a prediction, or assessment of the chances, of hostile reaction to deviation, and our own contention that though this statement presupposes a background in which deviations from rules are generally met by hostile reactions, yet its characteristic use is not to predict this but to say that a person's case falls under such a rule. In fact, however, this difference is not a slight one. Indeed, until its importance is grasped, we cannot properly understand the whole distinctive style of human thought, speech, and action which is involved in the existence of rules and which constitutes the normative structure of society.

The following contrast again in terms of the "internal" and "external" aspect of rules may serve to mark what gives this distinction its great importance for the understanding not only of law but of the structure of any society. When a social group has certain rules of conduct, this fact affords an opportunity for many closely related yet different kinds of assertion; for it is possible to be concerned with the rules, either merely as an observer who does not himself accept them, or as a member of the group which accepts and uses them as guides to conduct. We may call these respectively the "external" and the "internal points of view." Statements made from the external point of view may themselves be of different kinds. For the observer may, without accepting the rules himself, assert that the group accepts the rules, and thus may from outside refer to the way in which *they* are concerned with them from the internal point of view. But whatever the rules are, whether they are those of games, like chess or cricket, or moral or legal rules, we can if we choose occupy the position of an observer who does not even refer in this way to the internal point of view of the group. Such an observer is content merely to record the regularities of observable behaviour in which conformity with the rules partly consists and those further regularities, in the form of the hostile reaction, reproofs, or punishments, with which deviations from the rules are met. After a time the external observer may, on the basis of the regularities observed, correlate deviation with hostile reaction, and be able to predict with a fair measure of success, and to assess the chances that a deviation from the group's normal behaviour will meet with hostile reaction or punishment. Such knowledge may not only reveal much about the group, but might enable him to live among them without unpleasant consequences which would attend one who attempted to do so without such knowledge.

If, however, the observer really keeps austerely to this extreme external point of view and does not give any account of the manner in which members of the group who accept the rules view their own regular behaviour, his description of their life cannot be in terms of rules at all, and so not in the terms of the rule-dependent notions of obligation or duty. Instead, it will be in terms of observable regularities of conduct, predictions, probabilities, and signs. For such an observer, deviations by a member of the group from normal conduct will be a sign that hostile reaction is likely to follow, and nothing more. His view will be like the view of one who, having observed the working of a traffic signal in a busy street for some time, limits himself to saying that when the light turns red there is a high probability that the traffic will stop. He treats the light merely as a natural *sign that* people will behave in certain ways, as clouds are a *sign that* rain will come. In so doing he will miss out a whole dimension of the social life of those whom he is watching, since for them the red light is not merely a sign that others will stop: they look upon it as a *signal for them to* stop, and so a reason for stopping in conformity to rules which make stopping when the light is red a standard of behaviour and an obligation. To mention this is to bring into the account the way in which the group regards its own behaviour. It is to refer to the internal aspect of rules seen from their internal point of view.

The external point of view may very nearly reproduce the way in which the rules function in the lives of certain members of the group, namely those who reject its rules and are only concerned with them when and because they judge that unpleasant consequences are likely to follow violation. Their point of view will need for its expression, "I was obliged to do it," "I am likely to suffer for it if . . . ," "You will probably suffer for it if . . . ," "They will do that to you if. . . . " But they will not need forms of expression like "I had an obligation" or "You have an obligation" for these are required only by those who see their own and other persons' conduct from the internal point of view. What the external point of view, which limits itself to the observable regularities of behaviour, cannot reproduce is the way in which the rules function as rules in the lives of those who normally are the majority of society. These are the officials, lawyers, or private persons who use them, in one situation after another, as guides to the conduct of social life, as the basis for claims, demands, admissions, criticism, or punishment, viz., in all the familiar transactions of life according to rules. For them the violation of a rule is not merely a basis for the prediction that a hostile reaction will follow but a *reason* for hostility.

At any given moment the life of any society which lives by rules, legal or not, is likely to consist in a tension between those who, on the one hand, accept and voluntarily co-operate in maintaining the rules, and so see their own and other persons' behaviour in terms of the rules, and those who, on the other hand, reject the rules and attend to them only from the external point of view as a sign of possible punishment. One of the difficulties facing any legal theory anxious to do justice to the complexity of the facts is to remember the presence of both these points of view and not to define one of them out of existence. Perhaps all our criticisms of the predictive theory of obligation may be best summarized as the accusation that this is what it does to the internal aspect of obligatory rules.

THE ELEMENTS OF LAW

It is, of course, possible to imagine a society without a legislature, courts or officials of any kind. Indeed, there are many studies of primitive communities which not only claim that this possibility is realized but depict in detail the life of a society where the only means of social control is that general attitude of the group towards its own standard modes of behaviour in terms of which we have characterized rules of obligation. A social structure of this kind is often referred to as one of "custom"; but we shall not use this term, because it often implies that the customary rules are very old and supported with less social pressure than other rules. To avoid these implications we shall refer to such a social structure as one of primary rules of obligation. If a society is to live by such primary rules alone, there are certain conditions which, granted a few of the most obvious truisms about human nature and the world we live in, must clearly be satisfied. The first of these conditions is that the rules must contain in some form restrictions on the free use of violence, theft, and deception to which human beings are tempted but which they must, in general, repress, if they are to coexist in close proximity to each other. Such rules are in fact always found in the primitive societies of which we have knowledge, together with a variety of others imposing on individuals various positive duties to perform services or make contributions to the common life. Secondly, though such a society may exhibit the tension, already described, between those who accept the rules and those who reject the rules except where fear of social pressure induces them to conform, it is plain that the latter cannot be more than a minority, if so loosely organized a society of persons, approximately equal in physical strength, is to endure: for otherwise those who reject the rules would have too little social pressure to fear. This too is confirmed by what we know of primitive communities where, though there are dissidents and malefactors, the majority live by the rules seen from the internal point of view.

More important for our present purpose is the following consideration. It is plain that only a small community closely knit by ties of kinship, common sentiment, and belief, and placed in a stable environment, could live successfully by such a régime of unofficial rules. In any other conditions such a simple form of social control must prove defective and will require supplementation in different ways. In the first place, the rules by which the group lives will not form a system, but will simply be a set of separate standards, without any identifying or common mark, except of course that they are the rules which a particular group of human beings accepts. They will in this respect resemble our own rules of etiquette. Hence if doubts arise as to what the rules are or as to the precise scope of some given rule, there will be no procedure for settling this doubt, either by reference to an authoritative text or to an official whose declarations on this point are authoritative. For, plainly, such a procedure and the acknowledgement of either authoritative text or persons involve the existence of rules of a type different from the rules of obligation or duty which *ex hypothesi* are all that the group has. This defect in the simple social structure of primary rules we may call its *uncertainty*.

A second defect is the *static* character of the rules. The only mode of change in the rules known to such a society will be the slow process of growth, whereby courses of conduct once thought optional become first habitual or usual, and then obligatory, and the converse process of decay, when deviations, once severely dealt with, are first tolerated and then pass unnoticed. There will be no means, in such a society, of deliberately adapting the rules to changing circumstances, either by eliminating old rules or introducing new ones: for, again, the possibility of doing this presupposes the existence of rules of a different type from the primary rules of obligation by which alone the society lives. In an extreme case the rules may be static in a more drastic sense. This, though never perhaps fully realized in any actual community, is worth considering because the remedy for it is something very characteristic of law. In this extreme case, not only would there be no way of deliberately changing the general rules, but the obligations which arise under the rules in particular cases could not be varied or modified by the deliberate choice of any individual. Each individual would simply have fixed obligations or duties to do or abstain from doing certain things. It might indeed very often be the case that others would benefit from the performance of these obligations; yet if there are only primary rules of obligation they would have no power to release those bound from performance or to transfer to others the benefits which would accrue from performance. For such operations of release or transfer create changes in the initial positions of individuals under the primary rules of obligation, and for these operations to be possible there must be rules of a sort different from the primary rules.

The third defect of this simple form of social life is the *inefficiency* of the diffuse social pressure by which the rules are maintained. Disputes as to whether an admitted rule has or has not been violated will always occur and will, in any but the smallest societies, continue interminably, if there is no agency specially empowered to ascertain finally, and authoritatively, the fact of violation. Lack of such final and authoritative determinations is to be distinguished from another weakness associated with it. This is the fact that punishments for violations of the rules, and other forms of social pressure involving physical effort or the use of force, are not administered by a special agency but are left to the individuals affected or to the group at large. It is obvious that the waste of time involved in the group's unorganized efforts to catch and punish offenders, and the smouldering vendettas which may result from self help in the absence of an official monopoly of "sanctions," may be serious. The history of law does, however, strongly suggest that the lack of official agencies to determine authoritatively the fact of violation of the rules is a much more serious defect; for many societies have remedies for this defect long before the other.

The remedy for each of these three main defects in this simplest form of social structure consists in supplementing the *primary* rules of obligation with *secondary* rules which are rules of a different kind. The introduction of the remedy for each defect might, in itself, be considered a step from the pre-legal into the legal world; since each remedy brings with it many elements that permeate law: certainly all three remedies together are enough to convert the régime of primary rules into what is indisputably a legal system. We shall consider in turn each of these remedies and show why law may most illuminatingly be characterized as a union of primary rules of obligation with such secondary rules. Before we do this, however, the following general points should be noted. Though the remedies consist in the introduction of rules which are certainly different from each other, as well as from the primary rules of obligation which they supplement, they have important features in common and are connected in various ways. Thus they may all be said to be on a different level from the primary rules, for they are all *about* such rules; in the sense that while primary rules are concerned with the actions that individuals must or must not do, these secondary rules are all concerned with the primary rules themselves. They specify the ways in which the primary rules may be conclusively ascertained, introduced, eliminated, varied, and the fact of their violation conclusively determined.

The simplest form of remedy for the *uncertainty* of the régime of primary rules is the introduction of what we shall call a "rule of recognition." This will specify some feature or features possession of which by a suggested rule is taken as a conclusive affirmative indication that it is a rule of the group to be supported by the social pressure it exerts. The existence of such a rule of recognition may take any of a huge variety of forms, simple or complex. It may, as in the early law of many societies, be no more than that an authoritative list or text of the rules is to be found in a written document or carved on some public monument. No doubt as a matter of history this step from the pre-legal to the legal may be accomplished in distinguishable stages, of which the first is the mere reduction to writing of hitherto unwritten rules. This is not itself the crucial step, though it is a very important one: what is crucial is the acknowledgement of reference to the writing or inscription as *authoritative,* i.e. as the *proper* way of disposing of doubts as to the existence of the rule. Where there is such an acknowledgement there is a very simple form of secondary rule: a rule for conclusive identification of the primary rules of obligation.

In a developed legal system the rules of recognition are of course more complex; instead of identifying rules exclusively by reference to a text or list they do so by reference to some general characteristic possessed by the primary rules. This may be the fact of their having been enacted by a specific body, or their long customary practice, or their relation to judicial decisions. Moreover, where more than one of such general characteristics are treated as identifying criteria, provision may be made for their possible conflict by their arrangement in an order of superiority, as by the common subordination of custom or precedent to statute, the latter being a "superior source" of law. Such complexity may make the rules of recognition in a modern legal system seem very different from the simple acceptance of an authoritative text: yet even in this simplest form, such a rule brings with it many elements distinctive of law. By providing an authoritative mark it introduces, although in embryonic form, the idea of a legal system: for the rules are now not just a discrete unconnected set but are, in a simple way, unified. Further, in the simple operation of identifying a given rule as possessing the required feature of being an item on an authoritative list of rules we have the germ of the idea of legal validity.

The remedy for the *static* quality of the régime of primary rules consists in the introduction of what we shall call "rules of change." The simplest form of such a rule is that which empowers an individual or body of persons to introduce new primary rules for the conduct of the life of the group, or of some class within it, and to eliminate old rules. As we have already argued in [a previous discussion] it is in terms of such a rule, and not in terms of orders backed by threats, that the ideas of legislative enactment and repeal are to be understood. Such rules of change may be very simple or very complex: the powers conferred may be unrestricted or limited in various ways: and the rules may, besides specifying the persons who are to legislate, define in more or less rigid terms the procedure to be followed in legislation. Plainly, there will be a very close connexion between the rules of change and the rules of recognition: for where the former exists the latter will necessarily incorporate a reference to legislation as an identifying feature of the rules, though it need not refer to all the details of procedure involved in legislation. Usually some official certificate or official copy will, under the rules of recognition, be taken as a sufficient proof of due enactment. Of course if there is a social structure so simple that the only "source of law" is legislation, the rule of recognition will simply specify enactment as the unique identifying mark or criterion of validity of the rules. This will be the case for example in the imaginary kingdom of Rex I depicted in [a previous discussion]: there the rule of recognition would simply be that whatever Rex I enacts is law.

We have already described in some detail the rules which confer on individuals power to vary their initial positions under the primary rules. Without such private power-conferring rules society would lack some of the chief amenities which law confers upon it. For the operations which these rules make possible are the making of wills, contracts, transfers of property, and many other voluntarily created structures of rights and duties which typify life under law, though of course an elementary form of power-conferring rule also underlies the moral institution of a promise. The kinship of these rules with the rules of change involved in the notion of legislation is clear, and as recent theory such as Kelsen's has shown, many of the features which puzzle us in the institutions of contract or property are clarified by thinking of the operations of making a contract or transferring property as the exercise of limited legislative powers by individuals.

The third supplement to the simple régime of primary rules, intended to remedy the *inefficiency* of its diffused social pressure, consists of secondary rules empowering individuals to make authoritative determinations of the question whether, on a particular occasion, a primary rule has been broken. The minimal form of adjudication consists in such determinations, and we shall call the secondary rules which confer the power to make them "rules of adjudication." Besides identifying the individuals who are to adjudicate, such rules will also define the procedure to be followed. Like the other secondary rules these are on a different level from the primary rules: though they may be reinforced by further rules imposing duties on judges to adjudicate, they do not impose duties but confer judicial powers and a special status on judicial declarations about the breach of obligations. Again these rules, like the other secondary rules, define a group of important legal concepts: in this case the concepts of judge or court, jurisdiction and judgment. Besides these resemblances to the other secondary rules, rules of adjudication have intimate connexions with them. Indeed, a system which has rules of adjudication is necessarily also committed to a rule of recognition of an elementary and imperfect sort. This is so because, if courts are empowered to make authoritative determinations of the fact that a rule has been broken, these cannot avoid being taken as authoritative determinations of what the rules are. So the rule which confers jurisdiction will also be a rule of recognition, identifying the primary rules through the judgments of the courts and these judgments will become a "source" of law. It is true that this form of rule of recognition, inseparable from the minimum form of jurisdiction, will be very imperfect. Unlike an authoritative text or a statute book, judgments may not be couched in general terms and their use as authoritative guides to the rules depends on a somewhat shaky inference from particular decisions, and the reliability of this must fluctuate both with the skill of the interpreter and the consistency of the judges.

It need hardly be said that in few legal systems are judicial powers confined to authoritative determinations of the fact of violation of the primary rules. Most systems have, after some delay, seen the advantages of further centralization of social pressure; and have partially prohibited the use of physical punishments or violent self help by private individuals. Instead they have supplemented the primary rules of obligation by further secondary rules, specifying or at least limiting the penalties for violation, and have conferred upon judges, where they have ascertained the fact of violation, the exclusive power to direct the application of penalties by other officials. These secondary rules provide the centralized official "sanctions" of the system.

If we stand back and consider the structure which has resulted from the combination of primary rules of obligation with the secondary rules of recognition, change and adjudication, it is plain that we have here not only the heart of a legal system, but a most powerful tool for the analysis of much that has puzzled both the jurist and the political theorist.

Not only are the specifically legal concepts with which the lawyer is professionally concerned, such as those of obligation and rights, validity and source of law, legislation and jurisdiction, and sanction, best elucidated in terms of this combination of elements. The concepts (which bestride both law and political theory) of the state, of authority, and of an official require a similar analysis if the obscurity which still lingers about them is to be dissipated. The reason why an analysis in these terms of primary and secondary rules has this explanatory power is not far to seek. Most of the obscurities and distortions surrounding legal and political concepts arise from the fact that these essentially involve reference to what we have called the internal point of view: the view of those who do not merely record and predict behaviour conforming to rules, but *use* the rules as standards for the appraisal of their own and others' behaviour. This requires more detailed attention in the analysis of legal and political concepts than it has usually received. Under the simple régime of primary rules the internal point of view is manifested in its simplest form, in the use of those rules as the basis of criticism, and as the justification of demands for conformity, social pressure, and punishment. Reference to this most elementary manifestation of the internal point of view is required for the analysis of the basic concepts of obligation and duty. With the addition to the system of secondary rules, the range of what is said and done from the internal point of view is much extended and diversified. With this extension comes a whole set of new concepts and they demand a reference to the internal point of view for their analysis. These include the notions of legislation, jurisdiction, validity and, generally, of legal powers, private and public. There is a constant pull towards an analysis of these in the terms of ordinary or "scientific," fact-stating or predictive discourse. But this can only reproduce their external aspect: to do justice to their distinctive, internal

aspect we need to see the different ways in which the law-making operations of the legislator, the adjudication of a court, the exercise of private or official powers, and other "acts-in-the-law" are related to secondary rules.

In [a subsequent discussion] we shall show how the ideas of the validity of law and sources of law, and the truths latent among the errors of the doctrines of sovereignty may be rephrased and clarified in terms of rules of recognition. But we shall conclude this chapter with a warning: though the combination of primary and secondary rules merits, because it explains many aspects of law, the central place assigned to it, this cannot by itself illuminate every problem. The union of primary and secondary rules is at the centre of a legal system; but it is not the whole, and as we move away from the centre we shall have to accommodate, in ways indicated in later chapters, elements of a different character.

THE FOUNDATIONS OF A LEGAL SYSTEM

RULE OF RECOGNITION AND LEGAL VALIDITY

According to the theory criticized in [a previous discussion] the foundations of a legal system consist of the situation in which the majority of a social group habitually obey the orders backed by threats of the sovereign person or persons, who themselves habitually obey no one. This social situation is, for this theory, both a necessary and a sufficient condition of the existence of law. We have already exhibited in some detail the incapacity of this theory to account for some of the salient features of a modern municipal legal system: yet nonetheless, as its hold over the minds of many thinkers suggests, it does contain, though in a blurred and misleading form, certain truths about certain important aspects of law. These truths can, however, only be clearly presented, and their importance rightly assessed, in terms of the more complex social situation where a secondary rule of recognition is accepted and used for the identification of primary rules of obligation. It is this situation which deserves, if anything does, to be called the foundations of a legal system. In this chapter we shall discuss various elements of this situation which have received only partial or misleading expression in the theory of sovereignty and elsewhere.

Wherever such a rule of recognition is accepted, both private persons and officials are provided with authoritative criteria for identifying primary rules of obligation. The criteria so provided may, as we have seen, take any one or more of a variety of forms: these include reference to an authoritative text; to legislative enactment; to customary practice; to general declarations of specified persons, or to past judicial decisions in particular cases. In a very simple system like the world of Rex I depicted in [a previous discussion], where only what he enacts is law and no legal limitations upon his legislative power are imposed by customary rule or constitutional document, the sole criterion for identifying the law will be a simple reference to fact of enactment by Rex I. The existence of this simple form of rule of recognition will be manifest in the general practice, on the part of officials or private persons, of identifying the rules by this criterion. In a modern legal system where there are a variety of "sources" of law, the rule of recognition is correspondingly more complex: the criteria for identifying the law are multiple and commonly include a written constitution, enactment by a legislature, and judicial precedents. In most cases, provision is made for possible conflict by ranking these criteria in an order of relative subordination and primacy. It is in this way that in our system "common law" is subordinate to "statute."

It is important to distinguish this relative subordination of one criterion to another from derivation, since some spurious support for the view that all law is essentially or "really" (even if only "tacitly") the product of legislation, has been gained from confusion of these two ideas. In our own system, custom and precedent are subordinate to legislation since customary and common law rules may be deprived of their status as law by statute. Yet they owe their status of law, precarious as this may be, not to a "tacit" exercise of legislative power but to the acceptance of a rule of recognition which accords them this independent though subordinate place. Again, as in the simple case, the existence of such a complex rule of recognition with this hierarchical ordering of distinct criteria is manifested in the general practice of identifying the rules by such criteria.

In the day-to-day life of a legal system its rule of recognition is very seldom expressly formulated as a rule; though occasionally, courts in England may announce in general terms the relative place of one criterion of law in relation to another, as when they assert the supremacy of Acts of Parliament over other sources or suggested sources of law. For the most part the rule of recognition is not stated, but its existence is shown in the way in which particular rules are identified, either by courts or other officials or private persons or their advisers. There is, of course, a difference in the use made by courts of the criteria provided by the rule and the use of them by others: for when courts reach a particular conclusion on the footing that a particular rule has been correctly identified as law, what they say has a special authoritative status conferred on it by other rules. In this respect, as in many others, the rule of recognition of a legal system is like the scoring rule of a game. In the course of the game the general rule defining the activities which constitute scoring (runs, goals, &c.) is seldom formulated; instead it is used by officials and players in identifying the particular phases which count towards winning. Here too, the declarations of officials (umpire or scorer) have a special authoritative status attributed to them by other rules. Further, in both cases there is the possibility of a conflict between these authoritative applications of the rule and the general understanding of what the rule plainly requires according to its terms. This, as we shall see later, is a complication which must be catered for in any account of what it is for a system of rules of this sort to exist.

The use of unstated rules of recognition, by courts and others, in identifying particular rules of the system is characteristic of the internal point of view. Those who use them in this way thereby manifest their own acceptance of them as guiding rules and with this attitude there goes a characteristic vocabulary different from the natural expressions of the external point of view. Perhaps the simplest of these is the expression, "It is the law that . . . ," which we may find on the lips not only of judges, but of ordinary men living under a legal system, when they identify a given rule of the system. This, like the expression "Out" or "Goal," is the language of one assessing a situation by reference to rules which he in common with others acknowledges as appropriate for this purpose. This attitude of shared acceptance of rules is to be contrasted with that of an observer who records *ab extra* the fact that a social group accepts such rules but does not himself accept them. The natural expression of this external point of view is not "It is the law that . . . " but "In England they recognize as law . . . whatever the Queen in Parliament enacts. . . ." The first of these forms of expression we shall call an *internal statement* because it manifests the internal point of view and is naturally used by one who, accepting the rule of recognition and without stating the fact that it is accepted, applies the rule in recognizing some particular rule of the system as valid. The second form of expression we shall call an *external statement* because it is the natural language of an external observer of the system who, without himself accepting its rule of recognition, states the fact that others accept it.

If this use of an accepted rule of recognition in making internal statements is understood and carefully distinguished from an external statement of fact that the rule is accepted, many obscurities concerning the notion of legal "validity" disappear. For the word "valid" is most frequently, though not always, used, in just such internal statements, applying to a particular rule of a legal system, an unstated but accepted rule of recognition. To say that a given rule is valid is to recognize it as passing all the tests provided by the rule of recognition and so as a rule of the system. We can indeed simply say that the statement that a particular rule is valid means that it satisfies all the criteria provided by the rule of recognition. This is incorrect only to the extent that it might obscure the internal character of such statements; for, like the cricketers' "Out," these statements of validity normally apply to a particular case a rule of recognition accepted by the speaker and others, rather than expressly state that the rule is satisfied.

Some of the puzzles connected with the idea of legal validity are said to concern the relation between the validity and the "efficacy" of law. If by "efficacy" is meant that the fact that a rule of law which requires certain behaviour is obeyed more often than not, it is plain that there is no necessary connexion between the validity of any particular rule and *its* efficacy, unless the rule of recognition of the system includes among its criteria, as some do, the provision (sometimes referred to as a rule of obsolescence) that no rule is to count as a rule of the system if it has long ceased to be efficacious.

From the inefficacy of a particular rule, which may or may not count against its validity, we must distinguish a general disregard of the rules of the system. This may be so complete in character and so protracted that we should say, in the case of a new system, that it had never established itself as the legal system of a given group, or, in the case of a once-established system, that it had ceased to be the legal system of the group. In either case, the normal context or background for making any internal statement in terms of the rules of the system is absent. In such cases it would be generally *pointless* either to assess the rights and duties of particular persons by reference to the primary rules of a system or to assess the validity of any of its rules by reference to its rules of recognition. To insist on applying a system of rules which had either never actually been effective or had been discarded would, except in special circumstances mentioned below, be as futile as to assess the progress of a game by reference to a scoring rule which had never been accepted or had been discarded.

One who makes an internal statement concerning the validity of a particular rule of a system may be said to *presuppose* the truth of the external statement of fact that the system is generally efficacious. For the normal use of internal statements is in such a context of general efficacy. It would however be wrong to say that statements of validity 'mean' that the system is generally efficacious. For though it is normally pointless or idle to talk of the validity of a rule of a system which has never established itself or has been discarded, none the less it is not meaningless nor is it always pointless. One vivid way of teaching Roman Law is to speak *as if* the system were efficacious still and to discuss the validity of particular rules and solve problems in their terms; and one way of nursing hopes for the restoration of an old social order destroyed by revolution, and rejecting the new, is to cling to the criteria of legal validity of the old régime. This is implicitly done by the White Russian who still claims property under some rule of descent which was a valid rule of Tsarist Russia.

A grasp of the normal contextual connexion between the internal statement that a given rule of a system is valid and the external statement of fact that the system is generally efficacious, will help us see in its proper perspective the common theory that to assert the validity of a rule is to predict that it will be enforced by courts or some other official action taken. In many ways this theory is similar to the predictive analysis of obligation which we considered and rejected in [a previous discussion]. In both cases alike the motive for advancing this predictive theory is the conviction that only thus can metaphysical interpretations be avoided: that either a statement that a rule is valid must ascribe some mysterious property which cannot be detected by empirical means or it must be a prediction of future behaviour of officials. In both cases also the plausibility of the theory is due to the same important fact: that the truth of the external statement of fact, which an observer might record, that the system is generally efficacious and likely to continue so, is normally presupposed by anyone who accepts the rules and makes an internal statement of obligation or validity. The two are certainly very closely associated. Finally, in both cases alike the mistake of the theory is the same: it consists in neglecting the special character of the internal statement and treating it as an external statement about official action.

This mistake becomes immediately apparent when we consider how the judge's own statement that a particular rule is valid functions in judicial decision; for, though here too, in making such a statement, the judge presupposes but does not state the general efficacy of the system, he plainly is not concerned to predict his own or others' official action. His statement that a rule is valid is an internal statement recognizing that the rule satisfies the tests for identifying what is to count as law in his court, and constitutes not a prophecy of but part of the *reason* for his decision. There is indeed a more plausible case for saying that a statement that a rule is valid is a prediction when such a statement is made by a private person; for in the case of conflict between unofficial statements of validity or invalidity and that of a court in deciding a case, there is often good sense in saying that the former must then be withdrawn. Yet even here, as we shall see when we come . . . to investigate the significance of such conflicts between official declarations and the plain requirements of the rules, it may be dogmatic to assume that it is withdrawn as a statement now shown to be *wrong,* because it has falsely *predicted* what a court would say. For there are more reasons for withdrawing statements than the fact that they are wrong, and also more ways of being wrong than this allows.

The rule of recognition providing the criteria by which the validity of other rules of the system is assessed is in an important sense, which we shall try to clarify, an *ultimate* rule: and where, as is usual, there are several criteria ranked in order of relative subordination and primacy one of them is *supreme.* These ideas of the ultimacy of the rule of recognition and the supremacy of one of its criteria merit some attention. It is important to disentangle them from the theory, which we have rejected, that somewhere in every legal system, even though it lurks behind legal forms, there must be a sovereign legislative power which is legally unlimited.

Of these two ideas, supreme criterion and ultimate rule, the first is the easiest to define. We may say that a criterion of legal validity or source of law is supreme if rules identified by reference to it are still recognized as rules of the system, even if they conflict with rules identified by reference to the other criteria, whereas rules identified by reference to the latter are not so recognized if they conflict with the rules identified by reference to the supreme criterion. A similar explanation in comparative terms can be given of the notions of "superior" and "subordinate" criteria which we have already used. It is plain that the notions of a superior and a supreme criterion merely refer to a *relative* place on a scale and do not import any notion of legally *unlimited* legislative power. Yet "supreme" and "unlimited" are easy to confuse—at least in legal theory. One reason for this is that in the simpler forms of legal system the ideas of ultimate rule of recognition, supreme criterion, and legally unlimited legislature seem to converge. For where there is a legislature subject to no constitutional limitations and competent by its enactment to deprive all other rules of law emanating from other sources of their status as law, it is part of the rule of recognition in such a system that enactment by that legislature is the supreme criterion of validity. This is, according to constitutional theory, the position in the United Kingdom. But even systems like that of the United States in which there is no such legally unlimited legislature may perfectly well contain an ultimate rule of recognition which provides a set of criteria of validity, one of which is supreme. This will be so, where the legislative competence of the ordinary legislature is limited by a constitution which contains no amending power, or places some clauses outside the scope of that power. Here there is no legally unlimited legislature, even in the widest interpretation of "legislature"; but the system of course contains an ultimate rule of recognition and, in the clauses of its constitution, a supreme criterion of validity.

The sense in which the rule of recognition is the *ultimate* rule of a system is best understood if we pursue a very familiar chain of legal reasoning. If the question is raised whether some suggested rule is legally valid, we must, in order to answer the question, use a criterion of validity provided by some other rule. Is this purported by-law of the Oxfordshire County Council valid? Yes: because it was made in exercise of the powers conferred, and in accordance with the procedure specified, by a statutory order made by the Minister of Health. At this first stage the statutory order provides the criteria in terms of which the validity of the by-law is assessed. There may be no practical need to go farther; but there is a standing possibility of doing so. We may query the validity of the statutory order and assess its validity in terms of the statute empowering the minister to make such orders. Finally when the validity of the statute has been queried and assessed by reference to the rule that what the Queen in Parliament enacts is law, we are brought to a stop in inquiries concerning validity; for we have reached a rule which, like the intermediate statutory order and statute, provides criteria for the assessment of the validity of other rules; but it is also unlike them in that there is no rule providing criteria for the assessment of its own legal validity.

There are, indeed, many questions which we can raise about this ultimate rule. We can ask whether it is the practice of courts, legislatures, officials, or private citizens in England actually to use this rule as an ultimate rule of recognition. Or has our process of legal reasoning been an idle game with the criteria of validity of a system now discarded? We can ask whether it is a satisfactory form of legal system which has such a rule at its root. Does it produce more good than evil? Are there prudential reasons for supporting it? Is there a moral obligation to do so? These are plainly very important questions; but, equally plainly, when we ask them about the rule of recognition, we are no longer attempting to answer the same kind of question about it as those which we answered about other rules with its aid. When we move from saying that a particular enactment is valid, because it satisfies the rule that what the Queen in Parliament enacts is law, to saying that in England this last rule is used by courts, officials, and private persons as the ultimate rule of recognition, we have moved from an internal statement of law asserting the validity of a rule of the system to an external statement of fact which an observer of the system might make even if he did not accept it. So too when we move from the statement that a particular enactment is valid,

to the statement that the rule of recognition of the system is an excellent one and the system based on it is one worthy of support, we have moved from a statement of legal validity to a statement of value.

Some writers, who have emphasized the legal ultimacy of the rule of recognition, have expressed this by saying that, whereas the legal validity of other rules of the system can be demonstrated by reference to it, its own validity cannot be demonstrated but is "assumed" or "postulated" or is a "hypothesis." This may, however, be seriously misleading. Statements of legal validity made about particular rules in the day-to-day life of a legal system whether by judges, lawyers, or ordinary citizens do indeed carry with them certain presuppositions. They are internal statements of law expressing the point of view of those who accept the rule of recognition of the system and, as such, leave unstated much that could be stated in external statements of fact about the system. What is thus left unstated forms the normal background or context of statements of legal validity and is thus said to be "presupposed" by them. But it is important to see precisely what these presupposed matters are, and not to obscure their character. They consist of two things. First, a person who seriously asserts the validity of some given rule of law, say a particular statute, himself makes use of a rule of recognition which he accepts as appropriate for identifying the law. Secondly, it is the case that this rule of recognition, in terms of which he assesses the validity of a particular statute, is not only accepted by him but is the rule of recognition actually accepted and employed in the general operation of the system. If the truth of this presupposition were doubted, it could be established by reference to actual practice: to the way in which courts identify what is to count as law, and to the general acceptance of or acquiescence in these identifications.

Neither of these two presuppositions are well described as "assumptions" of a "validity" which cannot be demonstrated. We only need the word "validity," and commonly only use it, to answer questions which arise *within* a system of rules where the status of a rule as a member of the system depends on its satisfying certain criteria provided by the rule of recognition. No such question can arise as to the validity of the very rule of recognition which provides the criteria; it can neither be valid nor invalid but is simply accepted as appropriate for use in this way. To express this simple fact by saying darkly that its validity is "assumed but cannot be demonstrated," is like saying that we assume, but can never demonstrate, that the standard metre bar in Paris which is the ultimate test of the correctness of all measurement in metres, is itself correct.

A more serious objection is that talk of the "assumption" that the ultimate rule of recognition is valid conceals the essentially factual character of the second presupposition which lies behind the lawyers' statements of validity. No doubt the practice of judges, officials, and others, in which the actual existence of a rule of recognition consists, is a complex matter. As we shall see later, there are certainly situations in which questions as to the precise content and scope of this kind of rule, and even as to its existence, may not admit of a clear or determinate answer. None the less it is important to distinguish "assuming the validity" from "presupposing the existence" of such a rule; if only because failure to do this obscures what is meant by the assertion that such a rule *exists*.

In the simple system of primary rules of obligation sketched in the last chapter, the assertion that a given rule existed could only be an external statement of fact such as an observer who did not accept the rules might make and verify by ascertaining whether or not, as a matter of fact, a given mode of behaviour was generally accepted as a standard and was accompanied by those features which, as we have seen, distinguish a social rule from mere convergent habits. It is in this way also that we should now interpret and verify the assertion that in England a

rule—though not a legal one—exists that we must bare the head on entering a church. If such rules as these are found to exist in the actual practice of a social group, there is no separate question of their validity to be discussed, though of course their value or desirability is open to question. Once their existence has been established as a fact we should only confuse matters by affirming or denying that they were valid or by saying that "we assumed" but could not show their validity. Where, on the other hand, as in a mature legal system, we have a system of rules which includes a rule of recognition so that the status of a rule as a member of the system now depends on whether it satisfies certain criteria provided by the rule of recognition, this brings with it a new application of the word "exist." The statement that a rule exists may now no longer be what it was in the simple case of customary rules—an external statement of the *fact* that a certain mode of behaviour was generally accepted as a standard in practice. It may now be an internal statement applying an accepted but unstated rule of recognition and meaning (roughly) no more than "valid given the systems criteria of validity." In this respect, however, as in others a rule of recognition is unlike other rules of the system. The assertion that it exists can only be an external statement of fact. For whereas a subordinate rule of a system may be valid and in that sense "exist" even if it is generally disregarded, the rule of recognition exists only as a complex, but normally concordant, practice of the courts, officials, and private persons in identifying the law by reference to certain criteria. Its existence is a matter of fact.

H. L. A. HART
Positivism and the Separation of Law and Morals*

In this article I shall discuss and attempt to defend a view which Mr. Justice Holmes, among others, held and for which he and they have been much criticized. But I wish first to say why I think that Holmes, whatever the vicissitudes of his American reputation may be, will always remain for Englishmen a heroic figure in jurisprudence. This will be so because he magically combined two qualities: One of them is imaginative power, which English legal thinking has often lacked; the other is clarity, which English legal thinking usually possesses. The English lawyer who turns to read Holmes is made to see that what he had taken to be settled and stable is really always on the move. To make this discovery with Holmes is to be with a guide whose words may leave you unconvinced, sometimes even repelled, but never mystified. Like our own Austin, with whom Holmes shared many ideals and thoughts, Holmes was sometimes clearly wrong; but again like Austin, when this was so he was always wrong clearly. This surely is a sovereign virtue in jurisprudence. Clarity I know is said not to be enough; this may be true, but there are still questions in jurisprudence where the issues are confused because they are discussed in a style which Holmes would have spurned for its obscurity. Perhaps this is inevitable: Jurisprudence trembles so uncertainly on the margin of many subjects that there will always be need for someone, in Bentham's phrase, "to pluck the mask of Mystery" from its face.[1] This is true, to a preeminent degree, of the subject of this article. Contemporary voices tell us we must recognize something obscured by the legal "positivists" whose day is now over: that there is a "point of intersection between law and morals,"[2] or that what *is* and what *ought* to be are somehow indissolubly fused or inseparable,[3] though the positivists denied it. What do these phrases mean? Or rather which of

the many things that they *could* mean, *do* they mean? Which of them do "positivists" deny and why is it wrong to do so?

I.

I shall present the subject as part of the history of an idea. At the close of the eighteenth century and the beginning of the nineteenth the most earnest thinkers in England about legal and social problems and the architects of great reforms were the great utilitarians. Two of them, Bentham and Austin, constantly insisted on the need to distinguish, firmly and with the maximum of clarity, law as it is from law as it ought to be. This theme haunts their work, and they condemned the natural-law thinkers precisely because they had blurred this apparently simple but vital distinction. By contrast, at the present time in this country and to a lesser extent in England, this separation between law and morals is held to be superficial and wrong. Some critics have thought that it blinds men to the true nature of law and its roots in social life.[4] Others have thought it not only intellectually misleading but corrupting in practice, at its worst apt to weaken resistance to state tyranny or absolutism,[5] and at its best apt to bring law into disrespect. The nonpejorative name "legal positivism," like most terms which are used as missiles in intellectual battles, has come to stand for a baffling multitude of different sins. One of them is the sin, real or alleged, of insisting, as Austin and Bentham did, on the separation of law as it is and law as it ought to be.

How then has this reversal of the wheel come about? What are the theoretical errors in this distinction? Have the practical consequences of stressing the distinction as Bentham and Austin did been bad? Should we now reject it or keep it? In considering these questions we should recall the social philosophy which went along with the utilitarians' insistence on this distinction. They stood firmly but on their own utilitarian ground for all the principles of liberalism in law and government. No one has ever combined, with such

*From 71 *Harvard Law Review* 593 (1958). Copyright © 1958 by The Harvard Law Review Association. Reprinted by permission of the author and the publisher.

even-minded sanity as the utilitarians, the passion for reform with respect for law together with a due recognition of the need to control the abuse of power even when power is in the hands of reformers. One by one in Bentham's works you can identify the elements of the *Rechtstaat* and all the principles for the defense of which the terminology of natural law has in our day been revived. Here are liberty of speech, and of press, the right of association,[6] the need that laws should be published and made widely known before they are enforced,[7] the need to control administrative agencies,[8] the insistence that there should be no criminal liability without fault,[9] and the importance of the principle of legality, *nulla poena sine lege.*[10] Some, I know, find the political and moral insight of the utilitarians a very simple one, but we should not mistake this simplicity for superficiality nor forget how favorably their simplicities compare with the profundities of other thinkers. Take only one example: Bentham on slavery. He says the question at issue is not whether those who are held as slaves can reason, but simply whether they suffer.[11] Does this not compare well with the discussion of the question in terms of whether or not there are some men whom Nature has fitted only to be the living instruments of others? We owe it to Bentham more than anyone else that we have stopped discussing this and similar questions of social policy in that form.

So Bentham and Austin were not dry analysts fiddling with verbal distinctions while cities burned, but were the vanguard of a movement which laboured with passionate intensity and much success to bring about a better society and better laws. Why then did they insist on the separation of law as it is and law as it ought to be? What did they mean? Let us first see what they said. Austin formulated the doctrine:

The existence of law is one thing; its merit or demerit is another. Whether it be or be not is one enquiry; whether it be or be not conformable to an assumed standard, is a different enquiry. A law, which actually exists, is a law, though we happen to dislike it, or though it vary from the text, by which we regulate our approbation and disapprobation. This truth, when formally announced as an abstract proposition, is so simple and glaring that it seems idle to insist upon it. But simple and glaring as it is, when enunciated in abstract expressions the enumeration of the instances in which it has been forgotten would fill a volume.

Sir William Blackstone, for example, says in his "Commentaries," that the laws of God are superior in obligation to all other laws; that no human laws should be suffered to contradict them; that human laws are of no validity if contrary to them; and that all valid laws derive their force from that Divine original.

Now, he *may* mean that all human laws ought to conform to the Divine laws. If this be his meaning, I assent to it without hesitation. . . . Perhaps, again, he means that human lawgivers are themselves obliged by the Divine laws to fashion the laws which they impose by that ultimate standard, because if they do not, God will punish them. To this also I entirely assent. . . .

But the meaning of this passage of Blackstone, if it has a meaning, seems rather to be this: that no human law which conflicts with the Divine law is obligatory or binding; in other words, that no human law which conflicts with the Divine law *is a law.* . . . [12]

Austin's protest against blurring the distinction between what law is and what it ought to be is quite general: it is a mistake, whatever our standard of what ought to be, whatever "the text by which we regulate our approbation or disapprobation." His examples, however, are always a confusion between law as it is and law as morality would require it to be. For him, it must be remembered, the fundamental principles of morality were God's commands, to which utility was an "index": besides this there was the actual accepted morality of a social group or "positive" morality.

Bentham insisted on this distinction without characterizing morality by reference to God but only, of course, by reference to the principles of utility. Both thinkers' prime reason for this insistence was to enable men to see steadily the precise issues posed by the existence of morally bad laws, and to understand the specific character of the authority of a legal order. Bentham's general recipe for life under the government of laws was simple: it was *"to obey punctually; to censure freely."*[13] But Bentham was especially aware, as an anxious spectator of the French revolution, that this was not enough: the time might come in any society when the law's commands were so evil that the question of resistance had to be faced, and it was then essential that the issues at stake at this point should neither be oversimplified nor obscured.[14] Yet, this was precisely what the confusion between law and morals had done and Bentham found that the confusion had spread symmetrically in two different directions. On the one hand Bentham had in mind the anarchist who argues thus: "This ought not to be the law, therefore it is not and I am free not merely to censure but to disregard it." On the other hand he thought of the reactionary who argues: "This is the law, therefore it is what it ought to be," and thus stifles criticism at its birth. Both errors, Bentham thought, were to be found in Blackstone: there was his incautious statement that human laws were invalid if contrary to the law of God,[15] and "that spirit of obsequious *quietism* that seems constitutional in our Author" which "will scarce ever let him recognise a difference" between what is and what ought to be.[16] This indeed was for Bentham the occupational disease of lawyers: "[I]n the eyes of lawyers—not to speak of their dupes—that is to say, as yet, the generality of non-lawyers—the *is* and *ought to be* ... were one and indivisible."[17] There are therefore two dangers between which insistence on this distinction will help us to steer: the danger that law and its authority may be dissolved in man's conceptions of what law ought to be and the danger that the existing law may supplant morality as a final test of conduct and so escape criticism.

In view of later criticisms it is also important to distinguish several things that the utilitarians did not mean by insisting on their separation of law and morals. They certainly accepted many of the things that might be called "the intersection of law and morals." First, they never denied that, as a matter of historical fact, the development of legal systems had been powerfully influenced by moral opinion, and, conversely, that moral standards had been profoundly influenced by law, so that the content of many legal rules mirrored moral rules or principles. It is not in fact always easy to trace this historical causal connection, but Bentham was certainly ready to admit its existence; so too Austin spoke of the "frequent coincidence"[18] of positive law and morality and attributed the confusion of what law is with what law ought to be to this very fact.

Secondly, neither Bentham nor his followers denied that by explicit legal provisions moral principles might at different points be brought into a legal system and form part of its rules, or that courts might be legally bound to decide in accordance with what they thought just or best. Bentham indeed recognized, as Austin did not, that even the supreme legislative power might be subjected to legal restraints by a constitution[19] and would not have denied that moral principles, like those of the Fifth Amendment, might form the content of such legal constitutional restraints. Austin differed in thinking that restraints on the supreme legislative power could not have the force of law, but would remain merely political or moral checks;[20] but of course he would have recognized that a statute, for example, might confer a delegated legislative power and restrict the area of its exercise by reference to moral principles.

What both Bentham and Austin were anxious to assert were the following two simple things: first, in the absence of an expressed constitutional or legal provision, it could not follow from the mere fact that a rule violated standards of morality that it was not a rule of law; and, conversely, it could not follow from the mere fact that a rule was morally desirable that it was a rule of law.

The history of this simple doctrine in the nineteenth century is too long and too intricate to trace here. Let me summarize it by saying that after it was propounded to the world by Austin it dominated English jurisprudence and constitutes part of the framework of most of those curiously English and perhaps unsatisfactory productions—the omnibus surveys of the whole field of jurisprudence. A succession of these were published after a full text of Austin's lectures finally appeared in 1863. In each of them the utilitarian separation of law and morals is treated as something that enables lawyers to attain a new clarity. Austin was said by one of his English successors, Amos, "to have delivered the law from the dead body of morality that still clung to it";[21] and even Maine, who was critical of Austin at many points, did not question this part of his doctrine. In the United States men like N. St. John Green,[22] Gray, and Holmes considered that insistence on this distinction had enabled the understanding of law as a means of social control to get off to a fruitful new start; they welcomed it both as self-evident and as illuminating—as a revealing tautology. This distinction is, of course, one of the main themes of Holmes' most famous essay "The Path of the Law,"[23] but the place it had in the estimation of these American writers is best seen in what Gray wrote at the turn of the century in *The Nature and Sources of the Law*. He said:

The great gain in its fundamental conceptions which Jurisprudence made during the last century was the recognition of the truth that the Law of a State ... is not an ideal, but something which actually exists.... [I]t is not that which ought to be, but that which is. To fix this definitely in the Jurisprudence of the Common Law, is the feat that Austin accomplished.[24]

II.

So much for the doctrine in the heyday of its success. Let us turn now to some of the criticisms. Undoubtedly, when Bentham and Austin insisted on the distinction between law as it is and as it ought to be, they had in mind *particular* laws the meanings of which were clear and so not in dispute, and they were concerned to argue that such laws, even if morally outrageous, were still laws. It is, however, necessary, in considering the criticisms which later developed, to consider more than those criticisms which were directed to this particular point if we are to get at the root of the dissatisfaction felt; we must also take account of the objection that, even if what the utilitarians said on this particular point were true, their insistence on it, in a terminology suggesting a general cleavage between what is and ought to be law, obscured the fact that at other points there is an essential point of contact between the two. So in what follows I shall consider not only criticisms of the particular point which the utilitarians had in mind, but also the claim that an essential connection between law and morals emerges if we examine how laws, the meanings of which are in dispute, are interpreted and applied in concrete cases; and that this connection emerges again if we widen our point of view and ask, not whether every particular rule of law must satisfy a moral minimum in order to be a law, but whether a system of rules which altogether failed to do this could be a legal system.

There is, however, one major initial complexity by which criticism has been much confused. We must remember that the utilitarians combined with their insistence on the separation of law and morals two other equally famous but distinct doctrines. One was the important truth that a purely analytical study of legal concepts, a study of the meaning of the distinctive vocabulary of the law, was as vital to our understanding of the nature of law as historical or sociological studies, though of course it could not supplant them. The other doctrine was the famous imperative theory of law—that law is essentially a command.

These three doctrines constitute the utilitarian tradition in jurisprudence; yet they are distinct doctrines. It is possible to endorse the separation between law and morals and to value analytical inquiries into the meaning of legal concepts and yet think it wrong to conceive of law as essentially a command. One source of great confusion in the criticism of the separation of law and morals was the belief that the falsity of any one of these three

doctrines in the utilitarian tradition showed the other two to be false; what was worse was the failure to see that there were three quite separate doctrines in this tradition. The indiscriminate use of the label "positivism" to designate ambiguously each one of these three separate doctrines (together with some others which the utilitarians never professed) has perhaps confused the issue more than any other single factor.[25] Some of the early American critics of the Austinian doctrine were, however, admirably clear on just this matter. Gray, for example, added at the end of the tribute to Austin, which I have already quoted, the words, "He may have been wrong in treating the Law of the State as being the command of the sovereign"[26] and he touched shrewdly on many points where the command theory is defective. But other critics have been less clearheaded and have thought that the inadequacies of the command theory which gradually came to light were sufficient to demonstrate the falsity of the separation of law and morals.

This was a mistake, but a natural one. To see how natural it was we must look a little more closely at the command idea. The famous theory that law is a command was a part of a wider and more ambitious claim. Austin said that the notion of a command was "the *key* to the sciences of jurisprudence and morals,"[27] and contemporary attempts to elucidate moral judgments in terms of "imperative" or "prescriptive" utterances echo this ambitious claim. But the command theory, viewed as an effort to identify even the quintessence of law, let along the quintessence of morals, seems breathtaking in its simplicity and quite inadequate. There is much, even in the simplest legal system, that is distorted if presented as a command. Yet the utilitarians thought that the essence of a legal system could be conveyed if the notion of a command were supplemented by that of a habit of obedience. The simple scheme was this: What is a command? It is simply an expression by one person of the desire that another person should do or abstain from some action, accompanied by a threat of punishment which is likely to follow disobedience. Commands are laws if two conditions are satisfied: First, they must be general; second, they must be commanded by what (as both Bentham and Austin claimed) exists in every political society whatever its constitutional form, namely, a person or a group of persons who are in receipt of habitual obedience from most of the society but pay no such obedience to others. These persons are its sovereign. Thus law is the command of the un-commanded commanders of society—the creation of the legally untrammelled will of the sovereign who is by definition outside the law.

It is easy to see that this account of a legal system is threadbare. One can also see why it might seem that its inadequacy is due to the omission of some essential connection with morality. The situation which the simple trilogy of command, sanction, and sovereign avails to describe, if you take these notions at all precisely, is like that of a gunman saying to his victim, "Give me your money or your life." The only difference is that in the case of a legal system the gunman says it to a large number of people who are accustomed to the racket and habitually surrender to it. Law surely is not the gunman situation writ large, and legal order is surely not to be thus simply identified with compulsion.

This scheme, despite the points of obvious analogy between a statute and a command, omits some of the most characteristic elements of law. Let me cite a few. It is wrong to think of a legislature (and a fortiori an electorate) with a changing membership, as a group of persons habitually obeyed: this simple idea is suited only to a monarch sufficiently long-lived for a "habit" to grow up. Even if we waive this point, nothing which legislators do makes law unless they comply with fundamental accepted rules specifying the essential lawmaking procedures. This is true even in a system having a simple unitary constitution like the British. These fundamental accepted rules specifying what the legislature must do to legislate are not commands habitually obeyed, nor can they be expressed as habits of obedience to persons. They lie at the root of a legal system, and what is most missing in the utilitarian scheme is an analysis of what it is for a social group and its officials to accept such rules. This notion, not that of a command as Austin claimed, is the "key to the science of jurisprudence," or at least one of the keys.

Again, Austin, in the case of a democracy, looked past the legislators to the electorate as "the sovereign" (or in England as part of it). He thought that in the United States the mass of the electors to the state and federal legislatures were the sovereign whose commands, given by their "agents" in the legislatures, were law. But on this footing the whole notion of the sovereign outside the law being "habitually obeyed" by the "bulk" of the population must go: for in this case the "bulk" obeys the bulk, that is, it obeys itself.

Plainly the general acceptance of the authority of a lawmaking procedure, irrespective of the changing individuals who operate it from time to time, can be only distorted by an analysis in terms of mass habitual obedience to certain persons who are by definition outside the law, just as the cognate but much simpler phenomenon of the general social acceptance of a rule, say of taking off the hat when entering a church, would be distorted if represented as habitual obedience by the mass to specific persons.

Other critics dimly sensed a further and more important defect in the command theory, yet blurred the edge of an important criticism by assuming that the defect was due to the failure to insist upon some important connection between law and morals. This more radical defect is as follows. The picture that the command theory draws of life under law is essentially a simple relationship of the commander to the commanded, of superior to inferior, of top to bottom; the relationship is vertical between the commanders or authors of the law conceived of as essentially outside the law and those who are commanded and subject to the law. In this picture no place, or only an accidental or subordinate place, is afforded for a distinction between types of legal rules which are in fact radically different. Some laws require men to act in certain ways or to abstain from acting whether they wish to or not. The criminal law consists largely of rules of this sort: like commands they are simply "obeyed" or "disobeyed." But other legal rules are presented to society in quite different ways and have quite different functions. They provide facilities more or less elaborate for individuals to create structures of rights and duties for the conduct of life within the coercive framework of the law. Such are the rules enabling individuals to make contracts, wills, and trusts, and generally to mould their legal relations with others. Such rules, unlike the criminal law, are not factors designed to obstruct wishes and choices of an antisocial sort. On the contrary, these rules provide facilities for the realization of wishes and choices. They do not say (like commands) "do this whether you wish it or not," but rather "if you wish to do this, here is the way to do it." Under these rules we exercise powers, make claims, and assert rights. These phrases mark off characteristic features of laws that confer rights and powers; they are laws which are, so to speak, put at the disposition of individuals in a way in which the criminal law is not. Much ingenuity has gone into the task of "reducing" laws of this second sort to some complex variant of laws of the first sort. The effort to show that laws conferring rights are "really" only conditional stipulations of sanctions to be exacted from the person ultimately under a legal duty characterizes much of Kelsen's work.[28] Yet to urge this is really just to exhibit dogmatic determination to suppress one aspect of the legal system in order to maintain the theory that the stipulation of a sanction, like Austin's command, represents the quintessence of law. One might as well urge that the rules of baseball were "really" only complex conditional directions to the scorer and that this showed their real or "essential" nature.

One of the first jurists in England to break with the Austinian tradition, Salmond, complained that the analysis in terms of commands left the notion of a right unprovided with a place.[29] But he confused the point. He argued first, and correctly, that if laws are merely commands it is inexplicable that we should have come to speak of legal rights and powers as conferred or arising under them, but then wrongly concluded that the rules of a legal system must necessarily be connected with moral rules or principles of justice and that only on this footing could the phenomenon of legal rights be explained. Otherwise, Salmond thought, we would have to say that a mere "verbal coincidence" connects the concepts of legal and moral right. Similarly, continental critics of the utilitarians, always alive to the complexity of the notion of a subjective right, insisted that the command theory gave it no place. Hägerström insisted that if laws were merely commands the notion of an individual's right was really inexplicable, for commands are, as he said, something which we either obey or we do not obey; they do not confer rights.[30] But he, too, concluded that moral, or, as he put it, commonsense, notions of justice must therefore be necessarily involved in the analysis of any legal structure elaborate enough to confer rights.[31]

Yet, surely these arguments are confused. Rules that confer rights, though distinct from commands, need not be moral rules or coincide with them. Rights, after all, exist under the rules of ceremonies, games, and in many other spheres regulated by rules which are irrelevant to the question of justice or what the law ought to be. Nor need rules which confer rights be just or morally good rules. The rights of a master over his slaves show us that. "Their merit or demerit," as Austin termed it, depends on how rights are distributed in society and over whom or what they are exercised. These critics indeed revealed the inadequacy of the simple notions of command and habit for the analysis of law; at many points it is apparent that the social acceptance of a rule or standard of authority (even if it is motivated only by fear or superstition or rests on inertia) must be brought into the analysis and cannot itself be reduced to the two simple terms. Yet nothing in this showed the utilitarian insistence on the distinction between the existence of law and its "merits" to be wrong.

III.

I now turn to a distinctively American criticism of the separation of the law that is from the law that ought to be. It emerged from the critical study of the judicial process with which American jurisprudence has been on the whole so beneficially occupied. The most skeptical of these critics—the loosely named "Realists" of the 1930s—perhaps too naïvely accepted the conceptual framework of the natural sciences as adequate for the characterization of law and for the analysis of rule-guided action of which a living system of law at least partly consists. But they opened men's eyes to what actually goes on when courts decide cases, and the contrast they drew between the actual facts of judicial decision and the traditional terminology for describing it as if it were a wholly logical operation was usually illuminating; for in spite of some exaggeration the "Realists" made us acutely conscious of one cardinal feature of human language and human thought, emphasis on which is vital not only for the understanding of law but in areas of philosophy far beyond the confines of jurisprudence. The insight of this school may be presented in the following example. A legal rule forbids you to take a vehicle into the public park. Plainly this forbids an automobile, but what about bicycles, roller skates, toy automobiles? What about airplanes? Are these, as we say, to be called "vehicles" for the purpose of the rule or not? If we are to communicate with each other at all, and if, as in the most elementary form of law, we are to express our intentions that a certain type of behavior be regulated by rules, then the general words we use—like "vehicle" in the case I consider—must have some standard instance in which no doubts are felt about its application. There must be a core of settled meaning, but there will be, as well, a penumbra of debatable cases in which words are neither obviously applicable nor obviously ruled out. These cases will each have some features in common with the standard case; they will lack others or be accompanied by features not present in the standard case. Human invention and natural processes continually throw up such variants on the familiar, and if we are to say that these ranges of facts do or do not fall under existing rules, then the classifier must make a decision which is not dictated to him, for the facts and phenomena to which we fit our words and apply our rules are as it were *dumb*. The toy automobile cannot speak up and say, "I am a vehicle for the purpose of this legal rule," nor can the roller skates chorus, "We are not a vehicle." Fact situations do not await us neatly labeled, creased, and folded, nor is their legal classification written on them to be simply read off by the judge. Instead, in applying legal rules, someone must take the responsibility of deciding that words do or do not cover some case in hand with all the practical consequences involved in this decision.

We may call the problems which arise outside the hard core of standard instances or settled meaning "problems of the penumbra"; they are always with us whether in relation to such trivial things as the regulation of the use of the public park or in relation to the multidimensional generalities of a constitution. If a penumbra of uncertainty must surround all legal rules, then their application to specific cases in the penumbral area cannot be a matter of logical deduction, and so deductive reasoning, which for generations has been cherished as the very perfection of human reasoning, cannot serve as a model for what judges, or indeed anyone, should do in bringing particular cases under general rules. In this area men cannot live by deduction alone. And it follows that if legal arguments and legal decisions of penumbral questions are to be rational, their rationality must lie in something other than a logical relation to premises. So if it is rational or "sound" to argue and to decide that for the purposes of this rule an airplane is not a vehicle, this argument must be sound or rational without being logically conclusive. What is it then that makes such decisions correct or at least better than alternative decisions? Again, it seems true to say that the criterion which makes a decision sound in such cases is some concept of what the law ought to be; it is easy to slide from that into saying that it must be a moral judgment about what law ought to be. So here we touch upon a point of necessary "intersection between law and morals" which demonstrates the falsity

or, at any rate, the misleading character of the utilitarians' emphatic insistence on the separation of law as it is and ought to be. Surely, Bentham and Austin could only have written as they did because they misunderstood or neglected this aspect of the judicial process, because they ignored the problems of the penumbra.

The misconception of the judicial process which ignores the problems of the penumbra and which views the process as consisting preeminently in deductive reasoning is often stigmatized as the error of "formalism" or "literalism." My question now is, how and to what extent does the demonstration of this error show the utilitarian distinction to be wrong or misleading? Here there are many issues which have been confused, but I can only disentangle some. The charge of formalism has been leveled both at the "positivist" legal theorist and at the courts, but of course it must be a very different charge in each case. Leveled at the legal theorist, the charge means that he has made a theoretical mistake about the character of legal decision; he has thought of the reasoning involved as consisting in deduction from premises in which the judges' practical choices or decision play no part. It would be easy to show that Austin was guiltless of this error; only an entire misconception of what analytical jurisprudence is and why he thought it important has led to the view that he, or any other analyst, believed that the law was a closed logical system in which judges deduced their decisions from premises.[32] On the contrary, he was very much alive to the character of language, to its vagueness or open character;[33] he thought that in the penumbral situation judges must necessarily legislate,[34] and, in accents that sometimes recall those of the late Judge Jerome Frank, he berated the common-law judges for legislating feebly and timidly and for blindly relying on real or fancied analogies with past cases instead of adapting their decisions to the growing needs of society as revealed by the moral standard of utility.[35] The villains of this piece, responsible for the conception of the judge as an automaton, are not the utilitarian thinkers. The responsibility, if it is to be laid at the door of any theorist, is with thinkers like Blackstone and, at an earlier stage, Montesquieu. The root of this evil is preoccupation with the separation of powers and Blackstone's "childish fiction" (as Austin termed it) that judges only "find," never "make," law.

But we are concerned with "formalism" as a vice not of jurists but of judges. What precisely is it for a judge to commit this error, to be a "formalist," "automatic," a "slot machine"? Curiously enough the literature which is full of the denunciation of these vices never makes this clear in concrete terms; instead we have only descriptions which cannot mean what they appear to say: it is said that in the formalist error courts make an excessive use of logic, take a thing to "a dryly logical extreme,"[36] or make an excessive use of analytical methods. But just how in being a formalist does a judge make an excessive use of logic? It is clear that the essence of his error is to give some general term an interpretation which is blind to social values and consequences (or which is in some other way stupid or perhaps merely disliked by critics). But logic does not prescribe interpretation of terms; it dictates neither the stupid nor intelligent interpretation of any expression. Logic only tells you hypothetically that *if* you give a certain term a certain interpretation then a certain conclusion follows. Logic is silent on how to classify particulars—and this is the heart of a judicial decision. So this reference to logic and to logical extremes is a misnomer for something else, which must be this. A judge has to apply a rule to a concrete case—perhaps the rule that one may not take a stolen "vehicle" across state lines, and in this case an airplane has been taken.[37] He either does not see or pretends not to see that the general terms of this rule are susceptible of different interpretations and that he has a choice left open uncontrolled by linguistic conventions. He ignores, or is blind to, the fact that he is in the area of the penumbra and is not dealing with a standard case. Instead of choosing in the light of social aims, the judge fixes the meaning in a different way. He either takes the meaning that the word most obviously suggests in its ordinary nonlegal context to ordinary men, or one which the word has been given in some other legal context, or, still worse, he thinks of a standard case and then arbitrarily identifies certain features in it—for example, in the case of a vehicle, (1) normally used on land, (2) capable of carrying a human person, (3) capable of being self-propelled—and treats these three as always necessary and always sufficient conditions for the use in all contexts of the word "vehicle," irrespective of the social consequences of giving it this interpretation. This choice, not "logic," would force the judge to include a toy motor car (if electrically propelled) and to exclude bicycles and the airplane. In all this there is possibly great stupidity but no more "logic," and no less, than in cases in which the interpretation given to a general term and the consequent application of some general rule to a particular case is consciously controlled by some identified social aim.

Decisions made in a fashion as blind as this would scarcely deserve the name of decisions; we might as well toss a penny in applying a rule of law. But it is at least doubtful whether any judicial decisions (even in England) have been quite as automatic as this. Rather either the interpretations stigmatized as automatic have resulted from the conviction that it is fairer in a criminal statute to take a meaning which would jump to the mind of the ordinary man at the cost even of defeating other values, and this itself is a social policy (though possibly a bad one); or much more frequently, what is stigmatized as "mechanical" and "automatic" is a determined choice made indeed in the light of a social aim but of a conservative social aim. Certainly many of the Supreme Court decisions at the turn of the century which have been so stigmatized[38] represent clear choices in the penumbral area to give effect to a policy of a conservative type. This is peculiarly true of Mr. Justice Peckham's opinions defining the spheres of police power and due process.[39]

But how does the wrongness of deciding cases in an automatic and mechanical way and the rightness of deciding cases by reference to social purposes show that the utilitarian insistence on the distinction between what the law is and what it ought to be is wrong? I take it that no one who wished to use these vices of formalism as proof that the distinction between what is and what ought to be is mistaken would deny that the decisions stigmatized as automatic are law; nor would he deny that the system in which such automatic decisions are made is a legal system. Surely he would say that they are law, but they are bad law, they ought not to be law. But this would be to use the distinction, not to refute it; and of course both Bentham and Austin used it to attack judges for failing to decide penumbral cases in accordance with the growing needs of society.

Clearly, if the demonstration of the errors of formalism is to show the utilitarian distinction to be wrong, the point must be drastically restated. The point must be not merely that a judicial decision to be rational must be made in the light of some conception of what ought to be, but that the aims, the social policies and purposes to which judges should appeal if their decisions are to be rational, are themselves to be considered as part of the law in some suitably wide sense of "law" which is held to be more illuminating than that used by the utilitarians. This restatement of the point would have the following consequence: Instead of saying that the recurrence of penumbral questions shows us that legal rules are essentially incomplete, and that, when they fail to determine decisions, judges must legislate and so exercise a creative choice between alternatives, we shall say that the social policies which guide the judges' choice are in a sense there for them to discover; the judges are only "drawing out" of the rule what, if it is properly understood, is "latent" within it. To call this judicial legislation is to obscure some essential continuity between the clear cases of the rule's application and the penumbral decisions. I shall question later whether this way of talking is salutary, but I wish at this time to point out something obvious, but likely, if not stated, to tangle the issues. It does not follow that, because the opposite of a decision reached blindly in the formalist or literalist manner is a decision intelligently reached by reference to some conception of what ought to be, we have a junction of law and morals. We must, I think, beware of thinking in a too simple-minded fashion about the word "ought." This is not because there is no distinction to be made between law as it is and ought to be. Far from it. It is because the distinction should be between what is and what from many different points of view ought to be. The word "ought" merely reflects the presence of some standard of criticism; one of these standards is a moral standard but not all standards are moral. We say to our neighbour, "You ought not to lie," and that may certainly be a moral judgment, but we should remember that the baffled poisoner may say, "I ought to have given her a second dose." The point here is that intelligent decisions which we oppose to mechanical or formal decisions are not necessarily identical with decisions defensible on moral grounds. We may say of many a decision: "Yes, that is right; that is as it ought to be," and we may mean only that some accepted purpose or policy has been thereby advanced; we may not mean to endorse the moral propriety of the policy or the decision. So the contrast between the mechanical decision and the intelligent one can be reproduced inside a system dedicated to the pursuit of the most evil aims. It does not exist as a contrast to be found only in legal systems which, like our own, widely recognize principles of justice and moral claims of individuals.

An example may make this point plainer. With us the task of sentencing in criminal cases is the one that seems most obviously to demand from the judge the exercise of moral judgment. Here the factors to be weighed seem clearly to be moral factors: society must not be exposed to wanton attack; too much misery must not be inflicted on either the victim or his dependents; efforts must be made to enable him to lead a better life and regain a position in the society whose laws he has violated. To a judge striking the balance among these claims, with all the discretion and perplexities involved, his task seems as plain an example of the exercise of moral judgment as could be; and it seems to be the polar opposite of some mechanical application of a tariff of penalties fixing a sentence careless of the moral claims which in our system have to be weighed. So here intelligent and rational decision is guided however uncertainly by moral aims. But we have only to vary the example to see that this need not necessarily be so and surely, if it need not necessarily be so, the utilitarian point remains unshaken. Under the Nazi regime men were sentenced by courts for criticism of the regime. Here the choice of sentence might be guided exclusively by consideration of what was needed to maintain the state's tyranny effectively. What sentence would both terrorize the public at large and keep the friends and family of the prisoner in suspense so that both hope and fear would cooperate as factors making for subservience? The prisoner of such a system would be regarded simply as an object to be used in pursuit of these aims. Yet, in contrast with a mechanical decision, decision on these grounds would be intelligent and purposive, and from one point of view the decision would be as it ought to be. Of course, I am not unaware that a whole philosophical tradition has sought to demonstrate the fact that we cannot correctly call decisions or behavior truly rational unless they are in conformity with moral aims and principles. But the example I have used seems to me to serve at least as a warning that we cannot use the errors of formalism as something which per se demonstrates the falsity of the utilitarian insistence on the distinction between law as it is and law as *morally* it ought to be.

We can now return to the main point. It is true that the intelligent decision of penumbral questions is one made not mechanically but in the light of aims, purposes, and policies, though not necessarily in the light of anything we would call moral principles, is it wise to express this important fact by saying that the firm utilitarian distinction between what the law is and what it ought to be should be dropped? Perhaps the claim that it is wise cannot be theoretically refuted for it is, in effect, an *invitation* to revise our conception of what a legal rule is. We are invited to include in the "rule" the various aims and policies in the light of which its penumbral cases are decided on the ground that these aims have, because of their importance, as much right to be called law as the core of legal rules whose meaning is settled. But though an invitation cannot be refuted, it may be refused and I would proffer two reasons for refusing this invitation. First, everything we have learned about the judicial process can be expressed in other less mysterious ways. We can say laws are incurably incomplete and we must decide the penumbral cases rationally by reference to social aims. I think Holmes, who had such a vivid appreciation of the fact that "general propositions do not decide concrete cases," would have put it that way. Second, to insist on the utilitarian distinction is to emphasize that the hard core of settled meaning is law in some centrally important sense and that even if there are borderlines, there must first be lines. If this were not so the notion of rules controlling courts' decisions would be senseless as some of the "Realists" —in their most extreme moods, and, I think, on bad grounds—claimed.[40]

By contrast, to soften the distinction, to assert mysteriously that there is some fused identity between law as it is and as it ought to be, is to suggest that all legal questions are fundamentally like those of the penumbra. It is to assert that there is no central element of actual law to be seen in the core of central meaning which rules have, that there is nothing in the nature of a legal rule inconsistent with *all* questions being open to reconsideration in the light of social policy. Of course, it is good to be occupied with the penumbra. Its problems are rightly the daily diet of the law schools. But to be occupied with the penumbra is one thing, to be preoccupied with it another. And preoccupation with the penumbra is, if I may say so, as rich a source of confusion in the American legal tradition as formalism in the English. Of course we might abandon the notion that rules have authority; we might cease to attach force or even meaning to an argument that a case falls clearly within a rule and the scope of a precedent. We might call all such reasoning "automatic" or "mechanical," which is already the routine invective of the courts. But until we decide that this *is* what we want; we should not encourage it by obliterating the utilitarian distinction.

IV.

The third criticism of the separation of law and morals is of a very different character; it certainly is less an intellectual argument against the utilitarian distinction than a passionate appeal supported not by detailed reasoning but by reminders of a terrible experience. For it consists of the testimony of those who have descended into Hell, and, like Ulysses or Dante, brought back a message for human beings. Only in this case the Hell was not beneath or beyond earth, but on it; it was a Hell created on earth by men for other men.

This appeal comes from those German thinkers who lived through the Nazi regime and reflected upon its evil manifestations in the legal system. One of these thinkers, Gustav Radbruch, had himself shared the "positivist" doctrine until the Nazi tyranny, but he was converted by this experience and so his appeal to other men to discard the doctrine of the separation of law and morals has the special poignancy of a recantation. What is important about this criticism is that it really does confront the particular point which Bentham and Austin had in mind in urging the separation of law as it is and as it ought to be. These German thinkers put their insistence on the need to join together what the utilitarians separated just where this separation was of most importance in the eyes of the utilitarians; for they were concerned with the problem posed by the existence of morally evil laws.

Before his conversion Radbruch held that resistance to law was a matter for the personal conscience, to be thought out by the individual as a moral problem, and the validity of a law could not be disproved by showing that the effect of compliance with the law would be more evil than the effect of disobedience. Austin, it may be recalled, was emphatic in condemning those who said that if human laws conflicted with the fundamental principles of morality then they cease to be laws, as talking "stark nonsense."

The most pernicious laws, and therefore those which are most opposed to the will of God, have been and are continually enforced as laws by judicial tribunals. Suppose an act innocuous, or positively beneficial, be prohibited by the sovereign under the penalty of death; if I commit this act, I shall be tried and condemned, and if I object to the sentence, that it is contrary to the law of God ... the court of justice will demonstrate the inconclusiveness of my reasoning by hanging me up, in pursuance of the law of which I have impugned the validity. An exception, demurrer, or plea, founded on the law of God was never heard in a Court of Justice, from the creation of the world down to the present moment.[41]

These are strong, indeed brutal words, but we must remember that they went along—in the case of Austin and, of course, Bentham—with the conviction that if laws reached a certain degree of iniquity then there would be a plain moral obligation to resist them and to withhold obedience. We shall see, when we consider the alternatives, that this simple presentation of the human dilemma which may arise has much to be said for it.

Radbruch, however, had concluded from the ease with which the Nazi regime had exploited subservience to mere law—or expressed, as he thought, in the "positivist" slogan "law is law" *(Gesetz als Gesetz)*—and from the failure of the German legal profession to protest against the enormities which they were required to perpetrate in the name of law, that "positivism" (meaning here the insistence on the separation of law as it is from law as it ought to be) had powerfully contributed to the horrors. His considered reflections led him to the doctrine that the fundamental principles of humanitarian morality were part of the very concept of *Recht* or Legality and that no positive enactment or statute, however clearly it was expressed and however clearly it conformed with the formal criteria of validity of a given legal system, could be valid if it contravened basic principles of morality. This doctrine can be appreciated fully only if the nuances imported by the German word *Recht* are grasped. But it is clear that the doctrine meant that every lawyer and judge should denounce statutes that transgressed the fundamental principles not as merely immoral or wrong but as having no legal character, and enactments which on this ground lack the quality of law should not be taken into account in working out the legal position of any given individual in particular circumstances. The striking recantation of his previous doctrine is unfortunately omitted from the translation of his works, but it should be read by all who wish to think afresh on the question of the interconnection of law and morals.[42]

It is impossible to read without sympathy Radbruch's passionate demand that the German legal conscience should be open to the demands of morality and his complaint that this has been too little the case in the German tradition. On the other hand there is an extraordinary naïveté in the view that insensitiveness to the demands of morality and subservience to state power in a people like the Germans should have arisen from the belief that law might be law though it failed to conform with the minimum requirements of morality. Rather this terrible history prompts inquiry into why emphasis on the slogan "law is law," and the distinction between law and morals, acquired a sinister character in Germany, but elsewhere, as with the utilitarians themselves, went along with the most enlightened liberal attitudes. But something more disturbing than naïveté is latent in Radbruch's whole presentation of the issues to which the existence of morally iniquitous laws give rise. It is not, I think, uncharitable to say that we can see in his argument that he has only half digested the spiritual message of liberalism which he is seeking to convey to the legal profession. For everything that he says is really dependent upon an enormous overvaluation of the importance of the bare fact that a rule may be said to be a valid rule of law, as if this, once declared, was conclusive of the final moral question: "Ought this rule of law to be obeyed?" Surely the truly liberal answer to any sinister use of the slogan "law is law" or of the distinction between law and morals is, "Very well, but that does not conclude the question. Law is not morality; do not let it supplant morality."

However, we are not left to a mere academic discussion in order to evaluate the plea which Radbruch made for the revision of the distinction between law and morals. After the war Radbruch's conception of law as containing in itself the essential moral principle of humanitarianism was applied in practice by German courts in certain cases in which local war criminals, spies, and informers under the Nazi regime were punished. The special importance of these cases is that the persons accused of these crimes claimed that what they had done was not illegal under the laws of the regime in force at the time these actions were performed. This plea was met with the reply that the laws upon which they relied were invalid as contravening the fundamental principles of morality. Let me cite briefly one of these cases.[43]

In 1944 a woman, wishing to be rid of her husband, denounced him to the authorities for insulting remarks he had made about Hitler while home on leave from the German army. The wife was under no legal duty to report his acts, though what he had said was apparently in violation of statutes making it illegal to make statements detrimental to the government of the Third Reich or to impair by any means the military defense of the

German people. The husband was arrested and sentenced to death, apparently pursuant to these statutes, though he was not executed but was sent to the front. In 1949 the wife was prosecuted in a West German court for an offense which we would describe as illegally depriving a person of his freedom *(rechtswidrige Freiheitsberaubung)*. This was punishable as a crime under the German Criminal Code of 1871 which had remained in force continuously since its enactment. The wife pleaded that her husband's imprisonment was pursuant to the Nazi statutes and hence that she had committed no crime. The court of appeal to which the case ultimately came held that the wife was guilty of procuring the deprivation of her husband's liberty by denouncing him to the German courts, even though he had been sentenced by a court for having violated a statute, since, to quote the words of the court, the statute "was contrary to the sound conscience and sense of justice of all decent human beings." This reasoning was followed in many cases which have been hailed as a triumph of the doctrines of natural law and as signaling the overthrow of positivism. The unqualified satisfaction with this result seems to me to be hysteria. Many of us might applaud the objective—that of punishing a woman for an outrageously immoral act—but this was secured only by declaring a statute established since 1934 not to have the force of law, and at least the wisdom of this course must be doubted. There were, of course, two other choices. One was to let the woman go unpunished; one can sympathize with and endorse the view that this might have been a bad thing to do. The other was to face the fact that if the woman were to be punished it must be pursuant to the introduction of a frankly retrospective law and with a full consciousness of what was sacrificed in securing her punishment in this way. Odious as retrospective criminal legislation and punishment may be, to have pursued it openly in this case would at least have had the merits of candour. It would have made plain that in punishing the woman a choice had to be made between two evils, that of leaving her unpunished and that of sacrificing a very precious principle of morality endorsed by most legal systems. Surely if we have learned anything from the history of morals it is that the thing to do with a moral quandary is not to hide it. Like nettles, the occasions when life forces us to choose between the lesser of two evils must be grasped with the consciousness that they are what they are. The vice of this use of the principle that, at certain limiting points, what is

utterly immoral cannot be law or lawful is that it will serve to cloak the true nature of the problems with which we are faced and will encourage the romantic optimism that all the values we cherish ultimately will fit into a single system, that no one of them has to be sacrificed or compromised to accommodate another.

"All Discord Harmony not understood
All Partial Evil Universal Good"

This is surely untrue and there is an insincerity in any formulation of our problem which allows us to describe the treatment of the dilemma as if it were the disposition of the ordinary case.

It may seem perhaps to make too much of forms, even perhaps of words, to emphasize one way of disposing of this difficult case as compared with another which might have led, so far as the woman was concerned, to exactly the same result. Why should we dramatize the difference between them? We might punish the woman under a new retrospective law and declare overtly that we were doing something inconsistent with our principles as the lesser of two evils; or we might allow the case to pass as one in which we do not point out precisely where we sacrifice such a principle. But candour is not just one among many minor virtues of the administration of law, just as it is not merely a minor virtue of morality. For if we adopt Radbruch's view, and with him the German courts make our protest against evil law in the form of an assertion that certain rules cannot be law because of their moral iniquity, we confuse one of the most powerful, because it is the simplest, forms of moral criticism. If with the utilitarians we speak plainly, we say that laws may be law but too evil to be obeyed. This is a moral condemnation which everyone can understand and it makes an immediate and obvious claim to moral attention. If, on the other hand, we formulate our objection as an assertion that these evil things are not law, here is an assertion which many people do not believe, and if they are disposed to consider it at all, it would seem to raise a whole host of philosophical issues before it can be accepted. So perhaps the most important single lesson to be learned from this form of the denial of the utilitarian distinction is the one that the utilitarians were most concerned to teach: when we have the ample resources of plain speech we must not present the moral criticism of institutions as propositions of a disputable philosophy.

V.

I have endeavored to show that, in spite of all that has been learned and experienced since the utilitarians wrote, and in spite of the defects of other parts of their doctrine, their protest against the confusion of what is and what ought to be law has a moral as well as an intellectual value. Yet it may well be said that, though this distinction is valid and important if applied to any particular law of a system, it is at least misleading if we attempt to apply it to "law," that is, to the notion of a legal system, and that if we insist, as I have, on the narrower truth (or truism), we obscure a wider (or deeper) truth. After all, it may be urged, we have learned that there are many things which are untrue of laws taken separately, but which are true and important in a legal system considered as a whole. For example, the connection between law and sanctions and between the existence of law and its "efficacy" must be understood in this more general way. It is surely not arguable (without some desperate extension of the word "sanction" or artificial narrowing of the word "law") that every law in a municipal legal system must have a sanction, yet it is at least plausible to argue that a legal system must, to be a legal system, provide sanctions for certain of its rules. So too, a rule of law may be said to exist though enforced or obeyed in only a minority of cases, but this could not be said of a legal system as a whole. Perhaps the differences with respect to laws taken separately and a legal system as a whole are also true of the connection between moral (or some other) conceptions of what law ought to be and law in this wider sense.

This line of argument, found (at least in embryo form) in Austin, where he draws attention to the fact that every developed legal system contains certain fundamental notions which are "necessary" and "bottomed in the common nature of man,"[44] is worth pursuing—up to a point —and I shall say briefly why and how far this is so.

We must avoid, if we can, the arid wastes of inappropriate definition, for, in relation to a concept as many-sided and vague as that of a legal system, disputes about the "essential" character, or necessity to the whole, of any single element soon begin to look like disputes about whether chess could be "chess" if played without pawns. There is a wish, which may be understandable, to cut straight through the question whether a legal system, to be a legal system, must measure up to some moral or other standard with simple statements of fact: for example, that no system which utterly failed in this respect has ever existed or could endure; that the normally fulfilled assumption that a legal system aims at some form of justice colours the whole way in which we interpret specific rules in particular cases, and if this normally fulfilled assumption were not fulfilled no one would have any reason to obey except fear (and probably not that) and still less, of course, any moral obligation to obey. The connection between law and moral standards and principles of justice is therefore as little arbitrary and as "necessary" as the connection between law and sanctions, and the pursuit of the question whether this necessity is logical (part of the "meaning" of law) or merely factual or causal can safely be left as an innocent pastime for philosophers.

Yet in two respects I should wish to go further (even though this involves the use of a philosophical fantasy) and show what could intelligibly be meant by the claim that certain provisions in a legal system are "necessary." The world in which we live, and we who live in it, may one day change in many different ways; and if this change were radical enough not only would certain statements of fact now true be false and vice versa, but whole ways of thinking and talking which constitute our present conceptual apparatus, through which we see the world and each other, would lapse. We have only to consider how the whole of our social, moral, and legal life, as we understand it now, depends on the contingent fact that though our bodies do change in shape, size, and other physical properties they do not do this so drastically nor with such quicksilver rapidity and irregularity that we cannot identify each other as the same persistent individual over considerable spans of time. Though this is but a contingent fact which may one day be different, on it at present rest huge structures of our thought and principles of action and social life. Similarly, consider the following possiblity (not because it is more than a possibility but because it reveals why we think certain things necessary in a legal system and what we mean by this): suppose that men were to become invulnerable to attack by each other, were clad perhaps like giant land crabs with an impenetrable carapace, and could extract the food they needed from the air by some internal chemical process. In such circumstances (the details of which can be left to science fiction) rules forbidding the free use of violence and rules constituting the minimum form of property—with its rights and duties sufficient to enable food to grow and be retained until eaten—would not have the necessary nonarbitrary status which they have for us, constituted as we are in a world like ours. At present, and until such radical changes supervene, such rules are so fundamental that if a legal system did not have them there would be no point in having any other rules at all. Such rules overlap with basic moral principles vetoing murder, violence, and theft; and so we can add to the factual statement that all legal systems in fact coincide with morality at such vital points, the statement that this is, in this sense, necessarily so. And why not call it a "natural" necessity?

Of course even this much depends on the fact that in asking what content a legal system must have we take this question to be worth asking only if we who consider it cherish the humble aim of survival in close proximity to our fellows. Natural-law theory, however, in all its protean guises, attempts to push the argument much further and to assert that human beings are equally devoted to and united in their conception of aims (the pursuit of knowledge, justice to their fellow men) other than that of survival, and these dictate a further necessary content to a legal system (over and above my humble minimum) without which it would be pointless. Of course we must be careful not to exaggerate the differences among human beings, but it seems to me that above this minimum the purposes men have for living in society are too conflicting and varying to make possible much extension of the argument that some fuller overlap of legal rules and moral standards is "necessary" in this sense.

Another aspect of the matter deserves attention. If we attach to a legal system the minimum meaning that it must consist of general rules—general both in the sense that they refer to courses of action, not single actions, and to multiplicities of men, not single individuals—this meaning connotes the principle of treating like cases alike, though the criteria of when cases are alike will be, so far, only the general elements specified in the rules. It is, however, true that *one* essential element of the concept of justice is the principle of treating like cases alike. This is justice in the administration of the law, not justice of the law. So there is, in the very notion of law consisting of general rules, something which prevents us from treating it as if morally it is utterly neutral, without any necessary contact with moral principles. Natural procedural justice consists therefore of those principles of objectivity and impartiality in the administration of the law which implement just this aspect of law and which are designed to ensure that rules are applied only to what are genuinely cases of the rule or at least to minimize the risks of inequalities in this sense.

These two reasons (or excuses) for talking of a certain overlap between legal and moral standards as necessary and natural, of course, should not satisfy anyone who is really disturbed by the utilitarian or "positivist" insistence that law and morality are distinct. This is so because a legal system that satisfied these minimum requirements might apply, with the most pedantic impartiality as between the persons affected, laws which were hideously oppressive, and might deny to a vast rightless slave population the minimum benefits of protection from violence and theft. The stink of such societies is, after all, still in our nostrils and to argue that they have (or had) no legal system would only involve the repetition of the argument. Only if the rules failed to provide these essential benefits and protection for anyone —even for a slave-owning group—would the minimum be unsatisfied and the system sink to the status of a set of meaningless taboos. Of course no one denied those benefits would have any reason to obey except fear and would have every moral reason to revolt.

VI.

I should be less than candid if I did not, in conclusion, consider something which, I suspect, most troubles those who react strongly against "legal positivism." Emphasis on the distinction between law as it is and law as it ought to be may be taken to depend upon and to entail what are called "subjectivist" and "relativist" or "noncognitive" theories concerning the very nature of moral judgments, moral distinctions, or "values." Of course the utilitarians themselves (as distinct from later positivists like Kelsen) did not countenance any such theories, however unsatisfactory their moral philosophy may appear to us now. Austin thought ultimate moral principles were the commands of God, known to us by revelation or through the "index" of utility, and Bentham thought they were verifiable propositions about utility. Nonetheless I think (though I cannot prove) that insistence upon the distinction between law as it is and ought to be has been, under the general head of "positivism," confused with a moral theory according to which statements of what is the case ("statements of fact") belong to a category or type radically different from statements of what ought to be ("value statements"). It may therefore be well to dispel this source of confusion.

There are many contemporary variants of this type of moral theory: according to some, judgments of what ought to be, or ought to be done, either are or include as essential elements expression of "feeling," "emotion," or "attitudes" or "subjective preferences"; in others such judgments both express feelings or emotions or attitudes and enjoin others to share them. In other variants such judgments indicate that a particular case falls under a general principle or policy of action which the speaker has "chosen" or to which he is "committed" and which is itself not a recognition of what is the case but analogous to a general "imperative" or command addressed to all including the speaker himself. Common to all these variants is the insistence that judgments of what ought to be done, because they contain such "non-cognitive" elements, cannot be argued for or established by rational methods as statements of fact can be, and cannot be shown to follow from any statement of fact but only from other judgments of what ought to be done in conjunction with some statement of fact. We cannot, on such a theory, demonstrate, for example, that an action was wrong, ought not to have been done, merely by showing that it consisted of the deliberate infliction of pain solely for the gratification of the agent. We only show it to be wrong if we add to those verifiable "cognitive" statements of fact a general principle not itself verifiable or "cognitive" that the infliction of pain in such circumstances is wrong, ought not to be done. Together with this general distinction between statements of what is and what ought to be go sharp parallel distinctions between statements about means and statements of moral ends. We can rationally discover and debate what are appropriate means to given ends, but ends are not rationally discoverable or debatable; they are "fiats of the will," expression of "emotions," "preferences," or "attitudes."

Against all such views (which are of course far subtler than this crude survey can convey) others urge that all these sharp distinctions between is and ought, fact and value, means and ends, cognitive and noncognitive, are wrong. In acknowledging ultimate ends or moral values we are recognizing something as much imposed upon us by the character of the world in which we live, as little a matter of choice, attitude, feeling, emotion

as the truth of factual judgments about what is the case. The characteristic moral argument is not one in which the parties are reduced to expressing or kindling feelings or emotions or issuing exhortations or commands to each other but one by which parties come to acknowledge after closer examination and reflection that an initially disputed case falls within the ambit of a vaguely apprehended principle (itself no more "subjective," no more a "fiat of our will" than any other principle of classification) and this has as much title to be called "cognitive" or "rational" as any other initially disputed classification of particulars.

Let us now suppose that we accept this rejection of "noncognitive" theories of morality and this denial of the drastic distinction in type between statements of what is and what ought to be, and that moral judgments are as rationally defensible as any other kind of judgments. What would follow from this as to the nature of the connection between law as it is and law as it ought to be? Surely, from this alone, nothing. Laws, however morally iniquitous, would still (so far as this point is concerned) be laws. The only difference which the acceptance of this view of the nature of moral judgments would make would be that the moral iniquity of such laws would be something that could be demonstrated; it would surely follow merely from a statement of what the rule required to be done that the rule was morally wrong and so ought not to be law or conversely that it was morally desirable and ought to be law. But the demonstration of this would not show the rule not to be (or to be) law. Proof that the principles by which we evaluate or condemn laws are rationally discoverable, and not mere "fiats of the will," leaves untouched the fact that there are laws which may have any degree of iniquity or stupidity and still be laws. And conversely there are rules that have every moral qualification to be laws and yet are not laws.

Surely something further or more specific must be said if disproof of "noncognitivism" or kindred theories in ethics is to be relevant to the distinction between law as it is and law as it ought to be, and to lead to the abandonment at some point or some softening of this distinction. No one has done more than Professor Lon Fuller of the Harvard Law School in his various writings to make clear such a line of argument and I will end by criticising what I take to be its central point. It is a point which again emerges when we consider not those legal rules or parts of legal rules the meanings of which are clear and excite no debate but the interpretation of rules in concrete cases where doubts are initially felt and argument develops about their meaning. In no legal system is the scope of legal rules restricted to the range of concrete instances which were present or are believed to have been present in the minds of legislators; this indeed is one of the important differences between a legal rule and a command. Yet, when rules are recognized as applying to instances beyond any that legislators did or could have considered, their extension to such new cases often presents itself not as a deliberate choice or fiat on the part of those who so interpret the rule. It appears neither as a decision to give the rule a new or extended meaning nor as a guess as to what legislators, dead perhaps in the eighteenth century, would have said had they been alive in the twentieth century. Rather, the inclusion of the new case under the rule takes its place as a natural elaboration of the rule, as something implementing a "purpose" which it seems natural to attribute (in some sense) to the rule itself rather than to any particular person dead or alive. The utilitarian description of such interpretative extension of old rules to new cases as judicial legislation fails to do justice to this phenomenon; it gives no hint of the differences between a deliberate fiat or decision to treat the new case in the same way as past cases and a recognition (in which there is little that is deliberate or even voluntary) that inclusion of the new case under the rule will implement or articulate a continuing and identical purpose, hitherto less specifically apprehended.

Perhaps many lawyers and judges will see in this language something that precisely fits their experience; others may think it a romantic gloss on facts better stated in the utilitarian language of judicial "legislation" or in the modern American terminology of "creative choice."

To make the point clear Professor Fuller uses a nonlegal example from the philosopher Wittgenstein which is, I think, illuminating.

Someone says to me: "Show the children a game." I teach them gaming with dice and the other says "I did not mean that sort of game." Must the exclusion of the game with dice have come before his mind when he gave me the order?[45]

Something important does seem to me to be touched on in this example. Perhaps there are the following (distinguishable) points. First, we nor-

mally do interpret not only what people are trying to do but what they say in the light of assumed common human objectives so that unless the contrary were expressly indicated we would not interpret an instruction to show a young child a game as a mandate to introduce him to gambling even though in other contexts the word "game" would be naturally so interpreted. Second, very often, the speaker whose words are thus interpreted might say: "Yes, that's what I mean [or "that's what I meant all along"] though I never thought of it until you put this particular case to me." Third, when we thus recognize, perhaps after argument or consultation with others, a particular case not specifically envisaged beforehand as falling within the ambit of some vaguely expressed instruction, we may find this experience falsified by description of it as a mere decision on our part so to treat the particular case, and that we can only describe this faithfully as coming to realize and to articulate what we "really" want or our "true purpose"—phrases which Professor Fuller uses later in the same article.[46]

I am sure that many philosophical discussions of the character of moral argument would benefit from attention to cases of the sort instanced by Professor Fuller. Such attention would help to provide a corrective to the view that there is a sharp separation between "ends" and "means" and that in debating "ends" we can only work on each other nonrationally, and that rational argument is reserved for dicussion of "means." But I think the relevance of his point to the issue whether it is correct or wise to insist on the distinction between law as it is and law as it ought to be is very small indeed. Its net effect is that in interpreting legal rules there are some cases which we find after reflection to be so natural an elaboration or articulation of the rule that to think of and refer to this as "legislation," "making law," or a "fiat" on our part would be misleading. So, the argument must be, it would be misleading to distinguish in such cases between what the rule is and what it ought to be—at least in some sense of ought. We think it ought to include the new case and come to see after reflection that it really does. But even if this way of presenting a recognizable experience as an example of a fusion between is and ought to be is admitted, two caveats must be borne in mind. The first is that "ought" in this case need have nothing to do with morals for the reasons explained already in section III: there may be just the same sense that a new case will implement and articulate the purpose of a rule in interpreting the rules of a game or some hideously immoral code of oppression whose immorality is appreciated by those called in to interpret it. They too can see what the "spirit" of the game they are playing requires in previously unenvisaged cases. More important is this: After all is said and done we must remember how rare in the law is the phenomenon held to justify this way of talking, how exceptional is this feeling that one way of deciding a case is imposed upon us as the only natural or rational elaboration of some rule. Surely it cannot be doubted that, for most cases of interpretation, the language of choice between alternatives, "judicial legislation" or even "fiat" (though not arbitrary fiat), better conveys the realities of the situation.

Within the framework of relatively well-settled law there jostle too many alternatives too nearly equal in attraction between which judge and lawyer must uncertainly pick their way to make appropriate here language which may well describe those experiences which we have in interpreting our own or others' principles of conduct, intention, or wishes, when we are not conscious of exercising a deliberate choice, but rather of recognizing something awaiting recognition. To use in the description of the interpretation of laws the suggested terminology of a fusion of inability to separate what is law and ought to be will serve (like earlier stories that judges only find, never make, law) only to conceal the facts, that here if anywhere we live among uncertainties between which we have to choose, and that the existing law imposes only limits on our choice and not the choice itself.

NOTES

1. Bentham, *A Fragment on Government,* in 1 Works 221, 235 (Bowring ed. 1859) (preface, 41st para.).
2. D'Entrèves, Natural Law 116 (2d ed. 1952).
3. Fuller, The Law in Quest of Itself 12 (1940); Brecht, *The Myth of Is and Ought,* 54 Harv. L. Rev. 811 (1941); Fuller, *Human Purpose and Natural Law,* 53 J. Philos 697 (1953).
4. See Friedmann, Legal Theory 154, 294–95 (3d ed. 1953). Friedmann also says of Austin that "by his sharp distinction between the science of legislation and the science of law," he "inaugurated an era of legal positivism and self-sufficiency which enabled the rising national State to assert its authority undisturbed by juristic doubts." *Id.* at 416. Yet, "the existence of a highly organised State which claimed sovereignty and unconditional obedience of the citizen" is said to be "the political condition which makes analytical positivism possible." *Id.* at 163. There is therefore some difficulty in determining which, in this account, is to be hen and which egg (analytical positivism or political condition). Apart from this,

there seems to be little evidence that any national State rising in or after 1832 (when the *Province of Jurisprudence Determined* was first published) was enabled to assert its authority by Austin's work or "the era of legal positivism" which he "inaugurated."
5. See Radbruch, *Die Erneuerung des Rechts,* 2 Die Wandlung 8 (Germany 1947); Radbruch, *Gesetzliches Unrecht und Übergesetzliches Recht,* I Süddeutsche Juristen-Zeitung 105 (Germany 1946) (reprinted in Radbruch, Rechtsphilosophie 347 (4th ed. 1950). Radbruch's views are discussed at pp. 617–21 *infra.*
6. Bentham, *A Fragment on Government,* in 1 Works 221, 230 (Bowring ed. 1859) (preface, 16th para.); Bentham, *Principles of Penal Law,* in 1 Works 365, 574–75, 576–78 (Bowring ed. 1859) (pt. III, c. XXI, 8th para., 12th para.).
7. Bentham, *Of Promulgation of the Laws,* in 1 Works 155 (Bowring ed. 1859); Bentham, *Principles of the Civil Code,* in 1 Works 297, 323 (Bowring ed. 1859) (pt. I, c. XVII, 2d para.); Bentham, *A Fragment on Government,* in 1 Works 221, 233 n.[*m*] (Bowring ed. 1859) (preface, 35th para.).
8. Bentham, *Principles of Penal Law,* in 1 Works 365, 576 (Bowring ed. 1859) (pt. III, c. XXI, 10th para., 11th para.).
9. Bentham, *Principles of Morals and Legislation,* in 1 Works I, 84 (Bowring ed. 1859) (c. XIII).
10. Bentham, *Anarchical Fallacies,* in 2 Works 489, 511–12 (Bowring ed. 1859) (art. VIII); Bentham, *Principles of Morals and Legislation,* in 1 Works 1, 144 (Bowring ed. 1859) (c. XIX, 11th para.).
11. *Id.* at 142 n.§ (c. XIX, 4th para. n.§).
12. Austin, The Province of Jurisprudence Determined 184–85 (Library of Ideas ed. 1954).
13. Bentham, *A Fragment on Government,* in 1 Works 221, 230 (Bowring ed. 1859) (preface, 16th para.).
14. See Bentham, *Principles of Legislation,* in The Theory of Legislation 1, 65 n.* (Ogden ed. 1931) (c. XII, 2d para. n.*).
Here we touch upon the most difficult of questions. If the law is not what it ought to be; if it openly combats the principle of utility; ought we to obey it? Ought we to violate it? Ought we to remain neuter between the law which commands an evil, and morality which forbids it?
See also Bentham, *A Fragment on Government,* in 1 Works 221, 287–88 (Bowring ed. 1859) (c. IV, 20th–25th paras.).
15. 1 Blackstone, Commentaries *41. Bentham criticized "this dangerous maxim," saying "the natural tendency of such a doctrine is to impel a man, by the force of conscience, to rise up in arms against any law whatever that he happens not to like." Bentham, *A Fragment on Government,* in 1 Works 221, 287 (Bowring ed. 1859) (c. IV, 19th para.). See also *Bentham, A Comment on the Commentaries* 49 (1928) (c. III). For an expression of a fear lest anarchy result from such a doctrine, combined with a recognition that resistance may be justified on grounds of utility, See Austin, *op. cit. supra* note 12, at 186.
16. Bentham, *A Fragment on Government,* in 1 Works 221, 294 (Bowring ed. 1859) (c. V, 10th para.).
17. Bentham, *A Commentary on Humphreys' Real Property Code,* in 5 Works 389 (Bowring ed. 1843).
18. Austin, *op. cit. supra* note 12, at 162.
19. Bentham, *A Fragment on Government,* in 1 Works 221, 289–90 (Bowring ed. 1859) (c. IV, 33d–34th paras.).
20. See Austin, *op. cit. supra* note 12, at 231.
21. Amos, The Science of Law 4 (5th ed. 1881). See also Markby, Elements of Law 4–5 (5th ed. 1896):
Austin, by establishing the distinction between positive law and morals, not only laid the foundation for a science of law, but cleared the conception of law . . . of a number of perni-

cious consequences to which . . . it had been supposed to lead. Positive laws, as Austin has shown, must be legally binding, and yet a law may be unjust. . . . He has admitted that law itself may be immoral, in which case it may be our moral duty to disobey it. . . .

Cf. Holland, Jurisprudence 1–20 (1880).

22. See Green, Book Review, 6 Am. L. Rev. 57, 61 (1871) (reprinted in Green, Essays and Notes on the Law of Tort and Crime 31, 35 (1933)).

23. 10 Harv. L. Rev. 457 (1897).

24. Gray, The Nature and Sources of the Law 94 (1st ed. 1909) (§ 213).

25. It may help to identify five (there may be more) meanings of "positivism" bandied about in contemporary jurisprudence:

(1) the contention that laws are commands of human beings, see pp. 602–06 *infra,*

(2) the contention that there is no necessary connection between law and morals or law as it is and ought to be, see pp. 594–600 *supra,*

(3) the contention that the analysis (or study of the meaning) of legal concepts is (a) worth pursuing and (b) to be distinguished from historical inquiries into the causes or origins of laws, from sociological inquiries into the relation of law and other social phenomena, and from the criticism or appraisal of law whether in terms of morals, social aims, "functions," or otherwise, see pp. 608–10 *infra,*

(4) the contention that a legal system is a "closed logical system" in which correct legal decisions can be deduced by logical means from predetermined legal rules without reference to social aims, policies, moral standards, see pp. 608–10 *infra,* and

(5) the contention that moral judgments cannot be established or defended, as statements of facts can, by rational argument, evidence, or proof ("noncognitivism" in ethics), see pp. 624–26 *infra.*

Bentham and Austin held the views described in (1), (2), and (3) but not those in (4) and (5). Opinion (4) is often ascribed to analytical jurists, see pp. 608–10 *infra,* but I know of no "analyst" who held this view.

26. Gray, The Nature and Sources of the Law 94–95 (2d ed. 1921).

27. Austin, *op. cit. supra* note 12, at 13.

28. See, *e.g.,* Kelsen, General Theory of Law and State 58–61, 143–44 (1945). According to Kelsen, all laws, not only those conferring rights and powers, are reducible to such "primary norms" conditionally stipulating sanctions.

29. Salmond, The First Principles of Jurisprudence 97–98 (1893). He protested against "the creed of what is termed the English school of jurisprudence," because it "attempted to deprive the idea of law of that ethical significance which is one of its most essential elements." *Id.* at 9, 10.

30. Hägerström, Inquiries Into the Nature of Law and Morals 217 (Olivecrona ed. 1953): "[T]he whole theory of the subjective rights of private individuals . . . is incompatible with the imperative theory." See also *id.* at 221:

The description of them [claims to legal protection] as rights is wholly derived from the idea that the law which is concerned with them is a true expression of rights and duties in the sense in which the popular notion of justice understands these terms.

31. *Id.* at 218.

32. This misunderstanding of analytical jurisprudence is to be found in, among others, Stone, The Province and Function of Law 141 (1950):

In short, rejecting the implied assumption that all propositions of all parts of the law must be logically consistent with

each other and proceed on a single set of definitions . . . he [Cardozo, J.,] denied that the law is actually what the analytical jurist, *for his limited purposes,* assumes it to be.

See also *id.* at 49, 52, 138, 140; Friedmann, Legal Theory 209 (3d ed. 1953). This misunderstanding seems to depend on the unexamined and false belief that analytical studies of the meaning of legal terms would be impossible or absurd if, to reach sound decisions in particular cases, more than a capacity for formal logical reasoning from unambiguous and clear predetermined premises is required.

33. See the discussion of vagueness and uncertainty in law, in Austin, *op. cit. supra* note 12, at 202–05, 207, in which Austin recognized that, in consequence of this vagueness, often only "fallible tests" can be provided for determining whether particular cases fall under general expressions.

34. See Austin, *op. cit. supra* note 12, at 191: "I cannot understand how any person who has considered the subject can suppose that society could possibly have gone on if judges had not legislated. . . ." As a corrective to the belief that the analytical jurist must take a "slot machine" or "mechanical" view of the judicial process it is worth noting the following observations made by Austin:

(1) Whenever law has to be applied, the " 'competition of opposite analogies' " may arise, for the case "may resemble in some of its points" cases to which the rule has been applied in the past and in other points "cases from which the application of the law has been withheld." 2 Austin, Lectures on Jurisprudence 633 (5th ed. 1885).

(2) Judges have commonly decided cases and so derived new rules by "building" on a variety of grounds including sometimes (in Austin's opinion too rarely) their views of what law ought to be. Most commonly they have derived law from preexisting law by "consequence founded on analogy," *i.e.,* they have made a new rule "in *consequence* of the existence of a similar rule applying to subjects which are *analogous.* . . ." 2 *id.* at 638–39.

(3) "[I]f every rule in a system of law were perfectly definite or precise," these difficulties incident to the application of law would not arise. "But the ideal completeness and correctness I now have imagined is not attainable in fact. . . . though the system had been built and ordered with matchless solicitude and skill." 2 *id.* at 997–98. Of course he thought that much could and should be done by codification to eliminate uncertainty. See 2 *id.* at 662–81.

35. 2 *id.* at 641:

Nothing, indeed, can be more natural, than that legislators, direct or judicial (especially if they be narrow-minded, timid and unskillful), should lean as much as they can on the examples set by their predecessors.

See also 2 *id.* at 647:

But it is much to be regretted that Judges of capacity, experience and weight, have not seized every opportunity of introducing a new rule (a rule beneficial for the future). . . . This is the reproach I should be inclined to make against Lord Eldon. . . . [T]he Judges of the Common Law Courts would not do what they ought to have done, namely to model their rules of law and of procedure to the growing exigencies of society, instead of stupidly and sulkily adhering to the old and barbarous usages.

36. Hynes v. New York Cent. R.R., 231 N.Y. 229, 235, 131 N.E. 898, 900 (1921); see Pound, Interpretations of Legal History 123 (2d ed. 1930); Stone, *op. cit. supra* note 32, at 140–41.

37. See McBoyle v. United States, 283 U.S. 25 (1931).

38. See, *e.g.,* Pound, *Mechanical Jurisprudence,* 8 Colum. L. Rev. 605, 615–16 (1908).

39. See, *e.g.,* Lochner v. New York, 198 U.S. 45 (1905).

Justice Peckham's opinion that there were no reasonable grounds for interfering with the right of free contract by determining the hours of labour in the occupation of a baker may indeed be a wrongheaded piece of conservatism but there is nothing automatic or mechanical about it.

40.   One recantation of this extreme position is worth mention in the present context. In the first edition of *The Bramble Bush,* Professor Llewellyn committed himself wholeheartedly to the view that "what these officials do about disputes is, to my mind, the law itself" and that "*rules* . . . are important so far as they help you . . . predict what judges will do. . . . That is all their importance, except as pretty playthings." Llewellyn, The Bramble Bush 3, 5 (1st ed. 1930). In the second edition he said that these were "unhappy words when not more fully developed, and they are plainly at best a very partial statement of the whole truth. . . . [O]ne office of law is to control officials in some part, and to guide them even . . . where no thoroughgoing control is possible, or is desired. . . . [T]he words fail to take proper account . . . of the office of the institution of law as an instrument of conscious shaping. . . ." Llewellyn, The Bramble Bush 9 (2d ed. 1951).

41.   Austin, the Province of Jurisprudence Determined 185 (Library of Ideas ed. 1954).

42.   See Radbruch, *Gesetzliches Unrecht und Übergesetzliches Recht,* 1 Süddeutsche Juristen-Zeitung 105 (Germany 1946) (reprinted in Radbruch, Rechts-philosophie 347 (4th ed. 1950)). I have used the translation of part of this essay and of Radbruch, *Die Erneuerung des Rechts,* 2 Die Wandlung 8 (Germany 1947), prepared by Professor Lon Fuller of the Harvard Law School as a mimeographed supplement to the readings in jurisprudence used in his course at Harvard.

43.   Judgment of July 27, 1949, Oberlandesgericht, Bamberg, 5 Süddeutsche Juristen-Zeitung 207 (Germany 1950), 64 Harv. L. Rev. 1005 (1951); See Freidmann, Legal Theory 457 (3d ed. 1953).

44.   Austin, *Uses of the Study of Jurisprudence,* in The Province of Jurisprudence Determined 365, 373, 367–69 (Library of Ideas ed. 1954).

45.   Fuller, *Human Purpose and Natural Law,* 53 J. Philos. 697, 700 (1956).

46   *Id.* at 701, 702.

LON L. FULLER

Positivism and Fidelity to Law—A Reply to Professor Hart*

Professor Hart has made an enduring contribution to the literature of legal philosophy. I doubt if the issues he discusses will ever again assume quite the form they had before being touched by his analytical powers. His argument is no mere restatement of Bentham, Austin, Gray, and Holmes. Their views receive in his exposition a new depth that are uniquely his own.

I must confess that when I first encountered the thoughts of Professor Hart's essay, his argument seemed to me to suffer from a deep inner contradiction. On the one hand, he rejects emphatically any confusion of "what is" with "what ought to be." He will tolerate no "merger" of law and conceptions of what law ought to be, but at the most an antiseptic "intersection." Intelligible communication on any subject, he seems to imply, becomes impossible if we leave it uncertain whether we are talking about "what is" or "what ought to be." Yet it was precisely this uncertainty about Professor Hart's own argument which made it difficult for me at first to follow the thread of his thought. At times he seemed to be saying that the distinction between law and morality is something that exists, and will continue to exist, however we may talk about it. It expresses a reality which, whether we like it or not, we must accept if we are to avoid talking nonsense. At other times, he seemed to be warning us that the reality of the distinction is itself in danger and that if we do not mend our ways of thinking and talking we may lose a "precious moral ideal," that of fidelity to law. It is not clear, in other words, whether in Professor Hart's own thinking the distinction between law and morality simply "is," or is something that "ought to be" and that we should join with him in helping to create and maintain.

These were the perplexities I had about Professor Hart's argument when I first encountered it. But on reflection I am sure any criticism of his essay as being self-contradictory would be both unfair and unprofitable. There is no reason why the argument for a strict separation of law and morality cannot be rested on the double ground that this separation serves both intellectual clarity and moral integrity. If there are certain difficulties in bringing these two lines of reasoning into proper relation to one another, these difficulties affect also the position of those who reject the views of Austin, Gray, and Holmes. For those of us who find the "positivist" position unacceptable do ourselves rest our argument on the double ground that its intellectual clarity is specious and that its effects are, or may be, harmful. On the one hand, we assert that Austin's definition of law, for example, violates the reality it purports to describe. Being false in fact, it cannot serve effectively what Kelsen calls "an interest of cognition." On the other hand, we assert that under some conditions the same conception of law may become dangerous, since in human affairs what men mistakenly accept as real tends, by the very act of their acceptance, to become real.

It is a cardinal virtue of Professor Hart's argument that for the first time it opens the way for a truly profitable exchange of views between those whose differences center on the distinction between law and morality. Hitherto there has been no real real joinder of issue between the opposing camps. On the one side, we encounter a series of definitional fiats. A rule of law is—that is to say, it really and simply and always is—the command of a sovereign, a rule laid down by a judge, a prediction of the future incidence of state force, a pattern of official behavior, etc. When we ask what purpose these definitions serve, we receive the answer, "Why, no purpose, except to describe accurately the social reality that corresponds to the word 'law.'" When we reply, "But

*From 71 *Harvard Law Review* 630 (1958). Copyright © 1958 by The Harvard Law Review Association. Reprinted by permission of the publisher.

it doesn't look like that to me," the answer comes back, "Well, it does to me." There the matter has to rest.

This state of affairs has been most unsatisfactory for those of us who are convinced that "positivistic" theories have had a distorting effect on the aims of legal philosophy. Our dissatisfaction arose not merely from the impasse we confronted, but because this impasse seemed to us so unnecessary. All that was needed to surmount it was an acknowledgment on the other side that its definitions of "what law really is" are not mere images of some datum of experience, but direction posts for the application of human energies. Since this acknowledgment was not forthcoming, the impasse and its frustrations continued. There is indeed no frustration greater than to be confronted by a theory which purports merely to describe, when it not only plainly prescribes, but owes its special prescriptive powers precisely to the fact that it disclaims prescriptive intentions. Into this murky debate, some shafts of light did occasionally break through, as in Kelsen's casual admission, apparently never repeated, that his whole system might well rest on an emotional preference for the ideal of order over that of justice.[1] But I have to confess that in general the dispute that has been conducted during the last twenty years has not been very profitable.

Now, with Professor Hart's paper, the discussion takes a new and promising turn. It is now explicitly acknowledged on both sides that one of the chief issues is how we can best define and serve the ideal of fidelity to law. Law, as something deserving loyalty, must represent a human achievement; it cannot be a simple fiat of power or a repetitive pattern discernible in the behavior of state officials. The respect we owe to human laws must surely be something different from the respect we accord to the law of gravitation. If laws, even bad laws, have a claim to our respect, then law must represent some general direction of human effort that we can understand and describe, and that we can approve in principle even at the moment when it seems to us to miss its mark.

If, as I believe, it is a cardinal virtue of Professor Hart's argument that it brings into the dispute the issue of fidelity to law, its chief defect, if I may say so, lies in a failure to perceive and accept the implications that this enlargement of the frame of argument necessarily entails. This defect seems to me more or less to permeate the whole essay, but it comes most prominently to the fore in his dis-

cussion of Gustav Radbruch and the Nazi regime.[2] Without any inquiry into the actual workings of whatever remained of a legal system under the Nazis, Professor Hart assumes that something must have persisted that still deserved the name of law in a sense that would make meaningful the ideal of fidelity to law. Not that the Professor Hart believes the Nazis' laws should have been obeyed. Rather he considers that a decision to disobey them presented not a mere question of prudence or courage, but a genuine moral dilemma in which the ideal of fidelity to law had to be sacrificed in favor of more fundamental goals. I should have thought it unwise to pass such a judgment without first inquiring with more particularity what "law" itself meant under the Nazi regime.

I shall present later my reasons for thinking that Professor Hart is profoundly mistaken in his estimate of the Nazi situation and that he gravely misinterprets the thought of Professor Radbruch. But first I shall turn to some preliminary definitional problems in which what I regard as the central defect in Professor Hart's thesis seems immediately apparent.

I. THE DEFINITION OF LAW

Throughout his essay Professor Hart aligns himself with a general position which he associates with the names of Bentham, Austin, Gray, and Holmes. He recognizes, of course, that the conceptions of these men as to "what law is" vary considerably, but this diversity he apparently considers irrelevant in his defense of their general school of thought.

If the only issue were that of stipulating a meaning for the word "law" that would be conducive to intellectual clarity, there might be much justification for treating all of these men as working in the same direction. Austin, for example, defines law as the command of the highest legislative power, called the sovereign. For Gray, on the other hand, law consists in the rules laid down by judges. A statute is, for Gray, not a law, but only a source of law, which becomes law only after it has been interpreted and applied by a court. Now if our only object were to obtain that clarity which comes from making our definitions explicit and then adhering strictly to those definitions, one could argue plausibly that either conception of the meaning of "law" will do. Both conceptions appear to avoid a confusion of morals and law, and both writers let the reader know what meaning they propose to attribute to the word "law."

The matter assumes a very different aspect, however, if our interest lies in the ideal of fidelity to law, for then it may become a matter of capital importance what position is assigned to the judiciary in the general frame of government. Confirmation for this observation may be found in the slight rumbling of constitutional crisis to be heard in this country today. During the past year readers of newspapers have been writing to their editors urging solemnly, and even apparently with sincerity, that we should abolish the Supreme Court as a first step toward a restoration of the rule of law. It is unlikely that this remedy for our governmental ills derives from any deep study of Austin or Gray, but surely those who propose it could hardly be expected to view with indifference the divergent definitions of law offered by those two jurists. If it be said that it is a perversion of Gray's meaning to extract from his writings any moral for present controversies about the role of the Supreme Court, then it seems to me there is equal reason for treating what he wrote as irrelevant to the issue of fidelity of law generally.

Another difference of opinion among the writers defended by Professor Hart concerns Bentham and Austin and their views on constitutional limitations on the power of the sovereign. Bentham considered that a constitution might preclude the highest legislative power from issuing certain kinds of laws. For Austin, on the other hand, any legal limit on the highest lawmaking power was an absurdity and an impossibility. What guide to conscience would be offered by these two writers in a crisis that might some day arise out of the provision of our constitution to the effect that the amending power can never be used to deprive any state without its consent of its equal representation in the Senate?[3] Surely it is not only in the affairs of everyday life that we need clarity about the obligation of fidelity to law, but most particularly and urgently in times of trouble. If all the positivist school has to offer in such times is the observation that, however you may choose to define law, it is always something different from morals, its teachings are not of much use to us.

I suggest, then, that Professor Hart's thesis as it now stands is essentially incomplete and that before he can attain the goals he seeks he will have to concern himself more closely with a definition of law that will make meaningful the obligation of fidelity to law.

II. THE DEFINITION OF MORALITY

It is characteristic of those sharing the point of view of Professor Hart that their primary concern is to preserve the integrity of the concept of law. Accordingly, they have generally sought a precise definition of law, but have not been at pains to state just what it is they mean to exclude by their definitions. They are like men building a wall for the defense of a village, who must know what it is they wish to protect, but who need not, and indeed cannot, know what invading forces those walls may have to turn back.

When Austin and Gray distinguish law from morality, the word "morality" stands indiscriminately for almost every conceivable standard by which human conduct may be judged that is not itself law. The inner voice of conscience, notions of right and wrong based on religious belief, common conceptions of decency and fair play, culturally conditioned prejudices—all of these are grouped together under the heading of "morality" and are excluded from the domain of law. For the most part Professor Hart follows in the tradition of his predecessors. When he speaks of morality he seems generally to have in mind all sorts of extra-legal notions about "what ought to be," regardless of their sources, pretensions, or intrinsic worth. This is particularly apparent in his treatment of the problem of interpretation, where uncodified notions of what ought to be are viewed as affecting only the penumbra of law, leaving its hard core untouched.

Toward the end of the essay, however, Professor Hart's argument takes a turn that seems to depart from the prevailing tenor of his thought. This consists in reminding us that there is such a thing as an immoral morality and that there are many standards of "what ought to be" that can hardly be called moral.[4] Let us grant, he says, that the judge may properly and inevitably legislate in the penumbra of a legal enactment, and that this legislation (in default of any other standard) must be guided by the judge's notions of what ought to be. Still, this would be true even in a society devoted to the most evil ends, where the judge would supply the insufficiencies of the statute with the iniquity that seemed to him most apt for the occasion. Let us also grant, says Professor Hart toward the end of his essay, that there is at times even something that looks like discovery in the judicial process, when a judge by restating a principle seems to bring more clearly to light what was really sought from the beginning. Again, he reminds us, this could happen in a society devoted to the highest refinements of sin, where the implicit demands of an evil rule might be a matter for discovery when the rule was applied to a situation not consciously considered when it was formulated.

I take it that this is to be a warning addressed to those who wish "to infuse more morality into the law." Professor Hart is reminding them that if their program is adopted the morality that actually gets infused may not be to their liking. If this is his point it is certainly a valid one, though one wishes it had been made more explicitly, for it raises much the most fundamental issue of his whole argument. Since the point is made obliquely, and I may have misinterpreted it, in commenting I shall have to content myself with a few summary observations and questions.

First, Professor Hart seems to assume that evil aims may have as much coherence and inner logic as good ones. I, for one, refuse to accept that assumption. I realize that I am here raising, or perhaps dodging, questions that lead into the most difficult problems of the epistemology of ethics. Even if I were competent to undertake an excursus in that direction, this is not the place for it. I shall have to rest on the assertion of a belief that may seem naïve, namely, that coherence and goodness have more affinity than coherence and evil. Accepting this belief, I also believe that when men are compelled to explain and justify their decisions, the effect will generally be to pull those decisions toward goodness, by whatever standards of ultimate goodness there are. Accepting these beliefs, I find a considerable incongruity in any conception that envisages a possible future in which the common law would "work itself pure from case to case" toward a more perfect realization of iniquity.

Second, if there is a serious danger in our society that a weakening of the partition between law and morality would permit an infusion of "immoral morality," the question remains, what is the most effective protection against this danger? I cannot myself believe it is to be found in the positivist position espoused by Austin, Gray, Holmes, and Hart. For those writers seem to me to falsify the problem into a specious simplicity which leaves untouched the difficult issues where real dangers lie.

Third, let us suppose a judge bent on realizing through his decisions an objective that most ordinary citizens would regard as mistaken or evil. Would such a judge be likely to suspend the letter of the statute by openly invoking a "higher law"? Or would he be more likely to take refuge behind the maxim that "law is law" and explain his decision in such a way that it would appear to be demanded by the law itself?

Fourth, neither Professor Hart nor I belong to anything that could be said in a significant sense to be a "minority group" in our respective countries. This has its advantages and disadvantages to one aspiring to a philosophic view of law and government. But suppose we were both transported to a country where our beliefs were anathemas, and where we, in turn, regarded the prevailing morality as thoroughly evil. No doubt in this situation we would have reason to fear that the law might be covertly manipulated to our disadvantage; I doubt if either of us would be apprehensive that its injunctions would be set aside by an appeal to a morality higher than law. If we felt that the law itself was our safest refuge, would it not be because even in the most perverted regimes there is a certain hesitancy about writing cruelties, intolerances, and inhumanities into law? And is it not clear that this hesitancy itself derives, not from a separation of law and morals, but precisely from an identification of law with those demands of morality that are the most urgent and the most obviously justifiable, which no man need be ashamed to profess?

Fifth, over great areas where the judicial process functions, the danger of an infusion of immoral, or at least unwelcome, morality does not, I suggest, present a real issue. Here the danger is precisely the opposite. For example, in the field of commercial law the British courts in recent years have, if I may say so, fallen into a "law-is-law" formalism that constitutes a kind of belated counterrevolution against all that was accomplished by Mansfield.[5] The matter has reached a stage approaching crisis as commercial cases are increasingly being taken to arbitration. The chief reason for this development is that arbitrators are willing to take into account the needs of commerce and ordinary standards of commercial fairness. I realize that Professor Hart repudiates "formalism," but I shall try to show later why I think his theory necessarily leads in that direction.[6]

Sixth, in the thinking of many there is one question that predominates in any discussion of the relation of law and morals, to the point of coloring everything that is said or heard on the subject. I refer to the kind of question raised by the Pope's pronouncement concerning the duty of Catholic judges in divorce actions.[7] This pronouncement does indeed raise grave issues. But it does not present a problem of the relation between law, on the one hand, and, on the other, generally shared views of right conduct that have grown spontaneously through experience and discussion. The issue is rather that of a conflict between two pronouncements, both of which claim to be authoritative; if you will, it is one kind of law against another. When this kind of issue is taken as the key to the whole problem of law and morality, the discussion is so denatured and distorted that profitable exchange becomes impossible. In mentioning this last aspect of the dispute about "positivism," I do not mean to intimate that Professor Hart's own discussion is dominated by any *arriére-pensée;* I know it is not. At the same time I am quite sure that I have indicated accurately the issue that will be uppermost in the minds of many as they read his essay.

In resting content with these scant remarks, I do not want to seem to simplify the problem in a direction opposite to that taken by Professor Hart. The questions raised by "immoral morality" deserve a more careful exploration than either Professor Hart or I have offered in these pages.

III. THE MORAL FOUNDATIONS OF A LEGAL ORDER

Professor Hart emphatically rejects "the command theory of law," according to which law is simply a command backed by a force sufficient to make it effective. He observes that such a command can be given by a man with a loaded gun, and "law surely is not the gunman situation writ large."[8] There is no need to dwell here on the inadequacies of the command theory, since Professor Hart has already revealed its defects more clearly and succinctly than I could. His conclusion is that the foundation of a legal system is not coercive power, but certain "fundamental accepted rules specifying the essential lawmaking procedures."[9]

When I reached this point in his essay, I felt certain that Professor Hart was about to acknowledge an important qualification on his thesis. I confidently expected that he would go on to say something like this: I have insisted throughout on the importance of keeping sharp the distinction between law and morality. The question may now be raised, therefore, as to the nature of these fundamental rules that furnish the framework within which the making of law takes place.

On the one hand, they seem to be rules, not of law, but of morality. They derive their efficacy from a general acceptance, which in turn rests ultimately on a perception that they are right and necessary. They can hardly be said to be law in the sense of an authoritative pronouncement, since their function is to state when a pronouncement is authoritative. On the other hand, in the daily functioning of the legal system they are often treated and applied much as ordinary rules of law are. Here, then, we must confess there is something that can be called a "merger" of law and morality, and to which the term "intersection" is scarcely appropriate.

Instead of pursuing some such course of thought, to my surprise I found Professor Hart leaving completely untouched the nature of the fundamental rules that make law itself possible, and turning his attention instead to what he considers a confusion of thought on the part of the critics of positivism. Leaving out of account his discussion of analytical jurisprudence, his argument runs something as follows: Two views are associated with the names of Bentham and Austin. One is the command theory of law, the other is an insistence on the separation of law and morality. Critics of these writers came in time to perceive—"dimly," Professor Hart says—that the command theory is untenable. By a loose association of ideas they wrongly supposed that in advancing reasons for rejecting the command theory they had also refuted the view that law and morality must be sharply separated. This was a "natural mistake," but plainly a mistake just the same.

I do not think any mistake is committed in believing that Bentham and Austin's error in formulating improperly and too simply the problem of the relation of law and morals was part of a larger error that led to the command theory of law. I think the connection between these two errors can be made clear if we ask ourselves what would have happened to Austin's system of thought if he had abandoned the command theory.

One who reads Austin's Lectures V and VI[10] cannot help being impressed by the way he hangs doggedly to the command theory, in spite of the fact that every pull of his own keen mind was toward abandoning it. In the case of a sovereign monarch, law is what the monarch commands. But what shall we say of the "laws" of succession which tell who the "lawful" monarch is? It is of the essence of a command that it be addressed by a superior to an inferior, yet in the case of a "sovereign many," say, a parliament, the sovereign seems to command itself since a member of parliament may be convicted under a law he himself drafted and voted for. The sovereign must be unlimited in legal power, for who could adjudicate the legal bounds of a supreme lawmaking power? Yet a "sovereign many" must accept the limitation of rules before it can make law at all. Such a body can gain the power to issue commands only by acting in a "corporate capacity"; this it can do only by proceeding "agreeably to the modes and forms" established and accepted for the making of law. Judges exercise a power delegated to them by the supreme lawmaking power, and are commissioned to carry out its "direct or circuitous commands." Yet in a federal system it is the courts which must resolve conflicts of competence between the federation and its components.

All of these problems Austin sees with varying degrees of explicitness, and he struggles mightily with them. Over and over again he teeters on the edge of an abandonment of the command theory in favor of what Professor Hart has described as a view that discerns the foundations of a legal order in "certain fundamental accepted rules specifying the essential lawmaking procedures." Yet he never takes the plunge. He does not take it because he had a sure insight that it would forfeit the black-and-white distinction between law and morality that was the whole object of his Lectures—indeed, one may say, the enduring object of a dedicated life. For if law is made possible by "fundamental accepted rules"—which for Austin must be rules, not of law, but of positive morality—what are we to say of the rules that the lawmaking power enacts to regulate its own lawmaking? We have election laws, laws allocating legislative representation to specific geographic areas, rules of parliamentary procedure, rules for the qualification of voters, and many other laws and rules of similar nature. These do not remain fixed, and all of them shape in varying degrees the lawmaking process. Yet how are we to distinguish between those basic rules that owe their validity to acceptance, and those which are properly rules of law, valid even when men generally consider them to be evil or ill-advised? In other words, how are we to define the words "fundamental" and "essential" in Professor Hart's own formulation: "certain fundamental accepted rules specifying the essential lawmaking procedure"?

The solution for this problem in Kelsen's theory is instructive. Kelsen does in fact take the plunge over which Austin hesitated too long. Kelsen realizes that before we can distinguish between what is law and what is not, there must be an acceptance of some basic procedure by which law is made. In any legal system there must be some fundamental rule that points unambiguously to the source from which laws must come in order to be laws. This rule Kelsen called "the basic norm." In his own words,

The basic norm is not valid because it has been created in a certain way, but its validity is assumed by virtue of its content. It is valid, then, like a norm of natural law.... The idea of a pure positive law, like that of natural law, has its limitations.[11]

It will be noted that Kelsen speaks, not as Professor Hart does, of "fundamental rules" that regulate the making of law, but of a single rule or norm. Of course, there is no such single rule in any modern society. The notion of the basic norm is admittedly a symbol, not a fact. It is a symbol that embodies the positivist quest for some clear and unambiguous test of law, for some clean, sharp line that will divide the rules which owe their validity to acceptance and intrinsic appeal. The difficulties Austin avoided by sticking with the command theory, Kelsen avoids by a fiction which simplifies reality into a form that can be absorbed by positivism.

A full exploration of all the problems that result when we recognize that law becomes possible only by virtue of rules that are not law, would require drawing into consideration the effect of the presence or absence of a written constitution. Such a constitution in some ways simplifies the problems I have been discussing, and in some ways complicates them. In so far as a written constitution defines basic lawmaking procedure, it may remove the perplexities that arise when a parliament in effect defines itself. At the same time, a legislature operating under a written constitution may enact statutes that profoundly affect the lawmaking procedure and its predictable outcome. If these statutes are drafted with sufficient cunning, they may remain within the frame of the constitution and yet undermine the institutions it was intended to establish. If the "court–packing" proposal of the thirties does not illustrate this danger unequivocally, it at least suggests that the fear of it is not fanciful. No written constitution can be self-executing. To be effective it requires not merely the respectful deference we show for ordinary legal enactments, but that willing convergence of effort we give to moral principles in which we have an active belief. One may properly work to amend a constitution, but so long as it remains unamended one must work with it, not against it or around it. All this amounts to saying that to be effective a written constitution must be accepted, at least provisionally, not just as law, but as good law.

What have these considerations to do with the ideal of fidelity to law? I think they have a great deal to do with it, and that they reveal the essential incapacity of the positivistic view to serve that ideal effectively. For I believe that a realization of this ideal is something for which we must plan, and that is precisely what positivism refuses to do.

Let me illustrate what I mean by planning for a realization of the ideal of fidelity to law. Suppose we are drafting a written constitution for a country just emerging from a period of violence and disorder in which any thread of legal continuity with previous governments has been broken. Obviously such a constitution cannot lift itself unaided into legality; it cannot be law simply because it says it is. We should keep in mind that the efficacy of our work will depend upon general acceptance and that to make this acceptance secure there must be a general belief that the constitution itself is necessary, right, and good. The provisions of the constitution should, therefore, be kept simple and understandable, not only in language, but also in purpose. Preambles and other explanations of what is being sought, which would be objectionable in an ordinary statute, may find an appropriate place in our constitution. We should think of our constitution as establishing a basic procedural framework for future governmental action in the enactment and administration of laws. Substantive limitations on the power of government should be kept to a minimum and should generally be confined to those for which a need can be generally appreciated. In so far as possible, substantive aims should be achieved procedurally, on the principle that if men are compelled to act in the right way, they will generally do the right things.

These considerations seem to have been widely ignored in the constitutions that have come into existence since World War II. Not uncommonly these constitutions incorporate a host of economic and political measures of the type one would ordinarily associate with statutory law. It is hardly likely that these measures have been written into the constitution because they represent aims that are generally shared. One suspects that the reason for their inclusion is precisely the opposite, namely, a fear that they would not be able to survive the vicissitudes of an ordinary exercise of parliamentary power. Thus, the divisions of opinion that are a normal accompaniment of lawmaking are written into the document that makes law itself possible. This is obviously a procedure that contains serious dangers for a future realization of the ideal of fidelity to law.

I have ventured these remarks on the making of constitutions not because I think they can claim any special profundity, but because I wished to illustrate what I mean by planning the conditions that will make it possible to realize the ideal of fidelity to law. Even within the limits of my modest purpose, what I have said may be clearly wrong. If so, it would not be for me to say whether I am also wrong clearly. I will, however, venture to assert that if I am wrong, I am wrong significantly. What disturbs me about the school of legal positivism is that it not only refuses to deal with problems of the sort I have just discussed, but bans them on principle from the province of legal philosophy. In its concern to assign the right labels to the things men do, this school seems to lose all interest in asking whether men are doing the right things.

IV. THE MORALITY OF LAW ITSELF

Most of the issues raised by Professor Hart's essay can be restated in terms of the distinction between order and good order. Law may be said to represent order *simpliciter*. Good order is law that corresponds to the demands of justice, or morality, or men's notions of what ought to be. This rephrasing of the issue is useful in bringing to light the ambitious nature of Professor Hart's undertaking, for surely we would all agree that it is no easy thing to distinguish order from good order. When it is said, for example, that law simply represents that public order which obtains under all governments—democratic, Fascist, or Communist [12]—the order intended is certainly not that of a morgue or cemetery. We must mean a functioning order, and such an order has to be at least good enough to be considered as functioning by some standard or other. A reminder that workable order usually requires some play in the joints, and therefore cannot be too orderly, is enough to suggest some of the complexities that would be involved in any attempt to draw a sharp distinction between order and good order.

For the time being, however, let us suppose we can in fact clearly separate the concept of order from that of good order. Even in this unreal and abstract form the notion of order itself contains what may be called a moral element. Let me illustrate this "morality of order" in its crudest and most elementary form. Let us suppose an absolute monarch, whose word is the only law known to his subjects. We may further suppose him to be utterly selfish and to seek in his relations with his subjects solely his own advantage. This monarch from time to time issues commands, promising rewards for compliance and threatening punishment for disobedience. He is, however, a dissolute and forgetful fellow, who never makes the slightest attempt to ascertain who have in fact followed his directions and who have not. As a result he habitually punishes loyalty and rewards disobedience. It is apparent that this monarch will never achieve even his own selfish aims until he is ready to accept that minimum self-restraint that will create a meaningful connection between his words and his actions.

Let us now suppose that our monarch undergoes a change of heart and begins to pay some attention to what he said yesterday when, today, he has occasion to distribute bounty or to order the chopping off of heads. Under the strain of this new responsibility, however, our monarch relaxes his attention in other directions and becomes hopelessly slothful in the phrasing of his commands. His orders become so ambiguous and are uttered in so inaudible a tone that his subjects never have any clear idea what he wants them to do. Here, again, it is apparent that if our monarch for his own selfish advantage wants to create in his realm anything like a system of law he will have to pull himself together and assume still another responsibility. Law, considered merely as order, contains, then, its own implicit morality. This morality of order must be respected if we are to create anything that can be called law, even bad law. Law by itself is powerless to bring this morality into existence. Until our monarch is really ready to face the responsibilities of his position, it will do no good for him to issue still another futile command, this time self-addressed and threatening himself with punishment if he does not mend his ways.

There is a twofold sense in which it is true that law cannot be built on law. First of all, the authority to make law must be supported by moral attitudes that accord to it the competency it claims. Here we are dealing with a morality external to law, which makes law possible. But this alone is not enough. We may stipulate that in our monarchy the accepted "basic norm" designates the monarch himself as the only possible source of law. We still cannot have law until our monarch is ready to accept the internal morality of law itself.

In the life of a nation these external and internal moralities of law reciprocally influence one another; a deterioration of the one will almost inevitably produce a deterioration in the other. So closely related are they that when the anthropologist Lowie speaks of "the generally accepted ethical postulates underlying our . . . legal institutions as their ultimate sanction and guaranteeing their smooth functioning,"[13] he may be presumed to have both of them in mind.

What I have called "the internal morality of law" seems to be almost completely neglected by Professor Hart. He does make brief mention of "justice in the administration of the law," which consists in the like treatment of like cases, by whatever elevated or perverted standards the word "like" may be defined.[14] But he quickly dismisses this aspect of law as having no special relevance to his main enterprise.

In this I believe he is profoundly mistaken. It is his neglect to analyze the demands of a morality of order that leads him throughout his essay to treat law as a datum projecting itself into human striving. When we realize that order itself is something that must be worked for, it becomes apparent that the existence of a legal system, even a bad or evil legal system, is always a matter of degree. When we recognize this simple fact of everyday legal experience, it becomes impossible to dismiss the problems presented by the Nazi regime with a simple assertion: "Under the Nazis there was law, even if it was bad law." We have instead to inquire how much of a legal system survived the general debasement and perversion of all forms of social order that occurred under the Nazi rule, and what moral implications this mutilated system had for the conscientious citizen forced to live under it.

It is not necessary, however, to dwell on such moral upheavals as the Nazi regime to see how completely incapable the positivistic philosophy is of serving the one high moral ideal it professes, that of fidelity to law. Its default in serving this ideal actually becomes most apparent, I believe, in the everyday problems that confront those who are earnestly desirous of meeting the moral demands of a legal order, but who have responsible functions to discharge in the very order toward which loyalty is due.

Let us suppose the case of a trial judge who has had an extensive experience in commercial matters and before whom a great many commercial disputes are tried. As a subordinate in a judicial hierarchy, our judge has of course the duty to follow the law laid down by his supreme court. Our imaginary Scrutton has the misfortune, however, to live under a supreme court which he considers woefully ignorant of the ways and needs of commerce. To his mind, many of this court's decisions in the field of commercial law simply do not make sense. If a conscientious judge caught in this dilemma were to turn to the positivistic philosophy what succor could he expect? It will certainly do no good to remind him that he has an obligation of fidelity to law. He is aware of this already and painfully so, since it is the source of his predicament. Nor will it help to say that if he legislates, it must be "interstitially," or that his contributions must be "confined from molar to molecular motions."[15] This mode of statement may be congenial to those who like to think of law, not as a purposive thing, but as an expression of the dimensions and directions of state power. But I cannot believe that the essentially trite idea behind this advice can be lifted by literary eloquence to the point where it will offer any real help to our judge; for one thing, it may be impossible for him to know whether his supreme court would regard any particular contribution of his as being wide or narrow.

Nor is it likely that a distinction between core and penumbra would be helpful. The predicament of our judge may well derive, not from particular precedents, but from a mistaken conception of the nature of commerce which extends over many decisions and penetrates them in varying degrees. So far as his problem arises from the use of particular words, he may well find that the supreme court often uses the ordinary terms of commerce in senses foreign to actual business dealings. If he interprets those words as a business executive or accountant would, he may well reduce the precedents he is bound to apply to a logical shambles. On the other hand, he may find great difficulty in discerning the exact sense in which the supreme court used those words, since in his mind that sense is itself the product of a confusion.

Is it not clear that it is precisely positivism's insistence on a rigid separation of law as it is from law as it ought to be that renders the positivistic philosophy incapable of aiding our judge? Is it not also clear that our judge can never achieve a satisfactory resolution of his dilemma unless he views his duty of fidelity to law in a context which also embraces his responsibility for making law what it ought to be?

The case I have supposed may seem extreme, but the problem it suggests pervades our whole legal system. If the divergence of views between our judge and his supreme court were less drastic, it would be more difficult to present his predicament graphically, but the perplexity of his position might actually increase. Perplexities of this sort are a normal accompaniment of the discharge of any adjudicative function; they perhaps reach their most poignant intensity in the field of administrative law.

One can imagine a case—surely not likely in Professor Hart's country or mine—where a judge might hold profound moral convictions that were exactly the opposite of those held, with equal attachment, by his supreme court. He might also be convinced that the precedents he was bound to apply were the direct product of a morality he considered abhorrent. If such a judge did not find the solution for his dilemma in surrendering his office, he might well be driven to a wooden and literal application of precedents which he could not otherwise apply because he was incapable of understanding the philosophy that animated them. But I doubt that a judge in this situation would need the help of legal positivism to find these melancholy escapes from his predicament. Nor do I think that such a predicament is likely to arise within a nation where both law and good law are regarded as collaborative human achievements in need of constant renewal, and where lawyers are still at least as interested in asking "What is good law?" as they are in asking "What is law?"

V. THE PROBLEM OF RESTORING RESPECT FOR LAW AND JUSTICE AFTER THE COLLAPSE OF A REGIME THAT RESPECTED NEITHER

After the collapse of the Nazi regime the German courts were faced with a truly frightful predicament. It was impossible for them to declare the whole dictatorship illegal or to treat as void every decision and legal enactment that had emanated from Hitler's government. Intolerable dislocations would have resulted from any such wholesale outlawing of all that occurred over a span of twelve years. On the other hand, it was equally impossible to carry forward into the new government the effects of every Nazi perversity that had been committed in the name of law; any such course would have tainted an indefinite future with the poisons of Nazism.

This predicament—which was, indeed, a pervasive one, affecting all branches of law—came to a dramatic head in a series of cases involving informers who had taken advantage of the Nazi terror to get rid of personal enemies or unwanted spouses. If all Nazi statutes and judicial decisions were indiscriminately "law," then these despicable creatures were guiltless, since they had turned their victims over to processes which the Nazis themselves knew by the name of law. Yet it was intolerable, especially for the surviving relatives and friends of the victims, that these people should go about unpunished, while the objects of their spite were dead, or were just being released after years of imprisonment, or, more painful still, simply remained unaccounted for.

The urgency of this situation does not by any means escape Professor Hart. Indeed, he is moved to recommend an expedient that is surely not lacking itself in a certain air of desperation. He suggests that a retroactive criminal statute would have been the least objectionable solution to the problem. This statute would have punished the informer, and branded him as a criminal, for an act which Professor Hart regards as having been perfectly legal when he committed it.[16]

On the other hand, Professor Hart condemns without qualification those judicial decisions in which the courts themselves undertook to declare void certain of the Nazi statutes under which the informer's victims had been convicted. One cannot help raising at this point the question whether the issue as presented by Professor Hart himself is truly that of fidelity to law. Surely it would be a necessary implication of a retroactive criminal statute against informers that, for purposes of that statute at least, the Nazi laws as applied to the informers or their victims were to be regarded as void. With this turn the question seems no longer to be whether what was once law can now be declared not to have been law, but rather who should do the dirty work, the courts or the legislature.

But, as Professor Hart himself suggests, the issues at stake are much too serious to risk losing them in a semantic tangle. Even if the whole question were one of words, we should remind ourselves that we are in an area where words have a powerful effect on human attitudes. I should

like, therefore, to undertake a defense of the German courts, and to advance reasons why, in my opinion, their decisions do not represent the abandonment of legal principle that Professor Hart sees in them. In order to understand the background of those decisions we shall have to move a little closer, within smelling distance of the witches' caldron, than we have been brought so far by Professor Hart. We shall have also to consider an aspect of the problem ignored in his essay, namely, the degree to which the Nazis observed what I have called the inner morality of law itself.

Throughout his discussion Professor Hart seems to assume that the only difference between Nazi law and, say, English law is that the Nazis used their laws to achieve ends that are odious to an Englishman. This assumption is, I think, seriously mistaken, and Professor Hart's acceptance of it seems to me to render his discussion unresponsive to the problem it purports to address.

Throughout their period of control the Nazis took generous advantage of a device not wholly unknown to American legislatures, the retroactive statute curing past legal irregularities. The most dramatic use of the curative powers of such a statute occurred on July 3, 1934, after the "Roehm purge." When this intraparty shooting affair was over and more than seventy Nazis had been —one can hardly avoid saying—"rubbed out," Hitler returned to Berlin and procured from his cabinet a law ratifying and confirming the measures taken between June 30, and July 1, 1934, without mentioning the names of those who were now considered to have been lawfully executed.[17] Some time later Hitler declared that during the Roehm purge "the supreme court of the German people ... consisted of myself,"[18] surely not an overstatement of the capacity in which he acted if one takes seriously the enactment conferring retroactive legality on "the measures taken."

Now in England and America it would never occur to anyone to say that "it is in the nature of law that it cannot be retroactive," although, of course, constitutional inhibitions may prohibit certain kinds of retroactivity. We would say it is normal for a law to operate prospectively, and that it may be arguable that it ought never operate otherwise, but there would be a certain occult unpersuasiveness in any assertion that retroactivity violates the very nature of law itself. Yet we have only to imagine a country in which all laws are retroactive in order to see that retroactivity presents a real problem for the internal morality of law. If we suppose an absolute monarch who allows his realm to exist in a constant state of anarchy, we would hardly say that he could create a regime of law simply by enacting a curative statute conferring legality on everything that had happened up to its date and by announcing an intention to enact similar statutes every six months in the future.

A general increase in the resort to statutes curative of past legal irregularities represents a deterioration in that form of legal morality without which law itself cannot exist. The threat of such statutes hangs over the whole legal system, and robs every law on the books of some of its significance. And surely a general threat of this sort is implied when a government is willing to use such a statute to transform into lawful execution what was simple murder when it happened.

During the Nazi regime there were repeated rumors of "secret laws." In the article criticized by Professor Hart, Radbruch mentions a report that the wholesale killings in concentration camps were made "lawful" by a secret enactment.[19] Now surely there can be no greater legal monstrosity than a secret statute. Would anyone seriously recommend that following the war the German courts should have searched for unpublished laws among the files left by Hitler's government so that citizens' rights could be determined by a reference to these laws?

The extent of the legislator's obligation to make his laws known to his subjects is, of course, a problem of legal morality that has been under active discussion at least since the Secession of the Plebs. There is probably no modern state that has not been plagued by this problem in one form or another. It is most likely to arise in modern societies with respect to unpublished administrative directions. Often these are regarded in quite good faith by those who issue them as affecting only matters of internal organization. But since the procedures followed by an administrative agency, even in its "internal" actions, may seriously affect the rights and interests of the citizen, these unpublished, or "secret," regulations are often a subject for complaint.

But as with retroactivity, what in most societies is kept under control by the tacit restraints of legal decency broke out in monstrous form under Hitler. Indeed, so loose was the whole Nazi morality of law that it is not easy to know just what should be regarded as an unpublished or secret law. Since unpublished instructions to those administering the law could destroy the letter of any published law by imposing on it an outrageous interpretation, there was a sense in which the meaning of every law was "secret." Even a verbal order from Hitler that a thousand prisoners in concentration camps be put to death was at once an administrative direction and a validation of everything done under it as being "lawful."

But the most important affronts to the morality of law by Hitler's government took no such subtle forms as those exemplified in the bizarre outcroppings I have just discussed. In the first place, when legal forms became inconvenient, it was always possible for the Nazis to bypass them entirely and "to act through the party in the streets." There was no one who dared bring them to account for whatever outrages might thus be committed. In the second place, the Nazi-dominated courts were always ready to disregard any statute, even those enacted by the Nazis themselves, if this suited their convenience or if they feared that a lawyer-like interpretation might incur displeasure "above."

This complete willingness of the Nazis to disregard even their own enactments was an important factor leading Radbruch to take the position he did in the articles so severely criticized by Professor Hart. I do not believe that any fair appraisal of the action of the postwar German courts is possible unless we take this factor into account, as Professor Hart fails completely to do.

These remarks may seem inconclusive in their generality and to rest more on assertion than evidentiary fact. Let us turn at once, then, to the actual case discussed by Professor Hart.[20]

In 1944 a German soldier paid a short visit to his wife while under travel orders on a reassignment. During the single day he was home, he conveyed privately to his wife something of his opinion of the Hitler government. He expressed disapproval of (*sich abfßllig geäussert über*) Hitler and other leading personalities of the Nazi party. He also said it was too bad Hitler had not met his end in the assassination attempt that had occurred on July 20th of that year. Shortly after his departure, his wife, who during his long absence on military duty "had turned to other men" and who wished to get rid of him reported his remarks to the local leader of the Nazi party, observing that "a man who would say a thing like that does not deserve to live." The result was a trial of the husband by a military tribunal and a sentence of death. After a short period of imprisonment, instead of being executed, he was sent to the front again. After the collapse of the Nazi regime, the wife was brought to trial for having procured the imprisonment of her husband. Her defense rested on the ground that her husband's statements to her about Hitler and the Nazis constituted a crime under the laws then in force. Accordingly, when she informed on her husband she was simply bringing a criminal to justice.

This defense rested on two statutes, one passed in 1934, the other in 1938. Let us first consider the second of these enactments, which was part of a more comprehensive legislation creating a whole series of special wartime criminal offenses. I reproduce below a translation of the only pertinent section:

The following persons are guilty of destroying the national power of resistance and shall be punished by death: Whoever publicly solicits or incites a refusal to fulfill the obligations of service in the armed forces of Germany, or in armed forces allied with Germany, or who otherwise publicly seeks to injure or destroy the will of the German people or an allied people to assert themselves stalwartly against their enemies.[21]

It is almost inconceivable that a court of present-day Germany would hold the husband's remarks to his wife, who was barred from military duty by her sex, to be a violation of the final catch-all provision of this statute, particularly when it is recalled that the test reproduced above was part of a more comprehensive enactment dealing with such things as harboring deserters, escaping military duty by self-inflicted injuries, and the like. The question arises, then, as to the extent to which the interpretive principles applied by the courts of Hitler's government should be accepted in determining whether the husband's remarks were indeed unlawful.

This question becomes acute when we note that the act applies only to *public* acts or utterances, whereas the husband's remarks were in the privacy of his own home. Now it appears that the Nazi courts (and it should be noted we are dealing with a special military court) quite generally disregarded this limitation and extended the act to all utterances, private or public.[22] Is Professor Hart prepared to say that the legal meaning of this statute is to be determined in the light of this apparently uniform principle of judicial interpretation?

Let us turn now to the other statute upon which Professor Hart relies in assuming that the husband's utterance was unlawful. This is the act of 1934, the relevant portions of which are translated below:

(1) Whoever publicly makes spiteful or provocative statements directed against, or statements which disclose a base disposition toward, the leading personalities of the nation or of the National Socialist German Workers' Party, or toward measures taken or institutions established by them, and of such a nature as to undermine the people's confidence in their political leadership, shall be punished by imprisonment.

(2) Malicious utterances not made in public shall be treated in the same manner as public utterances when the person making them realized or should have realized they would reach the public.

(3) Prosecution for such utterances shall be only on the order of the National Minister of Justice; in case the utterance was directed against a leading personality of the National Socialist German Workers' Party, the Minister of Justice shall order prosecution only with the advice and consent of the Representative of the Leader.

(4) The National Minister of Justice shall, with the advice and consent of the Representative of the Leader, determine who shall belong to the class of leading personalities for purposes of Section 1 above.[23]

Extended comment on this legislative monstrosity is scarcely called for, overlarded and undermined as it is by uncontrolled administrative discretion. We may note only: first, that it offers no justification whatever for the death penalty actually imposed on the husband, though never carried out; second, that if the wife's act in informing on her husband made his remarks "public," there is no such thing as a private utterance under this statute. I should like to ask the reader whether he can actually share Professor Hart's indignation that, in the perplexities of the postwar reconstruction, the German courts saw fit to declare this thing not a law. Can it be argued seriously that it would have been more beseeming to the judicial process if the postwar courts had undertaken a study of "the interpretative principles" in force during Hitler's rule and had then solemnly applied those "principles" to ascertain the meaning of this statute? On the other hand, would the courts really have been showing respect for Nazi law if they had construed the Nazi statutes by their own, quite different, standards of interpretation? Professor Hart castigates the German courts and Radbruch, not so much for what they believed had to be done, but because they failed to see that they were confronted by a moral dilemma of a sort that would have been immediately apparent to Bentham and Austin. By the simple dodge of saying, "When a statute is sufficiently evil it ceases to be law," they ran away from the problem they should have faced.

This criticism is, I believe, without justification. So far as the courts are concerned, matters certainly would not have been helped if, instead of saying, "This is not law," they had said, "This is law but it is so evil we will refuse to apply it." Surely moral confusion reaches its height when a court refuses to apply something it admits to be law, and Professor Hart does not recommend any such "facing of the true issue" by the courts themselves. He would have preferred a retroactive statute. Curiously, this was also the preference of Radbruch.[24] But unlike Professor Hart, the German courts and Gustav Radbruch were living participants in a situation of drastic emergency. The informer problem was a pressing one, and if legal institutions were to be rehabilitated in Germany it would not do to allow the people to begin taking the law into their own hands, as might have occurred while the courts were waiting for a statute.

As for Gustav Radbruch, it is, I believe, wholly unjust to say that he did not know he was faced with a moral dilemma. His postwar writings repeatedly stress the antinomies confronted in the effort to rebuild decent and orderly government in Germany. As for the ideal of fidelity to law, I shall let Radbruch's own words state his position:

We must not conceal from ourselves—especially not in the light of our experiences during the twelve-year dictatorship—what frightful dangers for the rule of law can be contained in the notion of "statutory lawlessness" and in refusing the quality of law to duly enacted statutes.[25]

The situation is not that legal positivism enables a man to know when he faces a difficult problem of choice, while Radbruch's beliefs deceive him into thinking there is no problem to face. The real issue dividing Professors Hart and Radbruch is: How shall we state the problem? What is the nature of the dilemma in which we are caught?

I hope I am not being unjust to Professor Hart when I say that I can find no way of describing the dilemma as he sees it but to use some such words as the following: On the one hand, we have an amoral datum called law, which has the peculiar quality of creating a moral duty to obey it. On the other hand, we have a moral duty to do what we think is right and decent. When we are confronted by a statute we believe to be thoroughly evil, we have to choose between those two duties.

If this is the positivist position, then I have no hesitancy in rejecting it. The "dilemma" it states has the verbal formulation of a problem, but the problem it states makes no sense. It is like saying I have to choose between giving food to a starving man and being mimsy with the borogoves. I do not think it is unfair to the positivistic philosophy to say that it never gives any coherent meaning to the moral obligation of fidelity to law. This obligation seems to be conceived as sui generis, wholly unrelated to any of the ordinary, extralegal ends of human life. The fundamental postulate of positivism—that law must be strictly severed from morality—seems to deny the possibility of any bridge between the obligation to obey law and other moral obligations. No mediating principle can measure their respective demands on conscience, for they exist in wholly separate worlds.

While I would not subscribe to all of Radbruch's postwar views—especially those relating to "higher law"—I think he saw, much more clearly than does Professor Hart, the true nature of the dilemma confronted by Germany in seeking to rebuild her shattered legal institutions. Germany had to restore both respect for law and respect for justice. Though neither of these could be restored without the other, painful antinomies were encountered in attempting to restore both at once, as Radbruch saw all too clearly. Essentially Radbruch saw the dilemma as that of meeting the demands of order, on the one hand, and those of good order, on the other. Of course no pat formula can be derived from this phrasing of the problem. But, unlike legal positivism, it does not present us with opposing demands that have no living contact with one another, that simply shout their contradictions across a vacuum. As we seek order, we can meaningfully remind ourselves that order itself will do us no good unless it is good for something. As we seek to make our order good, we can remind ourselves that justice itself is impossible without order, and that we must not lose order itself in the attempt to make it good.

VI. THE MORAL IMPLICATIONS OF LEGAL POSITIVISM

We now reach the question whether there is any ground for Gustav Radbruch's belief that a general acceptance of the positivistic philosophy in pre-Nazi Germany made smoother the route to dictatorship. Understandably, Professor Hart regards this as the most outrageous of all charges against positivism.

Here indeed we enter upon a hazardous area of controversy, where ugly words and ugly charges have become commonplace. During the last half century in this country no issue of legal philosophy has caused more spilling of ink and adrenalin than the assertion that there are "totalitarian" implications in the views of Oliver Wendell Holmes, Jr. Even the most cautiously phrased criticisms of that grand old figure from the age of Darwin, Huxley, and Haeckel seem to stir the reader's mind with the memory of past acerbities.[26] It does no good to suggest that perhaps Holmes did not perceive all the implications of his own philosophy, for this is merely to substitute one insult for another. Nor does it help much to recall the dictum of one of the closest companions of Holmes' youth—surely no imperceptive observer—that Holmes was "composed of at least two and a half different people rolled into one, and the way he keeps them together in one tight skin, without quarreling any more than they do, is remarkable."[27]

In the venturing upon these roughest of all jurisprudential waters, one is not reassured to see even so moderate a man as Professor Hart indulging in some pretty broad strokes of the oar. Radbruch disclosed "an extraordinary naïveté" in assessing the temper of his own profession in Germany and in supposing that its adherence to positivism helped the Nazis to power.[28] His judgment on this and other matters shows that he had "only half–digested the spiritual message of liberalism he mistakenly thought he was conveying to his countrymen."[29] A state of "hysteria"[30] is revealed by those who see a wholesome reorientation of German legal thinking in such judicial decisions as were rendered in the informer cases.

Let us put aside at least the blunter tools of invective and address ourselves as calmly as we can to the question whether legal positivism, as practiced and preached in Germany, had, or could have had, any causal connection with Hitler's ascent to power. It should be recalled that in the seventy-five years before the Nazi regime the positivistic philosophy had achieved in Germany a standing such as it enjoyed in no other country. Austin praised a German scholar for bringing international law within the clarity-producing restraints of positivism.[31] Gray reported with pleasure that the "abler" German jurists of his time

were "abjuring all *'nicht positivisches Recht,'*" and cited Bergbohm as an example.[32] This is an illuminating example, for Bergbohm was a scholar whose ambition was to make German positivism live up to its own pretensions. He was distressed to encounter vestigial traces of natural-law thinking in writings claiming to be positivistic. In particular, he was disturbed by the frequent recurrence of such notions as that law owes its efficacy to a perceived moral need for order, or that it is in the nature of man that he requires a legal order, etc. Bergbohm announced a program, never realized, to drive from positivistic thinking these last miasmas from the swamp of natural law.[33] German jurists generally tended to regard the Anglo-American common law as a messy and unprincipled conglomerate of law and morals.[34] Positivism was the only theory of law that could claim to be "scientific" in an Age of Science. Dissenters from this view were characterized by positivists with that epithet modern man fears above all others: "naïve." The result was that it could be reported by 1927 that "to be found guilty of adherence to natural law theories is a kind of social disgrace."[35]

To this background we must add the observation that the Germans seem never to have achieved that curious ability possessed by the British, and to some extent by the Americans, of holding their logic on short leash. When a German defines law, he means his definition to be taken seriously. If a German writer had hit upon the slogan of American legal realism, "Law is simply the behavior patterns of judges and other state officials," he would not have regarded this as an interesting little conversation-starter. He would have believed it and acted on it.

German legal positivism not only banned from legal science any consideration of the moral ends of law, but it was also indifferent to what I have called the inner morality of law itself. The German lawyer was therefore peculiarly prepared to accept as "law" anything that called itself by that name, was printed at government expense, and seemed to come "*von oben herab.*"

In the light of these considerations I cannot see either absurdity or perversity in the suggestion that the attitudes prevailing in the German legal profession were helpful to the Nazis. Hitler did not come to power by a violent revolution. He was Chancellor before he became the Leader. The exploitation of legal forms started cautiously and became bolder as power was consolidated. The first attacks on the established order were on ramparts which, if they were manned by anyone, were manned by lawyers and judges. These ramparts fell almost without a struggle.

Professor Hart and others have been understandably distressed by references to a "higher law" in some of the decisions concerning informers and in Radbruch's postwar writings. I suggest that if German jurisprudence had concerned itself more with the inner morality of law, it would not have been necessary to invoke any notion of this sort in declaring void the more outrageous Nazi statutes.

To me there is nothing shocking in saying that a dictatorship which clothes itself with a tinsel of legal form can so far depart from the morality of order, from the inner morality of law itself, that it ceases to be a legal system. When a system calling itself law is predicated upon a general disregard by judges of the terms of the laws they purport to enforce, when this system habitually cures its legal irregularities, even the grossest, by retroactive statutes, when it has only to resort to forays of terror in the streets, which no one dares challenge, in order to escape even those scant restraints imposed by the pretence of legality—when all these things have become true of a dictatorship, it is not hard for me, at least, to deny to it the name of law.

I believe that the invalidity of the statutes involved in the informer cases could have been grounded on considerations such as I have just outlined. But if you were raised with a generation that said "law is law" and meant it, you may feel the only way you can escape one law is to set another off against it, and this perforce must be a "higher law." Hence these notions of "higher law," which are a justifiable cause for alarm, may themselves be a belated fruit of German legal positivism.

It should be remarked at this point that it is chiefly in Roman Catholic writings that the theory of natural law is considered, not simply as a search for those principles that will enable men to live together successfully, but as a quest for something that can be called "a higher law." This identification of natural law with a law that is above human laws seems in fact to be demanded by any doctrine that asserts the possibility of an authoritative pronouncement of the demands of natural law. In those areas affected by such pronouncements as have so far been issued, the conflict between Roman Catholic doctrine and opposing views seems to me to be a conflict between two forms of positivism. Fortunately, over

most of the area with which lawyers are concerned, no such pronouncements exist. In these areas I think those of us who are not adherents of its faith can be grateful to the Catholic Church for having kept alive the rationalistic tradition in ethics.

I do not assert that the solution I have suggested for the informer cases would not have entailed its own difficulties, particularly the familiar one of knowing where to stop. But I think it demonstrable that the most serious deterioration in legal morality under Hitler took place in branches of the law like those involved in the informer cases; no comparable deterioration was to be observed in the ordinary branches of private law. It was in those areas where the ends of law were most odious by ordinary standards of decency that the morality of law itself was most flagrantly disregarded. In other words, where one would have been most tempted to say, "This is so evil it cannot be a law," one could usually have said instead, "This thing is the product of a system so oblivious to the morality of law that it is not entitled to be called a law." I think there is something more than accident here, for the overlapping suggests that legal morality cannot live when it is severed from a striving toward justice and decency.

But as an actual solution for the informer cases, I, like Professors Hart and Radbruch, would have preferred a retroactive statute. My reason for this preference is not that this is the most nearly lawful way of making unlawful what was once law. Rather I would see such a statute as a way of symbolizing a sharp break with the past, as a means of isolating a kind of cleanup operation from the normal functioning of the judicial process. By this isolation it would become possible for the judiciary to return more rapidly to a condition in which the demands of legal morality could be given proper respect. In other words, it would make it possible to plan more effectively to regain for the ideal of fidelity to law its normal meaning.

VII. THE PROBLEM OF INTERPRETATION: THE CORE AND THE PENUMBRA

It is essential that we be just as clear as we can be about the meaning of Professor Hart's doctrine of "the core and the penumbra,"[36] because I believe the casual reader is likely to misinterpret what he has to say. Such a reader is apt to suppose that Professor Hart is merely describing something that is a matter of everyday experience for the lawyer, namely, that in the interpretation of legal rules it is typically the case (though not universally so) that there are some situations which will seem to fall rather clearly within the rule, while others will be more doubtful. Professor Hart's thesis takes no such jejune form. His extended discussion of the core and the penumbra is not just a complicated way of recognizing that some cases are hard, while others are easy. Instead, on the basis of a theory about language meaning generally, he is proposing a theory of judicial interpretation which is, I believe, wholly novel. Certainly it has never been put forward in so uncompromising a form before.

As I understand Professor Hart's thesis (if we add some tacit assumptions implied by it, as well as some qualifications he would no doubt wish his readers to supply) a full statement would run something as follows: The task of interpretation is commonly that of determining the meaning of the individual words of a legal rule, like "vehicle" in a rule excluding vehicles from a park. More particularly, the task of interpretation is to determine the range of reference of such a word, or the aggregate of things to which it points. Communication is possible only because words have a "standard instance," or a "core of meaning" that remains relatively constant, whatever the context in which the word may appear. Except in unusual circumstances, it will always be proper to regard a word like "vehicle" as embracing its "standard instance," that is, that aggregate of things it would include in all ordinary contexts, within or without the law. This meaning the word will have in any legal rule, whatever its purpose. In applying the word to its "standard instance," no creative role is assumed by the judge. He is simply applying the law "as it is."

In addition to a constant core, however, words also have a penumbra of meaning which, unlike the core, will vary from context to context. When the object in question (say, a tricycle) falls within this penumbral area, the judge is forced to assume a more creative role. He must now undertake, for the first time, an interpretation of the rule in the light of its purpose or aim. Having in mind what was sought by the regulation concerning parks, ought it to be considered as barring tricycles? When questions of this sort are decided there is at least an "intersection" of "is" and "ought," since the judge, in deciding what the rule "is," does so in the light of his notions of what "it ought to be" in order to carry out its purpose.

If I have properly interpreted Professor Hart's theory as it affects the "hard core," then I think it is quite untenable. The most obvious defect of his theory lies in its assumption that problems of interpretation typically turn on the meaning of individual words. Surely no judge applying a rule of the common law ever followed any such procedure as that described (and, I take it, prescribed) by Professor Hart; indeed, we do not normally even think of his problem as being one of "interpretation." Even in the case of statutes, we commonly have to assign meaning, not to a single word, but to a sentence, a paragraph, or a whole page or more of text. Surely a paragraph does not have a "standard instance" that remains constant whatever the context in which it appears. If a statute seems to have a kind of "core meaning" that we can apply without a too precise inquiry into its exact purpose, this is because we can see that, however one might formulate the precise objective of the statute, *this* case would still come within it.

Even in situations where our interpretive difficulties seem to head up in a single word, Professor Hart's analysis seems to me to give no real account of what does or should happen. In his illustration of the "vehicle," although he tells us this word has a core of meaning that in all contexts defines unequivocally a range of objects embraced by it, he never tells us what these objects might be. If the rule excluding vehicles from parks seems easy to apply in some cases, I submit this is because we can see clearly enough what the rule "is aiming at in general" so that we know there is no need to worry about the difference between Fords and Cadillacs. If in some cases we seem to be able to apply the rule without asking what its purpose is, this is not because we can treat a directive arrangement as if it had no purpose. It is rather because, for example, whether the rule be intended to preserve quiet in the park, or to save carefree strollers from injury, we know, "without thinking," that a noisy automobile must be excluded.

What would Professor Hart say if some local patriots wanted to mount on a pedestal in the park a truck used in World War II, while other citizens, regarding the proposed memorial as an eyesore, support their stand by the "no vehicle" rule? Does this truck, in perfect working order, fall within the core or the penumbra?

Professor Hart seems to assert that unless words have "standard instances" that remain constant regardless of context, effective communication would break down and it would become impossible to construct a system of "rules which have authority."[37] If in every context words took on a unique meaning, peculiar to that context, the whole process of interpretation would become so uncertain and subjective that the ideal of a rule of law would lose its meaning. In other words, Professor Hart seems to be saying that unless we are prepared to accept his analysis of interpretation, we must surrender all hope of giving an effective meaning to the ideal of fidelity to law. This presents a very dark prospect indeed, if one believes, as I do, that we cannot accept his theory of interpretation. I do not take so gloomy a view of the future of the ideal of fidelity to law.

An illustration will help to test, not only Professor Hart's theory of the core and the penumbra, but its relevance to the ideal of fidelity to law as well. Let us suppose that in leafing through the statutes, we come upon the following enactment: "It shall be a misdemeanor, punishable by a fine of five dollars, to sleep in any railway station." We have no trouble in perceiving the general nature of the target toward which this state is aimed. Indeed, we are likely at once to call to mind the picture of a disheveled tramp, spread out in an ungainly fashion on one of the benches of the station, keeping weary passengers on their feet and filling their ears with raucous and alcoholic snores. This vision may fairly be said to represent the "obvious instance" contemplated by the statute, though certainly it is far from being the "standard instance" of the physiological state called "sleep."

Now let us see how this example bears on the ideal of fidelity to law. Suppose I am a judge, and that two men are brought before me for violating this statute. The first is a passenger who was waiting at 3 A.M. for a delayed train. When he was arrested he was sitting upright in an orderly fashion, but was heard by the arresting officer to be gently snoring. The second is a man who had brought a blanket and pillow to the station and had obviously settled himself down for the night. He was arrested, however, before he had a chance to go to sleep. Which of these cases presents the "standard instance" of the word "sleep"? If I disregard that question, and decide to fine the second man and set free the first, have I violated a duty of fidelity to law? Have I violated that duty if I interpret the word "sleep" as used in this statute to mean something like "to spread oneself out on a bench or floor to spend the night, or as if to spend the night"?

Testing another aspect of Professor Hart's theory, is it really ever possible to interpret a word in a statute without knowing the aim of the statute? Suppose we encounter the following incomplete sentence: "All improvements must be promptly reported to . . ." Professor Hart's theory seems to assert that even if we have only this fragment before us we can safely construe the word "improvement" to apply to its "standard instance," though we would have to know the rest of the sentence before we could deal intelligently with "problems of the penumbra." Yet surely in the truncated sentence I have quoted, the word "improvement" is almost as devoid of meaning as the symbol "X."

The word "improvement" will immediately take on meaning if we fill out the sentence with the words, "the head nurse," or, "the Town Planning Authority," though the two meanings that come to mind are radically dissimilar. It can hardly be said that these two meanings represent some kind of penumbral accretion to the word's "standard instance." And one wonders, parenthetically, how helpful the theory of the core and the penumbra would be in deciding whether, when the report is to be made to the planning authorities, the word "improvement" includes an unmortgageable monstrosity of a house that lowers the market value of the land on which it is built.

It will be instructive, I think, to consider the effect of other ways of filling out the sentence. Suppose we add to, "All improvements must be promptly reported to . . ." the words, "the Dean of the Graduate Division." Here we no longer seem, as we once did, to be groping in the dark; rather, we seem now to be reaching into an empty box. We achieve a little better orientation if the final clause reads, "to the Principal of the School," and we feel completely at ease if it becomes, "to the Chairman of the Committee on Relations with the Parents of Children in the Primary Division."

It should be noted that in deciding what the word "improvement" means in all these cases, we do not proceed simply by placing the word in some general context, such as hospital practice, town planning, or education. If this were so, the "improvement" in the last instance might just as well be that of the teacher as that of the pupil. Rather, we ask ourselves, What can this rule be for? What evil does it seek to avert? What good is it intended to promote? When it is "the head nurse" who receives the report, we are apt to find ourselves asking, "Is there, perhaps, a shortage of hospital space, so that patients who improve sufficiently are sent home or are assigned to a ward where they will receive less attention?" If "Principal" offers more orientation than "Dean of the Graduate Division," this must be because we know something about the differences between primary education and education on the postgraduate university level. We must have some minimum acquaintance with the ways in which these two educational enterprises are conducted, and with the problems encountered in both of them, before any distinction between "Principal" and "Dean of the Graduate Division" would affect our interepretation of "improvement." We must, in other words, be sufficiently capable of putting ourselves in the position of those who drafted the rule to know what they thought "ought to be." It is in the light of this "ought" that we must decide what the rule "is."

Turning now to the phenomenon Professor Hart calls "preoccupation with the penumbra," we have to ask ourselves what is actually contributed to the process of interpretation by the common practice of supposing various "borderline" situations. Professor Hart seems to say, "Why, nothing at all, unless we are working with problems of the penumbra." If this is what he means, I find his view a puzzling one, for it still leaves unexplained why, under this theory, if one is dealing with a penumbral problem, it could be useful to think about other penumbral problems.

Throughout his whole discussion of interpretation, Professor Hart seems to assume that it is a kind of cataloguing procedure. A judge faced with a novel situation is like a library clerk who has to decide where to shelve a new book. There are easy cases: the *Bible* belongs under Religion, *The Wealth of Nations* under Economics, etc. Then there are hard cases, when the librarian has to exercise a kind of creative choice, as in deciding whether *Das Kapital* belongs under Politics or Economics, *Gulliver's Travels* under Fantasy or Philosophy. But whether the decision where to shelve is easy or hard, once it is made all the librarian has to do is to put the book away. And so it is with judges, Professor Hart seems to say, in all essential particulars. Surely the judicial process is something more than a cataloguing procedure. The judge does not discharge his responsibility when he pins an apt diagnostic label on the case. He has to do something about it, to treat it, if you will. It is this larger responsibility which explains why interpretative problems

almost never turn on a single word, and also why lawyers for generations have found the putting of imaginary borderline cases useful, not only "on the penumbra," but in order to know where the penumbra begins.

These points can be made clear, I believe, by drawing again on our example of the statutory fragment which reads, "All improvements must be promptly reported to. . . ." Whatever the concluding phrase may be, the judge has not solved his problems simply by deciding what kind of improvement is meant. Almost all of the words in the sentence may require interpretation, but most obviously this is so of "promptly" and "reported." What kind of "report" is contemplated: a written note, a call at the office, entry in a hospital record? How specific must it be? Will it be enough to say "a lot better," or "a big house with a bay window"?

Now it should be apparent to any lawyer that in interpreting words like "improvement," "prompt," and "report," no real help is obtained by asking how some extralegal "standard instance" would define these words. But, much more important, when these words are all parts of a single structure of thought, they are in interaction with one another during the process of interpretation. "What is an 'improvement'? Well, it must be something that can be made the subject of a report. So, for purposes of this statute 'improvement' really means 'reportable improvement.' What kind of 'report' must be made? Well, that depends upon the sort of 'improvement' about which information is desired and the reasons for desiring the information."

When we look beyond individual words to the statute as a whole, it becomes apparent how the putting of hypothetical cases assists the interpretative process generally. By pulling our minds first in one direction, then in another, these cases help us to understand the fabric of thought before us. This fabric is something we seek to discern, so that we may know truly what it is, but it is also something that we inevitably help to create as we strive (in accordance with our obligation of fidelity to law) to make the statute a coherent, workable whole.

I should have considered all these remarks much too trite to put down here if they did not seem to be demanded in an answer to the theory of interpretation proposed by Professor Hart, a theory by which he puts such store that he implies we cannot have fidelity to law in any meaningful sense unless we are prepared to accept it.

Can it be possible that the positivistic philosophy demands that we abandon a view of interpretation which sees as its central concern, not words, but purpose and structure? If so, then the stakes in this battle of schools are indeed high.

I am puzzled by the novelty Professor Hart attributes to the lessons I once tried to draw from Wittgenstein's example about teaching a game to children.[38] I was simply trying to show the role reflection plays in deciding what ought to be done. I was trying to make such simple points as that decisions about what ought to be done are improved by reflection, by an exchange of views with others sharing the same problems, and by imagining various situations that might be presented. I was assuming that all of these innocent and familiar measures might serve to sharpen our perception of what we were trying to do, and that the product of the whole process might be, not merely a more apt choice of means for the end sought, but a clarification of the end itself. I had thought that a famous judge of the English bench had something like this in mind when he spoke of the common law as working "itself pure."[39] If this view of the judicial process is no longer entertained in the country of its origin, I can only say that, whatever the vicissitudes of Lord Mansfield's British reputation may be, he will always remain for us in this country a heroic figure of jurisprudence.

I have stressed here the deficiencies of Professor Hart's theory as that theory affects judicial interpretation. I believe, however, that its defects go deeper and result ultimately from a mistaken theory about the meaning of language generally. Professor Hart seems to subscribe to what may be called "the pointer theory of meaning,"[40] a theory which ignores or minimizes the effect on the meaning of words of the speaker's purpose and the structure of language. Characteristically, this school of thought embraces the notion of "common usage." The reason is, of course, that it is only with the aid of this notion that it can seem to attain the inert datum of meaning it seeks, a meaning isolated from the effects of purpose and structure.

It would not do to attempt here an extended excursus into linguistic theory. I shall have to content myself with remarking that the theory of meaning implied in Professor Hart's essay seems to me to have been rejected by three men who stand at the very head of modern developments in logical analysis: Wittgenstein, Russell, and Whitehead. Wittgenstein's posthumous *Philo-* *sophical Investigations* constitutes a sort of running commentary on the way words shift and transform their meanings as they move from context to context. Russell repudiates the cult of "common usage," and asks what "instance" of the word "word" itself can be given that does not imply some specific intention in the use of it.[41] Whitehead explains the appeal that "the deceptive identity of the repeated word" has for modern philosophers; only by assuming some linguistic constant (such as the "core of meaning") can validity be claimed for procedures of logic which of necessity move the word from one context to another.[42]

VIII. THE MORAL AND EMOTIONAL FOUNDATIONS OF POSITIVISM

If we ignore the specific theories of law associated with the positivistic philosophy, I believe we can say that the dominant tone of positivism is set by a fear of a purposive interpretation of law and legal institutions, or at least by a fear that such an interpretation may be pushed too far. I think one can find confirmatory traces of this fear in all of those classified as "positivists" by Professor Hart, with the outstanding exception of Bentham, who is in all things a case apart and who was worlds removed from anything that could be called *ethical* positivism.

Now the belief that many of us hold, that this fear of purpose takes a morbid turn in positivism, should not mislead us into thinking that the fear is wholly without justification, or that it reflects no significant problem in the organization of society.

Fidelity to law *can* become impossible if we do not accept the broader responsibilities (themselves purposive, as all responsibilities are and must be) that go with a purposive interpretation of law. One can imagine a course of reasoning that might run as follows: This statute says absinthe shall not be sold. What is its purpose? To promote health. Now, as everyone knows, absinthe is a sound, wholesome, and beneficial beverage. Therefore, interpreting the statute in the light of its purpose, I construe it to direct a general sale and consumption of that most healthful of beverages, absinthe.

If the risk of this sort of thing is implicit in a purposive interpretation, what measures can we take to eliminate it, or to reduce it to bearable proportions? One is tempted to say. "Why, just use ordinary common sense." But this would be an evasion, and would amount to saying that although we know the answer, we cannot say what it is. To give a better answer, I fear I shall have to depart from those high standards of clarity Professor Hart so rightly prizes and so generally exemplifies. I shall have to say that the answer lies in the concept of *structure*. A statute or a rule of common law has, either explicitly, or by virtue of its relation with other rules, something that may be called a structural integrity. This is what we have in mind when we speak of "the intent of the statute," though we know it is men who have intentions and not words on paper. Within the limits of that structure, fidelity to law not only permits but demands a creative role from the judge, but beyond that structure it does not permit him to go. Of course, the structure of which I speak presents its own "problems of the penumbra." But the penumbra in this case surrounds something real, somthing that has a meaning and integrity of its own. It is not a purposeless collocation of words that gets its meaning on loan from lay usage.

It is one of the great virtues of Professor Hart's essay that it makes explicit positivism's concern for the ideal of fidelity to law. Yet I believe, though I cannot prove, that the basic reason why positivism fears a purposive interpretation is not that it may lead to anarchy, but that it may push us too far in the opposite direction. It sees in a purposive interpretation, carried too far, a threat to human freedom and human dignity.

Let me illustrate what I mean by supposing that I am a man without religious beliefs living in a community of ardent Protestant Christian faith. A statute in this community makes it unlawful for me to play golf on Sunday. I find this statute an annoyance and accept its restraints reluctantly. But the annoyance I feel is not greatly different from that I might experience if, though it were lawful to play on Sunday, a power failure prevented me from taking the streetcar I would normally use in reaching the course. In the vernacular, "it is just one of those things."

What a different complexion the whole matter assumes if a statute compels me to attend church, or, worse still, to kneel and recite prayers! Here I may feel a direct affront to my integrity as a human being. Yet the purpose of both statutes may well be to increase church attendance. The difference may even seem to be that the first statute seeks its end slyly and by indirection, the second, honestly and openly. Yet surely this is a case in which indirection has its virtues and honesty its heavy price in human dignity.

Now I believe that positivism fears that a too explicit and uninhibited interpretation in terms of purpose may well push the first kind of statute in the direction of the second. If this is a basic concern underlying the positivistic philosophy, that philosophy is dealing with a real problem, however inept its response to the problem may seem to be. For this problem of the impressed purpose is a crucial one in our society. One thinks of the obligation to bargain "in good faith" imposed by the National Labor Relations Act.[43] One recalls the remark that to punish a criminal is less of an affront to his dignity than to reform and improve him. The statutory preamble comes to mind: the increasing use made of it, its legislative wisdom, the significance that should be accorded to it in judicial interpretation. The flag salute cases[44] will, of course, occur to everyone. I myself recall the splendid analysis by Professor von Hippel of the things that were fundamentally wrong about Nazism, and his conclusion that the grossest of all Nazi perversities was that of coercing acts, like the putting out of flags and saying, "Heil Hitler!" that have meaning only when done voluntarily, or, more accurately, have a meaning when coerced that is wholly parasitic on an association of them with past voluntary expressions.[45]

Questions of this sort are undoubtedly becoming more acute as the state assumes a more active role with respect to economic activity. No significant economic activity can be organized exclusively by "don'ts." By its nature economic production requires a co-operative effort. In the economic field there is special reason, therefore, to fear that "This you may not do" will be transformed into "This you must do—but willingly." As we all know, the most tempting opportunity for effecting this transformation is presented by what is called in administrative practice "the prehearing conference," in which the negative threat of a statute's sanctions may be used by its administrators to induce what they regard, in all good conscience, as "the proper attitude."

I look forward to the day when legal philosophy can address itself earnestly to issues of this sort, and not simply exploit them to score points in favor of a position already taken. Professor Hart's essay seems to me to open the way for such a discussion, for it eliminates from the positivistic philosophy a pretense that has hitherto obscured every issue touched by it. I mean, of course, the pretense of the ethical neutrality of positivism. That is why I can say in all sincerity that, despite my almost paragraph-by-paragraph disagreement with the views expressed in his essay, I believe Professor Hart has made an enduring contribution to legal philosophy.

NOTES

1. Kelsen, *Die Idee des Naturrechtes*, 7 ZEITSCHRIFT FÜR ÖFFENTLICHES RECHT 221, 248 (Austria 1927).

2. Hart, *Positivism and the Separation of Law and Morals*, 71 HARV. L. REV. 593, 615–21 (1958).

3. U. S. CONSTITUTION art. V.

4. Hart, *supra* note 2, at 624.

5. For an outstanding example, see G. Scammell and Nephew, Ltd. v. Custom, [1941] A.C.251 (1940). I personally would be inclined to put under the same head Victoria Laundry, Ltd. v. Newman Industries, Ltd., [1949] 2 K.B. 528 (C.A.).

6. See Hart, *supra* note 2, at 608–12.

7. See N.Y. Times, Nov. 8, 1949, p. 1, col. 4 (late city ed.) (report of a speech made on November 7, 1949 to the Central Committee of the Union of Catholic Italian Lawers).

8. Hart, *supra* note 2, at 603.

9. *Ibid.*

10. I AUSTIN, LECTURES ON JURISPRUDENCE 167–341 (5th ed. 1885).

11. KELSEN, GENERAL THEORY OF LAW AND STATE 401 (3d ed. 1949).

12. *E.g.,* Friedmann, *The Planned State and the Rule of Law*, 22 AUSTR. L. J. 162, 207 (1948).

13. LOWIE, THE ORIGIN OF THE STATE 113 (1927).

14. Hart, *supra* note 2, at 623–24.

15. Southern Pacific Co. v. Jensen, 244 U.S. 205, 221 (1917) (Holmes J., dissenting), paraphrasing Storti v. Commonwealth, 178 Mass. 549, 554, 60 N.E. 210, 211 (1901) (Holmes, C.J.) in which it was held that a statute providing for electrocution as a means of inflicting the punishment of death was not cruel or unusual punishment within the Massachusetts Declaration of Rights, MASS. CONST. pt. First, art. XXVI, simply because it accomplished its object by molecular, rather than molar, motions.

16. See Hart, *supra* note 2, at 619–20.

17. N.Y. Times, July 4, 1934, p. 3, col. 3 (late city ed.).

18. See N.Y. Times, July 14, 1934, p.5, col. 2 (late city ed.).

19. Radbruch, *Die Erneuerung des Rechts*, 2 DIE WANDLUNG 8, 9 (Germany 1947). A useful discussion of the Nazi practice with reference to the publicity given laws will be found in Giese, *Verkündung und Gesetzeskraft*, 76 ARCHIV DES ÖFFENTLICHEN RECHTS 464, 471–72 (Germany 1951). I rely on this article for the remarks that follow in the text.

20. Judgment of July 27, 1949, Oberlandesgericht, Bamberg, 5 SÜDDEUTSCHE JURISTEN-ZEITUNG 207 (Germany 1950), 64 HARV. L. REV. 1005 (1951).

21. The passage translated is § 5 of a statute creating a Kriegssonderstrafrecht. Law of Aug. 17, 1938, [1939] 2 REICHSGESETZBLATT pt. 1, at 1456. The translation is mine.

22. See 5 SÜDDEUTSCHE JURISTEN-ZEITUNG 207, 210 (Germany 1950).

23. The translated passage is article II of A Law Against Malicious Attacks on the State and the Party and for the Protection of the Party Uniform, Law of Dec. 20, 1934, [1934] 1 REICHSGESETZBLATT 1269. The translation is mine.

24. See Radbruch, *Die Erneuerung des Rechts*, 2 DEI WANDLUNG 8, 10 (Germany 1947).

25. Radbruch, *Gesetzliches Unrecht und Übergesetzliches Recht*, 1 SÜDDEUTSCHE JURISTEN-ZEITUNG 105, 107 (Germany 1946) (reprinted in RADBRUCH, RECHTSPHILOSOPHIE

347, 354 (4th ed. 1950)). The translation is mine.

26. See, *e.g.*, Howe, *The Positivism of Mr. Justice Holmes*, 64 HARV. L. REV. 529 (1951).

27. See 1 PERRY, THE THOUGHT AND CHARACTER OF WILLIAM JAMES 297 (1935) (quoting a letter written by William James in 1869).

28. Hart, *supra* note 2, at 617–18.

29. *Id.* at 618.

30. *Id.* at 619.

31. 1 AUSTIN, LECTURES ON JURISPRUDENCE 173 (5th ed. 1885) (Lecture V).

32. GRAY, THE NATURE AND SOURCES OF THE LAW 96 (2d ed.1921).

33. 1 BERGBOHM, JURISPRUDENZ UND RECHTSPHILOSOPHIE 355–552 (1892).

34. See, *e.g.* Heller, *Die Krisis der Staatslehre*, 55 ARCHIV FÜR SOZIALWISSENSCHAFT UND SOZIALPOLITIK 289, 309 (Germany 1926).

35. Voegelin, *Kesen's Pure Theory of Law*, 42 POL. SCI. Q. 268, 269 (1927).

36. Hart, *supra* note 2, at 606–08.

37. See *id.* at 607.

38. Fuller, *Human Purpose and Natural Law*, 53 J. PHILOS. 697, 700 (1956).

39. Omychund v. Barker, 1 Atk. 21, 33, 26 Eng. Rep. 15, 22–23 (Ch. 1744) (argument of Solicitor-General Murray, later Lord Mansfield): "All occasions do not arise at once; . . . a statute very seldom can take in all cases, therefore the common law, *that works itself pure* by rules drawn from the fountain of justice, is for this reason superior to an act of Parliament."

40. I am speaking of the linguistic theory that seems to be implied in the essay under discussion here. In Professor Hart's brilliant inaugural address, *Definition and Theory in Jurisprudence*, 70, L.Q. REV. 37 (1954), the most important point made is that terms like "rule," "right," and "legal person" cannot be defined by pointing to correspondent things or actions in the external world, but can only be understood in terms of the function performed by them in the larger system, just as one cannot understand the umpire's ruling, "You're out!" without having at least a general familiarity with the rules of baseball. Even in the analysis presented in the inaugural address, however, Professor Hart seems to think that the dependence of meaning on function and context is a peculiarity of formal and explicit systems, like those of a game or a legal system. He seems not to recognize that what he has to say about explicit systems is also true of the countless informal and overlapping systems that run through language as a whole. These implicit systematic or structural elements in language often enable us to understand at once the meaning of a word used in a wholly novel sense, as in the statement, "Experts regard the English Channel as the most difficult swim in the world." In the essay now being discussed, Professor Hart seems nowhere to recognize that a rule or statute has a structural or systematic quality that reflects itself in some measure into the meaning of every principal term in it.

41. RUSSELL, *The Cult of "Common Usage,"* in PORTRAITS FROM MEMORY AND OTHER ESSAYS 166, 170–71 (1956).

42. WHITEHEAD, *Analysis of Meaning*, in ESSAYS IN SCIENCE AND PHILOSOPHY 122, 127 (1947).

43. § 8 (d), added by 61 Stat. 142 (1947), 29 U.S.C. § 158 (d) (1952): see NLRA §§ 8(a) (5), (b) (3), as amended, 61 Stat. 141 (1947), 29 U.S.C. §§ 158 (a) (5), (b) (3) (1952).

44. Minersville School Dist. v. Gobitis, 310 U.S. 586 (1940), *overruled*, West Virginia State Bd. of Educ. v. Barnette, 319 U.S. 624 (1943).

45. VON HIPPEL DIE NATIONALSOZIALISTISCHE HERRSCHAFISORDNUNG ALS WARNUNG UND LHERE 6–7 (1946).

GUSTAV RADBRUCH

Five Minutes of Legal Philosophy*

FIRST MINUTE

"An order is an order," the soldier is told. "A law is a law," says the jurist. The soldier, however, is required neither by duty nor by law to obey an order that he knows to have been issued with a felony or misdemeanor in mind, while the jurists, since the last of the natural law theorists among them disappeared a hundred years ago, have recognized no such exceptions to the validity of a law or to the requirement of obedience by those subject to it. A law is valid because it is a law, and it is a law if in the general run of cases it has the power to prevail.

This view of the nature of a law and of its validity (we call it the positivistic theory) has rendered the jurist as well as the people defenseless against laws, however arbitrary, cruel, or criminal they may be. In the end, the positivistic theory equates the law with power; there is law only where there is power.

SECOND MINUTE

There have been attempts to supplement or replace this tenet with another: Law is what benefits the people.

That is, arbitrariness, breach of contract, and illegality, provided only that they benefit the people, are law. Practically speaking, that means that every whim and caprice of the despot, punishment without laws or judgment, lawless killing of the sick—whatever the state authorities deem to be of benefit to the people—is law. That *can* mean that the private benefit of those in power is regarded as a public benefit. The equating of the law with supposed or ostensible benefits to the people thus transformed a *Rechtsstaat* into a state of lawlessness.

*   "Fünf Minuten Rechtsphilosophie," translated by Stanley L. Paulson, first appeared in the Rhein-Neckar-Zeitung, September 12, 1945, and was reprinted in the 8th edition of Gustav Radbruch's *Rechtsphilosophie,* edited by Erik Wolf and Hans-Peter Schneider (Stuttgart: K. F. Koehler Verlag, 1973), pp. 327-29. The translation is printed with the kind permission of the K. F. Koehler Verlag.

No, this tenet should not be read as: Whatever benefits the people is law. Rather, it is the other way around: Only what is law benefits the people.

THIRD MINUTE

Law is the will to justice, and justice means: To judge without regard to the person, to treat everyone according to the same standard.

If one applauds the assassination of political opponents and orders the murder of those of another race while meting out the most cruel, degrading punishments for the same acts committed against those of one's own persuasion, that is neither justice nor law.

If laws consciously deny the will to justice, if, for example, they grant and deny human rights arbitrarily, then these laws lack validity, the people owe them no obedience, and even the jurists must find the courage to deny their legal character.

FOURTH MINUTE

Surely public benefit, along with justice, is an end of the law. Surely laws as such, even bad laws, have value nonetheless—the value of safeguarding the law against doubt. And surely, owing to human imperfection, the three values of the law—public benefit, legal certainty, and justice—cannot always be united harmoniously in laws. It remains, then, only to consider whether validity is to be granted to bad, detrimental, or unjust laws for the sake of legal certainty or whether it is to be denied them because they are unjust or socially detrimental. One thing, however, must be indelibly impressed on the consciousness of the people and the jurists: there *can* be laws that are so unjust, so socially detrimental that their validity, indeed their very character as laws, must be denied.

FIFTH MINUTE

There are, therefore, principles of law that are stronger than any statute, so that a law conflicting with these principles is devoid of validity. One calls these principles the natural law or the law of reason. To be sure, their details remain somewhat doubtful, but the work of centuries has established a solid core of them and they have come to enjoy such a far-reaching consensus in the declarations of human and civil rights that only the deliberate skeptic can still entertain doubts about some of them.

In religious language the same thoughts have been recorded in two biblical passages. On the one hand it is written that you are to obey the authorities who have power over you. But then on the other, it is also written that you are to obey God before man—and this is not simply a pious wish, but a valid proposition of law. The tension between these two directives cannot, however, be relieved by appealing to a third—say, to the maxim: Render unto Caesar the things that are Caesar's and unto God the things that are God's. For this directive too, leaves the boundary in doubt. Rather, it leaves the solution to the voice of God, which speaks to the conscience of the individual only in the exceptional case.

JOHN RAWLS
Civil Disobedience*

THE DEFINITION OF CIVIL DISOBEDIENCE

I now wish to illustrate the content of the principles of natural duty and obligation by sketching a theory of civil disobedience. As I have already indicated, this theory is designed only for the special case of a nearly just society, one that is well-ordered for the most part but in which some serious violations of justice nevertheless do occur. Since I assume that a state of near justice requires a democratic regime, the theory concerns the role and the appropriateness of civil disobedience to legitimately established democratic authority. It does not apply to the other forms of government nor, except incidentally, to other kinds of dissent or resistance. I shall not discuss this mode of protest, along with militant action and resistance, as a tactic for transforming or even overturning an unjust and corrupt system. There is no difficulty about such action in this case. If any means to this end are justified, then surely nonviolent opposition is justified. The problem of civil disobedience, as I shall interpret it, arises only within a more or less just democratic state for those citizens who recognize and accept the legitimacy of the constitution. The difficulty is one of a conflict of duties. At what point does the duty to comply with laws enacted by a legislative majority (or with executive acts supported by such a majority) cease to be binding in view of the right to defend one's liberties and the duty to oppose injustice? This question involves the nature and limits of majority rule. For this reason the problem of civil disobedience is a crucial test case for any theory of the moral basis of democracy.

A constitutional theory of civil disobedience has three parts. First, it defines this kind of dissent and separates it from other forms of opposition to democratic authority. These range from legal demonstrations and infractions of law designed to raise test cases before the courts to militant action and organized resistance. A theory specifies the place of civil disobedience in this spectrum of possibilities. Next, it sets out the grounds of civil disobedience and the conditions under which such action is justified in a (more or less) just democratic regime. And finally, a theory should explain the role of civil disobedience within a constitutional system and account for the appropriateness of this mode of protest within a free society.

Before I take up these matters, a word of caution. We should not expect too much of a theory of civil disobedience, even one framed for special circumstances. Precise principles that straightway decide actual cases are clearly out of the question. Instead, a useful theory defines a perspective within which the problem of civil disobedience can be approached; it identifies the relevant considerations and helps us to assign them their correct weights in the more important instances. If a theory about these matters appears to us, on reflection, to have cleared our vision and to have made our considered judgments more coherent, then it has been worthwhile. The theory has done what, for the present, one may reasonably expect it to do: namely, to narrow the disparity between the conscientious convictions of those who accept the basic principles of a democratic society.

I shall begin by defining civil disobedience as a public, nonviolent, conscientious yet political act contrary to law usually done with the aim of bringing about a change in the law or policies of the government.[1] By acting in this way one addresses the sense of justice of the majority of the community and declares that in one's considered opinion the principles of social cooperation among free and equal men are not being respected. A preliminary gloss on this definition is that it does not require that the civilly disobedient act breach the same law that is being protested.[2] It allows for what some have called indirect as well as direct civil disobedience. And this a definition should do, as there are sometimes strong

*Reprinted by permission of the publishers from *A Theory of Justice* by John Rawls, Cambridge, Mass.: The Belknap Press of Harvard University Press, copyright © 1971 by the President and Fellows of Harvard College.

reasons for not infringing on the law or policy held to be unjust. Instead, one may disobey traffic ordinances or laws of trespass as a way of presenting one's case. Thus, if the government enacts a vague and harsh statute against treason, it would not be appropriate to commit treason as a way of objecting to it, and in any event, the penalty might be far more than one should reasonably be ready to accept. In other cases there is no way to violate the government's policy directly, as when it concerns foreign affairs, or affects another part of the country. A second gloss is that the civilly disobedient act is indeed thought to be contrary to law, at least in the sense that those engaged in it are not simply presenting a test case for a constitutional decision; they are prepared to oppose the statute even if it should be upheld. To be sure, in a constitutional regime, the courts may finally side with the dissenters and declare the law or policy objected to unconstitutional. It often happens, then, that there is some uncertainty as to whether the dissenters' action will be held illegal or not. But this is merely a complicating element. Those who use civil disobedience to protest unjust laws are not prepared to desist should the courts eventually disagree with them, however pleased they might have been with the opposite decision.

It should also be noted that civil disobedience is a political act not only in the sense that it is addressed to the majority that holds political power, but also because it is an act guided and justified by political principles, that is, by the principles of justice which regulate the constitution and social institutions generally. In justifying civil disobedience one does not appeal to principles of personal morality or to religious doctrines, though these may coincide with and support one's claims; and it goes without saying that civil disobedience cannot be grounded solely on group or self-interest. Instead one invokes the commonly shared conception of justice that underlies the political order. It is assumed that in a reasonably just democratic regime there is a public conception of justice by reference to which citizens regulate their political affairs and interpret the constitution. The persistent and deliberate violation of the basic principles of this conception over any extended period of time, especially the infringement of the fundamental equal liberties, invites either submission or resistance. By engaging in civil disobedience a minority forces the majority to consider whether it wishes to have its actions construed in this way, or whether, in view

of the common sense of justice, it wishes to acknowledge the legitimate claims of the minority.

A further point is that civil disobedience is a public act. Not only is it addressed to public principles, it is done in public. It is engaged in openly with fair notice; it is not covert or secretive. One may compare it to public speech, and being a form of address, an expression of profound and conscientious political conviction, it takes place in the public forum. For this reason, among others, civil disobedience is nonviolent. It tries to avoid the use of violence, especially against persons, not from the abhorrence of the use of force in principle, but because it is a final expression of one's case. To engage in violent acts likely to injure and to hurt is incompatible with civil disobedience as a mode of address. Indeed, any interference with the civil liberties of others tends to obscure the civilly disobedient quality of one's act. Sometimes if the appeal fails in its purpose, forceful resistance may later be entertained. Yet civil disobedience is giving voice to conscientious and deeply held convictions; while it may warn and admonish, it is not itself a threat.

Civil disobedience is nonviolent for another reason. It expresses disobedience to law within the limits of fidelity to law, although it is at the outer edge thereof.[3] The law is broken, but fidelity to law is expressed by the public and nonviolent nature of the act, by the willingness to accept the legal consequences of one's conduct.[4] This fidelity to law helps to establish to the majority that the act is indeed politically conscientious and sincere, and that it is intended to address the public's sense of justice. To be completely open and nonviolent is to give bond of one's sincerity, for it is not easy to convince another that one's acts are conscientious, or even to be sure of this before oneself. No doubt it is possible to imagine a legal system in which conscientious belief that the law is unjust is accepted as a defense for noncompliance. Men of great honesty with full confidence in one another might make such a system work. But as things are, such a scheme would presumably be unstable even in a state of near justice. We must pay a certain price to convince others that our actions have, in our carefully considered view, a sufficient moral basis in the political convictions of the community.

Civil disobedience has been defined so that it falls between legal protest and the raising of test cases on the one side, and conscientious refusal and the various forms of resistance on the other. In this range of possibilities it stands for that form of dissent at the boundary of fidelity to law. Civil disobedience, so understood, is clearly distinct from militant action and obstruction; it is far removed from organized forcible resistance. The militant, for example, is much more deeply opposed to the existing political system. He does not accept it as one which is nearly just or reasonably so; he believes either that it departs widely from its professed principles or that it pursues a mistaken conception of justice altogether. While his action is conscientious in its own terms, he does not appeal to the sense of justice of the majority (or those having effective political power), since he thinks that their sense of justice is erroneous, or else without effect. Instead, he seeks by well-framed militant acts of disruption and resistance, and the like, to attack the prevalent view of justice or to force a movement in the desired direction. Thus the militant may try to evade the penalty, since he is not prepared to accept the legal consequences of his violation of the law; this would not only be to play into the hands of forces that he believes cannot be trusted, but also to express a recognition of the legitimacy of the constitution to which he is opposed. In this sense militant action is not within the bounds of fidelity to law, but represents a more profound opposition to the legal order. The basic structure is thought to be so unjust or else to depart so widely from its own professed ideals that one must try to prepare the way for radical or even revolutionary change. And this is to be done by trying to arouse the public to an awareness of the fundamental reforms that need to be made. Now in certain circumstances militant action and other kinds of resistance are surely justified. I shall not, however, consider these cases. As I have said, my aim here is the limited one of defining a concept of civil disobedience and understanding its role in a nearly just constitutional regime.

THE DEFINITION OF CONSCIENTIOUS REFUSAL

Although I have distinguished civil disobedience from conscientious refusal, I have yet to explain the latter notion. This will now be done. It must be recognized, however, that to separate these two ideas is to give a narrower definition to civil disobedience than is traditional; for it is customary to think of civil disobedience in a broader sense as any noncompliance with law for conscientious reasons, at least when it is not covert and does not involve the use of force. Thoreau's essay is characteristic, if not definitive, of the tradi-

tional meaning.[5] The usefulness of the narrower sense will, I believe, be clear once the definition of conscientious refusal is examined.

Conscientious refusal is noncompliance with a more or less direct legal injunction or administrative order. It is refusal since an order is addressed to us and, given the nature of the situation, whether we accede to it is known to the authorities. Typical examples are the refusal of the early Christians to perform certain acts of piety prescribed by the pagan state, and the refusal of the Jehovah's Witnesses to salute the flag. Other examples are the unwillingness of a pacifist to serve in the armed forces, or of a soldier to obey an order that he thinks is manifestly contrary to the moral law as it applies to war. Or again, in Thoreau's case, the refusal to pay a tax on the grounds that to do so would make him an agent of grave injustice to another. One's action is assumed to be known to the authorities, however much one might wish, in some cases, to conceal it. Where it can be covert, one might speak of conscientious evasion rather than conscientious refusal. Covert infractions of a fugitive slave law are instances of conscientious evasion.[6]

There are several contrasts between conscientious refusal (or evasion) and civil disobedience. First of all, conscientious refusal is not a form of address appealing to the sense of justice of the majority. To be sure, such acts are not generally secretive or covert, as concealment is often impossible anyway. One simply refuses on conscientious grounds to obey a command or to comply with a legal injunction. One does not invoke the convictions of the community, and in this sense conscientious refusal is not an act in the public forum. Those ready to withhold obedience recognize that there may be no basis for mutual understanding; they do not seek out occasions for disobedience as a way to state their cause. Rather, they bide their time hoping that the necessity to disobey will not arise. They are less optimistic than those undertaking civil disobedience and they may entertain no expectation of changing laws or policies. The situation may allow no time for them to make their case, or again there may not be any chance that the majority will be receptive to their claims.

Conscientious refusal is not necessarily based on political principles; it may be founded on religious or other principles at variance with the constitutional order. Civil disobedience is an appeal to a commonly shared conception of justice, whereas conscientious refusal may have other grounds. For example, assuming that the early Christians would not justify their refusal to comply with the religious customs of the Empire by reasons of justice but simply as being contrary to their religious convictions, their argument would not be political; nor, with similar qualifications, are the views of a pacifist, assuming that wars of self-defense at least are recognized by the conception of justice that underlies a constitutional regime. Conscientious refusal may, however, be grounded on political principles. One may decline to go along with a law thinking that it is so unjust that complying with it is simply out of the question. This would be the case if, say, the law were to enjoin our being the agent of enslaving another, or to require us to submit to a similar fate. These are patent violations of recognized political principles.

It is a difficult matter to find the right course when some men appeal to religious principles in refusing to do actions which, it seems, are required by principles of political justice. Does the pacifist possess an immunity from military service in a just war, assuming that there are such wars? Or is the state permitted to impose certain hardships for noncompliance? There is a temptation to say that the law must always respect the dictates of conscience, but this cannot be right. As we have seen in the case of the intolerant, the legal order must regulate men's pursuit of their religious interests so as to realize the principle of equal liberty; and it may certainly forbid religious practices such as human sacrifice, to take an extreme case. Neither religiosity nor conscientiousness suffices to protect this practice. A theory of justice must work out from its own point of view how to treat those who dissent from it. The aim of a well-ordered society, or one in a state of near justice, is to preserve and strengthen the institutions of justice. If a religion is denied its full expression, it is presumably because it is in violation of the equal liberties of others. In general, the degree of tolerance accorded opposing moral conceptions depends upon the extent to which they can be allowed an equal place within a just system of liberty.

If pacifism is to be treated with respect and not merely tolerated, the explanation must be that it accords reasonably well with the principles of justice, the main exception arising from its attitude toward engaging in a just war (assuming here that in some situations wars of self-defense are justified). The political principles recognized by the community have a certain affinity with the doctrine the pacifist professes. There is a common abhorrence of war and the use of force, and a belief in the equal status of men as moral persons. And given the tendency of nations, particularly great powers, to engage in war unjustifiably and to set in motion the apparatus of the state to suppress dissent, the respect accorded to pacifism serves the purpose of alerting citizens to the wrongs that governments are prone to commit in their name. Even though his views are not altogether sound, the warnings and protests that a pacifist is disposed to express may have the result that on balance the principles of justice are more rather than less secure. Pacifism as a natural departure from the correct doctrine conceivably compensates for the weakness of men in living up to their professions.

It should be noted that there is, of course, in actual situations no sharp distinction between civil disobedience and conscientious refusal. Moreover the same action (or sequence of actions) may have strong elements of both. While there are clear cases of each, the contrast between them is intended as a way of elucidating the interpretation of civil disobedience and its role in a democratic society. Given the nature of this way of acting as a special kind of political appeal, it is not usually justified until other steps have been taken within the legal framework. By contrast this requirement often fails in the obvious cases of legitimate conscientious refusal. In a free society no one may be compelled, as the early Christians were, to perform religious acts in violation of equal liberty, nor must a soldier comply with inherently evil commands while awaiting an appeal to higher authority. These remarks lead up to the question of justification.

THE JUSTIFICATION OF CIVIL DISOBEDIENCE

With these various distinctions in mind, I shall consider the circumstances under which civil disobedience is justified. For simplicity I shall limit the discussion to domestic institutions and so to injustices internal to a given society. The somewhat narrow nature of this restriction will be mitigated a bit by taking up the contrasting problem of conscientious refusal in connection with the moral law as it applies to war. I shall begin by setting out what seem to be reasonable conditions for engaging in civil disobedience, and then later connect these conditions more systematically with the place of civil disobedience in a state of near justice. Of course, the conditions enumerated should be taken as presumptions; no doubt there will be situations when they do not hold, and other arguments could be given for civil disobedience.

The first point concerns the kinds of wrongs that are appropriate objects of civil disobedience. Now if one views such disobedience as a political act addressed to the sense of justice of the community, then it seems reasonable, other things equal, to limit it to instances of substantial and clear injustice, and preferably to those which obstruct the path to removing other injustices. For this reason there is a presumption in favor of restricting civil disobedience to serious infringements of the first principle of justice, the principle of equal liberty, and to blatant violations of the second part of the second principle, the principle of fair equality of opportunity. Of course, it is not always easy to tell whether these principles are satisfied. Still, if we think of them as guaranteeing the basic liberties, it is often clear that these freedoms are not being honored. After all, they impose certain strict requirements that must be visibly expressed in institutions. Thus when certain minorities are denied the right to vote or to hold office, or to own property and to move from place to place, or when certain religious groups are repressed and others denied various opportunities, these injustices may be obvious to all. They are publicly incorporated into the recognized practice, if not the letter, of social arrangements. The establishment of these wrongs does not presuppose an informed examination of institutional effects.

By contrast infractions of the difference principle are more difficult to ascertain.* There is usually a wide range of conflicting yet rational opinion as to whether this principle is satisfied. The reason for this is that it applies primarily to economic and social institutions and policies. A choice among these depends upon theoretical and speculative beliefs as well as upon a wealth of statistical and other information, all of this seasoned with shrewd judgment and plain hunch. In view of the complexities of these questions, it is difficult to check the influence of self-interest and prejudice; and even if we can do this in our own case, it is another matter to convince others of our good faith. Thus unless tax laws, for example, are

clearly designed to attack or to abridge a basic equal liberty, they should not normally be protested by civil disobedience. The appeal to the public's conception of justice is not sufficiently clear. The resolution of these issues is best left to the political process provided that the requisite equal liberties are secure. In this case a reasonable compromise can presumably be reached. The violation of the principle of equal liberty is, then, the more appropriate object of civil disobedience. This principle defines the common status of equal citizenship in a constitutional regime and lies at the basis of the political order. When it is fully honored the presumption is that other injustices, while possibly persistent and significant, will not get out of hand.

A further condition for civil disobedience is the following. We may suppose that the normal appeals to the political majority have already been made in good faith and that they have failed. The legal means of redress have proved of no avail. Thus, for example, the existing political parties have shown themselves indifferent to the claims of the minority or have proved unwilling to accommodate them. Attempts to have the laws repealed have been ignored and legal protests and demonstrations have had no success. Since civil disobedience is a last resort, we should be sure that it is necessary. Note that it has not been said, however, that legal means have been exhausted. At any rate, further normal appeals can be repeated; free speech is always possible. But if past actions have shown the majority immovable or apathetic, further attempts may reasonably be thought fruitless, and a second condition for justified civil disobedience is met. This condition is, however, a presumption. Some cases may be so extreme that there may be no duty to use first only legal means of political opposition. If, for example, the legislature were to enact some outrageous violation of equal liberty, say by forbidding the religion of a weak and defenseless minority, we surely could not expect that sect to oppose the law by normal political procedures. Indeed, even civil disobedience might be much too mild, the majority having already convicted itself of wantonly unjust and overtly hostile aims.

The third and last condition I shall discuss can be rather complicated. It arises from the fact that while the two preceding conditions are often sufficient to justify civil disobedience, this is not always the case. In certain circumstances the natural duty of justice may require a certain restraint. We can see this as follows. If a certain

---

*The "difference principle" (which Rawls explains elsewhere) is the principle that inequalities in the distribution of goods are justified only if they contribute to the well being of the worst off party. [Eds.]

minority is justified in engaging in civil disobedience, then any other minority in relevantly similar circumstances is likewise justified. Using the two previous conditions as the criteria of relevantly similar circumstances, we can say that, other things equal, two minorities are similarly justified in resorting to civil disobedience if they have suffered for the same length of time from the same degree of injustice and if their equally sincere and normal political appeals have likewise been to no avail. It is conceivable, however, even if it is unlikely, that there should be many groups with an equally sound case (in the sense just defined) for being civilly disobedient; but that, if they were all to act in this way, serious disorder would follow which might well undermine the efficacy of the just constitution. I assume here that there is a limit on the extent to which civil disobedience can be engaged in without leading to a breakdown in the respect for law and the constitution, thereby setting in motion consequences unfortunate for all. There is also an upper bound on the ability of the public forum to handle such forms of dissent; the appeal that civilly disobedient groups wish to make can be distorted and their intention to appeal to the sense of justice of the majority lost sight of. For one or both of these reasons, the effectiveness of civil disobedience as a form of protest declines beyond a certain point; and those contemplating it must consider these constraints.

The ideal solution from a theoretical point of view calls for a cooperative political alliance of the minorities to regulate the overall level of dissent. For consider the nature of the situation: there are many groups each equally entitled to engage in civil disobedience. Moreover they all wish to exercise this right, equally strong in each case; but if they all do so, lasting injury may result to the just constitution to which they each recognize a natural duty of justice. Now when there are many equally strong claims which if taken together exceed what can be granted, some fair plan should be adopted so that all are equitably considered. In simple cases of claims to goods that are indivisible and fixed in number, some rotation or lottery scheme may be the fair solution when the number of equally valid claims is too great.[7] But this sort of device is completely unrealistic here. What seems called for is a political understanding among the minorities suffering from injustice. They can meet their duty to democratic institutions by coordinating their actions so that

while each has an opportunity to exercise its right, the limits on the degree of civil disobedience are not exceeded. To be sure, an alliance of this sort is difficult to arrange; but with perceptive leadership, it does not appear impossible.

Certainly the situation envisaged is a special one, and it is quite possible that these sorts of considerations will not be a bar to justified civil disobedience. There are not likely to be many groups similarly entitled to engage in this form of dissent while at the same time recognizing a duty to a just constitution. One should note, however, that an injured minority is tempted to believe its claims as strong as those of any other; and therefore even if the reasons that different groups have for engaging in civil disobedience are not equally compelling, it is often wise to presume that their claims are indistinguishable. Adopting this maxim, the circumstance imagined seems more likely to happen. This kind of case is also instructive in showing that the exercise of the right to dissent, like the exercise of rights generally, is sometimes limited by others having the very same right. Everyone's exercising this right would have deleterious consequences for all, and some equitable plan is called for.

Suppose that in the light of the three conditions, one has a right to appeal one's case by civil disobedience. The injustice one protests is a clear violation of the liberties of equal citizenship, or of equality of opportunity, this violation having been more or less deliberate over an extended period of time in the face of normal political opposition, and any complications raised by the question of fairness are met. These conditions are not exhaustive; some allowance still has to be made for the possibility of injury to third parties, to the innocent, so to speak. But I assume that they cover the main points. There is still, of course, the question whether it is wise or prudent to exercise this right. Having established the right, one is now free, as one is not before, to let these matters decide the issue. We may be acting within our rights but nevertheless unwisely if our conduct only serves to provoke the harsh retaliation of the majority. To be sure, in a state of near justice, vindictive repression of legitimate dissent is unlikely, but it is important that the action be properly designed to make an effective appeal to the wider community. Since civil disobedience is a mode of address taking place in the public forum, care must be taken to see that it is understood. Thus the exercise of the right to civil disobedience should, like any other right, be rationally framed to advance one's ends or the ends of those one wishes to assist. The theory of justice has nothing specific to say about these practical considerations. In any event questions of strategy and tactics depend upon the circumstances of each case. But the theory of justice should say at what point these matters are properly raised.

Now in this account of the justification of civil disobedience I have not mentioned the principle of fairness.* The natural duty is the of justice primary basis of our political ties to a constitutional regime. As we noted before ... only the more favored members of society are likely to have a clear political obligation as opposed to a political duty. They are better situated to win public office and find it easier to take advantage of the political system. And having done so, they have acquired an obligation owed to citizens generally to uphold the just constitution. But members of subjected minorities, say, who have a strong case for civil disobedience will not generally have a political obligation of this sort. This does not mean, however, that the principle of fairness will not give rise to important obligations in their case.[8] For not only do many of the requirements of private life derive from this principle, but it comes into force when persons or groups come together for common political purposes. Just as we acquire obligations to others with whom we have joined in various private associations, those who engage in political action assume obligatory ties to one another. Thus while the political obligation of dissenters to citizens generally is problematical, bonds of loyalty and fidelity still develop between them as they seek to advance their cause. In general, free association under a just constitution gives rise to obligations provided that the ends of the group are legitimate and its arrangements fair. This is as true of political as it is of other associations. These obligations are of immense significance and they constrain in many ways what individuals can do. But they are distinct from an obligation to comply with a just constitution. My discussion of civil disobedience is in terms of the duty of justice alone; a fuller view would note the place of these other requirements.

*The principle of fairness is the principle that "when a number of persons engage in a mutually advantageous cooperative venture according to rules, those who submit have a right to similar acquiescence from the others." [Eds.]

THE JUSTIFICATION OF CONSCIENTIOUS REFUSAL

In examining the justification of civil disobedience I assumed for simplicity that the laws and policies protested concerned domestic affairs. It is natural to ask how the theory of political duty applies to foreign policy. Now in order to do this it is necessary to extend the theory of justice to the law of nations. I shall try to indicate how this can be done. To fix ideas I shall consider briefly the justification of conscientious refusal to engage in certain acts of war, or to serve in the armed forces. I assume that this refusal is based upon political and not upon religious or other principles; that is, the principles cited by way of justification are those of the conception of justice underlying the constitution. Our problem, then, is to relate the just political principles regulating the conduct of states to the contract doctrine and to explain the moral basis of the law of nations from this point of view.

Let us assume that we have already derived the principles of justice as these apply to societies as units and to the basic structure. Imagine also that the various principles of natural duty and of obligation that apply to individuals have been adopted. Thus the persons in the original position have agreed to the principles of right as these apply to their own society and to themselves as members of it. Now at this point one may extend the interpretation of the original position and think of the parties as representatives of different nations who must choose together the fundamental principles to adjudicate conflicting claims among states. Following out the conception of the initial situation, I assume that these representatives are deprived of various kinds of information. While they know that they represent different nations each living under the normal circumstances of human life, they know nothing about the particular circumstances of their own society, its power and strength in comparison with other nations, nor do they know their place in their own society. Once again the contracting parties, in this case representatives of states, are allowed only enough knowledge to make a rational choice to protect their interests but not so much that the more fortunate among them can take advantage of their special situation. This original position is fair between nations; it nullifies the contingencies and biases of historical fate. Justice between states is determined by the principles that would be chosen in the original position so interpreted. These principles are political principles, for they govern public policies toward other nations.

I can give only an indication of the principles that would be acknowledged. But, in any case, there would be no surprises, since the principles chosen would, I think, be familar ones.[9] The basic principle of the law of nations is a principle of equality. Independent peoples organized as states have certain fundamental equal rights. This principle is analogous to the equal rights of citizens in a constitutional regime. One consequence of this equality of nations is the principle of self-determination, the right of a people to settle its own affairs without the intervention of foreign powers. Another consequence is the right of self-defense against attack, including the right to form defensive alliances to protect this right. A further principle is that treaties are to be kept, provided they are consistent with the other principles governing the relations of states. Thus treaties for self-defense, suitably interpreted, would be binding, but agreements to cooperate in an unjustified attack are void *ab initio*.

These principles define when a nation has a just cause in war or, in the traditional phrase, its *jus ad bellum*. But there are also principles regulating the means that a nation may use to wage war, its *jus in bello*.[10] Even in a just war certain forms of violence are strictly inadmissible; and where a country's right to war is questionable and uncertain, the constraints on the means it can use are all the more severe. Acts permissible in a war of legitimate self-defense, when these are necessary, may be flatly excluded in a more doubtful situation. The aim of war is a just peace, and therefore the means employed must not destroy the possibility of peace or encourage a contempt for human life that puts the safety of ourselves and of mankind in jeopardy. The conduct of war is to be constrained and adjusted to this end. The representatives of states would recognize that their national interest, as seen from the original position, is best served by acknowledging these limits on the means of war. This is because the national interest of a just state is defined by the principles of justice that have already been acknowledged. Therefore such a nation will aim above all to maintain and to preserve its just institutions and the conditions that make them possible. It is not moved by the desire for world power or national glory; nor does it wage war for purposes of economic gain or the acquisition of territory. These ends are contrary to the conception of justice that defines a society's legitimate interest, however prevalent they have been in the actual conduct of states. Granting these presumptions, then, it seems reasonable to suppose that the traditional prohibitions incorporating the natural duties that protect human life would be chosen.

Now if conscientious refusal in time of war appeals to these principles, it is founded upon a political conception, and not necessarily upon religious or other notions. While this form of denial may not be a political act, since it does not take place in the public forum, it is based upon the same theory of justice that underlies the constitution and guides its interpretation. Moreover, the legal order itself presumably recognizes in the form of treaties the validity of at least some of these principles of the law of nations. Therefore if a soldier is ordered to engage in certain illicit acts of war, he may refuse if he reasonably and conscientiously believes that the principles applying to the conduct of war are plainly violated. He can maintain that, all things considered, his natural duty not to be made the agent of grave injustice and evil to another outweighs his duty to obey. I cannot discuss here what constitutes a manifest violation of these principles. It must suffice to note that certain clear cases are perfectly familiar. The essential point is that the justification cites political principles that can be accounted for by the contract doctrine. The theory of justice can be developed, I believe, to cover this case.

A somewhat different question is whether one should join the armed forces at all during some particular war. The answer is likely to depend upon the aim of the war as well as upon its conduct. In order to make the situation definite, let us suppose that conscription is in force and that the individual has to consider whether to comply with his legal duty to enter military service. Now I shall assume that since conscription is a drastic interference with the basic liberties of equal citizenship, it cannot be justified by any needs less compelling than those of national security.[11] In a well-ordered society (or in one nearly just) these needs are determined by the end of preserving just institutions. Conscription is permissible only if it is demanded for the defense of liberty itself, including here not only the liberties of the citizens of the society in question, but also those of persons in other societies as well. Therefore if a conscript army is less likely to be an instrument of unjustified foreign adventures, it may be justified on this basis alone despite the fact that conscription infringes upon the equal liberties of citizens. But in any case, the priority of liberty (assuming serial order to obtain) requires that conscription be used only as the security of liberty necessitates. Viewed from the standpoint of the legislature (the appropriate stage for this question), the mechanism of the draft can be defended only on this ground. Citizens agree to this arrangement as a fair way of sharing in the burdens of national defense. To be sure, the hazards that any particular individual must face are in part the result of accident and historical happenstance. But in a well-ordered society anyway, these evils arise externally, that is, from unjustified attacks from the outside. It is impossible for just institutions to eliminate these hardships entirely. The most that they can do is to try to make sure that the risks of suffering from these imposed misfortunes are more or less evenly shared by all members of society over the course of their life, and that there is no avoidable class bias in selecting those who are called for duty.

Imagine, then, a democratic society in which conscription exists. A person may conscientiously refuse to comply with his duty to enter the armed forces during a particular war on the ground that the aims of the conflict are unjust. It may be that the objective sought by war is economic advantage or national power. The basic liberty of citizens cannot be interfered with to achieve these ends. And, of course, it is unjust and contrary to the law of nations to attack the liberty of other societies for these reasons. Therefore a just cause for war does not exist, and this may be sufficiently evident that a citizen is justified in refusing to discharge his legal duty. Both the law of nations and the principles of justice for his own society uphold him in this claim. There is sometimes a further ground for refusal based not on the aim of the war but upon its conduct. A citizen may maintain that once it is clear that the moral law of war is being regularly violated, he has a right to decline military service on the ground that he is entitled to insure that he honors his natural duty. Once he is in the armed forces, and in a situation where he finds himself ordered to do acts contrary to the moral law of war, he may not be able to resist the demand to obey. Actually, if the aims of the conflict are sufficiently dubious and the likelihood of receiving flagrantly unjust commands is sufficiently great, one may have a duty and not only a right to refuse. Indeed, the conduct and aims of states in waging war, especially large and powerful ones, are in some

circumstances so likely to be unjust that one is forced to conclude that in the foreseeable future one must abjure military service altogether. So understood a form of contingent pacifism may be a perfectly reasonable position: the possibility of a just war is conceded but not under present circumstances.[12]

What is needed, then, is not a general pacifism but a discriminating conscientious refusal to engage in war in certain circumstances. States have not been loath to recognize pacifism and to grant it a special status. The refusal to take part in all war under any conditions is an unworldly view bound to remain a sectarian doctrine. It no more challenges the state's authority than the celibacy of priests challenges the sanctity of marriage.[13] By exempting pacifists from its prescriptions the state may even seem to display a certain magnanimity. But conscientious refusal based upon the principles of justice between peoples as they apply to particular conflicts is another matter. For such refusal is an affront to the government's pretensions, and when it becomes widespread, the continuation of an unjust war may prove impossible. Given the often predatory aims of state power, and the tendency of men to defer to their government's decision to wage war, a general willingness to resist the state's claims is all the more necessary.

THE ROLE OF CIVIL DISOBEDIENCE

The third aim of a theory of civil disobedience is to explain its role within a constitutional system and to account for its connection with a democratic polity. As always, I assume that the society in question is one that is nearly just; and this implies that it has some form of democratic government, although serious injustices may nevertheless exist. In such a society I assume that the principles of justice are for the most part publicly recognized as the fundamental terms of willing cooperation among free and equal persons. By engaging in civil disobedience one intends, then, to address the sense of justice of the majority and to serve fair notice that in one's sincere and considered opinion the conditions of free cooperation are being violated. We are appealing to others to reconsider, to put themselves in our position, and to recognize that they cannot expect us to acquiesce indefinitely in the terms they impose upon us.

Now the force of this appeal depends upon the democratic conception of society as a system of cooperation among equal persons. If one thinks of society in another way, this form of protest may be out of place. For example, if the basic law is thought to reflect the order of nature and if the sovereign is held to govern by divine right as God's chosen lieutenant, then his subjects have only the right of suppliants. They can plead their cause but they cannot disobey should their appeal be denied. To do this would be to rebel against the final legitimate moral (and not simply legal) authority. This is not to say that the sovereign cannot be in error but only that the situation is not one for his subjects to correct. But once society is interpreted as a scheme of cooperation among equals, those injured by serious injustice need not submit. Indeed, civil disobedience (and conscientious refusal as well) is one of the stabilizing devices of a constitutional system, although by definition an illegal one. Along with such things as free and regular elections and an independent judiciary empowered to interpret the constitution (not necessarily written), civil disobedience used with due restraint and sound judgment helps to maintain and strengthen just institutions. By resisting injustice within the limits of fidelity to law, it serves to inhibit departures from justice and to correct them when they occur. A general disposition to engage in justified civil disobedience introduces stability into a well-ordered society, or one that is nearly just.

It is necessary to look at this doctrine from the standpoint of the persons in the original position. There are two related problems which they must consider. The first is that, having chosen principles for individuals, they must work out guidelines for assessing the strength of the natural duties and obligations, and, in particular, the strength of the duty to comply with a just constitution and one of its basic procedures, that of majority rule. The second problem is that of finding reasonable principles for dealing with unjust situations, or with circumstances in which the compliance with just principles is only partial. Now it seems that given the assumptions characterizing a nearly just society, the parties would agree to the presumptions (previously discussed) that specify when civil disobedience is justified. They would acknowledge these criteria as spelling out when this form of dissent is appropriate. Doing this would indicate the weight of the natural duty of justice in one important special case. It would also tend to enhance the realization of justice throughout the society by strengthening men's self-esteem as well as their respect for one another. As the contract doctrine emphasizes, the principles of justice are the principles of willing cooperation among equals. To deny justice to another is either to refuse to recognize him as an equal (one in regard to whom we are prepared to constrain our actions by principles that we would choose in a situation of equality that is fair), or to manifest a willingness to exploit the contingencies of natural fortune and happenstance for our own advantage. In either case deliberate injustice invites submission or resistance. Submission arouses the contempt of those who perpetuate injustice and confirms their intention, whereas resistance cuts the ties of community. If after a decent period of time to allow for reasonable political appeals in the normal way, citizens were to dissent by civil disobedience when infractions of the basic liberties occurred, these liberties would, it seems, be more rather than less secure. For these reasons, then, the parties would adopt the conditions defining justified civil disobedience as a way of setting up, within the limits of fidelity to law, a final device to maintain the stability of a just constitution. Although this mode of action is strictly speaking contrary to law, it is nevertheless a morally correct way of maintaining a constitutional regime.

In a fuller account the same kind of explanation could presumably be given for the justifying conditions of conscientious refusal (again assuming the context of a nearly just state). I shall not, however, discuss these conditions here. I should like to emphasize instead that the constitutional theory of civil disobedience rests solely upon a conception of justice. Even the features of publicity and nonviolence are explained on this basis. And the same is true of the account of conscientious refusal, although it requires a further elaboration of the contract doctrine. At no point has a reference been made to other than political principles; religious or pacifist conceptions are not essential. While those engaging in civil disobedience have often been moved by convictions of this kind. there is no necessary connection between them and civil disobedience. For this form of political action can be understood as a way of addressing the sense of justice of the community, an invocation of the recognized principles of cooperation among equals. Being an appeal to the moral basis of civic life, it is a political and not a religious act. It relies upon common sense principles of justice that men can require one another to follow and not upon the affirmations of religious faith and love which they cannot demand that everyone accept. I do not mean, of course, that nonpolitical conceptions have no validity. They may, in fact, confirm our judgment and support our acting in ways known on other grounds to be just. Nevertheless, it is not these principles but the principles of justice, the fundamental terms of social cooperation between free and equal persons, that underlie the constitution. Civil disobedience as defined does not require a sectarian foundation but is derived from the public conception of justice that characterizes a democratic society. So understood a conception of civil disobedience is part of the theory of free government.

One distinction between medieval and modern constitutionalism is that in the former the supremacy of law was not secured by established institutional controls. The check to the ruler who in his judgments and edicts opposed the sense of justice of the community was limited for the most part to the right of resistance by the whole society, or any part. Even this right seems not to have been interpreted as a corporate act; an unjust king was simply put aside.[14] Thus the Middle Ages lacked the basic ideas of modern constitutional government, the idea of the sovereign people who have final authority and the institutionalizing of this authority by means of elections and parliaments— and other constitutional forms. Now in much the same way that the modern conception of constitutional government builds upon the medieval, the theory of civil disobedience supplements the purely legal conception of constitutional democracy. It attempts to formulate the grounds upon which legitimate democratic authority may be dissented from in ways that while admittedly contrary to law nevertheless express a fidelity to law and appeal to the fundamental political principles of a democratic regime. Thus to the legal forms of constitutionalism one may adjoin certain modes of illegal protest that do not violate the aims of a democratic constitution in view of the principles by which such dissent is guided. I have tried to show how these principles can be accounted for by the contract doctrine.

Some may object to this theory of civil disobedience that it is unrealistic. It presupposes that the majority has a sense of justice, and one might reply that moral sentiments are not a significant political force. What moves men are various interests, the desires for power, prestige, wealth, and the like. Although they are clever at producing moral arguments to support their claims, between one situation and another their opinions do not fit into a coherent conception of justice. Rather their views at any given time are occasional pieces calculated to advance certain interests. Unquestionably there is much truth in this contention, and in some societies it is more true than in others. But the essential question is the relative strength of the tendencies that oppose the sense of justice and whether the latter is ever strong enough so that it can be invoked to some significant effect.

A few comments may make the account presented more plausible. First of all, I have assumed throughout that we have to do with a nearly just society. This implies that there exists a constitutional regime and a publicly recognized conception of justice. Of course, in any particular situation certain individuals and groups may be tempted to violate its principles but the collective sentiment in their behalf has considerable strength when properly addressed. These principles are affirmed as the necessary terms of cooperation between free and equal persons. If those who perpetrate injustice can be clearly identified and isolated from the larger community, the convictions of the greater part of society may be of sufficient weight. Or if the contending parties are roughly equal, the sentiment of justice of those not engaged can be the deciding factor. In any case, should circumstances of this kind not obtain, the wisdom of civil disobedience is highly problematic. For unless one can appeal to the sense of justice of the larger society, the majority may simply be aroused to more repressive measures if the calculation of advantages points in this direction. Courts should take into account the civilly disobedient nature of the protester's act, and the fact that it is justifiable (or may seem so) by the political principles underlying the constitution, and on these grounds reduce and in some cases suspend the legal sanction.[15] Yet quite the opposite may happen when the necessary background is lacking. We have to recognize then that justifiable civil disobedience is normally a reasonable and effective form of dissent only in a society regulated to some considerable degree by a sense of justice.

There may be some misapprehension about the manner in which the sense of justice is said to work. One may think that this sentiment expresses itself in sincere professions of principle and in actions requiring a considerable degree of self-sacrifice. But this supposition asks too much. A community's sense of justice is more likely to be revealed in the fact that the majority cannot bring itself to take the steps necessary to suppress the minority and to punish acts of civil disobedience as the law allows. Ruthless tactics that might be contemplated in other societies are not entertained as real alternatives. Thus the sense of justice affects, in ways we are often unaware of, our interpretation of political life, our perception of the possible courses of action, our will to resist the justified protests of others, and so on. In spite of its superior power, the majority may abandon its position and acquiesce in the proposals of the dissenters; its desire to give justice weakens its capacity to defend its unjust advantages. The sentiment of justice will be seen as a more vital political force once the subtle forms in which it exerts its influence are recognized, and in particular its role in rendering certain social positions indefensible.

In these remarks I have assumed that in a nearly just society there is a public acceptance of the same principles of justice. Fortunately this assumption is stronger than necessary. There can, in fact, be considerable differences in citizens' conceptions of justice provided that these conceptions lead to similar political judgments. And this is possible, since different premises can yield the same conclusion. In this case there exists what we may refer to as overlapping rather than strict consensus. In general, the overlapping of professed conceptions of justice suffices for civil disobedience to be a reasonable and prudent form of political dissent. Of course, this overlapping need not be perfect; it is enough that a condition of reciprocity is satisfied. Both sides must believe that however much their conceptions of justice differ, their views support the same judgment in the situation at hand, and would do so even should their respective positions be interchanged. Eventually, though, there comes a point beyond which the requisite agreement in judgment breaks down and society splits into more or less distinct parts that hold diverse opinions on fundamental political questions. In this case of strictly partitioned consensus, the basis for civil disobedience no longer obtains. For example, suppose those who do not believe in toleration, and who would not tolerate others had they the power, wish to protest their lesser liberty by appealing to the sense of justice of the majority which holds the principle of equal liberty. While those who accept this principle should, as we have seen, tolerate the intolerant as far as the safety of free institutions permits, they are likely to resent being reminded of this duty by the intolerant who would, if positions were switched, establish their own dominion. The majority is bound to feel that their allegiance to equal liberty is being exploited by others for unjust ends. This situation illustrates once again the fact that a common sense of justice is a great collective asset which requires the cooperation of many to maintain. The intolerant can be viewed as free-riders, as persons who seek the advantages of just institutions while not doing their share to uphold them. Although those who acknowledge the principles of justice should always be guided by them, in a fragmented society as well as in one moved by group egoisms, the conditions for civil disobedience do not exist. Still, it is not necessary to have strict consensus, for often a degree of overlapping consensus allows the reciprocity condition to be fulfilled.

There are, to be sure, definite risks in the resort to civil disobedience. One reason for constitutional forms and their judicial interpretation is to establish a public reading of the political conception of justice and an explanation of the application of its principles to social questions. Up to a certain point it is better that the law and its interpretation be settled than that it be settled rightly. Therefore it may be protested that the preceding account does not determine who is to say when circumstances are such as to justify civil disobedience. It invites anarchy by encouraging everyone to decide for himself, and to abandon the public rendering of political principles. The reply to this is that each person must indeed make his own decision. Even though men normally seek advice and counsel, and accept the injunctions of those in authority when these seem reasonable to them, they are always accountable for their deeds. We cannot divest ourselves of our responsibility and transfer the burden of blame to others. This is true of any theory of political duty and obligation that is compatible with the principles of a democratic constitution. The citizen is autonomous yet he is held responsible for what he does . . . If we ordinarily think that we should comply with the law, this is because our political principles normally lead to this conclusion. Certainly in a state of near justice there is a presumption in favor of compliance in the absence of strong reasons to the contrary. The many free and reasoned decisions of individuals fit together into an orderly political regime.

But while each person must decide for himself whether the circumstances justify civil disobedience, it does not follow that one is to decide as one pleases. It is not by looking to our personal interests, or to our political allegiances narrowly construed, that we should make up our minds. To act autonomously and responsibly a citizen must look to the political principles that underlie and guide the interpretation of the constitution. He must try to assess how these principles should be applied in the existing circumstances. If he comes to the conclusion after due consideration that civil disobedience is justified and conducts himself accordingly, he acts conscientiously. And though he may be mistaken, he has not done as he pleased. The theory of political duty and obligation enables us to draw these distinctions.

There are parallels with the common understandings and conclusions reached in the sciences. Here, too, everyone is autonomous yet responsible. We are to assess theories and hypotheses in the light of the evidence by publicly recognized principles. It is true that there are authoritative works, but these sum up the consensus of many persons each deciding for himself. The absence of a final authority to decide, and so of an official interpretation that all must accept, does not lead to confusion, but is rather a condition of theoretical advance. Equals accepting and applying reasonable principles need have no established superior. To the question, who is to decide? The answer is: all are to decide, everyone taking counsel with himself, and with reasonableness, comity, and good fortune, it often works out well enough.

In a democratic society, then, it is recognized that each citizen is responsible for his interpretation of the principles of justice and for his conduct in the light of them. There can be no legal or socially approved rendering of these principles that we are always morally bound to accept, not even when it is given by a supreme court or legislature. Indeed each constitutional agency, the legislature, the executive, and the court, puts forward its interpretation of the constitution and the political ideals that inform it.[16] Although the court may have the last say in settling any particular case, it is not immune from powerful political influences that may force a revision of its reading of the constitution. The court presents its doctrine by reason and argument; its conception of the constitution must, if it is to endure, persuade the major part of the citizens of its soundness. The final court of appeal is not the court, nor the executive or the legislature, but the electorate as a whole. The civilly disobedient appeal in a special way to this body. There is no danger of anarchy so long as there is a sufficient working agreement in citizens' conceptions of justice and the conditions for resorting to civil disobedience are respected. That men can achieve such an understanding and honor these limits when the basic political liberties are maintained is an as-

sumption implicit in a democratic polity. There is no way to avoid entirely the danger of divisive strife, any more than one can rule out the possibility of profound scientific controversy. Yet if justified civil disobedience seems to threaten civic concord, the responsibility falls not upon those who protest but upon those whose abuse of authority and power justifies such opposition. For to employ the coercive apparatus of the state in order to maintain manifestly unjust institutions is itself a form of illegitimate force that men in due course have a right to resist.

NOTES

1. Here I follow H. A. Bedau's definition of civil disobedience. See his "On Civil Disobedience," *Journal of Philosophy*, vol. 58 (1961), p. 653–661. It should be noted that this definition is narrower that the meaning suggested by Thoreau's essay, as I note in the next section. A statement of a similar view is found in Martin Luther King's "Letter from Birmingham City Jail" (1963), reprinted in H. A. Bedau, ed., *Civil Disobedience* (New York: Pegasus, 1969), pp. 72–89. The theory of civil disobedience in the text tries to set this sort of conception into a wider framework. Some recent writers have also defined civil disobedience more broadly. For example, Howard Zinn, *Disobedience and Democracy* (New York: Random House, 1968), pp. 119f., defines it as "the deliberate, discriminate violation of law for a vital social purpose." I am concerned with a more restricted notion. I do not at all mean to say that only this form of dissent is ever justified in a democratic state.

2. This and the following gloss are from Marshall Cohen, "Civil Disobedience in a Constitutional Democracy," *The Massachusetts Review*, vol. 10 (1969), pp. 224–226, 218–221, respectively.

3. For a fuller discussion of this point, see Charles Fried, "Moral Causation," *Harvard Law Review*, vol. 77 (1964), pp. 1268f. For clarification below of the notion of militant action, I am indebted to Gerald Loev.

4. Those who define civil disobedience more broadly might not accept this description. See for example, Zinn, *Disobedience and Democracy*, pp. 27–31, 39, 119f. Moreover, he denies that civil disobedience need be nonviolent. Certainly one does not accept the punishment as right, that is as deserved for an unjustified act. Rather one is willing to undergo the legal consequences for the sake of fidelity to law, which is a different matter. There is room for latitude here in that the definition allows that the charge may be contested in court, should this prove appropriate. But there comes a point beyond which dissent ceases to be civil disobedience as defined here.

5. See Henry David Thoreau, "Civil Disobedience" (1848) reprinted in H. A. Bedau, ed., *Civil Disobedience*, pp. 27–48. For a critical discussion, see Bedau's remarks, pp. 15–26.

6. For these distinctions I am indebted to Burton Drebin.

7. For a discussion of the conditions when some fair arrangement is called for, see Kurt Baier, *The Moral Point of View* (Ithaca, N.Y.: Cornell University Press, 1958), pp. 207–213; and David Lyons, *Forms and Limits of Utilitarianism* (Oxford: The Clarendon Press, 1965), pp. 160–176. Lyons gives an example of a fair rotation scheme and he also observes that (waiving costs of setting them up) such fair proce-

dures may be reasonably efficient. See pp. 169–171. I accept the conclusions of his account, including his contention that the notion of fairness cannot be explained by assimilating it to utility, p. 176f. The earlier discussion by C. D. Broad, "On the Function of False Hypotheses in Ethics," *International Journal of Ethics*, vol. 26 (1916), esp. pp. 385–390, should also be noted here.

8.   For a discussion of these obligations, see Michael Walzer, *Obligations: Essays on Disobedience, War, and Citizenship* (Cambridge: Harvard University Press, 1970), chap. III.

9.   See J. L. Brierly, *The law of Nations*, 6th ed. (Oxford: The Clarendon Press, 1963), especially chapters IV–V. This work contains all that we need here.

10.   For a recent discussion, see Paul Ramsey, *War and the Christian Conscience* (Durham, N.C.: The Duke University Press, 1961); and also R. B. Potter, *War and Moral Discourse* (Richmond, Va.: John Knox Press, 1969). The latter contains a useful bibliographical essay, pp. 87–123.

11.   I am indebted to R. G. Albritton for clarification on this and other matters in this paragraph.

12.   See *Nuclear Weapons and Christian Conscience*, ed., Walter Stein (London: The Merlin Press, 1965), for a presentation of this sort of doctrine in connection with nuclear war.

13.   I borrow this point from Walzer, *Obligations*, p. 127.

14.   See J. H. Franklin, ed., *Constitutionalism and Resistance in the Sixteenth Century* (New York: Pegasus, 1969), in the introduction, pp. 11–15.

15.   For a general discussion, see Ronald Dworkin, "On Not Prosecuting Civil Disobedience," *The New York Review of Books*, June 6, 1968.

16.   For a presentation of this view, to which I am indebted, see A. M. Bickel, *The Least Dangerous Branch* (New York: Bobbs-Merrill, 1962), especially chapters V and VI.

JOEL FEINBERG

Civil Disobedience in the Modern World*

The common element among the various kinds of actions that have been called "civilly disobedient" is, as Professor Daube puts it, "an offense against human authority, committed openly in a higher cause, or a cause thought to be higher."[1] The focus of the modern discussion of civil disobedience, however, is somewhat narrower, since it is restricted to disobedience of political authority, usually by acts that violate the law of the state and thereby incur criminal sanctions. In Western countries in the nineteenth and twentieth centuries the focus is narrower still. Civilly disobedient acts do not aim to overthrow whole régimes thought to be illegitimate; nor do they reject an accepted principle of legitimacy itself, like that of "the divine right of kings" or "the consent of the governed." They occur in post-revolutionary countries against a background of acknowledged just constitutions, democratic parliaments, and valid laws; and their purpose is not to undermine authority but to protest its misuse.

Closely related to civil disobedience but properly distinguishable from it are rule departures by state officials, those of policemen who do not arrest lawbreakers, prosecutors who don't prosecute them, jurors who acquit obviously guilty defendants, judges who depart from judicial rules—in general, deliberate failures, often for conscientious reasons, to discharge the duties of one's office. Such official derelictions resemble civil disobedience in important ways, but they do not normally render officials liable to criminal punishment, so I won't consider them to be civilly disobedient, even though when their intended beneficiary is himself an avowed civil disobedient, refusal to arrest, prosecute, or convict him form part of the complete treatment of our subject. In this article I shall not discuss the official's problem but shall concentrate on civil disobedience as a moral problem for the private citizen. My question will be, When, if ever, is there a moral right to commit civil disobedience? and not the closely related derivative question, What are the moral duties of legal officials toward the civilly disobedient lawbreakers?

Civil disobedience, however, is not just *any* kind of deliberate infraction of valid penal law; so it will be useful, at the outset, to distinguish it from other sorts of lawbreaking with which it can be confused. First of all, the common crimes of robbers, muggers, burglars, killers, rapists, and con artists, though they are instances of deliberate lawbreaking, have no other resemblance to the acts with which we are concerned. Civil disobedience is lawbreaking from certain motives only and in certain circumstances only. The common crimes are committed from such familiar motives as personal gain, malice, and hate; their specific intent is to harm the interests of others; and they are accompanied either by a desire to escape apprehension or an emotionally induced indifference to the risk of apprehension. In all of these ways they differ from civil disobedience. In other respects civil disobedience contrasts with acts of "warfare against the state"—assassination, sabotage, terrorism, riot, insurrection, avowed revolution—since civil disobedience is a kind of resistance within the accepted political structure, a violation of the law without loss of respect for law and the other basic political institutions, which are acknowledged to be, by and large, fair.

When the only alternative in the circumstances to the evil of lawbreaking is to permit an evil that is greater still, a desperate choice of the illegal "lesser evil" may often look like civil disobedience, but since most modern legal systems accept the defense of "necessity" as a complete justification, it is not really "disobedience" at all. I have in mind such examples as borrowing a stranger's car without his permission in order to get a heart attack victim quickly to the hospital, destroying another's property to prevent the spread of a raging fire, violating the speed limit in pursuit of an escaping criminal, and so on. The traditional attitude of the Anglo-American law toward such actions is well expressed in the words of the judge in the sixteenth-century criminal case: "An act may break the words of

* From *Humanities in Society*, Vol. 2, No. 1, Winter, 1979, pp. 37–60. Reprinted by permission of the publisher.

the law and yet not break the law itself." The defense of necessity is a generalized justification based on two judgments, first, that when the evil produced by breaking a rule is likely to be substantially less than the evil that would result in a given case from complying with it, then it is reasonable to breach it and, second, that it is unfair to impose criminal liability on objectively reasonable conduct. Rule departures resulting from such forced choices of a lesser evil, then, are not examples of civil disobedience. But if our legal system did not recognize the defense of necessity and remained rigidly and stupidly literalistic, then exceeding the speed limit to get a wife in labor to the maternity ward might well count as civilly disobedient, dissimilar though it may be to the acts of disinterested political protest that are the most familiar examples, in our time, of that broad genre.

Even closer to civil disobedience, but probably still worth distinguishing from it, are deliberately created test cases for statutes of doubtful validity. These phenomena are a peculiar feature of the American system, in which private citizens can get constitutionally suspect laws overthrown by the tactic of getting themselves convicted for disobeying them and then launching an appeal upward through the courts. "You pays your money and you takes your chances," as carnival barkers used to say. You violate the explicit prohibitions of the suspect law; you are found guilty; you get an expensive constitutional lawyer, and proceed through the appellate system perhaps even to the Supreme Court, arguing always that the reason why you are innocent is not that you didn't do what the prosecution alleges that you did, but rather that the statute you violated was not a valid law in the first place. If you win, then you are a public benefactor, for you have effectively employed what is virtually the only way in our system to get rid of popular but unconstitutional pseudo-laws, and you have paid a price in money, time, and anxiety in order to do that public service. But if you lose, and the Supreme Court does not accept your arguments, you are as unlucky as any losing gambler, and the law may treat you no differently from any common criminal. In addition to all the previously mentioned personal costs, you may be sent to prison for a while as a reward for your public service. Such test cases raise moral issue similar to those we shall be considering, but I still wish to distinguish them from genuine civil disobedience because the "lawbreaker" is not intentionally vio-

lating a law. He thinks that what he is doing is entirely within his legal rights, an opinion that happens to disagree with that of the local police, the prosecutor, and the courts. He wants the appellate courts to settle the disagreement, and "disobedience" is the only way *he* can get them to do so, since he must have "standing" if he is to use the courts for that purpose, and one cannot acquire standing by complying with the law in question. Of course, he may want to repeat his behavior even after the Supreme Court has declared it illegal once and for all, as an act of public protest against an unfair law, and that would begin to look like civil disobedience proper.

Three types of lawbreaking remain to be discussed: conscientious evasion, conscientious refusal, and disobedience as moral protest. Many writers, following John Rawls, speak of the third of these (moral protests) as civil disobedience proper and contrast it with acts of conscientious evasion and refusal. There are differences, of course, among these three forms of disobedience, and clarity is always served by a recognition of dissimilarities among classes otherwise easily confused. But since the three types of conduct raise importantly similar moral questions, we can lump them together, along with forced choices of the lesser evil in a system that does not recognize the necessity defense, under the generic label "civil disobedience in the wide sense" and reserve the label "civil disobedience in the narrow sense" for moral protests, those acts of lawbreaking that Rawls thinks of as "civil disobedience proper." Our concern in the second half of this essay will be with the moral justification of civil disobedience in the broad sense.

Acts of conscientious evasion might be thought of as borderline cases of civil disobedience since they share with covert crimes the hope of escaping apprehension and arrest. Their impelling motives, however, are strikingly different from those of most ordinary crimes. The conscientious evader genuinely believes that the law he violates is morally wrong, even though validly enacted, and personal gain is not a large element—if it is present at all—in his motivation for violating it. He thinks that he can do more good for the cause of justice by remaining free to violate the iniquitous law some more than by making a martyr of himself. The clearest historical examples of what I have in mind were the covert infractions by white northerners of the fugitive slave laws before the Civil War.

"Conscientious refusal" is the term Rawls uses to describe deliberate "noncompliance with a more or less direct legal injunction or administrative order,"[2] where one's action is assumed to be known to the authorities, however much one might wish, in some cases, to conceal it. Among the examples cited by Rawls are the refusal of Jehovah's Witnesses to salute the flag, the refusal of pacifists to serve in the armed forces, and Thoreau's famous refusal to pay his taxes during the Mexican War on the ground that payment would make him a participant in a great evil. Conscientious refusal resembles civil disobedience in the narrow sense in that its motives are conscientious. It is not done from the desire for personal gain, and there is little hope of escaping apprehension. But neither is it impelled by a desire to act as a form of public protest. Rather one acts either to avert an evil close at hand or else simply to keep one's own hands, morally speaking, clean. (Thoreau had no hope of stopping the Mexican War, but at least he could avoid having guilt on *his* hands.)

Civil disobedience (in what I call the "narrow sense") is defined by Rawls as "a public, nonviolent, conscientious yet political act contrary to law usually done with the aim of bringing about a change in the law or policies of the government."[3] Rawls here describes a kind of conduct that was frequently engaged in by moral protestors in the 1960s, first against racial discrimination and then against the Vietnamese War. Let us briefly consider the defining elements of this form of protest, one by one.

Civil disobedience is *public*—engaged in openly, often even with prior notice, since the protestor wants as much publicity and attention as possible for his tactical purposes. Civil disobedience is *nonviolent* for the simple tactical reason that injury to others, harm to property, and extreme inconvenience to others, are likely to be self-defeating, since they can obscure one's message, cause bitter resentment, and distract public attention from what is vital. The main reason, in short, why the civil disobedient wants his act to be nonviolent is the same as his reason for wanting it to be public—so that he can convince the majority of his fellow citizens that the act is indeed conscientious and sincere and intended to address the public's sense of justice. Indeed it is absolutely essential to civil disobedience as Rawls conceives it that it is a form of address, a symbolic way of making a statement, in his words "an expression of profound and conscientious political conviction . . .

in the public forum."[4] As such it can be valued on the one hand as an end in itself, either a kind of "bearing witness" to a moral truth for its own sake, or a disavowal of responsibility, or on the other hand (what is more likely) as a *tactic*. When it is meant to be a method for producing reform, it must be distinguished from *intimidation*. It is in essential contrast to such tactics as disruption of traffic, strikes, boycotts, and political pressure. It does not say "Give us our way or else." That sort of threat often backfires. The only pressure involved is "moral pressure"—dramatically sincere appeal to the public's sense of justice.

The third defining characteristic in Rawls's account is *deliberate unlawfulness*. Under this heading two types of civil disobedience must be distinguished. *Direct* civil disobedience violates the very law that is the target of the protest, whereas *indirect* civil disobedience violates some other law whose reasonableness is not in question. As Rawls points out, civil disobedience cannot always be direct: "If the government enacts a vague and harsh statute against treason, it would not be appropriate to commit treason as a way of objecting to it."[5] To which Carl Cohen adds the observation that one doesn't protest capital punishment for rape by committing rape. In fact it is surprisingly difficult to protest the most likely sorts of unjust laws and policies by direct civil disobedience. White men sitting in the black sections of segregated buses in the 1950s and war protestors burning their draft cards are good examples, but more characteristically, acts of civil disobedience in recent years have been indirect, the most familiar being those that violate local trespass ordinances, for example, "sitting in" at an atomic energy site until one must be forcibly carried away by the police in order to protest, not trespass laws, but rather the policy of building atomic power plants.

Finally, civilly disobedient acts in Rawls' conception must be *conscientious*. The main point of this part of the definition presumably is to rule out the motives of private or personal gain or malicious emotion as primary and immediate. Insofar as those motives, which are characteristic of ordinary crimes, are present at all, we should hesitate to classify an infraction as "civil disobedience." Rawls reminds us that the civil disobedient suffers inconvenience, expense, taunts, threats, real danger, and eventually punishment. His willingness, in the typical case, to suffer these consequences helps to demonstrate that his purpose is to protest an injustice or a wrong—not to achieve some *immediate* gain for himself. He suffers for a *cause,* some larger goal or principle for whose sake he breaks the law publicly and thereby sacrifices at least his short-run interests. While all of this is true, the word "conscientious," as we shall see, may be a misleading way of expressing it.

What does it mean to act conscientiously? I shall want to qualify the following answer shortly, but let me begin by giving what might be called "the strongest account of conscientiousness," namely that to act conscientiously is to act because of one's honest and sincere conviction that what one is doing is right, not merely in the sense of "all right," but rather in the sense of "morally mandatory"—the uniquely correct thing to do, whatever the cost. "Here I stand; I can do no other," said Luther. "Here I sit; I can do no other" might have been said during the Southern sit-ins of the early 1960s. There are two important, though obvious, things to say about conscientiousness so construed: (1) people can be wrong in their conscientious convictions as in any other ones; but (2) insofar as convictions are genuinely conscientious, in this strong sense, they deserve respect from everyone and respectful treatment, insofar as that is consistent with other goals, from the law. Conscientious motives have a very special kind of moral value.

There is no denying that the motives of many acts of civil disobedience fit the above description, but if the strong account of conscientiousness is included in our definition, then many apparent examples of civil disobedience are not civil disobedience at all, because they are *not* "conscientious." I have in mind not acts done from a sense of duty, but rather acts done because the actor wishes to stand on his *rights*—to affirm them, vindicate them, and demand their recognition and enforcement. These are acts done *in* a clear conscience, but not *from* conscientiousness (in the strong sense). Publicly drinking beer during Prohibition and attending a marijuana smoke-in are examples. The drinker may well have been affirming thereby his moral right to drink beer, but he was not doing what he did because his conscience required beer drinking. One can hardly compare him with Luther! When one is prepared to sacrifice one's short-run interests in order to secure one's rights and acts out of genuine conviction that moral principle does indeed confer those rights,

then there is a sense in which one's action is disinterested, at least more so than actions that demand, in the absense of moral deliberation or conviction of any kind, that others simply "gimme, gimme, gimme, gimme, what I cry for." We can even call them "conscientious" in a weaker sense of that term. It is important, however, to understand that civil disobedience (in the wide sense that includes principled protest, evasion, and refusal) need not be conscientious in the usual strong sense. To persist in the contrary view may be to fall into a serious muddle about the very concept of a *conscience*. It is essential to the idea of a person's conscience that it is a faculty of self-address concerned only with the duties of its possessor. My conscience tells *me* what it is right for *me* to do, what I must do, what it is my duty to do, and not merely what I may do if I wish. If we say, on the contrary, that my conscience tells me what my *rights* are, then we are committed logically to the view that one person's conscience can tell him what other people's duties are, which is not only conceptually odd, but politically dangerous as well.

The modern discussion among philosophers of the justifiability of civil disobedience has at least a dual source, partly in democratic political theory and partly in philosophical jurisprudence. On the one hand, the problem civil disobedience raises for our moral judgments derives from the almost universal belief that every citizen in a constitutional democracy with at least approximately just institutions has a general obligation to obey the valid laws and lawful commands of his government. Civil disobedience by definition is a violation of those laws or commands. How then can it be justified? Duties of course can be overridden in particular cases by a "higher duty," or in a "higher cause." What then must these higher principles be like, and when are they strong enough, to override the general moral obligation to be law abiding? That in turn depends, at least in part, on the grounds, strength, and limits of the latter obligation. In this way the question of civil disobedience draws philosophers into the venerable problem of the nature of political obligation.

There is also a path through the philosophy of law to the same destination. The period during which civil disobedience began to challenge modern thinkers largely corresponded with the rise of the doctrine called "legal positivism" and the decline of the traditional doctrines of natural law. According to the natural law theory, the validity of humanly made coercive laws depends in part on their *content*, that is, on what they require or prohibit. If they are, in the appropriate way, arbitrary, unjust, cruel, pointless, or immoral, then they have no authority or force of law whatever, in which case there is no more moral obligation to obey them than there is to comply with any pseudolaw or mere masquerade as law. To the legal positivists that view was intolerably paradoxical. The validity of law, they insisted, is one thing; its justice or morality is another; so there can be no contradiction in characterizing a statute as an unjust valid law. The validity of law, on their view, stems from its proper *enactment*. All valid law is enacted law. So-called laws of nature may be standards for distinguishing good from bad law, but law is law, whether good or bad. It is the pedigree of a law (where it comes from) rather than its content (what it commands) that determines its validity.

The positivist account of legal validity obviously gains much support from common sense, but historically the legal positivists have often held another doctrine that is hard to reconcile with the first, namely that valid law as such, no matter what its content, deserves our respect and our general fidelity. Even if valid law is bad law, we have some obligation to obey it simply because it is law. But how can this be so if a law's validity has nothing to do with its content? Why should I have *any* respect or duty of fidelity toward a statute with a wicked or stupid content just because it was passed into law by a bunch of men (possibly very wicked men like the Nazi legislators) according to the accepted recipes for making law? Thus Lon Fuller, the leading American critic of legal positivism, triumphantly springs his trap: the positivist cannot explain how "laws, even bad laws, have a claim to our respect."[6] The two doctrines of validity by pedigree and respect for law as such yield in combination an unstable conception of law as "an amoral datum" that has a kind of magical capacity to generate moral obligations. One easy way out for the positivist, and I think the only way, is to abandon the second doctrine and admit that there is no moral duty whatever to obey law simply because it is valid law. To support that startlingly radical proposition the positivist must cast his skeptical eye on the variously alleged grounds for "the moral obligation

to obey the law as such," and soon he is likely to encounter the political theorist exploring the possible grounds for a perfectly general moral obligation to obey the democratic state and the moralist puzzled about the moral justifiability of civil disobedience.

The standard way of characterizing the individual citizen's moral problem concerning civil disobedience is as a conflict of reasons of basically different types. According to this conception, the question, Is it ever right to disobey a law, and if so, under what conditions? is exactly the same in form as the question(s), Is it ever right to break a promise, tell a lie, inflict pain on others . . . etc., and if so, under what conditions? This approach to the problem assumes that there is (to use philosophical jargon that I don't altogether like) a "*prima facie* obligation" to obey the law that can in principle conflict with, override, or be overridden by "*prima facie* obligations" of other kinds. I would prefer to speak of "reasons for" and "reasons against," but since the term *prima facie obligation* has become fixed by a strong convention, it will be well to come to terms with it. So for the moment let us see what philosophers have meant by *prima facie* obligation, or PFO, as I shall abbreviate it.

In explaining what they mean by a PFO, some philosophers resort to an analogy with the idea of a vector of forces that is used in physics. The analogy is useful up to a point. We do feel "pulled in both ways," as we say, when we are in situations like that which Plato describes in the *Republic,* in which we have promised a neighbor to keep a weapon for him and return it when he requests and he then comes back in a furious homicidal rage against another party and demands that we return his property to him. Thinking no doubt of cases of this sort, Carl Cohen writes:

One's ultimate or actual obligation in any morally complex situation will require the careful weighing of several, even many, *prima facie* obligations, some of which may conflict head-on with others. We may think of such *prima facie* obligations as components, or vectors, pushing us in different directions with differing degrees of force, the morally correct outcome of the set being our resultant obligation.[7]

Despite the intuitively familiar points of resemblance between PFOs and physical forces, this analogy is more misleading than helpful. In physics, a resultant force compounded out of component forces is always a kind of splitting of the difference, not always right down the middle of course, but a result determined in some measure by each of its components. When two forces act on a body, the resultant direction and velocity of that object will be a kind of "compromise." Its resultant direction, if the two forces are equal and at right angles to one another, will be at a 45° angle, splitting the difference between where it would have gone if only the one force were acting on it and where it would have gone if only the other force were acting on it. But in morals there is often no way of splitting the difference, in which case one must do the one duty or the other, rather than do a part of each. Plato's householder could hardly solve his problem by means of a compromise between the moral demand that he keep his promise to return another's lethal weapon and the moral demand that he protect a third party from harm. It would not do, for example, to substitute a less lethal weapon—say a somewhat brittle wooden club—for the original sword.

I think that we can avoid this difficulty and achieve greater clarity by thinking of PFOs and resultant obligations simply in terms of supporting and conclusive reasons. Then we can say that one's having promised to do an act A (say) is always a reason of direct relevance and at least some cogency in favor of doing A and one's promise not to do B is a reason against doing B, and in the absence of other reasons having a bearing on the situation, either would be a conclusive reason. Further, a PFO (general type of supporting reason) is not in every case a decisive reason, but it is always a relevant one and one which would be conclusive if no other relevant reason of greater strength applied to the situation. Thus if Jones has a PFO to do A, then he has a moral reason to do A which is such that unless he has a moral reason *not* to do A that is at least as strong, then not doing A is wrong, and he has an actual obligation to do A.[8]

Philosophers have differed over the question of how many general kinds of PFOs there are and over which are basic and which derivative. The following list of basic PFOs is, I think, representative and plausible, though I can make no stronger claim for it here:

1. The PFO of fidelity: to keep promises.
2. The PFO of veracity: to tell the truth (or better—not to tell lies).
3. The PFO of fair play: not to exploit, cheat, or "free load" on others.
4. The PFO of gratitude: to return favors.
5. The PFO of nonmaleficence: not to cause pain or suffering to others.
6. The PFO of beneficence: to help others in distress when this involves no great danger to oneself or third parties.
7. The PFO of reparation: to repair harms to others that are one's own fault.
8. The PFO not to kill others (except in self-defense).
9. The PFO not to deprive others of their property.
10. The PFO to oppose injustices when this involves no great cost to oneself.
11. The PFO to promote just institutions and to work toward their establishment, maintenance, and improvement.

Insofar as a given act is an instance of one of the above eleven kinds, that is a moral reason in favor of doing it, and if it is not, at the same time, a negative instance of one of the other categories on the list, then it is a decisive reason. If it is a positive instance of one type and a negative instance of another, say a promise that can only be kept by telling a lie, then one's actual duty will be to perform the PFO which is the more stringent in the circumstances. That is all that a moralist can say in the abstract with any degree of certainty.

In addition to the list of eleven PFOs, is there also a PFO to obey the law? Is the fact that a contemplated act would be illegal a reason against doing it? Of course it might always be a prudential reason of some weight against doing it. You might get caught, and the risk is always a consideration to be weighed carefully by any reasonable person. But that is not what we are concerned about. We wish to know whether illegality is also a type of *moral reason*, a consideration that tends to bind us morally to refrain from the act and will ground an actual obligation to refrain if no other conflicting PFOs are pulling us even harder in the opposite direction. Philosophers have differed sharply over this question. Few are tempted these days to hold the view, so effectively demolished by Richard Wasserstrom,[9] that it can *never* be right to disobey a law, that "X is illegal" is always a decisive moral reason against doing X. But a growing number of philosophers hold the very opposite and surprisingly plausible view that "X

is illegal" is no kind of reason at all, that there isn't even a PFO to obey the law. (We do, of course, have a PFO not to do many of the things prohibited by law—not to kill, steal, etc. —but because these things are *mala in se,* not because they are illegal.) These philosophers usually argue that there is no sort of reason why anyone ought to obey a rotten rule created in a rotten system under an authoritarian régime or a thoroughly iniquitous constitution. Nazi rules against helping Jews were "valid laws" in Germany, all right, and duly enacted by Nazi legislatures. Their ruthless enforcement, moreover, gave every German citizen a prudential reason for obeying them. But the fact that helping Jews was illegal was itself morally irrelevant, neither here nor there in the moral universe, utterly beside the point. Surely, these philosophers conclude, not just *any* legal obligation in *any* legal system imposes a moral PFO, giving us a moral reason of any strength at all for obedience.

Philosophers on the other side usually grant the point and make a small strategic retreat. If there is a PFO to obey the law as such, they concede, it can only be in a reasonably just society, under a reasonably just constitution, with fair (presumably democratic) procedures for making and changing laws. But in such a state, they insist, the fact that *X* is illegal is always a moral reason, of some discernible weight at least, against doing *X*. But even that reasonably modified position no longer gains unanimous assent, and more and more philosophers, myself included, are coming to question it.

There is a dilemma for adherents of even the weakest version of the doctrine that there is a moral PFO to obey the law. (I refer to the version that restricts the PFO to valid laws in the citizen's own legal system when that system is democratic and by and large just.) Either this alleged PFO is one of the basic ones, on the same level as the eleven on our list, or it is derivative from some one or combination of them. If basic, it can only be defended by an appeal to self-evidence, for *ex hypothesi* there is no more basic ethical principle from which it follows. But whereas that kind of appeal is plausible in the other eleven cases (who could deny, for example, that "you promised" is always *a* reason, at the very least, for doing what was promised?), it seems much less so in this case. In any event when so many astute philosophers[10] are saying "I don't see it," it certainly lacks argumentative force to rest one's case on the insistence that it

is just obviously so. But if, on the other hand, the PFO to obey the law is derivative from one or more of the basic ones, one must be able to show how it is derived, and that is a notoriously difficult undertaking, not yet successfully done.[11]

Almost all of the basic PFOs on our list have been thought by one philosopher or another to be the ground, or part of the ground, for a derivative PFO to obey the law, but the most interesting attempts to derive such a PFO, and the most popular, invoke numbers 4 (gratitude), 1 (fidelity), 3 (fair play), and 10–11 (justice). Let us examine each of these attempts briefly but critically.

The argument from gratitude proceeds as follows. In general, by accepting benefits from others we incur "debts of gratitude." Many moralists derive the PFO to help one's parents from this basic one, and indeed Socrates, in Plato's dialogue the *Crito,* likens his own relation to the Athenian state to that of a son to his parents and declines to resist even a fatally unjust application of its laws on that ground. We do accept the protection of the police, the armed forces, and the Public Health Service, and the benefits of the money system, the postal service, public schools, and so on; therefore we are said to have a debt of gratitude to the state and a PFO to obey its laws. Not to do so would be ungrateful.

What are we to make of this curious argument? In the first place, it should be observed that debts of gratitude don't have anything to do with gratitude in the usual sense, which is a certain motive, attitude, or feeling. There can be no duty to have a particular feeling or to act from a certain motive, for the pinpoint control over our emotions that would be required by such a duty is beyond our powers of self-manipulation. Our only plausible duties are to do, or to omit doing, certain things (from whatever motive). A duty to repay services is less paradoxically called a "duty of reciprocation" than a duty of gratitude. Indeed, so separate are the ideas of reciprocation and gratitude that sometimes the former is taken as a sign of the *absence* of the latter, as was noted by St. Thomas Aquinas, who quotes with approval a passage from Seneca that "a person who wants to repay a gift too quickly with a gift in return is an unwilling debtor and an ungrateful person."[12] Nevertheless a duty of reciprocation is fully discharged by appropriate payment even when done in a grudging spirit of ungrateful resentment, and gratitude without suitable repayment, however commendable for its own sake, cannot discharge a duty of reciprocation.

A stronger and more relevant point is also yielded by the example of the gift. Unlike formal loans and contractual performances, a gift is not the sort of thing that one has a duty to "repay." Gratitude may be appropriate though it is not the sort of thing that can be exacted, but repayment is not the sort of concept that has any application at all to the gift situation. There can no more be a duty of reciprocation than a duty of gratitude to return gratuitous gifts and favors. Suppose that the Joneses, obscure acquaintances of yours, invite you to dinner, and you accept, to your later regret. Do you have a PFO to reciprocate by inviting them to dinner? Would you be blamably "ungrateful" if you did not? Would a cash payment sent later through the mails be an acceptable mode of repayment? Suppose that Jones is a rich man or the president of your university, someone who entertains others constantly and lavishly and is more than occupied by his own busy social schedule. Are you torn over your duty to reciprocate? Or, to take examples of another kind, suppose that a young woman receives flowers from an admirer, then candy, then dresses, then electrical appliances, despite her continued efforts to discourage him. Finally she begins to "doubt his motives." Is there even a trace of a moral reason here for reciprocation? cooperation? obedience? Or suppose that a college teacher gives a pretty coed a good grade when the student knows that her work is poor. She might well wonder "What is he up to anyway?" but certainly not "What should I do for him?" In the latter two cases not only is a duty of reciprocation out of the question; it is also the case that one of the psychologically necessary conditions for the emergence of the feeling of gratitude itself is absent, namely, the belief that the gratuitous gift or favor was offered from genuinely disinterested friendship or benevolence, with no "ulterior motive." In any event, even if we are grateful—let us suppose for a good dinner given us by well-meaning but very boring persons who wished only to please us—it does not follow that we have a moral PFO to reciprocate, but at most that we may feel some trace of a desire or inclination to do so. (If only they weren't so boring!)

The case for deriving a PFO to obey the laws of the state from a basic PFO of "gratitude" collapses completely in the light of the above observations. If the argument is meant only to establish a ground for the feeling of gratitude, then it needs to be supplemented by a showing that the state's undoubted services and protections are genuine gifts rather than contractual performances and, further, that its motive was personal benevolence or disinterested friendship (an unenviable task); and even if there is a ground for gratitude, there can be no duty to *feel* grateful; and even if there were such a duty, it could not in turn ground a duty of reciprocation. Finally, and most conclusively, even if there is some sort of duty of repayment (which is most implausible), it could not take the form required by the argument, namely faithful obedience to commands, for as M. B. E. Smith puts it, "The mere fact that a person has conferred benefits on me, even the most momentous benefits conferred from genuinely benevolent motives, doesn't establish his right to dictate all my behavior."[13] The benefits are no reason at all in support of *that* PFO. A fifty-year-old son may have numerous duties toward his eighty-year-old parents, but they will all be duties to help them, not to obey them. No matter how grateful he is to them for their past services, he can have no duty to let them determine, for example, what hour he must come home at night or what foods he may eat.

Like any theory that has been defended by great philosophers in the past, the gratitude theory does have a grain of truth. There is a more plausible interpretation of something that can be called a duty of gratitude, and no doubt such a duty can yield, under very special circumstances, something like a PFO to comply with the laws of a state and even to perform certain positive services for it. If there is such a thing in ordinary interpersonal relations as a PFO of gratitude, it is not an obligation to reciprocate favor for favor, service for service, benefit for benefit, but rather an obligation to stand ready, in case one's benefactor should ever falter, to help him too. If a wealthy friend of his father gives a young person enough money to pay for his whole college education, he will appropriately feel grateful, especially if he believes that the gift was a genuine expression of benevolence or friendship without ulterior motive. But insofar as the payment was a genuine gift and not a loan, the young person will have no burdensome duty to repay a like sum during his postgraduate years. Presumably if the benefactor had intended to impose such a burden, he would have explicitly described his transfer of funds as a *loan,* not a gift. Suppose, however, that years later it comes to the attention of the younger man, now middle-aged and comfortable, that the elderly benefactor has come upon hard times, having lost all his money through unlucky investments, and now is suffering from bad health. Not to help him *now,* if he can, would indeed be ungrateful and a violation of a moral duty to reciprocate the old man's earlier favors. Similarly, an expatriate living happily abroad, though with warm feelings toward his native land and "gratitude" for having learned its language and culture and for having been shaped by its institutions, might feel morally impelled to come to the aid of his country in its time of dire need and pay taxes and bear arms in its defense. On the other hand, an Englishman at the start of World War II or an Israeli at the outset of the Yom Kippur War who takes all of his goods and flees to Geneva or Cuernavaca would rightly be thought a morally derelict ingrate by his countrymen. In such cases one has a moral duty to come to the aid of one's country, a duty derived perhaps in part from having benefited from its laws and services in the past. But that is quite another thing than a general duty in good or hard times to obey each and every law or order.

The second way of deriving a moral PFO of obedience to law bases it on a deliberate undertaking of the citizen, a kind of formal promise to comply with laws, or at least a voluntary granting of one's consent to the lawmaker's authority, which amounts to the same thing. Thus the PFO of obedience is like the obligation to discharge one's part of a bargain; the state provides its benefits *in exchange for which* the citizen provides his constant fidelity to law. (State benefits, on this view, are more like loans than gifts.) The argument can be stated simply: (1) a person can have no obligation to obey or support the state unless he has personally granted his consent to its authority, but once that consent is granted or promise made, a duty of obedience has been assumed; (2) we all have granted that consent; therefore, (3) we all have the standing duty (like all general duties, a PFO) to obey the law of the state.

The most doubtful part of the argument, of course, is its second premise. The reader might well claim that he (for one) never granted consent of the sort required by the argument. In

fact, no representative of the state ever asked him to do so. His friend Angelo did so at the naturalization ceremony as part of a solemn oath with his hand on a Bible. But most of us native-born citizens never did anything of the kind. It won't do to say in reply to this that the reader's ancestors took the oath, either at the time of "the original contract" or at later naturalization proceedings, for there is no way to explain how a person can be bound morally by a promise made by another person at a time before he even came into existence.

A more plausible rejoinder than the "inherited obligation" ploy is that for which John Locke is famous: Of course the reader gave no explicit statement of consent; rather he granted a "tacit consent," not in language but in conduct from which the consent can be inferred. A. John Simmons, in an important article, has given a definitive refutation of this claim.[14] He points out first that there *is* a kind of behavior that can be called "tacit consent," but that it is not "unexpressed consent deduced from conduct," but rather "consent expressed in a certain way—by silence."[15] For an example he has us imagine a board meeting at which the chairman announces: "We will meet again next Thursday unless there are objections to that date. Does anyone have objections?" There is silence for one full minute, at the conclusion of which the chairman notes that all have agreed (consented) to his proposal. The reader will recognize this familiar notion of consent by silence but strenuously resist its application to his own case. How could anyone think that he consented to the authority of his government simply by being silent? No one in authority ever asked him if he consented. He was never presented with options and alternatives and asked to decide. He was no more aware that his silence on this question constituted consent than he is that his silence about network TV scheduling constitutes an agreement to watch all the shows.

Simmons point out, however, that Locke surely did not mean by "tacit consent" the familiar notion of consent by silence. Rather he argued in two other ways, first, that our consent is implied by our acceptance of government benefits and, second, by our continued residence in the country of our citizenship. The odd thing about these closely interrelated arguments is that they imply that we can given our binding consent by accident, so to speak, unknowingly and unintentionally. Perhaps if I had known that I was assuming a lifelong obligation of fidelity I would at least have hesitated before accepting benefits. As it is, Locke puts me in the position that would be occupied by the lady in our earlier example if she learned belatedly that her acceptance of gifts from her suitor was a way of getting married and that he is now her husband come what may, for better or worse.

Elsewhere Locke writes that a sure sign of consent to governmental authority (whatever the consenter's actual intentions) is one's continued residence in a country. But in the absence of a clearly presented choice and a formal convention for indicating consent (like the board meeting described above), this too would be an "unknowing or unintentional consent," which is to say an absurdity. In modern nations at the present time, at least, there is no such general procedure; no genuine choice is ever made available to most of us. The reader might complain that he did not know that he was incurring a permanent obligation of obedience when he chose to settle down in his native land until he read Locke, and by then it was too late!

Perhaps it is possible in principle, however, though not presently the case, to design a political procedure that would make residence a sign of "tacit consent" to a country's laws. Simmons reminds us that Socrates in the *Crito* claimed that such formal procedures *were* available to every Athenian on attaining the "age of manhood." The Athenian state in effect told every young man that he could take all his property and "go wherever you wish with our blessing, if you don't like it here. Your silence will be taken as an acknowledgment of a lifelong obligation to obey our laws." Assuming that this was an accurate account of things in at least one ancient Greek city-state and that young Athenians were able to make a *truly voluntary choice* of political allegiance, we must now ask whether it is possible to design such a procedure for the modern state.

Surely the difficulties would be formidable. Perhaps it was not very difficult, economically or psychologically, for free Hellenic Greeks to change their residence from one city-state to another. All moves are disruptive, of course, but in total impact on the lives of the movers, a change from Athens to Corinth was probably no harder than a change from New York to California today. But now, the "option" for a twenty-one-year-old American youth to say good-bye to his family and friends, pack his bags, change his money, and board a jet plane for a new life in whatever alien land would deign to receive him is hardly a genuine "choice" at all. Simmons is hardly less scathing than David Hume had been in his eighteenth-century reply to Locke[16] when he (Simmons) writes that "our most precious 'possessions' are not movable property that can be put on the boat with one's books and TV set."[17] The legal opportunity to emigrate then hardly provides a procedure for voluntarily expressing one's consent by silence. Simmons' example of the opportunity at the board meeting to express an objection, freely and knowingly, by the easy and conventionally understood device of raising one's arm in response to a question bears little analogy to the forced and dangerous expedient of emigrating. The latter, Simmons tells us, is more like the case of the boss at the board meeting inviting all those who object to so signify by lopping off their right arms or implying by his manner that objection however expressed carries a high risk of demotion or firing.[18]

The third way of basing a PFO to obey the law is to derive it from the PFO of fair play. This argument was well formulated (and first named) in an influential article of John Rawls, which was later severely qualified and even renamed in Rawls's book.[19] A PFO of fair play comes into existence not only in sports and competitive games (as its name suggests) but also in a large variety of social settings. Its principal home, in fact, is in cooperative rather than competitive joint undertakings, in voluntary rule-structured associations like clubs, teams, partnerships, political parties, and the like, and in more informal joint enterprises, like voluntary clean-up or repair work among a group of friends who possess a car in common. Each person has his own share to do if all are to gain, but it is possible for a given person to *cheat,* not do his share, and thus take his benefit as "free" only because the others are doing *their* shares. The "free rider" doesn't "play fair." He may not harm anybody directly, but by cheating he *exploits* the others' cooperativeness to his own benefit. He "takes advantage of them," as we say. A paradigmatic example is not paying one's fare on a railroad train. The others pay in full confidence that everyone will, and the free rider takes advantage of that trust. So he gains at their expense. It is not that he *harms* them; that is not the gravamen of their grievance. Their share of the costs of the railroad (reflected in the owners' adjusted prices) may go up only a tiny fraction of a penny because of his nonpayment. But they have voluntarily foregone the benefits he got in expectation that he would forego them too. Their grievance is that he took advantage of them.

That complaint can just as well be expressed in the language of rights and duties. Adapting one of Simmons's examples, we can consider a community scheme to preserve water pressure during a dry spell by prohibiting the watering of lawns in the evening, although the facts are such that if as many as five percent of the homeowners watered their lawns, there would be no lowering of the pressure. Jones waters his lawn in the evening. He causes no harm to anyone because noncompliance has not passed the five percent threshold. Nevertheless, his neighbors are understandably indignant. They see that Jones profits *only because they forebear.* They cooperated and discharged their duties of fair play, and they had a right that Jones do so too.

Perhaps the most apt and familiar example is drawn from one of the largest of all the collective activities of our time, the cooperative movement of automobiles in all directions through a modern nation's highway system. Suppose that there is a restricted lane reserved for emergency vehicles on the right shoulder of a multilaned road. We are creeping along bumper to bumper in heavy traffic returning from a well-attended football game. You look in your rearview mirror and see a car pull into that forbidden lane and accelerate rapidly by the line of cars jammed in the permitted lanes. Generously you infer that there is some extreme emergency that has impelled this motorist to so desperate a course. But as he passes on your right you note that his car is packed with spirited revelers; there are pennants flying from all the windows, and lusty voices are singing the college fight song. The rest of us have stayed out of the restricted lane and because—only because—of our obedience, the disobedient motorist profits. He has exploited our good faith for his own benefit.

If a general PFO to obey the law can be derived from the basic PFO of fair play, then each individual citizen's duty of obedience is owed ultimately, not to the state, but to the other citizens, for it is essentially a duty not to take advantage of them even in "harmless" ways. There are indeed many examples of legal disobedience that does exploit unfairly the law-abidingness of

others. Traffic infractions of course provide one class of examples. Income tax evasion provides another. But there are too many counterexamples for there to be a perfectly general PFO of obedience derived from the basic PFO of fair play. There are many types of cases where violating the law doesn't take advantage of anyone, and since the element of exploitation is not involved *necessarily* in every instance of law breaking, "fair play" is by no means a perfect model. In those cases where exploitation of other citizens is involved (and indeed they are common), we have a PFO to obey the law not simply because it *is* the law, but rather because it would be unfair exploitation not to, just as in other cases, we may have a duty to obey the law, not because it is the law, but because it would harm someone, or break a promise to someone, or so on, not to.

Examples of nonexploitative lawbreaking may not be typical instances of crimes in a democracy, but they are not so rare as to seem exotic. Most traffic violations either endanger or take advantage of others, but particular instances even of generally dangerous or exploitative types do neither—running a red light on empty streets late at night under perfect conditions of visability, for example, or exceeding the speed limit on an empty stretch of highway when it is perfectly safe (except for the possibility of apprehension by a traffic cop) to do so. Whatever the reasons for avoiding such conduct, there is surely no one who can complain that he has been taken advantage of by it. Such lawbreaking is neither harmful nor dangerous nor exploitative. What then could be the basis of a moral PFO to abstain from it? Then there are examples of so-called victimless crimes like smoking marijuana or cohabitation which abound in almost all penal codes. Not only do they not harm (or at least not *wrong*) anyone; they don't take advantage of anyone either. Surely the models of driving in a restricted lane and cheating on one's income tax do not apply to them.

Most deliberate lawbreaking is obviously harmful to someone, namely, its victims. But even much wrongful lawbreaking of that class cannot be thought of as exploitative of other parties who are *not* its victims. When *A* rapes *B* may all of the rest of us males complain that *A* took unfair advantage of our compliance with the rape law to benefit at our expense? When *B* murders her husband in a fit of wrathful jealousy, may all the other married people complain that she was able to get her way only because of their forebearance, that it is unfair to *them* that she acted on her wrath when they must repress theirs? Not very likely.

It is *prima facie* more plausible, however, to claim that civil disobedience in the narrow sense (political protest) does invariably have the characteristic of unfair play and that exploitation is at least one of its inevitable moral costs even when it is justified on balance. If that is so, then there is always *some* reason against that kind of disobedience (a PFO to refrain from it) even when counterbalanced by reasons on the other side. When you sit in at the atomic energy site, for example, your fellow citizens might all be entitled to say: "You are able to violate the trespass laws to further your favorite moral cause *only* because we don't do the same every time we think we have a higher moral cause. If all our moral causes were promoted in your fashion, the costs to our democratic institutions, our public civility, and our domestic tranquility would be disastrous." This is often a quite proper thing to say to the rash civil disobedient whose political anger is more like self-righteousness than genuinely disinterested indignation. Civil disobedience is often *not* justified precisely on the ground that it is not fair play and is made possible only by the self-sacrificial forebearance of others. There is in fact a moral PFO of fair play, and when civil disobedience violates that PFO, it is usually unjustified. But some disobedience does not violate that PFO, and if it also does not violate any other basic and obvious PFO, there can be no grounds for calling it unjustified, except perhaps its contravention of an alleged PFO to obey the law as such. Civil disobedience in the narrow sense can be justified, as Rawls has insisted all along,[20] only when (1) it is done sincerely for a "higher moral cause," (2) when there are no other legal means available (when all democratic remedies have been exhausted), and (3) when civil disobedience is not yet so widespread as to be self-defeating and dangerous to the survival of mutually beneficial institutions. When it is done under these conditions, it retains its character as an unusual and extreme step and is not "exploitative" of anyone. To the question, What if everyone did it? the justified civil disobedient can answer that if every one did it (where by "it" we mean disobedience that satisfies the above condition), the results would not be bad at all.

There is one further respect in which some lawbreaking departs from the unfair play models, and this too has been emphasized by Rawls, especially in his book, in which he severely qualifies his earlier view of the importance of the fair play analogy. The benefits of government and the rule of law are not as equally distributed among the citizens of a modern industrial state as the benefits of traffic laws, for example, are distributed among motorists. So long as there is economic deprivation, social discrimination, and unequal access to powerful offices, society is not a "mutually advantageous" cooperative venture. If there is a PFO of obedience derived from the basic PFO of fair play, therefore, it could apply at most to the more favored members of society.

The final argument for a PFO of obedience to law derives it from what Rawls in his more mature work called the "natural duty to uphold just institutions."[21] This argument has the advantage over his earlier reliance on "fair play" in that the basic PFO in question is one we *all* share, regardless of our position in society and the degree to which we share the benefits of common undertakings. Rawls begins by distinguishing technical senses of *obligation* and *duty* (terms which I have treated here, for reasons of convenience, as synonyms). Obligations are incurred only by one's own voluntary acts, for example the obligations to keep one's promises, pay one's debts, and honor one's agreements. Duties typically attach to special stations, offices, or roles, whether or not we voluntarily occupy them; but our "natural duties" are those that everyone has, regardless of his jobs or roles—for example, duties to be generally friendly, helpful to those in need, and not to be cruel. Among our other natural duties, Rawls reports, is a duty to work toward the establishment of just institutions and to strengthen and support them once they are established.

Rawls's account of these matters has much to recommend it. I think that there clearly is a "natural duty," in his sense, to uphold just institutions, and that it is one of the basic PFOs in our sense. Individual justice is much less likely to be done in general in the absence of strong and reliable just institutions that are constituted by clear and reasonable rules. I have in mind especially such political institutions and constitutive rules as the jury system, the universal franchise, free speech, majority rule in legislatures, and courts organized on the principle of due process. Insofar as one damages these institutional practices, one harms the cause of justice generally. That we are morally bound not to do such harm is as self-evident, I think, as that we are bound not to harm the cause of human happiness in general. Nevertheless, I doubt that a general PFO to obey valid laws can be derived from the basic PFO to support just institutions. Much lawbreaking does damage or threaten just institutions, but equally certainly much lawbreaking (including much unjustified lawbreaking) has no damaging effect on them whatever—for example, running a red light at three in the morning, cohabiting, playing poker at home with friends (where this is illegal). These examples are of actions that do not generate "disrespect for law," because they are unwitnessed or done in private. Perhaps many open and public acts of civil disobedience do damage just institutions, but there is no necessity that this be so. Rawls himself writes that civil disobedience, when it satisfies certain minimal conditions of reasonableness (including the circumstantial condition that such acts have not already become so common as to threaten to poison public discourse and lower standards of civility), actually functions as "a final device to maintain the stability of a just constitution,"[22] because it is an escape valve for pent-up indignations and is "disobedience to law within the framework of fidelity to law, although at the outer edge thereof."[23] Warfare against the state, covert subversion, disruption, violent intimidation, and the like do always carry the high risk of weakening just institutions, but civil disobedience, paradoxically, can actually strengthen them.

There could be a derivative moral PFO to obey the law only if, of necessity, every individual instance of deliberate disobedience were a violation of some basic PFO, but that seems to be no more true of the PFO to uphold just institutions than of the PFOs of gratitude, promise keeping, and fair play. The fact that an act would be illegal then, we may conclude, has no tendency whatever to make that act wrong. Why, in that case, does our conclusion seem, at first sight, so startling? That may be because in our legal system, as well as in many others that we can imagine, most of the actions that are legally prohibited also happen to be wrong on other grounds. The typical crimes of fraud and violence are wrong because they harm or endanger other people; they would be no less wrong if they were perfectly legal. Other prohibited acts, like driving in restricted lanes, are wrong even when harmless in the given case because they

unfairly take advantage of the forebearance of others. If we knew that ninety percent of all illegal acts in our country are in similar ways wrong on grounds independent of their illegality and all we knew of a given act is that it is illegal, then we would be entitled to infer, with a degree of confidence proportioned to the evidence, that the given act is wrong too. That is to say that illegal acts are "*prima facie* wrong" in a sense different from the one we have been considering, namely, that there is a *statistical presumption* that they are, in any given case, wrong. But that is not to say that it is their character as illegal that makes them wrong or contributes in any degree to their wrongness. Rather their illegality is a characteristic contingently linked to the other properties that truly make them wrong; so that its presence may be a more or less reliable index or clue to the presence of wrongness, not its ground or basis.

The conclusions of this essay can now be stated tersely:

1. There is no general moral PFO to obey valid law, even in a democratic state with a just constitution.
2. The individual's moral problem in civil disobedience is not that of choosing between his higher moral cause and the PFO of obedience to law, but rather it is either
   a) no problem at all since his civil disobedience will not violate any PFOs but *only* break the law; or
   b) the problem of choosing between his higher moral cause and prudence (for example, personal safety), or
   c) the moral problem of choosing between conflicting PFOs, one which supports his loyalty to the higher moral cause and another basic PFO (such as the PFO of fair play or the PFO to support just institutions) that may in this particular case be in conflict with it.

In case (*c*) no *general* advice from a moral philosopher is possible except to weigh sensitively the two conflicting PFOs and act in accordance with the one that seems weightier in the present circumstances.

3. Legal positivists should drop their assumption that even bad laws deserve respect simply because they are laws and that they impose some small obligation, at least, of obedience. Then, having no more problem of reconciliation, they can hold to

their primary contention that all properly enacted law is valid law.

4. The ancient quest for a perfectly general ground of political obligation can be abandoned.

NOTES

1. David Daube, *Civil Disobedience in Antiquity* (Edinburgh, 1972), p. 1.

2. John Rawls, *A Theory of Justice* (Cambridge, Mass., 1971), p. 368.

3. Ibid., p. 364.

4. Ibid., p. 366.

5. Ibid., p. 365.

6. Lon L. Fuller, "Positivism and Fidelity to Law: A Reply to Professor Hart," *Harvard Law Review* 71 (1958): 630.

7. Carl Cohen, *Civil Disobedience: Conscience, Tactics, and the Law* (New York, 1971), p. 6.

8. Compare M. B. E. Smith, "Is There a Prima Facie Obligation to Obey the Law?," *The Yale Law Journal* 82 (1973): 950.

9. Richard Wasserstrom, "The Obligation to Obey the Law," *UCLA Law Review* 10 (1963).

10. For example, Rolf Sartorius, *Individual Conduct and Social Norms* (Belmont, Calif., 1975), chap. 6; A. John Simmons, *Moral Principles and Political Obligations* (Princeton, N.J., 1979), Chap. 8; Smith, "Prima Facie Obligation." I have found Simmons's brilliant new book especially useful.

11. One early sketchy attempt was that of W. D. Ross, *The Right and the Good* (Oxford, 1930), pp. 27-28, who derived the PFO to obey laws of one's country "partly (as Socrates contends in the *Crito*) from the duty of gratitude for the benefits one has received from it, partly from the implicit promise to obey which seems to be involved in permanent residence in a country whose laws we know we are *expected* to obey, and still more clearly involved when we ourselves invoke the protection of its law . . .; and partly (if we are fortunate in our country) from the fact that its laws are potent instruments for the general good."

12. As quoted by Josef Pieper, *Justice* (London, 1957), p. 107.

13. Smith, "Prima Facie Obligation." p. 952.

14. A. John Simmons, "Tacit Consent and Political Obligation," *Philosophy and Public Affairs* 5 (1976).

15. Ibid., p. 279.

16. David Hume, "Of the Original Contract," first published in his *Essays Moral and Political* (1748).

17. Simmons, *Moral Principles*, p. 99.

18. Ibid.

19. The earlier formulation is in John Rawls, "Legal Obligation and the Duty of Fair Play" in *Law and Philosophy*, edited by Sidney Hook (New York, 1964), pp. 3-18. Rawls' second thoughts are found in his *Theory of Justice*, pp. 342-49 *et passim*. In the book Rawls refers to "the principle of fairness" rather than "the principle of fair play," in part, apparently, to avoid the suggestion that all life is a game.

20. *Theory of Justice*, pp. 371-77.

21. Ibid., 333-41.

22. Ibid., p. 384.

23. Ibid., p. 366.

H. L. A. HART
Problems of Legal Reasoning*

Since the early twentieth century, the critical study of the forms of reasoning by which courts decide cases has been a principal concern of writers on jurisprudence, especially in America. From this study there has emerged a great variety of theories regarding the actual or proper place in the process of adjudication of what has been termed, often ambiguously, "logic." Most of these theories are skeptical and are designed to show that despite appearances, deductive and inductive reasoning play only a subordinate role. Contrasts are drawn between "logic" and "experience" (as in Holmes's famous dictum that "the life of the law has not been logic; it has been experience") or between "deductivism" or "formalism" on the one hand and "creative choice" or "intuitions of fitness" on the other. In general, such theories tend to insist that the latter members of these contrasted sets of expressions more adequately characterize the process of legal adjudication, despite its appearance of logical method and form. According to some variants of these theories, although logic in the sense of deductive and inductive reasoning plays little part, there are other processes of legal reasoning or rational criteria which courts do and should follow in deciding cases. According to more extreme variants, the decisions of courts are essentially arbitrary.

LEGISLATION AND PRECEDENT

In Anglo-American jurisprudence the character of legal reasoning has been discussed chiefly with reference to the use of the courts of two "sources" of law: (1) the general rules made by legislative bodies (or by other rule-making agencies to which legislative powers have been delegated) and (2) particular precedents or past decisions of courts which are treated as material from which legal rules may be extracted al-

though, unlike legislative rules, there is no authoritative or uniquely correct formulation of the rules so extracted. Conventional accounts of the reasoning involved in the application of legislative rules to particular cases have often pictured it as exclusively a matter of deductive inference. The court's decision is represented as the conclusion of a syllogism in which the major premise consists of the rule and the minor premise consists of the statement of the facts which are agreed or established in the case. Similarly, conventional accounts of the use of precedents by courts speak of the courts' extraction of a rule from past cases as inductive reasoning and the application of that rule to the case in hand as deductive reasoning.

In their attack on these conventional accounts of judicial reasoning, skeptical writers have revealed much that is of great importance both to the understanding and to the criticism of methods of legal adjudication. There are undoubtedly crucially important phases in the use of legal rules and precedents to decide cases which do not consist merely of logical operations and which have long been obscured by the traditional terminology adopted both by the courts themselves in deciding cases and by jurists in describing the activities of courts. Unfortunately, the general claim that logic has little or no part to play in the judicial process is, in spite of its simple and monolithic appearance, both obscure and ambiguous; it embraces a number of different and sometimes conflicting contentions which must be separately investigated. The most important of these issues are identified and discussed below. There are, however, two preliminary issues of peculiar concern to philosophers and logicians which demand attention in any serious attempt to characterize the forms of legal reasonings.

DEDUCTIVE REASONING

It has been contended that the application of legal rules to particular cases cannot be regarded as a syllogism or any other kind of deductive inference, on the grounds that neither general

*From "Philosophy of Law, Problems of Legal Reasoning" by H. L. A. Hart. Reprinted with permission of the publisher from *The Encyclopedia of Philosophy*, Paul Edwards, Editor in Chief. Volume 6, pp. 268–272. Copyright © 1967 by Macmillan, Inc.

legal rules nor particular statements of law (such as those ascribing rights or duties to individuals) can be characterized as either true or false and thus cannot be logically related either among themselves or to statements of fact; hence, they cannot figure as premises or conclusions of a deductive argument. This view depends on a restrictive definition, in terms of truth and falsehood, of the notion of a valid deductive inference and of logical relations such as consistency and contradiction. This would exclude from the scope of deductive inference not only legal rules or statements of law but also commands and many other sentential forms which are commonly regarded as susceptible of logical relations and as constituents of valid deductive arguments. Although considerable technical complexities are involved, several more general definitions of the idea of valid deductive inference that render the notion applicable to inferences the constituents of which are not characterized as either true or false have now been worked out by logicians. In what follows, as in most of contemporary jurisprudential literature, the general acceptability of this more generalized definition of valid inference is assumed.

INDUCTIVE REASONING

Considerable obscurity surrounds the claim made by more conventional jurisprudential writers that inductive reasoning is involved in the judicial use of precedents. Reference to induction is usually made in this connection to point a contrast with the allegedly deductive reasoning involved in the application of legislative rules to particular cases. "Instead of starting with a general rule the judge must turn to the relevant cases, discover the general rule implicit in them. . . . The outstanding difference between the two methods is the source of the major premise—the deductive method assumes it whereas the inductive sets out to discover it from particular instances" (G. W. Paton, *A Textbook of Jurisprudence,* 2d ed., Oxford, 1951, pp. 171–172).

It is of course true that courts constantly refer to past cases both to discover rules and to justify their acceptance of them as valid. The past cases are said to be "authority" for the rules "extracted" from them. Plainly, one necessary condition must be satisfied if past cases are in this way to justify logically the acceptance of a rule: the past case must be an instance of the rule in the sense that the decision in the case could be deduced from a statement of the rule together with

a statement of the facts of the case. The reasoning insofar as the satisfaction of this necessary condition is concerned is in fact an inverse application of deductive reasoning. But this condition is, of course, only one necessary condition and not a sufficient condition of the court's acceptance of a rule on the basis of past cases, since for any given precedent there are logically an indefinite number of alternative general rules which can satisfy the condition. The selection, therefore, of one rule from among these alternatives as the rule for which the precedent is taken to be authority must depend on the use of other criteria limiting the choice, and these other criteria are not matters of logic but substantive matters which may vary from system to system or from time to time in the same system. Thus, some theories of the judicial use of precedent insist that the rule for which a precedent is authority must be indicated either explicitly or implicitly by the court through its choice of facts to be treated as "material" to a case. Other theories insist that the rule for which a precedent is authority is the rule which a later court considering the precedent would select from the logically possible alternatives after weighing the usual moral and social factors.

Although many legal writers still speak of the extraction of general rules from precedents, some would claim that the reasoning involved in their use of precedents is essentially reasoning from case to case "by example": A court decides the present case in the same way as a past case if the latter "sufficiently" resembles the former in "relevant" respects, and thus makes use of the past case as a precedent without first extracting from it and formulating any general rule. Nevertheless, the more conventional accounts, according to which courts use past cases to discover and justify their acceptance of general rules, are sufficiently widespread and plausible to make the use of the term "induction" in this connection worth discussing.

The use of "induction" to refer to the inverse application of deduction involved in finding that a past case is the instance of a general rule may be misleading: it suggests stronger analogies than exist with the modes of probabilistic inference used in the sciences when general propositions of fact or statements about unobserved particulars are inferred from or regarded as confirmed by observed particulars. "Induction" may also invite confusion with the form of deductive inference known as perfect induction, or with real or alleged methods of discovering generalizations sometimes referred to as intuitive induction.

It is however, true that the inverse application of deduction involved in the use of precedents is also an important part of scientific procedure, where it is known as hypothetic inference or hypotheticodeductive reasoning. Hence, there are certain interesting analogies between the interplay of observation and theory involved in the progressive refining of a scientific hypothesis to avoid its falsification by contrary instances and the way in which a court may refine a general rule both to make it consistent with a wide range of different cases and to avoid a formulation which would have unjust or undesirable consequences.

Notwithstanding these analogies, the crucial difference remains between the search for general propositions of fact rendered probable by confirming instances but still falsifiable by future experience, and rules to be used in the decision of cases. An empirical science of the judicial process is of course possible: it would consist of factual generalization about the decisions of courts and might be an important predictive tool. However, it is important to distinguish the general propositions of such an empirical science from the rules formulated and used by courts.

DESCRIPTIVE AND PRESCRIPTIVE THEORIES

The claim that logic plays only a subordinate part in the decision of cases is sometimes intended as a corrective to misleading descriptions of the judicial process, but sometimes it is intended as a criticism of the methods used by courts, which are stigmatized as "excessively logical," "formal," "mechanical," or "automatic." Descriptions of the methods actually used by courts must be distinguished from prescriptions of alternative methods and must be separately assessed. It is, however, notable that in many discussions of legal reasoning these two are often confused, perhaps because the effort to correct conventional misdescriptions of the judicial process and the effort to correct the process itself have been inspired by the realization of the same important but often neglected fact: the relative indeterminacy of legal rules and precedents. This indeterminacy springs from the fact that it is impossible in framing general rules to anticipate and provide for every possible combination of circumstances which the future may bring. For any rule, however precisely formulated, there will always be some factual situations in which the question whether the situations fall within the scope of the general classificatory terms of the rule cannot be settled by appeal to linguistic rules or conventions or to canons of statutory interpretation, or even by reference to the manifest or assumed purposes of the legislature. In such cases the rules may be found either vague or ambiguous. A similar indeterminacy may arise when two rules apply to a given factual situation and also where rules are expressly framed in such unspecific terms as "reasonable" or "material." Such cases can be resolved only by methods whose rationality cannot lie in the logical relations of conclusions to premises. Similarly, because precedents can logically be subsumed under an indefinite number of general rules, the identification of *the* rule for which a precedent is an authority cannot be settled by an appeal to logic.

These criticisms of traditional descriptions of the judicial process are in general well taken. It is true that both jurists and judges, particularly in jurisdictions in which the separation of powers is respected, have frequently suppressed or minimized the indeterminancy of legal rules or precedents when giving an account of the use of them in the process of decision. On the other hand, another complaint often made by the same writers, that there is an excess of logic or formalism in the judicial process, is less easy to understand and to substantiate. What the critics intend to stigmatize by these terms is the failure of courts, when applying legal rules or precedents, to take advantage of the relative indeterminacy of the rules or precedents to give effect to social aims, policies, and values. Courts, according to these critics, instead of exploiting the fact that the meaning of a statutory rule is indeterminate at certain points, have taken the meaning to be determinate simply because in some different legal context similar wording has been interpreted in a certain way or because a given interpretation is the "ordinary" meaning of the words used.

This failure to recognize the indeterminacy of legal rule (often wrongly ascribed to analytical jurisprudence and stigmatized as conceptualism) has sometimes been defended on the ground that it maximizes certainty and the predictability of decisions. It has also sometimes been welcomed as furthering an ideal of a legal system in which there are a minimum number of independent rules and categories of classification.

The vice of such methods of applying rules is that their adoption prejudges what is to be done in ranges of different cases whose composition cannot be exhaustively known beforehand: rigid classification and divisions are set up which ignore differences and similarities of social and moral importance. This is the burden of the complaint that there is an excessive use of logic in the judicial process. But the expression "an excessive use of logic" is unhappy, for when social values and distinctions of importance are ignored in the interpretation of legal rules and the classification of particulars, the decision reached is not more logical than decisions which give due recognition to these factors: logic does not determine the interpretation of words or the scope of classifications. What is true is that in a system in which such rigid modes of interpretation are common, there will be more occasions when a judge can treat himself as confronted with a rule whose meaning has been predetermined.

METHODS OF DISCOVERY AND STANDARDS OF APPRAISAL

In considering both descriptive and prescriptive theories of judicial reasoning, it is important to distinguish (1) assertions made concerning the usual processes or habits of thought by which judges actually reach their decisions, (2) recommendations concerning the processes to be followed, and (3) the standards by which judicial decisions are to be appraised. The first of these concerns matters of descriptive psychology, and to the extent that assertions in this field go beyond the descriptions of examined instances, they are empirical generalizations or laws of psychology; the second concerns the art or craft of legal judgment, and generalizations in this field are principles of judicial technology; the third relates to the assessment or justification of decisions.

These distinctions are important because it has sometimes been argued that since judges frequently arrive at decisions without going through any process of calculation or inference in which legal rules or precedents figure, the claim that deduction from legal rules plays any part in decision is mistaken. This argument is confused, for in general the issue is not one regarding the manner in which judges do, or should, come to their decisions; rather, it concerns the standards they respect in justifying decisions, however reached. The presence or absence of logic in the appraisal of decisions may be a reality whether the decisions are reached by calculation or by an intuitive leap.

CLEAR CASES AND INDETERMINATE RULES

When the various issues identified above are distinguished, two sets of questions emerge. The first of these concerns the decisions of courts in "clear" cases where no doubts are felt about the meaning and applicability of a single legal rule, and the second concerns decisions where the indeterminacy of the relevant legal rules and precedents is acknowledged.

CLEAR CASES

Even where courts acknowledge that an antecedent legal rule uniquely determines a particular result, some theorists have claimed that this cannot be the case, that courts always "have a choice," and that assertions to the contrary can only be ex post facto rationalizations. Often this skepticism springs from the confusion of the questions of methods of discovery with standards of appraisal noted above. Sometimes, however, it is supported by references to the facts that even if courts fail to apply a clearly applicable rule using a determinate result, this is not a punishable offense, and that the decision given is still authoritative and, if made by a supreme tribunal, final. Hence, it is argued that although courts may show a certain degree of regularity in decision, they are never bound to do so: they always are free to decide otherwise than they do. These last arguments rest on a confusion of finality with infallibility in decisions and on a disputable interpretation of the notion of "being bound" to respect legal rules.

Yet skepticism of this character, however unacceptable, does serve to emphasize that it is a matter of some difficulty to give any exhaustive account of what makes a "clear case" clear or makes a general rule obviously and uniquely applicable to a particular case. Rules cannot claim their own instances, and fact situations do not await the judge neatly labeled with the rule applicable to them. Rules cannot provide for their own application, and even in the clearest case a human being must apply them. The clear cases are those in which there is general agreement that they fall within the scope of a rule, and it is tempting to ascribe such agreements simply to the fact that there are necessarily such agreements in the use of the shared conventions of language. But this would be an oversimplification because it does not allow for the special conventions of the legal use of words, which may diverge from their common use, or for the way in which the meanings of words may be clearly controlled by reference to the purpose of a statutory enactment which itself may be either explicitly stated or generally agreed. A full exploration of these questions is the subject matter of the study of the interpretation of statute.

INDETERMINATE RULES

The decisions of cases which cannot be exhibited as deductions from determinate legal rules have often been described as arbitrary. Although much empirical study of the judicial process remains to be done, it is obvious that this description and the dichotomy of logical deduction and arbitrary decision, if taken as exhaustive, is misleading. Judges do not generally, when legal rules fail to determine a unique result, intrude their personal preferences or blindly choose among alternatives; and when words like "choice" and "discretion," or phrases such as "creative activity" and "interstitial legislation" are used to describe decisions, these do not mean that courts do decide arbitrarily without elaborating reasons for their decisions—and still less that any legal system authorizes decisions of this kind.

It is of crucial importance that cases for decision do not arise in a vacuum but in the course of the operation of a working body of rules, an operation in which a multiplicity of diverse considerations are continuously recognized as good reasons for a decision. These include a wide variety of individual and social interests, social and political aims, and standards of morality and justice; and they may be formulated in general terms as principles, policies, and standards. In some cases only one such consideration may be relevant, and it may determine decision as unambiguously as a determinate legal rule. But in many cases this is not so, and judges marshal in support of their decisions a plurality of such considerations which they regard as jointly sufficient to support their decision, although each separately would not be. Frequently these considerations conflict, and courts are forced to balance or weigh them and to determine priorities among them. The same considerations (and the same need for weighing them when they conflict) enter into the use of precedents when courts must choose between alternative rules which can be extracted from them, or when courts consider whether a present case sufficiently resembles a past case in relevant respects.

Perhaps most modern writers would agree up to this point with this account of judicial decision where legal rules are indeterminate, but beyond this point there is a divergence. Some theorists claim that notwithstanding the heterogeneous and often conflicting character of the factors which are relevant to decision, it is still meaningful to speak of a decision as *the* uniquely correct decision in any case and of the duty of the judge to discover it. They would claim that a judicial choice or preference does not become rational because it is deferred until after the judge has considered the factors that weigh for and against it.

Other theorists would repudiate the idea that in such cases there is always a decision which is uniquely correct, although they of course agree that many decisions can be clearly ruled out as incorrect. They would claim that all that courts do and can do at the end of the process of coolly and impartially considering the relevant considerations is to choose one alternative which they find the most strongly supported, and that it is perfectly proper for them to concede that another equally skilled and impartial judge might choose the other alternative. The theoretical issues are not different from those which arise at many points in the philosophical discussions of moral argument. It may well be that terms like "choice," "discretion," and "judicial legislation" fail to do justice to the phenomenology of considered decision: its felt involuntary or even inevitable character which often marks the termination of deliberation on conflicting considerations. Very often the decision to include a new case in the scope of a rule or to exclude it is guided by the sense that this is the "natural" continuation of a line of decisions or carries out the "spirit" of a rule. It is also true that if there were not also considerable agreement in judgment among lawyers who approach decisions in these ways, we should not attach significance and value to them or think of such decisions as reached through a rational process. Yet however it may be in moral argument, in the law it seems difficult to substantiate the claim that a judge confronted with a set of conflicting considerations must always assume that there is a single uniquely correct resolution of the conflict and attempt to demonstrate that he has discovered it.

RULES OF EVIDENCE

Courts receive and evaluate testimony of witnesses, infer statements of fact from other statements, and accept some statements as probable or more probable than others or as "beyond reasonable doubt." When it is said that in these activities special modes of legal reasoning are exhibited and that legal proof is different from ordinary proof, reference is usually intended to the exclusionary rules of the law of evidence (which frequently require courts, in determining questions of fact, to disregard matters which are logically relevant), or to various presumptions which assign greater or lesser weight to logically relevant considerations than ordinary standards of reasoning do.

The most famous examples of exclusionary rules are those against "hearsay," which (subject to certain exceptions) make inadmissible, as evidence of the facts stated, reports tendered by a witness, however credible, of statements made by another person. Another example is the rule that when a person is charged with a crime, evidence of his past convictions and disposition to commit similar crimes is not admissible as evidence to show that he committed the crime charged. An example of a rule which may give certain facts greater or less probative weight than ordinary standards do is the presumption that unless the contrary is proved beyond reasonable doubt, a child born to a woman during wedlock is the child of both parties to the marriage.

The application of such rules and their exceptions gives rise to results which may seem paradoxical, even though they are justifiable in terms of the many different social needs which the courts must satisfy in adjudicating cases. Thus, one consequence of the well-known exception to the hearsay rule that a report of a statement is admissible as evidence of a fact stated if it is made against the interest of the person who stated it, is that a court may find that a man committed adultery with a particular woman but be unable to draw the conclusion that she committed adultery with him. A logician might express the resolution of the paradox by saying that from the fact that p entails q it does not follow that "it is legally proved that p" entails "it is legally proved that q".

Apart from such paradoxes, the application of the rules of evidence involves the drawing of distinctions of considerable philosophical importance. Thus, although in general the law excludes reports of statements as evidence of the facts stated, it may admit such reports for other purposes, and in fact draws a distinction between statements of fact and what J. L. Austin called performatory utterances. Hence, if the issue is whether a given person made a promise or placed a bet, reports that he uttered words which in the context amounted to a promise or a bet are admissible. So, too, reports of a person's statement of his contemporary mental states or sensations are admissible, and some theorists justify this on the ground that such first-person statements are to be assimilated to behavior manifesting the mental state or sensation in question.

RONALD M. DWORKIN
The Model of Rules*

EMBARRASSING QUESTIONS

Lawyers lean heavily on the connected concepts of legal right and legal obligation. We say that someone has a legal right or duty, and we take that statement as a sound basis for making claims and demands, and for criticizing the acts of public officials. But our understanding of these concepts is remarkably fragile, and we fall into trouble when we try to say what legal rights and obligations are. We say glibly that whether someone has a legal obligation is determined by applying "the law" to the particular facts of this case, but this is not a helpful answer, because we have the same difficulties with the concept of law.

We are used to summing up our troubles in the classic questions of jurisprudence: What is "the law"? When two sides disagree, as often happens, about a proposition "of law," what are they disagreeing about, and how shall we decide which side is right? Why do we call what "the law" says a matter of legal "obligation"? Is "obligation" here just a term of art, meaning only "what the law says"? Or does legal obligation have something to do with moral obligation? Can we say that we have, in principle at least, the same reasons for meeting our legal obligations that we have for meeting our moral obligations?

These are not puzzles for the cupboard, to be taken down on rainy days for fun. They are sources of continuing embarrassment, and they nag at our attention. They embarrass us in dealing with particular problems that we must solve, one way or another. Suppose a novel right-of-privacy case comes to court, and there is no statute or precedent either granting or denying the particular right of anonymity claimed by the plaintiff. What role in the court's decision should be played by the fact that most people in the community think that private individuals are "morally" entitled to that particular privacy? Suppose the Supreme Court orders some prisoner

freed because the police used procedures that the Court now says are constitutionally forbidden, although the Court's earlier decisions upheld these procedures. Must the Court, to be consistent, free all other prisoners previously convicted through these same procedures?[1] Conceptual puzzles about "the law" and "legal obligation" become acute when a court is confronted with a problem like this.

These eruptions signal a chronic disease. Day in and day out we send people to jail, or take money away from them, or make them do things they do not want to do, under coercion of force, and we justify all of this by speaking of such persons as having broken the law or having failed to meet their legal obligations, or having interfered with other people's legal rights. Even in clear cases (a bank robber or a willful breach of contract), when we are confident that someone had a legal obligation and broke it, we are not able to give a satisfactory account of what that means, or why that entitles the state to punish or coerce him. We may feel confident that what we are doing is proper, but until we can identify the principles we are following we cannot be sure that they are sufficient, or whether we are applying them consistently. In less clear cases, when the issue of whether an obligation has been broken is for some reason controversial, the pitch of these nagging questions rises, and our responsibility to find answers deepens.

Certain lawyers (we may call them "nominalists") urge that we solve these problems by ignoring them. In their view the concepts of "legal obligation" and "the law" are myths, invented and sustained by lawyers for a dismal mix of conscious and subconscious motives. The puzzles we find in these concepts are merely symptoms that they are myths. They are unsolvable because unreal, and our concern with them is just one feature of our enslavement. We would do better to flush away the puzzles and the concepts altogether, and pursue our important social objectives without this excess baggage.

*From 35 *University of Chicago Law Review* 14 (1967). Reprinted by permission of the author and the publisher.

This is a tempting suggestion, but it has fatal drawbacks. Before we can decide that our concepts of law and of legal obligation are myths, we must decide what they are. We must be able to state, at least roughly, what it is we all believe that is wrong. But the nerve of our problem is that we have great difficulty in doing just that. Indeed, when we ask what law is and what legal obligations are, we are asking for a theory of how we use these concepts and of the conceptual commitments our use entails. We cannot conclude, before we have such a general theory, that our practices are stupid or superstitious.

Of course, the nominalists think they know how the rest of us use these concepts. They think that when we speak of "the law," we mean a set of timeless rules stocked in some conceptual warehouse awaiting discovery by judges, and that when we speak of legal obligation we mean the invisible chains these mysterious rules somehow drape around us. The theory that there are such rules and chains they call "mechanical jurisprudence," and they are right in ridiculing its practitioners. Their difficulty, however, lies in finding practitioners to ridicule. So far they have had little luck in caging and exhibiting mechanical jurisprudents (all specimens captured—even Blackstone and Joseph Beale—have had to be released after careful reading of their texts).

In any event, it is clear that most lawyers have nothing like this in mind when they speak of the law and of legal obligation. A superficial examination of our practices is enough to show this, for we speak of laws changing and evolving, and of legal obligation sometimes being problematical. In these and other ways we show that we are not addicted to mechanical jurisprudence.

Nevertheless, we do use the concepts of law and legal obligation, and we do suppose that society's warrant to punish and coerce is written in that currency. It may be that when the details of this practice are laid bare, the concepts we do use will be shown to be as silly and as thick with illusion as those the nominalists invented. If so, then we shall have to find other ways to describe what we do, and either provide other justifications or change our practices. But until we have discovered this and made these adjustments, we cannot accept the nominalists' premature invitation to turn our backs on the problems our present concepts provide.

Of course the suggestion that we stop talking about "the law" and "legal obligation" is mostly bluff. These concepts are too deeply cemented into the structure of our political practices—they cannot be given up like cigarettes or hats. Some of the nominalists have half-admitted this and said that the myths they condemn should be thought of as Platonic myths and retained to seduce the masses into order. This is perhaps not so cynical a suggestion as it seems; perhaps it is a covert hedging of a dubious bet.

If we boil away the bluff, the nominalist attack reduces to an attack on mechanical jurisprudence. Through the lines of the attack, and in spite of the heroic calls for the death of law, the nominalists themselves have offered an analysis of how the terms "law" and "legal obligation" should be used which is not very different from that of more classical philosophers. Nominalists present their analysis as a model of how legal institutions (particularly courts) "really operate." But their model differs mainly in emphasis from the theory first made popular by the nineteenth century philosopher John Austin, and now accepted in one form or another by most working and academic lawyers who hold views on jurisprudence. I shall call this theory, with some historical looseness, "positivism." I want to examine the soundness of positivism, particularly in the powerful form that Professor H. L. A. Hart of Oxford has given to it. I choose to focus on his position, not only because of its clarity and elegance, but because here, as almost everywhere else in legal philosophy, constructive thought must start with a consideration of his views.

POSITIVISM

Positivism has a few central and organizing propositions as its skeleton, and though not every philosopher who is called a positivist would subscribe to these in the way I present them, they do define the general position I want to examine. These key tenets may be stated as follows:

(a) The law of a community is a set of special rules used by the community directly or indirectly for the purpose of determining which behavior will be punished or coerced by the public power. These special rules can be identified and distinguished by specific criteria, by tests having to do not with their content but with their *pedigree* or the manner in which they were adopted or developed. These tests of pedigree can be used to distinguish valid legal rules from spurious legal rules (rules which lawyers and litigants wrongly argue are rules of law) and also from other sorts of social rules (generally lumped together as "moral rules") that the community follows but does not enforce through public power.

(b) The set of these valid legal rules is exhaustive of "the law," so that if someone's case is not clearly covered by such a rule (because there is none that seems appropriate, or those that seem appropriate are vague, or for some other reason) then that case cannot be decided by "applying the law." It must be decided by some official, like a judge, "exercising his discretion," which means reaching beyond the law for some other sort of standard to guide him in manufacturing a fresh legal rule or supplementing an old one.

(c) To say that someone has a "legal obligation" is to say that his case falls under a valid legal rule that requires him to do or to forbear from doing something. (To say he has a legal right, or has a legal power of some sort, or a legal privilege or immunity, is to assert, in a shorthand way, that others have actual or hypothetical legal obligations to act or not to act in certain ways touching him.) In the absence of such a valid legal rule there is no legal obligation; it follows that when the judge decides an issue by exercising his discretion, he is not enforcing a legal obligation as to that issue.

This is only the skeleton of positivism. The flesh is arranged differently by different positivists, and some even tinker with the bones. Different versions differ chiefly in their description of the fundamental test of pedigree a rule must meet to count as a rule of law.

Austin, for example, framed his version of the fundamental test as a series of interlocking definitions and distinctions.[2] He defined having an obligation as lying under a rule, a rule as a general command, and a command as an expression of desire that others behave in a particular way, backed by the power and will to enforce that expression in the event of disobedience. He distinguished classes of rules (legal, moral or religious) according to which person or group is the author of the general command the rule represents. In each political community, he thought, one will find a sovereign—a person or a determinate group whom the rest obey habitually, but who is not in the habit of obeying anyone else. The legal rules of a community are the general commands its sovereign has deployed. Austin's definition of legal obligation followed from this definition of law. One has a legal obligation, he thought, if one is among the addressees of some general order of the sovereign, and is in danger of suffering a sanction unless he obeys that order.

Of course, the sovereign cannot provide for all contingencies through any scheme of orders, and some of his orders will inevitably be vague or have furry edges. Therefore (according to Austin) the sovereign grants those who enforce the law (judges) discretion to make fresh orders when novel or troublesome cases are presented. The judges then make new rules or adapt old rules, and the sovereign either overturns their creations, or tacitly confirms them by failing to do so.

Austin's model is quite beautiful in its simplicity. It asserts the first tenet of positivism, that the law is a set of rules specially selected to govern public order, and offers a simple factual test— what has the sovereign commanded?— as the sole criterion for identifying those special rules. In time, however, those who studied and tried to apply Austin's model found it too simple. Many objections were raised, among which were two that seemed fundamental. First, Austin's key assumption that in each community a determinate group or institution can be found, which is in ultimate control of all other groups, seemed not to hold in a complex society. Political control in a modern nation is pluralistic and shifting, a matter of more or less, of compromise and cooperation and alliance, so that it is often impossible to say that any person or group has that dramatic control necessary to qualify as an Austinian sovereign. One wants to say, in the United States for example, that the "people" are sovereign. But this means almost nothing, and in itself provides no test for determining what the "people" have commanded, or distinguishing their legal from their social or moral commands.

Second, critics began to realize that Austin's analysis fails entirely to account for, even to recognize, certain striking facts about the attitudes we take toward "the law." We make an important distinction between law and even the general orders of a gangster. We feel that the law's strictures—and its sanctions—are different in that they are obligatory in a way that the outlaw's commands are not. Austin's analysis has no place for any such distinction, because it defines an obligation as subjection to the threat of force, and so founds the authority of law entirely on the sovereign's ability and will to harm those who disobey. Perhaps the distinction we make is illusory—perhaps our feelings of some special authority attaching to the law is based on religious hangover or another sort of mass self-deception. But Austin does not demonstrate this, and we are entitled to insist that an analysis of our concept of law either acknowledge and explain our attitudes, or show why they are mistaken.

H. L. A. Hart's version of positivism is more complex than Austin's, in two ways. First, he recognizes, as Austin did not, the rules are of different logical kinds (Hart distinguishes two kinds, which he calls "primary" and "secondary" rules). Second, he rejects Austin's theory that a rule is a kind of command, and substitutes a more elaborate general analysis of what rules are. We must pause over each of these points, and then note how they merge in Hart's concept of law.

Hart's distinction between primary and secondary rules is of great importance.[3] Primary rules are those that grant rights or impose obligations upon members of the community. The rules of the criminal law that forbid us to rob, murder or drive too fast are good examples of primary rules. Secondary rules are those that stipulate how, and by whom, such primary rules may be formed, recognized, modified or extinguished. The rules that stipulate how Congress is composed, and how it enacts legislation, are examples of secondary rules. Rules about forming contracts and executing wills are also secondary rules because they stipulate how very particular rules governing particular legal obligations (that is, the terms of a contract or the provisions of a will) come into existence and are changed.

His general analysis of rules is also of great importance.[4] Austin had said that every rule is a general command, and that a person is obligated under a rule if he is liable to be hurt should he disobey it. Hart points out that this obliterates the distinction between being *obliged* to do something and being *obligated* to do it. If one is bound by a rule he is obligated, not merely obliged, to do what it provides, and therefore being bound by a rule must be different from being subject to an injury if one disobeys an order. A rule differs from an order, among other ways, by being *normative,* by setting a standard of behavior that has a call on its subject beyond the threat that may enforce it. A rule can never be binding just because some person with physical power wants it to be so. He must have *authority* to issue the rule or it is no rule, and such authority can only come from another rule which is already binding on those to whom he speaks. That is the difference between a valid law and the orders of a gunman.

So Hart offers a general theory of rules that does not make their authority depend upon the physical power of their authors. If we examine the way different rules come into being, he tells us, and attend to the distinction between primary and secondary rules, we see that there are two possible sources of a rule's authority.[5]

(a) A rule may become binding upon a group of people because that group through its practices *accepts* the rule as a standard for its conduct. It is not enough that the group simply conforms to a pattern of behavior: even though most Englishmen may go to the movies on Saturday evening, they have not accepted a rule requiring that they do so. A practice constitutes the acceptance of a rule only when those who follow the practice regard the rule as binding, and recognize the rule as a reason or justification for their own behavior and as a reason for criticizing the behavior of others who do not obey it.

(b) A rule may also become binding in quite a different way, namely by being enacted in conformity with some *secondary* rule that stipulates that rules so enacted shall be binding. If the constitution of a club stipulates, for example, that by-laws may be adopted by a majority of the members, then particular by-laws so voted are binding upon all the members, not because of any practice of acceptance of these particular by-laws, but because the constitution says so. We use the concept of *validity* in this connection: rules binding because they have been created in a manner stipulated by some secondary rule are called "valid" rules. Thus we can record Hart's fundamental distinction this way: a rule may be binding (a) because it is accepted or (b) because it is valid.

Hart's concept of law is a construction of these various distinctions.[6] Primitive communities have only primary rules, and these are binding entirely because of practices of acceptance. Such communities cannot be said to have "law," because there is no way to distinguish a set of legal rules from amongst other social rules, as the first tenet of positivism requires. But when a particular community has developed a fundamental secondary rule that stipulates how legal rules are to be identified, the idea of a distinct set of legal rules, and thus of law, is born.

Hart calls such a fundamental secondary rule a "rule of recognition." The rule of recognition of a given community may be relatively simple ("What the king enacts is law") or it may be very complex (the United States Constitution, with all its difficulties of interpretation, may be considered a single rule of recognition). The demonstration that a particular rule is valid may therefore require tracing a complicated chain of validity back from that particular rule ultimately to the fundamental rule. Thus a parking ordinance of the city of New Haven is valid because it is adopted by a city council, pursuant to the procedures and within the competence specified by the municipal law adopted by the state of Connecticut, in conformity with the procedures and within the competence specified by the constitution of the state of Connecticut, which was in turn adopted consistently with the requirements of the United States Constitution.

Of course, a rule of recognition cannot itself be valid, because by hypothesis it is ultimate, and so cannot meet tests stipulated by a more fundamental rule. The rule of recognition is the sole rule in a legal system whose binding force depends upon its acceptance. If we wish to know what rule of recognition a particular community has adopted or follows, we must observe how its citizens, and particularly its officials, behave. We must observe what ultimate arguments they accept as showing the validity of a particular rule, and what ultimate arguments they use to criticize other officials or institutions. We can apply no mechanical test, but there is no danger of our confusing the rule of recognition of a community with its rules of morality. The rule of recognition is identified by the fact that its province is the operation of the governmental apparatus of legislatures, courts, agencies, policemen, and the rest.

In this way Hart rescues the fundamentals of positivism from Austin's mistakes. Hart agrees with Austin that valid rules of law may be created through the acts of officials and public institutions. But Austin thought that the authority of these institutions lay only in their monopoly of power. Hart finds their authority in the background of constitutional standards against which they act, constitutional standards that have been accepted, in the form of a fundamental rule of recognition, by the community which they govern. This background legitimates the decisions of government and gives them the cast and call of obligation that the naked commands of Austin's sovereign lacked. Hart's theory differs from Austin's also, in recognizing that different communities use different ultimate tests of law, and that some allow other means of creating law than the deliberate act of a legislative institution. Hart mentions "long customary practice" and "the relation [of a rule] to judicial decisions" as other criteria that are often used, though generally along with and subordinate to the test of legislation.

So Hart's version of positivism is more complex than Austin's, and his test for valid rules of law is more sophisticated. In one respect, however, the two models are very similar. Hart, like Austin, recognizes that legal rules have fuzzy edges (he speaks of them as having "open texture") and, again like Austin, he accounts for troublesome cases by saying that judges have had exercise discretion to decide these cases by fresh legislation.[7] (I shall later try to show why one who thinks of law as a special set of rules is almost inevitably drawn to account for difficult cases in terms of someone's exercise of discretion.)

RULES, PRINCIPLES, AND POLICIES

I want to make a general attack on positivism, and I shall use H. L. A. Hart's version as a target, when a particular target is needed. My strategy will be organized around the fact that when lawyers reason or dispute about legal rights and obligations, particularly in those hard cases when our problems with these concepts seem most acute, they make use of standards that do not function as rules, but operate differently as principles, policies, and other sorts of standards. Positivism, I shall argue, is a model of and for a system of rules, and its central notion of a single fundamental test for law forces us to miss the important roles of these standards that are not rules.

I just spoke of "principles, policies, and other sorts of standards." Most often I shall use the term "principle" generically, to refer to the whole set of these standards other than rules; occasionally, however, I shall be more precise, and distinguish between principles and policies. Although nothing in the present argument will turn on the distinction, I should state how I draw it. I call a "policy" that kind of standard that sets out a goal to be reached, generally an improvement in some economic, political, or social feature of the community (though some goals are negative, in that they stipulate that some present feature is to be protected from adverse change). I call a "principle" a standard that is to be observed, not because it will advance or secure an economic, political, or social situation deemed desirable, but because it is a requirement of justice or fairness or some other dimension of morality. Thus the standard that automobile accidents are to be decreased is a policy, and the standard that no man may profit by his own wrong a principle. The distinction can be collapsed by construing a principle as stating a social goal (that is, the goal of a society in which no man profits by his own wrong), or by construing a policy as stating a principle (that is, the principle that the goal the policy embraces is a worthy one) or by adopting the utilitarian thesis that principles of justice are disguised statements of goals (securing the greatest happiness of the greatest number). In some contexts the distinction has uses which are lost if it is thus collapsed.[8]

My immediate purpose, however, is to distinguish principles in the generic sense from rules, and I shall start by collecting some examples of the former. The examples I offer are chosen haphazardly; almost any case in a law school casebook would provide examples that would serve as well. In 1889 a New York court, in the famous case of *Riggs v. Palmer,*[9] had to decide whether an heir named in the will of his grandfather could inherit under that will, even though he had murdered his grandfather to do so. The court began its reasoning with this admission: "It is quite true that statutes regulating the making, proof and effect of wills, and the devolution of property, if literally construed, and if their force and effect can in no way and under no circumstances be controlled or modified, give this property to the murderer."[10] But the court continued to note that "all laws as well as all contracts may be controlled in their operation and effect by general, fundamental maxims of the common law. No one shall be permitted to profit by his own fraud, or to take advantage of his own wrong, or to found any claim upon his own iniquity, or to acquire property by his own crime."[11] The murderer did not receive his inheritance.

In 1960, a New Jersey court was faced, in *Henningsen v. Bloomfield Motors, Inc.,*[12] with the important question of whether (or how much) an automobile manufacturer may limit his liability in case the automobile is defective. Henningsen had bought a car, and signed a contract which said that the manufacturer's liability for defects was limited to "making good" defective parts—"this warranty being expressly in lieu of all other warranties, obligations or liabilities." Henningsen argued that, at least in the circumstances of his case, the manufacturer ought not to be protected by this limitation, and ought to be liable for the medical and other expenses of persons injured in a crash. He was not able to point to any statute, or to any established rule of law, that prevented the manufacturer from standing on the contract. The court nevertheless agreed with Henningsen. At various points in the court's argument the following appeals to standards are made: (a) "[W]e must keep in mind the general principle that, in the absence of fraud, one who

does not choose to read a contract before signing it cannot later relieve himself of its burdens."[13] (b) "In applying that principle, the basic tenet of freedom of competent parties to contract is a factor of importance."[14] (c) "Freedom of contract is not such an immutable doctrine as to admit of no qualification in the area in which we are concerned."[15] (d) "In a society such as ours where the automobile is a common and necessary adjunct of daily life, and where its use is so fraught with danger to the driver, passengers and the public, the manufacturer is under a special obligation in connection with the construction, promotion and sale of his cars. Consequently, the courts must examine purchase agreements closely to see if consumer and public interests are treated fairly."[16] (e) " '[I]s there any principle which is more familiar or more firmly embedded in the history of Anglo-American law than the basic doctrine that the courts will not permit themselves to be used as instruments of inequity and injustice?' "[17] (f) " 'More specifically, the courts generally refuse to lend themselves to the enforcement of a "bargain" in which one party has unjustly taken advantage of the economic necessities of other. . . .' "[18]

The standards set out in these quotations are not the sort we think of as legal rules. They seem very different from propositions like "The maximum legal speed on the turnpike is sixty miles an hour" or "A will is invalid unless signed by three witnesses." They are different because they are legal principles rather than legal rules.

The difference between legal principles and legal rules is a logical distinction. Both sets of standards point to particular decisions about legal obligation in particular circumstances, but they differ in the character of the direction they give. Rules are applicable in an all-or-nothing fashion. If the facts a rule stipulates are given, then either the rule is valid, in which case the answer it supplies must be accepted, or it is not, in which case it contributes nothing to the decision.

This all-or-nothing is seen most plainly if we look at the way rules operate, not in law, but in some enterprise they dominate—a game, for example. In baseball a rule provides that if the batter has had three strikes, he is out. An official cannot consistently acknowledge that this is an accurate statement of a baseball rule, and decide that a batter who has had three strikes is not out. Of course, a rule may have exceptions (the batter who has taken three strikes is not out if the catcher drops the third strike.) However, an accurate statement of the rule would take this exception into account, and any that did not would be incomplete. If the list of exceptions is very large, it would be too clumsy to repeat them each time the rule is cited; there is, however, no reason in theory why they could not all be added on, and the more that are, the more accurate is the statement of the rule.

If we take baseball rules as a model, we find that rules of law, like the rule that a will is invalid unless signed by three witnesses, fit the model well. If the requirement of three witnesses is a valid legal rule, then it cannot be that a will has been signed by only two witnesses and is valid. The rule might have exceptions, but if it does then it is inaccurate and incomplete to state the rule so simply, without enumerating the exceptions. In theory, at least, the exceptions could all be listed, and the more of them that are, the more complete is the statement of the rule.

But this is not the way the sample principles in the quotations operate. Even those which look most like rules do not set out legal consequences that follow automatically when the conditions provided are met. We say that our law respects the principle that no man may profit from his own wrong, but we do not mean that the law never permits a man to profit from wrongs he commits. In fact, people often profit, perfectly legally, from their legal wrongs. The most notorious case is adverse possession—if I trespass on your land long enough, some day I will gain a right to cross your land whenever I please. There are many less dramatic examples. If a man leaves one job, breaking a contract, to take a much higher paying job, he may have to pay damages to his first employer, but he is usually entitled to keep his new salary. If a man jumps bail and crosses state lines to make a brilliant investment in another state, he may be sent back to jail, but he will keep his profits.

We do not treat these—and countless other counter-instances that can easily be imagined—as showing that the principle about profiting from one's wrongs is not a principle of our legal system, or that it is incomplete and needs qualifying exceptions. We do not treat counter-instances as exceptions (at least not exceptions in the way in which a catcher's dropping the third strike is an exception) because we could not hope to capture these counter-instances simply by a more extended statement of the principle. They are not, even in theory, subject to enumeration, because we would have to include not only these cases

(like adverse possession) in which some institution has already provided that profit can be gained through a wrong, but also those numberless imaginary cases in which we know in advance that the principle would not hold. Listing some of these might sharpen our sense of the principle's weight (I shall mention that dimension in a moment), but it would not make for a more accurate or complete statement of the principle.

A principle like "No man may profit from his own wrong" does not even purport to set out conditions that make its application necessary. Rather, it states a reason that argues in one direction, but does not necessitate a particular decision. If a man has or is about to receive something, as a direct result of something illegal he did to get it, then that is a reason which the law will take into account in deciding whether he should keep it. There may be other principles or policies arguing in the other direction—a policy of securing title, for example, or a principle limiting punishment to what the legislature has stipulated. If so, our principle may not prevail, but that does not mean that it is not a principle of our legal system, because in the next case, when these contravening considerations are absent or less weighty, the principle may be decisive. All that is meant, when we say that a particular principle is a principle of our law, is that the principle is one which officials must take into account, if it is relevant, as a consideration inclining in one direction or another.

The logical distinction between rules and principles appears more clearly when we consider principles that do not even look like rules. Consider the proposition, set out under "(d)" in the excerpts from the *Henningsen* opinion, that "the manufacturer is under a special obligation in connection with the construction, promotion and sale of his cars." This does not even purport to define the specific duties such a special obligation entails, or to tell us what rights automobile consumers acquire as a result. It merely states—and this is an essential link in the *Henningsen* argument—that automobile manufacturers must be held to higher standards than other manufacturers, and are less entitled to rely on the competing principle of freedom of contract. It does not mean that they may never rely on that principle, or that courts may rewrite automobile purchase contracts at will; it means only that if a particular clause seems unfair or burdensome, courts have less reason to enforce the clause than if it were for the purchase of neckties. The "special obligation" counts in favor, but does not in itself necessitate, a decision refusing to enforce the terms of an automobile purchase contract.

This first difference between rules and principles entails another. Principles have a dimension that rules do not—the dimension of weight or importance. When principles intersect (the policy of protecting automobile consumers intersecting with principles of freedom of contract, for example), one who must resolve the conflict has to take into account the relative weight of each. This cannot be, of course, an exact measurement, and the judgment that a particular principle or policy is more important than another will often be a controversial one. Nevertheless, it is an integral part of the concept of a principle that it has this dimension, that it makes sense to ask how important or how weighty it is.

Rules do not have this dimension. We can speak of rules as being *functionally* important or unimportant (the baseball rule that three strikes are out is more important than the rule that runners may advance on a balk, because the game would be much more changed with the first rule altered than the second). In this sense, one legal rule may be more important than another because it has a greater or more important role in regulating behavior. But we cannot say that one rule is more important than another within the system of rules, so that when two rules conflict one supersedes the other by virtue of its greater weight. If two rules conflict, one of them cannot be a valid rule. The decision as to which is valid, and which must be abandoned or recast, must be made by appealing to considerations beyond the rules themselves. A legal system might regulate such conflicts by other rules, which prefer the rule enacted by the higher authority, or the rule enacted later, or the more specific rule, or something of that sort. A legal system may also prefer the rule supported by the more important principles. (Our own legal system uses both of these techniques.)

It is not always clear from the form of a standard whether it is a rule or a principle. "A will is invalid unless signed by three witnesses" is not very different in form from "A man may not profit from his own wrong," but one who knows something of American laws knows that he must take the first as stating a rule and the second as stating a principle. In many cases the distinction is difficult to make—it may not have been settled how the standard should operate, and this issue may itself be a focus of controversy. The First

Amendment to the United States Constitution contains the provision that Congress shall not abridge freedom of speech. Is this a rule, so that if a particular law does abridge freedom of speech, it follows that it is unconstitutional? Those who claim that the first amendment is "an absolute" say that it must be taken in this way, that is, as a rule. Or does it merely state a principle, so that when an abridgement of speech is discovered, it is unconstitutional unless the context presents some other policy or principle which in the circumstances is weighty enough to permit the abridgement? That is the position of those who argue for what is called the "clear and present danger" test or some other form of "balancing."

Sometimes a rule and a principle can play much the same role, and the difference between them is almost a matter of form alone. The first section of the Sherman Act states that every contract in restraint of trade shall be void. The Supreme Court had to make the decision whether this provision should be treated as a rule in its own terms (striking down every contract "which restrains trade," which almost any contract does) or as a principle, providing a reason for striking down a contract in the absence of effective contrary policies. The Court construed the provision as a rule, but treated that rule as containing the word "unreasonable," and as prohibiting only "unreasonable" restraints of trade.[19] This allowed the provision to function logically as a rule (whenever a court finds that the restraint is "unreasonable" it is bound to hold the contract invalid) and substantially as a principle (a court must take into account a variety of other principles and policies in determining whether a particular restraint in particular economic circumstances is "unreasonable").

Words like "reasonable," "negligent," "unjust," and "significant" often perform just this function. Each of these terms makes the application of the rule which contains it depend to some extent upon principles or policies lying beyond the rule, and in this way makes that rule itself more like a principle. But they do not quite turn the rule into a principle, because even the least confining of these terms restricts the *kind* of other principles and policies on which the rule depends. If we are bound by a rule that says that "unreasonable" contracts are void, or that grossly "unfair" contracts will not be enforced, much more judgment is required than if the quoted terms were omitted. But suppose a case in which some consideration of policy or principle suggests that a contract should be enforced even though its restraint is not reasonable, or even though it is grossly unfair. Enforcing these contracts would be forbidden by our rules, and thus permitted only if these rules were abandoned or modified. If we were dealing, however, not with a rule but with a policy against enforcing unreasonable contracts, or a principle that unfair contracts ought not to be enforced, the contracts could be enforced without alteration of the law.

PRINCIPLES AND THE CONCEPT OF LAW

Once we identify legal principles as separate sorts of standards, different from legal rules, we are suddenly aware of them all around us. Law teachers teach them, lawbooks cite them, legal historians celebrate them. But they seem most energetically at work, carrying most weight, in difficult lawsuits like *Riggs and Henningsen*. In cases like these principles play an essential part in arguments supporting judgments about particular legal rights and obligations. After the case is decided, we may say that the case stands for a particular rule (that is, the rule that one who murders is not eligible to take under the will of his victim). But the rule does not exist before the case is decided; the court cites principles as its justification for adopting and applying a new rule. In *Riggs,* the court cited the principle that no man may profit from his own wrong as a background standard against which to read the statute of wills and in this way justified a new interpretation of that statute. In *Henningsen,* the court cited a variety of intersecting principles and policies as authority for a new rule respecting manufacturer's liability for automobile defects.

An analysis of the concept of legal obligation must therefore account for the important role of principles in reaching particular decisions of law. There are two very different tacks we might take.

(a) We might treat legal principles the way we treat legal rules and say that some principles are binding as law and must be taken into account by judges and lawyers who make decisions of legal obligation. If we took this tack, we should say that in the United States, at least, the "law" includes principles as well as rules.

(b) We might, on the other hand, deny that principles can be binding the way some rules are.

We would say, instead, that in cases like *Riggs* or *Henningsen* the judge reaches beyond the rules that he is bound to apply (reaches, that is, beyond the "law") for extralegal principles he is free to follow if he wishes.

One might think that there is not much difference between these two lines of attack, that it is only a verbal question of how one wants to use the word "law." But that is a mistake, because the choice between these two accounts has the greatest consequences for an analysis of legal obligation. It is a choice between two *concepts* of a legal principle, a choice we can clarify by comparing it to a choice we might make between two concepts of a legal rule. We sometimes say of someone that he "makes it a rule" to do something, when we mean that he has chosen to follow a certain practice. We might say that someone has made it a rule, for example, to run a mile before breakfast because he wants to be healthy and believes in a regimen. We do not mean, when we say this, that he is *bound* by the rule that he must run a mile before breakfast, or even that he regards it as binding upon him. Accepting a rule as binding is something different from making it a rule to do something. If we use Hart's example again, there is a difference between saying that Englishmen make it a rule to see a movie once a week, and saying that the English have a rule that one must see a movie once a week. The second implies that if an Englishman does not follow the rule, he is subject to criticism or censure, but the first does not. The first does not exclude the possibility of a *sort* of criticism—we can say that one who does not see movies is neglecting his education—but we do not suggest that he is doing something wrong *just* in not following the rule.[20]

If we think of the judges of a community as a group, we could describe the rules of law they follow in these two different ways. We could say, for instance, that in a certain state the judges make it a rule not to enforce wills unless there are three witnesses. This would not imply that the rare judge who enforces such a will is doing anything wrong just for that reason. On the other hand we can say that in that state a rule of law requires judges not to enforce such wills; this does imply that a judge who enforces them is doing something wrong. Hart, Austin and other positivists, of course, would insist on this latter account of legal rules; they would not at all be satisfied with the "make it a rule" account. It is not a verbal question of which account is right. It is a question of which describes the social situation more accurately. Other important issues turn on which description we accept. If judges simply "make it a rule" not to enforce certain contracts, for example, then we cannot say, before the decision, that anyone is "entitled" to that result, and that proposition cannot enter into any justification we might offer for the decision.

The two lines of attack on principles parallel these two accounts of rules. The first tack treats principles as binding upon judges, so that they are wrong not to apply the principles when they are pertinent. The second tack treats principles as summaries of what most judges "make it a principle" to do when forced to go beyond the standards that bind them. The choice between these approaches will affect, perhaps even determine, the answer we can give to the question whether the judge in a hard case like *Riggs* or *Henningsen* is attempting to enforce preexisting legal rights and obligations. If we take the first tack, we are still free to argue that because such judges are applying binding legal standards they are enforcing legal rights and obligations. But if we take the second, we are out of court on that issue, and we must acknowledge that the murderer's family in *Riggs* and the manufacturer in *Henningsen* were deprived of their property by an act of judicial discretion applied *ex post facto.* This may not shock many readers—the notion of judicial discretion has percolated through the legal community—but it does illustrate one of the most nettlesome of the puzzles that drive philosophers to worry about legal obligation. If taking property away in cases like these cannot be justified by appealing to an established obligation, yet another justification must be found, and nothing satisfactory has yet been supplied.

In my skeleton diagram of positivism, previously set out, I listed the doctrine of judicial discretion as the second tenet. Positivists hold that when a case is not covered by a clear rule, a judge must exercise his discretion to decide that case by what amounts to a fresh piece of legislation. There may be an important connection between this doctrine and the question of which of the two approaches to legal principles we must take. We shall therefore want to ask whether the doctrine is correct, and whether it implies the second approach, as it seems on its face to do. En route to these issues, however, we shall have to polish our understanding of the concept of discretion. I shall try to show how certain confusions about that concept, and in particular a failure to discriminate different senses in which it is used, account for the popularity of the doctrine of discretion. I

shall argue that in the sense in which the doctrine does have a bearing on our treatment of principles, it is entirely unsupported by the arguments the positivists use to defend it.

DISCRETION

The concept of discretion was lifted by the positivists from ordinary language, and to understand it we must put it back *in habitat* for a moment. What does it mean, in ordinary life, to say that someone "has discretion"? The first thing to notice is that the concept is out of place in all but very special contexts. For example, you would not say that I either do or do not have discretion to choose a house for my family. It is not true that I have "no discretion" in making that choice, and yet it would be almost equally misleading to say that I do have discretion. The concept of discretion is at home in only one sort of context: when someone is in general charged with making decisions subject to standards set by a particular authority. It makes sense to speak of the discretion of a sergeant who is subject to orders of superiors, or the discretion of a sports official or contest judge who is governed by a rule book or the terms of the contest. Discretion, like the hole in a doughnut, does not exist except as an area left open by a surrounding belt of restriction. It is therefore a relative concept. It always makes sense to ask, "Discretion under which standards?" or "Discretion as to which authority?" Generally the context will make the answer to this plain, but in some cases the official may have discretion from one standpoint though not from another.

Like almost all terms, the precise meaning of "discretion" is affected by features of the context. The term is always colored by the background of understood information against which it is used. Although the shadings are many, it will be helpful for us to recognize some gross distinctions.

Sometimes we use "discretion" in a weak sense, simply to say that for some reason the standards an official must apply cannot be applied mechanically but demand the use of judgment. We use this weak sense when the context does not already make that clear, when the background our audience assumes does not contain that piece of information. Thus we might say, "The sergeant's orders left him a great deal of discretion," to those who do not know what the sergeant's orders were or who do not know something that made those orders vague or hard to carry out. It would make perfect sense to add, by way of amplification, that the lieutenant had ordered the sergeant to take his five most experienced men on patrol but that it was hard to determine which were the most experienced.

Sometimes we use the term in a different weak sense, to say only that some official has final authority to make a decision and cannot be reviewed and reversed by any other official. We speak this way when the official is part of a hierarchy of officials structured so that some have higher authority but in which the patterns of authority are different for different classes of decision. Thus we might say that in baseball certain decisions, like the decision whether the ball or the runner reached second base first, are left to the discretion of the second base umpire, if we mean that on this issue the head umpire has no power to substitute his own judgment if he disagrees.

I call both of these senses weak to distinguish them from a stronger sense. We use "discretion" sometimes not merely to say that an official must use judgment in applying the standards set him by authority, or that no one will review that exercise of judgment, but to say that on some issue he is simply not bound by standards set by the authority in question. In this sense we say that a sergeant has discretion who has been told to pick any five men for patrol he chooses or that a judge in a dog show has discretion to judge airedales before boxers if the rules do not stipulate an order of events. We use this sense not to comment on the vagueness or difficulty of the standards, or on who has the final word in applying them, but on their range and the decisions they purport to control. If the sergeant is told to take the five most experienced men, he does not have discretion in this strong sense because that order purports to govern his decision. The boxing referee who must decide which fighter has been the more aggressive does not have discretion, in the strong sense, for the same reason.[21]

If anyone said that the sergeant or the referee had discretion in these cases, we should have to understand him, if the context permitted, as using the term in one of the weak senses. Suppose, for example, the lieutenant ordered the sergeant to select the five men he deemed most experienced, and then added that the sergeant had discretion to choose them. Or the rules provided that the referee should award the round to the more aggressive fighter, with discretion in selecting him. We should have to understand these statements in the second weak sense, as speaking to the ques-

tion of review of the decision. The first weak sense —that the decisions take judgment—would be otiose, and the third, strong sense is excluded by the statements themselves.

We must avoid one tempting confusion. The strong sense of discretion is not tantamount to license, and does not exclude criticism. Almost any situation in which a person acts (including those in which there is no question of decision under special authority, and so no question of discretion) makes relevant certain standards of rationality, fairness and effectiveness. We criticize each other's acts in terms of these standards, and there is no reason not to do so when the acts are within the center rather than beyond the perimeter of the doughnut of special authority. So we can say that the sergeant who was given discretion (in the strong sense) to pick a patrol did so stupidly or maliciously or carelessly, or that the judge who had discretion in the order of viewing dogs made a mistake because he took boxers first although there were only three airedales and many more boxers. An official's discretion means not that he is free to decide without recourse to standards of sense and fairness, but only that his decision is not controlled by a standard furnished by the particular authority we have in mind when we raise the question of discretion. Of course this latter sort of freedom is important; that is why we have the strong sense of discretion. Someone who has discretion in this third sense can be criticized, but not for being disobedient, as in the case of the soldier. He can be said to have made a mistake, but not to have deprived a participant of a decision to which he was entitled, as in the case of a sports official or contest judge.

We may now return, with these observations in hand, to the positivists' doctrine of judicial discretion. That doctrine argues that if a case is not controlled by an established rule, the judge must decide it by exercising discretion. We want to examine this doctrine and to test its bearing on our treatment of principles; but first we must ask in which sense of discretion we are to understand it.

Some nominalists argue that judges always have discretion, even when a clear rule is in point, because judges are ultimately the final arbiters of the law. This doctrine of discretion uses the second weak sense of that term, because it makes the point that no higher authority reviews the decisions of the highest court. It therefore has no bearing on the issue of how we account for principles, any more than it bears on how we account for rules.

The positivists do not mean their doctrine this way, because they say that a judge has no discretion when a clear and established rule is available. If we attend to the positivists' arguments for the doctrine, we may suspect that they use discretion in the first weak sense to mean only that judges must sometimes exercise judgment in applying legal standards. Their arguments call attention to the fact that some rules of law are vague (Professor Hart, for example, says that all rules of law have "open texture"), and that some cases arise (like *Henningsen*) in which no established rule seems to be suitable. They emphasize that judges must sometimes agonize over points of law, and that two equally trained and intelligent judges will often disagree.

These points are easily made; they are commonplace to anyone who has any familiarity with law. Indeed, that is the difficulty with assuming that positivists mean to use "discretion" in this weak sense. The proposition that, when no clear rule is available discretion in the sense of judgment must be used, is a tautology. It has no bearing, moreover, on the problem of how to account for legal principles. It is perfectly consistent to say that the judge in *Riggs,* for example, had to use judgment, and that he was bound to follow the principle that no man may profit from his own wrong. The positivists speak as if their doctrine of judicial discretion is an insight rather than a tautology, and as if it does have a bearing on the treatment of principles. Hart, for example, says that when the judge's discretion is in play, we can no longer speak of his being bound by standards, but must speak rather of what standards he "characteristically uses."[22] Hart thinks that when judges have discretion, the principles they cite must be treated on our second approach, as what courts "make it a principle" to do.

It therefore seems that positivists, at least sometimes, take their doctrine in the third, strong sense of discretion. In that sense it does bear on the treatment of principles; indeed, in that sense it is nothing less than a restatement of our second approach. It is the same thing to say that when a judge runs out of rules he has discretion, in the sense that he is not bound by any standards from the authority of law, as to say that the legal standards judges cite other than rules are not binding on them.

So we must examine the doctrine of judicial discretion in the strong sense. (I shall henceforth use the term "discretion" in that sense.) Do the principles judges cite in cases like *Riggs* or *Henningsen* control their decisions, as the sergeant's orders to take the most experienced men or the referee's duty to choose the more aggressive fighter control the decisions of these officials? What arguments could a positivist supply to show that they do not?

(1) A positivist might argue that principles cannot be binding or obligatory. That would be a mistake. It is always a question, of course, whether any particular principle is *in fact* binding upon some legal official. But there is nothing in the logical character of a principle that renders it incapable of binding him. Suppose that the judge in *Henningsen* had failed to take any account of the principle that automobile manufacturers have a special obligation to their consumers, or the principle that the courts seek to protect those whose bargaining position is weak, but had simply decided for the defendant by citing the principle of freedom of contract without more. His critics would not have been content to point out that he had not taken account of considerations that other judges have been attending to for some time. Most would have said that it was his duty to take the measure of these principles and that the plaintiff was entitled to have him do so. We mean no more, when we say that a *rule* is binding upon a judge, than that he must follow it if it applies, and that if he does not he will on that account have made a mistake.

It will not do to say that in a case like *Henningsen* the court is only "morally" obligated to take particular principles into account, or that it is "institutionally" obligated, or obligated as a matter of judicial "craft," or something of that sort. The question will still remain why this type of obligation (whatever we call it) is different from the obligation that rules impose upon judges, and why it entitles us to say that principles and policies are not part of the law but are merely extralegal standards "courts characteristically use."

(2) A positivist might argue that even though some principles are binding, in the sense that the judge must take them into account, they cannot determine a particular result. This is a harder argument to assess because it is not clear what it means for a standard to "determine" a result. Perhaps it means that the standard *dictates* the result whenever it applies so that nothing else counts. If so, then it is certainly true that individual principles do not determine results, but that

is only another way of saying that principles are not rules. Only rules dictate results, come what may. When a contrary result has been reached, the rule has been abandoned or changed. Principles do not work that way; they incline a decision one way, though not conclusively, and they survive intact when they do not prevail. This seems no reason for concluding that judges who must reckon with principles have discretion because a set of principles *can* dictate a result. If a judge believes that principles he is bound to recognize point in one direction and that principles pointing in the other direction, if any, are not of equal weight, then he must decide accordingly, just as he must follow what he believes to be a binding rule. He may, of course, be wrong in his assessment of the principles, but he may also be wrong in his judgment that the rule is binding. The sergeant and the referee, we might add, are often in the same boat. No one factor dictates which soldiers are the most experienced or which fighter the more aggressive. These officials must make judgments of the relative weights of these various factors; they do not on that account have discretion.

(3) A positivist might argue that principles cannot count as law because their authority, and even more so their weight, are congenitally *controversial.* It is true that generally we cannot *demonstrate* the authority or weight of a particular principle as we can sometimes demonstrate the validity of a rule by locating it in an act of Congress or in the opinion of an authoritative court. Instead, we make a case for a principle, and for its weight, by appealing to an amalgam of practice and other principles in which the implications of legislative and judicial history figure along with appeals to community practices and understandings. There is no litmus paper for testing the soundness of such a case—it is a matter of judgment, and reasonable men may disagree. But again this does not distinguish the judge from other officials who do not have discretion. The sergeant has no litmus paper for experience, the referee none for aggressiveness. Neither of these has discretion, because he is bound to reach an understanding, controversial or not, of what his orders or the rules require, and to act on that understanding. That is the judge's duty as well.

Of course, if the positivists are right in another of the doctrines—the theory that in each legal system there is an ultimate *test* for binding law like Professor Hart's rule of recognition—it follows that principles are not binding law. But the incompatibility of principles with the positivists' theory can hardly be taken as an argument that principles must be treated any particular way. That begs the question; we are interested in the status of principles because we want to evaluate the positivists' model. The positivist cannot defend his theory of a rule of recognition by fiat; if principles are not amenable to a test he must show some other reason why they cannot count as law. Since principles seem to play a role in arguments about legal obligation (witness, again *Riggs* and *Henningsen*), a model that provides for that role has some initial advantage over one that excludes it, and the latter cannot properly be inveighed in its own support.

These are the most obvious of the arguments a positivist might use for the doctrine of discretion in the strong sense, and for the second approach to principles. I shall mention one strong counterargument against that doctrine and in favor of the first approach. Unless at least some principles are acknowledged to be binding upon judges, requiring them as a set to reach particular decisions, then no rules, or very few rules, can be said to be binding upon them either.

In most American jurisdictions, and now in England also, the higher courts not infrequently reject established rules. Common law rules—those developed by earlier court decisions—are sometimes overruled directly, and sometimes radically altered by further development. Statutory rules are subjected to interpretation and reinterpretation, sometimes even when the result is not to carry out what is called the "legislative intent."[23] If courts had discretion to change established rules, then these rules would of course not be binding upon them, and so would not be law on the positivists' model. The positivist must therefore argue that there are standards, themselves binding upon judges, that determine when a judge may overrule or alter an established rule, and when he may not.

When, then, is a judge permitted to change an existing rule of law? Principles figure in the answer in two ways. First, it is necessary, though not sufficient, that the judge find that the change would advance some policy or serve some principle, which policy or principle thus justifies the change. In *Riggs* the change (a new interpretation of the statute of wills) was justified by the principle that no man should profit from his own wrong; in *Henningsen* certain rules about automobile manufacturer's liability were altered on the basis of the principles and policies I quoted from the opinion of the court.

But not any principle will do to justify a change, or no rule would ever be safe. There must be some principles that count and others that do not, and there must be some principles that count for more than others. It could not depend on the judge's own preferences amongst a sea of respectable extralegal standards, any one in principle eligible, because if that were the case we could not say that any rules were binding. We could always imagine a judge whose preferences amongst extralegal standards were such as would justify a shift or radical reinterpretation of even the most entrenched rule.

Second, any judge who proposes to change existing doctrine must take account of some important standards that argue against departures from established doctrine, and these standards are also for the most part principles. They include the doctrine of "legislative supremacy," a set of principles and policies that require the courts to pay a qualified deference to the acts of the legislature. They also include the doctrine of precedent, another set of principles and policies reflecting the equities and efficiencies of consistency. The doctrines of legislative supremacy and precedent incline toward the *status quo,* each within its sphere, but they do not command it. Judges are not free, however, to pick and choose amongst the principles and policies that make up these doctrines—if they were, again, no rule could be said to be binding.

Consider, therefore, what someone implies who says that a particular rule is binding. He may imply that the rule is affirmatively supported by principles the court is not free to disregard, and which are collectively more weighty than other principles that argue for a change. If not, he implies that any change would be condemned by a combination of conservative principles of legislative supremacy and precedent that the court is not free to ignore. Very often, he will imply both, for the conservative principles, being principles and not rules, are usually not powerful enough to save a common law rule or an aging statute that is entirely unsupported by substantive principles the court is bound to respect. Either of these implications, of course, treats a body of principles and policies as law in the sense that rules are; it treats them as standards binding upon the officials of a community, controlling their decisions of legal right and obligation.

We are left with this issue. If the positivists' theory of judicial discretion is either trivial because it uses "discretion" in a weak sense, or

unsupported because the various arguments we can supply in its defense fall short, why have so many careful and intelligent lawyers embraced it? We can have no confidence in our treatment of that theory unless we can deal with that question. It is not enough to note (although perhaps it contributes to the explanation) that "discretion" has different senses that may be confused. We do not confuse these senses when we are not thinking about law.

Part of the explanation, at least, lies in a lawyer's natural tendency to associate laws and rules, and to think of "the law" as a collection or system of rules. Roscoe Pound, who diagnosed this tendency long ago, thought that English-speaking lawyers were tricked into it by the fact that English uses the same word, changing only the article, for "a law" and "the law."[24] (Other languages, on the contrary, use two words: "loi" and "droit," for example, and "Gesetz" and "Recht.") This may have had its effect, with the English speaking positivists, because the expression "a law" certainly does suggest a rule. But the principal reason for associating law with rules runs deeper, and lies, I think, in the fact that legal education has for a long time consisted of teaching and examining those established rules that form the cutting edge of law.

In any event, if a lawyer thinks of law as a system of rules, and yet recognizes, as he must, that judges change old rules and introduce new ones, he will come naturally to the theory of judicial discretion in the strong sense. In those other systems of rules with which he has experience (like games), the rules are the only special authority that govern official decisions, so that if an umpire could change a rule, he would have discretion as to the subject matter of that rule. Any principles umpires might mention when changing the rules would represent only their "characteristic" preferences. Positivists treat law like baseball revised in this way.

There is another, more subtle consequence of this initial assumption that law is a system of rules. When the positivists do attend to principles and policies, they treat them as rules *manque.* They assume that *if* they are standards of law they must be rules, and so they read them as standards that are trying to be rules. When a positivist hears someone argue that legal principles are part of the law, he understands this to be an argument for what he calls the "higher law" theory, that these principles are the rules of a law above the law.[25] He refutes this theory by pointing out that these "rules" are sometimes followed and sometimes not, that for every "rule" like "no man shall profit from his own wrong" there is another competing "rule" like "the law favors security of title," and that there is no way to test the validity of "rules" like these. He concludes that these principles and policies are not valid rules of a law above the law, which is true, because they are not rules at all. He also concludes that they are extralegal standards which each judge selects according to his own lights in the exercise of his discretion, which is false. It is as if a zoologist had proved that fish are not mammals, and then concluded that they are really only plants.

THE RULE OF RECOGNITION

This discussion was provoked by our two competing accounts of legal principles. We have been exploring the second account, which the positivists seem to adopt through their doctrine of judicial discretion, and we have discovered grave difficulties. It is time to return to the fork in the road. What if we adopt the first approach? What would the consequences of this be for the skeletal structure of positivism? Of course we should have to drop the second tenet, the doctrine of judicial discretion (or, in the alternative, to make plain that the doctrine is to be read merely to say that judges must often exercise judgment). Would we also have to abandon or modify the first tenet, the proposition that law is distinguished by tests of the sort that can be set out in a master rule like Professor Hart's rule of recognition? If principles of the *Riggs* and *Henningsen* sort are to count as law, and we are nevertheless to preserve the notion of a master rule for law, then we must be able to deploy some test that all (and only) the principles that do count as law meet. Let us begin with the test Hart suggests for identifying valid *rules* of law, to see whether these can be made to work for principles as well.

Most rules of law, according to Hart, are valid because some competent institution enacted them. Some were created by a legislature, in the form of statutory enactments. Others were created by judges who formulated them to decide particular cases, and thus established them as precedents for the future. But this test of pedigree will not work for the *Riggs* and *Henningsen* principles. The origin of these as legal principles lies not in a particular decision of some legislature or court, but in a sense of appropriateness developed in the profession and the public over time. Their continued power depends upon this sense of appropriateness being sustained. If it no longer seemed unfair to allow people to profit by their wrongs, or fair to place special burdens upon oligopolies that manufacture potentially dangerous machines, these principles would no longer play much of a role in new cases, even if they had never been overruled or repealed. (Indeed, it hardly makes sense to speak of principles like these as being "overruled" or "repealed." When they decline they are eroded, not torpedoed.)

True, if we were challenged to back up our claim that some principle is a principle of law, we would mention any prior cases in which that principle was cited, or figured in the argument. We would also mention any statute that seemed to exemplify that principle (even better if the principle was cited in the preamble of the statute, or in the committee reports or other legislative documents that accompanied it). Unless we could find some such institutional support, we would probably fail to make out our case, and the more support we found, the more weight we could claim for the principle.

Yet we could not devise any formula for testing how much and what kind of institutional support is necessary to make a principle a legal principle, still less to fix its weight at a particular order of magnitude. We argue for a particular principle by grappling with a whole set of shifting, developing and interacting standards (themselves principles rather than rules) about institutional responsibility, statutory interpretation, the persuasive force of various sorts of precedent, the relation of all these to contemporary moral practices, and hosts of other such standards. We could not bolt all of these together into a single "rule," even a complex one, and if we could the result would bear little relation to Hart's picture of a rule of recognition, which is the picture of a fairly stable master rule specifying "some feature or features possession of which by a suggested rule is taken as a conclusive affirmative indicating that it is a rule. . . ."[26]

Moreover, the techniques we apply in arguing for another principle do not stand (as Hart's rule of recognition is designed to) on an entirely different level from the principles they support. Hart's sharp distinction between acceptance and validity does not hold. If we are arguing for the principle that a man should not profit from his own wrong, we could cite the acts of courts and legislatures that exemplify it, but this speaks as much to the principle's acceptance as its validity. (It seems odd to speak of a principle as being valid at all, perhaps because validity is an all-or-nothing concept, appropriate for rules, but inconsistent with a principle's dimension of weight.) If we are asked (as we might well be) to defend the particular doctrine of precedent, or the particular technique of statutory interpretation, that we used in this argument, we should certainly cite the practice of others in using that doctrine or technique. But we should also cite other general principles that we believe support that practice, and this introduces a note of validity into the chord of acceptance. We might argue, for example, that the use we make of earlier cases and statutes is supported by a particular analysis of the point of practice of legislation or the doctrine of precedent, or by the principles of democratic theory, or by a particular position on the proper division of authority between national and local institutions, or something else of that sort. Nor is this path of support a one-way street leading to some ultimate principle resting on acceptance alone. Our principles of legislation, precedent, democracy, or federalism might be challenged too; and if they were we should argue for them, not only in terms of practice, but in terms of each other and in terms of the implications of trends of judicial and legislative decisions, even though this last would involve appealing to those same doctrines of interpretation we justified through the principles we are now trying to support. At this level of abstraction, in other words, principles rather hang together than link together.

So even though principles draw support from the official acts of legal institutions, they do not have a simple or direct enough connection with these acts to frame that connection in terms of criteria specified by some ultimate master rule of recognition. Is there any other route by which principles might be brought under such a rule?

Hart does say that a master rule might designate as law not only rules enacted by particular legal institutions, but rules established by *custom* as well. He has in mind a problem that bothered other positivists, including Austin. Many of our most ancient legal rules were never explicitly created by a legislature or a court. When they made their first appearance in legal opinions and texts, they were treated as already being part of the law because they represented the customary practice of the community, or some specialized part of it, like the business community. (The examples ordinarily given are rules of mercantile practice, like the rules governing what rights arise under a standard form of commercial paper.)[27] Since Austin thought that all law was the command of a determinate sovereign, he held that

these customary practices were not law until the courts (as agents of the sovereign) recognized them, and that the courts were indulging in a fiction in pretending otherwise. But that seemed arbitrary. If everyone thought custom might in itself be law, the fact that Austin's theory said otherwise was not persuasive.

Hart reversed Austin on this point. The master rule, he says, might stipulate that some custom counts as law even before the courts recognize it. But he does not face the difficulty this raises for this general theory, because he does not attempt to set out the criteria a master rule might use for this purpose. It cannot use, as its only criterion, the provision that the community regard the practice as *morally* binding, for this would not distinguish legal customary rules from moral customary rules, and of course not all of the community's long-standing customary moral obligations are enforced at law. If, on the other hand, the test is whether the community regards the customary practice as *legally* binding, the whole point of the master rule is undercut, at least for this class of legal rules. The master rule, says Hart, marks the transformation from a primitive society to one with law, because it provides a test for determining social rules of law other than by measuring their acceptance. But if the master rule says merely that whatever other rules the community accepts as legally binding are legally binding, then it provides no such test at all, beyond the test we should use were there no master rule. The master rule becomes (for these cases) a nonrule of recognition; we might as well say that every primitive society has a secondary rule of recognition, namely the rule that whatever is accepted as binding is binding. Hart himself, in discussing international law, ridicules the idea that such a rule could be a rule of recognition, by describing the proposed rule as "an empty repetition of the mere fact that the society concerned . . . observes certain standards of conduct as obligatory rules."[28]

Hart's treatment of custom amounts, indeed, to a confession that there are at least some rules of law that are not binding because they are valid under standards laid down by a master rule but are binding—like the master rule—because they are accepted as binding by the community. This chips at the neat pyramidal architecture we admired in Hart's theory: we can no longer say that only the master rule is binding because of its acceptance, all other rules being valid under its terms.

This is perhaps only a chip, because the customary rules Hart has in mind are no longer a very significant part of the law. But it does suggest that Hart would be reluctant to widen the damage by bringing under the head of "custom" all those crucial principles and policies we have been discussing. If he were to call these part of the law and yet admit that the only test of their force lies in the degree to which they are accepted as law by the community or some part thereof, he would very sharply reduce that area of the law over which his master rule held any dominion. It is not just that all the principles and policies would escape its sway, though that would be bad enough. Once these principles and policies are accepted as law, and thus as standards judges must follow in determining legal obligations, it would follow that *rules* like those announced for the first time in *Riggs* and *Henningsen* owe their force at least in part to the authority of principles and policies, and so not entirely to the master rule of recognition.

So we cannot adapt Hart's version of positivism by modifying his rule of recognition to embrace principles. No tests of pedigree, relating principles to acts of legislation, can be formulated, nor can his concept of customary law, itself an exception to the first tenet of positivism, be made to serve without abandoning that tenet altogether. One more possibility must be considered, however. If no rule of recognition can provide a test for identifying principles, why not say that principles are ultimate, and *form* the rule of recognition of our law? The answer to the general question "What is valid law in an American jurisdiction?" would then require us to state all the principles (as well as ultimate constitutional rules) in force in that jurisdiction at the time, together with appropriate assignments of weight. A positivist might then regard the complete set of these standards as the rule of recognition of the jurisdiction. This solution has the attraction of paradox, but of course it is an unconditional surrender. If we simply designate our rule of recognition by the phrase "the complete set of principles in force," we achieve only the tautology that law is law. If, instead, we tried actually to list all the principles in force we would fail. They are controversial, their weight is all important, they are numberless, and they shift and change so fast that the start of our list would be obsolete before we reached the middle. Even if we succeeded, we would not have a key for law because there would be nothing left for our key to unlock.

I conclude that if we treat principles as law we must reject the positivists' first tenet, that the law of a community is distinguished from other social standards by some test in the form of a master rule. We have already decided that we must then abandon the second tenet—the doctrine of judicial discretion—or clarify it into triviality. What of the third tenet, the positivists' theory of legal obligation?

This theory holds that a legal obligation exists when (and only when) an established rule of law imposes such an obligation. It follows from this that in a hard case—when no such established rule can be found—there is no legal obligation until the judge creates a new rule for the future. The judge may apply that new rule to the parties in the case, but this is *ex post facto* legislation, not the enforcement of an existing obligation.

The positivists' doctrine of discretion (in the strong sense) required this view of legal obligation, because if a judge has discretion there can be no legal right or obligation—no entitlement—that he must enforce. Once we abandon that doctrine, however, and treat principles as law, we raise the possibility that a legal obligation might be imposed by a constellation of principles as well as by an established rule. We might want to say that a legal obligation exists whenever the case supporting such an obligation, in terms of binding legal principles of different sorts, is stronger than the case against it.

Of course, many questions would have to be answered before we could accept that view of legal obligation. If there is no rule of recognition, no test for law in that sense, how do we decide which principles are to count, and how much, in making such a case? How do we decide whether one case is better than another? If legal obligation rests on an undemonstrable judgment of that sort, how can it provide a justification for a judicial decision that one party had a legal obligation? Does this view of obligation square with the way lawyers, judges and laymen speak, and is it consistent with our attitudes about moral obligation? Does this analysis help us to deal with the classical jurisprudential puzzles about the nature of law?

These questions must be faced, but even the questions promise more than positivism provides. Positivism, on its own thesis, stops short of just those puzzling, hard cases that send us to look for theories of law. When we reach these cases, the positivist remits us to a doctrine of discretion that leads nowhere and tells nothing. His picture of law as a system of rules has exercised a tenacious hold on our imagination, perhaps through its very simplicity. If we shake ourselves loose from this model of rules, we may be able to build a model truer to the complexity and sophistication of our own practices.

NOTES

1. *See* Linkletter v. Walker, 381 U.S. 618 (1965).
2. J. Austin, The Province of Jurisprudence Determined (1832).
3. *See* H. L. A. Hart, The Concept of Law 89–96 (1961).
4. *Id.* at 79–88.
5. *Id.* at 97–107.
6. *Id. passim,* particularly ch. VI.
7. *Id.* ch. VII.
8. *See* Dworkin, *Wasserstrom: The Judicial Decision,* 75 Ethics 47 (1964), reprinted as *Does Law Have a Function?,* 74 Yale L. J. 640 (1965).
9. 115 N.Y. 506, 22 N.E. 188 *1889).
10. *Id.* at 509, 22 N.E. at 189.
11. *Id.* at 511, 22 N.E. at 190.
12. 32 N.J. 358, 161 A.2d 69 (1960).
13. *Id.* at 386, 161 A.2d at 84.
14. *Id.*
15. *Id.* at 388, 161 A.2d at 86.
16. *Id.* at 387, 161 A.2d at 85.
17. *Id.* at 389, 161 A.2d at 86 (quoting Frankfurter, J., in United States v. Bethlehem Steel, 315 U.S. 289, 326 (1942).
18. *Id.*
19. Standard Oil v. United States, 221 U.S. 1, 60 (1911); United States v. American Tobacco Co., 221 U.S. 106, 180 (1911).
20. The distinction is in substance the same as that made by Rawls, *Two Concepts of Rules,* 64 Philosophical Rev. 3 (1955).
21. I have not spoken of that jurisprudential favorite, "limited" discretion, because that concept presents no special difficulties if we remember the relativity of discretion. Suppose the sergeant is told to choose from "amongst" experienced men, or to "take experience into account." We might say either that he has (limited) discretion in picking his patrol, or (full) discretion to either pick amongst experienced men or decide what else to take into account.
22. H. L. A. Hart, The Concept of Law 144 (1961).
23. *See* Wellington & Albert, *Statutory Interpretation and the Political Process: A Comment on Sinclair v. Atkinson,* 72 Yale L. J. 1547 (1963).
24. R. Pound, An Introduction to the Philosophy of Law 56 (rev. ed. 1954).
25. *See, e.g.,* Dickinson, *The Law Behind Law* (pts. 1 & 2), 29 Colum. L. Rev. 112, 254 (1929).
26. H. L. A. Hart, The Concept of Law 92 (1961).
27. *See* Note, *Custom and Trade Usage: Its Application to Commercial Dealings and the Common Law,* 55 Colum. L. Rev. 1192 (1955), and materials cited therein at 1193 n.1. As that note makes plain, the actual practices of courts in recognizing trade customs follow the pattern of applying a set of general principles and policies rather than a test that could be captured as part of a rule of recognition.
28. H. L. A. Hart, The Concept of Law 230 (1961).

RIGGS v. PALMER

Court of Appeals of New York, 1889*

RIGHTS OF LEGATEES—MURDER OF TESTATOR

The law of New York relating to the probate of wills and the distributions of estates will not be construed so as to secure the benefit of a will to a legatee who has killed the testator in order to prevent a revocation of the will. GRAY and DANFORTH, JJ., dissenting.

Appeal from supreme court, general term, third department.

Leslie W. Russell, for appellants. *W. M. Hawkins*, for respondents.

EARL, J. On the 13th day of August 1880, Francis B. Palmer made his last will and testament, in which he gave small legacies to his two daughters, Mrs. Riggs and Mrs. Preston, the plaintiffs in this action, and the remainder of his estate to his grandson, the defendant Elmer E. Palmer, subject to the support of Susan Palmer, his mother, with a gift over to the two daughters, subject to the support of Mrs. Palmer in case Elmer should survive him and die under age, unmarried, and without any issue. The testator, at the date of his will, owned a farm, and considerable personal property. He was a widower, and thereafter, in March, 1882, he was married to Mrs. Bresee, with whom, before his marriage, he entered into an ante-nuptial contract, in which it was agreed that in lieu of dower and all other claims upon his estate in case she survived him she should have her support upon his farm during her life, and such support was expressly charged upon the farm. At the date of the will, and subsequently to the death of the testator, Elmer lived with him as a member of his family, and at his death was 16 years old. He knew of the provisions made in his favor in the will, and, that he might prevent his grandfather from revoking such provisions, which he had manifested some intention to do, and to obtain the speedy enjoyment and immediate possession of his property, he willfully murdered him by poisoning him. He now claims the property, and the sole question for our determination is, can he have it?

The defendants say that the testator is dead; that his will was made in due form, and has been admitted to probate; and that therefore it must have effect according to the letter of the law. It is quite true that statutes regulating the making, proof, and effect of wills and the devolution of property, if literally construed, and if their force and effect can in no way and under no circumstances be controlled or modified, give this property to the murderer. The purpose of those statutes was to enable testators to dispose of their estates to the objects of their bounty at death, and to carry into effect their final wishes legally expressed; and in considering and giving effect to them this purpose must be kept in view. It was the intention of the law-makers that the donees in a will should have the property given to them. But it never could have been their intention that a donee who murdered the testator to make the will operative should have any benefit under it. If such a case had been present to their minds, and it had been supposed necessary to make some provision of law to meet it, it cannot be doubted that they would have provided for it. It is a familiar canon of construction that a thing which is within the intention of the makers of a statute is as much within the statute as if it were within the letter; and a thing which is within the letter of the statute is not within the statute unless it be within the intention of the makers. The writers of laws do not always express their intention perfectly, but either exceed it or fall short of it, so that judges are to collect it from probable or rational conjectures only, and this is called "rational interpretation;" and Rutherford, in his Institutes, (page 420) says: "Where we make use of rational interpretation, sometimes we restrain the meaning of the writer so as to take in less, and sometimes we extend or enlarge his meaning so as to take in more, than his words express." Such a construction ought to be put upon a statute as will best answer the intention which the makers had in view, for *qui hæret in litera, hæret in cortice*. In Bac. Abr. "Statutes," 1, 5; Puff. Law Nat. bk. 5, c. 12; Ruth. Inst. 422, 427, and in Smith's Commentaries, 814, many cases are mentioned where it was held that matters embraced in the general words of statutes nevertheless were not within the statutes, because it could not have been the intention of the law-makers that they should be included.

*22 N.E. 188 (1889).

They were taken out of the statutes by an equitable construction; and it is said in Bacon: "By an equitable construction a case not within the letter of a statute is sometimes holden to be within the meaning, because it is within the mischief for which a remedy is provided. The reason for such construction is that the law-makers could not set down every case in express terms. In order to form a right judgment whether a case be within the equity of a statute, it is a good way to suppose the law-maker present, and that you have asked him this question: Did you intend to comprehend this case? Then you must give yourself such answer as you imagine he, being an upright and reasonable man, would have given. If this be that he did mean to comprehend it, you may safely hold the case to be within the equity of the statute; for while you do no more than he would have done, you do not act contrary to the statute, but in conformity thereto." 9 Bac. Abr. 248. In some cases the letter of a legislative act is restrained by an equitable construction; in others, it is enlarged; in others, the construction is contrary to the letter. The equitable construction which restrains the letter of a statute is defined by Aristotle as frequently quoted in this manner: *Æquitas est correctio legis generaliter latæ qua parte deficit.* If the law-makers could, as to this case, be consulted, would they say that they intended by their general language that the property of a testator or of an ancestor should pass to one who had taken his life for the express purpose of getting his property? In 1 Bl. Comm. 91, the learned author, speaking of the construction of statutes, says: "If there arise out of them collaterally any absurd consequences manifestly contradictory to common reason, they are with regard to those collateral consequences void. * * * Where some collateral matter arises out of the general words, and happens to be unreasonable, there the judges are in decency to conclude that this consequence was not foreseen by the parliament, and therefore they are at liberty to expound the statute by equity, and only *quoad hoc* disregard it;" and he gives as an illustration, if an act of parliament gives a man power to try all causes that arise within his manor of Dale, yet, if a cause should arise in which he himself is party, the act is construed not to extend to that, because it is unreasonable that any man should determine his own quarrel. There was a statute in Bologna that whoever drew blood in the streets should be severely punished, and yet it was held not to apply to the case of a barber who opened a vein in the street. It is commanded in the decalogue that no work shall be done upon the Sabbath, and yet giving the command a rational interpretation founded upon its design the Infallible Judge

held that it did not prohibit works of necessity, charity, or benevolence on that day.

What could be more unreasonable than to suppose that it was the legislative intention in the general laws passed for the orderly peaceable, and just devolution of property that they should have operation in favor of one who murdered his ancestor that he might speedily come into the possession of his estate? Such an intention is inconceivable. We need not, therefore, be much troubled by the general language contained in the laws. Besides, all laws, as well as all contracts, may be controlled in their operation and effect by general, fundamental maxims of the common law. No one shall be permitted to profit by his own fraud, or to take advantage of his own wrong, or to found any claim upon his own iniquity, or to acquire property by his own crime. These maxims are dictated by public policy, have their foundation in universal law administered in all civilized countries, and have nowhere been superseded by statutes. They were applied in the decision of the case of Insurance Co. v. Armstrong, 117 U. S. 599, 6 Sup. Ct. Rep. 877. There it was held that the person who procured a policy upon the life of another, payable at his death, and then murdered the assured to make the policy payable, could not recover thereon, Mr. Justice FIELD, writing the opinion, said: "Independently of any proof of the motives of Hunter in obtaining the policy, and even assuming that they were just and proper, he forfeited all rights under it when, to secure its immediate payment, he murdered the assured. It would be a reproach to the jurisprudence of the country if one could recover insurance money payable on the death of a party whose life he had feloniously taken. As well might he recover insurance money upon a building that he had willfully fired." These maxims, without any statute giving them force or operation, frequently control the effect and nullify the language of wills. A will procured by fraud and deception, like any other instrument, may be decreed void, and set aside; and so a particular portion of a will may be excluded from probate, or held inoperative, if induced by the fraud or undue influence of the person in whose favor it is. Allen v. McPherson, 1 H. L. Cas. 191; Harrison's Appeal, 48 Conn. 202. So a will may contain provisions which are immoral, irreligious, or against public policy, and they will be held void.

Here there was no certainty that this murderer would survive the testator, or that the testator would not change his will, and there was no certainty that he would get this property if nature was allowed to take its course. He therefore murdered the testator expressly to vest himself with an estate. Under such circumstances, what law, human or divine, will allow him to take the estate and enjoy the fruits of his crime? The will spoke and became operative at the death of the testator. He caused that death, and thus by his crime made it speak and have operation. Shall it speak and operate in his favor? If he had met the testator, and taken his property by force, he would have had no title to it. Shall he acquire title by murdering him? If he had gone to the testator's house, and by force compelled him, or by fraud or undue influence had induced him, to will him his property, the law would not allow him to hold it. But can he give effect and operation to a will by murder, and yet take the property? To answer these questions in the affirmative it seems to me would be a reproach to the jurisprudence of our state, and an offense against public policy. Under the civil law, evolved from the general principles of natural law and justice by many generations of jurisconsults, philosophers, and statesmen, one cannot take property by inheritance or will from an ancestor or benefactor whom he has murdered. Dom. Civil Law, pt. 2, bk. 1, tit. 1, § 3; Code Nap. § 727; Mack. Rom. Law, 530, 550. In the Civil Code of Lower Canada the provisions on the subject in the Code Napoleon have been substantially copied. But, so far as I can find, in no country where the common law prevails has it been deemed important to enact a law to provide for such a case. Our revisers and law-makers were familiar with the civil law, and they did not deem it important to incorporate into our statutes it provisions upon this subject. This is not a *casus omissus*. It was evidently supposed that the maxims of the common law were sufficient to regulate such a case, and that a specific enactment for that purpose was not needed. For the same reasons the defendant Palmer cannot take any of this property as heir. Just before the murder he was not an heir, and it was not certain that he ever would be. He might have died before his grandfather, or might have been disinherited by him. He made himself an heir by the murder, and he seeks to take property as the fruit of his crime. What has before been said as to him as legatee applies to him with equal force as an heir. He cannot vest himself with title by crime. My view of this case does not inflict upon Elmer any greater or other punishment for his crime than the law specifies. It takes from him no property, but simply holds that he shall not acquire property by his crime, and thus be rewarded for its commission.

Our attention is called to Owens v. Owens, 100 N. C. 240, 6 S. E. Rep. 794, as a case quite like this. There a wife had been convicted of being an accessory before the fact to the murder of her husband, and it was held that she was nevertheless entitled to dower. I am unwilling to assent to the doctrine of that

case. The statutes provide dower for a wife who has the misfortune to survive her husband, and thus lose his support and protection. It is clear beyond their purpose to make provision for a wife who by her own crime makes herself a widow, and willfully and intentionally deprives herself of the support and protection of her husband. As she might have died before him, and thus never have been his widow, she cannot by her crime vest herself with an estate. The principle which lies at the bottom of the maxim *volenti non fit injuria* should be applied to such a case, and a widow should not, for the purpose of acquiring, as such, property rights, be permitted to allege a widowhood which she has wickedly and intentionally created.

The facts found entitled the plaintiffs to the relief they seek. The error of the referee was in his conclusion of law. Instead of granting a new trial, therefore, I think the proper judgment upon the facts found should be ordered here. The facts have been passed upon twice with the same result,—first upon the trial of Palmer for murder, and then by the referee in this action. We are therefore of opinion that the ends of justice do not require that they should again come in question. The judgment of the general term and that entered upon the report of the referee should therefore be reversed, and judgment should be entered as follows: That Elmer E. Palmer and the administrator be enjoined from using any of the personalty or real estate left by the testator for Elmer's benefit; that the devise and bequest in the will to Elmer be declared ineffective to pass the title to him; that by reason of the crime of murder committed upon the grandfather he is deprived of any interest in the estate left by him; that the plaintiffs are the true owners of the real and personal estate left by the testator, subject to the charge in favor of Elmer's mother and the widow of the testator, under the antenuptial agreement, and that the plaintiffs have costs in all the courts against Elmer. All concur, except GRAY, J., who reads dissenting opinion, and DANFORTH, J., concurs.

GRAY, J., (*dissenting.*) This appeal represents an extraordinary state of facts, and the case, in respect to them, I believe, is without precedent in this state. The respondent, a lad of 16 years of age, being aware of the provisions in his grandfather's will, which constituted him the residuary legatee of the testator's estate, caused his death by poison, in 1882. For this crime he was tried, and was convicted of murder in the second degree, and at the time of the commencement of this action he was serving out his sentence in the state reformatory. This action was brought by two of the children of the testator for the purpose of having those provisions of the will in the respondent's favor canceled and annulled. The apellants' argument for a reversal of the judgment, which dismissed their complaint, is that the respondent unlawfully prevented a revocation of the existing will, or a new will from being made, by his crime; and that he terminated the enjoyment by the testator of his property, and effected his own succession to it, by the same crime. They say that to permit the respondent to take the property willed to him would be to permit him to take advantage of his own wrong. To sustain their position the appellants' counsel has submitted an able and elaborate brief, and, if I believed that the decision of the question could be effected by considerations of an equitable nature, I should not hesitate to assent to views which commend themselves to the conscience. But the matter does not lie within the domain of conscience. We are bound by the rigid rules of law, which have been established by the legislature, and within the limits of which the determination of this question is confined. The question we are dealing with is whether a testamentary disposition can be altered, or a will revoked, after the testator's death, through an appeal to the courts, when the legislature has by its enactments prescribed exactly when and how wills may be made, altered, and revoked, and apparently, as it seems to me, when they have been fully complied with, has left no room for the exercise of an equitable jurisdiction by courts over such matters. Modern jurisprudence, in recognizing the right of the individual, under more or less restrictions, to dispose of his property after his death, subjects it to legislative control, both as to extent and as to mode of exercise. Complete freedom of testamentary disposition of one's property has not been and is not the universal rule, as we see from the provisions of the Napoleonic Code, from the systems of jurisprudence in countries which are modeled upon the Roman law, and from the statutes of many of our states. To the statutory restraints which are imposed upon the disposition of one's property by will are added strict and systematic statutory rules for the execution, alteration, and revocation of the will, which must be, at least substantially, if not exactly, followed to insure validity and performance. The reason for the establishment of such rules, we may naturally assume, consists in the purpose to create those safeguards about these grave and important acts which experience has demonstrated to be the wisest and surest. That freedom which is permitted to be exercised in the testamentary disposition of one's estate by the laws of the state is subject to its being exercised in conformity with the regulations of the statutes. The capacity and the power of the individual to dispose of his property after death, and the mode by which that power can be exercised, are matters of which the legislature has assumed the entire control, and has undertaken to regulate with comprehensive particularity.

The appellants' argument is not helped by reference to those rules of the civil law, or to those laws of other governments, by which the heir, or legatee, is excluded from benefit under the testament if he has been convicted of killing, or attempting to kill, the testator. In the absence of such legislation here, the courts are not empowered to institute such a system of remedial justice. The deprivation of the heir of his testamentary succession by the Roman law, when guilty of such a crime, plainly was intended to be in the nature of a punishment imposed upon him. The succession, in such a case of guilt, escheated to the exchequer. See Dom. Civil Law, pt. 2, bk.1, tit.1, § 3. I concede that rules of law which annul testamentary provisions made for the benefit of those who have become unworthy of them may be based on principles of equity and of natural justice. It is quite reasonable to suppose that a testator would revoke or alter his will, where his mind has been so angered and changed as to make him unwilling to have his will executed as it stood. But these principles only suggest sufficient reasons for the enactment of laws to meet such cases.

The statutes of this state have prescribed various ways in which a will may be altered or revoked; but the very provision defining the modes of alteration and revocation implies a prohibition of alteration or revocation in any other way. The words of the section of the statute are: "No will in writing, except in the cases hereinafter mentioned, nor any part thereof, shall be revoked or altered otherwise," etc. Where, therefore, none of the cases mentioned are met by the facts, and the revocation is not in the way described in the section, the will of the testator is unalterable. I think that a valid will must continue as a will always, unless revoked in the manner provided by the statutes. Mere intention to revoke a will does not have the effect of revocation. The intention to revoke is necessary to constitute the effective revocation of a will, but it must be demonstrated by one of the acts contemplated by the statute. As WOODWORTH, J., said in Dan v. Brown, 4 Cow. 490; "Revocation is an act of the mind, which must be demonstrated by some outward and visible sign of revocation." The same learned judge said in that case: "The rule is that if the testator lets the will stand until he dies, it is his will; if he does not suffer it to do so, it is not his will." And see Goodright v. Glazier, 4 Burrows, 2512, 2514; Pemberton v. Pemberton, 13 Ves. 290. The finding of fact of the referee that presumably the testator would have altered his will had he known of his grandson's murderous intent cannot affect the question. We may concede it to the fullest extent; but still the cardinal objection is undisposed of,—that the making and the revocation of a will are purely matters of statutory regulation, by which the court is bound in the determination of questions relating to these acts.

Two cases,—in this state and in Kentucky,—at an early day, seem to me to be much in point. Gains v. Gains, 2 A. K. Marsh. 190, was decided by the Kentucky court of appeals in 1820. It was there urged that the testator intended to have destroyed his will, and that he was forcibly prevented from doing so by the defendant in error or devisee; and it was insisted that the will, though not expressly, was thereby virtually, revoked. The court held, as the act concerning wills prescribed the manner in which a will might be revoked, that, as none of the acts evidencing revocation were done, the intention could not be substituted for the act. In that case the will was snatched away, and forcibly retained. In 1854, Surrogate BRADFORD, whose opinions are entitled to the highest consideration, decided the case of Leaycraft v. Simmons, 3 Bradf. Sur. 35. In that case the testator, a man of 89 years of age, desired to make a codicil to his will, in order to enlarge the provisions for his daughter. His son, having the custody of the instrument, and the one to be prejudiced by the change, refused to produce the will at testator's request, for the purpose of alteration. The learned surrogate refers to the provisions of the civil law for such and other cases of unworthy conduct in the heir or legatee, and says: "Our statute has undertaken to prescribe the mode in which wills can be revoked [citing the statutory provision.] This is the law by which I am governed in passing upon questions touching the revocation of wills. The whole of this subject is now regulated by statute; and a mere intention to revoke, however well authenticated, or however defeated, is not sufficient." And he held that the will must be admitted to probate. I may refer also to a case in the Pennsylvania courts. In that state the statute prescribed the mode for repealing or altering a will, and in Clingan v. Micheltree, 31 Pa. St. 25, the supreme court of the state held, where a will was kept from destruction by the fraud and misrepresentation of the devisee, that

to declare it canceled as against the fraudulent party would be to enlarge the statute.

I cannot find any support for the argument that the respondent's succession to the property should be avoided because of his criminal act, when the laws are silent. Public policy does not demand it; for the demands of public policy are satisfied by the proper execution of the laws and the punishment of the crime. There has been no convention between the testator and his legatee; nor is there any such contractual element, in such a disposition of property by a testator, as to impose or imply conditions in the legatee. The appellants' argument practically amounts to this: that, as the legatee has been guilty of a crime, by the commission of which he is placed in a position to sooner receive the benefits of the testamentary provision, his rights to the property should be forfeited, and he should be divested of his estate. To allow their argument to prevail would involve the diversion by the court of the testator's estate into the hands of persons whom, possibly enough, for all we know, the testator might not have chosen or desired as its recipients. Practically the court is asked to make another will for the testator. The laws do not warrant this judicial action, and mere presumption would not be strong enough to sustain it. But, more than this, to concede the appellants' views would involve the imposition of an additional punishment or penalty upon the respondent. What power or warrant have the courts to add to the respondent's penalties by depriving him of property? The law has punished him for his crime, and we may not say that it was an insufficient punishment. In the trial and punishment of the respondent the law has vindicated itself for the outrage which he committed, and further judicial utterance upon the subject of punishment or deprivation of rights is barred. We may not, in the language of the court in People v. Thornton, 25 Hun, 456, "enhance the pains, penalties, and forfeitures provided by law for the punishment of crime." The judgment should be affirmed, with costs.

DANFORTH, J., concurs.

RONALD M. DWORKIN

Hard Cases*

1. INTRODUCTION

Legal positivism provides a theory of hard cases. When a particular lawsuit cannot be brought under a clear rule of law, laid down by some institution in advance, then the judge has, according to that theory, a 'discretion' to decide the case either way. His opinion is written in language that seems to assume that one or the other party had a preexisting right to win the suit, but that idea is only a fiction. In reality he has legislated new legal rights, and then applied them retrospectively to the case at hand. In the last two chapters I argued that this theory of adjudication is wholly inadequate; in this chapter I shall describe and defend a better theory.

I shall argue that even when no settled rule disposes of the case, one party may nevertheless have a right to win. It remains the judge's duty, even in hard cases, to discover what the rights of the parties are, not to invent new rights retrospectively. I should say at once, however, that it is no part of this theory that any mechanical procedure exists for demonstrating what the rights of parties are in hard cases. On the contrary, the argument supposes that reasonable lawyers and judges will often disagree about legal rights, just as citizens and statesmen disagree about political rights. This chapter describes the questions that judges and lawyers must put to themselves, but it does not guarantee that they will all give these questions the same answer.

Some readers may object that, if no procedure exists, even in principle, for demonstrating what legal rights the parties have in hard cases, it follows that they have none. That objection presupposes a controversial thesis of general philosophy, which is that no proposition can be true unless it can, at least in principle, be demonstrated to be true. There is no reason to accept that thesis as part of a general

theory of truth, and good reason to reject its specific application to propositions about legal rights.

2. THE RIGHTS THESIS

PRINCIPLES AND POLICIES

Theories of adjudication have become more sophisticated, but the most popular theories still put judging in the shade of legislation. The main outlines of this story are familiar. Judges should apply the law that other institutions have made; they should not make new law. That is the ideal, but for different reasons it cannot be realized fully in practice. Statutes and common law rules are often vague and must be interpreted before they can be applied to novel cases. Some cases, moreover, raise issues so novel that they cannot be decided even by stretching or reinterpreting existing rules. So judges must sometimes make new law, either covertly or explicitly. But when they do, they should act as deputy to the appropriate legislature, enacting the law that they suppose the legislature would enact if seized of the problem.

That is perfectly familiar, but there is buried in this common story a further level of subordination not always noticed. When judges make law, so the expectation runs, they will act not only as deputy to the legislature but as a deputy legislature. They will make law in response to evidence and arguments of the same character as would move the superior institution if it were acting on its own. This is a deeper level of subordination, because it makes any understanding of what judges do in hard cases parasitic on a prior understanding of what legislators do all the time. This deeper subordination is thus conceptual as well as political.

In fact, however, judges neither should be nor are deputy legislators, and the familiar assumption, that when they go beyond political decisions already made by someone else they are legislating, is misleading. It misses the importance of a fundamental distinction within

*From Ronald Dworkin, ''Hard Cases,'' 88 *Harvard Law Review* (1975). Reprinted by permission of the author and The Harvard Law Review.

political theory, which I shall now introduce in a crude form. This is the distinction between arguments of principle on the one hand and arguments of policy on the other.

Arguments of policy justify a political decision by showing that the decision advances or protects some collective goal of the community as a whole. The argument in favor of a subsidy for aircraft manufacturers, that the subsidy will protect national defense, is an argument of policy. Arguments of principle justify a political decision by showing that the decision respects or secures some individual or group right. The argument in favor of antidiscrimination statutes, that a minority has a right to equal respect and concern, is an argument of principle. These two sorts of argument do not exhaust political argument. Sometimes, for example, a political decision, like the decision to allow extra income tax exemptions for the blind, may be defended as an act of public generosity or virtue rather than on grounds of either policy or principle. But principle and policy are the major grounds of political justification.

The justification of a legislative program of any complexity will ordinarily require both sorts of argument. Even a program that is chiefly a matter of policy, like a subsidy program for important industries, may require strands of principle to justify its particular design. It may be, for example, that the program provides equal subsidies for manufacturers of different capabilities, on the assumption that weaker aircraft manufacturers have some right not to be driven out of business by government intervention, even though the industry would be more efficient without them. On the other hand, a program that depends chiefly on principle, like an antidiscrimination program, may reflect a sense that rights are serious. The program may provide, for example, that fair employment practice rules do not apply when they might prove especially disruptive or dangerous. In the subsidy case we might say that the rights conferred are generated by policy and qualified by principle; in the antidiscrimination case they are generated by principle and qualified by policy.

It is plainly competent for the legislature to pursue arguments of policy and to adopt programs that are generated by such arguments. If courts are deputy legislators, then it must be competent for them to do the same. Of course, unoriginal judicial decisions that merely enforce the clear terms of some plainly valid stat-

ute are always justified on arguments of principle, even if the statute itself was generated by policy. Suppose an aircraft manufacturer sues to recover the subsidy that the statute provides. He argues his right to the subsidy; his argument is an argument of principle. He does not argue that the national defense would be improved by subsidizing him; he might even concede that the statute was wrong on policy grounds when it was adopted, or that it should have been repealed, on policy grounds, long ago. His right to a subsidy no longer depends on any argument of policy because the statute made it a matter of priciple.

But if the case at hand is a hard case, when no settled rule dictates a decision either way, then it might seem that a proper decision could be generated by either policy or principle. Consider, for example, the problem of the recent *Spartan Steel* case.[1] The defendant's employees had broken an electrical cable belonging to a power company that supplied power to the plaintiff, and the plaintiff's factory was shut down while the cable was repaired. The court had to decide whether to allow the plaintiff recovery for economic loss following negligent damage to someone else's property. It might have proceeded to its decision by asking either whether a firm in the position of the plaintiff had a right to a recovery, which is a matter of principle, or whether it would be economically wise to distribute liability for accidents in the way the plaintiff suggested, which is a matter of policy.

If judges are deputy legislators, then the court should be prepared to follow the latter argument as well as the former, and decide in favor of the plaintiff if that argument recommends. That is, I suppose, what is meant by the popular idea that a court must be free to decide a novel case like *Spartan Steel* on policy grounds; and indeed Lord Denning described his own opinion in that case in just that way. I do not suppose he meant to distinguish an argument of principle from an argument of policy in the technical way I have, but he in any event did not mean to rule out an argument of policy in that technical sense.

I propose, nevertheless, the thesis that judicial decisions in civil cases, even in hard cases like *Spartan Steel,* characteristically are and should be generated by principle not policy. That thesis plainly needs much elaboration, but we may notice that certain arguments of political theory and jurisprudence support the thesis even in its abstract form. These arguments are not decisive, but they are sufficiently powerful to suggest the importance of the thesis, and to justify the attention that will be needed for a more careful formulation. . . .

JURISPRUDENCE

We have, therefore, in these political considerations, a strong reason to consider more carefully whether judicial arguments cannot be understood, even in hard cases, as arguments generated by principle. We have an additional reason in a familiar problem of jurisprudence. Lawyers believe that when judges make new law their decisions are constrained by legal traditions but are nevertheless personal and original. Novel decisions, it is said, reflect a judge's own political morality, but also reflect the morality that is embedded in the traditions of the common law, which might well be different. This is, of course, only law school rhetoric, but it nevertheless poses the problem of explaining how these different contributions to the decision of a hard case are to be identified and reconciled.

One popular solution relies on a spatial image; it says that the traditions of the common law contract the area of a judge's discretion to rely upon his personal morality, but do not entirely eliminate that area. But this answer is unsatisfactory on two grounds. First, it does not elucidate what is at best a provocative metaphor, which is that some morality is embedded in a mass of particular decisions other judges have reached in the past. Second, it suggests a plainly inadequate phenomenological account of the judicial decision. Judges do not decide hard cases in two stages, first checking to see where the institutional constraints end, and then setting the books aside to stride off on their own. The institutional constraints they sense are pervasive and endure to the decision itself. We therefore need an account of the interaction of personal and institutional morality that is less metaphorical and explains more successfully that pervasive interaction.

The rights thesis, that judicial decisions enforce existing political rights, suggests an explanation that is more successful on both counts. If the thesis holds, then institutional history acts not as a constraint on the political judgment of judges but as an ingredient of that judgment, because institutional history is part of the background that any plausible judgment

about the rights of an individual must accommodate. Political rights are creatures of both history and morality: what an individual is entitled to have, in civil society, depends upon both the practice and the justice of its political institutions. So the supposed tension between judicial originality and institutional history is dissolved: judges must make fresh judgments about the rights of the parties who come before them, but these political rights reflect, rather than oppose, political decisions of the past. When a judge chooses between the rule established in precedent and some new rule thought to be fairer, he does not choose between history and justice. He rather makes a judgment that requires some compromise between considerations that ordinarily combine in any calculation of political right, but here compete.

The rights thesis therefore provides a more satisfactory explanation of how judges use precedent in hard cases than the explanation provided by any theory that gives a more prominent place to policy. Judges, like all political officials, are subject to the doctrine of political responsibility. This doctrine states, in its most general form, that politial officials must make only such political decisions as they can justify within a political theory that also justifies the other decisions they propose to make. The doctrine seems innocuous in this general form; but it does, even in this form, condemn a style of political administration that might be called, following Rawls, intuitionistic. It condemns the practice of making decisions that seem right in isolation, but cannot be brought within some comprehensive theory of general principles and policies that is consistent with other decisions also thought right. Suppose a Congressman votes to prohibit abortion, on the ground that human life in any form is sacred, but then votes to permit the parents of babies born deformed to withhold medical treatment that will keep such babies alive. He might say that he feels that there is some difference, but the principle of responsibility, strictly applied, will not allow him these two votes unless he can incorporate the difference within some general political theory he sincerely holds.

The doctrine demands, we might say, articulate consistency. But this demand is relatively weak when policies are in play. Policies are aggregative in their influence on political decisions and it need not be part of a responsible strategy for reaching a collective goal that individuals be treated alike. It does not follow from the doctrine of responsibility, therefore, that if the legislature awards a subsidy to one aircraft manufacturer one month it must award a subsidy to another manufacturer the next. In the case of principles, however, the doctrine insists on distributional consistency from one case to the next, because it does not allow for the idea of a strategy that may be better served by unequal distribution of the benefit in question. If an official, for example, believes that sexual liberty of some sort is a right of individuals, then he must protect that liberty in a way that distributes the benefit reasonably equally over the class of those whom he supposes to have the right. If he allows one couple to use contraceptives on the ground that this right would otherwise be invaded, then he must, so long as he does not recant that earlier decision, allow the next couple the same liberty. He cannot say that the first decision gave the community just the amount of sexual liberty it needed, so that no more is required at the time of the second.

Judicial decisions are political decisions, at least in the broad sense that attracts the doctrine of political responsibility. If the rights thesis holds, then the distinction just made would account, at least in a very general way, for the special concern that judges show for both precedents and hypothetical examples. An argument of principle can supply a justification for a particular decision, under the doctrine of responsibility, only if the principle cited can be shown to be consistent with earlier decisions not recanted, and with decisions that the institution is prepared to make in the hypothetical circumstances. That is hardly surprising, but the argument would not hold if judges based their decisions on arguments of policy. They would be free to say that some policy might be adequately served by serving it in the case at bar, providing, for example, just the right subsidy to some troubled industry, so that neither earlier decisions nor hypothetical future decisions need be understood as serving the same policy.

Consistency here, of course, means consistency in the application of the principle relied upon, not merely in the application of the particular rule announced in the name of that principle. If, for example, the principle that no one has the duty to make good remote or unexpected losses flowing from his negligence is relied upon to justify a decision for the defendant in *Spartan Steel,* then it must be shown that the rule laid down in other cases, which allows recovery for negligent misstatements, is consistent with that principle; not merely that the rule about negligent misstatement is a different rule from the rule in *Spartan Steel.* . . .

4. INSTITUTIONAL RIGHTS

The rights thesis provides that judges decide hard cases by confirming or denying concrete rights. But the concrete rights upon which judges rely must have two other characteristics. They must be institutional rather than background rights, and they must be legal rather than some other form of institutional rights. We cannot appreciate or test the thesis, therefore, without further elaboration of these distinctions.

Institutional rights may be found in institutions of very different character. A chess player has a 'chess' right to be awarded a point in a tournament if he checkmates an opponent. A citizen in a democracy has a legislative right to the enactment of statutes necessary to protect his free speech. In the case of chess, institutional rights are fixed by constitutive and regulative rules that belong distinctly to the game, or to a particular tournament. Chess is, in this sense, an autonomous institution; I mean that it is understood, among its participants, that no one may claim an institutional right by direct appeal to general morality. No one may argue, for example, that he has earned the right to be declared the winner by his general virtue. But legislation is only partly autonomous in that sense. There are special constitutive and regulative rules that define what a legislature is, and who belongs to it, and how it votes, and that it may not establish a religion. But these rules belonging distinctly to legislation are rarely sufficient to determine whether a citizen has an institutional right to have a certain statute enacted; they do not decide, for example, whether he has a right to minimum wage legislation. Citizens are expected to repair to general considerations of political morality when they argue for such rights.

The fact that some institutions are fully and others partly autonomous has the consequence . . . , that the institutional rights a political theory acknowledges may diverge from the background rights it provides. Institutional rights are nevertheless genuine rights. Even if we suppose that the poor have an abstract background right to money taken from the rich, it would be wrong, not merely unexpected, for the referees of a chess tournament to award the prize money to the poorest contestant rather than the contestant with the most points. It would provide no excuse to say that since tournament rights merely describe the conditions necessary for calling the tournament a chess tournament, the referee's act is justified so long as he does not use the word 'chess' when he hands out the award. The participants entered the tournament with the understanding that chess rules would apply; they have genuine rights to the enforcement of these rules and no others.

Institutional autonomy insulates an official's institutional duty from the greater part of background political morality. But how far does the force of this insulation extend? Even in the case of a fully insulated institution like chess some rules will require interpretation or elaboration before an official may enforce them in certain circumstances. Suppose some rule of a chess tournament provides that the referee shall declare a game forfeit if one player 'unreasonably' annoys the other in the course of play. The language of the rule does not define what counts as 'unreasonable' annoyance; it does not decide whether, for example, a player who continually smiles at his opponent in such a way as to unnerve him, as the Russian grandmaster Tal once smiled at Fischer, annoys him unreasonably.

The referee is not free to give effect to his background convictions in deciding this hard case. He might hold, as a matter of political theory, that individuals have a right to equal welfare without regard to intellectual abilities. It would nevertheless be wrong for him to rely upon that conviction in deciding difficult cases under the forfeiture rule. He could not say, for example, that annoying behavior is reasonable so long as it has the effect of reducing the importance of intellectual ability in deciding who will win the game. The participants, and the general community that is interested, will say that his duty is just the contrary. Since chess is an intellectual game, he must apply the forfeiture rule in such a way as to protect, rather than jeopardize, the role of intellect in the contest.

We have, then, in the case of the chess referee, an example of an official whose decisions about institutional rights are understood to be governed by institutional constraints even when the force of these constraints is not clear. We do not think that he is free to legislate interstitially within the 'open texture' of imprecise rules.[2] If one interpretation of the forfeiture rule will protect the character of the game, and another will not, then the participants have a right to the first interpretation. We may hope to find, in this relatively simple case, some general feature of institutional rights in hard cases that will bear on the decision of a judge in a hard case at law.

I said that the game of chess has a character that the referee's decisions must respect. What does that mean? How does a referee know that chess is an intellectual game rather than a game of chance or an exhibition of digital ballet? He may well start with what everyone knows. Every institution is placed by its participants in some very rough category of institution; it is taken to be a game rather than a religious ceremony or a form of exercise or a political process. It is, for that reason, definitional of chess that it is a game rather than an exercise in digital skill. These conventions, exhibited in attitudes and manners and in history, are decisive. If everyone takes chess to be a game of chance, so that they curse their luck and nothing else when a piece *en prise* happens to be taken, then chess is a game of chance, though a very bad one . . .

5. LEGAL RIGHTS

A. LEGISLATION

Legal argument, in hard cases, turns on contested concepts whose nature and function are very much like the concept of the character of a game. These include several of the substantive concepts through which the law is stated, like the concepts of a contract and of property. But they also include two concepts of much greater relevance to the present argument. The first is the idea of the 'intention' or 'purpose' of a particular statute or statutory clause. This concept provides a bridge between the political justification of the general idea that statutes create rights and those hard cases that ask what rights a particular statute has created. The second is the concept of principles that 'underlie' or are 'embedded in' the positive rules of law. This concept provides a bridge between the political justification of the doctrine that like cases should be decided alike and those hard cases in which it is unclear what that general doctrine requires. These concepts together define legal rights as a function, though a very special function, of political rights. If a judge accepts the settled practices of his legal system—if he accepts, that is, the autonomy provided by its distinct constitutive and regulative rules—then he must, according to the doctrine of political responsibility, accept some general political theory that justifies these practices. The concepts of legislative purpose and common law principles are devices for applying that general political theory to controversial issues about legal rights.

We might therefore do well to consider how a philosophical judge might develop, in appropriate cases, theories of what legislative purpose and legal principles require. We shall find that he would construct these theories in the same manner as a philosophical referee would construct the character of a game. I have invented, for this purpose, a lawyer of superhuman skill, learning, patience, and acumen, whom I shall call Hercules. I suppose that Hercules is a judge in some representative American jurisdiction. I assume that he accepts the main uncontroversial constitutive and regulative rules of the law in his jurisdiction. He accepts, that is, that statutes have the general power to create and extinguish legal rights, and that judges have the general duty to follow earlier decisions of their court or higher courts whose rationale, as lawyers say, extends to the case at bar.

1. THE CONSTITUTION. Suppose there is a written constitution in Hercules' jurisdiction which provides that no law shall be valid if it establishes a religion. The legislature passes a law purporting to grant free busing to children in parochial schools. Does the grant establish a religion?[3] The words of the constitutional provision might support either view. Hercules must nevertheless decide whether the child who appears before him has a right to her bus ride.

He might begin by asking why the constitution has any power at all to create or destroy rights. If citizens have a background right to salvation through an established church, as many believe they do, then this must be an important right. Why does the fact that a group of men voted otherwise several centuries ago prevent this background right from being made a legal right as well? His answer must take some form such as this. The constitution sets out a general political scheme that is sufficiently just to be taken as settled for reasons of fairness. Citizens take the benefit of living in a society whose institutions are arranged and governed in accordance with that scheme, and they must take the burdens as well, at least until a new scheme is put into force either by discrete amendment or general revolution. But Hercules must then ask just what scheme of principles has been settled. He must construct, that is, a constitutional theory; since he is Hercules we may suppose that he can develop a full political theory that justifies the constitution as a whole. It must be a scheme that fits the particular rules of this constitution, of course. It cannot include a powerful background right to an established church. But more than one fully specified theory may fit the specific provision about religion sufficiently well. One theory might provide, for example, that it is wrong for the government to enact any legislation that will cause great social tension or disorder; so that since the establishment of a church will have that effect, it is wrong to empower the legislature to establish one. Another theory will provide a background right to religious liberty, and therefore argue that an established church is wrong, not because it will be socially disruptive, but because it violates that background right. In that case Hercules must turn to the remaining constitutional rules and settled practices under these rules to see which of these two theories provides a smoother fit with the constitutional scheme as a whole.

But the theory that is superior under this test will nevertheless be insufficiently concrete to decide some cases. Suppose Hercules decides that the establishment provision is justified by a right to religious liberty rather than any goal of social order. It remains to ask what, more precisely, religious liberty is. Does a right to religious liberty include the right not to have one's taxes used for any purpose that helps a religion to survive? Or simply not to have one's taxes used to benefit one religion at the expense of another? If the former, then the free transportation legislation violates that right, but if the latter it does not. The institutional structure of rules and practice may not be sufficiently detailed to rule out either of these two conceptions of religious liberty, or to make one a plainly superior justification of that structure. At some point in his career Hercules must therefore consider the question not just as an issue of fit between a theory and the rules of the institution, but as an issue of political philosophy as well. He must decide which conception is a more satisfactory elaboration of the general idea of religious liberty. He must decide that question because he cannot otherwise carry far enough the project he began. He cannot answer in sufficient detail the question of what political scheme the constitution establishes.

So Hercules is driven, by this project, to a process of reasoning that is much like the process of the self-conscious chess referee. He must develop a theory of the constitution, in the shape of a complex set of principles and policies that justify that scheme of government, just as the chess referee is driven to develop a theory about the character of his game. He must develop that theory by referring alternately to political philosophy and institutional detail. He must generate possible theories justifying different aspects of the scheme and test the theories against the broader institution. When the discriminating power of that test is exhausted, he must elaborate the contested concepts that the successful theory employs.

2. STATUTES. A statute in Hercules' jurisdiction provides that it is a federal crime for someone knowingly to transport in interstate commerce 'any person who shall have been unlawfully seized, confined, inveigled, decoyed, kidnapped, abducted, or carried away by any means whatsoever. . . .' Hercules is asked to decide whether this statute makes a federal criminal of a man who persuaded a young girl that it was her religious duty to run away with him, in violation of a court order, to consummate what he called a celestial marriage.[4] The statute had been passed after a famous kidnapping case, in order to enable federal authorities to join in the pursuit of kidnappers. But its words are sufficiently broad to apply to this case, and there is nothing in the legislative record or accompanying committee reports that says they do not.

Do they apply? Hercules might himself despise celestial marriage, or abhor the corruption of minors, or celebrate the obedience of children to their parents. The groom nevertheless has a right to his liberty, unless the statute properly understood deprives him of that right; it is inconsistent with any plausible theory of the constitution that judges have the power retroactively to make conduct criminal. Does the statute deprive him of that right? Hercules must begin by asking why any statute has the power

to alter lgeal rights. He will find the answer in his constitutional theory: this might provide, for example, that a democratically elected legislature is the appropriate body to make collective decisions about the conduct that shall be criminal. But that same constitutional theory will impose on the legislature certain responsibilities: it will impose not only constraints reflecting individual rights, but also some general duty to pursue collective goals defining the pubilc welfare. That fact provides a useful test for Hercules in this hard case. He might ask which interpretation more satisfactorily ties the language the legislature used to its constitutional responsibilities. That is, like the referee's question about the character of a game. It calls for the construction, not of some hypothesis about the mental state of particular legislators, but of a special political theory that justifies this statute, in the light of the legislature's more general responsibilities, better than any alternative theory.[5]

Which arguments of principle and policy might properly have persuaded the legislature to enact just that statute? It should not have pursued a policy designed to replace state criminal enforcement by federal enforcement whenever constitutionally possible. That would represent an unnecessary interference with the principle of federalism that must be part of Hercules' constitutional theory. It might, however, responsibly have followed a policy of selecting for federal enforcement all crimes with such an interstate character that state enforcement was hampered. Or it could responsibly have selected just specially dangerous or widespread crimes of that character. Which of these two responsible policies offers a better justification of the statute actually drafted? If the penalties provided by the statute are large, and therefore appropriate to the latter but not the former policy, the latter policy must be preferred. Which of the different interpretations of the statute permitted by the language serves that policy better? Plainly a decision that inveiglement of the sort presented by the case is not made a federal crime by the statute.

I have described a simple and perhaps unrepresentative problem of statutory interpretation, because I cannot now develop a theory of statutory interpretation in any detail. I want only to suggest how the general claim, that calculations judges make about the purposes of statutes are calculations about political rights, might be defended. There are, however, two points that must be noticed about even this simple example. It would be inaccurate, first, to say that Hercules supplemented what the legislature did in enacting the statute, or that he tried to determine what it would have done if it had been aware of the problem presented by the case. The act of a legislature is not, as these descriptions suggest, an event whose force we can in some way measure so as to say it has run out at a particular point; it is rather an event whose content is contested in the way in which the content of an agreement to play a game is contested. Hercules constructs his political theory as an argument about what the legislature has, on this occasion, done. The contrary argument, that it did not actually do what he said, is not a realistic piece of common sense, but a competitive claim about the true content of that contested event.

Second, it is important to notice how great a role the canonical terms of the actual statute play in the process described. They provide a limit to what must otherwise be, in the nature of the case, unlimited. The political theory Hercules developed to interpret the statute, which featured a policy of providing federal enforcement for dangerous crimes, would justify a great many decisions that the legislature did not, on any interpretation of the language, actually make. It would justify, for example, a statute making it a federal crime for a murderer to leave the state of his crime. The legislature has no general duty to follow out the lines of any particular policy, and it would plainly be wrong for Hercules to suppose that the legislature had in some sense enacted that further statute. The words of the statute they did enact enables this process of interpretation to operate without absurdity; it permits Hercules to say that the legislature pushed some policy to the limits of the language it used, without also supposing that it pushed that policy to some indeterminate further point.

B. THE COMMON LAW

1. PRECEDENT. One day lawyers will present a hard case to Hercules that does not turn upon any statute; they will argue whether earlier common law decisions of Hercules' court, properly understood, provide some party with a right to a decision in his favor. *Spartan Steel* was such a case. The plaintiff did not argue that any statute provided it a right to recover its economic damages; it pointed instead to certain earlier judicial decisions that awarded recovery for other sorts of damage, and argued that the principle behind these cases required a decision for it as well.

Hercules must begin by asking why arguments of that form are ever, even in principle, sound. He will find that he has available no quick or obvious answer. When he asked himself the parallel question about legislation he found, in general democratic theory, a ready reply. But the details of the practices of precedent he must now justify resist any comparably simple theory.

He might, however, be tempted by this answer. Judges, when they decide prticular cases at common law, lay down general rules that are intended to benefit the community in some way. Other judges, deciding later cases, must therefore enforce these rules so that the benefit may be achieved. If this account of the matter were a sufficient justification of the practices of precedent, then Hercules could decide these hard common law cases as if earlier decisions were statutes, using the techniques he worked out for statutory interpretation. But he will encounter fatal difficulties if he pursues that theory very far. It will repay us to consider why, in some detail, because the errors in the theory will be guides to a more successful theory.

Statutory interpretation, as we just noticed, depends upon the availability of a canonical form of words, however vague or unspecific, that set limits to the political decisions that the statute may be taken to have made. Hercules will discover that many of the opinions that litigants cite as precedents do not contain any special propositions taken to be a canonical form of the rule that the case lays down. It is true that it was part of Anglo-American judicial style, during the last part of the nineteenth century and the first part of this century, to attempt to compose such canonical statements, so that one could thereafter refer, for example, to the rule in *Rylands v. Fletcher.*[6] But even in this period, lawyers and textbook writers disagreed about which parts of famous opinions should be taken to have that character. Today, in any case, even important opinions rarely attempt that legislative sort of draftsmanship. They cite reasons, in the form of precedents and principles, to justify a decision, but it is the decision, not some new and stated rule of law, that these precedents and principles are taken to justify. Sometimes a judge will acknowledge openly that it lies to later cases to determine the full effect of the case he has decided.

Of course, Hercules might well decide that when he does find, in an earlier case, a canonical form of words, he will use his techniques of statutory interpretation to decide whether the rule composed of these words embraces a novel case.[7] He might well acknowledge what could be called an enactment force of precedent. He will nevertheless find that when a precedent does have enactment force, its influence on later cases is not taken to be limited to that force. Judges and lawyers do not think that the force of precedents is exhausted, as a statute would be, by the linguistic limits of some particular phrase. If *Spartan Steel* were a New York case, counsel for the plaintiff would suppose that Cardozo's earlier decision in *MacPherson v. Buick,*[8] in which a woman recovered damages for injuries from a negligently manufactured automobile, counted in favor of his client's right to recover, in spite of the fact that the earlier decision contained no language that could plausibly be interpreted to enact that right. He would urge that the earlier decision exerts a gravitational force on later decisions even when these later decisions lie outside its particular orbit.

This gravitational force is part of the practice Hercules' general theory of precedent must capture. In this important respect, judicial practice differs from the practice of officials in other institutions. In chess, officials conform to established rules in a way that assumes full institutional autonomy. They exercise originality only to the extent required by the fact that an occasional rule, like the rule about forfeiture, demands that originality. Each decision of a chess referee, therefore, can be said to be directly required and justified by an established rule of chess, even though some of these decisions must be based on an interpretation, rather than on simply the plain and unavoidable meaning, of that rule.

Some legal philosophers write about common law adjudication as if it were in this way like chess, except that legal rules are much more likely than chess rules to require interpretation. That is the spirit, for example, of Professor Hart's argument that hard cases arise only because legal rules have what he calls 'open texture'.[9] In fact, judges often disagree not simply about how some rule or principle should be interpreted, but whether the rule or principle one judge cites should be acknowl-edged to be a rule or principle at all. In some cases both the majority and the dissenting opinions recognize the same earlier cases as relevant, but disagree about what rule or principle these precedents should be understood to have established. In adjudication, unlike chess, the argument *for* a particular rule may be more important than the argument *from* that rule to the particular case; and while the chess referee who decides a case by appeal to a rule no one has ever heard of before is likely to be dismissed or certified, the judge who does so is likely to be celebrated in law school lectures.

Nevertheless, judges seem agreed that earlier decisions do contribute to the formulation of new and controversial rules in some way other than by interpretation; they are agreed that earlier decisions have gravitational force even when they disagree about what that force is. The legislator may very often concern himself only with issues of background morality or policy in deciding how to cast his vote on some issue. He need not show that his vote is consistent with the votes of his colleagues in the legislature, or with those of past legislatures. But the judge very rarely assumes that character of independence. He will always try to connect the justification he provides for an original decision with decisions that other judges or officials have taken in the past.

In fact, when good judges try to explain in some general way how they work, they search for figures of speech to describe the constraints they feel even when they suppose that they are making new law, constraints that would not be appropriate if they were legislators. They say, for example, that they find new rules immanent in the law as a whole, or that they are enforcing an internal logic of the law through some method that belongs more to philosophy than to politics, or that they are the agents through which the law works itself pure, or that the law has some life of its own even though this belongs to experience rather than logic. Hercules must not rest content with these famous metaphors and personifications, but he must also not be content with any description of the judicial process that ignores their appeal to the best lawyers.

The gravitational force of precedent cannot be captured by any theory that takes the full force of precedent to be its enactment force as a piece of legislation. But the inadequacy of that approach suggests a superior theory. The gravitational force of a precedent may be explained by appeal, not to the wisdom of enforcing enactments, but to the fairness of treating like cases alike. A precedent is the report of an earlier political decision; the very fact of that decision, as a piece of political history, provides some reason for deciding other cases in a similar way in the future. This general explanation of the gravitational force of precedent accounts for the feature that defeated the enactment theory, which is that the force of a precedent escapes the language of its opinion. If the government of a community has forced the manufacturer of defective motor cars to pay damages to a woman who was injured because of the defect, then that historical fact must offer some reason, at least, why the same government should require a contractor who has caused economic damage through the defective work of his employees to make good that loss. We may test the weight of that reason, not by asking whether the language of the earlier decision, suitably interpreted, requires the contractor to pay damages, but by asking the different question whether it is fair for the government, having intervened in the way it did in the first case, to refuse its aid in the second.

Hercules will conclude that this doctrine of fairness offers the only adequate account of the full practice of precedent. He will draw certain further conclusions about his own responsibilities when deciding hard cases. The most important of these is that he must limit the gravitational force of earlier decisions to the extension of the arguments of principle necessary to justify those decisions. If an earlier decision were taken to be entirely justified by some argument of policy, it would have no gravitational force. Its value as a precedent would be limited to its enactment force, that is, to further cases captured by some particular words of the opinion. The distributional force of a collective goal, as we noticed earlier, is a matter of contingent fact and general legislative strategy. If the government intervened on behalf of Mrs. MacPherson, not because she had any right to its intervention, but only because wise strategy suggested that means of pursuing some collective goal like economic efficiency, there can be no effective argument of fairness that it therefore ought to intervene for the plaintiff in *Spartan Steel*.

We must remind ourselves, in order to see why this is so, of the slight demands we make upon legislatures in the name of consistency when their decisions are generated by arguments of policy.[10] Suppose the legislature wishes to stimulate the economy and might do so, with roughly the same efficiency, either by subsidizing housing or by increasing direct government spending for new roads. Road construction companies have no right that the legislature choose road construction; if it does, then home construction firms have no right, on any principle of consistency, that the legislature subsidize housing as well. The legislature may decide that the road construction program has stimulated the economy just enough, and that no further programs are needed. It may decide this even if it now concedes that subsidized housing would have been the more efficient decision in the first place. Or it might concede even that more stimulation of the economy is needed, but decide that it wishes to wait for more evidence—perhaps evidence about the success of the road program—to see whether subsidies provide an effective stimulation. It might even say that it does not now wish to commit more of its time and energy to economic policy. There is, perhaps, some limit to the arbitrariness of the distinctions the legislature may make in its pursuit of collective goals. Even if it is efficient to build all shipyards in southern California, it might be thought unfair, as well as politically unwise, to do so. But these weak requirements, which prohibit grossly unfair distributions, are plainly compatible with providing sizeable incremental benefits to one group that are withheld from others.

There can be, therefore, no general argument of fairness that a government which serves a collective goal in one way on one occasion must serve it that way, or even serve the same goal, whenever a parallel opportunity arises. I do not mean simply that the government may change its mind, and regret either the goal or the means of its earlier decision. I mean that a responsible government may serve different goals in a piecemeal and occasional fashion, so that even though it does not regret, but continues to enforce, one rule designed to serve a particular goal, it may reject other rules that would serve that same goal just as well. It might legislate the rule that manufacturers are responsible for damages flowing from defects in their cars, for example, and yet properly refuse to legislate the same rule for manufacturers of washing machines, let alone contractors who cause economic damage like the damage of *Spartan Steel*. Government must, of course, be rational and fair; it must make decisions that overall serve a justifiable mix of collective goals and nevertheless respect whatever rights citizens have. But that general requirement would not support anything like the gravitational force that the judicial decision in favour of Mrs. MacPherson was in fact taken to have.

So Hercules, when he defines the gravitational force of a particular precedent, must take into account only the arguments of principle that justify that precedent. If the decision in favour of Mrs. MacPherson supposes that she has a right to damages, and not simply that a rule in her favor supports some collective goal, then the argument of fairness, on which the practice of precedent relies, takes hold. It does not follow, of course, that anyone injured in any way by the negligence of another must have the same concrete right to recover that she has. It may be that competing rights require a compromise in the later case that they did not require in hers. But it might well follow that the plaintiff in the later case has the same abstract right, and if that is so then some special argument citing the competing rights will be required to show that a contrary decision in the later case would be fair.

2. THE SEAMLESS WEB. Hercules' first conclusion, that the gravitational force of a precedent is defined by the arguments of principle that support the precedent, suggest a second. Since judicial practice in his community assumes that earlier cases have a *general* gravitational force, then he can justify that judicial practice only by supposing that the rights thesis holds in his community. It is never taken to be a satisfactory argument against the gravitational force of some precedent that the goal that precedent served has now been served sufficiently, or that the courts would now be better occupied in serving some other goal that has been relatively neglected, possibly returning to the goal the precedent served on some other occasion. The practices of precedent do not suppose that the *rationales* that recommend judicial decisions can be served piecemeal in that way. If it is acknowledged that a particular precedent is justified for a particular reason; if that reason would also recommend a particular result in the case at bar; if the earlier decision has not been recanted or in some other way taken as a matter of institutional regret; then that decision must be reached in the later case.

Hercules must suppose that it is understood in his community, though perhaps not explicitly recognized, that judicial decisions must be taken to be justified by arguments of principle rather than arguments of policy. He now sees that the familiar concept used by judges to explain their reasoning from precedent, the concept of certain principles that underlie or are embedded in the common law, is itself only a metaphorical statement of the rights thesis. He may henceforth use that concept in his decisions of hard common law cases. It provides a general test for deciding such cases that is like the chess referee's concept of the character of a game, and like his own concept of a legislative purpose. It provides a question—What set of principles best justifies the precedents?— that builds a bridge between the general justification of the practice of precedent, which is fairness, and his own decision about what that general justification requires in some particular hard case.

Hercules must now develop his concept of principles that underlie the common law by assigning to each of the relevant precedents some scheme of principle that justifies the decision of that precedent. He will now discover a further important difference between this concept and the concept of statutory purpose that he used in statutory interpretation. In the case of statutes, he found it necessary to choose some theory about the purpose of the particular statute in question, looking to other acts of the legislature only insofar as these might help to select between theories that fit the statute about equally well. But if the gravitational force of precedent rests on the idea that fairness requires the consistent enforcement of rights, then Hercules must discover principles that fit, not only the particular precedent to which some litigant directs his attention, but all other judicial decisions within his general jurisdiction and, indeed, statutes as well, so far as these must be seen to be generated by principle rather than policy. He does not satisfy his duty to show that his decision is consistent with established principles, and therefore fair, if the principles he cites as established are themselves inconsistent with other decisions that his court also proposes to uphold.

Suppose, for example, that he can justify Cardozo's decision in favor of Mrs. MacPherson by citing some abstract principle of equality, which argues that whenever an accident occurs then the richest of the various persons whose acts might have contributed to the accident must bear the loss. He nevertheless cannot show that that principle has been respected in other accident cases, or, even if he could, that it has been respected in other branches of the law, like contract, in which it would also have great impact if it were recognized at all. If he decides against a future accident plaintiff who is richer than the defendant, by appealing to this alleged right of equality, that plaintiff may properly complain that the decision is just as inconsistent with government's behavior in other cases as if *MacPherson* itself had been ignored. The law may not be a seamless web; but the plaintiff is entitled to ask Hercules to treat it as if it were.

 You will now see why I called our judge Hercules. He must construct a scheme of abstract and concrete principles that provides a coherent justification for all common law precedents and, so far as these are to be justified on principle, constitutional and statutory provisions as well. We may grasp the magnitude of this enterprise by distinguishing, within the vast material of legal decisions that Hercules must justify, a vertical and a horizontal ordering. The vertical ordering is provided by distinguishing layers of authority; that is, layers at which official decisions might be taken to be controlling over decisions made at lower levels. In the United States the rough character of the vertical ordering is apparent. The constitutional structure occupies the highest level, the decision of the Supreme Court and perhaps other courts interpreting that structure the next, enactments of the various legislatures the next and decisions of the various courts developing the common law different levels below that. Hercules must arrange justification of principle at each of these levels so that the justification is consistent with principles taken to provide the justification of higher levels. The horizontal ordering simply requires that the principles taken to justify a decision at one level must also be consistent with the justification offered for other decisions at that level.

Suppose Hercules, taking advantage of his unusual skills, proposed to work out this entire scheme in advance, so that he would be ready to confront litigants with an entire theory of law should this be necessary to justify any particular decision. He would begin, deferring to vertical ordering, by setting out and refining the constitutional theory he has already used. That constitutional theory would be more or less

different from the theory that a different judge would develop, because a constitutional theory requires judgments about complex issues of institutional fit, as well as judgments about political and moral philosophy, and Hercules' judgments will inevitably differ from those other judges would make. These differences at a high level of vertical ordering will exercise considerable force on the scheme each judge would propose at lower levels. Hercules might think, for example, that certain substantive constitutional constraints on legislative power are best justified by postulating an abstract right to privacy against the state, because he believes that such a right is a consequence of the even more abstract right to liberty that the constitution guarantees. If so, he would regard the failure of the law of tort to recognize a parallel abstract right to privacy against fellow citizens, in some concrete form, as an inconsistency. If another judge did not share his beliefs about the connection between privacy and liberty, and so did not accept his constitutional interpretation as persuasive, that judge would also disagree about the proper development of tort.

So the impact of Hercules' own judgments will be pervasive, even though some of these will be controversial. But they will not enter his calculations in such a way that different parts of the theory he constructs can be attributed to his independent convictions rather than to the body of law that he must justify. He will not follow those classical theories of adjudication I mentioned earlier, which suppose that a judge follows statutes or precedent until the clear direction of these runs out, after which he is free to strike out on his own. His theory is rather a theory about what the statute or the precedent itself requires, and though he will, of course, reflect his own intellectual and philosophical convictions in making that judgment, that is a very different matter from supposing that those convictions have some independent force in his argument just because they are his.

3. MISTAKES. I shall not now try to develop, in further detail, Hercules' theory of law. I shall mention, however, two problems he will face. He must decide, first, how much weight he must give, in constructing a scheme of justification for a set of precedents, to the arguments that the judges who decided these cases attached to their decisions. He will not always find in these opinions any proposition precise enough to serve as a statute he might then interpret. But the opinions will almost always contain argument, in the form of propositions that the judge takes to recommend his decision. Hercules will decide to assign these only an initial or prima facie place in his scheme of justification. The purpose of that scheme is to satisfy the requirement that the government must extend to all, the rights it supposes some to have. The fact that one officer of the government offers a certain principle as the ground of his decision, may be taken to establish prima facie that the government does rely that far upon that principle.

But the main force of the underlying argument of fairness is forward-looking, not backward-looking. The gravitational force of Mrs. MacPherson's case depends not simply on the fact that she recovered for her Buick, but also on the fact that the government proposes to allow others in just her position to recover in the future. If the courts proposed to overrule the decision, no substantial argument of fairness, fixing on the actual decision in the case, survives in favor of the plaintiff in *Spartan Steel*. If, therefore, a principle other than the principle Cardozo cited can be found to justify *MacPherson*, and if this other principle also justifies a great deal of precedent that Cardozo's does not, or if it provides a smoother fit with arguments taken to justify decisions of a higher rank in vertical order, then this new principle is a more satisfactory basis for further decisions. Of course, this argument for not copying Cardozo's principle is unnecessary if the new principle is more abstract, and if Cardozo's principle can be seen as only a concrete form of that more abstract principle. In that case Hercules incorporates, rather than rejects, Cardozo's account of his decision. Cardozo, in fact, used the opinion in the earlier case of *Thomas v. Winchester*,[11] on which case he relied, in just that fashion. It may be, however, that the new principle strikes out on a different line, so that it justifies a precedent or a series of precedents on grounds very different from what their opinions propose. Brandeis and Warren's famous argument about the right to privacy[12] is a dramatic illustration: they argued that this right was not unknown to the law but was, on the contrary, demonstrated by a wide variety of decisions, in spite of the fact that the judges who decided these cases mentioned no such right. It may be that their argument, so conceived, was unsuccessful, and that Her-

cules in their place, would have reached a different result. Hercules' theory nevertheless shows why their argument, sometimes taken to be a kind of brilliant fraud, was at least sound in its ambition.

Hercules must also face a different and a greater problem. If the history of his court is at all complex, he will find, in practice, that the requirement of total consistency he has accepted will prove too strong, unless he develops it further to include the idea that he may, in applying this requirement, disregard some part of institutional history as a mistake. For he will be unable, even with his superb imagination, to find any set of principles that reconciles all standing statutes and precedents. This is hardly surprising: the legislators and judges of the past did not all have Hercules' ability or insight, nor were they men and women who were all of the same mind and opinion. Of course, any set of statutes and decisions can be explained historically, or psychologically, or sociologically, but consistency requires justification, not explanation, and the justification must be plausible and not sham. If the justification he constructs makes distinctions that are arbitrary and deploys principles that are unappealing, then it cannot count as a justification at all.

Suppose the law of negligence and accidents in Hercules' jurisdiction has developed in the following simplified and imaginary way. It begins with specific common law decisions recognizing a right to damages for bodily injury caused by very dangerous instruments that are defectively manufactured. These cases are then reinterpreted in some landmark decision, as they were in *MacPherson*, as justified by the very abstract right of each person to the reasonable care of others whose actions might injure his person or property. This principle is then both broadened and pinched in different ways. The courts, for example, decide that no concrete right lies against an accountant who has been negligent in the preparation of financial statements. They also decide that the right cannot be waived in certain cases; for example, in a standard form contract of automobile purchase. The legislature adds a statute providing that in certain cases of industrial accident, recovery will be allowed unless the defendant affirmatively establishes that the plaintiff was entirely to blame. But it also provides that in other cases, for example in airplane accidents, recovery will be limited to a stipulated amount, which might be much less than the actual loss; and it later adds that the guest in an automobile cannot sue his host even if the host drives negligently and the guest is injured. Suppose now, against this background, that Hercules is called upon to decide *Spartan Steel*.

Can he find a coherent set of principles that justifies this history in the way fairness requires? He might try the proposition that individuals have no right to recover for damages unless inflicted intentionally. He would argue that they are allowed to recover damages in negligence only for policy reasons, not in recognition of any abstract right to such damages, and he would cite the statutes limiting liability to protect airlines and insurance companies, and the cases excluding liability against accountants, as evidence that recovery is denied when policy argues the other way. But he must concede that this analysis of institutional history is incompatible with the common law decisions, particularly the landmark decision recognizing a general right to recovery in negligence. He cannot say, compatibly with the rest of his theory, that these decisions may themselves be justified on policy grounds, if he holds, by virtue of the rights thesis, that courts may extend liability only in response to arguments of principle and not policy. So he must set these decisions aside as mistakes.

He might try another strategy. He might propose some principle according to which individuals have rights to damages in just the circumstances of the particular cases that decided they did, but have no general right to such damages. He might concede, for example, a legal principle granting a right to recover for damages incurred within an automobile owned by the plaintiff, but deny a principle that would extend to other damage. But though he could in this way tailor his justification of institutional history to fit that history exactly, he would realize that this justification rests on distinctions that are arbitrary. He can find no room in his political theory for a distinction that concedes an abstract right if someone is injured driving his own automobile but denies it if he is a guest or if he is injured in an airplane. He has provided a set of arguments that cannot stand as a coherent justification of anything.

He might therefore concede that he can make no sense of institutional history except by supposing some general abstract right to recover for negligence; but he might argue that it is a relatively weak right and so will yield to policy

considerations of relatively minor force. He will cite the limiting statutes and cases in support of his view that the right is a weak one. But he will then face a difficulty if, though the statute limiting liability in airplane accidents has never been repealed, the airlines have become sufficiently secure, and the mechanisms of insurance available to airlines so efficient and inexpensive, that a failure to repeal the statute can only be justified by taking the abstract right to be so weak that relatively thin arguments of policy are sufficient to defeat it. If Hercules takes the right to be that weak then he cannot justify the various common law decisions that support the right, as a concrete right, against arguments of policy much stronger than the airlines are now able to press. So he must choose either to take the failure to repeal the airline accident limitation statute, or the common law decisions that value the right much higher, as mistakes.

In any case, therefore, Hercules must expand his theory to include the idea that a justification of institutional history may display some part of that history as mistaken. But he cannot make impudent use of this device, because if he were free to take any incompatible piece of institutional history as a mistake, with no further consequences for his general theory, then the requirement of consistency would be no genuine requirement at all. He must develop some theory of institutional mistakes, and this theory of mistakes must have two parts. It must show the consequences for further arguments of taking some institutional event to be mistaken; and it must limit the number and character of the events than can be disposed of in that way.

He will construct the first part of this theory of mistakes by means of two sets of distinctions. He will first distinguish between the specific authority of any institutional event, which is its power as an institutional act to effect just the specific institutional consequences it describes, and its gravitational force. If he classifies some event as a mistake, then he does not deny its specific authority but he does deny its gravitational force, and he cannot consistently appeal to that force in other arguments. He will also distinguish between embedded and corrigible mistakes; embedded mistakes are those whose specific authority is fixed so that it survives their loss of gravitational force; corrigible mistakes are those whose specific authority depends on gravitational force in such a way that it cannot survive this loss.

The constitutional level of his theory will determine which mistakes are embedded. His theory of legislative supremacy, for example, will insure that any statutes he treats as mistakes will lose their gravitational force but not their specific authority. If he denies the gravitational force of the aircraft liability limitation statute, the statute is not thereby repealed; the mistake is embedded so that the specific authority survives. He must continue to respect the limitations the statute imposes upon liability, but he will not use it to argue in some other case for a weaker right. If he accepts some strict doctrine of precedent, and designates some judicial decision, like the decision denying a right in negligence against an accountant, a mistake, then the strict doctrine may preserve the specific authority of that decision, which might be limited to its enactment force, but the decision will lose its gravitational force; it will become in Justice Frankfurter's phrase, a piece of legal flotsam or jetsam. It will not be necessary to decide which.

That is fairly straightforward, but Hercules must take more pains with the second part of his theory of mistakes. He is required, by the justification he has fixed to the general practice of precedent, to compose a more detailed justification, in the form of a scheme of principle, for the entire body of statutes and common law decisions. But a justification that designates part of what is to be justified as mistaken is prima facie weaker than one that does not. The second part of his theory of mistakes must show that it is nevertheless a stronger justification than any alternative that does not recognize any mistakes, or that recognizes a different set of mistakes. That demonstration cannot be a deduction from simple rules of theory construction, but if Hercules bears in mind the connection he earlier established between precedent and fairness, this connection will suggest two guidelines for his theory of mistakes. In the first place, fairness fixes on institutional history, not just as history but as a political program that the government proposed to continue into the future; it seizes, that is, on forward-looking, not the backward-looking implications of precedent. If Hercules discovers that some previous decision, whether a statute or a judicial decision, is now widely regretted within the pertinent branch of the profession, that fact in itself distinguishes that decision as vulnerable. He must remember, second, that the argument from fairness that

demands consistency is not the only argument from fairness to which government in general, or judges in particular, must respond. If he believes, quite apart from any argument of consistency, that a particular statute or decision was wrong because unfair, within the community's own concept of fairness, then that belief is sufficient to distinguish the decision, and make it vulnerable. Of course, he must apply the guidelines with a sense of the vertical structure of his overall justification, so that decisions at a lower level are more vulnerable than decisions at a higher.

Hercules will therefore apply at least two maxims in the second part of his theory of mistakes. If he can show, by arguments of history or by appeal to some sense of the legal community, that a particular principle, though it once had sufficient appeal to persuade a legislature or court to a legal decision, has now so little force that it is unlikely to generate any further such decisions, then the argument from fairness that supports that principle is undercut. If he can show by arguments of political morality that such a principle, apart from its popularity, is unjust, then the argument from fairness that supports that principle is overridden. Hercules will be delighted to find that these discriminations are familiar in the practice of other judges. The jurisprudential importance of his career does not lie in the novelty, but just in the familiarity, of the theory of hard cases that he has now created.

NOTES

1. *Spartan Steel & Alloys Ltd. v. Martin & Co.*, [1973] 1 Q.B. 27.

2. See generally H.L.A. Hart, *The Concept of Law* (1961): 121–32.

3. See *Everson v. Board of Educ.*, 330 U.S. 1 (1947).

4. See *Chatwin v. United States*, 326 U.S. 455 (1946).

5. One previous example of the use of policy in statutory interpretations illustrates this form of constitution. In *Charles River Bridge v. Warren Bridge*, 24 Mass. (7 Pick.) 344 (1830), *aff'd*, 36 U.S. (11 Pet.) 420 (1837), the court had to decide whether a charter to construct a bridge across the Charles River was to be taken as exclusive, so that no further charters could be granted. Justice Morton of the Supreme Judicial Court held that the grant was not to be taken as exclusive, and argued, in support of that interpretation, that: [I]f consequences so inconsistent with the improvement and prosperity of the state result from the liberal and extended construction of the charters which have been granted, we ought, if the terms used will admit of it, rather to adopt a more limited and restricted one, than to impute such improvidence to the legislature. . . . . . .[Construing the grant as exclusive] would amount substantially to a cove-

nant, that during the plaintiffs' charter an important portion of our commonwealth, as to facilities for travel and transportation, should remain *in statu quo*. I am on the whole irresistibly brought to the conclusion, that this construction is neither consonant with sound reason, with judicial authorities, with the course of legislation, nor with the principles of our free institutions. Ibid. 460.

6.   [1866] L.R. 1 Ex. 265, *aff'd*, (1868) L.R. 3 H.L. 330.

7.   But since Hercules will be led to accept the rights thesis, see pp. 115–16 *infra*, his 'interpretation' of judicial enactments will be different from his interpretation of statutes in one important respect. When he interprets statutes he fixes to some statutory language, as we saw, arguments of principle or policy that provide the best justification of that language in the light of the legislature's responsibilities. His argument remains an argument of principle; he uses policy to determine what rights the legislature has already created. But when he 'interprets' judicial enactments he will fix to the relevant language only arguments of principle, because the rights thesis argues that only such arguments acquit the responsibility of the 'enacting' court.

8.   *MacPherson v. Buick Motor Co.*, 217 N.Y. 382, 111 N.E. 1050 (1916).

9.   H. L. A. Hart, *The Concept of Law*, 121–32.

10.   In *Williamson v. Lee Optical Co.*, 348 U.S. 483 (1955), Justice Douglas suggested that legislation generated by policy need not be uniform or consistent: The problem of legislative classification is a perennial one, admitting of no doctrinaire definition. Evils in the same field may be of different dimensions and proportions, requiring different remedies. Or so the legislature may think. Or the reform may take one step at a time, addressing itself to the phase of the problem which seems most acute to the legislative mind. The legislature may select one phase of one field and apply a remedy there, neglecting the others. The prohibition of the Equal Protection Clause goes no further than the invidious discrimination. Ibib. 489 (citations omitted). Of course the point of the argument here, that the demands of consistency are different in the cases of principle and policy, is of great importance in understanding the recent history of the equal protection clause. It is the point behind attempts to distinguish 'old' from 'new' equal protection, or to establish 'suspect' classifications, and it provides a more accurate and intelligible distinction than these attempts have furnished.

11.   6 N.Y. 397 (1852).

12.   Warren & Brandeis, "The Right of Privacy," 4 *Harv. L. Rev.* (1890) 193.

RONALD M. DWORKIN

The Law of the Slave-Catchers*

Justice Accused by Robert M. Cover is an excellent book about a fascinating historical and legal puzzle. In the years before the American Civil War a considerable number of very able judges decided problematical law suits in such a way as to promote slavery, in spite of the fact that these judges were themselves opposed to that institution and in some cases passionately so. Most of these cases arose under the Fugitive Slave Acts. The Constitution, as part of the grand compromise between slave and free states, had provided if a "Person held to Service of Labour in one State" escapes to another, he shall not, in consequence of any law or regulation of the latter, be discharged from that service, "but shall be delivered up on Claim of the Party to whom such Service of Labour may be due." Congress, in 1793 and 1850, enacted procedures through which a slave who had escaped to a free state might be arrested by a slave-catcher without a warrant, brought before federal officials, and then returned to his master.

These statutes, particularly the latter, offended ordinary notions of due process in several ways: the federal official was a mere commissioner who received a higher fee if the alleged slave was sent back than if he was not, there was no question of jury trial, and the defendant was not allowed to contest whether he was in fact a slave, that issue being left to be decided in the slave state after his return. The statutes also left open many questions of procedure, particularly about the power of the free states themselves to impose restrictions on the process in the interests of the alleged slave.

The statutes were hated and often evaded in the Northern states. Many anti-slavery lawyers said that they were unconstitutional; others argued that they should be narrowly applied against the slave-catchers and, where ambiguous, interpreted so as to defeat them. With the exception of one decision in Wisconsin, all these liberal arguments lost in the courts. Judges like the famous Joseph Story and Lemuel Shaw, who revolutionized the common law with his progressive and policy-minded decisions, said that they were duty-bound to enforce the law as it was, against the slaves, rather than to follow their own moral convictions.

They did not take these decisions to please any crowd or to advance their own political or judicial careers; on the contrary, their decisions were enormously unpopular and the career of one judge, at least, was destroyed by his decisions in the slave cases.

There are two directions we might follow in looking for a reason for these decisions. The first is psychological. Can we find, in the character of men like Story and Shaw, some complexity to explain why they might want to see themselves as unflinching servants of a harsh law? The second is jurisprudential. Can we find, in the reigning legal philosophy, some explanation of why they conceived of their duty as they did?

Professor Cover does not discuss the psychological question at length, but he offers an intriguing literary hypothesis. Herman Melville was Shaw's son-in-law, and Shaw might have been the model for Captain Vere in *Billy Budd*, who thought that Billy was an innocent "angel of God" and yet ordered him to be hanged for killing under extreme provocation. The comparison seems superficial because the law of mutiny that Vere enforced was clear and admitted no excuse, so that Vere, unlike Shaw, had a clear decision between law and morality.

But it is Vere's response to his own decision, not the decision itself that is suggestive. Like the biblical Abraham, he found satisfaction in the very idea of a power so strong that it can exact obligation, not simply obedience, no matter how unjust its command. There may always be, in lawyers and judges, a taint of satisfaction in that idea, which makes them officers and priests in a powerful mystery. But

*Ronald Dworkin, "The Law of the Slave-Catchers," A review of *Justice Accused: Antislavery and the Judicial Process* by Robert M. Cover, December 5, 1975, p. 1437. Reprinted by permission of *The Times Literary Supplement*, London.

though Melville, if Professor Cover is right, may have sensed that pleasure in his father-in-law, it could not have been so widespread among all the abolitionist judges as to explain the unanimity of their decisions.

The book explores the jurisprudential question at much greater length. Professor Cover says that the judges found themselves in what he calls a moral-formal dilemma, and that they chose to conform to formal constraints rather than to follow morality. He does not mean (though he sometimes suggests he does) that the judges were formalistic, in the sense in which judges, particularly in England, are often accused of that vice. There was nothing mechanical or legalistic about their decisions. The anti-slavery judges suffered not from too much formalism but from too little.

They looked, not to the technical language, but to the purpose of the provisions they were called upon to interpret. They understood that the constitutional provision and the congressional statutes were designed to appease the South and preserve the Union, and they cut through any number of narrowly legalistic and verbal arguments, which would have justified decisions for the slaves, to promote that purpose. They were in this way progressive and policy-minded judges, very much in the spirit of Oliver Wendell Holmes who, a generation later, led a revolt against formalism and who also, incidentally, hated many of the policies his progressive jurisprudence required him to promote.

Professor Cover means that the judges were formalistic in a different sense: they saw a conflict between their own moral principles and their institutional duty as judges, and they preferred institutional duty to independent principle. That is, however, hardly surprising, for it seems quite normal and right for judges to do their duty even when they find it distasteful.

If the slavery cases had been easy cases from the legal point of view—if the legal issues really were already settled in favour of the slave-catchers—then it would not have been surprising that the judges would have enforced that law even though they disapproved it. The slavery cases are interesting and puzzling only because they were not easy cases; the law was not already settled against the slaves, though the judges said it was. The important question is not, therefore, why the judges decided to follow their sense of the institutional duty, but rather why they thought their institutional duty required them to decide that way.

Jurisprudence played an important part. In the early nineteenth century the philosophical tradition of natural law was still alive. Many lawyers, for whom William Blackstone was the principal spokesman, accepted the idea of a body of law that exists by virtue of objective morality rather than the positive enactments of legislatures or other human agencies. Some lawyers thought that this body of natural law was superior to any positive law, so that the pro-slavery provisions of the Constitution and the Fugitive Slave Acts, which violated the natural rights of men to be free, were invalid as a matter of law.

Others thought that natural law acted, not as a test of positive law in this way, but as a reserve body of law available to fill in the gaps when positive law was incomplete or unclear. They argued that this reserve of natural law required a liberal rather than a pro-slavery interpretation of the unclear constitutional and statutory provisions.

These different natural-law arguments were made to the judges. If they had accepted these arguments, they would not have thought that their judicial duty required them to hold against the slaves, because their general duty—to apply the law—would have dictated the opposite. But the judges, as a matter of legal philosophy, rejected the idea of natural law entirely. Professor Cover says that they were legal positivists in the manner of Bentham; if so, they thought that the positive law exhausted the law, so that if positive law is unsettled, and does not dictate a decision one way or another in a hard case, there is no other source of law to which judges may turn. They must, in that situation, exercise their discretion to develop the law as their sense of justice or policy suggests.

But if the judges were Benthamite positivists, it is more rather than less puzzling that they decided the slavery cases against the slaves. If they believed that the positive law did not require those decisions, why did they think that their institutional duty, as judges, required them to decide that way? If they believed that they had to exercise a legislative discretion to make new law, why did they believe they had to make new law that they thought was immoral?

Professor Cover thinks that they believed that their legislative role was necessarily a subordinate role. They thought that their duty required them to legislate so as to advance whatever policies the superior institutions—the Constitutional Convention and the Congress—had set in train, and not to attempt to interfere with these policies no matter how wrong they seemed. But why did the judges conceive their institutional duty that way? They thought that the legislative policies in question violated the most fundmental of human rights. Why should they reject the competing idea that their formal responsibility as judges required that they protect individual right against misguided public policy?

That competing idea is not, after all, a bizarre or alien theory of judicial responsibility. It has dominated the Supreme Court, in the person of John Marshall, years before the slavery cases, just as it was to dominate the Conservative Court of the early 1930s and the liberal Warren Court of the 1960s. Professor Cover supposes that the judges had a sense of democracy that obliged them to defer to the policies of elected officials. But there are difficulties in that hypothesis too. The Constitution reflected an eighteenth-century conception of democracy, which was as concerned to limit power of the people, so as to protect the rights of individuals, as to extend the power. In any case, the Fugitive Slave Acts were wildly unpopular with the general public in the states in which these judges sat.

There is, perhaps, a simpler explanation of why the judges could not accept that their formal role required them to defend the individual rights in which they believed. The rights in which they believed were accepted locally, but they were also the subject of a national political controversy so violent that it would end in war.

The judges could not easily accept that the judicial branch should be institutionally committed to one side or another of such a controversy, and the more passionate were the moral convictions of a particular judge, the more might he suspect any suggestion that an official supposed to be impartial should impose these convictions from the bench. Such a judge saw, on one side of the legislative scales, a policy that could be called public because it had been embodied in a constitutional provision and a series of national statutes. He found, on the other side, a passion that, however fervent, he could not count as public but only as personal.

But if that is how the judges saw their predicament, then a failure in jurisprudence contributed to their dilemma. The debate between natural law and positivism had squeezed out a third theory of law according to which the rights of the slaves were as much institutional, and much more the responsibility of judges to protect, than the national policies of appeasement.

This is the theory that the law of a community consists not simply in the discrete statutes and rules that its official enact but in the general principles of justice and fairness that these statutes and rules, taken together, presuppose by way of implicit justfication. The general structure of the American Constitution presupposed a conception of individual freedom antagonistic to slavery, a conception of procedural justice that condemned the procedures established by the Fugitive Slave Acts, and a conception of federalism inconsistent with the idea that the State of Massachusetts had no power to supervise the capture of men and women within its territory. These principles were not simply the personal morality of a few judges, which they set aside in the interests of objectivity. They were rather, on this theory of what law is, more central to the law than were the particular and transitory policies of the slavery compromise.

That theory was not set out in any influential work of jurisprudence, but it was not unknown or foreign to contemporary lawyers.

It is, in fact, the theory of law on which the idea of the common law is based. Story himself relied on a similar theory in a famous opinion in the conflict of laws, an opinion that years later Holmes himself rejected because it was based on the idea that law is, as this theory supposes, a "brooding omnipresence" of principle. Nevertheless Story and the others rejected the theory as the basis of the law of slavery, and endured instead the agony of serving an institution they deplored. Whatever the reason, these judges missed a chance to develop an alternative to both natural law and policy-orientated positivism, and that omission is an important part of American legal and intellectual history.

Professor Cover's book is splendid in many ways. His legal history and legal philosphy are both first class; he is a good enough historian to tell more of a story than he needs to prove a point, and a good enough philosopher to understand how complex are the points he wishes to prove. This is, for a change, an interdisciplinary work that is a credit to both disciplines.

J. L. MACKIE

The Third Theory of Law*

I have resisted the temptation to entitle this paper "Taking Rights Seriously and Playing Fast and Loose with the Law." But it will become plain, as I go on, why I was tempted.

Professor Dworkin's theory of law is now well known, especially since the publication of his book, *Taking Rights Seriously*.[1] But it may be as well to review it, and show how some of his main theses fit together.

I call it the third theory of law because it contrasts both with legal positivism and with the doctrine of natural law, and is in some ways intermediate between the two. The natural law doctrine is well summarized by Blackstone: "This law of nature being coeval with mankind and dictated by God himself is of course superior in obligation to any other. It is binding over the whole globe, in all countries and at all times. No human laws are of any validity if contrary to this, and such of them as are valid derive their force and all their authority, mediately or immediately, from this original."[2] This entails that a judge, relying on his rational knowledge of natural law, may overrule even what appears to be the settled law of the land—unambiguous and regularly enacted statutes or clearly relevant and unopposed precedents—and declare that the apparently settled law is not the law. Against this, I think that Professor Dworkin would concede that all law is made somehow by human beings, and that the (detailed) question, What is the law? makes sense only if construed as asking, What is at a certain time the law of England, or of France, or of the United States, or of South Dakota? The validity of a law is wholly relative to the legal system to which it belongs. Consequently the finding out of what is the law is an empirical task, not a matter of *a priori* reasoning. But, this being conceded, Professor Dworkin stresses a series of contrasts between his view and legal positivism, even such a cautious form of positivism as Professor Hart's.

First, he holds that the law consists not only of rules but also of principles, the distinction between these being logical: "Rules are applicable in an all-or-nothing fashion," whereas principles have the extra dimension of weight (*TRS,* pp. 22–28).

Secondly, he rejects the positivist notion of a single ultimate or fundamental test for law, such as Professor Hart's "rule of recognition." In its place he puts the sort of reasoning that he ascribes, in "Hard Cases," to his imaginary judge, Hercules. Some parts of the law in a certain jurisdiction are settled and relatively uncontroversial, in the constitution or statutes or precedents. Hercules uses these as data, seeking the theory, in terms of further rights and principles, which best explains and justifies this settled law. Having developed this theory, he then applies it to the hard case (*TRS,* pp. 105–123).

Thirdly, and as a result of this method, Professor Dworkin holds that in any sufficiently rich legal system (notably in that of England no less than in that of the United States) the question, What is the law on this issue? always has a right answer, discoverable in principle, and it is the duty of the judge to try to discover it. One of the parties will always have a right to a decision in his favor. "Judicial decisions enforce existing political rights." There is a theoretical possibility of a tie, a dead heat, between competing sets of principles when all relevant considerations have been taken into account, but this is so unlikely that it may in practice be ignored. (See *TRS,* pp. 81, 279–290, esp. 286–287.)

Consequently, and fourthly, though judges in hard or controversial cases have discretion in the weak sense that they are called upon to exercise judgment—they are not supplied with any cut and dried decision procedure—they never have discretion in the strong sense which would exclude a duty to decide the case one way rather than the other (*TRS,* pp. 31–35, 68–71).

Fifthly, though it is really only another way of making the same point, Professor Dworkin holds that even in a hard case one does not reach a stage where the law has run out before it has yielded a decision, and the judge has to make some new law to deal with a new problem. Judges never need to act, even surreptitiously,

*From J. L. Mackie, "The Third Theory of Law," *Philosophy & Public Affairs,* Vol. 7, No. 1 (Fall 1977). Copyright © 1977 by Princeton University Press. Reprinted by permission of Princeton University Press.

as legislators, though he has allowed that they may in fact do so as they sometimes do when they make a mistake or when they prospectively overrule a clear precedent.[3]

A sixth point is a further consequence of this. If judges were in effect legislating, it would be appropriate for them to do so in the light of considerations of policy—in particular, of utility or the general welfare of the community or the known will of the majority of the people. But if they are not legislating but still discovering an already existing law, they must confine themselves to considerations of principle; if they let policy outweigh principle, they will be sacrificing someone's rights in order to benefit or satisfy others, and this is unjust. There is, however, an exception to this point. It holds uniformly in civil cases, Professor Dworkin says, but only asymmetrically in criminal cases. The accused may have a right to be acquitted, but the prosecution never has a right to a conviction. So a court may sometimes justly acquit, for reasons of policy, someone who is in fact guilty (TRS, pp. 82–100).

Seventhly, Professor Dworkin rejects the traditional positivist separation of law from morality. However, this is a tricky issue. The legal positivism he has explicitly taken as his main target is that of Professor Hart, and Professor Hart recognizes many ways in which law and morality are closely linked. For example, he says, "In some systems, as in the United States, the ultimate criteria of legal validity explicitly incorporate principles of justice or substantive moral values . . ." " . . . statutes may be a mere legal shell and demand by their express terms to be filled out with the aid of moral principles; the range of enforceable contracts may be limited by reference to conceptions of morality and fairness . . . " and "Judicial decision, especially on matters of high constitutional import, often involves a choice between moral values . . . " But one point on which Professor Hart stands firm is that we can sometimes say, "This is law but too iniquitous to obey or apply," rather than, "Because this is iniquitous it is not law." He argues (against supporters of natural law) that it is both more clearheaded and morally better to allow that something can be valid law and yet evil.[4] It is not clear to me whether Professor Dworkin would deny this. But he makes the following important point. The task which he assigns to Hercules in "Hard Cases" is to find the theory that best explains and justifies the settled law, and to use this theory to decide

otherwise unsettled issues. He construes the phrase "best explains and justifies" as including a moral dimension; Hercules has to find the morally best justification of the constitution, statutes, practices, and so on which are not in dispute. In doing this, Hercules must himself make substantive moral judgments, and not merely take account of conventional morality, of widely accepted social rules (TRS, pp. 123–128; cf. pp. 206–222).

This third theory of law combines descriptive with prescriptive elements. On the one hand, Professor Dworkin is claiming that it gives the best theoretical understanding of legal procedures and legal reasoning actually at work in such systems as those of England and the United States. But on the other, he wants it to be more explicitly accepted and more consciously followed. He wants it to become a truer description than it yet is, whereas some views that might count as interpretations of the positivist model—for example, the "strict constructionist" view favored by ex-President Nixon—would, he thinks, have deplorable results (TRS, pp. 131–149).

It follows that discussion of this theory must also be on more than one level. We are concerned with both its truth as a description and its merit as a recommendation. Let us consider it first as a description. Professor Dworkin argues that courts do, in fact, appeal to principles as distinct from rules and that no coherent description of their procedures can be given by a theory which recognizes only rules as constituting the law. This must, I think, be conceded. But he further maintains that the way in which judges reason in hard cases is some approximation to that which he ascribes to his superhuman judge, Hercules; and such a view is much more controversial. Along with other aspects of his descriptive theory it needs to be checked empirically and in detail. But some general preliminary comments can be made.

First, there is a distinction—and there may be a divergence—between what judges say they are doing, what they think they are doing, and the most accurate objective description of what they actually are doing. They may say and even believe that they are discovering and applying an already existing law, they may be following procedures which assume this as their aim, and yet they may in fact be making new law. Such a divergence is not even improbable, because even where new law is being made, it will seem fairer if this fact is concealed and the decision is believed to enforce only presently existing rights; and because the making of new law will usually mean only that existing rules or principles are extended somewhat beyond their previous field of application.

Secondly, even though legal reasoning in hard cases involves appeals to principles and rights and is affected by "the gravitational force of precedents," it does not follow that it does or must or even should work in terms of a complete theory of the underlying law for the jurisdiction in question. The superhuman Hercules is, as his name indicates, a mythical figure, and human judges will always operate in a more limited way. However, the practical force of Professor Dworkin's account is that it allows and encourages judges to bring to bear upon a controversial case general considerations and notions about rights which are supported by elements in the settled law that are remote from the case in hand. We may or may not want this; but I would stress that this holistic treatment of the law is in no way required by the admission that legal reasoning appeals to principles as well as to rules. That admission allows such remote control, but does not require it.

Thirdly, though legal reasoning in hard cases refers to rights, this does not entail that it can take no account of interests. Admittedly, to take rights seriously is to see them as having some resistance to interests; in particular, it is to recognize that the rights of an individual will often justify a decision in his favor which is against the interests of the community as a whole. However, Professor Dworkin himself does not regard all rights as absolute, but admits that they may sometimes be overruled by community interest. And when rights conflict with one another, interests may help to determine which right is the stronger in the particular circumstances.

There is no doubt that judges sometimes argue in this way, as in *Miller* v. *Jackson and Another,* heard in the British Court of Appeal—reported in *The Times,* 7 April 1977. The plaintiff lived in a house built in 1972 near a village cricket ground which had been used for over seventy years. He sought an injunction to prevent the club members from playing cricket unless they took adequate steps to prevent stray balls from hitting his house and garden. There is a conflict of rights here: *prima facie* the club has a right to go on playing cricket and the plaintiff has a right to enjoy his home and garden in safety. The court refused, by two to one, to grant the injunction. The judges on the majority side spoke of the public interest and also stressed that the injunction sought was a discretionary remedy. Lord Denning said that the public interest lay in protecting the environment by preserving playing fields in the face of mounting development and enabling our youth to enjoy the benefits of outdoor games, in contrast to the private interest, which lay in securing the privacy of a home and garden without intrusion or interference. Lord Justice Cumming-Bruce said that in considering whether to exercise a judicial discretion to grant an injunction the court was under a duty to consider the interests of the public. That is, they seemed to think that while each party had a *prima facie* right, when these rights came into conflict the importance of the public interest made the cricket club's right the stronger. Professor Dworkin may deplore such reasoning, but he can hardly deny that it occurs, nor can he argue that it should not occur merely because in a hard case there are appeals to principles and rights.

Fourthly, it would be a mere fallacy (which I want to guard against, but do not accuse Professor Dworkin of committing) to argue from the premise that hard cases should be reasoned (partly) in terms of rights—including *prima facie,* non-absolute rights—to the conclusion that in such a case one party must have a (final or resultant) right to a decision in his favor.

Fifthly, there is a weakness in the argument that an exactly equal balance between the considerations on either side is so unlikely that it is almost certain that one party will have an antecedent right to win (*TRS,* pp. 286–287). This argument assumes too simple a metric for the strength of considerations, that such strengths are always commensurable on a linear scale, so that the strength of the case for one side must be either greater than that of the case for the other side, or less, or else they must be equal in the sense of being so finely balanced that even the slightest additional force on either side would make it the stronger. But in fact considerations may be imperfectly commensurable, so that neither of the opposing cases is stronger than the other, and yet they are not finely balanced. Consider the analogous question about three brothers: Is Peter more like James than he is like John? There may be an objectively right and determinable answer to this question, but again there may not. It may be that the only correct reply is that Peter is more like James in some ways and more like John in others, and that there is no objective reason for putting more weight on the former points of resemblance than on the latter or vice versa. While we might say that Peter's likeness to James is equal to his likeness to John (because neither is determinately the greater), this does not mean that any slight additional resemblance to either would decide the issue; hence, it does not mean that this equality expresses an improbably exact balance.

Sixthly, we must note an implication of Professor Dworkin's inclusion of a moral dimension in the reasoning he assigns to Hercules. Hercules' judgment about what the law is on some specific issue depends on what he finds to be the best explanatory and justificatory theory of the settled law. So what the law is, on Professor Dworkin's view, may crucially depend on what is morally best—what is best, not what is conventionally regarded as best in that society. Now I would argue, though I cannot do so here, that moral judgments of this kind have an irreducibly subjective element.[5] If so, then Professor Dworkin's theory automatically injects a corresponding subjectivity into statements about what the law is. Of course, Professor Dworkin is right in arguing that the moral judgments people make—and this may also be true for those that Hercules can be presumed to make—are not, in general, reports of socially established rules or even such reports conjoined with the speaker's acceptance or endorsement of those rules (TRS, pp. 45-58). Moral judgments typically include what I call a claim to objectivity and to the objectivity precisely of their prescriptive authority. But these claims, I maintain, are always false. Prescriptive moral judgments are really subjective, though those who make them commonly think that they are objectively valid and mean them to be objectively valid. Suppose Hercules and another judge in the same jurisdiction, both following Professor Dworkin's methods, reach different conclusions about what the law on some issue is because each has reasoned coherently in the light of his own moral views. Though each of them will sincerely and consistently believe that the law already is as he determines it, I maintain that they will both be wrong. The grounds on which they rely fail to determine an objective preexisting law. Whichever judge's opinion wins the day in the final court of appeal will become the law and will then be the law. The judges who finally decide the case will have been legislating, though they will sincerely, consistently, and ra-

tionally believe that they have not. By making a choice determined by their subjective moral judgments for which they honestly but mistakenly claim objective validity, they will have been making law on an issue on which there was previously no determinate law, on which they had no antecedent duty to decide one way rather than the other, and on which neither party had a right to a decision in his favor.

These six general points cast doubt on some parts of Professor Dworkin's descriptive theory, but they should be tested along with the theory, against actual examples of hard cases. I now want to leave the question of description and consider the merits of the third theory as a recommendation. I can do this best by going straight to a concrete example, taken from the legal history of the United States. Professor Dworkin, in a review of Robert M. Cover's book *Justice Accused,* applies his theory to cases which arose before the American Civil War under the Fugitive Slave Acts.[6]

He finds it puzzling that such judges as Joseph Story and Lemuel Shaw, though themselves strongly opposed to slavery, enforced these acts, sending alleged runaway slaves back from states in which slavery was not permitted to states where it still existed and from which they were alleged to have escaped. But why is there a puzzle? Were these judges not, as they themselves said, simply doing their legal duty of enforcing what was then the law of the land, despite the fact that it conflicted with their own moral views? Professor Dworkin argues that it is not so simple. The relevant law was not settled: these cases were controversial. Though the judges in question explicitly denied this, in their deeper thinking they admitted it. But then, being legal positivists, they concluded that they had to legislate, to make new law by their findings. But why, then, did they not make the law in accordance with their moral convictions and their sense of justice? Because, says Professor Dworkin, following Cover, they saw themselves as subordinate legislators only, bound to make the law in harmony with the discoverable intentions of the superior legislators in Congress and, earlier, in the Constitutional Convention. These legislators had, in their several enactments, created and maintained a compromise between the slave states and the nonslave states; therefore, sending an alleged slave back to the state from which he had come was the natural fulfilment of that compromise.

According to Professor Dworkin, the reason-

ing of these judges was a "failure of jurisprudence." If they had been adherents, not of positivism, but of the third theory, they could have
found in the general structure of the American
Constitution "a conception of individual freedom antagonistic to slavery, a conception of
procedural justice that condemned the procedures established by the Fugitive Slave Acts,
and a conception of federalism inconsistent
with the idea that the State of Massachusetts
had no power to supervise the capture of men
and women within its territory." These principles were "more central to the law than were the
particular and transitory policies of the slavery
compromise."

It is not in dispute that if these judges had
been adherents of the natural law doctrine—as
evidently they were not—they might have refused to enforce the Fugitive Slave Acts. Then
the judges would have held that even if the Acts
were settled law in the sense of being unambiguous and regularly enacted statutes, they were
not genuine law because they violated principles
of justice and natural right which were prior to
any man-made system of law. The problem is
whether the third theory would have yielded the
same result.

First, was the law really not settled? Professor
Dworkin says that the (federal) Fugitive Slave
Acts "left open many questions of procedure,
particularly about the power of the free states
themselves to impose restrictions on the process
in the interests of the alleged slave." And Massachusetts had enacted such restrictions. However, the judges held that these restrictions were
overruled by the federal laws, and this seems to
follow from a straightforward interpretation of
Article VI of the United States Constitution:
"This Constitution, and the laws of the United
States which shall be made in pursuance
thereof, . . . shall be the supreme law of the
land; and the judges in every State shall be
bound thereby, anything in the constitution or
laws of any State notwithstanding." Professor
Dworkin refers also to "narrowly legalistic and
verbal arguments" on behalf of the alleged
slaves, but arguments of that description, too
easily produced, will not show that the law was
not, for all that, settled. The only ground on
which he can claim, in a way that is even initially plausible, that the law was not settled, is
that the procedures laid down in these acts "offended ordinary notions of due process." The
federal official who returned the alleged slave to
his purported master was "a mere commissioner

who received a higher fee if the alleged slave
was sent back than if he was not, there was no
question of a jury trial, and the defendant was
not allowed to contest whether he was in fact a
slave, that issue being left to be decided in the
slave state after his return."

But it is far from clear that these provisions
offend against due process. They would be defended on the ground that these proceedings
were only preliminary: the legal issue about the
fugitive's status was still to be decided in the
state from which he had come, and that, surely,
was where witnesses to his identity and status
would be available. He was not being deprived
of liberty without due process of law; the due
process would take place in, say, Virginia. This
argument could be rebutted only by casting
doubt on the legal respectability of the Virginia
courts, and whatever private doubts the Massachusetts judges may have had about this, it was
an essential part of the federal compromise that
they should not be guided by such doubts in
their legal decisions. Article IV, Section I, of the
Constitution says that "full faith and credit
shall be given in each State to the public acts,
records, and judicial proceedings of any other
State." The Virginian slave-owner could have
argued that if he were not allowed to get his
slave back without bringing a large number of
witnesses five hundred miles so as to have his
claim heard before a Massachusetts jury which
was likely to be hostile to the very institution of
slavery on which his claim was based, he would
be, in effect, being deprived of his property,
namely the slave, without due process of law.
Article IV, Section 2, of the Constitution is
quite explicit: "No person held to service or labor in one State, under the laws thereof, escaping into another, shall, in consequence of any
law or regulation therein, be discharged from
such service or labor, but shall be delivered up
on claim of the party to whom such service or
labor may be due."

That, in the face of all this, Professor
Dworkin can hold that the law was not settled
brings out an important characteristic of his
theory, highly relevant to the assessment of its
merits as a recommendation: the third theory
often takes as unsettled issues which on a legal
positivist view belong clearly to the realm of settled law.

But suppose that the law was not settled, and
that a judge at the time had tried to decide these
cases by Professor Dworkin's method. What
conclusion would he have reached? Hercules,

being a product of Professor Dworkin's imagination, would no doubt have argued as Professor Dworkin does. But let us invent another mythical judge, say Rhadamanthus.[7] He might have argued as follows:

What principles that are relevant to this case are implicit in the settled law? The fundamental fact is the Union itself, which arose out of an alliance, against Britain, of thirteen separate and very different colonies. It was recognized from the start that these colonies, and the states which they have become, have diverse institutions and ways of life. The Union exists and can survive only through compromises on issues where these differing institutions and ways of life come into conflict. One salient principle, then, enshrined as clearly as anything could be in the federal Constitution and in various statutes, is that the rights which individuals have by virtue of the institutions of the states in which they live are to be protected throughout the Union. A Virginian slave-owner's property in his slaves is one of these rights; the clear intention of Article IV, Section 2, of the Constitution and of the Fugitive Slave Acts is to protect this right. Therefore, whatever merely technical defects may be found in them the law of the land, as determined by the third theory of law which I hold, is that the alleged slave should be returned from Massachusetts to Virginia, where it can be properly decided, by the evidence of many witnesses, whether he is in fact the slave of the man who claims him.

The contrary view, that the Constitution presupposes a conception of freedom antagonistic to slavery, cannot be upheld. Jefferson, who actually wrote the Declaration of Independence, and who later was mainly responsible for the amendments which most strongly assert individual rights, was himself a slave-owner. The individual freedom which the Constitution presupposes was never intended to apply to slaves. Nor will the requirements of procedural justice, which can indeed be seen as principles enshrined in the settled law, support a finding in favor of the alleged slave. On the presumption that slave-owners have legally valid property rights in their slaves, procedural justice will best be secured by sending the alleged slave back. The conception of federalism does no doubt give the state of Massachusetts the power to supervise the capture of men and women in its territory, but this power must be exercised in ways that respect the institutions of Virginia and the rights of citizens of Virginia, especially as these are further protected by federal law.

Even if Joseph Story and Lemuel Shaw had shared Professor Dworkin's theory of jurisprudence, they might still have followed Rhadamanthus rather than Hercules and, without for a moment abandoning their reliance on principles or their concern for rights, might have reached just those decisions they did reach by a more positivistic route. This brings out a second characteristic of the third theory, highly relevant to the assessment of its merits as a recommendation: the rights thesis, like the natural law doctrine that it in some ways resembles, is a two-edged weapon. It is particularly risky for an opponent of slavery and of racial discrimination to appeal to states' rights within a federal system. The special importance which Professor Dworkin, in his essays on applied jurisprudence (*TRS,* pp. 206–258), gives to the right to equality is not a necessary consequence of the rights thesis as such.

A third important characteristic of Professor Dworkin's theory is that its adoption would tend to make the law not only less certain but also less determinate than it would be on the rival positivist view. Of course, it is never completely determinate. Reasonable judges may well disagree on hard cases, whatever theory of jurisprudence they hold. But the third theory introduces a further source of indeterminacy. It is well known that the inference from a precedent to a general rule supposed to be implicit in it is not watertight; but a much larger degree of freedom is introduced if the judge has to frame hypotheses, not merely about rules which apply directly to cases, but also about far more general and abstract principles of justice and their implications.

Professor Dworkin would deny this. He would say that it is legal positivism that would make the law in hard cases indeterminate, since it envisages situations in which the law as a whole, not merely the settled law, has run out. Judges are then called upon to legislate, bringing in considerations of policy as well as morality, and it tells judges that they thus have discretion in the strong sense. His theory, on the other hand, holds that there is on every issue a determinate and, in principle, discoverable, though perhaps not settled or certain, law.

This is why I am tempted to speak of Professor Dworkin playing fast and loose with the law.[8] The alleged determinacy of the law in hard cases is a myth, and the practical effect of the acceptance of this myth would be to give, in three ways, a larger scope for what is in reality judicial legislation. First, it would shift the boundary between the settled and the unsettled law, it would make what on another view would be easy cases into hard ones. Secondly, this approach would encourage a holistic treatment of the law, letting very general principles and remote parts of the law bear upon each specific issue. Thirdly, it would encourage judges, in this holistic treatment, to rely upon their necessarily subjective views about a supposedly objective morality.

The third theory of law is thus a plea for a more speculative and enterprising handling by judges of their traditional materials and data. Like the natural law doctrine, this theory allows the consciences and the speculations of judges to intervene more significantly between what the legislative and executive branches try to do—or, for whatever reason, leave undone—and the law as it actually operates. We know well that people's prejudices, training, and social position—the movements in which they are caught up and the ideologies linked with these—strongly influence their consciences and their speculations. Whether we consider this a merit or a demerit depends upon our judgment of the judges, and particularly upon comparative judgments we make between them, the legislators, and the holders of executive office. Which of these three, with their characteristic methods and the influences to which they are exposed or from which they are sheltered, are

the more to be trusted with the opportunity for partly independent decision in the making and remaking of the law? Should we give up some certainty and determinacy about what the law is, and some freedom for legislators to decide what it shall be, in order to give greater weight to what judges will see as people's rights or just claims? I do not know what answer to give, but I want it to be clear that this is the choice.

NOTES

1. Ronald Dworkin, *Taking Rights Seriously* (London, 1977).
2. *Commentaries,* quoted by Julius Stone, *The Providence and Function of Law* (Sydney, 1946), p. 227.
3. *TRS,* pp. 82–84. Professor Dworkie gave this clarification in reply to a question from Professor Sir Rupert Cross at a seminar on Hard Cases in Oxford, 12 May 1976.
4. H. L. A. Hart, *The Concept of Law* (Oxford, 1961), pp. 181–207, esp. 199–200 and 205–207.
5. I have argued for this view in Chapter 1 of my *Ethics: Inventing Right and Wrong* (Harmondsworth, 1977).
6. *The Times Literary Supplement,* 5 December 1975.
7. Cf. Plato, *The Apology of Socrates* 40e–41a: "Would it be such a bad journey if one arrived in Hades, having got rid of the self-styled judges here, and found the true judges who are said to have jurisdiction there, Minos and Rhadamanthus and Aeacus and Triptolemus and such other demigods as were just during their lives?"
8. Cf. *Oxford English Dictionary:* "Fast and loose: A cheating game played with a stick and a belt or string, so arranged that a spectator would think he could make the latter fast by placing a stick through its intricate folds, whereas the operator could detach it at once."

ANDREW ALTMAN

Legal Realism, Critical Legal Studies, and Dworkin*

I

In contemporary Anglo-American legal philosophy, little attention has been paid to the work in legal theory carried out in this country during the first half of the century. Indeed, it would be only a slight exaggeration to say that legal theory prior to the publication of H. L. A. Hart's classic *The Concept of Law,* is generally treated as belonging to a kind of prehistorical legal philosophy.[1] Contemporary authors feel it unnecessary to grapple with the theories belonging to this prehistory, as it is widely viewed that such theories have been transcended by the work of Hart and those who followed in his wake.

Nowhere is this attitude toward the legal theories of the first half of the century more evident than in the contemporary treatment of American legal realism. Attention to the realist movement is, to say the least, scanty. Ronald Dworkin devotes approximately one page to the movement in the more than three hundred pages of *Taking Rights Seriously.*[2] Theodore Benditt is more generous in the space he devotes to discussing realism: two chapters of his *Law as Rule and Principle.* Yet, Benditt treats realism as little more than a historical relic.[3] To be sure, realism is regarded as having had its insights, but they are thought of as having been long ago recognized and absorbed into mainstream legal philosophy, while the deficiencies have been presumably identified and repudiated. Such is the dominant message about realism transmitted by most current work in legal philosophy.[4]

A principal part of the explanation for why most current legal philosophers seem to accept this message lies, I believe, in the apparently cogent critique of realism offered by Hart in *The Concept of Law.* Hart's theory absorbed many of the claims associated with the realist movement. At the same time, he repudiated what were called the "excesses" of realism by invoking a well worked out conception of law as a system of rules. Among those so-called excesses was the idea that the law was shot through with indeterminacy, so that in almost any dispute which reached the stage of litigation the law failed to dictate any specific outcome. Hart's theoretical strategy was to admit that there was a significant amount of indeterminacy in the law, but to argue that such indeterminacy necessarily occupied a peripheral zone in the work of the legal system. Hart thus domesticated the realist indeterminacy thesis. Subsequently, under the influence of Ronald Dworkin, mainstream legal philosophy became preoccupied with the issue of whether or not Hart had himself exaggerated the zone of legal indeterminacy. The more radical indeterminacy of the realist was consigned to the category of realist excesses which everyone now recognized and repudiated.

In this article, I shall begin by examining the realist indeterminacy thesis. Hart's criticisms of realism, I argue, do not come to grips with the most radical source of legal indeterminacy posited by realism. The same may be said for the extensive set of criticisms offered by Benditt. Dworkin's jurisprudence will then be analyzed as an effort to provide a superior response to realism than that offered by Hart. In assessing the Dworkinian approach, I shall be especially concerned to explore its relations to the only contemporary school of legal thought which has tried to utilize and expand upon the realist indeterminacy analysis, namely, the Critical Legal Studies movement (hereafter referred to as CLS). Although it will prove impossible to resolve the basic disagreements between Dworkin and CLS in the context of this article, I shall try to show that CLS does raise some very serious and unanswered questions about the soundness of Dworkinian jurisprudence and of mainstream legal philosophy in general.

*Andrew Altman, ''Legal Realism, Critical Legal Studies, and Dworkin,'' *Philosophy & Public Affairs*, Vol. 15, No. 3 (1986), pp. 205–236. Copyright © 1986 Princeton University Press. Reprinted with permission of Princeton University Press.

II

One of the now familiar theses defended by Hart in *The Concept of Law* is that there are some cases in which the rules of a legal system do not clearly specify the correct legal outcome.[5] Hart claims that such cases arise because of the ineliminable open-texture of natural language: all general terms have a penumbral range in which it is unclear and irresolvably controversial as to whether the term applies to some particular. Yet, this penumbral range of extensional indeterminacy is necessarily much smaller than the core extension in which the term's application is clear and uncontroversial. For Hart, then, the indeterminacy of law is a peripheral phenomenon in a system of rules which, by and large, does provide specific outcomes to cases.

The realist analysis of indeterminacy sees it as both more pervasive and deeper than the indeterminacy Hart attributes to the legal order. For the realist, there is no way to confine indeterminacy to some peripheral region of the law. For my purposes here, I shall be concerned mainly with the realist analysis of common-law adjudication. It should not be forgotten, however, that the realists could and did extend their analysis to all types of adjudication found in our legal system, including those involving statutory and constitutional issues.[6]

The realist analysis of indeterminacy can be presented in two stages.[7] The first stage proceeded from the idea that there was always a cluster of rules relevant to the decision in any litigated case. Thus, deciding whether an uncle's promise to pay his nephew a handsome sum of money if he refrained from smoking, drinking, and playing pool was enforceable brought into play a number of rules, for example, rules regarding offer, acceptance, consideration, revocation, and so on.[8] The realists understood that the vagueness of any one of these rules could affect the outcome of the case. In any single case, then, there were multiple potential points of indeterminacy due to rule vagueness, not a single point as Hart's account sometimes seems to suggest.

The second stage of the realist analysis began with the rejection of a distinction central to the doctrine of precedent, namely, that between holding and dictum.[9] The holding in a case referred to the essential grounds of the decision and thus what subsequent judges were bound by. The dicta were everything in an opinion not essential to the decision, for example, comments about points of law not treated as the basis of the outcome. The realists argued that in its actual operation the common-law system treated the distinction as a vague and shifting one. Even when the judge writing an opinion characterized part of it as "the holding," judges writing subsequent opinions were not bound by the original judge's perception of what was essential for the decision. Subsequent judges were indeed bound by the decision itself, that is, by the finding for or against the plaintiff, and very rarely was the decision in a precedent labeled as mistaken. But this apparently strict obligation to follow precedent was highly misleading, according to the realists. For later judges had tremendous leeway in being able to redefine the holding and the dictum in the precedential cases. This leeway enabled judges, in effect, to rewrite the rules of law on which earlier cases had been decided. The upshot was that in almost any case which reached the state of litigation, a judge could find opinions which read relevant precedents as stating a contrary rule. The common-law judge thus faced an indeterminate legal situation in which he had to render a decision by choosing which of the competing rules was to govern the case. In other words, while the realists claimed that all cases implicated a cluster of rules, they also contended that in any cluster there were competing rules leading to opposing outcomes.[10]

It is this second form of indeterminacy which the realist saw as the deepest and most pervasive. Depending upon how a judge would read the holdings in the cases deemed to be precedents, she would extract different rules of law capable of generating conflicting outcomes in the case before her. In the common-law system, it was left undetermined as to which rules, of a number of incompatible rules, were to govern a case. This type of indeterminacy cuts a much deeper and wider path than the kind Hart was willing to acknowledge. For Hart, the cases afflicted with indeterminacy are the ones in which we know which rule applies but are uncertain over the outcome because the rule contains some vague general term. This second type of realist indeterminacy stems from the fact that the choice of which rules to apply in the first place is not dictated by the law and that competing rules will be available in almost any case which reaches the stage of litigation.

In discussing realism, Hart makes three concessions to realist indeterminacy claims, while at the same time coupling each claim with a major qualification designed to show that actual indeterminacy is far less radical than realism suggests. First, Hart concedes that "there is no single method of determining the rule for which a given authoritative precedent is an authority." But he quickly adds: "Notwithstanding this, in the vast majority of decided cases, there is very little doubt. The headnote is usually correct enough."[11] It is simply question begging, though, for Hart to assert that the headnote usually provides a sufficiently accurate statement of the correct rule. The realist point is that there is nothing that can be thought of as "the correct rule" for which a precedent stands, and so there is no standard against which one can say that a given rule is "correct enough." On the realist analysis, the headnote, or indeed a later opinion, states only one of any number of competing rules which may, with equal legitimacy, be said to constitute the holding of a case. Hart's assertions do nothing to show that this analysis is wrong; they merely presuppose that it is wrong.

Hart's second concession to realism is that "there is no authoritative or uniquely correct formulation of any rule to be extracted from cases." But then he adds that "there is often very general agreement, when the bearing of a precedent on a later case is in issue, that a given formulation is adequate."[12] Hart seems to be saying here that lawyers may disagree on the precise formulation of a rule but still agree on the correct outcome of a case and so be able to accept, for the purposes of the case, a formulation which, in the given instance, straddles the different versions of the rule. This claim may very well be accurate, but it fails to defeat the realist indeterminacy claims for two reasons. It assumes that the problem of being able to extract conflicting rules from the same line of precedents has been resolved, and, as I argued in connection with Hart's first pair of points, that assumption is question begging. Second, even if there is general agreement on the outcome of a case and on some rough statement of the governing rule (and this, of course, ignores the disagreement which will always be found between the attorneys for the litigants), it does not follow that they agree on the outcome because they agree (roughly) on the legal rule which is said to govern the case. In other words, it does not follow that the law deter-

mines the outcome. Agreement on the outcome and on the rough statement of the rule used to justify the outcome may both be the result of some more fundamental political value choice which is agreed upon. Indeed, this is exactly what the realist analysis would suggest by way of explaining broad agreement on outcomes and rules. Realism is not committed to denying broad agreement. It is simply committed to the view that the agreement cannot be explained by the determinacy of the law. Thus, Hart's invocation of agreement here does nothing to defeat the realist's indeterminacy thesis.

Hart's third concession to realism is that courts invariably engage in narrowing and widening the rules which precedents lay down. Yet he says that, despite this, the doctrine of precedent has produced "a body of rules of which a vast number, of both major and minor importance, are as determinate as any statutory rule."[13] The problem with this claim, though, is that it misses the crucial realist point regarding the availability of competing rules: let each legal rule be as precise as is humanly possible, the realists insist that the legal system contains competing rules which will be available for a judge to choose in almost any litigated case. The claims made by Hart in his effort to domesticate the realist notion of legal indeterminacy all systematically fail to deal with this crucial realist point.

Benditt's arguments against realism are similarly flawed: none of them directly attack the problem of competing rules.[14] Indeed, this is not surprising, since Benditt's entire account of realism is distorted by his insistence on interpreting realism as denying the existence of authoritative legal rules.[15] While such "rule nihilism" may be suggested in some of the remarks of some realists, the more influential members and allies of the movement were clear that it is precisely the existence of competing *authoritative* rules which creates the radical indeterminacy problem. Llewellyn, perhaps the principal spokesperson for realism during its heyday, characterizes the problem as due to the fact that there are opposing "authoritative premises" for any case.[16] And Dewey's highly influential piece, "Logical Method and Law," stresses the problem of choice among competing rules, rather than denying the existence of authoritative rules.[17] Realists were undoubtedly a very heterogeneous group, at least when measured by their ideas about law, and some of the criticisms made by Hart and Benditt against some realist claims are persuasive.[18] But the standard criticisms do not touch the realist thesis that there is a pervasive indeterminacy in the legal system owing to the existence of competing rules of law.

III

To this point, I have portrayed the realists as focusing upon the choice of competing legal rules which judges in common-law cases must make. This may seem to leave the realist open to one of the principal criticisms which Dworkinians have made of Hart: the law is more than just legal rules. It is also the ethical principles and ideals of which the rules are an (albeit imperfect) expression, and it is these principles and ideals which help to guide judges to a determinate outcome.[19] Indeed, the Dworkinian might try to use the realist indeterminacy analysis to his advantage: if the law were simply a collection of rules, as Hart thinks, it would be afflicted by exactly the kind of deep and pervasive indeterminacy which the realist posits. Yet, if the law were indeterminate to the degree suggested by the realist analysis, it would not be much more than a pious fraud: judges would be "legislating" not only in penumbral cases, but in all cases. Judges would always be creating law, in flagrant violation of their institutional duty to apply preexisting law. The Dworkinian may conclude that we face this choice: either include principles and ideals as part of the law in order to contain (and, perhaps, eliminate) the indeterminacy it would have were it simply a collection of rules or admit that common-law adjudication is a fraud. Although the latter choice is logically possible, assumptions shared by both Dworkin and his positivist critics make it an entirely implausible one from their point of view. The only plausible alternative may thus seem to be the acceptance of Dworkin's important idea that ethical principles be understood as part of the law even when they are not explicitly formulated in some authoritative legal text or clearly identifiable by the application of some noncontroversial, positivist rule for specifying authoritative legal norms in terms of their source. Thus, Dworkin argues that adjudication requires the invocation of principles which take judges "well past the point where it would be accurate to say that any 'test' of pedigree exists. . . ."[20] Moreover, such principles are, on Dworkin's view, binding on judges and so

we must realize that "legal obligation . . .[is] . . . imposed by a constellation of principles as well as by an established rule."[21] Indeed, it is this constellation of principles which must guide the judge to a determinate outcome when the relevant legal rules are in competition with one another. For instance, the principles could indicate to the judge the proper scope of application of each of the competing rules and thus resolve any apparent conflict by showing that just one of the rules was properly applicable in the case at hand.

Yet, which principles are legally binding? Dworkin's answer is that they are those which belong to the "soundest theory of the settled law."[22] The settled law consists of those legal rules and doctrines which would be accepted as authoritative by the consensus of the legal community. The soundest theory is the most defensible ethical and political theory which coheres with and justifies those legal rules and doctrines. The coherence does not have to be perfect, for Dworkin allows that the soundest theory may characterize some rules and legal outcomes as mistakes, but coherence with most of the settled law is demanded. In principle, the soundest theory is to encompass every area of law: every branch of the common law, all statutes, the whole body of administrative law, and the entire range of constitutional law. Of course, Dworkin recognizes that no merely human judge could ever formulate and defend such a theory. But his character, Hercules, is intended to show us that, in principle, such a theory could be formulated and defended by a sufficiently great intelligence.[23] Even though the fictional, judicial Hercules has powers far beyond those of mortal judges, Dworkin tells us that mortal judges are committed both the the logical possibility of such a character and to the task of trying to arrive at the outcome he would arrive at were he to be hearing their cases. Mortal judges thus can and do appeal to principles in reaching determinate outcomes, and, in doing so, they are giving force to preexisting legal obligations, and not simply making a political choice among competing legal rules.

It should be noted that the realists were not blind to seeing legal rules as expressions of ethical principles. Nonetheless, there are tremendous differences between the way in which a realist such as Thurman Arnold viewed these principles and the way in which Dworkin and his followers see them. Arnold was thoroughly cynical about the ethical ideals in terms of which the law was understood: they were high-sounding phrases which appealed to people's emotions and satisfied their need to think of the legal order as more than just some arbitrary and contingent setup. But they had no meaning other than this emotive one and could not be the subject of any rational discussion or defense.[24] Other realists, such as Felix Cohen, were not at all cynical and believed that ethical principles were amenable to rational discussion. Yet they did little to analyze carefully the ethical principles embedded in law or to examine the implications of the existence of such principles for the problem of indeterminacy.[25]

In this section, I have raised the possibility that Dworkin's jurisprudential project succeeds where Hart failed in defeating the radical realist indeterminacy thesis. However, it would be premature to make a judgment regarding the success of Dworkin's project in this respect, for scholars in the Critical Legal Studies movement have picked up and elaborated realist ideas in a way that seriously threatens the foundations of Dworkinian jurisprudence. It is to CLS that I shall turn presently. One important point should be made before I do that, however. For the most part, proponents of CLS and Dworkinians have ignored one another's positions. There are some passing references to CLS in some pieces by avowed Dworkinians, such as Charles Fried.[26] And there is some treatment of Dworkin in the CLS literature.[27] Yet, neither side seems to do anything more than make very superficial, highly polemical points against the other. The interchange of ideas between Dworkinians and CLSers is one which I have constructed with the deliberate aim of avoiding the superficial polemics which have thus far characterized the few occasions on which the one side has deigned in print to deal with the position of the other.

IV

CLS scholars accept the Dworkinian idea that legal rules are infused with ethical principles and ideals.[28] Moreover, they take such principles as seriously as Dworkinians in that they conceive of the articulation and examination of such principles to be one of the major tasks of legal theory.[29] Thus, Duncan Kennedy has analyzed the role in the form and content of legal doctrine of what he characterizes as "individualist" and "altruist" ethical conceptions.

And Roberto Unger has examined the normative principles which he takes to be embodied in the common law of contracts.[30] Yet, one of the main themes of CLS work is that the incorporation of ethical principles and ideals into the law cuts against Dworkinian efforts to rescue legal determinacy. The operative claim in CLS analysis is that the law is infused with irresolvably opposed principles and ideals. Kennedy writes that the opposing ethical conceptions which inform legal doctrine "reflect a deeper level of contradiction. At this deeper level, we are divided, among ourselves and also within ourselves, between irreconcilable visions of humanity and society, and between radically different aspirations for our common future."[31] While the realists stress competing rules, CLSers stress competing, and indeed irreconcilable, principles and ideals. Yet, the basic theme is the same: the judge must make a choice which is not dictated by the law. In the CLS analysis, the choice is one of several competing principles or ideals to be used in guiding her to a decision. Different choices lead to different outcomes. Thus, from the CLS perspective, the jurisprudential invocation of principles only serves to push back to another stage the point at which legal indeterminacy enters and judicial choice takes place.

The Dworkinian response would be to deny that legal indeterminacy follows from the fact that the law contains principles which pull in opposing directions. One of Dworkin's major points in his account of principles is that they have differing weights.[32] Thus, even if we have a case in which two competing principles appear applicable, for example, "A person should not be held liable unless she was at fault" versus "As between two innocents, the one who caused the harm should pay," Dworkin will argue that, in all likelihood, one of those principles will carry greater weight in the case at hand and it is that principle which determines the correct legal outcome. Dworkin does allow for the possibility that there may be a case in which the weights of all applicable principles are exactly equal, leaving the legal outcome truly indeterminate, but goes on to claim that such cases will be extremely rare in any developed legal system.

It must be noted here that Dworkin's conception of the soundest theory of the settled law assumes that there is some metalevel principle for determining the appropriate weights to be assigned to the different principles which may be applicable in a given case. This assumption becomes clear once we see that Dworkin's conception of the soundest theory rejects intuitionism, according to which relative weights are intuited in each case without there being any higher order standard in virtue of which each principle has its particular weight. Dworkin's position is that there is a legal fact of the matter regarding the weight of a given principle in a given case, and this fact is determined by the weight that principle receives according to the standards of the soundest theory of the settled law. Moreover, this rejection of intuitionism is firmly rooted in a commitment to the rule of law ideal.[33] That ideal requires that legal decisions be the outcome of reasoning that can be reconstructed according to principles which can be articulated and understood. To use a term which has been popular among legal theorists, judicial decision must be "principled."[34] This means that the judge cannot simply appeal to his inarticulate sense that a particular principle is weightier than some competing principle in the case before him. He must believe that there is some higher order principle which makes the one weightier than the other, and he must at least try to figure out and articulate what that higher order principle is.

Now, one line of CLS attack against Dworkin is to argue that there is no discoverable metaprinciple for assigning weights. Duncan Kennedy suggests this line in discussing the possibility of using moral theory to justify legal doctrine. Kennedy admits that, in the context of the fact situation of a particular case, opposing principles do not necessarily carry the same weight: "we are able to distinguish particular fact situations in which one side is more plausible than the other. The difficulty, the mystery, is that there are no available metaprinciples to explain just what it is about these particular situations that make them ripe for resolution."[35] Actually, Kennedy's point should be put in a less sweeping way: no one has come up with such metaprinciples, and it is implausible to think that it can be done. When put in these terms, the CLS position becomes an essentially reactive one which awaits Dworkinian efforts and then reacts against them: Dworkinians put forth their rational/ethical reconstructions of the law (or some portion of it), complete with metaprinciples for assigning weights to principles, and then CLSers and others attempt to show that the reconstruction is inadequate and incoherent. The burden of production thus seems to be on the Dworkinians. What have they produced?

The closest thing we have from them of a Dworkinian reconstruction of a portion of the settled law is Charles Fried's effort to reconstruct contract law on the basis of the principle that one ought to keep one's promises and related conceptions from a liberal individualist philosophy.[36] Yet, Fried sought to avoid the problem of developing metaprinciples by narrowly defining the body of law which he attempted to reconstruct. Thus, he did not attempt to incorporate collective bargaining law with its decidedly greater collectivist orientation than the common law of contracts, and he even banished to other fields of law doctrines which are standardly treated as part of the common law of contracts but which do not fit neatly with the individualist principles animating his reconstruction.[37] This is not to imply any assessment regarding the success or failure of Fried's effort to reconstruct his highly streamlined body of contract law. For now my point is the modest one that by gerrymandering doctrine, he attempted, in effect, to evade the difficulty of developing higher order standards to harmonize the competing principles which infuse the law of contracts, and so he simply delayed tackling one of the principal obstacles in the path of constructing the kind of theory which Dworkinian jurisprudence presumes we can and should build.

It is important to recognize here that I am not talking about the theory which Dworkin's Hercules would try to construct, one encompassing the entire body of the law. Rather, what is at issue is a theory for some connected but limited portion of the law, such as the law of contracts. Both CLS and I assume that Dworkinians are committed to the notion that such limited theories can be built by humans, not merely by gods. For if humans cannot construct even such modest theories, the problem of legal indeterminacy will be irresolvable from a human point of view, no matter what may be true from a divine point of view. If the rule of law is to be a guiding ideal for humans, and not just gods, then the problem of legal indeterminacy must be resolvable from a human point of view. Moreover, Dworkinian jurisprudence itself prohibits evasion of the problem of competing principles by so gerrymandering doctrine that one never has to harmonize such principles. Dworkin is clear that different parts of the law have to be understood in terms of each other, for example, a statute affecting tort liability will properly play a role in a judge's decision in a common-law tort action.[38] The judge cannot ignore the statute on the ground that it embodies principles in some tension with common-law principles and thus is difficult to reconcile with them. The judge is supposed to (try to) reconcile the tension and not avoid facing it.

CLS scholars would clearly go further than I have so far and reject as wrongheaded even the relatively modest project Fried has undertaken to reconstruct common-law contract doctrine from the promise principle. In addition, CLS-ers would judge as totally implausible the belief that any coherent Dworkinian theory, complete with metaprinciples, can be developed for any significant portion of the settled law. Yet, the CLS claims in this regard are unpersuasive, given the argument that has been adduced in their behalf to this point. Even if it is admitted that there are difficulties in the way of constructing a Dworkinian theory for any significant portion of the settled law because such a portion will invariably embody principles in tension with one another, surely no argument has yet been given that makes it implausible to believe that such a theory can be constructed. Nonetheless, the points made so far do not by any means exhaust the potential CLS critique of Dworkinian jurisprudence. While CLS rhetoric often does make the invalid leap from the premise that there are competing principles which infuse settled doctrine to the conclusion that there must be pervasive legal indeterminacy, there are within CLS distinct and more powerful lines of reasoning against the viability of the Dworkinian project.

The additional lines of reasoning are premised on the idea that the settled law is the transitory and contingent outcome of ideological struggles among social factions in which conflicting conceptions of justice, goodness, and social and political life get compromised, truncated, vitiated, and adjusted.[39] The point here is not simply that there are competing principles embodied in settled doctrine, although that is a starting point for the statement of the problem. More fundamentally, the point is that these principles have their weight and scope of application in the settled law determined, not by some metalevel philosophical principle which imposes order and harmony, but by an ideological power struggle in which coherent theories become compromised and

truncated as they fit themselves into the body of law. The settled law as a whole, and each field within it, represents the (temporary) outcome of such an ideological conflict. This is, to be sure, a causal claim about the genesis of legal doctrines and principles, rather than a logical one regarding the lack of amenability of such doctrines and principles to rational reconstruction. But the CLS positions can be interpreted as linking the logical claim to the causal one. The position is that it is implausible to believe that any system of norms generated by such a process of struggle and compromise will be capable of an ethically principled reconstruction. Unger summarizes the CLS view this way:

> . . . it would be strange if the results of a coherent, richly developed normative theory were to coincide with a major portion of any extended branch of law. The many conflicts of interest and vision that lawmaking involves, fought out by countless minds and wills working at cross purposes, would have to be the vehicle of an immanent moral rationality whose message could be articulated by a single cohesive theory. This daring and implausible sanctification of the actual is in fact undertaken by the dominant legal theories. . . .[40]

This idea that the law is a patchwork quilt, as it were, of irreconcilably opposed ideologies is tied to CLS's version of the repudiation of the distinction between law (adjudication) and politics. Sometimes CLS scholars suggest that the distinction unravels principally because of the fact that controversial normative and descriptive judgments are just as much an ineliminable part of adjudication as they are of politics. Yet, I think that there is a more important, though related, way in which the distinction is thought to unravel. The idea is this: all of those ideological controversies which play a significant part in the public debate of our political culture are replicated in the argument of judicial decision. In other words, the spectrum of ideological controversy in politics is reproduced in the law. Of course, CLS recognizes that in legal argument the controversies will often be masked or hidden by talk of the intent of the framers, the requirements of *stare decisis,* and so on. The point is that the same ideological debates which fragment political discourse are replicated in one form or another in a legal argument. As a patchwork quilt of irreconcilable ideologies, the law is a mirror which faithfully reflects the fragmentation of our political culture. Such, at least, is a principal CLS theme.

How is it possible to parlay these CLS ideas regarding the patchwork-quilt character of doctrine and the unraveling of the law/politics distinction into a cogent argument against Dworkinian jurisprudence? I think there are two principal lines of argument. The first seeks to show that it makes no sense to think there is any soundest theory of the settled law. The second seeks to show that the Dworkinian theory fails on its own terms to provide a satisfactory account of the legitimacy of judicial decision making. Let us explore each of these lines of argument in turn.

V

One possible line of CLS argument is that legal doctrine is so internally inconsistent that it is implausible to believe that there is any single, coherent theory capable of justifying enough of it to satisfy the Dworkinian fit requirement. Consistently applying any of the theories embodied in some significant portion of the law across the entire body of doctrine would, the argument goes, involve such substantial doctrinal reconstruction that it would violate the Dworkinian mandate that any theory invoked to decide cases fit or cohere with the bulk of the settled law. Thus, ethically principled reconstruction of any substantial portion of doctrine is ruled out by the law's internal contradictions, such contradictions being symptomatic of the law's conception in ideological compromise and struggle and of its tendency to reflect the range of political conflict present in the culture. This means that there simply is no soundest theory of the settled law, and so the Dworkinian efforts to rescue legal determinacy by appealing to such a notion fail.

It may be helpful in clarifying this CLS argument to show how Dworkin's responses to more conventional criticisms of his jurisprudence completely fail to come to grips with the central claim of this argument. A typical conventional criticism will claim that legal indeterminacy survives the Dworkinian efforts to erase it because there are multiple, conflicting theories no one of which can be cogently established as providing an account of the settled law which is superior to that of any of the other theories. In other words, the concept of the soundest theory really has more than one referent, and

they provide different answers to questions regarding who should win cases.[41]

Dworkin's response to this type of criticism is in two stages. First, he argues that, although there may be several theories which fit the settled law well enough when one is talking about the settled law of a simple, undeveloped legal system, the probability of that happening in a complex and developed system such as we have is very small. Second, he claims that even if there were several theories which fit well enough, that would not defeat his claims since the soundest theory would be the one from those several which is most defensible on the grounds of political and ethical philosophy. Thus, he concludes that two claims must be sustained in order to defeat his position: that there are multiple theories which fit the settled law well enough, and that political and ethical philosophy suffer from an indeterminacy (or an irremediable subjectivity) which makes it impossible to choose just one of those theories as the most defensible.[42]

However convincing this Dworkinian argument may be against conventional legal philosophers, it does not even begin to join the issue with CLS. For the CLS patchwork-quilt argument is not that there is legal indeterminacy due to the fact that there are several "soundest theories"; rather the argument is that there is indeterminacy because there are none. Or, more accurately, the argument is that there is indeterminacy because of what excludes the possibility of any soundest theory, namely, the internally incoherent character of legal doctrine. This argument makes it completely beside the point whether ethical and political philosophy is indeterminate or subjective. If doctrine is as internally contradictory as CLS claims, then Dworkinian jurisprudence fails to rescue legal determinacy even if there is a uniquely and objectively true ethical and political philosophy.

Dworkin's replies to conventional critics of his jurisprudence are essentially irrelevant here because those critics share Dworkin's assumption that doctrine is by and large coherent. More generally, the conventional critics share Dworkin's assumption that legal doctrine and argument are largely in good logical order, though they believe that indeterminacy has a somewhat broader toehold in the law than Dworkin is willing to admit. CLS dissents from these assumptions. In this respect the CLS position may be usefully analogized with Alasdair

MacIntyre's diagnosis of the ethical thought of modern culture.[43] MacIntyre argues that such thought is internally incoherent. This state of incoherence is due to the fact that modern ethical thought amounts to an amalgam of fragments of irreconcilable ethical views. Conventional philosophers not only fail to perceive the utter incoherence of modern ethical thought, but operate on the assumption that it is largely in good order. For them the issue is the best way to systematize that thought, not whether it is so self-contradictory that systematization is impossible. The result is that the debates fought out among conventional ethical philosophers, such as Rawls and Nozick, do not join the issue with MacIntyre's position. He repudiates the assumptions which the conventional antagonists share. In a very similar way, the debate between Dworkin and his conventional critics fails to join the issue with CLS. They assume a doctrinal coherence which CLS repudiates, and so the conventional debate takes place in terms which are largely irrelevant to the CLS position.

Duncan Kennedy makes the CLS position on doctrinal incoherence plain in his description of a private law field which he takes to be representative of doctrine in general:

In contract law, for example, there are *two* principles: there is a reliance, solidarity, joint enterprise concept, and there is a hands-off, arms length, expectancy-oriented, "no flexibility and no excuses" orientation. They can be developed very coherently, but only if one accepts that they are inconsistent. There are fifteen or twenty contract doctrines about which there is a conflict. . . . That is the structure of contract doctrine, and it's typical. Doctrine is not consistent or coherent. The outcomes of these conflicts form a patchwork, rather than following straight lines.[44]

Given the terms in which the CLS position has been stated, it is clear what the Dworkinian reply must be in order to join the issue: that doctrine is not as internally contradictory as CLS claims. The main argument would have to be that any internal inconsistencies in legal doctrine are merely marginal, capable of characterization as "mistakes" without any substantial rupture to the fabric of doctrine. This argument would be supplemented, I think, by one to the effect that CLS exaggerates the degree to which theory must fit the settled law in order to be said to fit well enough. To make out these arguments would not be at all easy. CLS

analyses have sought to exhibit the deep and pervasive incoherence of doctrine in such areas as constitutional law, labor law, contract law, administrative law, and criminal law, to name only a few.[45] Indeed, I think it is accurate to say that CLS has, through these analyses, made a much more thorough and stronger case for the incoherence of legal doctrine than MacIntyre has made for the incoherence of ethical thought. Meanwhile, Dworkinians have done little to respond to these CLS analyses. Moreover, Dworkin's most recent efforts to clarify the character of the fit test provide little ammunition against the CLS argument. Let us briefly examine those efforts in order to see why this is so.

Dworkin's recent writing indicates that the fit test is more sophisticated than some of his critics have taken it to be.[46] He tells us that the degree of fit is not just a matter of adding up the number of precedents and rules for which a given theory accounts. One must also take into consideration such factors as the trend of recent decisions. Two theories may account for the same number of precedents and rules, but, if one accounts for more of the recent decisions and the other for more of the older decisions, then the former has a better fit, according to Dworkin.

Dworkin does not indicate how much weight should be given to the capacity to account for recent trends. Nor does he explain why accounting for a trend in new decisions makes for a better fit than accounting for the pre-trend pattern of old ones. Moreover, he ignores the point that the question of what counts as a significant trend and what counts as an insignificant blip or anomaly is not a theory-neutral one. What counts as a trend from the perspective of one theory may count as an anomaly to be ignored from the perspective of another. It does no good to be told here that the soundest theory of the law determines what is a trend and what is an anomaly, since the fit test is supposed to help us figure out which theory is the soundest one. But, more to the point for the doctrinal incoherence issue, the CLS contention is that the patchwork character of law is manifested within the body of recent decisions and not just between recent ones and old ones. There may be trends but there are countertrends as well. Some decisions may introduce or expand new lines of doctrine, but other recent decisions will continue the older lines. By characterizing the former as "trends" and giving their line of doctrine greater weight, Dworkin is merely picking out one line of doctrine for favored status from among several conflicting lines. His aim does seem to be to reduce doctrinal dissonance, but he provides no argument for giving greater importance to trends than countertrends and so he does not succeed.

Even if Dworkin were able to provide some convincing argument for according greater importance to trends, it is not at all obvious that he would thereby solve the problem of doctrinal incoherence. His recent writing explicitly states that there is some threshold level of fit which any theory must satisfy in order to be the soundest theory of the law.[47] Presumably, this threshold would require a theory to account for most, but not all, of the doctrinal materials. However, CLS analyses suggest that doctrinal incoherence is so deep and pervasive that, even if one grants that accounting for certain doctrinal lines (the trends) gives somewhat better fit than accounting for others (the countertrends), any coherent theory will prove incompatible with such a broad range of doctrine as to make implausible the notion that it has satisfied the threshold. These analyses do not conclusively establish the point, but they do raise a strong prima facie case to which there has been only the most meager response by conventional legal philosophers of any stripe, Dworkinian or otherwise.

It seems to me, then, that the patchwork-quilt line of argument presents unmet and serious challenges to the viability of the Dworkinian jurisprudential project, as well as to other conventional legal philosophies. Even if this CLS argument is met by some cogent conventional response, however, there is an independent line of CLS argument against another key Dworkinian position. Let us now turn to that position.

VI

Dworkin is concerned to defend the legitimacy of judicial decision making that invokes controversial principles of ethical or political philosophy. The Dworkinian judge is licensed to rely on such principles because, as Dworkin well realizes, it is inevitable that a judge who, in a hard case, seeks to enunciate and invoke the principles embodied in the settled law will fail to find principles on which everyone can agree. If the judge is to guide her decision by the principles she thinks are embodied in the

law, then the reliance of adjudication on controversial principles is inescapable, at least for many cases. In this sense, Dworkin is willing to acknowledge that adjudication is "political."[48] Yet, he thinks that such an acknowledgment does nothing to impugn the legitimacy of the adjudication.

Dworkin's arguments in favor of the legitimacy of such admittedly "political adjudication" are not entirely clear. Let me suggest the following as the principal Dworkinian argument on this point. The invocation of controversial ethical or political principles in adjudication is constrained by the judicial duty to decide a hard case according to the dictates of the soundest theory of the settled law. Thus, the "political" reasoning and choice of the judge take place within much narrower confines than if she were a legislator deciding what sort of legislative enactment was best. As Dworkin says in his discussion of a judge deciding an abortion case, it is one thing for her to decide whether political philosophy dictates that government should acknowledge a right to an abortion, and it is quite another for her to decide whether the settled law of our legal/political system is best accounted for by a theory incorporating a conception of dignity which entails such a right.[49] The former decision is, of course, appropriate for a legislature, not a court. Yet, it is the latter decision, not the former, which the Dworkinian judge is under a duty to make, and it is a decision which is made within much narrower confines than the former. Thus, it is misguided to think that the kind of "political adjudication" endorsed by Dworkinian jurisprudence constitutes an illegitimately broad exercise of judicial power and is tantamount to judicial legislation. Such adjudication is inevitably controversial, but it is substantially constrained by the duty under which judges, but not legislators, act.

Certain CLS claims regarding the law/politics distinction can be parlayed into an argument against this Dworkinian defense of the legitimacy of adjudication in hard cases. What makes this CLS argument particularly interesting for current purposes is that it does not hinge on the adequacy of the patchwork-quilt argument examined in the preceding section. Indeed, it can be construed as granting, *arguendo,* that there is a unique soundest theory of the law which does dictate the correct legal outcomes in hard cases. Let us set the stage for such a CLS argument.

In trying to undo the law/politics distinction, CLS claims that the spectrum of ideological controversy in the political arena is replicated in the legal forum. The claim means that all of the arguments and ideologies which are a significant part of political debate in our culture are to be found, in one form or another, in legal argument and doctrine. It is undoubtedly true that certain ideological viewpoints are foreclosed from the legal arena. Thus, the ideology of Islamic theocracy is to be found embodied nowhere in our legal doctrine. But such ideologies also play no significant role in the internal political debates of our polity.

It is also undeniable that the canons of legal argument place certain formal constraints on the ideological controversies which manifest themselves within judicial decision making. Judges cannot ignore the authoritative texts of the legal culture: the Constitution, statutes, case law, and so on. And legal argument is constrained by the need to phrase itself in terms of the framer's intent, *stare decisis,* and so on. Controversy in the political arena is not bound as strongly by such formal constraints, even though the language of legal opinion does often spill over into the political arena. CLS does not deny any of these distinctive, formal marks of legal argument. What they do claim is that beneath these legal forms one can find all of the significant ideological controversies of the political culture. The substance of the political debates is replicated in judicial argument, even if the form of the debates is distinctive. Legal form fails to screen out or significantly reduce the range of ideological conflict present within the general political culture.

CLS supports these contentions regarding the range of ideological conflict within legal doctrine and argument by analyses of doctrinal principles and the kinds of arguments found in judicial decisions. Consider again Kennedy's description of the structure of contract law. Doctrines from the "solidarity" side of contract law, for example, those of duress, unconscionability, and reasonable reliance, are taken to embody the principles of the political left: welfare-state liberals and, to some extent, left-wing egalitarians. Doctrines from the "individualist" side, such as those of consideration, the revocability of an offer until there is acceptance, and the demand that acceptance be a mirror image of the offer, are taken to embody the principles of the political right: free-marketeers and libertarians. The political

middle is represented by attempts to mix the two sides of doctrine in varying proportions (attempts which, in CLS eyes, are doomed to logical incoherence for reasons made clear in the patchwork-quilt argument). A hard case emerges when the two sides of doctrine collide in a single fact situation: there was no consideration, but there was reliance; or there was consideration, but it was quite disproportionate in value to what was received in exchange. The CLS view is that such cases implicate doctrinal materials and arguments representing the spectrum of conflicting political viewpoints.

The CLS claim that the range of ideological conflict in the political arena is replicated in legal doctrine and argument can be viewed in two ways. On the first, it is taken as reinforcing the patchwork-quilt argument against Dworkin. To the extent that one documents the claim, one lends support to the idea that doctrine is a patchwork quilt of inconsistent political ideologies of which no single, coherent political theory could ever capture very much. Take Kennedy's account of contract law. The CLS argument can be put this way: to the extent that we have no reason to believe that the political philosophy of a welfare-state liberal can be reconciled with that of a libertarian, we have no reason to think that the opposing doctrines of contract law can be logically reconciled with one another, for those doctrines are the legal embodiment of just those opposing political philosophies (or something close to them). The position is then generalized to cover all fields of law. This way of setting up the CLS argument is, at bottom, another effort to show that the law is too internally incoherent for there to be any soundest theory of it and thereby to discredit Dworkin's attempts to defend judicial legitimacy by invoking a judicial duty to decide according to the dictates of the soundest theory.

There is, however, another way to view the CLS claim about the range of ideological conflict embodied in legal doctrine. This alternate reading leads to a line of argument whose key contention is that, even if there were a Dworkinian soundest theory, it would impose no practical constraint on judges whose favored political ideology is in conflict with the one embodied in that theory. The theory would exert no effective pull or tug on the decisions of judges who fail to share its ideology. This is because judges who conscientiously attempt to carry out their Dworkinian duty to decide a hard case according to the soundest theory of the law will read their favored ideology into the settled and see it as the soundest theory. This would happen, the argument goes, because the authoritative legal materials, in replicating the ideological conflicts of the political arena, contain a sufficient number of doctrines, rules, and arguments representing any politically significant ideology that a judge who conscientiously consults the materials would find his favored ideology in some substantial portion of the settled law and conclude that it was the soundest theory of the law.

Of course, no one expects that the true soundest theory of law will have the power to persuade all conscientious judges of its status. However, the Dworkinian argument for the legitimacy of adjudication in hard cases does presuppose that the theory imposes some practical constraint on judicial decision making by exerting a kind of gravitational pull on those judges who recognize their abstract duty to decide according to the soundest theory but who are in fact in ideological disagreement with the principles of the true theory. (Keep in mind that this judicial duty is abstract in the sense that the statement of the duty contains no specification of the particular theory which is the soundest one, and so recognition of the duty, by itself, does nothing to insure that a judge's decisions will be pulled in any particular direction.) The pull of the true soundest theory doesn't have to be an irresistible one, but, for the Dworkinian legitimacy argument to work, it must be substantial enough to make a difference to the decisions of conscientious judges who in fact hold to an ideology which conflicts with the soundest theory. Many of the decisions of these judges would have to be different from what they would be if there were no soundest theory, and the difference has to be explainable in terms of the pull of the theory. If the soundest theory were to lack any such pull, then the constraint imposed by the duty to decide according to the soundest theory would be illusory, and the Dworkinian defense of judicial legitimacy would fall apart. The CLS argument is that the constraint is an illusion. Judges holding to virtually any ideology which is of significance in the American political arena will simply read their favored ideology into the settled law as its soundest theory. This can be and is done, even by the most conscientious judge, because each view on the political spectrum is embodied in some substantial portion of the authoritative materials.

It should be noted that the CLS view on this point is not the same as a view often expressed by mainstream critics of Dworkin and against which Dworkin has directed several arguments. That view consists of the idea that in a hard case, the law "runs out" and the judge makes her decision in a kind of legal vacuum. Dworkin has argued quite forcefully that this gives us a false picture of how judges should and characteristically do go about deciding hard cases.[50] It leads us to think that judges first consult the authoritative materials, find that there is no unambiguous answer there, and then proceed to forget the legal materials and decide by some wholly extralegal criterion. Dworkin counters with a picture of judges who search for the most cogent principles and theories which can be thought of as embodied in the relevant authoritative materials and who decide according to such principles and theories. This is, in Dworkin's eyes, the search for (the relevant portion of) the soundest theory of the settled law.

CLS can agree with Dworkin's important point that judges do not leave the authoritative materials behind when they make a decision in a case where those materials fail to dictate unambiguously an answer to the case. It can also agree with Dworkin that in such cases judges look for the most convincing principles and theories embodied in the materials.[51] The point of the present CLS argument is that, even though judges typically do decide in such Dworkinian fashion and even if there happens to be a soundest theory dictating the correct legal outcome, the existence of such a theory makes no practical difference because a judge will typically see her favored ideology as constituting that theory. The soundest theory is not some brooding omnipresence in the sky, but rather a brooding irrelevance in the sky (assuming it is anywhere at all).

There are two potential lines of response for the Dworkinian to this CLS argument. The first is to deny that the full spectrum of ideological controversy in politics is to be found in legal doctrine and decision and so to hold on to the idea that legal form, particularly the fit requirement, does screen out a significant range of political controversy. This line of response does not appear to me to be very promising. There are a host of CLS analyses of both private and public law, making quite persuasive its contention regarding the extent of ideological controversy within legal doctrine and argument.

A second line of response is to deny that the legitimacy of "political adjudication" in hard cases hinges on whether or not ideological controversy within the law is as wide as it is in the political arena. The idea is that Dworkin's defense of adjudication works, even if the law/politics distinction unravels in precisely the way CLS asserts. In fact, we can find in Dworkin's work two arguments which can be construed in this way. They concern the issue of whether courts have correctly held that there is a legal right to an abortion under our constitutional arrangements. Dworkin imagines the issue turning on the question of whether the concept of dignity implicit in our legal and political institutions implies the existence of such a right.[52] He then examines the suggestion that legislatures, which reflect the will and ideas of the ordinary person, rather than courts, are the most appropriate forum in which to find the answer to such a question. In other words, the suggestion is the positivist one that in hard cases courts should act as legislatures would.

Dworkin claims that there are two arguments against such a suggestion and, by implication, in favor of the judge deciding the issue by what she thinks the (soundest theory of the) law dictates, and not by what (she thinks) the legislature thinks it ought to be.[53] The first argument is that judges think more carefully about the meaning our institutions give to the idea of dignity when they decide cases than ordinary folks do when they cast their ballots (or politicians do when they vote on legislation). Judges are thus thought to have greater competence in handling such hard cases than legislatures do. The second arggument is that a Dworkinian judge will legitimately refuse to defer to legislative judgment, even if she thinks that it does reflect the considered opinion of the ordinary person, when she thinks that the opinion is inconsistent with the soundest theory of the law. This is legitimate because such a judge believes that the law really does have a determinate answer to the hard case before her and that it is her duty to discover and announce it, whatever anyone else thinks. By doing so she is acting no differently from a positivist judge in an easy case, who would certainly refrain from a decision contrary to his legal judgment, no matter what the ordinary person/legislature may think.

Neither one of these arguments provides a convincing response to the CLS position. The first would justify the most far-reaching judicial usurpations on the grounds that judges have thought more carefully about the issue in question than did the electorate or their representatives. There is virtually no legislative enactment or policy which is safe from such reasoning. The second argument clearly begs the whole question of whether the law is determinate in hard cases. The Dworkinian judge may believe that it is, but, if that belief is incorrect or even unjustified, it can hardly be claimed that her refusal to defer to legislative judgment in a hard case is analogous to the positivist judge's refusal to do so in an easy case. Yet, even granting the law's determinacy, Dworkin's argument presumes that the soundest theory of the law does impose some effective constraints on judicial decision making. For otherwise there will be no practical difference between a legal regime in which judges have no duty to decide hard cases according to the dictates of (the soundest theory of) the law but may decide such cases on the basis of their favored ideology, and one in which they do have such a duty. Dworkin's views commit him to the claim that there is not only a difference between the two regimes, but that the latter sort of regime alone can be legitimated in terms of the priciples of liberal democracy.

Let me hasten to add that CLS does not accept an important assumption shared by both Dworkinians and their positivist critics, namely, that the exercise of judicial power, even in hard cases, is largely legitimate and that the issue is over how to account for that legitimacy. For CLSers, the legitimacy of the exercise of judicial power is not something that can be assumed but is deeply problematic. Thus, they are no more persuaded by the positivist's efforts to wrap judicial decision in the cloak of legislative legitimacy than they are by Dworkin's invocation of the duty to decide by the soundest theory of law. From the CLS perspective, the positivist injuction to decide according to the will of the legislature leaves as much room for judges to make their favored ideology the basis of decision as does the Dworkinian injunction to decide according to the soundest theory. My principal point here, though, concerns Dworkinian jurisprudence. Dworkinians must show that the soundest theory of law is not only a logical possiblity, given the tensions existing within doctrine, but that it can exert an effective practical constraint on judges who hold conflicting ideological views. CLS's law/politics argument raises serious doubts about whether the theory, even conceding its existence, would exert any such constraint, and thus far Dworkinians have done little to assuage such doubts.

VII

In this article, I have not aimed at providing the last word on the points of contention between CLS and Dworkinian jurisprudence. I have tried to locate some of the more important issues within a frame that recognizes the influence of legal realism on contemporary legal thought. CLS has picked up and elaborated upon the realist contention that the law largely fails to determine the outcome in cases which are brought to litigation. Among the important advances of the CLS analysis over that of their realist forerunners are: the effort to take seriously and to analyze the conflicting ethical visions and principles which infuse legal doctrine; the painstaking attempts to display doctrinal inconsistencies and incoherencies; and the effort to show how debates in the political arena are replicated in unsuspected corners of private-law doctrine. I believe that these are substantial advances on the realist position and that they can be parlayed into powerful arguments which are thus far unmet by Dworkinians or indeed by conventional legal philosophers of any stripe. It is well past the time when legal philosophers can justifiably ignore the body of work associated with the Critical Legal Studies movement.

NOTES

For illuminating discussions of many of the issues treated in this article, I would like to thank Lewis Sargentich, Duncan Kennedy, Morton Horwitz, and John Fellas. Comments and suggestions made by the Editors of *Philosophy & Public Affairs* helped me improve my arguments at several points. The article was conceived and written while I was a liberal arts fellow at Harvard Law School, 1984–5. I am greatly indebted to the John Dewey Foundation for its generous financial support during that time.

1. H. L. A. Hart, *The Concept of Law* (Oxford: Oxford University Press, 1961).

2. Ronald Dworkin, *Taking Rights Seriously* (Cambridge, MA: Harvard University Press, 1977), pp. 3–4; also see pp. 15–16.

3. Theodore Benditt, *Law as Rule and Principle* (Stanford: Stanford University Press, 1978), chaps. 1–2. In his preface,

Benditt says that his reason for such an extended treatment of realism is that "students find [it] interesting and persuasive." (p. vii.) It is difficult for me to interpret the remark as anything but a put-down of both realism and any contemporary theorists who find it both interesting and persuasive.

4. A principal exception to the general failure to treat realism as having contemporary significance is R. S. Summers, *Instrumentalism and American Legal Theory* (Ithaca, NY: Cornell University Press, 1982). Also see the articles in the "Symposium on American Legal Theory," *Cornell Law Review* 66 (1981): 860. It is useful to think of the realist movement as constituted by six distinct themes. First, there is the instrumentalist theme, according to which law should be understood and evaluated as animated by social purposes and policies. This theme has been absorbed into much mainstream legal thinking. Second, there is the behaviorist theme, which reduces the meaning of legal concepts and doctrines to the particular actions of legal officials. Such a theory of meaning stands repudiated by virtually all contemporary theorists. (See footnote 18 below.) The third theme is that of legal indeterminacy, which is the focus of this article. Fourth, there is the anticonceptualist theme, according to which legal thinking should always take place at a very low level of abstraction and should never stray very far from the particular fact pattern presented by a case. (See footnote 28 below.) Fifth, there is the realist idea that private law concepts and doctrines ought to be reconceptualized so that they are understood as instruments of state imposed regulatory policies. This theme, which is clearly related to the instrumentalist one, has been a major influence on contemporary legal scholars working in the area of contract law. See Patrick Atiyah, *The Rise and Fall of Freedom of Contract* (Oxford: Oxford University Press, 1979), pp. 405–419, and Grant Gilmore, *The Death of Contract* (Columbus, Ohio: Ohio State University Press, 1974). Finally, there is the master theme of legal realism, that of the breakdown of any sharp distinction between law (adjudication) and politics. Each of the five previous themes can be understood as various ways in which the realists tried to unravel that distinction.

5. Hart, *The Concept of Law*, pp. 119, 123–25.

6. A provocative realist analysis of constitutional adjudication is found in George Braden, "The Search for Objectivity in Constitutional Law," *Yale Law Journal* 57 (1948): 571. The classic realist statement of the indeterminacy of statutory interpretation is found in Appendix C of Karl Llewellyn, *The Common Law Tradition* (Boston: Little, Brown, 1960), pp. 521–35. Also see his *The Bramble Bush* (New York: Oceana, 1960), pp. 88–90.

7. On the indeterminacy of the common-law system, see Llewellyn, *The Bramble Bush*, pp. 61–77; also see the chapter, "The Leeways of Precedent," in *The Common Law Tradition*.

8. The facts in this example are from *Hamer v. Sidway* 124 NY 538 (1891).

9. For a general historical discussion of *stare decisis*, see Harold J. Berman and William R. Greiner, *The Nature and Functions of Law*, 4th ed. (Mineola, NY: Foundation Press, 1980), pp. 587–88. For a realist critique of the distinction between holding and dictum, see Felix Cohen, "The Ethical Basis of Legal Criticism," *Yale Law Journal* 41 (1931): 201.

10. Llewellyn, "Some Realism About Realism," *Harvard Law Review* 44 (1931): 1222, 1252.

11. Hart, *The Concept of Law*, p. 131.

12. Ibid.

13. Ibid., p. 132.

14. Benditt, *Law as Rule and Principle*, pp. 25–42.

15. Ibid., pp. 10–11, 22.

16. Llewellyn, "Some Realism About Realism," p. 1252. Llewellyn takes fellow realist Jerome Frank to task for suggesting that rules and precedents lack authoritative status; see his contribution to "*Law and the Modern Mind*: A Symposium," *Columbia Law Review* 31 (1931): 82, 90.

17. John Dewey, "Logical Method and Law," *Cornell Law Quarterly* 10 (1924): 17.

18. For example, the criticism Hart and Benditt make of the theory of the meaning endorsed by realists is extremely persuasive. The theory is asserted in Felix Cohen, "Transcendental Nonsense and the Functional Approach," *Columbia Law Review* 35 (1935): 809. The seminal statement of the position is in Oliver Wendell Holmes, *The Path of the Law, Collected Papers* (New York: Harcourt, Brace, 1921), p. 173. For the criticisms, see Hart, *The Concept of Law*, pp. 39, 88; Benditt, *Law as Rule and Principle*, pp. 46–50.

19. Dworkin, *Taking Rights Seriously*, pp. 25–26, 36, 44–45, 67–68, 71–80, 82–90, 96–97, 105ff.

20. Ibid., p. 67.

21. Ibid., p. 44.

22. Ibid., pp. 67–68, 79, 283, and 340.

23. Ibid., pp. 105ff.

24. Thurman Arnold, "Law Enforcement: An Attempt at Social Dissection," *Yale Law Journal* 42 (1932); 1, 12–13, 23. *Symbols of Government* (New Haven: Yale University Press, 1935), pp. 71, 125, 248–249.

25. Felix Cohen was the realist most concerned with ethical issues in the law. See almost any of his essays in Lucy K. Cohen, ed., *The Legal Conscience: Selected Papers of Felix S. Cohen* (New Haven: Yale University Press, 1960). There is, however, a considerable tension between Cohen's highly reductionist theory of the meaning of legal concepts, on the one hand, and his efforts to see the law as infused with cognitively meaningful ethical ideals, on the other. That kind of theory makes it very difficult to explain how ideals can impose any cognitively meaningful, normative constraints on the operation of the legal system and leads quite readily to Arnold's kind of cynical emotivism. For a closely related criticism of Cohen, see Martin Godling, "Realism and Functionalism in the Legal Thought of Felix S. Cohen," *Cornell Law Review* 66 (1981): 1032, 1054.

26. Charles Fried, "The Laws of Change: The Cunning of Reason in Moral and Legal History," *Journal of Legal Studies* 9 (1980): 335, and *Contract as Promise* (Cambridge, MA: Harvard University Press, 1981), pp. 2–3, 90–91, and 149. It is interesting that Fried gives endorsement to Dworkin's jurisprudence even though his political commitments are decidedly less liberal than those of Dworkin. I characterize Fried as a Dworkinian on account of his endorsement of Dworkin's ideas that legal doctrine is animated by and derivable from moral principles, that judges are obligated to resolve cases in the light of such principles, that the law has a determinate answer for all cases which come before it, and that it is only because the law is animated by moral principles that it has determinate answers for such disputes. See *Contract as Promise*, pp. 67–69.

27. See Elizabeth Mensch, "The History of Mainstream Legal Thought," in David Kairys, ed., *The Politics of Law* (New York: Pantheon, 1982), p. 19, and Peter Gabel, "Review of *Taking Rights Seriously*," *Harvard Law Review* 91 (1977): 302. Mensch dismissed Dworkin's theory in six lines of a footnote, characterizing his contribution to jurisprudence as "vastly overrated." Gabel's treatment is more extended, and yet he never really joins the issue with Dworkin. He simply assumes that judges pervasively exercise political choice in a way that is inconsistent with Dworkin's theory. Instead of meeting Dworkin on his own terms, Gabel takes for granted the truth of an orthodox version of historical materialism and seeks to expose Dworkin's jurisprudence as just the latest in a series of theoretical efforts to justify capitalism.

It is important to realize that Critical Legal Studies embraces a substantial variety of conflicting theoretical approaches, many of them quite hostile to anything similar to orthodox Marxist theory. (See footnote 39 below.) In this article, I shall be able to touch upon only a few of the more important themes developed in the literature. Among the important themes which will be left untreated are the critique of social hierarchy and the rather vigorous "left-wing" egalitarianism which accompany many CLS writings. It is often pointed out, correctly I believe, that there is no necessary connection between CLS claims regarding legal indeterminacy and its egalitarian political vision. But this simply means that the one does not logically stand or fall with the other. There is, however, a kind of strategic connection: CLS's political vision requires that one see the current legal order as essentially illegitimate. CLS's claims regarding legal indeterminacy serve to delegitimate that order by undercutting that order's own conception of why it is legitimate. See Duncan Kennedy, "The Political Significance of the Structure of the Law School Curriculum," *Seton Hall Law Review* 14 (1983): 1, 14. For an extensive bibliography of CLS writings, see *Yale Law Journal* 94 (1984): 464.

28. A seminal CLS text on this theme is Duncan Kennedy: "Form and Substance in Private Law Adjudication," *Harvard Law Review* 89 (1976): 1685. This text and other CLS writings exhibit an important difference with realism on the so-called issue of "conceptualism." Several realists argued that legal thinking should take place at a very low level of abstraction. Abstractions, especially those purporting to represent ethical ideals, were rejected as useless or worse in the conduct of legal thinking. CLS scholars have not followed these realists on the point. It is true that some, such as Kennedy, have suggested that judicial decisions rest on an appreciation of the peculiar fact pattern of the case at bar, rather than any effort to see the result as following from highly abstract principles which transcend that fact pattern. This is because Kennedy believes that ascending to higher levels of abstraction does not add to the cogency of arguments made in terms of the case's particular fact pattern. Disagreements which arise at the lower levels of abstraction will, in his view, simply be replicated at the higher level. And yet much of Kennedy's work, as well as that of other CLS theorists, is premised on the assumption that very high level abstractions have tremendous heuristic value in thinking about the law. Kennedy's "Form and Substance in Private Law Adjudication" is an extended examination of two abstractions which he calls "individualism" and "altruism." The premise is that the abstractions, each representing a competing ideal for human social life, will help us better grasp the terrain of legal doctrine, even if it will not help us in the end make a clinching legal argument. Moreover, some CLS writers clearly believe that such systematic thinking can be of far more than heuristic importance and teach us something crucial about the historical development of legal doctrine and its connection to social transformation generally. See Morton Horwitz, "Review of G. Gilmore, *The Ages of American Law*," *Buffalo Law*

Review 27 (1977): 47, and *The Transformation of American Law, 1780–1860* (Cambridge, MA: Harvard University Press, 1977).

29.   There is some disagreement within CLS regarding the task of constructing a defensible ethical theory. Roberto Unger considers it desirable to undertake the task and thinks there is no good reason to believe that it will never succeed. His most recent steps in carrying out the task are in *Passion: An Essay on Personality* (New York: Free Press, 1984). Duncan Kennedy is skeptical about the value, and prospects for success, of any such ethical theorizing. See his *Legal Education and the Reproduction of Hierarchy* (Cambridge: Afar, 1983), pp. 82–83. It would be a mistake, however, to infer from this that Kennedy is an ethical subjectivist of some sort. See "Form and Substance in Private Law Adjudication," pp. 1771–72.

30.   Kennedy, "Form and Substance in Private Law Adjudication"; Unger, "Critical Legal Studies Movement," *Harvard Law Review* 96 (1983): 561, 616–46. Also see Kennedy, "The Structure of Blackstone's Commentaries," *Buffalo Law Review* 28 (1978): 205. Morton Horwitz, *The Transformation of American Law: 1780–1860* (Cambridge, MA: Harvard University Press, 1977); and Mark Kelman, "Interpretive Construction in the Substantive Criminal Law," *Stanford Law Review* 33 (1981): 591.

31.   Kennedy, "Form and Substance in Private Law Adjudication," p. 1685.

32.   Dworkin, *Taking Rights Seriously*, p. 26.

33.   Dworkin, "A Reply by Ronald Dworkin," in M. Cohen, ed., *Ronald Dworkin and Contemporary Jurisprudence* (Totowa, NJ: Rowman and Allanheld, 1984), pp. 278–79.

34.   Articulating the dominant view of his time, and one which is still widely held, Herbert Wechsler wrote that "the main constituent of the judicial process is that it must be genuinely principled, resting on analyses and reasons quite transcending the immediate result that is achieved." "Toward Neutral Principles of Constitutional Law," *Harvard Law Review* 73 (1959): 1, 15. Dworkin is clearly a direct heir of this view, although I believe that his effort to draw a sharp distinction between principle and policy for the purpose of distinguishing the legal from the legislative process goes beyond what the main legal theorists of the 1950s would have endorsed. See *Taking Rights Seriously*, pp. 82–84 and contrast with Henry Hart and Albert Sacks, *The Legal Process* (tent. ed. 1958), pp. 158–71.

35.   Kennedy, "Form and Substance in Private Law Adjudication," p. 1724.

36.   Fried, *Contract as Promise*.

37.   Among the best CLS analyses of labor law are Karl Klare, "Judicial Deradicalization of the Wagner Act and the Origins of Modern Legal Consciousness, 1937–1941," *Minnesota Law Review* 62 (1978): 265, and "Critical Legal Theory and Labor Relations Law," in Kairys, ed., *The Politics of Law*, pp. 65–88. In *Contract as Promise,* Fried does not discuss labor law or collective bargaining at all, except to mention that they do not fit his model of obligations willed by the individual upon himself (p. 2). For Fried's discussion of the doctrines which he expels from contract law, see his remarks on unjust enrichment and reasonable reliance, pp. 23–26.

38.   Dworkin, *Taking Rights Seriously*, pp. 119–20.

39.   Unger, "The Critical Legal Studies Movement," p. 571. This line of CLS argument presumes the falsity of the thesis of orthodox Marxism that law is a superstructural phenomenon which merely reinforces the existing relations of production by giving expression to the ideology of the dominant economic class. Many CLS writers repudiate this Marxist position. They see law and ideology generally as much more complex than can be captured by notions such as "capitalist," and they see causation in social life as much more complex than theories regarding superstructure and base can suggest. See, for example, Kennedy, "The Structure of Blackstone's Commentaries," pp. 362–63, fn. 56, and Klare, "Critical Theory and Labor Relations Law." For a CLS description of modern Western society as more complicated than that portrayed in the class analysis of orthodox Marxism, see Unger, *Knowledge and Politics* (New York: Free Press, 1975), pp. 151–85, and *Law in Modern Society* (New York: Free Press, 1976), pp. 66–76, 171.

40.   Unger, "The Critical Legal Studies Movement," p. 571.

41.   For such a conventional criticism of Dworkin, see Neil MacCormick, "Dworkin as Pre-Benthamite," in Cohen, ed., *Ronald Dworkin and Contemporary Jurisprudence,* pp. 184–85, 192.

42.   Dworkin, "No Right Answer?" *New York University Law Review* 53 (1978): 1, 31–33; also see "A Reply by Ronald Dworkin," in Cohen, ed., *Ronald Dworkin and Contemporary Jurisprudence,* pp. 278–79.

43.   Alasdair MacIntyre, *After Virtue* (Notre Dame, IN: University of Notre Dame Press, 1981), see esp. pp. 2–4, 227–37.

44.   Kennedy, "The Political Significance of the Structure of the Law School Curriculum," p. 15.

45.   See, e.g., Mark Tushnet, "Critical Legal Studies and Constitutional Law: An Essay in Deconstruction," *Stanford Law Review* 36 (1984): 623; Paul Brest, "State Action and Liberal Theory: A Casenote on *Flagg Brothers v. Brooks,*" *University of Pennsylvania Law Review* 130 (1982): 130; Richard Parker, "The Past of Constitutional Theory—And Its Future," *Ohio State Law Journal* 42 (1981): 223; Karl Klare, "The Public/Private Distinction in Labor Law," *University of Pennsylvania Law Review* 130 (1982): 1358; Gerald Frug, "The Ideology of Bureaucracy in American Law," *Harvard Law Review* 97 (1984): 1276; Unger, "The Critical Legal Studies Movement," pp. 602–47, and Kelman, "Interpretive Construction in the Substantive Criminal Law."

46.   Dworkin, "A Reply By Ronald Dworkin," p. 272.

47.   Ibid.

48.   Dworkin, *Taking Rights Seriously,* p. 127.

49.   Ibid.

50.   Ibid., pp. 35–45, 81–130.

51.   CLS would naturally add that, to the extent that judges think that there is a soundest theory of the law, they are victims of legal false-consciousness.

52.   Dworkin, *Taking Rights Seriously*, pp. 127–29.

53.   Ibid., p. 129.

PART 2

Liberty

For what purposes can the state rightly interfere with the liberty of individual citizens to do as they please? This central question of political theory becomes a vital question in legal philosophy by virtue of the fact that, in democracies, the legal system is the primary means by which restraints on liberty are imposed. Certain kinds of conduct are directly prohibited by criminal statutes which threaten punishment, typically fines or imprisonment, for noncompliance. Other kinds of undesirable behavior are controlled by regulatory devices which employ the criminal law only indirectly, as a kind of "sanction of last resort."[1] Citizens must be licensed, for example, to drive automobiles or to practice medicine, a requirement that permits the state to regulate these dangerous activities carefully and to withdraw licenses from those who fail to conform to reasonable standards. Withdrawal of license is itself an administrative penalty diminishing the liberty of those subjected to it, but it is not a criminal penalty. The criminal sanction is reserved as a backup threat to prevent persons from driving or practicing medicine without a license. Similarly, "cease and desist" orders and other injunctions restrict the liberty of those to whom they are addressed without any recourse to the criminal law, which comes into play only to prevent or to punish disobedience. Still another form of administrative or noncriminal restriction of liberty is the civil commitment procedure by which mentally disturbed persons judged dangerous to others or incompetent to govern themselves are compelled to reside in hospitals or other nonpenal institutions. For some classes of harmful conduct—for example, defamatory statements, invasions of privacy, and certain kinds of trespass and nuisance—the civil law seems better suited than the criminal law to provide threatened parties with protection. Our liberty to tell damaging lies about our neighbors, to prevent them from enjoying their property, or to tap their telephone lines, is restricted by their legal power to bring a civil suit against us which can culminate in a judgment directing us to pay compensatory or punitive damages to them. Again, the criminal law is not involved except as a backup sanction to enforce court orders.

Most writers agree that restrictions of individual liberty, whether by direct criminal prohibition or by some other legal instrumentality, always need some special justification. That is, other things being equal, it is always preferable that individuals be left free to make their own choices. Undesirable conduct, then, is discouraged by such noncoercive measures as education, exhortation, taxation (of undesirable conduct) or provision of positive incentives such as economic subsidies or rewards (for alternatives to undesirable conduct). It is not easy to state the grounds of this presumption in favor of liberty. Various philosophers, in making the presumptive case for liberty, have argued that absence of coercion is a necessary (though certainly not a sufficient) condition for individual self-realization and social progress, and for such specific goods as individual spontaneity, social diversity, and the full flowering of various moral and intellectual virtues. In any case, most of us are fully convinced that our own personal liberty is a precious thing, and consistency inclines us to suppose that it is equally precious, and equally worth respecting, in others.

The value of liberty, however, is easily overstated. Liberty may be precious but it is by no means the only thing of value. Contentment and happiness, while difficult in the absence of freedom, are not impossible. Moreover, one can have perfect political liberty and feel alienated and discontented. Obviously, no matter how intimately they may be related, freedom and contentment are distinct values not reducible one to the other. Similarly, a given society may enjoy political liberty and still permit large-scale social injustice, a possibility which indicates that liberty and justice are distinct social values. Failure to appreciate these distinctions has led hasty thinkers to make certain familiar errors in their discussions of liberty. Some have argued that any liberty conflicting with contentment or with justice is not "true liberty," but rather some beguiling counterfeit. It is more accurate to say that liberty is but one value among many, that it is vitally important but not sufficient, that it can conflict with other values, and even that it may not, in some circumstances, be worth its price as measured against other values.

Other writers have argued that political liberty in the absence of certain specific powers and opportunities is not "true liberty" at all, but a sham and a deceit. If an invalid confined to his bed were to scoff at a legal system that grants him freedom of movement, we should no doubt reply to him that our politically guaranteed liberty to move about at will is a genuine liberty and a genuine good, even though it may be worthless to a paralyzed person. The invalid's plight shows that health and mobility are also important and independent goods, not that political liberty is a sham. Similarly, the political radical in a capitalist bourgeois society might deny that he has true liberty of speech because he does not have fair access to the communications media which are dominated by wealthy corporations. This shows that his freedom of expression is not worth as much as a wealthier person's, and that economic power is also an important good, not that he is not "really" at liberty to speak his mind. His complaint shows us that it is possible to praise liberty too much, but if he claims further that he would be no worse off if his political opinions were criminally proscribed, he is either disingenuous or naively under-appreciative of liberty's actual value.

It must be acknowledged, however, that a given person's lack of power or opportunity—his or her poverty, ignorance, or poor health—may be the *indirect result* of a structure of coercive laws. To take a crude and obvious hypothetical example, racial laws on the South African model might explicitly prohibit blacks from engaging in certain renumerative occupations. As a result, blacks would be poorer than other citizens, perhaps undernourished and undereducated as well. In that case there would be a very real point in describing a given black's lack of power or opportunity to make his views heard and considered as a diminished liberty. Political liberty is best understood as the absence of political coercion (typically, the absence of criminal prohibitions and other coercive legal instrumentalities), and not simply as *de facto* ability or opportunity. But where a law preventing a class of citizens from doing *X* leads indirectly to an absence of ability or opportunity for members of that class to do *Y,* there is a clear reason to describe the latter as a negation of the *liberty* to do *Y.*

CHALLENGES TO SELF-DETERMINATION: LEGAL PATERNALISM AND LEGAL MORALISM

Under what conditions, and for what reasons, can the presumption in favor of political liberty be overridden? This is not merely an abstract question addressed to philosophers, but an unavoidable practical question to be faced by every democratic legislator. In effect, it is a question of the limits beyond which restrictive lawmaking is morally illegitimate. John Stuart Mill, the first essayist presented in this part, gives the classic liberal answer to the question. Restriction of the liberty of one citizen, he argues, can be justified only to prevent harm to others. We can refer to Mill's position as the "harm to others principle," or more succinctly, the "harm principle." Several things should be noted about this principle at the outset. First, by "harm," Mill means not only direct personal injury such as broken bones or the loss of money, but also more diffuse social harms such as air pollution or the impairment of public institutions. Second, the principle does not propose a sufficient condition for the restriction of liberty, because some harms to others are too slight to outbalance the very real harm or danger involved in the restriction of liberty. Thus, in close cases, legislators must balance the value of the interests to be restricted by proposed coercive legislation *and* the collateral costs of enforcing any coercive law on the one hand against the value of the interests to be protected by the proposed legislation on the other. It is only when the probable harms prevented by the statute are greater than those that it will cause that the legislation is justified. Finally, the harm principle should be interpreted as a claim about *reasons:* Only one *kind* of consideration is ever morally relevant to the justification of coercion, namely, that it is necessary to prevent harm to others. It is never a relevant reason that the conduct to be restricted is merely offensive (as opposed to harmful) or even that it is intrinsically immoral, nor is it relevant that coercion is necessary to prevent a person from harming himself or herself (as opposed to others).

No one would disagree that prevention of harm to others is always *a* relevant reason for coercion, but many disagree with Mill's contention that it is the *only* relevant consideration. Thus, no one will seriously suggest that laws against battery, larceny, and homicide are unjustified, but many maintain that the state is also justified, at least in some circumstances, in prohibiting (1) "immoralities" even when they harm no one but their perpetrators (the principle of legal moralism), (2) actions that hurt or endanger the actor himself or herself (the principle of legal paternalism), or (3) conduct that is offensive though not harmful to others (the offense principle). These rival doctrines cannot easily be proved or refuted in the abstract. Rather, they are best judged by how faithfully they reflect, and how systematically they organize, our considered judgments in particular cases; for such principles, after all, purport to be explicit renderings of the axioms to which we are committed by the most confident judgments we make in everyday discourse about problems of liberty. The main areas of controversy in which such problems arise are those concerning unorthodox expressions of opinion, "morals offenses" in the criminal law (especially when committed in private by solitary individuals or among consenting adults), pornography and obscenity (when offered or displayed to the public or to nonconsenting individuals), activities that are harmful or dangerous to those who voluntarily engage in them, voluntary suicide and euthanasia, otherwise harmless invasions of the privacy of others, and conscientious acts of civil disobedience. The cautious theorist will begin with Mill's harm principle as an account of at least one set of reasons that is always relevant in such controversies, and then apply it to the various problem areas to determine the extent, if any, to which it must be supplemented to provide solutions that are both plausible and consistent. In particular, we must decide, in each area, whether we need have recourse to the offense principle, legal moralism, or legal paternalism.

Under most of the problem area headings, there is still another kind of controversy to be settled, namely, whether even the unsupplemented harm principle can justify *too much* coercion, and whether, therefore, doing justice to our considered judgments requires also a doctrine of *natural rights* limiting the applicability of the harm principle (or any of the other liberty-limiting principles that might apply at all). Perhaps this kind of question arises most prominently in the area of free expression of opinion. There is no doubt that expression of opinion, in speech or writing, do often cause vast amounts of harm. Politicians sometimes advocate policies that would lead to disastrous consequences if adopted, and scientists sometimes defend theories that are false and detrimental to scientific progress. If we apply the harm principle in a straightforward, unqualified way by prohibiting all particular expressions which seem, on the best evidence, likely to cause more harm than good, we might very well justify widespread invasions of what we should naturally take to be a moral right of free speech. Quite clearly, if he or she is to avoid this embarrassing consequence, the partisan of the harm principle will have to propose subtle refinements and mediating norms for the application of this principle, weighing such matters as the balancing of rival interests and social costs, and the measurements of probabilities, dangers, and risks.

In a broader analysis of paternalism, Gerald Dworkin considers in a comprehensive and systematic way the question of whether paternalistic statutes (defined roughly as those interfering with a person's liberty "for his own good") are ever justified. He treats Mill's absolutistic position with respect, but points out how widespread paternalistic restrictions are, and how drastic their total elimination would be. Laws requiring hunters to wear red caps and motorcyclists to wear helmets, or those requiring medical prescriptions for certain therapeutic drugs, for example, seem innocuous to most of us. Even more so are laws that actually protect children and incompetents from their own folly, and those which persons regard as "social insurance" against their own future decisions that might be not only dangerous but also irreversible. Dworkin then attempts to find criteria that can be used to separate unjustified paternalistic restrictions from those he thinks any rational man would welcome. Dworkin's "second thoughts," written fifteen years after the original essay, is also included.

In *Rogers* v. *Okin* both voluntary and involuntary patients in state psychiatric hospitals claim that their civil rights are violated when antipsychotic drugs are administered without their consent. The court's opinion addresses in a particularly thoughtful way the difficult questions of legal paternalism and autonomy that arise when a person is not only (arguably) in need of medical care but suffers from the sort of disability that may make it impossible for him to appreciate the condition he is in. Cases of enforced medical treatment frequently present interesting dilemmas, but in this case there is the additional problem of medication administered with an eye to protecting other patients and maintaining a more manageable institutional regime.

The liberalism of John Stuart Mill has come under attack not only from legal paternalists, but from those loosely grouped under the rubric "legal moralism." Patrick Devlin, not the purest example of a legal moralist, argues for the enforcement of a society's moral code, but not as an end in itself. He identifies the conventions of one time and place not as commandments of true morality, but rather as means of preventing the social and personal *harms* that would result from the weakening of social cohesion. "An established morality," he insists, "is as necessary as good government to the welfare of society." On that ground, Devlin would justify the legal enforcement even of those parts of the established morality which forbid actions that are not in themselves directly harmful to anyone, for example, homosexual sex acts performed by consenting adults in private.

For over a decade beginning in the mid 1950s, a committee of the American Law Institute (an elite group of lawyers, judges, and law professors) worked on a massive rewriting of the criminal law. Their goal was to produce a model penal code that might influence legislatures to rewrite the codes then in effect in most of the fifty states. The main "reporters" for this project, and the authors of the numerous tentative drafts, were Herbert Wechsler of the Columbia University Law School and Louis B. Schwartz of the University of Pennsylvania Law School. In his article included here, Professor Schwartz turns his attention to a class of crimes in our codes that are very difficult to justify by the unsupplemented harm principle. These so-called "offenses against morality" include not only tabooed sexual behavior, but also a somewhat puzzling miscellany of nonsexual conduct including mistreatment of corpses and desecration of the flag. The offense principle provides a rationale for judging some of these as crimes (for example, "open lewdness"), even when they cause no one any injury. Other morals offenses (for example, homosexual relations between consenting adults in private) can be defended only by recourse to the principle of legal moralism, which maintains that the law may properly be used to enforce the prevailing morality as such, even in the absence of harm or offense.

The Model Penal Code recommendations about morals offenses are the work of a group of enlightened "would-be lawmakers" who are very much opposed to legal moralism but unwilling, if only on grounds of political realism, to urge extremely radical departures from the past ways of the law. Sexual behavior that is immoral by conventional standards should not be made criminal, according to the code, unless it involves violence or exploitation of children and other incompetents; and the traditional crimes of fornication, adultery, and sodomy are to be wiped from the books. In the absence of harm to others, Schwartz and his colleagues insist, the sexual behavior of individuals is no one else's business. "Open lewdness," on the other hand, like other "flagrant affronts" to the sensibilities of others, is another matter. Not only conventionally "immoral" sexual acts but even perfectly "normal" ones can be criminally proscribed if done in *public,* not because public sex acts harm anyone, but because they cause *offense* (quite another thing) to the unwilling observer. Thus, the Model Penal Code, while rejecting legal moralism, seems to endorse the offense principle.

This combination of principles seems to have rather clear implications in respect to obscenity control. Freely consenting adults, one would think, would be given the unfettered liberty to read or witness anything they choose, provided only that they do not display offensive materials in public or impose them on unsuspecting passersby or children. The Model Penal Code, however, while approximating this position, prefers a more "oblique approach." The code would ban not only public exhibitions but also advertising and sale of materials "whose predominant appeal is to prurient interest." The target of this restriction, Schwartz assures us, is not "the sin of obscenity" but rather a kind of unfair business practice: "Just as merchants may be prohibited from selling their wares by appeal to the public's weakness for gambling, so they may be restrained from purveying books, movies, or other commercial exhibition by exploiting the well-nigh universal weakness for a look behind the curtain of modesty." This commercial approach to the problem of obscenity apparently influenced the Supreme Court in the famous case that sent Ralph Ginzburg to prison. With the benefit of hindsight, one can wonder whether the Model Penal Code's "oblique approach" is not simply a less direct way of accomplishing what legal moralism would do forthrightly. Is not the legal judgment that prurient interest in sex is a moral "weakness" itself a way of enveloping the conventional morality in the law?

The idea of privacy made a major new entry into American constitutional law through the celebrated case of *Griswold* v. *Connecticut,* decided by the United States Supreme Court in 1965. The opinions in that case raise a variety of genuinely philosophical issues, and might well have been included with equal relevance in any of the first three sections of this anthology. The decision overturned a Connecticut statute making the use of contraceptives by "any person" a criminal offense. That statute was unconstitutional, Mr. Justice Douglas wrote, because it violated a right of marital privacy, "older than the Bill of Rights," but included in the "penumbra" of the First, Fourth, Fifth, Eighth, Ninth, and Fourteenth Amendments. A "penumbra" of a right is a set of further rights not specifically guaranteed in so many words, but properly inferrable from the primary right either as necessary means for its fulfillment or as implied by it in certain factual circumstances not necessarily foreseen by those who formulated it.

Still, the Constitution does not specifically spell out a right of marital privacy, and the dissenters on the Court (Justices Stewart and Black) were suspicious of the technique of finding anything a judge thinks just and reasonable in the penumbra of a specific guarantee. Justice Goldberg in his concurring opinion had rested his case for a constitutional right of marital privacy on the Ninth Amendment's reference to fundamental rights "retained by the people," and Justices Harlan and White in their concurring opinions (not reprinted here) derived the unconstitutionality of the anti-contraception statute from its capriciousness, irrationality, and offensiveness to a "sense of fairness and justice." A careful reader of Part One of this book will recognize here the overtones of the natural law tradition, whereas in Justice Black's skeptical stricture on the "catchwords" of "natural justice"in his dissenting opinion, there is the powerful echo of the tradition of legal positivism.

In *Bowers* v. *Hardwick* a majority of the United States Supreme Court defended the right of a state to have a law on its books that purported to regulate commonplace sexual practices. The state's liberty to regulate within constitutional limits is the issue the Court addresses, rather than the issue of what limits the constitution itself must respect. The main dissenting opinion develops the conception of a fundamental right to be left alone that is enjoyed in the area of sexual activity by those who are not acting within the family, as well as those who are. Paternalistic and moralistic arguments are woven together to provide the fabric of the Court's opinion, while the dissent rests its case broadly on the protection of individual liberty that marks in a very fundamental way the political culture of the nation.

No contemporary issue of public important has more sharply divided public opinion in the United States than abortion, and none has produced a richer philosophical literature. The personal autonomy of women appears to be in conflict with the protection of human life, but no such simple characterization of the question will suffice. The deepest moral convictions of many people are engaged on one side or the other, and without great enthusiasm anywhere for the compromise that the Supreme Court's *Roe* v. *Wade* decision represents. Ronald Dworkin's essay, "The Great Abortion Case," was published shortly before *Webster* v. *Reproductive Health Services* was decided. The decision in that case maintained the basic position of *Roe* v. *Wade,* but allowed the state to curtail the public provision of medical facilities for abortion. In arguing that *Roe* v. *Wade* should not be overturned, Dworkin presents the issues and analyzes the abortion arguments from a perspective that is philosophically uncompromised by the author's partisan position. It is very difficult to defend *Roe* v. *Wade* as a decision based on principle rather than a decision representing judicious political compromise, but Dworkin does regard it as sound in principle. In arguing that the state has a right to restrict abortion within limits, he suggests that the emotional and moral significance of the fetus in our culture cannot be ignored, and that the state has a right to protect the community from the dangerous insensitivity that might well be promoted by unrestricted abortion.

One might ask why such relatively remote and general consequences, which are not clear and present dangers, should override the right a woman would otherwise have to terminate a pregnancy in its later stages. Is the position that Dworkin takes impervious to the sort of criticism that might be directed against the position taken by Patrick Devlin? It is interesting to consider also what Mill might have to say about the decision in *Roe* v. *Wade* and the intriguing defense of it mounted here by Dworkin.

FREEDOM OF EXPRESSION AND ITS LIMITS

In the first essay in this section, Joel Feinberg considers further how the harm principle must be qualified if it is to guarantee free expression of opinion in a morally satisfactory way. He examines first the relatively noncontroversial limits on free speech imposed by Anglo-American law: civil liability for defamatory utterances and for nondefamatory statements that reveal information which is properly private, criminal liability for irresponsible statements that cause panics or riots, laws against incitements to crime and (more controversially) sedition. They are considered in part because each raises its own questions of interest for the philosophy of law, and in part because each provides a challenge for the harm principle to provide a rationale for sensible restrictions on liberty that will not at the same time justify restrictions on free speech unacceptable to Mill and other liberals. Feinberg then attempts to provide a philosophical rationale for Justice Holmes's "clear and present danger" test, and concludes with comments on the inevitable "balancing of interests" so central to the harm principle approach to problems of liberty.

In *Village of Skokie* v. *National Socialist Party of America* the Supreme Court of Illinois carries out the mandate of a previous United States Supreme Court decision allowing a demonstration march by the American Nazi Party through a predominantly Jewish suburb of Chicago. The focal issue is whether the use of swastikas by the marchers is protected by the First Amendment's protection of free speech. The court regards the swastikas as a form of protected symbolic expression that cannot be banned because of the offense it may cause, or even because of the violence it may provoke. The "fighting words" exception to First Amendment protection is held not to apply here, and the fact that those who may be upset by the sight of swastikas can avoid that sight without any great inconvenience distinguishes this case from other cases in which there is intrusion into the home or in which there is a captive audience. Throughout the court's opinion the judicial posture seems understandably defensive, and there is a suggestion at several points that it is only inability to formulate the distinctive features of this case that requires the court to allow the use of the swastika in the way the marchers wish to use it. Granted that the display of symbols such as swastikas is a form of political expression entitled to protection, does that display in this case confer a broad protection on the whole enterprise of which it is a part? How might that enterprise be described by constitutionally sensitive objectors who think it ought to be subject to restriction? And what sort of principle might be formulated to protect the display of swastikas and other political symbols without compromising either First Amendment freedoms or the legitimate interests of members of the community?

A different aspect of the problem of obscenity was dramatically illustrated in the United States Supreme Court case of *Cohen* v. *California* in 1971. This case raised issues that connect the themes of the articles by Schwartz and Feinberg. Cohen was convicted by a Los Angeles municipal court for lingering in the corridors of a public building while wearing a jacket emblazoned with the words "Fuck the Draft." In his appeal to the Supreme Court of California and later to the United States Supreme

Court, Cohen claimed that his right to free speech guaranteed by the First and Fourteenth Amendments had been violated, whereas the California authorities argued that they had properly applied against him a valid statute forbidding "willfully . . . offensive conduct." Now there are two ways in which a written or spoken statement can be offensive: It can express an opinion that some auditors might find offensive or it can express an opinion in language that is itself offensive independently of the "substantive message it conveys." Neither the United States Constitution nor the libertarian principles of free expression of opinion espoused by Mill and Feinberg would permit legal interference with free speech to prevent the expression of an "offensive opinion." However, restrictions on obscene, scurrilous, and incitive words, quite apart from their role in the expression of unpopular opinions, might well be justified by the offense principle, and indeed by the Constitution itself insofar as it tacitly employs the offense principle to mark out a class of exceptions to the free speech guarantee. Justice Harlan, however, rejected this approach to the case. The free expression of opinion protected by the Constitution, he argued, extends not merely to the proposition declared by a statement, but also to the speaker's (or writer's) emotions, or the intensity of his attitudes—in the case at hand "the depths of his feelings against the Vietnam War and the draft." Harlan's distinction points to an important function of what are ordinarily called obscene words. "Unseemly epithets" can shock and jolt, and in virtue of their very character as socially unacceptable, give expression to intense feelings more accurately than any other words in the language.

Texas v. *Johnson* in some ways looks like *Skokie* stood on its head. Instead of the flaunting of an abhorrent political symbol, the swastika, we now have the public burning of a generally respected political symbol, the American flag. In this case the United States Supreme Court considers whether such an act is entitled to be protected under the First Amendment. The first question to be considered is whether flag burning qualifies constitutionally as expression. After that issue is dealt with, the question of whether the act may be prohibited as a breach of the peace is considered, as well as the question of whether flag burning may be prohibited to preserve the flag as a symbol of nationhood and national unity. The arguments in this case rely on some of the same First Amendment cases that were used in *Skokie*, even though the arguments here make rather different use of them. In this case, however, a more subtle analysis of expression and its effects is undertaken in the Court's opinion. Perhaps the most interesting point that emerges is best put in a hypothetical mode. If it were quite clear that unrestrained flag burning had the effect of changing the attitude of the community toward the flag, would the state be justified in prohibiting such activity despite principles of First Amendment protection?

Injury to reputation or emotional distress may be the consequence of some publication that ridicules or defames a person. Having the privilege to express ourselves freely does not imply that we cannot ever be called to account by others for injuries that may result from what we say. Clearly the same rules cannot be applied to public figures as are applied to ordinary members of the community since the very fact of being a public figure means one is noticed and spoken of freely by the world at large. Unlike private citizens, public figures do not retain a substantial measure of control over what others know. *Hustler Magazine* v. *Falwell* addresses a fairly outrageous and quite unbelievable advertising parody that uses the well-known minister and commentator Jerry Falwell as its object of ridicule. Falwell seeks damages both for emotional distress and for libel. A unanimous United States Supreme Court denies there is any liability, since a mock advertisement cannot be judged outrageous with sufficient objectivity to say there has been intentional infliction of emotional distress, and the depiction of Falwell could not reasonably be thought to be intended as a true account. This case raises interesting questions about the character of expressions that may enjoy First Amendment protection. There are very important reasons why public figures often are not able to seek redress when those not in the public eye would certainly have a legal remedy. What exactly are those reasons, and how do they apply (if they do) in this case?

Unlike the authors preceding him in this section, Irving Kristol is primarily concerned not with expressions of opinion or attitude, but rather with expression in works of drama and literature and their counterfeits. Moreover, he gives a spirited defense of a kind of censorship which he claims is quite consistent with a generally liberal attitude toward state coercion. His explicit target is the prevailing liberal view that consenting adults should be permitted to see or read anything they please and that censorship and prior restraint are justified only to protect children and unwilling witnesses. Censorship, he argues, is required for at least two additional kinds of reasons: (1) to protect the general quality of life, indeed our civilized institutions themselves (an appeal to the harm principle); and (2) to exclude practices that "brutalize and debase our citizenry" (an appeal to a kind of "moral paternalism," the need to protect even adults from moral corruption). One of the more difficult challenges Kristol poses for the liberal view he is attacking consists of an embarrassing hypothetical example. Suppose an enterprising promoter sought to stage gladiatorial contests like those of Ancient Rome in Yankee Stadium, in which well-paid gladiators fought to the death to the roars of large crowds. How could he be prevented from doing this on liberal grounds? Presumably the spectacle would be restricted to consenting adults so that interference would not be necessary to protect children and offended witnesses. The gladiators too would be consenting adults, fully prepared to shoulder enormous risks to life and limb, supposedly for the sake of money. (We can imagine that, with closed circuit TV, the promoter could offer the winning gladiator some twenty million dollars.) To interfere with the liberty of the gladiators to make agreements with promoters on the ground that the rewards they seek are not worth the risks they *voluntarily* assume would be to invoke the principle of legal paternalism, which is anathema to liberals who follow Mill. Kristol himself is not so much interested in protecting his hypothetical gladiators from death or physical harm as she is in defending the audience from a kind of moral harm, or harm to character.

PRIVACY

The relation of liberty to privacy is often obscured by subtle differences of sense and nuance in various applications of those abstract words. Privacy is often contrasted with liberty, or cited (as in Feinberg's article) as one of the moral limits to free activity. In this sense, one person's privacy is a limit to *another* person's liberty.

Privacy so described is common to a set of claims citizens have, not only against one another, but also against policemen and other agents of the state. In other contexts privacy is spoken of as itself a kind of liberty—a liberty to be left alone, to enjoy one's solitude, not to be intruded upon or even known about in certain respects. Expressed in this way, privacy is a negative sort of freedom, a freedom (indeed, a right) *not* to be treated in certain ways. Thus one person's right to privacy characteristically conflicts wih more active liberties of movement and surveillance by others. So conceived, privacy is not one of the "liberties" normally ascribed to the state. Some state officials and agencies, to be sure, enjoy immunities and privileges of nondisclosure, but these forms of protected secrecy characteristically have as their rationales the need to enhance efficient functioning, not the need to protect privacy. Only persons have private thoughts, inner lives, and unknown histories that in virtue of their intimate character essentially merit protection from unwanted scrutiny; and the state, as such, is not a genuine person.

The notion of privacy first entered American law in the law of torts where it served to protect a miscellany[2] of personal interests against invasions by private individuals or groups by authorizing law suits for damages. Yet, in an implicit way, the idea of a private realm into which the state cannot legitimately penetrate, a domain which is simply not the state's proper business, is both ancient and ubiquitous. In the fictitious "Invitation to Dinner Case" included in this section, all of the legal requirements for an action for breach of contract appear to have been met, yet it is questionable whether such an action should be entertained. A dinner party, the judge might well be expected to say, is a householder's private affair and no proper concern of the courts. Here in a civil contest is the suggestion, normally made only with regard to criminal prohibitions, that public authority has no business interfering in private affairs.

What is this privacy which, in some cultures at least, is held so dear, and which is so easily confused with the privileges of property, the residue of shame, or the essence of personal autonomy, among other things? By sorting out various separable elements, Hyman Gross makes a strong start on a philosophical analysis of the concept. A central theme in his account is that the loss of privacy is a loss of *control* over information about and impressions of oneself. Gross then proceeds to illuminate the connections between this aspect of privacy and self-determination, self-respect, and moral responsibility—connections that help explain the high value put on privacy, both by citizens and (now) by the law.

In the brief selection entitled "The Theatrical Model and Concern for Privacy" Alan Ryan provides an account of the concern for privacy that stresses a widespread and frequent need in life to dissemble, to withdraw, to hide, and to create particular impressions for particular purposes. The self behind the performance is the private self, and the importance of preserving that self is the measure of how important it is to protect privacy. Legal protection of privacy in this aspect would seem to be mainly protection against exposure of calculated deceits in personal relations, and against intrusion into the safe houses that family life and other private enclaves represent. The first suggests the vast area of legally untrammeled privilege in which, for example, the "Invitation to Dinner Case" takes place, while the second points to those legal protections that are suggested by the phrase "in the privacy of . . . ."

Richard Posner presents an economic theory of privacy that attempts to account for the value of privacy instrumentally. Both privacy and the prying whose aim is to defeat it are viewed as goods that are used to produce income or some other form of utility or welfare. Economic efficiency is the crucial consideration in deciding questions of protectability. Not surprisingly, one conclusion drawn here is that in general the case for protecting business privacy is stronger than the case for protecting individual privacy. In the development of legal protection of privacy the common law, rather than legislation, has reflected the truths of economic value, according to Posner. It is useful to consider generally whether Posner's examples of people's behavior are sufficiently comprehensive to support the general conclusions he draws, or indeed even whether the examples he provides are typical and so satisfactory for the purposes at hand.

RIGHTS

Discussions of liberty can hardly avoid using the terminology of rights, and indeed the concepts of "liberty" and "right" are so intimately intertwined that clarification of either without understanding of the other is next to impossible. Where one can speak of a liberty to do, to be, or to possess something, one might also speak of a right to do, be, or possess that thing, except that the right, in most usage, is a stronger kind of liberty, an open option that is guaranteed, or reinforced, by a corresponding duty imposed on other parties not to interfere or else to provide necessary means. A liberty and a right to a given X, then, are different ways of having an open option with respect to that X. Sometimes, however, we speak of liberty itself as something people have a right to. In this case, we mean not merely that certain basic options *ought* to be left open, but rather that the state is *bound* by moral principle to keep those options open by imposing legal duties both on itself and on others not to interfere.

By far the most ingenious and influential work of conceptual analysis in jurisprudence is *Fundamental Legal Conceptions* by the former Yale University law professor Wesley Hohfeld, first published in 1919. Hohfeld surveyed all of the various sorts of "jural relations" that can hold between two persons (e.g., "master-servant," "principal-agent," "husband-wife") and found that they could be reduced to four different kinds of underlying normative relationships, the basic building blocks out of which all jural relations can be constructed. Each of these basic relations is sometimes described by the word "right," so it might be maintained that "right" as used in the law is a highly ambiguous term referring to any one of a cluster of four distinct relations. Hohfeld thinks, however, that this apparent ambiguity is largely the product of careless usage, and that only one of the four kinds of rights can claim the title of "right in the strict sense." A right in this sense (sometimes called a "claim" or "claim right") is logically correlated with the duties of one or more other people. If Jones owes one thousand dollars to Smith, then he has a duty to pay the money to Smith, which seen from another vantage point is simply Smith's right to that money. Smith's right and Jones's duty are equivalent ways of describing one "jural relation" that holds between them. Smith has a legally enforcible claim against Jones, corresponding to Jones's legal duty to Smith.

Sometimes, however, we use the word "right" (somewhat loosely, Hohfeld would say) to refer to a *privilege* or a *liberty* of a person that is not correlated with the duties of any one else. To say that Smith has a privilege to X, or is at liberty to X, is to say that he has *no duty not* to X. That in turn implies nothing whatever about any other person's duties toward Smith in respect to X. Normally Smith has a duty not to strike Jones with his fist, but if Jones attacks Smith and strikes him first, then the legal situation changes and Smith no longer has a duty to refrain from punching Jones, which is to say that he has the legal privilege of striking back or (equivalently) that he is at liberty to strike back. That statement implies nothing about Jones's duties to Smith, but it does entail that Jones no longer has a claim on Smith's forbearance. Thus the statement of Smith's liberty ("no duty not . . . ") does entail the negative statement that Jones has "no right" that Smith not hit him.

The third basic jural relation is that connected with the idea of a legal *power* (also loosely called a "right"). Smith has a legal power with respect to Jones insofar as he has the ability to bring into existence, by his own voluntary behavior, new legal relations involving Jones, or to alter or extinguish existing relations. Thus if Smith strikes Jones, he creates the privilege in Jones, which otherwise would not exist, of striking Smith. If Jones has made Smith an offer, then Smith has the *power* of creating a claim-duty contractual relation with Jones by accepting. If he accepts, then Jones will have a duty, which he would not otherwise have, of doing his side of the bargain. The correlative to Smith's power, in these examples, is Jones's *liability* to changes in his legal position. The fourth basic relation is that associated with the idea of an *immunity* (also sometimes loosely called a "right"). Smith has an immunity with respect to Jones just insofar as his legal relations are not subject to alteration by Jones. In some states Mrs. Smith can change Mr. Smith's legal status simply by filing for a "no-fault" divorce, but Jones lacks this power of Mrs. Smith; no voluntary act of his can have the immediate legal effect of making Smith divorced. Jones is under a legal disability in this respect, which is the *correlative* to Smith's immunity.

Hohfeld then can sum up the basic jural relations in the following manner. Smith's claim-right against Jones is correlated with Jones's duty to Smith. The opposite of such a claim-right is a "no-right." Smith's privilege or liberty to act in a certain way toward Jones is correlated with Jones's "no-right" against Smith. The opposite of such a liberty is a duty. Smith's legal power over Jones is correlated with Jones's liability in respect to Smith. The opposite of such a power is a disability. Finally, Smith's immunity in some respect to Jones is correlated with Jones's disability in that respect toward Smith. The opposite of such an immunity is a liability. The system is worked out with perfect symmetry and great elegance.

Carl Wellman also endorses the Hohfeldian analysis of legal rights, but adds some important twists of his own. A legal right, in his view, is a *cluster* of liberties, claims, powers, and/or immunities around a central core element, itself one of the Hohfeldian elements. Depending on the content of the specific right in question, the clustered and core elements may vary in composition. The Hohfeldian distinctions are especially useful in enabling us to specify, in all relevant terms, precisely what the content of a given legal right is. Legal rights are invariably *complex*; what unites the diverse elements is their common function: to enlarge and strengthen one's area of autonomous self-government. An original feature of Wellman's analysis is his extension of the Hohfeldian legal model to moral and human rights by the recognition of ethical analogues to legal liberties, claims, powers, and immunities. He then defines "human rights" as a cluster of such ethical elements possessed by an individual simply by virtue of his humanity and held against the state. Finally, he applies his analysis to the "human right to privacy," bringing us back full circle to that elusive but fundamental notion.

The right of self-defense is commonly invoked when death or injury occurs in a situation of some hostility. Its limits are not entirely clear, and the class of cases in which it will provide a defense in law is still unsettled. In "Self-Defense and Rights" Judith Thomson analyzes the right and suggests several kinds of qualification to make its operation fit our moral intuitions. In the end she reminds us that we need an account of how our appeal to rights functions in ethical discussion, and suggests that the right of self-defense is a case in point. In the critical spirit of her observation it may be useful to ask first what (if anything) would be missing if arguments for or against liability in any case of self-defense made no mention of rights, but sought to justify the harm done to another person by an appeal to vicarious experience as the facts of the case (including the state of mind of the defendant) are presented in far greater detail than in Thomson's description of the events, and are considered in the light of established principles such as reasonable force in the circumstances, no safe retreat, reasonable apprehension of the danger, and other textbook qualifications. When the discourse of rights is refined perhaps we shall be able to say more exactly how rights are transformed in changed circumstances and what happens when rights are in collision. But it may turn out that we then know nothing more than we do now about who ought to prevail when claims are in conflict. The correct resolution of such disputes depends on things other than getting right our conception of rights.

NOTES

1. The phrase is Herbert Packer's. See his *The Limits of the Criminal Sanction* (Stanford, Calif.: Stanford University Press, 1968), pp. 253–56.

2. Cf. Prosser on *Torts*, 2nd ed. (St. Paul, Minn.: West Publishing Co., 1955), chap. 20.

CHALLENGES TO SELF-DETERMINATION: LEGAL PATERNALISM AND LEGAL MORALISM

JOHN STUART MILL

On Liberty*

The object of this Essay is to assert one very simple principle, as entitled to govern absolutely the dealings of society with the individual in the way of compulsion and control, whether the means used be physical force in the form of legal penalties, or the moral coercion of public opinion. That principle is, that the sole end for which mankind are warranted, individually or collectively, in interfering with the liberty of action of any of their number, is self-protection. That the only purpose for which power can be rightfully exercised over any member of a civilized community, against his will, is to prevent harm to others. His own good, either physical or moral, is not a sufficient warrant. He cannot rightfully be compelled to do or forbear because it will be better for him to do so, because it will make him happier, because, in the opinions of others, to do so would be wise, or even right. These are good reasons for remonstrating with him, or reasoning with him, or persuading him, or entreating him, but not for compelling him, or visiting him with any evil, in case he do otherwise. To justify that, the conduct from which it is desired to deter him must be calculated to produce evil to some one else. The only part of the conduct of any one, for which he is amenable to society, is that which concerns others. In the part which merely concerns himself, his independence is, of right, absolute. Over himself, over his own body and mind, the individual is sovereign.

It is, perhaps, hardly necessary to say that this doctrine is meant to apply only to human beings in the maturity of their faculties. We are not speaking of children, or of young persons below the age which the law may fix as that of manhood or womanhood. Those who are still in a state to require being taken care of by others, must be protected against their own actions as well as against external injury. For the same reason, we may leave out of consideration those backward states of society in which the race itself may be considered as in its nonage. The early difficulties in the way of spontaneous progress are so great, that there is seldom any choice of means for overcoming them; and a ruler full of the spirit of improvement is warranted in the use of any expedients that will attain an end, perhaps otherwise unattainable. Despotism is a legitimate mode of government in dealing with barbarians, provided the end be their improvement, and the means justified by actually effecting that end. Liberty, as a principle, has no application to any state of things anterior to the time when mankind have become capable of being improved by free and equal discussion. Until then, there is nothing for them but implicit obedience to an Akbar or a Charlemagne, if they are so fortunate as to find one. But as soon as mankind have attained the capacity of being guided to their own improvement by conviction or persuasion (a period long since reached in all nations with whom we need here concern ourselves), compulsion, either in the direct form or in that of pains and penalties for non-compliance, is no longer admissible as a means to their own good, and justifiable only for the security of others.

It is proper to state that I forego any advantage which could be derived to my argument from the idea of abstract right, as a thing independent of utility. I regard utility as the ultimate appeal on all ethical questions; but it must be utility in the largest sense, grounded on the permanent interests of man as a progressive being. Those interests, I contend, authorize the subjection of individual spontaneity to external control, only in respect to those actions of each, which concern the interest of other people. If any one does an act hurtful to others, there is a *primâ facie* case for punishing him, by law, or, where legal penalties are not safely applicable, by general disapprobation. There are also many positive acts for the benefit of others, which he may rightfully be compelled to perform; such as, to give evidence in a court of justice; to bear his fair share in the com-

*From *On Liberty*. Excerpts from Chapters I and II, and all of Chapter IV. First published in 1859.

mon defence, or in any other joint work necessary to the interest of the society of which he enjoys the protection; and to perform certain acts of individual beneficence, such as saving a fellow creature's life, or interposing to protect the defenceless against ill-usage, things which whenever it is obviously a man's duty to do, he may rightfully be made responsible to society for not doing. A person may cause evil to others not only by his actions but by his inaction, and in either case he is justly accountable to them for the injury. The latter case, it is true, requires a much more cautious exercise of compulsion than the former. To make any one answerable for doing evil to others, is the rule; to make him answerable for not preventing evil, is, comparatively speaking, the exception. Yet there are many cases clear enough and grave enough to justify that exception. In all things which regard the external relations of the individual, he is *de jure* amenable to those whose interests are concerned, and if need be, to society as their protector. There are often good reasons for not holding him to the responsibility; but these reasons must arise from the special expediencies of the case: either because it is a kind of case in which he is on the whole likely to act better, when left to his own discretion, than when controlled in any way in which society have it in their power to control him; or because the attempt to exercise control would produce other evils, greater than those which it would prevent. When such reasons as these preclude the enforcement of responsibility, the conscience of the agent himself should step into the vacant judgment-seat, and protect those interests of others which have no external protection; judging himself all the more rigidly, because the case does not admit of his being made accountable to the judgment of his fellow-creatures.

But there is a sphere of action in which society, as distinguished from the individual, has, if any, only an indirect interest; comprehending all that portion of a person's life and conduct which affects only himself, or, if it also affects others, only with their free, voluntary, and undeceived consent and participation. When I say only himself, I mean directly, and in the first instance: for whatever affects himself, may affect others *through* himself; and the objection which may be grounded on this contingency, will receive consideration in the sequel. This, then, is the appropriate region of human liberty. It comprises, first, the inward domain of consciousness; demanding liberty of conscience, in the most comprehensive sense; liberty of thought and feeling; absolute freedom of opinion and sentiment on all subjects, practical or speculative, scientific, moral, or theological. The liberty of expressing and publishing opinions may seem to fall under a different principle, since it belongs to that part of the conduct of an individual which concerns other people; but, being almost of as much importance as the liberty of thought itself, and resting in great part on the same reasons, is practically inseparable from it. Secondly, the principle requires liberty of tastes and pursuits; of framing the plan of our life to suit our own character; of doing as we like, subject to such consequences as may follow; without impediment from our fellow-creatures, so long as what we do does not harm them, even though they should think our conduct foolish, perverse, or wrong. Thirdly, from this liberty of each individual, follows the liberty, within the same limits, of combination among individuals; freedom to unite, for any purpose not involving harm to others: the persons combining being supposed to be of full age, and not forced or deceived.

No society in which these liberties are not, on the whole, respected, is free, whatever may be its form of government; and none is completely free in which they do not exist absolute and unqualified. The only freedom which deserves the name, is that of pursuing our own good in our own way, so long as we do not attempt to deprive others of theirs, or impede their efforts to obtain it. Each is the proper guardian of his own health, whether bodily, or mental and spiritual. Mankind are greater gainers by suffering each other to live as seems good to themselves, than by compelling each to live as seems good to the rest . . .

We have now recognized the necessity to the mental well-being of mankind (on which all their other well-being depends) of freedom of opinion, and freedom of the expression of opinion, on four distinct grounds; which we will now briefly recapitulate.

First, if any opinion is compelled to silence, that opinion may, for aught we can certainly know, be true. To deny this is to assume our own infallibility.

Secondly, though the silenced opinion be an error, it may, and very commonly does, contain a portion of truth; and since the general or prevailing opinion on any subject is rarely or never the whole truth, it is only by the collision of adverse opinions that the remainder of the truth has any chance of being supplied.

Thirdly, even if the received opinion be not only true, but the whole truth; unless it is suffered to be, and actually is vigorously and earnestly contested, it will, by most of those who receive it, be held in the manner of a prejudice, with little comprehension or feeling of its rational grounds. And not only this, but fourthly, the meaning of the doctrine itself will be in danger of being lost, or enfeebled, and deprived of its vital effect on the character and conduct: the dogma becoming a mere formal profession, inefficacious for good, but cumbering the ground, and preventing the growth of any real and heartfelt conviction from reason or personal experience . . .

OF THE LIMITS TO THE AUTHORITY OF SOCIETY OVER THE INDIVIDUAL

What, then, is the rightful limit to the sovereignty of the individual over himself? Where does the authority of society begin? How much of human life should be assigned to individuality, and how much to society?

Each will receive its proper share, if each has that which more particularly concerns it. To individuality should belong the part of life in which it is chiefly the individual that is interested; to society, the part which chiefly interests society.

Though society is not founded on a contract, and though no good purpose is answered by inventing a contract in order to deduce social obligations from it, every one who receives the protection of society owes a return for the benefit, and the fact of living in society renders it indispensable that each should be bound to observe a certain line of conduct towards the rest. This conduct consists, first, in not injuring the interests of one another; or rather certain interests, which, either by express legal provision or by tacit understanding, ought to be considered as rights; and secondly, in each person's bearing his share (to be fixed on some equitable principle) of the labors and sacrifices incurred for defending the society or its members from injury and molestation. These conditions society is justified in enforcing, at all costs to those who endeavor to withhold fulfillment. Nor is this all that society may do. The acts of an individual may be hurtful to others, or wanting in due consideration for their welfare, without going the length of violating any of their constituted rights. The offender may then be justly punished by opinion, though not by law. As soon as any part of a person's conduct affects prejudicially the interests of others, society has jurisdiction over it, and the question whether the general welfare will or will not be promoted by interfering with it, becomes open to discussion. But there is no room for entertain-

ing any such question when a person's conduct affects the interests of no persons besides himself, or needs not affect them unless they like (all the persons concerned being of full age, and the ordinary amount of understanding). In all such cases there should be perfect freedom, legal and social, to do the action and stand the consequences.

It would be a great misunderstanding of this doctrine, to suppose that it is one of selfish indifference, which pretends that human beings have no business with each other's conduct in life, and that they should not concern themselves about the well-doing or well-being of one another, unless their own interest is involved. Instead of any diminution, there is need of a great increase of disinterested exertion to promote the good of others. But disinterested benevolence can find other instruments to persuade people to their good, than whips and scourges, either of the literal or the metaphorical sort. I am the last person to undervalue the self-regarding virtues; they are only second in importance, if even second, to the social. It is equally the business of education to cultivate both. But even education works by conviction and persuasion as well as by compulsion, and it is by the former only that, when the period of education is past, the self-regarding virtues should be inculcated. Human beings owe to each other help to distinguish the better from the worse, and encouragement to choose the former and avoid the latter. They should be forever stimulating each other to increased exercise of their higher faculties, and increased direction of their feelings and aims towards wise instead of foolish, elevating instead of degrading, objects and contemplations. But neither one person, nor any number of persons, is warranted in saying to another human creature of ripe years, that he shall not do with his life for his own benefit what he chooses to do with it. He is the person most interested in his own well-being: the interest which any other person, except in cases of strong personal attachment, can have in it, is trifling, compared with that which he himself has; the interest which society has in him individually (except as to his conduct to others) is fractional, and altogether indirect: while, with respect to his own feelings and circumstances, the most ordinary man or woman has means of knowledge immeasurably surpassing those that can be possessed by anyone else. The interference of society to overrule his judgment and purposes in what only regards himself, must be grounded on general presumptions; which may be altogether wrong, and even if right, are as likely as not to be misapplied to individual cases, by persons no better acquainted with the circumstances of such cases than those are who look at them merely from without. In this department, therefore, of human affairs, Individuality has its proper field of action. In the conduct of human beings towards one another, it is necessary that general rules should for the most part be observed, in order that people may know what they have to expect; but in each person's own concerns, his individual spontaneity is entitled to free exercise. Considerations to aid his judgment, exhortations to strengthen his will, may be offered to him, even obtruded on him, by others; but he, himself, is the final judge. All errors which he is likely to commit against advice and warning, are far outweighed by the evil of allowing others to constrain him to what they deem his good.

I do not mean that the feelings with which a person is regarded by others, ought not to be in any way affected by his self-regarding qualities or deficiencies. This is neither possible nor desirable. If he is eminent in any of the qualities which conduce to his own good, he is, so far, a proper object of admiration. He is so much the nearer to the ideal perfection of human nature. If he is grossly deficient in those qualities, a sentiment the opposite of admiration will follow. There is a degree of folly, and a degree of what may be called (though the phrase is not unobjectionable) lowness or depravation of taste, which, though it cannot justify doing harm to the person who manifests it, renders him necessarily and properly a subject of distaste, or, in extreme cases, even of contempt: a person would not have the opposite qualities in due strength without entertaining these feelings. Though doing no wrong to anyone, a person may so act as to compel us to judge him, and feel to him, as a fool, or as a being of an inferior order: and since this judgment and feeling are a fact which he would prefer to avoid, it is doing him a service to warn him of it beforehand, as of any other disagreeable consequence to which he exposes himself. It would be well, indeed, if this good office were much more freely rendered than the common notions of politeness at present permit, and if one person could honestly point out to another that he thinks him in fault, without being considered unmannerly or presuming. We have a right, also, in various ways, to act upon our unfavorable opinion of any one, not to the oppression of his individuality, but in the exercise of ours. We are not bound, for example, to seek his society; we have a right to avoid it (though not to parade the avoidance), for we have a right to choose the society most acceptable to us. We have a right, and it may be our duty to caution others against him, if we think his example or conversation likely to have a pernicious effect on those with whom he associates. We may give others a preference over him in optional good offices, except those which tend to his improvement. In these various modes a person may suffer very severe penalties at the hands of others, for faults which directly concern only himself; but he suffers these penalties only in so far as they are the natural, and, as it were, the spontaneous consequences of the faults themselves, not because they are purposely inflicted on him for the sake of punishment. A person who shows rashness, obstinacy, self-conceit—who cannot live within moderate means—who cannot restrain himself from hurtful indulgences—who pursues animal pleasures at the expense of those of feelings and intellect—must expect to be lowered in the opinion of others, and to have a less share of their favorable sentiments, but of this he has no right to complain, unless he has merited their favor by special excellence in his social relations, and has thus established a title to their good offices, which is not affected by his demerits towards himself.

What I contend for is, that the inconveniences which are strictly inseparable from the unfavorable judgment of others, are the only ones to which a person should ever be subjected for that portion of his conduct and character which concerns his own good, but which does not affect the interests of others in their relations with him. Acts injurious to others require a totally different treatment. Encroachment on their rights; infliction on them of any loss or damage not justified by his own rights; falsehood or duplicity in dealing with them; unfair or ungenerous use of advantages over them; even selfish abstinence from defending them against injury—these are fit objects of moral reprobation, and, in grave cases, of moral retribution and punishment. And not only these acts, but the dispositions which lead to them, are properly immoral, and fit subjects of disapprobation which may rise to abhorrence. Cruelty of disposition; malice and ill-nature; that most anti-social and odious of all passions, envy; dissimulation and insincerity; irascibility on insufficient cause, and resentment disproportioned to the provocation; the love of domineering over others; the desire to engross more than one's share of advantages (the πλε νεξῖα of the Greeks); the pride which derives gratification from the abasement of others; the egotism which thinks self and its concerns more important than everything else, and decides all doubtful questions in his own favor—these are moral vices, and constitute a bad and odious moral character: unlike the self-regarding faults previously mentioned, which are not properly immoralities, and to whatever pitch they may be carried, do not constitute wickedness. They may be proofs of any amount of folly, or want of personal dignity and self-respect; but they are only a subject or moral reprobation when they involve a breach of duty to others, for whose sake the individual is bound to have care for himself. What are called duties to ourselves are not socially obligatory, unless circumstances render them at the same time duties to others. The term duty to oneself, when it means anything more than prudence, means self-respect or self-development; and for none of these is any one accountable to his fellow-creatures, because for none of them is it for the good of mankind that he be held accountable to them.

The distinction between the loss of consideration which a person may rightly incur by defect of prudence or of personal dignity, and the reprobation which is due to him for an offence against the rights of others, is not a merely nominal distinction. It makes a vast difference both in our feelings and in our conduct towards him, whether he displeases us in things in which we think we have a right to control him, or in things in which we know that we have not. If he displeases us, we may express our distaste, and we may stand aloof from a person as well as from a thing that displeases us; but we shall not therefore feel called on to make his life uncomfortable. We shall reflect that he already bears, or will bear, the whole penalty of his error; if he spoils his life by mismanagement, we shall not, for that reason, desire to spoil it still further: instead of wishing to punish him, we shall rather endeavor to alleviate his punishment, by showing him how he may avoid or cure the evils his conduct tends to bring upon him. He may be to us an object of pity, perhaps of dislike, but not of anger or resentment; we shall not treat him like an enemy of society: the worst we shall think ourselves justified in doing is leaving him to himself, if we do not interfere benevolently by showing interest or concern for him. It is far otherwise if he has infringed the rules necessary for the protection of his fellow-creatures, individually or collectively. The evil consequences of his acts do not then fall on himself, but on others; and society, as the protector of all its members, must retaliate on him; must inflict pain on him for the express purpose of punishment,

and must take care that it be sufficiently severe. In the one case, he is an offender at our bar, and we are called on not only to sit in judgment on him, but, in one shape or another, to execute our own sentence: in the other case, it is not our part to inflict any suffering on him, except what may incidentally follow from our using the same liberty in the regulation of our own affairs, which we allow to him in his.

The distinction here pointed out between the part of a person's life which concerns only himself, and that which concerns others, many persons will refuse to admit. How (it may be asked) can any part of the conduct of a member of society be a matter of indifference to the other members? No person is an entirely isolated being; it is impossible for a person to do anything seriously or permanently hurtful to himself, without mischief reaching at least to his near connections, and often far beyond them. If he injures his property, he does harm to those who directly or indirectly derived support from it, and usually diminishes, by a greater or less amount, the general resources of the community. If he deteriorates his bodily or mental faculties, he not only brings evil upon all who depended on him for any portion of their happiness, but disqualifies himself for rendering the services which he owes to his fellow-creatures generally; perhaps becomes a burden on their affection or benevolence; and if such conduct were very frequent, hardly any offence that is committed would detract more from the general sum of good. Finally, if by his vices or follies a person does no direct harm to others, he is nevertheless (it may be said) injurious by his example; and ought to be compelled to control himself, for the sake of those whom the sight or knowledge of his conduct might corrupt or mislead.

And even (it will be added) if the consequences of misconduct could be confined to the vicious or thoughtless individual, ought society to abandon to their own guidance those who are manifestly unfit for it? If protection against themselves is confessedly due to children and persons under age, is not society equally bound to afford it to persons of mature years who are equally incapable of self-government? If gambling, or drunkenness, or incontinence, or idleness, or uncleanliness, are as injurious to happiness, and as great a hindrance to improvement, as many or most of the acts prohibited by law, why (it may be asked) should not law, so far as is consistent with practicability and social convenience, endeavor to repress these also? And as a supplement to the unavoidable imperfections of law, ought not opinion at least to organize a powerful police against these vices, and visit rigidly with social penalties those who are known to practise them? There is no question here (it may be said) about restricting individuality, or impeding the trial of new and original experiments in living. The only things it is sought to prevent are things which have been tried and condemned from the beginning of the world until now; things which experience has shown not to be useful or suitable to any person's individuality. There must be some length of time and amount of experience, after which a moral or prudential truth may be regarded as established: and it is merely desired to prevent generation after generation from falling over the same precipice which has been fatal to their predecessors.

I fully admit that the mischief which a person does to himself, may seriously affect, both through their sympathies and their interests, those nearly connected with him, and in a minor degree, society at large. When, by conduct of this sort, a person is led to violate a distinct and assignable obligation to any other person or persons, the case is taken out of the self-regarding class, and becomes amenable to moral disapprobation in the proper sense of the term. If, for example, a man, through intemperance or extravagance, becomes unable to pay his debts, or, having undertaken the moral responsibility of a family, becomes from the same cause incapable of supporting or educating them, he is deservedly reprobated, and might be justly punished; but it is for the breach of duty to his family or creditors, not for the extravagance. If the resources which ought to have been devoted to them, had been diverted from them for the most prudent investment, the moral culpability would have been the same. George Barnwell murdered his uncle to get money for his mistress, but if he had done it to set himself up in business, he would equally have been hanged. Again, in the frequent case of a man who causes grief to his family by addiction to bad habits, he deserves reproach for his unkindness or ingratitude; but so he may for cultivating habits not in themselves vicious, if they are painful to those with whom he passes his life, or who from personal ties are dependent on him for their comfort. Whoever fails in the consideration generally due to the interests and feelings of others, not being compelled by some more imperative duty, or justified by allowable self-preference, is a subject of moral disapprobation for that failure, but not for the cause of it, nor for the errors, merely

personal to himself, which may have remotely led to it. In like manner, when a person disables himself, by conduct purely self-regarding, from the performance of some definite duty incumbent on him to the public, he is guilty of a social offence. No person ought to be punished simply for being drunk; but a soldier or a policeman should be punished for being drunk on duty. Whenever, in short, there is a definite damage, or a definite risk of damage, either to an individual or to the public, the case is taken out of the province of liberty, and placed in that of morality or law.

But with regard to the merely contingent, or, as it may be called, constructive injury which a person causes to society, by conduct which neither violates any specific duty to the public, nor occasions perceptible hurt to any assignable individual except himself; the inconvenience is one which society can afford to bear, for the sake of the greater good of human freedom. If grown persons are to be punished for not taking proper care of themselves, I would rather it were for their own sake, than under pretence of preventing them from impairing their capacity of rendering to society benefits which society does not pretend it has a right to exact. But I cannot consent to argue the point as if society had no means of bringing its weaker members up to its ordinary standard of rational conduct, except waiting till they do something irrational, and then punishing them, legally or morally, for it. Society has had absolute power over them during all the early portion of their existence: it has had the whole period of childhood and nonage in which to try whether it could make them capable of rational conduct in life. The existing generation is master both of the training and the entire circumstances of the generation to come; it cannot indeed make them perfectly wise and good, because it is itself so lamentably deficient in goodness and wisdom; and its best efforts are not always, in individual cases, its most successful ones; but it is perfectly well able to make the rising generation, as a whole, as good as, and a little better than, itself. If society lets any considerable number of its members grow up mere children, incapable of being acted on by rational consideration of distant motives, society has itself to blame for the consequences. Armed not only with all the powers of education, but with the ascendency which the authority of a received opinion always exercises over the minds who are least fitted to judge for themselves; and aided by the *natural* penalties which cannot be prevented from falling on those who incur the distaste or the contempt of those who know them; let not society pretend that it needs, besides all this, the power to issue commands and enforce obedience in the personal concerns of individuals, in which, on all principles of justice and policy, the decision ought to rest with those who are to abide the consequences. Nor is there anything which tends more to discredit and frustrate the better means of influencing conduct, than a resort to the worse. If there be among those whom it is attempted to coerce into prudence or temperance, any of the material of which vigorous and independent characters are made, they will infallibly rebel against the yoke. No such person will ever feel that others have a right to control him in his concerns, such as they have to prevent him from injuring them in theirs; and it easily comes to be considered a mark of spirit and courage to fly in the face of such usurped authority, and do with ostentation the exact opposite of what it enjoins; as in the fashion of grossness which succeeded, in the time of Charles II, to the fanatical moral intolerance of the Puritans. With respect to what is said of the necessity of protecting society from the bad example set to others by the vicious or the self-indulgent; it is true that bad example may have a pernicious effect, especially the example of doing wrong to others with impunity to the wrongdoer. But we are now speaking of conduct which, while it does no wrong to others, is supposed to do great harm to the agent himself: and I do not see how those who believe this, can think otherwise than that the example, on the whole, must be more salutary than hurtful, since, if it displays the misconduct, it displays also the painful or degrading consequences which, if the conduct is justly censured, must be supposed to be in all or most cases attendant on it.

But the strongest of all the arguments against the interference of the public with purely personal conduct, is that when it does interfere, the odds are that it interferes wrongly, and in the wrong place. On questions of social morality, of duty to others, the opinion of the public, that is, of an overruling majority, though often wrong, is likely to be still oftener right; because on such questions they are only required to judge of their own interests; of the manner in which some mode of conduct, if allowed to be practised, would affect themselves. But the opinion of a similar majority, imposed as a law on the minority, on questions of self-regarding conduct, is quite as likely to be wrong as right; for in these cases public opinion means, at the best, some people's opinion of what is good or bad for other people;

while very often it does not even mean that; the public, with the most perfect indifference, passing over the pleasure or convenience of those whose conduct they censure, and considering only their own preference. There are many who consider as an injury to themselves any conduct which they have a distaste for, and resent it as an outrage to their feelings; as a religious bigot, when charged with disregarding the religious feelings of others, has been known to retort that they disregard his feelings, by persisting in their abominable worship or creed. But there is no parity between the feeling of a person for his own opinion, and the feeling of another who is offended at his holding it; no more than between the desire of a thief to take a purse, and the desire of the right owner to keep it. And a person's taste is as much his own peculiar concern as his opinion or his purse. It is easy for any one to imagine an ideal public, which leaves the freedom and choice of individuals in all uncertain matters undisturbed, and only requires them to abstain from modes of conduct which universal experience has condemned. But where has there been seen a public which set any such limit to its censorship? or when does the public trouble itself about universal experience? In its interferences with personal conduct it is seldom thinking of anything but the enormity of acting or feeling differently from itself; and this standard of judgment, thinly disguised, is held up to mankind as the dictate of religion and philosophy, by nine tenths of all moralists and speculative writers. These teach that things are right because they are right; because we feel them to be so. They tell us to search in our own minds and hearts for laws of conduct binding on ourselves and on all others. What can the poor public do but apply these instructions, and make their own personal feelings of good and evil, if they are tolerably unanimous in them, obligatory on all the world?

The evil here pointed out is not one which exists only in theory; and it may perhaps be expected that I should specify the instances in which the public of this age and country improperly invests its own preferences with the character of moral laws. I am not writing an essay on the aberrations of existing moral feeling. That is too weighty a subject to be discussed parenthetically, and by way of illustration. Yet examples are necessary, to show that the principle I maintain is of serious and practical moment, and that I am not endeavoring to erect a barrier against imaginary evils. And it is not difficult to show, by abundant instances, that to extend the bounds of what may be called moral police, until it encroaches on the most unquestionably legitimate liberty of the individual, is one of the most universal of all human propensities.

As a first instance, consider the antipathies which men cherish on no better grounds than that persons whose religious opinions are different from theirs, do not practise their religious observances, especially their religious abstinences. To cite a rather trivial example, nothing in the creed or practice of Christians does more to envenom the hatred of Mahomedans against them, than the fact of their eating pork. There are few acts which Christians and Europeans regard with more unaffected disgust, than Mussulmans regard this particular mode of satisfying hunger. It is, in the first place, an offence against their religion; but this circumstance by no means explains either the degree or the kind of their repugnance; for wine also is forbidden by their religion, and to partake of it is by all Mussulmans accounted wrong, but not disgusting. Their aversion to the flesh of the "unclean beast" is, on the contrary, of that peculiar character, resembling an instinctive antipathy, which the idea of uncleanness, when once it thoroughly sinks into the feelings, seems always to excite even in those whose personal habits are anything but scrupulously cleanly, and of which the sentiment of religious impurity, so intense in the Hindoos, is a remarkable example. Suppose now that in a people, of whom the majority were Mussulmans, that majority should insist upon not permitting pork to be eaten within the limits of the country. This would be nothing new in Mahomedan countries.* Would it be a legitimate exercise of the moral authority of public opinion? and if not, why not? The practice is really revolting to such a public. They also sincerely think that it is forbidden and abhorred by the Deity. Neither could the prohibition be censured as religious persecution. It might be religious in its origin, but it would not be persecution for religion, since nobody's religion makes it a duty to eat pork. The only tenable ground of condemnation would be, that with the

*The case of the Bombay Parsees is a curious instance in point. When this industrious and enterprising tribe, the descendants of the Persian fire-worshippers, flying from their native country before the Caliphs, arrived in Western India, they were admitted to toleration by the Hindoo sovereigns, on condition of not eating beef. When those regions afterwards fell under the dominion of Mahomedan conquerors, the Parsees obtained from them a continuance of indulgence, on condition of refraining from pork. What was at first obedience to authority became a second nature, and the Parsees to this day abstain both from beef and pork. Though not required by their religion, the double abstinence has had time to grow into a custom of their tribe; and custom, in the East, is a religion.

personal tastes and self-regarding concerns of individuals the public has no business to interfere.

To come somewhat nearer home: the majority of Spaniards consider it a gross impiety, offensive in the highest degree to the Supreme Being, to worship him in any other manner than the Roman Catholic; and no other public worship is lawful on Spanish soil. The people of all Southern Europe look upon a married clergy as not only irreligious, but unchaste, indecent, gross, disgusting. What do Protestants think of these perfectly sincere feelings, and of the attempt to enforce them against non-Catholics? Yet, if mankind are justified in interfering with each other's liberty in things which do not concern the interests of others, on what principle is it possible consistently to exclude these cases? or who can blame people for desiring to suppress what they regard as a scandal in the sight of God and man? No stronger case can be shown for prohibiting anything which is regarded as a personal immorality, than is made out for suppressing these practices in the eyes of those who regard them as impieties; and unless we are willing to adopt the logic of persecutors, and to say that we may persecute others because we are right, and that they must not persecute us because they are wrong, we must beware of admitting a principle of which we should resent as a gross injustice the application to ourselves.

The preceding instances may be objected to, although unreasonably, as drawn from contingencies impossible among us: opinion, in this country, not being likely to enforce abstinence from meats, or to interfere with people for worshipping, and for either marrying or not marrying, according to their creed or inclination. The next example, however, shall be taken from an interference with liberty which we have by no means passed all danger of. Wherever the puritans have been sufficiently powerful, as in New England, and in Great Britain at the time of the Commonwealth, they have endeavored, with considerable success, to put down all public, and nearly all private, amusements: especially music, dancing, public games, or other assemblages for purposes of diversion, and the theatre. There are still in this country large bodies of persons by whose notions of morality and religion these recreations are condemned; and those persons belonging chiefly to the middle class, who are the ascendant power in the present social and political condition of the kingdom, it is by no means impossible that persons of these sentiments may at some time or other command a majority in Parliament. How will the remaining portion of the community like to have the amusements that shall be permitted to them regulated by the religious and moral sentiments of the stricter Calvinists and Methodists? Would they not, with considerable peremptoriness, desire these intrusively pious members of society to mind their own business? This is precisely what should be said to every government and every public, who have the pretension that no person shall enjoy any pleasure which they think wrong. But if the principle of the pretension be admitted, no one can reasonably object to its being acted on in the sense of the majority, or other preponderating power in the country; and all persons must be ready to conform to the idea of a Christian commonwealth, as understood by the early settlers in New England, if a religious profession similar to theirs should ever succeed in regaining its lost ground, as religions supposed to be declining have so often been known to do.

To imagine other contingency, perhaps more likely to be realized than the one last mentioned. There is confessedly a strong tendency in the modern world towards a democratic constitution of society, accompanied or not by popular political institutions. It is affirmed that in the country where this tendency is most completely realized —where both society and the government are most democratic—the United States—the feeling of the majority, to whom any appearance of a more showy or costly style of living than they can hope to rival is disagreeable, operates as a tolerably effectual sumptuary law, and that in many parts of the Union it is really difficult for a person possessing a very large income, to find any mode of spending it, which will not incur popular disapprobation. Though such statements as these are doubtless much exaggerated as a representation of existing facts, the state of things they describe is not only a conceivable and possible, but a probable result of democratic feeling, combined with the notion that the public has a right to a veto on the manner in which individuals shall spend their incomes. We have only further to suppose a considerable diffusion of Socialist opinions, and it may become infamous in the eyes of the majority to possess more property than some very small amount, or any income not earned by manual labor. Opinions similar in principle to these, already prevail widely among the artisan class, and weigh oppressively on those who are amenable to the opinion chiefly of that class, namely, its own members. It is known that the bad workmen who form the majority of the operatives in many branches of industry, are decid-

edly of opinion that bad workmen ought to receive the same wages as good, and that no one ought to be allowed, through piecework or otherwise, to earn by superior skill or industry more than others can without it. And they employ a moral police, which occasionally becomes a physical one, to deter skilful workmen from receiving, and employers from giving, a larger remuneration for a more useful service. If the public have any jurisdiction over private concerns, I cannot see that these people are in fault, or that any individual's particular public can be blamed for asserting the same authority over his individual conduct, which the general public asserts over people in general.

But, without dwelling upon suppositious cases, there are, in our own day, gross usurpations upon the liberty of private life actually practised, and still greater ones threatened with some expectation of success, and opinions proposed which assert an unlimited right in the public not only to prohibit by law everything which it thinks wrong, but in order to get at what it thinks wrong, to prohibit any number of things which it admits to be innocent.

Under the name of preventing intemperance, the people of one English colony, and of nearly half the United States, have been interdicted by law from making any use whatever of fermented drinks, except for medical purposes: for prohibition of their sale is in fact, as it is intended to be, prohibition of their use. And though the impracticability of executing the law has caused its repeal in several of the States which had adopted it, including the one from which it derives its name, an attempt has notwithstanding been commenced, and is prosecuted with considerable zeal by many of the professed philanthropists, to agitate for a similar law in this country. The association, or "Alliance" as it terms itself, which has been formed for this purpose, has acquired some notoriety through the publicity given to a correspondence between its Secretary and one of the very few English public men who hold that a politician's opinions ought to be founded on principles. Lord Stanley's share in this correspondence is calculated to strengthen the hopes already built on him, by those who know how rare such qualities as are manifested in some of his public appearances, unhappily are among those who figure in political life. The organ of the Alliance, who would "deeply deplore the recognition of any principle which could be wrested to justify bigotry and persecution," undertakes to point out the "broad and impassable barrier" which divides such principles from those of the association. "All matters relating to thought, opinion, conscience, appear to me," he says, "to be without the sphere of legislation; all pertaining to social act, habit, relation, subject only to a discretionary power vested in the State itself, and not in the individual, to be within it." No mention is made of a third class, different from either of these, viz., acts and habits which are not social, but individual; although it is to this class, surely, that the act of drinking fermented liquors belongs. Selling fermented liquors, however, is trading, and trading is a social act. But the infringement complained of is not on the liberty of the seller, but on that of the buyer and consumer; since the State might just as well forbid him to drink wine, as purposely make it impossible for him to obtain it. The Secretary, however, says, "I claim, as a citizen, a right to legislate whenever my social rights are invaded by the social act of another." And now for the definition of these "social rights." "If anything invades my social rights, certainly the traffic in strong drink does. It destroys my primary right of security, by constantly creating and stimulating social disorder. It invades my right of equality, by deriving a profit from the creation of a misery, I am taxed to support. It impedes my right to free moral and intellectual development, by surrounding my path with dangers, and by weakening and demoralizing society, from which I have a right to claim mutual aid and intercourse." A theory of "social rights," the like of which probably never before found its way into distinct language—being nothing short of this—that it is the absolute social right of every individual, that every other individual shall act in every respect exactly as he ought; that whosoever fails thereof in the smallest particular, violates my social right, and entitles me to demand from the legislature the removal of the grievance. So monstrous a principle is far more dangerous than any single interference with liberty; there is no violation of liberty which it would not justify; it acknowledges no right to any freedom whatever, except perhaps to that of holding opinions in secret, without ever disclosing them: for the moment an opinion which I consider noxious, passes any one's lips, it invades all the "social rights" attributed to me by the Alliance. The doctrine ascribes to all mankind a vested interest in each other's moral, intellectual, and even physical perfection, to be defined by each claimant according to his own standard.

Another important example of illegitimate interference with the rightful liberty of the individual, not simply threatened, but long since carried into triumphant effect, is Sabbatarian legislation. Without doubt, abstinence on one day in the week, so far as the exigencies of life permit, from the usual daily occupation, though in no respect religiously binding on any except Jews, it is a highly beneficial custom. And inasmuch as this custom cannot be observed without a general consent to that effect among the industrious classes, therefore, in so far as some persons by working may impose the same necessity on others, it may be allowable and right that the law should guarantee to each, the observance by others of the custom, by suspending the greater operations of industry on a particular day. But this justification, grounded on the direct interest which others have in each individual's observance of the practice, does not apply to the self-chosen occupations in which a person may think fit to employ his leisure; nor does it hold good, in the smallest degree, for legal restrictions on amusements. It is true that the amusement of some is the day's work of others; but the pleasure, not to say the useful recreation, of many, is worth the labor of a few, provided the occupation is freely chosen, and can be freely resigned. The operatives are perfectly right in thinking that if all worked on Sunday seven days' work would have to be given for six days' wages: but so long as the great mass of employments are suspended, the small number who for the enjoyment of others must still work, obtain a proportional increase of earnings; and they are not obliged to follow those occupations, if they prefer leisure to emolument. If a further remedy is sought, it might be found in the establishment by custom of a holiday on some other day of the week for those particular classes of persons. The only ground, therefore, on which restrictions on Sunday amusements can be defended, must be that they are religiously wrong; a motive of legislation which never can be too earnestly protested again. "Deorum injuriæ Diis curæ." It remains to be proved that society or any of its officers holds a commission from on high to avenge any supposed offence to Omnipotence, which is not also a wrong to our fellow-creatures. The notion that it is one man's duty that another should be religious, was the foundation of all the religious persecutions ever perpetrated, and if admitted, would fully justify them. Though the feeling which breaks out in the repeated attempts to stop railway travelling on Sunday, in the resistance to the opening of Museums, and the like, has not the cruelty of the old persecutors, the state of mind indicated by it is fundamentally the same. It is a determination not to tolerate others in doing what is permitted by their religion, because it is not permitted by the persecutor's religion. It is a belief that God not only abominates the act of the misbeliever, but will not hold us guiltless if we leave him unmolested.

I cannot refrain from adding to these examples of the little account commonly made of human liberty, the language of downright persecution which breaks out from the press of this country, whenever it feels called on to notice the remarkable phenomenon of Mormonism. Much might be said on the unexpected and instructive fact, that an alleged new revelation, and a religion founded on it, the product of palpable imposture, not even supported by the *prestige* of extraordinary qualities in its founder, is believed by hundreds of thousands, and has been made the foundation of a society, in the age of newspapers, railways, and the electric telegraph. What here concerns us is, that this religion, like other and better religions, has its martyrs; that its prophet and founder was, for his teaching, put to death by a mob; that others of its adherents lost their lives by the same lawless violence; that they were forcibly expelled, in a body, from the country in which they first grew up; while, now that they have been chased into a solitary recess in the midst of a desert, many of this country openly declare that it would be right (only that it is not convenient) to send an expedition against them, and compel them by force to conform to the opinion of other people. The article of the Mormonite doctrine which is the chief provocative to the antipathy which thus breaks through the ordinary restraints of religious tolerance, is its sanction of polygamy; which, though permitted to Mahomedans, and Hindoos, and Chinese, seems to excite unquenchable animosity when practised by persons who speak English, and profess to be a kind of Christians. No one has a deeper disapprobation than I have of this Mormon institution; both for other reasons, and because, far from being in any way countenanced by the principle of liberty, it is a direct infraction of that principle, being a mere riveting of the chains of one half of the community, and an emancipation of the other from reciprocity of obligation towards them. Still, it must be remembered that this relation is as much voluntary on the part of the women concerned in it, and who may be deemed the sufferers by it, as is the case with any other form of the marriage institution; and however surprising this fact may appear, it has its explanation in the common ideas and customs of the world, which teaching women to think marriage the one thing needful, make it intelligible that many a woman should prefer being one of several wives, to not being a wife at all. Other countries are not asked to recognize such unions, or release any portion of their inhabitants from their own laws on the score of Mormonite opinions. But when the dissentients have conceded to the hostile sentiments of others, far more than could justly be demanded; when they have left the countries to which their doctrines were unacceptable, and established themselves in a remote corner of the earth, which they have been the first to render habitable to human beings; it is difficult to see on what principles but those of tyranny they can be prevented from living there under what laws they please, provided they commit no aggression on other nations, and allow perfect freedom of departure to those who are dissatisfied with their ways. A recent writer, in some respects of considerable merit, proposes (to use his own words) not a crusade, but a *civilizade,* against this polygamous community, to put an end to what seems to him a retrograde step in civilization. It also appears so to me, but I am not aware that any community has a right to force another to be civilized. So long as the sufferers by the bad law do not invoke assistance from other communities, I cannot admit that persons entirely unconnected with them ought to step in and require that a condition of things with which all who are directly interested appear to be satisfied, should be put and end to because it is a scandal to persons some thousands of miles distant, who have no part or concern in it. Let them send missionaries, if they please, to preach against it; and let them, by any fair means (of which silencing the teachers is not one), oppose the progress of similar doctrines among their own people. If civilization has got the better of barbarism when barbarism had the world to itself, it is too much to profess to be afraid lest barbarism, after having been fairly got under, should revive and conquer civilization. A civilization that can thus succumb to its vanquished enemy must first have become so degenerate, that neither its appointed priests and teachers, nor anybody else, has the capacity, or will take the trouble, to stand up for it. If this be so, the sooner such a civilization receives notice to quit, the better. It can only go on from bad to worse, until destroyed and regenerated (like the Western Empire) by energetic barbarians.

GERALD DWORKIN

Paternalism*

Neither one person, nor any number of persons, is warranted in saying to another human creature of ripe years, that he shall not do with his life for his own benefit what he chooses to do with it. [Mill]

I do not want to go along with a volunteer basis. I think a fellow should be compelled to become better and not let him use his discretion whether he wants to get smarter, more healthy or more honest. [General Hershey]

I take as my starting point the "one very simple principle" proclaimed by Mill *On Liberty* . . .

That principle is, that the sole end for which mankind are warranted, individually or collectively, in interfering with the liberty of action of any of their number, is self-protection. That the only purpose for which power can be rightfully exercised over any member of a civilized community, against his will, is to prevent harm to others. He cannot rightfully be compelled to do or forbear because it will be better for him to do so, because it will make him happier, because, in the opinion of others, to do so would be wise, or even right.

This principle is neither "one" nor "very simple." It is at least two principles; one asserting that self-protection or the prevention of harm to others is sometimes a sufficient warrant and the other claiming that the individual's own good is *never* a sufficient warrant for the exercise of compulsion either by the society as a whole or by its individual members. I assume that no one, with the possible exception of extreme pacifists or anarchists, questions the correctness of the first half of the principle. This essay is an examination of the negative claim embodied in Mill's principle—the objection to paternalistic interferences with a man's liberty.

*From *Morality and the Law* edited by Richard A. Wasserstrom. Copyright © 1971 by Wadsworth Publishing Company, Inc., Belmont, California 94002. Reprinted by permission of the publisher and the author.

I

By paternalism I shall understand roughly the interference with a person's liberty of action justified by reasons referring exclusively to the welfare, good, happiness, needs, interests or values of the person being coerced. One is always well-advised to illustrate one's definitions by examples but it is not easy to find "pure" examples of paternalistic interferences. For almost any piece of legislation is justified by several different kinds of reasons and even if historically a piece of legislation can be shown to have been introduced for purely paternalistic motives, it may be that advocates of the legislation with an antipaternalistic outlook can find sufficient reasons justifying the legislation without appealing to the reasons which were originally adduced to support it. Thus, for example, it may be that the original legislation requiring motorcyclists to wear safety helmets was introduced for purely paternalistic reasons. But the Rhode Island Supreme Court recently upheld such legislation on the grounds that it was "not persuaded that the legislature is powerless to prohibit individuals from pursuing a course of conduct which could conceivably result in their becoming public charges," thus clearly introducing reasons of a quite different kind. Now I regard this decision as being based on reasoning of a very dubious nature but it illustrates the kind of problem one has in finding examples. The following is a list of the kinds of interferences I have in mind as being paternalistic.

II

1. Laws requiring motorcyclists to wear safety helmets when operating their machines.
2. Laws forbidding persons from swimming at a public beach when lifeguards are not on duty.
3. Laws making suicide a criminal offense.
4. Laws making it illegal for women and children to work at certain types of jobs.

5. Laws regulating certain kinds of sexual conduct, for example, homosexuality among consenting adults in private.
6. Laws regulating the use of certain drugs which may have harmful consequences to the user but do not lead to antisocial conduct.
7. Laws requiring a license to engage in certain professions with those not receiving a license subject to fine or jail sentence if they do engage in the practice.
8. Laws compelling people to spend a specified fraction of their income on the purchase of retirement annuities (Social Security).
9. Laws forbidding various forms of gambling (often justified on the grounds that the poor are more likely to throw away their money on such activities than the rich who can afford to).
10. Laws regulating the maximum rates of interest for loans.
11. Laws against duelling.

In addition to laws which attach criminal or civil penalties to certain kinds of action there are laws, rules, regulations, decrees which make it either difficult or impossible for people to carry out their plans and which are also justified on paternalistic grounds. Examples of this are:

1. Laws regulating the types of contracts which will be upheld as valid by the courts, for example, (an example of Mill's to which I shall return) no man may make a valid contract for perpetual involuntary servitude.
2. Not allowing assumption of risk as a defense to an action based on the violation of a safety statute.
3. Not allowing as a defense to a charge of murder or assault the consent of the victim.
4. Requiring members of certain religious sects to have compulsory blood transfusions. This is made possible by not allowing the patient to have recourse to civil suits for assault and battery and by means of injunctions.
5. Civil commitment procedures when these are specifically justified on the basis of preventing the person being committed from harming himself. The D.C. Hospitalization of the Mentally Ill Act provides for involuntary hospitalization of a person who "is mentally ill, and because of that illness, is likely to injure himself or others if allowed to remain at liberty." The term injure in this context applies to unintentional as well as intentional injuries.

All of my examples are of existing restrictions on the liberty of individuals. Obviously one can think of interferences which have not yet been imposed. Thus one might ban the sale of cigarettes, or require that people wear safety belts in automobiles (as opposed to merely having them installed), enforcing this by not allowing motorist to sue for injuries even when caused by other drivers if the motorist was not wearing a seat belt at the time of the accident.

I shall not be concerned with activities which though defended on paternalistic grounds are not interferences with the liberty of persons, for example, the giving of subsidies in kind rather than in cash on the grounds that the recipients would not spend the money on the goods which they really need, or not including a $1,000 deductible provision in a basic protection automobile insurance plan on the ground that the people who would elect it could least afford it. Nor shall I be concerned with measures such as "truth-in-advertising" acts and Pure Food and Drug legislation which are often attacked as paternalistic but which should not be considered so. In these cases all that is provided—it is true by the use of compulsion—is information which it is presumed that rational persons are interested in having in order to make wise decisions. There is no interference with the liberty of the consumer unless one wants to stretch a point beyond good sense and say that his liberty to apply for a loan without knowing the true rate of interest is diminished. It is true that sometimes there is sentiment for going further than providing information, for example when laws against usurious interest are passed preventing those who might wish to contract loans at high rates of interest from doing so, and these measures may correctly be considered paternalistic.

III

Bearing these examples in mind, let me return to a characterization of paternalism. I said earlier that I meant by the term, roughly, interference with a person's liberty for his own good. But, as some of the examples show, the class of persons whose good is involved is not always identical with the class of persons whose freedom is restricted. Thus, in the case of professional licensing it is the practitioner who is directly interfered with but it is the would-be patient whose interests are presumably being served. Not allowing the consent of the victim to be a defense to certain types of crime primarily affects the would-be aggressor but it is the interests of the willing victim that we are trying to protect. Sometimes a person may fall into both classes as would be the case if we banned the manufacture and sale of cigarettes and a given manufacturer happened to be a smoker as well.

Thus we may first divide paternalistic interferences into "pure" and "impure" cases. In "pure" paternalism the class of persons whose freedom is restricted is identical with the class of persons whose benefit is intended to be promoted by such restrictions. Examples: the making of suicide a crime, requiring passengers in automobiles to wear seat belts, requiring a Christian Scientist to receive a blood transfusion. In the case of "impure" paternalism in trying to protect the welfare of a class of persons we find that the only way to do so will involve restricting the freedom of other persons besides those who are benefitted. Now it might be thought that there are no cases of "impure" paternalism since any such case could always be justified on nonpaternalistic grounds, that is, in terms of preventing harm to others. Thus we might ban cigarette manufacturers from continuing to manufacture their product on the grounds that we are preventing them from causing illness to others in the same way that we prevent other manufacturers from releasing pollutants into the atmosphere, thereby causing danger to the members of the community. The difference is, however, that in the former but not the latter case the harm is of such a nature that it could be avoided by those individuals affected if they so chose. The incurring of the harm requires, so to speak, the active cooperation of the victim. It would be mistaken theoretically and hypocritical in practice to assert that our interference in such cases is just like our interference in standard cases of protecting others from harm. At the very least someone interfered with in this way can reply that no one is complaining about his activities. It may be that impure paternalism requires arguments or reasons of a stronger kind in order to be justified, since there are persons who are losing a portion of their liberty and they do not even have the solace of having it be done "in their own interest." Of course in some sense, if paternalistic justifications are ever correct, then we are protecting others, we are preventing some from injuring others, but it is important to see the differences between this and the standard case.

Paternalism then will always involve limitations on the liberty of some individuals in their own interest but it may also extend to interferences with the liberty of parties whose interests are not in question.

IV

Finally, by way of some more preliminary analysis, I want to distinguish paternalistic interference with liberty from a related type with which it is often confused. Consider, for example, legislation which forbids employees to work more than, say, forty hours per week. It is sometimes argued that such legislation is paternalistic for if employees desired such a restriction on their hours of work they could agree among themselves to impose it voluntarily. But because they do not the society imposes its own conception of their best interests upon them by the use of coercion. Hence this is paternalism.

Now it may be that some legislation of this nature is, in fact, paternalistically motivated. I am not denying that. All I want to point out is that there is another possible way of justifying such measures which is not paternalistic in nature. It is not paternalistic because, as Mill puts it in a similar context, such measures are "required not to overrule the judgment of individuals respecting their own interest, but to give effect to that judgment: they being unable to give effect to it except by concert, which concert again cannot be effectual unless it receives validity and sanction from the law." (*Principles of Political Economy*).

The line of reasoning here is a familiar one first found in Hobbes and developed with great sophistication by contemporary economists in the last decade or so. There are restrictions which are in the interests of a class of persons taken collectively but are such that the immediate interest of each individual is furthered by his violating the rule when others adhere to it. In such cases the individuals involved may need the use of compulsion to give effect to their collective judgment of their own interest by guaranteeing each individual compliance by the others. In these cases compulsion is not used to achieve some benefit which is not recognized to be a benefit by those concerned, but rather because it is the only feasible means of achieving some benefit which *is* recognized as such by all concerned. This way of viewing matters provides us with another characterization of paternalism in general. Paternalism might be thought of as the use of coercion to achieve a good which is not recognized as such by those persons for whom the good is intended. Again while this formulation captures the heart of the matter—it is surely what Mill is objecting to in *On Liberty*—the matter is not always quite like that. For example, when we force motorcyclists to wear helmets we are trying to promote a good—the protection of the person from injury—which is surely recognized by most of the individuals concerned. It is not that a cyclist doesn't value his bodily integrity; rather, as a supporter of such legislation would put it, he either places, perhaps irrationally, another value or good (freedom from wearing a helmet) above that of physical well-being or, perhaps, while recognizing the danger in the abstract, he either does not fully appreciate it or he underestimates the likelihood of its occurring. But now we are approaching the question of possible justifications of paternalistic measures and the rest of this essay will be devoted to that question.

V

I shall begin for dialectical purposes by discussing Mill's objections to paternalism and then go on to discuss more positive proposals.

An initial feature that strikes one is the absolute nature of Mill's prohibitions against paternalism. It is so unlike the carefully qualified admonitions of Mill and his fellow utilitarians on other moral issues. He speaks of self-protection as the *sole* end warranting coercion, of the individual's own goals as *never* being a sufficient warrant. Contrast this with his discussion of the prohibition against lying in *Utilitarianism:*

Yet that even this rule, sacred as it is, admits of possible exception, is acknowledged by all moralists, the chief of which is where the with-holding of some fact . . . would save an individual . . . from great and unmerited evil.

The same tentativeness is present when he deals with justice:

It is confessedly unjust to break faith with any one: to violate an engagement, either express or implied, or disappoint expectations raised by our own conduct, at least if we have raised these expectations knowingly and voluntarily. Like all the other obligations of justice already spoken of, this one is not regarded as absolute, but as capable of being overruled by a stronger obligation of justice on the other side.

This anomaly calls for some explanation. The structure of Mill's argument is as follows:

1. Since restraint is an evil the burden of proof is on those who propose such restraint.
2. Since the conduct which is being considered is purely self-regarding, the normal appeal to the protection of the interests of others is not available.
3. Therefore we have to consider whether reasons involving reference to the individual's own good, happiness, welfare, or interests are sufficient to overcome the burden of justification.
4. We either cannot advance the interests of the individual by compulsion, or the attempt to do so involves evils which outweigh the good done.
5. Hence the promotion of the individual's own interests does not provide a sufficient warrant for the use of compulsion.

Clearly the operative premise here is (4), and it is bolstered by claims about the status of the individual as judge and appraiser of his welfare, interests, needs, et cetera.:

With respect to his own feelings and circumstances, the most ordinary man or woman has means of knowledge immeasurably surpassing those that can be possessed by any one else.

He is the man most interested in his own well-being: the interest which any other person, except in cases of strong personal attachment, can have in it is trifling, compared to that which he himself has.

These claims are used to support the following generalizations concerning the utility of compulsion for paternalistic purposes.

The interferences of society to overrule his judgment and purposes in what only regards himself must be grounded on general presumptions; which may be altogether wrong, and even if right, are as likely as not to be missapplied to individual cases.

But the strongest of all the arguments against the interference of the public with purely personal conduct is that when it does interfere, the odds are that it interferes wrongly and in the wrong place.

All errors which the individual is likely to commit against advice and warning are far outweighed by the evil of allowing others to constrain him to what they deem his good.

Performing the utilitarian calculation by balancing the advantages and disadvantages, we find that: "Mankind are greater gainers by suffering each other to live as seems good to themselves, than by compelling each other to live as seems good to the rest." Ergo, (4).

This classical case of a utilitarian argument with all the premises spelled out is not the only line of reasoning present in Mill's discussion. There are asides, and more than asides, which look quite different and I shall deal with them later. But this is clearly the main channel of Mill's thought and it is one which has been subjected to vigorous attack from the moment it appeared— most often by fellow utilitarians. The link that they have usually seized on is, as Fitzjames Stephen put it in *Liberty, Equality, Fraternity,* the absence of proof that the "mass of adults are so well acquainted with their own interests and so much disposed to pursue them that no compulsion or restraint put upon them by any others for the purpose of promoting their interest can really promote them." Even so sympathetic a critic as H. L. A. Hart is forced to the conclusion that:

In Chapter 5 of his essay [On Liberty] Mill carried his protests against paternalism to lengths that may now appear to us as fantastic . . . No doubt if we no longer sympathise with this criticism this is due, in part, to a general decline in the belief that individuals know their own interest best.

Mill endows the average individual with "too much of the psychology of a middle-aged man whose desires are relatively fixed, not liable to be artificially stimulated by external influences; who knows what he wants and what gives him satisfaction or happiness; and who pursues these things when he can."

Now it is interesting to note that Mill himself was aware of some of the limitations on the doctrine that the individual is the best judge of his own interests. In his discussion of government intervention in general (even where the intervention does not interfere with liberty but provides alternative institutions to those of the market) after making claims which are parallel to those just discussed, for example, "People understand their own business and their own interests better, and care for them more, than the government does, or can be expected to do," he goes on to an intelligent discussion of the "very large and conspicuous exceptions" to the maxim that:

Most persons take a juster and more intelligent view of their own interest, and of the means of promoting it than can either be prescribed to them by a general enactment of the legislature, or pointed out in the particular case by a public functionary.

Thus there are things

of which the utility does not consist in ministering to inclinations, nor in serving the daily uses of life, and the want of which is least felt where the need is greatest. This is peculiarly true of those things which are chiefly useful as tending to raise the character of human beings. The uncultivated cannot be competent judges of cultivation. Those who most need to be made wiser and better, usually desire it least, and, if they desire it, would be incapable of finding the way to it by their own lights.

. . . A second exception to the doctrine that individuals are the best judges of their own interest, is when an individual attempts to decide irrevocably now what will be best for his interest at some future and distant time. The presumption in favor of individual judgment is only legitimate, where the judgment is grounded on actual, and especially on present, personal experience; not where it is formed antecedently to experience, and not suffered to be reversed even after experience has condemned it.

The upshot of these exceptions is that Mill does not declare that there should never be government interference with the economy but rather that

. . . in every instance, the burden of making out a strong case should be thrown not on those who resist but those who recommend government interference. Letting alone, in short, should be the general practice: every departure from it, unless required by some great good, is a certain evil.

In short, we get a presumption, not an absolute prohibition. The question is why doesn't the argument against paternalism go the same way?

I suggest that the answer lies in seeing that in addition to a purely utilitarian argument Mill uses another as well. As a utilitarian, Mill has to show, in Fitzjames Stephen's words, that: "Self-protection apart, no good object can be attained by any compulsion which is not in itself a greater evil than the absence of the object which the compulsion obtains." To show this is impossible, one reason being that it isn't true. Preventing a man from selling himself into slavery (a paternalistic measure which Mill himself accepts as legitimate), or from taking heroin, or from driving a car without wearing seat belts may constitute a lesser evil than allowing him to do any of these things. A consistent utilitarian can only argue against paternalism on the grounds that it (as a matter of fact) does not maximize the good. It is always a contingent question that may be returned by the evidence. But there is also a non-contingent argument which runs through *On Liberty*. When Mill states that "there is a part of the life of every person who has come to years of discretion, within which the individuality of that person ought to reign uncontrolled either by any other person or by the public collectively," he is saying something about what it means to be a person, an autonomous agent. It is because coercing a person for his own good denies this status as an independent entity that Mill objects to it so strongly and in such absolute terms. To be able to choose is a good that is independent of the wisdom of what is chosen. A man's "mode of laying out his existence is the best, not because it is the best in itself, but because it is his own mode." It is the privilege and proper condition of a human being, arrived at the maturity of his faculties, to use and interpret experience in his own way.

As further evidence of this line of reasoning in Mill, consider the one exception to his prohibition against paternalism.

In this and most civilised countries, for example, an engagement by which a person should sell himself, or allow himself to be sold, as a slave, would be null and void; neither enforced by law nor by opinion. The ground for thus limiting his power of voluntarily disposing of his own lot in life, is apparent, and is very clearly seen in this extreme case. The reason for not interfering, unless for the sake of others, with a person's voluntary acts, is consideration for his liberty. His voluntary choice is evidence that what he so chooses is desirable, or at least endurable, to him, and his good is on the whole best provided for by allowing him to take his own means of pursuing it. But by selling himself for a slave, he abdicates his liberty; he foregoes any future use of it beyond that single act. He therefore defeats, in his own case, the very purpose which is the justification of allowing him to dispose of himself. He is no longer free; but is thenceforth in a position which has no longer the presumption in its favour, that would be afforded by his voluntarily remaining in it. The principle of freedom cannot require that he should be free not to be free. It is not freedom to be allowed to alienate his freedom.

Now leaving aside the fudging on the meaning of freedom in the last line, it is clear that part of this argument is incorrect. While it is true that *future* choices of the slave are not reasons for thinking that what he chooses then is desirable for him, what is at issue is limiting his immediate choice; and since this choice is made freely, the individual may be correct in thinking that his interests are best provided for by entering such a contract. But the main consideration for not allowing such a contract is the need to preserve the liberty of the person to make future choices. This gives us a principle—a very narrow one—by which to justify some paternalistic interferences. Paternalism is justified only to preserve a wider range of freedom for the individual in question. How far this principle could be extended, whether it can justify all the cases in which we are inclined upon reflection to think paternalistic measures justified, remains to be discussed. What I have tried to show so far is that there are two strains of argument in Mill—one a straight-forward utilitarian mode of reasoning and one which relies not on the goods which free choice leads to but on the absolute value of the choice itself. The first cannot establish any absolute prohibition but at most a presumption and indeed a fairly weak one given some fairly plausible assumptions about human psychology; the second, while a stronger line of argument, seems to me to allow on its own grounds a wider range of paternalism than might be suspected. I turn now to a consideration of these matters.

VI

We might begin looking for principles governing the acceptable use of paternalistic power in cases where it is generally agreed that it is legitimate. Even Mill intends his principles to be applicable only to mature individuals, not those in what he calls "non-age." What is it that justifies us in interfering with children? The fact that they lack some of the emotional and cognitive capacities required in order to make fully rational decisions. It is an empirical question to just what extent children have an adequate conception of their own present and future interests but there is not much doubt that there are many deficiencies. For example, it is very difficult for a child to defer gratification for any considerable period of time. Given these deficiencies and given the very real and permanent dangers that may befall the child, it becomes not only permissible but even a duty of the parent to restrict the child's freedom in various ways. There is however an important moral limitation on the exercise of such parental power which is provided by the notion of the child eventually coming to see the correctness of his parent's interventions. Parental paternalism may be thought of as a wager by the parent on the child's subsequent recognition of the wisdom of the restrictions. There is an emphasis on what could be called future-oriented consent—on what the child will come to welcome, rather than on what he does welcome.

The essence of this idea has been incorporated by idealist philosophers into various types of "real-will" theory as applied to fully adult persons. Extensions of paternalism are argued for by claiming that in various respects, chronologically mature individuals share the same deficiencies in knowledge, capacity to think rationally, and the ability to carry out decisions that children possess. Hence in interfering with such people we are in effect doing what they would do if they were fully rational. Hence we are not really opposing their will, hence we are not really interfering with their freedom. The dangers of this move have been sufficiently exposed by Berlin in his Two Concepts of Liberty. I see no gain in theoretical clarity nor in practical advantage in trying to pass over the real nature of the interferences with liberty that we impose on others. Still the basic notion of consent is important and seems to me the only acceptable way of trying to delimit an area of justified paternalism.

Let me start by considering a case where the consent is not hypothetical in nature. Under certain conditions it is rational for an individual to agree that others should force him to act in ways which, at the time of action, the individual may not see as desirable. If, for example, a man knows that he is subject to breaking his resolves when temptation is present, he may ask a friend to refuse to entertain his requests at some later stage.

A classical example is given in the Odyssey when Odysseus commands his men to tie him to the mast and refuse all future orders to be set free, because he knows the power of the Sirens to enchant men with their songs. Here we are on relatively sound ground in later refusing Odysseus' request to be set free. He may even claim to have changed his mind but, since it is *just* such changes that he wished to guard against, we are entitled to ignore them.

A process analogous to this may take place on a social rather than individual basis. An electorate may mandate its representatives to pass legislation which when it comes time to "pay the price" may be unpalatable. I may believe that a tax increase is necessary to halt inflation though I may resent the lower pay check each month. However in both this case and that of Odysseus, the measure to be enforced is specifically requested by the party involved and at some point in time there is genuine consent and agreement on the part of those persons whose liberty is infringed. Such is not the case for the paternalistic measures we have been speaking about. What must be involved here is not consent to specific measures but rather consent to a system of government, run by elected representatives, with an understanding that they may act to safeguard our interests in certain limited ways.

I suggest that since we are all aware of our irrational propensities, deficiencies in cognitive and emotional capacities, and avoidable and unavoidable ignorance, it is rational and prudent for us to in effect take out "social insurance policies." We may argue for and against proposed paternalistic measures in terms of what fully rational individuals would accept as forms of protection. Now clearly, since the initial agreement is not about specific measures we are dealing with a more-or-less blank check and therefore there have to be carefully defined limits. What I am looking for are certain kinds of conditions which make it plausible to suppose that rational men could reach agreement to limit their liberty even when other men's interest are not affected.

Of course as in any kind of agreement schema there are great difficulties in deciding what rational individuals would or would not accept. Particularly in sensitive areas of personal liberty, there is always a danger of the dispute over agreement and rationality being a disguised version of evaluative and normative disagreement.

Let me suggest types of situations in which it seems plausible to suppose that fully rational individuals would agree to having paternalistic restrictions imposed upon them. It is reasonable to suppose that there are "goods" such as health which any person would want to have in order to pursue his own good—no matter how that good is conceived. This is an argument used in connection with compulsory education for children but it seems to me that it can be extended to other goods which have this character. Then one could agree that the attainment of such goods should be promoted even when not recognized to be such, at the moment, by the individuals concerned.

An immediate difficulty arises from the fact that men are always faced with competing goods and that there may be reasons why even a value such as health—or indeed life—may be overridden by competing values. Thus the problem with the Christian Scientist and blood transfusions. It may be more important for him to reject "impure substances" than to go on living. The difficult problem that must be faced is whether one can give sense to the notion of a person irrationally attaching weights to competing values.

Consider a person who knows the statistical data on the probability of being injured when not wearing seat belts in an automobile and knows the types and gravity of the various injuries. He also insists that the inconvenience attached to fastening the belt every time he gets in and out of the car outweighs for him the possible risks to himself. I am inclined in this case to think that such a weighing is irrational. Given his life plans, which we are assuming are those of the average person, his interests and commitments already undertaken, I think it is safe to predict that we can find inconsistencies in his calculations at some point. I am assuming that this is not a man who for some conscious or unconscious reasons is trying to injure himself nor is he a man who just likes to "live dangerously." I am assuming that he is like us in all the relevant respects but just puts an enormously high negative value on inconvenience—one which does not seem comprehensible or reasonable.

It is always possible, of course, to assimilate this person to creatures like myself. I, also, neglect to fasten my seat belt and I concede such behavior is not rational but not because I weigh the inconvenience differently from those who fasten the belts. It is just that having made (roughly) the same calculation as everybody else, I ignore it in my actions. [Note: a much better case of weakness of the will than those usually given in ethics tests.] A plausible explanation for this deplorable habit is that although I know in some intellectual sense what the probabilities and risks are I do not fully appreciate them in an emotionally genuine manner.

We have two distinct types of situation in which a man acts in a nonrational fashion. In one case he attaches incorrect weights to some of his values; in the other he neglects to act in accordance with his actual preferences and desires. Clearly there is a stronger and more persuasive argument for paternalism in the latter situation. Here we are really not—by assumption—imposing a good on another person. But why may we not extend our interference to what we might call evaluative delusions? After all, in the case of cognitive delusions we are prepared, often, to act against the expressed will of the person involved. If a man believes that when he jumps out the

window he will float upwards—Robert Nozick's example—would not we detain him, forcibly if necessary? The reply will be that this man doesn't wish to be injured and if we could convince him that he is mistaken as to the consequences of his action, he would not wish to perform the action. But part of what is involved in claiming that the man who doesn't fasten his seat-belts is attaching an incorrect weight to the inconvenience of fastening them is that if he were to be involved in an accident and severely injured he would look back and admit that the inconvenience wasn't as bad as all that. So there is a sense in which, if I could convince him of the consequences of his action, he also would not wish to continue his present course of action. Now the notion of consequences being used here is covering a lot of ground. In one case it's being used to indicate what will or can happen as a result of a course of action and in the other it's making a prediction about the future evaluation of the consequences—in the first sense —of a course of action. And whatever the difference between facts and values—whether it be hard and fast or soft and slow—we are genuinely more reluctant to consent to interferences where evaluative differences are the issue. Let me now consider another factor which comes into play in some of these situations which may make an important difference in our willingness to consent to paternalistic restrictions.

Some of the decisions we make are of such a character that they produce changes which are in one or another way irreversible. Situations are created in which it is difficult or impossible to return to anything like the initial stage at which the decision was made. In particular, some of these changes will make it impossible to continue to make reasoned choices in the future. I am thinking specifically of decisions which involve taking drugs that are physically or psychologically addictive and those which are destructive of one's mental and physical capacities.

I suggest we think of the imposition of paternalistic interferences in situations of this kind as being a kind of insurance policy which we take out against making decisions which are far-reaching, potentially dangerous and irreversible. Each of these factors is important. Clearly there are many decisions we make that are relatively irreversible. In deciding to learn to play chess, I could predict in view of my general interest in games that some portion of my free time was going to be preempted and that it would not be easy to give up the game once I acquired a certain competence. But my whole life style was not going to be jeopardized in an extreme manner. Further it might be argued that even with addictive drugs such as heroin one's normal life plans would not be seriously interfered with if an inexpensive and adequate supply were readily available. So this type of argument might have a much narrower scope than appears to be the case at first.

A second class of cases concerns decisions which are made under extreme psychological and sociological pressures. I am not thinking here of the making of the decision as being something one is pressured into—for example, a good reason for making duelling illegal is that unless this is done many people might have to manifest their courage and integrity in ways in which they would rather not do so—but rather of decisions, such as that to commit suicide, which are usually made at a point where the individual is not thinking clearly and calmly about the nature of his decision. In addition, of course, this comes under the previous heading of all-too-irrevocable decisions. Now there are practical steps which a society could take if it wanted to decrease the possibility of suicide—for example not paying social security benefits to the survivors or, as religious institutions do, not allowing persons to be buried with the same status as natural deaths. I think we may count these as interferences with the liberty of persons to attempt suicide and the question is whether they are justifiable.

Using my argument schema the question is whether rational individuals would consent to such limitations. I see no reason for them to consent to an absolute prohibition but I do think it is reasonable for them to agree to some kind of enforced waiting period. Since we are all aware of the possibility of temporary states, such as great fear of depression, that are inimical to the making of well-informed and rational decisions, it would be prudent for all of us if there were some kind of institutional arrangement whereby we were restrained from making a decision which is so irreversible. What this would be like in practice is difficult to envisage and it may be that if no practical arrangements were feasible we would have to conclude that there should be no restriction at all on this kind of action. But we might have a "cooling off" period, in much the same way that we now require couples who file for divorce to go through a waiting period. Or, more far-fetched, we might imagine a Suicide Board composed of a psychologist and another member picked by the applicant. The Board would be required to meet and talk with the person proposing to take his life, though its approval would not be required.

A third class of decisions—these classes are not supposed to be disjoint—involves dangers which are either not sufficiently understood or appreciated correctly by the persons involved. Let me illustrate, using the example of cigarette smoking, a number of possible cases.

1. A man may not know the facts—for example, smoking between one and two packs a day shortens life expectancy 6.2 years, the costs and pain of the illness caused by smoking, et cetera.
2. A man may know the facts, wish to stop smoking, but not have the requisite will-power.
3. A man may know the facts but not have them play the correct role in his calculation because, say, he discounts the danger psychologically since it is remote in time and/or inflates the attractiveness of other consequences of his decision which he regards as beneficial.

In case 1 what is called for is education, the posting of warnings, et cetera. In case 2 there is no theoretical problem. We are not imposing a good on someone who rejects it. We are simply using coercion to enable people to carry out their own goals. (Note: There obviously is a difficulty in that only a subclass of the individuals affected wish to be prevented from doing what they are doing.) In case 3 there is a sense in which we are imposing a good on someone in that given his current appraisal of the facts he doesn't wish to be restricted. But in another sense we are not imposing a good since what is being claimed—and what must be shown or at least argued for—is that an accurate accounting on his part would lead him to reject his current course of action. Now we all know that such cases exist, that we are prone to disregarding dangers that are only possibilities, that immediate pleasures are often magnified and distorted.

If in addition the dangers are severe and far-reaching, we could agree to allow the state a certain degree of power to intervene in such situations. The difficulty is in specifying in advance, even vaguely, the class of cases in which intervention will be legitimate.

A related difficulty is that of drawing a line so that it is not the case that all ultra-hazardous activities are ruled out, for example, mountain-climbing, bull-fighting, sports-car racing, et cetera. There are some risks—even very great ones —which a person is entitled to take with his life.

A good deal depends on the nature of the deprivation—for example, does it prevent the person from engaging in the activity completely or merely limit his participation—and how important to the nature of the activity is the absence of restriction when this is weighed against the role that the activity plays in the life of the person. In the case of automobile seat belts, for example, the restriction is trivial in nature, interferes not at all with the use or enjoyment of the activity, and does, I am assuming, considerably reduce a high risk of serious injury. Whereas, for example, making mountain-climbing illegal completely prevents a person from engaging in an activity which may play an important role in his life and his conception of the person he is.

In general, the easiest cases to handle are those which can be argued about in the terms which Mill thought to be so important—a concern not just for the happiness or welfare, in some broad sense, of the individual but rather a concern for the autonomy and freedom of the person. I suggest that we would be most likely to consent to paternalism in those instances in which it preserves and enhances for the individual his ability to rationally consider and carry out his own decisions.

I have suggested in this essay a number of types of situations in which it seems plausible that rational men would agree to granting the legislative powers of a society the right to impose restrictions on what Mill calls "self-regarding" conduct. However, rational men knowing something about the resources of ignorance, ill-will and stupidity available to the lawmakers of a society—a good case in point is the history of drug legislation in the United States—will be concerned to limit such intervention to a minimum. I suggest in closing two principles designed to achieve this end.

In all cases of paternalistic legislation there must be a heavy and clear burden of proof placed on the authorities to demonstrate the exact nature of the harmful effects (or beneficial consequences) to be avoided (or achieved) and the probability of their occurrence. The burden of proof here is twofold—what lawyers distinguish as the burden of going forward and the burden of persuasion. That the authorities have the burden of going forward means that it is up to them to raise the question and bring forward evidence of the evils to be avoided. Unlike the case of new drugs, where the manufacturer must produce some evidence that the drug has been tested and found not harmful, no citizen has to show with respect to self-regarding conduct that it is not harmful or promotes his best interest. In addition the nature and cogency of the evidence for the harmfulness of the course of action must be set at a high level. To paraphrase a formulation of the burden of proof for criminal proceedings—better ten men ruin themselves than one man be unjustly deprived of liberty.

Finally, I suggest a principle of the least restrictive alternative. If there is an alternative way of accomplishing the desired end without restricting liberty although it may involve great expense, inconvenience, et cetera, the society must adopt it.

GERALD DWORKIN

Paternalism: Some Second Thoughts*

"I changed my mind."
"Oh, yeah? Does it work any better?"
—FROM A MAE WEST MOVIE

I

As seems appropriate for second thoughts, I shall begin at the beginning—the definition of paternalism. Earlier, I defined the concept as

interference with a person's liberty of action justified by reasons referring exclusively to the welfare, good, happiness, needs, interests, or values of the person being coerced.[1]

A number of critics have objected that confining the concept to interferences with liberty is too restrictive in scope.[2] Given the problem I was interested in, i.e., the proper limits of state coercion, this restriction was reasonable, although even here one ought to be aware that the state has other ways of influencing people's behavior. It may refuse to enforce contracts, give in-kind rather than cash aid, set up licensing boards, require manufacturers to install seat-belts as original equipment, and so forth.

If, however, one wishes to consider the issue of paternalism in other contexts, for example, in the professions, one will need a broader definition. Not all paternalistic acts are acts of the state. Not all paternalistic acts involve interference with liberty. The doctor who lies to her terminally ill patients, the parent who stipulates in her will that a child may not inherit an estate before the age of thirty, the psychiatrist who tells his adolescent patient that he must inform her parents of her drug usage, the professor who refuses to recommend her Ph.D. student to a certain university because he will be "out of his league"—these are all cases of paternalism that do not involve the use of coercion or force and, therefore, on standard views of liberty do not involve restrictions on liberty.

How should one broaden the definition? One way is to include such specific elements as deception. Buchanan, for example, characterizes paternalism as

interference with a person's freedom of action or freedom of information, or the deliberate dissemination of misinformation.[3]

Given a suitably broad notion of freedom of information, this definition will include not only the case of a doctor acting paternalistically toward a patient by misinforming him or by not revealing information, but also the case of a doctor telling the patient more than he wants to know. A patient may make it quite clear that he does not want to know something about his condition and a doctor may insist on telling him the whole truth for his own good.

Still this definition seems too restrictive in scope. There are other ways to paternalize besides coercing or manipulating one's information set. Suppose, for example, we play tennis together and I realize that you are getting upset about the frequency with which you lose to me. So, for your own good and against your wishes, I refuse to play with you. My refusal to engage in a form of social cooperation does not seem to me an infringement of your liberty. But it also seems to me a case of paternalism.

On the other hand, the attempt to broaden the notion by including any violation of a moral rule is too restrictive because it will not cover cases such as the following.[4] A husband who knows his wife is suicidal hides his sleeping pills. He violates no moral rule. They are his pills and he can put them wherever he wishes.

This example, as well as that of the doctor who tells the patient the truth against his wishes, also works against defining paternalism in terms of acts that violate the rights of the person in question. The wife does not have a right to those pills, nor does the patient have a right not to be told the truth.

It begins to look as if the only condition that will work is one that depends upon the fact that the person who is being treated paternalistically does not wish to be treated that way. The wife has no right to the pills, but she does not want

*From *Paternalism,* ed. by Rolf Sartorius (Minneapolis: University of Minnesota Press, 1983), pp. 105–12. Reprinted by permission of the publisher.

her husband to hide them. The patient has no right to not be told the truth, but he doesn't want to hear it. But something more must be present in order to include a case like the following:

Consider a father (a lawyer) who wants his daughter to become a lawyer. The daughter believes that she would make a very good lawyer. Indeed, she believes it likely that she would be more successful professionally than her father, who has managed to survive only on a marginal basis. Because she believes that such success would make her father very unhappy, the daughter decides to become a doctor instead. Here is a decision made against the wishes of another person for that person's own good. Yet, I think that this is not a case of paternalism. The daughter does nothing to interfere with the self-determination of the father. She does not act in accordance with her father's judgment, but neither does she act in such a fashion as to substitute her judgment for that of her father.

There must be a violation of a person's autonomy (which I conceive as a distinct notion from that of liberty) for one to treat another paternalistically. There must be a usurpation of decision-making, either by preventing people from doing what they have decided or by interfering with the way in which they arrive at their decisions.

An implication of this view is that there are no methods of influencing people that are necessarily immune to being used paternalistically. It is not as if rational argument cannot be paternalistic while brute force must be. Some people may want to make their decisions impulsively, without rational deliberation; insisting that they hear arguments (for their own good) is paternalism. On the other hand, brute force used to prevent someone from crossing a washed-out bridge need not be paternalism.

What we must ascertain in each case is whether the act in question constitutes an attempt to substitute one person's judgment for another's, to promote the latter's benefit.

It is because of the violation of the autonomy of others that normative questions about the justification of paternalism arise. The denial of autonomy is inconsistent with having others share the ends of one's actions—for if they would share the end, it would not be necessary to usurp their decision-making powers. At one level, therefore, paternalism seems to treat others as means (with the important difference that it is as a means to their ends, not ours). But, at the same time, because we know that the relation between the good of a person and what that person wants is not a simple one, because what is in a person's interests is not always what satisfies his or her current desires, and because we can conceive of situations in which we would want to have our autonomy denied, the possibility of justifying some paternalistic intervention emerges.

One useful heuristic to guide our judgments about the justifiability of such interventions is to ask under what conditions does A's attempt to substitute his or her judgment for B's consitute treating B as less than a moral equal.

II

It is useful to distinguish between "hard" and "soft" paternalism. By soft paternalism, I mean the view that (1) paternalism is sometimes justified, and (2) it is a necessary condition for such justification that the person for whom we are acting paternalistically is in some way not competent. This is the view defended by Feinberg in his article "Legal Paternalism."[5] More precisely, his view is slightly stronger since the necessary condition is either that the conduct in question be substantially nonvoluntary, or that we need time to determine whether the conduct is voluntary or not. By hard paternalism, I mean the view that paternalism is sometimes justified even if the action is fully voluntary.

In arguing for a "hypothetical consent" scheme for justifying paternalism, I did not make clear whether I regarded the argument as *always* resting upon some deficiency in competence against which we wished to protect ourselves. I spoke of "irrational propensities, deficiencies in cognition and emotional capacities, and avoidable and unavoidable ignorance[6] as being rational reasons for agreeing (hypothetically) to limitations of our conduct, even when others' interest are not affected. I also spoke of insuring ourselves against making decisions which are "far-reaching, potentially dangerous, and irreversible." One set of considerations focuses on the agent; the other on the character of the decision. The former raises questions of rationality and competence; the latter of danger and harm.

The example of forcing people to wear seatbelts illustrates the difficulty I felt both about the correctness of paternalistic intervention and about the proper basis for its justification in such cases. Since I felt that intervention was legitimate, I sought to show that persons who do not fasten their seat-belts (at least most of them) are in some way failing in rationality. They either put an unreasonably high negative weight on what is at most an inconvenience, or discount unreasonably the probability or seriousness of future injury.

I think now that the issue must be faced more squarely. While it is possible to relate such cases to the soft paternalist thesis by claiming ignorance or weakness of the will, the strategy seems too ad hoc to be convincing. In any case, there will be other situations (for example, not allowing individuals to become slaves) in which this approach seems implausible. I propose, therefore, to consider three cases which are difficult for the soft paternalist, and to examine the strategies for dealing with them.

The first set of cases I shall call "safety cases." These include requiring motorcyclists to wear helmets, hunters to wear brightly colored jackets, sailors to carry life-preservers, and drivers to wear seat-belts. These are all instances of making people buy and use various items. They also include cases of preventing people from buying and using various things—bans on Red Dye No. 2, firecrackers, heroin.

The second set of cases is illustrated by the issue of putting fluoride in the community water supply. These cases differ from safety cases since, for example, we do not *require* anybody to drink fluoridated water. We just make it easy for those who wish to receive fluoride to do so and we make it correspondingly more difficult for those who do not wish to do so to avoid it. Since the argument for such measures involves a claim that there are certain actions that should be done collectively, I shall refer to these cases as "collective decisions."

The third set of cases are those forbidding people to sell themselves into slavery or to sell body parts to others. I shall refer to such cases as "slavery cases."

For all three types of cases I shall be making the assumption that there is no convincing reason for regarding the actions of the parties (not to wear helmets, not to be fluoridated, to enter into slavery) as necessarily less than voluntary.

Therefore, if one believes that the restrictive actions are justified, and if one believes that the justification is at least in part paternalistic, we have test cases for soft paternalism.

Of course, one can reject these as counterexamples by claiming that it would be wrong or unjustifiable to prevent people from becoming slaves or to force sailors to carry life-preservers.

I confess that I do not see how to progress further with the argument if this is the point of disagreement. These judgments (that it is wrong to prevent people from becoming slaves, etc.) are part of a perfectly consistent positon and one that is not in any way crazy. Of course, those who accept this consequence may do so because they are convinced on independent grounds that hard paternalism is unjustifiable. If so, one may be able to show that their arguments are not sound. But if the disagreement centers on these intuitions, I find it hard to see how it can be resolved.

The first strategy is to argue that the assumption I make about these cases is not valid. Anybody who would agree to become a slave or who would object to carrying a life-preserver must be in some way distracted, misinformed, impetuous, weak-willed, self-destructive, or so forth. In effect, this move denies that these are test-cases for soft paternalism. The contention seems implausible. One cannot argue *a priori* that persons who do such things are acting nonvoluntarily. Nothing in the concept of becoming a slave prohibits one doing this freely.

While there might be empirical evidence for the nonvoluntary character of many such actions, it is unlikely that all such acts will be nonvoluntary. I do not see how one can rule out the possibility that hard paternalism may be the only position which can justify restrictions on such actions.

The most likely response is that while interference may be justified in such cases, it may be for nonpaternalistic reasons. The justification is based on the interests of third parties who are affected in ways that they have a right to be protected against.

The argument in the "safety" cases is that persons who are injured or killed because of their risky behavior impose costs on the rest of us. When the costs are economic, such as the costs of medical care, the obvious reply is that this might show that we can require such individuals to purchase medical insurance, but it does not show that we can require them to actually wear safety helmets.

Note that in purely economic terms it is quite likely that the effect of requiring motorcycle helmets is to cause badly injured persons to survive (requiring costly medical care) who might otherwise might have died from head injuries!

If the costs result from the efforts involved in rescue operations and so forth, one could again require compensation for such effort as a matter of contract or tort law. But there will be certain individuals who intentionally or otherwise will not insure themselves and who may not be in a position to make financial compensation.

What do we do in the case of such individuals? The libertarian answer is that we announce ahead of time that such individuals will not be aided by us. But surely this imposes a psychic cost on us—that of ignoring or abandoning people in distress. There does seem to be an argument for interference here, because the rest of us do not want to be put in such a position.

In the case of hunters who are shot by other hunters because they do not wear brightly-colored clothing, there is another kind of cost. People have to bear the knowledge that they have caused harm (perhaps death) to another.

Ultimately I am left with the feeling that these arguments either are not relevant to justifying restrictions on behavior (although they may justify compulsory insurance) or, if they are relevant, do not seem strong enough to tip the scale by themselves. In the final analysis, I think we are justified in requiring sailors to take along life-preservers because it minimizes the risk of harm to them at the cost of a trivial interference with their freedom.

The second set of cases, those of "collective decisions," create difficulties for any consent scheme that requires unanimous consent; it is implausible to suppose that one can argue for the rationality of such consent without making various ad hoc assumptions about the extent to which we share common values, religious outlooks, and risk-taking preferences.

We are faced with the following problem. Suppose that most people in a community would consent to a certain practice, but that a minority would not. Although the best solution would be to exempt the minority, considerations of administrative and economic efficiency may make this solution very expensive. It is both more effective and cheaper to put flouride in the community water supply than it is to distribute fluoride pills to those who want them or to supply nonfluoridated water to those who do not want fluoride.

If justice takes precedence over efficiency, the solution is clear. But this is not a question of determining the basic structure of society. It is more a constitutional question of deciding what powers to give the legislature. I am inclined to think that some balancing of interests is appropriate here. Knowing that we will be in the mi-

nority on some issues, and in the majority on others, it is reasonable not to demand unanimity for certain issues.

The relevant conditions are: (1) that the majority interest must be important (such as health); (2) that the imposition on the minority must be relatively minor (they have to buy their own water); and (3) that the administrative and economic costs of not imposing on the minority would be very high. However, fairness requires that if there are economic costs to the minority (such as purchasing nonfluoridated water), they should be borne by those who gain.

In this analysis, the restriction on the minority is not motivated by paternalistic considerations, but by the interests of a majority who wish to promote their own welfare. Hence, these are not paternalistic decisions, and do not count against soft paternalism.

Finally, we come to "slavery cases," in which people are not allowed to enter into certain voluntary agreements that would result in great loss of liberty or serious risk of bodily injury. While there may be a presumption in light of what we know about human nature that such choices are usually not fully voluntary, this is a presumption that may be rebutted in particular cases. These are also difficult cases for soft paternalism.

In these cases, however, there is a different line of argument open to the soft paternalist. Since the issue is whether a certain contract will be enforced rather than whether there will be a first-order restriction on the conduct itself, one might argue that different principles apply. Refusal to enforce such agreements may frustrate desires, but it is not a direct interference with liberty.

Again, one may look for third-party considerations. Most of us do not want to live in a society in which, for example, we are legally obligated to return runaway slaves to their owners. Such considerations underlie the general doctrine in contract law which does not require specific performance for the breach of a personal-service contract.

In my original paper, I argued that our objection to allowing voluntary slavery was linked to the promotion of the very value against which paternalism offends—autonomy. If we conceive of autonomy as the capacity of individuals to critically reflect on and take responsibility for the kind of persons they want to be, then we stop people from becoming slaves in order to preserve their future ability to define the kind of lives they want to lead. While I still find this argument plausible, my more recent reflections on autonomy raise the following theoretical problem. There is nothing in the idea of autonomy which precludes a person from saying:

I want to be the kind of person who acts at the command of others. I define myself as a slave and endorse those attitudes and preferences. My autonomy consists in being a slave.

If this is coherent, and I think it is, one cannot argue against such slavery on grounds of autonomy. The argument will have to appeal to some idea of what is a fitting life for a person and, thus, be a direct attempt to impose a conception of what is "good" on another person.

If, as I suspect, any person who adopted the above attitude would argue for it on grounds of maximizing some other good, the case may reduce to a safety-case as one of mistaken calculation about the best way of securing a person's good as conceived by her or him. The hard theoretical position may never be reached.

NOTES

1. Gerald Dworkin, "Paternalism," *The Monist* 56, no. 1, January 1972, p. 65.

2. See, for example, Bernard Gert and Charles Culver, "Paternalistic Behavior," *Philosophy and Public Affairs* 6, no. 1 (Fall, 1976), pp. 45–57.

3. Allen Buchanan, "Medical Paternalism," *Philosophy and Public Affairs* 7, no. 4 (Summer, 1978), p. 372.

4. This condition is Gert and Culver's.

5. Joel Feinberg, "Legal Paternalism," *Canadian Journal of Philosophy* 1, no. 1, pp. 106–24.

6. I would like to thank Daniel Brock, Leslie Francis, and Eric Mack for helpful comments on an earlier draft.

ROGERS v. OKIN

United States Court of Appeals. First Circuit, 1980

COFFIN, Chief Judge.

These appeals are the latest stage in a lengthy and complex civil rights action concerning the practices at Massachusetts state mental health facilities. Plaintiffs are voluntary and involuntary psychiatric patients at Massachusetts state mental health facilities. Defendants are the state Commissioner of Mental Health and various hospital officials and physicians responsible for plaintiffs' care. The full factual background and procedural history are set forth in the published opinion of the district court, *Rogers* v. *Okin,* 478 F.Supp. 1342 (D.Mass.1979), and will not be repeated here. Two chief issues are raised in these cross-appeals from the district court judgment: I. Under what circumstances may state officials forcibly administer antipsychotic drugs to mental health patients without violating the Fourteenth Amendment? II. Did the district court correctly find that an award of monetary damages to plaintiffs under 42 U.S.C. § 1983 or various state causes of action was not warranted? On the latter issue, we fully concur with the judgment of the district court. With regard to the former, we are in substantial agreement with portions of the district court's reasoning, but find that several important aspects of the court's ruling require modification.

I.

A. NATURE OF THE INDIVIDUAL RIGHT

We begin our analysis with what seems to us to be an intuitively obvious proposition: a person has a constitutionally protected interest in being left free by the state to decide for himself whether to submit to the serious and potentially harmful medical treatment that is represented by the administration of antipsychotic drugs.[1] The precise textual source in the Constitution of the protection of this interest is unclear, and the authorities directly supportive of the proposition itself are surprisingly few. Nevertheless, we are convinced that the proposition is correct and

*634 F. 2d. 650 (1st Cir. 1980).

that a source in the Due Process Clause of the Fourteenth Amendment for the protection of this interest exists, most likely as part of the penumbral right to privacy, bodily integrity, or personal security. . . .

None of the parties or *amici* in this suit contest the correctness of this general proposition. With regard to the treatment of the mentally ill in state run institutions, however, defendants point to several state interests that, they claim, override the individual's protected interest and justify the forced administration of drugs. Additionally, defendants contend that within this context, the interests of the individuals to whom the state wishes to administer drugs are fundamentally different from those of individuals who are not mentally ill, and are not in fact inconsistent with the interests of the state. Plaintiffs, on the other hand, while conceding that the interests of the individual are not absolute and can be overridden in certain circumstances, argue that the mere fact that an individual suffers from mental illness and resides in a mental health facility does not constitute such a circumstance. In order to resolve this dispute between the parties, we first examine the various state interests involved.

B. STATE INTERESTS

As we have indicated, neither defendants nor their *amici* argue that the state could forcibly administer antipsychotic drugs to a randomly selected "normal" individual. Unfortunately, the plaintiffs in this suit are far from "normal." Instead, suffering from various mental illnesses, they are in the words of the district court "victims of fate shortchanged by life." 478 F.Supp. at 1369. As a result of their afflictions, they are in many instances in desperate need of care and treatment, and, in some cases, are dangerous to either themselves or others. Because of their illnesses, some of these individuals are unable to make any meaningful choice as to whether they should accept treatment, including the administration of drugs. Given these circumstances, the state asserts primarily its police power and its *parens partiae* power as justifications for the forcible administration of antipsychotic drugs to those individuals who are in state run hospitals as a result of mental illness.

1. POLICE POWER. The parties agree that the state has a legitimate interest in protecting persons from physical harm at the hands of the mentally ill. They also agree that this interest can justify the forcible administration of drugs to a mentally ill person whether or not that person has been adjudicated incompetent to make his own treatment decisions. The district court accordingly held that "a committed mental patient may be forcibly medicated in an emergency situation in which a failure to do so would result in a substantial likelihood of physical harm to that patient, other patients, or to staff members of the institution." 478 F.Supp. at 1365.[2] Plaintiffs have no complaint with this ruling. Defendants, however, have two basic complaints, which they raise on this appeal. First, defendants contend that the district court's definition of emergency is too narrow and should include situations in which "a patient requires the prompt initiation of medication to prevent further suffering by that patient or the rapid worsening of that person's clinical state." Since the state interests sought to be furthered by this proffered definition are its *parens patriae* interests—the desire to treat the patient effectively—we shall address that part of defendants' argument in Part I.B.2 of this opinion, *infra*.

Defendants' second basic complaint is that the necessity of finding a "substantial likelihood of physical harm . . . " (*see* note 2, *supra*) is an overly rigid and unworkable requirement. Defendants argue that some mentally ill patients have an identifiable capacity for spontaneous acts of violence but that it is not always possible to determine beforehand whether a specific patient is likely to commit such acts. This problem of prediction is increased, defendants claim, by the prospect that doctors will be second-guessed in section 1983 suits for damages. In sum, defendants assert that the overall effect of following the district court's standard is to increase the incidence of violent acts that otherwise would not occur had a less restrictive standard been used.

The district court rejected this complaint, finding that the actual experience of operating under the standard during the period covered by a temporary restraining order showed defendants' "gloomy forecast" to be "more dramatic than factual." To a certain extent it is clear that throughout this litigation defendants and their supporting *amici* have erroneously attributed acts of violence to the strictness of the court's standard. Nevertheless, it does appear that the district court may have overlooked or misconstrued evidence of specific acts of violence occurring as a result of defendants' difficulty in applying the court's standard.

For example, at one point during the trial, defendant Gill, director of the Austin Unit of the state hospital, testified that a particular patient on one occasion displayed indications of a possible proclivity towards violence. Defendant, who was aware of the patient's previous favorable medical reaction to the administration of drugs, testified that he would have forcibly medicated the patient as a precaution had he been free to do so. He stated, however, that the indications were not sufficiently clear to enable him to predict that the patient would be likely to commit violence without the medication. He therefore did not medicate the patient, who subsequently seriously injured a staff member during a spontaneous violent outburst. The district court dismissed this incident simply by finding that the defendant doctor had erred in his medical prognosis: he should have realized that violence was likely to occur.

This rather typical dialogue reveals, we think, the inaptness in this context of a clear-cut unitary standard of quantitative likelihood that violence would occur if no medication is administered. In the first place, a unitary standard assumes that there is only one kind of probability to be tested: e.g., a likelihood that an individual has committed or is committing a crime, a likelihood that certain contraband will be found on described premises, or a likelihood that A is right and B is wrong. Here, however, there are two sets of interests, each capable of being compelling and, most importantly, each capable of varying from case to case. On the institutional side, we deal with an institution to which many individuals are involuntarily committed because of a demonstrated proclivity for committing acts of violence outside the hospital community, *see* Mass.Gen.Laws Ann. ch. 123 §§ 7, 8 & 1, a proclivity that the record shows often carries over after commitment. The volatility of a large concentration of such individuals adds substance and immediacy to the state's concern in preventing violence. This concern takes on an added dimension when we consider that patients themselves are the likely victims of any violence. These mental patients are persons who, as we have noted, have "a right, under the Fourteenth Amendment, to be secure in [their] life and person while confined under state authority." . . . On the individual's side, we deal with the concededly substantial right of competent patients to be free from the forcible administration of antipsychotics, the violation of which right may not only occasion temporary distress but possibly aftereffects as well.

The professional judgment-call required in balancing these varying interests and determining whether a patient should be subjected to forcible administering of antipsychotic drugs demands an *individualized* estimation of the possibility and type of violence, the likely effects of particular drugs on a particular individual, and an appraisal of alternative, less restrictive courses of action. Thus, for example, if the violence feared is potentially life-threatening, and the patient's prior experience with antipsychotics favorable, it would be patently unreasonable to require that defendants determine that the probability of the feared violence occurring is greater than fifty percent before they can act. By contrast, if the patient has experienced severe adverse side-effects from antipsychotics, it would be only reasonable to expect defendants to explore less harmful alternatives much more vigorously than in the former case.

Not only do we deem out of place a simplistic unitary standard for police power emergency drug administration, but we see particular problems in adopting such a standard that can be interpreted as requiring a prediction of more-probable-than-not violent behavior. While lawyers and judges may assure themselves that such a standard allows adequate scope for discretion, the important fact is that trained psychiatrists, who possess expert qualifications and experience that the judge lacks, find that in many situations they cannot make predictions that, to their science oriented minds, meet a quantitative level of probability. Instead of second-guessing defendants, the court should have taken as true their asserted difficulties in applying the court's general formulation (at least in the absence of a finding that defendants were lying), and fashioned a ruling that took these difficulties into consideration. "[N]either judges nor administrative hearing officers are better qualified than psychiatrists to render psychiatric judgments." . . .

Moreover, the array of relevant factors bearing on a quantitative judgment in this institutional setting almost defies prediction or reviewability. For example, we suspect that the likelihood of a violence-prone patient's losing control of himself may often depend on the provocation of others. The difficulty of factoring such possibilities into an individual determination makes a preponderance prediction fall short of being practical, not to mention short of being constitutionally mandated.

In so holding, we do not imply that the Constitution places no limits on the discretion of the defendants. The state's purpose in administering drugs forcibly must be to further its police power interests, i.e., the decision must be the result of a determination that the need to prevent violence in a particular situation outweighs the possibility of harm to the medicated individual. Thus, medication cannot be forcibly administered solely for treatment purposes absent a finding of incompetency. *See* Part I.B.2 of this opinion, *infra*. Additionally, reasonable alternatives to the administration of antipsychotics must be ruled out. Otherwise, the administration of the drugs

would not be necessary to accomplish the state's objective. Indeed, it may be possible that in most situations less restrictive means will be available. On remand, the district court should explore this possibility. Finally, given the interests involved, the Fourteenth Amendment requires the imposition of procedures whereby the necessary determinations can be made with due process. Thus, for example, it would seem that at a minimum the determination that medication is necessary must be made by a qualified physician as to each individual patient to be medicated. What additional procedures might be warranted we leave to the district court on remand, noting only that our admonitions concerning the creation of general, *substantive* standards for weighing the competing interests should not be construed as limiting the ability of the court to be creative in designing procedural mechanisms whereby it can be reasonably sure that the interests of the patients are taken into consideration.

In sum, we hold that the district court should not attempt to fashion a single "more-likely-than-not" standard as a substitute for an individualized balancing of the varying interests of particular patients in refusing antipsychotic medication against the equally varying interests of patients—and the state—in preventing violence. Because we recognize the legitimacy of both of these interests, we conclude that neither should be allowed necessarily to override the other in a blanket fashion. Instead, the court should leave this difficult, necessarily *ad hoc* balancing to state physicians and limit its own role to designing procedures for ensuring that the patients' interests in refusing antipsychotics are taken into consideration and that antipsychotics are not forcibly administered absent a finding by a qualified physician that those interests are outweighed in a particular situation and less restrictive alternatives are unavailable.

2. PARENS PATRIAE POWERS. The concept of *parens patriae,* which developed with reference to the power of the sovereign to act as "the general guardian of all infants, idiots, and lunatics," . . . is clearly applicable to the facts of this case. There is no doubt that "[t]he state has a legitimate interest under its *parens patriae* powers in providing care to its citizens who are unable to care for themselves. . . ." The use of these powers to go beyond the mere protection of the mentally ill from harm to the forcible administration of treatment thought curative is regarded as having its origins in the Massachusetts case of *In re Oates,* 8 Law Rep. 122 (Mass. 1845), *see Developments, supra* at 1209. Such use of the powers is implicit in their very nature.

"Inherent in an adjudication that an individual should be committed under the state's *parens patriae* power is the decision that he can be forced to accept the treatments found to be in his best interest; it would be incongruous if an individual who lacks the capacity to make a treatment decision could frustrate the very justification for the state's action by refusing such treatments." *Id.* at 1344.

In *Oakes* the treatment administered consisted largely of rehabilitative incarceration, which unfortunately was largely ineffective. Today, however, due in large part to the development of numerous drugs for treating mental illness, the possibility of improvement as a result of forced treatment is relatively substantial. Given such a possibility, and confronted with the often severe suffering of individuals afflicted with mental illness, the state today finds its interest in being able to offer meaningful assistance to the individual even more substantial than it was in previous times. However, for the state to invoke this interest as a justification for the administration of treatment that could represent substantial intrusions upon the individual, the individual himself must be incapable of making a competent decision concerning treatment on his own. Otherwise, the very justification for the state's purported exercise of its *parens patriae* power—its citizen's inability to care for himself . . . would be missing. Therefore, the *sine qua non* for the state's use of its *parens patriae* power as justification for the forceful administration of mind-affecting drugs is a determination that the individual to whom the drugs are to be administered lacks the capacity to decide for himself whether he should take the drugs. . . .

For the most part, the parties do not contest this conclusion. Instead, their dispute concerns whether or not such a determination has in fact been properly made with respect to the plaintiffs. Defendants assert that the judicial commitment proceedings conducted under Massachusetts law, Mass.Gen.Laws Ann. ch. 123 (1979), constitute the determination of incapacity necessary for the state to provide treatment over the objections of the patient. "Given that these patients have already been recognized as so mentally ill that their decision to reject voluntary hospitalization and its treatment has been overridden, it is illogical to accept the patient's same objections to treatment once hospitalized."[3] To demonstrate why the district court was correct in rejecting this assertion, we turn our focus to the Massachusetts commitment scheme.

The predicate to the prolonged involuntary commitment of an individual under Massachusetts law is a judicial determination that the individual is mentally ill and that failure to hospitalize him would create a "likelihood of serious harm." *Id.* §§ 7, 8. Within the bounds of certain administrative requirements, an individual may be committed without his consent for shorter periods of up to ten days upon a determination by one or more physicians that "failure to hospitalize such person would create a likelihood of serious harm by reason of mental illness." In either situation, "likelihood of serious harm" is defined as:

"(1) a substantial risk of physical harm to the person himself as manifested by evidence of threats of, or attempts at, suicide or serious bodily harm; (2) a substantial risk of physical harm to other persons as manifested by evidence of homicidal or other violent behavior or evidence that others are placed in reasonable fear of violent behavior and serious physical harm to them; or (3) a very substantial risk of physical impairment or injury to the person himself as manifested by evidence that such person's judgment is so affected that he is unable to protect himself in the community and that reasonable provision for his protection is not available in the community." *Id.* § 1.

When we scrutinize this statutory scheme in search of a judicial determination of *incapacity,* we find no direct inference of such. We can conceive of a logical step that could be taken—inferring from an adjudication that an individual was incompetent to make a decision concerning his commitment that he was incompetent to make decisions concerning his treatment. But even on this basis we see such a nexus only where a finding of "likelihood of serious harm" concerning an individual is based on the third definition of that term in section 1 of the statute. That is, an adjudication that an individual's judgment is so affected that he cannot protect himself in the community may well justify the conclusion that he has also been adjudged incapable of making his own decision concerning his commitment and—to complete the chain of inference—treatment. In such a situation the commitment adjudication may well imply the incapacity to make treatment decisions that justifies the state's assumption of its *parens patriae* role regarding treatment. But adjudications under the first two definitions of section 1 provide no adjudication of judgmental capacity; commitment is based on a determination of risk of physical harm to the individual or to others.

We see no systematic means whereby we might identify those individuals whose commitment is based upon the third statutory definition of "likelihood of serious harm," and appellants point to no such means. It is therefore possible that many or all involuntary patients might have been committed pursuant to the first or second definitions. In short, under the statutory scheme any given individual might have been committed despite the fact that he competently believed that treatment was not in his best interests.

Defendants contest the correctness of this conclusion by pointing to the fact that the statutory scheme does require a finding that the committed individual suffers from mental illness. This finding, defendants argue, is a sufficient predicate to state action based on its *parens patriae* power. Nothing in the statutory scheme, however, suggests that a finding of mental illness is equivalent to a finding that the individual is incapable of deciding for himself whether commitment and treatment are in his own best interest. Indeed, as the district court noted, the fact that Massachusetts law provides for a separate proceeding for determinations of legal incompetency, Mass.Gen.Laws Ann. ch. 123 § 25, strongly implies that the commitment proceeding itself is not intended to be a determination that the individual lacks the capacity to make his own treatment decisions. . . . This implication is explicitly confirmed in another section of the statute that recognizes the ability and right of a committed patient to refuse electroconvulsion treatment and lobotomies. Mass.Gen.Laws Ann. ch. 123 § 23. Finally, as a factual matter, the district court found, 478 F.Supp. at 1364, and defendants concede, that not all patients institutionalized for mental illness are incapable of making their own treatment decisions.[4]

The foregoing analysis is not intended to suggest that the Massachusetts commitment scheme is unconstitutional. To the contrary, in many respects the Massachusetts scheme goes well beyond the minimum requirements mandated by the Fourteenth Amendment.[5] The point of our analysis is instead to demonstrate that the commitment decision itself is an inadequate predicate to the forcible administration of drugs to an individual where the purported justification for that action is the state's *parens patriae* power.

In so ruling, we recognize that there is a need for some procedure whereby the state can provide needed treatment to an objecting individual who lacks the capacity to make meaningful treatment decisions on his own. The district court, pointing to the powers and proceedings of the Massachusetts Probate Courts . . . found that such a procedure exists in Massachusetts and that it is constitutionally sound. Plaintiffs concurred in this judgment. Defendants, however, contend that the probate proceedings and the use of a guardian are too cumbersome to serve as a necessary predicate to forcible medication for treatment purposes.[6] In so arguing, defendants for the most part misconstrue the import of the district court's reasoning. The court did not hold that fullblown probate proceedings are constitutionally required. Rather, the court held that some determination of incompetency must be made, and found that

probate proceedings under section 25 of chapter 123 sufficed. The court specifically advised defendants to aim their complaint concerning the efficacy of these proceedings to the state legislature.

We do agree with defendants, however, that there are two aspects of the district court's ruling that require some modification. First, the district court held that absent an "emergency" defendants can never forcibly medicate an individual without an adjudication of incompetency and approval by the appointed guardian. The court defined an emergency as "circumstances in which a failure to [forcibly medicate] would bring about a substantial likelihood of physical harm to the patient or others." In so restricting the definition to instances in which immediate action is required to prevent physical harm the district court rejected defendants' claim that an emergency should also include situations in which the immediate administration of drugs is reasonably believed to be necessary to prevent further deterioration in the patient's mental health.

The district court did not proffer any explanation for requiring an actual adjudication of incompetency in such circumstances. While judicial determinations are certainly preferable in general, room must be left for responsible state officials to respond to exigencies that render totally impractical recourse to traditional forms of judicial process.

"The judicial model of fact finding for all constitutionally protected interests, regardless of their nature, can turn rational decisionmaking into an unmanageable enterprise." . . .

Moreover, in the particular situation presented here, it cannot be said that the interests of the patient himself would be furthered by requiring responsible physicians to stand by and watch him slip into possibly chronic illness while awaiting an adjudication of incompetency. *Cf. Coll* v. *Hyland*, 411 F.Supp. 905, 910 (D.N.J.1976) (three judge court, *per curiam*) ("When the choice is between loss of life or health and a loss of liberty for a brief period of time, the preferable alternative is apparent"). Instead, the interests of the individual in such a situation coincide with those of the state and mandate decisive, immediate action. We therefore vacate the district court's limited definition of the emergency circumstances in which adjudications are not required and remand the case for consideration of alternative means for making incompetency determinations in situations where any delay could result in significant deterioration of the patient's mental health.

Second, it is possible to read the district court's opinion as implying that once a determination of incompetency has been made, a traditional, individual guardian must make all treatment decisions involving the use of antipsychotic drugs. To the extent that the district court's opinion might be so read, we reject that part of its holding.

The district court focused extensively on the harmful side effects that the various medications can produce. Its findings concerning these effects are supported by the record. However, the record also shows that in many situations, despite the risks of harmful side effects, the administration of drugs to an individual is clearly in his best interests because of the beneficial effects that the drugs can have, including the amelioration of the patient's illness. In such situations, the *failure* to medicate an incompetent patient could have side effects—e.g., the unnecessary and possibly irreversible continuation of his illness—far more harmful, and probable, than any that might result from the drugs themselves.

Thus, any treatment decision, including the decision not to treat, brings with it the potential for serious harm to the patient. Accordingly, if we were to adopt what is arguably the district court's reasoning concerning guardians, we would be led to the conclusion that appellants must consult a guardian whenever they decide not to administer drugs to an incompetent patient.[7] Such a requirement would, we think, be impractical and largely incapable of enforcement.

Of course the mere fact that it would be impractical to have a guardian make all significant treatment decisions for an incompetent patient does not itself indicate that it is undesirable to have a guardian make those decisions that can be made practically. Our concern, however, is that the requirement of individualized guardian review on only some aspects of significant treatment decisions might in the long run create a tendency for patients to receive other treatment, i.e., no treatment, in situations where the best interests of the patient would dictate otherwise.[8] While we cannot be certain that such a result would occur, we do think that the nature of the problem presented is such that it is unwise to declare that the Constitution requires that state officials must receive guardian approval for individual treatment decisions simply because the administration of drugs is recommended.

In so holding, we do not imply that the Constitution places no limits whatsoever on the manner in which the state may decide how to treat incompetent patients. Following a determination of incompetency, state actions based on *parens patriae* interests must be taken with the aim of making treatment decisions as the individual himself would were he competent to do so. *Cf. Superintendent of Belchertown* v. *Saikewicz, supra,* 373 Mass. at 745–55, 370 N.E.2d 417 ("substituted judgment" standard). Furthermore, in order to ensure compliance with this requirement, some minimum procedural requirements would seem to be necessary. Thus, for example, at a minimum there might be some mechanism for periodic review by nontreating physicians of the full treatment history of patients to ensure that the treating physicians are in fact attempting to make treatment decisions as the patients themselves would were they competent.

Appellants claim that they employ such procedures, and ask us to declare them sufficient. We hesitate, however, to make such a finding. Despite our intensive review of this case, our familiarity with the factual details of the functioning of the hospitals and the needs of the patients does not approach that of the district court. Moreover, neither the district court nor the parties have had the opportunity to evaluate the present procedures in terms of the criteria we set forth today. For the purposes of this appeal, we therefore rest on our holding that, absent an emergency, a judicial determination of incapacity to make treatment decisions must be made before the state may rely on its *parens patriae* powers to forcibly medicate a patient, but, as a constitutional matter, the state is not required to seek individualized guardian approval for decisions to treat incompetent patients with antipsychotic drugs. What procedural safeguards might be required, short of individualized guardian review, we leave for the present to the district court.

C. VOLUNTARY PATIENTS

One point that our analysis leaves unaddressed is whether patients who voluntarily enter a state mental health facility have a right to refuse antipsychotic medication. The district court held that "the voluntary patient has the same right to refuse treatment in a non-emergency as does the involuntary patient." 478 F.Supp. at 1368. The court apparently rejected defendants' argument that voluntary patients can be forced to choose between leaving the hospital and accepting prescribed treatment.

In so holding, the district court in effect found that Massachusetts citizens have a constitutional right upon voluntary admittance to state facilities to dictate to the hospital staff the treatment that they are given. The district court cited no authority for this finding, and we know of none. Massachusetts law provides for the voluntary admission of mental health patients who are "in need of care and treatment . . . providing the admitting facility is suitable for such care and treatment." Mass.Gen.Laws Ann. ch. 123 § 10(a). The statute does not guarantee voluntary patients the treatment of their choice. Instead, it offers a treatment regimen that state doctors and staff determine is best, and if the patient thinks otherwise, he can leave.[9] We can find nothing even arguably unconstitutional in such a statutory scheme. . . .

In conclusion, we find it worth noting that in an important respect this case differs from the traditional, adversary model of private litigation. Plaintiffs and defendants, as well as the various *amici*, share in large part the primary goal of assuring that adequate care and treatment are provided to patients in state hospitals. As is evident from this opinion, we have not accepted absolutist positions advanced by either the parties or *amici*. Accepting the premise that application of the Constitution to the setting of a state mental health institution requires the most sensitive combination of deference to professional judgment and respect for competent individual judgment as to personal autonomy, we have demonstrated our conviction that such a balance is most likely to be achieved through a variety of procedural devices designed for their suitability to this kind of institutional life rather than for their similarity to judicial models. The record of exploration and evaluation of such safeguards has yet to be made. And the making of a record that will advance the interests of all concerned demands that the parties, despite their differences in views, work together on remand in a less absolutist and more pragmatic way to develop constitutionally valid, mutually acceptable, and workable solutions to the difficult issues remaining in this case.

Judgment affirmed in part, reversed in part, and vacated and remanded for further proceedings in accordance with this opinion.

NOTES

1.   We use the term "antipsychotic drugs" to refer to medications such as Thorazine, Mellaril, Prolixis and Haldol that are used in treating psychoses, particularly schizophrenia. The district court used this term interchangeably with the apparently broader term "psychotropic drugs," which may include antidepressants and lithium, and which as far as the record shows do not have as substantial a potential for serious side effects as do the antipsychotics. Both the parties and the district court have throughout this litigation focused exclusively on the antipsychotics, *see, e.g.,* 478 F.Supp. at 1359–60. Accordingly, we interpret the district court's use of the term "psychotropic drugs" to mean antipsychotic drugs. The potentially harmful side effects of these drugs are set forth in detail in the record, and described in part in the district court opinion. Foremost among them is tardive dyskinesia, a painful, disfiguring, and sometimes disabling neurological affliction which all parties in this case concede might be caused by the use of antipsychotic drugs.

2.   The exact meaning of the term "substantial likelihood" is unclear on its face. Elsewhere in its opinion, however, the district court suggests that in using this term it means "more likely than not." 478 F.Supp. at 1364. The parties have apparently so construed the term, and so shall we.

3.   Amicus American Psychiatric Association similarly argues that "[t]he fatal flaw in the district court's analysis is its failure to explain why the decision to commit a person against his will is not a sufficient constitutional predicate to justify the provision of that treatment for which the individual was committed to receive."

4.   It is also worth noting that appellants issue patients an "Admission packet" informing them that they may make their own treatment decisions.

5.   For example, the federal Constitution does not mandate a reasonable doubt standard for commitment proceedings, *Addington* v. *Texas,* 441 U.S. 418, 99 S.Ct. 1804, 60 L.Ed.2d 323 (1979), yet Massachusetts employs such a standard. *Superintendent of Worcester State Hospital* v. *Hagburg,* 374 Mass. 271, 372 N.E.2d 242 (1978).

6.   The district court did find, with ample justifications, that defendants' assertions of impracticality were a bit overblown, noting that "there is statutory authority for 'immediate appointment [of guardians] . . . ' " 478 F.Supp. at 1363 n. 15.

7.   At least in the case of individuals declared incompetent and denied the right of acting or choosing on their own, we see no relevant distinction between state action and inaction.

8.   This result would occur to the extent that any physicians were deterred, either consciously or unconsciously, from recommending drug treatment due to the need to seek the approval of a guardian. Physicians acting in good faith could nevertheless be so deterred by the need to limit the amount of time spent on administrative matters.

9.   To the extent that patients might be prevented from leaving, they become involuntary patients whose rights are as set forth in the preceding parts of this opinion.

PATRICK DEVLIN

Morals and the Criminal Law*

I think it is clear that the criminal law as we know it is based upon moral principle. In a number of crimes its function is simply to enforce a moral principle and nothing else. The law, both criminal and civil, claims to be able to speak about morality and immorality generally. Where does it get its authority to do this and how does it settle the moral principles which it enforces? Undoubtedly, as a matter of history, it derived both from Christian teaching. But I think that the strict logician is right when he says that the law can no longer rely on doctrines in which citizens are entitled to disbelieve. It is necessary therefore to look for some other source.

In jurisprudence . . . everything is thrown open to discussion and, in the belief that they cover the whole field, I have framed three interrogatories addressed to myself to answer:

1. Has society the right to pass judgement at all on matters of morals? Ought there, in other words, to be a public morality, or are morals always a matter for private judgement?
2. If society has the right to pass judgement, has it also the right to use the weapon of the law to enforce it?
3. If so, ought it to use that weapon in all cases or only in some; and if only in some, on what principles should it distinguish?

[1] I shall begin with the first interrogatory and consider what is meant by the right of society to pass a moral judgement, that is, a judgement about what is good and what is evil. The fact that a majority of people may disapprove of a practice does not of itself make it a matter for society as a whole. Nine men out of ten may disapprove of what the tenth man is doing and still say that it is not their business. There is a case for a collective judgement (as distinct from

a large number of individual opinions which sensible people may even refrain from pronouncing at all if it is upon somebody else's private affairs) only if society is affected. Without a collective judgement there can be no case at all for intervention. Let me take as an illustration the Englishman's attitude to religion as it is now and as it has been in the past. His attitude now is that a man's religion is his private affair; he may think of another man's religion that it is right or wrong, true or untrue, but not that it is good or bad. In earlier times that was not so; a man was denied the right to practise what was thought of as heresy, and heresy was thought of as destructive of society.

The language [in] the Wolfenden Report suggests the view that there ought not to be a collective judgement about immorality *per se*. Is this what is meant by "private morality" and "individual freedom of choice and action"? Some people sincerely believe that homosexuality is neither immoral nor unnatural. Is the "freedom of choice and action" that is offered to the individual, freedom to decide for himself what is moral or immoral, society remaining neutral; or is it freedom to be immoral if he wants to be? The language of the Report may be open to question, but the conclusions at which the Committee arrive answer this question unambiguously. If society is not prepared to say that homosexuality is morally wrong, there would be no basis for a law protecting youth from "corruption" or punishing a man for living on the "immoral" earnings of a homosexual prostitute, as the Report recommends.[1] This attitude the Committee make even clearer when they come to deal with prostitution. In truth, the Report takes it for granted that there is in existence a public morality which condemns homosexuality and prostitution. What the Report seems to mean by private morality might perhaps be better described as private behaviour in matters of morals.

This view—that there is such a thing as public morality—can also be justified by *a priori* argument. What makes a society of any sort is community of ideas, not only political ideas but also ideas about the way its members should behave and govern their lives; these latter ideas are its morals. Every society has a moral structure as well as a political one: or rather, since that might suggest two independent systems, I should say that the structure of every society is made up both of politics and morals. Take, for example, the institution of marriage. Whether a man should be allowed to take more than one wife is something about which every society has to make up its mind one way or the other. In England we believe in the Christian idea of marriage and therefore adopt monogamy as a moral principle. Consequently the Christian institution of marriage has become the basis of family life and so part of the structure of our society. It is there not because it is Christian. It has got there because it is Christian, but it remains there because it is built into the house in which we live and could not be removed without bringing it down. The great majority of those who live in this country accept it because it is the Christian idea of marriage and for them the only true one. But a non-Christian is bound by it, not because it is part of Christianity but because, rightly or wrongly, it has been adopted by the society in which he lives. It would be useless for him to stage a debate designed to prove that polygamy was theologically more correct and socially preferable; if he wants to live in the house, he must accept it as built in the way in which it is.

We see this more clearly if we think of ideas or institutions that are purely political. Society cannot tolerate rebellion; it will not allow argument about the rightness of the cause. Historians a century later may say that the rebels were right and the Government was wrong and a percipient and conscientious subject of the State may think so at the time. But it is not a matter which can be left to individual judgement.

The institution of marriage is a good example for my purpose because it bridges the division, if there is one, between politics and morals. Marriage is part of the structure of our society and it is also the basis of a moral code which condemns fornication and adultery. The institution of marriage would be gravely threatened if individual judgements were permitted about the morality of adultery; on these points there must be a public morality. But public morality is not to be confined to those moral principles which support institutions such as marriage. People do not think of monogamy as something which has to be supported because our society has chosen to organize itself upon it; they think of it as something that is good in itself and offering a good way of life and that it is for that reason that our society has adopted it. I return to the statement that I have already made, that society means a community of ideas; without shared ideas on politics, morals, and ethics no society can exist. Each one of us has ideas about what is good and what is evil; they cannot be kept private from the society in which we live. If men and women try to create a society in which there is no fundamental agreement about good and evil they will fail; if, having based it on common agreement, the agreement goes, the society will disintegrate. For society is not something that is kept together physically; it is held by the invisible bonds of common thought. If the bonds were too far relaxed the members would drift apart. A common morality is part of the bondage. The bondage is part of the price of society; and mankind, which needs society, must pay its price. . . .

[2] You may think that I have taken far too long in contending that there is such a thing as public morality, a proposition which most people would readily accept, and may have left myself too little time to discuss the next question which to many minds may cause greater difficulty: to what extent should society use the law to enforce its moral judgements? But I believe that the answer to the first question determines the way in which the second should be approached and may indeed very nearly dictate the answer to the second question. If society has no right to make judgements on morals, the law must find some special justification for entering the field of morality: if homosexuality and prostitution are not in themselves wrong, then the onus is very clearly on the lawgiver who wants to frame a law against certain aspects of them to justify the exceptional treatment. But if society has the right to make a judgement and has it on the basis that a recognized morality is as necessary to society as, say, a recognized government, then society may use the law to preserve morality in the same way as it uses it to safeguard anything else that is essential to its existence. If therefore the first proposition is securely established with all its implications, society has a *prima facie* right to legislate against immorality as such.

The Wolfenden Report, notwithstanding that it seems to admit the right of society to condemn homosexuality and prostitution as immoral, requires special circumstances to be shown to justify the intervention of the law. I think that this is wrong in principle and that any attempt to approach my second interrogatory on these lines is bound to break down. I think that the attempt by the Committee does break down and that this is shown by the fact that it has to define or describe its special circumstances so widely that they can be supported only if it is accepted that the law is concerned with immorality as such.

The widest of the special circumstances are described as the provision of "sufficient safeguards against exploitation and corruption of others, particularly those who are specially vulnerable because they are young, weak in body or mind, inexperienced, or in a state of special physical, official or economic dependence."[2] The corruption of youth is a well-recognized ground for intervention by the State and for the purpose of any legislation the young can easily be defined. But if similar protection were to be extended to every other citizen, there would be no limit to the reach of the law. The "corruption and exploitation of others" is so wide that it could be used to cover any sort of immorality which involves, as most do, the co-operation of another person. Even if the phrase is taken as limited to the categories that are particularized as "specially vulnerable," it is so elastic as to be practically no restriction. This is not merely a matter of words. For if the words used are stretched almost beyond breaking-point, they still are not wide enough to cover the recommendations which the Committee make about prostitution.

Prostitution is not in itself illegal and the Committee do not think that it ought to be made so.[3] If prostitution is private immorality and not the law's business, what concern has the law with the ponce or the brothel-keeper or the householder who permits habitual prostitution? The Report recommends that the laws which make these activities criminal offences should be maintained or strengthened and brings them (so far as it goes into principle; with regard to brothels it says simply that the law rightly frowns on them) under the head of exploitation.[4] There may be cases of exploitation in this trade, as there are or used to be in many others, but in general a ponce exploits a prostitute no more than an impresario exploits an actress. The Report finds that "the great majority of prostitutes are women whose psychological makeup is such that they choose this life because they find in it a style of living which is to them easier, freer and more profitable than

would be provided by any other occupation. . . ." In the main the association between prostitute and ponce is voluntary and operates to mutual advantage.[5] The Committee would agree that this could not be called exploitation in the ordinary sense. They say: "It is in our view an oversimplification to think that those who live on the earnings of prostitution are exploiting the prostitute as such. What they are really exploiting is the whole complex of the relationship between prostitute and customer; they are, in effect, exploiting the human weaknesses which cause the customer to seek the prostitute to meet the demand."[6]

All sexual immorality involves the exploitation of human weaknesses. The prostitute exploits the lust of her customers and the customer the moral weakness of the prostitute. If the exploitation of human weaknesses is considered to create a special circumstance, there is virtually no field of morality which can be defined in such a way as to exclude the law.

I think, therefore, that it is not possible to set theoretical limits to the power of the State to legislate against immorality. It is not possible to settle in advance exceptions to the general rule or to define inflexibly areas of morality into which the law is in no circumstances to be allowed to enter. Society is entitled by means of its laws to protect itself from dangers, whether from within or without. Here again I think that the political parallel is legitimate. The law of treason is directed against aiding the king's enemies and against sedition from within. The justification for this is that established government is necessary for the existence of society and therefore its safety against violent overthrow must be secured. But an established morality is as necessary as good government to the welfare of society. Societies disintegrate from within more frequently than they are broken up by external pressures. There is disintegration when no common morality is observed and history shows that the loosening of moral bonds is often the first stage of disintegration, so that society is justified in taking the same steps to preserve its moral code as it does to preserve its government and other essential institutions.[7] The suppression of vice is as much the law's business as the suppression of subversive activities; it is no more possible to define a sphere of private morality than it is to define one of private subversive activity. It is wrong to talk of private morality or of the law not being concerned with immorality as such or to try to set rigid bounds to the part which the law may play in the suppression of vice. There are no theoretical limits to the power of the State to legislate treason and sedition, and likewise I think there can be no theoretical limits to legislation against immorality. You may argue that if a man's sins affect only himself it cannot be the concern of society. If he chooses to get drunk every night in the privacy of his own home, is any one except himself the worse for it? But suppose a quarter or a half of the population got drunk every night, what sort of society would it be? You cannot set a theoretical limit to the number of people who can get drunk before society is entitled to legislate against drunkenness. The same may be said of gambling. The Royal Commission on Betting, Lotteries, and Gaming took as their test the character of the citizen as a member of society. They said: "Our concern with the ethical significance of gambling is confined to the effect which it may have on the character of the gambler as a member of society. If we were convinced that whatever the degree of gambling this effect must be harmful we should be inclined to think that it was the duty of the state to restrict gambling to the greatest extent practicable."[8]

[3] In what circumstances the State should exercise its power is the third of the interrogatories I have framed. But before I get to it I must raise a point which might have been brought up in any one of the three. How are the moral judgements of society to be ascertained? By leaving it until now, I can ask it in the more limited form that is now sufficient for my purpose. How is the law-maker to ascertain the moral judgements of society? It is surely not enough that they should be reached by the opinion of the majority; it would be too much to require the individual assent of every citizen. English law has evolved and regularly uses a standard which does not depend on the counting of heads. It is that of the reasonable man. He is not to be confused with the rational man. He is not expected to reason about anything and his judgement may be largely a matter of feeling. It is the viewpoint of the man in the street—or to use an archaism familiar to all lawyers—the man in the Clapham omnibus. He might also be called the right-minded man. For my purpose I should like to call him the man in the jury box, for the moral judgement of society must be something about which any twelve men or women drawn at random might after discussion be expected to be unanimous. This was the

standard the judges applied in the days before Parliament was as active as it is now and when they laid down rules of public policy. They did not think of themselves as making law but simply as stating principles which every right-minded person would accept as valid. It is what Pollock called "practical morality," which is based not on theological or philosophical foundations but "in the mass of continuous experience half-consciously or unconsciously accumulated and embodied in the morality of common sense." He called it also "a certain way of thinking on questions of morality which we expect to find in a reasonable civilized man or a reasonable Englishman, taken at random."[9]

Immorality then, for the purpose of the law, is what every right-minded person is presumed to consider to be immoral. Any immorality is capable of affecting society injuriously and in effect to a greater or lesser extent it usually does; this is what gives the law its *locus standi*. It cannot be shut out. But—and this brings me to the third question—the individual has a *locus standi* too; he cannot be expected to surrender to the judgement of society the whole conduct of his life. It is the old and familiar question of striking a balance between the rights and interests of society and those of the individual. . . .

. . . It is possible to make general statements of principle which it may be thought the legislature should bear in mind when it is considering the enactment of laws enforcing morals.

I believe that most people would agree upon the chief of these elastic principles. There must be toleration of the maximum individual freedom that is consistent with the integrity of society. It cannot be said that this is a principle that runs all through the criminal law. Much of the criminal law that is regulatory in character—the part of it that deals with *malum prohibitum* rather than *malum in se*—is based upon the opposite principle, that is, that the choice of the individual must give way to the convenience of the many. But in all matters of conscience the principle I have stated is generally held to prevail. It is not confined to thought and speech; it extends to action, as is shown by the recognition of the right to conscientious objection in war-time; this example shows also that conscience will be respected even in times of national danger. The principle appears to me to be peculiarly appropriate to all questions of morals. Nothing should be punished by the law that does not lie beyond the limits of tolerance. It is not nearly enough to say that a majority dislike a practice; there must be a real feeling of reprobation. Those who are dissatisfied with the present law on homosexuality often say that the opponents of reform are swayed simply by disgust. If that were so it would be wrong, but I do not think one can ignore disgust if it is deeply felt and not manufactured. Its presence is a good indication that the bounds of toleration are being reached. Not everything is to be tolerated. No society can do without intolerance, indignation, and disgust [citation omitted]; they are the forces behind the moral law, and indeed it can be argued that if they or something like them are not present, the feelings of society cannot be weighty enough to deprive the individuals of freedom of choice. I suppose that there is hardly anyone nowadays who would not be disgusted by the thought of deliberate cruelty to animals. No one proposes to relegate that or any other form of sadism to the realm of private morality or to allow it to be practised in public or in private. It would be possible no doubt to point out that until a comparatively short while ago nobody thought very much of cruelty to animals and also that pity and kindliness and the unwillingness to inflict pain are virtues more generally esteemed now than they have ever been in the past. But matters of this sort are not determined by rational argument. Every moral judgement, unless it claims a divine source, is simply a feeling that no right-minded man could behave in any other way without admitting that he was doing wrong. It is the power of a common sense and not the power of reason that is behind the judgements of society. But before a society can put a practice beyond the limits of tolerance there must be a deliberate judgement that the practice is injurious to society. There is, for example, a general abhorrence of homosexuality. We should ask ourselves in the first instance whether, looking at it calmly and dispassionately, we regard it as a vice so abominable that its mere presence is an offence. If that is the genuine feeling of the society in which we live, I do not see how society can be denied the right to eradicate it. Our feeling may not be so intense as that. We may feel about it that, if confined, it is tolerable, but that if it spread it might be gravely injurious; it is in this way that most societies look upon fornication, seeing it as a natural weakness which must be kept within bounds but which cannot be rooted out. It becomes then a question of balance, the danger to society in one scale and the extent of the restriction in the other. On this sort of point

the value of an investigation by such a body as the Wolfenden Committee and of its conclusions is manifest.

The limits of tolerance shift. This is supplementary to what I have been saying but of sufficient importance in itself to deserve statement as a separate principle which lawmakers have to bear in mind. I suppose that moral standards do not shift; so far as they come from divine revelation they do not, and I am willing to assume that the moral judgements made by a society always remain good for that society. But the extent to which society will tolerate—I mean tolerate, not approve—departures from moral standards varies from generation to generation. It may be that over-all tolerance is always increasing. The pressure of the human mind, always seeking greater freedom of thought, is outwards against the bonds of society forcing their gradual relaxation. It may be that history is a tale of contraction and expansion and that all developed societies are on their way to dissolution. I must not speak of things I do not know; and anyway as a practical matter no society is willing to make provision for its own decay. I return therefore to the simple and observable fact that in matters of morals the limits of tolerance shift. Laws, especially those which are based on morals, are less easily moved. It follows as another good working principle that in any new matter of morals the law should be slow to act. By the next generation the swell of indignation may have abated and the law be left without the strong backing which it needs. But it is then difficult to alter the law without giving the impression that moral judgement is being weakened. This is now one of the factors that is strongly militating against any alteration to the law on homosexuality.

A third elastic principle must be advanced more tentatively. It is that as far as possible privacy should be respected. This is not an idea that has ever been made explicit in the criminal law. Acts or words done or said in public or in private are all brought within its scope without distinction in principle. But there goes with this a strong reluctance on the part of judges and legislators to sanction invasions of privacy in the detection of crime. The police have no more right to trespass than the ordinary citizen has; there is no general right of search; to this extent an Englishman's home is still his castle. The Government is extremely careful in the exercise even of those powers which it claims to be undisputed. Telephone tapping and interference with the mails afford a good illustration of this. . . .

This indicates a general sentiment that the right to privacy is something to be put in the balance against the enforcement of the law. Ought the same sort of consideration to play any part in the formation of the law? Clearly only in a very limited number of cases. When the help of the law is invoked by an injured citizen, privacy must be irrelevant; the individual cannot ask that his right to privacy should be measured against injury criminally done to another. But when all who are involved in the deed are consenting parties and the injury is done to morals, the public interest in the moral order can be balanced against the claims of privacy. The restriction on police powers of investigation goes further than the affording of a parallel; it means that the detection of crime committed in private and when there is no complaint is bound to be rather haphazard and this is an additional reason for moderation. These considerations do not justify the exclusion of all private immorality from the scope of the law. I think that, as I have already suggested, the test of "private behaviour" should be substituted for "private morality" and the influence of the factor should be reduced from that of a definite limitation to that of a matter to be taken into account. Since the gravity of the crime is also a proper consideration, a distinction might well be made in the case of homosexuality between the lesser acts of indecency and the full offence, which on the principle of the Wolfenden Report it would be illogical to do.

NOTES

1. The Wolfenden Report (New York: Stein and Day, 1963), Para. 76.
2. The Wolfenden Report (New York: Stein and Day, 1963), Para. 13.
3. The Wolfenden Report (New York: Stein and Day, 1963), Paras. 224, 285, and 318.
4. The Wolfenden Report (New York: Stein and Day, 1963), Paras. 302 and 320.
5. The Wolfenden Report (New York: Stein and Day, 1963), Para. 223.
6. The Wolfenden Report (New York: Stein and Day, 1963), Para. 306.

7. It is somewhere about this point in the argument that Professor Hart in *Law, Liberty and Morality* discerns a proposition which he describes as central to my thought. He states the proposition and his objection to it as follows (p. 51). "He appears to move from the acceptable proposition that *some* shared morality is essential to the existence of any society [this I take to be the proposition on p. 12] to the unacceptable proposition that a society is identical with its morality as that is at any given moment of its history, so that a change in its morality is tantamount to the destruction of a society. The former proposition might be even accepted as a necessary rather than an empirical truth depending on a quite plausible definition of society as a body of men who hold certain moral views in common. But the latter proposition is absurd. Taken strictly, it would prevent us saying that the morality of a given society had changed, and would compel us instead to say that one society had disappeared and another one taken its place. But it is only on this absurd criterion of what it is for the same society to continue to exist that it could be asserted without evidence that any deviation from a society's shared morality threatens its existence." In conclusion (p. 82) Professor Hart condemns the whole thesis in the lecture as based on "a confused definition of what a society is".

I do not assert that *any* deviation from a society's shared morality threatens its existence any more than I assert that *any* subversive activity threatens its existence. I assert that they are both activities which are capable in their nature of threatening the existence of society so that neither can be put beyond the law.

For the rest, the objection appears to me to be all a matter of words. I would venture to assert, for example, that you cannot have a game without rules and that if there were no rules there would be no game. If I am asked whether that means that the game is "identical" with the rules, I would be willing for the question to be answered either way in the belief that the answer would lead to nowhere. If I am asked whether a change in the rules means that one game has disappeared and another has taken its place, I would reply probably not, but that it would depend on the extent of the change.

Likewise I should venture to assert that there cannot be a contract without terms. Does this mean that an "amended" contract is a "new" contract in the eyes of the law? I once listened to an argument by an ingenious counsel that a contract, because of the substitution of one clause for another, had "ceased to have effect" within the meaning of a statutory provision. The judge did not accept the argument; but if most of the fundamental terms had been changed, I dare say he would have done.

The proposition that I make in the text is that if (as I understand Professor Hart to agree, at any rate for the purposes of the argument) you cannot have a society without morality, the law can be used to enforce morality as something that is essential to a society. I cannot see why this proposition (whether it is right or wrong) should mean that morality can never be changed without the destruction of society. If morality is changed, the law can be changed. Professor Hart refers (p. 72) to the proposition as "the use of legal punishment to freeze into immobility the morality dominant at a particular time in a society's existence." One might as well say that the inclusion of a penal section into a statute prohibiting certain acts freezes the whole statute into immobility and prevents the prohibitions from ever being modified.

8. (1951) Cmd. 8190, para. 159.
9. *Essays in Jurisprudence and Ethics* (1882), Macmillan, pp. 278 and 353.

LOUIS B. SCHWARTZ

Morals Offenses and the Model Penal Code*

What are the "offenses against morals"? One thinks first of the sexual offenses, adultery, fornication, sodomy, incest, and prostitution, and then, by easy extension, of such sex-related offenses as bigamy, abortion, open lewdness, and obscenity. But if one pauses to reflect on what sets these apart from offenses "against the person," or "against property," or "against public administration," it becomes evident that sexual offenses do not involve violation of moral principles in any peculiar sense. Virtually the entire penal code expresses the community's ideas of morality, or at least of the most egregious immoralities. To steal, to kill, to swear falsely in legal proceedings —these are certainly condemned as much by moral and religious as by secular standards. It also becomes evident that not all sexual behavior commonly condemned by prevailing American penal laws can be subsumed under universal moral precepts. This is certainly the case as to laws regulating contraception and abortion. But it is also true of such relatively uncontroversial (in the Western World) "morals" offenses as bigamy and polygamy; plural marriage arrangements approved by great religions of the majority of mankind can hardly be condemned out-of-hand as "immoralities."

What truly distinguishes the offenses commonly thought of as "against morals" is not their relation to morality but the absence of ordinary justification for punishment by a nontheocratic state. The ordinary justification for secular penal controls is preservation of public order. The king's peace must not be disturbed, or, to put the matter in the language of our time, public security must be preserved. Individuals must be able to go about their lawful pursuits without fear of attack, plunder, or other harm. This is an interest that only organized law enforcement can effectively safeguard. If individuals had to protect themselves by restricting their movements to

avoid dangerous persons or neighborhoods, or by restricting their investments for fear of violent dispossession, or by employing personal bodyguards and armed private police, the economy would suffer, the body politic would be rent by conflict of private armies, and men would still walk in fear.

No such results impend from the commission of "morals offenses." One has only to stroll along certain streets in Amsterdam to see that prostitution may be permitted to flourish openly without impairing personal security, economic prosperity, or indeed the general moral tone of a most respected nation of the Western World. Tangible interests are not threatened by a neighbor's rash decision to marry two wives or (to vary the case for readers who may see this as economic suicide) by a lady's decision to be supported by two husbands, assuming that the arrangement is by agreement of all parties directly involved. An obscene show, the predilection of two deviate males for each other, or the marriage of first cousins— all these leave nonparticipants perfectly free to pursue their own goals without fear or obstacle. The same can be said of certain nonsexual offenses, which I shall accordingly treat in this paper as "morals offenses": cruelty to animals, desecration of a flag or other generally venerated symbol, and mistreatment of a human corpse. What the dominant lawmaking groups appear to be seeking by means of morals legislation is not security and freedom in their own affairs but restraint of conduct by others that is regarded as offensive.

Accordingly, Professor Louis Henkin has suggested[1] that morals legislation may contravene constitutional provisions designed to protect liberty, especially the liberty to do as one pleases without legal constraints based solely on religious beliefs. There is wisdom in his warning, and it is the purpose of this article to review in the light of that warning some of the Model Penal Code[2] sections that venture into the difficult area of morals legislation. Preliminarily, I offer some

*From *Columbia Law Review*, Vol. 63, p. 669 (1963). Reprinted by permission of the author and the publisher.

general observations on the point of view that necessarily governed the American Law Institute as a group of would-be lawmakers. We were sensitive, I hope, to the supreme value of individual liberty, but aware also that neither legislatures nor courts will soon accept a radical change in the boundary between permissible social controls and constitutionally protected nonconformity.

I. CONSIDERATIONS IN APPRAISING MORALS LEGISLATION

The first proposition I would emphasize is that a statute appearing to express nothing but religious or moral ideas is often defensible on secular grounds.[3] Perhaps an unrestricted flow of obscenity *will* encourage illicit sexuality or violent assaults on women, as some proponents of the ban believe. Perhaps polygamy and polyandry as well as adultery are condemnable on Benthamite grounds. Perhaps tolerance of homosexuality *will* undermine the courage and discipline of our citizen militia, notwithstanding contrary indications drawn from the history of ancient Greece. The evidence is hopelessly inconclusive. Professor Henkin and I may believe that those who legislate morals are minding other people's business, not their own, but the great majority of people believe that morals of "bad" people do, at least in the long run, threaten the security of the "good" people. Thus, *they* believe that it is their own business they are minding. And that belief is not demonstrably false, any more than it is demonstrably true. It is hard to deny people the right to legislate on the basis of their beliefs not demonstrably erroneous, especially if these beliefs are strongly held by a very large majority. The majority cannot be expected to abandon a credo and its associated sensitivities, however irrational, in deference to a minority's skepticism.

The argument of the preceding paragraph does not mean that all laws designed to enforce morality are acceptable or constitutionally valid if enough people entertain a baseless belief in their social utility. The point is rather that recognizing irrational elements in the controversy over morals legislation, we ought to focus on other elements, about which rational debate and agreement are possible. For example, one can examine side effects of the effort to enforce morality by penal law. One can inquire whether enforcement will be so difficult that the offense will seldom be prosecuted and, therefore, risk of punishment will not in fact operate as a deterrent. One can ask whether the rare prosecutions for sexual derelictions are arbitrarily selected, or facilitate private blackmail or police discriminations more often than general compliance with legal norms. Are police forces, prosecution resources, and court time being wastefully diverted from the central insecurities of our metropolitan life—robbery, burglary, rape, assault, and governmental corruption?

A second proposition that must be considered in appraising morals legislation is that citizens may legitimately demand of the state protection of their psychological as well as their physical integrity. No one challenges this when the protection takes the form of penal laws guarding against fear caused by threat or menace. This is probably because these are regarded as incipient physical attacks. Criminal libel laws are clearly designed to protect against psychic pain;[4] so also are disorderly conduct laws insofar as they ban loud noises, offensive odors, and tumultuous behavior disturbing the peace. In fact, laws against murder, rape, arson, robbery, burglary, and other violent felonies afford not so much protection against direct attack—that can be done only by self-defense or by having a policeman on hand at the scene of the crime—as psychological security and comfort stemming from the knowledge that the probabilities of attack are lessened by the prospect of punishment and, perhaps, from the knowledge that an attacker will be condignly treated by society.

If, then, penal law frequently or typically protects us from psychic aggression, there is basis for the popular expectation that it will protect us also from blasphemy against a cherished religion, outrage to patriotic sentiments, blatant pornography, open lewdness affronting our sensibilities in the area of sexual mores, or stinging aspersions against race or nationality. Psychiatrists might tell us that the insecurities stirred by these psychic aggressions are deeper and more acute than those involved in crimes of physical violence. Physical violence is, after all, a phenomenon that occurs largely in the domain of the ego; we can rationally measure the danger and its likelihood, and our countermeasures can be proportioned to the threat. But who can measure the dark turbulences of the unconscious when sex, race, religion or patriotism (that extension of father-reverence) is the concern?

If unanimity of strongly held moral views is approached in a community, the rebel puts himself, as it were, outside the society when he arraigns himself against those views. Society owes debt to martyrs, madmen, criminals, and professors who occasionally call into question its fundamental assumptions, but the community cannot be expected to make their first protests respectable or even tolerated by law. It is entirely understandable and in a sense proper that blasphemy should have been criminal in Puritan Massachusetts, and that cow slaughter in a Hindu state, hog-raising in a theocratic Jewish or Moslem state, or abortion in a ninety-nine per cent Catholic state should be criminal. I do not mean to suggest a particular percentage test of substantial unanimity. It is rather a matter of when an ancient and unquestioned tenet has become seriously debatable in a given community. This may happen when it is discovered that a substantial, although inarticulate, segment of the population has drifted away from the old belief. It may happen when smaller numbers of articulate opinion-makers launch an open attack on the old ethic. When this kind of a beach-head has been established in the hostile country of traditional faith, then, and only then, can we expect constitutional principles to restrain the fifty-one per cent majority from suppressing the public flouting of deeply held moral views.

Some may find in all this an encouragement or approval of excessive conservatism. Societies, it seems, are by this argument morally entitled to use force to hold back the development of new ways of thought. I do not mean it so. Rather, I see this tendency to enforce old moralities as an inherent characteristic of organized societies, and I refrain from making moral judgments on group behavior that I regard as inevitable. If I must make a moral judgment, it is in favor of the individual visionaries who are willing to pay the personal cost to challenge the old moral order. There is a morality in some lawbreaking, even when we cannot condemn the law itself as immoral, for it enables conservative societies to begin the re-examination of even the most cherished principles.

Needless to say, recognizing the legitimacy of the demand for protection against psychic discomfort does not imply indiscriminate approval of laws intended to give such protection. Giving full recognition to that demand, we may still find that other considerations are the controlling ones. Can we satisfy the demand without impairing other vital interests? How can we protect religious feelings without "establishing" religion or impairing the free exercise of proselytizing faiths? How can we protect racial sensibilities without exacerbating race hatreds and erecting a government censorship of discussion?[5] How shall we prevent pain and disgust to many who are deeply offended by portrayal of sensuality without stultifying our artists and writers?

A third aspect of morals legislation that will enter into the calculations of the rational legislator is that some protection against offensive immorality may be achieved as a by-product of legislation that aims directly at something other than immorality. We may be uneasy about attempting to regulate private sexual behavior, but we will not be so hesitant in prohibiting the commercialization of vice. This is a lesser intrusion on freedom of choice in personal relations. It presents a more realistic target for police activity. And conceptually such regulation presents itself as a ban on a form of economic activity rather than a regulation of morals. It is not the least of the advantages of this approach that it preserves to some extent the communal disapproval of illicit sexuality, thus partially satisfying those who would really prefer outright regulation of morality. So also, we may be reluctant to penalize blasphemy or sacrilege, but feel compelled to penalize the mischievous or zealous blasphemer who purposely disrupts a religious meeting or procession with utterances designed to outrage the sensibilities of the group and thus provoke a riot.[6] Reasonable rules for the maintenance of public peace incidentally afford a measure of protection against offensive irreligion. Qualms about public "establishment" of religion must yield to the fact that the alternative would be to permit a kind of violent private interference with freedom to conduct religious ceremonies.

It remains to apply the foregoing analysis to selected provisions of the Model Penal Code.

II. THE MODEL PENAL CODE APPROACH

A. FLAGRANT AFFRONTS AND PENALIZATION OF PRIVATE IMMORALITY

The Model Penal Code does not penalize the sexual sins, fornication, adultery, sodomy or other illicit sexual activity not involving violence or imposition upon children, mental incompetents, wards, or other dependents. This decision to keep penal law out of the area of private sexual relations approaches Professor Henkin's suggestion that private morality be immune from secular regulation. The Comments in Tentative Draft No. 4 declared:

The Code does not attempt to use the power of the state to enforce purely moral or religious standards. We deem it inappropriate for the government to attempt to control behavior that has no substantial significance except as to the morality of the actor. Such matters are best left to religious, educational and other social influences. Apart from the question of constitutionality which might be raised against legislation avowedly commanding adherence to a particular religious or moral tenet, it must be recognized, as a practical matter, that in a heterogeneous community such as ours, different individuals and groups have widely divergent views of the seriousness of various moral derelictions.[7]

Although this passage expresses doubt as to the constitutionality of state regulation of morals, it does so in a context of "widely divergent views of the seriousness of various moral derelictions." Thus, it does not exclude the use of penal sanctions to protect a "moral consensus" against flagrant breach. The Kinsey studies and others are cited to show that sexual derelictions are widespread and that the incidence of sexual dereliction varies among social groups. The Comments proceed to discuss various secular goals that might be served by penalizing illicit sexual relations, such as promoting the stability of marriage, preventing illegitimacy and disease, or forestalling private violence against seducers. The judgment is made that there is no reliable basis for believing that penal laws substantially contribute to these goals. Punishment of private vice is rejected on this ground as well as on grounds of difficulty of enforcement and the potential for blackmail and other abuse of rarely enforced criminal statutes.[8] The discussion with regard to homosexual offenses follows a similar course.[9]

The Code does, however, penalize "open lewdness"—"any lewd act which [the actor] . . . knows is likely to be observed by others who would be affronted or alarmed."[10] The idea that "flagrant affront to commonly held notions of morality" might have to be differentiated from other sorts of immorality appeared in the first discussions of the Institute's policy on sexual offenses, in connection with a draft that would have penalized "open and notorious" illicit relations.[11] Eventually, however, the decision was against establishing a penal offense in which guilt would depend on the level of gossip to which the moral transgression gave rise. Guilt under the open lewdness section turns on the likelihood that the lewd act itself will be observed by others who would be affronted.

Since the Code accepts the propriety of penalizing behavior that affects others only in flagrantly affronting commonly held notions of morality, the question arises whether such repression of offensive immorality need be confined to acts done in public where others may observe and be outraged. People may be deeply offended upon learning of private debauchery. The Code seems ready at times to protect against this type of "psychological assault," at other times not. Section 250.10 penalizes mistreatment of a corpse "in a way that [the actor] . . . knows would outrage ordinary family sensibilities," although the actor may have taken every precaution for secrecy. Section 250.11 penalizes cruel treatment of an animal in private as well as in public. On the other hand, desecration of the national flag or other object of public veneration, an offense under section 250.9, is not committed unless others are likely to "observe or discover." And solicitation of deviate sexual relations is penalized only when the actor "loiters in or near any public place" for the purpose of such solicitation.[12] The Comments make it clear that the target of this legislation is not private immorality but a kind of public "nuisance" caused by congregation of homosexuals offensively flaunting their deviance from general norms of behavior.[13]

As I search for the principle of discrimination between the morals offenses made punishable only when committed openly and those punishable even when committed in secrecy, I find nothing but differences in the intensity of the aversion with which the different kinds of behavior are regarded. It was the intuition of the draftsman and his fellow lawmakers in the Institute that disrespectful behavior to a corpse and cruelty to animals were more intolerable affronts to ordinary feelings than disrespectful behavior to a flag. Therefore, in the former cases, but not the latter, we overcame our general reluctance to extend penal controls of immorality to private behavior that disquiets people soley because they learn that things of this sort are going on.

Other possible explanations do not satisfy me. For example, it explains nothing to say that we wish to "protect" the corpse or the mistreated dog, but not the flag itself. The legislation on its face seeks to deter mistreatment of all three. All three cases involve interests beyond, and merely represented by, the thing that is immediately "protected." It is not the mistreated dog who is the ultimate object of concern; his owner is entirely free to kill him (though not "cruelly") without interference from other dog owners. Our concern is for the feelings of other human beings, a large proportion of whom, although accustomed to the slaughter of animals for food, readily identify themselves with a tortured dog or horse and respond with great sensitivity to its sufferings. The desire to protect a corpse from degradation is not a deference to this remnant of a human being—the dead have no legal rights and no legislative lobby—but a protection of the feelings of the living. So also in the case of the flag, our concern is not for the bright bit of cloth but for what it symbolizes, a cluster of patriotic emotions. I submit that legislative tolerance for private flag desecration is explicable by the greater difficulty an ordinary man has in identifying with a country and all else that a flag symbolizes as compared with the ease in identifying with a corpse or a warm-blooded domestic animal. This is only an elaborate way of saying that he does not feel the first desecration as keenly as the others. Perhaps also, in the case of the flag, an element of tolerance is present for the right of political dissent when it goes no further than private disrespect for the symbol of authority.[14]

A penal code's treatment of private homosexual relations presents the crucial test of a legislator's views on whether a state may legimately protect people from "psychological assault" by repressing not merely overt affront to consensus morals but also the most secret violation of that moral code. As is often wise in legislative affairs, the Model Penal Code avoids a clear issue of principle. The decision against penalizing deviate sexuality is rested not merely on the idea of immunity from regulation of private morality, but on a consideration of practical difficulties and evils in attempting to use the penal law in this way.[15] The Comments note that existing laws dealing with homosexual relations are nullified in practice, except in cases of violence, corruption of children, or public solicitation. Capricious selection of a few cases for prosecution, among millions of infractions, is unfair and chiefly benefits extortioners and seekers of private vengeance. The existence of the criminal law prevents some deviates from seeking psychiatric aid. Furthermore, the pursuit of homosexuals involves policemen in degrading entrapment practices, and diverts attention and effort that could be employed more usefully against the crimes of violent aggression, fraud, and government corruption, which are the overriding concerns of our metropolitan civilization.

If state legislators are not persuaded by such arguments to repeal the laws against private deviate sexual relations among adults, the constitutional issue will ultimately have to be faced by the courts. When that time comes, one of the important questions will be whether homosexuality is in fact the subject of a "consensus." If not, that is, if a substantial body of public opinion regards homosexuals' private activity with indifference, or if homosexuals succeed in securing recognition as a considerable minority having otherwise "respectable" status, this issue of private morality may soon be held to be beyond resolution by vote of fifty-one per cent of the legislators.[16] As to the status of homosexuality in this country, it is significant that the Supreme Court has reversed an obscenity conviction involving a magazine that was avowedly published by, for, and about homosexuals and that carried on a ceaseless campaign against the repressive laws.[17] The much smaller group of American polygamists have yet to break out of the class of idiosyncratic heretic-martyrs[18] by bidding for public approval in the same group-conscious way.

B. THE OBSCENITY PROVISIONS

The obscenity provisions of the Model Penal Code best illustrate the Code's preference for an oblique approach to morals offenses, that is, the effort to express the moral impulses of the community in a penal prohibition that is nevertheless pointed at and limited to something else than sin. In this case the target is not the "sin of obscenity," but primarily a disapproved form of economic activity—commercial exploitation of the widespread weakness for titillation by pornography. This is apparent not only from the narrow definition of "obscene" in section 251.4 of the Code, but even more from the narrow definition of the forbidden behavior; only sale, advertising, or public exhibition are forbidden, and noncommercial dissemination within a restricted circle of personal associates is expressly exempt.[19]

Section 251.4 defines obscenity as material whose "predominant appeal is to prurient interest. . . ."[20] The emphasis is on the "appeal" of the material, rather than on its "effect," an emphasis designed explicitly to reject prevailing definitions of obscenity that stress the "effect."[21] This effect is traditionally identified as a tendency to cause "sexually impure and lustful thoughts" or to "corrupt or deprave."[22] The Comments on section 251.4 take the position that repression of sexual thoughts and desires is not a practicable or legitimate legislative goal. Too many instigations to sexual desire exist in a society like ours, which approves much eroticism in literature, movies, and advertising, to suppose that any conceivable repression of pornography would substantially diminish the volume of such impulses. Moreover, "thoughts and desires not manifested in overt antisocial behavior are generally regarded as the exclusive concern of the individual and his spiritual advisors."[23] The Comments, rejecting also the test of tendency to corrupt or deprave, point out that corruption or depravity are attributes of character inappropriate for secular punishment when they do not lead to misconduct, and there is a paucity of evidence linking obscenity to misbehavior.[24]

The meretricious "appeal" of a book or picture is essentially a question of the attractiveness of the merchandise from a certain point of view: what makes it sell. Thus, the prohibition of obscenity takes on an aspect of regulation of unfair business or competitive practices. Just as merchants may be prohibited from selling their wares by appeal to the public's weakness for gambling,[25] so they may be restrained from purveying books, movies, or other commercial exhibition by exploiting the well-nigh universal weakness for a look behind the curtain of modesty. This same philosophy of obscenity control is evidenced by the Code provision outlawing advertising appeals that attempt to sell material "whether or not obscene, by representing or suggesting that it is obscene."[26] Moreover, the requirement under section 251.4 that the material go "substantially beyond customary limits of candor" serves to exclude from criminality the sorts of appeal to eroticism that, being prevalent, can hardly give a particular purveyor a commercial advantage.

It is important to recognize that material may predominantly "appeal" to prurient interest notwithstanding that ordinary adults may actually respond to the material with feelings of aversion or disgust. Section 251.4 explicitly encompasses material dealing with excretory functions as well as sex, which the customer is likely to find *both* repugnant and "shameful" and yet attractive in a morbid, compelling way. Not recognizing that material may be repellent and appealing at the same time, two distinguished commentators on the Code's obscenity provisions have criticized the "appeal" formula, asserting that "hard core pornography," concededly the main category we are trying to repress, has no appeal for "ordinary adults," who instead would be merely repelled by the material.[27] Common experience suggests the contrary. It is well known that policemen, lawyers, and judges involved in obscenity cases not infrequently regale their fellows with viewings of the criminal material. Moreover, a poll conducted by this author among his fellow law

professors—"mature" and, for the present purposes, "ordinary" adults—evoked uniformly affirmative answers to the following question: "Would you look inside a book that you had been certainly informed has grossly obscene hard-core pornography if you were absolutely sure that no one else would ever learn that you had looked?" It is not an answer to this bit of amateur sociological research to say that people would look "out of curiosity." It is precisely such shameful curiosity to which "appeal" is made by the obscene, as the word "appeal" is used in section 251.4.

Lockhart and McClure, the two commentators referred to above, prefer a "variable obscenity" concept over the Institute's "constant obscenity" concept. Under the "constant obscenity" concept, material is normally judged by reference to "ordinary adults."[28] The "variable obscenity" concept always takes account of the nature of the comtemplated audience; material would be obscene if it is "primarily directed to an audience of the sexually immature for the purpose of satisfying their craving for erotic fantasy."[29] The preference for "variable obscenity" rests not only on the mistaken view that hard-core pornography does not appeal to ordinary adults, but also on the ground that this concept facilitates the accomplishment of several ancillary legislative goals, namely, exempting transactions in "obscene" materials by persons with scholarly, scientific, or other legitimate interests in the obscene and prohibiting the advertising of material "not intrinsically pornographic as if it were hard-core pornography."[30] The Code accomplishes these results by explicit exemption for justifiable transactions in the obscene and by specific prohibition of suggestive advertising.[31] This still seems to me the better way to draft a criminal statute.

The Code's exemption for justifiable dealing in obscene material provides a workable criterion of public gain in permitting defined categories of transactions. It requires no analysis of the psyche of customers to see whether they are sexually immature or given to unusual craving for erotic fantasy. It makes no impractical demand on the sophistication of policemen, magistrates, customs officers, or jurymen. The semantics of the variable obscenity concept assumes without basis that the Kinsey researchers were immune to the prurient appeal of the materials with which they worked.[32] Would it not be a safe psychiatric guess that some persons are drawn into research of this sort precisely to satisfy in a socially approved way the craving that Lockhart and McClure deplore? In any event, it seems a confusing distortion of language to say that a pornographic picture is not obscene as respects the blasé [sexually mature?] shopkeeper who stocks it, the policeman who confiscates it, or the Model Penal Code reporter who appraises it.

As for the prohibition against suggestive advertising, this is certainly handled more effectively by explicitly declaring the advertisement criminal without regard to the "obscene" character of the material advertised than by the circumlocution that an advertisement is itself to be regarded as obscene if it appeals to the cravings of the sexually immature. That kind of test will prove more than a little troublesome for the advertising departments of some respectable literary journals.

If the gist of section 251.4 is, as suggested above, commercial exploitation of the weakness for obscenity, the question arises whether the definition of the offense should not be formulated in terms of "pandering to an interest in obscenity," that is, "exploiting such an interest primarily for pecuniary gain. . . ."[33] This proposal, made by Professor Henry Hart, a member of the Criminal Law Advisory Committee, was rejected because of the indefiniteness of "exploiting . . . primarily for pecuniary gain," and because it would clearly authorize a bookseller, for example, to procure any sort of hard-core pornography upon the unsolicited order of a customer. "Exploiting . . . primarily for pecuniary gain" is not a formula apt for guiding either judicial interpretation or merchants' behavior. It is not clear what the prosecution would have to prove beyond sale of the objectionable item. Would advertising or an excessive profit convert sale into "exploitation"? Would the formula leave a bookseller free to enjoy a gradually expanding trade in obscenity so long as he kept his merchandise discreetly under the counter and let word-of-mouth publicize the availability of his tidbits? Despite these difficulties, it may well be that the Code section on obscenity has a constitutional infirmity of the sort that concerned Professor Henkin insofar as the section restricts the freedom of an adult to buy, and thus to read, whatever he pleases. This problem might be met by framing an appropriate exemption for such transactions to be added to those now set forth in subsection (3).

The rejection of the Hart "pandering" formulation highlights another aspect of section 251.4, namely, its applicability to a class of completely noncommercial transactions that could not conceivably be regarded as "pandering." This ban on certain noncommercial disseminations results from the fact that subsection (2) forbids every

dissemination except those exempted by subsection (3), and subsection (3) exempts noncommercial dissemination only if it is limited to "personal associates of the actor." Thus, a general distribution or exhibition of obscenity is prohibited even though no one is making money from it: a zealot for sex education may not give away pamphlets at the schoolyard gates containing illustrations of people engaged in erotic practices; a rich homosexual may not use a billboard on Times Square to promulgate to the general populace the techniques and pleasures of sodomy. Plainly, this is not the economic regulation to which I have previously tried to assimilate the Code's antiobscenity regulations. But equally, it is not merely sin-control of the sort that evoked Professor Henkin's constitutional doubts. Instead, the community is merely saying: "Sin, if you must, in private. Do not flaunt your immoralities where they will grieve and shock others. If we do not impose our morals upon you, neither must you impose yours upon us, undermining the restraints we seek to cultivate through family, church, and school." The interest being protected is not, directly or exclusively, the souls of those who might be depraved or corrupted by the obscenity, but the right of parents to shape the moral notions of their children, and the right of the general public not to be subjected to violent psychological affront.

C. PROSTITUTION

The prostitution provisions of the Model Penal Code, like the obscenity provisions, reflect the policy of penalizing not sin but commercial exploitation of a human weakness, or serious affront to public sensibilities. The salient features of section 251.2 are as follows. Sexual activity is penalized only when carried on as a business or for hire. The section covers any form of sexual gratification. "Promoters" of prostitution—that is, procurers, pimps, keepers of houses of prostitution—are penalized more severely than the prostitutes. The patron of the prostitute is subject to prosecution for a "violation" only, that is, he may be fined but not jailed, and the offense is, by definition, not a "crime." Dependents of a prostitute are not declared to be criminals by virtue of the fact that they live off the proceeds of prostitution, as under many present laws, but the circumstance of being supported by a prostitute is made presumptive evidence that the person supported is engaged in pimping or some other form of commercial exploitation of prostitution.

The main issues in the evolution of the Institute's position on prostitution were, on the one hand, whether to penalize all "promiscuous" intercourse even if not for hire or, on the other hand, whether even intercourse for hire should be immune from prosecution when it is carried on discreetly out of the public view. Those who favored extending the criminal law to promiscuous noncommercial sexuality did so on secular, not moral, grounds. They pointed to the danger that promiscuous amateurs would be carriers of venereal disease, and they argued that law enforcement against hire-prostitution would be facilitated if the law, proceeding on the basis that most promiscuity is accompanied by hire, dispensed with proof of actual hire. Others doubted the utility or propriety of the law's intervening in private sexual relations on the basis of a vague and moralistic judgment of promiscuity; and these doubts prevailed.

It was more strenuously contended that the Model Penal Code should, following the English pattern, penalize prostitution only when it manifests itself in annoying public solicitation.[34] This position was defeated principally by the argument that "call-houses" were an important cog in the financial machine of the underworld, linked to narcotics peddling and other "rackets." I find more interesting and persuasive the parallel between this problem of the discreet exploitation of sex and the suggestion in the obscenity and context that discreet sale of obscene books to patrons who request them might not constitute "pandering." Both distinctions present the difficulty of drawing an administrable line between aggressive merchandising and passive willingness to make profits by catering to a taste for spicy life or literature.

Other provisions of section 251.2 also demonstrate its basic orientation against undesirable commerce rather than sin. The grading of offenses under the section ranges from the classification of the patron's guilt as a noncriminal "violation," through the "petty misdemeanor" classification (thirty-day maximum imprisonment) for the prostitute herself, and the "misdemeanor" classification (one year maximum) for minor participation in the promotion of prostitution, to the "third degree felony" classification (five year maximum) for owning or managing a prostitution business, bringing about an association between a prostitute and a house of prostitution, or recruiting persons into prostitution. Clearly, from the point of view of the sinfulness of illicit sexual relations, the patron's guilt is equal to that of the prostitute, but it is the seller rather than the sinful customer who is labelled a criminal. And the higher the rank in the selling organization, the graver the penalty—a significant departure from the normal assimilation of accessorial guilt to that of the principal offender. This emphasis on the businessman in sex is underscored by the fact that the higher penalties applicable to him do not depend on whether he is the instigator of the relationship; if a prostitute persuades someone to manage her illicit business or to accept her in a house of prostitution, it is he, not she, who incurs the higher penalty.

In one respect, the Code's provisions against illicit sexual activity depart from the regulation of commerce. Section 251.3 makes it a petty misdemeanor to loiter "in or near any public place for the purpose of soliciting or being solicited to engage in deviate sexual relations." This extension is explained as follows in the accompanying status note:

[T]he main objective is to suppress the open flouting of prevailing moral standards as a sort of nuisance in public thoroughfares and parks. In the case of females, suppression of professionals is likely to accomplish that objective. In the case of males, there is a greater likelihood that non-professional homosexuals will congregate and behave in a manner grossly offensive to other users of public facilities.[35]

The situation is analogous to that of noncommercial dissemination of obscenity by billboard publication or indiscriminate gratuitous distribution of pornography. In a community in which assemblages of "available" women evoke the same degree of violent resentment as assemblages of homosexuals, it would be consistent with this analysis to make public loitering to solicit illicit heterosexual relations an offense regardless of proof of "hire." On the other hand, the legislator may well decide that even in such a community it is not worth risking the possibility of arbitrary police intrusion into dance halls, taverns, corner drug stores, and similar resorts of unattached adolescents, on suspicion that some of the girls are promiscuous, though not prostitutes in the hire sense . . .

NOTES

1. See Henkin, *Morals and the Constitution: The Sin of Obscenity,* 63 Colum. L. Rev. 391 (1963), to which the present article is a companion piece. Controversy on the role of the state in the enforcement of morals has recently reached a new pitch of intensity. See Hart, *Law, Liberty, and Morality* (1963); Devlin, *The Enforcement of Morals* (1959); Devlin, *Law, Democracy, and Morality,* 110 U. Pa. L. Rev. 635

(1962). I shall not attempt to judge this debate, cf. Rostow, the Sovereign Prerogative 45–80 (1962), and I leave it to others to align the present essay with one or another of the sides. The recent controversy traverses much the same ground as was surveyed in the nineteenth century. See Mill *On Liberty* (1859); Stephen, *Liberty, Equality, Fraternity* (1873).

2. The Model Penal Code is hereinafter cited as MPC. Unless otherwise indicated, all citations are to the 1962 Official Draft.

3. See McGowan v. Maryland, 366 U.S. 420 (1961). The Supreme Court upheld the constitutionality of a law requiring business establishments to close on Sunday, on the ground that such regulation serves the secular goal of providing a common day of rest and recreation, notwithstanding that the statute proscribed profanation of "the Lord's day."

4. The Model Penal Code does not make libel a criminal offense. But this decision rests upon a judgment that the penal law is not a useful or safe instrument for repressing defamation; by no means is it suggested that the hurt experienced by one who is libelled is an inappropriate concern of government. See MPC § 250.7, comment 2 (Tent. Draft No. 13, 1961).

5. See MPC § 250.7 & comments 1–4 (Tent. Draft No. 13, 1961) ("Fomenting Group Hatred"). The section was not included in the Official Draft of 1962.

6. See MPC §§ 250.8, 250.3 & comment (Tent. Draft No. 13, 1961).

7. MPC § 207.1, comment at 207 (Tent. Draft No. 4, 1955).

8. MPC § 207.1, comment at 205–10 (Tent. Draft No. 4, 1955).

9. MPC § 207.5, comment at 278–79 (Tent. Draft NO. 4, 1955). "No harm to the secular interests of the community is involved in atypical sex practice in private between consenting adult partners. This area of private morals is the distinctive concern of spiritual authorities. . . . [T]here is the fundamental question of the protection to which every individual is entitled against state interference in his personal affairs when he is not hurting others." MPC § 207.5, comment at 277–78 (Tent. Draft No. 4, 1955).

10. MPC § 251.1; *cf.* MPC § 213.5, which penalizes exposure of the genitals for the purpose of arousing or gratifying sexual desire in circumstances likely to cause affront or alarm. This later offense carries a heavier penalty than open lewdness, "since the behavior amounts to, or at least is often taken as, threatening sexual aggression." MPC § 213.4 & 251.1, comment at 82 (Tent. Draft No. 13, 1961).

11. MPC § 207.1 & comment at 209 (Tent. Draft No. 4, 1955).

12. MPC § 251.3; see text accompanying note 35 *infra.*

13. MPC § 251.3, status note at 237.

14. Not all legislatures are so restrained. See, e.g., Pa. Stat. Ann. tit. 18, § 4211 (1945) ("publicly or privately mutilates, defaces, defiles or tramples upon, or casts contempt either by words or act upon, any such flag"). Query as to the constitutionality of this effort to repress a private expression of political disaffection.

15. MPC § 207.5, comment 278–79 (Tent. Draft No. 4, 1955).

16. *Cf.* Robinson v. California, 371 U.S. 905 (1962) (invalidating statute that penalized addiction to narcotics).

17. One, Inc. v. Oleson, 355 U.S. 371 (1958), *reversing* 241 F.2d 772 (9th Cir. 1957). On the "homosexual community" see Helmer, *New York's "Middle-class" Homosexuals,* Harper's, March 1963, p. 85 (evidencing current nonshocked attitude toward this minority group).

18. See Cleveland v. United States, 329 U.S. 14 (1946); Reynolds v. United States, 98 U.S. 145 (1878).

19. MPC § 251.4(2), (3).

20. (1) *Obscene Defined.* Material is obscene if, considered as a whole, its predominant appeal is to prurient interest, that is, a shameful or morbid interest, in nudity, sex or excretion, and if in addition it goes substantially beyond customary limits of candor in describing or representing such matters. Predominant appeal shall be judged with reference to ordinary adults unless it appears from the character of the material or the circumstances of its dissemination to be designed for children or other specially susceptible audience. . . . MPC § 251.4(1).

21. See MPC § 207.10, comment 6 at 19, 29 (Tent. Draft No. 6, 1957) (§ 207.10 was subsequently renumbered § 251.4).

22. See MPC § 207.10, comment 6 at 19 n.21, 21 (Tent. Draft No. 6, 1957).

23. MPC § 207.10, comment 6 at 20 (Tent. Draft No. 6, 1957).

24. MPC § 207.10, comment 6 at 22–28 (Tent. Draft No. 6, 1957).

25. See FTC v. R. F. Keppel & Brother, 291 U.S. 304 (1934) (sale of penny candy by device of awarding prizes to lucky purchasers of some pieces). The opinion of the Court declares that Section 5 of the Federal Trade Commission Act, proscribing unfair methods of competition, "does not authorize business men," *ibid.,* p. 313, but that the Commission may prevent exploitation of consumers by the enticement of gambling, as well as imposition upon competitors by use of a morally obnoxious selling appeal.

26. MPC § 251.4(2)(e). Equivalent provisions appear in some state laws. E.g., N.Y. Pen. Law § 1141. There is some doubt whether federal obscenity laws reach such advertising. See Manual Enterprises, Inc. v. Day, 370 U.S. 478. 491 (1962). *But see* United States v. Hornick, 229 F.2d 120, 121 (3d Cir. 1956).

27. See Lockhart & McClure, *Censorship of Obscenity: The Developing Constitutional Standards,* 45 Minn. L. Rev. 72–73 (1960).

28. The Model Penal Code employs the "variable obscenity" concept in part, since § 251.4(1) provides that "appeal" shall be judged with reference to the susceptibilities of children or other specially susceptible audience when it appears that the material is designed for or directed to such an audience.

29. Lockhart & McClure, *supra* note 27, at 79.

30. *Ibid.*

31. MPC § 251.4(2)(e), (3)(a).

32. *Cf.* United States v. 31 Photographs, 156 F. Supp. 350 (S.D.N.Y. 1957), in which, absent a statutory exemption, the court was compelled to rely on variable obscenity in order to sanction import of obscene pictures by the [Kinsey] Institute for Sex Research.

33. MPC § 207.10(1) (Tent. Draft No. 6, 1957) (alternative).

34. See Street Offenses Act, 1959, 7 & 8 Eliz. 2, c. 57.

GRISWOLD v. CONNECTICUT

United States Supreme Court, 1965*

Mr. Justice Douglas delivered the opinion of the Court.

Appellant Griswold is Executive Director of the Planned Parenthood League of Connecticut. Appellant Buxton is a licensed physician and a professor at the Yale Medical School who served as Medical Director for the League at its Center in New Haven—a center open and operating from November 1 to November 10, 1961, when appellants were arrested.

They gave information, instruction, and medical advice to *married persons* as to the means of preventing conception. They examined the wife and prescribed the best contraceptive device or material for her use. Fees were usually charged, although some couples were serviced free.

The statutes whose constitutionality is involved in this appeal are §§ 53–32 and 54–196 of the General Statutes of Connecticut (1958 rev.). The former provides:

"Any person who uses any drug, medicinal article or instrument for the purpose of preventing conception shall be fined not less than fifty dollars or imprisoned not less than sixty days nor more than one year or be both fined and imprisoned."

Section 54–196 provides:

"Any person who assists, abets, counsels, causes, hires or commands another to commit any offense may be prosecuted and punished as if he were the principal offender."

The appellants were found guilty as accessories and fined $100 each, against the claim that the accessory statute as so applied violated the Fourteenth Amendment. The Appellate Division of the Circuit Court affirmed. The Supreme Court of Errors affirmed that judgment.*

We think that appellants have standing to raise the constitutional rights of the married people with whom they had a professional relationship. . . . Certainly the accessory should have standing to assert that the offense which he is charged with assisting is not, or cannot constitutionally be, a crime . . .

*381 U.S. 479 (1965). Excerpts only. Footnotes renumbered.

*Citation omitted (Eds.)

Coming to the merits, we are met with a wide range of questions that implicate the Due Process Clause of the Fourteenth Amendment. Overtones of some arguments suggest that *Lochner* v. *New York,* 198 U.S. 45, should be our guide. But we decline that invitation.* We do not sit as a super-legislature to determine the wisdom, need, and propriety of laws that touch economic problems, business affairs, or social conditions. This law, however, operates directly on an intimate relation of husband and wife and their physician's role in one aspect of that relation.

The association of people is not mentioned in the Constitution nor in the Bill of Rights. The right to educate a child in a school of the parents' choice—whether public or private or parochial—is also not mentioned. Nor is the right to study any particular subject or any foreign language. Yet the First Amendment has been construed to include certain of those rights.

By *Pierce* v. *Society of Sisters,* * the right to educate one's children as one chooses is made applicable to the States by the force of the First and Fourteenth Amendments. By *Meyer* v. *Nebraska,* * the same dignity is given the right to study the German language in a private school. In other words, the State may not, consistently with the spirit of the First Amendment, contract the spectrum of available knowledge. The right of freedom of speech and press includes not only the right to utter or to print, but the right to distribute, the right to receive, the right to read* and freedom of inquiry, freedom of thought, and freedom to teach*—indeed the freedom of the entire university community.* Without those peripheral rights the specific rights would be less secure . . .

In *NAACP* v. *Alabama,* 357 U.S. 449, 462, we protected the "freedom to associate and privacy in one's associations," noting that freedom of association was a peripheral First Amendment right. Disclosure of membership lists of a constitutionally valid association, we held, was invalid "as entailing the likelihood of a substantial restraint upon the exercise by petitioner's members of their right to freedom of association." *Ibid.* In other words, the First Amendment has a penumbra where privacy is protected from governmental intrusion. In like context, we have protected forms of "association" that are not political in the customary sense but pertain to the social, legal, and economic benefit of the members.* In *Schware* v. *Board of Bar Examiners,* 353 U.S. 232, we held it not permissible to bar a lawyer from practice, because he had once been a member of the Communist Party. The man's "association with that Party" was not shown to be "anything more than a political faith in a political party"* and was not action of a kind proving bad moral character.*

Those cases involved more than the "right of assembly"—a right that extends to all irrespective of their race or ideology.* The right of "association," like the right of belief,* is more than the right to attend a meeting; it includes the right to express one's attitudes or philosophies by membership in a group or by affiliation with it or by other lawful means. Association in that context is a form of expression of opinion; and while it is not expressly included in the First Amendment its existence is necessary in making the express guarantees fully meaningful.

The foregoing cases suggest that specific guarantees in the Bill of Rights have penumbras, formed by emanations from those guarantees that help give them life and substance.* Various guarantees create zones of privacy. The right of association contained in the penumbra of the First Amendment is one, as we have seen. The Third Amendment in its prohibition against the quartering of soldiers "in any house" in time of peace without the consent of the owner is another facet of that privacy. The Fourth Amendment explicitly affirms the "right of the people to be secure in their persons, houses, papers, and effects, against unreasonable searches and seizures." The Fifth Amendment in its Self-Incrimination Clause enables the citizen to create a zone of privacy which government may not force him to surrender to his detriment. The Ninth Amendment provides: "The enumeration in the Constitution, of certain rights, shall not be construed to deny or disparage others retained by the people."

The Fourth and Fifth Amendments were described in *Boyd* v. *United States,* 116 U.S. 616, 630, as protection against all governmental invasions "of the sanctity of a man's home and the privacies of life." We recently referred in *Mapp* v. *Ohio,* 367 U.S. 643, 656, to the Fourth Amendment as creating a "right to privacy, no less important than any other right carefully and particularly reserved to the people."* These cases bear witness that the right of privacy which presses for recognition here is a legitimate one.

The present case, then, concerns a relationship lying within the zone of privacy created by several fundamental constitutional guarantees. And it concerns a law which, in forbidding the *use* of contraceptives rather than regulating their manufacture or sale, seeks to achieve its goals by means having a maximum destructive impact upon that relationship. Such a law cannot stand in light of the familiar principle, so often applied by this Court, that a "governmental purpose to control or prevent activities constitutionally subject to state regulation may not be achieved by means which sweep unnecessarily broadly and thereby invade the area of protected freedoms." *NAACP* v. *Alabama,* 377 U.S. 288, 307. Would we allow the police to search the sacred precincts of marital bedrooms for telltale signs of the use of contraceptives? The very idea is repulsive to the notions of privacy surrounding the marriage relationship.

We deal with a right of privacy older than the Bill of Rights—older than our political parties, older than our school system. Marriage is a coming together for better or for worse, hopefully enduring, and intimate to the degree of being sacred. It is an association that promotes a way of life, not causes; a harmony in living, not political faiths; a bilateral loyalty, not commercial or social projects. Yet it is an association for as noble a purpose as any involved in our prior decisions.

Reversed.

Mr. Justice Goldberg, whom The Chief Justice and Mr. Justice Brennan join, concurring . . . My Brother Stewart dissents on the ground that he "can find no . . . general right of privacy in the Bill of Rights, in any other part of the Constitution, or in any case ever before decided by this Court." He would require a more explicit guarantee than the one which the Court derives from several constitutional amendments. This Court, however, has never held that the Bill of Rights or the Fourteenth Amendment protects only those rights that the Constitution specifically mentions by name . . .

My Brother Stewart, while characterizing the Connecticut birth control law as "an uncommonly silly law," would nevertheless let it stand on the ground that it is not for the courts to " 'substitute their social and economic beliefs for the judgment of legislative bodies, who are elected to pass laws.' " Elsewhere, I have stated that "[w]hile I quite agree with Mr. Justice Brandeis that . . . 'a . . . State may . . . serve as a laboratory; and try novel social and economic experiments,'* I do not believe that this includes the power to experiment with the fundamental liberties of citizens. . . ." The vice of the dissenters' views is that it would permit such experimentation by the States in the area of the fundamental personal rights of its citizens. I cannot agree that the Constitution grants such either to the States or to the Federal Government.

The logic of the dissents would sanction federal or state legislation that seems to me even more plainly

*Citation omitted [Eds.]

unconstitutional than the statute before us. Surely the Government, absent a showing of a compelling subordinating state interest, could not decree that all husbands and wives must be sterilized after two children have been born to them. Yet by their reasoning such an invasion of marital privacy would not be subject to constitutional challenge because, while it might be "silly," no provision of the Constitution specifically prevents the Government from curtailing the marital right to bear children and raise a family. While it may shock some of my Brethren that the Court today holds that the Constitution protects the right of marital privacy in my view it is far more shocking to believe that the personal liberty guaranteed by the Constitution does not include protection against such totalitarian limitation of family size, which is at complete variance with our constitutional concepts. Yet, if upon a showing of a slender basis of rationality, a law outlawing voluntary birth control by married persons is valid, then, by the same reasoning a law requiring compulsory birth control also would seem to be valid. In my view, however, both types of law would unjustifiably intrude upon rights of marital privacy which are constitutionally protected.

In a long series of cases this Court has held that where fundamental personal liberties are involved, they may not be abridged by the States simply on a showing that a regulatory statute has some rational relationship to the effectuation of a proper state purpose. "Where there is a significant encroachment upon personal liberty, the State may prevail only upon showing a subordinating interest which is compelling," *Bates* v. *Little Rock*, 361 U.S. 516, 524. The law must be shown "necessary, and not merely rationally related, to the accomplishment of a permissible state policy." *McLaughlin* v. *Florida*, 379 U.S. 184, 196.*

Although the Connecticut birth-control law obviously encroaches upon a fundamental personal liberty, the State does not show that the law serves any "subordinating [state] interest which is compelling" or that it is "necessary . . . to the accomplishment of a permissible state policy." The State, at most, argues that there is some rational relation between this statute and what is admittedly a legitimate subject of state concern—the discouraging of extra-marital relations. It says that preventing the use of birth-control devices by married persons helps prevent the indulgence by some in such extra-marital relations. The rationality of this justification is dubious, particularly in light of the admitted widespread availability to all persons in the State of Connecticut, unmarried as well as married, of birth-control devices for the prevention of disease, as distin-

guished from the prevention of conception.* But, in any event, it is clear that the state interest in safeguarding marital fidelity can be served by a more discriminately tailored statute, which does not, like the present one, sweep unnecessarily broadly, reaching far beyond the evil sought to be dealt with and intruding upon the privacy of all married couples.* Here, as elsewhere, "[p]recision of regulation must be the touchstone in an area so closely touching our most precious freedoms." *NAACP* v. *Button*, 371 U.S. 415, 438. The State of Connecticut does have statutes, the constitutionality of which is beyond doubt, which prohibit adultery and fornication.* These statutes demonstrate that means for achieving the same basic purpose of protecting marital fidelity are available to Connecticut without the need to "invade the area of protected freedoms." *NAACP* v. *Alabama, supra,* at 307.*

Finally, it should be said of the Court's holding today that it in no way interferes with a State's proper regulation of sexual promiscuity or misconduct. As my Brother Harlan so well stated in his dissenting opinion in *Poe* v. *Ullman,*

"Adultery, homosexuality and the like are sexual intimacies which the State forbids . . . but the intimacy of husband and wife is necessarily an essential and accepted feature of the institution of marriage, an institution which the State not only must allow, but which always and in every age it has fostered and protected. It is one thing when the State exerts its power either to forbid extra-marital sexuality . . . or to say who may marry, but it is quite another when, having acknowledged a marriage and the intimacies inherent in it, it undertakes to regulate by means of the criminal law the details of that intimacy."

In sum, I believe that the right of privacy in the marital relation is fundamental and basic—a personal right "retained by the people" within the meaning of the Ninth Amendment. Connecticut cannot constitutionally abridge this fundamental right, which is protected by the Fourteenth Amendment from infringement by the States. I agree with the Court that petitioners' convictions must therefore be reversed . . .

Mr. Justice Black, with whom Mr. Justice Stewart joins, dissenting.

I agree with my Brother Stewart's dissenting opinion. And like him I do not to any extent whatever base my view that this Connecticut law is constitutional on a belief that the law is wise or that its policy is a good one. In order that there may be no room at all to doubt why I vote as I do, I feel constrained to add that the law is every bit as offensive to me as it is to my Brethren of the majority and my Brothers Harlan, White and Goldberg who, reciting reasons why it is offensive to them, hold it unconstitutional. There is no single one of the graphic and eloquent strictures and criticisms fired at the policy of this Connecticut law either by the Court's opinion or by those of my concurring Brethren

*Citation omitted [Eds.]

to which I cannot subscribe—except their conclusion that the evil qualities they see in the law make it unconstitutional . . .

The Court talks about a constitutional "right of privacy" as though there is some constitutional provision or provisions forbidding any law ever to be passed which might abridge the "privacy" of individuals. But there is not. There are, of course, guarantees in certain specific constitutional provisions which are designed in part to protect privacy at certain times and places with respect to certain activities. Such, for example, is the Fourth Amendment's guarantee against "unreasonable searches and seizures." But I think it belittles that Amendment to talk about it as though it protects nothing but "privacy." To treat it that way is to give it a niggardly interpretation, not the kind of liberal reading I think any Bill of Rights provision should be given. The average man would very likely not have his feelings soothed any more by having his property seized openly than by having it seized privately and by stealth. He simply wants his property left alone. And a person can be just as much, if not more, irritated, annoyed and injured by an unceremonious public arrest by a policeman as he is by a seizure in the privacy of his office or home.

One of the most effective ways of diluting or expanding a constitutionally guaranteed right is to substitute for the crucial word or words of a constitutional guarantee another word or words, more or less flexible and more or less restricted in meaning. This fact is well illustrated by the use of the term "right of privacy" as a comprehensive substitute for the Fourth Amendment's guarantee against "unreasonable searches and seizures." "Privacy" is a broad, abstract and ambiguous concept which can easily be shrunken in meaning but which can also, on the other hand, easily be interpreted as a constitutional ban against many things other than searches and seizures. I have expressed the view many times that First Amendment freedoms, for example, have suffered from a failure of the courts to stick to the simple language of the First Amendment in construing it, instead of invoking multitudes of words substituted for those the Framers used.* For these reasons I get nowhere in this case by talk about a constitutional "right of privacy" as an emanation from one or more constitutional provisions. I like my privacy as well as the next one, but I am nevertheless compelled to admit that government has a right to invade it unless prohibited by some specific constitutional provision. For these reasons I cannot agree with the Court's judgment and the reasons it gives for holding this Connecticut law unconstitutional . . .

The due process argument which my Brothers Harlan and White adopt here is based, as their opinions indicate, on the premise that this Court is vested with power to invalidate all state laws that it considers to be arbitrary, capricious, unreasonable, or oppressive, or on this Court's belief that a particular state law under scrutiny has no "rational or justifying" purpose, or is offensive to a "sense of fairness and justice." If these formulas based on "natural justice," or others which mean the same thing,[1] are to prevail, they require judges to determine what is or is not constitutional on the basis of their own appraisal of what laws are unwise or unnecessary. The power to make such decisions is of course that of a legislative body. Surely it has to be admitted that no provision of the Constitution specifically gives such blanket power to courts to exercise such a supervisory veto over the wisdom and value of legislative policies and to hold unconstitutional those laws which they believe unwise or dangerous. I readily admit that no legislative body, state or national, should pass laws that can justly be given any of the invidious labels invoked as constitutional excuses to strike down state laws. But perhaps it is not too much to say that no legislative body ever does pass laws without believing that they will accomplish a sane, rational, wise and justifiable purpose. While I completely subscribe to the holding of *Marbury* v. *Madison,* and subsequent cases, that our Court has constitutional power to strike down statutes, state or federal, that violate commands of the Federal Constitution, I do not believe that we are granted power by the Due Process Clause or any other constitutional provision or provisions to measure constitutionality by our belief that legislation is arbitrary, capricious or unreasonable, or accomplishes no justifiable purpose, or is offensive to our own notions of "civilized standards of conduct."[2] Such an appraisal of the wisdom of legislation is an attribute of the power to make laws, not of the power to interpret them. The use by federal courts of such a formula or doctrine or whatnot to veto federal or state laws simply takes away from Congress and States the power to make laws based on their own judgment of fairness and wisdom and transfers that power to this Court for ultimate determination—a power which was specifically denied to federal courts by the convention that framed the Constitution. . . .

My Brother Goldberg has adopted the recent discovery[3] that the Ninth Amendment as well as the Due Process Clause can be used by this Court as authority to strike down all state legislation which this Court thinks violates "fundamental principles of liberty and justice," or is contrary to the "traditions and [collective] conscience of our people." He also states, without proof satisfactory to me, that in making decisions on this basis judges will not consider "their personal and private notions." One may ask how they can avoid

*Citations omitted [Eds.]

considering them. Our Court certainly has no machinery with which to take a Gallup Poll.[4] And the scientific miracles of this age have not yet produced a gadget which the Court can use to determine what traditions are rooted in the "[collective] conscience of our people." Moreover, one would certainly have to look far beyond the language of the Ninth Amendment[5] to find that the Framers vested in this Court any such awesome veto powers over lawmaking, either by the States or by the Congress. Nor does anything in the history of the Amendment offer any support for such a shocking doctrine. The whole history of the adoption of the Constitution and Bill of Rights points the other way, and the very material quoted by my Brother Goldberg shows that the Ninth Amendment was intended to protect against the idea that "by enumerating particular exceptions to the grant of power" to the Federal Government, "those rights which were not singled out, were intended to be assigned into the hands of the General Government [the United States], and were consequently insecure."[6] That Amendment was passed, not to broaden the powers of this Court or any other department of "the General Government," but, as every student of history knows, to assure the people that the Constitution in all its provisions was intended to limit the Federal Government to the powers granted expressly or by necessary implication. If any broad, unlimited power to hold laws unconstitutional because they offend what this Court conceives to be the "[collective] conscience of our people" is vested in this Court by the Ninth Amendment, the Fourteenth Amendment, or any other provision of the Constitution, it was not given by the Framers, but rather has been bestowed on the Court by the Court. This fact is perhaps responsible for the peculiar phenomenon that for a period of a century and a half no serious suggestion was ever made that the Ninth Amendment, enacted to protect state powers against federal invasion, could be used as a weapon of federal power to prevent state legislatures from passing laws they consider appropriate to govern local affairs. Use of any such broad, unbounded judicial authority would make of this Court's members a day-to-day constitutional convention.

NOTES

1.   A collection of the catchwords and catch phrases invoked by judges who would strike down under the Fourteenth Amendment laws which offend their notions of natural justice would fill many pages. Thus it has been said that this Court can forbid state action which "shocks the conscience," *Rochin* v. *California,* 342 U.S. 165, 172, sufficiently to "shock itself into the protective arms of the Constitution," *Irvine* v. *California,* 347 U.S. 128, 138 (concurring opinion). It has been urged that States may not run counter to the "decencies of civilized conduct," *Rochin, supra,* at 173, or "some principle of justice so rooted in the traditions, and conscience of our people as to be ranked as fundamental," *Snyder* v. *Massachusetts,* 291 U.S. 97, 105, or to "those canons of decency and fairness which express the notions of justice of English-speaking peoples," *Malinski* v. *New York,* 324 U.S. 401, 417 (concurring opinion), or to "the community's sense of fair play and decency," *Rochin, supra,* at 173. It has been said that we must decide whether a state law is "fair, reasonable and appropriate," or is rather "an unreasonable, unnecessary and arbitrary interference with the right of the individual to his personal liberty or to enter into . . . contracts," *Lochner* v. *New York,* 198 U.S. 45, 56. States, under this philosophy, cannot act in conflict with "deeply rooted feelings of the community," *Haley* v. *Ohio,* 332 U.S. 596, 604 (separate opinion), or with "fundamental notions of fairness and justice," *id.,* 607. See also, e.g., *Wolf* v. *Colorado,* 338 U.S. 25, 27 ("rights . . . basic to our free society"); *Hebert* v. *Louisiana,* 272 U.S. 312, 316 ("fundamental principles of liberty and justice"); *Adkins* v. *Children's Hospital,* 261 U.S. 525, 561 ("arbitrary restraint of . . . liberties"); *Betts* v. *Brady,* 316 U.S. 455, 462 ("denial of fundamental fairness, shocking to the universal sense of justice"); *Poe* v. *Ullman,* 367 U.S. 497, 539 (dissenting opinion) ("intolerable and unjustifiable"). Perhaps the clearest, frankest and briefest explanation of how this due process approach works is the statement in another case handed down today that this Court is to invoke the Due Process Clause to strike down state procedures or laws which it can "not tolerate." *Linkletter* v. *Walker, post,* p. 618, at 631.

2.   See Hand, The Bill of Rights (1958) 70: "[J]udges are seldom content merely to annul the particular solution before them; they do not, indeed they may not, say that taking all things into consideration, the legislators' solution is too strong for the judicial stomach. On the contrary they wrap up their veto in a protective veil of adjectives such as 'arbitrary,' 'artificial,' 'normal,' 'reasonable,' 'inherent,' 'fundamental,' or 'essential,' whose office usually, though quite innocently, is to disguise what they are doing and impute to it a derivation far more impressive than their personal preferences, which are all that in fact lie behind the decision." [Citations omitted—Eds.]

3.   See Patterson, The Forgotten Ninth Amendment (1955). Mr. Patterson urges that the Ninth Amendment be used to protect unspecified "natural and inalienable rights." P. 4. The Introduction by Roscoe Pound states that "there is a marked revival of natural law ideas throughout the world. Interest in the Ninth Amendment is a symptom of that revival." P. iii.

4.   Of course one cannot be oblivious to the fact that Mr. Gallup has already published the results of a poll which he says show that 46% of the people in this country believe schools should teach about birth control. Washington Post, May 21, 1965, p. 2, col. 1. I can hardly believe, however, that Brother Goldberg would view 46% of the persons polled as so overwhelming a proportion that this Court may now rely on it to declare that the Connecticut law infringes "fundamental" rights, and overrule the long-standing view of the people of Connecticut expressed through their elected representatives.

5.   U.S. Const., Amend. IX, provides: "The enumeration in the Constitution, of certain rights, shall not be construed to deny or disparage others retained by the people."

6.   Annuals of Congress 439.

BOWERS v. HARDWICK

United States Supreme Court, 1986*

Justice WHITE delivered the opinion of the Court.

In August 1982, respondent was charged with violating the Georgia statute criminalizing sodomy[1] by committing that act with another adult male in the bedroom of respondent's home. After a preliminary hearing, the District Attorney decided not to present the matter to the grand jury unless further evidence developed.

Respondent then brought suit in the Federal District Court, challenging the constitutionality of the statute insofar as it criminalized consensual sodomy.[2] He asserted that he was a practicing homosexual, that the Georgia sodomy statute, as administered by the defendants, placed him in imminent danger of arrest, and that the statute for several reasons violates the Federal Constitution. The District Court granted the defendants' motion to dismiss for failure to state a claim, relying on *Doe* v. *Commonwealth's Attorney for the City of Richmond,* 403 F.Supp. 1199 (ED Va.1975), which this Court summarily affirmed, 425 U.S. 901, 96 S.Ct. 1489, 47 L.Ed.2d 751 (1976).

A divided panel of the Court of Appeals for the Eleventh Circuit reversed. . . . The court first held that, because *Doe* was distinguishable and in any event had been undermined by later decisions, our summary affirmance in that case did not require affirmance of the District Court. Relying on our decisions in *Griswold* v. *Connecticut,* . . . *Eisenstadt* v. *Baird,* . . . *Stanley* v. *Georgia,* . . . and *Roe* v. *Wade,* . . . the court went on to hold that the Georgia statute violated respondent's fundmental rights because his homosexual activity is a private and intimate association that is beyond the reach of state regulation by reason of the Ninth Amendment and the Due Process Clause of the Fourteenth Amendment. The case was remanded for trial, at which, to prevail, the State would have to prove that the statute is supported by a compelling interest and is the most narrowly drawn means of achieving that end.

Because other Courts of Appeals have arrived at judgments contrary to that of the Eleventh Circuit in this case,[3] we granted the State's petition for certiorari questioning the holding that its sodomy statute violates the fundmental rights of homosexuals. We agree with the State that the Court of Appeals erred, and hence reverse its judgment.[4]

This case does not require a judgment on whether laws against sodomy between consenting adults in general, or between homosexuals in particular, are wise or desirable. It raises no question about the right or propriety of state legislative decisions to repeal their laws that criminalize homosexual sodomy, or of state court decisions invalidating those laws on state constitutional grounds. The issue presented is whether the Federal Constitution confers a fundamental right upon homosexuals to engage in sodomy and hence invalidates the laws of the many States that still make such conduct illegal and have done so for a very long time. The case also calls for some judgment about the limits of the Court's role in carrying out its constitutional mandate.

We first register our disagreement with the Court of Appeals and with respondent that the Court's prior cases have construed the Constitution to confer a right of privacy that extends to homosexual sodomy and for all intents and purposes have decided this case. The reach of this line of cases was sketched in *Carey* v. *Population Services International,* . . . *Pierce* v. *Society of Sisters,* . . . and *Meyer* v. *Nebraska,* . . . were described as dealing with child rearing and education; *Prince* v. *Massachusetts,* . . . with family relationships; *Skinner* v. *Oklahoma ex xel. Williamson,* . . . with procreation; *Loving* v. *Virginia,* . . . with marriage; *Griswold* v. *Connecticut, supra,* and *Eisenstadt* v. *Baird, supra,* with contraception; and *Roe* v. *Wade,* . . . with abortion. The latter three cases were interpreted as construing the Due Process Clause of the Fourteenth Amendment to confer a fundamental individual right to decide whether or not to beget or bear a child. . . .

Accepting the decisions in these cases and the above description of them, we think it evident that none of the rights announced in those cases bears any resemblance to the claimed constitutional right of homosexuals to engage in acts of sodomy that is asserted in this case. No connection between family, marriage, or procreation on the one hand and homosexual activity on the other has been demonstrated, either by the Court of Appeals or by respondent. Moreover, any claim that these cases nevertheless stand for the proposition that any kind of private sexual conduct between consenting adults is constitutionally insulated from state proscription is unsupportable. Indeed, the Court's opinion in Carey twice asserted that the privacy right, which the *Griswold* line of cases found to be one of the protections provided by the Due Process Clause, did not reach so far. . . .

Precedent aside, however, respondent would have us announce, as the Court of Appeals did, a fundamental right to engage in homosexual sodomy. This we are quite unwilling to do. It is true that despite the language of the Due Process Clauses of the Fifth and Fourteenth Amendments, which appears to focus only on the processes by which life, liberty, or property is taken, the cases are legion in which those Clauses have been interpreted to have substantive content, subsuming rights that to a great extent are immune from federal or state regulation or proscription. Among such cases are those recognizing rights that have little or no textual support in the constitutional language. *Meyer, Prince,* and *Pierce* fall in this category, as do the privacy cases from *Griswold* to *Carey.*

Striving to assure itself and the public that announcing rights not readily identifiable in the Constitution's text involves much more than the imposition of the Justices' own choice of values on the States and the Federal government, the Court has sought to identify the nature of the rights qualifying for heightened judicial protection. In *Palko* v. *Connecticut,* . . . it was said that this category includes those fundamental liberties that are "implicit in the concept of ordered liberty," such that "neither liberty nor justice would exist if [they] were sacrificed." A different description of fundamental liberties appeared in *Moore* v. *East Cleveland,* . . . (opinion of POWELL, J.), where they are characterized as those liberties that are "deeply rooted in this Nation's history and tradition." . . .

It is obvious to us that neither of these formulations would extend a fundamental right to homosexuals to engage in acts of consensual sodomy. Proscriptions against that conduct have ancient roots. See generally, Survey on the Constitutional Right to Privacy in the Context of Homosexual Activity, 40 U.Miami L.Rev. 521, 525 (1986). Sodomy was a criminal offense at common law and was forbidden by the laws of the original thirteen States when they ratified the Bill of Rights.[5] In 1868, when the Fourteenth Amendment was ratified, all but 5 of the 37 States in the Union had criminal sodomy laws.[6] In fact, until 1961,[7] all 50 States outlawed sodomy, and today, 24 States and the District of Columbia continue to provide criminal penalties for sodomy performed in private and between consent-

ing adults. Survey, U.Miami L.Rev., *supra,* at 524, n. 9. Against this background, to claim that a right to engage in such conduct is "deeply rooted in this Nation's history and tradition" or "implicit in the concept of ordered liberty" is, at best, facetious.

Nor are we inclined to take a more expansive view of our authority to discover new fundamental rights imbedded in the Due Process Clause. The Court is most vulnerable and comes nearest to illegitimacy when it deals with judge-made constitutional law having little or no cognizable roots in the language or design of the Constitution. That this is so was painfully demostrated by the face-off between the Executive and the Court in the 1930s, which resulted in the repudiation of much of the substantive gloss that the Court had placed on the Due Process Clause of the Fifth and Fourteenth Amendments. There should be, therefore, great resistance to expand the substantive reach of those Clauses, particularly if it requires redefining the category of rights deemed to be fundamental. Otherwise, the Judiciary necessarily takes to itself further authority to govern the country without express constitutional authority. The claimed right pressed on us today falls far short of overcoming this resistance.

Respondent, however, asserts that the result should be different where the homosexual conduct occurs in the privacy of the home. He relies on *Stanley* v. *Georgia,* . . . where the Court held that the First Amendment prevents conviction for possessing and reading obscene material in the privacy of his home: "If the First Amendment means anything, it means that a State has no business telling a man, sitting alone in his house, what books he may read or what films he may watch." . . .

Stanley did protect conduct that would not have been protected outside the home, and it partially prevented the enforcement of state obscenity laws; but the decision was firmly grounded in the First Amendment. The right pressed upon us here has no similar support in the text of the Constitution, and it does not qualify for recognition under the prevailing principles for construing the Fourteenth Amendment. Its limits are also difficult to discern. Plainly enough, otherwise illegal conduct is not always immunized whenever it occurs in the home. Victimless crimes, such as the possession and use of illegal drugs do not escape the law where they are committed at home. *Stanley* itself recognized that its holding offered no protection for the possession in the home of drugs, firearms, or stolen goods. *Id.,* at 568, n. 11, 89 S.Ct., at 1249, n. 11. And if respondent's submission is limited to the voluntary sexual conduct between consenting adults, it would be difficult, except by fiat, to limit the claimed right to homosexual conduct while leaving exposed to prosecution adultery, incest, and other sexual crimes even though they are committed in the home. We are unwilling to start down that road.

Even if the conduct at issue here is not a fundamental right, respondent asserts that there must be a rational basis for the law and that there is none in this case other than the presumed belief of a majority of the electorate in Georgia that homosexual sodomy is immoral and unacceptable. This is said to be an inadequate rationale to support the law. The law, however, is constantly based on notions of morality, and if all laws representing essentially moral choices are to be invalidated under the Due Process Clause, the courts will be very busy indeed. Even respondent makes no such claim, but insists that majority sentiments about the morality of homosexuality should be declared inadequate. We do not agree, and are unpersuaded that the sodomy laws of some 25 States should be invalidated on this basis.[8]

Accordingly, the judgment of the Court of Appeals is

Reversed.

Chief Justice BURGER, concurring.

I join the Court's opinion, but I write separately to underscore my view that in constitutional terms there is no such thing as a fundamental right to commit homosexual sodomy.

As the Court notes, *ante* at —, the proscriptions against sodomy have very "ancient roots." Decisions of individuals relating to homosexual conduct have been subject to state intervention throughout the history of Western Civilization. Condemnation of those practices is firmly rooted in Judaeo-Christian moral and ethical standards. Homosexual sodomy was a capital crime under Roman law. See Code Theod. 9.7.6; Code Just. 9.9.31. See also D. Bailey, Homosexuality in the Western Christian Tradition 70–81 (1975). During the English Reformation when powers of the ecclesiastical courts were transferred to the King's Courts, the first English statute criminalizing sodomy was passed. 25 Hen. VIII, c. 6. Blackstone described "the infamous crime against nature" as an offense of "deeper malignity" than rape, an heinous act "the very mention of which is a disgrace to human nature," and "a crime not fit to be named." Blackstone's Commentaries *215. The common law of England, including its prohibition of sodomy, became the received law of Georgia and the other Colonies. In 1816 the Georgia Legislature passed the statute at issue here, and that statute has been continuously in force in one form or another since that time. To hold that the act of homosexual sodomy is some-

how protected as a fundamental right would be to cast aside millennia of moral teaching.

This is essentially not a question of personal "preferences" but rather of the legislative authority of the State. I find nothing in the Constitution depriving a State of the power to enact the statute challenged here.

Justice POWELL, concurring.

I join the opinion of the Court. I agree with the Court that there is no fundamental right—*i.e.,* no substantive right under the Due Process Clause— such as that claimed by respondent, and found to exist by the Court of Appeals. This is not to suggest, however, that respondent may not be protected by the Eighth Amendment of the Constitution. The Georgia statute at issue in this case, Ga.Code Ann. § 16–6–2, authorizes a court to imprison a person for up to 20 years for a single private, consensual act of sodomy. In my view, a prison sentence for such conduct—certainly a sentence of long duration—would create a serious Eighth Amendment issue. Under the Georgia statute a single act of sodomy, even in the private setting of a home, is a felony comparable in terms of the possible sentence imposed to serious felonies such as aggravated battery, § 16–5–24, first degree arson, § 16–7–60 and robbery, § 16–8–40.[9]

In this case, however, respondent has not been tried, much less convicted and sentenced.[10] Moreover, respondent has not raised the Eighth Amendment issue below. For these reasons this constitutional argument is not before us.

Justice BLACKMUN, with whom Justice BRENNAN, Justice MARSHALL, and Justice STEVENS join, dissenting.

This case is no more about "a fundamental right to engage in homosexual sodomy," as the Court purports to declare, . . . than *Stanley* v. *Georgia,* . . . was about a fundamental right to watch obscene movies, or *Katz* v. *United States,* . . . was about a fundamental right to place interstate bets from a telephone booth. Rather, this case is about "the most comprehensive of rights and the right most valued by civilized men," namely, "the right to be let alone." *Olmstead* v. *United States,* 277 U.S. 438, 478, 48 S.Ct. 564, 572, 72 L.Ed. 944 (1928) (Brandeis, J., dissenting).

The statute at issue, Ga.Code Ann. § 16–6–2, denies individuals the right to decide for themselves whether to engage in particular forms of private, consensual sexual activity. The Court concludes that § 16–6–2 is valid essentially because "the laws of . . . many States . . . still make such conduct illegal and have done so for a very long time." . . . But the fact that the moral judgments expressed by statutes like § 16–6–2 may be "natural and familiar . . . ought not to conclude our judgment upon the question whether statutes embodying them conflict with the Constitution of the United States." *Roe* v. *Wade*, . . . quoting *Lochner* v. *New York*, . . . (Holmes, J., dissenting). Like Justice Holmes, I believe that "[i]t is revolting to have no better reason for a rule of law than that so it was laid down in the time of Henry IV. It is still more revolting if the grounds upon which it was laid down have vanished long since, and the rule simply persists from blind imitation of the past." Holmes, The Path of the Law, 10 Harv.L.Rev. 457, 469 (1897). I believe we must analyze respondent's claim in the light of the values that underlie the constitutional right to privacy. If that right means anything, it means that, before Georgia can prosecute its citizens for making choices about the most intimate aspects of their lives, it must do more than assert that the choice they have made is an " 'abominable crime not fit to be named among Christians,' " . . .

I

In its haste to reverse the Court of Appeals and hold that the Constitution does not confe[r] a fundamental right upon homosexuals to engage in sodomy," *ante*, at 2843, the Court relegates the actual statute being challenged to a footnote and ignores the procedural posture of the case before it. A fair reading of the statute and of the complaint clearly reveals that the majority has distorted the question this case presents.

First, the Court's almost obsessive focus on homosexual activity is particularly hard to justify in light of the broad language Georgia has used. Unlike the Court, the Georgia Legislature has not proceeded on the assumption that homosexuals are so different from other citizens that their lives may be controlled in a way that would not be tolerated if it limited the choices of those other citizens. . . . Rather, Georgia has provided that "[a] person commits the offense of sodomy when he performs or submits to any sexual act involving the sex organs of one person and the mouth or anus of another." Ga.Code Ann. § 16–6–2(a). The sex or status of the persons who engage in the act is irrelevant as a matter of state law. In fact, to the extent I can discern a legislative purpose for Georgia's 1968 enactment of § 16–6–2, that purpose seems to have been to broadened the coverage of the law to reach heterosexual as well as homosexual activity.[11] I therefore see no basis for the Court's decision to treat this case as an "as applied" challenge to § 16–6–2, . . . or for Georgia's attempt, both in

its brief and at oral argument, to defend § 16–6–2 solely on the grounds that it prohibits homosexual activity. Michael Hardwick's standing may rest in significant part on Georgia's apparent willingness to enforce against homosexuals a law it seems not to have any desire to enforce against heterosexuals. . . . But his claim that § 16–6–2 involves an unconstitutional intrusion into his privacy and his right of intimate association does not depend in any way on his sexual orientation.

Second, I disagree with the Court's refusal to consider whether § 16–6–2 runs afoul of the Eighth or Ninth Amendments or the Equal Protection Clause of the Fourteenth Amendment. . . . Respondent's complaint expressly invoked the Ninth Amendment, see App. 6, and he relied heavily before this Court on *Griswold* v. *Connecticut*, . . . which identifies that Amendment as one of the specific constitutional provisions giving "life and substance" to our understanding of privacy. . . . More importantly, the procedural posture of the case requires that we affirm the Court of Appeals' judgment if there is *any* ground on which respondent may be entitled to relief. This case is before us on petitioner's motion to dismiss for failure to state a claim. . . . It is a well-settled principle of law that "a complaint should not be dismissed merely because a plaintiff's allegations do not support the particular legal theory he advances, for the court is under a duty to examine the complaint to determine if the allegations provide for relief on any possible theory." . . . Thus, even if respondent did not advance claims based on the Eighth or Ninth Amendments, or on the Equal Protection Clause, his complaint should not be dismissed if any of those provisions could entitle him to relief. I need not reach either the Eighth Amendment or the Equal Protection Clause issues because I believe that Hardwick has stated a cognizable claim that § 16–6–2 interferes with constitutionally protected interests in privacy and freedom of intimate association. But neither the Eighth Amendment nor the Equal Protection Clause is so clearly irrelevant that a claim resting on either provision should be peremptorily dismissed.[12] The Court's cramped reading of the issue before it makes for a short opinion, but it does little to make for a persuasive one.

II

"Our cases long have recognized that the Constitution embodies a promise that a certain private sphere of individual liberty will be kept largely beyond the reach of government." *Thornburgh* v. *American Coll. of Obst. & Gyn.*, . . . In construing the right to privacy, the Court has proceeded along two somewhat distinct, albeit complementary, lines. First, it has recognized a privacy interest with reference to certain *decisions* that are properly for the individual to make. . . . Second, it has recognized a privacy interest with reference to certain *places* without regard for the particular activities in which the individuals who occupy them are engaged. . . . The case before us implicates both the decisional and the spatial aspects of the right to privacy.

A

The Court concludes today that none of our prior cases dealing with various decisions that individuals are entitled to make free of governmental interference "bears any resemblance to the claimed constitutional right of homosexuals to engage in acts of sodomy that is asserted in this case." . . . While it is true that these cases may be characterized by their connection to protection of the family, . . . the Court's conclusion that they extend no further than this boundary ignores the warning in *Moore* v. *East Cleveland,* . . . against "clos[ing] our eyes to the basic reasons why certain rights associated with the family have been accorded shelter under the Fourteenth Amendment's Due Process Clause." We protect those rights not because they contribute, in some direct and material way, to the general public welfare, but because they form so central a part of an individual's life. "[T]he concept of privacy embodies the 'moral fact that a person belongs to himself and not others nor to society as a whole)' " . . . And so we protect the decision whether to marry precisely because marriage "is an association that promotes a way of life, not causes; a harmony in living, not political faiths; a bilateral loyalty, not commercial or social projects." *Griswold* v. *Connecticut.* . . . We protect the decision whether to have a child because parenthood alters so dramatically an individual's self-definition, not because of demographic considerations or the Bible's command to be fruitful and multiply. Cf. *Thornburgh* v. *American Coll. of Obst. & Gyn., supra,* — U.S., at —,n. 6, 106 S.Ct., at 2188, n. 6 (STEVENS, J., concurring). And we protect the family because it contributes so powerfully to the happiness of individuals, not because of a preference for stereotypical households. . . . The Court recognized in *Roberts* . . . that (the "ability independently to define one's identity that is central to any concept of liberty" cannot truly be exercised in a vacuum; we all depend on the "emotional enrichment of close ties with others." . . .

Only the most willful blindness could obscure the fact that sexual intimacy is "a sensitive, key relationship of human existence, central to family life, com-munity welfare, and the development of human personality," . . . The fact that individuals define themselves in a significant way through their intimate sexual relationships with others suggests, in a Nation as diverse as ours, that there may be many "right" ways of conducting those relationships, and that much of the richness of a relationship will come from the freedom an individual has to *choose* the form and nature of these intensely personal bonds. See Karst, The Freedom of Intimate Association, 89 Yale L.J. 624, 637 (1980) . . .

In a variety of circumstances we have recognized that a necessary corollary of giving individuals freedom to choose how to conduct their lives is acceptance of the fact that different individuals will make different choices. For example, in holding that the clearly important state interest in public education should give way to a competing claim by the Amish to the effect that extended formal schooling threatened their way of life, the Court declared: "There can be no assumption that today's majority is 'right' and the Amish and others like them are 'wrong.' A way of life that is odd or even erratic but interferes with no rights or interests of others is not to be condemned because it is different." *Wisconsin* v. *Yoder,* . . . The Court claims that its decision today merely refuses to recognize a fundamental right to engage in homosexual sodomy; what the Court really has refused to recognize is the fundamental interest all individuals have in controlling the nature of their intimate associations with others.

B

The behavior for which Hardwick faces prosecution occurred in his own home, a place to which the Fourth Amendment attaches special significance. The Court's treatment of this aspect of the case is symptomatic of its overall refusal to consider the broad principles that have informed our treatment of privacy in specific cases. Just as the right to privacy is more than the mere aggregation of a number of entitlements to engage in specific behavior, so too, protecting the physical integrity of the home is more than merely a means of protecting specific activities that often take place there. Even when our understanding of the contours of the right to privacy depends on "reference to a 'place,' " . . . "the essence of a Fourth Amendment violation is 'not the breaking of [a person's] doors, and the rummaging of his drawers,' but rather is 'the invasion of his indefeasible right of personal security, personal liberty and private property.' " . . .

The Court's interpretation of the pivotal case of *Stanley* v. *Georgia,* . . . is entirely unconvincing.

Stanley held that Georgia's undoubted power to punish the public distribution of constitutionally unprotected, obscene material did not permit the State to punish the private possession of such material. According to the majority here, *Stanley* relied entirely on the First Amendment, and thus, it is claimed, sheds no light on cases not involving printed materials. . . . But that is not what *Stanley* said. Rather, the *Stanley* Court anchored its holding in the Fourth Amendment's special protection for the individual in his home:

" 'The makers of our Constitution undertook to secure conditions favorable to the pursuit of happiness. They recognized the significance of man's spiritual nature, of his feelings and of his intellect. They knew that only a part of the pain, pleasure and satisfactions of life are to be found in material things. They sought to protect Americans in their beliefs, their thoughts, their emotions and their sensations.'

"These are the rights that appellant is asserting in the case before us. He is asserting the right to read or observe what he pleases—the right to satisfy his intellectual and emotional needs in the privacy of his own home." . . .

The central place that *Stanley* gives Justice Brandeis' dissent in *Olmstead*, a case raising *no* First Amendment claim, shows that *Stanley* rested as much on the Court's understanding of the Fourth Amendment as it did on the First. Indeed, in *Paris Adult Theatre I* v. *Slaton*, . . . suggested that reliance on the Fourth Amendment not only supported the Court's outcome in *Stanley* but actually was *necessary* to it: "If obscene material unprotected by the First Amendment in itself carried with it a 'penumbra' of constitutionally protected privacy, this Court would not have found it necessary to decide *Stanley* on the narrow basis of the 'privacy of the home,' which was hardly more than a reaffirmation that 'a man's home is his castle.' " . . . "The right of the people to be secure in their . . . houses," expressly guaranteed by the Fourth Amendment, is perhaps the most "textual" of the various constitutional provisions that inform our understanding of the right to privacy, and thus I cannot agree with the Court's statement that "[t]he right pressed upon us here has no . . . support in the text of the Constitution," . . . Indeed, the right of an individual to conduct intimate relationships in the intimacy of his or her own home seems to me to be the heart of the Constitution's protection of privacy.

III

The Court's failure to comprehend the magnitude of the liberty interests at stake in this case leads it to slight the question whether petitioner, on behalf of the State, has justified Georgia's infringement on these interests. I believe that neither of the two general justifications for § 16–6–2 that . . . advanced warrants dismissing resp . . . lenge for failure to state a claim.

First, petitioner asserts that the acts . . . by the statute may have serious a . . . quences for "the general public health . . . such as spreading communicable dise. . . ing other criminal activity. . . . Inasmuch as this case was dismissed by the District Court on the pleadings, it is not surprising that the record before us is barren of any evidence to support petitioner's claim.[13] In light of the state of the record, I see no justification for the Court's attempt to equate the private, consensual sexual activity at issue here with the "possession in the home of drugs, firearms, or stolen goods," . . . to which *Stanley* refused to extend its protection. . . . None of the behavior so mentioned in *Stanley* can properly be viewed as "[v]ictimless," . . . drugs and weapons are inherently dangerous, . . . and for property to be "stolen," someone must have been wrongfully deprived of it. Nothing in the record before the Court provides any justification for finding the activity forbidden by § 16–6–2 to be physically dangerous, either to the persons engaged in it or to others.[14]

The core of petitioner's defense of § 16–6–2, however, is that respondent and others who engage in the conduct prohibited by § 16–6–2 interfere with Georgia's exercise of the " 'right of the Nation and of the States to maintain a decent society,' " . . . Essentially, petitioner argues, and the Court agrees, that the fact that the acts described in § 16–6–2 "for hundreds of years, if not thousands, have been uniformly condemned as immoral" is a sufficient reason to permit a State to ban them today. . . .

I cannot agree that either the length of time a majority has held its convictions or the passions with which it defends them can withdraw legislation from this Court's scrutiny. . . . As Justice Jackson wrote so eloquently for the Court in *West Virginia Board of Education* v. *Barnette*, . . . "we apply the limitations of the Constitution with no fear that freedom to be intellectually and spiritually diverse or even contrary will disintegrate the social organization. . . . [F]reedom to differ is not limited to things that do not matter much. That would be a mere shadow of freedom. The test of its substance is the right to differ as to things that touch the heart of the existing order." See also Karst, 89 Yale L.J., at 627. It is precisely because the issue raised by this case touches the heart of what makes individuals what they are that we should be especially sensitive to the rights of those whose choices upset the majority.

The assertion that "traditional Judeo-Christian values proscribe" the conduct involved, Brief for

ioner 20, cannot provide an adequate justifica-
on for § 16–6–2. That certain, but by no means all,
religious groups condemn the behavior at issue gives
the State no license to impose their judgments on the
entire citizenry. The legitimacy of secular legislation
depends instead on whether the State can advance
some justification for its law beyond its conformity
to religious doctrine. . . . Thus, far from buttressing
his case, petitioner's invocation of Leviticus, Romans, St. Thomas Aquinas, and sodomy's heretical
status during the Middle Ages undermines his suggestion that § 16–6–2 represents a legitimate use of
secular coercive power.[15] A State can no more punish
private behavior because of religious intolerance
than it can punish such behavior because of racial
animus. "The Constitution cannot control such prejudices, but neither can it tolerate them. Private biases
may be outside the reach of the law, but the law
cannot, directly or indirectly give them effect." . . .
No matter how uncomfortable a certain group may
make the majority of this Court, we have held that
"[m]ere public intolerance or animosity cannot constitutionally justify the deprivation of a person's
physical liberty." . . .

Nor can § 16–6–2 be justified as a "morally neutral" exercise of Georgia's power to "protect the
public environment," . . . Certainly, some private
behavior can affect the fabric of society as a whole.
Reasonable people may differ about whether particular sexual acts are moral or immoral, but "we have
ample evidence for believing that people will not
abandon morality, will not think any better of murder, cruelty and dishonesty, merely because some
private sexual practice which they abominate is not
punished by the law." H.L.A. Hart, Immorality and
Treason, reprinted in The Law as Literature 220, 225
(L. Blom-Cooper ed. 1961). Petitioner and the Court
fail to see the difference between laws that protect
public sensibilities and those that enforce private
morality. Statutes banning public sexual activity are
entirely consistent with protecting the individual's
liberty interest in decisions concerning sexual relations: the same recognition that those decisions are
intensely private which justifies protecting them
from governmental interference can justify protecting individuals from unwilling exposure to the sexual
activities of others. But the mere fact that intimate
behavior may be punished when it takes place in
public cannot dictate how States can regulate intimate behavior that occurs in intimate places. See
Paris Adult Theatre I, . . . ("marital intercourse on
a street corner or a theater stage" can be forbidden
despite the constitutional protection identified in
Griswold v. *Connecticut,* . . . [16]

This case involves no real interference with the
rights of others, for the mere knowledge that other
individuals do not adhere to one's value system cannot be a legally cognizable interest, . . . let alone an
interest that can justify invading the houses, hearts,
and minds of citizens who choose to live their lives
differently.

IV

It took but three years for the Court to see the error
in its analysis in *Minersville School District* v. *Gobitis* . . . and to recognize that the threat to national
cohesion posed by a refusal to salute the flag was
vastly outweighed by the threat to those same values
posed by compelling such a salute. . . . I can only
hope that here, too, the Court soon will reconsider
its analysis and conclude that depriving individuals
of the right to choose for themselves how to conduct
their intimate relationships poses a far greater threat
to the values most deeply rooted in our Nation's
history than tolerance of nonconformity could ever
do. Because I think the Court today betrays those
values, I dissent.

Justice STEVENS, with whom Justice BREN-
NAN and Justice MARSHALL join, dissenting.

Like the statute that is challenged in this case,[17]
the rationale of the Court's opinion applies equally
to the prohibited conduct regardless of whether the
parties who engage in it are married or unmarried, or
are of the same or different sexes.[18] Sodomy was
condemned as an odious and sinful type of behavior
during the formative period of the common law.[19]
That condemnation was equally damning for heterosexual and homosexual sodomy.[20] Moreover, it provided no special exemption for married couples.[21]
The license to cohabit and to produce legitimate
offspring simply did not include any permission to
engage in sexual conduct that was considered a
"crime against nature."

The history of the Georgia statute before us clearly
reveals this traditional prohibition of heterosexual,
as well as homosexual, sodomy.[22] Indeed, at one
point in the 20th century, Georgia's law was construed to permit certain sexual conduct between homosexual women even though such conduct was
prohibited between heterosexuals.[23] The history of
the statutes cited by the majority as proof for the
proposition that sodomy is not constitutionally protected, . . . similarly reveals a prohibition on heterosexual, as well as homosexual, sodomy.[24]

Because the Georgia statute expresses the traditional view that sodomy is an immoral kind of conduct regardless of the identity of the persons who

engage in it, I believe that a proper analysis of its constitutionality requires consideration of two questions: First, may a State totally prohibit the described conduct by means of a neutral law applying without exception to all persons subject to its jurisdiction? If not, may the State save the statute by announcing that it will only enforce the law against homosexuals? The two questions merit separate discussion.

I

Our prior cases make two propositions abundantly clear. First, the fact that the governing majority in a State has traditionally viewed a particular practice as immoral is not a sufficient reason for upholding a law prohibiting the practice; neither history nor tradition could save a law prohibiting miscegenation from constitutional attack.[25] Second, individual decisions by married persons, concerning the intimacies of their physical relationship, even when not intended to produce offspring, are a form of "liberty" protected by the Due Process Clause of the Fourteenth Amendment. *Griswold* v. *Connecticut.* . . . Moreover, this protection extends to intimate choices by unmarried as well as married persons. . . .

In consideration of claims of this kind, the Court has emphasized the individual interest in privacy, but its decisions have actually been animated by an even more fundamental concern. As I wrote some years ago:

"These cases do not deal with the individual's interest in protection from unwarranted public attention, comment, or exploitation. They deal, rather, with the individual's right to make certain unusually important decisions that will affect his own, or his family's, destiny. The Court has referred to such decisions as implicating 'basic values,' as being 'fundamental,' and as being dignified by history and tradition. The character of the Court's language in these cases brings to mind the origins of the American heritage of freedom—the abiding interest in individual liberty that makes certain state intrusions on the citizen's right to decide how he will live his own life intolerable. Guided by history, our tradition of respect for the dignity of individual choice in matters of conscience and the restraints implicit in the federal system, federal judges have accepted the responsibility for recognition and protection of these rights in appropriate cases." . . .

Society has every right to encourage its individual members to follow particular traditions in expressing affection for one another and in gratifying their personal desires. It, of course, may prohibit an individual from imposing his will on another to satisfy his own selfish interests. It also may prevent an individual from interfering with, or violating, a legally sanctioned and protected relationship, such as marriage. And it may explain the relative advantages and disadvantages of different forms of intimate expres-

sion. But when individual married couples are isolated from observation by others, the way in which they voluntarily choose to conduct their intimate relations is a matter for them—not the State—to decide.[26] The essential "liberty" that animated the development of the law in cases like *Griswold,* *Eisenstadt,* and *Carey* surely embraces the right to engage in nonreproductive, sexual conduct that others may consider offensive or immoral.

Paradoxical as it may seem, our prior cases thus establish that a State may not prohibit sodomy within "the sacred precincts of marital bedrooms," *Griswold,* . . . or, indeed, between unmarried heterosexual adults. *Eisenstadt.* . . . In all events, it is perfectly clear that the State of Georgia may not totally prohibit the conduct proscribed by § 16–6–2 of the Georgia Criminal Code.

II

If the Georgia statute cannot be enforced as it is written—if the conduct it seeks to prohibit is a protected form of liberty for the vast majority of Georgia's citizens—the State must assume the burden of justifying a selective application of its law. Either the persons to whom Georgia seeks to apply its statute do not have the same interest in "liberty" that others have, or there must be a reason why the State may be permitted to apply a generally applicable law to certain persons that it does not apply to others.

The first possibility is plainly unacceptable. Although the meaning of the principle that "all men are created equal" is not always clear, it surely must mean that every free citizen has the same interest in "liberty" that the members of the majority share. From the standpoint of the individual, the homosexual and the heterosexual have the same interest in deciding how he will live his own life, and, more narrowly, how he will conduct himself in his personal and voluntary associations with his companions. State intrusion into the private conduct of either is equally burdensome.

The second possibility is similarly unacceptable. A policy of selective application must be supported by a neutral and legitimate interest—something more substantial than a habitual dislike for, or ignorance about, the disfavored group. Neither the State nor the Court has identified any such interest in this case. The Court has posited as a justification for the Georgia statute "the presumed belief of a majority of the electorate in Georgia that homosexual sodomy is immoral and unacceptable." . . . But the Georgia electorate has expressed no such belief—instead, its representatives enacted a law that presumably reflects the belief that *all sodomy* is immoral and unacceptable. Unless the Court is prepared to conclude that such a law is constitutional, it may not rely on the work product of the Georgia Legislature to support its holding. For the Georgia statute does not single out homosexuals as a separate class meriting special disfavored treatment.

Nor, indeed, does the Georgia prosecutor even believe that all homosexuals who violate this statute should be punished. This conclusion is evident from the fact that the respondent in this very case has formally acknowledged in his complaint and in court that he has engaged, and intends to continue to engage, in the prohibited conduct, yet the State has elected not to process criminal charges against him. As Justice POWELL points out, moreover, Georgia's prohibition on private, consensual sodomy has not been enforced for decades.[27] The record of nonenforcement, in this case and in the last several decades, belies the Attorney General's representations about the importance of the State's selective application of its generally applicable law.[28]

Both the Georgia statute and the Georgia prosecutor thus completely fail to provide the Court with any support for the conclusion that homosexual sodomy, *simpliciter,* is considered unacceptable conduct in that State, and that the burden of justifying a selective application of the generally applicable law has been met.

III

The Court orders the dismissal of respondent's complaint even though the State's statute prohibits all sodomy; even though that prohibition is concededly unconstitutional with respect to heterosexuals; and even though the State's *post hoc* explanations for selective application are belied by the State's own actions. At the very least, I think it clear at this early stage of the litigation that respondent has alleged a constitutional claim sufficient to withstand a motion to dismiss.[29]

I respectfully dissent.

NOTES

1. Ga.Code Ann. § 16–6–2 (1984) provides, in pertinent part, as follows:

"(a) A person commits the offense of sodomy when he performs or submits to any sexual act involving the sex organs of one person and the mouth or anus of another. . . .

"(b) A person convicted of the offense of sodomy shall be punished by imprisonment for not less than one nor more than 20 years. . . . "

2. John and Mary Doe were also plaintiffs in the action. They alleged that they wished to engage in sexual activity proscribed by § 16–6–2 in the privacy of their home, App. 3,

and that they had been "chilled and deterred" from engaging in such activity by both the existence of the statute and Hardwick's arrest. *Id.,* at 5. The District Court held, however, that because they had neither sustained, nor were in immediate danger of sustaining, any direct injury from the enforcement of the statute, they did not have proper standing to maintain the action. *Id.,* at 18. The Court of Appeals affirmed the District Court's judgment dismissing the Does' claim for lack of standing. 760 F.2d 1202, 1206–1207 (1985), and the Does do not challenge that holding in this Court.

The only claim properly before the Court, therefore, is Hardwick's challenge to the Georgia statute as applied to consensual homosexual sodomy. We express no opinion on the constitutionality of the Georgia statute as applied to other acts of sodomy.

3. See *Baker* v. *Wade,* 769 F.2d 289, reh'g denied, 774 F.2d 1285 (CA5 1985) (en banc). *Dronenburg* v. *Zech,* 239 U.S.App.D.C. 229, 741 F.2d 1388, reh'g denied, 241 U.S.App.D.C. 262, 746 F.2d 1579 (1984).

4. The State also submits that the Court of Appeals erred in holding that the District Court was not obligated to follow our summary affirmance in *Doe.* We need not resolve this dispute, for we prefer to give plenary consideration to the merits of this case rather than rely on our earlier action in *Doe.* See *Usery* v. *Turner Elkhorn Mining Co.,* 428 U.S. 1, 14, 96 S.Ct. 2882, 2891, 49 L.Ed.2d 752 (1976); *Massachusetts Board of Retirement* v. *Murgia,* 427 U.S. 307, 309, n. 1, 96 S.Ct. 2562, 2565, n. 1, 49 L.Ed.2d 520 (1976); *Edelman* v. *Jordan,* 415 U.S. 651, 671, 94 S.Ct. 1347, 1359, 39 L.Ed.2d 662 (1974). Cf. *Hicks* v. *Miranda,* 422 U.S. 332, 344, 95 S.Ct. 2281, 2289, 45 L.Ed.2d 223 (1975).

5. Criminal sodomy laws in effect in 1791:
Connecticut: Public Statute Laws of the State of Connecticut, 1808, Title LXVI, Ch. 1, § 2 (rev. 1672).
Delaware: 1 Laws of the State of Delaware, 1797, ch. 22, § 5 (passed 1719).
Georgia had no criminal sodomy statute until 1816, but sodomy was a crime at common law, and the General Assembly adopted the Common Law of England as the law of Georgia in 1784. The First Laws of the State of Georgia, pt. 1 (1981).
Maryland had no criminal sodomy statute in 1791. Maryland's Declaration of Rights, passed in 1776, however, stated that "the inhabitants of Maryland are entitled to the common law of England," and sodomy was a crime at common law. 4 Sources and Documents of United States Constitutions 372 (W. Swindler ed. 1975).
Massachusetts: Acts and Laws passed by the General Court of Massachusetts, ch. 14, Act of March 3, 1785.
New Hampshire passed its first sodomy statute in 1718. Acts and Laws of New Hampshire 1680–1726, p. 141 (1978).
Sodomy was a crime at common law in New Jersey at the time of the ratification of the Bill of Rights. The State enacted its first criminal sodomy law five years later. Acts of the Twentieth General Assembly, March 18, 1796, Ch. DC, § 7, p. 93.
New York: Laws of New York, ch. 21, p. 391 (passed 1787).
At the time of ratification of the Bill of Rights, North Carolina had adopted the English statute of Henry III outlawing sodomy. See Collection of the Statutes of the Parliament of England in Force in the State of North Carolina 314 (1792).
Pennsylvania: Laws of the Fourteenth General Assembly of the Commonwealth of Pennsylvania, ch. CLIV, § 2, p. 293 (passed 1790).
Rhode Island passed its first sodomy law in 1662. The Earliest Acts and Laws of the Colony of Rhode Island and Providence Plantations 1647–1719 142 (1977).

South Carolina: Public Laws of the State of South Carolina, p. 49 (1790).

At the time of the ratification of the Bill of Rights, Virginia had no specific statute outlawing sodomy, but had adopted the English common law. 9 Hening's Laws of Virginia, ch. 5, § 6, p. 127 (1821) (passed 1776).

6. Criminal sodomy statutes in effect in 1868:

Alabama: Ala.Code, § 3604 (1867).
Arizona (Terr.): Howell Code, ch. 10, § 48 (1865).
Arkansas: Ark.Stat., ch. 51, Art. IV, § 5 (1858).
California: 1 Cal.Gen.Laws, ch. 99, § 48 (1865).
Colorado (Terr.): Colo.Rev.Stat., ch. 22, §§ 45, 46 (1868).
Connecticut: Conn.Gen.Stat., Tit. 122, ch. 7, § 124 (1866).
Delaware: Del.Code Ann., Tit. 20, ch. 131, § 7 (1852).
Florida: Acts and Resolutions, ch. 8, § 17 (1868).
Georgia: Ga.Code §§ 4286, 4287, 4290 (1867).
Kingdom of Hawaii: Hawaii Penal Code, ch. 13, § 11 (1868).
Illinois: Ill.Rev.Stat., div. 5, §§ 49, 50 (1845).
Kansas: Kan. (Terr.) Stat., ch. 53, § 7 (1855).
Kentucky: 1 Ky.Rev.Stat., ch. 28, Art. IV, § 11 (1860).
Louisiana: La.Rev.Stat., Crimes and Offences, § 5 (1856).
Maine: Me.Rev.Stat., tit. XII, ch. 160 § 4 (1847).
Maryland: 1 Md.Code, Art. 30, § 201 (1860).
Massachusetts: Mass.Gen.Laws, ch. 165, § 18 (1860).
Michigan: Mich.Rev.Stat., Tit. 30, ch. 158, § 16 (1846).
Minnesota: Minn.Stat., ch. 96, § 13 (1859).
Mississippi: Miss.Rev.Code, ch. 64, Art. 238, § LII, art. 238 (1857).
Missouri: 1 Mo.Rev.Stat., ch. 50, Art. VIII, § 7 (1856).
Montana (Terr.): Mont.Laws, Criminal Practice Acts, ch. IV, § 44 (1864).
Nebraska (Terr.): Neb.Rev.Stat., Crim.Code, ch. 4, § 47 (1866).
Nevada (Terr.): Nev.Comp.Laws, ch. 28, § 45 (1862).
New Hampshire: N.H.Rev.Laws, Act of June 19, 1812, § 5 (1815).
New Jersey: N.J.Rev.Stat., Tit. 8, ch. 1, § 9 (1847).
New York: 3 N.Y.Rev.Stat., pt. 4, ch. 1, tit. 5, art. 3, § 20 (1858).
North Carolina: N.C.Rev.Code, ch. 34, § 6 (1854).
Oregon: Laws of Ore., Crimes—Against Morality, etc., ch. 7, § 655 (1874).
Pennsylvania: Act of March 31, 1860, § 32, Pub.Law 392, in 1 Digest of Statute Law of Pa. 1700–1903 1011 (Purdon 1905).
Rhode Island: R.I.Gen.Stat., ch. 232, § 12 (1872).
South Carolina: Act of 1712, in 2 Stat. at Large of S.C. 1682–1716, p. 493 (1837).
Tennessee: Tenn.Code, ch. 8, Art. 1, § 4843 (1858).
Texas: Tex.Rev.Stat., Penal Code, tit. 10, ch. 5, Art. 342 (1887) (passed 1860).
Vermont: Laws of the State of Vermont (1779).
Virginia: Va.Code, ch. 149, § 12 (1868).
West Virginia: W.Va.Code, ch. 149, § 12 (1860).
Wisconsin (Terr.): Wis.Stat., § 14 (1839).

7. In 1961, Illinois adopted the American Law Institute's Model Penal Code, which decriminalized adult, consensual, private, sexual conduct. Criminal Code of 1961, §§ 11–2, 11–3, 1961 Ill. Laws 1985, 2006 (codified as amended at Ill. Rev.Stat., ch. 38, ¶¶ 11–2, 11–3 (1983) (repealed 1984). See American Law institute, Model Penal Code § 213.2 (Proposed Official Draft 1962).

8. Respondent does not defend the judgment below based on the Ninth Amendment, the Equal Protection Clause or the Eighth Amendment.

9. Among those States that continue to make sodomy a crime, Georgia authorizes one of the longest possible sentences. See Ala.Code § 13A–6–65(a)(3) (1982) (1-year maximum); Ariz.Rev.Stat.Ann. §§ 13–1411, 13–1412 (West Supp.1985) (30 days); Ark.Stat.Ann. § 41–1813 (1977) (1-year maximum); D.C.Code § 22–3502 (1981) (10-year maximum); Fla.Stat. § 800.02 (1985) (60-day maximum); Ga.Code § 16–6–2 (1984) (1 to 20 years); Idaho Code § 18–6605 (1979) (5-year minimum); Kan.Stat.Ann. § 21–3505 (Supp.1985) (6-month maximum); Ky.Rev.Stat. § 510.100 (1985) (90 days to 12 months); La.Rev.Stat.Ann. §§ 14:89 (West Supp.1986) (5-year maximum); Md.Code Art. 27, §§ 553–554 (1982) (10-year maximum); Mich.Comp.Laws §§ 750.158 (15-year maximum); 750.338a–750.338b (1968) (5-year maximum); Minn.Stat. § 609.293 (1984) (1-year maximum); Miss.Code Ann. § 97–29–59 (1973) (10-year maximum); Mo.Rev.Stat. § 566.090 (1978) (1-year maximum); Mont.Code Ann. § 45–5–505 (1985) (10-year maximum); Nev.Rev.Stat. § 201.190 (1985) (6-year maximum); N.C.Gen.Stat. § 14–177 (1981) (10-year maximum); Okla.Stat. Tit. 21, § 886 (1983) (10-year maximum); R.I.Gen.Laws § 11–10–1 (1981) (7 to 20 years); S.C.Code § 16–15–120 (1985) (5-year maximum); Tenn.Code Ann. § 39–2–612 (1982) (5 to 15 years); Tex.Penal Code Ann. § 21.06 (1974) ($200 maximum fine); Utah Code Ann. § 76–5–403 (1983) (6-month maximum); Va.Code § 18.2–361 (1982) (5-year maximum).

10. It was conceded at oral argument that, prior to the complaint against respondent Hardwick, there had been no reported decision involving prosecution for private homosexual sodomy under this statute for several decades. See *Thompson* v. *Aldredge,* 187 Ga. 467, 200 S.E. 799 (1939). Moreover, the State has declined to present the criminal charge against Hardwick to a grand jury, and this is a suit for declaratory judgment brought by respondents challenging the validity of the statute. The history of nonenforcement suggests the moribund character today of laws criminalizing this type of private, consensual conduct. Some 26 states have repealed similar statutes. But the constitutional validity of the Georgia statute was put in issue by respondents, and for the reasons stated by the Court, I cannot say that conduct condemned for hundreds of years has now become a fundamental right.

11. Until 1968, Georgia defined sodomy as "the carnal knowledge and connection against the order of nature, by man with man, or in the same unnatural manner with woman." Ga. Crim.Code § 26–5901 (1933). In *Thompson* v. *Aldredge,* 187 Ga. 467, 200 S.E. 799 (1939), the Georgia Supreme Court held that § 26–5901 did not prohibit lesbian activity. And in *Riley* v.*Garrett,* 219 Ga. 345, 133 S.E.2d 367 (1963), the Georgia Supreme Court held that § 26–5901 did not prohibit heterosexual cunnilingus. Georgia passed the act-specific statute currently in force "perhaps in response to the restrictive court decisions such as *Riley*," Note, The Crimes Against Nature, 16 J.Pub.L. 159, 167, n. 47 (1967).

12. In *Robinson* v. *California,* 370 U.S. 660, 82 S.Ct. 1417, 8 L.Ed.2d 758 (1962), the Court held that the Eighth Amendment barred convicting a defendant due to his "status" as a narcotics addict, since that condition was "apparently an illness which may be contracted innocently or involuntarily." *Id.,* at 667, 82 S.Ct., at 1420. In *Powell* v. *Texas,* 392 U.S. 514, 88 S.Ct. 2145, 20 L.Ed.2d 1254 (1968), where the Court refused to extend *Robinson* to punishment of public drunkenness by a chronic alcoholic, one of the factors relied on by Justice MARSHALL, in writing the plurality opinion, was that Texas had not "attempted to regulate appellant's behavior in the privacy of his own home." *Id.,* at 532, 88 S.Ct., at 2154. Justice WHITE wrote separately:

"Analysis of this difficult case is not advanced by preoccupation with the label 'condition.' In *Robinson* the Court dealt with 'a statute which makes the "status" of narcotic addition a criminal offense. . . . ' 370 U.S., at 666 [82 S.Ct., at 1420]. By precluding criminal conviction for such a 'status' the Court was dealing with a condition brought about by acts remote in time from the application of the criminal sanctions contemplated, a condition which was relatively permanent in duration, and a condition of great magnitude and significance in terms of human behavior and values. . . . If it were necessary to distinguish between 'acts' and 'conditions' for purposes of the Eighth Amendment, I would adhere to the concept of 'condition' implicit in the opinion in *Robinson*. . . . The proper subject of inquiry is whether volitional acts brought about the 'condition' and whether those acts are sufficiently proximate to the 'condition' for it to be permissible to impose penal sanctions on the 'condition.' " *Id.*, 392 U.S., at 550–551, n. 2, 88 S.Ct., at 2163, n. 2.

Despite historical views of homosexuality, it is no longer viewed by mental health professionals as a "disease" or disorder. See Brief for American Psychological Association and American Public Health Association as *Amici Curiae* 8–11. But, obviously, neither is it simply a matter of deliberate personal election. Homosexual orientation may well form part of the very fiber of an individual's personality. Consequently, under Justice WHITE's analysis in *Powell*, the Eighth Amendment may pose a constitutional barrier to sending an individual to prison for acting on that attraction regardless of the circumstances. An individual's ability to make constitutionally protected "decisions concerning sexual relations," *Carey* v. *Population Services International*, 431 U.S. 678, 711, 97 S.Ct. 2010, 2029, 52 L.Ed.2d 675 (1977) (POWELL, J., concurring in part and concurring in the judgment), is rendered empty indeed if he or she is given no real choice but a life without any physical intimacy.

With respect to the Equal Protection Clause's applicability to § 16–6–2, I note that Georgia's exclusive stress before this Court on its interest in prosecuting homosexual activity despite the gender-neutral terms of the statute may raise serious questions of discriminatory enforcement, questions that cannot be disposed of before this Court on a motion to dismiss. See *Yick Wo* v. *Hopkins*, 118 U.S. 356, 373–374, 6 S.Ct. 1064, 1072–1073, 30 L.Ed. 220 (1886). The legislature having decided that the sex of the participants is irrelevant to the legality of the acts, I do not see why the State can defend § 16–6–2 on the ground that individuals singled out for prosecution are of the same sex as their partners. Thus, under the circumstances of this case, a claim under the Equal Protection Clause may well be available without having to reach the more controversial question whether homosexuals are a suspect class. See, *e.g.*, *Rowland* v. *Mad River Local School District*, — U.S. —, —, 105 S.Ct. 1373, —, 84 L.Ed.2d 392 (1985) (BRENNAN, J., dissenting from denial of certiorari); Note, The Constitutional Status of Sexual Orientation: Homosexuality as a Suspect Classification, 98 Harv.L.Rev. 1285 (1985).

13.   Even if a court faced with a challenge to § 16–6–2 were to apply simple rational-basis scrutiny to the statute, Georgia would be required to show an actual connection between the forbidden acts and the ill effects it seeks to prevent. The connection between the acts prohibited by § 16–6–2 and the harms identified by petitioner in his brief before this Court is a subject of hot dispute, hardly amenable to dismissal under Federal Rule of Civil Procedure 12(b)(6). Compare, *e.g.*, Brief for Petitioner 36–37 and Brief for David Robinson, Jr., as *Amicus Curiae* 23–28, on the one hand, with *People* v. *Onofre*, 51 N.Y.2d 476, 489, 434 N.Y.S.2d 947, 951–952, 415 N.E.2d 936, 941 (1980); Brief for the Attorney General of the State of New York, joined by the Attorney General of the State of California, as *Amici Curiae* 11–14; and Brief for the American Psychological Association and American Public Health Association as *Amici Curiae* 19–27, on the other.

14.   Although I do not think it necessary to decide today issues that are not even remotely before us, it does seem to me that a court could find simple, analytically sound distinctions between certain private, consensual sexual conduct, on the one hand, and adultery and incest (the only two vaguely specific "sexual crimes" to which the majority points, *ante*, at 2846), on the other. For example, marriage, in addition to its spiritual aspects, is a civil contract that entitles the contracting parties to a variety of governmentally provided benefits. A State might define the contractual commitment necessary to become eligible for these benefits to include a commitment of fidelity and then punish individuals for breaching that contract. Moreover, a State might conclude that adultery is likely to injure third persons, in particular, spouses and children of persons who engage in extramarital affairs. With respect to incest, a court might well agree with respondent that the nature of familial relationships renders true consent to incestuous activity sufficiently problematical that a blanket prohibition of such activity is warranted. See Tr. of Oral Arg. 21–22. Notably, the Court makes no effort to explain why it has chosen to group private, consensual homosexual activity with adultery and incest rather than with private, consensual heterosexual activity by unmarried persons or, indeed, with oral or anal sex within marriage.

15.   The theological nature of the origin of Anglo-American antisodomy statutes is patent. It was not until 1533 that sodomy was made a secular offense in England. 25 Hen. VIII, cap. 6. Until that time, the offense was, in Sir James Stephen's words, "merely ecclesiastical." 2 J. Stephen, A History of the Criminal Law of England 430 (1883). Pollock and Maitland similarly observed that "[t]he crime against nature . . . was so closely connected with heresy that the vulgar had but one name for both." 2 F. Pollock & F. Maitland, The History of English Law 554 (1895). The transfer of jurisdiction over prosecutions for sodomy to the secular courts seems primarily due to the alteration of ecclesiastical jurisdiction attendant on England's break with the Roman Catholic Church, rather than to any new understanding of the sovereign's interest in preventing or punishing the behavior involved. Cf. E. Coke, The Third Part of the Institutes of the Laws of England, ch. 10 (4th ed. 1797).

16.   At oral argument a suggestion appeared that, while the Fourth Amendment's special protection of the home might prevent the State from enforcing § 16–6–2 against individuals who engage in consensual sexual activity there, that protection would not make the statute invalid. See Tr. of Oral Arg. 10–11. The suggestion misses the point entirely. If the law is not invalid, then the police *can* invade the home to enforce it, provided, of course, that they obtain a determination of probable cause from a neutral magistrate. One of the reasons for the Court's holding in *Griswold* v. *Connecticut*, 381 U.S. 479, 85 S.Ct. 1678, 14 L.Ed.2d 510 (1965), was precisely the possibility, and repugnancy, of permitting searches to obtain evidence regarding the use of contraceptives. *Id.*, at 485–486, 85 S.Ct., at 1682. Permitting the kinds of searches that might be necessary to obtain evidence of the sexual activity banned by § 16–6–2 seems no less intrusive, or repugnant. Cf. *Winston* v. *Lee*, — U.S. —, 105 S.Ct. 1611, 84 L.Ed.2d 662 (1985); *Mary Beth G.* v. *City of Chicago*, 723 F.2d 1263, 1274 (CA7 1983).

17.   See Ga.Code Ann. § 16–6–2(a) (1984) ("A person commits the offense of sodomy when he performs or submits

to any sexual act involving the sex organs of one person and the mouth or anus of another").

18.   The Court states that the "issue presented is whether the Federal Constitution confers a fundamental right upon homosexuals to engage in sodomy and hence invalidates the laws of the many States that still make such conduct illegal and have done so for a very long time." *Ante,* at 2843. In reality, however, it is the indiscriminate prohibition of sodomy, heterosexual as well as homosexual, that has been present "for a very long time." See nn. 3, 4, and 5, *infra.* Moreover, the reaonsing the Court employs would provide the same support for the statute as it is written as it does for the statute as it is narrowly construed by the Court.

19.   See, *e.g.,* 1 W. Hawkins, Pleas of the Crown 9 (6th ed. 1787) ("All unnatural carnal copulations, whether with man or beast, seem to come under the notion of sodomy, which was felony by the antient common law, and punished, according to some authors, with burning; according to others, . . . with burying alive"); 4 W. Blackstone, Commentaries *215 (discussing "the infamous *crime against nature,* committed either with man or beast; a crime which ought to be strictly and impartially proved, and then as strictly and impartially punished").

20.   See 1 E.H. East, Pleas of the Crown 480 (1803) ("This offence, concerning which the least notice is the best, consists in a carnal knowledge committed against the order of nature by man with man, or in the same unnatural manner with woman, or by man or woman in any manner with beast"); J. Hawley & M. McGregor, the Criminal Law 287 (3d ed. 1899) ("Sodomy is the carnal knowledge against the order of nature by two persons with each other, or of a human being with a beast. . . . The offense may be committed between a man and a woman, or between two male persons, or between a man or a woman and a beast").

21.   See J. May, The Law of Crimes § 203 (2d ed. 1893) ("Sodomy, otherwise called buggery, bestiality, and the crime against nature, is the unnatural copulation of two persons with each other, or of a human being with a beast. . . . It may be committed by a man with a man, by a man with a beast, or by a woman with a beast, or by a man with a woman—his wife, in which case, if she consents, she is an accomplice").

22.   The predecessor of the current Georgia statute provided, "Sodomy is the carnal knowledge and connection against the order of nature, by man with man, or in the same unnatural manner with woman." Ga.Code, Tit. 1, Pt. 4, § 4251 (1861). This prohibition of heterosexual sodomy was not purely hortatory. See, *eg., Comer* v. *State,* 21 Ga.App. 306, 94 S.E. 314 (1917) (affirming prosecution for consensual heterosexual sodomy).

23.   See *Thompson* v. *Aldredge,* 187 Ga 467, 200 S.E. 799 (1939).

24.   A review of the statutes cited by the majority discloses that, in 1791, in 1868, and today, the vast majority of sodomy statutes do not differentiate between homosexual and heterosexual sodomy.

25.   See *Loving* v. *Virginia,* 388 U.S. 1, 87 S.Ct. 1817, 18 L.Ed.2d 1010 (1967). Interestingly, miscegenation was once treated as a crime similar to sodomy. See Hawley & McGregor, The Criminal Law, at 287 (discussing crime of sodomy); *id.,* at 288 (discussing crime of miscegenation).

26.   Indeed, the Georgia Attorney General concedes that Georgia's statute would be unconstitutional if applied to a married couple. See. Tr. of Oral Arg. 8 (stating that application of the statute to a married couple "would be unconstitutional" because of the "right of marital privacy as identified by the Court in Griswold"). Significantly, Georgia passed the current statute three years after the Court's decision in *Griswold.*

27.   *Ante,* at 2848, n. 2 (POWELL, J., concurring). See also Tr. of Oral Arg., at 4–5 (argument of Georgia Attorney General) (noting, in response to question about prosecution "where the activity took place in a private residence," the "last case I can recall was back in the 1930s or '40s").

28.   It is, of course, possible to argue that a statute has a purely symbolic role. Cf. *Carey* v. *Population Services International,* 431 U.S. 678, 715, n. 3, 97 S.Ct. 2010, 2031, n. 3, 52 L.Ed.2d 675 (1977) (STEVENS, J., concurring in part and concurring in judgment) ("The fact that the State admittedly has never brought a prosecution under the statute . . . is consistent with appellants' position that the purpose of the statute is merely symbolic"). Since the Georgia Attorney General does not even defend the statute as written, however, see n. 26, *supra,* the State cannot possibly rest on the notion that the statute may be defended for its symbolic message.

29.   Indeed, at this stage, it appears that the statute indiscriminately authorizes a policy of selective prosecution that is neither limited to the class of homosexual persons nor embraces all persons in that class, but rather applies to those who may be arbitrarily selected by the prosecutor for reasons that are not revealed either in the record of this case or in the text of the statute. If that is true, although the text of the statute is clear enough, its true meaning may be "so intolerably vague that evenhanded enforcement of the law is a virtual impossibility." *Marks* v. *United States,* 430 U.S. 188, 198, 97 S.Ct. 990, 996, 51 L.Ed.2d 260 (1977) (STEVENS, J., concurring in part and dissenting in part).

RONALD M. DWORKIN

The Great Abortion Case*

1.

No judicial decision in our time has aroused as much sustained public outrage, emotion, and physical violence, or as much intemperate professional criticism, as the Supreme Court's 1973 decision in *Roe* v. *Wade,* which declared, by a seven to two majority, that women have a constitutionally protected right to abortion in the early stages of pregnancy.[1] For sixteen years anti-abortion groups and political conservatives have campaigned with single-minded conviction to reverse that decision. They proposed without success a series of constitutional amendments, sponsored unsuccessful bills asking Congress to declare that a fetus's life begins at conception, persuaded President Reagan to appoint anti-abortion judges to the federal courts, waged single-issue political campaigns against candidates who support a right to abortion, and disrupted and bombed abortion clinics.[2] The public at large is divided in different ways about different aspects of the abortion issue. A *Los Angeles Times* national survey reported that 61 percent of Americans think abortion morally wrong—57 percent think it murder—and yet 74 percent nevertheless believe that "abortion is a decision that has to be made by every woman for herself."

The composition of the Supreme Court has changed dramatically since 1973,[3] and now, in *Webster* v. *Reproductive Health Services,* the State of Missouri and the Bush administration ask the Court to reverse *Roe* v. *Wade.* The Missouri legislature had enacted a statute designed to discourage abortions in spite of that decision. The statute, among other things, declared that human life begins at conception; it required doctors, as part of determining whether a fetus is viable before undertaking an abortion, to perform expensive, often irrelevant, and sometimes dangerous tests; and it

*Ronald M. Dworkin, "The Great Abortion Case," *The New York Review of Books,* June 29, 1989, pp. 49–54. Reprinted with permission from *The New York Review of Books.* Copyright © 1989 Nyrev, Inc.

prohibited any abortion in hospitals or medical facilities that employ assets owned, leased, or controlled by the state. Lower federal courts declared all these provisions unconstitutional under *Roe* v. *Wade*. Missouri appealed to the Supreme Court, asking the Court to overrule that decision or, failing that, to curtail or restrict it in such a way that the Missouri statute would then be constitutional.

Oral argument was heard on April 26, while protesters on both sides of the issue organized long and noisy demonstrations outside the Court. Charles Fried, who was solicitor general in the Reagan administration and has now returned to the Harvard Law School faculty, defended in a brief and in oral argument the Bush administration's claim that *Roe* v. *Wade* should now be discarded. Seventy-eight other briefs—more than in any previous case—were filed by a wide variety of concerned groups. These include, for example, briefs on various aspects of the litigation on behalf of 25 United States senators and 115 congressmen, the American Medical Association and other medical groups, 281 academic historians, 885 law professors, and a large number of anti-abortion groups. The Court is expected to hand down its decision before it adjourns in July, though it might wait until next year. Whatever decision it reaches will frustrate and anger millions of Americans.

Is the human fetus a person from the moment of conception? That question has been argued by theologians and moral philosophers and ordinary people for many centuries. It cannot be resolved by legal research or scientific evidence or conceptual analysis; it will continue to divide people, as it divides Americans now, so long as deep disagreements remain about God and morals and metaphysics. It therefore seems an exceptionally poor issue to ask any court, including the Supreme Court, to decide, and that fact best explains, I think, the immediate appeal many people feel in the idea that the abortion issue is best decided politically, through the ordinary processes of legislation. It seems offensive that a majority of judges on a single court should declare one answer for everyone. It seems more democratic, and also better suited to the inherent complexity of the issue, that different groups of Americans should be permitted to decide, in politics, state by state, which solution fits their own convictions and needs best.

That first impression is misguided in several ways, however. Leaving the abortion issue to state-by-state politics will not, of course, mean that each woman will be able to decide which solution best fits *her* convictions and needs. It means that if the anti-abortion lobby is sufficiently powerful in a particular state, the women of that state will be denied that opportunity, as they were before *Roe* v. *Wade*.[4] It is doubtful that there were fewer abortions then, relative to the number of pregnancies, even though most of them were illegal. But there were many more deaths: abortion-related fatalities were 40 percent higher before *Roe* v. *Wade*.[5] Blacks suffered most. In New York, for example, a black woman was nine times as likely to die in an illegal abortion as a white one. Of course, if *Roe* v. *Wade* were reversed women who were rich and knowledgeable enough could still decide to have an abortion by traveling to the nearest or most convenient place where it was legal, as thousands did before 1973 by traveling to Britain, for example. But a poor woman who found herself pregnant might have to choose between the danger of illegal abortion and the misery imposed by and on a child she could not support or raise.

The first impression is misguided not just practically, but legally and logically as well. The key question in the debate over *Roe* v. *Wade* is not a metaphysical question about the concept of personhood or a theological question about whether a fetus has a soul, but a legal question about the correct interpretation of the Constitution which in our political system *must* be settled one way or the other judicially, by the Supreme Court, rather than politically. It is the question whether the fetus is a *constitutional* person, that is, a person whose rights and interests must be ranked equally important with those of other people in the scheme of individual rights the Constitution establishes. That is a complex and difficult question, and it does involve moral issues. But it is nevertheless different from the metaphysical question philosophers and theologians debate; it is entirely consistent to think, for example, that a fetus is just as much a human being as an adult, or that

it has a soul from the moment of conception, and yet that the Constitution, on the best interpretation, does not grant a fetus rights competitive with the rights it grants other people.

Courts cannot avoid deciding the legal question whether a fetus is a constitutional person because it makes no sense to consider what constitutional rights some people do or do not have, in any area of constitutional law, without first deciding who *else* has rights a state must or may also recognize. The Supreme Court has held, for example, that the citizens of each state have a constitutional right that state elections be conducted under districting arrangements that ensure one person one vote, and a state could not undermine that principle by counting as people whole classes of entities that the Constitution, properly interpreted, does not. A state could not declare corporations persons, for instance, by providing separate votes for them, and cut down the voting power of real people. The question of whether and in what sense corporations are constitutional persons, with rights of their own, has been much debated throughout constitutional history. But it has never been doubted that because that question affects the rights of everyone else, it must be decided judicially, at the national constitutional level. Of course a state may promote the interests of its corporations in a wide variety of ways. But it cannot endow them with rights whose force is to curtail the constitutional rights enjoyed by others. Only the Constitution can do that.[6]

So the question of who is a constitutional person must be settled at the constitutional level, by the Supreme Court, as part of deciding what constitutional rights anyone has, and the question whether a fetus is a constitutional person is pivotal to the abortion debate. In *Roe* v. *Wade* the Court decided that a fetus is not a constitutional person before birth, and though its opinion has been criticized by several academic lawyers, it is largely persuasive once that premise is accepted. Earlier Supreme Court decisions had established that a person has a fundamental constitutional right to control his or her own role in procreation—the Court had decided, for example, that for this reason a state may not prohibit the sale of contraceptives. If a fetus is not a constitutional person, then a fetus's right to live cannot be cited as a justification for denying that right after pregnancy begins, though of course a state can nevertheless protect the fetus's interests in a great variety of other ways.

But if the fetus is a constitutional person then *Roe* v. *Wade* is plainly wrong, as the Court's opinion in that case conceded. The Fourteenth Amendment declares that no state may deny any person "equal protection of the laws." If the fetus is protected by that clause, then of course a state is entitled to protect its life in the same way it protects the lives of other prople under its care, and for that reason is entitled to say that a woman's right to control the use of her body for procreation ends, at least when her health is not at stake, when pregnancy begins. Indeed it would be difficult to resist a very much stronger conclusion: that a state is not only entitled but *required* to take that view, so that states like New York, which decided to permit abortion in early pregnancy even before *Roe* v. *Wade* was decided, would be constitutionally *prohibited* from doing so.

The equal protection clause requires states to extend the protection of their laws against murder and assault equally to all persons, and if fetuses were constitutional persons any state legislation that discriminated against them in that respect, by permitting abortion, would be "suspect," under equal protection principles, and the Supreme Court would have an obligation to review such legislation to determine whether the state's justification for that discrimination was "compelling." In some cases it would be: when a state permitted abortion to protect the health of a mother, for example, or perhaps in cases of rape or incest. But if a woman is well aware of the physical and emotional consequences of pregnancy and voluntarily has sexual intercourse knowing that she risks becoming pregnant, a state that permits her or her doctor to abort her fetus has no compelling justification for doing so if the fetus is entitled to equal protection of the laws. For a state fails to show equal concern for both mother and fetus when it allows the mother to regain the freedom of her body at the expense of the fetus's life.

It is true, as a number of legal scholars have pointed out, that the law does not generally require people to make any sacrifice at all to save the life of another person who needs their aid. A person ordinarily has no legal duty to save a stranger from drowning even if he can do so at no risk to himself and with minimal effort.[7] But abortion normally requires a physical attack on a fetus, not just the failure to come to its aid. And in any case parents are invariably made an exception to the general doctrine under which people are not required to save others. Parents have a legal duty to care for their children, and if a fetus is a constitutional person from conception a state would not be justified in discriminating between fetuses and infants. If it did not permit killing infants or abandoning them in circumstances in which they would inevitably die, it could not permit abortion either.[8] The physical and emotional and economic burdens of pregnancy are intense, of course, but so are the parallel burdens of parenthood.

I stress this point because it is important to notice that those who urge the Supreme Court to leave the question of abortion to the states, to decide as their politics dictate, have in effect conceded that a fetus is *not* a constitutional person. In oral argument, Justice White asked Charles Fried whether in his view there is "some problem about the state permitting abortion." Fried replied, "Oh, no," and said very firmly that it would be a serious mistake for the Court to "constitutionalize" the issue at any "point in the spectrum" by requiring constitutional scrutiny of permissive abortion legislation by a state. That position is preposterous except on the assumption that the Constitution itself offers a fetus's life no protection at all.[9]

But Fried could hardly have given White's question any other answer. It would be political madness for the Court to try to force unwilling states to outlaw abortion; and neither the government nor any other responsible group has asked it to do so. The damage to the community, to the Court's authority, and to the Constitution would be far greater if it did try to force the states to outlaw abortion, than if it simply left the law where it stands. But the Court can avoid that inconceivable decision, legitimately, only by confirming *Roe* v. *Wade*'s explicit decision that a fetus is not a constitutional person. So the most complex and difficult of the legal issues in the abortion dispute has been removed from the controversy by a kind of practical necessity. I do not mean to suggest, by emphasizing these practical arguments for the view, that it is not the correct view in law. On the contrary, I think that it is.

The question is one of legal interpretation. The principle that the fetus is not a constitutional person fits better with other parts of our law and also with our sense of how related issues would and should be decided if they arose than the rival principle that it is. Even if the fetus is a human being, it is in a unique situation politically as well as biologically for a reason that could properly be thought sufficient to deny it constitutional status. The state can take action that affects it, in order to protect or advance its interests, only through its mother, and only through means that would necessarily restrict her freedom in ways no man or other woman's freedom could constitutionally be limited: by dictating her diet and other personal and intimate behavior, for example. Apart from anti-abortion statues, there are few signs in our law of the kind of regulation of pregnancy that would be appropriate if the fetus were a constitutional person, and the Supreme Court has never suggested any constitutional requirement of such protection.

The best historical evidence shows, moreover, that even anti-abortion laws, which were not prevalent in the United States before the middle of the nineteenth century, were adopted to protect the health of the mother and the privileges of the medical profession, not out of any recognition of a fetus's rights.[10] Even states that had the most stringent anti-abortion laws before *Roe* v. *Wade,* moreover, did not punish abortion as severely as murder, as they should have done if they thought a fetus a constitutional person. Nor did they try to outlaw or penalize a woman procuring an abortion in another state or abroad.

So the better interpretation of our constitutional law and practice holds that a fetus is not a constitutional person. That conclusion could be accepted, as I suggested, even by someone who thinks abortion a heinous sin: not every sin is or could be punished by law. But it will of course be easier to accept for someone who believes that a human being has no moral right to life until it has developed self-consciousness as a being whose life extends over time.[11] On the assumption that this condition is not reached until some time after birth the interpretive conclusion, that a human being becomes a constitutional person no earlier than at that point, seems even sounder.

2.

It is therefore not an acceptable argument, against the claim that women have a constitutional right to choose an abortion in early pregnancy, that the fetus is a constitutional person whose competing right to live would overcome any such right. I have already mentioned the argument for the claim that women do have a constitutional right of that character. In a series of previous cases relating to sterilization, marriage, and contraception, the Supreme Court recognized that all citizens have a general right, based in the Fourteenth Amendment's guarantee of due process of law, to decide for themselves ethical and personal issues arising from marriage and procreation.[12] Justice Blackmun relied heavily on these previous decisions, which have come to be called "privacy" decisions, in his opinion for the Court in *Roe* v. *Wade.* He argued that though abortion raises questions different from those raised by these other issues, the general principle that people have a right to control their own role in procreation plainly applied to abortion as well.[13] Neither Missouri nor the Bush administration has argued that these precedents should be overruled.[14] Fried, in oral argument, said that the case of *Griswold* v. *Connecticut,* which upheld a right of contraception, was correct and should not be disturbed. He said that *Roe* v. *Wade* could be overruled without affecting that case or the other privacy precedents, that *Roe* v. *Wade* could be pulled from the fabric woven by these past decisions like a single thread.

Abortion cannot be disentagled from contraception even medically, however, because both the IUD and the most popular and safest birth-control pills act as abortifacients, that is, they destroy fertilized ova. So the Court could not hold that a woman's right to control her role in procreation ends with fertilization without permitting states to outlaw the contraceptives now in use. That would be in effect to overrule *Griswold,* which Fried said was a correct decision. Even if contraception and abortion did not overlap medically in that way, they could not be distinguished in principle, once it is assumed that a fetus is not a constitutional person.

The Court's previous privacy decisions can be justified only on the assumption that decisions affecting marriage and childbirth are so important, so intimate and personal, so crucial to the development of personality and sense of moral responsibility, and so closely tied to religious and ethical convictions protected by the First Amendment, that people must be allowed to make these decisions for themselves, consulting their own conscience, rather than allowing society to thrust its collective decision on them. The abortion decision is at least as much a private decision in that sense as any other the Court has protected. In many ways it is more private, because the decision involves a woman's control not just of her connections to others, but of the use of her own body, and the Constitution recognizes in a variety of ways the special intimacy of a person's connection to her own physical integrity.[15]

If a fetus were a constitutional person, then abortion could of course be distinguished from at least contraception that did not involve abortifacients, because a state could properly cite a compelling interest in protecting the fetus's right to life and to be treated with equal concern. But given the assumption that a fetus is not a constitutional person, that reason for distinguishing abortion from contraception, and from the other activities permitted by decisions protecting privacy, fails. Fried tried to distinguish the contraception cases on the ground that *Griswold* v. *Connecticut* was based not on any general right to control one's own procreation, but on the different basis that the police could enforce a prohibition on the use of contraceptives only by searching the marital bedroom, which would be offensive. It is true that one opinion in *Griswold* v. *Connecticut* mentioned that reason for invalidating a prohibition on married couples using contraceptives. But it is a silly reason, not only because prohibitions on the use of contraceptives could be enforced without breaking down bedroom doors, but because the Court has upheld other criminal statutes that might be thought just as difficult to enforce without offensive and impermissible searches.[16]

In any case, the later contraception cases rejected that interpretation of *Griswold* v. *Connecticut,* and they are inconsistent with it. In *Eisenstadt* v. *Baird,* Justice Brennan, for the Court, stated the point of the past privacy cases this way:

If the right of privacy means anything, it is the right of the *individual,* married or not, to be free from government intrusion into matters so fundamentally affecting a person as the decision whether to bear or beget a child.

And one of the justices who dissented in the *Griswold* case, Potter Stewart, joined the majority in *Roe* v. *Wade* on the ground that if one accepts the *Griswold* decision, as he then did on grounds of precedent, one has to accept *Roe* v. *Wade* as well. Fried's claim that the privacy decisions were really only about searching bedrooms proved too bizarre for him to defend with any confidence. When Justice O'Connor asked a direct question, "Do you say there is no fundamental right to decide whether to have a child or not?" he could only answer, "I would hesitate to formulate the right in such abstract terms."

So the argument from precedent in favor of *Row* v. *Wade* seems a strong one: Supreme Court precedents established a constitutional right of control over one's own role in childbirth, and, if a fetus is not a constitutional person, that right naturally extends to abortion. But we must now consider the opposing arguments made by those lawyers, including the justices dissenting in that case, who insist it was wrong and should now be discarded. They say that the right to abortion is "judge-made" and has "little or no cognizable roots in the language or design of the Constitution."[17] Or that the right has "no moorings in the text of our Constitution or in familiar constitutional doctrine," and cannot be sustained by "the interpretive tradition of the legal community."[18] Or that the right does not exist because the subject of abortion is "one upon which the Constitution is silent."[19]

But these various complaints beg the question. Of course, if the judges who decided *Roe* v. *Wade* made up the constitutional rights they announced, or if those rights have no roots in the language or design of the Constitution, or if they cannot be established as drawn from the Constitution by interpretive methods traditional to legal reasoning, then the decision was certainly wrong. But we cannot decide whether these complaints are justified without some theory of how judges *should* interpret the abstract provisions of the Constitution, such as the provision that requires due process of law. How should judges decide which rights do and which do not have "roots" in the abstract language?

The various government briefs in *Webster* sometimes suggest an answer to that question which our legal tradition has decisively rejected: that abstract language should never be interpreted to yield a right that the historical framers who enacted the abstract provision did not accept themselves. The briefs argue that the Fourteenth Amendment cannot be thought to include a right to abortion because abortion laws were being enacted by states throughout the country when that amendment was added to the Constitution.[20] But the Congress that enacted the Fourteenth Amendment itself segregated the public schools of the District of Columbia, and no one now argues that *Brown* v. *Board of Education,* which held that segregation violated the rights provided by that amendment, was wrong.

The briefs of the Bush administration and the state of Missouri also rely on a variety of other interpretative suggestions. They propose that the Constitution should be understood to contain only "enumerated" rights, that is, rights explicitly mentioned in the text. But that ignores the fact that the same legal situation can be described in different ways. The Supreme Court decided, in 1952, that the police may not pump out a suspect's stomach for evidence. Shall we say that the Court decided that the right to due process of law, which is mentioned in the text of the Constitution, applied to the particular facts of that case? Or that it decided that people have a right not to have their stomachs pumped, which is derived from the due process clause but which is not itself mentioned in the text? There is only a verbal difference between the two formulations and neither is more accurate than the other.

In any case, if we must reject the right to an abortion because abortion is not mentioned in the Constitution, then we must also reject a great number of other, unquestioned constitutional rights that lawyers frequently describe in language not to be found there either. These include the right to use contraceptives, which the government now argues is part of the Constitution in spite of the fact that contraception is not mentioned. They also include the right to vote, to marry, to travel between states, to live with one's extended family, to educate one's children privately in schools meeting educational standards, and to attend racially desegregated schools. If these are all "unenumerated" rights, and so "judge-made" constitutional law,

it hardly counts against *Roe* v. *Wade* that it falls into the same category.

One of the government briefs replies to that objection with a metaphor. It says that the supposed right of abortion "travels further from its point of departure in the text" than these other rights. But how do we measure the distance between a right and the constitutional language from which it is drawn? How can we tell whether the distance between abortion and the constitutional language of due process is greater than the distance between contraception or stomach pumping and that language? Or the distance between the other "unenumerated" rights I listed and the constitutional language in which these were rooted?

Our legal tradition gives a very different, less metaphorical and superficial, answer to the question how abstract constitutional provisions should be interpreted. Judges should seek to identify the principles latent in the Constitution as a whole, and in past judicial decisions applying the Constitution's abstract language, in order to enforce the same principles in new areas and so make the law steadily more coherent. In that way, the principles that have been relied on to justify rights for one group or in one situation are extended, so far as that is possible, to everyone else to whom they equally apply. That common-law process was used in *Roe* v. *Wade* to argue that the principles latent in the earlier privacy decisions about sterilization and family and contraception must be applied to the abortion case as well. These earlier privacy decisions can themselves be defended in a similar way, as part of a broader project of the Court, begun earlier in the century, to identify and enforce the principles implicit in what the Court called "the concept of ordered liberty," which means the principle a society truly committed to individual liberty and dignity must recognize. A right to control one's part in procreation finds support in that general project, as well as in the more closely related decisions protecting privacy, because that right is crucially important to the moral, social, and economic freedom of women.

These are the arguments that the opponents of *Roe* v. *Wade* must meet, and they should try to meet them in the traditional way, by explaining why different principles from those mentioned, which do not yield a right to abortion, provide a more satisfactory interpretation of the Constitution as a whole and the Court's past decisions under it. Of course different judges will come to very different conclusions about which principles provide the best interpretation of the Constitution, and since there is no neutral standpoint from which it can be proved which side is right, each justice must in the end rely on his or her convictions about which argument is best. But that is an inevitable feature of a political system like ours, which conceives of its constitution as a charter of principle rather than a particular collection of political settlements.

Certainly the present critics of *Roe* v. *Wade* offer no alternative. Since their question-begging rhetoric about "judge-made law" and "new rights" rests on no reasoned intellectual basis, it provides even less discipline than the traditional interpretive method, because the latter does demand coherent and extended argument, not just name-calling. The question-begging rhetoric, on the contrary, leaves lawyers free to accept constitutional rights now popular in the community, such as the right to legally integrated education and to use contraceptives, and to oppose rights politically more troublesome, such as the right to abortion, without having to explain what the difference between the constitutional standing of these rights actually is.

3.

Though *Roe* v. *Wade* held that women have a right in principle to control their part in procreation, it added that states have a legitimate interest in protecting "potential life," and that any statement of a woman's constitutional right to an abortion must take that interest into account. It decided that the state's interest becomes compelling enough in late pregnancy, when the fetus has become viable, to permit the state to regulate or prohibit abortions after that point, except as necessary to protect the mother's health. Unfortunately, the Court did not satisfactorily explain what kind of interest a state is permitted to take in "potential life," or why its concern grows stronger or more legitimate after a fetus becomes viable.

The Court did not mean, of course, that a state has a legitimate interest in increasing the birthrate, because that interest would apply with equal strength at all times in pregnancy and, indeed, would justify a state's opposing contraception as vigorously as abortion. Nor did the Court mean that a state may legitimately decide that a being with potential life has rights of its own which the state may take an interest in protecting. As we saw, the Court rightly held that the question whether a fetus is a constitutional person, and thus a person whose rights are competitive with the constitutional rights of others, must be settled at the constitutional level, not be state legislation, and it then held that the fetus is not such a person. What else could a state's interest in "potential life" mean?

The most persuasive answer, which takes the Court's subsequent decisions into account, is, I believe, the following. Even though a fetus is not a constitutional person, it is nevertheless an entity of considerable moral and emotional significance in our culture, and a state may recognize and try to protect that significance in ways that fall short of any substantial abridgment of a woman's constitutional right over the use of her own body. A state might properly fear the impact of widespread abortion on its citizens' instinctive respect for the value of human life and their instinctive horror at human destruction or suffering, which are values essential for the maintenance of a just and decently civil society. A political community in which abortion became commonplace and a matter of ethical indifference, like appendectomy, would certainly be a more callous and insensitive community, and it might be a more dangerous one as well.

A state's concern for the moral significance of a fetus increases as pregnancy advances, and it is particularly intense after viability when the fetus has assumed a postnatal baby's form. This is a matter of resemblance.[21] People's instinctive respect for life is unlikely to be lessened significantly if they come to regard the abortion of a just-fertilized ovum as permissible, any more than it is lessened when they accept contraception. But the assault on instinctive values is likely to be almost as devastating when a nearly full-term baby is aborted as when a week-old child is killed.

So the state's concern is greatest after the point at which a fetus, under present technology, is viable, and a prohibition on elective abortion after that time will not significantly burden or compromise a woman's constitutional right.[22] Her right is a right to make fundamental decisions for herself, and that right is satisfied when she has had ample time after discovering her pregnancy to consider whether she wishes to continue it, and to arrange a safe and convenient abortion if she does not.[23] *Roe v. Wade,* understood in that way, did not balance a woman's rights against the competing rights of a fetus or of anyone else. Rather it identified a scheme of regulation that could meet a state's most powerful needs without substantially compromising a woman's rights at all.

The Court had to pick a particular event or period of pregnancy in constructing that scheme in order to make it clear enough to be administered by officials and judges.[24] If the Court had said simply that a state must allow a woman "ample" or "reasonable" time after the discovery of pregnancy to decide about abortion, it would have faced a succession of test cases provoked by state legislatures defining the cutoff line earlier and earlier, so that it would eventually have been forced to draw a line in any case. The Court's decision to make the crucial event viability, which occurs at approximately twenty-three or twenty-four weeks, has much to recommend it. Viability marks a distinct stage of pregnancy after which the difference between a fetus and a premature infant is not a matter of development but only of environment. Since viability follows "quickening," or the point at which a pregnant woman feels movement in her womb, it is late enough to provide her a reasonable opportunity for an abortion after pregnancy is discovered. (Teenage women, particularly, may easily be unaware of pregnancy before quickening; their periods may have been erratic or missing before pregnancy and they may not "show," or look pregnant, before then.)

Some critics feared that advances in medical technology would make fetuses viable much earlier, and thus require the Court to change its standard; in an earlier case Justice O'Connor said that *Roe v. Wade* was for that reason on "a collision course" with itself. But a consensus of medical opinion now declares that fear unfounded: there is, according to the brief filed in the *Webster* case by the American Medical Association and other medical groups, an "anatomical threshhold for fetal survival of about twenty-three to twenty-four weeks of gestation . . . because the fetal lung does not mature sufficiently to permit normal or even mechanically-assisted respiration before [that time]."

An established Supreme Court decision, particularly one that recognizes individual constitutional rights, should not be overruled unless it is clearly wrong or has proved thoroughly unworkable.[25] *Roe v. Wade* is not wrong, and it certainly is not clearly wrong. Justice Blackmun's opinion might have been clearer in some respects, and the Court might have chosen an event in pregnancy other than viability but which occurs at roughly the same time, such as neocortical functioning, to mark the point at which abortion might be prohibited.[26] But these are hardly reasons to tear apart constitutional law by overturning the decision now. The Court should refuse to nourish the cynical view, already popular among its critics, that constitutional law is only a matter of which president appointed the last few justices.

4.

If the Court declines to overrule or substantially restrict *Roe v. Wade,* as it should, it must decide the more limited constitutional issues raised by the *Webster* case. As I said, the lower courts declared unconstitutional a variety of clauses in Missouri's statute. The state does not now contest some of these rulings, and urges implausible but benign interpretations of others in order to save them from unconstitutionality. The important remaining controversy concerns the state's ban on the use of public facilities in connection with abortion even when the abortion is performed by a private doctor and paid for by private funds.

The statute defines public facilities very broadly as "any public institution, public facility, public equipment, or any physical asset owned, leased, or controlled by this state or any agency or political subdivision thereof." So it would forbid abortion in the Truman Medical Center in Kansas City—where 97 percent of all hospital abortions at sixteen weeks or later in Missouri were performed in 1985—in spite of the fact that the center is a private hospital staffed mainly by private doctors, and administered by private corporations, just because that hospital is located on ground leased from a political subdivision of the state.[27]

Missouri defends the provision by appealing to earlier decisions of the Supreme Court. In *Maber v. Roe,*[28] the Court sustained a state's right to provide medical assistance funds for childbirth but not for abortion, and in *Poelker v. Doe*[29] it allowed a state to provide childbirth but not abortion facilities in a public city hospital. The Court said that although a state may not forbid abortions, it need not go into the abortion business itself. It might constitutionally adopt a preference for childbirth to abortion, and provide funds only for the former.

The decisions in the *Maber* and *Poelker* cases have been criticized because they permit states to take action to discourage people from exercising their constitutional rights. But even if we accept these decisions as sound they do not support Missouri's broad prohibition. Of course a state need not subsidize or support the exercise of every constitutional right, and it may pursue policies of its own choice in the benefits it awards. It may without violating anyone's rights to free speech publish literature encouraging conservation while refusing to distribute other political material.

But Missouri's argument overlooks a crucial distinction. It is one thing for a state to decline to participate in some act it disapproves in circumstances in which it would itself be the author of the act, or would plausibly be taken to be, if it did. A state, for example, may refuse to distribute political criticism of its own government without violating anyone's rights to free speech. It is quite another thing for a state to use its economic power or control of crucial resources to discourage citizens from exercising their constitutional rights when there is no question of the state being seen as the author of, or as in any way supporting, what they do. A city cannot force newsstands in shopping centers built on public land to sell only papers it approves. It cannot force theaters it supplies with water and power and police protection to perform only plays it likes.

Perhaps a state that itself pays for abortions, or provides them in free public hospitals, will in effect have declared itself neutral between abortion and childbirth, or will be understood to have done so. For the state is necessarily the author of its own public funding and public medical provision. But it is preposterous that a state should be understood as itself performing abortions carried out by private doctors on their own initiative and paid for with private funds, just because the hospital in which this is done is in other ways state-supported, or because it is on land the state, as it happens, owns.

The true explanation of why Missouri adopted its stringent prohibition is not, of course, that it wants to avoid declaring itself neutral about abortion, but that it wants to make abortion as difficult and as expensive as possible, in order to discourage its residents from exercising their constitutional rights. It enacts whatever measures to that end its officials can devise and the federal courts have not yet condemned, including measures so obviously unconstitutional that its lawyers do not seriously defend them when they are challenged. That is impermissible: a state must not declare war on its own people because it is angry that the law is on their side.

Unhappily, if the Court in any way now signals itself more ready to accept constraints on abortion than it has been in the past, that dismal spectacle will continue. Other states will adopt more and more restrictive statutes to provoke more and more test cases to see how far the Court will actually go. Charles Fried anticipated exactly that at the close of his oral argument. He asked the justices, even if they did not overrule *Roe* v. *Wade,* at least not to say anything "that would further entrench this decision as a secure premise for reasoning in future cases." The justices would do best for constitutional order and decorum, as well as principle, if they refused to take that bad advice.

NOTES

1. It held that abortions could not be made criminal in the first three months of pregnancy and could be made criminal before the fetus became viable only when necessary to protect the health of the mother.

2. For a general discussion of the character and effect of the controversy, see Jane Maslow Cohen, "Comparison-shopping in the Marketplace of Rights," *Yale Law Journal,* Vol. 98 (1989), p. 1235.

3. Of the seven justices in the majority in *Roe* v. *Wade,* only three remain: Blackmun, who wrote the opinion, Brennan, and Marshall. Justice Stevens, who joined the Court later, has indicated his full support for the decision. The two Roe dissenters, Justices Rehnquist, who is now Chief Justice, and White, have recently repeated their view that it is unsound, and Justice Scalia has often expressed himself as skeptical of rights with no "textual" basis. Justice O'Connor dissented in two later cases in which anti-abortion groups unsuccessfully sought to limit Roe's force, but she has not suggested that the decision should be reversed. She and Justice Kennedy, Reagan's final appointment, hold the balance of power.

4. Some states have already adopted strong anti-abortion laws to take effect after any weakening of *Roe* v. *Wade* by the Supreme Court, and several others have declared their intention of doing so. Even if the Court does not reverse that case outright, but either weakens the rights it guaranteed or accepts Missouri's constraints on abortion as consistent with those rights, a rash of new state legislation, once again testing the boundaries of the Court's willingness to retreat, is expected. Only a clear reaffirmation of the basic *Roe* v. *Wade* principles could remove the issue from the political front burner.

5.   Erwin Chemrinsky, "Rationalizing the Abortion Debate: Legal Rhetoric and the Abortion Controversy," *Buffalo Law Review*, Vol. 31 (1982), p. 106.

6.   Of course I do not mean to suggest that fetuses are no more important or sacred than corporations. As I insist later, the moral significance of a fetus should be clear and justifies whatever state regulation of abortion is consistent with constitutional rights. My point is only that no state is free to deny or substantially curtail rights the Constitution does establish by recognizing rights, or right bearers, that it does not. John Hart Ely pointed out, in an influential early attack on *Roe* v. *Wade*, that even though dogs are not persons under the equal protection clause, a state can stop demonstrators from killing dogs without violating the demonstrators' First Amendment rights (Ely, "The Wages of Crying Wolf: A Comment on *Roe* v. *Wade*," *Yale Law Journal*, Vol. 92, 1973, p. 920). But, as Laurence Tribe pointed out, no one has to kill animals to exercise his right to free speech, though a pregnant woman does need to abort her fetus to retain control over her part in procreation. See Tribe, *American Constitutional Law*, Second Edition (Foundation Press, 1987), p. 1349.

7.   These scholars argue that for that reason anti-abortion laws are unconstitutional even if a fetus is considered a person, and they would certainly reject my much stronger claim that in that event many laws permitting abortion would be unconstitutional. The legal arguments rely on a famous and influential article about the morality of abortion by Judith Jarvis Thomson ("A Defense of Abortion," *Philosophy and Public Affairs*, Vol. 1, No. 1, Fall 1971). Thomson does not argue that every pregnant woman has a right to an abortion, even if a fetus is a person, but only that some do, and she recognizes that a woman who voluntarily risks pregnancy may not have such a right. The legal arguments applying Thomson's views to constitutional law are best and most persuasively presented in Donald Regan, "Rewriting *Roe* v. *Wade*," *Michigan Law Review*, Vol. 77 (1979), p. 1569.

8.   In the article cited in the preceding note, Donald Regan questions the analogy between abortion and infanticide on the ground that parents have the option of arranging an adoption for their child. But that is not inevitably true: infants from poor minority families, in particular, may not be able to find adoptive homes, and their parents, of course, are not permitted to kill them or abandon them in circumstances that will inevitably lead to their death even when they can in fact make no other arrangement.

9.   In oral argument Fried said that the Fourteenth Amendment does not "take any position" on the question whether a fetus "is not merely potential life but actual human life." That is true, as I said earlier. But it does not follow that the amendment takes no view on the different question I distinguished, which is whether the fetus is a *constitutional* person, that is, a person within the meaning of the requirement that a state accord every person equal protection. The Constitution, properly interpreted, must take a position on *that* point, because defining the range of its key concepts is part of what interpreting the Constitution is. And Fried's position is defensible only if, on the best interpretation, a fetus is not a constitutional person.

10.   See "Brief of 281 American Historians as Amici Curiae Supporting Appellees" in *Webster* v. *Reproductive Health Services*. It is worth noticing that the historian cited in the government's brief to support the claim that anti-abortion laws are traditional in America, James Mohr, is one of the signers of this brief.

11.   For an account and defense of this view, see Michael Tooley, "Abortion and Infanticide," *Philosophy and Public Affairs*, Vol. 2, No. 1 (Fall 1972). The view has important implications, of course, for the end of the right to life as well as the beginning. See my monograph, "Philosophical Issues in Senile Dementia," published by Office of Technology Assessment, U.S. Congress (U.S. Government Printing Office, 1987).

12.   See, for example, *Skinner* v. *Oklahoma*, 316 U.S. 535 (1942), *Griswold* v. *Connecticut*, 381 U.S. 479 (1965), *Eisenstadt* v. *Baird*, 405 U.S. 438 (1972). See also *Carey* v. *Population Services International*, 431 U.S. 678 (1977). In *Griswold* v. *Connecticut*, the Court held that no state could forbid married people the use of contraceptives. It expanded that holding in *Eisenstadt* v. *Baird* to include unmarried people as well, and in *Carey* v. *Population Services International* it held that a state could not prohibit the sale of contraceptives even to teen-agers.

13.   Many lawyers believe that an equally or even more powerful argument for the result in *Roe* v. *Wade* can be based not on the due process clause and the privacy precedents, but on the equal protection clause I mentioned earlier. They argue that anti-abortion laws should be considered suspect under that clause because such laws cause very great disadvantage to women, in some circumstances destroying their opportunity to lead lives routinely available to men. Legislatures are still dominated by men, many of whom believe unmarried pregnant women deserve punishment rather than sympathy, and few of whom could fully appreciate the misery of their situation even if they wished to do so. For a particularly effective account of this argument, and of the special impact of abortion law on women, see Silvia A. Law, "Rethinking Sex and the Constitution," *University of Pennsylvania Law Review*, Vol. 132 (1984), p. 955.

14.   *Griswold* v. *Connecticut* and the other contraception cases figured prominently in the 1987 debates over the unsuccessful nomination of Robert Bork to the Supreme Court. Bork had written that these cases should be overruled, and the enormous unpopularity of that suggestion helped persuade public opinion to oppose his nomination.

15.   See the article by Donald Regan cited in note 7 above.

16.   The Court recently upheld a statute that made homosexual acts of sodomy a crime. (*Bowers* v. *Hardwick*, 106 S.Ct. 2841, 1986). Justice White's opinion for the Court said that the fact that homosexual acts may take place in the privacy of the home was irrelevant, and that the contraception cases were not about private acts in that sense but "were interpreted . . . to confer a fundamental individual right to decide whether or not to beget or bear a child," and hence were irrelevant to the question of homosexual sodomy.

17.   Justice White, in *Bowers* v. *Hardwick*. See the preceding note. White dissented in *Griswold* v. *Connecticut* as well as in *Roe* v. *Wade*. The acting solicitor general's brief in *Webster* v. *Reproductive Health Services* quoted these remarks.

18.   See the brief filed by then acting Solicitor General Fried in *Thornburgh* v. *American College of Obstetricians & Gynecologists*, 416 U.S. 747 (1986).

19.   Fried, in the same brief.

20.   The historians' brief described in note 10 above argues that these statutes were motivated by concern for the safety of women, for doctors, and for the birth rate of nonimmigrants, which would not be permissible justifications for anti-abortion laws now.

21. The importance of resemblance and of understanding the Court's concern with viability in that light is skillfully analyzed by Nancy Rhoden in "Trimesters and Technology: Revamping *Roe* v. *Wade*," *Yale Law Journal*, Vol. 95 (1986), p. 639.

22. Cases in which a threat to the mother's life or the fetus's development is noticed only after viability require different constitutional treatment, as the Court noticed in *Roe* v. *Wade*.

23. Ninety percent of abortions are performed during the first trimester of pregnancy, only 1 percent after twenty weeks, only .01 percent in the third trimester. See "Brief of the American Medical Association (and several other medical groups) as Amici Curiae in Support of Appellees."

24. For an account of the courts' traditional role in making principle administrable as a matter of strategy, see Lawrence Sager, "State Courts and the Strategic Space Between the Norms and Rules of Constitutional Law," *Texas Law Review*, Vol. 63, p. 959.

25. One hundred and forty United States senators and congressmen filed an amicus brief in *Webster* v. *Reproductive Health Services* arguing that respect for law would be weakened if *Roe* v. *Wade* were overruled.

26. See Gary B. Gertler, "Brain Birth: A Proposal for Defining When a Fetus Is Entitled to Human Life Status," *Southern California Law Review*, Vol. 59, p. 1061.

27. See Brief for the Appellees in *Webster* v. *Reproductive Health Services*, p. 48.

28. *Maber* v. *Roe*, 432 U.S. 464 (1977).

29. *Poelker* v. *Doe*, 432 U.S. 519 (1977).

JOEL FEINBERG

Limits to the Free Expression of Opinion*

The purpose of this essay is to determine how the liberal principles that support free expression of opinion generally also define the limits to what the law can permit to be said. The liberal principle in question, put vaguely, is that state coercion is justified only to prevent personal or public harm. That more harm than good can be expected to come from suppression of dissenting opinions in politics and religion has been amply documented by experience and argument, but concentration on this important truth, despite its salutary practical effects, is likely to mislead us into thinking that the liberal "harm principle" is simple in its meaning and easy in its application. For that reason, this essay will only summarize (in Part I) the impressive case for total freedom of expression of opinions of certain kinds in normal contexts, and concentrate instead (in Part II) on the types of expressions *excluded* by the harm principle: defamation and "malicious truth," invasions of privacy, and expressions that cause others to do harm (those that cause panics, provoke retaliatory violence, or incite others to crime or insurrection). Part III will examine the traditional crime of "sedition," and conclude that it is not properly among the categories of expressions excluded by the harm principle. Among the other lessons that will emerge from these exercises, I hope, is that the harm principle is a largely empty formula in urgent need of supplementation by tests for determining the relative importance of conflicting interests and by measures of the degree to which interests are endangered by free expressions.

I THE CASE FOR FREEDOM

The classic case for free expression of opinion was made by John Stuart Mill.[1] Mill's purpose in his famous chapter "Of the Liberty of Thought and Discussion" was to consider, as a beginning, just one class of actions and how his "harm principle" applied to them. The actions in question were instances of expressing orally or in print opinions about matters of fact, and about historical, scientific, theological, philosophical, political, and moral questions. Mill's conclusion was that suppressing such expressions is always more harmful than the expressions themselves would be and therefore is never justified. But don't expressions of opinion *ever* harm others? Of course they do, and it would be silly to ascribe to Mill the absurd contrary view. Expressions of opinion harm others when they are: defamatory (libelous or slanderous), seditious, incitive to violence, malicious publications of damaging or embarrassing truths, or invasions of privacy. In fact, in classifying an expression under one of these headings, we are *ipso facto* declaring that it is harmful. Mill is not radical about this. Putting these obviously harmful expressions to one side (he is best understood as asking) is there any [further] ground for suppressing mere "opinions"? To *this* question Mill's answer is radical and absolutist: If an expression cannot be subsumed under one of these standard headings for harmfulness, then it can never be sufficiently injurious to be justifiably suppressed. Apart from direct harm to assignable persons, no other ground is ever a sufficient reason for overriding the presumption in favor of liberty. One may *never* properly suppress an expression on the grounds, for example, that it is immoral, shocking to sensibilities, annoying, heretical, unorthodox, or "dangerous," and especially not on the ground simply that it is false.

Expressions of opinion thus occupy a very privileged position, in Mill's view. That is because their suppression, he contends, is not only a private injury to the coerced party but also and inevitably a very serious harm to the public in general. The argument has two distinct branches. The first has us consider the possibility that the suppressed opinion is wholly or partially true. On this assumption, of course, repression will have the harmful social consequence of loss of truth.

The crucial contention in this wing of the argument, however, is much stronger than that. Mill

*This essay was written expressly for this book, and has not been published elsewhere.

contends that there is *always* a chance, for all we can know, that the suppressed opinion is at least partially true, so that the act of repression itself necessarily involves some risk. Moreover, the risk is always an unreasonable one, never worth taking, since the risk of its alternative—permitting free expression generally—to our interest in acquiring knowledge and avoiding error, is negligible. By letting every opinion, no matter how "certainly true," be challenged, we minimize the risk of permanent commitment to falsehood. In the process, of course, we allow some falsehoods to be expressed, but since the truth is not denied its champions either, there is very little risk that the tolerated falsehood will become permanently enthroned. The balance of favorable risks then is clearly on the side of absolute freedom of expression.

This argument is especially convincing in the world of science, where no hypothesis bears its evidence on its face, and old errors are continually exposed by new and easily duplicable evidence and by more careful and refined experimental techniques. Even totalitarian regimes have learned that it is in their own interest to permit physicists and plant geneticists to go their theoretical ways unencumbered by ideological restrictions. Sometimes, to be sure, the truth of a scientific theory is so apparent that it is well worth acting on even though it strains governmental priorities to do so and requires large investment of funds; but this very confidence, Mill argued, is justified only when every interested party has had an opportunity to refute the theory. In respect at least to scientific theories, the more open to attack an opinion is, the more confident we can eventually be of its truth. That "no one has disproved it yet" is a convincing reason for accepting a theory only when everyone has been free to try.

To deny that it is possible for a given opinion to be true, Mill maintained, is to assume one's own infallibility. This is no doubt an overstatement, but what does seem clear is that to deny that a given proposition can possibly be true is to assume one's own infallibility with respect to *it,* though of course not one's infallibility generally. To say that one cannot possibly be wrong in holding a given belief is to say that one knows that one's knowledge of its truth is authentic. We claim to know infallibly when we claim to know that we know. It is also clear, I think, that we are sometimes justified in making such claims. I know that I know that $2 + 3 = 5$, that I am seated at my desk writing, and that New York is in the United States. In the face of challenges from the relentless epistemological skeptic, I may have to admit that I don't know *how* I know these things, but it doesn't follow from that that I don't know them. It seems then that there is no risk, after all, in suppressing some opinions, namely, the denials of such truisms.

Yet what could ever be the point of forbidding persons from denying that $2 + 3 = 5$ or that New York is in the United States? There is surely no danger that general confidence in these true propositions would be undermined. There is no risk of loss of truth, I suppose, in suppressing their denials, but also no risk in allowing them free circulation. Conceding that we can know truisms infallibly, therefore, can hardly commit us to approve of the suppression of their denials, at least so long as we adhere, with Mill, exclusively to the harm principle. More importantly, there are serious risks involved in granting any mere man or group of men the power to draw the line between those opinions that are known infallibly to be true and those not so known, in order to ban expression of the former. Surely, if there is one thing that is *not* infallibly known, it is how to draw *that* line.

In any case, when we leave tautologies and truisms behind and consider only those larger questions of substance, doctrines about which have in fact been banned by rulers in the past as certainly false (for example, the shape of the earth, the cause of disease, the wisdom of certain wars or economic policies, and the morality of certain kinds of conduct) our own fallibility is amply documented by history. The sad fact is that at every previous stage of history including the recent past there have been questions of the highest importance about which nearly *everyone,* including the wisest and most powerful, has been dead wrong. The more important the doctrines, then, the greater the risk we run in forbidding expressions of disagreement.

Mill's account, in this first wing of his argument, of the public interest in the discovery and effective dissemination of truth has many important practical implications. Mill himself thought that we should seek out our ideological enemies and offer them public forums in which to present and defend their views, or failing that, hire "devil's advocates" to defend unpopular positions in schools and in popular debates. Mill's reasons for these proposals also provide the grounding for the so-called "adversary theory of politics." The argument is (in the words of Zechariah Chafee): "Truth can be sifted out from falsehood only if the government is vigorously and constantly cross-examined . . . Legal proceedings prove that an opponent makes the best cross-examiner."[2] This states the rationale of the two-party system exactly. The role of the out-party is like that of the prosecutor in a criminal trial, or plaintiff in a civil action. It is a vitally important role too. Numerous historical instances suggest that we are in grave danger when both parties agree. Witness, for example, the Vietnam debacle, which was the outcome of a twenty-year "bipartisan foreign policy." Foreign policy decisions are as difficult as they are important; hence the need for constant reexamination, probing for difficulties and soft spots, bringing to light new and relevant facts, and subjecting to doubt hitherto unquestioned first premises. Without these aids, we tend to drift quite complacently into dead ends and quagmires.[3]

The second branch of the argument has us assume that the unorthodox opinion we are tempted to suppress really is false anyway. Even in this case, Mill insists, we will all be the losers, in the end, for banning it. When people are not forced by the stimulus of dissent to rethink the grounds of their convictions, then their beliefs tend to wither and decay. The rationales of the tenets are forgotten, their vital direction and value lost, their very meaning altered, until at last they are held in the manner of dead dogmas rather than living truths.

No part of Mill's argument in *On Liberty* is more impressive than his case for totally free expression of opinion. It is especially ingenious in that it rests entirely on social advantages and foregoes all help that might come from appeals to "the inalienable right to say what one pleases whether it's good for society or not." But that very utilitarian ingenuity may be its Achilles heel; for if liberty of expression is justified only because it is socially useful, then some might think that it is justified only *when* it is socially useful. The possibility of special circumstances in which repression is still *more* useful is real enough to disturb allies of Mill who love liberty fully as much as he and would seek therefore a still more solid foundation for it. But even if the case for absolute liberty of opinion must rest ultimately on some theory of natural rights, Mill has given that case powerful utilitarian reinforcement.

II LIMITS TO FREEDOM

Despite the impressive case for complete liberty of expression, there are obvious instances where permitting a person to speak his mind

freely will cause more harm than good all around. These instances have been lumped together in various distinct legal categories whose names have come to stand for torts or crimes and to suggest, by a powerful linguistic convention, unpermitted wrongdoing. Thus, there can be no more right to defame or to incite to riot than there can be a right way, in Aristotle's example,[4] to commit adultery. Underlying these linguistic conventions, however, are a settled residue of interest weightings as well as actual and hypothetical applications of the harm principle, often filled in or mediated in various ways by principles of other kinds. The various categories of excluded expressions are worth examining not only for the light they throw on the harm principle, but also for the conceptual and normative problems each raises on its own for political theory.

1. *Defamation and "Malicious Truth."* Defamatory statements are those that damage a person's reputation by their expression to third parties in a manner that "tends to diminish the esteem in which the plaintiff is held, or to excite adverse feelings or opinions against him."[5] The primary mode of discouraging defamers in countries adhering to the common law has been the threat of civil liability to a court-enforced order to pay cash to the injured party in compensation for the harm done his reputation. In cases of especially malicious defamation, the defendant may be ordered to pay a stiff fine ("punitive damages") to the plaintiff as well. Only in the most egregious cases (and rarely even then) has criminal liability been imposed for defamation, but nevertheless the threat of civil suit as sufficient to entitle us to say that our law does not leave citizens (generally) free to defame one another. Here then is one clear limit to our freedom of expression.

Not all expressions that harm another's reputation, of course, are legally forbidden. Even when damaging defamation has been proved by the plaintiff, the defendant may yet escape liability by establishing one of two kinds of defense. He may argue that his utterance or publication was "privileged," or simply that it is *true*. The former defense is established by showing either that the defendant, in virtue of his public office or his special relation to the plaintiff, has been granted an absolute immunity from liability for defamation (for example, he spoke in a judicial or legislative proceeding, or he had the prior consent of the plaintiff), or that he had a prior immunity contingent on the reasonableness of his conduct. Examples of this category of privilege are the immunity of a person protecting himself or another by a warning that someone is of poor character, or of a drama, literary, or political critic making "fair comment" of an extremely unfavorable kind about a performance, a book, or a policy. These immunities are still other examples of public policies that protect an interest (in this case, the interest in reputation) just to the point where the protection interferes with interests deemed more important—either to the public in general or to other private individuals. These policies imply that a person's reputation is a precious thing that deserves legal protection just as his life, health, and property do, but on the other hand, a certain amount of rough handling of reputations is to be expected in courtrooms, in the heated spontaneous debates of legislative chambers, in reviews of works presented to the public for critical comment, and in the rough-and-tumble competition among eminent persons for power or public acclaim. To withhold immunities in these special contexts would be to allow nervous inhibitions to keep hard truths out of law courts to the detriment of justice, or out of legislatures to the detriment of the laws themselves; or to make critics overly cautious, to the detriment of those who rely on their judgments; or to make political commentators overly deferential to power and authority, to the detriment of reform.

There is, however, no public interest in keeping those who are not in these special contexts uninhibited when they speak or write about others. Indeed, we should all be nervous when we make unfavorable comments, perhaps not on the ground that feelings and reputations will simply be damaged (there may be both justice and social gain in such damage), but at least on the ground that the unfavorable comment may be *false*. In a way, the rationale for the defamation action at law is the opposite of Mill's case for the free expression of opinion. The great public interest in possessing the truth in science, philosophy, politics, and so on, is best served by keeping everyone uninhibited in the expression of his views; but there are areas where there is a greater interest in avoiding falsehood than in acquiring truth, and here we are best served by keeping people very nervous indeed when they are tempted to speak their minds.

Once the plaintiff has proved that the defendant has published a defamatory statement about him, the defendant may avoid liability in another way, namely, by showing that the statement in question is *true*. "Out of a tender regard for reputations," writes Professor Prosser, "the law presumes in the first instance that all defamation is false, and the defendant has the burden of pleading and proving its truth."[6] In the large majority of American jurisdictions, truth is a "complete defense" which will relieve the defendant of liability even when he published his defamation merely out of spite, in the absence of any reasonable social purpose. One wonders why this should be. Is the public interest in "the truth" so great that it should always override a private person's interest in his own reputation? An affirmative answer, I should think, would require considerable argument.

Most of the historical rationales for the truth defense worked out in the courts and in legal treatises will not stand scrutiny. They all founder, I think, on the following kind of case. A New York girl supports her drug addiction by working as a prostitute in a seedy environment of crime and corruption. After a brief jail sentence, she decides to reform, and travels to the Far West to begin her life anew. She marries a respectable young man, becomes a leader in civic and church affairs, and raises a large and happy family. Then twenty years after her arrival in town, her neurotically jealous neighbor learns of her past, and publishes a lurid but accurate account of it for the eyes of the whole community. As a consequence, her "friends" and associates snub her; she is asked to resign her post as church leader; gossipmongers prattle ceaselessly about her; and obscene inscriptions appear on her property and in her mail. She dare not sue her neighbor for defamation since the defamatory report is wholly true. She has been wronged, but she has no legal remedy.

Applied to this case the leading rationales for the truth defense are altogether unconvincing. One argument claims that the true gravamen of the wrong in defamation is the deception practiced on the public in misrepresenting the truth, so that where there is no misrepresentation there is no injury—as if the injury to the reformed sinner is of no account. A variant of this argument holds the reformed sinner to be deserving of exposure on the ground that he (or she) in covering up his past deceives the public, thereby compounding the earlier delinquency. If this sort of "deception" is morally blameworthy, then so is every form of 'covering up the truth,' from cosmetics to window blinds! Others have argued that a delinquent plaintiff should not be allowed any standing in court because of his established bad character. A related contention is that "a person is in no position to complain of a reputation which is consistent with his actual character and behavior."[7] Both of these rationales apply well enough to the unrepentant sinner, but work nothing but injustice and suffering on the reformed person, on the plaintiff defamed in some way that does not reflect upon his character, or on the person whose "immoralities" have been wholly private and scrupulously kept from the public eye. It does not follow from the fact that a person's reputation is consistent with the truth that it is "deserved."

The most plausible kind of argument for the truth defense is that it serves some kind of overriding public interest. Some have argued that fear of eventual exposure can serve as effectively as the threat of punishment to *deter* wrongdoing. This argument justifies a kind of endless social penalty and is therefore more cruel than a system of criminal law, which usually permits a wrongdoer to wipe his slate clean. Others have claimed that exposure of character flaws and past sins protects the community by warning it of dangerous or untrustworthy persons. That argument is well put (but without endorsement) by Harper and James when they refer to ". . . the social desirability as a general matter, of leaving individuals free to warn the public of antisocial members of the community, provided only that the person furnishing the information take the risk of its being false."[8] (Blackstone went so far as to assert that the defendant who can show the truth of his defamatory remarks has rendered a public service in exposing the plaintiff and deserves the public's gratitude.)[9] This line of argument is convincing enough when restricted to public-spirited defamers and socially dangerous plaintiffs; but it lacks all plausibility when applied to the malicious and useless exposure of past misdeeds, or to nonmoral failings and "moral" flaws of a wholly private and well-concealed kind.

How precious a thing, after all, is this thing denoted by the glittering abstract noun, the "Truth"? The truth in general is a great and noble cause, a kind of public treasury more important than any particular person's feelings; but the truth about a particular person may be of no great value at all except to that person. When the personal interest in reputation outweighs the dilute public interest in truth (and there is no doubt that this is sometimes the case) then it must be protected even at some cost to our general knowledge of the truth. The truth, like any other commodity, is not so valuable that it is a bargain at *any* cost. A growing number of American states have now modified the truth defense so that it applies only when the defamatory statement has been published with good motives, or is necessary for some reasonable public purpose, or (in some cases) both. The change is welcome.

In summary, the harm principle would permit all harmless statements about others whether true or false (harmless statements by definition are not defamatory), but it would impose liability for all defamatory false statements and all seriously defamatory true statements except those that serve (or seem likely to serve) some beneficial social purpose.

2. *Invasions of Privacy*. Still other expressions are neither defamatory nor false, and yet they can unjustly wound the persons they describe all the same. These do not invade the interest in a good reputation so much as a special kind of interest in peace of mind, sometimes called a sense of dignity, sometimes the enjoyment of solitude, but most commonly termed the interest in personal privacy. As the legal "right to privacy" is now understood, it embraces a miscellany of things, protecting the right-holder not only from "physical intrusions upon his solitude" and "publicity given to his name or likeness or to private information about him" without his permission, but also from being placed "in a false light [but without defamation] in the public eye" and from the "commercial appropriation of elements of his personality."[10] (Some of these are really invasions of one's property rights through unpermitted commercial exploitation of one's name, image, personality, and so on. For that reason it has been urged that the invaded right in these cases be called "the right to publicity.") What concerns us here are statements conveying true and nondefamatory information about the plaintiff, of a very intimate and properly private kind, gathered and published without his consent, often to his shame and mortification. Business advantage and journalistic profit have become ever stronger motives for such statements, and the invention of tiny, very sensitive snooping devices has made the data easier than ever to come by.

Since the "invasion of privacy" tort has been recognized, plaintiffs have recovered damages from defendants who have shadowed them, looked into their windows, investigated their bank accounts, and tapped their telephone wires. In many of these cases, the court's judgment protected the plaintiff's interest in "being let alone," but in other cases the interest protected was not merely this, or not this at all, but rather the interest in *not being known about.* If there is a right not to be known about in some respects by anyone, then *a fortiori* there is a right not to be known about, in those respects, by nearly everyone. Privacy law has also protected the interests of those who don't want details of their lives called to the public's attention and made the subject of public wonder, amusement, discussion, analysis, or debate. Hence some plaintiffs have recovered from defendants who have published embarrassing details of their illness or physical deformity; their personal letters or unpublished notes, or inventories of their possessions; their photographs in a "good looks" popularity contest, or in a "before and after" advertisement for baldness or obesity cures, or on the labels of tomato cans; and from defendants who have published descriptions of the plaintiffs' sexual relations, hygienic habits, and other very personal matters. No life, of course, can be kept wholly private, or immune from public inspection even in some of its most personal aspects. "No one enjoys being stared at," Harper and James remind us, yet if a person "goes out on the street he [can have] no legal objection to people looking at him."[11] On the other hand, life would be hardly tolerable if there were no secrets we could keep (away from "the street"), no preserve of dignity, no guaranteed solitude.

There would probably be very little controversy over the existence of a right to privacy were it not the case that the interest in being let alone is frequently in conflict with other interests that seem at least equally deserving of protection. Even where the right is recognized by law, it is qualified by the recognition of very large classes of privileged expressions. First of all, like most other torts and crimes, the charge of invasion of privacy is completely defeated by proof that the plaintiff gave his consent to the defendant's conduct. Secondly, and more interestingly, the right of privacy can conflict with the constitutionally guaranteed freedom of the press, which, according to Prosser, "justifies the publication of news and all other matters of legitimate public interest and concern."[12] For a court to adjudicate between a paper's right to publish and an individual's right to privacy then, it must employ some standard for determining what is of legitimate public concern or, what amounts to the same thing, which news about a person is "fit to print." Such legal standards are always in the making, never finished, but the standard of "legitimate interest" has begun to take on a definite shape. American courts have decided, first of all, that "the person who intentionally puts himself in the public eye . . . has no right to complain of any publicity which reasonably bears on his activ-

ity."[13] The rationale for this judgment invokes the maxim that a person is not wronged by that to which he consents, or by that the risk of which he has freely assumed. The person who steps into the public spotlight ought to know what he is letting himself in for; hence the law presumes that he *does* know, and therefore that he is asking for it. Much the same kind of presumption lies behind the "fair comment" defense in defamation cases: The person who voluntarily publishes his own work is presumed to be inviting criticism and is therefore not entitled to complain when the criticism is adverse or harsh, providing only that it is relevant and not personally abusive. One can put oneself voluntarily into the public eye by running for or occupying public office; by becoming an actor, musician, entertainer, poet, or novelist; by inventing an interesting device or making a geographical or scientific discovery; or even by becoming wealthy. Once a person has become a public figure, he has sacrificed much of his right of privacy to the public's legitimate curiosity. Of course, one never forfeits *all* rights of privacy; even the public figure has a right to the privacy of his very most intimate affairs. (This may, however, be very small consolation to him.)

One cannot always escape the privilege of the press to invade one's privacy simply by avoiding public roles and offices, for the public spotlight can catch up with anyone. "Reluctant public characters" are nonetheless public and therefore, according to the courts, as legitimate objects of public curiosity as the voluntary public figures. Those unfortunates who attract attention unwillingly by becoming involved, even as victims, in accidents, or by being accused of crimes, or even as innocent bystanders to interesting events, have become "news," and therefore subject to the public's right to know. They maintain this unhappy status "until they have reverted to the lawful and unexciting life led by the great bulk of the community," but until then, "they are subject to the privileges which publishers have to satisfy the curiosity of the public as to their leaders, heroes, villains, and victims."[14] Again, the privilege to publish is not unlimited so that "the courts must somehow draw the distinction between conduct which outrages the common decencies and goes beyond what the public mores will tolerate, and that which the plaintiff must be expected in the circumstances to endure."[15]

When interests of quite different kinds head toward collisions, how can one determine which has the right of way? This problem, which lies behind the most puzzling questions about the grounds for liberty and coercion, tends to be concealed by broadly stated principles. The conflict between the personal interest in privacy and the public curiosity is one of the best illustrations of the problem, but it is hardly unique. In defamation cases, as we have seen, there is often a conflict between the public interest in truth and the plaintiff's interest in his own good name. In nuisance law, there is a conflict between the plaintiff's interest in the peaceful enjoyment of his land and the defendant's interest in keeping a hogpen, or a howling dog, or a small boiler factory. In suburban neighborhoods, the residents' interest in quiet often conflicts with motorcyclists' interest in cheap and speedy transportation. In buses and trains, one passenger's interest in privacy[16] can conflict with another's interest in listening to rock and roll music on a portable radio, or for that matter, with the interests of two nearby passengers in making unavoidably audible, but avoidably inane, conversation. The principle of "the more freedom the better" doesn't tell us whose freedom must give way in these competitive situations.

The invasion of privacy cases are among the very clearest examples of the inevitable clash of interests in populous modern communities. They are, moreover, examples that show that solving the problem is not just a matter of minimizing harm all around. Harm is the invasion of an interest, and invasions do differ in degree, but when interests of radically different kinds are invaded to the same degree, where is the greater harm? Perhaps we should say that some interests are more important than others in the sense that harm to them is likely to lead to greater damage to the whole economy of personal (or as the case may be, community) interests than harm to the lesser interest, just as harm to one's heart or brain will do more damage to one's bodily health than an "equal degree" of harm to less vital organs. Determining which interests are more "vital" in an analogous sense would be no easy task, but even if we could settle this matter, there would remain serious difficulties. In the first place, interests pile up and reinforce one another. My interest in peace and quiet may be more vital in my system than the motorcyclist's interests in speed, excitement, and economy are in his, but there is also the interest of the cyclists' employer in having workers efficiently transported to his factory, and the economic interest of the community in general (including me) in the flourishing of the factory owner's business; the interest of the motorcycle manufacturers in their own profits; the

interest of the police and others (perhaps including me) in providing a relatively harmless outlet for adolescent exuberance, and in not having a difficult rule to enforce. There may be nowhere near so great a buildup of reinforcing interests, personal and public, in the quietude of my neighborhood.

There is still another kind of consideration that complicates the delicate task of interest-balancing. Interests differ not only in the extent to which they are thwarted, in their importance or "vitality," and the degree to which they are backed up by other interests, but also in their inherent moral quality. Some interests, simply by reason of their very natures, we might think better worth protecting than others. The interest in knowing the intimate details of Brigitte Bardot's married sex life (the subject of a sensational law suit in France) is a morally repugnant peeping tom's interest. The sadist's interest in having others suffer pain is a morbid interest. The interest in divulging a celebrity's private conversations is a busybody's interest. It is probably not conducive to the public good to encourage development of the character flaws from which these interests spring, but even if there were social advantage in the individual vices, there would be a case against protecting their spawned interests, based upon their inherent unworthiness. The interests in understanding, diagnosing, and simply being apprised of newsworthy events might well outbalance a given individual's reluctance to be known about, but photographs and descriptions with no plausible appeal except to the morbid and sensational can have very little weight in the scales.

3. *Causing Panic.* Defamatory statements, "malicious truths," and statements that wrongfully invade privacy do harm to the persons they are about by conveying information or falsehood to third parties. Their publication tends to instill certain beliefs in others, and the very existence of those beliefs constitutes a harm to the person spoken or written about. Other classes of injurious expressions do harm in a rather different way, namely, by causing those who listen to them (or more rarely, those who read them) to act in violent or otherwise harmful ways. In these cases, the expressions need not be about any specifiable persons, or if they are about persons, those individuals are not necessarily the victims of the subsequent harm. When spoken words cause panic, breach the peace, or incite to crime or revolt, a variety of important interests, personal and social, will be seriously harmed. Such expres-

sions, therefore, are typically proscribed by the criminal, and not merely the civil, law.

"The most stringent protection of free speech," wrote Holmes in his most celebrated opinion, "would not protect a man in falsely shouting fire in a theatre and causing a panic."[17] In some circumstances a person can cause even more harm by *truthfully* shouting "Fire!" in a crowded theater, for the flames and smoke might reinforce the tendency of his words to cause panic, and the fire itself might block exits, leading the hysterical crowds to push and trample. But we do not, and cannot fairly, hold the excited alarm sounder criminally responsible for his warning when it was in fact true and shouted with good intentions. We can hardly demand on pain of punishment that persons pick their words carefully in emergencies, when emotions naturally run high and there is no time for judicious deliberation. A person's warning shout in such circumstances is hardly to be treated as a full-fledged voluntary act at all. Perhaps it can be condemned as negligent, but given the mitigating circumstances, such negligence hardly amounts to the gross and wanton kind that can be a basis of criminal liability. The law, then, can only punish harmful words of this class when they are spoken or written with the intention of causing the harm that in fact ensues, or when they are spoken or written in conscious disregard of a high and unreasonable risk that the harm will ensue. The practical joker in a crowded auditorium who whispers to his comrade, "Watch me start a panic," and then shouts "Fire!" could be convicted for using words intentionally to cause a panic. The prankster who is willing to risk a general panic just for the fun of alarming one particular person in the audience could fairly be convicted for the grossly reckless use of dangerous words. Indeed, his recklessness is akin to that of the motorist who drives at an excessive speed just to frighten a timorous passenger.

Suppose, however, that the theater is virtually empty, and as the lights come on at the end of the film, our perverse or dim-witted jokester shouts "Fire! Fire!" just for the sake of confusing the three or four other patrons and alarming the ushers. The ushers quickly see through the ruse and suffer only a few moments of anxiety, and the patrons walk quickly to the exits and depart. No harm to speak of has been done; nor could any have reasonably been anticipated. This example shows how very important are the surrounding circumstances of an utterance to the question of its permissibility. Given the presumptive case for

liberty in general, and especially the powerful social interest in leaving persons free to use *words* as they see fit, there can be a countervailing case for suppression on the grounds of the words' dangerous tendency only when the danger in fact is great and the tendency immediate. These matters are determined not only by the particular words used, but by the objective character of the surrounding circumstances—what lawyers call "the time, place, and manner" of utterance.

The question of legal permissibility should not be confused with that of moral blameworthiness or even with civil liability. The practical joker, even in relatively harmless circumstances, is no moral paragon. But then neither are the liar, the vulgarian, the rude man, and the scandalmonger, most of whose faults are not fit subjects for penal legislation. We cannot make every instance of mendacity, rudeness, and malicious gossip criminal, but we can protect people from the serious injury that comes from fraud, battery, or defamation. Similarly, practical jokers should be blamed but not punished, unless their tricks reach the threshold of serious danger to others. On the other hand, almost all lies, bad tales, jokes, and tricks create some risk, and there is no injustice in making the perpetrator compensate (as opposed to being punished) even his unlikely victim. Thus, if a patron in the nearly empty theater described above sprains an ankle in hurrying towards an exit, there is no injustice in requiring the jokester to pay the medical expenses.

It is established in our law that when words did not in fact cause harm the speaker may nevertheless be punished for having uttered them only if there was high danger when they were spoken that serious harm would result. This condition of course could be satisfied even though the harm in fact was averted: Not everything probable becomes actual. Similarly, for a person rightly to be punished even for harm in fact caused by his words, the harm in its resultant magnitude must have been an objectively probable consequence of the spoken words in the circumstances; otherwise the speaker will be punished for an unforeseeable fluke. In either case, then, the clear and present danger that serious harm will follow a speaker's words is necessary if he is rightly to be punished.

As we have seen, punishment for the harm caused by words is proper only if the speaker caused the harm either *intentionally* or *recklessly*. Both of these "mental conditions" of guilt require the satisfaction of the clear and present danger formula, or something like it. Consider recklessness first. For there to be recklessness there must really be a substantial risk consciously and unreasonably run. A speaker is not being reckless if he utters words that have only a remote and speculative tendency to cause panics or riots.

Intentional harm-causing by words raises more complications. Suppose an evil-minded person wishes to cause a panic and believes what is false and wholly unsupported by any real evidence, namely, that his words will have that effect. Imagine that he attends a meeting of the Policemen's Benevolent Association and, at what he takes to be the strategic moment, he stands up and shrieks, "There's a mouse under my chair!" Perhaps these words would cause a panic at a meeting of Girl Scouts but it merely produces a round of contemptuous laughter here. Wanting a panic and sincerely believing that one is causing a panic by one's words, then, are not sufficient. Suppose however we complicate the story so that by some wholly unforeseeable fluke the spoken words do precipitate a panic. The story is hard to invent at this point, but let us imagine that one patrolman laughs so hard that he tips over his chair causing another to drop his pipe, starting a fire, igniting live bullets, et cetera. Now, in addition to evil desire, and conscious belief in causal efficacy, we have a third important element: The words actually do initiate a causal process resulting in the desired panic. But these conditions still are not sufficient to permit us to say that the speaker *intentionally caused* a panic. Without the antecedent objective probability that a panic would follow these words in these circumstances, we have only a bizarre but tragic coincidence.

We would say much the same thing of a superstitious lady who "attempts" to start a riot by magic means. In an inconspicuous corner of a darkened theater, she sticks pins into a doll and mutters under her breath a magic incantation designed to produce a panic. Of course this doesn't work in the way intended, but a nearsighted and neurotic passerby observes her, takes the doll to be a real baby, and screams. The hoped-for panic then really follows. The evil lady cannot be found guilty of intentionally causing a panic, even though she intended to cause one and really did cause (or at least initiate a causal process that resulted in) one. She can be condemned for having very evil motives. But if people are sufficiently ignorant and impotent, the law, applying the harm principle, allows them to be as evil as they wish.

4. *Provoking Retaliatory Violence.* Suppose a person utters words which have as their unhappy effects violence directed *at him* by his angry audience, counterviolence by his friends and protectors, and escalation into a riotous breach of the peace. This is still another way of causing harm by words. Should the speaker be punished? In almost every conceivable case, the answer should be No. There is a sense, of course, in which the speaker did not start the physical violence. He used only words, and while words can sting and infuriate, they are not instruments of violence in the same sense that fists, knives, guns, and clubs are. If the law suppresses public speech, either by withholding permits in advance or punishing afterwards, simply on the ground that the expressed views are so unpopular that some auditors can be expected to start fighting, then the law punishes some for the criminal proclivities of others. "A man does not become a criminal because someone else assaults him . . .," writes Zechariah Chafee. Moreover, he continues, on any such theory, "a small number of intolerant men . . . can prevent *any kind* of meeting . . . A gathering which expressed the sentiment of a majority of law-abiding citizens would become illegal because a small gang of hoodlums threatened to invade the hall."[18] When violent response to speech threatens, the obvious remedy is not suppression, but rather increased police protection.

So much seems evident, but there may be some exceptions. Some words uttered in public places in the presence of many unwilling auditors may be so abusive or otherwise offensive as to be "reasonably considered a direct provocation to violence."[19] The captive auditor, after all, is not looking for trouble as he walks the public streets intent on his private errands. If he is forced to listen, as he walks past a street meeting, to speakers denouncing and ridiculing his religion, and forced to notice a banner with a large and abusive caricature of the Pope,[20] his blood might reasonably be expected to boil. Antireligious and anticlerical opinions, of course, no matter how unpopular, are entitled to the full protection of the law. Even abusive, virulent, and mocking expressions of such views are entitled to full protection if uttered to private gatherings, in private or privately reserved places. Such expressions become provocative only when made in public places to captive auditors.

What makes an expression "provocative?" Surely, if words are to be suppressed on the ground that they are provocative of violence, they must be more than merely "provoking," else all unpopular opinions will be suppressed, to the great public loss. As far as I know, the concept of provocation has received thorough legal elaboration only in the law of homicide, where provocation reduces a charge of murder to that of manslaughter, thus functioning as a kind of mitigating consideration rather than as a justification or complete excuse. In the common law, for there to be sufficient provocation to mitigate: (1) The behavior of the victim must have been so aggravating that it would have produced "such excitement and passion as would obscure the reason of an ordinary man and induce him . . . to strike the blow."[21] (2) There must not have elapsed so much time between the provocation and the violence that a reasonable man's blood would have cooled. (3) But for the victim's provocation the violence would not have occurred. In short, provocation mitigates only when it in fact produces a reason-numbing rage in the attacker and is such that it could be expected to produce such a rage in any normal person in his circumstances. Nazi emblems might be expected to have this effect on a former inmate of a Nazi death camp, but the Democratic party line cannot be sufficiently provocative to excuse a violent Republican, and similarly the other way round. Indeed, in the law of homicide, *no mere words alone,* no matter how abusive or scurrilous, can be adequate provocation to justify or totally excuse killing as a response.

There would seem to be equally good reason not to consider mere words either as justifying or totally excusing nonlethal acts of violence. The "reasonable person" in a democracy must be presumed to have enough self-control to refrain from violent responses to odious words and doctrines. If he is followed, insulted, taunted, and challenged, he can get injunctive relief, or bring charges against his tormentor as a nuisance; if there is no time for this and he is backed to the wall he may be justified in using "reasonable force" in self-defense; or if he is followed to his own home, he can use the police to remove the nuisance. But if he is not personally harrassed in these ways, he can turn on his heels and leave the provocation behind, and this is what the law, perhaps, should require of him.

Only when public speech satisfies stringent tests qualifying it as "direct provocation to violence," (if that is possible at all) will the harm principle justify its suppression. But there are many possible modes of suppression, and some are far more restrictive of liberty than others. Orders to cease and desist on pain of arrest are most economical, for they permit the speaker to continue to air his views in a nonprovocative way or else retire with his audience to a less public place. Lawful removal of the provocation (as a public nuisance) may be more satisfactory than permitting violent response to it, and is infinitely preferable to punishing the speaker. Nowhere in the law where provocation is considered as a defense do the rules deem the proven provoker (the victim) a criminal himself! At best his conduct mitigates the crime of his attacker, who is the only criminal.

One final point. While it is conceivable that some public *speech* can satisfy the common law test for provocation by being so aggravating that even a reasonable person could be expected to lose control of his reason when exposed to it, this can never be true of books. One can always escape the provocation of the printed word simply by declining to read it, and where escape from provocation is that easy, no "reasonable person" will succumb to it.

5. *Incitement to Crime or Insurrection.* In the criminal law, anyone who "counsels, commands, or encourages another to commit a crime" is himself guilty of the resultant crime as an "accessory before the fact." Counseling, commanding, and encouraging, however, must consist in more than merely uttering certain words in the presence of others. Surely there must also be serious (as opposed to playful) intent and some possibility at least of the words having their desired effect. It is not possible that these conditions can be satisfied if I tell my secretary that she should overthrow the United States government, or if a speaker tells an audience of bank presidents that they should practice embezzlement whenever they can. These situations are analogous to the efforts to start a panic by magical means or to panic policemen with words about mice.

The problem of interpreting the meaning of a rule making the counseling of crime itself a crime is similar, I should think, to that raised by a statute forbidding the planting of a certain kind of plant. One does not violate such a statute if he scatters the appropriate kind of seeds on asphalt pavement or in barren desert, even with evil intent. (Again, if you are stupid enough, the law—insofar as it derives from the harm principle—can allow you to be as evil as you wish.) To violate the statute, either one would have to dig a little hole in the appropriate sort of soil, deposit the appropriate seeds, cultivate, fertilize, allow for sufficient water, protect against winds, worms, and dogs; *or* one would have to find suitable conditions ready-made, where the soil is already receptive and merely dropping the seeds will create a substantial likelihood that plants will grow and thrive. By analogy, even words of advice, if they are to count as incitements to crime, must fall on reasonably receptive ears. The harm principle provides a ready rationale for this requirement. If we permit coercive repression of nondangerous words we will confer such abundant powers on the repressive organs of the state that they are certain to be abused. Moreover, we will so inhibit persons in their employment of language as to discourage both spontaneity and serious moral discussion, thus doing a great deal of harm and virtually no good at all. (The only "gain," if it is that, to be expected from looser standards of interpretation would be that nondangerous persons with evil motives could be scooped up in the state's tighter nets and punished.)

Counseling others to crime is not the only use of speech that can be described as incitement. We must also come to terms with instigating, egging on, and inflaming others to violence. Even Mill conceded that the opinion that "corn dealers are starvers of the poor," which deserves protection when published in the press, may nevertheless "justly incur punishment when delivered orally to an excited mob assembled before the house of a corn dealer . . ."[22] The metaphor of planting seeds in receptive soil is perhaps less apt for this situation than the commonly employed "spark and tinder" analogy. Words which merely express legitimate though unpopular opinion in one context become "incendiary" when addressed to an already inflammable mob. As Chafee put it: "Smoking is all right, but not in a powder magazine."[23] Of course the man who carries a cigar into a powder magazine may not know that the cigar he is carrying is lighted, or he may not know that he has entered a powder magazine. He may plead his lack of intention afterward (if he is still alive) as a defense. Similarly, the man who speaks his opinion to what he takes to be a calm audience, or an excited audience with *different* axes all ground fine, may plead his ignorance in good faith as a defense. But "the law" (as judges are fond of saying) "presumes that a man intends the natural and probable consequences of his actions," so that a defendant who denies that he intended to cause a riot may have the burden of proving his innocent intention to the jury.

In summary, there are two points to emphasize in connection with the punishment of inflammatory incitements. First, the audience must really be tinder, that is to say not merely sullen, but angry to the point of frenzy, and so predisposed to violence. A left-wing radical should be permitted to deliver a revolutionary tirade before the ladies of the D.A.R., even if his final words are "to the barricades!", for that would be to light a match not in a powder magazine but in a Turkish steam bath. Second, no one should be punished for inciting others to violence unless he used words intentionally, or at least recklessly, with respect to that consequence. Otherwise at best a speaker will be punished for his mere negligence, and at worst he will be punished though perfectly innocent.

There is one further problem raised by the concept of incitement as a crime. It might well be asked how one person—the inciter—can be held criminally responsible for the free and deliberate actions of another person—the one who is incited by his words. This problem is common to both kinds of incitement, counseling and inflaming or egging on, but it seems especially puzzling in the case of advising and persuading; for the deliberate, thoughtful, unforced, and undeceived acceptance of the advice of another person is without question itself a voluntary act. Yet there may well be cases which are such that had not the advice been given, the crime would never have been perpetrated, so that the advisor can truly be said to have "got" the advisee to do something he might otherwise never have done. In this case, the initiative was the advisor's, and his advice was the crucial causal factor that led to the criminal act, so that it would be no abuse of usage to call it "the cause." And yet, for all of that, no one *forced* the advisee to act; he could have rejected the advice, but he didn't.

If there is the appearance of paradox in this account, or in the very idea of one person's causing another to act voluntarily, it is no doubt the result of an unduly restrictive conception of what a cause is. There are, of course, a great many ways of causing another person to behave in a given way by the use of words. If we sneak up behind him and shout "boo!" we may startle him so that he jumps and shrieks. In this case our word functioned as a cause not in virtue of its meaning or the mediation of the other person's understanding, but simply as a noise, and the person's startled reaction to this physical stimulus was as involuntary as an eye-twitch or a knee-jerk. Some philosophers would restrict the notion of causing behavior to cases of this kind, but there is no good reason for such a restriction, and a strong case can be built against it based both on its capacity to breed paradox and on common sense and usage. I can "get" an acquaintance to say "Good morning" by putting myself directly in his line of vision, smiling, and saying "Good morning" to him. If I do these things and he predictably responds in the way I intended, I can surely say that my behavior was the cause, in those circumstances, of his behavior; for my conduct is not only a circumstance but for which his action would not have occurred, it is also a circumstance which, when added to those already present, made the difference between his speaking and remaining silent. Yet I did not force him to speak; I did not deceive him; I did not trick him. Rather I exploited those of his known policies and dispositions that made him antecedently "receptive" to my words. To deny that I caused him to act voluntarily, in short, is either to confuse causation with compulsion (a venerable philosophical mistake) or to regard one person's initiative as incompatible with another person's responsibility.[24]

In any case, where one person causes another to act voluntarily either by giving him advice or information or by otherwise capitalizing on his carefully studied dispositions and policies, there is no reason why *both* persons should not be held responsible for the act if it should be criminal. It is just as if the law made it criminal to contribute to a human explosion either by being human dynamite or by being a human spark: either by being predisposed by one's character to crime or by one's passions to violence, or else by providing the words or materials which could fully be anticipated to incite the violent or criminal conduct of others. It is surely no reasonable defense of the spark to say that but for the dynamite there would have been no explosion. Nor is it any more reasonable to defend the dynamite by arguing that but for the spark it should have remained forever quiescent.

There is probably even less reason for excluding from responsibility the speaker haranguing an inflammable mob on the grounds that the individuals in the throng are free adults capable of refraining from violence in the circumstances. A mob might well be understood as a kind of fictitious collective person whose passions are much more easily manipulated and whose actions more easily maneuvered than those of individual persons. If one looks at it this way, the caused behavior of an inflamed mob may be a good deal less than fully voluntary, even though the component individuals in it, being free adults, are all acting voluntarily on their own responsibility.

III SEDITION

Causing panic, provoking violence, and inciting to crime or insurrection are all made punishable by what Chafee calls "the normal criminal law of words."[25] The relevant common law categories are riot, breach of the peace, solicitation, and incitement. All these crimes, as we have seen, require either intentionally harmful or reckless conduct, and all of them require, in addition—and for reasons partly derived from and explicable by the harm principle—that there be some objective likelihood that the relevant sort of harm will be produced by the words uttered in the circumstances. In addition to these traditional common law crimes, many governments have considered it necessary to create statutes making *sedition* a crime. It will be useful to consider the question of sedition against the background of the normal criminal law of words, for this will lead us quickly to two conclusions. The first is that sedition laws are wholly unnecessary to avert the harm they are ostensibly aimed at. The second is that if we must nevertheless put up with sedition laws, they must be applied by the courts in accordance with the same standards of objective likelihood and immediate danger that govern the application of the laws against provoking and inciting violence. Otherwise sedition statutes are likely to do far more social harm than good. Such laws when properly interpreted by enforcers and courts are at best legal redundancies. At worst they are corrosive of the values normally protected by freedom of expression.

The word "sedition," which in its oldest, prelegal sense meant simply divisiveness and strife, has never been the name of a crime in the English common law. Rather the adjective "seditious" forms part of the name of the common law crimes of "seditious words," "seditious libel," and "seditious conspiracy." Apparently the common ingredient in these offenses was so-called "seditious intent." The legal definition of "seditious intent" has changed over the centuries. In the beginning any spoken or written words which in fact had a tendency, however remote, to cause dissension or to weaken the grip of governmental authorities, and were spoken or published intentionally (with or without the further purpose of weakening the government or causing dissension) were held to manifest the requisite intent. In the fifteenth and sixteenth centuries, for example, publicly to call the king a fool, even in jest, was to risk capital punishment. There was to be less danger somewhat later for authors of *printed* words; for all books and printed papers had to be submitted in advance to the censorship (a practice denounced in Milton's eloquent *Areopagitica*), so that authors of politically dangerous words risked not punishment but only prior restraint. There is little evidence, however, that many of them felt more free as a consequence of this development.

The abandonment of the censorship in 1695 was widely hailed as a triumph for freedom of the press, but it was soon replaced by an equally repressive and far more cruel series of criminal trials for "seditious libel." Juries were permitted to decide only narrow factual questions, whereas the matter of "seditious intent" was left up to very conservative judges who knew well where their own personal interests lay. Moreover, truth was not permitted as a defense[26]—a legal restriction which in effect destroyed all right of adverse political criticism. Zechariah Chafee[27] has argued convincingly that the First Amendment to the United States Constitution was proposed and adopted by men who were consciously reacting against the common law of seditious libel, and in particular against the applications of that law in the English trials of the time. "Reform" (of sorts) came in England through Fox's Libel Act of 1792, which allowed juries to decide the question of seditious intent and permitted the truth defense if the opinions were published with good motives. (The ill-advised and short-lived American Sedition Act of 1798 was modeled after this act.) In the hysterical reaction to the French Revolution and the Napoleonic Wars, however, juries proved to be even more savage than judges, and hundreds were punished even for the mildest political unorthodoxy.

Throughout most of the nineteenth century, the prevailing definition of seditious intent in English law derived from a statute passed during the repressive heyday of the Fox Act sedition trials. Men were punished for publishing any words with:

the intention of (1) exciting disaffection, hatred, or contempt against the sovereign, or the government and constitution of the kingdom, or either house of parliament, or the administration of justice, *or* (2) exciting his majesty's subjects to attempt, otherwise than by lawful means, the alteration of any matter in church or state by law established, *or* (3) to promote feelings of ill will and hostility between different classes.[28]

In short, the three possible modes of seditious libel were defamation of the institutions or officers of the government, incitement to unlawful acts, and a use of language that tends toward the breach of the peace "between classes." The normal criminal law of words sufficiently covers the last two modes; and the civil law of defamation would apply to the first. The criminal law, as we have seen, employs a clear and present danger test for incitement and breach of peace, and does so for good reasons derived from the harm principle and the analysis of "intentional causing." For other good reasons, also derived from the harm principle, the law of defamation privileges fair comment on public officials, and gives no protection at all to institutions. So there would seem to be no further need, at least none demonstrated by the harm principle, for a criminal law of sedition.[29]

Still, many have thought that the harm principle requires sedition laws, and some still do. The issue boils down to the question of whether the normal law of words with its strict standard of immediate danger is too lax to prevent serious harms, and whether, therefore, it needs supplementing by sedition laws employing the looser standards of "bad tendency" and "presumptive intent." By the standard of bad tendency, words can be punished for their dangerous propensity "long before there is any probability that they will break out into unlawful acts";[30] and by the test of presumptive intent, it is necessary only that the defendant intended to publish his words, not that he intended further harm by them. It is clear that most authors of sedition statutes have meant them to be interpreted by the courts in accordance with the tests of bad tendency and presumptive intent (although the United States Supreme Court has in recent decades declared that such interpretations are contrary to the First Amendment of the Constitution). Part of the rationale for the older tests was that if words make a definite contribution to a situation which is on its way to being dangerous, it is folly not to punish them well before that situation reaches the threshold of actual harm. There may seem to be no harm in piling up twigs as such, but if this is done with the purpose (or even the likely outcome) of starting a fire eventually, why not stop it now before it is too late? Those who favor this argument have often employed the harm principle also to defend laws against institutional defamation. The reason why it should be unlawful to bring the Constitution or the courts (or even the *flag*) into disrepute by one's words, they argue, is not simply that such words are offensive, but rather that they tend to undermine respect and loyalty and thereby contribute to more serious harm in the long run.

The focus of the disagreement over sedition laws is the status of *advocacy*. The normal law of words quite clearly outlaws counseling, urging, or demanding (under certain conditions) that others resort to crime or engage in riots, assassinations, or insurrections. But what if a person uses language not directly to counsel or call for violence but rather (where this is different) to *advocate* it? In the wake of the Russian Revolution, many working class parties in America and Europe adopted some variant of an ideology which declared that the propertied classes derived their wealth from the systematic exploitation of the poor; capitalists controlled the major media of news and opinion as well as parliaments and legislators; the grievances of the workers therefore could not be remedied through normal political channels but required instead direct pressure through such means as general strikes, boycotts, and mass demonstrations; and that the working class would inevitably be triumphant in its struggle, expropriate the exploiters, and itself run industry. Spokesmen for this ideology were known for their flamboyant rhetoric, which invariably contained such terms as "arise," "struggle," "victory," and "revolution." Such persons were commonly charged with violations of the Federal Espionage Act during and after World War I, of state sedition laws during the 1920s, and, after World War II, of the Smith Act. Often the key charge in the indictment was "teaching or advocating" riot, assassination, or the violent overthrow of the government.

Trials of Marxists for advocacy of revolution tended to be extremely difficult and problematic partly because it was never clear whether revolution in any usual sense was something taught and approved by them, and partly because it was unclear whether the form of reference to revolution in the Marxist ideology amounted to "advocacy" of it. Marxists disagreed among themselves over the first point. Many thought that forms of group pressure well short of open violence would be sufficient to overturn the capitalists; others thought that "eventually" (when is that?), when conditions were at last ripe, a brief violent seizure of power might be necessary. Does this, in any case, amount to the advocacy of revolution? If it is criminal advocacy to teach that there are conceivable circumstances under which revolution would be justified, then almost everyone, including this author, "advocates" revolution. Suppose one holds further that the "conceivable justifying conditions" may one day become actual, or that it is even probable that they will be actual at some indeterminate future time. Is this to count as criminal advocacy?

Not according to Justice Holmes in his famous opinion in *U.S. v. Schenk.* Schenk and others had encouraged draft resistance in 1917 by mailing circulars denouncing conscription as unconstitutional and urging in very emotional prose that draft-eligible men "assert their rights." The lower court found this to be advocacy of unlawful conduct, a violation, in particular, of the Espionage Act of 1917. The Supreme Court upheld the conviction but nevertheless laid down in the words of O. W. Holmes the test which was to be applied, in a more generous spirit, in later cases: "The question in every case is whether the words . . . are used in such circumstances and are of such a nature as to create a clear and present danger that they will bring about the substantive evils that Congress has a right to prevent." Since Congress has the right to raise armies, any efforts to interfere by words or action with the exercise of that right are punishable. But the clear and present danger standard brings advocacy under the same kind of test as that used for incitement in the normal law of words. One can "advocate" draft resistance over one's breakfast table to one's daughter (though perhaps not to one's son), but not to a sullen group waiting to be sworn in at the induction center.

There is, on the other hand, never any real danger in this country in permitting the open advocacy of *revolution,* except, perhaps, as Chafee puts it, "in extraordinary times of great tension." He continues:

The chances of success are so infinitesimal that the probability of any serious attempt following the utterances seems too slight to make them punishable. . . . This is especially true if the speaker urges revolution at some future day, so that no immediate check is needed to save the country.[31]

Advocacy of assassination, on the other hand, is less easily tolerated. In the first place, the soil is always more receptive to that seed. It is not that potential assassins are more numerous than potential revolutionaries, although at most times that is true. Potential assassins include among their number persons who are contorted beyond reason by hate, mentally unstable persons, and unpredictable crackpots. Further, a successful assassination requires only one good shot. Since it is more likely to be tried and easier to achieve, its danger is always more "clear and present." There will be many circumstances, therefore, in which Holmes's test would permit advocacy of revolution but punish advocacy of assassination. Still in most contexts of utterance it would punish neither. It should no doubt be criminal for a prominent politician to advocate assassination of the president in a talk over national television, or in a letter to the *New York Times*,[32] but when a patron of a neighborhood tavern heatedly announces to his fellow drinkers that "the bum ought to be shot," the president's life will not be significantly endangered. There are times and places where it doesn't matter in the slightest how carelessly one chooses one's words, and others where one's choice of words can be a matter of life and death.

I shall, in conclusion, sketch a rationale for the clear and present danger test, as a kind of mediating standard for the application of the harm principle in the area of political expression. The natural challenge to the use of that test has been adumbrated above. It is true, one might concede, that the teaching of Communist ideology here and now will not create a clear and present danger of violent revolution. Every one knows that, including the Communists. Every trip, however, begins with some first steps, and that includes trips to forbidden destinations. The beginning steps are meant to increase numbers, add strength, and pick up momentum at later stages. To switch the metaphor to one used previously, the Communists are not just casting seeds on barren ground; their words are also meant to cultivate the ground and irrigate it. If the law prohibits planting a certain kind of shrub and we see people storing the forbidden seeds, garden tools, and fertilizer, and actually digging trenches for irrigation pipes, why wait until they are ready to plant the seed before stopping them? Even at these early stages of preparation, they are clearly attempting to achieve what is forbidden. So the argument goes.

The metaphor employed by the argument, however, is not very favorable to its cause. There is a world of difference between making plans and preparations for a future crime and actually launching an attempt, and this distinction has long been recognized by the ordinary criminal law. Mere preparations without actual steps in the direction of perpetration are not sufficient for the crime of attempt (though if preparation involves talking with collaborators, it may constitute the crime of conspiracy). Not even preliminary "steps" are sufficient; for "the act must reach far enough toward the accomplishment of the desired result to amount to the commencement of the consummation."[33] So the first

faltering steps of a surpassingly difficult fifty-year trip toward an illegal goal can hardly qualify as an "attempt" in either the legal or the everyday sense.

If the journey is a collective enterprise, the participants could be charged with *conspiracy* without any violation of usage. The question is whether it would be sound public policy to suppress dissenting voices in this manner so long before they reach the threshold of public danger. The argument to the contrary has been given very clear statement in our time by Zechariah Chafee. Consider what interests are involved when the state employs some coercive technique to prevent a private individual or group from expressing an opinion on some issue of public policy, or from teaching or advocating some political ideology. Chafee would have us put these various interests in the balance to determine their relative weights. In the one pan of the scale, there are the private interests of the suppressed individual or group in having their opinions heard and shared, and in winning support and eventual acceptance for them. These interests will be effectively squelched by state suppression. In the other pan is the public interest in peace and order, and the preservation of democratic institutions. These interests may be endangered to some degree by the advocacy of radical ideologies. Now if these are the only interests involved, there is no question that the public interest (which after all includes all or most private interests) sits heavier in the pan. There is, however, another public interest involved of very considerable weight. That is the public interest in the discovery and dissemination of all information that can have any bearing on public policy, and of all opinions about what public policy should be. The dangers that come from neglecting *that* interest are enormous at all times. (See Part I above.) And the more dangerous the times—the more serious the questions before the country's decision makers (and *especially* when these are questions of war and peace)—the more important it is to keep open all the possible avenues to truth and wisdom.

Only the interest in national safety can outweigh the public interest in open discussion, but *it sits in the scale only to the degree that it is actually imperiled.* From the point of view of the public interest alone, with no consideration whatever of individual rights, it would be folly to sacrifice the social benefits of free speech for the bare possibility that the public safety may be somewhat affected. The greater the certainty and imminence of danger, however, the more the interest in public safety moves on to the scale, until at the point of clear and present danger it is heavy enough to tip the scales its way.

The scales analogy, of course, is only an elaborate metaphor for the sorts of deliberations that must go on among enforcers and interpreters of the law when distinct public interests come into conflict. These clashes of interest are most likely to occur in times of excitement and stress when interest "balancing" calls for a clear eye, a sensitive scale, and a steady hand. At such times the clear and present danger rule is a difficult one to apply, but other guides to decision have invariably gone wrong, while the clear and present danger test has hardly ever been seriously tried. Perhaps that helps account, to some degree, for the sorry human record of cruelty, injustice, and war.

NOTES

1. In Chapter Two of *On Liberty,* not reprinted in this volume.

2. Zechariah Chafee, Jr., *Free Speech in the United States* (1941), p. 33.

3. This point applies especially to discussions of moral, social, political, legal, and economic questions, as well as matters of governmental policy, domestic and foreign. "Cross-examination" in science and philosophy is perhaps less important.

4. Aristotle, *Nicomachean Ethics,* Bk. II, Chap. 6, 1107 ª. "When a man commits adultery, there is no point in asking whether it was with the right woman or at the right time or in the right way, for to do anything like that is simply wrong."

5. William L. Prosser, *Handbook of the Law of Torts,* 2nd ed. (St. Paul: West Publishing Co., 1955), p. 584.

6. *Ibid.,* p. 631.

7. Fowler V. Harper and Fleming James, Jr., *The Law of Torts* (Boston: Little, Brown and Co., 1956), Vol. I, p. 416. The authors do not endorse this view.

8. *Ibid.*

9. William Blackstone, *Commentaries on the Laws of England,* Vol. III, 1765 Reprint (Boston: Beacon Press, 1962), p. 125.

10. Prosser, *op. cit.,* p. 644.

11. Harper and James, *op. cit.,* p. 680.

12. Prosser, *op. cit.,* p. 642.

13. *Loc. cit.*

14. American Law Institute, *Restatement of the Law of Torts* (St. Paul, 1934) § 867, comment c.

15. Prosser, *op. cit.,* p. 644.

16. "There are two aspects of the interest in seclusion. First, the interest in preventing others from seeing and hearing what one does and says. Second, *the interest in avoiding seeing and hearing what other people do and say.* . . . It may be as distasteful to suffer the intrusions of a garrulous and unwelcome guest as to discover an eavesdropper or peeper." Harper and James, *op. cit.,* p. 681. (Emphasis added.)

17. Schenck v. United States, 249 U.S. 47 (1919).

18. Chafee, *op. cit.,* pp. 152, 161, 426. cf. Terminiello v. Chicago 337 U.S. 1, (1949).

19. Chafee, *op. cit.,* p. 426.

20. *Ibid.,* p. 161.

21. Toler v. State, 152 Tenn. 1, 13, 260 S.W. 134 (1923).

22. Mill, *op. cit.,* pp. 67–8.

23. Chafee, *op. cit.,* p. 397.

24. For a more detailed exposition of this view see my "Causing Voluntary Actions" in *Doing and Deserving* (Princeton, N.J.: Princeton University Press, 1970), p. 152.

25. Chafee, *op. cit.,* p. 149.

26. In the words of the great common law judge, William Murray, First Earl of Mansfield, "The Greater the Truth, the Greater the Libel," hence Robert Burns's playful lines in his poem, "The Reproof":

"Dost not know that old Mansfield
    Who writes like the Bible,
Says the more 'tis a truth, sir,
    The more 'tis a libel?"

27. Chafee, *op. cit.,* pp. 18–22.

28. *Ibid.,* p. 506.

29. Such things, however, as patriotic sensibilities are capable of being highly *offended* by certain kinds of language. The rationale of sedition laws, therefore, may very well derive from the "offense-principle," which warrants prohibition of offensive behavior even when it is (otherwise) harmless.

30. Chafee, *op. cit.,* p. 24.

31. *Ibid.,* p. 175.

32. In which case the newspaper too would be criminally responsible for publishing the letter.

33. Lee v. Commonwealth, 144 Va. 594, 599, 131 S.E. 212, 214 (1926) as quoted in Rollin M. Perkins, *Criminal Law* (Brooklyn Foundation Press, 1957), p. 482.

VILLAGE OF SKOKIE v. NATIONAL SOCIALIST PARTY OF AMERICA

Supreme Court of Illinois, 1978*

PER CURIAM:

Plaintiff, the village of Skokie, filed a complaint in the circuit court of Cook County seeking to enjoin defendants, the National Socialist Party of America (the American Nazi Party) and 10 individuals as "officers and members" of the party, from engaging in certain activities while conducting a demonstration within the village. The circuit court issued an order enjoining certain conduct during the planned demonstration. The appellate court modified the injunction order, and, as modified, defendants are enjoined from "[i]ntentionally displaying the swastika on or off their persons, in the course of a demonstration, march, or parade." . . . We allowed defendants' petition for leave to appeal. . . .

The pleadings and the facts adduced at the hearing are fully set forth in the appellate court opinion, and only those matters necessary to the discussion of the issues will be repeated here. The facts are not disputed.

It is alleged in plaintiff's complaint that the "uniform of the National Socialist Party of America consists of the storm trooper uniform of the German Nazi Party embellished with the Nazi swastika"; that the plaintiff village has a population of about 70,000 persons of which approximately 40,500 persons are of "Jewish religion or Jewish ancestry" and of this latter number 5,000 to 7,000 are survivors of German concentration camps; that the defendant organization is "dedicated to the incitation of racial and religious hatred directed principally against individuals of Jewish faith or ancestry and non-Caucasians"; and that its members "have patterned their conduct, their uniform, their slogan and their tactics along the pattern of the German Nazi Party * * *."

Defendants moved to dismiss the complaint. In an affidavit attached to defendants' motion to dismiss, defendant Frank Collin, who testified that he was "party leader," stated that on or about March 20,

1977, he sent officials of the plaintiff village a letter stating that the party members and supporters would hold a peaceable, public assembly in the village on May 1, 1977, to protest the Skokie Park District's requirement that the party procure $350,000 of insurance prior to the party's use of the Skokie public parks for public assemblies. The demonstration was to begin at 3 p.m., last 20 to 30 minutes, and consist of 30 to 50 demonstrators marching in single file, back and forth, in front of the village hall. The marchers were to wear uniforms which include a swastika emblem or armband. They were to carry a party banner containing a swastika emblem and signs containing such statements as "White Free Speech," "Free Speech for the White Man," and "Free Speech for White America." The demonstrators would not distribute handbills, make any derogatory statements directed to any ethnic or religious group, or obstruct traffic. They would cooperate with any reasonable police instructions or requests.

At the hearing on plaintiff's motion for an "emergency injunction" a resident of Skokie testified that he was a survivor of the Nazi holocaust. He further testified that the Jewish community in and around Skokie feels the purpose of the march in the "heart of the Jewish population" is to remind the two million survivors "that we are not through with you" and to show "that the Nazi threat is not over, it can happen again." Another resident of Skokie testified that as the result of defendants' announced intention to march in Skokie, 15 to 18 Jewish organizations, within the village and surrounding area, were called and a counterdemonstration of an estimated 12,000 to 15,000 people was scheduled for the same day. There was opinion evidence that defendants' planned demonstration in Skokie would result in violence.

The circuit court entered an order enjoining defendants from "marching, walking or parading in the uniform of the National Socialist Party of America; marching, walking or parading or otherwise displaying the swastika on or off their person; distributing pamphlets or displaying any materials which incite

*373 N.E. 2d 21 (Ill. 1978). Citation details deleted throughout.

or promote hatred against persons of Jewish faith or ancestry or hatred against persons of any faith or ancestry, race or religion" within the village of Skokie. The appellate court, as earlier noted, modified the order so that defendants were enjoined only from intentional display of the swastika during the Skokie demonstration.

The appellate court opinion adequately discussed and properly decided those issues arising from the portions of the injunction order which enjoined defendants from marching, walking, or parading, from distributing pamphlets or displaying materials, and from wearing the uniform of the National Socialist Party of America. The only issue remaining before this court is whether the circuit court order enjoining defendants from displaying the swastika violates the first amendment rights of those defendants.

In defining the constitutional rights of the parties who come before this court, we are, of course, bound by the pronouncements of the United States Supreme Court in its interpretation of the United States Constitution. The decisions of that court, particularly *Cohen* v. *California* . . . in our opinion compel us to permit the demonstration as proposed, including display of the swastika.

"It is firmly settled that under our Constitution the public expression of ideas may not be prohibited merely because the ideas are themselves offensive to some of their hearers" . . . and it is entirely clear that the wearing of distinctive clothing can be symbolic expression of a thought or philosophy. The symbolic expression of thought falls within the free speech clause of the first amendment . . . and the plaintiff village has the heavy burden of justifying the imposition of a prior restraint upon defendants' right to freedom of speech. . . . The village of Skokie seeks to meet this burden by application of the "fighting words" doctrine first enunciated in *Chaplinsky* v. *New Hampshire* (1942), . . . That doctrine was designed to permit punishment of extremely hostile personal communication likely to cause immediate physical response, "no words being 'forbidden except such as have a direct tendency to cause acts of violence by the persons to whom, individually, the remark is addressed.' " . . . In *Cohen* the Supreme Court restated the description of fighting words as "those personally abusive epithets which, when addressed to the ordinary citizen, are, as a matter of common knowledge, inherently likely to provoke violent reaction." . . . Plaintiff urges, and the appellate court has held, that the exhibition of the Nazi symbol, the swastika, addresses to ordinary citizens a message which is tantamount to fighting words. Plaintiff further asks this court to extend *Chaplinsky*, which upheld a statute punishing the use of such

words, and hold that the fighting-words doctrine permits a prior restraint on defendants' symbolic speech. In our judgment we are precluded from doing so.

In *Cohen*, defendant's conviction stemmed from wearing a jacket bearing the words "Fuck the Draft" in a Los Angeles County courthouse corridor. The Supreme Court for reasons we believe applicable here refused to find that the jacket inscription constituted fighting words. That court stated:

"The constitutional right of free expression is powerful medicine in a society as diverse and populous as ours. It is designed and intended to remove governmental restraints from the arena of public discussion, putting the decision as to what views shall be voiced largely into the hands of each of us, in the hope that use of such freedom will ultimately produce a more capable citizenry and more perfect polity and in the belief that no other approach would comport with the premise of individual dignity and choice upon which our political system rests. . . .

To many, the immediate consequence of this freedom may often appear to be only verbal tumult, discord, and even offensive utterance. These are, however, within established limits, in truth necessary side effects of the broader enduring values which the process of open debate permits us to achieve. That the air may at times seem filled with verbal cacophony is, in this sense not a sign of weakness but of strength. We cannot lose sight of the fact that, in what otherwise might seem a trifling and annoying instance of individual distasteful abuse of a privilege, these fundamental societal values are truly implicated. * * * 'so long as the means are peaceful, the communication need not meet standards of acceptability,' . . .

Against this perception of the constitutional policies involved, we discern certain more particularized considerations that peculiarly call for reversal of this conviction. First, the principle contended for by the State seems inherently boundless. How is one to distinguish this from any other offensive word [emblem]? Surely the State has no right to cleanse public debate to the point where it is grammatically palatable to the most squeamish among us. Yet no readily ascertainable general principle exists for stopping short of that result were we to affirm the judgment below. For, while the particular four-letter word [emblem] being litigated here is perhaps more distasteful than most others of its genre, it is nevertheless often true that one man's vulgarity is another's lyric. Indeed, we think it is largely because governmental officials cannot make principled distinctions in this area that the Constitution leaves matters of taste and style so largely to the individual.

*   *   *   *   *   *

Finally, and in the same vein, we cannot indulge the facile assumption that one can forbid particular words without also running a substantial risk of suppressing ideas in the process. Indeed, governments might soon seize upon the censorship of particular words [emblems] as a convenient guise for banning the expression of unpopular views. We have been able, as noted above, to discern little social benefit that might result from running the risk of opening the door to such grave results." . . .

The display of the swastika, as offensive to the principles of a free nation as the memories it recalls may be, is symbolic political speech intended to convey to the public the beliefs of those who display it. It does not, in our opinion, fall within the definition of "fighting words," and that doctrine cannot be used here to overcome the heavy presumption against the constitutional validity of a prior restraint.

Nor can we find that the swastika, while not representing fighting words, is nevertheless so offensive and peace threatening to the public that its display can be enjoined. We do not doubt that the sight of this symbol is abhorrent to the Jewish citizens of Skokie, and that the survivors of the Nazi persecutions, tormented by their recollections, may have strong feelings regarding its display. Yet it is entirely clear that this factor does not justify enjoining defendants' speech. The *Cohen* court spoke to this subject:

"Finally, in arguments before this Court much has been made of the claim that Cohen's distasteful mode of expression was thrust upon unwilling or unsuspecting viewers, and that the State might therefore legitimately act as it did in order to protect the sensitive from otherwise unavoidable exposure to appellant's crude form of protest. Of course, the mere presumed presence of unwitting listeners or viewers does not serve automatically to justify curtailing all speech capable of giving offense. . . . While this Court has recognized that government may properly act in many situations to prohibit intrusion into the privacy of the home of unwelcome views and ideas which cannot be totally banned from the public dialogue, *e.g.,* Rowan v. *Post Office Dept.,* 397 U.S. 728, 90 S.Ct. 1484, 25 L.Ed.2d 736 (1970), we have at the same time consistently stressed that 'we are often "captives" outside the sanctuary of the home and subject to objectionable speech.' *Id.,* at 738, 90 S.Ct. at 1491. The ability of government, consonant with the Constitution, to shut off discourse solely to protect others from hearing it is, in other words, dependent upon a showing that substantial privacy interests are being invaded in an essentially intolerable manner. Any broader view of this authority would effectively empower a majority to silence dissidents simply as a matter of personal predilections." . . .

Similarly, the Court of Appeals for the Seventh Circuit, in reversing the denial of defendant Collin's application for a permit to speak in Chicago's Marquette Park, noted that courts have consistently refused to ban speech because of the possibility of unlawful conduct by those opposed to the speaker's philosophy.

"Starting with *Terminiello* v. *City of Chicago,* . . . and continuing to *Gregory* v. *City of Chicago,* . . . it has become patent that a hostile audience is not a basis for restraining otherwise legal First Amendment activity. As with many of the cases cited herein, if the actual behavior is not sufficient to sustain a conviction under a statute, then certainly the anticipation of such events cannot sustain the burden necessary to justify a prior restraint." . . .

Rockwell v. *Morris* . . . also involved an American Nazi leader, George Lincoln Rockwell, who challenged a bar to his use of a New York City park to hold a public demonstration where anti-Semitic speeches would be made. Although approximately 2 1/2 million Jewish New Yorkers were hostile to Rockwell's message, the court ordered that a permit to speak be granted, stating:

"A community need not wait to be subverted by street riots and storm troopers; but, also, it cannot, by its policemen or commissioners, suppress a speaker, in prior restraint, on the basis of news reports, hysteria, or inference that what he did yesterday, he will do today. Thus, too, if the speaker incites others to immediate unlawful action he may be punished—in a proper case, stopped when disorder actually impends; but this is not to be confused with unlawful action from others who seek unlawfully to suppress or punish the speaker.

So, the unpopularity of views, their shocking quality, their obnoxiousness, and even their alarming impact is not enough. Otherwise, the preacher of any strange doctrine could be stopped; the anti-racist himself could be suppressed, if he undertakes to speak in 'restricted' areas; and one who asks that public schools be open indiscriminately to all ethnic groups could be lawfully suppressed, if only he choose to speak where persuasion is needed most." . . .

In summary, as we read the controlling Supreme Court opinions, use of the swastika is a symbolic form of free speech entitled to first amendment protections. Its display on uniforms or banners by those engaged in peaceful demonstrations cannot be totally precluded solely because that display may provoke a violent reaction by those who view it. Particularly is this true where, as here, there has been advance notice by the demonstrators of their plans so that they have become, as the complaint alleges, "common knowledge" and those to whom sight of the swastika banner or uniforms would be offense are forewarned and need not view them. A speaker who gives prior notice of his message has not compelled a confrontation with those who voluntarily listen.

As to those who happen to be in a position to be involuntarily confronted with the swastika, the following observations from *Erznoznik* v. *City of Jacksonville* . . . are appropriate:

"The plain, if at all times disquieting, truth is that in our pluralistic society, constantly proliferating new and ingenious forms of expression, 'we are inescapably captive audiences for many purposes.' . . . Much that we encounter offends our esthetic, if not our political and moral, sensibilities. Nevertheless, the Constitution does not permit government to decide which types of otherwise protected speech are sufficiently offensive to require protection for the unwilling listener or viewer. Rather, absent the narrow circumstances described above [home intrusion or captive audience], the burden normally falls upon the viewer to 'avoid further bombardment of [his] sensibilities simply by averting [his] eyes.' . . .

Thus by placing the burden upon the viewer to avoid further bombardment, the Supreme Court has permitted speakers to justify the initial intrusion into the citizen's sensibilities.

We accordingly, albeit reluctantly, conclude that the display of the swastika cannot be enjoined under the fighting-words exception to free speech, nor can anticipation of a hostile audience justify the prior restraint. Furthermore, *Cohen* and *Erznoznik* direct the citizens of Skokie that it is their burden to avoid the offensive symbol if they can do so without unreasonable inconvenience. Accordingly, we are constrained to reverse that part of the appellate court judgment enjoining the display of the swastika. That judgment is in all other respects affirmed.

Affirmed in part and reversed in part.

CLARK, Justice, dissenting.

COHEN v. CALIFORNIA
United States Supreme Court, 1971*

OPINION OF THE COURT

Mr. Justice Harlan delivered the opinion of the Court.

This case may seem at first blush too inconsequential to find its way into our books, but the issue it presents is of no small constitutional significance.

Appellant Paul Robert Cohen was convicted in the Los Angeles Municipal Court of violating that part of California Penal Code § 415 which prohibits "maliciously and willfully disturb[ing] the peace or quiet of any neighborhood or person . . . by . . . offensive conduct . . . "[1] He was given 30 days' imprisonment. The facts upon which his conviction rests are detailed in the opinion of the Court of Appeal of California, Second Appellate District, as follows:

"On April 26, 1968, the defendant was observed in the Los Angeles County Courthouse in the corridor outside of division 20 of the municipal court wearing a jacket bearing the words 'Fuck the Draft' which were plainly visible. There were women and children present in the corridor. The defendant was arrested. The defendant testified that he wore the jacket knowing that the words were on the jacket as a means of informing the public of the depth of his feelings against the Vietnam War and the draft.

"The defendant did not engage in, nor threaten to engage in, nor did anyone as the result of his conduct in fact commit or threaten to commit any act of violence. The defendant did not make any loud or unusual noise, nor was there any evidence that he uttered any sound prior to his arrest."*

In affirming the conviction the Court of Appeal held that "offensive conduct" means "behavior which has a tendency to provoke *others* to acts of violence or to in turn disturb the peace," and that the State had proved this element because, on the facts of this case, "[i]t was certainly reasonably foreseeable that such conduct might cause others to rise up to commit a violent act against the person of the defendant or attempt to forceably remove his jacket."* The California Supreme Court declined review by a divided vote. We brought

*408 U.S. 15 (1971). Some footnotes omitted.
*Citation omitted [Eds.]

the case here, postponing the consideration of the question of our jurisdiction over this appeal to a hearing of the case on the merits.* We now reverse.

I

In order to lay hands on the precise issue which this case involves, it is useful first to canvass various matters which this record does *not* present.

The conviction quite clearly rests upon the asserted offensiveness of the *words* Cohen used to convey his message to the public. The only "conduct" which the State sought to punish is the fact of communication. Thus, we deal here with a conviction resting solely upon "speech",* not upon any separately identifiable conduct which allegedly was intended by Cohen to be perceived by others as expressive of particular views but which, on its face, does not necessarily convey any message and hence arguably could be regulated without effectively repressing Cohen's ability to express himself.* Further, the State certainly lacks power to punish Cohen for the underlying content of the message the inscription conveyed. At least so long as there is no showing of an intent to incite disobedience to or disruption of the draft, Cohen could not, consistently with the First and Fourteenth Amendments, be punished for asserting the evident position on the inutility or immorality of the draft his jacket reflected.*

Appellant's conviction, then, rests squarely upon his exercise of the "freedom of speech" protected from arbitrary governmental interference by the Constitution and can be justified, if at all, only as a valid regulation of the manner in which he exercised that freedom, not as a permissible prohibition on the substantive message it conveys. This does not end the inquiry, of course, for the First and Fourteenth Amendments have never been thought to give absolute protection to every individual to speak whenever or wherever he pleases, or to use any form of address in any circumstances that he chooses. In this vein, too, however, we think it important to note that several issues typically associated with such problems are not presented here.

In the first place, Cohen was tried under a statute applicable throughout the entire State. Any attempt to support this conviction on the ground that the statute seeks to preserve an appropriately decorous atmosphere in the courthouse where Cohen was arrested must fail in the absence of any language in the statute that would have put appellant on notice that certain kinds of otherwise permissible speech or conduct would nevertheless, under California law, not be tolerated in certain places.* No fair reading of the phrase "offensive conduct" can be said sufficiently to inform the ordinary person that distinctions between certain locations are thereby created.[2]

In the second place, as it comes to us, this case cannot be said to fall within those relatively few categories of instances where prior decisions have established the power of government to deal more comprehensively with certain forms of individual expression simply upon a showing that such a form was employed. This is not, for example, an obscenity case. Whatever else may be necessary to give rise to the States' broader power to prohibit obscene expression, such expression must be, in some significant way, erotic.* It cannot plausibly be maintained that this vulgar allusion to the Selective Service System would conjure up such psychic stimulation in anyone likely to be confronted with Cohen's crudely defaced jacket.

This Court has also held that the States are free to ban the simple use, without a demonstration of additional justifying circumstances, of so-called "fighting words," those personally abusive epithets which, when addressed to the ordinary citizen, are, as a matter of common knowledge, inherently likely to provoke violent reaction.* While the four-letter word displayed by Cohen in relation to the draft is not uncommonly employed in a personally provocative fashion, in this instance it was clearly not "directed to the person of the hearer."* No individual actually or likely to be present could reasonably have regarded the words on appellant's jacket as a direct personal insult. Nor do we have here an instance of the exercise of the State's police power to prevent a speaker from intentionally provoking a given group to hostile reaction.* There is, as noted above, no showing that anyone who saw Cohen was in fact violently aroused or that appellant intended such a result.

Finally, in arguments before this Court much has been made of the claim that Cohen's distasteful mode of expression was thrust upon unwilling or unsuspecting viewers, and that the State might therefore legitimately act as it did in order to protect the sensitive from otherwise unavoidable exposure to appellant's crude form of protest. Of course, the mere presumed presence of unwitting listeners or viewers does not serve automatically to justify curtailing all speech capable of giving offense.* While this Court has recognized that government may properly act in many situations to prohibit intrusion into the privacy of the home of unwelcome views and ideas which cannot be totally banned from the public dialogue,* we have at the same time consistently stressed that "we are often 'captives' outside the sanctuary of the home and subject to objectionable speech."* The ability of government, consonant with the Constitution, to shut off discourse solely to protect others from hearing it is, in other words, dependent upon a showing that substantial privacy interests are being invaded in an essentially intolerable manner. Any broader view of this authority would effectively empower a majority to silence dissidents simply as a matter of personal predilections.

In this regard, persons confronted with Cohen's jacket were in a quite different posture than, say, those subjected to the raucous emissions of sound trucks blaring outside their residences. Those in the Los Angeles courthouse could effectively avoid further bombardment of their sensibilities simply by averting their eyes. And, while it may be that one has a more substantial claim to a recognizable privacy interest when walking through a courthouse corridor than, for example, strolling through Central Park, surely it is nothing like the interest in being free from unwanted expression in the confines of one's own home.* Given the subtlety and complexity of the factors involved, if Cohen's "speech" was otherwise entitled to constitutional protection, we do not think the fact that some unwilling "listeners" in a public building may have been briefly exposed to it can serve to justify this breach of the peace conviction where, as here, there was no evidence that persons powerless to avoid appellant's conduct did in fact object to it, and where that portion of the statute upon which Cohen's conviction rests evinces no concern, either on its face or as construed by the California courts, with the special plight of the captive auditor, but, instead, indiscriminately sweeps within its prohibitions all "offensive conduct" that disturbs "any neighborhood or person."*

II

Against this background, the issue flushed by this case stands out in bold relief. It is whether California can excise, as "offensive conduct," one particular scurrilous epithet from the public discourse, either upon the theory of the court below that its use is inherently likely to cause violent reaction or upon a more general assertion that the States, acting as guardians of public morality, may properly remove this offensive word from the public vocabulary.

The rationale of the California court is plainly untenable. At most it reflects an "undifferentiated fear or apprehension of disturbance [which] is not enough to overcome the right to freedom of expression."* We have been shown no evidence that substantial numbers of citizens are standing ready to strike out physically at whoever may assault their sensibilities with execrations like that uttered by Cohen. There may be some persons about with such lawless and violent proclivities, but that is an insufficient base upon which to erect, consistently with constitutional values, a governmental power to force persons who wish to ventilate their dissident views into avoiding particular forms of expression. The argument amounts to little more than the self-defeating proposition that to avoid physical censorship of one who has not sought to provoke such a response by a hypothetical coterie of the violent and lawless, the States may more appropriately effectuate that censorship themselves.*

Admittedly, it is not so obvious that the First and Fourteenth Amendments must be taken to disable the States from punishing public utterance of this unseemly expletive in order to maintain what they regard as a suitable level of discourse within the body politic. We think, however, that examination and reflection will reveal the shortcomings of a contrary viewpoint.

At the outset, we cannot overemphasize that, in our judgment, most situations where the State has a justifiable interest in regulating speech will fall within one or more of the various established exceptions, discussed above but not applicable here, to the usual rule that governmental bodies may not prescribe the form or content of individual expression. Equally important to our conclusion is the constitutional backdrop against which our decision must be made. The constitutional right of free expression is powerful medicine in a society as diverse and populous as ours. It is designed and intended to remove governmental restraints from the arena of public discussion, putting the decision as to what views shall be voiced largely into the hands of each of us, in the hope that use of such freedom will ultimately produce a more capable citizenry and more perfect polity and in the belief that no other approach would comport with the premise of individual dignity and choice upon which our political system rests.*

To many, the immediate consequence of this freedom may often appear to be only verbal tumult, discord, and even offensive utterance. These are, however, within established limits, in truth necessary side effects of the broader enduring values which the process of open debate permits us to achieve. That the air may at times seem filled with verbal cacophony is, in this sense not a sign of weakness but of strength. We cannot lose sight of the fact that, in what otherwise might seem a

trifling and annoying instance of individual distasteful abuse of a privilege, these fundamental societal values are truly implicated. That is why "[w]holly neutral futilities . . . come under the protection of free speech as fully as do Keats' poems or Donne's sermons," Winters v New York, (1948)* (Frankfurter, J., dissenting), and why "so long as the means are peaceful, the communication need not meet standards of acceptability," Organization for a Better Austin v Keefe, (1971).*

Against this perception of the constitutional policies involved, we discern certain more particularized considerations that peculiarly call for reversal of this conviction. First, the principle contended for by the State seems inherently boundless. How is one to distinguish this from any other offensive word? Surely the State has no right to cleanse public debate to the point where it is grammatically palatable to the most squeamish among us. Yet no readily ascertainable general principle exists for stopping short of that result were we to affirm the judgment below. For, while the particular four-letter word being litigated here is perhaps more distasteful than most others of its genre, it is nevertheless often true that one man's vulgarity is another's lyric. Indeed, we think it is largely because governmental officials cannot make principled distinctions in this area that the Constitution leaves matters of taste and style so largely to the individual.

Additionally, we cannot overlook the fact, because it is well illustrated by the episode involved here, that much linguistic expression serves a dual communicative function: it conveys not only ideas capable of relatively precise, detached explication, but otherwise inexpressible emotions as well. In fact, words are often chosen as much for their emotive as their cognitive force. We cannot sanction the view that the Constitution, while solicitous of the cognitive content of individual speech, has little or no regard for that emotive function which, practically speaking, may often be the more important element of the overall message sought to be communicated. Indeed, as Mr. Justice Frankfurter has said, "[o]ne of the prerogatives of American citizenship is the right to criticize public men and measures—and that means not only informed and responsible criticism but the freedom to speak foolishly and without moderation." Baumgartner v United States, (1944).*

Finally, and in the same vein, we cannot indulge the facile assumption that one can forbid particular words without also running a substantial risk of suppressing ideas in the process. Indeed, governments might soon seize upon the censorship of particular words as a convenient guise for banning the expression of unpopular

*Citation omitted [Eds.]

*Citation omitted [Eds.]

views. We have been able, as noted above, to discern little social benefit that might result from running the risk of opening the door to such grave results.

It is, in sum, our judgment that, absent a more particularized and compelling reason for its actions, the State may not, consistently with the First and Fourteenth Amendments, make the simple public display here involved of this single four-letter expletive a criminal offense. Because that is the only arguably sustainable rationale for the conviction here at issue, the judgment below must be reversed.

SEPARATE OPINION

Mr. Justice **Blackmun,** with whom The **Chief Justice** and Mr. Justice **Black** join.

I dissent, and I do so for two reasons:

1. Cohen's absurd and immature antic, in my view, was mainly conduct and little speech.* The California Court of Appeal appears so to have described it,* and I cannot characterize it otherwise. Further, the case appears to me to be well within the sphere of Chaplinsky v New Hampshire,* where Mr. Justice Murphy, a known champion of First Amendment freedoms, wrote for a unanimous bench. As a consequence, this

*Citation omitted [Eds.]

Court's agonizing First Amendment values seems misplaced and unnecessary.

2. I am not at all certain that the California Court of Appeal's construction of § 415 is now the authoritative California construction . . .

NOTES

1. The statute provides in full:

"Every person who maliciously and willfully disturbs the peace or quiet of any neighborhood or person, by loud or unusual noise, or by tumultuous or offensive conduct, or threatening, traducing, quarreling, challenging to fight, or fighting, or who, on the public streets of any unincorporated town, or upon the public highways in such unincorporated town, run any horse race, either for a wager or for amusement, or fire any gun or pistol in such unincorporated town, or use any vulgar language within the presence or hearing of women or children, in a loud and boisterous manner, is guilty of a misdemeanor, and upon conviction by any Court of competent jurisdiction shall be punished by fine not exceeding two hundred dollars, or by imprisonment in the County Jail for not more than ninety days, or by both fine and imprisonment, or either, at the discretion of the Court."

2. It is illuminating to note what transpired when Cohen entered a courtroom in the building. He removed his jacket and stood with it folded over his arm. Meanwhile, a policeman sent the presiding judge a note suggesting that Cohen be held in contempt of court. The judge declined to do so and Cohen was arrested by the officer only after he emerged from the courtroom.

TEXAS v. JOHNSON

United States Supreme Court, 1989*

JUSTICE BRENNAN delivered the opinion of the Court.

After publicly burning an American flag as a means of political protest, Gregory Lee Johnson was convicted of desecrating a flag in violation of Texas law. This case presents the question whether his conviction is consistent with the First Amendment. We hold that it is not.

I

While the Republican National Convention was taking place in Dallas in 1984, respondent Johnson participated in a political demonstration dubbed the "Republican War Chest Tour." As explained in literature distributed by the demonstrators and in speeches made by them, the purpose of this event was to protest the policies of the Reagan administration and of certain Dallas-based corporations. The demonstrators marched through the Dallas streets, chanting political slogans and stopping at several corporate locations to stage "die-ins" intended to dramatize the consequences of nuclear war. On several occasions they spray-painted the walls of buildings and overturned potted plants, but Johnson himself took no part in such activities. He did, however, accept an American flag handed to him by a fellow protestor who had taken it from a flag pole outside one of the targeted buildings.

The demonstration ended in front of Dallas City Hall, where Johnson unfurled the American flag, doused it with kerosene, and set it on fire. While the flag burned, the protestors chanted, "America, the red, white, and blue, we spit on you." After the demonstrators dispersed, a witness to the flag-burning collected the flag's remains and buried them in his backyard. No one was physically injured or threatened with injury, though several witnesses testified that they had been seriously offended by the flag-burning.

Of the approximately 100 demonstrators, Johnson alone was charged with a crime. The only criminal offense with which he was charged was the desecration of a venerated object in violation of Tex. Penal

Code Ann. §42.09 (a)(3) (1989).[1] After a trial, he was convicted, sentenced to one year in prison, and fined $2,000. The Court of Appeals for the Fifth District of Texas at Dallas affirmed Johnson's conviction, . . . but the Texas Court of Criminal Appeals reversed, . . . holding that the State could not, consistent with the First Amendment, punish Johnson for burning the flag in these circumstances.

The Court of Criminal Appeals began by recognizing that Johnson's conduct was symbolic speech protected by the First Amendment: "Given the context of an organized demonstration, speeches, slogans, and the distribution of literature, anyone who observed appellant's act would have understood the message that appellant intended to convey. The act for which appellant was convicted was clearly 'speech' contemplated by the First Amendment." *Id.*, at 95. To justify Johnson's conviction for engaging in symbolic speech, the State asserted two interests: preserving the flag as a symbol of national unity and preventing breaches of the peace. The Court of Criminal Appeals held that neither interest supported his conviction.

Acknowledging that this Court had not yet decided whether the Government may criminally sanction flag desecration in order to preserve the flag's symbolic value, the Texas court nevertheless concluded that our decision in *West Virginia Board of Education* v. *Barnette*, . . . (1943), suggested that furthering this interest by curtailing speech was impermissible. "Recognizing that the right to differ is the centerpiece of our First Amendment freedoms," the court explained, "a government cannot mandate by fiat a feeling of unity in its citizens. Therefore, that very same government cannot carve out a symbol of unity and prescribe a set of approved messages to be associated with that symbol when it cannot mandate the status or feeling the symbol purports to represent." . . . Noting that the State had not shown that the flag was in "grave and immediate danger," *Barnette, supra*, . . . of being stripped of its symbolic value, the Texas court also decided that the flag's special status was not endangered by Johnson's conduct. . . .

As to the State's goal of preventing breaches of the peace, the court concluded that the flag-desecration statute was not drawn narrowly enough to encompass

*109 S.Ct. 2533 (1989). Only an excerpt has been included here from the dissenting opinion.

only those flag-burnings that were likely to result in a serious disturbance of the peace. And in fact, the court emphasized, the flag-burning in this particular case did not threaten such a reaction. " 'Serious offense' occurred," the court admitted, "but there was no breach of peace nor does the record reflect that the situation was potentially explosive. One cannot equate 'serious offense' with incitement to breach the peace." . . . The court also stressed that another Texas statute, Tex. Penal Code Ann. §42.01 (1989), prohibited breaches of the peace. Citing *Boos* v. *Barry,* . . . the court decided that §42.01 demonstrated Texas' ability to prevent disturbances of the peace without punishing this flag desecration.

Because it reversed Johnson's conviction on the ground that §42.09 was unconstitutional as applied to him, the state court did not address Johnson's argument that the statute was, on its face, unconstitutionally vague and overbroad. We granted certiorari, . . . and now affirm.

II

Johnson was convicted of flag desecration for burning the flag rather than for uttering insulting words.[2] This fact somewhat complicates our consideration of his conviction under the First Amendment. We must first determine whether Johnson's burning of the flag constituted expressive conduct, permitting him to invoke the First Amendment in challenging his conviction. . . . If his conduct was expressive, we next decide whether the State's regulation is related to the suppression of free expression. . . . If the State's regulation is not related to expression, then the less stringent standard we announced in *United States* v. *O'Brien* for regulations of noncommunicative conduct controls. . . . If it is, then we are outside of *O'Brien*'s test, and we must ask whether this interest justifies Johnson's conviction under a more demanding standard.[3] . . . A third possibility is that the State's asserted interest is simply not implicated on these facts, and in that event the interest drops out of the picture.

The First Amendment literally forbids the abridgement only of "speech," but we have long recognized that its protection does not end at the spoken or written word. While we have rejected "the view that an apparently limitless variety of conduct can be labeled 'speech' whenever the person engaging in the conduct intends thereby to express an idea," . . . we have acknowledged that conduct may be "sufficiently imbued with elements of communication to fall within the scope of the First and Fourteenth Amendments."

In deciding whether particular conduct possesses sufficient communicative elements to bring the First Amendment into play, we have asked whether "[a]n intent to convey a particularized message was present, and [whether] the likelihood was great that the message would be understood by those who viewed it." . . . Hence, we have recognized the expressive nature of students' wearing of black armbands to protest American military involvement in Vietnam, . . . of a sit-in by blacks in a "whites only" area to protest segregation, . . . of the wearing of American military uniforms in a dramatic presentation criticizing American involvement in Vietnam, . . . and of picketing about a wide variety of causes. . . .

Especially pertinent to this case are our decisions recognizing the communicative nature of conduct relating to flags. Attaching a peace sign to the flag, . . . saluting the flag, . . . and displaying a red flag, . . . we have held, all may find shelter under the First Amendment. See also *Smith* v. *Goguen* . . . (treating flag "contemptuously" by wearing pants with small flag sewn into their seat is expressive conduct). That we have had little difficulty identifying an expressive element in conduct relating to flags should not be surprising. The very purpose of a national flag is to serve as a symbol of our country; it is, one might say, "the one visible manifestation of two hundred years of nationhood."

Thus, we have observed:

"[T]he flag salute is a form of utterance. Symbolism is a primitive but effective way of communicating ideas. The use of an emblem or flag to symbolize some system, idea, institution, or personality, is a short cut from mind to mind. Causes and nations, political parties, lodges and ecclesiastical groups seek to knit the loyalty of their followings to a flag or banner, a color or design."

. . . Pregnant with expressive content, the flag as readily signifies this Nation as does the combination of letters found in "America."

We have not automatically concluded, however, that any action taken with respect to our flag is expressive. Instead, in characterizing such action for First Amendment purposes, we have considered the context in which it occurred. In *Spence,* for example, we emphasized that Spence's taping of a peace sign to his flag was "roughly simultaneous with and concededly triggered by the Cambodian incursion and the Kent State tragedy." . . . The State of Washington had conceded, in fact, that Spence's conduct was a form of communication, and we stated that "the State's concession is inevitable on this record."

The State of Texas conceded for purposes of its oral argument in this case that Johnson's conduct was expressive conduct, . . . and this concession seems to us as prudent as was Washington's in *Spence.*

Johnson burned an American flag as part—indeed, as the culmination—of a political demonstration that coincided with the convening of the Republican Party and its renomination of Ronald Reagan for President. The expressive, overtly political nature of this conduct was both intentional and overwhelmingly apparent. At his trial, Johnson explained his reasons for burning the flag as follows: "The American Flag was burned as Ronald Reagan was being renominated as President. And a more powerful statement of symbolic speech, whether you agree with it or not, couldn't have been made at that time. It's quite a just position [juxtaposition]. We had new patriotism and no patriotism." . . . In these circumstances, Johnson's burning of the flag was conduct "sufficiently imbued with elements of communication, . . . to implicate the First Amendment.

III

The Government generally has a freer hand in restricting expressive conduct than it has in restricting the written or spoken word. . . . It may not, however, proscribe particular conduct *because* it has expressive elements. "[W]hat might be termed the more generalized guarantee of freedom of expression makes the communicative nature of conduct an inadequate *basis* for singling out that conduct for proscription. A law *directed at* the communicative nature of conduct must, like a law directed at speech itself, be justified by the substantial showing of need that the First Amendment requires." . . . It is, in short, not simply the verbal or nonverbal nature of the expression, but the governmental interest at stake, that helps to determine whether a restriction on that expression is valid.

Thus, although we have recognized that where " 'speech' and 'nonspeech' elements are combined in the same course of conduct, a sufficiently important governmental interest in regulating the nonspeech element can justify incidental limitations on First Amendment freedoms," . . . we have limited the applicability of *O'Brien*'s relatively lenient standard to those cases in which "the governmental interest is unrelated to the suppression of free expression." . . . In stating, moreover, that *O'Brien*'s test "in the last analysis is little, if any, different from the standard applied to time, place, or manner restrictions," . . . we have highlighted the requirement that the governmental interest in question be unconnected to expression in order to come under *O'Brien*'s less demanding rule.

In order to decide whether *O'Brien*'s test applies here, therefore, we must decide whether Texas has asserted an interest in support of Johnson's conviction that is unrelated to the suppression of expression. If we find that an interest asserted by the State is simply not implicated on the facts before us, we need not ask whether *O'Brien*'s test applies. . . . The State offers two separate interests to justify this conviction: preventing breaches of the peace, and preserving the flag as a symbol of nationhood and national unity. We hold that the first interest is not implicated on this record and that the second is related to the suppression of expression.

A

Texas claims that its interest in preventing breaches of the peace justifies Johnson's conviction for flag desecration.[4] However, no disturbance of the peace actually occurred or threatened to occur because of Johnson's burning of the flag. Although the State stresses the disruptive behavior of the protestors during their march toward City Hall, . . . it admits that "no actual breach of the peace occurred at the time of the flagburning or in response to the flagburning." . . . The State's emphasis on the protestors' disorderly actions prior to arriving at City Hall is not only somewhat surprising given that no charges were brought on the basis of this conduct, but it also fails to show that a disturbance of the peace was a likely reaction to Johnson's conduct. The only evidence offered by the State at trial to show the reaction to Johnson's actions was the testimony of several persons who had been seriously offended by the flag-burning.

The State's position, therefore, amounts to a claim that an audience that takes serious offense at particular expression is necessarily likely to disturb the peace and that the expression may be prohibited on this basis.[5] Our precedents do not countenance such a presumption. On the contrary, they recognize that a principal "function of free speech under our system of government is to invite dispute. It may indeed best serve its high purpose when it induces a condition of unrest, creates dissatisfaction with conditions as they are, or even stirs people to anger." . . . It would be odd indeed to conclude *both* that "if it is the speaker's opinion that gives offense, that consequence is a reason for according it constitutional protection," . . . *and* that the Government may ban the expression of certain disagreeable ideas on the unsupported presumption that their very disagreeableness will provoke violence.

Thus, we have not permitted the Government to assume that every expression of a provocative idea will incite a riot, but have instead required careful consideration of the actual circumstances surrounding such expression, asking whether the expression "is directed to inciting or producing imminent law-less action and is likely to incite or produce such action." *Brandenburg* v. *Ohio,* . . . (reviewing circumstances surrounding rally and speeches by Ku Klux Klan). To accept Texas' arguments that it need only demonstrate "the potential for a breach of the peace, . . . and that every flag-burning necessarily possesses that potential, would be to eviscerate our holding in *Brandenburg.* This we decline to do.

Nor does Johnson's expressive conduct fall within that small class of "fighting words" that are "likely to provoke the average person to retaliation, and thereby cause a breach of the peace." . . . No reasonable onlooker would have regarded Johnson's generalized expression of dissatisfaction with the policies of the Federal Government as a direct personal insult or an invitation to exchange fisticuffs. . . .

We thus conclude that the State's interest in maintaining order is not implicated on these facts. The State need not worry that our holding will disable it from preserving the peace. We do not suggest that the First Amendment forbids a State to prevent "imminent lawless action." . . . And, in fact, Texas already has a statute specifically prohibiting breaches of the peace, Tex. Penal Code Ann. § 42.01 (1989), which tends to confirm that Texas need not punish this flag desecration in order to keep the peace. . . .

B

The State also asserts an interest in preserving the flag as a symbol of nationhood and national unity. In *Spence,* we acknowledged that the Government's interest in preserving the flag's special symbolic value "is directly related to expression in the context of activity" such as affixing a peace symbol to a flag. . . . We are equally persuaded that this interest is related to expression in the case of Johnson's burning of the flag. The State, apparently, is concerned that such conduct will lead people to believe either that the flag does not stand for nationhood and national unity, but instead reflects other, less positive concepts, or that the concepts reflected in the flag do not in fact exist, that is, we do not enjoy unity as a Nation. These concerns blossom only when a person's treatment of the flag communicates some message, and thus are related "to the suppression of free expression" within the meaning of *O'Brien.* We are thus outside of *O'Brien*'s test altogether.

IV

It remains to consider whether the State's interest in preserving the flag as a symbol of nationhood and national unity justifies Johnson's conviction.

As in *Spence,* "[w]e are confronted with a case of prosecution for the expression of an idea through activity," and "[a]ccordingly, we must examine with particular care the interests advanced by [petitioner] to support its prosecution." 418 U.S., at 411. Johnson was not, we add, prosecuted for the expression of just any idea; he was prosecuted for his expression of dissatisfaction with the policies of this country, expression situated at the core of our First Amendment values. . . .

Moreover, Johnson was prosecuted because he knew that his politically charged expression would cause "serious offense." If he had burned the flag as a means of disposing of it because it was dirty or torn, he would not have been convicted of flag desecration under this Texas law: federal law designates burning as the preferred means of disposing of a flag "when it is in such condition that it is no longer a fitting emblem for display," . . . and Texas has no quarrel with this means of disposal. . . . The Texas law is thus not aimed at protecting the physical integrity of the flag in all circumstances, but is designed instead to protect it only against impairments that would cause serious offense to others.[6] Texas concedes as much: "Section 42.09(b) reaches only those severe acts of physical abuse of the flag carried out in a way likely to be offensive. The statute mandates intentional or knowing abuse, that is, the kind of mistreatment that is not innocent, but rather is intentionally designed to seriously offend other individuals." . . .

Whether Johnson's treatment of the flag violated Texas law thus depended on the likely communicative impact of his expressive conduct.[7] Our decision in *Boos* v. *Barry* . . . tells us that this restriction on Johnson's expression is content-based. In *Boos,* we considered the constitutionality of a law prohibiting "the display of any sign within 50 feet of a foreign embassy if that sign tends to bring that foreign government into 'public odium' or 'public disrepute.' " . . . Rejecting the argument that the law was content-neutral because it was justified by "our international law obligation to shield diplomats from speech that offends their dignity," . . . we held that a "[t]he emotive impact of speech on its audience is not a 'secondary effect' " unrelated to the content of the expression itself. . . .

According to the principles announced in *Boos,* Johnson's political expression was restricted because of the content of the message he conveyed. We must therefore subject the State's asserted interest in preserving the special symbolic character of the flag to "the most exacting scrutiny."[8] . . .

Texas argues that its interest in preserving the flag as a symbol of nationhood and national unity survives this close analysis. Quoting extensively from the writings of this Court chronicling the flag's historic and symbolic role in our society, the State emphasizes the " 'special place' " reserved for the flag in our Nation. . . . The State's argument is not that it has an interest simply in maintaining the flag as a symbol of *something,* no matter what it symbolizes; indeed, if that were the State's position, it would be difficult to see how that interest is endangered by highly symbolic conduct such as Johnson's. Rather, the State's claim is that it has an interest in preserving the flag as a symbol of *nationhood* and *national unity,* a symbol with a determinate range of meanings. . . . According to Texas, if one physically treats the flag in a way that would tend to cast doubt on either the idea that nationhood and national unity are the flag's referents or that national unity actually exists, the message conveyed thereby is a harmful one and therefore may be prohibited.[9]

If there is a bedrock principle underlying the First Amendment, it is that the Government may not prohibit the expression of an idea simply because society finds the idea itself offensive or disagreeable. . . .

We have not recognized an exception to this principle even where our flag has been involved. In *Street* v. *New York,* . . . we held that a State may not criminally punish a person for uttering words critical of the flag. Rejecting the argument that the conviction could be sustained on the ground that Street had "failed to show the respect for our national symbol which may properly be demanded of every citizen," we concluded that "the constitutionally guaranteed 'freedom to be intellectually . . . diverse or even contrary,' and the 'right to differ as to things that touch the heart of the existing order,' encompass the freedom to express publicly one's opinions about our flag, including those opinions which are defiant or contemptuous." . . . Nor may the Government, we have held, compel conduct that would evince respect for the flag. "To sustain the compulsory flag salute we are required to say that a Bill of Rights which guards the individual's right to speak his own mind, left it open to public authorities to compel him to utter what is not in his mind." . . .

In holding in *Barnette* that the Constitution did not leave this course open to the Government, Justice Jackson described one of our society's defining principles in words deserving of their frequent repetition: "If there is any fixed star in our constitutional constellation, it is that no official, high or petty, can prescribe what shall be orthodox in politics, nationalism, religion, or other matters of opinion or force citizens to confess by word or act their faith therein." . . . In *Spence,* we held that the same interest asserted by Texas here was insufficient to support a

criminal conviction under a flag-misuse statute for the taping of a peace sign to an American flag. "Given the protected character of [Spence's] expression and in light of the fact that no interest the State may have in preserving the physical integrity of a privately owned flag was significantly impaired on these facts," we held, "the conviction must be invalidated." . . . See also *Goguen,* . . . (to convict person who had sewn a flag onto the seat of his pants for "contemptuous" treatment of the flag would be "[t]o convict not to protect the physical integrity or to protect against acts interfering with the proper use of the flag, but to punish for communicating ideas unacceptable to the controlling majority in the legislature").

In short, nothing in our precedents suggests that a State may foster its own view of the flag by prohibiting expressive conduct relating to it.[10] To bring its argument outside our precedents, Texas attempts to convince us that even if its interest in preserving the flag's symbolic role does not allow it to prohibit words or some expressive conduct critical of the flag, it does permit it to forbid the outright destruction of the flag. The State's argument cannot depend here on the distinction between written or spoken words and nonverbal conduct. That distinction, we have shown, is of no moment where the nonverbal conduct is expressive, as it is here, and where the regulation of that conduct is related to expression, as it is here. . . . In addition, both *Barnette* and *Spence* involved expressive conduct, not only verbal communication, and both found that conduct protected.

Texas' focus on the precise nature of Johnson's expression, moreover, misses the point of our prior decisions: their enduring lesson, that the Government may not prohibit expression simply because it disagrees with its message, is not dependent on the particular mode in which one chooses to express an idea.[11] If we were to hold that a State may forbid flag-burning wherever it is likely to endanger the flag's symbolic role, but allow it wherever burning a flag promotes that role—as where, for example, a person ceremoniously burns a dirty flag—we would be saying that when it comes to impairing the flag's physical integrity, the flag itself may be used as a symbol—as a substitute for the written or spoken word or a "short cut from mind to mind"—only in one direction. We would be permitting a State to "prescribe what shall be orthodox" by saying that one may burn the flag to convey one's attitude toward it and its referents only if one does not endanger the flag's representation of nationhood and national unity.

We never before have held that the Government may ensure that a symbol be used to express only one view of that symbol or its referents. Indeed, in *Schacht* v. *United States,* we invalidated a federal statute permitting an actor portraying a member of one of our armed forces to " 'wear the uniform of that armed force if the portrayal does not tend to discredit that armed force.' " . . . This proviso, we held, "which leaves Americans free to praise the war in Vietnam but can send persons like Schacht to prison for opposing it, cannot survive in a country which has the First Amendment." . . .

We perceive no basis on which to hold that the principle underlying our decision in *Schacht* does not apply to this case. To conclude that the Government may permit designated symbols to be used to communicate only a limited set of messages would be to enter territory having no discernible or defensible boundaries. Could the Government, on this theory, prohibit the burning of state flags? Of copies of the Presidential seal? Of the Constitution? In evaluating these choices under the First Amendment, how would we decide which symbols were sufficiently special to warrant this unique status? To do so, we would be forced to consult our own political preferences, and impose them on the citizenry, in the very way that the First Amendment forbids us to do. . . .

There is, moreover, no indication—either in the text of the Constitution or in our cases interpreting it—that a separate juridical category exists for the American flag alone. Indeed, we would not be surprised to learn that the persons who framed our Constitution and wrote the Amendment that we now construe were not known for their reverence for the Union Jack. The First Amendment does not guarantee that other concepts virtually sacred to our Nation as a whole—such as the principle that discrimination on the basis of race is odious and destructive—will go unquestioned in the marketplace of ideas. . . . We decline, therefore, to create for the flag an exception to the joust of principles protected by the First Amendment.

It is not the State's ends, but its means, to which we object. It cannot be gainsaid that there is a special place reserved for the flag in this Nation, and thus we do not doubt that the Government has a legitimate interest in making efforts to "preserv[e] the national flag as an unalloyed symbol of our country." . . . We reject the suggestion, urged at oral argument by counsel for Johnson, that the Government lacks "any state interest whatsoever" in regulating the manner in which the flag may be displayed. . . . Congress has, for example, enacted precatory regulations describing the proper treatment of the flag, see 36 U.S.C.§§173–177, and we cast no doubt on the legitimacy of its interest in making such recommendations. To say that the Government has an interest in

encouraging proper treatment of the flag, however, is not to say that it may criminally punish a person for burning a flag as a means of political protest. "National unity as an end which officials may foster by persuasion and example is not in question. The problem is whether under our Constitution compulsion as here employed is a permissible means for its achievement." . . .

We are fortified in today's conclusion by our conviction that forbidding criminal punishment for conduct such as Johnson's will not endanger the special role played by our flag or the feelings it inspires. To paraphrase Justice Holmes, we submit that nobody can suppose that this one gesture of an unknown man will change our Nation's attitude towards its flag. . . . Indeed, Texas' argument that the burning of an American flag " 'is an act having a high likelihood to cause a breach of the peace,' " . . . and its statute's implicit assumption that physical mistreatment of the flag will lead to "serious offense," tend to confirm that the flag's special role is not in danger; if it were, no one would riot or take offense because a flag had been burned.

We are tempted to say, in fact, that the flag's deservedly cherished place in our community will be strengthened, not weakened, by our holding today. Our decision is a reaffirmation of the principles of freedom and inclusiveness that the flag best reflects, and of the conviction that our toleration of criticism such as Johnson's is a sign and source of our strength. Indeed, one of the proudest images of our flag, the one immortalized in our own national anthem, is of the bombardment it survived at Fort McHenry. It is the Nation's resilience, not its rigidity, that Texas sees reflected in the flag—and it is that resilience that we reassert today.

The way to preserve the flag's special role is not to punish those who feel differently about these matters. It is to persuade them that they are wrong. "To courageous, self-reliant men, with confidence in the power of free and fearless reasoning applied through the processes of popular government, no danger flowing from speech can be deemed clear and present, unless the incidence of the evil apprehended is so imminent that it may befall before there is opportunity for full discussion. If there be time to expose through discussion the falsehood and fallacies, to avert the evil by the processes of education, the remedy to be applied is more speech, not enforced silence." . . . And, precisely because it is our flag that is involved, one's response to the flag-burner may exploit the uniquely persuasive power of the flag itself. We can imagine no more appropriate response to burning a flag than waving one's own, no better way to counter a flag-burner's message than by saluting the flag that burns, no surer means of preserving the dignity even of the flag that burned than by—as one witness here did—according its remains a respectful burial. We do not consecrate the flag by punishing its desecration, for in doing so we dilute the freedom that this cherished emblem represents.

V

Johnson was convicted for engaging in expressive conduct. The State's interest in preventing breaches of the peace does not support his conviction because Johnson's conduct did not threaten to disturb the peace. Nor does the State's interest in preserving the flag as a symbol of nationhood and national unity justify his criminal conviction for engaging in political expression. The judgment of the Texas Court of Criminal Appeals is therefore

Affirmed.

CHIEF JUSTICE REHNQUIST, with whom JUSTICE WHITE and JUSTICE O'CONNOR join, dissenting.

In holding this Texas statute unconstitutional, the Court ignores Justice Holmes' familiar aphorism that "a page of history is worth a volume of logic." . . . For more than 200 years, the American flag has occupied a unique position as the symbol of our Nation, a uniqueness that justifies a governmental prohibition against flag burning in the way respondent Johnson did here. . . .

The Court concludes its opinion with a regrettably patronizing civics lecture, presumably addressed to the Members of both Houses of Congress, the members of the 48 state legislatures that enacted prohibitions against flag burning, and the troops fighting under that flag in Vietnam who objected to its being burned: "The way to preserve the flag's special role is not to punish those who feel differently about these matters. It is to persuade them that they are wrong." . . . The Court's role as the final expositor of the Constitution is well established, but its role as a platonic guardian admonishing those responsible to public opinion as if they were truant school children has no similar place in our system of government. The cry of "no taxation without representation" animated those who revolted against the English Crown to found our Nation—the idea that those who submitted to government should have some say as to what kind of laws would be passed. Surely one of the high purposes of a democratic society is to legislate against conduct that is regarded as evil and profoundly offensive to the majority of people—whether it be murder, embezzlement, pollution, or flag burning.

Our Constitution wisely places limits on powers of legislative majorities to act, but the declaration of such limits by this Court "is, at all times, a question of much delicacy, which ought seldom, if ever, to be decided in the affirmative, in a doubtful case." *Fletcher* v. *Peck,* 6 Cranch 87, 128 (1810) (Marshall, C. J.). Uncritical extension of constitutional protection to the burning of the flag risks the frustration of the very purpose for which organized governments are instituted. The Court decides that the American flag is just another symbol, about which not only must opinions pro and con be tolerated, but for which the most minimal public respect may not be enjoined. The government may conscript men into the Armed Forces where they must fight and perhaps die for the flag, but the government may not prohibit the public burning of the banner under which they fight. I would uphold the Texas statute as applied in this case.[12]

NOTES

1. Tex. Penal Code Ann. § 42.09 (1989) provides in full:
"§ 42.09. Desecration of Venerated Object
"(a) A person commits an offense if he intentionally or knowingly desecrates:
"(1) a public monument;
"(2) a place of worship or burial; or
"(3) a state or national flag.
"(b) For purposes of this section, 'desecrate' means deface, damage, or otherwise physically mistreat in a way that the actor knows will seriously offend one or more persons likely to observe or discover his action.
"(c) An offense under this section is a Class A misdemeanor."

2. Because the prosecutor's closing argument observed that Johnson had led the protestors in chants denouncing the flag while it burned, Johnson suggests that he may have been convicted for uttering critical words rather than for burning the flag. Brief for Respondent 33–34. He relies on *Street* v. *New York,* 394 U.S. 576, 578 (1969), in which we reversed a conviction obtained under a New York statute that prohibited publicly defying or casting contempt on the flag "either by words or act" because we were persuaded that the defendant may have been convicted for his words alone. Unlike the law we faced in *Street,* however, the Texas flag-desecration statute does not on its face permit conviction for remarks critical of the flag, as Johnson himself admits. See Brief for Respondent 34. Nor was the jury in this case told that it could convict Johnson of flag desecration if it found only that he had uttered words critical of the flag and its referents.
Johnson emphasizes, though, that the jury was instructed—according to Texas' law of parties—that " 'a person is criminally responsible for an offense committed by the conduct of another if acting with intent to promote or assist the commission of the offense, he solicits, encourages, directs, aids, or attempts to aid the other person to commit the offense.' " Brief for Respondent 2, n. 2, quoting 1 Record 49. The State offered this instruction because Johnson's defense was that he was not the person who had burned the flag. Johnson did not object to this instruction at trial, and although he challenged it on direct appeal, he did so only on the ground that there was insufficient evidence to support it. 706 S. W. 2d 120, 124 (Tex. App. 1986). It is only in this Court that Johnson has argued that the

law-of-parties instruction might have led the jury to convict him for his words alone. Even if we were to find that this argument is properly raised here, however, we would conclude that it has no merit in these circumstances. The instruction would not have permitted a conviction merely for the pejorative nature of Johnson's words, and those words themselves did not encourage the burning of the flag as the instruction seems to require. Given the additional fact that "the bulk of the State's argument was premised on Johnson's culpability as a sole actor," *ibid.*, we find it too unlikely that the jury convicted Johnson on the basis of this alternative theory to consider reversing his conviction on this ground.

3.   Although Johnson has raised a facial challenge to Texas' flag-desecration statute, we choose to resolve this case on the basis of his claim that the statute as applied to him violates the First Amendment. Section 42.09 regulates only physical conduct with respect to the flag, not the written or spoken word, and although one violates the statute only if one "knows" that one's physical treatment of the flag "will seriously offend one or more persons likely to observe or discover his action," Tex. Penal Code Ann. § 42.09(b) (1989), this fact does not necessarily mean that the statute applies only to *expressive* conduct protected by the First Amendment. *Cf. Smith* v. *Goguen,* 415 U.S. 566, 588 (1974) (WHITE, J., concurring in judgment) (statute prohibiting "contemptuous" treatment of flag encompasses only expressive conduct). A tired person might, for example, drag a flag through the mud, knowing that this conduct is likely to offend others, and yet have no thought of expressing any idea; neither the language nor the Texas courts' interpretations of the statute precludes the possibility that such a person would be prosecuted for flag desecration. Because the prosecution of a person who had not engaged in expressive conduct would pose a different case, and because we are capable of disposing of this case on narrower grounds, we address only Johnson's claim that § 42.09 as applied to political expression like his violates the First Amendment.

4.   Relying on our decision in *Boos* v. *Barry,* 485 U.S. 312 (1988), Johnson argues that this state interest is related to the suppression of free expression within the meaning of *United States* v. *O'Brien,* 391 U.S. 367 (1968). He reasons that the violent reaction to flag-burnings feared by Texas would be the result of the message conveyed by them, and that this fact connects the State's interest in the suppression of expression. Brief for Respondent 12, n. 11. This view has found some favor in the lower courts. See *Monroe* v. *State Court of Fulton County,* 739 F. 2d 568, 574–575 (CA11 1984). Johnson's theory may overread *Boos* insofar as it suggests that a desire to prevent a violent audience reaction is "related to expression" in the same way that a desire to prevent an audience from being offended is "related to expression." Because we find that the State's interest in preventing breaches of the peace is not implicated on these facts, however, we need not venture further into this area.

5.   There is, of course, a tension between this argument and the State's claim that one need not actually cause serious offense in order to violate § 42.09. See Brief for Petitioner 44.

6.   *Cf. Smith* v. *Goguen,* 415 U.S., at 590–591 (BLACKMUN, J., dissenting) (emphasizing that lower court appeared to have construed state statute so as to protect physical integrity of the flag in all circumstances); *id.,* at 597–598 (REHNQUIST, J., dissenting) (same).

7.   Texas suggests that Johnson's conviction did not depend on the onlookers' reaction to the flag-burning because § 42.09 is violated only when a person physically mistreats the flag in a way that he "*knows* will seriously offend one or more persons

likely to observe or discover his action." Tex. Penal Code Ann. § 42.09(b) (1969) (emphasis added). "The 'serious offense' language of the statute," Texas argues, "refers to an individual's intent and to the manner in which the conduct is effectuated, not to the reaction of the crowd." Brief for Petitioner 44. If the statute were aimed only at the actor's intent and not at the communicative impact of his actions, however, there would be little reason for the law to be triggered only when an audience is "likely" to be present. At Johnson's trial, indeed, the State itself seems not to have seen the distinction between knowledge and actual communicative impact that it now stresses; it proved the element of knowledge by offering the testimony of persons who had in fact been seriously offended by Johnson's conduct. *Id.,* at 6–7. In any event, we find the distinction between Texas' statute and one dependent on actual audience reaction too precious to be of constitutional significance. Both kinds of statutes clearly are aimed at protecting onlookers from being offended by the ideas expressed by the prohibited activity.

8.   Our inquiry is, of course, bounded by the particular facts of this case and by the statute under which Johnson was convicted. There was no evidence that Johnson himself stole the flag he burned, Tr. of Oral Arg. 17, nor did the prosecution or the arguments urged in support of it depend on the theory that the flag was stolen. *Ibid.* Thus, our analysis does not rely on the way in which the flag was acquired, and nothing in our opinion should be taken to suggest that one is free to steal a flag so long as one later uses it to communicate an idea. We also emphasize that Johnson was prosecuted *only* for flag desecration—not for trespass, disorderly conduct, or arson.

9.   Texas claims that "Texas is not endorsing, protecting, avowing or prohibiting any particular philosophy." Brief for Petitioner 29. If Texas means to suggest that its asserted interest does not prefer Democrats over Socialists, or Republicans over Democrats, for example, then it is beside the point, for Johnson does not rely on such an argument. He argues instead that the State's desire to maintain the flag as a symbol of nationhood and national unity assumes that there is only one proper view of the flag. Thus, if Texas means to argue that its interest does not prefer *any* viewpoint over another, it is mistaken; surely one's attitude towards the flag and its referents is a viewpoint.

10.   Our decision in *Halter* v. *Nebraska,* 205 U.S. 34 (1907), addressing the validity of a state law prohibiting certain commercial uses of the flag, is not to the contrary. That case was decided "nearly 20 years before the Court concluded that the First Amendment applies to the States by virtue of the Fourteenth Amendment." *Spence* v. *Washington,* 418 U.S. 405, 413, n. 7 (1974). More important, as we continually emphasized in *Halter* itself, that case involved purely commercial rather than political speech. 205 U.S., at 38, 41, 42, 45.

Nor does *San Francisco Arts & Athletics* v. *Olympic Committee,* 483 U.S. 522, 524 (1987), addressing the validity of Congress' decision to "authoriz[e] the United States Olympic Committee to prohibit certain commercial and promotional uses of the word 'Olympic,' " relied upon by the dissent, *post,* at 9, even begin to tell us whether the Government may criminally punish physical conduct towards the flag engaged in as a means of political protest.

11.   The dissent appears to believe that Johnson's conduct may be prohibited and, indeed, criminally sanctioned, because "his act . . . conveyed nothing that could not have been conveyed and was not conveyed just as forcefully in a dozen different ways." *Post,* at 10. Not only does this assertion sit uneasily next to the dissent's quite correct reminder that the flag occupies a unique position in our society—which demonstrates

that messages conveyed without use of the flag are not "just as forcefu[l]" as those conveyed with it—but it also ignores the fact that, in *Spence, supra,* we "rejected summarily" this very claim. See 418 U.S., at 411, n. 4.

12.   In holding that the Texas statute as applied to Johnson violates the First Amendment, the Court does not consider Johnson's claims that the statute is unconstitutionally vague or overbroad. Brief for Respondent 24–30. I think those claims are without merit. In *New York State Club Assn.* v. *City of New York,* 487 U.S. —, —(1988), we stated that a facial challenge is only proper under the First Amendment when a statute can never be applied in a permissible manner or when, even if it may be validly applied to a particular defendant, it is so broad as to reach the protected speech of third parties. While Tex. Penal Code Ann. § 42.09 (1989) "may not satisfy those intent on finding fault at any cost, [it is] set out in terms that the ordinary person exercising ordinary common sense can sufficiently understand and comply with." *CSC* v. *Letter Carriers,* 413 U.S. 548, 579 (1973). By defining "desecrate" as "deface," "damage" or otherwise "physically mistreat" in a manner that the actor knows will "seriously offend" others, § 42.09 only prohibits flagrant acts of physical abuse and destruction of the flag of the sort at issue here—soaking a flag with lighter fluid and igniting it in public—and not any of the examples of improper flag etiquette cited in Respondent's brief.

HUSTLER MAGAZINE v. FALWELL

United States Supreme Court, 1988*

...[a suit against *Hustler* magazine and its publisher, Larry] Flynt, to recover damages for invasion of privacy, libel, and intentional infliction of emotional distress. The District Court directed a verdict against respondent on the privacy claim, and submitted the other two claims to a jury. The jury found for petitioners on the defamation claim, but found for respondent on the claim for intentional infliction of emotional distress and awarded damages. We now consider whether this award is consistent with the First and Fourteenth Amendments of the United States Constitution.

The inside front cover of the November 1983 issue of Hustler Magazine featured a "parody" of an advertisement for Campari Liqueur that contained the name and picture of respondent and was entitled "Jerry Falwell talks about his first time." This parody was modeled after actual Campari ads that included interviews with various celebrities about their "first times." Although it was apparent by the end of each interview that this meant the first time they sampled Campari, the ads clearly played on the sexual double entendre of the general subject of "first times." Copying the form and layout of these Campari ads, Hustler's editors chose respondent as the featured celebrity and drafted an alleged "interview" with him in which he states that his "first time" was during a drunken incestuous rendezvous with his mother in an outhouse. The Hustler parody portrays respondent and his mother as drunk and immoral, and suggests that respondent is a hypocrite who preaches only when he is drunk. In small print at the bottom of the page, the ad contains the disclaimer, "ad parody— not to be taken seriously." The magazine's table of contents also lists the ad as "Fiction; Ad and Personality Parody."

Soon after the November issue of Hustler became available to the public, respondent brought this diversity action in the United States District Court for the Western District of Virginia against Hustler Magazine, Inc., Larry C. Flynt, and Flynt Distributing Co. Respondent stated in his complaint that publica-

*485 U.S. 46 (1988).

tion of the ad parody in Hustler entitled him to recover damages for libel, invasion of privacy, and intentional infliction of emotional distress. The case proceeded to trial.[1] At the close of the evidence, the District Court granted a directed verdict for petitioners on the invasion of privacy claim. The jury then found against respondent on the libel claim, specifically finding that the ad parody could not "reasonably be understood as describing actual facts about [respondent] or actual events in which [he] participated." App. to Pet. for Cert. C1. The jury ruled for respondent on the intentional infliction of emotional distress claim, however, and stated that he should be awarded $100,000 in compensatory damages, as well as $50,000 each in punitive damages from petitioners.[2] Petitioners' motion for judgment notwithstanding the verdict was denied.

On appeal, the United States Court of Appeals for the Fourth Circuit affirmed the judgment against petitioners. . . . The court rejected petitioners' argument that the "actual malice" standard of *New York Times Co.* v. *Sullivan*, . . . must be met before respondent can recover for emotional distress. The court agreed that because respondent is concededly a public figure, petitioners are "entitled to the same level of first amendment protection in the claim for intentional infliction of emotional distress that they received in [respondent's] claim for libel." . . . But this does not mean that a literal application of the actual malice rule is appropriate in the context of an emotional distress claim. In the court's view, the *New York Times* decision emphasized the constitutional importance not of the falsity of the statement or the defendant's disregard for the truth, but of the heightened level of culpability embodied in the requirement of "knowing . . . or reckless" conduct. Here, the *New York Times* standard is satisfied by the state-law requirement, and the jury's finding, that the defendants have acted intentionally or recklessly.[3] The Court of Appeals then went on to reject the contention that because the jury found that the ad parody did not describe actual facts about respondent, the ad was an opinion that is protected by the First Amendment. As the court put it, this was "irrelevant," as the issue is "whether [the ad's] publication was sufficiently outrageous to constitute intentional infliction of emotional distress."

. . . Petitioners then filed a petition for rehearing en banc, but this was denied by a divided court. Given the importance of the constitutional issues involved, we granted certiorari.

This case presents us with a novel question involving First Amendment limitations upon a State's authority to protect its citizens from the intentional infliction of emotional distress. We must decide whether a public figure may recover damages for emotional harm caused by the publication of an ad parody offensive to him, and doubtless gross and repugnant in the eyes of most. Respondent would have us find that a State's interest in protecting public figures from emotional distress is sufficient to deny First Amendment protection to speech that is patently offensive and is intended to inflict emotional injury, even when that speech could not reasonably have been interpreted as stating actual facts about the public figure involved. This we decline to do.

At the heart of the First Amendment is the recognition of the fundamental importance of the free flow of ideas and opinions on matters of public interest and concern. "[T]he freedom to speak one's mind is not only an aspect of individual liberty—and thus a good unto itself—but also is essential to the common quest for truth and the vitality of society as a whole." . . . We have therefore been particularly vigilant to ensure that individual expressions of ideas remain free from governmentally imposed sanctions. The First Amendment recognizes no such thing as a "false" idea. . . . As Justice Holmes wrote, "[W]hen men have realized that time has upset many fighting faiths, they may come to believe even more than they believe the very foundations of their own conduct that the ultimate good desired is better reached by free trade in ideas—that the best test of truth is the power of the thought to get itself accepted in the competition of the market. . . . "

The sort of robust political debate encouraged by the First Amendment is bound to produce speech that is critical of those who hold public office or those public figures who are "intimately involved in the resolution of important public questions or, by reason of their fame, shape events in areas of concern to society at large." . . . Justice Frankfurter put it succinctly in *Baumgartner* v. *United States*, . . . when he said that "[o]ne of the prerogatives of American citizenship is the right to criticize public men and measures." Such criticism, inevitably, will not always be reasoned or moderate; public figures as well as public officials will be subject to "vehement, caustic, and sometimes unpleasantly sharp attacks," . . .

"[T]he candidate who vaunts his spotless record and sterling integrity cannot convincingly cry 'Foul!' when an opponent or an industrious reporter attempts to demonstrate the contrary." . . .

Of course, this does not mean that *any* speech about a public figure is immune from sanction in the form of damages. Since *New York Times Co.* v. *Sullivan, supra,* we have consistently ruled that a public figure may hold a speaker liable for the damage to reputation caused by publication of a defamatory falsehood, but only if the statement was made "with knowledge that it was false or with reckless disregard of whether it was false or not." . . . False statements of fact are particularly valueless; they interfere with the truth-seeking function of the marketplace of ideas, and they cause damage to an individual's reputation that cannot easily be repaired by counterspeech, however persuasive or effective. . . .

But even though falsehoods have little value in and of themselves, they are "nevertheless inevitable in free debate," . . . and a rule that would impose strict liability on a publisher for false factual assertions would have an undoubted "chilling" effect on speech relating to public figures that does have constitutional value. "Freedoms of expression require 'breathing space.' "

. . . This breathing space is provided by a constitutional rule that allows public figures to recover for libel or defamation only when they can prove *both* that the statement was false and that the statement was made with the requisite level of culpability.

Respondent argues, however, that a different standard should apply in this case because here the State seeks to prevent not reputational damage, but the severe emotional distress suffered by the person who is the subject of an offensive publication. . . . In respondent's view, and in the view of the Court of Appeals, so long as the utterance was intended to inflict emotional distress, was outrageous, and did in fact inflict serious emotional distress, it is of no constitutional import whether the statement was a fact or an opinion, or whether it was true or false. It is the intent to cause injury that is the gravamen of the tort, and the State's interest in preventing emotional harm simply outweighs whatever interest a speaker may have in speech of this type.

Generally speaking the law does not regard the intent to inflict emotional distress as one which should receive much solicitude, and it is quite understandable that most if not all jurisdictions have chosen to make it civilly culpable where the conduct in question is sufficiently "outrageous." But in the world of debate about public affairs, many things done with motives that are less than admirable are protected by the First Amendment. In *Garrison* v. *Louisiana*, . . . we held that even when a speaker or writer is motivated by hatred or ill-will his expression was protected by the First Amendment:

"Debate on public issues will not be uninhibited if the speaker must run the risk that it will be proved in court that he spoke out of hatred; even if he did speak out of hatred, utterances honestly believed contribute to the free interchange of ideas and the ascertainment of truth."

Thus while such a bad motive may be deemed controlling for purposes of tort liability in other areas of the law, we think the First Amendment prohibits such a result in the area of public debate about public figures.

Were we to hold otherwise, there can be little doubt that political cartoonists and satirists would be subjected to damages awards without any showing that their work falsely defamed its subject. Webster's defines a caricature as "the deliberately distorted picturing or imitating of a person, literary style, etc. by exaggerating features or mannerisms for satirical effect." . . . The appeal of the political cartoon or caricature is often based on exploration of unfortunate physical traits or politically embarrassing events—an exploration often calculated to injure the feelings of the subject of the portrayal. The art of the cartoonist is often not reasoned or evenhanded, but slashing and one-sided. One cartoonist expressed the nature of the art in these words:

"The political cartoon is a weapon of attack, of scorn and ridicule and satire; it is least effective when it tries to pat some politician on the back. It is usually as welcome as a bee sting and is always controversial in some quarters."

Several famous examples of this type of intentionally injurious speech were drawn by Thomas Nast, probably the greatest American cartoonist to date, who was associated for many years during the post-Civil War era with Harper's Weekly. In the pages of that publication Nast conducted a graphic vendetta against William M. "Boss" Tweed and his corrupt associates in New York City's "Tweed Ring." It has been described by one historian of the subject as "a sustained attack which in its passion and effectiveness stands alone in the history of American graphic art." M. Keller, The Art and Politics of Thomas Nast 177 (1968). Another writer explains that the success of the Nast cartoon was achieved "because of the emotional impact of its presentation. It continuously goes beyond the bounds of good taste and conventional manners." C. Press, The Political Cartoon 251 (1981).

Despite their sometimes caustic nature, from the early cartoon portraying George Washington as an ass down to the present day, graphic depictions and satirical cartoons have played a prominent role in public and political debate. Nast's castigation of the Tweed Ring, Walt McDougall's characterization of presidential candidate James G. Blaine's banquet with the millionaires at Delmonico's as "The Royal Feast of Belshazzar," and numerous other efforts have undoubtedly had an effect on the course and outcome of contemporaneous debate. Lincoln's tall, gangling posture, Teddy Roosevelt's glasses and teeth, and Franklin D. Roosevelt's jutting jaw and cigarette holder have been memorialized by political cartoons with an effect that could not have been obtained by the photographer or the portrait artist. From the viewpoint of history it is clear that our political discourse would have been considerably poorer without them.

Respondent contends, however, that the caricature in question here was so "outrageous" as to distinguish it from more traditional political cartoons. There is no doubt that the caricature of respondent and his mother published in Hustler is at best a distant cousin of the political cartoons described above, and a rather poor relation at that. If it were possible by laying down a principled standard to separate the one from the other, public discourse would probably suffer little or no harm. But we doubt that there is any such standard, and we are quite sure that the pejorative description "outrageous" does not supply one. "Outrageousness" in the area of political and social discourse has an inherent subjectiveness about it which would allow a jury to impose liability on the basis of the jurors' tastes or views, or perhaps on the basis of their dislike of a particular expression. An "outrageousness" standard thus runs afoul of our longstanding refusal to allow damages to be awarded because the speech in question may have an adverse emotional impact on the audience. . . . *NAACP* v. *Claiborne Hardware Co.*, . . . ("Speech does not lose its protected character . . . simply because it may embarrass others or coerce them into action"). And, as we stated in *FCC* v. *Pacifica Foundation*. . . .

"[T]he fact that society may find speech offensive is not a sufficient reason for suppressing it. Indeed, if it is the speaker's opinion that gives offense, that consequence is a reason for according it constitutional protection. For it is a central tenet of the First Amendment that the government must remain neutral in the marketplace of ideas."

See also *Street* v. *New York*, . . . ("It is firmly settled that . . . the public expression of ideas may not be prohibited merely because the ideas are themselves offensive to some of their hearers.")

Admittedly, these oft-repeated First Amendment principles, like other principles, are subject to limitations. We recognized in *Pacifica Foundation*, that speech that is " 'vulgar,' 'offensive,' and 'shocking' " is "not entitled to absolute constitutional protection under all circumstances." . . . In . . . *Chaplinsky* v. *New Hampshire*, we held that a state could lawfully punish an individual for the use of insulting

" 'fighting' words—those which by their very utterance inflict injury or tend to incite an immediate breach of the peace." . . . These limitations are but recognition of the observation in *Dun & Bradstreet, Inc.* v. *Greenmoss Builders, Inc.,* . . . that this Court has "long recognized that not all speech is of equal First Amendment importance." But the sort of expression involved in this case does not seem to us to be governed by any exception to the general First Amendment principles stated above.

We conclude that public figures and public officials may not recover for the tort of intentional infliction of emotional distress by reason of publications such as the one here at issue without showing in addition that the publication contains a false statement of fact which was made with "actual malice," *i.e.,* with knowledge that the statement was false or with reckless disregard as to whether or not it was true. This is not merely a "blind application" of the *New York Times* standard, . . . it reflects our considered judgment that such a standard is necessary to give adequate "breathing space" to the freedoms protected by the First Amendment.

Here it is clear that respondent Falwell is a "public figure" for purposes of First Amendment law.[4] The jury found against respondent on his libel claim when if decided that the Hustler ad parody could not "reasonably be understood as describing actual facts about [respondent] or actual events in which [he] participated."

. . . The Court of Appeals interpreted the jury's finding to be that the ad parody "was not reasonably believable," . . . and in accordance with our custom we accept this finding. Respondent is thus relegated to his claim for damages awarded by the jury for the intentional infliction of emotional distress by "outrageous" conduct. But for reasons heretofore stated this claim cannot, consistently with the First Amendment, form a basis for the award of damages when the conduct in question is the publication of a caricature such as the ad parody involved here. The judgment of the Court of Appeals is accordingly

Reversed.

NOTES

1.   While the case was pending, the ad parody was published in Hustler magazine a second time.

2.   The jury found no liability on the part of Flynt Distributing Co., Inc. It is consequently not a party to this appeal.

3.   Under Virginia law, in an action for intentional infliction of emotional distress a plaintiff must show that the defendant's conduct (1) is intentional or reckless; (2) offends generally accepted standards of decency or morality; (3) is causally connected with the plaintiff's emotional distress; and (4) caused emotional distress that was severe. 797 F.2d, at 1275, n. 4 (citing *Womack* v. *Eldridge,* 215 Va. 338, 210 S.E.2d 145 (1974)).

4.   Neither party disputes this conclusion. Respondent is the host of a nationally syndicated television show and was the founder and president of a political organization formerly known as the Moral Majority. He is also the founder of Liberty University in Lynchburg, Virginia, and is the author of several books and publications. Who's Who in America 849 (44th ed. 1986–1987).

IRVING KRISTOL

"Pornography, Obscenity, and the Case for Censorship"*

Being frustrated is disagreeable, but the real disasters in life begin when you get what you want. For almost a century now, a great many intelligent, well-meaning, and articulate people—of a kind generally called liberal or intellectual, or both—have argued eloquently against any kind of censorship of art and/or entertainment. And within the past ten years, the courts and the legislatures of most Western nations have found these arguments persuasive—so persuasive that hardly a man is now alive who clearly remembers what the answers to these arguments were. Today, in the United States and other democracies, censorship has to all intents and purposes ceased to exist.

Is there a sense of triumphant exhilaration in the land? Hardly. There is, on the contrary, a rapidly growing unease and disquiet. Somehow, things have not worked out as they were supposed to, and many notable civil libertarians have gone on record as saying this was not what they meant at all. They wanted a world in which "Desire Under the Elms" could be produced, or "Ulysses" published, without interference by philistine busybodies holding public office. They have got that, of course; but they have also got a world in which homosexual rape takes place on the stage, in which the public flocks during lunch hours to witness varieties of professional fornication, in which Times Square has become little more than a hideous market for the sale and distribution of printed filth that panders to all known (and some fanciful) sexual perversions.

But disagreeable as this may be, does it really matter? Might not our unease and disquiet be merely a cultural hangover—a "hangup," as they say? What reason is there to think that anyone was ever corrupted by a book?

This last question, oddly enough, is asked by the very same people who seem convinced that advertisements in magazines or displays of violence on television do indeed have the power to corrupt. It is also asked, incredibly enough and in all sincerity, by people—e.g., university professors and school teachers—whose very lives provide all the answers one could want. After all, if you believe that no one was ever corrupted by a book, you have also to believe that no one was ever improved by a book (or a play or a movie). You have to believe, in other words, that all art is morally trivial and that, consequently, all education is morally irrelevant. No one, not even a university professor, really believes that.

To be sure, it is extremely difficult, as social scientists tell us, to trace the effects of any single book (or play or movie) on an individual reader or any class of readers. But we all know, and social scientists know it too, that the ways in which we use our minds and imaginations do shape our characters and help define us as persons. That those who certainly know this are nevertheless moved to deny it merely indicates how a dogmatic resistance to the idea of censorship can—like most dogmatism—result in a mindless insistence on the absurd.

I have used these harsh terms—"dogmatism" and "mindless"—advisedly. I might also have added "hypocritical." For the plain fact is that none of us is a complete civil libertarian. We all believe that there is some point at which the public authorities ought to step in to limit the "self-expression" of an individual or a group, even where this might be seriously intended as a form of artistic expression, and even where the artistic transaction is between consenting adults. A playwright or theatrical director might, in this crazy world of ours, find someone willing to commit suicide on the stage, as called for by the script. We would not allow that—any more than we would permit scenes of real physical torture on the stage, even if the victim were a willing masochist. And I know of no one, no matter how free in spirit, who argues that we ought to permit gladiatorial contests in Yankee Stadium, similar to those once performed in the Colosseum at Rome—even if only consenting adults were involved.

*From *The New York Times Magazine,* March 28, 1971. Reprinted by permission of the author.

The basic point that emerges is one that Prof. Walter Berns has powerfully argued: No society can be utterly indifferent to the ways its citizens publicly entertain themselves.* Bearbaiting and cockfighting are prohibited only in part out of compassion for the suffering animals; the main reason they were abolished was because it was felt that they debased and brutalized the citizenry who flocked to witness such spectacles. And the question we face with regard to pornography and obscenity is whether, now that they have such strong legal protection from the Supreme Court, they can or will brutalize and debase our citizenry. We are, after all, not dealing with one passing incident—one book, or one play, or one movie. We are dealing with a general tendency that is suffusing our entire culture.

I say pornography *and* obscenity because, though they have different dictionary definitions and are frequently distinguishable as "artistic" genres, they are nevertheless in the end identical in effect. Pornography is not objectionable simply because it arouses sexual desire or lust or prurience in the mind of the reader or spectator; this is a silly Victorian notion. A great many nonpornographic works—including some parts of the Bible—excite sexual desire very successfully. What is distinctive about pornography is that, in the words of D. H. Lawrence, it attempts "to do dirt on [sex] . . . [It is an] insult to a vital human relationship."

In other words, pornography differs from erotic art in that its whole purpose is to treat human beings obscenely, to deprive human beings of their specifically human dimension. That is what obscenity is all about. It is light-years removed from any kind of carefree sensuality—there is no continuum between Fielding's "Tom Jones" and the Marquis de Sade's "Justine." These works have quite opposite intentions. To quote Susan Sontag: "What pornographic literature does is precisely to drive a wedge between one's existence as a full human being and one's existence as a sexual being—while in ordinary life a healthy person is one who prevents such a gap from opening up." This definition occurs in an essay *defending* pornography—Miss Sontag is a candid as well as gifted critic—so the definition, which I accept, is neither tendentious nor censorious.

Along these same lines, one can point out—as C. S. Lewis pointed out some years back—that it is no accident that in the history of all literatures obscene words—the so-called "four-letter words" —have always been the vocabulary of farce or vituperation. The reason is clear—they reduce men and women to some of their mere bodily functions—they reduce man to his animal component, and such a reduction is an essential purpose of farce or vituperation.

Similarly, Lewis also suggested that it is not an accident that we have no offhand, colloquial, neutral terms—not in any Western European language at any rate—for our most private parts. The words we do use are either (a) nursery terms, (b) archaisms, (c) scientific terms or (d) a term from the gutter (that is, a demeaning term). Here I think the genius of language is telling us something important about man. It is telling us that man is an animal with a difference: he has a unique sense of privacy, and a unique capacity for shame when this privacy is violated. Our "private parts" are indeed private, and not merely because convention prescribes it. This particular convention is indigenous to the human race. In practically all primitive tribes, men and women cover their private parts; and in practically all primitive tribes, men and women do not copulate in public.

It may well be that Western society, in the latter half of the 20th century, is experiencing a drastic change in sexual mores and sexual relationships. We have had many such "sexual revolutions" in the past—and the bourgeois family and bourgeois ideas of sexual propriety were themselves established in the course of a revolution against 18th century "licentiousness"—and we shall doubtless have others in the future. It is, however, highly improbable (to put it mildly) that what we are witnessing is the Final Revolution which will make sexual relations utterly unproblematic, permit us to dispense with any kind of ordered relationships between the sexes, and allow us freely to redefine the human condition. And so long as humanity has not reached that utopia, obscenity will remain a problem.

One of the reasons it will remain a problem is that obscenity is not merely about sex, any more than science fiction is about science. Science fiction, as every student of the genre knows, is a peculiar vision of power: what it is really about is politics. And obscenity is a peculiar vision of humanity: what it is really about is ethics and metaphysics.

*This is as good a place as any to express my profound indebtedness to Walter Berns's superb essay, "Pornography vs. Democracy," in the winter, 1971, issue of The Public Interest.

Imagine a man—a well-known man, much in the public eye—in a hospital ward, dying an agonizing death. He is not in control of his bodily functions, so that his bladder and his bowels empty themselves of their own accord. His consciousness is overwhelmed and extinguished by pain, so that he cannot communicate with us, nor we with him. Now, it would be, technically, the easiest thing in the world to put a television camera in his hospital room and let the whole world witness this spectacle. We don't do it—at least we don't do it as yet—because we regard this as an *obscene* invasion of privacy. And what would make the spectacle obscene is that we would be witnessing the extinguishing of humanity in a human animal.

Incidentally, in the past our humanitarian crusaders against capital punishment understood this point very well. The abolitionist literature goes into great physical detail about what happens to a man when he is hanged or electrocuted or gassed. And their argument was—and is—that what happens is shockingly obscene, and that no civilized society should be responsible for perpetrating such obscenities, particularly since in the nature of the case there must be spectators to ascertain that this horror was indeed being perpetrated in fulfillment of the law.

Sex—like death—is an activity that is both animal and human. There are human sentiments and human ideals involved in this animal activity. But when sex is public, the viewer does not see—cannot see—the sentiments and the ideals. He can only see the animal coupling. And that is why, when men and women make love, as we say, they prefer to be alone—because it is only when you are alone that you can make love, as distinct from merely copulating in an animal and casual way. And that, too, is why those who are voyeurs, if they are not irredeemably sick, also feel ashamed at what they are witnessing. When sex is a public spectacle, a human relationship has been debased into a mere animal connection.

It is also worth noting that this making of sex into an obscenity is not a mutual and equal transaction, but is rather an act of exploitation by one of the partners—the male partner. I do not wish to get into the complicated question as to what, if any, are the essential differences—as distinct from conventional and cultural differences—between male and female. I do not claim to know the answer to that. But I do know—and I take it as a sign which has meaning—that pornography is, and always has been, a man's work; that women rarely write pornography; and that women tend to be indifferent consumers of pornography.* My own guess, by way of explanation, is that a woman's sexual experience is ordinarily more suffused with human emotion than is man's, that men are more easily satisfied with autoerotic activities, and that men can therefore more easily take a more "technocratic" view of sex and its pleasures. Perhaps this is not correct. But whatever the explanation, there can be no question that pornography is a form of "sexism," as the Women's Liberation Movement calls it, and that the instinct of Women's Lib has been unerring in perceiving that, when pornography is perpetrated, it is perpetrated against them, as part of a conspiracy to deprive them of their full humanity.

But even if all this is granted, it might be said —and doubtless will be said—that I really ought not to be unduly concerned. Free competition in the cultural marketplace—it is argued by people who have never otherwise had a kind word to say for laissez-faire—will automatically dispose of the problem. The present fad for pornography and obscenity, it will be asserted, is just that, a fad. It will spend itself in the course of time; people will get bored with it, will be able to take it or leave it alone in a casual way, in a "mature way," and, in sum, I am being unnecessarily distressed about the whole business. The New York Times, in an editiorial, concludes hopefully in this vein.

"In the end . . . the insensate pursuit of the urge to shock, carried from one excess to a more abysmal one, is bound to achieve its own antidote in total boredom. When there is no lower depth to descend to, ennui will erase the problem."

I would like to be able to go along with this line of reasoning, but I cannot. I think it is false, and for two reasons, the first psychological, the second political.

The basic psychological fact about pornography and obscenity is that it appeals to and provokes a kind of sexual regression. The sexual pleasure one gets from pornography and obscenity is autoerotic and infantile; put bluntly, it is a masturbatory exercise of the imagination,

*There are, of course, a few exceptions—but of a kind that prove the rule. "L'Histoire d'O," for instance, written by a woman, is unquestionably the most *melancholy* work of pornography ever written. And its theme is precisely the dehumanization accomplished by obscenity.

when it is not masturbation pure and simple. Now, people who masturbate do not get bored with masturbation, just as sadists don't get bored with sadism, and voyeurs don't get bored with voyeurism.

In other words, infantile sexuality is not only a permanent temptation for the adolescent or even the adult—it can quite easily become a permanent, self-reinforcing neurosis. It is because of an awareness of this possibility of regression toward the infantile condition, a regression which is always open to us, that all the codes of sexual conduct ever devised by the human race take such a dim view of autoerotic activities and try to discourage autoerotic fantasies. Masturbation is indeed a perfectly natural autoerotic activity, as so many sexologists blandly assure us today. And it is precisely because it is so perfectly natural that it can be so dangerous to the mature or maturing person, if it is not controlled or sublimated in some way. That is the true meaning of Portnoy's complaint. Portnoy, you will recall, grows up to be a man who is incapable of having an adult sexual relationship with a woman; his sexuality remains fixed in an infantile mode, the prison of his autoerotic fantasies. Inevitably, Portnoy comes to think, in a perfectly *infantile* way, that it was all his mother's fault.

It is true that, in our time, some quite brilliant minds have come to the conclusion that a reversion to infantile sexuality is the ultimate mission and secret destiny of the human race. I am thinking in particular of Norman O. Brown, for whose writings I have the deepest respect. One of the reasons I respect them so deeply is that Mr. Brown is a serious thinker who is unafraid to face up to the radical consequences of his radical theories. Thus, Mr. Brown knows and says that for his kind of salvation to be achieved, humanity must annul the civilization it has created—not merely the civilization we have today, but all civilization —so as to be able to make the long descent backwards into animal innocence.

What is at stake is civilization and humanity, nothing less. The idea that "everything is permitted," as Nietzsche put it, rests on the premise of nihilism and has nihilistic implications. I will not pretend that the case against nihilism and for civilization is an easy one to make. We are here confronting the most fundamental of philosophical questions, on the deepest levels. But that is precisely my point—that the matter of pornography and obscenity is not a trivial one, and that only superficial minds can take a bland and untroubled view of it.

In this connection, I might also point out those who are primarily against censorship on liberal grounds tell us not to take pornography or obscenity seriously, while those who are for pornography and obscenity, on radical grounds, take it very seriously indeed. I believe the radicals— writers like Susan Sontag, Herbert Marcuse, Norman O. Brown, and even Jerry Rubin—are right, and the liberals are wrong. I also believe that those young radicals at Berkeley, some five years ago, who provoked a major confrontation over the public use of obscene words, showed a brilliant political instinct. Once the faculty and administration had capitulated on this issue— saying: "Oh, for God's sake, let's be adult: what difference does it make anyway?"—once they said that, they were bound to lose on every other issue. And once Mark Rudd could publicly ascribe to the president of Columbia a notoriously obscene relationship to his mother, without provoking any kind of reaction, the S.D.S. had already won the day. The occupation of Columbia's buildings merely ratified their victory. Men who show themselves unwilling to defend civilization against nihilism are not going to be either resolute or effective in defending the university against anything.

I am already touching upon a political aspect of pornography when I suggest that it is inherently and purposefully subversive of civilization and its institutions. But there is another and more specifically political aspect, which has to do with the relationship of pornography and/or obscenity to democracy, and especially to the quality of public life on which democratic government ultimately rests.

Though the phrase, "the quality of life," trips easily from so many lips these days, it tends to be one of those clichés with many trivial meanings and no large, serious one. Sometimes it merely refers to such externals as the enjoyment of cleaner air, cleaner water, cleaner streets. At other times it refers to the merely private enjoyment of music, painting or literature. Rarely does it have anything to do with the way the citizen in a democracy views himself—his obligations, his intentions, his ultimate self-definition.

Instead, what I would call the "managerial" conception of democracy is the predominant opinion among political scientists, sociologists and economists, and has, through the untiring efforts of these scholars, become the conventional journalistic opinion as well. The root idea behind this "managerial" conception is that democracy is a "political system" (as they say) which can be adequately defined in terms of—can be fully reduced to—its mechanical arrangements. Democracy is then seen as a set of rules and procedures, and *nothing but* a set of rules and procedures, whereby majority rule and minority rights are reconciled into a state of equilibrium. If everyone follows these rules and procedures, then a democracy is in working order. I think this is a fair description of the democratic idea that currently prevails in academia. One can also fairly say that it is now the liberal idea of democracy par excellence.

I cannot help but feel that there is something ridiculous about being this kind of a democrat, and I must further confess to having a sneaking sympathy for those of our young radicals who also find it ridiculous. The absurdity is the absurdity of idolatry—of taking the symbolic for the real, the means for the end. The purpose of democracy cannot possibly be the endless functioning of its own political machinery. The purpose of any political regime is to achieve some version of the good life and the good society. It is not at all difficult to imagine a perfectly functioning democracy which answers all questions except one—namely, why should anyone of intelligence and spirit care a fig for it?

There is, however, an older idea of democracy —one which was fairly common until about the beginning of this century—for which the conception of the quality of public life is absolutely crucial. This idea starts from the proposition that democracy is a form of self-government, and that if you want it to be a meritorious polity, you have to care about what kind of people govern it. Indeed, it puts the matter more strongly and declares that, if you want self-government, you are only entitled to it if that "self" is worthy of governing. There is no inherent right to self-government if it means that such government is vicious, mean, squalid and debased. Only a dogmatist and a fanatic, an idolater of democratic machinery, could approve of self-government under such conditions.

And because the desirability of self-government depends on the character of the people who govern, the older idea of democracy was very solicitous of the condition of this character. It was solicitous of the individual self, and felt an obligation to educate it into what used to be called "republican virtue." And it was solicitous of that collective self which we call public opinion and which, in a democracy, governs us collectively. Perhaps in some respects it was nervously

oversolicitous—that would not be surprising. But the main thing is that it cared, cared not merely about the machinery of democracy but about the quality of life that this machinery might generate.

And because it cared, this older idea of democracy had no problem in principle with pornography and/or obscenity. It censored them—and it did so with a perfect clarity of mind and a perfectly clear conscience. It was not about to permit people capriciously to corrupt themselves. Or, to put it more precisely: in this version of democracy, the people took some care not to let themselves be governed by the more infantile and irrational parts of themselves.

I have, it may be noticed, uttered that dreadful word, "censorship." And I am not about to back away from it. If you think pornography and/or obscenity is a serious problem, you have to be for censorship. I'll go even further and say that if you want to prevent pornography and/or obscenity from becoming a problem, you have to be for censorship. And lest there be any misunderstanding as to what I am saying, I'll put it as bluntly as possible: if you care for the quality of life in our American democracy, then you have to be for censorship.

But can a liberal be for censorship? Unless one assumes that being a liberal *must* mean being indifferent to the quality of American life, then the answer has to be: yes, a liberal can be for censorship—but he ought to favor a liberal form of censorship.

Is that a contradiction in terms? I don't think so. We have no problem in contrasting *repressive* laws governing alcohol and drugs and tobacco with laws *regulating* (that is, discouraging the sale of) alcohol and drugs and tobacco. Laws encouraging temperance are not the same thing as laws that have as their goal prohibition or abolition. We have not made the smoking of cigarettes a criminal offense. We have, however, and with good liberal conscience, prohibited cigarette advertising on television, and may yet, again with good liberal conscience, prohibit it in newspapers and magazines. The idea of restricting individual freedom, in a liberal way, is not at all unfamiliar to us.

I therefore see no reason why we should not be able to distinguish repressive censorship from liberal censorship of the written and spoken word. In Britain, until a few years ago, you could perform almost any play you wished—but certain plays, judged to be obscene, had to be performed in private theatrical clubs which were deemed to have a "serious" interest in theater. In the U.S. all of us who grew up using public libraries are familiar with the circumstances under which certain books could be circulated only to adults, while still other books had to be read in the library reading room, under the librarian's skeptical eye. In both cases, a small minority that was willing to make a serious effort to see an obscence play or read an obscene book could do so. But the impact of obscenity was circumscribed and the quality of public life was only marginally affected.*

I am not saying it is easy in practice to sustain a distinction between liberal and repressive censorship, especially in the public realm of a democracy, where popular opinion is so vulnerable to demagoguery. Moreover, an acceptable system of liberal censorship is likely to be exceedingly difficult to devise in the United States today, because our educated classes, upon whose judgment a liberal censorship must rest, are so convinced that there is no such thing as a problem of obscenity, or even that there is no such thing as obscenity at all. But, to counterbalance this, there is the further, fortunate truth that the tolerable margin for error is quite large, and single mistakes or single injustices are not all that important.

This possibility, of course, occasions much distress among artists and academics. It is a fact, one that cannot and should not be denied, that any system of censorship is bound, upon occasion, to treat unjustly a particular work of art—to find pornography where there is only gentle eroticism, to find obscenity where none really exists, or to find both where its existence ought to be tolerated because it serves a larger moral purpose. Though most works of art are not obscene, and though most obscenity has nothing to do with art, there are some few works of art that are, at least in part, pornographic and/or obscene. There are also some few works of art that are in the special category of the comic-ironic "bawdy" (Boccaccio, Rabelais). It is such works of art that are likely to suffer at the hands of the censor. That is the price one has to be prepared to pay for censorship—even liberal censorship.

But just how high is this price? If you believe, as so many artists seem to believe today, that art

is the only sacrosanct activity in our profane and vulgar world—that any man who designates himself an artist thereby acquires a sacred office—then obviously censorship is an intolerable form of sacrilege. But for those of us who do not subscribe to this religion of art, the costs of censorship do not seem so high at all.

If you look at the history of American or English literature, there is precious little damage you can point to as a consequence of the censorship that prevailed throughout most of that history. Very few works of literature—of real literary merit, I mean—ever were suppressed; and those that were, were not suppressed for long. Nor have I noticed, now that censorship of the written word has to all intents and purposes ceased in this country, that hitherto suppressed or repressed masterpieces are flooding the market. Yes, we can now read "Fanny Hill" and the Marquis de Sade. Or, to be more exact, we can now openly purchase them, since many people were able to read them even though they were publicly banned, which is as it should be under a liberal censorship. So how much have literature and the arts gained from the fact that we can all now buy them over the counter, that, indeed, we are all now encouraged to buy them over the counter? They have not gained much that I can see.

And one might also ask a question that is almost never raised: how much has literature lost from the fact that everything is now permitted? It has lost quite a bit, I should say. In a free market, Gresham's Law can work for books or theater as efficiently as it does for coinage—driving out the good, establishing the debased. The cultural market in the United States today is being preempted by dirty books, dirty movies, dirty theater. A pornographic novel has a far better chance of being published today than a nonpornographic one, and quite a few pretty good novels are not being published at all simply because they are not pornographic, and are therefore less likely to sell. Our cultural condition has not improved as a result of the new freedom. American cultural life wasn't much to brag about 20 years ago; today one feels ashamed for it.

Just one last point which I dare not leave untouched. If we start censoring pornography or obscenity, shall we not inevitably end up censoring political opinion? A lot of people seem to think this would be the case—which only shows the power of doctrinaire thinking over reality. We had censorship of pornography and obscenity for

---

*It is fairly predictable that some one is going to object that this point of view is "elitist"—that, under a system of liberal censorship, the rich will have privileged access to pornography and obscenity. Yes, of course they will—just as at present, the rich have privileged acess to heroin if they want it. But one would have to be an egalitarian maniac to object to this state of affairs on the grounds of equality.

150 years, until almost yesterday, and I am not aware that freedom of opinion in this country was in any way diminished as a consequence of this fact. Fortunately for those of us who are liberal, freedom is not indivisible. If it were, the case for liberalism would be indistinguishable from the case for anarchy; and they are two very different things.

But I must repeat and emphasize: What kind of laws we pass governing pornography and obscenity, what kind of censorship—or, since we are still a federal nation—what kinds of censorship we institute in our various localities may indeed be difficult matters to cope with; nevertheless the real issue is one of principle. I myself subscribe to the liberal view of the enforcement problem: I think that pornography should be illegal and available to anyone who wants it so badly as to make a pretty strenuous effort to get it. We have lived with under-the-counter pornography for centuries now, in a fairly comfortable way. But the issue of principle, of whether it should be over or under the counter, has to be settled before we can reflect on the advantages and disadvantages of alternative modes of censorship. I think the settlement we are living under now, in which obscenity and democracy are regarded as equals, is wrong; I believe it is inherently unstable; I think it will, in the long run, be incompatible with any authentic concern for the quality of life in our democracy.

HENRY M. HART, JR., and ALBERT M. SACKS

The Invitation to Dinner Case*

On the way home for lunch on Friday, January 6, 1956, Mr. Patrick met Mr. David, an acquaintance of his. Mr. Patrick told Mr. David that he expected Professor Thomas for dinner and would like Mr. David to join them both for dinner and for bridge afterward. Mr. Patrick explained to Mr. David that he must be sure about coming so that there would be enough persons for bridge. Bridge, he said, was a favorite game of Professor Thomas's, and he wanted to humor the professor because he needed his help in getting a job. Mr. David asked what there would be for dinner, and Mr. Patrick promised to have planked steak, which he knew to be a favorite dish of Mr. David's. On hearing this, Mr. David promised firmly to be there at 7 P.M.

At 6:30 P.M., while Mr. David was dressing, the telephone rang. On the line was his friend, Mr. Jack, who asked him to come over for a game of poker. Mr. David agreed at once, and left soon for Jack's house, telling his wife that he was going to Patrick's.

At 9 P.M. the telephone rang in Jack's house, and a voice asked for Mr. David. Mr. David answered, fearful that it was his wife, but it was Mr. Patrick, who could hardly talk from anger. He said: "So I knew where to find you, you . . . If you do not come over to my place at once, I'll sue you in court." Mr. David hung up the phone without answering, and told the story to Jack and his friends who had a good laugh. All of them kept on playing until the early morning hours.

Mr. Patrick was as good as his word, and his lawyer filed an action against Mr. David. He claimed damages for breach of contract, including the price of a portion of planked steak specially prepared for the defendant; $2,500 compensation for not getting a job (Professor Thomas having left in dudgeon immediately after dinner); and $1,000 for mental suffering.

Mr. Patrick's lawyer claimed that there had been a legally binding contract, supported by consideration, and that the defendant had wilfully and maliciously failed to fulfill his legal and moral obligation. While acknowledging that he could find no case directly in point, he argued that the common law is elastic, and capable of developing a remedy for every wrong, especially in a case such as this where there was reliance on a promise made upon consideration, damage suffered because of malicious default, and warning to the defendant that the matter would be taken to court.

Mr. David appeared without a lawyer, telling the judge that he never thought he could be summoned to court over a social dinner invitation, and asked that the case be dismissed.

How should the judge decide?

*From *The Legal Process* by Henry M. Hart, Jr. and Albert M. Sacks (Cambridge, Mass.: Tentative Edition, 1958), pp. 477–78. Copyright © 1958 by Henry M. Hart, Jr. and Albert M. Sacks. Reprinted by permission of Albert M. Sacks. (This problem was suggested by Mr. Y. Dror, LL.M. Harvard, 1955, and a candidate for the degree of S. J. D. at the Harvard Law School during the academic year 1955–56.)

HYMAN GROSS

Privacy and Autonomy*

Why is privacy desirable? When is its loss objectionable and when is it not? How much privacy is a person entitled to? These questions challenge at the threshold our concern about protection of privacy. Usually they are pursued by seeking agreement on the boundary between morbid and healthy reticence, and by attempting to determine when unwanted intrusion or notoriety is justified by something more important than privacy. Seldom is privacy considered as the condition under which there is *control* over acquaintance with one's personal affairs by the one enjoying it, and I wish here to show how consideration of privacy in this neglected aspect is helpful in answering the basic questions. First I shall attempt to make clear this part of the idea of privacy, next suggest why privacy in this aspect merits protection, then argue that some important dilemmas are less vexing when we do get clear about these things, and finally offer a cautionary remark regarding the relation of privacy and autonomy.

I

What in general is it that makes certain conduct offensive to privacy? To distinguish obnoxious from innocent interference with privacy we must first see clearly what constitutes loss of privacy at all, and then determine why loss of privacy when it does occur is sometimes objectionable and sometimes not.

Loss of privacy occurs when the limits one has set on acquaintance with his personal affairs are not respected. Almost always we mean not respected by *others,* though in unusual cases we might speak of a person not respecting his own privacy—he is such a passionate gossip, say, that he gossips even about himself and later regrets it. Limits on acquaintance may be maintained by the physical insulation of a home, office, or other private place within which things that are to be private may be confined. Or such bounds may exist by virtue of exclusionary social conventions, for example those governing a private conversation in a public place; or through restricting conventions which impose an obligation to observe such limits, as when disclosure is made in confidence. Limits operate in two ways. There are restrictions on what is known, and restrictions on who may know it. Thus, a curriculum vitae furnished to or for a prospective employer is not normally an invitation to undertake a detective investigation using the items provided as clues. Nor is there normally license to communicate to others the information submitted. In both instances there would be disregard of limitations implied by considerations of privacy, unless the existence of such limitations is unreasonable under the circumstances (the prospective employer is the CIA, or the information is furnished to an employment agency). But there is no loss of privacy when such limits as do exist are respected, no matter how ample the disclosure or how extensive its circulation. If I submit a detailed account of my life while my friend presents only the barest résumé of his, I am not giving up more of privacy than he. And if I give the information to a hundred employers, I lose no more in privacy than my friend who confides to only ten, provided those informed by each of us are equally restricted. More people know more about me, so my *risk* of losing privacy is greater and the threatened loss more serious. Because I am a less private person than my friend, I am more willing to run that risk. But until there is loss of control over what is known, and by whom, my privacy is uncompromised—though much indeed may be lost in secrecy, mystery, obscurity, and anonymity.

Privacy is lost in either of two ways. It may be given up, or it may be taken away. Abandonment of privacy (though sometimes undesired) is an inoffensive loss, while deprivation by others is an offensive loss.

*From *Nomos XIII, Privacy,* ed. by John Chapman and J. Roland Pennock (New York: Lieber-Atherton, 1971), pp. 169–182. Reprinted by permission of the publisher.

If one makes a public disclosure of personal matters or exposes himself under circumstances that do not contain elements of restriction on further communication, there is loss of control for which the person whose privacy is lost is himself responsible. Such abandonment may result from indifference, carelessness, or a positive desire to have others become acquainted. There are, however, instances in which privacy is abandoned though this was not intended. Consider indiscrete disclosures while drunk which are rued when sober. If the audience is not under some obligation (perhaps the duty of a confidant) to keep dark what was revealed, there has been a loss of privacy for which the one who suffers it is responsible. But to constitute an abandonment, the loss of privacy must result from voluntary conduct by the one losing it, and the loss must be an expectable result of such conduct. If these two conditions are not met, the person who suffers the loss cannot be said to be responsible for it. Accordingly, a forced revelation, such as an involuntary confession, is not an abandonment of privacy, because the person making it has not given up control but has had it taken from him.

Regarding the requirement of expectability, we may see its significance by contrasting the case of a person whose conversation is overheard in Grand Central Station with the plight of someone made the victim of eavesdropping in his living room. In a public place loss of control is expectable by virtue of the circumstances of communication: part of what we mean when we say a place is public is that there is not present the physical limitation upon which such control depends. But a place may be called private only when there is such limitation, so communication in it is expectably limited and the eavesdropping an offensive violation for which the victim is not himself responsible. And consider the intermediate case of eavesdropping on a conversation in a public place —a distant parabolic microphone focused on a street-corner conversation, or a bugging device planted in an airplane seat. The offensive character of such practices derives again from their disregard of expectable limitations, in this instance the force of an exclusionary social convention which applies to all except those whose immediate presence enables them to overhear.

So far there has been consideration of what constitutes loss of privacy, and when it is objectionable. But to assess claims for protection of privacy we must be clear also about *why* in general loss of privacy is objectionable. This becomes especially important when privacy and other things we value are in competition, one needing to be sacrificed to promote the other. It becomes important then to understand what good reasons there are for valuing privacy, and this is our next item of business.

II

There are two sorts of things we keep private, and with respect to each, privacy is desirable for somewhat different reasons. Concern for privacy is sometimes concern about which facts about us can become known, and to whom. This includes acquaintance with all those things which make up the person as he may become known—identity, appearance, traits of personality and character, talents, weaknesses, tastes, desires, habits, interests—in short, things which tell us who a person is and what he's like. The other kind of private matter is about our lives—what we've done, intend to do, are doing now, how we feel, what we have, what we need—and concern about privacy here is to restrict acquaintance with these matters. Together these two classes of personal matters comprise all those things which can be private. Certain items of information do indeed have aspects which fit them for either category. For example, a person's belief is something which pertains to him when viewed as characteristic of him, but pertains to the events of his life when viewed as something he has acquired, acts on, and endeavors to have others adopt.

Why is privacy of the person important? This calls mainly for consideration of what is necessary to maintain an integrated personality in a social setting. Although we are largely unaware of what influences us at the time, we are constantly concerned to control how we appear to others, and act to implement this concern in ways extremely subtle and multifarious. Models of image and behavior are noticed, imitated, adopted, so that nuances in speech, gesture, facial expression, *politesse,* and much more become a person as known on an occasion. The deep motive is to influence the reactions of others, and this is at the heart of human social accommodation. Constraints to imitation and disguise can become a pathological problem of serious proportions when concern with appearances interferes with normal functioning, but normal behavior allows, indeed requires, that we perform critically in presenting and withholding in order to effect certain appearances. If these editorial efforts are not to be wasted, we must have a large measure of control over what of us is seen and heard, when, where, and by whom. For this reason we see as offensive the candid camera which records casual behavior with the intention of later showing it as entertainment to a general audience. The victim is not at the time aware of who will see him and so does not have the opportunity to exercise appropriate critical restraint in what he says and does. Although subsequent approval for the showing eliminates grounds for objection to the publication as an offense to privacy, there remains the lingering objection to the prior disregard of limits of acquaintance which are normal to the situation and so presumably relied on by the victim at the time. The nature of the offense is further illuminated by considering its aggravation when the victim has been deliberately introduced unawares into the situation for the purpose of filming his behavior, or its still greater offensiveness if the setting is a place normally providing privacy and assumed to be private by the victim. What we have here are increasingly serious usurpations of a person's prerogative to determine how he shall appear, to whom, and on what occasion.

The same general objection applies regarding loss of privacy where there is information about our personal affairs which is obtained, accumulated, and transmitted by means beyond our control. It is, however, unlike privacy of personality in its untoward consequences. A data bank of personal information is considered objectionable, but not because it creates appearances over which we have no control. We are willing to concede that acquaintance with our reputation is in general not something we are privileged to control, and that we are not privileged to decide just what our reputation shall be. If the reputation is correct we cannot object because we do not appear as we would wish. What then are the grounds of objection to a data bank, an objection which indeed persists even if its information is correct and the inferences based on the information are sound? A good reason for objecting is that a data bank is an offense to self-determination. We are subject to being acted on by others because of conclusions about us which we do not know and whose effect we have no opportunity to counteract. There is a loss of control over reputation which is unacceptable because we no longer have the ability to try to change what is believed about us. We feel entitled to know what others believe, and why, so that we may try to change misleading impressions and on occasion show why a decision about us ought not to be based on reputation even if the reputation is justified. If our account in the data bank were made known to us and opportunity given to change its effect, we should drop

most (though not all) of our objection to it. We might still fear the danger of abuse by public forces concerned more with the demands of administrative convenience than justice, but because we could make deposits and demand a statement reflecting them, we would at least no longer be in the position of having what is known and surmised about us lie beyond our control.

Two aspects of privacy have been considered separately, though situations in which privacy is violated sometimes involve both. Ordinary surveillance by shadowing, peeping, and bugging commonly consists of observation of personal behavior as well as accumulation of information. Each is objectionable for its own reasons, though in acting against the offensive practice we protect privacy in both aspects. Furthermore, privacy of personality and of personal affairs have some common ground in meriting protection, and this has to do with a person's role as a responsible moral agent.

In general we do not criticize a person for untoward occurrences which are a result of his conduct if (through no fault of his own) he lacked the ability to do otherwise. Such a person is similarly ineligible for applause for admirable things which would not have taken place but for his conduct. In both instances we claim that he is not responsible for what happened, and so should not be blamed or praised. The principle holds true regarding loss of privacy. If a person cannot control how he is made to appear (nor could he have prevented his loss of control), he is not responsible for how he appears or is thought of, and therefore cannot be criticized as displeasing or disreputable (nor extolled as the opposite). He can, of course, be condemned for conduct which is the basis of the belief about him, but that is a different matter from criticism directed solely to the fact that such a belief exists. Personal gossip (even when believed) is not treated by others as something for which the subject need answer, because its existence defies his control. Responsible appraisal of anyone whose image or reputation is a matter of concern requires that certain private items illicitly in the public domain be ignored in the assessment. A political figure may, with impunity, be known as someone who smokes, drinks, flirts, and tells dirty jokes, so long (but only so long) as this is not the public image *he* presents. The contrasting fortunes of recent political leaders remind us that not being responsible for what is believed by others can be most important. If such a man is thought in his private life to engage in discreet though illicit liaisons he is not held accountable for rumors without more. However, once he has allowed himself to be publicly exposed in a situation which is in the slightest compromising, he must answer for mere appearances. And on this same point, we might consider why a woman is never held responsible for the way she appears in the privacy of her toilette.

To appreciate the importance of this sort of disclaimer of responsibility we need only imagine a community in which it is not recognized. Each person would be accountable for himself however he might be known, and regardless of any precautionary seclusion which was undertaken in the interest of shame, good taste, or from other motives of self-regard. In such a world modesty is sacrificed to the embarrassment of unwanted acclaim, and self-criticism is replaced by the condemnation of others. It is part of the vision of Orwell's *1984,* in which observation is so thorough that it forecloses the possibility of a private sector of life under a person's exclusionary control, and so makes him answerable for everything observed without limits of time or place. Because of this we feel such a condition of life far more objectionable than a community which makes the same oppressive social demands of loyalty and conformity but with the opportunity to be free of concern about appearances in private. In a community without privacy, furthermore, there can be no editorial privilege exercised in making oneself known to others. Consider, for example, the plight in which Montaigne would find himself. He observed that "No quality embraces us purely and universally. If it did not seem crazy to talk to oneself, there is not a day when I would not be heard growling at myself: 'Confounded fool!' And yet I do not intend that to be my definition." Respect for privacy is required to safeguard our changes of mood and mind, and to promote growth of the person through self-discovery and criticism. We want to run the risk of making fools of ourselves and be free to call ourselves fools, yet not be fools in the settled opinion of the world, convicted out of our own mouths.

III

Privacy is desirable, but rights to enjoy it are not absolute. In deciding what compromises must be made some deep quandaries recur, and three of them at least seem more manageable in light of what has been said so far.

In the first place, insistence on privacy is often taken as implied admission that there is cause for shame. The assumption is that the only reason for keeping something from others is that one is ashamed of it (although it is conceded that sometimes there is in fact no cause for shame even though the person seeking privacy thinks there is). Those who seek information and wish to disregard interests in privacy often play on this notion by claiming that the decent and the innocent have no cause for shame and so no need for privacy: "Only those who have done or wish to do something shameful demand privacy." But it is unsound to assume that demands for privacy imply such an admission. Pride, or at least wholesome self-regard, is the motive in many situations. The famous Warren and Brandeis article on privacy which appeared in the *Harvard Law Review* in 1890 was impelled in some measure, we are told, by Samuel Warren's chagrin. His daughter's wedding, a very social Boston affair, had been made available to the curious at every newsstand by the local press. Surely he was not ashamed of the wedding even though outraged by the publicity. Or consider Miss Roberson, the lovely lady whose picture was placed on a poster advertising the product of Franklin Mills with the eulogistic slogan "Flour of the family," thereby precipitating a lawsuit whose consequences included the first statutory protection of privacy in the United States. What was exploited was the lady's face, undoubtedly a source of pride.

Both these encroachments on privacy illustrate the same point. Things which people like about themselves are taken by them to belong to them in a particularly exclusive way, and so control over disclosure or publication is especially important to them. The things about himself which a person is most proud of he values most, and thus are things over which he is most interested to exercise exclusive control. It is true that shame is not infrequently the motive for privacy, for often we do seek to maintain conditions necessary to avoid criticism and punishment. But since it is not the only motive, the quest for privacy does not entail tacit confessions. Confusion arises here in part because an assault on privacy always does involve humiliation of the victim. But this is because he has been deprived of control over something personal which is given over to the control of others. In short, unwilling loss of privacy always results in the victim being shamed, not because of what others learn, but because they and not he may then determine who else shall know it and what use shall be made of it.

Defining the privilege to make public what is otherwise private is another source of persistent difficulty. There is a basic social interest in making available information about people, in exploring the personal aspects of human affairs, in stimulating and satisfying curiosity about others. The countervailing interest is in allowing people who have not offered themselves for public scrutiny to remain out of sight and out of mind. In much of the United States the law has strained with the problem of drawing a line of protection which accords respect to both interests. The result, broadly stated, has been recognition of a privilege to compromise privacy for news and other material whose primary purpose is to impart information, but to deny such privileged status to literary and other art, to entertainment, and generally to any appropriation for commercial purposes. Development of the law in New York after Miss Roberson's unsuccessful attempt to restrain public display of her picture serves as a good example. A statute was enacted prohibiting unauthorized use of the name, portrait, or picture of any living person for purposes of trade or advertising, and the legislation has been interpreted by the courts along the general lines indicated. But it is still open to speculation why a writer's portrayal of a real person as a character in a novel could qualify as violative, while the same account in biographical or historical work would not. It has not been held that history represents a more important social interest than art and so is more deserving of a privileged position in making known personal matters, or, more generally, that edification is more important than entertainment. Nor is the question ever raised, as one might expect, whether an item of news is sufficiently newsworthy to enjoy a privilege in derogation of privacy. Further, it was not held that the implied statutory criterion of intended economic benefit from the use of a personality would warrant the fundamental distinctions. Indeed, the test of economic benefit would qualify both television's public affairs programs and its dramatic shows as within the statute, and the reportage of *Life* Magazine would be as restricted as the films of De Mille or Fellini. But in each instance the former is in general free of the legal prohibition while the latter is not. What, then, is the basis of distinction? Though not articulated, a sound criterion does exist.

Unauthorized *use* of another person—whether for entertainment, artistic creation, or economic gain—is offensive. So long as we remain in charge of how we are used, we have no cause for complaint. In those cases in which a legal wrong is recognized, there has been use by others in disregard of this authority, but in those cases in which a privilege is found, there is not *use* of personality or personal affairs at all, at least not use in the sense of one person assuming control over another, which is the gist of the offense to autonomy. We do indeed suffer a loss of autonomy whenever the power to place us in free circulation is exercised by others, but we consider such loss offensive only when another person assumes the control of which we are deprived, when we are used and not merely exposed. Failure to make clear this criterion of offensiveness has misled those who wish to define the protectable area, and they conceive the problem as one of striking an optimal balance between two valuable interests, when in fact it is a matter of deciding whether the acts complained of are offensive under a quite definite standard of offensiveness. The difficult cases here have not presented a dilemma of selecting the happy medium, but rather the slippery job of determining whether the defendant had used the plaintiff or whether he had merely caused things about him to become known, albeit to the defendant's profit. The difference is between managing another person as a means to one's own ends, which is offensive, and acting merely as a vehicle of presentation (though not gratuitously) to satisfy established social needs, which is not offensive. Cases dealing with an unauthorized biography that was heavily anecdotal and of questionable accuracy, or with an entertaining article that told the true story of a former child prodigy who became an obscure eccentric, are perplexing ones because they present elements of both offensive and inoffensive publication, and a decision turns on which is predominant.

There remains another balance-striking quandary to be dismantled. It is often said that privacy as an interest must be balanced against security. Each, we think, must sacrifice something of privacy to promote the security of all, though we are willing to risk some insecurity to preserve a measure of privacy. Pressure to reduce restrictions on wiretapping and searches by police seeks to push the balance toward greater security. But the picture we are given is seriously misleading. In the first place we must notice the doubtful assumption on which the argument rests. It may be stated this way: the greater the ability to watch what is going on, or obtain evidence of what has gone on, the greater the ability to prevent crime. It is a notion congenial to those who believe that more efficient law enforcement contributes significantly to a reduction in crime. We must, however, determine if such a proposition is in fact sound, and we must see what crimes are suppressible, even in principle, before any sacrifice of privacy can be justified. There is, at least *in limine,* much to be said for the conflicting proposition that, once a generally efficient system of law enforcement exists, an increase in its efficiency does not result in a corresponding reduction in crime, but only in an increase in punishments. Apart from that point, there is an objection relating more directly to what has been said here about privacy. Security and privacy are both desirable, but measures to promote each are on different moral footing. Men ought to be secure, we say, because only in that condition can they live a good life. Privacy, however, like peace and prosperity, is itself part of what we mean by a good life, a part having to do with self-respect and self-determination. Therefore, the appropriate attitudes when we are asked to sacrifice privacy for security are first a critical one which urges alternatives that minimize or do not at all require the sacrifice, and ultimately regret for loss of a cherished resource if the sacrifice proves necessary.

IV

In speaking of privacy and autonomy, there is some danger that privacy may be conceived as autonomy. Such confusion has been signaled in legal literature by early and repeated use of the phrase "right to be let alone" as a synonym for "right of privacy." The United States Supreme Court succumbed completely in 1965 in its opinion in *Griswold v. Connecticut,* and the ensuing intellectual disorder warrants comment.

In that case legislative prohibition of the use of contraceptives was said to be a violation of a constitutional right of privacy, at least when it affected married people. The court's opinion relied heavily on an elaborate *jeu de mots,* in which different senses of the word "privacy" were punned upon, and the legal concept generally mismanaged in ways too various to recount here. In the *Griswold* situation there had been an attempt by government to regulate personal affairs, not get acquainted with them, and so there was an issue regarding autonomy and not privacy. The opinion was not illuminating on the question of what are proper bounds for the exercise of legislative power, which was the crucial matter before the court. It is precisely the issue of what rights to autonomous determination of his affairs are enjoyed by a citizen. The *Griswold* opinion not only failed to take up that question in a forthright manner, but promoted confusion about privacy in the law by unsettling the intellectual focus on it which had been developed in torts and constitutional law. If the confusion in the court's argument was inadvertent, one may sympathize with the deep conceptual difficulties which produced it, and if it was deliberately contrived, admire its ingenuity. Whatever its origin, its effect is to muddle the separate issues, which must be analyzed and argued along radically different lines when protection is sought either for privacy or for autonomy. Hopefully, further developments will make clear that while an offense to privacy is an offense to autonomy, not every curtailment of autonomy is a compromise of privacy.

ALAN RYAN

The Theatrical Model and Concern for Privacy*

THE THEATRICAL MODEL AND CONCERN FOR PRIVACY

The concern with autonomy recovers a good deal of what we ordinarily know about human behaviour, but not all of it. Some of the rest, at least, is picked up by an emphasis on the theatrical model. Indeed, the sociologists' talk of roles suggests we ought never to have neglected the ability to *play* parts and *manage* appearances, that is, to lay on performances of what Goffman sometimes calls 'strips' of social interaction. That the theatrical metaphor is both inescapable and elusive is not only noticed by the writer with whom it is currently associated, Erving Goffman, but was a matter of some discussion in the eighteenth century and even before.[1] Detaching the idea from any particular writer, we plainly have to begin with the observation that a great deal of behaviour is not just doing but saying. Our actions in a given role do more than merely fulfil whatever requirements of a successful performance they do fulfil; crucially, they tell the audience something about us and how we relate to the role.[2]

Two ideas much at home in this account, and nowhere else, are the concept of role-distance and the explanation of tact—of the sort of forbearance that one might call allowing people some privacy even in public. Armed with these insights we have another way of considering the importance of privacy in general. The kind of phenomenon which role-distance is adduced to illuminate is the behaviour of parents on children's rides at a fairground, say, where parents habitually go to great lengths to make it clear that they are there only *qua* parent, that they wouldn't spend their time on the rides if they weren't compelled to, and so on. In essence, what the parent does is make it clear that he is not really the sort of person who *wants* to

do frivolous and childish things. What the parent can do is employ the known obligations of the role to subvert inferences about *him*. The ability to play a role in such a way as to communicate any number of different things about ourselves while we do it may be used for altruistic and public-spirited ends—the surgeon who pretends that he would rather be on the golf course is not trying to get his colleagues to believe that he really is an idle beast who cannot distinguish a scalpel from a niblick. He is reassuring them that he is so much in control of his bit of the team's task that they can safely relax and not worry about him. Lightheartedness and conscientiousness may, agreeably, be allies.

Now, since people will always draw inferences about *us* from the performances we give, we can finally move to say a little about privacy. I take it that a central element in the idea of privacy is that we have the right to control what information people possess about certain areas of our lives, and that other people have a duty to skirt round those areas—not that they have a duty not to *know* about us, but that they have a duty not to try to find out. And a central concern of the theatrical model is precisely with how we control what others do know about us. The assumption is that other people inevitably want to know a good deal about us, since they have projects at risk if we are unreliable or deviate from their expectations. Much of the time we shall want to make our private selves public for precisely this reason—we shall want to reassure others. Of course, this cannot be done by direct means; people look at our conduct to decide how far they can really trust our direct assurances.

All this, however, is inevitably somewhat wearing. Moreover, everyone knows that not every moment can be spent in whole-hearted commitment to being a sincere and committed player in the social game. Played too rigorously, the whole thing would become impossible, too many lapses would be detected, too large a gap between private profession and pub-

*Alan Ryan, from "Private Selves and Public Parts," in *Public and Private in Social Life*, edited by S. I. Benn and G. F. Gaus (London and Canberra: Croom Helm, 1983 and New York: St. Martins Press, 1983), pp. 150–153. Reprinted by permission of the publishers.

lic performance. If people were checked and rebuked each time such a gap was suspected, or even known, cooperation would collapse. So we work with a lighter touch than that and avoid impugning the quality of the underlying self except when matters become particularly serious. Just as we affect not to hear the rumblings of guests' stomachs at dinner, treating these as hazards not to be held against them, so a good many quirks of taste and temperament are treated as hazards not to be held against a man. He keeps his self-respect, we keep a partner in social enterprises.

This, pressed a little further, illuminates the need for privacy with friends and families. Although a family *can* be 'the public' before which we enact our roles as fathers and sons or whatever, it is also true that at least in our sort of society the family is private, a sort of backstage area where one can wipe off the greasepaint, complain about the audience, worry about one's performance and so on. In their company we can engage in repairs and rehabilitation, chew over performances and think how to improve them, and even rethink the whole play in which we are engaged. Of course, we *may* wish to do all this even more completely on our own, either merely thinking things through, or fantasising new scripts, or simply engaging in activities we want nobody else to know about, and want to answer to nobody for. Family life and marriage or prolonged affairs are all of them full of examples of this.

One other aspect of the theatrical picture may also be connected with this—though less directly. An emphasis on theatricality is partly an emphasis on style, and a worry about privacy may partly be a recognition that style matters, and that people need to be able to keep at least enough distance between themselves and their audience to plan their performance. A feeling for the essential privacy of the actor and for style as the way that private self comes out into the public arena is something to which the theatrical model calls attention. Whether this is an attractive phenomenon is something on which opinions divide sharply. One (gloomy) view might be that society is so efficient at finding slots for us to fill that we can safely be consoled by being allowed to weave roses round our chains—so where one observer might notice the variety and gaiety of American office-workers' clothes, another might notice that their clothes were the only gay and varied

things in their lives. The America-domiciled exiles from the Frankfurt School notoriously went in different directions on this sort of issue.[3]

The elaboration of these remarks is best left for empirical research, of which there is a good deal already available. The final question we ought to address here is whether any of this emphasis on the theatrical capacity of the self raises philosophical or conceptual problems. On one view, it surely cannot. What is mostly at stake is simply the fact that when we discuss the way people set about filling the roles they are called on to fill, we need to invoke information-passing, appearance-managing, self-protecting skills in our analysis. That people do use such skills is indubitable; the question is how they do it. The answer will vary from one situation to another, no doubt, but none of it demands any drastic rethinking of the nature of the self and its capacities.

On another view, we may need to revise our conceptions of the self more drastically. If theatrical skills are central, a great deal of social life will be very poorly explained in 'materialist' terms. It seems likely that human beings will be more concerned to put on a good show, even at the price of a good meal, than most materialist theories can cope with. This suggests that the explanation of human behaviour in human terms may simply stop at the communicative and expressive levels, without there being any pressure to find more basic functions for such behaviour to fulfil.[4] This in turn would detach the human sciences from studies of animal behaviour and cast doubt on the utility of sociobiology. But this would be no bad thing, since it is human beings alone who have the sort of self-consciousness which is a precondition of any idea of privacy. Animals may be said in a loose way to have private lives, but this is either a coy way of talking about their sexual activities or a reference to what they do in hiding from possible predators. The distinctively human conception of privacy is detachable from sexual matters; and the monitoring self we carry about with us wherever we go is clearly a private rather than a hidden possession. If having such a self is tied in so closely with our ability to act in a particular style, and with our ability to communicate something special about ourselves, then it seems that either in addition to a capacity for autonomy or as an aspect of that capacity, the self's dramatic capacities must be regarded as essential, central and as yet not very well understood.

NOTES

1. See Trilling, *Sincerity and Authenticity*, p. 10.

2. Goffman, *Encounters,* pp. 102–3.

3. Herbert Marcuse, *One Dimensional Man* (Routledge and Kegan Paul, London, 1964), pp. 57–77.

4. Rom Harré, *Social Being* (Basil Blackwell, Oxford, 1979), pp. 10ff.

RICHARD A. POSNER

An Economic Theory of Privacy*

Much ink has been spilled in trying to clarify the elusive and ill-defined concept of "privacy." I will sidestep the definitional problem by simply noting that one aspect of privacy is the withholding or concealment of information. This aspect is of particular interest to the economist now that the study of information has become an important field of economics. It is also of interest to the regulator, and those affected by him, because both the right to privacy and the "right to know" are becoming more and more the subject of regulation.

Heretofore the economics of information has been limited to topics relating to the dissemination and, to a lesser extent, the concealment of information in explicit (mainly labor and consumer-good) markets—that is, to such topics as advertising, fraud, price dispersion, and job search. But it is possible to use economic analysis to explore the dissemination and withholding of information in personal as well as business contexts, and thus to deal with such matters as prying, eavesdropping, "self-advertising," and gossip. Moreover, the same analysis may illuminate questions of privacy within organizations, both commercial and noncommercial.

I shall first attempt to develop a simple economic theory of privacy. I shall then argue from this theory that, while personal privacy seems today to be valued more highly than organizational privacy (if one may judge by current legislative trends), a reverse ordering would be more consistent with the economics of the problem.

Theory

People invariably possess information, including the contents of communications and facts about themselves, that they will incur costs to conceal. Sometimes such information

*Richard A. Posner, ''An Economic Theory of Privacy,'' *Regulation* (May/June, 1978) 19–26. Copyright 1978 by American Enterprise Institute for Public Policy Research. Reprinted by permission of the publisher.

is of value to other people—that is, other people will incur costs to discover it. Thus we have two economic goods, "privacy" and "prying." We could regard them as pure consumption goods, the way turnips or beer are normally regarded in economic analysis, and we would then speak of a "taste" for privacy or for prying. But this would bring the economic analysis to a grinding halt because tastes are unanalyzable from an economic standpoint. An alternative is to regard privacy and prying as intermediate rather than final goods—instrumental rather than final values. Under this approach, people are assumed not to desire or value privacy or prying in themselves but to use these goods as inputs into the production of income or some other broad measure of utility or welfare. This is the approach that I take here; the reader will have to decide whether it captures enough of the relevant reality to be enlightening.

NOT SO IDLE CURIOSITY

Now the demand for private information (viewed, as it is here, as an intermediate good) is readily understandable where the existence of an actual or potential relationship, business or personal, creates opportunities for gain by the demander. These opportunities obviously exist in the case of information sought by the tax collector, fiancé, partner, creditor, competitor, and so on. Less obviously, much of the casual prying (a term not used here with any pejorative connotation) into the private lives of friends and colleagues that is so common a feature of social life is, I believe, motivated—to a greater extent than we usually think—by rational considerations of self-interest. Prying enables one to form a more accurate picture of a friend or colleague, and the knowledge gained is useful in one's social or professional dealings with that friend or colleague. For example, one wants to know in choosing a friend whether he will be discreet or indiscreet, selfish or generous. These qualities are not necessarily apparent on initial acquaintance. Even a pure altruist needs to know the (approximate) wealth of any prospective beneficiary of his altruism in order to be able to gauge the value of a gift or transfer to him.

The other side of the coin is that social dealings, like business dealings, present opportunities for exploitation through misrepresentation. Psychologists and sociologists have pointed out that even in everyday life people try to manipulate other people's opinion of them, using misrepresentation. The strongest defenders of privacy usually define the individual's right to privacy as the right to control the flow of information about him. A seldom-remarked corollary to a right to misrepresent one's character is that others have a legitimate interest in unmasking the misrepresentation.

Yet some of the demand for private information about other people seems mysteriously disinterested—for example, that of the readers of newspaper gossip columns, whose "idle curiosity" has been deplored, groundlessly in my opinion. Gossip columns recount the personal lives of wealthy and successful people whose tastes and habits offer models—that is, yield information—to the ordinary person in making consumption, career, and other decisions. The models are not always positive. The story of Howard Hughes, for example, is usually told as a morality play, warning of the pitfalls of success. That does not make it any less educational. The fascination with the notorious and the criminal—with John Profumo and with Nathan Leopold—has a similar basis. Gossip columns open people's eyes to opportunities and dangers; they are genuinely informative.

Moreover, the expression "idle curiosity" is misleading. People are not given to random undifferentiated curiosity. Why is there less curiosity about the lives of the poor (as measured, for example, by the infrequency with which poor people figure as central characters in popular novels) than about those of the rich? One reason is that the lives of the poor do not provide as much useful information for the patterning of our own lives. What interest there is in the poor is focused on people who were like us but who became poor, rather than on those who were always poor; again, the cautionary function of such information should be evident.

Samuel Warren and Louis Brandeis once attributed the rise of curiosity about people's lives to the excesses of the press (in an article in the *Harvard Law Review,* 1890). The economist does not believe, however, that supply creates demand. A more persuasive explanation for the rise of the gossip column is the increase in personal income over time. There is apparently very little privacy in poor societies, where, consequently, people can readily observe at first hand the intimate lives of others. Personal surveillance is costlier in wealthier societies, both because people live in conditions that give them greater privacy and because the value (and hence opportunity cost) of time is greater—too great, in fact, to make the expenditure of a lot of it in watching the neighbors a worthwhile pursuit. An alternative method of informing oneself about how others live was sought by the people and provided by the press. A legitimate and important function of the press is to provide specialization in prying in societies where the costs of obtaining information have become too great for the Nosy Parker.

The fact that disclosure of personal information is resisted by (is costly to) the person to whom the information pertains, yet is valuable to others, may seem to argue for giving people property rights in information about themselves and letting them sell those rights freely. The process of voluntary exchange would then ensure that the information was put to its most valuable use. The attractiveness of this solution depends, however, on (1) the nature and source of the information and (2) transaction costs.

The strongest case for property rights in secrets is presented where such rights are necessary in order to encourage investment in the production of socially valuable information. This is the rationale for giving legal protection to the variety of commercial ideas, plans, and information encompassed by the term "trade secret." It also explains why the "shrewd bargainer" is not required to tell the other party to the bargain his true opinion of the values involved. A shrewd bargainer is, in part, one who invests resources in obtaining information about the true values of things. Were he forced to share this information with potential sellers, he would get no return on his investment and the process—basic to a market economy—by which goods are transferred through voluntary exchange into successively more valuable uses would be impaired. This is true even though the lack of candor in the bargaining process deprives it of some of its "voluntary" character.

At some point nondisclosure becomes fraud. One consideration relevant to deciding whether the line has been crossed is whether the information sought to be concealed by one of the transacting parties is a product of significant investment. If not, the social costs of nondisclosure are reduced. This may be decisive, for example, on the question whether the owner of a house should be required to disclose latent (nonobvious) defects to a purchaser. The ownership and maintenance of a house are costly and productive activities. But since knowledge of the house's defects is acquired by the owner costlessly (or nearly so), forcing him to disclose these defects will not reduce his incentive to invest in discovering them.

As examples of cases where transaction-cost considerations argue against assigning a property right to the possessor of a secret, consider (1) whether the Bureau of the Census should be required to *buy* information from the firms or households that it interviews and (2) whether a magazine should be allowed to sell its subscriber list to another magazine without obtaining the subscribers' consent. Requiring the Bureau of the Census to pay (that is, assigning the property right in the information sought to the interviewee) would yield a skewed sample: the poor would be overrepresented, unless the bureau used a differentiated price schedule based on the different costs of disclosure (and hence prices for cooperating) to the people sampled. In the magazine case, the costs of obtaining subscriber approval would be high relative to the value of the list. If, therefore, we are confident that these lists are generally worth more to the purchasers than being shielded from possible unwanted solicitations is worth to the subscribers, we should assign the property right to the magazine, and this is what the law does.

The decision to assign the property right away from the individual is further supported, in both the census and subscription-list cases, by the fact that the costs of disclosure to the individual are low. They are low in the census case because the government takes precautions against disclosure of the information collected to creditors, tax collectors, or others who might have transactions with the individual in which they could use the information to gain an advantage over him. They are low in the subscription-list case because the information about the subscribers that is disclosed to the list purchaser is trivial and cannot be used to impose substantial costs on them.

Even though the type of private information discussed thus far is not in general discreditable

to the individual to whom it pertains, we have seen that there may still be strong reasons for assigning the property right away from that individual. Much of the demand for privacy, however, concerns discreditable information— often information concerning past or present criminal activity or moral conduct at variance with a person's professed moral standards— and often the motive for concealment is, as suggested earlier, to mislead others. People also wish to conceal private information that, while not strictly discreditable, would if revealed correct misapprehensions that the individual is trying to exploit—as when a worker conceals a serious health problem from his employer or a prospective husband conceals his sterility from his fiancée. It is not clear why society in these cases should assign the property right in information to the individual to whom it pertains; and under the common law, generally it does not. A separate question, taken up a little later, is whether the decision to assign the property right away from the possessor of guilty secrets implies that any and all methods of uncovering those secrets should be permitted.

An analogy to the world of commerce may clarify why people should not—on economic grounds in any event—have a right to conceal material facts about themselves. We think it wrong (and inefficient) that a seller in hawking his wares should be permitted to make false or incomplete representations as to their quality. But people "sell" themselves as well as their goods. A person professes high standards of behavior in order to induce others to engage in social or business dealings with him from which he derives an advantage, but at the same time conceals some of the facts that the people with whom he deals need in order to form an accurate picture of his character. There are practical reasons for not imposing a general legal duty of full and frank disclosure of one's material personal shortcomings—a duty not to be a hypocrite. But each of us should be allowed to protect ourselves from disadvantageous transactions by ferreting out concealed facts about other individuals that are material to their implicit or explicit self-representations.

It is no answer that, in Brandeis's phrase, people have "the right to be let alone." Few people want to be let alone. They want to manipulate the world around them by selective disclosure of facts about themselves. Why should others be asked to take their self-serving claims at face value and prevented from obtaining the information necessary to verify or disprove these claims?

Some private information that people desire to conceal is not discreditable. In our culture, for example, most people do not like to be seen naked, quite apart from any discreditable fact that such observation might reveal. Since this reticence, unlike concealment of discreditable information, is not a source of social costs and since transaction costs are low, there is an economic case for assigning the property right in this area of private information to the individual; and this is what the common law does. I do not think, however, that many people have a *general* reticence that makes them wish to conceal nondiscrediting personal information. Anyone who has sat next to a stranger on an airplane or a ski lift knows the delight that some people take in talking about themselves to complete strangers. Reticence appears when one is speaking to people—friends, family, acquaintances, business associates—who might use information about him to gain an advantage in business or social transactions with him. Reticence is generally a means rather than an end.

The reluctance of many people to reveal their income is sometimes offered as an example of a desire for privacy that cannot be explained in purely instrumental terms. But I suggest that people conceal an unexpectedly low income because being thought to have a high income has value in credit markets and elsewhere, and they conceal an unexpectedly high income in order to (1) avoid the attention of tax collectors, kidnappers, and thieves, (2) fend off solicitations from charities and family members, and (3) preserve a reputation of generosity that would be shattered if the precise fraction of their income that was being given away were known. Points (1) and (2) may explain anonymous gifts to charity.

PRYING, EAVESDROPPING, AND FORMALITY

To the extent that personal information is concealed in order to mislead, the case for giving it legal protection is, I have argued, weak. Protection would simply increase transaction costs, much as if we permitted fraud in the sale of goods. However, it is also necessary to consider the *means* by which personal information is obtained. Prying by means of casual interrogation of acquaintances of the object of the prying must be distinguished from eavesdropping (electronically or otherwise) on a person's conversations. A in conversation with B disparages C. If C has a right to hear this conversation, A, in choosing the words he uses to B, will have to consider the possible reactions of C. Conversation will be more costly because of the external effects and this will result in less—and less effective—communication. After people adjust to this new world of public conversation, even the Cs of the world will cease to derive much benefit in the way of greater information from conversational publicity: people will be more guarded in their speech. The principal effect of publicity will be to make conversation more formal and communication less effective rather than to increase the knowledge of interested third parties.

Stated differently, the costs of defamatory utterances and hence the cost-justified level of expenditures on avoiding defamation are greater the more publicity given the utterance. If every conversation were public, the time and other resources devoted to ensuring that one's speech was free from false or unintended slanders would rise. The additional costs are avoided by the simple and inexpensive expedient of permitting conversations to be private.

It is relevant to observe that language becomes less formal as society evolves. The languages of primitive peoples are more elaborate, more ceremonious, and more courteous than that of twentieth-century Americans. One reason may be that primitive people have little privacy. There are relatively few private conversations because third parties are normally present and the effects of the conversation on them must be taken into account. Even today, one observes that people speak more formally the greater the number of people present. The rise of privacy has facilitated private conversation and thereby enabled us to economize on communication—to speak with a brevity and informality apparently rare among primitive peoples. This valuable economy of communication would be undermined by allowing eavesdropping.

In some cases, to be sure, communication is not related to socially productive activity. Communication among criminal conspirators is an example. In these cases—where limited eavesdropping is indeed permitted—the effect of eavesdropping in reducing communication is not an objection to, but an advantage of, the eavesdropping.

The analysis here can readily be extended to efforts to obtain people's notes, letters, and other private papers; communication would be inhibited by such efforts. A more complex question is presented by photographic surveillance—for example, of the interior of a person's home. Privacy enables a person to dress and otherwise disport himself in his home without regard to the effect on third parties. This economizing property would be lost if the interior of the home were in the public domain. People dress not merely because of the effect on others but also because of the reticence, noted earlier, concerning nudity and other sensitive states. This is another reason for giving people a privacy right with regard to the places in which these sensitive states occur.

ENDS AND MEANS

The two main strands of my argument—relating to personal facts and to communications, respectively—can be joined by remarking the difference in this context between ends and means. With regard to ends, there is a prima facie case for assigning the property right in a secret that is a by-product of socially productive activity to the individual if its compelled disclosure would impair the incentives to engage in that activity; but there is a prima facie case for assigning the property right away from the individual if secrecy would reduce the social product by misleading others. However, the fact that under this analysis most facts about people belong in the public domain does not imply that intrusion on private communications should generally be permitted, given the effects of such intrusions on the costs of legitimate communications.

Admittedly, the suggested dichotomy between facts and communications is too stark. If you are allowed to interrogate my acquaintances about my income, I may take steps to conceal it that are analogous to the increased formality of conversation that would ensue from abolition of the right to conversational privacy, and the costs of these steps are a social loss. The difference is one of degree. Because eavesdropping and related modes of intrusive surveillance are such effective ways of eliciting

private information and are at the same time relatively easy to thwart, we can expect that evasive maneuvers, costly in the aggregate, would be undertaken if conversational privacy were compromised. It is more difficult to imagine people taking effective measures against casual prying. An individual is unlikely to alter his income or style of living drastically in order to better conceal his income or private information from casual or journalistic inquiry. (Howard Hughes was a notable exception to this generalization.)

We have now sketched the essential elements of an economically based legal right of privacy: (1) Trade and business secrets by which businessmen exploit their superior knowledge or skills would be protected. (The same principle would be applied to the personal level and would thus, for example, entitle the social host or hostess to conceal the recipe of a successful dinner.) (2) Facts about people would generally not be protected. My ill health, evil temper, even my income would not be facts over which I had property rights, though I might be able to prevent their discovery by methods unduly intrusive under the third category. (3) Eavesdropping and other forms of intrusive surveillance would be limited (so far as possible) to the discovery of illegal activities.

Application

To what extent is the economic theory developed above reflected in public policy? To answer this question, it is necessary to distinguish sharply between common law and statutory responses to the privacy question.

THE COMMON LAW

The term common law refers to the body of legal principles evolved by English and American appellate judges in the decision of private suits over a period of hundreds of years. I believe, and have argued in greater detail elsewhere, that the common law of privacy is strongly stamped by the economic principles (though nowhere explicitly recognized by the judges) developed in this article. That law contains the precise elements that an economically based right of privacy would include. Trade secrets and commercial privacy generally are well protected. It has been said by one court: "almost any knowledge or information used in the conduct of one's business may be held by its possessor secret." In another well-known case, aerial photography of a competitor's plant under construction was held to be unlawful, and the court used the term "commercial privacy" to describe the interest it was protecting.

An analogy in the personal area is the common law principle that a person's name or photograph may not be used in advertising without his consent. The effect is to create a property right which ensures that a person's name or likeness (O. J. Simpson's, for example) will be allocated to the advertising use in which it is most valuable. Yet, consistent with the economics of the problem, individuals have in general no right in common law to conceal discrediting information about themselves. But, again consistent with the economics of the problem, they do have a right to prevent eavesdropping, photographic surveillance of the interior of a home, the ransacking of private records to discover information about an individual, and similarly intrusive methods of penetrating the wall of privacy that people build about themselves. The distinction is illustrated by Ralph Nader's famous suit against General Motors. The court affirmed General Motors' right to have Nader followed about, to question his acquaintances, and, in short, to ferret out personal information about Nader that the company might have used to undermine his public credibility. Yet I would expect a court to enjoin any attempt through such methods to find out what Nader was about to say on some subject in order to be able to plagiarize his ideas.

When, however, we compare the implications of the economic analysis not with the common law relating to privacy but with recent legislation in the privacy area, we are conscious not of broad concordance but of jarring incongruity. As noted, from the economic standpoint, private business information should in general be accorded greater legal protection than personal information. Secrecy is an important method of appropriating social benefits to the entrepreneur who creates them, while in private life it is more likely simply to conceal legitimately discrediting or deceiving facts. Communications within organizations, whether public or private, should receive the same protection as communications among individuals, for in either case the effect of publicity would be to encumber and retard communication.

THE TREND IN LEGISLATION

But in fact the legislative trend is toward giving individuals more and more privacy protection with respect to facts and communications, and business firms and other organizations (including government agencies, universities, and hospitals) less and less. The Freedom of Information Act, sunshine laws opening the deliberations of administrative agencies to the public, and the erosion of effective sanctions against breach of government confidences have greatly reduced the privacy of communications within the government. Similar forces are at work in private institutions such as business firms and private universities (note, for example, the Buckley Amendment and the opening of faculty meetings to student observers). Increasingly, moreover, the facts about an individual—arrest record, health, credit-worthiness, marital status, sexual proclivities—are secured from involuntary disclosure, while the facts about business corporations are thrust into public view by the expansive disclosure requirements of the federal securities laws (to the point where some firms are "going private" in order to secure greater confidentiality for their plans and operations), the civil rights laws, "line of business" reporting, and other regulations. A related trend is the erosion of the privacy of government officials through increasingly stringent ethical standards requiring disclosure of income.

The trend toward elevating personal and downgrading organizational privacy is mysterious to the economist (as are other recent trends in public regulation). To repeat, the economic case for privacy of *communications* seems unrelated to the nature of the communicator, whether a private individual or the employee of a university, corporation, or government agency, while so far as *facts* about people or organizations are concerned, the case for protecting business privacy is stronger, in general, than that for protecting individual privacy.

Some of the differences in the protection accorded to governmental and personal privacy may, to be sure, simply reflect a desire to reduce the power of government. Viewed in this light, the Freedom of Information Act is perhaps supported by the same sorts of considerations that are believed by some to justify wiretapping in national security or organized crime cases. But only a small part of the recent legislative output in the privacy area can be explained in such terms.

A good example of legislative refusal to respect the economics of the privacy problem is the Buckley Amendment, which gives students (and their parents) access to their school records. The amendment permits students to waive, in writing, their right to see letters of recommendation, and most students do so. They do so because they know that letters of recommendation to which they have access convey no worthwhile information to the recipient. The effect on the candor and value of communication is the same as would be that of a rule that allowed C to hear A and B's conversations about him. Throwing open faculty meetings or congressional conferences to the public has the identical effect of reducing the value of communication without benefitting the public, for the presence of the public deters the very communication they want to hear.

As another example of an economically perverse legislative response to privacy issues, consider the different treatment of disclosures of corporate and of personal crime. The corporation that bribes foreign officials must make public disclosure of the fact, even though the crime may benefit the corporation, its shareholders, the United States as a whole, and even the citizens of the foreign country in question. Yet the convicted rapist, the recidivist con artist, and even the murderer "acquitted" by reason of insanity are not only under no duty to reveal to new acquaintances their criminal activities but are often assisted by law in concealing these activities.

Through the Fair Credit Reporting Act, credit bureaus are forbidden to report to their customers a range of information concerning applicants for credit—for instance, bankruptcies more than fourteen years old and all other adverse information (including criminal convictions and civil judgments) more than seven years old. These restrictions represent an extraordinary intervention in the credit process that could be justified only if credit bureaus systematically collected and reported information that, because of its staleness, had negligible value to its customers in deciding whether credit should be extended. No such assumption of economic irrationality is possible.

These examples could be multiplied, but the main point should be clear enough. Legislatures are increasingly creating rights to conceal information that is material to prospective creditors and employers, and at the same time forcing corporations and other organizations to publicize information whose confidentiality is necessary to their legitimate operation.

A CONTRARY VIEW

I know of only one principled effort to show that individual privacy claims are stronger than those of businesses and other organizations. Professors Kent Greenawalt and Eli Noam of Columbia, in an unpublished paper, offer two distinctions between a business's (or other organization's) interest in privacy and an individual's interest. First, they say that the latter is a matter of rights and that the former is based merely on instrumental, utilitarian considerations. The reasons they offer for recognizing a right of personal privacy are, however, utilitarian—that people need an opportunity to "make a new start" (that is, to conceal embarrassing or discreditable facts about their past), that people cannot preserve their sanity without privacy, and so on. Yet Greenawalt and Noam disregard the utilitarian justification for secrecy as an incentive to investment in productive activity—the strongest justification for secrecy and one mainly relevant, as I have argued, in business contexts.

The second distinction they suggest between the business and personal claims to privacy is a strangely distorted mirror of my argument for entrepreneurial or productive secrecy. They argue that it is difficult to establish property rights in information and even remark that secrecy is one way of doing so. But they do not draw the obvious conclusion that secrecy can promote productive activity by creating property rights in valuable information. Instead they use the existence of imperfections in the market for information as a justification for government regulation designed to extract private information from business firms. They do not explain, however, how the government could, let alone demonstrate that it would, use this information more productively than firms, and they do not consider the impact of this form of public prying on the incentive to produce the information in the first place.

Conclusion

Discussions of the privacy question have contained a high degree of cant, sloganeering, emotion, and loose thinking. A fresh perspective on the question is offered by economic analysis, and by a close examination of the common law principles that have evolved under the influence (perhaps unconsciously) of economic perceptions. In the perspective offered by economics and by the common law, the recent legislative emphasis on favoring individual and denigrating corporate and organizational privacy stands revealed as still another example of perverse government regulation of social and economic life.

WESLEY NEWCOMB HOHFELD
Rights and Jural Relations*

FUNDAMENTAL JURAL RELATIONS CONTRASTED WITH ONE ANOTHER

One of the greatest hindrances to the clear understanding, the incisive statement, and the true solution of legal problems frequently arises from the express or tacit assumption that all legal relations may be reduced to "rights" and "duties," and that these latter categories are therefore adequate for the purpose of analyzing even the most complex legal interests, such as trusts, options, escrows, "future" interests, corporate interests, etc. Even if the difficulty related merely to inadequacy and ambiguity of terminology, its seriousness would nevertheless be worthy of definite recognition and persistent effort toward improvement; for in any closely reasoned problem, whether legal or non-legal, chameleon-hued words are a peril both to clear thought and to lucid expression. As a matter of fact, however, the above mentioned inadequacy and ambiguity of terms unfortunately reflect, all too often, corresponding paucity and confusion as regards actual legal conceptions. That this is so may appear in some measure from the discussion to follow.

The strictly fundamental legal relations are, after all, *sui generis;* and thus it is that attempts at formal definition are always unsatisfactory, if not altogether useless. Accordingly, the most promising line of procedure seems to consist in exhibiting all of the various relations in a scheme of "opposites" and "correlatives," and then proceeding to exemplify their individual scope and application in concrete cases.... [Basic legal relations are of four kinds, and for each kind there are two legal terms ("correlatives"), one describing the relation from the point of view of one person, and one from that of the other.

*From Wesley Newcomb Hohfeld, *Fundamental Legal Conceptions,* edited by Walter Wheeler Cook (New Haven and London: Yale University Press, 1919), pp. 35-64. Reprinted by permission of the Yale University Press. Footnotes have been edited and renumbered.

Moreover, for each term there is another standing for its "opposite," or contradictory. The four basic relations can be illustrated as follows:

	Person *A*	Person *B*
I.	Right (or Claim) ⟷	Duty
	OPPOSITE: No - Right	
II.	Privilege ⟷	No - Right
	OPPOSITE: Duty	
III.	Power ⟷	Liability
	OPPOSITE: Disability	
IV.	Immunity ⟷	Disability
	OPPOSITE: Liability]	

Rights and Duties. As already intimated, the term "rights" tends to be used indiscriminately to cover what in a given case may be a privilege, a power, or an immunity, rather than a right in the strictest sense; and this looseness of usage is occasionally recognized by the authorities. As said by Mr. Justice Strong in *People v. Dikeman.*[1]

The word "right" is defined by lexicographers to denote, among other things, *property, interest, power, prerogative, immunity, privilege* (Walker's Dict. word "Right"). In law it is most frequently applied to property in its restricted sense, but it is often used to designate *power, prerogative, and privilege.*

Recognition of this ambiguity is also found in the language of Mr. Justice Jackson, in *United States v. Patrick.*[2]

The words "right" or "privilege" have, of course, a variety of meanings, according to the connection or context in which they are used. Their definition, as given by standard lexicographers, includes "that which one has a *legal claim to do,*" "*legal power,*" "*authority,*" "*immunity* granted by authority," "the investiture with special or peculiar rights."

And, similarly, in the language of Mr. Justice Sneed, in *Lonas v. State.*[3]

The state, then, is forbidden from making and enforcing any law which shall abridge the *privileges* and *immunities* of citizens of the United States. It is said that the words *rights, privileges* and *immunities,* are abusively used, as if they were synonymous. The word *rights* is generic, common, embracing whatever may be lawfully claimed.

It is interesting to observe, also, that a tendency toward discrimination may be found in a number of important constitutional and statutory provisions. Just how accurate the distinctions in the mind of the draftsman may have been it is, of course, impossible to say.

Recognizing, as we must, the very broad and indiscriminate use of the term "right," what clue do we find, in ordinary legal discourse, toward limiting the word in question to a definite and appropriate meaning? That clue lies in the correlative "duty," for it is certain that even those who use the word and the conception "right" in the broadest possible way are accustomed to thinking of "duty" as the invariable correlative. As said in *Lake Shore & M. S. R. Co. v. Kurtz.*[4]

A duty or a legal obligation is that which one ought or ought not to do. "Duty" and "right" are correlative terms. When a right is invaded, a duty is violated.

In other words, if X has a right against Y that he shall stay off the former's land, the correlative (and equivalent) is that Y is under a duty toward X to stay off the place. If, as seems desirable, we should seek a synonym for the term "right" in this limited and proper meaning, perhaps the word "claim" would prove the best. The latter has the advantage of being a monosyllable. In this connection, the language of Lord Watson in *Studd v. Cool*[5] is instructive:

Any words which in a settlement of movables would be recognized by the law of Scotland as sufficient to create a right or *claim* in favor of an executor ... must receive effect if used with reference to lands in Scotland.

Privileges and "No-Rights." As indicated in the above scheme of jural relations, a privilege is the opposite of a duty, and the correlative of a "no-right." In the example last put, whereas X has a *right* or *claim* that Y, the other man, should stay off the land, he himself has the *privilege* of entering on the land; or, in equivalent words, X does not have a duty to stay off. The privilege of entering is the negation of a duty to stay off. As indicated by this case, some caution is necessary at

this point; for, always, when it is said that a given privilege is the mere negation of a *duty,* what is meant, of course, is a duty having a content or tenor precisely *opposite* to that of the privilege in question. Thus, if, for some special reason, X has contracted with Y to go on the former's own land, it is obvious that X has, as regards Y, both the privilege of entering and the *duty of entering.* The privilege is perfectly consistent with this sort of duty,—for the latter is of the *same* content or tenor as the privilege;—but it still holds good that, as regards Y, X's privilege of entering is the precise negation of a duty *to stay off.* Similarly, if A has not contracted with B to perform certain work for the latter, A's privilege of *not* doing so is the very negation of a duty of *doing* so. Here again the duty contrasted is of a content or tenor exactly opposite to that of the privilege.

Passing now to the question of "correlatives," it will be remembered, of course, that a duty is the invariable correlative of that legal relation which is most properly called a right or claim. That being so, if further evidence be needed as to the fundamental and important difference between a right (or claim) and a privilege, surely it is found in the fact that the correlative of the latter relation is a "no-right," there being no single term available to express the latter conception. Thus, the correlative of X's right that Y shall not enter on the land is Y's duty not to enter; but the correlative of X's privilege of entering himself is manifestly Y's "no-right" that X shall not enter.

In view of the considerations thus far emphasized, the importance of keeping the conception of a right (or claim) and the conception of a privilege quite distinct from each other seems evident; and, more than that, it is equally clear that there should be a separate term to represent the latter relation. No doubt, as already indicated, it is very common to use the term "right" indiscriminately, even when the relation designated is really that of privilege; and only too often this identity of terms has involved for the particular speaker or writer a confusion or blurring of ideas. Good instances of this may be found even in unexpected places. Thus Professor Holland, in his work on *Jurisprudence,* referring to a different and well-known sort of ambiguity inherent in the Latin *"Ius,"* the German *"Recht,"* the Italian *"Diritto,"* and the French *"Droit,"*—terms used to express "not only 'a right,' but also 'Law' in the abstract,"—very aptly observes:

If the expression of widely different ideas by one and the same term resulted only in the necessity for ...

clumsy paraphrases, or obviously inaccurate paraphrases, no great harm would be done; but unfortunately the identity of terms seems irresistibly to suggest an identity between the ideas expressed by them.

Curiously enough, however, in the very chapter where this appears,—the chapter on "Rights,"—the notions of right, privilege and power seem to be blended, and that, too, although the learned author states that "the correlative of . . . legal right is legal duty," and that "these pairs of terms express . . . in each case the same state of facts viewed from opposite sides." While the whole chapter must be read in order to appreciate the seriousness of this lack of discrimination, a single passage must suffice by way of example:

If . . . the power of the State will protect him in so carrying out his wishes, and will compel such acts or forbearances on the part of other people as may be necessary in order that his wishes may be so carried out, then he has a "legal right" so to carry out his wishes.[7]

The first part of this passage suggests privileges, the middle part rights (or claims), and the last part privileges.

Similar difficulties seem to exist in Professor Gray's able and entertaining work on *The Nature and Sources of Law.* In his chapter on "Legal Rights and Duties" the distinguished author takes the position that a right always has a duty as its correlative;[8] and he seems to define the former relation substantially according to the more limited meaning of "claim." Legal privileges, powers, and immunities are *prima facie* ignored, and the impression conveyed that all legal relations can be comprehended under the conceptions "right" and "duty." But, with the greatest hesitation and deference, the suggestion may be ventured that a number of his examples seem to show the inadequacy of such mode of treatment. Thus, e.g., he says:

The eating of shrimp salad is an interest of mine, and, if I can pay for it, the law will protect that interest, and it is therefore a right of mine to eat shrimp salad which I have paid for, although I know that shrimp salad always gives me the colic.[9]

This passage seems to suggest primarily two classes of relations: *first,* the party's respective privileges, as against A, B, C, D and others in relation to eating the salad, or, correlatively, the respective "no-rights" of A, B, C, D and others that the party should not eat the salad; *second,* the party's respective rights (or claims) as against A, B, C, D and others that they should not interfere with the physical act of eating the salad, or, correlatively, the respective duties of A, B, C, D and others that they should not interfere.

These two groups of relations seem perfectly distinct; and the privileges could, in a given case, exist even though the rights mentioned did not. A, B, C and D, being the owners of the salad, might say to X: "Eat the salad, if you can; you have our license to do so, but we don't agree not to interfere with you." In such a case the privileges exist, so that if X succeeds in eating the salad, he has violated no rights of any of the parties. But it is equally clear that if A had succeeded in holding so fast to the dish that X couldn't eat the contents, no right of X would have been violated.

Perhaps the essential character and importance of the distinction can be shown by a slight variation of the facts. Suppose that X, being already the legal owner of the salad, contracts with Y that he (X) will never eat this particular food. With A, B, C, D and others no such contract has been made. One of the relations now existing between X and Y is, as a consequence, fundamentally different from the relation between X and A. As regards Y, X has no privilege of eating the salad; but as regards either A or any of the others, X has such a privilege. It is to be observed incidentally that X's right that Y should not eat the food persists even though X's own privilege of doing so has been extinguished.

On grounds already emphasized, it would seem that the line of reasoning pursued by Lord Lindley in the great case of *Quinn v. Leathem*[10] is deserving of comment:

The plaintiff had the ordinary *rights* of the British subject. He was *at liberty* to earn his living in his own way, provided he did not violate ome special law prohibiting him from so doing, and provided he did not infringe the rights of other people. This *liberty* involved *the liberty* to deal with other persons who were willing to deal with him. *This liberty* is *a right* recognized by law; its *correlative* is the general *duty* of every one not to prevent the free exercise of this *liberty* except so far as his own liberty of action may justify him in so doing. But a person's *liberty* or *right* to deal with others is nugatory unless they are at liberty to deal with him if they choose to do so. Any interference with their liberty to deal with him affects him.

A "liberty" considered as a legal relation (or "right" in the loose and generic sense of that term) must mean, if it have any definite content at all, precisely the same thing as *privilege;* and certainly that is the fair connotation of the term as used the first three times in the passage quoted. It is equally clear, as already indicated, that such a privilege or liberty to deal with others at will might very conceivably exist without any peculiar concomitant rights against "third parties" as regards certain kinds of interference. Whether there should be such concomitant rights (or claims) is ultimately a question of justice and policy; and it should be considered, as such, on its merits. The only correlative logically implied by the privileges or liberties in question are the "no-rights" of "third parties." It would therefore be a *non sequitur* to conclude from the mere existence of such liberties that "third parties" are under a *duty* not to interfere, etc. Yet in the middle of the above passage from Lord Lindley's opinion there is a sudden and question-begging shift in the use of terms. First, the "liberty" in question is transmuted into a "right"; and then, possibly under the seductive influence of the latter word, it is assumed that the "correlative" must be "the general duty of every one not to prevent," etc.

Another interesting and instructive example may be taken from Lord Bowen's oft-quoted opinion in *Mogul Steamship Co. v. McGregor.*[11]

We are presented in this case with an apparent conflict or antinomy between two rights that are equally regarded by the law—the right of the plaintiffs to be protected in the legitimate exercise of their trade, and the right of the defendants to carry on their business as seems best to them, provided they commit no wrong to others.

As the learned judge states, the conflict or antinomy is only apparent; but this fact seems to be obscured by the very indefinite and rapidly shifting meanings with which the term "right" is used in the above quoted language. Construing the passage as a whole, it seems plain enough that by "the right of the plaintiffs" in relation to the defendants a legal right or claim in the strict sense must be meant; whereas by "the right of the defendants" in relation to the plaintiffs a legal privilege must be intended. That being so, the "two rights" mentioned in the beginning of the passage, being respectively claim and privilege, could not be in conflict with each other. To the extent that the defendants have privileges the plaintiffs have no rights; and, conversely, to the extent that the plaintiffs have rights the defendants have no privileges ("no-privilege" equals duty of opposite tenor).

Thus far it has been assumed that the term "privilege" is the most appropriate and satisfactory to designate the mere negation of duty. Is there good warrant for this?

In Mackeldey's *Roman Law*[12] it is said:

Positive laws either contain general principles embodied in the rules of law . . . or for especial reasons they establish something that differs from those general principles. In the first case they contain a common law *(jus commune),* in the second a special law *(jus singulare s. exorbitans).* The latter is either favorable or unfavorable . . . according as it enlarges or restricts, in opposition to the common rule, the rights of those for whom it is established. The favorable special law *(jus singulare)* as also the right created by it . . . in the Roman law is termed benefit of the law *(beneficium juris)* or privilege *(privilegium)* . . .

First a special law, and then by association of ideas, a special advantage conferred by such a law. With such antecedents, it is not surprising that the English word "privilege" is not infrequently used, even at the present time, in the sense of a special or peculiar legal advantage (whether right, privilege, power or immunity) belonging either to some individual or to some particular class of persons. There are, indeed, a number of judicial opinions recognizing this as one of the meanings of the term in question. That the word has a wider signification even in ordinary non-technical usage is sufficiently indicated, however, by the fact that the term *"special* privileges" is so often used to indicate a contrast to ordinary or general privileges. More than this, the dominant specific connotation of the term as used in popular speech seems to be mere *negation of duty.* This is manifest in the terse and oft-repeated expression, "That is your privilege,"—meaning, of course, "You are under no duty to do otherwise."

Such being the case, it is not surprising to find, from a wide survey of judicial precedents, that the *dominant* technical meaning of the term is, similarly, negation of *legal duty.* There are two very common examples of this, relating respectively to "privileged communications" in the law of libel and to "privileges against self-crimination" in the law of evidence. As regards the first case, it is elementary that if a certain group of operative facts are present, a privilege exists which, without such facts, would not be recognized. It is, of course, equally clear that even though all such facts be present as last supposed, the superadded fact of malice will, in cases of so-called "conditional privilege," negative the privilege that otherwise would exist. It must be evident also, that whenever the privilege does exist, it is not special in the sense of arising from a special law, or of being conferred as a special favor on a particular individual. The same privilege would exist, by virtue of general rules, for any person whatever under similar circumstances. So, also, in the law of evidence, the privilege against self-crimination signifies the mere negation of a duty to testify,— a duty which rests upon a witness in relation to all ordinary matters; and, quite obviously, such privilege arises, if at all, only by virtue of general laws.

As already intimated, while both the conception and the term "privilege" find conspicuous exemplification under the law of libel and the law of evidence, they nevertheless have a much wider significance and utility as a matter of judicial usage. To make this clear, a few miscellaneous judicial precedents will now be noticed. In *Dowman's Case,* [13] decided in the year 1583, and reported by Coke, the court applied the term to the subject of waste:

And as to the objection which was made, that the said privilege to be without impeachment of waste can not be without deed, etc. To that it was answered and resolved, that if it was admitted that a deed in such case should be requisite, yet within question all the estates limited would be good, although it is admitted, that the clause concerning the said privilege would be void.

In the great case of *Allen v. Flood* [14] the opinion of Mr. Justice Hawkins furnishes a useful passage for the purpose now in view:

Every person has a privilege . . . in the interests of public justice to put the criminal law in motion against another whom he *bona fide,* and upon reasonable and probable cause, believes to have been guilty of a crime . . . It must not, however, be supposed that hatred and ill-will existing in the mind of a prosecutor must of necessity *destroy* the *privilege,* for it is not impossible that such hatred and ill-will may have very natural and pardonable reasons for existing.

Applying the term in relation to the subject of property, Mr. Justice Foster, of the Supreme Court of Maine, said in the case of *Pulitzer v. Livingston.* [15]

It is contrary to the policy of the law that there should be any outstanding titles, estates, or powers, by the existence, operation or exercise of which, at a period of time beyond lives in being and twenty-one years and a fraction thereafter, the complete and unfettered enjoyment of an estate, *with all the rights, privileges and powers incident to ownership,* should be qualified or impeded.

As a final example in the present connection, the language of Baron Alderson in *Hilton v. Eckerly* [16] may be noticed:

Prima facie it is the privilege of a trader in a free country, in all matters not contrary to law, to regulate his own mode of carrying them on according to his discretion and choice.

The closest synonym of legal "privilege" seems to be legal "liberty" or legal "freedom." This is sufficiently indicated by an unusually discriminating and instructive passage in Mr. Justice Cave's opinion in *Allen v. Flood.* [17]

The personal rights with which we are most familiar are: 1. Rights of reputation; 2. Rights of bodily safety and freedom; 3. Rights of property; or, in other words, rights relating to mind, body and estate, . . .

In my subsequent remarks the word "right" will, as far as possible, always be used in the above sense; and it is the more necessary to insist on this as during the argument at your Lordship's bar it was frequently used in a much wider and more indefinite sense. Thus it was said that a man has a perfect right to fire off a gun, when all that was meant, apparently, was that a man has a *freedom* or *liberty* to fire off a gun, so long as he does not violate or infringe any one's rights in doing so, which is a very different thing from a right, the violation or disturbance of which can be remedied or prevented by legal process.

While there are numerous other instances of the apt use of the term "liberty," both in judicial opinions and in conveyancing documents, it is by no means so common or definite a word as "privilege." The former term is far more likely to be used in the sense of physical or personal freedom (i.e., absence of physical restraint), as distinguished from a legal relation; and very frequently there is the connotation of *general* political liberty, as distinguished from a particular relation between two definite individuals. Besides all this, the term "privilege" has the advantage of giving us, as a variable, the adjective "privileged." Thus, it is frequently convenient to speak of a privileged act, a privileged transaction, a privileged conveyance, etc.

The term "license," sometimes used as if it were synonymous with "privilege," is not strictly appropriate. This is simply another of those innumerable cases in which the mental and physical facts are so frequently confused with the legal relation which they create. Accurately used, "license" is a generic term to indicate a group of *operative* facts required to create a particular privilege,—this being especially evident when the word is used in the common phrase "leave and license." This point is brought out by a passage from Mr. Justice Adam's opinion in *Clifford v. O'Neill.* [18]

A license is merely a *permission* to do an act which, *without such permission,* would be amount to a trespass ... nor will the continuous enjoyment of the *privilege conferred,* for any period of time cause it to ripen into a tangible interest in the land affected.

Powers and Liabilities. As indicated in the preliminary scheme of jural relations, a legal power (as distinguished, of course, from a mental or physical power) is the opposite of legal disability, and the correlative of legal liability. But what is the intrinsic nature of a legal power as such? Is it possible to analyze the conception represented by this constantly employed and very important term of legal discourse? Too close an analysis might seem metaphysical rather than useful; so that what is here presented is intended only as an approximate explanation, sufficient for all practical purposes.

A change in a given legal relation may result (1) from some superadded fact or group of facts not under the volitional control of a human being (or human beings); or (2) from some superadded fact or groups of facts which are under the volitional control of one or more human beings. As regards the second class of cases, the person (or persons) whose volitional control is paramount may be said to have the (legal) power to effect the particular change of legal relations that is involved in the problem.

This second class of cases—powers in the technical sense—must now be further considered. The nearest synonym for any ordinary case seems to be (legal) "ability"—the latter being obviously the opposite of "inability," or "disability." The term "right," so frequently and loosely used in the present connection is an unfortunate term for the purpose,—a not unusual result being confusion of thought as well as ambiguity of expression. The term "capacity" is equally unfortunate; for, as we have already seen, when used with discrimination, this word denotes a particular group of operative facts, and not a legal relation of any kind.

Many examples of legal powers may readily be given. Thus, X, the owner of ordinary personal property "in a tangible object" has the power to extinguish his own legal interest (rights, powers, immunities, etc.) through that totality of operative facts known as abandonment; and—simultaneously and correlatively—to create in other persons privileges and powers relating to the abandoned object,—e. g., the power to acquire title to the latter by appropriating it. *Similarly,* X has the power to transfer his interest to Y,—that is to extinguish his own interest and concomitantly create in Y a new and corresponding interest. So also X has the power to create contractual obligations of various kinds. Agency cases are likewise instructive. By the use of some *metaphorical* expression such as the Latin, *qui facit per alium, facit per se** the true nature of agency relations is only too frequently obscured. The creation of an agency relation involves, *inter alia,* the grant of legal powers to the so-called agent, and the creation of correlative liabilities in the principal. That is to say, one party, P, has the power to create agency powers in another party, A,—for example, the power to convey P's property, the power to impose (so called) contractual obligations on P, the power to discharge a debt owing to P, the power to "receive" title to property so that it shall vest in P, and so forth. In passing, it may be well to observe that the term "authority," so frequently used in agency cases, is very ambiguous and slippery in its connotation. Properly employed in the present connection, the word seems to be an abstract or qualitative term corresponding to the concrete "authorization,"—the latter consisting of a particular group of operative facts taking place between the principal and the agent. All too often, however, the term in question is so used as to blend and confuse these operative facts with the powers and privileges thereby created in the agent. A careful discrimination in these particulars would, it is submitted, go far toward clearing up certain problems in the law of agency.

Essentially similar to the powers of agents are powers of appointment in relation to property interests. So, too, the powers of public officers are, intrinsically considered, comparable to those of agents,—for example, the power of a sheriff to sell property under a writ of execution. The power of a donor, in a gift *causa mortis,* to revoke the gift and divest the title of the donee is another clear example of the legal quantities now being considered; also a pledgee's statutory power of sale.

There are, on the other hand, cases where the true nature of the relations involved has not, perhaps, been so clearly recognized. Thus, in the case of a conditional sale of personalty, assuming the vendee's agreement has been fully performed ex-

*"He who acts through another acts himself." That is, the acts of a person's legal agent may be attributed to the person (the principal) himself.

cept as to the payment of the last instalment and the time for the latter has arrived, what is the interest of such vendee as regards the property? Has he, as so often assumed, merely a contractural *right* to have title passed to him by consent of the vendor, on final payment being made; or has he, irrespective of the consent of the vendor the power to divest the title of the latter and to acquire a perfect title for himself? Though the language of the cases is not always so clear as it might be, the vendee seems to have precisely that sort of power. Fundamentally considered, the typical escrow transaction in which the performance of conditions is within the volitional control of the grantee, is somewhat similar to the conditional sale of personalty; and, when reduced to its lowest terms, the problem seems easily to be solved in terms of legal powers. Once the "escrow" is formed, the grantor still has the legal title; but the grantee has an irrevocable power to divest that title by performance of certain conditions (i. e., the addition of various operative facts), and concomitantly to vest title in himself. While such power is outstanding, the grantor is, of course, subject to a correlative liability to have his title divested. Similarly, in the case of a conveyance of land in fee simple subject to condition subsequent, after the condition has been performed, the original grantor is commonly said to have a "*right* of entry." If, however, the problem is analyzed, it will be seen that, as of primary importance, the grantor has two legal quantities, (1) the privilege of entering, and (2) the power, by means of such entry, to divest the estate of the grantee. The latter's estate endures, subject to the correlative liability of being divested, until such power is actually exercised.

Passing now to the field of contracts, suppose A mails a letter to B offering to sell the former's land, Whiteacre, to the latter for ten thousand dollars, such letter being duly received. The operative facts thus far mentioned have created a power as regards B and a correlative liability as regards A. B, by dropping a letter of acceptance in the box, has the power to impose a potential or inchoate obligation *ex contractu* on A and himself; and, assuming that the land is worth fifteen thousand dollars, that particular legal quantity— the "power *plus* liability" relation between A and B—seems to be worth about five thousand dollars to B. The liability of A will continue for a reasonable time unless, in exercise of his power to do so, A previously extinguishes it by that series of operative facts known as "revocation." These last matters are usually described by saying that A's "offer" will "continue" or "remain open" for a reasonable time, or for the definite time actually specified, unless A previously "withdraws" or "revokes" such offer. While, no doubt, in the great majority of cases no harm results from the use of such expressions, yet these forms of statement seem to represent a blending of non-legal and legal quantities which, in any problem requiring careful reasoning, should preferably be kept distinct. An offer, considered as a series of physical and mental operative facts, has spent its force and become *functus officio* as soon as such series has been completed by the "offeree's receipt." The real question is therefore as to the *legal effect,* if any, at that moment of time. If the latter consist of B's power and A's correlative liability, manifestly it is those *legal relations* that "continue" or "remain open" until modified by revocation or other operative facts. What has thus far been said concerning contracts completed by mail would seem to apply, *mutatis mutandis,* to every type of contract. Even where the parties are in the presence of each other, the offer creates a liability against the offerer, together with a correlative power in favor of the offeree. The only distinction for present purposes would be in the fact that such power and such liability would expire within a very short period of time.

Perhaps the practical justification for this method of analysis is somewhat greater in relation to the subject of options. In his able work on *Contracts,* [19] Langdell says:

If the offerer stipulates that his offer shall remain open for a specified time, the first question is whether such stipulation constitutes a binding contract . . . When such a stipulation is binding, the further question arises, whether it makes the offer irrevocable. It has been a common opinion that it does, but that is clearly a mistake. . . . An offer is merely one of the elements of a contract; and it is indispensable to the making of a contract that the wills of the contracting parties do, in legal contemplation, concur at the moment of making it. An offer, therefore, which the party making it has no power to revoke, is a legal impossibility. Moreover, if the stipulation should make the offer irrevocable, it would be a contract incapable of being broken; which is also a legal impossibility. The only effect, therefore, of such a stipulation is to give the offeree a claim for damages if the stipulation be broken by revoking the offer.

The foregoing reasoning ignores the fact that an ordinary offer *ipso facto* creates a legal relation —a legal power and a legal liability,—and that it is this relation (rather than the physical and mental facts constituting the offer) that "remains open." If these points be conceded, there seems no difficulty in recognizing a unilateral option agreement supported by consideration or embodied in a sealed instrument as creating in the optionee an irrevocable power to create, at any time within the period specified, a bilateral obligation as between himself and the giver of the option. Correlatively to that power, there would of course, be a liability against the option-giver which he himself would have no power to extinguish. The courts seem to have no difficulty in reaching precisely this result as a matter of substance; though their explanations are always in terms of "withdrawal of offer," and similar expressions savoring of physical and mental quantities.

In connection with the powers and liabilities created respectively by an ordinary offer and by an option, it is interesting to consider the liabilities of a person engaged in a "public calling"; for, as it seems, such a party's characteristic position is, one might almost say, intermediate between that of an ordinary contractual offerer and that of an option-giver. It has indeed been usual to assert that such a party is (generally speaking) under a present *duty* to all other parties; but this is believed to be erroneous. Thus, Professor Wyman, in his work on *Public Service Companies,*[20] says:

The duty placed upon every one exercising a public calling is primarily a *duty* to serve every man who is a member of the public. . . . It is somewhat difficult to place this exceptional duty in our legal system. . . . The truth of the matter is that the obligation resting upon one who has undertaken the performance of public duty is *sui generis.*

It is submitted that the learned writer's difficulties arise primarily from a failure to see that the innkeeper, the common carrier and others similarly "holding out" are under present *liabilities* rather than present *duties*. Correlative to those liabilities are the respective powers of the various members of the public. Thus, for example, a traveling member of the public has the legal power, by making proper application and sufficient tender, to impose a duty on the innkeeper to receive him as a guest. For breach of the duty *thus* created an action would of course lie. It would therefore seem that the innkeeper is, to some extent, like one who had given an option to every traveling member of the public. He differs as regards net legal effect, only because he can extinguish his present liabilities and the correlative powers of the traveling members of the public *by*

going out of business. Yet, on the other hand, his liabilities are more onerous than that of an ordinary contractual offerer, for he cannot extinguish his liabilities by any simple performance akin to revocation of offer.

As regards all the "legal powers" thus far considered, possibly some caution is necessary. If, for example, we consider the ordinary property owner's power of alienation, it is necessary to distinguish carefully between the *legal* power, the *physical* power to do the things necessary for the "exercise" of the legal power, and, finally, the *privilege* of doing these things—that is, if such privilege does really exist. It may or may not. Thus, if X, a landowner, has contracted with Y that the former will not alienate to Z, the acts of *X* necessary to exercise the power of alienating to Z are privileged as between X and every party other than Y; but, obviously, as between X and Y, the former has no privilege of doing the necessary acts; or conversely, he is under a duty to Y not to do what is necessary to exercise the power.

In view of what has already been said, very little may suffice concerning a *liability* as such. The latter, as we have seen, is the correlative of power, and the opposite of immunity (or exemption). While no doubt the term "liability" is often loosely used as a synonym for "duty," or "obligation," it is believed, from an extensive survey of judicial precedents, that the connotation already adopted as most appropriate to the word in question is fully justified. A few cases tending to indicate this will now be noticed. In *McNeer v. McNeer,*[21] Mr. Justice Magruder balanced the conceptions of power and liability as follows:

So long as she lived, however, his interest in her land lacked those *elements of property,* such as *power of disposition* and *liability to sale on* execution which had formerly given it the character of a vested estate.

In *Booth v. Commonwealth,*[22] the court had to construe a Virginia statute providing "that all free white male persons who are twenty-one years of age and not over sixty, shall be *liable* to serve as jurors, except as hereinafter provided." It is plain that this enactment imposed only a *liability* and not a *duty*. It is a liability to have a duty created. The latter would arise only when, in exercise of their powers, the parties litigant and the court officers had done what was necessary to impose a specific duty to perform the functions of a juror. The language of the court, by Moncure, J., is particularly apposite as indicating that liability is the opposite, or negative, of immunity (or exemption):

The word both expressed and implied is "liable," which has a very different meaning from "qualified" . . . Its meaning is "bound" or "obliged." . . . A person exempt from serving on juries is not liable to serve, and a person not liable to serve is exempt from serving. The terms seem to be convertible.

A further good example of judicial usage is to be found in *Emery v. Clough*.[23] Referring to a gift *causa mortis* and the donee's liability to have his already vested interest divested by the donor's exercise of his power of revocation, Mr. Justice Smith said:

The title to the gift *causa mortis* passed by the delivery, defeasible only in the lifetime of the donor, and his death perfects the title in the donee by terminating the donor's right or *power of defeasance*. The property passes from the donor to the donee directly . . . and after his death it is *liable* to be *divested* only in favor of the donor's creditors. . . . His right and power ceased with his death.

Perhaps the nearest synonym is "subjection" or "responsibility." As regards the latter word, a passage from Mr. Justice Day's opinion in *McElfresh* v. *Kirkendall* is interesting:

The words "debt' and "liability" are not synonymous, and they are not commonly so understood. As applied to the pecuniary relations of the parties, liability is a term of broader significance than debt. . . . Liability is responsibility.

While the term in question has the broad generic connotation already indicated, no doubt it very frequently indicates that specific form of liability (or complex of liabilities) that is correlative to a power (or complex of powers) vested in a party litigant and the various court officers. Such was held to be the meaning of a certain California statute involved in the case of *Lattin v. Gillette*.[25] Said Mr. Justice Harrison:

The word "liability" is the condition in which an individual is placed after a breach of his contract, or a violation of any obligation resting upon him. It is defined by Bouvier to be responsibility.

Immunities and Disabilities. As already brought out, immunity is the correlative of disability ("no-power"), and the opposite, or negation, of liability. Perhaps it will also be plain, from the preliminary outline and from the discussion down to this point, that a power bears the same general contrast to an immunity that a right does to a privilege. A right is one's affirmative claim against another, and a privilege is one's freedom from the right or claim of another. Similarly, a power is one's affirmative "control" over a given legal relation as against another; whereas an immunity is one's freedom from the legal power or "control" of another as regards some legal relation.

A few examples may serve to make this clear. X, a landowner, has, as we have seen, power to alienate to Y or to any other ordinary party. On the other hand, X has also various immunities as against Y, and all other ordinary parties. For Y is under a disability (i.e., has no power) so far as shifting the legal interest either to himself or to a third party is concerned; and what is true of Y applies similarly to every one else who has not by virtue of special operative facts acquired a power to alienate X's property. If, indeed, a sheriff has been duly empowered by a writ of execution to sell X's interest, that is a very different matter: correlative to such sheriff's power would be the *liability* of X,—the very opposite of immunity (or exemption). It is elementary, too, that as against the sheriff, X might be immune or exempt in relation to certain parcels of property, and be liable as to others. Similarly, if an agent has been duly appointed by X to sell a given piece of property, then, as to the latter, X has, in relation to such agent, a liability rather than an immunity.

For over a century there has been, in this country, a great deal of important litigation involving immunities from powers of taxation. If there be any lingering misgivings as to the "practical" importance of accuracy and discrimination in legal conceptions and legal terms, perhaps some of such doubts would be dispelled by considering the numerous cases on valuable taxation exemptions coming before the United States Supreme Court. Thus, in *Phoenix Ins. Co. v. Tennessee*,[26] Mr. Justice Peckham expressed the views of the court as follows:

In granting to the De Soto Company "all the rights, privileges, and immunities" of the Bluff City Company, all words are used which could be regarded as necessary to carry the exemption from taxation possessed by the Bluff City Company; while in the next following grant, that of the charter of the plaintiff in error, the word "immunity" is omitted. Is there any meaning to be attached to that omission, and if so, what? We think some meaning is to be attached to it. The word "immunity" expresses more clearly and definitely an intention to include therein an exemption from taxation than does either of the other words. Exemption from taxation is more accurately described as an "immunity" than as a privilege, although it is not to be denied that the latter word may sometimes and under some circumstances include such exemptions.

In *Morgan v. Louisiana*[27] there is an instructive discussion from the pen of Mr. Justice Field. In holding that on a foreclosure sale of the franchise and property of a railroad corporation an immunity from taxation did not pass to the purchaser, the learned judge said:

As has been often said by this court, the whole community is interested in retaining the power of taxation undiminished. . . . The exemption of the property of the company from taxation, and the exemption of its officers and servants from jury and military duty, were both intended for the benefit of the company, and its benefit alone. In their personal character they are analogous to exemptions from execution of certain property of debtors, made by laws of several of the states.

So far as immunities are concerned, the two judicial discussions last quoted concern respectively problems of interpretation and problems of alienability. In many other cases difficult constitutional questions have arisen as the result of statutes impairing or extending various kinds of immunities. Litigants have, from time to time, had occasion to appeal both to the clause against impairment of the obligation of contracts and to the provision against depriving a person of property without due process of law. This has been especially true as regards exemptions from taxation and exemptions from execution.

If a word may now be permitted with respect to mere terms as such, the first thing to note is that the word "right" is overworked in the field of immunities as elsewhere. As indicated, however, by the judicial expressions already quoted, the best synonym is, of course, the term "exemption." It is instructive to note, also, that the word "impunity" has a very similar connotation. This is made evident by the interesting discriminations of Lord Chancellor Finch in *Skelton v. Skelton,*[28] a case decided in 1677:

But this I would be no means allow, that equity should enlarge the restraints of the disabilities introduced by act of parliament; and as to the granting of injunctions to stay waste, I took a distinction where tenant hath only *impunitatem,* and where he hath *jus in arboribus.* If the tenant have only a bare indemnity or *exemption* from an action (at law), if he committed waste, there it is fit he should be restrained by injuction from committing it.

In the latter part of the preceding discussion, eight conceptions of the law have been analyzed and compared in some detail, the purpose having been to exhibit not only their intrinsic meaning and scope, but also their relations to one another and the methods by which they are applied, in judicial reasoning, to the solution of concrete problems of litigation. Before concluding this branch of the discussion a general suggestion may be ventured as to the great practical importance of a clear appreciation of the distinctions and discriminations set forth. If a homely metaphor be permitted, these eight conceptions,—rights and duties, privileges and no-rights, powers and liabilities, immunities and disabilities,—seem to be what may be called "the lowest common denominators of the law." Ten fractions (1/3, 2/5, etc.) may, *superficially,* seem so different from one another as to defy comparison. If, however, they are expressed in terms of their lowest common denominators (5/15, 6/15, etc.), comparison becomes easy, and fundamental similarity may be discovered. The same thing is of course true as regards the lowest generic conceptions to which any and all "legal quantities" may be reduced.

Reverting, for example, to the subject of powers, it might be difficult at first glance to discover any essential and fundamental similarity between conditional sales of personalty, escrow transactions, option agreements, agency relations, powers of appointment, etc. But if all these relations are reduced to their lowest generic terms, the conceptions of legal power and legal liability are seen to be dominantly, though not exclusively, applicable throughout the series. By such a process it becomes possible not only to discover essential similarities and illuminating analogies in the midst of what appears superficially to be infinite and hopeless variety, but also to discern common principles of justice and policy underlying the various jural problems involved. An indirect, yet very practical, consequence is that it frequently becomes feasible, by virtue of such analysis, to use as persuasive authorities judicial precedents that might otherwise seem altogether irrelevant. If this point be valid with respect to powers, it would seem to be equally so as regards all of the other basic conceptions of the law. In short, the deeper the analysis, the greater becomes one's perception of fundamental unity and harmony in the law.

NOTES

1. (1852) 7 How. Pr., 124, 130.
2. (1893) 54 Fed. Rep., 338, 348.
3. (1871) 3 Heisk. (Tenn.), 287, 306–307.
4. (1894) 10 Ind. App., 60; 37 N.E., 303, 304.
5. (1883) 8 App. Cas., at p. 597.
6. *Elements of Jurisprudence* (10th ed.), 83.
7. *Ibid.*, 82.
8. See *Nature and Sources of Law* (1909), secs. 25, 45, 184.
9. *Nature and Sources of Law (1909) sec. 48.*
10. (1901) A.C., 495, 534.
11. (1889) 23 Q.B.D., 59.
12. (Dropsie trans.) secs. 196–197.
13. (1583) 9 Coke, 1.
14. (1898) A.C., 1, 19.
15. (1896) 89 Me., 359.
16. (1856) 6 E. & B., 47, 74.
17. (1898) A.C., 1, 29.
18. (1896) 12 App. Div., 17; 42 N.Y. Sup., 607, 609.
19. Langdell, *Summary of Contracts* (2d ed., 1880) Sec. 178.
20. Secs. 330–333.
21. (1892) 142 Ill., 388, 397.
22. (1861) 16 Grat., 519, 525.
23. (1885) 63 N.H., 552.
24. (1873) 36 Ia., 224, 226.
25. (1892) 95 Cal., 317, 319.
26. (1895) 161 U.S., 174, 177.
27. (1876) 93 U.S., 217, 222.
28. (1677) 2 Swanst., 170.

CARL WELLMAN

A New Conception of Human Rights*

The demand that individual privacy be respected is becoming more common and more insistent in our age. This probably reflects a rapidly increasing need for privacy arising from converging ecological, cultural, technical and social changes. The population explosion together with modern urbanization have made it much more difficult for the individual to get away, physically and psychologically, from the crowd of strangers around him. The growing allegiance to political individualism and moral autonomy have caused the individual to resent and resist legal regulation and social interference more intensely. At a time when bugging and other techniques of surveillance have been perfected to an alarming degree, the development of computers enables us to store and retrieve vastly increased amounts of information about any specified individual in even very large populations. Finally, as organizations have grown larger in size and more bureaucratic in structure, their tendency to invade the life of the individual has grown apace.

In the United States, whatever may be the case in other societies, the legal system has responded to these changes by relying more and more heavily upon the constitutional right to privacy. Only recently has the student's right to privacy been protected by legal restrictions upon the kinds of information that may be put into his academic file, the length of time potentially adverse material may be kept in his file, and the conditions under which it may be released without his written consent. The bugging of one's premises or telephone is now recognized as a violation of the prohibition in the Fourth Amendment against unreasonable searches and seizures. And in the landmark decision of *Roe* v. *Wade* (410 US 113), the Supreme Court found state laws prohibiting abortion during the first six months of pregnancy a violation of the pregnant woman's constitutional right to privacy.

Since the constitution does not explicitly mention any right to privacy, one may wonder why the Supreme Court has repeatedly recognized it as a fundamental legal right. In the earlier case of *Griswold* v. *Connecticut* (381 US 479), it had been successfully argued that the right to privacy is one of the unenumerated rights retained by the people and guaranteed to them by the Ninth Amendment. Since these rights are said to be "retained by" the people, they are taken to be rights prior to and independent of the constitution and to any laws made pursuant thereto. In short, the legal right to privacy is legally and morally grounded in the human right to privacy.

Unfortunately, any such appeal to human rights, whether made within a legal system or in the arena of political debate, raises at least three awkward philosophical questions. First, how do we know that there really is any human right to privacy? It is not just that there is widespread disagreement about the assertion, "there is a human right to privacy"; philosophers and jurists have not given us any convincing account of the kind of evidence that could establish rationally the truth or falsehood of this statement. Second, assuming that there is a human right to privacy, what duties or obligations does it imply? It might imply that the state ought to establish and enforce a legal right to privacy or merely that it ought to refrain from invading the privacy of those subject to its jurisdiction. It might or might not imply that one state has an obligation to put economic or political pressure upon another state to cause that state to respect the privacy of the citizens of that second state. The legal philosopher has provided no helpful principles or method for determining just what the practical implications of any human right are. Third, precisely how is the content of the human right to privacy to be defined? Not only is the concept of privacy obscure and unexplained, it is far from clear what it means to say that someone has a *right to* privacy. Does this mean that second parties ought not to invade one's privacy or that it is never wrong to resist

* From *Human Rights,* ed. by E. Kamenka and A. E. S. Tay (London: Edward Arnold, and New York: St. Martin's Press, 1978). © E. Kamenka and A. E. S. Tay 1978 and reprinted by permission of St. Martin's Press, Inc.

such invasions or both or neither of these things?

In this chapter, I propose to focus my attention on the third problem: how is the content of the human right to privacy to be defined? What concerns me is not so much the correct definition of this particular human right as the understanding of the way in which the content of any human right may best be conceived. For only if we can achieve a clear conception of the content of any specified human right can we fully understand what it means to assert or deny the existence of that right. And understanding what assertions of human rights mean is an essential preliminary to understanding what sort of evidence is required to establish their truth and what they logically imply.

The problem of defining the precise content of a mentioned right occurs in the law much as it does in the appeal to human rights. Just as we speak glibly of the human rights to privacy, security of person and an adequate standard of living, so we speak of the legal rights to life, free speech, and the equal protection of the laws. How, then, does the practising lawyer or presiding judge know precisely what in every detail is meant by such mere names and catch phrases? Often he does not; that is what lawsuits are all about. Nevertheless, this problem is much less serious in the law than in the sphere of human rights. Why?

The law provides two reasonably effective solutions to this problem of defining the content of any legal right, one practical and the other theoretical. Legal rights are institutional; they are created, defined and maintained by the legal system in some society. Hence, whenever their content proves to be insufficiently defined to cope with some new situation or case, they can be *re*defined by the legal institutions, particularly the legislature and the courts, that originally created them and continue to sustain them. Thus through a growing body of statutes and precedents, legal rights gradually achieve a precision and specificity sadly lacking in human rights. This sort of practical solution is not possible in the case of human rights. Since these rights, if they exist at all, exist prior to and independently of society and its institutions, they cannot be rendered determinate by the vote of any philosophical congress or the definition of any jurist. Fortunately, jurisprudence also offers a more theoretical solution to this problem. Wesley Hohfeld has identified certain legal conceptions that can be used to define, precisely and unambiguously, the content of any legal right.

Hohfeld identified and illustrated, but refused to define, eight fundamental legal conceptions—four conceptions of legal advantages and four of legal disadvantages. Since possessing a legal right is obviously having some sort of advantage in the law, it is the first four that primarily concern us here. Let us review them briefly. Our review is at one and the same time an articulation of four legal concepts and a characterization of four legal realities. They are:

1. *A legal liberty.* One party x has a legal liberty in face of some second party y to perform some action A if and only if x has no legal duty to y to refrain from doing A. I have, for example, the legal liberty in face of Professor Tay to use her name in this example; I do not, however, have the legal liberty of referring to her in any libellous manner. Let us suppose that I have secretly, and profitably, contracted with Professor Kamenka to mention him rather than Professor Tay at this point. I would still have the legal liberty in face of Professor Tay to use her name here, for I have no legal duty *to her* to refrain from doing so. But I would not have the legal liberty vis-à-vis Professor Kamenka to mention Professor Tay here, for under our contract I have a legal duty to him not to do so.

2. *A legal claim.* One party x has a legal claim against some second party y that y do some action A if and only if y has a legal duty to x to do A. Thus, I have a legal claim against Jones, to whom I loaned ten dollars on the understanding that he repay me today, that he repay me today; similarly, I have a legal claim against Smith, whoever Smith may be, that he not strike me.

3. *A legal power.* One party x has a legal power over some second party y to bring about some specific legal consequence C for y if and only if some voluntary action of x would be legally recognized as having this consequence for y. For example, a policeman has the legal power over a fleeing suspect to place him under arrest, and the owner of a car has the legal power over someone offering to buy his car of making him the new owner of the car.

4. *A legal immunity.* One party x has a legal immunity against some second party y

from some specified legal consequence *C* if and only if *y* lacks the legal power to do any action whatsoever that would be recognized by the law as having the consequence *C* for *x*. Thus, I have a legal immunity against my wife's renouncing my United States citizenship, but I lack a legal immunity against her spending the monies in our joint bank account. These, roughly indicated and briefly illustrated, are the four legal advantages Hohfeld takes to be fundamental in the law. (The four corresponding legal disadvantages are a legal no-claim, a legal duty, a legal liability and a legal disability.)

Hohfeld shows us in quotation after quotation how the expression "a right" is used almost indiscriminately to refer to any one of these four legal advantages. No one who has studied Hohfeld can imagine for a moment that the content of the right to life is simply life. He forces us to ask whether the right to life is essentially the liberty to defend one's life when under attack or the claim against being killed by another or the power to sue in the courts for legal protection of one's life or all of these or none of them. His conceptual analysis does not, of course, tell us precisely what the content of this or any other legal right is; only a detailed study of the law of the land can tell us that. What his fundamental legal conceptions do for us is to show us what questions we must ask in order to arrive at a clear understanding of the content of any legal right and to provide us with a terminology in which we can formulate our answers in the most helpful way. There are two very important reasons why it is particularly helpful to define the content of any legal right in Hohfeld's terms. First, such a formulation renders the modality or modalities of any right unambiguous. There is a very real legal difference between a liberty and a claim, or a liberty and a power, or a claim and an immunity. Any vocabulary that does not distinguish between liberty-rights and claim-rights, power-rights and immunity-rights, describes the legal realities inadequately and invites conceptual confusion. Secondly, such a formulation translates the content of any right into practical terms. Each of Hohfeld's fundamental legal conceptions refers to some action. For instance, a legal liberty is a liberty to do some action *A* and a legal power is the power to perform some action with the legal consequence *C*. Because Hohfeld's conceptions

focus upon actions, they are especially appropriate to the law, which regulates and facilitates human actions.

Reflection upon considerations like these has led me to formulate two heuristic principles to guide my investigation of human rights. Since the law has solved the problem of defining the content of its rights better than ethics has, I will take legal rights as my model of human rights. And since Hohfeld provides a terminology for defining legal rights in unambiguous and practical terms, the most theoretically precise and practically fruitful conception of legal rights will be articulated in terms of his fundamental legal conceptions.

Precisely how one can best translate the language of legal rights into Hohfeld's legal advantages is a matter for much debate. Presumably we would like our philosophical analysis of the concept of a legal right to preserve all or most of those features of legal rights we presuppose in our pre-philosophical thinking about them. For one thing, a legal right seems to be permissive for its possessor. In contrast with my legal duty to pay my taxes whether I wish to do so or not, my right to free speech permits, but does not require, me to speak out on controversial political issues. It is this feature that Thomas Hobbes tries to capture by defining a right as a liberty. Again, a legal right of one party imposes one or more duties upon some second party. Thus, the creditor's right to be repaid imposes a duty upon the debtor to repay him. On this model, Wesley Hohfeld identifies a legal right with a legal claim of *x* against *y,* the correlative of corresponding legal duty of *y* to *x*. Third, the possessor of any legal right can typically choose to have his right enforced by society. Thomas Holland accordingly defines a legal right as the power of influencing the acts of another by the force of society, specifically through its legal system. The most obvious instance is the legal power of the possessor to sue in the courts for remedy in the event that his right is threatened or violated. Fourth, a legal right is usually secured to its possessor by society. At the very least, the possessor must be legally immune to the annihilation of his right at the mere whim of any second party. Jurists have tended to fasten on one of these features of our thinking about legal rights and build it into their definitions of "a right," thereby ignoring or rejecting the other aspects of our pre-philosophical thinking. Debate then centres on the issue of which one of these features is most important, even essential, to legal rights. I propose to preserve all four of these features, if I can, because all four are normally taken for granted in our thinking about rights and all four are important in the legal reality to which "a right" refers. Rather than cut our conception of a legal right down to a single fundamental legal conception, I conceive of a legal right as a cluster of legal liberties, claims, powers, and immunities.

But how can anything as complex as this constitute *a* legal right? What unifies any right is its core. At the centre of any legal right stand one or more legal advantages that define the essential content of the right. Change the core and any remaining right would no longer be this same right. At the core of my right to be repaid is my legal claim to repayment. At the core of my right to free speech is my legal liberty of speaking out on controversial issues. At the core of my right to sell my car is my legal power of transferring ownership in my car to the second party of my choice. When we classify rights as claim-, power- or immunity-rights, it is to their defining cores that we refer. Whatever other legal elements may be contained in any right, they belong to this right because of their relation to its core. Thus, a legal right is not a mere aggregate or collection of disparate legal liberties, claims, powers and immunities; it is a system of legal advantages tied to its defining core.

What are the strings that tie some legal advantage to the core of a right? Upon reflection, it seems to me that every associated liberty, claim, power or immunity contributes some measure of freedom or control over the core to the possessor of the right. Thus, my legal liberty of accepting repayment from the debtor gives me the freedom to cooperate with my debtor should he choose to fulfil my core claim against him. My immunity from having my core claim terminated at the whim of my debtor and my power to sue him should he refuse to repay me both give me control over my legal claim against him, but in different ways. How many such associated elements there are and of what sorts is not a matter to be decided by philosophical analysis; that all depends on the detailed facts of the legal system. Clustered around the core of any legal right, then, are a number of associated legal advantages that give various sorts of freedom and control with respect to that core to the possessor of the right.

Freedom and control are not unrelated; they are two aspects of a single phenomenon. There can be no genuine freedom without control and no real control without freedom. It is not just that I am not free to do or refrain from doing something as long as my action is under the control of others; it is also that my freedom to do or refrain from doing requires that I have some measure of control over their attempts to prevent me from acting or to force me to act against my will. Again, I cannot have control over some part of my life without the freedom to choose and act in this area. Perhaps the most apt label for this totality of freedom and control is "autonomy" in the sense of self-government. Accordingly, I conceive of a legal right as a system of legal autonomy, a cluster of legal elements that together give its possessor legal freedom with respect to and control over its defining core.

Taking legal rights, thus conceived, as my model, my plan is to develop an analogous conception of human rights. My first step must be to identify and define ethical analogues of Hohfeld's fundamental legal conceptions. Just as he distinguished between legal liberties, claims, powers and immunities, so I hope to define ethical liberties, claims, powers and immunities.

1. *An ethical liberty.* A party has an ethical liberty to perform some action *A* if and only if he does not have any duty not to do *A*. I shall not attempt to define the word "duty" here, but I do wish to point out that a duty, in the strict sense, must be grounded in specifically moral reasons and that it need not be a duty *to* any assignable second party. I have the ethical liberties of dressing as I please, within the bounds of decency, of spending my spare cash as I wish, and of attending the church of my choice.

2. *An ethical claim.* One party *x* has an ethical claim against some second party *y* that *y* perform some action *A* if and only if *y* has a duty to *x* to do *A*. Again, I shall leave the word "duty" undefined, but I must say a word about what makes a duty a duty *to* some second party. A duty is a duty to whoever would be seriously injured by its non-performance. Thus my duty to refrain from striking you is a duty to you because you are the party who would be seriously injured were I to punch you in the nose or kick you in the stomach. Again, my ethical duty to support my child financially is primarily a duty to my child, for it is he who would in the first

instance be harmed were I to fail to support him; it may secondarily be a duty to my wife, for she would also suffer seriously were she forced to become both breadwinner and housemother by my failure to perform my duty. Accordingly, you have an ethical claim against me that I not strike you, and my child has an ethical claim against me that I support him.

3. *An ethical power.* A party has the ethical power to bring about some ethical consequence C if and only if that party possesses the competence required for performing some act with this ethical consequence. For example, I have the ethical power of making a promise, an act that brings into existence an obligation to do what I have promised, and the promisee has the ethical power to release me from my promise if he so chooses. Notice that not everyone is competent to make promises or release promises. Children too young to understand what it is to commit themselves to future undertakings cannot promise, even if they have learned to parrot the words "I promise" in the appropriate linguistic context; similarly, the mentally deranged husband who says to his wife "I release you from your marriage vows" does not thereby release her from her promise to him. By "competence" I refer to the qualifications or characteristics one must possess in order that one's action can actually bring about some sort of ethical consequence. What, then, do I mean by "bringing about some sort of ethical consequence"? To say that some act A brings about some ethical consequence C is to say that the statement "act A has been done" implies as a consequence that the ethical statement "C is the case" is true. Thus, my act of promising to submit this paper before 1 June brought about my obligation to do so just because "Carl Wellman promised to submit this paper before 1 June" implies "Carl Wellman had an obligation to submit this paper before 1 June." Precisely what kinds of sentences are ethical sentences is a question best left for discussion on another occasion.

4. *An ethical immunity.* A party is immune from some specified ethical consequence C if and only if there is no other party who is competent to perform any action with this ethical consequence. For example, I am immune from the loss through any act of another of my ethical claim against second parties that they refrain from striking me and equally immune from being morally bound by promises made by others on my behalf—unless, of course, I have authorized some second party to act for me in such ways.

My next step is to articulate a conception of ethical rights analogous to my conception of legal rights. Just as a legal right is a complex system of legal advantages, so an ethical right is a complex system of ethical advantages, a cluster of ethical liberties, claims, powers and immunities. At the centre of every ethical right stands some unifying core, one or more ethical advantages that define the essential content of the right. Thus, at the centre of my ethical right to dress as I please is my ethical liberty of wearing in public any decent clothing I wish, and the core of my ethical right to equal protection of the laws is my ethical claim against the state that its legal system afford me just as much protection as it affords any other individual subject to it. Around the core of any ethical right cluster an assortment of associated ethical liberties, claims, powers and immunities. What ties these ethical elements together into a single right is the way in which each associated element contributes some sort of freedom or control with respect to the defining core to the possessor of the right. Because freedom and control are two aspects of autonomy, any ethical right can accurately be thought of as a system of ethical autonomy.

My third and last step is to distinguish human rights from other species of ethical rights. It would be at least confusing, and probably an abuse of language, to describe as "human rights" the ethical rights that any individual human being has by virtue of being a promisee, a wife, or a citizen, for these are not rights one has simply by virtue of being human. Traditionally, human rights have been thought of as those ethical rights that every human being must possess simply because he or she is human. Thus, human rights are the rights any individual possess *as* a human being. Although this seems to capture current usage pretty well, I propose a more narrow conception of human rights. I define a human right as an ethical right of the individual as human being vis-à-vis the state. Excluded by this definition are the ethical rights one has as a human being that hold against other individuals or against organizations other than the state. I propose this restriction for two reasons. For one thing, all the important human rights documents, and the declarations of natural rights that preceded them, have been essentially political documents; their primary and definitive purpose has traditionally been to proclaim the rights of the individual human being in face of the state. For another thing, the fundamental ethical relations of any individual human being to the state must surely be very different from his or her ethical relations to other individuals just because the state is a special sort of organization with a distinctive role to play in human affairs. Therefore, the ethical rights of an individual against the state will be rather different from his or her rights against other individuals or organizations. To mark this difference I propose to reserve the expression "a human right" to refer to a right any individual has *as* a human being *in face of* the state.

In three swift steps we have moved from an interpretation of legal rights in terms of Hohfeld's fundamental legal conceptions to a new conceptions of human rights. A human right is a cluster of ethical liberties, claims, powers and immunities that together constitute a system of ethical autonomy possessed by an individual as a human being vis-à-vis the state. Let me illustrate this new conception by showing how one might use it to interpret the human right to privacy. I shall not pretend to give any complete or precise analysis of this sample right, but my partial description will serve to illustrate a new and helpful way of thinking about human rights.

As the United Nations Declaration of Human Rights recognizes, the core of the human right to privacy is complex. It contains both a claim to freedom from invasions of one's privacy and a claim to legal protection from invasions of one's privacy by the state or other individuals. Both of these are ethical claims of the individual as human being against the state, primarily against his or her own state, but secondarily against other politically organized societies. I would add a third core claim, the ethical claim of the individual against the state that it sustain the conditions necessary for the existence of privacy for the individual.

To define these core claims more fully, it is necessary to say something about the nature of privacy and the areas within which one has justified ethical claims to privacy. Privacy is the state of being unobserved or unknown, confidential, undisturbed or secluded. It is the opposite of being public, and hence the condition of not being open to or shared with the public. One's privacy is invaded when peeping Tom watches one undress, when an entire family must live in a single crowded room, when one's personal letters are published, and when one receives a threatening or obscene telephone call.

Areas within which the claim to privacy are justified include the home, the family, personal correspondence, and certain relationships such as that of husband and wife or doctor and patient. What is it about these areas that singles them out as areas where privacy ought to be respected and protected? In areas such as these, privacy is essential for the preservation of one's sense of security, the development of one's individual personality, and the maintenance of extremely important human relationships. The privacy of the home, for example, is clearly of tremendous value in all three ways: it provides a haven from the dangers, the crowds, and simply the confusions of the public world; it gives one an area where one can be oneself more fully and freely than when subject to alien scrutiny, criticism and even punishment; and it affords an environment in which the intimate relations of husband and wife or parent and child can flourish. The three core claims to privacy are limited to areas where privacy is important in these ways.

Around this complex core cluster a number of associated ethical elements, including at least the following:

1. The ethical liberty of the state to perform its duties corresponding with the three core claims of the individual human being. If the state had any genuine duty not to do these things, then the defining core of the human right to privacy would be vacuous or illusory.
2. The ethical claim of the possessor of the human right to privacy against other individuals that they take political action to ensure that the state perform its duties to meet his core claims. The same considerations that justify the ethical claims of the individual human being concerning privacy against the state justify his claim against other human beings that they intervene on his behalf should the state fail or refuse to perform its core duties to him.
3. The ethical power of the individual to waive his core claims to privacy against

the state. For example, it is no longer wrong for a policeman to search a house without a warrant if the owner has freely given his permission to enter and search; and when one marries, one is normally relieving the state of any ethical duty to protect one from invasions of one's privacy by one's spouse.

4. The ethical liberty of the possessor of the right to exercise his ethical power of waiving his core claims to privacy. Although there probably are instances in which one can, but has a duty not to, waive some core claim to privacy, there are many instances in which the exercise of this ethical power is ethically permitted.

5. The ethical immunity of the individual human being against having his core claims to privacy extinguished, suspended or reduced by any action of the state. For example, the state cannot diminish in the least its duty to refrain from invading my privacy by proclaiming a public breakdown of law and order and announcing its intention to search my house or person at any time it sees fit. Each of these associated ethical elements belong to the human right to privacy because each of them contributes some sort of ethical freedom or control over the core claims to the possessor of that right. Therefore, the core claims together with these, and other, associated elements constitute a system of ethical autonomy with respect to privacy.

I do not insist that my analysis of the human right to privacy is correct in every detail. I do suggest that it illustrates the fruitfulness of a new conception of human rights simply because it is detailed. We tend to speak and think human rights in terms of mere names or noun phrases that obscure their full and precise content by their very brevity. It is a considerable merit in this conception of a human right that it provides the vocabulary in which one can spell out, explicitly and in detail, the exact content of any right. Another advantage of this conception is that it renders the modality or modalities of any right unambiguous. In this case, it shows us that the core of the human right to privacy is a triple claim and that some associated elements are liberties, others powers and so on. Finally, it translates the content of any human right into practical terms. Since the description of any ethical liberty, claim, power or immunity includes the specification of some sort of action, to think of human rights as clusters of ethical advantages is to think of them in terms of human actions. This is a theoretical virtue for those who believe that the theory of human rights ought to be relevant to moral choice and a practical asset for those who wish to appeal to human rights in taking political action to reform the law to fit a changing society.

JUDITH JARVIS THOMSON

Self-Defense and Rights*†

1. Suppose Aggressor has got hold of a tank. He had told Victim that if he gets a tank, he's going to get in it and run Victim down. Victim sees Aggressor get in his tank and start towards Victim. It is open country, and Victim can see that there is no place to hide, and nothing he can put between himself and Aggressor which Aggressor cannot circle round. Fortunately, Victim happens to have an anti-tank gun with him, and it is in good working order, so he can use it to blow up the tank, thereby saving his life, but of course thereby also killing Aggressor. I think that most people would say that it is morally permissible for Victim to use that anti-tank gun: surely it is permissible to kill a man if that is the only way in which you can prevent him from killing you!

On the other hand, one of the things we are firmly wedded to is the belief that human beings have a right to life, and this presumably includes the right to not be killed. Aggressor is a human being; so he, like the rest of us, has a right to life, and presumably, therefore, the right to not be killed. So how *can* Victim kill him? Precisely *why* is it permissible for Victim to use that anti-tank gun on Aggressor? I propose we look at three replies which I think come fairly readily to mind.

2. The first reply I am going to call "forfeit," and it goes like this. "We good folk all do have a right to life, and that does include the right to not be killed. But there is such a thing as forfeiting a right. We say such things as that the right to life, liberty, and the pursuit of happiness are 'natural rights,' and therefore unconditionally possessed by all people; but that is just so much high-minded rhetoric. What has happened in the case described is that Aggressor, by virtue of his attack on Victim, has forfeited his right to not be killed, and therefore

his right to life. And *that* is why Victim may use his anti-tank gun on Aggressor, thereby killing him; he violates no right of Aggressor's in doing so."

But the fact is that this very natural first reply is not at all satisfactory. Suppose that as Victim raises his anti-tank gun to fire it, Aggressor's tank stalls. Aggressor gets out to examine the engine, but falls and breaks both ankles in the process. Victim (let us suppose) now has time to get away from Aggressor, and is in no danger. I take it you will not think that Victim may all the same go ahead and kill Aggressor. But why not—if Aggressor really has forfeited his right to not be killed by virtue of his attack on Victim.[1]

It could, of course, be said that at this point utilitarian considerations come into play. I.e., it could be said that yes, Aggressor has forfeited his right to life, but no, Victim cannot now kill him, and that this latter is true because Victim now has no need to kill Aggressor—indeed, because killing Aggressor would mean the loss of a life, whereas not killing Aggressor would mean no loss at all.

But I think this cannot be right. Suppose Victim is a great transplant surgeon. There is Aggressor, lying helpless next to his tank, with two broken ankles—but the rest of him physically fine and healthy. Can Victim now cart Aggressor off to surgery, cut him up, and give his one heart, two kidneys, and two lungs to five who need the parts? If Aggressor now has no right to not be killed (having forfeited it by his attack on Victim), so that utilitarian considerations are all we have to weigh here, it is hard to see why not. After all, five lives would be saved at a cost of only one. Yet surely Victim cannot do this.

I am inclined to think that it would no more be permissible for Victim to cut Aggressor up and parcel out his parts to save five than it would be for Victim to cut *you* up and parcel out *your* parts to save five. He cannot do this to you; and it is often said that the reason why he cannot (despite the fact that utilities might be maximized by doing so) is the fact that you have a right to life, and thus, presumably, the

*Judith J. Thomson, "Self-Defense and Rights," The Lindley Lecture, University of Kansas, 1976. Reprinted by permission of the Department of Philosophy, The University of Kansas.

†I am indebted to the students and faculty of the Department of Philosophy at the University of Kansas, and to the members of the Society for Ethical and Legal Philosophy, for criticisms of earlier versions of the following paper.

right to not be killed.[2] I should imagine that the very same thing makes it impermissible for Victim to do this to Aggressor, viz., the fact that Aggressor, now helpless and no danger to anyone, has a right to life, and thus, presumably, the right to not be killed.

There are, of course, those who think it permissible for a state to impose death, as a penalty, on one who commits one or another very serious crime. If any one of them is a friend of the reply I am calling "forfeit," he will no doubt say that what makes it permissible is the fact that one who commits such a crime has forfeited his right to not be killed. But in the first place, I doubt that those who think of death as an acceptable penalty would think it an acceptable penalty for an (unsuccessful) attempt on the life of another, and it will be remembered that an (unsuccessful) attempt is all that Aggressor is guilty of. More important, even if it could be made out that it *will* be permissible, after trial and conviction, for an agent of the state to kill Aggressor, no agent of the state can kill him *now* (prior to trial and conviction). And Victim not only cannot kill him now, Victim—unless he is himself an agent of the state—is not going to be able to kill him at any time. So while it is (I suppose) open to those who regard death as an acceptable penalty for Aggressor's crime to say that he *will* (after trial and conviction) have no right to not be killed by an agent of the state, he at any rate *now* has a right to not be killed by Victim, indeed a right to not be killed by anybody at all, and thus a right to not be killed.

There are two moves open to a friend of 'forfeit.' He can say (1) that the fact that the tank stalled and Aggressor broke both ankles shows that it never was necessary for Victim to kill Aggressor, so that Aggressor never did forfeit his right to not be killed. Or he can say (2) that Aggressor did forfeit his right to not be killed when he launched his attack on Victim, but that he regained this right at the moment at which he ceased to pose a threat to Victim's life.

(1) would be an unfortunate choice for the purpose of 'forfeit.' For surely Victim could, permissibly, have killed Aggressor at any time between the launching of Aggressor's attack and the stall of the tank. (Who in such circumstances could be expected to know that the tank would stall? Who in such circumstances could be expected to wait in hopes of so freakish an accident?) That indeed was where we began:

i.e., with the fact that it was then permissible for Victim to shoot. 'Forfeit' proposed to explain this fact by saying that Aggressor forfeited a right; yet (1) denies that he did.

(2) seems preferable for the purposes of this reply. If Aggressor did forfeit his right to not be killed when he launched the attack, that would explain why, between the launching of it and the stall of the tank, Victim could shoot; and if Aggressor re-acquired that right when he ceased to pose a threat to Victim, that would explain why, after the stall of the tank, Victim could no longer shoot.

But it is a far from happy choice. If it were by virtue just of the launching of that attack that Aggressor forfeited his right, then it would seem possible to say that when the attack ceases, Aggressor re-acquires his right—the right being, as it were, in abeyance throughout the time of the attack. But it surely cannot be said to have been by virtue *just* of the launching of that attack that Aggressor forfeited his right. Compare a second aggressor and a second victim. Suppose that Second Aggressor launches a similar attack on Second Victim, but that Second Aggressor (by contrast with Aggressor) is innocent: Second Aggressor, let us suppose, is a schizophrenic, and he is under a hallucination that Second Victim is in a tank of his own, driving towards Second Aggressor's home and family, so that, as Second Aggressor sees it, he is merely trying to ward off an attack. Morality may not protect us from getting run down by lunatics in tanks, but it does permit our protecting ourselves from such a fate; and it seems plain that poor Second Victim, who is himself innocent, may permissibly use his anti-tank gun on Second Aggressor. Why is this permissible? It is an excellent question. But presumably 'forfeit' would be a most implausible reply in this case.[3] Perhaps Aggressor, being a villain, can be thought to have forfeited a right; Second Aggressor, however, being himself innocent, cannot. But then it is not by virtue *just* of launching an attack on Victim that Aggressor forfeits his right; Aggressor's bad intention figures too. Yet Aggressor's bad intention may be supposed to remain, even after he becomes helpless—we may imagine him continuing to plot as he is carried off to jail—and if that remains, how can he be thought to have re-acquired the right he forfeited at least in part because of that bad intention?

There is room for maneuver here. It could be said that the point is this: both Aggressor and

Second Aggressor simply cease to have a right to not be killed when they launch their attacks on their victims, and both of them re-acquire that right when their tanks stall. (On this view, while Aggressor is guilty and Second Aggressor is not, this does not matter: launching an attack by itself—whether guilty or not—is what makes one lose the right to not be killed.) I shall come back to this idea later. For the moment, it should be noted that saying that Aggressor simply ceased to have the right is not the same as saying that Aggressor has forfeited the right. That is, *this* reply is entailed by the reply that I am calling "forfeit," but is not identical with it.

3. The second reply I am going to call "specification." In fact, I mean to use the term "specification" so as to cover two connected replies. Both begin in the same way. "You only think there's a problem here because you think that 'Aggressor has a right to life' entails 'Aggressor has a right to not be killed.' But it doesn't. We all do have a right to life, but that right to life *doesn't* include having a right to not be killed. Indeed, *nobody* has a right to not be killed: all you have is—" and here there are two ways in which the speaker may go on. I will call the first "moral specification": ". . . all you have is the right to not be wrongly, unjustly killed." I will call the second "factual specification": ". . . all you have is the right to not be killed if you are not in process of trying to kill a person, where that person has every reason to believe he can preserve his life only by killing you." There is what seems to me a serious objection, which bears against both of these equally. But first let us look at difficulties specific to each.

I used to think that the reply I have called "moral specification" was the right reply to make in the case I described, as in other, similar, cases. That is, I used to think it just a mistake to suppose that anyone has a right to not be killed. It is so obvious that there are cases in which it is permissible, and therefore no violation of anyone's rights, to kill a person that it seems right to say that the most we can plausibly be thought to have is a right to not be wrongly or unjustly killed. But if so, then it is hard to see how appeal to rights which we do or do not have can *explain* why it is or is not permissible for a person to kill. Consider Victim. We were asked to explain why it is permissible for Victim to use his anti-tank gun on

Aggressor, thereby killing him; and consider the following answer: "The reason why it is permissible for Victim to kill Aggressor is that Aggressor has no right to not be killed—he only has a right to not be killed wrongly or unjustly—and in killing Aggressor, Victim would not be killing Aggressor wrongly or unjustly." One does not mind all circles, but this circle is too small. For it to be permissible for Victim to kill Aggressor *is* for it to be the case that in killing Aggressor, Victim does not act wrongly or unjustly; and we cannot say that the reason *why* Victim is not acting wrongly or unjustly in killing Aggressor is the fact that in killing Aggressor, Victim is not acting wrongly or unjustly.

The reply I have called "factual specification" is, I think, even less satisfactory. Let us look at it again. "Nobody has a right to not be killed: all you have is a right to not be killed if you are not in process of trying to kill a person, where that person has every reason to believe he can preserve his life only by killing you." Hence Victim can kill Aggressor. For Victim violates no right of Aggressor's in killing him, for Aggressor *is* in process of trying to kill Victim, where Victim has every reason to believe that he can preserve his life only by killing Aggressor.

But the fact is that there are a great many other cases in which it is permissible to kill a man—defense of your life against a villain is by no means the only one. Consider Second Aggressor again. Second Aggressor is no villain; yet Second Victim can shoot to kill.

Again, consider a case which involves what Robert Nozick calls "an innocent shield of a threat."[4] Third Aggressor is driving his tank at you. But he has taken care to arrange that a baby is strapped to the front of the tank, so that if you use your anti-tank gun, you will not only kill Third Aggressor, you will kill the baby. Now Third Aggressor, admittedly, is in process of trying to kill you; but that baby isn't. Yet you can presumably go ahead and use the gun, even though this involves killing the baby as well as Third Aggressor.

It would, of course, be consistent to opt for 'factual specification' in the original case of Aggressor and Victim, and yet not opt for a similar reply in these other cases. Yet it is hard to see what reason there could be for distinguishing. And if a similar reply is opted for in these other cases, we shall find ourselves having to say, not only that nobody has a right to not be killed, but also that you do not even have a right to not be killed if you are not in process of trying to kill a person, where that person has every reason to believe he can preserve his life only by killing you. We shall find ourselves having to say that the most you have is a right to not be killed if (a) you are not a villain who is trying to kill a person, and (b) you are not a schizophrenic who is trying to (as he sees it) ward off an attack on his home and family, and (c) you are not tied to a tank which will kill a person—where the threatened person in (a), (b), and (c) has every reason to believe he can preserve his life only by killing you.

And this is obviously not the end of it. Consider a case of a quite different kind, which I borrow from Philippa Foot.[5] You are the driver of a trolley. On the track ahead of you are five track workmen. The banks are very steep at that point, and they are not able to get off the track. Well, it is plain enough: you had better put on your brakes. Alas, the brakes do not work. You notice just then that there is a spur of track leading off to the right, and your wheel works so that you can turn off onto it. But again alas, you can see that there is one track workman on the track on the right, and he too cannot get off the track. So you can do nothing, in which case you kill five; or you can turn off to the right, in which case you kill one. Presumably it is morally permissible—some would even say it was morally required—that you turn the trolley off to the right, thereby killing one. But *why* is it permissible to kill that one? Does he not have a right to life?[6] Notice that *he* is not threatening anybody at all; nor is he an innocent shield of a threat. A friend of 'factual specification' will then presumably have to expand still further his list of conditions under which killing is permissible, and thus make still more complicated the right which—as he says—is the most we have in respect of life.

Where is this to end? Is there anybody who knows what right it is which (it is here suggested) is the most we have in respect of life?

Moreover, it is worth noticing that a kind of circle is going to turn up here too. What the friend of 'factual specification' has to do is to figure out when it is permissible to kill, and then tailor, accordingly, his account of what right it is which is the most we have in respect of life. But if that is the only way anyone can have of finding out what right it is we have in respect of life, how can anyone then *explain* its being permissible to kill in such and such circumstances by appeal

to the fact that killing in those circumstances does not violate the right which is the most the victim has in respect of life?

But I think there is a more serious objection, which bears equally against both 'moral specification' and 'factual specification.' What I have in mind is that both replies issue from what I think is an incorrect view of rights: neither would be opted for by anyone who did not take the view that rights are, in a certain sense, *absolute*. What this sense is may best be brought out if we make a terminological distinction. Suppose a man has a right that something or other shall be the case; let us say he has a right that p, where p is some statement or other. And now suppose that we make p false. So, for example, if his right is the right that he is not punched in the nose, we make that false, i.e., we bring about that he *is* punched in the nose. Then, as I shall say, we *infringe* his right. But I shall say that we *violate* his right if and only if we do not merely infringe his right, but more, are acting wrongly, unjustly in doing so. Now the view that rights are 'absolute' in the sense I have in mind is the view that every infringing of a right is a violating of a right.

This view of rights seems to me, as I said, to be incorrect. That it is comes out in the following case. You are rich, and therefore own lots of steak, which you keep in a locked freezer on your back porch. Here is a child with a terrible protein deficiency: he will die if I do not get some protein into him fast. I have none myself at the moment. I call you to see if you will lend or sell me a steak, but your answering service says you are out of town for the weekend, and they do not know where. The only way in which I can get some protein for that child is to break into your freezer and take a steak. Now most people would say it is okay, I can go ahead. But why? Don't you have a right that people will not break into your freezer and take a steak? If anyone thinks that rights are 'absolute,' then he is committed to saying that you do not after all have a right that people will not break into your freezer and take a steak, and this on the ground that I do not act wrongly or unjustly if I do so—and I surely do not act wrongly or unjustly if I do so, since it is permissible for me to do so. This is not to say he has to deny you have *any* rights over your freezer and your steak. We are all familiar by now with the kind of right he can say you have. He can engage in moral specification: he can say that although you do not have a right that people will not break into your freezer and take a steak, you do have a right that people will not do this wrongly or unjustly. Or, alternatively, he can engage in factual specification: he can say that the right you do have is that people will not do this except where they have in hand a child with a protein deficiency, who will die if it is not done. But the point, I think, is that the wrong move was made from the start. Surely you *do* have a right that people will not break into your freezer and take a steak. If you had no such right, why would I have to compensate you later for having done so? And surely I do have to compensate you: I have to pay for the damage I caused to the freezer, and I have to replace, or pay you for, the steak I took.

If all you had was a right that I not wrongly or unjustly break into the freezer and take a steak, then I would have done nothing at all you have a right I not do; in which case, why would I owe you anything for what I did? Similarly, if all you had was a right that I not break into the freezer and take a steak when I do not have a starving child to feed, then since I did have a starving child to feed, I would have done nothing at all you had a right I not do; so once again, no compensation would be owing. The fact that compensation *is* owing shows (and it seems to me, shows conclusively) that I did do something you had a right that I not do. How are we to square this fact with the fact that I did not act wrongly or unjustly in doing so? I think we had better allow that there are cases in which a right may be infringed without being violated—i.e., cases in which one does a thing another has a right he not do, and yet in which one does not violate a right.

Now I do not suppose that if Victim kills Aggressor in the circumstances I described at the outset, then Victim must pay compensation to Aggressor's heirs. I do not suppose that if the trolley-driver turns off to the right, killing the one, then he must pay compensation to the one's heirs. But there surely are cases in which it is permissible to kill, and in which compensation *is* owed. If you are an "innocent threat"[7] to my life (you threaten it through no fault of your own), and I can save my life only by killing you, and therefore do kill you, I think I do owe compensation, for I take your life to save mine. If so, I infringe a right of yours but do not violate it. And this means that at least some rights in respect of life—as well as at least some rights in respect of property—are not absolute.

It could, of course, be insisted that Victim (supposing he killed Aggressor) not only violated no right of Aggressor's, but also infringed no right of Aggressor's. And as I said, there is not need for Victim to compensate Aggressor's heirs, so there is not available *that* ground for saying that Victim infringed a right of Aggressor's. On the other hand, if we do say that Victim infringed a right of Aggressor's (and that the trolley-driver infringed a right of the one on the right-hand track, and . . .), then it is open to us to say—what had certainly seemed plausible at the outset—that we all of us do have a right to not be killed. Quite simply: a right to not be killed. Not an absolute right to not be killed, of course, only a non-absolute right to not be killed. And saying this would be entirely consistent with saying that we also have the (absolute) right to not be killed wrongly or unjustly, which the moral specifier attributes to us, and the (absolute) right to not be killed if (a) we are not a villain who is trying to kill a person, and (b) we are not a schizophrenic who . . . , which the factual specifier will attribute to us if and when he ever finishes specifying it.

It is not surprising that people are inclined to opt for the view that rights are absolute: if a person has a *right* to such and such how can it be that anyone may, permissibly, deprive him of it? Isn't a right something one can positively *demand* accordance with? But the fact is that there are occasions on which a right is infringed but not violated; and a moral philosopher has to find some way of explaining what makes this be the case when it is. A move which is familiar enough is to say that what makes this be the case when it is is the fact that the right in question is 'over-ridden.' It is a natural idea, then, that we should make the same move in respect of Victim and Aggressor. This brings us to the third of the three replies to the question I asked: for obvious reasons, I will call it "over-riding."

4. An over-rider begins as follows. "Yes, Aggressor does, like the rest of us, have a right to not be killed. A non-absolute right is all it is, however. And the reason why it is permissible for Victim to kill Aggressor is the fact that, the circumstances being what they are, Aggressor's right to not be killed is over-ridden." But what does "His right is over-ridden" mean? If it means only "It is permissible to infringe his right," then—so far as explanatory force is concerned—the over-rider might as

well have instead said "And the reason why it is permissible for Victim to kill Aggressor is the fact that, the circumstances being what they are, it is permissible for Victim to kill Aggressor."

Moreover, by what is Aggressor's right supposed to be over-ridden? That is (as I take it), what is it in the circumstances such that, that thing being in the circumstances, it is permissible for Victim to kill Aggressor? An over-rider may be expected to answer in one or another of two ways. He may say "Aggressor's right to not be killed is over-ridden by the fact that a great lot of utility will get produced if Victim kills Aggressor—much more utility than if Victim does not kill Aggressor." Or he may instead say "Aggressor's right to not be killed is over-ridden by a more stringent right of Victim's." I find the first of these two answers uninteresting: it is easy enough to add details to the story which, *prima facie,* at any rate, suggest that the utilities are not as the answer claims they are, and I think that a dispute as to whether or not they really do is not theoretically fruitful. So I shall attend only to the second of the two answers.

The answer obviously invites a question: "What makes one right be 'more stringent than' another?" If what makes Victim's right (whatever it is) be more stringent than Aggressor's right to not be killed is merely the very fact that it is permissible for Victim to kill Aggressor, then it is hard to see how we can explain the fact that it is permissible for Victim to kill Aggressor by appeal to a right in Victim which is more stringent than Aggressor's right to not be killed. I do not say that no independent account of relative 'stringency' among rights can be given; I say only that an over-rider plainly needs one.

Moreover, there is a second question which the answer invites, and which we should take note of, namely the question "*What* right is it which Victim has, and which is more stringent than Aggressor's right to not be killed, and which is such that, the circumstances containing the fact that that right of Victim's is more stringent than Aggressor's right to not be killed, it is permissible for Victim to kill Aggressor?" It is a good question, I think.

We might begin with this: the right which Victim has, and which meets those further conditions, is the right to preserve his life. But *is* Victim's right to preserve his life more stringent than Aggressor's right to not be killed?

Certainly it just is not the case, quite generally, that one person's right to preserve his life is more stringent than another person's right to not be killed. Suppose I am starving, and need food or else I die. Suppose further that the only available food is *you.* I should imagine I do have a right to preserve my life; but surely your right to not be killed is more stringent than my right to preserve my life—surely it is not permissible for me to kill you to preserve my life!

Well, perhaps we simply fastened on the wrong right; perhaps we should instead have said that the right which Victim has, and which meets those further conditions, is the right to self-defense—more precisely, perhaps, the right to preserve his life against an attack on it. (Your being the only available food does not make it be the case that you are *attacking* me.) But *is* Victim's right to preserve his life against an attack on it more stringent than Aggressor's right to not be killed? Certainly it just is not the case, quite generally, that one person's right to preserve his life against an attack on it is more stringent than another person's right to not be killed. Suppose I am being threatened with a gun, and the only way in which I can preserve my life against that attack on it is by grabbing some innocent bystander and shoving him in front of me. I should imagine I do have a right to preserve my life against an attack on it; but surely the innocent bystander's right to not be killed is more stringent than my right to preserve my life against an attack on it—surely it is not permissible for me to shove the innocent bystander in front of me!

I suppose it could be said that Aggressor's right to not be killed is less stringent than yours is, and than the innocent bystander's is, and that that is why Victim may act though I may not. Aggressor is a villain, after all, and neither you nor the innocent bystander is.

But then are we to suppose that after the stall of the tank, and Aggressor's breaking of his ankles, Aggressor's right to not be killed sweeps back to being just as stringent as yours is, and as the innocent bystander's is? For after that time, Victim may not kill Aggressor on any weaker grounds than would permit of his killing you or an innocent bystander.

The right to not be killed (as well as the right to preserve one's life, the right to preserve one's life against an attack on it, and the right to life itself) is traditionally thought to be a 'natural right,' i.e., a right a human being has simply by virtue of being a human being.[8] Now if a right is a right which we have simply by virtue of being human beings, it is not possible that some human beings possess it and others do not. Moreover, it is not possible that a human being possesses it at one time and not at another, so long as he remains a human being throughout.

Suppose the time now is after the start of Aggressor's attack on Victim, but before the time at which Aggressor ceases to pose a threat to Victim. If the right to not be killed is a natural right, so defined (henceforth I shall take this qualification to be understood), then we plainly cannot say

(1) Aggressor had (before launching his attack) and will again have (after breaking his ankles) a right to not be killed, but he does not have this right now. *That* is why Victim may now kill him.

But *is* the right to not be killed a natural right? It is by no means obvious that it is. Perhaps the right to not be killed is forfeitable. Hobbes thought that the right to not be killed is inalienable, but perhaps even this is wrong. Could one not voluntarily relinquish one's right to not be killed? Suppose I am terminally ill, and want to be able to provide for my children. Here is a rich man, who likes to kill. I say "For so and so much, to be given to my children, you may kill me now." Suppose, then, that he accepts my offer, and kills me. No doubt he does not act *well*. Perhaps he does what it is impermissible for him to do. But I think it arguable that he violates—even that he infringes—no right of mine, and that if he does act impermissibly, it is nothing to do with my rights that makes this so.

Moreover, even if the right to not be killed is a natural right, this does not settle what we are to say about the case in hand. Of course we may not say (1). I should imagine also that we cannot say

(2) Aggressor has (at all times) a right to not be killed, but Aggressor's right to not be killed is (at all times) less stringent than any innocent person's is—so much less stringent as to be less stringent than Victim's right to preserve his life against an attack on it. *That* is why Victim may now kill him.

It is not inconsistent to suppose that a certain right is a right which we all have by virtue of being human beings, and nevertheless that it varies in stringency between human beings—in particular, between the innocent and the villains. We do of course say about natural rights that they are 'equal' in both of the following two senses: every human being has them, and no one human being's are any more stringent than any other human being's. But only the first follows from the definition of "natural right" which I gave above. So taking the right to not be killed to be a natural right does not rule out opting for (2). But I take it that what I drew attention to a moment ago *does* rule out opting for (2). What I have in mind is the fact that after the stall of the tank, and Aggressor's breaking of his ankles, Aggressor's right to not be killed is surely just as stringent as yours is, and as the innocent bystander's is—for after that time, Victim may not kill Aggressor on any weaker grounds than would permit of his killing you or an innocent bystander.

This points, however, to a further possibility. It is not inconsistent to suppose that a certain right is a right which we all have by virtue of being human beings, and nevertheless that it sweeps back and forth from one degree of stringency to another in one human being—according as he is or is not threatening another. I do not think it is as commonly said that natural rights are also 'equal' in the following (third) sense: no one human being's are any more stringent at one time than they are at any other time. That they are 'equal' in this sense certainly does not follow from the definition of "natural right" I gave, or even from their being 'equal' in either of the two senses I pointed to. So it would be consistent to say that the right to not be killed is a natural right, and yet also opt for

(3) Aggressor has (at all times) a right to not be killed, and Aggressor's right to not be killed was (before launching his attack) and will again be (after breaking his ankles) as stringent as any innocent person's is, but it is less stringent now—so much less stringent now as to be less stringent than Victim's right to preserve his life against an attack on it. *That* is why Victim may now kill him.

So far as I can see, nothing in the case rules this out.

But there is plainly yet another alternative. Don't we all of us have a right to kill a person who is currently giving us every reason to believe that he will kill us unless we kill him? And isn't this right as good a candidate for the status of 'natural right' as the right to not be killed is? And isn't it, moreover, *always* more stringent than the right to not be killed? If so, there is a fourth alternative:

(4) Aggressor has (at all times) an equally stringent right to not be killed, but that right is (always) less stringent than the right—possessed by Victim—to kill a person who is currently giving every reason to believe that he will kill Victim unless Victim kills him. *That* is why Victim may now kill him.

Is there any principled ground for choosing between (3) and (4)? Indeed, between (1), (3), and (4)—since, as I said, it is by no means obvious that the right to not be killed is a natural right.

The other side of the same coin is that (1), (3), and (4) are marvelously *ad hoc*. Consider the appeal in (1) to loss of, and then re-acquisition of, the right to not be killed; is there any reason to opt for (1) other than the fact that if we do, we seem to have in hand an explanation of why Victim may kill Aggressor? Similarly for the appeal in (3) to difference in stringency in one person across time. And what of that right to kill a person who is currently giving every reason to believe that he will kill you unless you kill him? Can there be any reason to suppose we have such a right other than the fact that it is permissible for a victim to kill an aggressor who is currently giving every reason to believe that he will kill the victim unless the victim kills him? Notice how carefully tailored to its explanatory purpose this right is.

Notice, moreover, how difficult it would be to find a lesson in any of this in respect of permitted killings generally. Take the case of the trolley driver I mentioned earlier. Surely the trolley driver may turn his trolley, to save five at a cost of one. Does it seem at all plausible to say that the reason why he may is that the one has ceased to have a right to not be killed, or that his right to not be killed is now less stringent than it was before he started work on that particular stretch of track? Of course we could say that the reason why the trolley driver may turn the trolley is that he has a right to turn his trolley onto one to save five, and that that right is always more stringent than the right to not be killed—cp. (4) above. But you might as well say: Leave me alone, I'm too busy to do moral philosophy this afternoon.

5. Many people who do moral philosophy these days appeal to rights to *explain* why this or that piece of behavior is or is not permissible. For example, it is common to say that the reason why you cannot maximize utility in such and such a case is the fact that the utility-maximizing course of action would involve infring-ing a right—indeed, violating a right, since the right in question is a stringent one, and the utility to be got not sufficiently great to over-ride the right. But when we say that, in that case, the utility-maximizing course of action would involve violating a right, *are* we saying anything more than that, in that case, it is not permissible to take the utility-maximizing course of action? If not, then we can hardly take ourselves to have explained why it is not per-missible, in that case, to take the utility-maxi-mizing course of action. It is arguable that if there is to be any point at all in appealing to rights in such discussions, there had better be something independent of permissibilities and impermissibilities which fixes their existence and degree of stringency. It is not obvious that this is true. I.e., it might be that to attribute a right is only to talk about permissibilities and impermissibilities, but in a way that groups or collects them, and brings whole clusters of cases to bear on each other. I do not for a moment think it a novel idea that we stand in need of an account of just how an appeal to a right may be thought to function in ethical dis-cussion. What strikes me as of interest, how-ever, is that the need for such an account shows itself even in a case which might have been thought to be transparent.

NOTES

1.   This question is asked by Sanford H. Kadish, in "Respect for Life and Regard for Rights in the Criminal Law," forthcom-ing. (In fact, this paper was caused by that one.)

2.   But it is not at all obvious that this is what explains the fact that Victim cannot cut you up and parcel out your parts to save five. Cf. footnote 7 below.

3.   Cf. again Kadish, *op. cit.*

4.   Cf. his *Anarchy, State, and Utopia* (New York: Basic Books, 1974), p. 35.

5.   Cf. her "Abortion and the Doctrine of the Double Ef-fect," *Oxford Review* 5 (1967).

6.   If the workman on the right-hand track has a right to life (and it seems plain that if we do, he does), then we cannot explain the fact that a surgeon cannot cut you up and parcel out your parts to save five by appeal to the fact that you have a right to life. For so does the workman; yet the driver *can* turn the trolley onto him to save five. Mrs. Foot (*op. cit.*) has an explanation; another may be found in J. J. Thomson, "Killing, Letting Die, and the Trolley Problem," *The Monist* 59 (1976).

7.   The term is Robert Nozick's: cf. *op. cit.*, p. 34.

8.   Cp. H. L. A. Hart's definition of "natural right" in "Are There Any Natural Rights?" *The Philosophical Review* 64 (1955). Cp. also Joel Feinberg's definition of what he calls "human rights" in *Social Philosophy* (Englewood Cliffs, New Jersey: Prentice-Hall, Inc., 1973).

PART 3

Justice

One of the very oldest conceptions of justice, which must be close to the original seed of the modern concept, derives from pre-Socratic Greek cosmology and its picture of a morally ordered universe in which everything has its assigned place, or natural role. Justice (*dike*) consisted of everything staying in that assigned place, and not usurping the place of another, which would throw the whole system out of kilter. Elements of this early notion survive in Plato's theory of justice as a virtue both of people and of states. Social justice, according to Plato, exists when every person performs the function for which he or she is best fitted by nature (his or her own proper business) and does not infringe upon the natural role of another. A corollary of this principle is that the rulers of the state should be those best fitted by their natures to rule; hence democracy, or rule by everybody, is inherently unjust.

The reason why people live in political communities in the first place, Plato argues in the *Republic,* is that no mere individual is self-sufficient. For all of us to satisfy our needs, we must divide our labors, with each person performing the task for which she is best fitted by their natural aptitudes. Instead of every person being her own carpenter, toolmaker, farmer, tailor, soldier, and police officer, each can work at the one thing he or she does best, while enjoying the benefits of the full-time labors of other specialists. The principle of cooperation by means of the specialization of labor explains what social organization is *for,* and why it should exist. There is justice in a society when all do their proper work: when square pegs are in square holes; when no talent is wasted or misused; when those who are naturally fit to rule do rule, and those who are naturally fit to obey, do obey. The sole criterion, then, for justice in assigning positions in society is *fitness for a function.* This in turn is best promoted, according to Plato, by fair educational and testing procedures that give each child, regardless of his race, sex, or the social rank of his parents, an equal opportunity to rise to his appropriate slot in the social hierarchy.

Aristotle, in the famous discussion of the virtue of justice, shares Plato's view that only the best should rule as well as Plato's disdain for perfect equality in the distribution of political burdens and benefits. His analysis of justice, however, is more subtle and more faithful to complexities in the concept's multifaceted employment. He acknowledges at the start that the word for justice is ambiguous, referring both to the whole of social virtue ("virtue in relation to our neighbor") and to one specific type of social virtue. The wider or generic concept Aristotle calls "universal justice"; the narrower he calls "particular justice." Unlike Plato in the *Republic,* Aristotle's chief concern is with the particular virtue that is only a part, not the whole, of social virtue. He does say of universal justice, however, that it coincides with conformity to *law.* He apparently means that the positive law of the state *should* aim at the enforcement of the social virtues (including not only "particular justice" but also benevolence, charity, fidelity, and so on), and that insofar as a given legal code does support social virtue, violation of "universal justice" will at the same time be violation of positive law.

Particular justice, as Aristotle understands it, is the same as *fairness.* The Greek word for fairness in Aristotle's time also meant *equality.* Thus, Aristotle's initial contention is that there are two concepts of justice: lawfulness and equality. Particular justice (fairness), he tells us, is of two kinds: *distributive* and *rectificatory justice.* His conviction that most fair distributions are unequal, held at a time when "just" meant or strongly suggested "equal," drove him (as Gregory Vlastos has put it) to "linguistic acrobatics."[1] Distributive justice, he argues ingeniously, does not consist in absolute equality (that is, perfectly equal shares for all those among whom something is to be distributed), but rather a proportionate equality, which is to say an equality of ratios. What justice requires, he insists, is that equal cases be treated alike (equally), and that unequal cases be treated unalike (unequally) in direct proportion to the differences (inequalities) between them, so that between any two persons the ratio between their shares ($S_1 : S_2$) should equal the ratio between their qualifying characteristics ($C_1 : C_2$).

Aristotle concedes that people disagree over which characteristics of persons should be taken into account in assessing their equality or the degree of their inequality, but all parties to these disagreements (except extreme democrats who insist upon absolute equality) employ tacitly the notion of proportionate equality. However "merit" is conceived, for example, those for whom it would be the sole criterion in awarding shares would give one person twice as large a share of some benefit as they would to any other person deemed only half as meritorious. The common object of these distributors, even when they disagree over what merit is, will be to divide shares into a ratio (2 : 1) equal to the ratio of the merits of the two persons (2 : 1). Such distributions are sometimes necessarily impressionistic (how can one person's merit be seen to be exactly one-half of another's?), but when the criterion of merit is exactly definable, and the shares themselves can be measured in terms of money, the calculations can sometimes achieve a mathematical precision. At times Aristotle seems to have in mind, for example, "the distribution of profits between partners in proportion to what each has put into the business."[2] Such contributions ("merits" in an extended, but properly Aristotelian, sense) as capital, time and labor are readily measurable.

Since any two persons will be unequal in some respects and equal in others, Aristotle's theory of distributive justice is incomplete until he tells us which personal characteristics are *relevant* factors to be considered in the balancing of ratios. Various criteria of relevance have been proposed by writers of different schools. Some have held that *A*'s share should be to *B*'s share as *A*'s ability is to *B*'s ability, or as *A*'s moral virtue is to *B*'s, or as *A*'s labor is to *B*'s, and so on. All the above maxims could be said to specify different forms of "merit," so that a *meritarian* theorist would be one who held that the only personal characteristics relevant to a just distribution of goods are such forms of personal "merit." Aristotle was undoubtedly a meritarian in this broad sense. Meritarian social philosophers, then, can disagree among themselves over which forms of merit are relevant and over criteria for assessing a given form of merit, or they might hold that some forms of merit are relevant to some types of distribution, and other merits to other types. A nonmeritarian theory would find exclusive relevance in personal characteristics (for example, needs) that are in no sense "merits," and of course mixed theories are also possible. Even a "democratic" or "equalitarian" theory, one which is wholly nonmeritarian, might plausibly be said to employ tacitly Aristotle's *analysis* of distributive justice as proportionate equality, while rejecting of course Aristotle's suggested criteria of relevance. Even a perfect equalitarian would presumably wish to endorse such maxims as: A's share should be to B's share as A's needs are to B's needs, or as A's "infinite human worth" is to B's "infinite human worth" (that is, the same). It seems likely, therefore, that all complete theories of social justice must contain maxims specifying relevant characteristics, and that all of them presuppose Aristotle's formal analysis of distributive justice as proportionate equality between shares and relevant characteristics.

Distributive justice applies to the distribution by statesmen of honors, rewards, public property (as, for example, land in a new Athenian or Macedonian colony), public assistance to the needy, or divisions of corporate profits or inheritances. Aristotle does not discuss the distribution of burdens such as taxation and military service, but his principle of proportionate equality presumably applies to them, too. The second kind of particular justice, *rectificatory justice*, applies to private transactions or business deals in which some unfair advantage or undeserved harm has occurred and one party sues for a "remedy." (Aristotle's phrase for rectificatory justice is sometimes translated as "remedial," as well as "corrective" or "compensatory" justice.) A judge then must assess the damages and order one party to make a payment to the other. These cases, Aristotle says, are of two kinds. In one type the harm to the plaintiff results from a transaction in which he voluntarily participated: buying, selling, loaning, pledging, depositing, hiring out, and the like. The law governing these cases corresponds roughly to our law of contracts. In the other type of case, the harm to the plaintiff results from a "transaction" in which he involuntarily participates as a victim from the start: fraud, theft, adultery, assault, imprisonment, or homicide. The law governing these cases, when the aim is to correct an unfairness by compensating a victim for his loss or injury, corresponds roughly to our law of torts.

Rectificatory justice, too, essentially involves the notion of equality. Its aim, Aristotle says, is to redress the "inequality" that results when one person profits unfairly at the expense of another. If A steals one hundred dollars from B, for example, he becomes one hundred dollars better off, an amount that is exactly equal to the amount by which B becomes worse off. The "equality" between A and B was their starting position before the "transaction," and that equality is restored by an order that requires A to pay to B exactly one hundred dollars. It is well to note that rectificatory justice, as Aristotle understands it, does not apply to the criminal law at all. If there is a justice in punishing A for his peculation beyond the penalty that merely restores the *status quo ante*, that must be justice of a different kind. Retributive justice, as such, does not receive a thorough discussion in Aristotle, and does not even receive a separate rubric in his classification of the types of justice.

Neither does Aristotle's analysis of rectificatory justice appear to be an adequate guide through the complexities of the law of torts. More than the restoration of equality by a simple arithmetical formula, at any rate, is involved in all but the simplest cases in deliberations aiming at the determination of compensatory damages. Suppose *A*'s wrongful act makes him $500 better off and *B* (the plaintiff) $200 worse off? What if *A*'s malevolence or spitefulness toward *B* is so great that he is willing to undergo a loss for himself in order to inflict one on *B*? Suppose, in that example, that *A*'s malicious act costs himself $500 and inflicts only a $100 loss on *B*. Or suppose, admittedly somewhat fanciful, that *A*'s wrongful act actually creates a $100 windfall for wholly innocent *B* while earning himself $1,000.

Some parts of Aristotle's discussion are primarily of antiquarian interest. His sketchy account in chapter 5, for example, of "Justice in Exchange" is one of the earliest discussions on record of economic justice. Several other sections of his treatment of justice are important both for their intrinsic interest and their historical influence. Chapter 7 on "Natural and Legal Justice," for instance, is a classical source for the long and still vital tradition of natural law, and the theory of Equity in chapter 10 has had a direct effect on the development of legal institutions that is still felt. In addition to the distinctions between equity and law, there is still another important distinction that Aristotle was the first to treat with great subtlety: the distinction between the just or unjust *quality* of an act and the just or unjust *effect* of an act on others. Injustice is always a violation of someone's rights or deserts, but such an effect can be brought about involuntarily. In such a case, the action that produced the effect cannot be unjust in itself, for normally to ascribe an unjust act to a person is to blame him or her, and involuntary acts are not blameworthy. Moreover, there are occasions, unhappily, in which a person can be fully justified in voluntarily producing an unjust effect on another; when that effect, for example, is the least evil result the actor could produce in the circumstances. *A* may be justified in violating *B*'s rights instead of *C*'s and *D*'s when there is no third alternative open to him, but that justification does not cancel the injustice done to *B*. In that case, we can say that *B* was unjustly *treated* although *A*'s act resulting in that effect was not an instance of unjust *behavior*. For an act to have an unjust quality (whatever its effects) it must be, objectively speaking, the wrong thing to do in the circumstances, unexcused and unjustified, voluntarily undertaken, and deliberately chosen by an unrushed actor who is well aware of the alternatives open to him. Other parties can be injured by unforeseeable accidents (mere mishaps), foreseeable accidents (blunders), by voluntary acts done in a fit of anger (*akrasia*), or by deliberate choice. Only in the last case is there unjust behavior, although there is blameworthiness of other kinds (negligence and hot-tempered impetuousness) in blunders and in angry violence, too.

THE MACHINERY OF JUSTICE

In the modern world (as in the ancient world) the principles of justice often seem far removed from the procedures of a legal system in operation. Attempts to do justice generate their own further problems of justice which philosophers of law can take up with equal relish.

The essay by John Langbein, "Torture and Plea Bargaining," presents with unusual clarity the very serious problems that surround the procedure employed to dispose of the great majority of criminal cases in America today. Criminal accusations are made the subject of negotiation rather than adjudication in most cases so that as little time, effort, and money as possible need be spent in dealing with criminal charges. Reducing the charge itself or reducing the sentence to be demanded on a particular charge is offered in exchange for a guilty plea in order to avoid the burdensome business of a trial. The accused is very rarely a free bargaining agent, and the result of frequently a coerced conviction. In other cases where there is serious crime, insupportable leniency to dispose of a case mocks the very reason for having a system of criminal justice. Those who commit crimes are encouraged by the system of plea bargaining to believe that after getting caught it is a matter mainly of whether one gets a good deal or not, and this must work against the cultivation of a general law-abiding attitude in the part of the community most prone to crime. The overdeveloped adversarial system makes plea-bargaining in some form necessary, in Langbein's view, and its evils can only be escaped by fundamental reforms that take the sort of approach to criminal justice that is seen in European countries. Regarding this last point, one wonders if the lack of certain traditional civil service standards in carrying on judicial and prosecutorial functions does not make a great difference to criminal justice on opposite sides of the Atlantic. Perhaps more elaborate protection against abuse of power is required in criminal procedures in America where success in carrying on the enterprise and the personal ambitions of those who carry it on are of much greater importance.

The technical difficulties of legal proceedings call for the professional services of a lawyer. The alternative would be to have laymen battle out the issue in a rather rough and tumble way before a judge or referee, as, for example, in small claims courts. But most people would not have the stomach for that in serious cases, and the opportunities for injustice would be very great. When the legal proceedings are criminal rather than civil, the services of a lawyer are an indispensable part of the system if there is to be any chance at all of justice being done. The U.S. Constitution recognizes this in the Sixth Amendment, and the law that has developed requires that there be effective assistance of counsel available to criminal defendants. Exactly what is required remains a matter of some doubt, however. In *United States* v. *DeCoster* Judge Bazelton's opinion provides a statement of the standard of representation adopted by the American Bar Association. With the resources normally available to criminal defendants, it can hardly surprise us that plea bargaining has become the usual method of disposing of cases. One wonders if the ABA recommended standards have been costed for typical criminal cases. And yet it seems unthinkable that any less diligent and comprehensive representation should be endorsed as adequate for purposes of procedural justice. It is useful to consider what the solution might be in a broader social perspective that subjects the criminal justice system to a vigorous public policy review and places the interests of justice on the same footing as law enforcement in deciding how tax money should be spent.

When a dispute arises and people have recourse to the law to settle it, it is the machinery of litigation that seems to be the means of producing justice. In fact a legal system allows for dispute resolution in ways other than adjudication of claims in a court through lawsuits. Reading many of the selections in Part One of this volume, one might well have the impression that it is courts adjudicating issues of law that is the most important feature of our legal system. In fact, alternative procedures, some formal and some informal, are far more important and account for dispute resolution in far more cases. An illuminating account of how this may take place is provided in the selection entitled "A Broad View of Dispute Resolution" by Henry Perritt. It might be well to consider whether justice is compromised in any way by these alternative procedures, or whether justice is better served by them. This will involve careful consideration of exactly what it is that we require for justice to be done in settling disputes.

JUSTICE AND COMPENSATION

Aristotle's concept of *corrective justice* (distinguished in the *Nichomachean Ethics* from *distributive justice*) is what we think of as the basis of compensation to an injured party when the one who injures him is required to pay it. Recently the foundations of the law of torts (and other areas of law) have been radically reinterpreted along lines of economic theory by certain legal theorists who suggest generally that notions of justice can be understood in terms of greater economic efficiency. In tort law perhaps more than in any other branch of law, the economic consequences of rules of liability seem to have great influence. Exactly what role, however, those consequences have played in the past or should play in the future is a matter of considerable controversy. In his article entitled "The Concept of Corrective Justice in Recent Theories of Tort Law," Richard Posner, the leading figure among modern economic revisionist scholars, argues that the theory of wealth maximization (his cardinal principle of economic interpretation) leads to results in tort law that are virtually the same as the orthodox theory of corrective justice propounded by Aristotle. Posner even suggests that economic theory may well provide the reason lacking in Aristotle's work for a duty to redress injuries. In his initial reply to various critics, he provides the reader with illuminating discussion not only of Aristotle's theory, but also of points that must be resolved by any comprehensive theory of compensation. It is natural to feel that somehow this economic interpretation misses the most important considerations in doing justice between the parties. Those who remain sceptical will be intrigued and challenged to explain the remarkable coincidence of considerations of justice and of economic efficiency in arriving at decisions in tort cases.

The arguments are drawn exceedingly fine, though the points made are substantial to the debate over how damages should be measured and where liability should be placed, which has important policy implications for the law itself. Professor Coleman's position allows the insights of those theorists who stress economic efficiency to be combined with legal theory that draws on more intuitive (albeit more mysterious) motives.

JUSTICE AND CONTRACT

Throughout its history, the law of contract has received a good deal of attention from legal scholars in search of theory to explain its principles. Even the most obvious features of contractual obligation become the subject of controversy when attempting to justify recognition of those rights, duties, and legal consequences that courts regularly consider when it is said that an agreement has been broken or in a dispute over the actual existence of an agreement in the first place. Philosophical analysis of the moral roots of such concepts, interest in the possibilities of economic interpretations, and the more general concerns of philosophers regarding justice, have recently moved the discussion to new levels of complexity and sophistication.

In the first of two selections dealing with the foundations of contract law, Anthony Kronman states that the aims of distributive justice should be pursued through the rules of contract law unless less costly or intrusive alternatives exist. Taken at face value, Professor Kronman's is especially bold since libertarian views such as Nozick's, as well as liberal views, such as Rawls's, stand in opposition. Kronman's strategy is to argue that the notion of a voluntary agreement, which is crucial in the libertarian theory of justice, cannot be understood except as a concept of distribution. The notion of individual liberty, upon which liberal theory relies, in itself offers no guidance in determining which circumstances render a contract involuntary because of the advantage one party enjoys over another.

A rather different approach to contracts is taken by Charles Fried in the chapter "Contract As Promise," reprinted here from his book of the same title. Professor Fried carefully analyzes the idea of a promise and the good moral reasons for the existence of promissory obligation. He takes these reasons to be the foundation of the law of contract, and, though not all of contract law can be derived from the principles of promissory obligation, they are nevertheless the main source of basic rules in contract law. In Fried's concept of contract law, the greatest emphasis is placed on certain social factors that are part of each community member's moral life, rather than on certain fundamental principles of justice in a political society, which should be furthered by the law. This point of view most dramatically reflects the contrasts between Kronman and Fried, and in turn brings to the surface some basic jurisprudential concerns about the role of law when there are disputes calling for invocation of rules of contract.

DISCRIMINATION AND REVERSE DISCRIMINATION

Invidiously discriminatory treatment in the distribution of benefits (including opportunities) and burdens is the essential feature of what Aristotle called "distributive injustice." In the United States grossly discriminatory rules and practices have only recently begun to crumble, and for the first time in centuries there is hope that the ideal of equal opportunity will one day be fulfilled. To expect the effects of racial and sexual discrimination to vanish overnight with the abrogation of ancient rules, however, would be exceedingly naive. Many reformers, in fact, have been urging that the elimination of discriminatory practices is not enough, and that a kind of "reverse discrimination," especially in the allocation of educational and professional opportunities for such groups as blacks and women, is required by social justice.

Louis Katzner, in his penetrating article, subjects this claim to close philosophical analysis, and concludes with a statement of four conditions which must be satisfied if reverse discrimination is to be justified. It is an interesting apparent consequence of Katzner's view that, while reverse discrimination in favor of blacks might in some circumstances be justified, reverse discrimination in favor of (all) women would likely not pass Katzner's test.

In the view of Lisa Newton, equality under the law is an ideal of political justice that is threatened with destruction by programs of reverse discrimination. If we do not regard everyone as entitled to equal consideration in the distribution of benefits, none of us may regard ourselves as the "bearer of rights—we are all petitioners for favors."

Newton's article suggests a number of questions of principle that reverse discrimination advocates must answer if their position is to enjoy moral respectability: Why are members of some historically disadvantaged groups and not others made beneficiaries under some programs? Why should the individual's personal history not confer entitlement if he or she has suffered personal disadvantage of the same sort? Why should those members of disadvantaged groups who have not themselves suffered such disadvantage nevertheless enjoy the benefits of reverse discrimination? Professor Newton's main concern addresses the practical effects of reverse discrimination programs upon the ideal of a rule of law that (1) prevents manipulation of political power and (2) ensures that all citizens are respected equally as objects of equal concern to government. Certainly the actual effects of favored treatment by government upon standards of political behavior is no insignificant matter. One wonders if recent adoption of criteria of entitlement based on group membership has had more baleful effects than in past times when the ideal of the rule of law seemed to flourish despite allowance by the law for invidious discrimination and which, not infrequently, put its force behind the prohibitions needed to accomplish it.

Thomas Nagel's "Equal Treatment and Compensatory Discrimination" is an extremely careful analysis of the various claims at the heart of the compensatory discrimination debate. Nagel addresses policies of compensatory discrimination in admissions to educational institutions, and concludes that they are not seriously unjust because the system from whose norms they depart, thereby giving rise to claims of injustice, is a system itself already seriously unjust for reasons of another sort. Careful attention to the subtle and complex argument well repays the reader's efforts. One important question to be considered is whether Nagel's account of the more fundamental systemic injustice represents the same sort of offense against justice as the one alleged by critics of the admissions policies in question. Can any individuals, either in their own right or as members of a group, claim to be victims of this systemic injustice and therefore entitled to compensation or other redress? If not, does this tend to undermine Nagel's position with regard to compensatory discrimination?

NOTES

1. Gregory Vlastos, "Justice and Equality," in *Social Justice*, ed., Richard B. Brandt (Englewood Cliffs, N.J.: Prentice-Hall, Inc., 1962), p. 32.

2. W. D. Ross, *Aristotle* (London: Metheun & Co., 1949), p. 210.

JOHN H. LANGBEIN

Torture and Plea Bargaining*

The American system of plea bargaining is becoming a subject of immense academic and public attention. A dozen books have appeared in the last year or so describing plea bargaining as observed in one forum or another. The law reviews are full of writing about the details; a special issue of the *Law and Society Review* is now offering 20 more articles. The general theme of much of the current writing is that although, arguably, plea bargaining might be in need of various operational reforms, the basic institution is natural, inevitable, universal, and just.

In this essay I shall set forth some of the case against plea bargaining from a perspective that must appear bizarre, although I hope to show that it is illuminating. I am going to contrast the modern American system of plea bargaining with the medieval European law of torture. My thesis is that there are remarkable parallels in origin, in function, and even in specific points of doctrine, between the law of torture and the law of plea bargaining. I shall suggest that these parallels expose some important truths about how criminal justice systems respond when their trial procedures fall into deep disorder.

THE LAW OF TORTURE

For about half a millennium, from the middle of the thirteenth century to the middle of the eighteenth, a system of judicial torture lay at the heart of Continental criminal procedure. In our own day the very word "torture" is, gladly enough, a debased term. It has come to mean anything unpleasant, and we hear people speak of a tortured interpretation of a poem, or the torture of a dull dinner party. In discussions of

*John H. Langbein, "Torture and Plea Bargaining," *The Public Interest,* No. 58, Winter, 1980, pp. 43–61. Reprinted by permission of *The Public Interest.*

contemporary criminal procedure we hear the word applied to describe illegal police practices or crowded prison conditions. But torture as the medieval European lawyers understood it had nothing to do with official misconduct or with criminal sanctions. Rather, the application of torture was a routine and judicially supervised feature of European criminal procedure. Under certain circumstances the law permitted the criminal courts to employ physical coercion against suspected criminals in order to induce them to confess. The law went to great lengths to limit this technique of extorting confessions to cases in which it was thought that the accused was highly likely to be guilty, and to surround the use of torture with other procedural safeguards that I shall discuss shortly.

This astonishing body of law grew up on the Continent as an adjunct to the law of proof—what we would call the system of trial—in cases of serious crime (for which the sanction was either death or severe physical maiming). The medieval law of proof was designed in the thirteenth century to replace an earlier system of proof, the ordeals, which the Roman Church effectively destroyed in the year 1215. The ordeals purported to achieve absolute certainty in criminal adjudication through the happy expedient of having the judgments rendered by God, who could not err. The replacement system of the thirteenth century aspired to achieve the same level of safeguard—absolute certainty—for human adjudication.

Although human judges were to replace God in the judgment seat, they would be governed by a law of proof so objective that it would make that dramatic substitution unobjectionable—a law of proof that would *eliminate human discretion* from the determination of guilt or innocence. Accordingly, the Italian Glossators who designed the system developed and entrenched the rule that conviction had to be based upon the testimony of two unimpeachable eyewitnesses to the gravamen of the crime—evidence that was, in the famous phrase, "clear as the noonday sun." Without these two eyewitnesses, a criminal court could not convict an accused who contested the charges against him. Only if the accused *voluntarily* confessed the offense could the court convict him without the eyewitness testimony.

Another way to appreciate the purpose of these rules is to understand their corollary: Conviction could not be based upon circumstantial evidence, because circumstantial evidence depends for its efficacy upon the subjective persuasion of the trier who decides whether to draw the inference of guilt from the evidence of circumstance. Thus, for example, it would not have mattered in this system that the suspect was seen running away from the murdered man's house and that the bloody dagger and the stolen loot were found in his possession. If no eyewitness saw him actually plunge the weapon into the victim, the court could not convict him.

In the history of Western culture no legal system has ever made a more valiant effort to perfect its safeguards and thereby to exclude completely the possibility of mistaken conviction. But the Europeans learned in due course the inevitable lesson. They had set the level of safeguard too high. They had constructed a system of proof that could as a practical matter be effective only in cases involving overt crime or repentant criminals. Because society cannot long tolerate a legal system that lacks the capacity to convict unrepentant persons who commit clandestine crimes, something had to be done to extend the system to those cases. The two-eyewitness rule was hard to compromise or evade, but the confession rule seemed to invite the subterfuge that in fact resulted. To go from accepting a voluntary confession to coercing a confession from someone against whom there was already strong suspicion was a step that began increasingly to be taken. The law of torture grew up to regulate this process of generating confessions.

The spirit of safeguard that had inspired the unworkable formal law of proof also permeated the subterfuge. The largest chapter of the European law of torture concerned the prerequisites for examination under torture. The European jurists devised what Anglo-American lawyers would today call a rule of probable cause, designed to assure that only persons highly likely to be guilty would be examined under torture. Thus, torture was permitted only when a so-called "half proof" had been established against the suspect. That meant either one eyewitness, or circumstantial evidence of sufficient gravity, according to a fairly elaborate tariff. In the example where a suspect was caught with the dagger and the loot, each of those indicia would be a quarter proof. Together they cumulated to a half proof, which was sufficient to permit the authorities to dispatch the suspect for a session in the local torture chamber.

In this way the prohibition against using circumstantial evidence was overcome. The law of torture found a place for circumstantial evidence, but a nominally subsidiary place. Circumstantial evidence was not consulted directly on the ultimate question, guilt or innocence, but on a question of interlocutory procedure—whether or not to examine the accused under torture. Even there the law attempted to limit judicial discretion by promulgating predetermined, ostensibly objective criteria for evaluating the indicia and assigning them numerical values (quarter proofs, half proofs, and the like). Vast legal treatises were compiled on this jurisprudence of torture to guide the examining magistrate in determining whether there was probable cause for torture.

In order to achieve a verbal or technical reconciliation with the requirement of the formal law of proof that the confession be voluntary, the medieval lawyers treated a confession extracted under torture as involuntary, hence ineffective, unless the accused repeated it free from torture at a hearing that was held a day or so later. Often enough the accused who had confessed under torture did recant when asked to confirm his confession. But seldom to avail: The examination under torture could thereupon be repeated. An accused who confessed under torture, recanted, and then found himself tortured anew, learned quickly enough that only a "voluntary" confession at the ratification hearing would save him from further agony in the torture chamber.

Fortunately, more substantial safeguards were devised to govern the actual application of torture. These were rules designed to enhance the reliability of the resulting confession. Torture was not supposed to be used to elicit an abject, unsubstantiated confession of guilt. Rather, torture was supposed to be employed in such a way that the accused would disclose the factual detail of the crime—information which, in the words of a celebrated German statute of the year 1532, "no innocent person can know." The examining magistrate was forbidden to engage in so-called suggestive questioning, in which the examiner supplied the accused with the detail he wanted to hear from him. Moreover, the information admitted under torture was supposed to be investigated and verified to the extent feasible. If the accused confessed to the slaying, he was supposed to be asked where he put the dagger. If he said he buried it under the old oak tree, the magistrate was supposed to send someone to dig it up.

Alas, these safeguards never proved adequate to overcome the basic flaw in the system. Because torture tests the capacity of the accused to endure pain, rather than his veracity, the innocent might (as one sixteenth-century commentator put it) yield to "the pain and torment and confess things that they never did." If the examining magistrate engaged in suggestive questioning, even accidentally, his lapse could not always be detected or prevented. If the accused knew something about the crime, but was still innocent of it, what he did know might be enough to give his confession verisimilitude. In some jurisdictions the requirement of verification was not enforced, or was enforced indifferently.

These shortcomings in the law of torture were identified even in the Middle Ages and were the subject of emphatic compliant in Renaissance and early modern times. The Europeans looked ever more admiringly at England, where the jury system—operating without the two-eyewitness rule—had never needed the law of torture. In the eighteenth century, as the law of torture was finally about to be abolished along with the system of proof that had required it, Beccaria and Voltaire became famous as critics of judicial torture; but they were latecomers to a critical legal literature nearly as old as the law of torture itself. Judicial torture survived the centuries not because its defects had been concealed, but in spite of their having been long revealed. The two-eyewitness rule had left European criminal procedure without a tolerable alternative. Having entrenched this unattainable level of safeguard in their formal trial procedure, the Europeans found themselves obliged to evade it through a subterfuge that they knew was defective. The coerced confession had to replace proof of guilt.

THE LAW OF PLEA BARGAINING

I am now going to cross the centuries and cross the Atlantic in order to speak of the rise of plea bargaining in twentieth-century America. The account of the European law of torture that I just presented (which is based upon my monograph *Torture and the Law of Proof,* 1977), should stir among American readers an unpleasant sensation of the familiar, for the parallels between our modern plea bargaining system and the ancient system of judicial torture are many and chilling.

Let us begin by recollecting the rudiments of the American system of plea bargaining in cases of serious crime. Plea bargaining occurs when the prosecutor induces an accused criminal to confess guilt and to waive his right to trial in exchange for a more lenient criminal sanction than would be imposed if the accused were adjudicated guilty following trial. The prosecutor offers leniency either directly, in the form of a charge reduction, or indirectly, through the connivance of the judge, in the form of a recommendation for reduced sentence that the judge will follow. In exchange for procuring this leniency for the accused, the prosecutor is relieved of the need to prove the accused's guilt, and the court is spared having to adjudicate it. The court condemns the accused on the basis of his confession, without independent adjudication.

Plea bargaining is, therefore, a nontrial procedure for convicting and condemning the accused criminal. If you turn to the American Constitution in search of authority for plea bargaining, you will look in vain. Instead, you will find—in no less hallowed a place than the Bill of Rights—an opposite guarantee, a guarantee of trial. The Sixth Amendment provides: "In *all* criminal prosecutions, the accused shall enjoy the right to . . . trial . . . by an impartial jury . . ." (emphasis added).

In our day, jury trial continues to occupy its central place both in the formal law and in the mythology of the law. The Constitution has not changed, the courts pretend to enforce the defendant's right to jury trial, and television transmits a steady flow of dramas in which a courtroom contest for the verdict of the jury leads inexorably to the disclosure of the true culprit. In truth, criminal jury trial has largely disappeared in America. The criminal justice system now disposes of virtually all cases of serious crime through plea bargaining. In the major cities between 95 and 99 percent of felony convictions are by plea. This nontrial procedure has become the ordinary dispositive procedure of American law.

Why has our formal system of proof been set out of force and this nontrial system substituted for the trial procedure envisaged by the Framers? Scholars are only beginning to investigate the history of plea bargaining, but enough is known to permit us to speak with some confidence about the broad outline. In the two centuries from the mid-eighteenth to the mid-twentieth, a vast transformation overcame the Anglo-American institution of criminal jury trial, rendering it absolutely unworkable as an ordinary dispositive procedure and requiring the development of an alternative procedure, which we now recognize to be the plea bargaining system.

In eighteenth-century England jury trial was still a *summary proceeding*. In the Old Bailey in the 1730s we know that the court routinely processed between 12 and 20 jury trials for felony in a single day. A single jury would be impaneled and would hear evidence in numerous unrelated cases before retiring to formulate verdicts in all. Lawyers were not employed in the conduct of ordinary criminal trials, either for the prosecution or the defense. The trial judge called the witnesses (whom the local justice of the peace had bound over to appear), and the proceeding transpired as a relatively unstructured altercation between the witnesses and the accused. Plea bargaining was unknown—indeed, judges actively discouraged pleas of guilty even from defendants who tendered them voluntarily and without hope of sentencing concessions. In the 1790s, when the Americans were constitutionalizing English jury trial, it was still rapid and efficient. The trial of Hardy for high treason in 1794 was the first that ever lasted more than one day, and the court seriously considered whether it had any power to adjourn. By contrast, we may note that the trial of Patricia Hearst for bank robbery in 1976 lasted 40 days and that the average felony jury trial in Los Angeles in 1968 required 7.2 days of trial time. In the eighteenth century the most characteristic (and time-consuming) features of modern jury trial, namely adversary procedure and the exclusionary rules of the law of criminal evidence, were still primitive and uncharacteristic. The accused's right to representation by retained counsel was not generalized to all felonies until the end of the

eighteenth century in America and the nineteenth century in England. Appellate review was very restricted into the twentieth century; counsel for indigent accused was not required until the middle of this century. The practices that so protract modern American jury trials—extended *voir dire* (pretrial probing of the views and backgrounds of individual jurors for juror challenges), exclusionary rules and other evidentiary barriers, motions designed to provoke and preserve issues for appeal, maneuvers and speeches of counsel, intricate and often incomprehensible instructions to the jury—all are late growths in the long history of common-law criminal procedure. No wonder, then, that plea bargaining appears to have been a late-nineteenth-century growth that was scarcely acknowledged to exist in the United States before the 1920s. (The English are only now facing up to the fact of their dependence on plea bargaining.)

Nobody should be surprised that jury trial has undergone great changes over the last two centuries. It desperately needed reform. The level of safeguard against mistaken conviction was in several respects below what civilized peoples now require. What we will not understand until there has been research directed to the question, is why the pressure for greater safeguards led in the Anglo-American procedure to the law of evidence and the lawyerization of the trial, reforms that ultimately destroyed the system in the sense that they made jury trial so complicated and time-consuming as to be unworkable as the routine dispositive procedure.

Similar pressures for safeguards were being felt on the Continent in the same period, but they led to reforms in nonadversarial procedure that preserved the institution of trial. In the middle of the nineteenth century, when Continental criminal procedure was being given its modern shape, the draftsmen of the European codes routinely studied Anglo-American procedure as a reform model. They found much to admire and to borrow, but they resisted the temptation to adversary domination. Their experience with the way that their medieval rules of evidence had led to the law of torture also left them unwilling to imitate the nascent Anglo-American law of evidence. And they were unanimous in rejecting the institution of the guilty plea. As early as the 1850s German writers were saying that it was wrong for a court to sentence an accused on mere confession, without satisfying itself of his guilt.

PARALLELS TO THE LAW OF TORTURE

Let me now turn to my main theme—the parallels in function and doctrine between the medieval European system of judicial torture and our plea bargaining system. The starting point, which will be obvious from what I have thus far said, is that each of these substitute procedural systems arose in response to the breakdown of the formal system of trial that it subverted. Both the medieval European law of proof and the modern Anglo-American law of jury trial set out to safeguard the accused by circumscribing the discretion of the trier in criminal adjudication. The medieval Europeans were trying to eliminate the discretion of the professional judge by requiring him to adhere to objective criteria of proof. The Anglo-American trial system has been caught up over the last two centuries in an effort to protect the accused against the dangers of the jury system, in which laymen ignorant of the law return a one- or two-word verdict that they do not explain or justify. Each system found itself unable to recant directly on the unrealistic level of safeguard to which it had committed itself, and each then concentrated on inducing the accused to tender a confession that would waive his right to the safeguards.

The European law of torture preserved the medieval law of proof undisturbed for those easy cases in which there were two eyewitnesses or voluntary confession. But in the more difficult cases (where, I might add, safeguard was more important), the law of torture worked an absolutely fundamental change within the system of proof: It largely *eliminated the adjudicative function*. Once probable cause had been determined, the accused was made to concede his guilt rather than his accusers to prove it.

In twentieth-century America we have duplicated the central experience of medieval European criminal procedure. We have moved from an adjudicatory to a concessionary system. We coerce the accused against whom we find probable cause to confess his guilt. To be sure, our means are much more polite; we use no rack, no thumbscrew, no Spanish boot to mash his legs. But like the Europeans of distant centuries who did employ those machines, we make

it terribly costly for an accused to claim his right to the constitutional safeguard of trial. We threaten him with a materially increased sanction if he avails himself of his right and is thereafter convicted. This sentencing differential is what makes plea bargaining coercive. There is, of course, a difference between having your limbs crushed if you refuse to confess, or suffering some extra years of imprisonment if you refuse to confess, but the difference is of degree, not kind. Plea bargaining, like torture, is coercive. Like the medieval Europeans, the Americans are now operating a procedural system that engages in condemnation without adjudication. The maxim of the medieval Glossators, no longer applicable to European law, now aptly describes American law: *Confessio est regina probationum,* confession is the queen of proof.

Supporters of plea bargaining typically maintain that a "mere" sentencing differential is not sufficiently coercive to pressure an innocent accused to convict himself. That point can be tested in the abstract simply by imagining a differential so great—for example, death versus a 50-cent fine—that any rational defendant would waive even the strongest defenses. The question of whether significant numbers of innocent people do plead guilty is not, of course, susceptible to empirical testing. It has been established that many of those who plead guilty claim that they are innocent. More importantly, prosecutors widely admit to bargaining hardest when the case is weakest, which is why the leading article on the subject, by Albert Alschuler ("The Prosecutor's Role in Plea Bargaining," University of Chicago Law Review, 1968), concluded that "the greatest pressures to plead guilty are brought to bear on defendants who may be innocent." Alschuler recounted one such case:

San Francisco defense attorney Benjamin M. Davis recently represented a man charged with kidnapping and forcible rape. The defendant was innocent, Davis says, and after investigating the case Davis was confident of an acquittal. The prosecutor, who seems to have shared the defense attorney's opinion on this point, offered to permit a guilty plea to simple battery. Conviction on this charge would not have led to a greater sentence than 30 days' imprisonment, and there was every likelihood that the defendant would be granted probation. When Davis informed his client of this offer, he emphasized that conviction at trial seemed highly improbable. The defendant's reply was simple: "I can't take the chance."

I do not think that great numbers of Americans plead guilty to offenses committed by strangers. (The European law of torture was also not supposed to apply in the easy cases where the accused could forthrightly explain away the evidence that might otherwise have given cause to examine him under torture.) I do believe that plea bargaining is used to coerce the waiver of tenable defenses, as in attorney Davis's example, and in cases where the offense has a complicated conceptual basis, as in tax and other white-collar crimes. Like the medieval law of torture, the sentencing differential in plea bargaining elicits confessions of guilt that would not be freely tendered, and some of the confessions are false. Plea bargaining is therefore coercive in the same sense as torture, although surely not in the same degree.

I do not mean to say that excesses of the plea bargaining system affect only the innocent who is coerced to plead guilty or the convict whose sentence is made more severe because he insisted on his right to trial. In other circumstances plea bargaining has been practiced in ways that result in unjustified leniency. Many observers have been struck by the extent of the concessions that prosecutors have been prepared to make in serious criminal cases in order to avoid having to go to trial. One Alaskan prosecutor told Alschuler in 1976 that "prosecutors can get rid of everything if they just go low enough. The police complained that we were giving cases away, and they were right."

I have said that European law attempted to devise safeguards for the use of torture that proved illusory; these measures bear an eerie resemblance to the supposed safeguards of the American law of plea bargaining. Foremost among the illusory safeguards of both systems is the doctrinal preoccupation with characterizing the induced waivers as voluntary. The Europeans made the torture victim repeat his confession "voluntarily," but under the threat of being tortured anew if he recanted. The American counterpart is Rule 11(d) of the Federal Rules of Criminal Procedure, which forbids the court from accepting a guilty plea without first "addressing the defendant personally in open court, determining that the plea is voluntary and not the result of force or threats or of promises *apart from a plea agreement.*" Of course, the plea agreement is the *source* of

the coercion and already embodies the involuntariness.

The architects of the European law of torture sought to enhance the reliability of a torture-induced confession with other safeguards designed to substantiate its factual basis. We have said that they required a probable-cause determination for investigation under torture and that they directed the court to take steps to verify the accuracy of the confession by investigating some of its detail. We have explained why these measures were inadequate to protect many innocent suspects from torture, confession, and condemnation. Probable cause is not the same as guilt, and verification, even if undertaken in good faith, could easily fail as a safeguard, either because the matters confessed were not susceptible of physical or testimonial corroboration, or because the accused might know enough about the crime to lend verisimilitude to his confession even though he was not in fact the culprit.

The American law of plea bargaining has pursued a similar chimera: the requirement of "adequate factual basis for the plea." Federal Rule 11(f) provides that "the court should not enter judgment upon [a guilty] plea without making such inquiry as shall satisfy it that there is a factual basis for the plea." As with the tortured confession, so with the negotiated plea: Any case that has resisted dismissal for want of probable cause at the preliminary hearing will rest upon enough inculpating evidence to cast suspicion upon the accused. The function of trial, which plea bargaining eliminates, is to require the court to adjudicate whether the facts proven support an inference of guilt beyond a reasonable doubt. Consider, however, the case of *North Carolina* v. *Alford,* decided in this decade, in which the U.S. Supreme Court found it permissible to condemn without trial a defendant who had told the sentencing court: "I pleaded guilty on second degree murder because they said there is too much evidence, but I ain't shot no man. . . . I just pleaded guilty because they said if I didn't they would gas me for it. . . . I'm not guilty but I plead guilty." I invite you to compare Alford's statement with the explanation of one Johannes Julius, seventeenth-century burgomaster of Bamberg, who wrote from his dungeon cell where he was awaiting execution, in order to tell his daughter why he had confessed to witchcraft "for which I must die. It is all falsehood and invention, so help me God. . . . They never cease to torture until one says something."

The tortured confession is, of course, markedly less reliable than the negotiated plea, because the degree of coercion is greater. An accused is more likely to bear false witness against himself in order to escape further hours on the rack than to avoid risking a longer prison term. But the resulting moral quandary is the same. Judge Levin of Michigan was speaking of the negotiated guilty plea, but he could as well have been describing the tortured confession when he said, "there is no way of knowing whether a particular guilty plea was given because the accused believed he was guilty, or because of the promised concession." Beccaria might as well have been speaking of the coercion of plea bargaining when he said of the violence of torture that it "confounds and obliterates those minute differences between things which enable us at times to know truth from falsehood." The doctrine of adequate factual basis for the plea is no better substitute for proof beyond reasonable doubt than was the analogous doctrine in the law of torture.

The factual unreliability of the negotiated plea has further consequences, quite apart from the increased danger of condemning an innocent man. In the plea bargaining that takes the form of charge bargaining (as opposed to sentence bargaining), the culprit is convicted not for what he did, but for something less opprobrious. When people who have murdered are said to be convicted of wounding, or when those caught stealing are nominally convicted of attempt or possession, cynicism about the processes of criminal justice is inevitably reinforced. This willful mislabelling plays havoc with our crime statistics, which explains in part why Americans—uniquely among Western peoples—attach so much importance to arrest records rather than to records of conviction. I think that the unreliability of the plea, the mislabelling of the offense, and the underlying want of adjudication all combine to weaken the moral force of the criminal law, and to increase the public's unease about the administration of criminal justice. The case of James Earl Ray is perhaps the best example of public dissatisfaction over the intrinsic failure of the plea bargaining system to establish the facts about crime and guilt in the forum of a public trial. Of course, not every trial resolves the question of guilt or innocence to public satisfaction. The Sacco-Vanzetti and Rosenberg cases continue to be relitigated in the forum of popular opinion. But plea bargaining leaves the public with what I believe to be a more pronounced sense of unease about the justness of results, because it avoids the open ventilation and critical evaluation of evidence that characterize public trial. (Just this concern appears to have motivated the government in the plea-bargained bribery case of Vice President Agnew to take extraordinary steps to assure the disclosure of the substance of the prosecution case.) It is interesting to remember that in Europe in the age of Beccaria and Voltaire, the want of adjudication and the unreliability of the law of torture had bred a strangely similar cynicism towards the criminal justice system of that day.

THE MORAL BLUNDER

Because plea bargaining involves condemnation without adjudication, it undermines a moral postulate of the criminal justice system so basic and elementary that in past centuries Anglo-American writers seldom bothered to express it: Serious criminal sanctions should only be imposed when the trier has examined the relevant evidence and found the accused guilty beyond reasonable doubt.

Why have we been able to construct a nontrial procedure that is irreconcilable with this fundamental proposition? A major reason is that we have been beguiled by the similarities between civil and criminal litigation in our lawyer-dominated procedural system. "What's wrong with settling cases?" the argument runs. "Surely society is correct not to insist on full-scale adjudication of every private grievance. If the parties are satisfied with their deal, there is no social interest in adjudication. Likewise in criminal adjudication: If the prosecutor and the accused can reach agreement about the sanction, hasn't the matter been satisfactorily concluded?"

The answer is that because the social interest in criminal adjudication differs importantly from that in civil cases, the deeply embedded policy in favor of negotiated (nontrial) settlement of civil disputes is misapplied when transposed to the criminal setting. There is good reason for treating adjudication as the norm in the criminal law, but as a last and exceptional resort in private law. Kenneth Kipnis has provided a wry illustration of the distinction with an example drawn from neither. Kipnis asks us to imagine a system of "grade bargaining," in which the teacher would offer a student a favorable grade in exchange for a waiver of the student's right to have the teacher read his examination paper. The teacher would save time, thus conserve his resources, and the student would not accept the teacher's grade offer unless he calculated it to be in his interest by comparison with his expected results from conventional grading.

We see instantly what is wrong with grade bargaining. Because third parties rely upon grades in admissions and hiring decisions, the grade bargain would adversely affect the legitimate interests of these outsiders. And because the grade is meant to inform the student about the teacher's perception of the comparative quality of his performance, the grade bargain would disserve the larger interest of the student.

Quite analogous objections apply to plea bargaining. Criminal sanctions are imposed for public purposes: certainly in order to deter future crime, probably still with the object of reforming at least some offenders, and perhaps still in the interest of retribution. Sentences that satisfy the accused's wish to minimize the sanction and the prosecutor's need to reduce his trial caseload are arrived at with only passing attention to these social interests. In particular, the enormous sentence differential needed to sustain the plea bargaining system is repugnant to any tenable theory of sentencing. We can scarcely claim to be tailoring the sentence to the crime when one of the largest aggravating factors we consult is whether the accused had the temerity to ask for his right to trial. The truth is that when an accused is convicted following jury trial, we customarily punish him twice: once for the crime, and then more severely for what the Constitution calls "enjoy[ing] the right to . . . trial . . . by an impartial jury."

Twenty years ago in a celebrated article the late Henry Hart compared so-called "civil commitment" for mental or contagious disease with imprisonment for criminal conviction. Many a prison is more pleasant than a nearby asylum. Why, then, do we treat the decision to imprison as the more serious and surround it with safeguards that, at least in theory, are more substantial than those for the civil-commitment process? Notwithstanding the operational similarity between civil and criminal sanctions, said Hart, there is a profound difference in purpose. "The core of the difference is that the patient has not incurred the moral condemnation of his community, whereas the convict has." The very stigma of criminal conviction is the source of much of the deterrent and retributive power of the criminal sanction. I believe that this moral force of the criminal sanction is partially dependent on the sanction having been imposed after rational inquiry and decision on the facts. Adjudication alone legitimates the infliction of serious criminal sanctions, because it alone is adequate to separate the innocent from the guilty and to establish the basis for proportioning punishment to the degree of culpability. To assert (as a defender of plea bargaining must) the equivalency of waiver and of adjudication is to overlook the distinctive characteristic of the criminal law.

THE PROSECUTOR

Our law of plea bargaining has not only recapitulated much of the doctrinal folly of the law of torture, complete with the pathetic safeguards of voluntariness and factual basis, but it has also repeated the main institutional blunder of the law of torture. Plea bargaining concentrates effective control of criminal procedure in the hands of a single officer. Our formal law of trial envisages a division of responsibility. We expect the prosecutor to make the charging decision, the judge and especially the jury to adjudicate, and the judge to set the sentence. Plea bargaining merges these accusatory, determinative, and sanctional phases of the procedure in the hands of the prosecutor. Students of the history of the law of torture are reminded that the great psychological fallacy of the European inquisitorial procedure of that time was that it concentrated in the investigating magistrate the powers of accusation, investigation, torture, and condemnation. The single inquisitor who wielded those powers needed to have what one recent historian has called "superhuman capabilities [in order to] . . . keep himself in his decisional function free from the predisposing influences of his own instigating and investigating activity."

The dominant version of American plea bargaining makes similar demands: It requires the prosecutor to usurp the determinative and sentencing functions, hence to make himself judge in his own cause. There are dangers in this concentration of prosecutorial power. One need not necessarily accept Jimmy Hoffa's view that Robert Kennedy was conducting a personal and political vendetta against him in order to appreciate the danger that he might have been. The power to prosecute as we know it carries within itself the power to persecute. The modern public prosecutor commands the vast resources of the state for gathering and generating accusing evidence. We allowed him this power in large part because the criminal trial interposed the safeguard of adjudication against the danger that he might bring those resources to bear against an innocent citizen—whether on account of honest error, arbitrariness, or worse. But the plea bargaining system has largely dissolved that safeguard.

While on the subject of institutional factors, I have one last comparison to advance. The point has been made, most recently by the Attorney General of Alaska, that preparing and taking cases to trial is much harder work than plea bargaining—for police, prosecutors, judges, and defense counsel. In short, convenience—or worse, sloth—is a factor that sustains plea bargaining. We suppose that this factor had a little to do with torture as well. As someone in India remarked to Sir James Fitzjames Stephen in 1872 about the proclivity of the native policemen for torturing suspects, "It is far pleasanter to sit comfortably in the shade rubbing red pepper into a poor devil's eyes than to go about in the sun hunting up evidence." If we were to generalize about this point, we might say that concessionary criminal-procedural systems like the plea bargaining system and the system of judicial torture may develop their own bureaucracies and constituencies. Here as elsewhere the old adage may apply that if necessity is the mother of invention, laziness is the father.

THE JURISPRUDENCE OF CONCESSION

Having developed these parallels between torture and plea bargaining, I want to draw some conclusions about what I regard as the lessons of the exercise. The most important is this: A legal system will do almost anything, tolerate almost anything, before it will admit the need for reform in its system of proof and trial. The law of torture endured for half a millennium although its dangers and defects had been understood virtually from the outset; and plea bargaining lives on although its evils are quite familiar to us all. What makes such shoddy subterfuges so tenacious is that they shield their legal systems from having to face up to the fact of breakdown in the formal law of proof and trial.

Why is it so hard for a legal system to reform a decadent system of proof? I think that there are two main reasons, one in a sense practical, the other ideological. From the standpoint of the practical, nothing seems quite so embedded in a legal system as the procedures for proof and trial, because most of what a legal system does is to decide matters of proof—what we call "fact finding." (Was the traffic light green or red? Was this accused the man who fired the shot or robbed the bank?) Blackstone emphasized this point in speaking of civil litigation, and it is even more true of criminal litigation. He said: "Experience will abundantly shew, that above a hundred of our lawsuits arise from disputed facts, for one where the law is doubted of." Every institution of the legal system is geared to the system of proof; forthright reconstruction would disturb, at one level or another, virtually every vested interest.

The inertia, the resistance to change that is associated with such deep-seated interests, is inevitably reinforced by the powerful ideological component that underlies a system of proof and trial. Adjudication, especially criminal adjudication, involves a profound intrusion into the lives of affected citizens. Consequently, in any society the adjudicative power must be rested on a theoretical basis that makes it palatable to the populace. Because the theory of proof purports to govern and explain the application of the adjudicative power, it plays a central role in legitimating the entire legal system. The medieval European law of proof assured people that the legal system would achieve certainty. The Anglo-American jury system invoked the inscrutable wisdom of the folk to justify its results. Each of these theories was ultimately untenable—the European theory virtually from its inception, the Anglo-American theory after a centuries-long transformation of jury procedure. Yet the ideological importance of these theories prevented either legal system from recanting them. For example, I have elsewhere pointed out how in the nineteenth century the ideological attachment to the jury retarded experimentation with juryless trial—that is, what we now call bench trial—while the plea bargaining system of juryless nontrial procedure was taking shape out of public sight. Like the medieval European lawyers before us, we have been unable to admit that our theory of proof has resulted in a level of procedural complexity and safeguard that renders our trial procedure unworkable in all but exceptional cases. We have responded to the breakdown of our formal system of proof by taking steps to perpetuate the ideology of the failed system, steps that closely resemble those taken by the architects of the law of torture. *Like the medieval Europeans, we have preserved an unworkable trial procedure in form, we have devised a substitute nontrial procedure to subvert the formal procedure, and we have arranged to place defendants under fierce pressure to "choose" the substitute.*

That this script could have been played out in a pair of legal cultures so remote from each other in time and place invites some suggestions about the adaptive processes of criminal procedural systems. First, there are intrinsic limits to the level of complexity and safeguard that even a civilized people can tolerate. If those limits are exceeded and the repressive capacity of the criminal justice system is thereby endangered, the system will respond by developing subterfuges that overcome the formal law. But subterfuges are intrinsically overbroad, precisely because they are not framed in a careful, explicit, and principled manner directed to achieving a proper balance between repression and safeguard. The upshot is that the criminal justice system is saddled with a lower level of safeguard than it could and would have achieved if it had not pretended to retain the unworkable formal system.

The medieval Europeans insisted on two eyewitnesses and wound up with a law of torture that allowed condemnation with no witnesses at all. American plea bargaining, in like fashion, sacrifices just those values that the unworkable system of adversary jury trial is meant to serve: lay participation in criminal adjudication, the presumption of innocence, the prosecutorial burden of proof beyond reasonable doubt, the right to confront and cross-examine accusers, the privilege against self-incrimination. Especially in its handling of the privilege against self-incrimination does American criminal procedure reach the outer bounds of incoherence. We have exaggerated the privilege to senseless lengths in formal doctrine, while in the plea bargaining system—which is our routine procedure for processing cases of serious crime—we have eliminated practically every trace of the privilege.

Furthermore, the sacrifice of our fundamental values through plea bargaining is needless.

In its sad plea bargaining opinions of the 1970s, the Supreme Court has effectively admitted that for reasons of expediency American criminal justice cannot honor its promise of routine adversary criminal trial, but the Court has simply assumed that the present nontrial plea bargaining procedure is the inevitable alternative. There is, however, a middle path between the impossible system of routine adversary jury trial and the disgraceful nontrial system of plea bargaining. That path is a streamlined nonadversarial trial procedure.

ROUTINE NONADVERSARIAL TRIALS

The contemporary nonadversarial criminal justice systems of countries like West Germany have long demonstrated that advanced industrial societies can institute efficient criminal procedures that nevertheless provide for lay participation and for full adjudication in every case of serious crime. I have described the German system in detail in my *Comparative Criminal Procedure: Germany* (1977), and I have made no secret of my admiration for the brilliant balance that it strikes between safeguard and procedural effectiveness. Not the least of its achievements is that in cases of serious crime it functions with no plea bargaining whatsoever. Confessions are still tendered in many cases (41 percent in one sample), but they are not and cannot be bargained for; nor does a confession excuse the trial court from hearing sufficient evidence for conviction on what amounts to a beyond-reasonable-doubt standard of proof. In a trial procedure shorn of all the excesses of adversary procedure and the law of evidence, the time difference between trial without confession and trial with confession is not all that great. Because an accused will be put to trial whether he confesses or not, he cannot inflict significant costs upon the prosecution by contesting an overwhelming case. Confessions are tendered at trial not because they are rewarded, but because there is no advantage to be wrung from the procedural system by withholding them.

Plea bargaining is all but incomprehensible to the Europeans, whose ordinary dispositive procedure is workable without such evasions. In the German press, the judicial procedure surrounding the criminal conviction and resignation of Vice President Agnew was viewed with the sort of wonder normally inspired by reports of the customs of primitive tribes. The

Badische Zeitung reported as the story unfolded in October 1973: "The resignation occurred as part of a 'cowtrade,' as it can only in the United States be imagined."

I hope that over the coming decades we who still live under criminal justice systems that engage in condemnation without adjudication will face up to the failure of adversary criminal procedure. I believe that we will find in modern Continental criminal procedure an irresistible model for reform. For the moment, however, I am left to conclude with a paradox. Today in lands where the law of torture once governed, peoples who live in contentment with their criminal justice systems look out across the sea in disbelief to the spectacle of plea bargaining in America, while American tourists come by the thousands each year to gawk in disbelief at the decaying torture chambers of medieval castles.

UNITED STATES v. DE COSTER

United States Court of Appeals, D.C. Circuit, 1978*

BAZELON, Chief Judge:

. . . The only serious issue in this case is whether appellant was denied his constitutionally guaranteed right to the effective assistance of counsel. . . .

I

The facts are relatively simple. The victim testified that he was accosted by appellant and two accomplices in a parking lot at about 6 p.m. He stated that one of the accomplices held him from behind, while the other stood in front of him with a knife and appellant went through his pockets. The robbers took a wallet containing $110, then fled when the police arrived.

Two policemen testified that they were cruising in an unmarked car when they saw the robbery in progress. The officers alighted from their vehicle and gave chase. One officer followed and arrested a man identified as Eley, and found a straight razor in his pocket. The second policeman and the victim chased appellant and his other cohort. When this pair of robbers split up, the policeman continued after appellant. The officer's quarry ran into a nearby hotel and the policeman followed; he found appellant standing at the desk in the lobby and arrested him. The victim immediately identified appellant as one of the robbers. A search of appellant turned up neither the stolen wallet nor any weapons. And neither officer had seen any weapon in use during the robbery.

Between the time of the offense and the time of trial, the victim was in a serious automobile accident, which caused lapses in his memory and damage to his eyesight. At trial, he was unable to identify either appellant or the straight razor taken from Eley.

Appellant testified that on the afternoon of the crime he met the victim for the first time at a bar near the parking lot where the robbery was alleged to have occurred. At around 6 p.m., after having a few drinks with the victim, appellant claims to have returned to his hotel, where he was arrested while trying to obtain his key from the desk. The victim was unsure whether he had met appellant before the robbery. The accomplice, Eley, testified that on the day of the

robbery he saw appellant and the victim drinking together at the bar and, later, fighting in a nearby parking lot when the police arrived.

. . . DeCoster was convicted by a jury of aiding and abetting in an armed robbery and an assault with a dangerous weapon. He was sentenced to 2–8 years on each count, to be served concurrently.

II

Several events and circumstances suggest that appellant may have been denied his sixth amendment right to the effective assistance of counsel:

(1) Although appellant, who failed to meet bail, was accepted for pretrial custody by Black Man's Development Center on October 12, counsel did not file a bond review motion until November 9. Even then, the motion did not mention the third party custody arrangement, and was filed in the wrong court. On November 13, DeCoster wrote to the court indicating that counsel had promised he would file a motion for his release. On December 8, counsel filed a motion in the proper court and defendant was released.

(2) It appears that defense counsel (who is not counsel on appeal) announced "ready" although he was not prepared to go to trial. As appellant's two day trial was about to begin, the following colloquy regarding the Government's alibi demand notice occurred:

Court: All right, are you ready for trial? If you are can you give the names and addresses [of your alibi witnesses] to the prosecutor? Are you prepared to give the names and addresses?

Defense: No, at the present time I am not. . . .

Court: Well are you here for trial?

Defense: I am here for trial but if the court pleases, under the statute we have 20 days.

Court: Are you asking for a continuance?

Defense: I would ask for a 4 or 5 day continuance for this trial which might give me an opportunity to give the prosecutor what we can in response to this notice.

Court: Well you did announce ready for trial, . . . and if you are going to rely on an alibi, then you must know the witnesses you are going to use as alibi witnesses. You announced ready.

*624 F.2d. 196 (D.C. Cir 1978).

. . .

Court: [I]t seems to me that if you have your witnesses ready for trial there seems to be no reason why you shouldn't be able to give the names of the people you intend to call as alibi witnesses at this time.

Defense: We will proceed without alibi witnesses. We will consider we don't have any alibi witnesses.

Court: You will not rely on an alibi defense?

Defense: That is correct.

(3) Counsel apparently made no effort to inquire into the disposition of the cases against appellant's two alleged accomplices. In fact, they had both already pled guilty before the same judge who was to sit on DeCoster's case. Thus, counsel agreed to waive a jury trial totally unaware that his client would, as the court pointed out, "be tried by a judge who has heard a portion of this evidence in connection with the other two defendants." (The Government, however, refused to waive a jury trial.)

(4) There are indications of a lack of communication between appellant and his trial counsel. When DeCoster personally requested the court to subpoena his two accomplices, counsel indicated that he had thought of calling them but "we have no address [*sic*] for them." Appellant immediately responded that one of the men was at the D.C. Jail under sentence for the instant offense. The other man had recently been placed on probation, also for his involvement in the instant offense, by the same judge who was presiding over DeCoster's case. This witness was never called.

Defendant informed the court, first by letter and then at the opening of trial, that he was dissatisfied with his appointed counsel. On the later occasion he pleaded:

Your honor, I feel that this case should be continued because this is, I can't get proper representation that I should be getting.

His request was denied without inquiry into the basis of his claim.

(5) The defense called only two witnesses: appellant and an alleged accomplice who contradicted appellant on a fundamental point. On direct examination, he placed DeCoster at the scene of the crime engaged in a fight with the victim at a time when DeCoster himself had testified he was at his hotel. This contradiction confused the defense case and stripped it of its credibility.

III

. . . This court does not sit to second guess strategic and tactical choices made by trial counsel. However, when counsel's choices are uninformed because of inadequate preparation, a defendant is denied the effective assistance of counsel. The pres-ent record, as is typical in cases raising a claim of ineffectiveness, poses more questions about counsel's preparation and investigation than it answers. For example, it is unclear whether an informed tactical judgment or a lack of preparation was at the root of counsel's inability to identify any alibi witnesses at the outset of trial, or his decision to call both DeCoster and his accomplice who contradicted him. Accordingly, the record is remanded for a supplemental hearing on counsel's preparation and investigation, and appellant's present counsel is given leave to file a motion for a new trial on remand.

IV

Since we remand for a determination of appellant's claim, it is necessary to discuss the governing principles. The effective assistance of counsel is a defendant's most fundamental right "for it affects his ability to assert any other right he may have." The Supreme Court has observed, "if the right to counsel guaranteed by the Constitution is to serve its purpose, defendants cannot be left to the mercies of incompetent counsel."

The first major ineffectiveness case in this Circuit was Jones v. Huff, . . . Applying a due process-fundamental fairness approach, we held the standard to be whether counsel's incompetence rendered the trial a "farce and a mockery." In Bruce v. United States, . . ., we reconsidered *Jones* and held that the "farce and mockery" language was "not to be taken literally, but rather as a vivid description of the principle that the accused has a heavy burden in showing requisite unfairness." The rule announced in *Bruce* required a defendant to prove:

both that there has been gross incompetence of counsel and that this has in effect blotted out the essence of a substantial defense . . . 379 F.2d at 116–117.

In *Bruce,* the claim of ineffective assistance arose on collateral attack. In several cases since then, when the ineffectiveness issue was raised on direct appeal, the court has silently ignored the *Bruce* requirement that the defendant has a "heavy burden" to show prejudice implying that a different test was applicable on direct appeal.

. . . Indeed, in *Bruce* itself the court pointed out that "a more powerful showing of inadequacy is necessary to sustain a collateral attack than to warrant an order for a new trial either by the District Court or by this court on direct appeal." . . . Since these decisions leave uncertain the correct standard to be applied when the question of ineffectiveness is raised on direct appeal, we now address that issue.

In this regard we are mindful that there have been several important developments since *Bruce.* The test there, with its requirement of a "heavy burden" to show "unfairness," appears to rest on the theory that an ineffectiveness claim is grounded in the due process clause. Since then, however, the Supreme Court has implied and this court has explicitly held, that effective assistance, like the right to counsel itself, derives not only from the due process clause, but from the sixth amendment's "more stringent requirements." Consistent with this recognition the Court has continued to repeat that the purpose of counsel is to "preserve the adversary process" and that counsel must act "in the role of an active advocate in behalf of his client." In the guilty plea context, the court has held that the accused's right to effective assistance is the right to "reasonably competent" representation. And the Third, Fourth, and Fifth Circuits have already realized that there is no reason to require less when the accused does not plead guilty. Accordingly, we adopt the following standard: *a defendant is entitled to the reasonably competent assistance of an attorney acting as his diligent conscientious advocate.*

. . . Since "reasonably competent assistance" is only a shorthand label, and not subject to ready application, we follow the approach adopted by the Fourth Circuit and set forth some of the duties owed by counsel to a client:

In General—Counsel should be guided by the American Bar Association Standards for the Defense Function. They represent the legal profession's own articulation of guidelines for the defense of criminal cases.

Specifically—(1) Counsel should confer with his client without delay and as often as necessary to elicit matters of defense, or to ascertain that potential defenses are unavailable. Counsel should discuss fully potential strategies and tactical choices with his client.

(2) Counsel should promptly advise his client of his rights and take all actions necessary to preserve them. Many rights can only be protected by prompt legal action. The Supreme Court has, for example, recognized the attorney's role in protecting the client's privilege against self-incrimination. . . . Counsel should also be concerned with the accused's right to be released from custody pending trial, and be prepared, where appropriate, to make motions for a pre-trial psychiatric examination or for the suppression of evidence.

(3) Counsel must conduct appropriate investigations, both factual and legal, to determine what matters of defense can be developed. The Supreme Court has noted that the adversary system requires that "all available defenses are raised" so that the government is put to its proof. This means that in most cases a defense attorney, or his agent, should interview not only his own witnesses but also those that the government intends to call, when they are accessible. The investigation should always include efforts to secure information in the possession of the prosecution and law enforcement

authorities. And, of course, the duty to investigate also requires adequate legal research.

. . . If a defendant shows a substantial violation of any of these requrements he has been denied effective representations unless the government, "on which is cast the burden of proof once a violation of these precepts is shown, can establish lack of prejudice thereby."

. . . Two factors justify this requirement. First, in our constitutionally prescribed adversary system the burden is on the government to prove guilt. A requirement that the defendant show prejudice, on the other hand, shifts the burden to him and makes him establish the likelihood of his innocence. It is no answer to say that the appellant has already had a trial in which the government was put to its proof because the heart of his complaint is that the absence of the effective assistance of counsel has deprived him of a full adversary trial.

Second, proof of prejudice may well be absent from the record precisely because counsel has been ineffective. For example, when counsel fails to conduct an investigation, the record may not indicate which witnesses he could have called, or defenses he would have raised.

V

. . . Much of the evidence of counsel's ineffectiveness is frequently not reflected in the trial record (*e.g.*, a failure to investigate the case, or to interview the defendant or a witness before trial). As a result, ineffectiveness cases have often evolved into tests of whether appellate judges can hypothesize a rational explanation for the apparent errors in the conduct of trial. But neither one judge's surmise nor another's doubt can take the place of proof. Thus, when a claim of ineffective assistance is contemplated, it should first be presented to the district court in a motion for a new trial. In such proceeding, evidence *dehors* the record may be submitted by affidavit, and when necessary the district judge may order a hearing or otherwise allow counsel to respond. If the trial court is willing to grant the motion, this court will remand. If the motion is denied, the appeal therefrom will be consolidated with the appeal from the conviction and sentence. The record of any hearing held on the motion, and any documents submitted below, will become part of the record on appeal.

Record remanded.

HENRY H. PERRITT, JR.

A Broad View of Dispute Resolution*

THEORY OF DISPUTE RESOLUTION

Meaningful evaluation of dispute resolution alternatives should work from some theoretical conception as to how private disputes are resolved. A body of literature on the theory of dispute resolution has developed during the last two decades. Generally, the commentators working in this area have sought to explain the dynamics of negotiation and settlement of disputes, to explain how the positions of the parties may be changed by litigation, and to identify the social costs of civil litigation.

A. TYPES OF DISPUTES

At the outset, one should distinguish between "interest disputes" and "rights disputes." The civil litigation system was designed to deal with rights disputes. Rights disputes presuppose an external principle or standard by which the claim can be settled. Interest disputes, in contrast, do not presuppose such a principle or standard. A simple negligence action or breach-of-contract claim are examples of rights disputes. Dean Hazard offers a good example of an interest dispute:

The type of dispute one gets into say, with one's friend, when you ask: Shall we go to the game or shall we stay at home and watch television? This kind of dispute requires a settlement procedure of some sort, but it is not the kind of dispute that is [suited for the courts].

B. BASIC PROCESSES FOR RESOLVING DISPUTES

1. DEFINITION OF TERMS. A discussion of dispute resolution theory can be enhanced by offering some definitions of basic dispute resolution procedures.

Negotiation is a process in which the parties to a dispute seek to resolve it themselves. Negotiation is the underlying, common process for most private disputes, and resolves about ninety percent of all civil cases filed in federal courts. The negotiation process is unlikely to be entirely absent in any form of private dispute, though negotiations may be suspended pending resort to other dispute resolution procedures. In negotiation, a rational party will accept any offer better than his Best Alternative To a Negotiated Agreement (BATNA). Settlement of a dispute through negotiation is possible when a "zone of agreement" exists. A zone of agreement exists when the claimant's BATNA is lower than his opponent's BATNA.

The availability of dispute resolution processes other than negotiation affects the BATNA's of the parties in the underlying negotiation, and therefore may create a zone of agreement when none would exist in the absence of the processes. For example, if a party is certain of obtaining a judgment of $10,000 in a trial, at a cost of $4,000, his BATNA in settlement negotiations will be $6,000. In the absence of any process for enforcing the claim (or some coercive power possessed by the claimant), the claimant's opponent's BATNA would be zero. A negotiated settlement is possible only because of the availability of a lawsuit or some other dispute resolution procedure. The availability of an enforcement process raises the opponent's BATNA above zero and, if it increases it at least to $6,000 in the example given, a zone of agreement exists.

Most alternatives to the trial offer lower costs, or a prediction of what payoff will result from a trial. Either lower costs or better predictions affect the BATNA's in settlement negotiations.

Adjudication is a formal process through which parties may obtain a third party decision about their dispute according to some pre-existing standard or principle. In the adjudication process, the parties seek to influence the decision maker in their favor by the

*Henry H. Perritt, Jr., "A Broad View of Dispute Resolution" (excerpt, footnotes omitted). Reprinted with permission from *Villanova Law Review*, Volume 29 #6, pp. 1229–1259. © Copyright 1984 by Villanova University.

presentation of logical arguments and the submission of factual proof linked to the pre-existing standard.

Adjudication is, of course, the protypical method of dispute resolution used by courts. It also is used by other dispute resolving institutions, such as arbitrators and administrative agencies. It is not, however, the only process other than negotiation for dispute resolution.

Arbitration is a process of dispute resolution in which a third party makes a decision. Arbitration may be more or less formal but usually it follows an adjudicatory model in which the disputing parties present their case through evidence and argument. In the pure form of arbitration, the third party decision maker is not a government official, and the decision is binding. So-called "nonbinding arbitration" is really fact finding.

Fact Finding is a process in which a third party to the dispute decides disputed facts in a nonbinding report. Fact finding usually resembles arbitration except that a fact finder's conclusions are not binding and an arbitrator's are. Fact finding does not directly resolve disputes because it is nonbinding; it can promote resolution of disputes by conditioning the expectations of the parties about what is obtainable in a binding process such as arbitration or a judicial trial. The survey results gathered in connection with a study of federal court-annexed arbitration are interesting in this respect. Counsel participating in this form of fact finding believed that settlement was promoted because the fact finding report became the focus of subsequent negotiations, or because the fact finding solution was perceived as reasonable. Fact finding, outside the special examples of court-annexed arbitration and public employee labor relations impasses, is used infrequently in two-party disputes. It can be useful, however, especially where counsel-negotiator perceptions are sufficiently close together to provide a zone of agreement, but client perceptions are sufficiently far apart to make negotiated settlement difficult or impossible. In order to change client perceptions about outcomes, though, the fact finding process must have characteristics that make it seem legitimate. This probably explains the attractiveness of court-annexed arbitration, and of rent-a-judge programs.

Mediation and *Conciliation* frequently are used to refer to the same process. In this process a third party assists the disputing parties in achieving a negotiated resolution of their dispute. To simplify the discussion, the term mediation will be used to refer to both mediation and conciliation. Mediation does not follow an adjudicatory model. Instead of aiming at a decision based on evidence and argument marshalled by the parties for their positions, the mediator aims at finding a solution that serves the underlying interests of the parties. Because mediation does not rely on proofs and argument, it does not depend for its legitimacy on the existence of a standard or principle according to which the dispute is to be resolved. Accordingly, it is inherently more suitable for interest disputes than any adjudicatory process.

Mediation also is useful in rights disputes. Frequently, mediation enhances integrative bargaining. In contrast, the adjudicatory methods of decision making enforce distributive or "zero-sum" bargaining. Eliminating the zero-sum constraint always makes settlement more likely.

Because adjudication is familiar to most lawyers and mediation is not, it is useful to elaborate on how mediation works. A mediator performs several different functions in a private dispute:

1. He may bring the parties together. This is a brokerage role. Brokerage is unnecessary when the parties have an ongoing relation, but it may be essential when the claimant is uncertain exactly who can take action that will satisfy his claim. This function is emphasized by Action Line and ombudsman programs. It is performed also in the common technique of the claimant's lawyer writing a letter to the person with whom his client has a dispute.

2. Establishing an atmosphere in which negotiations can proceed. Frequently two-party negotiations cannot proceed meaningfully because of interpersonal tensions or lack of structure for substantive communication. The mediator, by serving as a neutral chairman for discussions, can reduce these barriers by helping to set the agenda for negotiations and by enforcing the rules for civilized debate. The civilizing element of this function is apparent from the transcript of a simulated mediation of a landlord-tenant dispute, in which the mediator frequently cautions, "One person speaking at a time."

3. Collecting and judiciously communicating selected confidential material. The function

usually is performed by the technique, familiar in labor dispute mediation, of caucusing separately with the parties. By communicating information about the other party's position, the mediator can assist a party in understanding his opponent's BATNA. An accurate perception of the BATNA's on both sides is necessary to determine whether there is a potential zone of agreement and to assess how much change in position would be necessary to create a zone of agreement.

4. Helping to clarify values and derive responsible reservation prices. A skillful mediator can assist the parties in bargaining over interests rather than positions, as Professors Fisher and Ury urge. Professor Lon Fuller has pointed out that mediation commonly is directed, not toward achieving conformity to pre-existing norms, but toward the creation of the relevant norms themselves. A clear example is where a mediator assists the parties in working out the terms of a contract that defines their rights and duties toward one another. In such a case, there are no pre-existing rules or principles to guide mediation; it is the mediation process that produces the values or principles by which an acceptable settlement is measured. This is what makes mediation more useful than adjudication in interest disputes. In both interest and rights disputes, unrealistic demands can be tempered because the mediator helps the party understand for himself the underlying interest he wants to pursue and the relationship between different positions and service to that interest. Interests can be redefined so that positions can be more flexible, or so that joint gains, or "integrative bargaining," can take place.

Litigation is not a separate process. It is a means of invoking the state's power to strengthen the other processes mentioned here. In the ninety percent of civil lawsuits that are settled rather than going to trial, the state's power has been invoked in a way that reinforces the negotiation, mediation or fact finding processes. The filing of a lawsuit changes BATNA's and thus may produce a zone of agreement in negotiations. Other litigation processes change expectations about judgments obtainable after trial and thus further influence BATNA's. For example, conferences presided over by a judge or a subordinate court official are a form of mediation. Summary trial alternatives such as Judge Lambros' summary jury trial, or the Philadelphia asbestos bench trial, are forms of fact finding.

2. COURTS AS INSTITUTIONS FOR RESOLVING CIVIL DISPUTES Civil disputes are private and could be resolved privately. But modern states provide institutions for resolving civil disputes. The paradigm institution is a court. According to several legal philosophers, society provides civil courts to resolve disputes that might threaten social order if they cannot be resolved privately. In all of the answers suggested by legal philosophers, however, civil courts are treated as institutions the use of which is *optional*. There is little basis—in this part of the literature at least—for any argument that voluntary settlement of disputes outside the court system offends any constitutional rights or public policy. Rather, courts are provided only to handle those disputes that cannot be resolved privately and therefore threaten social order.

Professor Raz has attempted a general classification of functions of law that illustrates why courts might be socially desirable. Raz identifies four primary functions of law; (1) preventing undesirable behavior and securing desirable behavior, (2) providing facilities for private arrangements between individuals, (3) providing services and redistributing goods, and (4) settling unregulated disputes. Courts relate to all four functions.

Raz postulates three types of legal systems, within which courts would have different roles. Type A provides norms fulfilling all or some of the first three functions. It does not have norms stipulating procedures by which disputes can be settled authoritatively, i.e., it does not have courts. "Such a normative system will guide behavior, and in doing so will prevent many potential disputes. When a dispute does arise, reference to the norms will often help in reaching an agreed solution." However, there would be no authoritative way of deciding the correct solution to disputes governed by the norms of the system, and there would be disputes which could not be solved by direct reference to the norms, either because the norms are vague or because the case is not dealt with by the norms. In other words, the coercive power of the state would not be available to settle private disputes, and interest disputes would be "unregulated," in the sense that norms to guide their resolution would not exist.

A system of type B is similar to type A except that it includes authorities for settling disputes and regulating their operation. A system of type B would have courts, albeit with a strictly circumscribed role.

These authorities, however, have only power to settle questions of fact and pronounce about the correct application of existing norms to the case. Faced with cases not governed by existing norms or cases with regard to which the existing norms are vague, (i.e., interest disputes), the authorities will simply decline to make any decisions.

A system of type C does not provide any norms guiding the behavior of ordinary people and performing any of the first three functions. All of the norms for this type of system are concerned only with defining organs for settling disputes and regulating their operation. Sometimes the norms include norms making it a duty to bring the disputes before the relevant organs. "When faced with a dispute the organ may decide it in any way it likes." It does not state the reasons and is not bound to reach similar decisions in similar cases. The organs in a type C system clearly would not be adjudicatory in nature as that term is used by Professor Fuller and in this article. In this system, there could be no rights disputes, only interest disputes, but the coercive power of the state would be available to force resolution of private disputes.

Professor Raz asserts that real-world legal systems are a combination of types B and C. They provide for the settlement of both regulated and unregulated disputes, through there are certain types of unregulated disputes with which legal systems will refuse to interfere. "Many legal systems by establishing some principle of *stare decisis* transform automatically every unregulated dispute once it is brought before the courts into a regulated or at least a partially regulated one." In other words, courts tend to transform interest disputes into rights disputes.

Dean Hazard suggests that a society which is interested in resolving private disputes would reject a Type A system since such systems do not have authorities for settling disputes. According to Dean Hazard, a third party is often necessary to settle a private dispute. Without such a third party, the disputants often cannot negotiate to a conclusion.

Professor Fuller offers a roughly similar explanation of why a Type A system would not serve a modern society well. He maintans that, although courts may not be necessary to settle disputes in a small society with relatively simple rules, they are essential in a complex society such as ours. Since some means of resolving disputes is necessary in a complex society, Professor Fuller contends that the most efficient means of fulfilling this function is through some form of judicial proceeding.

The conclusion that a modern society needs courts to address some private disputes does not, however, presuppose a particular procedural system for those courts. Neither does the existence of courts imply that all private disputes ought to be resolved judicially.

Professor Raz's types B and C system are distinguished according to whether their state-sponsored tribunals are designed to apply pre-existing norms to disputes or to deal with disputes on an *ad hoc* basis, without reference to pre-existing norms. The adjudicatory court systems in modern American society are designed primarily to apply pre-existing norms or rules of decision to disputes brought before them. In this respect, they represent a system predominantly of type B. Unregulated, or interest, disputes are handled by a finding that "no claim upon which relief can be granted" is presented. Some type C characteristics are present, of course, in that courts have power to develop new causes of action, and to expand existing ones to encompass previously unregulated disputes. Nevertheless, adjudication is designed primarily to deal with rights disputes.

C. CHARACTERISTICS OF ADJUDICATION

The contemporary judicial system is largely adjudicatory; it functions in order to permit pre-existing rules of decision to be applied to facts as they are found to exist in the proceeding. The emphasis is on procedures that assure accuracy in finding facts. Accuracy is expensive. For some disputes, improved accuracy is worth higher cost to the parties or to society. For other disputes the need for factual accuracy is not so great as to justify the expense of the procedures designed to secure accuracy. The parties would be willing to accept a greater risk of an inaccurate decision in exchange for lower cost.

In cases involving interest disputes, suitable pre-existing rules for decision do not exist, and therefore accuracy is not a goal. The parties need to be provided a procedure that facilitates development of rules of decision that meet their needs and that each is willing to accept.

The alternative dispute resolution inquiry should begin at this point. Assuming that society needs to provide institutions for resolving private disputes, it still must decide the cost-accuracy tradeoff for the resolution of major classes of rights disputes, and to provide procedures other than adjudication to assist in resolving interest disputes.

The outer limits of the cost-accuracy tradeoff are defined by the concept of procedural due process, when the decision making institutions is provided by the state. The United States Supreme Court, in *Mathews* v. *Eldridge,* held that procedural due process is flexible, involving a determination of (1) the private interest that is affected by the legal action, (2) the chance of a mistaken deprivation of such interest through the procedures used, and the potential values, if any, of additional or different procedural safeguards, and (3) the Government's interest, including the function involved and the administrative and fiscal burdens that would result from the additional or different safeguards. In this cost-effectiveness formula, the first two criteria relate to effectiveness, and the third relates to cost.

Judge Friendly has offered a menu, from which elements of adjudicatory process can be selected.

1. An unbiased tribunal.
2. Notice of the proposed action and ground asserted for it.
3. An opportunity to present reasons why the proposed action should not be taken.
4. The right to present evidence, including the right to call witnesses.
5. The right to know opposing evidence.
6. The right to have the decision based only on the evidence presented.
7. The right to counsel.
8. A requirement that the tribunal prepare a record of the evidence presented.
9. A requirement that the tribunal prepare written findings of fact and reasons for its decision.
10. Public attendance.
11. Judicial review.

All of these elements are present in the traditional civil jury trial. Some are absent or present in weaker form in more simplified procedures. Making the cost-effectiveness tradeoff, and selecting among the items on Judge Friendly's list, are essential parts of making the choice among rights dispute resolution processes, whether the choice is made by the parties to the dispute or by designers of new dispute resolution processes.

D. DYNAMICS OF PARTY CHOICE

An intrinsic characteristic of private disputes is that they may be resolved privately, if neither party wants to participate in the dispute resolution procedures provided by society. Accordingly, if one wishes to understand the frequency with which the parties will resort to third-party dispute resolution procedures and when they will abandon their disputes or revert to private settlement, one needs to understand the choices available to them. A significant amount of theoretical literature, and some empirical literature, exists on party choice.

1. COMPELLING PARTICIPATION. Some choices may be foreclosed entirely for one or both parties. A central feature of litigation in the civil courts is that participation by the defendant is not voluntary. This feature has important implications for the choices available to the claimant.

Professor Posner contends that, in a purely private system of dispute resolution, the main difficulty is in compelling parties to submit themselves to the dispute resolution process, particularly when a party anticipates losing. He notes that this is not a problem when a state is administering the judicial system since the force of the state can be employed to compel submission. According to Posner, one sanction that often is successful in a private system of dispute resolution is expulsion from an organization.

During the early development of English civic procedure, obtaining participation by the defendant was a major problem. Today, the problem has been resolved in court procedure by the device of the default judgment, but it remains with respect to private means of dispute resolution. Most private means of resolving disputes operate against a backdrop of interdependence between the parties that militates toward participation by both in resolving the dispute outside the courts.

The social or economic interdependence between the parties that makes private dispute resolution possible is illustrated with two examples, one relating to religious disputes, and one related to family disputes. In religious courts, excommunication is the sanction that makes it effective, and that sanction represents a serious cost to members of the religious group.

Professor Posner also maintains that the family provides a good illustration of private adjudication. As he points out, family members are often compelled to submit to the jurisdiction of the family by the head of the family. For example, in the modern family, parents often provide incentives to force their children to resolve disputes.

The likelihood that the claimant will be more interested than the other party in resolving, rather than abandoning, the dispute means that selection of a dispute resolution process usually is determined in part by the means available to compel participation by the reluctant party. Dean Hazard suggests that certain alternatives to adjudication may avoid this difficulty. Although adjudication may be disagreeable to one of the parties, Dean Hazard maintains that negotiation can be voluntary and private and can bring about results catered to the parties' specific needs. According to Dean Hazard, another method of dispute resolution is coercion, which is used when one party believes that there is no reason to use persuasion to reach an agreement. Coercion as a means of compelling participation requires that interdependence between the parties exist.

In procedures that are adjuncts to court procedures, the defendant is compelled to participate—though not necessarily to accept the adjunct's result—by legal process and the possibility of a default judgment or other sanctions imposed by the court. If the case is settled in conciliation, conference or other pretrial proceeding, the settlement agreement frequently is embodied in a consent decree or judgment, in which case enforcement proceeds just as it would on a judgment or decree obtained after a traditional trial.

In private procedures, participation is either wholly voluntary or backed by the possibility of sanctions imposed in a collateral proceeding. The effectiveness of the private procedure may be affected by the speed and expense of the ultimate sanctions. For example, the Uniform Arbitration Act permits summary enforcement, by injunction, of agreements to arbitrate, and permits summary entry of judgment on an arbitration award.

2. VALUES AFFECTING CHOICES AMONG PROCESSES. Once a means is found of compelling participation by the reluctant party, other values affect choice among dispute resolution processes. Professor Carrington begins with three moral premises for dispute resolution:

1. Coercion by the government should be minimized.
2. Responsibility for the exercise of public power ought to be diffused as much as possible.
3. All formal procedures are inherently undesirable.

These premises lead him to conclude that any procedure that enables parties to a dispute to work out their own solutions by their own initiative is inherently desirable.

He notes that the least costly dispute resolution mechanism is simple forebearance by the party who is otherwise aggrieved. According to Carrington, there are some circumstances where the legal system should encourage people to forebear from suit because there is no means of dealing with the grievances that is not more burdensome than the grievance itself.

Professor Carrington also identifies a social value that constrains the search for litigation alternatives, assuming that forebearance or abandonment is not appropriate. Systems that follow familiar procedures are seen as more legitimate than entirely new procedures. One reason that arbitration procedure resembles formal adjudication is that adjudication is familiar and legitimate, and therefore is a way of securing mutual understanding between the parties who are agreeing to the process.

Another fundamental goal affecting choices among alternative processes is to provide for a way in which interest disputes—the type described by Professor Raz as "unregulated"—can be resolved more satisfactorily to the parties than by judicial applications of existing formal norms. This felt need supposes that the parties are better off if they can make up their own norms in the process of resolving the dispute as opposed to having an external set of norms imposed on them. This goal is served by ensuring the availability of nonadjudicatory, as well as adjudicatory, processes.

Empirical evidence on the handling of minor personal disputes shows that citizens tend to avoid the courts. Two possible reasons for this exist, which relate to the values suggested in this section. The first reason is that citizens like to avoid involving the government in their disputes, if possible. This is consistent with Professor Carrington's premise that government coercion ought to be minimized. The second reason is that real-world disputes usually do not fit legal pigeonholes precisely. Some can be shoe-horned into recognized forms of action without too much difficulty; these are characterized as rights disputes. Others cannot be conformed to recognized forms of action at all; these are characterized as interest disputes. In both cases, however, some simplification of the real nature of the dispute is required if it is to be decided by the formal court machinery. Therefore, party satisfaction is likely to be higher if dispute resolution methods are available which permit disputes to be addressed and resolved in a flexible, private manner.

3. EMPIRICAL EVIDENCE ON DISPUTANT BEHAVIOR
The limited empirical data on the universe of private disputes say that only a miniscule portion of such disputes is litigated. A study of consumer complaints was conducted from 1978 to 1982 in Milwaukee, Wisconsin. These complaints were examined to see how the complainant sought to resolve them. Several different possibilities were considered, including abandonment of the claim, consultation with a "broker" (an individual with perceived expertise), presentation of the claim to a private forum such as Action Line, and presentation to a government agency including small claims court and the district attorney's consumer fraud unit.

About twenty-three percent of the perceived problems did not result in claims. Seventy percent of the problems were resolved entirely or partially, but only three percent of the unresolved claims were presented to third parties for resolution. Of the claims presented to third parties, most were presented in informal networks of friends and associates, directly to producers, or to forums such as insurance companies or the Better Business Bureau. Very few claimants presented complaints to governmental agencies, and a miniscule proportion resorted to small claims court.

4. INCENTIVES AND DISINCENTIVES TO SETTLE It is well established that fewer than ten percent of the civil lawsuits filed are resolved by a judgment entered after a trial. Most lawsuits are settled through negotiation. This fact, combined with the likelihood that a far greater number of claims are abandoned or resolved through negotiation without ever reaching the judicial system, means that an inquiry into dispute resolution must concentrate on the incentives to settle claims. Incentives to settle can be understood best by drawing on analytical models developed in the theoretical literature.

The underlying premise of virtually all the theoretical models is Professor Fisher's concept that a rational negotiating position depends upon the "Best Alternative to a Negotiated Settlement" (BATNA): no party will settle for a figure below his or her BATNA at any point in time.

Lawsuits are filed to change BATNA's. Alternative dispute resolution methods can be evaluated by using the dynamics of a lawsuit as a baseline. Once one understands how lawsuits change BATNA's, one can consider how alternative dispute resolution methods change BATNA's.

Consider the defendant's negotiating position. A necessary consequence of being a defendant is that any negotiated settlement will impose a cost on the defendant. In other words, the defendant's benefit will be negative. If we assume that the plaintiff is a stranger, the defendant's BATNA when the dispute arises is zero. Therefore a rational defendant will make no positive offer and there is no zone of agreement. But if the plaintiff files suit, the defendant's BATNA changes to a nonzero (minus) quantity. If suit is filed, the plaintiff's BATNA becomes greater than zero, and the defendant's becomes less than zero. Thus the plaintiff can control the defendant's BATNA as well as his own. Whether this change in BATNA's produces a zone of agreement depends on the components of the respective BATNA's, and those components are in turn determined by the litigation process.

If suit is filed, the defendant's changed BATNA can be disaggregated into two components: (1) the economic value of a judgment in the lawsuit, and (2) the cost of defending the lawsuit. Both components have negative value to the defendant.

The plaintiff's perspective is the converse of the defendant's. If he files suit, his BATNA also may be disaggregated into two major components: (1) the economic value of a judgment, and (2) the cost of litigation. For the plaintiff, the value of the first component is positive, and the value of the second component is negative.

The economic value of a judgment obtainable in the litigation can be decomposed into a function of four variables: (1) the expected value of the judgment, (2) the variance around that expected value, (3) the length of time that will elapse before judgment is entered, and (4) a discount factor. In the aggregate, these variables will be referred to as the "outcome value."

The two components of party BATNA's can be explored by further elaboration of the example given above. If a plaintiff is certain of obtaining a judgment of $10,000 in a trial that will cost $4,000, his BATNA in settlement negotiations will be $6,000. Of course, in the real world no claimant is *certain* of receiving a judgment of any amount; rather his BATNA is determined by his *expectations* about the judgment he will receive if he tries the case. Expectations are inherently uncertain. The availability of ADR processes alter the claimant's BATNA in two possible ways: by changing his expectations about trial judgment, and/or by changing the costs of obtaining that judgment.

For example, suppose a claimant thinks he has a ninety percent chance of obtaining a $10,000 judgment, and a ten percent chance of obtaining a zero judgment, and that the cost of litigation will be $4,000 in either event. His BATNA in settlement negotiations will be $5,000 (.9 times $10,000, minus $4,000). Then suppose he is required to present his case in a summary jury trial, which results in a verdict of $8,000. This well may alter his expectations about the judgment obtainable from a full-blown trial to a ninety percent probability of obtaining $8,000 and a ten percent probability of obtaining zero. If his expectations are altered thus, his BATNA will be reduced to $3,200 by the availability of the summary jury trial procedure. The effect of an alternative procedure that reduces costs below $4,000 is more difficult to quantify in simple terms.

Costs of litigation can be decomposed into four variables: (1) the cost of filing suit, (2) the cost of discovery and other pretrial preparation, (3) the cost of trial, and (4) any fees imposed by the judicial system for moving from one step to another in the procedure. In most cases, the amount of attorney's fees will far exceed any other costs. The plaintiff has control, at least at the outset of the litigation, over his own litigation costs. Additionally, he can determine a "floor" for the defendant's litigation costs.

Filing a lawsuit requires the other party to address the dispute, if only by filing a respon-

sive pleading. This costs money. Filing also confronts the other party with the potential costs of obtaining legal representation and participating in discovery. If the other party is an institution with substantial resources already committed to handling litigation, these costs may be small. If the other party is an individual or an institution with few resources, however, these costs may be substantial. Accordingly, filing changes the BATNA of the defendant and therefore may produce a zone of agreement where none existed before suit. Any litigation alternative must be measured in part by how effectively it forces the unwilling party to address the dispute.

Once a lawsuit is filed, other litigation initiatives may be undertaken that further increase the costs to the other side. Probably the best example is discovery. Certain forms of discovery, such as depositions, are expensive for both sides. The relative cost burdens of taking a deposition may be greater for the initiating party than for the opponent. In contrast, the cost of propounding interrogatories is usually low, while the cost of answering them may be substantial. The same cost relationship obtains for production of documents. Therefore, once litigation has begun, both parties may have a rational incentive to proceed with certain types of discovery in order to increase the costs of not settling for the other side. In choosing discovery methods, they have an incentive to use procedures that have asymmetric costs.

Judicial and nonjudicial pretrial procedures affect more than costs; they also change the magnitude, and reduce the variance, of estimates about trial outcome. Understanding the interrelationships between negotiated resolution of disputes and the availability of dispute resolution institutions of different types requires a deeper understanding of two processes: the dynamics of negotiations and the characteristics of the institutions.

To resume the quantitiative hypothetical, recall that the plaintiff's BATNA after an advisory verdict had changed from $5,000 to $3,200. Consider the defendant's perspective. The defendant may have believed at the outset that he enjoyed a fifty percent probability of a $1,000 award in the plaintiff's favor. If he expected litigation costs of $500 (much lower than the plaintiff's) his BATNA would have been $1,000, and he would not have settled for the plaintiff's BATNA of $5,000. The advisory verdict could change the defendant's BATNA by changing his expectations about the probable jury verdict, say to the same expectations as the plaintiff's: $7,200. Then, even if he expects his further litigation costs to remain at $500, his BATNA will have been changed to $7,700, and he will settle for the plaintiff's new BATNA of $3,200.

Even if both parties' expectations about trial outcome remain disparate after the advisory verdict, however, the costs of proceeding further can produce a zone of agreement. Suppose that the plaintiff's expectations of the trial outcome are $7,200, as before, and that the plaintiff expects the costs of further litigation to be $2,000. Suppose the defendant's expectations of trial outcome, after receiving the advisory verdict, are $2,500, and that he also expects further litigation costs of $2,000. The plaintiff's BATNA will be $5,200, and the defendant's BATNA will be $4,500, and there will be no settlement. Suppose however, that both parties expect further litigation costs of $3,000. Then the plaintiff's BATNA will be $4,200, and the defendant's BATNA will be $5,500, and there is a zone of agreement. Accordingly, an alternative dispute resolution procedure can promote settlement by bringing the parties' estimates of trial outcome somewhat closer together when substantial costs will be incurred by both parties by litigating further. Generally, it can be shown that a zone of agreement will exist in this simple model whenever the cost of further litigation exceeds the difference between the parties' expectations about trial outcome.

5. ATTORNEY-CLIENT DIFFERENCES AND DEADLINES

Professor Dunlop's article identifies dynamic characteristics of negotiations, two of which are especially important for exploring party preferences in relatively simple disputes: the existence of differences between negotiators and constituents, and the importance of deadlines.

As in the negotiations between representatives of fairly stable or continuing organizations, discussed by Professor Dunlop, negotiations between attorneys may produce a zone of agreement between the attorneys but not between their clients because the clients continue to have substantially different expectations about trial outcome. The availability of an advisory verdict of some kind may be essential to close this client-to-client gap and thus permit the attorneys to settle the dispute on terms which the attorneys agree are reasonable.

Also, deadlines resulting from an early submission to advisory forum can stimulate settlement by forcing the parties to evaluate the strength of their positions.

6. OTHER LITERATURE ON PARTY BEHAVIOR

Gordon Tullock has made a useful conceptual contribution that aids in understanding these characteristics. He applies the principles of economic decision theory to a comprehensive model of civil litigation. In the basic Tullock model, the trial is represented as an imperfect random variable that will produce a correct decision with a probability of less than 100%, as a function of the quality of evidence presented to it.

In this model, the plaintiff, viewing the trial *ex ante,* will settle for any offer greater than his BATNA determined by the economic gain from trial (post-trial award less litigation costs), and will go to trial in the absence of such offer as long as his BATNA is greater than zero. If the plaintiff's BATNA is zero or negative, as it would be if the economic payoff from trial were less than litigation costs, he will abandon his claim. The defendant will settle for any figure less than his expected loss (post-trial award plus litigation costs). The defendant will defend at trial any case in which the expected loss is less than simply paying the plaintiff's demand.

The relationship between the parties' expectations about trial outcome and Tullock's model of the trial can now be explained. The parties know that trial is an imperfect process, and even if they have perfect knowledge about the information that would be presented at trial, they cannot be completely certain about trial outcome. In the real world, the parties not only face this uncertainty resulting from imperfections in the trial process, they also lack perfect knowledge about the information that will be presented at trial. Improving their knowledge about the information to be presented is, of course, one motivation for discovery. Under the Tullock model, the settlement range, and the prospects of trial, thus depend on two institutional characteristics of the litigation system and two characteristics of the particular dispute. The two institutional characteristics are (1) cost of trial, and (2) accuracy of decision making. The two dispute characteristics are (1) the nature of the available evidence, and (2) the cost of obtaining better evidence.

Higher trial costs *borne by the parties* will reduce the number of cases that go to trial, but will increase social costs. Lower trial costs will increase the number of cases that go to trial, but will reduce social costs. Improved evidence, that both parties know about, will reduce the chance of a particular case going to trial, because it reduces party uncertainty about trial outcome. These three variables, accuracy, cost and evidence quality, are not independent, however. Improving the quality of evidence may also increase costs.

Discovery is a good example of a procedural device that affects more than one variable, but that also increases cost. Informal procedure (for example, relaxation of the hearsay rule) is another good example. Presumably this would reduce accuracy, but it also reduces cost.

Some reasonable assumptions can be made about the nature of the interdependence among the variables that facilitate a search for the optimal theoretical combination. One can assume a diminishing marginal return for investment of additional resources. In other words, at some point as costs of the trial are increased, for each unit increase in cost, there will be less than one unit improvement in accuracy. Likewise, at some point as costs of discovery are increased, for each unit increase in cost, there will be less than one unit improvement in evidence quality.

There is therefore always a tradeofff in selecting among processes for dispute resolution. Accuracy of decision, or of forecasts about the probable decision, can be purchased only at a price. Cheaper processes produce less accurate decisions. Cheap final decision processes may be so inaccurate that they are unacceptable to the parties or to society. Cheap nonbinding decisions, intended to facilitate settlement by improving a party's ability to project ultimate trial outcome, may be so inaccurate that they do not promote settlement.

Other commentators have offered basically similar models of the dispute resolution process.

Professor Landes identifies factors that determine the choice between pretrial settlement and a trial in an economic model of the criminal justice system. Appendix A of his article extends his model to civil cases. In this appendix he concludes that the following factors make settlement likely:

- Both parties have similar expectations about the probability that the defendant would be found liable at trial;

- Both parties have similar estimates of damages given that the defendant is found liable at trial;
- Neither party has a strong preference for risk; and
- The costs of a trial to the plaintiff and defendant, including attorney's fees, court fees, and their own time exceed the cost of settlement.

The following factors make settlement before trial unlikely:

- Dissimilar estimates of liability and damages by the plaintiff and defendant, *if* the plaintiff's estimates are higher;
- Lower risk averseness; and
- Lower court costs relative to settlement costs.

Professor Landes concludes that increased costs of access to the courts would increase the incidence of settlement. He also concludes that differences in the rate at which the plaintiff and defendant discount future damages awarded at a trial can give rise to different settlement rates as a function of delay. According to Professor Landes, the higher the plaintiff's discount rate in relation to the defendant's, the greater the plaintiff's losses and the smaller the defendant's gains from an increase in delay.

Cootner and Marks have developed a theoretical model of bargaining in a litigation context. They predict the effect on the probability of settlement of changes in various parameters.

- An increase in the urgency of resolution resulting from a higher discount rate makes settlement more likely.
- An improvement in only one party's expectation about trial outcome makes settlement less likely.
- An increase in the transaction costs of continuing the dispute makes settlement more likely.
- An increase in spitefulness toward opponents makes settlement less likely.
- Lower risk aversion makes settlement less likely.
- An increase in the familiarity of the opponents with each other makes settlement more likely because it reduces uncertainty.

A recent article by Danzon and Lillard applied three theoretical models to data on medical malpractice suits in all fifty states. The key theoretical prediction of their model is that the sample of cases going to verdict will be a "small atypical group in which the plaintiff's overestimate or the defendant's underestimate of the payoff at verdict is large relative to the costs of litigation." Their data showed that fifty percent of the cases settled before suit was filed, forty percent settled after suit was filed but before a verdict was reached, and that less than ten percent of the cases went to verdict. Their study conclusions generally validate the theoretical model of disputant behavior.

This literature produces no single model of dispute resolution; nor does it permit a sufficiently sophisticated set of equations to represent the tradeoffs involved in party choice. Therefore no useful attempt can be made to propose a rigorous framework for the quantitative assessment of dispute resolution processes. The theoretical literature does reveal, however, virtual unanimity on the following propositions that are useful in evaluating alternative processes.

First, the higher the costs for the next procedural step, the greater the likelihood of settlement at that point.

Second, the more accurate—and similar—the parties' perceptions of the outcome ultimately obtainable from trial, the greater the chances of settlement.

All dispute resolution methods that seek to promote settlement rather than further litigation can be evaluated according to these two criteria.

III. INTEREST DISPUTES

Interest disputes are those for which there is no pre-existing rule or principles by which the dispute can be resolved. Traditionally, interest disputes have been thought unsuitable for resolution through litigation. Rather, private negotiation or public "negotiation" as a part of the legislative process were relied upon to deal with these types of disputes. In recent years, however, courts have become increasingly involved in addressing interest disputes. Therefore any inquiry into dispute resolution methods that seeks to divert disputes from the civil trial process must consider certain types of interest disputes.

Some types of interest disputes have been handled by the courts because of a failure of other political institutions to deal with them effectively. School integration disputes are a prominent example. Other types of interest disputes have been addressed judicially but the development of alternative institutions better suited for resolving them suggests that judicial involvement can be lessened. Environmental disputes are an example. Other interest disputes are handled almost entirely outside judicial institutions, with the judicial resources being applied only to ensure the integrity of the nonjudicial institutions developed to handle the underlying disputes. Labor disputes are the paradigm of this class. A final class of interest disputes are handled in administrative forums, but frequently spill over into the courts because of imperfections in the administrative institutions to deal with them effectively.

Simple interest disputes, such as Dean Hazard's dispute over whether to go to a ball game or to watch television, can be resolved without permanent machinery. More complex interest disputes, in contrast, require some institutional structure within which certain prerequisites to dispute resolution must take place. Legislatures provide one such structure that is relatively well accepted. American labor law, by institutionalizing and channeling the strike and lockout, provides another such structure that is well accepted by the parties to collective bargaining. Unfortunately, interest disputes that are not dealt with by legislatures, and that cannot be dealt with through traditional collective bargaining, cannot be referred to an institutional mechanism that is at all well suited to dealing with them. The rulemaking process under the Administrative Procedure Act, and similar state statutes, provides a starting point for developing such an institutional mechanism in administrative agencies, but frequently the disputing parties have escaped this mechanism and gone to the courts, where they have succeeded to a large degree in forcing the agencies to engage in adjudication, as though they are confronted with rights disputes rather than with interest disputes.

Recently, policy makers have come to realize that adjudicatory models are not well suited for resolving interest disputes, and have turned their attention to developing other institutional and procedural models. One of the most comprehensive is Phil Harter's regulatory negotiations model. Other models have been suggested in connection with environmental disputes. Still others, less visible because they have been developed as adjuncts to court systems at the local level, have been developed to deal with family disputes. William Kraut addresses one of these.

Most of these models concentrate on institutional ways to ensure the presence of the prerequisites for effective negotiation of interest disputes: (1) identifying the affected interests, (2) ensuring the adequacy of representation for these interests, (3) enforcing the duty to bargain in good faith, (4) and defining or limiting the types of pressure the parties may utilize to promote acceptance of their views.

In substance, these are the same issues that are addressed by labor law. Efforts to provide effective institutions for resolving interest disputes modelled on collective bargaining also, however, must seek to replicate the strike or lockout. The theory of negotiations says that a zone of agreement, and therefore the potential for settlement, does not exist unless the parties' BATNA's are nonzero. Adjudication of rights disputes in the civil courts often provides nonzero BATNA's resulting in a zone of agreement because of the costs of litigation. In any event, the traditional adjudicatory means of resolving rights disputes leads to a final decision that will be imposed by the state absent private agreement. It is more difficult to affect BATNA's or to provide for a final decision in interest disputes because such disputes, by definition, cannot be decided by reference to pre-existing principles. Most labor disputes are resolved because the continuing cost of a strike or lockout on both sides changes BATNA's until the parties adjust their position to produce a zone of agreement. Most of the interest dispute resolution machinery developed so far to address nonlabor interest disputes depends on the unattractiveness of a resolution through adjudicatory means to produce a zone of agreement. Thus, in custody conciliation, for example, the mediator says to the parties: "If you do not work this out for yourselves, the judge will impose a solution that neither of you may like."

It is appropriate to support continued efforts to refine these models and to force interest disputes to be addressed through them rather than through adjudication.

RICHARD POSNER

The Concept of Corrective Justice in Recent Theories of Tort Law*

For the last 100 years, which is to say since the publication of Holmes's *The Common Law*,[1] most tort scholars have thought that tort doctrines were, and should be, based on utilitarian (or, more recently, economic) concepts.[2] This was the view of Holmes, of Ames, and of Terry; of the draftsmen of the first and second *Restatement of Torts;* and of the legal realists who thought the focus of tort law should be on loss spreading rather than on assessment of fault.[3] It is also the view of economic analysts of tort law such as Guido Calabresi and myself. Writing in 1972 about tort scholarship, George Fletcher declared that "the fashionable questions of the time are instrumentalist: What social value does the rule of liability further in this case? Does it advance a desirable goal, such as compensation, deterrence, risk-distribution, or minimization of accident costs?"[4] It would be easy to show that the goals which he listed were regarded by their advocates as utilitarian, or sometimes economic, goals. Since he wrote, the economic approach to tort law has developed apace; at the same time, several scholars have joined Fletcher both in questioning the proposition that tort doctrines are or should be based on utilitarian or economic ideas, and in arguing that the tort law should be, and perhaps already is, based on the idea of corrective justice.

This article will examine the concept of corrective justice and its application to theories of tort law. Part I explains how the concept was defined by its inventor, Aristotle, whose treatment is still the "classic analysis."[5] Part II examines the use of the concept by recent torts scholars—besides Fletcher, by Richard Epstein, John Borgo, Jules Coleman, and Frederick

Sharp. Borgo, Fletcher, and Sharp refer to Aristotle explicitly; Coleman and Epstein do not, but they echo the Aristotelian definition. All five scholars, I contend, misapply the Aristotelian concept to a greater or lesser extent. Part III of the article argues that the Aristotelian concept is compatible with, and indeed required by, the economic theory of tort and, incidentally, contract and criminal law. Parts II and III illustrate the analysis with the question of no-fault automobile accident compensation plans.

The advocates of the corrective justice approach contend variously that corrective justice is and that it should be the basis of tort law. While ordinarily the difference between positive and normative analysis is of great importance in discussions of law, it is in this instance irrelevant. My argument is not that the theory of corrective justice provides either an inaccurate description of or an unsound guide to principles of tort liability, but that those who believe it is necessarily a rival to the economic approach are mistaken; the Aristotelian concept, at least, is not.

Appearances to the contrary notwithstanding, this paper is not an essay in antiquarianism. The idea of corrective justice, stated by Aristotle and accepted by later writers in the Aristotelian sense, continues to exercise a powerful hold over the imagination of legal scholars. It is for some of these scholars a ground for rejecting a utilitarian or economic conception of law. It is in short a part of the contemporary debate over legal theory.

I. ARISTOTLE'S CONCEPT OF CORRECTIVE JUSTICE

In Book V, Chapter 4, of the *Nicomachean Ethics*, Aristotle develops the concept of corrective justice.[6] He had discussed, in Chapter 3, distributive justice—that is, justice in the distri-

* Richard Posner, "The Concept of Corrective Justice in Recent Theories of Tort Law," *Journal of Legal Studies,* Vol. 10, No. 1 (1981), pp. 187–206. Reprinted by permission of The University of Chicago Press.

bution by the state of money, honors, and other things of value—saying that such awards should be made according to merit (*kat' axian*). Chapter 4 discusses a contrasting concept of justice, the rectificatory or corrective (*diorthōtikos*—literally "making straight"), which he says applies to transactions (*sunallagmata*), both voluntary (*hekosia*) and involuntary (*akosia*); the distinction is roughly that between contracts and torts.[7] The crucial passage in Chapter 4 is the following:

. . . it makes no difference [from a corrective justice standpoint] whether a good man has defrauded a bad man or a bad man a good one, nor whether it is a good or a bad man that has committed adultery; the law looks only to the distinctive character of the injury, and treats the parties as equal, if one is in the wrong and the other is being wronged, and if one inflicted injury and the other has received it.[8]

As far as remedy is concerned, Aristotle says that

the judge tries to equalize things by means of the penalty, taking away from the gain of the assailant. For the term 'gain' [*kerdos*] is applied generally to such cases—even if it be not a term appropriate to certain cases, e.g. to the person who inflicts a wound—and 'loss' [*zēmia*] to the sufferer; at all events, when the suffering has been estimated, the one is called loss and the other gain. . . . Therefore the just . . . consists in having an equal amount before and after the transaction.[9]

There is more, but the chapter is short, and the part I have summarized and especially the passages I have quoted contain the gist of Aristotle's concept.

The *Nicomachean Ethics,* consisting as they do of classroom notes of Aristotle's lectures, are notoriously obscure and there is a fair amount of exegetic literature on Book V, Chapter 4.[10] But there is little controversy with regard to the basic features of his concept of corrective justice, summarized above. As paraphrased by Joachim,

If, for example, the thief was a gentleman and the injured party a beggar—a member of an inferior class in the State—this difference of rank is nothing to the law. . . . All that the law is concerned with is that, of two parties before it, one has got an unfair advantage and the other has suffered an unfair disadvantage. There is, therefore, a wrong which needs redress—an inequality which needs to be equalized.[11]

Three points should be noted about Aristotle's concept of corrective justice:

1. The duty to rectify is based not on the fact of injury but on the conjunction of injury and wrongdoing. The injurer must do wrong (*adikei*) as well as do harm (*eblapsen*), and the victim must be wronged (*adiketei*) as well as harmed (*beblaptai*). Not all departures from distributive justice call for correction. Someone who voluntarily makes a bad bargain may end up worse off than the principles of distributive justice would, but for the bad bargain, dictate. But he has not been wronged, and he is not entitled to rectification. Moreover, what is wrongful or unjust—*adikos*—is not defined in Chapter 4; it is assumed. In Chapter 8 of Book V we learn that "Whether an act is or is not one of injustice (or of justice) is determined by its voluntariness or involuntariness."[12] But even within the class of voluntary acts, only those that are deliberate can be acts of injustice. Those done by misadventure (where "the injury takes place contrary to reasonable expectation") or by mistake (where, for example, "he threw not with intent to wound but only to prick") are not.[13]

2. The idea that distributive considerations do not count in a setting of corrective justice ("it makes no difference whether a good man has defrauded a bad man or a bad man a good one . . . ") is a procedural principle. It is not equivalent to saying that distributive notions should not affect the definition of rights or even that they should not enter into the determination of what sorts of acts are unjust or wrongful. The point, rather, is that the judge is interested only in the character—whether it is wrongful—of the injury, rather than in the character of the parties apart from that of the injury: "the moral worth of persons . . . is ignored."[14]

3. Aristotle was writing against the background of the Athenian legal system of his day, where even suits to redress crimes were (with rare exceptions) instituted and prosecuted by private individuals, the victim or a member of his family, rather than by the state.[15] So he naturally assumed that redress for wrongful injuries was by means of private actions. But there is no

indication in Chapter 4 that he thought there could be only one mode of rectification consistent with the concept of corrective justice—namely, a tort action, in which the judge orders the wrongdoer to pay a damages judgment to the victim. In fact, as we shall see in Part III, it is not even certain that Aristotle required that rectification involve full compensation of the victim.

To summarize, the main point in Chapter 4 is that if someone injures another wrongfully, he has behaved unjustly irrespective of his merit, relative to the victim's, evaluated apart from the wrongful injury itself. Chapter 4 is thus a corollary to Chapter 3, which discusses distributive justice. Chapter 4 makes clear that the rights of the superior individual do not include the right to injure an inferior person through wrongful conduct. This idea of "impartial legal correction"[16] is important, but it is more limited than the corrective justice concepts of recent tort scholars, to which I turn next. It is limited because it is part of what Aristotle called "particular" justice (in Chapter 2 of Book V), in contrast to universal justice which he equates to virtue in general.

II. MODERN TORT SCHOLARS ON CORRECTIVE JUSTICE

Professor Fletcher analyzes tort law under two competing "paradigms"—the "paradigm of reciprocity" and the "paradigm of reasonableness."[17] The former is derived from notions of corrective justice that Fletcher locates in Book V, Chapter 4 of the *Nicomachean Ethics,*[18] and the latter from utilitarian ideas. The paradigm of reasonableness corresponds in a rough way to the negligence standard, with its implicit (sometimes explicit[19]) balancing of the costs and benefits of risky activity. Under the paradigm of reciprocity, in contrast, "a victim has a right to recover for injuries caused by a risk greater in degree and different in order from those created by the victim and imposed on the defendant,"[20] irrespective of the social value of the defendant's or the plaintiff's activity giving rise to the injury. The choice between the two paradigms depends on "whether judges should look solely at the claims and interests of the parties before the court . . . without looking beyond the case at hand" (as corrective justice requires, according to Fletcher)—in which event they should choose

the paradigm of reciprocity—or whether judges should "resolve seemingly private disputes in a way that serves the interests of the community as a whole,"[21] in which event they should choose the paradigm of reasonableness.

Fletcher's suggested rule of reciprocity has no basis in the concept of corrective justice expounded by Aristotle, the only authority on corrective justice to whom Fletcher refers. Nowhere does Aristotle suggest that the concept of wrongful or unjust conduct excludes consideration of the social value of conduct. To be sure, the Aristotelian judge is not to look "beyond the case at hand," but only in the sense that he is not to consider whether the defendant is a better man than the plaintiff, evaluated apart from the character of the injury; it does not follow that the social utility of the defendant's conduct that gave rise to the injury is irrelevant to whether the injury was wrongful.[22] There is no basis in the Aristotelian concept of corrective justice for Fletcher's conclusion that negligence is an inappropriate standard when the victim's conduct is less dangerous to the injurer than the injurer's is to the victim.

Professor Epstein began publishing articles on tort law the year after Fletcher wrote his article. Epstein initially did not base his concept of tort liability on corrective justice; the only reference to the term in the first article is in a footnote criticizing Fletcher—who Epstein, at this point at least, seems to have thought was playing a different sort of game.[23] Epstein's first article bases his idea that tort liability is, *prima facie,* strict liability on notions variously described as causation, common sense, ordinary language, liberty, and free will—not corrective justice. But the term is used repeatedly in the next article,[24] and by 1979, writing on nuisance, Epstein describes his "basic . . . framework" or "conceptual . . . ideal" as one based on the "principles of corrective justice: rendering to each person whatever redress is required because of the violation of his rights by another."[25] This is an acceptable paraphrase of the Aristotelian concept, but reading on one realizes that corrective justice means something different to Epstein from what it meant to Aristotle. Epstein speaks of "the distribution of vested rights demanded by a corrective justice theory" and says that "corrective justice principles still help us decide who is a wrongdoer and who is an innocent driver," and again that "corrective justice arguments identify the wrongdoer."[26] But the Aristotelian concept of corrective justice does not tell us who is a wrongdoer or who has vested rights; all it tells us is that a wrongful injury is not excused by the moral superiority of the injurer to the victim. More recently Epstein has described his conceptual ideal as "straight corrective justice-libertarian theory."[27] But unless the Aristotelian notion is to be abandoned completely, "corrective justice" and "libertarian" cannot be yoked in this way—the former referring as it does to the rectification of a wrong, the latter to a particular theory of wrongful conduct.

Epstein seems to associate two fundamental ideas with corrective justice. The first is that the victim of wrongdoing has a right to be compensated by the wrongdoer for injury resulting from the invasion.[28] The second is that the fact of injury "permits the plaintiff to show that the initial balance between the two parties is in need of redress because of the defendant's conduct."[29] The first idea, that of the wrongdoer's duty to compensate the victim of wrong, is certainly found in Book V, Chapter 4 of the *Nicomachean Ethics,* but I think as background rather than as a central principle of corrective justice. If one had said to Aristotle, "the best way to deal with wrongful conduct is to deter it through a heavy criminal penalty, rather than to allow private damage actions," there is no evidence that he would have regarded such a substitution as unjust. As to the second point, while the ideas of balance and redress are part of Aristotle's concept of corrective justice, Epstein's idea that the balance is disturbed by injury alone is not. Aristotle requires, as the predicate for redress under a corrective justice theory, that the injurer be acting wrongfully *and* that the victim be harmed. These are two distinct requirements in Aristotle, not one as in Epstein.[30]

I do not criticize Epstein for not being an Aristotelian. But since the idea of corrective justice remains closely associated with the Aristotelian concept, it would promote clarity if modern writers wishing to use the term in a different sense would explain their meaning. No doubt they like the favorable connotations of the term "corrective justice"—why else use it? —but these favorable connotations properly belong to the Aristotelian usage, if only because the subsequent philosophical tradition accepted, and to this day accepts, that usage.[31]

I shall skip over Professor Coleman for a moment, though he is next chronologically, to discuss Professor Borgo, who builds his analysis of corrective justice on Epstein's. Borgo describes Epstein's concept of corrective justice as "the notion that when one man harms another the victim has a moral right to demand, and the injurer a moral duty to pay him, compensation for the harm,"[32] and Borgo accepts this as a correct statement of the Aristotelian concept, citing Book V, Chapter 4 of the *Nicomachean Ethics.*[33] But Aristotle does not suggest that a duty to compensate arises from the fact of harm; he states explicitly that the harm must be wrongful.

Borgo's mistake warps his entire analysis. Having defined the idea of corrective justice as requiring compensation paid for harm done, Borgo must do handsprings to come up with an idea of causation that will carry the moral freight that he associates with the idea of corrective justice. He states: "the linchpin of a system of corrective justice is a nonorthodox doctrine of causation. Such a doctrine makes it possible to focus analysis on the causal relation between the defendant's conduct and the plaintiff's harm. That relation in turn provides the basis for ascribing moral, and therefore legal, responsibility for harm."[34] If causation is defined as moral responsibility, so that the idea of harm is equated to the idea of wrongful harm, the Aristotelian concept is obtained. But this extraordinarily indirect route to the correct conclusion is necessary only because Borgo misreads Aristotle.

It is easy to see how Borgo was inveigled into taking this path by Professor Epstein, who uses the term corrective justice repeatedly, states that corrective justice principles require that a person be prima facie liable for any injury that he causes, and then, through the idea of "causal paradigms," imposes limitations on the meaning of "cause." In Epstein's view, the basic meaning of cause is captured in the paradigmatic example "*A* hit *B.*" To be considered causal, a relationship must resemble closely this example. Using this method, Esptein can show, for example, that competition is not a tort, because the way in which harm occurs when one rival offers a lower price or superior product than another does not involve the use of force or anything enough like force to be assimilated to the *A*-hit-*B* example.[35]

Epstein's idea of causation is an unusual one, for there is no linguistic or conceptual difficulty in regarding a successful competitor as having "caused" the business losses of his less successful rival, and an unnecessary one, for it does not follow from the idea of corrective justice that competition is a tort merely because it causes injury; the idea of corrective justice does not imply that merely causing a harm creates a right to redress or rectification. But because Borgo thinks Epstein has defined the Aristotelian notion of corrective justice correctly, and hence that merely causing harm *does* entitle the victim to redress, Borgo must find some other, non-Epsteinian method of limiting the idea of cause, in order to avoid unacceptable results such as liability in the competition case. Borgo's method is to equate causation in tort law to moral or legal responsibility.[36] It is as curious a way of limiting the idea of causation as Epstein's. It is true that conclusions about causation are frequently influenced by normative considerations: that we may single out one necessary condition from all the others as "the cause" because it is the thing we want to change. But causation and responsibility are not synonyms. The competition example shows this. The successful competitor has indeed "caused" his rival's business losses, but no moral opprobrium, or legal liability, attaches to this injury, because social welfare is enhanced by competition. Only a misreading of Aristotle could make Borgo think it important to pour the idea of moral responsibility into the idea of causation in order to avoid unacceptable results.

Another way to read Epstein is that he believes the duty of corrective justice is triggered not by causing harm but by causing harm through the use of physical force or some closely related modality such as fraud.[37] In this reading Aristotle's distinction between the wrong and the injury is preserved, and the wrong is the use of force or fraud. But in not making this distinction explicit Epstein merges the issues of wrong and injury, with the result that the ethical basis of his system is unclear.[38] Early Epstein is a "responsibility" theorist,[39] as is Borgo; later Epstein, and Fletcher, are "rights" theorists.[40] Although Epstein has used the term corrective justice to describe both stages of his thought, neither responsibility theories nor rights theories are theories of corrective justice. They are theories about the holdings or entitlements that people can legitimately claim. They belong to distributive rather than corrective justice.

Professor Jules Coleman has written a series of articles on tort law emphasizing what he calls compensatory or sometimes rectificatory justice, a term equivalent to Aristotle's corrective justice. Coleman states that "compensatory justice is concerned with eliminating undeserved or otherwise unjustifiable gains and losses. Compensation is therefore a matter of justice because it protects a distribution of wealth—resources or entitlements to them—from distortion through unwarranted gains and losses. It does so by requiring annulment of both."[41] Coleman recognizes that a duty of corrective justice is compatible with a substantive concept of unjust conduct based on economics or utilitarianism. The "distortion" of which he speaks comes about because the injurer has violated a standard of conduct and the standard could be "one of maximizing social utility."[42] This is an important point that is easily missed. If one equates retributive justice to punishment based on a nonutilitarian theory of desert, in the manner of Kant, and then equates retributive to corrective justice, then corrective justice will indeed seem necessarily inconsistent with utilitarianism. But even if the Kantian concept of retributive justice is accepted, the further step of equating retributive and corrective justice is unwarranted; Aristotle himself rejects retribution as a basis for punishment in Chapter 5 of Book V.

The twist that Coleman gives the concept of corrective justice is to emphasize the victim's deserts more than the injurer's guilt. If an injury is wrongful, the victim is entitled to be compensated, but not necessarily by the injurer; if the injurer did not gain from his wrongful act, corrective justice does not require that he be the source of the victim's compensation. But there is a problem: if the injurer is not the source of the compensation, then someone else, who is innocent, must be, and why is not that innocent party a victim of the wrongdoer's injurious conduct?

Defending no-fault automobile accident compensation plans against arguments based on corrective justice notions, Coleman argues that the victim of an accident in which the injurer was at fault is entitled to compensation and receives it under a no-fault system, but the injurer is not required as a matter of justice to be the source of the compensation because he does not gain by his wrongful act, as he would if we were speaking of a theft rather than an accident.[43] Both propositions—that the victim is compensated, and that the wrongdoer does not gain—can be questioned. Take the second first. The injurer avoids the costs of taking care. This cost saving is a gain to him; if his conduct (driving too fast, for example) is wrongful, it is a wrongful gain. Negligence under the Hand formula is a failure to take cost-justified precautions, and this failure involves a cost savings to the injurer which is a wrongful gain to him. Coleman has made not only a mistake in economics but a mistake about Aristotle, who used "gain" and "loss" to describe the relation between injurer and victim even when the term "gain" was (he thought) not quite appropriate, as in the case of a wounding.[44]

And is the victim really compensated? He receives the insurance proceeds, and let us assume they are sufficient to make him whole; but he paid for the insurance, so he just receives what is his. Potential victims as a class are clearly harmed by people who cause accidents; accident insurance premiums will be higher the higher the accident rate, and there will be no compensation by the wrongdoers for these higher premiums. Therefore, no-fault automobile accident compensation plans, which amount to eliminating liability and compelling potential victims to insure (at their own cost) against being hurt in automobile accidents, would appear to violate corrective justice because they do not redress injuries caused by wrongdoing.[45]

It does not follow that allowing people to buy *liability* insurance is inconsistent with the Aristotelian concept of corrective justice. It might appear that the effect of liability insurance is to shift the victim's costs resulting from the wrongdoer's action to the other members of the wrongdoer's risk pool, who become in effect uncompensated victims of his action. But they are compensated, albeit *ex ante,* by the opportunity which insurance affords them to shift some of their accident costs to other members of the risk pool. There is nothing in Aristotle to preclude this mode of compensation, indirect as it may seem; it is the principle of rectification, rather than the form it takes, that Aristotle insists on.

I come finally to Frederick Sharp, who has written an article applying "the ethical categories of Aristotle" to the question whether tort law should adopt "enterprise liability," defined as "liability without fault imposed on enterprises."[46] Corrective justice is one of these categories, but Sharp realizes that the Aristotelian concept of justice is not exhausted by the discussion of corrective justice in Chapter 4 of Book V.

Sharp's discussion of *Rylands* v. *Fletcher*[47] illustrates his method and its shortcomings. He begins by suggesting that there is a problem in applying the Aristotelian categories to the case because, he says, the injury involved a loss to the victim but no gain to the injurer. This is the same economic error that Coleman made, but Sharp, here a sharper reader of Aristotle than Coleman, notes that Aristotle said that there is a duty of corrective justice even in cases where there is no apparent gain to the injurer. But Sharp faces another problem: "although the defendant [in *Rylands* v. *Fletcher*] inflicted injury on the plaintiff, he did not do so 'wrongfully' since [according to Book V, Chapter 8 of the *Nicomachean Ethics*] this requires knowledge."[48]

Sharp nevertheless concludes that corrective justice supports the result in *Rylands* v. *Fletcher*. His reasoning is complex, and as the only extended attempt among the writers we are considering to extract a substantive principle of justice from Aristotle's discussion of corrective justice deserves quotation in full:

Between all citizens there is proportionality, which is altered when one suffers injury. It is unjust to suffer injury at the hands of another, and thus important that the injury be recompensed. But what to do if no one has gained by the injury? Mr. Justice Blackburn [in *Rylands* v. *Fletcher*] justified imposing liability on the defendant by the nature of his activity; "anything likely to do mischief if it escapes." Put in extended Aristotelian terms, anyone who carries on a hazardous activity which alters the social proportion of benefits by inflicting injury must bear the burden, because the nature of the activity has brought "gain" to the enterpriser. This is corrective justice in the sense that hazardous enterprises can cause injury disproportionate to the expectations of citizens living together by agreement in a commonwealth. A "gain" is imputed to the defendant in this case, since he departed from the restrictive standard of conduct owing to one's neighbours, and so potentially violated the social proportionality from the moment he embarked on the dangerous activity. It is thus that I argue Aristotle's support for the doctrine of enterprise liability for ultrahazardous activities, on the basis that industry must pay its own way.[49]

The key idea is that of proportion. There is indeed much discussion in Book V of the *Nicomachean Ethics,* as elsewhere in this great work, of proportion, balance, mean, and related terms. In particular, Aristotle makes a distinction between what he calls the "geometrical mean" and the "arithmetical mean,"[50] relating the first concept to distributive justice and the second to corrective justice. If there is some amount of money or of honors to be distributed by the state, it should be distributed in proportion to the relative merits of the citizens. Thus if A is twice as virtuous as B, and virtue is the standard of merit in the society, A should receive two-thirds of the distribution. This is the "geometrical mean." But if A steals a drachma from B, B is entitled to the return of the drachma—not just to one-third of a drachma. This is the "arithmetical mean."

In short, corrective justice requires annulling a departure from the preexisting distribution of money or honors in accordance with merit, but only when the departure is the result of *an act of injustice*, causing injury. Sharp omits this qualification. When he states, "It is unjust to suffer injury at the hands of another, and thus important that the injury be recompensed," he departs from the Aristotelian concept of corrective justice by failing to distinguish injury from wrong. The problem is not that the defendants in *Rylands* v. *Fletcher* did not gain from the injury—they did, at least in an economic analysis. The problem is that there is no basis in Aristotelian thought for regarding an injury that occurs without fault as unjust, and therefore as triggering a duty of corrective justice.[51] So we have a paradox: Epstein and Sharp (and also Fletcher) invoke corrective justice in support of enlarging the scope of strict liability as a principle of tort law, but if anything the Aristotelian concept suggests narrowing it, because the concept requires wrongful conduct as well as harmful result.

One could, I think, argue that strict liability would be consistent with the Aristotelian concept if it were shown to be simply a more efficient method of compensating the victims of wrongdoers; the fact that some injurers who were not wrongdoers would be mulcted in damages would not necessarily invalidate the argument. Yet Aristotle, with all the emphasis he places on the greatest good for man being happiness in activity, and not merely in disposition,[52] would probably have thought it odd to penalize the man of action by requiring him to compensate someone whom he injured while using due care. But this point, having to do with Aristotle's substantive conception of the good for man, cannot be adequately developed in the compass of this paper.

III. THE ECONOMIC BASIS OF CORRECTIVE JUSTICE

Once the concept of corrective justice is given its correct Aristotelian meaning, it becomes possible to show that it is not only compatible with, but required by, the economic theory of law. In that theory, law is a means of bringing about an efficient (in the sense of wealth-maximizing) allocation of resources by correcting externalities and other distortions in the market's allocation of resources.[53] The idea of rectification in the Aristotelian sense is implicit in this theory. If A fails to take precautions that would cost less than their expected benefits in accident avoidance, thus causing an accident in which B is injured, and nothing is done to rectify this wrong, the concept of justice as efficiency will be violated. The reason is discovered by considering the consequences of doing nothing. Since A does not bear the cost (or the full cost) of his careless behavior, he will have no incentive to take precautions in the future, and there will be more accidents than is optimal. Since B receives no compensation for his injury, he may be induced to adopt in the future precautions which by hypothesis (the hypothesis that the accident was caused by A's wrongful conduct, in an economic sense of "wrongful") are more costly than the precaution that A failed to take. B's precautions will reduce the number of accidents, thus partially offsetting the adverse consequences of A's continuing failure to take the precaution, but aggregate social welfare will be diminished by this allocation of care between the parties.

The substantive concept of "wrongful" conduct in this example is of course different from Aristotle's substantive concept of wrongful conduct as set forth in Chapter 8 of Book V. He did not consider negligence the kind of wrongful conduct that triggers a duty of rectification, because negligence is not a deliberate wrong; the negligent injurer does not desire to cause an injury. But the idea of corrective justice as redress for wrongful injury (Chapter 4) is logically separable from the idea of wrongful injury as *deliberately* wrongful (Chapter 8). By the same token, the act of injustice that triggers the duty of corrective justice could be defined more broadly than Aristotle, or a normative economist, would define it.

Although the economic theory of justice requires rectification in the above example and thus implies the Aristotelian concept of corrective justice, the precise mode of rectification remains, for the economist as for Aristotle, a secondary question having to do with the practical advantages and disadvantages of alternative modes. Aristotle assumed that the method of rectification would involve private actions, mainly for damages, because that was how things were done in his day. The situation today remains much the same and economists have presented arguments why the private damage action continues to be the cornerstone of the system of redress in most tort (and contract) settings.[54] But where private tort remedies are infeasible, as where injurers have no assets to levy on—not even what they wrongfully took from the victim—there is nothing in Aristole to imply that an alternative mode of rectification, such as criminal punishment, would be unjust.

A more difficult case is where tort remedies, while feasible, are more costly than the alternatives. Suppose the advocates of no-fault automobile accident compensation plans are correct that a combination of criminal penalties for dangerous driving and compulsory accident insurance for potential victims would be a more efficient method of accident control, considering all relevant social costs—the costs of accidents, the costs of accident avoidance, and the costs of administering the accident-control system itself—than the present tort system. If the criminal penalties deterred all negligent driving, there would be no victims of wrongful conduct and so no problem with the abolition of liability. But not all negligent injuries would be deterred, so some victims of wrongful injury would go uncompensated. Would the no-fault system therefore violate corrective justice? Not necessarily. The concept of *ex ante* compensation, introduced earlier, is again relevant. If the no-fault system is really cheaper, potential victims (who are also drivers) may prefer to buy accident insurance and forgo their tort rights in exchange for not having to buy liability insurance.

But there is a simpler route to the conclusion that a no-fault plan would not necessarily violate the concept of corrective justice. If there are good reasons, grounded in considerations of social utility, for abolishing the wrong of negligently injuring another, then the failure to compensate for such an injury is not a failure to compensate for *wrongful* injury. To repeat an earlier point, corrective justice is a procedural principle; the meaning of wrongful conduct must be sought elsewhere.

Let us consider another example of arguable conflict between corrective justice and economics. Suppose a favorite idea of economists was adopted, and a very high fine was set for some offense coupled with a very low probability of apprehension and conviction. Say the fine was $100—although the social cost of the offense was only $1—and the probability of apprehending and convicting an offender was set at one percent. Then in 99 out of 100 cases the offender would go scot-free. Would such a penalty scheme, though economically optimal, violate the principles of corrective justice? I think not. The expected cost of the offense is $1, which we said was its social cost. The offender has paid for the offense—in advance. To be sure, *ex post* there will be unequal treatment of offenders; *ex post,* some really will get off scot-free; but unless the *ex ante* perspective is inconsistent with the Aristotelian idea of corrective justice (and why should it be?), a failure of redress *ex post* is not necessarily a failure to do corrective justice.

Book V, Chapter 4 of the *Nicomachean Ethics* makes the point not only that a wrongful and injurious act requires rectification in some unspecified form—a point perilously close to being a tautology—but also, and more interestingly, that the duty of rectification is unaffected by the relative merit of injurer and victim considered apart from the injury; unaffected, that is, by distributive considerations. Distributive neutrality is also required by the economic analysis of law. Consider two otherwise identical accident cases, but in one the injurer and the victim have incomes of 100 (in present-value terms) and in the other the victim's income is only 60. The accident is the result of a wrong (in the economic sense of a failure to take a cost-justified precaution) by the injurer, and the victim is totally disabled from gainful work by the accident but not otherwise injured. Under the economic approach as under the Aristotelian, and assuming rectification takes the form of private damages actions, the first victim would be entitled to damages of 100 and the second to 60. If the second victim's damages were reduced by a further 60 percent—say on the ground that he is only 60 percent as meritorious as the injurer—there would be underdeterrence of accidents from an economic standpoint, because the injurer would not bear the full social costs of his accidents. Similarly, it would be wrong as a matter both of economics and corrective justice to award the same damages to both victims—notwithstanding the difference in their incomes—on the ground, for example, that they were in some sense equally good people. To adjust the compensation according to the relative merit of the injurer and the victim as persons would be contrary to Aristotle's concept of corrective justice, and it would also be inefficient because it would induce an inefficient level of precautions by one of the victims, or by both, or even by the injurer. For example, if victim A receives only 60 in damages, and victim B also 60, A will be undercompensated and will be led to take excessive precautions. If A and B each receive 100, there will be overdeterrence of injurers; in addition, B will have an incentive to act carelessly since he profits from being disabled. If each receives 80 (one-half their combined loss), then A will be undercompensated and B overcompensated, with inefficient results as just described. Thus, the distributive neutrality of the economic analysis of torts is not a merely adventitious characteristic of that analysis. Neutrality is required as a matter of justice, where justice is defined in terms of economic efficiency.

I am not arguing that Aristotle anticipated the economic analysis of law. He did not. Not only was his substantive concept of wrongful conduct too narrow from an economic standpoint, because limited to deliberate wrongs, but it is not clear whether his idea of corrective justice required that the victim of wrongful conduct be correctly (from an economic standpoint) compensated. The problem is most acute in the case where the wrongdoer's gain is less than the victim's loss. One commentator has suggested that if the wrongdoer gained 3 and the victim lost 7, Aristotle would have wanted the judge to award damages of 5.[55] Another commentator thinks Aristotle would have required full compensation.[56] The first suggestion would involve giving the victim an incentive to overinvest in safety.

The problem of asymmetrical gain and loss is common in contract as well as tort cases and helps explain why specific performance, as distinct from damages, is not necessarily required by the principles of corrective justice. At first glance it might seem that if someone has breached his contract, ordering him to perform it—specific performance—is the natural method of rectification. But suppose the reason he breached was that the cost of performance had become prohibitive; then specific performance would impose a cost on the wrongdoer that might be much greater than the loss to the victim of the breach, while a damages remedy might (depending on the rules of damages) compensate the victim fully.

Various rules of standing may seem to raise questions of conflict between corrective justice principles and economic principles. Take the rule that only a direct purchaser from a seller who is charging a price in violation of antitrust law can maintain a damages action against the seller. A purchaser from that purchaser—an indirect purchaser, in other words—is not allowed to sue even though the first purchaser may have passed on most of the overcharge to him.[57] The indirect purchaser is injured, and he is injured as the result of a wrongful act: must he not, therefore, be allowed to sue, if corrective justice is to be done? Professor Landes and I have argued that even in this case there is compensation *ex ante*.[58] If the direct purchaser has a right to collect the entire overcharge, the net cost to him of buying the good in question is lower, and he will pass on the saving to the indirect purchaser (or so much of the saving as he would pass on of the overcharge). Therefore, the indirect purchaser is compensated in advance for the expected cost of the antitrust overcharge passed on to him, by paying a lower price for the good. And the wrongdoer is punished, since he pays damages to the direct purchaser. The essentials of corrective justice are preserved.

But we also argued that the costs of allowing indirect purchasers to maintain damage actions provided an independent ground for denying such purchasers standing. Is cost a proper ground for refusing to do corrective justice? Consider this case. The theory of the second best teaches that sometimes the optimal way to improve the allocation of resources is to allow a compensating distortion. Suppose there is a cartel of widget producers, and they maintain a price far above cost, inducing some purchasers to switch to other products; this switching results in what the economist calls a "deadweight loss." One way of reducing the deadweight loss would be to raise the price of substitute products; then there would be less switching and less deadweight loss. Yet it would strain the ordinary meaning of the word "wrong" to say that the cartel's behavior was not wrongful, simply because society had decided to offset the wrong rather than correct it directly. Perhaps even in this case an argument based on *ex ante* compensation could be used, as in the earlier example of no-fault automobile accident compensation, to preserve corrective justice. But the more interesting question is whether corrective justice imposes duties regardless of cost. There is nothing in Aristotle to suggest that it does.

To all that I have said in this part of the paper two possible responses remain to be considered. The first is that I have limited discussion to *Aristotle's* concept of corrective justice and other concepts might lead to other results, perhaps inconsistent with the economic approach. This is of course possible, but while Aristotle's concept is not always followed, as I tried to show in Part II of this article, no alternative concept has, to my knowledge at least, been elaborated. Second, it may be argued that while both the Aristotelian concept and economic analysis result in the same or at least similar systems of redress, they do so for different reasons: the Aristotelian to carry out some ideal of justice, and the economic to maximize the wealth of society. But Aristotle did not explain *why* he thought there was a duty of corrective justice; he merely explained what that duty was.[59] Economic analysis supplies a reason why the duty to rectify wrongs, and the corollary principle of distributive neutrality in rectification, is (depending on the cost of rectification) a part of the concept of justice. Corrective justice is an instrument for maximizing wealth, and in the normative economic theory of the state—or at least in that version of the theory that I espouse—wealth maximization is the ultimate objective of the just state.

To summarize, my argument is not that Aristotle advocated an economic approach to law; it is that the concept of corrective justice in Book V, Chapter 4 of the *Nicomachean Ethics* is, and must be, a component of the economic theory of law. But whether this point is correct or not, those scholars who view the term "corrective justice" in a sense different from Aristotle's should explain and justify their unorthodox usage.

NOTES

1. See Oliver Wendell Holmes, Jr., The Common Law (1881), especially at pp. 94-96.

2. On the utilitarian tradition in tort law see William M. Landes & Richard A. Posner, The Economic Structure of Tort Law, ch. 1 (1980) (unpublished manuscript at the Univ. of Chicago). I have argued that the law is economic rather than utilitarian, that what is and should be maximized by judges applying that law is wealth rather than utility; but wealth and utility are both aggregate measures of social welfare, and my normative economic approach can be described as one of constrained utilitarianism. See Richard A. Posner, The Value of Wealth: A Comment on Dworkin and Kronman, 9 J. Legal Stud. 243, 248 (1980); cf. Richard A. Posner, Utilitarianism, Economics, and Legal Theory, 8 J. Legal Stud. 103 (1979); Richard A. Posner, The Economics of Justice, chs. 3-4 (Harvard University Press, forthcoming 1981).

3. The usual justification of loss spreading, as by making business enterprises strictly liable for injuries caused by their defective products, is a utilitarian (or economic) one: that given diminishing marginal utility of income, and assuming that victims and nonvictims of accidents have on average the same utility functions, distributing a loss over a large number of consumers or shareholders of the enterprise that causes the injury will result in less disutility than if the same loss is concentrated on the victim of the injury. This is the economic rationale of insurance; and enterprise liability, in the usual form in which it is advocated, is defended primarily as a desirable method of insuring against accidents caused by defective products. Similar justifications are offered for no-fault automobile insurance.

4. George P. Fletcher, Fairness and Utility in Tort Theory, 85 Harv. L. Rev. 537, 538 (1972) (footnote omitted).

5. John Borgo, Causal Paradigms in Tort Law 8 J. Legal Stud. 419 n.3 (1979).

6. He introduces it briefly in Chapter 2.

7. Voluntary transactions he instances by "sale, purchase, loan for consumption, pledging, loan for use, depositing, letting"; involuntary by "theft, adultery, poisoning, procuring, enticement of slaves, assassination, false witness [,] assault, murder, robbery with violence, mutilation, abuse, insult." Aristotle, The Nicomachean Ethics 111-12 (David Ross trans., rev. ed. 1980).

8. Id. at 114-15. The Greek (transliterated) is *ouden gar diapherei, ei epieikēs phaulon apesterēsen ē phaulos epieikē, oud' ei emoicheusen epieikēs ē phaulos; alla pros tou blabous tēn diaphoran monon blepei ho nomos, kai chrētai hōs isois, ei ho men adikei ho d' adikeitai, kai ei eblapsen ho de beblaptai.* Aristotelis, Ethica Nicomachea 96 (I. Bywater ed. 1894). Rendered more or less literally, this means: "for it makes no difference whether a fair [moderate, upper class, good, reasonable] man robs [bereaves, defrauds] a man of low [bad, inferior] station or a man of low station robs a fair man, or whether a fair man commits adultery [against a man of low station] or a man of low station [commits adultery against a fair man]; the law looks to the distinction alone of the injury, and treats as equals, if one acts unjustly and the other is wronged, and if one injures and the other is injured."

9. Aristotle, supra note 7, at 115, 117.

10. See 2 The Ethics of Aristotle 112-16 (Alexander Grant ed., 4th rev. ed. 1885); The Ethics of Aristotle 217-23 (John Burnet ed. 1904); The Fifth Book of the Nicomachean Ethics of Aristotle 82-86 (Henry Jackson ed. 1879); W. F. R. Hardie, Aristotle's Ethical Theory 192-95 (1968); H. H. Joachim, Aristotle: The Nicomachean Ethics: A Commentary 136-47 (D.A. Rees ed. 1951); D. G. Ritchie, Aristotle's Subdivisions of 'Particular Justice,' 8 Classical Rev. 185 (1894); J. A. Stewart, 1 Notes on the Nicomachean Ethics of Aristotle 430-41 (1973). See also Max Hamburger, Morals and Law: The Growth of Aristotle's Legal Theory 46-47, 51 (1951); Konrad Marc-Wogau, Aristotle's Theory of Corrective Justice and Reciprocity, in Philosophical Essays 21-30 (1967).

11. Joachim, supra note 10, at 144.

12. Aristotle, supra note 7, at 125.

13. Id. at 126-27. Hamburger, supra note 10, at 70, equates the mistake category to negligence. See Edgar Bodenheimer, Treatise on Justice 210-13 (1967), for a discussion of the state-of-mind requirement in Aristotle's concept of acting unjustly.

14. 2 The Ethics of Aristotle 113 n.3 (Alexander Grant ed., 4th rev. ed. 1885).

15. See A. R. W. Harrison, Aristotle's Nicomachean Ethics, Book V, and the Law of Athens, 77 J. Hellenic Stud. 42, 45-46 (1957); Joachim, supra note 10, at 137; Richard A. Posner, Retribution and Related Concepts of Punishment, 9 J. Legal Stud. 71, 85 (1980), and references cited therein; 2 Paul Vinogradoff, Outlines of Historical Jurisprudence 45-51 (1922). See generally H. D. P. Lee, The Legal Background of Two Passages in the *Nicomachean Ethics,* 31 Classical Q. 129 (1937).

16. Delba Winthrop, Aristotle and Theories of Justice, 72 Am. Pol. Sci. Rev. 1201, 1205 (1978). See also Morris Ginsberg, The Concept of Justice, 38 Philosophy 99, 105 (1963); H. L. A. Hart, The Concept of Law 158-61 (1961).

17. Fletcher, supra note 4, at 540-42.

18. Or so I infer from a comparison of id. at 538 with id. at 547 n.40.

19. As in the Hand formula. See id. at 542 n.19; Richard A. Posner, A Theory of Negligence, 1 J. Legal Stud. 29, 32 (1972).

20. Fletcher, supra note 4, at 542.

21. Id. at 540.

22. As Rawls states:

"The more specific sense that Aristotle gives to justice, and from which the most familar formulations derive, is that of refraining from *pleonexia,* that is, from gaining some advantage for oneself by seizing what belongs to another, his property, his reward, his office, and the like, or by denying a person that which is due to him, the fulfillment of a promise, the repayment of a debt, the showing of proper respect and so on. It is evident that this definition is framed to apply to actions, and persons are thought to be just insofar as they have, as one of the permanent elements of their character, a steady and effective desire to act justly. Aristotle's definition clearly presupposes, however, an account of what properly belongs to a person and of what is due to him. Now such entitlements are, I believe, very often derived from social institutions and the legitimate expectations to which they give rise. There is no reason to think that Aristotle would disagree with this, and certainly he has a conception of social justice to account for these claims."

John Rawls, A Theory of Justice 10-11 (1971) (footnote omitted). J. R. Lucas, On Justice 13-14 (1980), makes the general point well:

"Although the reasons on which a just decision is based have to be individualised reasons, they do not therefore have to exclude all general considerations. General considerations, e.g., of expediency or utility, can justify there being one general rule rather than another: what justice requires is that any such general considerations shall issue in rules that apply generally, and that their application in the individual case must be justified by reference to the facts of that case."

23. See Richard A. Epstein, A Theory of Strict Liability, 2 J. Legal Stud. 151, 165 n.42 (1973).

24. See Richard A. Epstein, Defenses and Subsequent Pleas in a System of Strict Liability, 3 J. Legal Stud. 165 (1974).

25. Richard A. Epstein, Nuisance Law: Corrective Justice and Its Utilitarian Constraints, 8 J. Legal Stud. 49, 50, 99 (1979).

26. Id. at 77, 101.

27. Richard A. Epstein, Causation and Corrective Justice: A Reply to Two Critics, 8 J. Legal Stud. 477, 496 (1979).

28. See Epstein, supra note 24, at 198-99 and n.87.

29. Id. at 167-68.

30. To be sure, Epstein's principle of strict liability is one only of *prima facie* liability, and he allows for various excuses. But if the defendant has no excuse (consent or self-defense or whatever), and he may not, then the fact of harm, by itself, is indeed a basis of redress. And this is not an Aristotelian idea.

31. See, e.g., William T. Blackstone, Reverse Discrimination and Compensatory Justice, 3 Soc. Theory & Practice 253, 254-55 (1975);

Ginsberg, supra note 16, at 111-12; Hart, supra note 16, at 158-61, 251:2 Vinogradoff, supra note 15, at 45.

32. Borgo, supra note 5, at 419-20. See also id. at 454: "the defendant's *prima facie* moral responsibility is determined exclusively by the existence *vel non* of a causal relation between his conduct and the plaintiff's harm."

33. See id. at 419 n.3.

34. Id. at 454.

35. See Richard A. Epstein, Intentional Harms, 4 J. Legal Stud. 391, 431-32 (1975).

36. See Borgo, supra note 5, at 444.

37. See the repeated equation of causation and use of force in Epstein, supra note 27, at 480-81.

38. As Joseph Steiner has said of Epstein's tort theory, "The physical descriptions which constitute the paradigms of causation either have no normative content and cannot lead to normative conclusions or they employ words with implicit normative content thereby incorporating unstated, independent, normative premises which are the very principles we are seeking. In neither case do the paradigms, per se, give guidance on the assignment of rights." Joseph M. Steiner, Economics, Morality, and the Law of Torts, 26 U. Toronto L. J. 227, 246 (1976).

39. That is, Epstein, in his early work, and Borgo believe that questions of legal liability can be answered within a more general theory of personal responsibility, a theory based on causation. I am indebted for the term to Jules Coleman.

40. On Epstein, see Richard A. Posner, Epstein's Tort Theory: A Critique, 8 J. Legal Stud. 457, 465-71 (1979); on Fletcher, see Jules Coleman, Justice and Reciprocity in Tort Theory, 14 W. Ontario L. Rev. 105, 117-18 (1975), explaining, and criticizing, Fletcher's derivation of the paradigm of reciprocity from a "security principle" analogous to one of John Rawls's principles of distributive justice.

41. Jules L. Coleman, Mental Abnormality, Personal Responsibility, and Tort Liability, in Mental Illness: Law and Public Policy 107, 123 (B. A. Brody & H. Tristam Engelhardt, Jr. eds. 1980) (reference omitted). For earlier discussion of his corrective justice approach to tort law see Jules L. Coleman, Justice and the Argument for No-Fault, 3 Soc. Theory & Practice 161, 173-78 (1975); Reply to Pilon, 59 The Personalist 307, 312-13 (1978); The Morality of Strict Tort Liability, 18 Wm. & Mary L. Rev. 259 (1976). Coleman acknowledges a debt to James W. Nickel, whose views may be found in Justice in Compensation, 18 Wm. & Mary L. Rev. 379 (1976).

42. Coleman, Mental Abnormality, Personal Responsibility, and Tort Liability, supra note 41, at 123.

43. "But in the case of accidental torts there is, in general, no gain on the wrongdoer's behalf that needs to be eliminated. That his conduct is wrongful supports the right of the victim to recompense, nothing more." Coleman, Justice and the Argument for No-Fault, supra note 41, at 177.

44. See text at note 9 supra. To be sure, as Coleman has pointed out to me, the gain in the negligence case is not triggered by the loss—it would be the same if the accident had not occurred—but I do not see what difference that makes so far as the wrongfulness of the injury is concerned. We would say that a robber who shot his victim injured him wrongfully, though it was no part of his plan to shoot him and he did so only because the victim resisted.

45. This assumes, of course, that negligence is wrongful. Aristotle would not have thought so, but, as Coleman and I both believe, Aristotle's idea of what constitutes wrongful conduct can be severed from his idea of corrective justice. More on this, and also on no-fault automobile accident compensation, in Part III.

46. Frederick L. Sharp, Aristotle, Justice and Enterprise Liability in the Law of Torts, 34 U. Toronto Faculty L. Rev. 84 and n.1 (1976).

47. (1868) L.R. 3 H.L. 330. This case imposed strict liability on the defendants for water damage to property caused by the collapse,

not due to the defendants' negligence or other wrongdoing, of a reservoir on the defendants' property.

48. Sharp, supra note 46, at 89.

49. Id. at 90 (footnotes omitted).

50. The term "mean" is not used in the mathematical sense of average.

51. As Coleman notes:

"the principle of strict liability is inadequate as a basis of justice in compensation. On the strict liability model, a victim is entitled to recompense even if his injurer is not at fault (usually negligent) in causing him harm. Thus, the strict liability rule does not restrict recompense to those who have absorbed *unjustifiable* losses, and though compensating the general category of victims *may* be justified as a matter of general welfare or benevolence, compensation is not a matter of justice their right. The rule of fault liability, on the other hand, enables us to identify those victims for whom recompense is a matter of justice."

Coleman, Reply to Pilon, supra note 41, at 315 n.31 (emphasis in original).

52. See the Nicomachean Ethics at bk. I, ch. 8 & bk. X, ch. 6.

53. See, e.g., Richard A. Posner, Economic Analysis of Law, pt. II (2d ed. 1977).

54. See William M. Landes & Richard A. Posner, The Private Enforcement of Law, 4 J. Legal Stud. 1, 32, 35 (1975); Posner, supra note 19, at 48-52. A parallel argument to that in the text is possible for breach of contract. See Landes & Posner, supra, at 36. In fact, Aristotle's treatment of torts and contracts as involuntary and voluntary transactions parallels the modern economic view of these sub-jects. See, e.g., Posner, supra note 53, at 179-80. Aristotle would apparently have regarded a breach of contract, if deliberate, as an act of injustice. Cf. note 7 supra. In the common law, breach of contract is a strict-liability concept by and large (some excuses are recognized, however—for example, where performance is impossible), but the difference between Aristotle's and the common law view has to do with the substantive concept of wrongdoing rather than with the duty to rectify a wrongful harm arising from a contractual relationship. The duty is common to both systems. Whether the wrong is a deliberate breach of contract, or any breach, does not affect the analysis of corrective justice.

55. See The Ethics of Aristotle 221n (John Burnet ed. 1904). In Burnet's actual example, the gain was 7 and the loss 3. In the example in the text I have reversed the numbers to make the example simpler to understand, but my basic analytical point is independent of this transposition. In Burnet's example, awarding the victim 5 would give him an incentive to be injured, since the injury would yield him a profit of 2.

56. See Harrison, supra note 15, at 45.

57. See Illinois Brick Co. v. Illinois, 431 U.S. 720 (1977).

58. See William M. Landes & Richard A. Posner, Should Indirect Purchasers Have Standing to Sue under the Antitrust Laws? An Economic Analysis of the Rule of *Illinois Brick,* 46 U. Chi. L. Rev. 602, 605-08 (1979).

59. In fact, because *adikos* means unlawful as well as unjust, it is unclear to what extent Aristotle thought he was doing more than describing legal concepts that happened to be prevalent in his society. See sources in note 15 supra.

JULES COLEMAN

Corrective Justice and Wrongful Gain*

Richard Posner's essay "The Concept of Corrective Justice in Recent Theories of Tort Law"[1] falls into three distinct but related sections. In the first part of the paper Posner attempts to characterize the principle(s) of corrective justice. In the second part, he criticizes the efforts of a number of other tort theorists, including George Fletcher, Richard Epstein, and myself, who have attempted to ground the law of torts on a foundation of corrective justice. Having himself previously advanced an efficiency-based conception of the law of torts, Posner goes on to argue in the third part of the essay that the principle of corrective justice is itself required by the principle of efficiency. By laying an economic foundation for the principle of corrective justice, Posner argues not only for the compatibility of the most promising line of moral defense of tort law with the dominant economic one, but for the primacy of the latter as well.

Posner has graciously provided me with the opportunity to respond to his paper. In a series of essays, some of which have appeared in philosophy journals,[2] others of which have surfaced in law reviews,[3] and one of which has appeared as a chapter in a very overpriced book,[4] I have explored the moral foundations of tort law. It would not be unfair—indeed, it may be too generous—to say that in these essays I have advanced a theory of torts based on the principle of corrective justice. In what follows I first summarize (in a very compressed fashion) my view of the role of corrective justice in tort theory, then briefly contrast it with those of Epstein and Fletcher, and finally consider Posner's objections to it.

I. LIABILITY, RECOVERY, AND A CONCEPTION OF CORRECTIVE JUSTICE

Central to my account of torts is the distinction between the grounds of liability and recovery—in other words, between the two questions

(1) What are the grounds necessary and sufficient to justify a victim's claim to recompense? and (2) Under what conditions ought an injurer be obligated to provide compensation to his victims?[5] That the grounds of recovery and liability are at least analytically distinguishable is illustrated by the fact that a society could establish an insurance scheme to compensate all accident victims, while only those injurers who are at fault in causing an accident would be required to contribute to the insurance pool. Were we to separate liability and recovery in this way, being at fault in causing harm would be a necessary condition of liability, but not of the victim's case for recovery. Whether a system that separated liability from recovery in this particular way would be just or efficient remains to be worked out. For now the point is simply that the considerations that ground a claim to recompense need not coincide with those that ground the obligation to repair.

Once the distinction between the foundations of recovery and liability is drawn, the next question concerns the role of corrective justice in each. This in turn requires a conception of corrective justice. In my view, corrective or compensatory justice is concerned with the category of wrongful gains and losses. Rectification, in this view, is a matter of justice when it is necessary to protect a distribution of holdings (or entitlements) from distortions which arise from unjust enrichments and wrongful losses. The principle of corrective justice requires the annulments of both wrongful gains and losses.[6]

This conception of corrective justice puts a great burden on the concepts of wrongful gain and wrongful loss. Without offering a set of conditions necessary and sufficient for a loss or gain to count as wrongful I have tried in my previous work to characterize the basic idea by examples. Within the category of wrongful losses are those one suffers through the fault or wrongful conduct of another; within the class of unjust enrichments are those one secures through one's wrongdoing, as in many instances of fraud and theft. A compensable or undeserved loss need not, however, be the result of another's wrongdoing. Sometimes the justifiable

* Jules Coleman, "Corrective Justice and Wrongful Gain," *Journal of Legal Studies,* Vol. 11, No. 2 (1982), pp. 421–440. Reprinted by permission of The University of Chicago Press.

(i.e., nonwrongful) taking of what another has a well-established right to justifies a claim to rectification.[7] An instance of a justifiable taking that creates a compensable loss is given by the following example of Joel Feinberg's:

Suppose that you are on a back-packing trip in the mountain country when an unanticipated blizzard strikes the area with such ferocity that your life is imperiled. Fortunately, you stumble onto an unoccupied cabin, locked and boarded up for the winter, clearly somebody else's private property. You smash in a window, enter, and huddle in a corner for three days until the storm abates. During this period you help yourself to your unknown benefactor's food supply and burn his wooden furniture in the fireplace to keep warm. Surely you are justified in doing all these things, and yet you have infringed the clear rights of another person.[8]

Feinberg argues, and I concur, that in spite of the justifiability of what you have done, you owe the owner of the cabin compensation for his food and furniture.

Though these examples do not define in any strict sense the operative notion of wrongfulness, they help to characterize it sufficiently to make the notion a useful one.

Given this general conception of corrective justice, the above examples of wrongful gain and loss, as well as the central distinction between the grounds of recovery and liability, we can begin to spell out my account of the role of corrective justice in tort theory.

In torts a distinction is drawn between the rules of fault (or conditional) and strict (or unconditional) liability. In fault liability, a victim is not entitled to recover his loss unless it is the result of another's fault, and an injurer is liable only for those harms that are his fault. In strict liability, neither the victim's claim to recompense nor the injurer's responsibility to make repair requires that the injurer's conduct be at fault.

A. CORRECTIVE JUSTICE AND THE FAULT PRINCIPLE

Consider first the role of corrective justice in grounding recovery and liability under the fault principle. Under the fault principle a victim is entitled to repair only if his loss results from another's fault. A loss that is the consequence of another's fault is, in the sense just characterized, a wrongful one. Since the principle of corrective justice requires annulling wrongful losses, it supports the victim's claim to recompense in fault liability.

The relationship between corrective justice and the principle that an individual ought to be liable for the untoward consequences of his fault is somewhat more complex. There are two kinds of cases in which the principle of corrective justice gives direct support to the principle of fault liability: (1) those cases in which an individual's fault results not only in another's loss, but in his gain as well; and (2) those cases in which an individual secures a wrongful gain through his fault, though his gain is not the result of another's loss. Unjust enrichment through fraud is an example of a wrongful gain secured at another's expense; non-harm-causing but nevertheless negligent motoring is often an example of conduct that creates wrongful gain in the absence of a corresponding wrongful loss.

Consider the case of negligent motoring more carefully. Negligent motoring may or may not result in an accident. Whether or not it does, individuals who drive negligently often secure a wrongful gain in doing so, namely, the "savings" from not taking adequate safety precautions—those required of the reasonable man of ordinary prudence. This form of wrongful gain is not, *ex hypothesi,* the result of anyone else's wrongful loss. On the other hand, if a negligent motorist causes another harm, he normally secures no *additional* wrongful gain in virtue of his doing so. In this respect faulty motoring differs from the usual case of fraud or theft. Because harmful, negligent motoring does not generally result in any wrongful gain (apart from that which is the result of negligence itself), the obligation to repair the victim's wrongful loss cannot be entirely grounded on a foundation of corrective justice. There is, in other words, no wrongful gain correlative of the wrongful loss the faulty injurer imposes upon his victim, and no reason, therefore, as a matter of corrective justice alone, for imposing the victim's loss upon his injurer. The wrongful gain negligent motorists secure is logically distinct from any loss they may cause others, and so the occasion of another's loss cannot be the moral basis for annulling these gains as a matter of justice.[9]

This is bound to appear controversial; some additional distinctions might make it appear less so. A full theory of justice in tort liability and recovery would distinguish among four issues: (1) the foundation of a claim that a person has suffered a compensable loss, or that he has secured an unjust gain; (2) the mode of rectification—that is, the manner in which unjust gains and losses are to be eliminated;[10] (3) the character of rectification—that is, whether a particular form of compensation (e.g., money) is always, sometimes, or rarely appropriate; and (4) the extent of rectification—that is, just how much of a person's loss (or gain) ought to be eliminated.[11]

The central claim of my thesis is the rather straightforward one (I believe) that determining whether a gain or loss is wrongful determines the answer only to the first of these issues. If there is a wrongful loss, it ought to be annulled; the same goes for wrongful or unwarranted gains. Nevertheless, the principle of corrective justice which enables us to identify compensable losses and unjust enrichments does not commit us to adopting any particular mode of rectification. The principle that determines which gains and losses are to be eliminated does not by itself specify a means for doing so. Presumably there is more than one way of rectifying undeserved gains and losses. So when I claim that if an injurer who through his fault imposes a wrongful loss on another but who does not thereby gain has an obligation to repair, his obligation cannot derive directly from the principle of corrective justice, I mean only to be emphasizing the obvious fact that he has secured no gain which would be the concern of corrective justice to rectify. His victim's claim to recompense is on the other hand a matter of corrective justice. And if we feel that the injurer should rectify his victim's loss, it must be for reasons other than the fact that doing so is required by justice in order to annul his gain.

Once we have adopted a system of tort liability we have committed ourselves to a particular mode of rectifying wrongful gains and losses—a method that imposes victims' losses on their injurers whether or not the loss occasions a wrongful gain. That particular mode of rectification is in no sense required by the principle of corrective justice. There may be reasons other than those which derive from a theory of corrective justice for imposing an innocent victim's loss on his injurer. Consider three such arguments. First, one might argue from the principle of retributive justice for the imposition of liability of faulty injurers. Such an argument would hold that wrongdoing, whether or not it secures personal gain, is sinful and ought to be punished or sanctioned. Imposing liability in torts is a way of sanctioning mischief. Therefore liability is imposed on the faulty injurer not to rectify his gain—of which there may be none— but to penalize his moral wrong.[12] Or one could argue from the principle that claim rights impose correlative duties to the conclusion that the victim's right, which is grounded in corrective justice, imposes a correlative duty to repair on his injurer.[13] Or one might take yet another tack and seek to ground the injurer's obligation to repair in considerations of deterrence or accident cost avoidance. This argument might take the following form. To be at fault is to act in an inefficient manner; it is to fail to take appropriate accident-avoidance measures when the cost of doing so is less than the cost of the harm to the victim discounted by the probability of its occurrence. An injurer who is at fault in harming another is obligated to make restitution because his doing so provides him with an incentive to take such precautions as are reasonable and necessary in the future, and because doing so in general has the long-term effect of reducing the sum of accident and accident-avoidance costs.[14] Were one to take an "economic approach" to the liability of the faulty injurer and a "corrective-justice" approach to the right of his victim to secure recompense, the net result would be a merger of economic and moral theories of fault liability, albeit a more narrowly defined one than Posner contemplates.

B. CORRECTIVE JUSTICE AND STRICT LIABILITY

Consider now the relationship between the principle of corrective justice and liability and recovery under the rule of unconditional or strict liability. The conception of unwarranted or wrongful gain and loss central to the principle of corrective justice includes losses and gains that result from justified "takings." Unlike the wrongful losses in fault liability, the unwarranted losses in these cases are not the result of wrongdoing in the ordinary sense. The "taking" itself may be reasonable or justified, as it is in Feinberg's example, and as it is in cases like *Vincent* v. *Lake Erie Transp. Co.*[15] Consequently, there is no wrong in the doing; were there any wrong at all it would consist in taking what another has a legitimate right to (under specifiable circumstances) and not rendering adequate compensation for having done so.

Understood in this way, corrective justice may explain those strict liability cases that can adequately be modeled on the idea of a taking.

Corrective justice might therefore explain *Vincent* v. *Lake Erie,* but probably not strict liability for either ultrahazardous activities or defective products. Just how much of strict liability the principle of corrective justice explains will depend on the proper analysis of what constitutes a taking—and that is no easy matter.

Again, one has to be careful to avoid misunderstanding the claim. It does not follow from what I have said that those areas of strict liability, like ultrahazardous or products liability, which do not involve takings in the ordinary sense cannot be justified or rationally explained. My point is simply that appealing to the principle of corrective justice—once it is properly understood—will not help to explain them. There may be other considerations, both of morality and economics, that neatly rationalize existing strict liability law. My purpose is simply to determine which, if any, of the existing law of torts might be defensible within a certain conception of corrective justice. If it turns out, as I think it does, that only certain well-defined areas of tort law can be comprehended by a single principle, so much the better for my view, for it demonstrates theoretically what we knew pretheoretically—namely, that the law of torts is extremely complex and that it resists simple analysis.[16]

II. EPSTEIN AND FLETCHER ON CORRECTIVE JUSTICE

Considerations of corrective justice ground four claims related to liability and recovery in torts: (1) the claim to recompense of a victim of another's fault, (2) the liability of a faulty injurer who gains through his mischief, (3) the claim of a victim in strict liability for a takings-like loss, and (4) the injurer's liability for a taking. In contrast, both Epstein and Fletcher appear to believe that all, or nearly all, of torts can be explained by subsumption under a theory of corrective justice. The interesting question concerns how it is that the three of us, each of whom believes that corrective justice is central to an adequate analysis of torts, reach such different conclusions.

There really is not much of a mystery, however. The key difference is that both Epstein and Fletcher share a strategy which is first to identify an element common to both strict and fault liability, then to argue that this common element is central to liability and recovery, then

finally to confer normativity upon this feature of both fault and strict liability by subsuming it under a particular conception of corrective justice. Fletcher and Epstein disagree about which element is the operative shared component in strict and fault liability. For Epstein it is the fact that in both fault and strict liability the injurer causes the victim's loss;[17] for Fletcher it is the fact that the injurer harmed the victim through his nonreciprocal risk taking.[18]

Epstein's arguments are motivated in part by a desire to deemphasize the role of fault in determining both liability and recovery. The desire to eliminate the centrality of fault to torts must be understood against the background of a failed moral theory of fault liability and an increasingly accepted economic account of it. Let me explain. At one time the prevailing moral theory of torts seized upon the introduction of the fault requirement in the mid nineteenth century as a shift away from the immoral criterion of strict liability to a moral foundation for liability. Instead of imposing liability without regard to the culpability or blameworthiness of the injurer—as was the case in strict liability—fault liability injected a concern for the moral character of the injurer's conduct into the formula that was to determine the appropriateness of imposing another's loss upon him.

The concern of torts for the moral character of the injurer's conduct has always been rather minimal, however. It is the lesson of *Vaughan* v. *Menlove*[19] that an individual may be at fault in torts even if he is not morally at fault for his conduct, his fault being determined by his failure to comply with a standard of reasonable care whether or not he is capable of compliance. Because moral culpability is not a condition of fault in torts, previous efforts to provide a moral account of fault liability have stalled. Moreover, by the early 1970s, the prevailing view had become that the only plausible, coherent account of fault in torts was an economic one: to be at fault is simply to fail to take the precautions necessary to avoid an inefficient (in cost/benefit terms) harm. In short, the standard of fault liability which moralists had hoped would anchor a moral theory of torts appeared not only to escape moral analysis, but to be firmly rooted in economic theory. Theorists intent on defending a moral account of torts were faced with a choice: either they could provide an alternative moral account of the fault principle, or they could reexamine, even eliminate, the role of fault in a moral theory of torts. (I have pursued the former route; Epstein and Fletcher have taken the latter.)

In reducing the role of fault liability Epstein focuses his attention on the fact that wherever liability is appropriate, someone has caused another harm. The moral freight which, in the traditional view, had been carried by the fault requirement is borne, in Epstein's view, by the causal condition. Unlike a theory of torts that relies on fault, the theory that relies on the causal condition can theoretically (at least) ground all of tort law under a comprehensive moral principle, since the causal condition, unlike the fault condition, is a necessary element in both fault and strict liability.

Though Epstein has always emphasized the causal condition as central to a moral account of tort liability, his view about the principle that confers moral significance on the causal condition has undergone subtle but significant changes.

In his early essay, "A Theory of Strict Liability,"[20] Epstein appears to have held the view that the best way to understand and (where possible) justify tort liability is by rooting it in a more comprehensive theory of personal responsibility. Tort liability is justly imposed provided the conditions of tort liability conform to the requirements of an agent's being responsible for his conduct. Epstein's view is that a satisfactory account of personal responsibility must be developed in terms of an analysis of causation and volition.

Running alongside the responsibility thesis in Epstein's early work is a very undeveloped argument which relies on corrective justice as the basis of tort liability. Prior to the incidence of harm, individuals are in a state of "equilibrium" or "balance." Liability in torts provides the mechanism for redressing imbalances caused by harmful conduct: liability and recovery in torts reestablish the previously existing equilibria. The causal condition remains central to a just theory of liability since the principle of corrective justice requires annulling gains and losses caused by harmful conduct.

Both the responsibility thesis and the simple corrective-justice accounts of tort liability are seriously flawed. I have argued that although considerations of personal responsibility are relevant to a full theory of torts, Epstein is mistaken in thinking that the analysis of responsibility (which would be a normative theory) could be adequately developed in terms of an analysis of causation (which would in-

volve a natural or scientific theory).[21] One can be responsible not only for what one does, but for what one fails to do as well. If an individual wrongly fails to act he may be culpable for his failure to prevent harm. Though it would be philosophically confused to say that his failure to act caused the harm, there might be sufficient reasons for ascribing the resulting harm to him as his responsibility.

The problem with the theory of corrective justice that relies on the fact that A caused B harm as sufficient both for (*prima facie*) liability and recovery (respectively) is simply that not every way in which A harms B is wrongful. Not every loss B suffers at A's hands is a wrongful one; not every gain A secures at B's expense is an unjust one.

Epstein's most recent view emerges from these lines of criticism. In answering the charge that A may have a duty to prevent harm to B so that his failure to do so may be both wrongful and the resulting harm to B his responsibility, Epstein denies that B has any *right* to rescue against A. And in answering the objection to the corrective-justice theory that not every harm creates a wrongful loss, Epstein's response is that only those harms that involve invasions of property *rights* are compensable. In short, the emerging Epstein view is that corrective justice requires annulling only gains and losses owing to the invasion of an individual's rights.[22]

This account of corrective justice maintains a commitment to the causal requirement as central to a just theory of liability not because causing harm is sufficient to trigger the principle's application, but because the concept of a "right invasion" is to be spelled out in causal terms. Causation, then, is necessary to liability but no longer sufficient to justify even the *prima facie* case. For it is also necessary that the injurer's conduct invade one or more of the victim's rights.

I take up Epstein's latest view elsewhere,[23] so I will confine these remarks to a few observations. One way of understanding this view is as follows: Epstein has simply adopted my general conception of corrective justice—that wrongful gains and losses are to be annulled. He has then chosen to analyze the difficult and troublesome notion of wrongfulness in terms of the more basic idea of a property-right violation. Wrongful losses are those that result from the invasion of a property right. So what a judge in a tort case is deciding upon is whether B has a property right against A which A has failed adequately to respect. If the claim "*A* invaded *B*'s right" is true, then it follows on this view that *B* has a further right against *A* to recompense for whatever loss *A*'s invasion occasioned.

My view, which I will not defend here, is that the latest Epstein account is both too strong and too weak. It is too strong because it makes the fact that the victim's loss resulted from a right invasion a necessary condition of liability, whereas in fact not every compensable loss requires that the harm for which one seeks recovery results from the invasion of a right. It is too weak because it maintains that if a person's property rights are violated it follows that he is entitled to recompense, whereas it does not follow either as a matter of logic or moral argument that every right violation triggers a right to repair.

For Fletcher, the guiding principle in determining liability and recovery is the principle of nonreciprocity of risk. A person is entitled to recover whenever he is the victim of harm caused by another's nonreciprocal risk taking; an individual is liable in torts whenever he has no excuse for having caused another harm through his nonreciprocal risk taking. An individual imposes a nonreciprocal risk on others whenever it is different in degree or kind from those risks others impose on him. Examples of nonreciprocal risk taking include engaging in ultrahazardous activities and keeping wild animals on one's property (while one's neighbors confine their affections to traditional domestic pets). The principle of nonreciprocity of risk therefore explains strict liability for harms that result from such activities. Strict liability is appropriate in those cases in which one risk taker imposes risks different from those others in general impose upon him.

There are other activities, however, in which individuals generally impose a certain level of risk on one another. Motoring is one. Liability is not imposed whenever an individual motorist harms another. In Fletcher's view that is because activities like motoring involve a level of reciprocal risk taking. For such activities liability is not strict. In order for liability to be imposed a motorist must negligently harm another. In other words, liability is appropriate only for risks that exceed the general level of shared risk. These nonreciprocal risks are all that is meant, in Fletcher's view, by negligence.

In fault as well as in strict liability, the key to recovery is nonreciprocity of risk. The difference between fault and strict liability is to be understood in terms of the level of risk that constitutes the "background" against which the criterion of nonreciprocity is to be applied. The fault criterion is appropriate to activities of mutual involvement, like motoring, in which there exists a shared level of background or reciprocal risk taking. A faulty or negligent risk is one that exceeds the level of common or background risk. In activities that do not by nature involve participants imposing similar risks on one another, activities like blasting, strict liability is the appropriate criterion.[24]

Fletcher is considerably less clear about what it is that confers moral significance on nonreciprocity of risk. He cites Aristotle on corrective justice as the source of nonreciprocity of risk's claim to moral significance, but the actual argument he advances on its behalf relies on Rawls. The difference is important. Whereas Aristotle is concerned with corrective justice, Rawls is concerned with principles of distributive justice.

Citing Rawls, Fletcher argues for nonreciprocity of risk by constructing a principle of distributive justice that he takes to be an analogue of Rawls's first principle of justice. Fletcher contends that each individual is entitled to the maximum degree of security compatible with a like level of security for all. (The "analogy" is to Rawls's principle that each individual is entitled to the most extensive liberty compatible with a like liberty for all.) Fletcher goes on to define security as freedom from harm without compensation. So defined, everyone has a right not to be harmed without being compensated. If we take Fletcher at his word, it is the fact that one has suffered harm that entitles one to recompense, not the fact that one's harm results from another's nonreciprocal risk taking. The principle that is supposed to impart moral significance on the criterion of nonreciprocity of risk actually has the effect of eliminating it. With nonreciprocity as a condition of liability out of the way, Fletcher's view collapses into Epstein's—in fact, into a less defensible version of Epstein's, since Epstein is committed to the weaker proposition that causing harm is sufficient to establish the *prima facie* case for liability only.

To maintain the centrality of nonreciprocity of risk in Fletcher's theory one must reformulate the principle that is to confer moral significance on it. This can be accomplished in a number of ways, each of which is problematic. First, one might redefine the notion of security more narrowly as freedom from exposure to nonreciprocal risk taking. An individual's right to security is then the freedom from having nonreciprocal risks imposed on him. If the right one has is to freedom from nonreciprocal risks, then the right to recover that is based upon it does not require that one actually suffer a harm. Exposure to nonreciprocal risk, whether or not it results in harm, triggers the right to recompense. The effect is to eliminate as central to liability what is currently necessary in both strict and fault liability: the requirement that one who seeks relief must establish a loss, not just the threat or risk of loss.

It will not do to redefine security even more narrowly as freedom from harm due to nonreciprocal risk, for that would trivialize the enterprise by restating the criterion of recovery as the principle that is supposed to justify it: people are entitled to recover for harms caused by nonreciprocal risk taking because there is a principle that people have such a right.

I want to develop a more sympathetic reading of Fletcher that involves ignoring his efforts to ground the principle of nonreciprocity of risk in a Rawlsian conception of distributive justice. I prefer to read Fletcher as follows: First, assume that he has adopted a conception of corrective justice like mine or Aristotle's. Then understand the criterion of nonreciprocity of risk as his way of characterizing wrongful gains and losses. In other words, ascribe to Fletcher the position that justice requires annulling wrongful gains and losses; then interpret his account of nonreciprocity of risk as a characterization of what it is that makes a gain or loss wrongful. Our views would then be much closer than they otherwise appear to be. The advantage of this would be that by identifying wrongful loss with losses that result from nonreciprocal risk taking, he can provide a criterion of wrongfulness that is applicable to all of tort law—both strict and fault liability. My conception of wrongfulness is considerably more narrow and explains only a small area of strict liability law. The problem with his view might then be that the notion of nonreciprocity of risk is too broad a characterization of wrongfulness to function within the principle of corrective justice.

To sum up: Epstein, Fletcher, and myself reach different conclusions regarding the extent to which the principle of corrective justice could figure in an adequate theory of liability and recovery in torts for the following reasons. Epstein advances both a simple and a more complex theory of corrective justice. According to the simple theory, corrective justice requires annulling losses caused by harmful conduct. This conception of corrective justice is broad enough to make the fact that A caused B harm sufficient to trigger its application. Since causing harm is (presumably) a necessary element in both strict and fault liability, Epstein's conception of corrective justice turns out to be sufficient to ground all of liability and recovery in torts.

According to the more complex theory of corrective justice, the facts that A harmed B and that in doing so A invaded a right of B's are both separately necessary and jointly sufficient to justify rectification. The best way to read this amendment to the simple view is as resulting from Epstein's sensitivity to the objection that not every harm one suffers at the hands of another creates a compensable loss. To meet that objection to the simple view Epstein restricts compensable losses to those occasioned by the invasion of a property right. Because Epstein must also believe that as a matter of fact all recoverable losses in torts involve property-right invasions, he can maintain the view that the principle of corrective justice grounds most, if not all, of tort law.

Fletcher does not explicitly put forward a conception of corrective justice, but it would be fair to ascribe to him a much narrower conception of it than the one Epstein first put forth, for example, one like mine or Aristotle's which requires that a loss or gain be wrongful in order to trigger its application. Fletcher and I differ because we have different conceptions of what makes a gain or loss a wrongful one. Because Fletcher believes that nonreciprocity of risk is central to both strict and fault liability, and because nonreciprocity of risk is one way of fleshing out the notion of wrongfulness in the principle of corrective justice, Fletcher, like Epstein (but for different reasons), is led to the conclusion that corrective justice explains most of torts.

When the emerging Epstein view and the principle of reciprocity are understood in the way in which I have been suggesting, it would be fair to ascribe to both Epstein and Fletcher the same conception of the principle of corrective justice I have advanced. The differences between us could be pinpointed as involving the ways which each of us analyzes the notion of wrongfulness. Whereas Fletcher and I may be said to adopt the same principle of corrective justice, the principle of nonreciprocity of risk constitutes a much broader conception of what makes a gain or loss compensable or wrongful than does the account I have been developing. Epstein's theory of wrongful losses as involving invasions of property rights is both broader and narrower than my own. It is narrower in the sense that my view allows compensation for losses even where the invasion of a property right is not established; it is broader in the sense that he believes that as a matter of fact every compensable loss in torts involves the invasion of a property right.

Let me close this section by saying something about the difference between my view and Aristotle's. In my view, the principle of corrective justice explains a good deal more of tort law than it would for Aristotle. While Aristotle's conception of corrective justice is very similar to mine, he appears to have held that a wrongful gain or loss requires that a wrong has been done. In that case, the principle of corrective justice could not explain any of strict liability. In contrast, my view is that a loss or gain may sometimes be wrongful, as in a justified taking, even if the conduct that creates it is not wrongful. Moreover, Aristotle appears to have further limited the notion of a wrong to deliberate or intentional wrongdoing. In that case the principle of corrective justice would be unable to account for much of fault liability in which liability is imposed for what one unintentionally but negligently does.

III. POSNER'S OBJECTIONS

I come finally to Posner's objections. Though Posner appears to find much to recommend the position he ascribes to me, he finds fault with three related components of my argument. Two of his objections concern the limitations I place on the argument for liability from the principle of corrective justice; the third concerns the question of whether requiring potential victims to purchase first-party insurance coverage actually enables them to secure full compensation in the event of injury.

One of the central points of my thesis is that, whereas the victim of another's fault has a claim as a matter of corrective justice to recompense, the obligation to make him whole may or may not be as a matter of corrective justice the injurer's responsibility. Objecting to this claim Posner asks rhetorically, "If the injurer is not the source of the compensation, someone else, who is innocent, must be, and why is not that

innocent party a victim of the wrongdoer's injurious conduct?"[25] Again, after ascribing to me the view that "the victim of an accident in which the injurer was at fault is entitled to compensation . . . the injurer is not required as a matter of justice to be the source of compensation because he does not gain by his wrongful act, as he would if we were speaking of a theft rather than an accident," Posner argues that because faulty injurers avoid the costs of taking adequate safety precautions, they in fact gain by their injurious conduct.[26] Because they gain by their wrongdoing, liability is appropriately imposed upon them.

In sum, Posner's objections are: (1) if a faulty injurer is not the source of compensation, some "innocent" third party must be, and this constitutes an injustice; and (2) each faulty injurer gains from his wrongdoing in a sense sufficient to warrant imposing the victim's loss upon him as a matter of corrective justice.

Taken together these points constitute a serious challenge to central features of my argument. Consider the second objection first. Surely Posner is right in thinking that by and large faulty injurers gain by their failing to satisfy the standard of reasonable care. In fact, their gain, the savings from failing to exercise the care required of others, is a wrongful one, since it is the consequence of their fault. Nevertheless, as I have already pointed out to Posner, and earlier in this paper, this gain in savings is secured by negligent individuals whether or not their negligence results in another's loss. The gain in savings is not triggered by the harm a particular individual's negligence causes another. In contrast to a theft, it is not a gain that results from another's loss. Posner acknowledges the distinction, but goes on to say that he fails to understand the importance of distinguishing between wrongful gains that result from another's loss and those which do not in determining whether an individual's conduct is wrongful.[27]

Posner's response misses the point, however. The distinction is not relevant to determining if an individual's gain from his actions is wrongful; I did not suggest that it was. The distinction may play an important role, however, in determining whether the victims's loss should be imposed upon his particular injurer. In making *that* determination it is relevant to inquire whether the injurer's gain is correlative of the victim's loss, for if the injurer's gain exists independently of the victim's loss, then it is not the victim's loss that provides the moral basis for annulling the injurer's gain.

Furthermore, there are ways other than imposing the victim's loss on him of annulling the gain faulty injurers secure by avoiding the costs of adequate precautions: for example, by imposing fines for negligence. Indeed, because the gains owing to taking inadequate precautions accrue to all negligent individuals, it is in fact more appropriate to annul the gain in savings by fines imposed on each. In this way we can treat this category of wrongful gains similarly by not imposing any additional burden on those particular faulty injurers who, though they do not gain further by their mischief, are unfortunate enough to cause another harm. In short, Posner is right to insist upon the fact that wrongful gain is sufficient to impose as a matter of corrective justice a victim's loss on his negligent injurer.

Posner's other objection is that if the faulty injurer is not required to compensate his victim, an innocent individual—either the victim or some third party—will be forced to do so, and that imposing the loss on an innocent individual constitutes an injustice. (Indeed, Posner goes so far as to refer to these innocent individuals as "victims" of the faulty party's conduct.) This objection goes astray from the start. It simply does not follow in a system in which faulty injurers were not made liable to victims of their mischief that innocent individuals would be coerced into doing so in their stead. Surely, it is at least logically possible that everyone would agree *ex ante* to distribute accident costs without regard to fault—for example, in accordance with a deep-pocket or risk-spreading principle. In such a system individuals other than those at fault in causing particular accidents would help to pay for the costs of accidents, though no injustice of the sort Posner imagines would exist. Alternatively, the costs of accidents as they accumulate over time could be allocated among faulty individuals—whether or not the fault of each results in harm—without any individual being liable to any particular victim of his fault. Instead, each negligent motorist, for example, would pay according to the degree of his fault rather than according to the extent of the damage his fault causes. (After all, minor faults often occasion major damage, and serious wrongdoing may result in little, if any, damage at all.) In both counterexamples to Posner's objection,

the negligent motorist is not obligated to his victim, yet the result is not that some innocent third party is unjustly held liable instead.

Both of these counterexamples imagine modes of rectifying wrongful losses other than the tort system. Perhaps Posner's objection is more telling if we limit ourselves to the tort system. Then his objection appears to be the following: In torts, the victim of another's wrongdoing has a right to recompense. This right constitutes a valid claim against someone. If the obligation to repair is not imposed upon the faulty injurer, the victim's loss will fall on some innocent party or other. According to Posner, my view is that if the faulty injurer does not gain from his conduct, he has no obligation as a matter of corrective justice to render compensation. Absent such an obligation, the victim's loss must indeed fall on someone else (i.e., an innocent person). Therefore (given the tort system as the appropriate mode of rectification), my position generates injustice.

Though more promising, this line of argument fails as well. The argument begins by assuming a particular mode of rectification, namely, that the desired way of annuling undeserved gains and losses is by conferring on victims a right to redress and by imposing on their injurers the corresponding obligation to repair. There is nothing in my view that is incompatible with establishing a tort system to annul wrongful losses. Given the tort system, it would be my view that the obligation to repair the victim's loss falls upon his faulty injurer. It is also my view, however, that it cannot logically be any part of the reason for imposing the duty to repair on the faulty victim in such cases that in doing so we rectify or annual his wrongful gain. He simply enjoys no gain that needs to be rectified. The duty to repair his victim's loss, in other words, may be rightly his responsibility in a tort system, though it is not a duty of corrective justice.

These objections to my view rest on an ambiguity concerning whether the tort system as a particular mode of rectification is to be assumed, or whether instead it needs some sort of justification. I take the latter approach; and because I do, I emphasize the fact that in the absence of wrongful gain the tort system will not be required by corrective justice. Some other principles must therefore ground our choice of this particular mode of rectification. Posner's last objection takes the tort system as given, then chides me for not being able to explain the faulty injurer's liability as rooted in corrective justice and accuses me of imposing the obligation to repair on an innocent third party. But if we take the tort system as given, my view does in fact impose the obligation to repair upon the faulty injurer; and though it imposes the obligation to repair upon the faulty injurer, it does not explain that obligation as required by the principle of corrective justice itself. Instead, whatever principle it is that leads us to adopt the tort system as the desired means of rectification (and I am not sure we should be driven in that direction) will be the principle that explains why we impose the victim's loss on his injurer. But to deny that the relevant principle is one of corrective justice is not tantamount to asserting that I cannot provide an explanation of the injurer's liability.

Given the tort system, one might object that I am making far too much of these subtle distinctions among the various ways of grounding the injurer's liability. After all, or so the argument might go, I am not denying that (under these circumstances) the faulty injurer has an obligation to make his victim whole. Provided the injurer is obligated to repair, why should it matter whether the duty derives from corrective justice, deterrence, or from a principle like Posner's? It does matter, however, for two very different reasons.

First, the concern of my work has been in part to explore the limits of the corrective-justice theory of torts. The limits on the role of corrective justice in imposing liability are therefore important. Second, it is important, I think, to distinguish between the question of whether a particular individual has a duty and the question of whether justice requires that the encumbered individual, rather than someone else, discharge the duty. If the faulty injurer's duty to repair is a matter of corrective justice, that means, in my view, that he has secured a wrongful gain. If someone else discharges the duty on his behalf, that is, compensates his victim, an injustice remains since the injurer's gain is left unrectified. In contrast, if the faulty injurer's duty does not derive from the principle of corrective justice, that means that his victim's loss does not translate into his wrongful gain. If someone other than the faulty injurer fully compensates the victim, no corrective injustice is done, since there exists no wrongful gain that is left unrectified.

The distinction I insist on among the various sources of one's obligation to repay is relevant in determining whether principles of justice permit or prohibit various means for compensating victims. Certain debts of repayment, like the criminal's debt to society, cannot, consistent with principles of justice, be discharged by others, for example, through an insurance scheme for criminal liability. The debt of repayment one has in virtue of the wrongful gain one secures at another's expense is another debt that must as a matter of justice be discharged by the encumbered party. Failure to do so leaves a wrongful gain unrectified. On the other hand, if I am right, the debt of repayment a faulty injurer who does not gain by his mischief owes his victim is one that can, consistent with the principle of corrective justice, be discharged by another. This feature of the debt of repayment in torts is, I have argued, central to any defense of no-fault insurance schemes.[28]

NOTES

1. Richard Posner, The Concept of Corrective Justice, 10 J. Legal Stud. 187 (1981).

2. Jules Coleman, On the Moral Argument for the Fault System, 71 J. Phil. 473 (1974), and Justice and the Argument for No-Fault, 3 Soc. Theory Practice 161 (1974).

3. Jules Coleman, The Morality of Strict Tort Liability, 18 Wm. & Mary L. Rev. 259 (1976).

4. Jules Coleman, Mental Abnormality, Personal Responsibility and Tort Liability, in Mental Illness: Law and Public Policy 107 (Baruch A. Brody & H. Tristram Engelhardt, Jr., eds. 1980).

5. The question of whether my analysis is intended to be normative or positive often comes up in connection with my insistence upon this distinction—a distinction which appears to play little role in existing tort practice. An honest answer is that my analysis is intended to be both normative and positive. It is normative in the sense that were I a legislator charged with the task of doing justice in the allocation of accident costs, I would be concerned first with identifying the relevant principles of justice, then with inquiring whether the current tort system or some alternative to it would best be able to meet the demands of justice. It is positive in that I believe many features of the existing law of torts can be understood as enforcing some plausible conception of corrective justice. I do not argue that the principle of corrective justice explains everything that goes on in torts, and to this extent my position is more modest than those of other proponents of corrective-justice accounts of tort law. Proponents of the economic analysis of torts, in particular, my friends Richard Posner and William Landes, have asked me why it is that I adhere to an account of torts that by my own admission explains only certain elements of the law, especially when there exists an alternative analysis—the economic one—that explains nearly all of tort law. This is a fair question that merits at least some response in the context of a reply to an essay by a major proponent of the economic analysis. First, I take as a starting point the common-sense view that in resolving disputes judges try to do justice—not economics—though they may fail to do either or both very well. Given the ordinary person's view that in resolving controversial disputes judges attempt to do justice, I have tried to get a handle on exactly what

sort of justice they do by developing an analysis of corrective justice that seems to make sense of a fair amount of what they do. Second, in response to the claim that economics makes sense out of more of what judges in torts do, my response is that it does not make better sense of it. The economic theory of adjudication is incompatible with any defensible analysis of judicial competence or authority. For it ascribes to judges the role of fixing rights and duties in particular disputes in order to serve the social goal of efficiency, when a proper theory of adjudication would (in my view anyway) restrict judicial authority to resolving disputes in terms of the respective claim litigants have against one another. Finally, the efficiency analysis of torts cannot explain why it is that judges impose the costs of harms on either of the litigants to the dispute. The efficient outcome might be secured by imposing the costs on some third party who, though not party to the dispute, may be the cheapest cost avoider. Economics, in other words, cannot explain the most basic feature of tort law, namely, the implicit decision to allocate losses as between respective litigants.

6. In my previous work I did not use the terms "wrongful gain" or "wrongful loss." Instead, I talked about unwarranted, undeserved, or unjustified losses and gains. I am using "wrongful" here as a catch phrase to cover all such compensable losses and rectifiable gains.

7. I owe the reader an account of how it is that justifiable or right conduct can sometimes create wrongful or compensable losses. That is, if what A does to B is justifiable or legitimate, why would we say that the losses B might suffer as a consequence are "wrongful" ones, or why would we feel that A has a duty to make good B's losses? I have suggested that the basic concept may be that of a "taking" which only shifts the burden to an analysis of which loss impositions are takings in the sense that requires compensation. I do not have a fully worked out analysis of a "taking," but I did not want the reader to think that I had not realized the importance of developing one.

8. Joel Feinberg, Voluntary Euthanasia and the Right to Life, 7 Phil. Pub. Aff. 93 (1978).

9. For a different view, see Posner, supra note 1, at 198 and n. 44.

10. There are means other than a tort system for rectifying wrongful gains and losses, for example, general insurance pools of the sort I have discussed elsewhere (On the Moral Argument for the Fault System, supra note 2). With respect to the matter of modes of rectification, I want to draw attention to a serious error in Posner's article. After noting the distinction between grounds and modes of rectification, Posner claims that there is nothing in Aristotle's view that would prohibit him from endorsing a system of penal sanctions as the best means of rectifying both wrongful losses and gains. Surely this is confused, since punishing an offender, by itself, does not annul his gain, and even if punishment deters future wrongs, reducing the incidence of wrongful gains is logically distinct from rectifying the gains and losses wrongs occasion.

11. Questions concerning the appropriate extent of rectification arise in determining damages and in explaining the principle of comparative negligence.

12. I have discussed and rejected the defense of fault liability in On the Moral Argument for the Fault System, supra note 2.

13. One obvious problem with this line of defense is that it assumes a particular mode of rectifying the innocent victim's wrongful loss, namely, by conferring upon him a claim right to recompense. Such a claim right logically imposes a duty on someone—usually the injurer. Assuming a system of correlative rights and duties, that is, a tort system, begs the justificatory question, namely, Why choose this rather than some other mode of rectification?

14. This line of argument is intended to be a "catchall" for the wide variety of economic analyses of fault liability. Whatever their differences, these accounts all believe that fault is a criterion of eco-

nomic efficiency and that liability is imposed on the basis of fault to reduce inefficient costs.

15. 10 Minn. 456, 124 NW 221 (1910).

16. When I presented a version of this paper at the University of Chicago Law School, Richard Posner expressed a powerful objection to my account which I want to share and discuss here. The objection relies on contrasting two cases. In the first case, Jones wrongfully injures Smith for no reason other than to have Smith suffer loss. Jones secures no gain in virtue of his misconduct; indeed, he may have arranged things to preclude the very possibility of his securing any gain other than the satisfaction he would derive from Smith's suffering. In the second case, in order to save valuable property (and perhaps life), Jones is compelled by good sense to harm Smith in some nontrivial but not terribly disastrous way. Suppose now that the second case falls within the takings analogy that I have suggested can be employed to explain aspects of strict tort liability. If that is the case, Jones is obligated to compensate Smith in the second case though he acted reasonably—even admirably. This obligation to render compensation is, in my view, apparently a matter of corrective justice. In the first case, however, Jones has no such obligation—since he did not gain in virtue of his mischief—though his conduct is hardly admirable, or even defensible. It (apparently) turns out that, in my view, right conduct may not free one from liability, but wrongful conduct can. Surely this is counterintuitive. The objection misses its mark, however. First, it is not my view that there are no grounds upon which to impose an obligation to repair in the first case. The fact that Jones intentionally injured Smith for no good reason may itself be reason enough for imposing Smith's loss upon him. But this response is inadequate, for Posner will argue that the real problem is not that we cannot develop some other reason for holding Jones liable in the first case; the problem is that my theory of corrective justice is unable to generate such an obligation. What's worse, corrective justice not only fails to impose an obligation where doing so is appropriate; it imposes one where doing so is inappropriate—in the second case. If this is the objection, then the problem with it is that it misunderstands my view. For my view need not impose an obligation in either case; that will depend on the mode of rectification. In the first case, there simply is no wrongful gain which it is the concern of corrective justice to rectify. There is, however, a wrongful loss. In this sort of case the appropriate mode of rectification may well be to impose the victim's loss on his injurer—though it is my view that the principle of corrective justice does not require that we do so. In the second case, there is once again wrongful loss. But is there wrongful gain as well? I am not sure. In Feinberg's example there is a gain that the mountain climber secures in virtue of his destroying the cabin owner's furniture and emptying his shelves: he stays alive. Does justice require that we annul *that* advantage—that we kill him? I do not think so. In *Vincent* v. *Lake Erie,* the ship and its goods were saved because the captain secured the boat to the dock, thereby causing the dock to suffer damage during the subsequent storm. Does justice require the ship owner to eliminate his gain in virtue of such conduct? I doubt it. So I am not clear that there is a wrongful gain in all such cases, though there is a gain that would not have occurred but for the loss others have suffered. (In some cases of nonwrongful conduct there can be wrongful gain or advantage which should as a matter of justice be annulled. Suppose unwittingly I wrongly step in front of you while we are queueing up for the theater. As it turns out, by stepping in front I get in and you do not. Justice does require that both my gain and your loss be rectified in some manner—probably by my getting out of and your getting into the theater.) When we have wrongful loss, but no wrongful gain, as we very well might in the second case, my view does not necessarily impose the victim's loss on the injurer. Indeed, even if we had both wrongful gain and loss in a case involving non-wrongful conduct, it still would not follow that on my view the "injurer"

would be obligated to his victim. Once again, that would depend on the chosen mode of rectification. It would be the case, in my view, that there is a gain and a loss to be rectified, but that would be the only way in which the first and second cases would differ. Whether there would be an obligation to repair imposed on the injurer in either, both, or neither of the cases is, I emphasize, another matter.

17.   Richard Epstein's views seem to have changed somewhat. See the discussion in text at notes 20-24.

18.   George Fletcher, Fairness and Utility in Tort Theory, 85 Harv. L. Rev. 537 (1972).

19.   3 Bing. (N.C.) 468 132 Eng. Rep. 490 (1837).

20.   Richard Epstein, A Theory of Strict Liability, 2 J. Legal Stud. 151 (1973).

21.   See my Mental Abnormality, Personal Responsibility and Tort Liability, supra note 4.

22.   Nuisance Law: Corrective Justice and Its Utilitarian Constraints, 8 J. Legal Stud. 49 (1979).

23.   See Jules Coleman, Moral Theories of Torts: Their Scope and Limits, Law & Philosophy, forthcoming.

24.   I raise doubts about the plausibility of nonreciprocity of risk as a standard of liability in Justice and Reciprocity in Tort Theory, 14 U. Western Ont. L. Rev. 105 (1975).

25.   Posner, supra note 1, at 197.

26.   Id. at 198.

27.   Id. at n. 44.

28.   See my Justice and the Argument for No-Fault, supra note 2.

ANTHONY T. KRONMAN
Contract Law and Distributive Justice*

Within broad limits, our legal system leaves individuals free to dispose of their property as they wish, either by giving it away or by transferring it in exchange for the property of others. The freedom individuals enjoy in this regard includes the power to make contracts, legally binding agreements that provide for the exchange of property on terms fixed by the parties. Among contract scholars, there is nearly universal agreement that the law of contracts, the tangled mass of legal rules that regulate the process of private exchange, has three legitimate functions: first, to specify which agreements are legally binding and which are not;[1] second, to define the rights and duties created by enforceable but otherwise ambiguous agreements;[2] and finally, to indicate the consequences of an unexcused breach.[3] Beyond this, however, it has sometimes been suggested that the law of contracts should also be used as an instrument of distributive justice and that those responsible for choosing or designing rules of contract law—courts and legislatures—should do so with an eye to their distributional effects in a self-conscious effort to achieve a fair division of wealth among the members of society.[4]

CONTRACT LAW AND DISTRIBUTIVE JUSTICE

There are, in fact, many rules of contract law that are deliberately intended to promote a distributional end of some sort. Obvious examples include: usury laws limiting the interest that can be charged on loans;[5] implied, but nevertheless nondisclaimable, warranties of quality or habitability;[6] and minimum wage laws.[7] The object of each of these rules is to shift wealth from one

group—lenders, sellers, landlords, employers—to another—borrowers, buyers, tenants, workers—presumably in accordance with some principle of distributive justice, by altering the terms on which individuals are allowed to contract. Can legal rules of this sort be defended? More generally, is it ever appropriate to use the law of contracts—understood in the broad sense in which I have been using the term—as an instrument of redistribution, or should the legal rules that govern the process of private exchange be fashioned without regard to their impact on the distribution of wealth in society?

Libertarians, who deny that the state is ever justified in forcibly redistributing wealth from one individual or group to another, answer this question in the negative.[8] Surprisingly, many liberals, who believe that at least some compulsory redistribution of wealth is morally acceptable, even required, give the same answer.[9] The libertarian's opposition to the use of contract law as a mechanism for redistribution derives from his general belief that the compulsory transfer of wealth is theft, regardless of how it is accomplished.[10] By contrast, liberals who oppose the use of contract law as a redistributive device do so because they believe that distributional objectives (whose basic legitimacy they accept) are always better achieved through the tax system than through the detailed regulation of individual transactions.[11]

Thus, despite their fundamentally different views regarding the moral legitimacy of forced redistribution, liberals and libertarians often find themselves defending a similar conception of contract law. While lawyers and philosophers in both camps approvingly describe the role that contract law plays in reducing the cost of the exchange process itself and emphasize the importance of protecting those engaged in the process against threats of physical violence and other unacceptable forms of coercion,[12] there also appears to be widespread agreement, on both sides, that the legal rules regulating volun-

* Reprinted by permission of The Yale Law Journal Company and Fred B. Rothman & Company. From Anthony T. Kronman, "Contract Law and Distributive Justice," *The Yale Law Journal*, Vol. 89 (1980), pp. 472–497.

tary exchanges between individuals should not be selected or designed with an eye to their distributional consequences. It is tempting to conclude that this conception of contract law, which I shall call the non-distributive conception, must be correct if those with such sharply divergent views on the most basic questions of distributive justice agree on its soundness.

In this Article, I argue that the non-distributive conception of contract law cannot be supported on either liberal or libertarian grounds, and defend the view that rules of contract law should be used to implement distributional goals whenever alternative ways of doing so are likely to be more costly or intrusive. The Article is divided into two parts. In the first part I examine the libertarian theory of contractual exchange and argue, against the standard libertarian view, that considerations of distributive justice not only *ought* to be taken into account in designing rules for exchange, but *must* be taken into account if the law of contracts is to have even minimum moral acceptability. My aim here is to show that the idea of voluntary agreement—an idea central to the libertarian theory of justice in exchange—cannot be understood except as a distributional concept, and to demonstrate that the notion of individual liberty, taken by itself, offers no guidance in determining which of the many forms of advantage-taking possible in exchange relations render an agreement involuntary and therefore unenforceable on libertarian grounds. Having established this general point, I propose a simple test, similar in form to Rawls's difference principle,[13] for deciding which kinds of advantage-taking should be permitted and which should not, and argue that this test is the one libertarians ought to accept as being most compatible with the moral premises of libertarianism itself.

In the second part of the Article, I challenge the standard liberal preference for taxation as a method of redistribution. The choice of a redistributive method involves moral issues as well as questions of expediency. In my view, however, a blanket preference for taxation is not justified by considerations of either sort. There is no reason to think that taxation is always the most neutral and least intrusive way of redistributing wealth, nor is there reason to think it is always the most efficient means of achieving a given distributive goal. Which method of redistribution has these desirable properties will depend, in any particular case, on circumstantial factors; neither method is inherently superior to the other. And while any redistributive scheme is bound to involve a conflict between distributive justice and individual liberty, the existence of this conflict, although it raises serious difficulties for liberal theory in general, does not provide a reason for adopting a non-distributive conception of contract law.

There are important, but different lessons to be learned from both the liberal and libertarian opposition to using the law of contracts for distributive purposes, and I shall attempt to clarify these in the course of my argument. However, while both views contribute to our understanding of the difficulties involved in treating the law of contracts as a mechanism for redistributing wealth, neither view justifies the claim, implicit in the writings of liberals and libertarians alike, that there is something *morally* wrong with using contract law in this way.[14]

I. DISTRIBUTIVE JUSTICE AND THE LIBERTARIAN THEORY OF EXCHANGE

A. VOLUNTARY EXCHANGE

The libertarian theory of contract law is premised upon the belief that individuals have a moral right to make whatever voluntary agreements they wish for the exchange of their own property, so long as the rights of third parties are not violated as a result. For a libertarian, there are only two grounds on which an agreement to exchange property may be impeached: first, that it infringes the rights of someone not a party to the agreement itself, and second, that one of the individuals agreeing to the exchange was coerced into doing so, and thus did not give his agreement voluntarily. Imagine a judge charged with responsibility for enforcing contracts between the members of a particular community. So long as the judge acts in a way consistent with libertarian principles, he need ask himself only two questions whenever a contract dispute arises: Did the party now said to be in breach voluntarily agree to do what the other party wants him to do? Will performance of the agreement violate the rights of third parties? If the answers are "yes" and "no," respectively, the contract must be enforced, regardless of its consequences for the welfare of the individuals involved. If the judge refuses to enforce a particular contract merely because it has certain distributional consequences, or if he adopts a general rule invalidating an entire class of contracts for similar reasons, his actions are indefensible on libertarian grounds. Taking distributional effects into account in this way is inconsistent with the libertarian conception of individual freedom and violates the basic entitlement on which that conception rests.

The question of when an agreement violates the rights of third parties—as opposed to merely diminishing their welfare—is a difficult and interesting one, but I shall say nothing about it here.[15] I want, instead, to focus on the second libertarian requirement for the enforcement of agreements—the requirement of voluntariness. Putting aside its effect on third party rights, the only thing about an agreement that matters, from a libertarian point of view, is the process by which it is reached. This is sometimes expressed by saying that the libertarian conception of contractual exchange is backward-looking or historical,[16] concerned with how agreements are made but not with their distributive consequences. There is, however, an ambiguity in this way of characterizing the libertarian theory of exchange. Imagine, for example, a legal system in which there is only one way of creating an enforceable contract—by pronouncing a sacred oath and then reciting the terms of the agreement. A judge in such a legal system might be instructed to base his decisions in disputed cases solely on whether the specified procedure had been complied with, and to ignore entirely the distributive consequences of his judgments. Whatever one thinks of its merits, this is a perfectly intelligible method of adjudication which can be described by saying that so far as the judge is concerned, it is only the process leading up to an agreement, and not its distributive effects, that matters. However, this method—which might be called pure proceduralism—ought not to be confused with libertarianism. It is not enough, for a libertarian, that the procedure for creating contracts (whatever it might be) has been complied with; it is necessary, in addition, that it has been complied with in a particular way, voluntarily rather than involuntarily. If someone has spoken the sacred oath with a gun at his head there is no justification, from a libertarian point of view, for enforcing his agreement even though every formality has been meticulously observed. Libertarians and pure proceduralists share a common unconcern with the distributive consequences of the private arrangements individuals make for exchanging their property: what distinguishes these two positions is that the lib-

ertarian cares about something which the pure proceduralist is in theory free to ignore, namely, the voluntariness of agreement itself.

More importantly, the distinction between these two views must be maintained so long as libertarianism purports to be a theory of *justice* in exchange. The mere fact that someone has observed a particular procedure in agreeing to do something does not explain why he should be required to abide by the terms of his agreement; to explain why he should, an appeal must be made to something other than the procedure itself.[17] Pure proceduralism is not a moral theory at all, although it may be part of one. By contrast, libertarianism is, or at least claims to be, a moral theory meant to vindicate the idea of individual freedom. A libertarian conception of contract law must therefore take the voluntariness of agreements, rather than their procedural correctness, as the ultimate touchstone of liability and disregard the latter where the two diverge.

But when is an agreement voluntary? For a libertarian, committed to the notion that all voluntary agreements must be enforced, the widest view of voluntariness is almost surely unacceptable. Suppose that I sign a contract to sell my house for $5,000 after being physically threatened by the buyer. It is possible to characterize my agreement as voluntary in one sense: after considering the alternatives, I have concluded that my self-interest is best served by signing and have deliberately implemented a perfectly rational decision by doing precisely that. Described in this general way, my agreement to sell appears in the same light that it would if, for example, I had not been threatened but signed the contract because I thought $5,000 a good price for the house. Under this description, however, my act of signing will be involuntary only if it is not motivated by a decision of any sort at all on my part. Such would be the case, for example, if the purchaser forcibly grabbed my hand and guided it over the document himself, or commanded me to sign the contract while I was in an hypnotic state.

There is, of course, nothing logically absurd about drawing the line between voluntary and involuntary agreements at this point, but I doubt most libertarians would wish to do so. Among other things, defining voluntariness in this way conflicts with deeply entrenched notions of moral responsibility. In assessing the voluntariness of an agreement, it is not enough merely to determine that the agreement was motivated by a deliberate decision of some sort; we also want to know something about the circumstances under which it was given. But if this is true, the problem of drawing a line between agreements that are voluntary and agreements that are not—a problem the libertarian must confront if the idea of voluntary exchange is to have any meaning at all—can be understood as the problem of specifying the conditions that must be present before we will consider an agreement to have been voluntarily concluded. Put differently, unless the libertarian is prepared to accept a very broad concept of voluntariness, which equates voluntary agreement with rational choice, he must specify the various circumstances under which even a deliberately given, rational agreement will be held to have been coerced.[18]

B. ADVANTAGE-TAKING

Whenever a promisor complains that his agreement was coerced and therefore ought not to be enforced, he should be understood as claiming that the agreement was given under circumstances that rendered it involuntary. In making an argument of this sort, a promisor may point to many different circumstances or conditions: he may say, for example, that his agreement was involuntary because he lacked the mental and emotional capacities required to appreciate its consequences;[19] or a promisor may claim that he was threatened or deceived by the other party,[20] or that his agreement was given at a time he was hard-pressed for cash and therefore had no choice but to accept the terms proposed by the promisee;[21] or a promisor may assert that his agreement was involuntary because he, unlike the other party, was ignorant of certain facts which, if known at the time of contracting, would have led him to make a different agreement or no agreement at all;[22] or he may say that the other party had a monopoly of some scarce resource—the only water hole or the best cow or the strongest shoulders in town—a monopoly which enabled him to dictate terms of sale to the promisor, making their agreement what is sometimes called a "contract of adhesion."[23]

In some of these cases, the circumstances allegedly making the promisor's agreement involuntary is an incapacity of the promisor himself—his insanity, youth, ignorance or impecuniousness. In others, the involuntariness of the promisor's agreement is attributable to an act by the other party—a fraudulent deception or threat of physical harm. Finally, in some cases, it is the other party's monopolization of a scarce resource and the market power he enjoys as a result which (it is claimed) renders the promisor's agreement involuntary. In each case, however, the promisor is asserting that his agreement, although deliberately given, lacked voluntariness because of the circumstances under which it was made—circumstances that in one way or another restricted his range of alternatives to a point where the promisor's choice could be said to be free in name only.[24]

The problem, of course, is to determine when the circumstances under which an agreement is given deprive it of its voluntariness in this sense. In my view, this problem is equivalent to another—the problem of determining which of the many forms of advantage-taking possible in exchange relationships are compatible with the libertarian conception of individual freedom. The latter way of stating the problem may appear to raise new and distinct issues but in fact it does not. In each of the hypothetical cases considered above, the promisee enjoys an advantage of some sort which he has attempted to exploit for his own benefit. The advantage may consist in his superior information, intellect, or judgment, in the monopoly he enjoys with regard to a particular resource, or in his possession of a powerful instrument of violence or a gift for deception. In each of these cases, the fundamental question is whether the promisee should be permitted to exploit his advantage to the detriment of the other party, or whether permitting him to do so will deprive the other party of the freedom that is necessary, from a libertarian point of view, to make his promise truly voluntary and therefore binding.[25]

The term "advantage-taking" is often used in a pejorative fashion, to refer to conduct we find morally objectionable or think the law should disallow. I mean the term to be understood in a broader sense, however, as including even those methods of gain the law allows and morality accepts (or perhaps even approves). In this broad sense, there is advantage-taking in every contractual exchange. Indeed, in mutually advantageous exchanges, there is advantage-taking by both parties. Suppose I have a cow you want, and you have a horse I want, and we agree to exchange our animals. The fact that you want my cow gives me an advantage I can exploit by insisting that you give me your horse in return. Your ownership of the horse gives you a symmetrical advantage over me. Each of us exploits the advantage we possess and—in this transaction at least—are both made better off as a result. This might seem to make my broad conception of advantage-taking empty or trivial. There is, however, an important reason for using the term in the unconventionally broad way that I do. By using the term to refer to *all* types of advantage-taking—those we tolerate as well as those we do not—attention is focused more sharply on the need to explain why the illicit methods of gain for which we normally reserve the term are thought to be objectionable.

In order to give meaningful content to the idea of voluntary exchange, a libertarian theory of contract law must provide an explanation of precisely this sort. However, although some principle or rule is needed as a basis for deciding which forms of advantage-taking should be allowed and which should not be, it is unclear what this principle or rule might be. Suppose, for example, that my neighbor threatens to shoot me unless I agree to buy his house. If there is one thing which must be treated as a condition for voluntary exchange, it is the absence of direct physical compulsion of the sort involved in this first case. But suppose that instead of threatening me with physical harm, the seller merely lies to me about the house—he tells me, for example, that water pipes inaccessibly buried beneath the basement are copper when in fact he knows them to be made of iron, an inferior material. Ought such advantage-taking be allowed?[26] While it is possible to justify advantage-taking of this sort on the grounds that only physical coercion should be disallowed, there is no good reason for making *this* distinction the decisive one. Moreover, even if one fastens on the physical nature of the advantage-taking act, explicit misrepresentation can be characterized in a way that gives it a physical character as well, for example by saying that the misrepresentation is communicated by soundwaves which stimulate an auditory response in the listener which in turn provokes a neutral change that causes him to sign the contract. This may be fanciful, but it suggests that with enough imagination any form of advantage-taking can be characterized as a physical intrusion,[27] and the question of when such a characterization is appropriate cannot be answered by simply repeating that it is the physical nature of the act which makes it objectionable.

At this point, many will be tempted to acknowledge explicit misrepresentation as an illegitimate form of advantage-taking, but insist that the line be drawn there—limiting the conditions necessary for voluntary exchange to two (absense of physical coercion and fraud). Suppose, however, that the seller makes no threats and tells no lies, but does say things that, although true, are meant to encourage me to draw a false conclusion about the condition of the house and to inspect the premises less carefully than I might otherwise. (The seller tells me, for example, that the house has been inspected by an exterminator from the Acme Termite Company every six months for the last ten years, which is true, but neglects to inform me that during his last visit the exterminator discovered a termite infestation which the seller has failed to cure.) By telling me only certain things about the house, and not others, the seller intends to throw me off the track and thereby take advantage of my ignorance and naiveté. The same is true if he tells me nothing at all, but simply fails to reveal a defect he knows I am unaware of—a case of pure nondisclosure.[28]

Should this last form of advantage-taking be allowed? At this point, undoubtedly, many will be inclined to say I have only myself to blame for drawing an incorrect inference from the seller's truthful representations and for failing to take precautionary measures such as having the house inspected by an expert. But why is this a good reason for holding me to my bargain here, but not in the previous cases as well? I can, for example, protect myself against the risk that I will be forced to sign a contract at gunpoint by hiring a bodyguard to accompany me wherever I go; and I can protect myself against the danger of explicit misrepresentation by requiring the other party to take a lie detector test or, more simply, by insisting that he warrant the house to be free of pests or any other possible defect that happens to concern me. Why isn't my failure to protect myself in these cases a good reason for enforcing the agreement I have made?

In attempting to sort out these various forms of advantage-taking, a number of distinctions suggest themselves—for example, the distinction between physical and non-physical advantage-taking, or between those forms of advantage-taking that can be prevented by the victim and those that cannot. None, however, provides a principled basis for determining which forms of advantage-taking ought to be allowed. Each can be interpreted in different ways, yielding different results, and the distinctions themselves provide no guidance in deciding which of the competing interpretations is the right one. An independent principle of some sort is required to determine the scope and relevance of these distinctions, and consequently it is that principle, whatever it might be, rather than the distinctions themselves that explains why we ought to allow some forms of advantage-taking but not others.

C. THE PRINCIPLE OF PARETIANISM

While there are many principles that might conceivably perform this function, the libertarian may be inclined to think that only one is morally acceptable. This principle, which I shall call the liberty principle, states that advantage-taking by one party to an agreement should be allowed unless it infringes the rights or liberty of the other party. The liberty principle has an appealing directness and simplicity. It does not, however, provide a satisfactory test for discriminating between acceptable and unacceptable forms of advantage-taking in the exchange process, but rather begs the question it is meant to answer.

For the liberty principle to be of any help at all, we must already know when an individual is entitled to complain that his liberty has been violated and to know this, we must know what rights he has. For example, we cannot say whether the liberty principle is violated if one person takes advantage of another by concealing valuable information in the course of an exchange, unless we have already decided that it is part of the first person's liberty that he be allowed to exploit the information he possesses in this way and not a part of the other person's liberty that he be free from such exploitation. The liberty principle does not purport to tell us what rights people actually have but assumes that we possess such knowledge independently of the principle itself.

How can we acquire the independent knowledge of rights needed to give the liberty principle meaning? Someone might claim that we can acquire such knowledge simply by looking to see what rights people have either by nature or convention. But rights cannot be ascertained in this way. Every claim concerning rights is necessarily embedded in a controversial theory: the only way to justify the claim that a person has a certain right is to argue that he does, and this means deploying a contestable theory[29] that cannot itself be verified or disproven by simply looking to see what is the case. In order to apply the liberty principle, we must already have a theory of rights. Because it does not itself supply such a theory, the liberty principle, standing alone, provides no guidance in deciding which forms of advantage-taking ought to be allowed.

If a direct appeal to the liberty principle is unhelpful, the libertarian is confronted with the problem of finding an alternative basis for distinguishing between acceptable and unacceptable forms of advantage-taking in the exchange process. A number of different principles suggest themselves, but three seem to me especially significant and I shall limit myself to these.

First, a libertarian might adopt the view that some people are simply better than others—more intelligent, beautiful, or noble—and argue that being a better person gives an individual the right to exploit his inferiors in certain ways.[30] A full elaboration of this view, which rests upon what may be called the doctrine of natural superiority, would require the following: a specification of the respects in which people differ as to their worth; a defense of the claim that worthiness is a legitimate ground for the assignment of rights and duties; and an account of the types of exploitation that can be justified by an appeal to the superiority of the exploiting party.

Second, a libertarian might attempt to justify certain forms of advantage-taking by arguing that they increase the total amount of some desired good such as happiness. Classical utilitarianism is the most familiar example of such a view; for convenience, I shall refer to the view itself as utilitarianism.[31]

Finally, a libertarian might attempt to distinguish between different forms of transactional advantage-taking by invoking the interest of the disadvantaged party himself. In some cases, it is reasonable to think that a person who has been taken advantage of in a particular way will be better off in the long run if the kind of advantage-taking in question is allowed than he would be were it prohibited. Whenever this is true, a libertarian might argue the advantage-taking should be permitted and in all other cases forbidden. I shall call this third view paretianism because of its close connection with the idea of Pareto efficiency.[32]

Each of these three principles provides an intelligible criterion for discriminating between acceptable and unacceptable forms of advantage-taking in the exchange process. Each leads to different results. All three rely upon something other than the bare idea of individual liberty and are therefore immune from the special criticisms to which the liberty principle is subject. Only the last of these three principles, however, is consistent with the basic ethical commitments of libertarianism; if a libertarian were required to choose among the three, the only one that he could choose without abandoning his most fundamental moral beliefs would be the third.[33]

In the first place, libertarianism is a strongly egalitarian theory. According to the libertarian, all individuals are equal in what, from a moral perspective, is the most important respect—in their basic right to freedom from the interference of others. This feature of libertarianism rules out the doctrine of natural superiority as a basis for discriminating between acceptable and unacceptable forms of advantage-taking. The doctrine of natural superiority not only leads to non-egalitarian results, as may libertarianism itself, but also rests upon a notion of differential worthiness wholly incompatible with the libertarian conception of individual equality. There is no way of incorporating the doctrine of natural superiority within the framework of a libertarian theory of rights.

In addition to being strongly egalitarian, libertarianism is also an individualistic theory in the sense that it assigns a unique value to the autonomy of the individual person. Any principle, such as utilitarianism, that purports to evaluate states of affairs solely on the basis of the total amount of some good they happen to contain is capable of taking the idea of autonomy into account only indirectly; utilitarianism can give weight to the independence of individuals only insofar as their independence contributes to something else which is taken to be good in itself.[34] Given the peculiar strength of his commitment to individual autonomy—to the idea that individuals have moral "boundaries" which must be respected even if more happiness or welfare could be produced by disregarding them[35]—the libertarian must also reject utilitarianism as a basis for distinguishing between acceptable and unacceptable forms of advantage-taking. This leaves only paretianism, which states that a particular form of advantage-taking should be allowed if it works to the longrun benefit of those disadvantaged by it, but not

otherwise—a principle that is neither anti-individualistic, since it does not make the sum or total of any impersonal good the touchstone of evaluation, nor anti-egalitarian.[36]

An important ambiguity in the principle of paretianism may seem to cast doubt on this claim, however. Suppose that Jim sells Fred a watch and lies to him about its condition. Should Jim be permitted to exploit Fred by deliberately defrauding him? On the assumption that paretianism is a strongly individualistic principle, one might conclude that it requires us to answer this question by considering the longrun effect of Jim's deceit on Fred's individual welfare. There are good reasons, however, for not interpreting the principle in this way. To begin with, it would probably be impossible for courts to make such highly individualized assessments, except in rare cases, and in any event, an approach of this sort would create uncertainty and deprive legal rules of their predictability. Moreover, unlike a court, a legislature must evaluate the effects of proposed rules on classes of persons rather than on particular, identifiable individuals. For these reasons, a strictly individualistic interpretation of paretianism is likely to make the principle unworkable in all but a few cases.

How should the principle be interpreted, then? Although the matter is by no means free from difficulty, one reasonable approach is to interpret paretianism as requiring only that the welfare of *most people* who are taken advantage of in a particular way be increased by the kind of advantage-taking in question.[37] If one adopts this view, in order to resolve the dispute between Jim and Fred, it is only necessary to decide whether most victims of fraud will be better off in the longrun, all things considered, if conduct such as Jim's is legally tolerated.

This interpretation of the principle of paretianism makes the principle easier to apply. At the same time, however, it appears to diminish the difference between paretianism and utilitarianism by substituting the overall welfare of a group for the welfare of a particular individual. But despite this appearance of similarity,[38] there are two related respects in which these principles remain distinguishable from one another. In the first place, paretianism and utilitarianism may lead to different results where the group of persons harmed by a particular form of advantage-taking represents a permanently distinct subset of society as a whole, since in cases of this sort, it is always possible that total welfare will increase while the welfare of the disadvantaged group declines. Assume, for example, that most people with low IQs are disadvantaged in their transactions with brighter people. Whether this kind of advantage-taking should be allowed depends entirely, for the utilitarian, on the total amount of welfare that it yields. If one adopts the principle of paretianism, on the other hand, advantage-taking by those with superior intellectual endowments can be justified only if it increases the longrun welfare of those with low IQs.

This points to a second and more fundamental difference between the two principles. The principle of paretianism ultimately rests on the notion that one person should be permitted to make himself better off at another's expense only if it is to the benefit of both that he be allowed to do so. By contrast, utilitarianism—as I use the term—is premised on the belief that more welfare is always better than less, regardless of how it is distributed. For a utilitarian, an increase in the total quantum of welfare is ethically significant in its own right; from the standpoint of paretianism, an increase of this sort has no meaning by itself. To be sure, a utilitarian may be driven to adopt paretianism as the best available method for measuring increases in total welfare,[39] but the principle of paretianism can never have independent ethical significance for the true utilitarian. Likewise, someone committed to paretianism may conclude that a simple summing of utilities is the only practical way of implementing *his* favored principle, but nevertheless reject the utilitarian notion that greater total welfare is a moral good in its own right, regardless of how it happens to be distributed among individuals. Thus, even where utilitarianism and paretianism converge to the same practical result, they do so for different reasons, arriving at a common conclusion from fundamentally different starting-points.

In comparing moral principles, it is important to consider the reasons they provide for acting in certain ways, as well as the actions they require and forbid.[40] Utilitarianism and paretianism offer strikingly different justifications for permitting certain forms of advantage-taking in the exchange process. Paretianism permits only those forms of advantage-taking that work to the benefit of all concerned, a requirement rooted in the conviction that every person has an equal right not to have his own welfare reduced for the sole purpose of increasing some-

one else's.[41] This constraint expresses, in a powerful way, respect for the integrity of individuals, and distinguishes paretianism from every ethical theory—including utilitarianism—that treats the maximization of some impersonal good as an end in itself. Since he is committed to the idea of individual integrity, the libertarian has good reason to prefer the principle of paretianism over utilitarianism and to adopt the former principle as a basis for discriminating between acceptable and unacceptable forms of advantage-taking in exchange transactions.

D. PARETIANISM APPLIED

I want now to indicate, in a more concrete way, how the principle of paretianism can be used to give meaningful content to the idea of voluntary exchange by helping us decide which kinds of advantage-taking should be permitted and which should not. Let me begin with a relatively easy case.[42] Suppose that *A* owns a piece of property that, unbeknownst to *A*, contains a rich mineral deposit of some sort. *B*, a trained geologist, inspects the property (from the air, let us assume), discovers the deposit, and without disclosing what he knows, offers to buy the land from *A* at a price well below its true value. *A* agrees, and then later attempts to rescind the contract on the ground that *B*'s failure to reveal what he knew about the property amounted to fraud. The general question here is whether buyers who have deliberately acquired superior information should be permitted to exploit their advantage by making contracts without revealing what they know or believe to be true. Except in special cases,[43] the law does not require disclosure by well-informed buyers, at least where their information is the product of a deliberate search. This rule can be defended in the following way. If *B* has made a deliberate investment in acquiring the information that gives him an advantage in his transaction with *A*, imposing a duty of disclosure will prevent him from reaping the fruits of his investment and thereby discourage others from making similar investments in the future. But this means that a smaller amount of useful geological information will be produced. As a result, the efficient allocation of land, the allocation of individual parcels to their best use, will be impaired. It is plausible to argue that this will hurt those at an informational disadvantage in particular exchanges more than they would be helped by imposing a duty of full disclosure in sale transactions such as the one involved here. For example, although imposing a duty of this sort will enable *A* to back out of a disadvantageous transaction with *B,* it will also increase the price *A* has to pay for oil and aluminum because the incentive to make the investment necessary to determine which pieces of land contain these resources in the first place will have been weakened as a result. Thus, a legal rule permitting *B* to buy *A*'s property without disclosing its true worth arguably works to *A*'s own benefit, since it provides a stimulus for the production of efficiency-enhancing information. This is, in any event, the kind of argument required by the principle of paretianism.

Although paretianism justifies certain types of advantage-taking,[44] it clearly rules out others. Suppose, for example, that *B* forces *A* to sell his property by threatening *A* with physical harm. If *B*'s behavior does not bar enforcement of the contract, *A* himself may on other occasions be able to benefit from such a rule by coercing others to make agreements against their will. In the long run, however, it is unlikely that *A* will be better off if physical coercion is permitted in the exchange process; as long as the means of violence are distributed in a relatively even fashion, there is no reason to think that *A*'s gains from such a rule will exceed his losses. More importantly, a rule of this sort would give people an incentive to shift scarce resources from productive uses—uses that increase everyone's level of material well-being—to non-productive ones (the development of more powerful weapons and better bulletproof vests) that improve no one's position but merely maintain the status quo. A legal rule permitting physical coercion in the exchange process would therefore have exactly the opposite effect of a rule permitting well-informed buyers to exploit deliberately acquired information.

The same is true of fraud (the deliberate production of misinformation).[45] If *B* agrees to purchase *A*'s automobile after *A* has lied to him about its mechanical condition, enforcing *B*'s agreement despite *A*'s fraud will hurt *B* and benefit *A*. The next time, however, *A* may be the victim and *B* the successful defrauder. Once again, there is no reason to think that most people will benefit from a rule permitting fraud; indeed, this is impossible, since total gains from such a rule will exactly equal total losses. Moreover, adopting a rule of this sort would give everyone an incentive to invest in the detection of fraudulent representations. Such investments

yield information, but only of a non-productive kind. It is to everyone's advantage that resources be devoted to other uses; a rule prohibiting fraud in exchange transactions encourages precisely that result.

Of course, the principle of paretianism does not always yield so clear an answer as these cases might suggest. Suppose, for example, that *A* is aware of an important defect in his own property—a termite infestation, say—and merely fails to inform *B* of the defect's presence. *A* is surely exploiting his superior information at *B*'s expense; in this respect, *A*'s conduct is indistinguishable from *B*'s in the situation described earlier—when *B* offers to buy *A*'s property without revealing what he knows about its true value. Moreover, *A*'s information, like *B*'s, is productive in nature, because it reveals a fact that must be taken into account if the allocation of scarce resources is to be as efficient as possible. Unlike *B*'s information, however, *A*'s knowledge regarding the termites may be the product of casual observations made while living in the house, rather than the result of a deliberate and costly search. If so, a rule requiring *A* to disclose what he knows about the termites will have no, or only a small, effect on the production of such information. Moreover, a rule of this sort will reduce *B*'s own inspection costs—which are likely to be higher than *A*'s given *B*'s unfamiliarity with the property.[46] Assuming that most people will be buyers about as often as they are sellers, one may perhaps tentatively conclude that their gains from a legal rule requiring sellers to disclose substantial, nonvisible defects will exceed the occasional losses they suffer as a result.

It does not follow, of course, that most people will be made better off if sellers of all sorts are required to disclose defects of every kind. Beyond a certain point, a rule requiring disclosure may have significant and undesirable incentive effects, and in some cases, the buyer's own search costs are likely to be so low as to trivialize the benefits he receives from disclosure. Even in this difficult area, however, the principle of paretianism provides guidance by indicating the kind of argument that must be made in order to justify any particular disclosure rule, whether it be a broad or narrow one.[47]

E. PARETIANISM AND EQUALITY

The principle of paretianism requires us to evaluate different kinds of advantage-taking by asking whether they make the disadvantaged themselves better off in the long run. But what is the baseline against which we are to measure changes in the welfare of the disadvantaged? Clearly, the baseline is represented by the situation in which the advantage-taking in question is legally forbidden: advantage-taking is to be allowed only if the disadvantaged are made better off than they would be were it prohibited. But the baseline situation, conceived in this way, is a situation of equality. Consequently, if a libertarian adopts paretianism as the basis for discriminating between acceptable and unacceptable forms of advantage-taking in the exchange process—and I have argued that he has good reasons for doing so—he will be endorsing a view that rests upon what, from a libertarian perspective, may seem to be a surprisingly strong egalitarian premise.

An example will help to clarify what I mean. Suppose that A possesses certain information but is forbidden to exploit it for his own benefit. If he wishes to make any use of the information in his transactions with others, A must reveal what he knows; a failure to do so, in any particular case, will render the other party's agreement unenforceable. When it is disclosed, A's information becomes a public asset which everyone has an equal right to use as he pleases. If A cannot make an enforceable contract without disclosing what he knows, he will be unable to exploit his informational advantage except on terms that benefit others equally. The alternative, of course, is to give A a property right in his information and permit him to exploit it as he would any other privately owned asset. The principle of paretianism states, however, that a property right of this sort should be granted only if those to whom the information is not disclosed will be even better off than they would be were the information treated as a public asset belonging to no one in particular and thus available for the equal use of all. It is the latter situation that provides the baseline against which we are to measure changes in the welfare of the disadvantaged.

The egalitarian nature of this baseline situation is illustrated, in a different way, by the rule forbidding the use of physical force in exchange relationships. Suppose that A has greater physical strength than his neighbors. If we refuse to give A the right to exploit his superior strength by threatening his neighbors with harm unless they agree to do what he wishes, we once again place everyone involved (the person who possesses the advantage as well as those who do not) in a situation of equality. Here, of course, equality is achieved not by forcing A to share his advantage with others, but by denying everyone, including A, a right to make use of the advantage in question, at least in this particular way.

Paretianism justifies divergence from this situation of equality only when A's weaker neighbors can be made better off if A is permitted to enforce agreements coerced by threats of physical force. The fact that A is not allowed to do so but is given the right to exploit his superior strength in other ways—for example, by insisting upon a higher price for his labor—only shows that the principle yields different results where different forms of advantage-taking are involved. In every case, however, the principle forbids us to grant the possessor of an advantage the exclusive right to exploit it for his own benefit unless those excluded from its ownership are thereby made better off than they would be if no one were given a greater right to the advantage than anyone else. Stating the principle in this way emphasizes its strongly egalitarian character and underscores its similarity to Rawls's test[48] for assessing the fairness of inequalities in the distribution of material wealth.

F. POSSESSION AND OWNERSHIP

Another way of representing the egalitarian character of paretianism is to imagine that all advantageous assets, including strength, intelligence and information, belong to a common pool or fund in which no one—not even the person who possesses the advantage—has any prior claim.[49] With regard to any advantage in the common pool, three possibilities exist: 1) the person possessing the advantage may be granted a right to exploit it for his own benefit; 2) the possessor may be allowed to exploit the advantage, but only in ways that benefit others equally; or 3) he may be forbidden to exploit the advantage at all. Paretianism is then to be viewed as a principle for determining which of these three alternatives ought to be adopted in any particular case, and thus for deciding who should be assigned the rights to different kinds of advantages.

Of course, many libertarians reject this way of thinking about the assignment of rights, claiming that attributes and advantages come into the world already attached to particular individuals and not as part of some common pool or fund.[50] Libertarians claim that mere possession of an advantage gives the possessor a right to exploit his advantage in any way he wishes, so long as the rights of others are not violated in the process. On this view, the fact that an individual possesses a particular advantage is held to give him a *prima facie* right to exploit it for his own benefit; his right to do so, however, may be defeated or overridden by the legitimate claims of others.[51]

This view implies that possession itself provides a moral reason—although only a defeasible one—for assigning property rights in particular advantages to those who possess them. In my judgment, however, the fact of possession fails to provide even a limited justification for assigning property rights in one way rather than another. Suppose that X possesses two advantages that Y lacks—greater physical strength and superior intelligence. Should we allow X to exploit these advantages in his transactions with Y, in whatever way he wishes? Most libertarians would answer this question in the negative: X should not be allowed to exploit his physical strength by threatening Y with harm, and he should not be permitted to exploit his intelligence by persuading Y to accept a believable lie, although he may be free to take advantage of his gifts in other ways. Presumably, the reason a libertarian will give for disallowing certain forms of advantage-taking on X's part is that they violate Y's right not to be coerced in these ways. But which types of coercion violate Y's right to non-interference? However one answers this question, the fact that X possesses the advantage he wants to exploit can never be an argument for defining the scope of Y's right in a certain way; that proposition will always be true and therefore cannot make the position of either party stronger (or weaker) than it would otherwise be. Likewise, it can never be an argument either for limiting or expanding the scope of Y's right to non-interference that Y himself possesses an interest that will be affected if others are allowed to take advantage of him, since this, too, is true in every case. The mere fact of possession—whether X's or Y's—provides no help whatsoever in deciding how Y's right to non-interference should be defined, or whether X should be assigned an exclusive right to the advantages he possesses.

Thus, it is a mistake to think that the fact of possession has any moral significance in itself, even of the limited sort claimed by libertarians, so far as the assignment of entitlements is concerned. By viewing individual advantages as if they were part of a common fund or pool, one eliminates the fact of possession as a relevant consideration and thereby avoids this mistake. The great attraction of viewing advantages in this way is that it forces us to clarify the underlying argument that must always provide the true foundation for protecting one set of possessory interests rather than another.

G. ADVANTAGE-TAKING AND DIFFERENCES IN WEALTH

At this point, most libertarians would probably respond by claiming that I have shown the libertarian theory of contract law to be a theory of distributive justice in only a limited or perhaps even trivial respect. While conceding that the notion of voluntary exchange cannot be given meaning without specifying how rights to transactional advantages *in the exchange process itself* are to be distributed, a libertarian might argue that this can be done without attaching any importance whatsoever to the distributional *consequences* of those exchanges in which there has been no impermissible advantage-taking. So long as there has been no advantage-taking of this sort, he might argue, agreements should be enforced regardless of their impact on the distribution of wealth in society. On this view, contractual limitations of the sort mentioned at the beginning of the Article—restrictions on interest rates, minimum wage laws, and nondisclaimable warranties—would be wholly unjustified if one assumes their purpose is not to insure voluntariness in exchange transactions, but to alter the distribution of wealth that results from the free exchange of property itself. In this way, a libertarian might concede that a limited theory of distributive justice is needed to explicate the notion of voluntary exchange, yet still maintain that his view is meaningfully different from that of anyone who believes it appropriate to manipulate the private law of contracts in order to achieve a more desirable distribution of wealth in society.

This position can be interpreted in one of two different ways. First, the claim may be that differences in wealth created or maintained by contractual exchange need not be justified by invoking the same principle of distributive justice, whatever it might be, that we appeal to in justifying various forms of advantage-taking in exchange relationships. On this view, differences in wealth that result from the free exchange of property are not to be thought of as requiring any justification at all, unlike the assignment of rights to transactional advantages in the exchange process; while the latter poses a problem of distributive justice, the former does not. I shall call this interpretation of the position the strong interpretation.

A second, weaker interpretation is also possible. Someone defending the position in question can be understood as claiming either that disparities in wealth which result from the free exchange of property *are* justified, on the same basis that certain forms of transactional advantage-taking are, or that existing disparities in wealth are *not* justified but should be corrected in some other way than by manipulating the rules for private exchange. I call this second interpretation weak because it accepts what the first interpretation questions—the claim that differences in wealth resulting from free exchange stand as much in need of justification as the exploitation of differential advantages in the exchange process itself.

In my view, the first of these two interpretations must be rejected since it rests upon an essentially arbitrary distinction between different kinds of wealth and the advantages associated with them, and fails to recognize that disparities in wealth resulting from one transaction become an advantage in the next. If we ask whether an individual should be permitted to exploit his superior information or intelligence in transactions with others, the answer—at least the answer the law gives[52]—is "sometimes and under certain circumstances." In order to explain why the possessor of these valuable resources should be allowed to exploit them in some ways but not others, appeal must be made to a principle of distributive justice. The same ought to be true if we ask whether someone with a substantial bank account should be allowed to take advantage of his superior wealth in transacting with other, less wealthy individuals. In the first place, if we define a person's wealth as comprising the sum total of revenue-generating assets which the law permits him to exploit for his own benefit, his wealth will include things like information, intelligence and physical strength, as well as dollars in the bank. If we prohibit someone from exploiting potentially valuable information or skills (for example, the skill of deception) we thereby decrease his wealth just as surely as if we were to take some money from his bank account and burn it or transfer it into

a common fund. Second, it is wrong to think of money—wealth in the narrow sense—as anything other than a transactional advantage, an advantage which gives its possessor a leg up in the exchange process. Money enables an individual to acquire other transactional advantages (for example, superior information), to withstand pressures that might otherwise force him to make agreements on less favorable terms, to outbid competitors, etc.; other things equal, the more money an individual has, the better he is likely to do in his transactions with other persons. In fact, money not only gives its possessor a transactional advantage: unlike intelligence or physical strength, it gives him nothing else. A sailor stranded alone on a desert island may benefit from his physical and mental abilities; unless he has someone to transact with, however, the money in his pocket does him no good at all.

For these reasons, no one should be allowed to exploit his financial resources in transactions with others to any greater extent than he should be allowed to exploit his superior intelligence, strength or information. It is true that each of these represents wealth of a different kind and gives its possessor a distinct advantage in transacting with others. But it is unclear why any importance should be attached to differences of this sort. If one kind of advantage-taking—that based on superior information, for example—must be justified by showing that it is consistent with a particular conception of distributive justice, other kinds of advantage-taking, including those attributable to inequalities of a financial sort, should be justified in the same way. It is simply arbitrary to assert that some forms of advantage-taking must be justified but others need not be.

It does not follow, of course, that the rich should be forbidden to exploit their financial power in transacting with the poor. Whether and to what extent they should will depend upon the principle of distributive justice one adopts and factual details relevant to the principle's application. There is, however, no *a priori* reason for regarding a rule of contract law that is intended to reduce inequalities of wealth (in the narrow sense) as any more objectionable than rules prohibiting fraud or requiring the disclosure of certain kinds of information, which also redistribute wealth (in the broad sense) from one group of individuals to another. Although there may be a sound reason for opposing a rule of contract law whose purpose is to shift resources from the rich to the poor,[53] the reason cannot be that the special financial advantages enjoyed by the rich fall outside the scope of the principle of distributive justice that controls the assignment of rights to other kinds of transactional advantages. Therefore, the only sensible interpretation of the libertarian's position is the second or weak interpretation: when a libertarian asserts that contract law should not be used to redistribute wealth from the rich to the poor, he must be claiming either that existing inequalities of wealth *are* justified (for example, on utilitarian or parentianist grounds) or that contract law is an unsuitable instrument for correcting those inequalities which are unjustifiable. Stating the libertarian position in this way, however, eliminates the most fundamental difference between liberal and libertarian theories of contract law.

NOTES

1. See 1 A. Corbin, Contracts 2 (1963); cf. U.C.C. § 1-201(11) (1972) ("'Contract' means the total legal obligation which results from the parties' agreement. . . . ")

2. See, e.g., G. Tullock, The Logic of the Law 47 (1971) (one function of contract law is to save parties inconvenience of drafting very long agreements by providing rules of interpretation); Farnsworth, *Disputes Over Omission in Contracts,* 68 Colum. L. Rev. 860, 860 n.2 (1968) (court, having determined a contract exists, cannot refuse to apply it even in case for which parties did not expressly provide); cf. U.C.C. §§ 2-310, 2-511(1) (1972) (prescribing certain conditions to be considered part of all contracts "unless otherwise agreed" by parties).

3. See, e.g., O. Holmes, The Common Law 227 (M. Howe ed. 1963); Farnsworth, *Legal Remedies for Breach of Contract,* 70 Colum. L. Rev. 1145, 1147 (1970). In recent years, a number of writers have advocated an economic approach to the problem of defining the appropriate remedies for breach. See, e.g., Barton, *The Economic Basis of Damages for Breach of Contract,* 1 J. Legal Stud. 277 (1972); Priest, *Breach and Remedy for the Tender of Nonconforming Goods Under the Uniform Commercial Code: An Economic Approach,* 91 Harv. L. Rev. 960 (1978).

4. See, e.g., Ackerman, *Regulating Slum Housing Markets on Behalf of the Poor: Of Housing Codes, Housing Subsidies and Income Redistribution Policy,* 80 Yale L. J. 1093, 1098 (1973) (housing codes, if properly enforced, can play important role in "war on poverty"); Kennedy, *Form and Substance in Private Law Adjudication,* 89 Harv. L. Rev. 1685, 1778 (1976) (contract law an "ideal context") for judicial task of creating "altruistic order"); Michelman, *Norms and Normativity in the Economic Theory of Law,* 62 Minn. L. Rev. 1015, 1016-37 (1978) (housing-code regulation of rental contracts justifiable as redistributive measure even if not demonstrably "efficient" in economic sense).

5. See, e.g., Conn. Gen. Stat. § 37-4 (1979); N. Y. Banking Law § 173-1 (McKinney 1971).

6. Javins v. First Nat'l Realty Corp., 428 F.2d 1071, 1079-82 (D.C. Cir.), cert. denied, 400 U.S. 925 (1970) (housing lease includes implied warranty of habitability).

7. See, e.g., 29 U.S.C. § 206(a)(1) (1976).

8. See F. Hayek, The Constitution of Liberty 93-102, 133-61 (1961) (redistribution of wealth restricts liberty and inappropriately attempts to align compensation with moral worth); R. Nozick, Anarchy, State and Utopia 149-53, 167-74 (1974) (property rights, established by principles of acquisition and transfer, should be inviolate); Buchanan, *Political Equality and Private Property: The Distributional Paradox,* in Markets and Morals 69-84 (G. Dworkin, G. Bennett, & P. Brown eds. 1977) (individual freedom inconsistent with forced economic equality); Epstein, *Unconscionability: A Critical Reappraisal,* 18 J. L. & Econ. 293, 293-94 (1975) (contract law provides individuals with a "sphere of influence" in which they are not required to justify their activity to the state).

9. See C. Fried, Right and Wrong 143-50 (1978); J. Rawls, A Theory of Justice 87-88, 274-79 (1971); Grey, *Property and Need: The Welfare State and Theories of Distributive Justice,* 28 Stan. L. Rev. 877, 890 n.38 (1976); Rawls, *The Basic Structure as Subject,* in Values and Morals 47, 54-55 (A. Golman & J. Kim eds. 1978) [hereinafter cited as *Basic Structure*]; C. DeMuth, Regulatory Costs and the "Regulatory Budget" 9 (Dec. 1979) (Discussion Paper, Faculty Project on Regulation, John F. Kennedy School of Government, Harvard University). But cf. Dworkin, *Liberalism,* in Public and Private Morality 133 (S. Hampshire ed. 1978) (preference for redistribution by taxation rather than regulation not essential to liberalism).

10. See, e.g., R. Nozick, supra note 8, at 172.

11. See, e.g., *Basic Structure,* supra note 9, at 55, 65.

12. Compare id. at 54-55 (fraud example) with R. Nozick, supra note 8, at 150 (same).

13. See, e.g., Epstein, supra note 8, at 293-95; *Basic Structure,* supra note 9, at 65.

14. See J. Rawls, supra note 9, at 60, 83, 302-03 (difference principle states that inequalities should be "arranged so that they are both to the greatest benefit of the least advantaged . . . and attached to offices and positions open to all").

15. The distinction between actions that violate a person's rights and those that merely reduce his welfare is developed in R. Nozick, supra note 8, at 57-84.

16. See id. at 153-55.

17. Thus, an advocate of pure proceduralism may attempt to defend his position on the ground that compliance with his favored procedure is the *best evidence* of voluntary consent, at which point his position becomes simply a more complicated version of libertarianism.

18. See generally Nozick, *Coercion,* in Philosophy, Science, and Method, Essays in Honor of Ernest Nagel (1969).

19. See, e.g., Faber v. Sweet Style Mfg. Corp., 242 N.Y.S.2d 763, 40 Misc. 2d 212 (1963) (plaintiff claimed to suffer from manic-depressive psychosis).

20. See, e.g., Schupp v. Davey Tree Expert Co., 235 Mich. 268, 209 N.W. 85 (1926) (plaintiff signed contract after being assured he would not be bound by its terms).

21. See, e.g., Hackley v. Headley, 45 Mich. 569, 8 N.W. 511 (1881) (plaintiff, unable to afford to sue for amount due him under contract, accepted note for lesser amount and gave receipt for full balance due).

22. See, e.g., Sherwood v. Walker, 66 Mich. 568, 33 N.W. 919 (1887) (sale of cow rescinded where the animal, assumed by both parties to be barren, later proved otherwise); Obde v. Schlemeyer, 56 Wash. 2d 449, 353 P.2d 672 (1960) (seller of home under duty to disclose termite infestation). For a theoretical discussion of the scope of the seller's duty to disclose, see Kronman, *Mistake, Disclosing Information, and the Law of Contracts,* 7 J. Legal Stud. 1 (1978).

23. Contracts of adhesion are standardized contracts characteristically used by large firms in every transaction for products or services of a certain kind. The use of such contracts can have profound implications for ordinary notions of freedom of contract:

"The weaker party, in need of the goods or services, is frequently not in a position to shop around for better terms, either because the author of the contract has a monopoly (natural or artificial) or because all competitors use the same clauses. His contractual intention is but a subjection more or less voluntary to terms dictated by the stronger party, terms whose consequences are often understood only in a vague way, if at all."

Kessler, *Contracts of Adhesion—Some Thoughts About Freedom of Contract,* 43 Colum. L. Rev. 629, 632 (1943). For a more recent discussion of adhesion contracts, see Leff, *Unconscionability and the Code—the Emperor's New Clause,* 115 U. Pa. L. Rev. 485, 504-08 (1967).

24. Cf. Scanlon, *Nozick on Rights, Liberty, and Property,* 6 Phil. & Pub. Affairs 3, 17 (1976) (idea of consent implies that choice occurs against some background of alternatives).

25. Cf. id. at 19 (adequate conceptions of "consent" and "freedom" would not legitimate loss of control over one's life resulting from unequal bargaining power).

26. This kind of advantage-taking does not differ significantly from deception that does not involve a spoken lie. Suppose that my neighbor makes no threats and tells no lies but merely covers over evidence of an existing termite infestation so completely that even an expert will now be unable to discover their presence in the house. See DeJoseph v. Zambelli, 392 Pa. 24, 139 A.2d 644 (1958). If I agree to buy the house after having had it inspected by an exterminator, should I be released from my agreement when the termites later make themselves known? It is difficult to see what reason there could be for not disallowing this form of advantage-taking if explicit misrepresentation is forbidden, other than the fact that here the deception is accomplished without a spoken lie. But this reason is hardly a good one since the seller has done things which are, in any meaningful sense, fully the equivalent of a deliberately uttered falsehood. So either it was a mistake to disallow one form of advantage-taking, or it is a mistake to permit the other: they ought to stand or fall together.

27. For an ingenious effort to assimilate verbal influence to physical action, see Epstein, *A Theory of Strict Liability,* 2 J. Legal Stud. 151, 172-74 (1973). According to Professor Epstein, defendants whose words frighten someone may thereby commit the tort of assault. If the frightened person suffers injury attributable to fright, or injuries someone else in an attempt to flee, his reactions are not "volitional" on Professor Epstein's view, and should therefore be regarded as the physical acts of the defendant.

28. In many jurisdictions, a seller is now required by law to disclose the presence of termites in a dwelling, despite the buyer's failure to make inquiries. See, e.g., Williams v. Benson, 3 Mich. App. 9, 141 N.W.2d 650 (1966); Cohen v. Blessing, 259 S.C. 400, 192 S.E.2d 204 (1972); Obde v. Schlemeyer, 56 Wash. 2d 449, 353 P.2d 672 (1960).

29. My argument here is that individual liberty is an "essentially contested concept," as that term is defined by W. B. Gallie. See Gallie, *Essentially Contested Concepts,* 56 Proc. Aristotelian Soc'y 167, 167-68 (1956). According to Gallie's formulation, a concept should be considered "essentially contestable" when it is evaluative as well as descriptive and has such diverse criteria of applicability that analysis of ordinary usage yields no single, preferred definition. The question which is the "best" definition is thus open to argument. The libertarian's failure to provide such an argument for his definition of individual liberty is criticized in Scanlon, supra note 24, at 3. For useful discussions of the disputable meaning of abstract concepts, see R. Dworkin, Taking Rights Seriously 134-35 (1977) (distinguishing concepts from "conceptions" offered as elucidations of them); S. Hampshire, Thought and Action 230-31 (1959) (disputes about boundaries necessarily involve disputes about host of connected notions).

30. See F. Nietzsche, The Will To Power §§901-902, 926 (Vintage ed. 1968).

31. For an energetic defense and an equally spirited critique of utilitarianism, see J. Smart & B. Williams, Utilitarianism: For and Against (1973).

32. Principles similar to paretianism have been discussed in connection with a range of legal problems. See, e.g., C. Fried, An Anatomy of Values 187-91 (1970) ("risk pool" concept in tort law); Epstein, *Nuisance Law: Corrective Justice and its Utilitarian Constraints,* 8 J. Legal Stud. 49, 77-78 (1979) (implicit in-kind compensation in nuisance law); Michelman, *Property, Utility, and Fairness: Comments on the Ethical Foundations of "Just Compensation" Law,* 80 Harv. L. Rev. 1165, 1194-96, 1222-24 (1967) (distribution of longrun benefits and losses in eminent domain law); Polinsky, *Probabilistic Compensation Criteria,* 86 Q. J. Econ. 407, 420-21 (1972) (paretian criterion defined in terms of longrun probabilities); Posner, *The Ethical and Political Basis of the Efficiency Norm in Common Law Adjudication* (forthcoming in 8 Hofstra L. Rev. (1980)) (ex ante compensation). For a discussion of the ethical implications of the Pareto principle, see Coleman, *Efficiency, Exchange and Auction: Philosophic Aspects of the Economic Approach to Law* (forthcoming in 68 Calif. L. Rev. (1980)).

33. Libertarians therefore face the following choice: show that the liberty principle does in fact yield a determinate solution to the problem of specifying which forms of advantage-taking are legitimate; acknowledge the vacuousness of the liberty principle but argue that some other principle, different from the three I have considered, is the best one; or, finally, accept paretianism as the appropriate standard by which to assess the legitimacy of the various kinds of advantage-taking possible in exchange transactions. Even from a libertarian point of view, the last alternative seems to me the most attractive of the three and in what follows I shall assume that this is in fact the choice most libertarians would make.

34. This is true even of utilitarian theories that treat individual autonomy as an intrinsic good to be maximized, perhaps along with other intrinsic goods. If autonomy is made a maxim and in this sense, then any limitations can be placed on a person's freedom so long as they yield a greater total amount of freedom overall. But this is to deny that persons have autonomy in the sense in which I am using the term. Respect for the autonomy of persons means that individuals cannot be restricted in their freedom solely for the purpose of increasing the overall amount of some desired good, including freedom itself.

35. Libertarian theorists often express the concept of individual autonomy in terms of the related notion of personal "boundaries." See R. Nozick, supra note 8, at 57-87; Epstein, supra note 32, at 50-54. The notion of boundaries suggests that each moral agent possesses a natural right to be free from violations of his body, and, more problematically, a similar right to be free from imposition of constraints on choice that are incompatible with moral personhood. His commitment to the idea of personal boundaries requires the libertarian to reject any theory, such as utilitarianism, that permits the violation of boundaries whenever the sum of some impersonal good can be advanced by doing so.

36. The latter point is developed more fully in a later section. See pp. 491-93 infra.

37. The practical necessity of evaluating rules by reference to their effects on classes rather than on particular individuals has been recognized previously. See J. Rawls, supra note 9, at 98. Rawls keys his difference principle to the welfare of the least advantaged class rather than the least advantaged person, and argues that a theory intended to protect individuals can employ general classifications with complete internal consistency when such classifications afford fuller protection to individuals than any other "practicable" scheme. See id.

38. For a fuller discussion of the differences between paretianism and utilitarianism as ethical theories, see Kronman, *Wealth Maximi-*

zation As a Normative Principle (forthcoming in 9 J. Legal Stud. (1980)).

39. See, e.g., Coleman, supra note 32; Posner, supra note 32.

40. See Kant's Critique of Practical Reason and Other Works on the Theory of Ethics 4-5 (6th ed. T. Abbott trans. 1909).

41. This conviction is an element of Rawls's theory as well. See J. Rawls, supra note 9, at 3-4, 22-27.

42. For a fuller discussion of this and similar cases, see Kronman, supra note 22, at 9-18.

43. An example of such a case is a situation in which there is a prior fiduciary relationship between the parties.

44. Arguments similar to the one in text can be made to justify taking advantage of superior acumen or intelligence. See J. Rawls, supra note 9, at 100-08.

45. See R. Posner, Economic Analysis of Law 80-84 (2d ed. 1977).

46. See Kronman, supra note 22, at 13-14.

47. Although the application of the principle of paretianism in difficult cases may require the resolution of factual questions that the professional economist is best equipped to answer, it would be a mistake to think that the principle states merely an economic test for assessing different forms of advantage-taking in exchange transactions. It would be more accurate to say that paretianism provides the morally inspired framework within which technical economic issues (for example, those regarding the incentive effects of a proposed disclosure rule) must be debated.

48. See note 14 supra.

49. This "common fund" notion is employed by Rawls. See J. Rawls, supra note 9, at 101-02, 107, 179, 278 (no one deserves greater natural capacity nor merits more favorable starting place in society). For my views on the reasonableness and utility of treating all personal assets as if they belonged to a common fund, see Kronman, *Talent Pooling* (forthcoming in Nomos).

50. See R. Nozick, supra note 8, at 228-31.

51. See R. Epstein, Possession as the Root of Title (unpublished paper on file with *Yale Law Journal*).

52. Compare Pratt Land & Improvement Co. v. McClain, 135 Ala. 452, 456, 33 So. 185, 187 (1902) "(a purchaser [of real estate] though having superior judgment of values, does not commit fraud merely by purchasing without disclosing his knowledge of value") with Equitable Life Assurance Soc'y of United States v. McElroy, 83 F. 631 (8th Cir. 1897) (insurance contract set aside due to nondisclosure of operation for appendicitis during period between signing of application and completion of contract).

53. See Schwartz, *A Reexamination of Nonsubstantive Unconscionability*, 63 Va. L. Rev. 1053, 1056-59 (1977).

CHARLES FRIED

Contract As Promise*

It is a first principle of liberal political morality that we be secure in what is ours—so that our persons and property not be open to exploitation by others, and that from a sure foundation we may express our will and expend our powers in the world. By these powers we may create good things or low, useful articles or luxuries, things extraordinary or banal, and we will be judged accordingly—as saintly or mean, skillful or ordinary, industrious and fortunate or debased, friendly and kind or cold and inhuman. But whatever we accomplish and however that accomplishment is judged, morality requires that we respect the person and property of others, leaving them free to make their lives as we are left free to make ours. This is the liberal ideal. This is the ideal that distinguishes between the good, which is the domain of aspiration, and the right, which sets the terms and limits according to which we strive. This ideal makes what we achieve our own and our failures our responsibility too—however much or little we may choose to share our good fortune and however we may hope for help when we fail.[1]

Everything must be available to us, for who can deny the human will the title to expand even into the remotest corner of the universe? And when we forbear to bend some external object to our use because of its natural preciousness we use it still, for it is to our judgment of its value that we respond, our own conception of the good that we pursue. Only other persons are not available to us in this way—they alone share our self-consciousness, our power of self-determination; thus to use them as if they were merely part of external nature is to poison the source of the moral power we enjoy. But others *are* part of the external world, and by denying ourselves access to their persons and powers, we drastically shrink the scope of our efficacy. So it was a crucial moral discovery that free men may yet freely serve each others' purposes: the discovery that beyond the fear of reprisal or the hope of reciprocal favor, morality itself might be enlisted to assure not only that you respect me and mine but that you actively serve my purposes.[2] When my confidence in your assistance derives from my conviction that you will do what is right (not just what is prudent), then I trust you, and trust becomes a powerful tool for our working our mutual wills in the world. So remarkable a tool is trust that in the end we pursue it for its own sake; we prefer doing things cooperatively when we might have relied on fear or interest or worked alone.[3]

The device that gives trust its sharpest, most palpable form is promise. By promising we put in another man's hands a new power to accomplish his will, though only a moral power: What he sought to do alone he may now expect to do with our promised help, and to give him this new facility was our very purpose in promising. By promising we transform a choice that was morally neutral into one that is morally compelled. Morality, which must be permanent and beyond our particular will if the grounds for our willing are to be secure, is itself invoked, molded to allow us better to work that particular will. Morality then serves modest, humdrum ends: We make appointments, buy and sell, harnessing this loftiest of all forces.

What is a promise, that by my words I should make wrong what before was morally indifferent? A promise is a communication—usually verbal; it says something. But how can my saying something put a moral charge on a choice that before was morally neutral? Well, by my misleading you, or by lying.[4] Is lying not the very paradigm of doing wrong by speaking? But this won't do, for a promise puts the moral charge on a *potential* act—the wrong is done later, when the promise is not kept—while a lie is a wrong committed at the time of its utterance. Both wrongs abuse trust, but in different ways. When I speak I commit myself to the truth of my utterance, but when I promise I commit myself to *act*, later. Though these two wrongs are thus quite distinct there has been a persistent tendency to run them together by treating a promise as a lie after all, but a par-

*From Charles Fried, *Contract As Promise, A Theory of Contractual Obligation* (Cambridge, Mass.: Harvard University Press, 1981). ©1981 by the President and Fellows of Harvard College. Reprinted by permission of the publisher.

ticular kind of lie: a lie about one's intentions. Consider this case:

I. I sell you a house, retaining an adjacent vacant lot. At the time of our negotiations, I state that I intend to build a home for myself on that lot. What if several years later I sell the lot to a person who builds a gas station on it? What if I sell it only one month later? What if I am already negotiating for its sale as a gas station at the time I sell the house to you?[5]

If I was already negotiating to sell the lot for a gas station at the time of my statement to you, I have wronged you. I have lied to you about the state of my intentions, and this is as much a lie as a lie about the state of the plumbing.[6] If, however, I sell the lot many years later, I do you no wrong. There are no grounds for saying I lied about my intentions; I have just changed my mind. Now if I had *promised* to use the lot only as a residence, the situation would be different. Promising is more than just truthfully reporting my present intentions, for I may be free to change my mind, as I am not free to break my promise.

Let us take it as given here that lying is wrong and so that it is wrong to obtain benefits or cause harm by lying (including lying about one's intentions). It does not at all follow that to obtain a benefit or cause harm by breaking a promise is also wrong. That my act procures me a benefit or causes harm all by itself proves nothing. If I open a restaurant near your hotel and prosper as I draw your guests away from the standard hotel fare you offer, this benefit I draw from you places me under no obligation to you. I should make restitution only if I benefit *unjustly,* which I do if I deceive you—as when I lie to you about my intentions in example I.[7] But where is the injustice if I honestly intend to keep my promise at the time of making it, and later change my mind? If we feel I owe you recompense in that case too, it cannot be because of the benefit I have obtained through my promise: We have seen that benefit even at another's expense is not alone sufficient to require compensation. If I owe you a duty to return that benefit it must be because of the promise. It is the promise that makes my enrichment at your expense unjust, and not the enrichment that makes the promise binding. And thus neither the statement of intention nor the benefit explains why, if at all, a promise does any moral work.

A more common attempt to reduce the force of a promise to some other moral category invokes the harm you suffer in relying on my promise. My statement is like a pit I have dug in the road, into which you fall. I have harmed you and should make you whole. Thus the tort principle might be urged to bridge the gap in the argument between a statement of intention and a promise: I have a duty just because I could have foreseen (indeed it was my intention) that you would rely on my promise and that you would suffer harm when I broke it. And this wrong then not only sets the stage for compensation of the harm caused by the misplaced reliance, but also supplies the moral predicate for restitution of any benefits I may have extracted from you on the strength of my promise.[8] But we still beg the question. If the promise is no more than a truthful statement of my intention, why am *I* responsible for harm that befalls you as a result of my change of heart? To be sure, it is not like a change in the weather—I might have kept to my original intention—but how does this distinguish the broken promise from any other statement of intention (or habit or prediction of future conduct) of mine of which you know and on which you choose to rely? Should your expectations of me limit my freedom of choice? If you rent the apartment next to mine because I play chamber music there, do I owe you more than an expression of regret when my friends and I decide to meet instead at the cellist's home? And in general, why should my liberty be constrained by the harm you would suffer from the disappointment of the expectations you choose to entertain about my choices?

Does it make a difference that when I promise you do not just happen to rely on me, that I communicate my intention to you and therefore can be taken to know that changing my mind may put you at risk? But then I might be aware that you would count on my keeping to my intentions even if I myself had not communicated those intentions to you. (*You* might have told me you were relying on me, or you might have overheard me telling some third person of my intentions.) It might be said that I become the agent of your reliance by telling you, and that this makes my responsibility clearer: After all, I can scarcely control all the ways in which you might learn of my intentions, but I *can* control whether or not I tell you of them. But we are still begging the question. If promising is no more than my telling you of my intentions, why do we both not know that I may yet change my mind? Perhaps, then, promising is like telling you of my intention and telling you that I don't intend to change my mind. But why can't I change my mind about the latter intention?

Perhaps the statement of intention in promising is binding because we not only foresee reliance, we invite it: We intend the promisee to rely on the promise. Yet even this will not do. If I invite reliance on my stated intention, then that is all I invite. Certainly I may hope and intend, in example I, that you buy my house on the basis of what I have told you, but why does that hope bind me to do more than state my intention honestly? And that intention and invitation are quite compatible with my later changing my mind. In every case, of course, I should weigh the harm I will do if I do change my mind. If I am a doctor and I know you will rely on me to be part of an outing on which someone may fall ill, I should certainly weigh the harm that may come about if that reliance is disappointed. Indeed I should weigh that harm even if you do not rely on me, but are foolish enough not to have made a provision for a doctor. Yet in none of these instances am I bound as I would be had I promised.[9]

A promise invokes trust in my future actions, not merely in my present sincerity. We need to isolate an additional element, over and above benefit, reliance, and the communication of intention. That additional element must *commit* me, and commit me to more than the truth of some statement. That additional element has so far eluded our analysis.

It has eluded us, I believe, because there is a real puzzle about how we can commit ourselves to a course of conduct that absent our commitment is morally neutral. The invocation of benefit and reliance are attempts to explain the force of a promise in terms of two of its most usual effects, but the attempts fail because these effects depend on the prior assumption of the force of the commitment. The way out of the puzzle is to recognize the bootstrap quality of the argument: To have force in *a particular case* promises must be assumed to have force generally. Once that general assumption is made, the effects we intentionally produce by a particular promise may be morally attributed to us. This recognition is not as paradoxical as its abstract statement here may make it seem. It lies, after all, behind every conventional structure: games,[10] institutions and practices, and most important, language.

Let us put to one side the question of how a convention comes into being, or of when and why we are morally bound to comply with its terms, while we look briefly at what a convention is and how it does its work. Take the classical example of a game. What the players do is defined by a system of rules—sometimes quite vague and informal, sometimes elaborate and codified. These rules apply only to the players—that is, to persons who invoke them. These rules are a human invention, and their consequences (castling, striking out, winning, losing) can be understood only in terms of the rules. The players may have a variety of motives for playing (profit, fun, maybe even duty to fellow players who need participants). A variety of judgments are applicable to the players—they may be deemed skillful, imaginative, bold, honest, or dishonest—but these judgments and motives too can be understood only in the context of the game. For instance, you can cheat only by breaking rules to which you pretend to conform.

This almost canonical invocation of the game example has often been misunderstood as somehow applying only to unserious matters, to play, so that it is said to trivialize the solemn objects (like law or promises) that it is used to explain. But this is a mistake, confusing the interests involved, the reasons for creating and invoking a particular convention, with the logical structure of conventions in general. Games are (often) played for fun, but other conventions—for instance religious rituals or legal procedures—may have most earnest ends, while still other conventions are quite general. To the last category belongs language. The conventional nature of language is too obvious to belabor. It is worth pointing out, however, that the various things we do with language—informing, reporting, promising, insulting, cheating, lying—all depend on the conventional structure's being firmly in place. You could not lie if there were not both understanding of the language you lied in and a general convention of using that language truthfully. This point holds irrespective of whether the institution of language has advanced the situation of mankind and of whether lying is sometimes, always, or never wrong.

Promising too is a very general convention—though less general than language, of course, since promising is itself a use of language.[11] The convention of promising (like that of language) has a very general purpose under which we may bring an infinite set of particular purposes. In order that I be as free as possible, that my will have the greatest possible range consistent with the similar will of others, it is necessary that there be a way in which I may commit myself. It is necessary that I be able to make nonoptional a course of conduct that would otherwise be optional for me. By doing this I can facilitate the projects of others, because I can make it possible for those others to count on my future conduct, and thus those others can pursue more intricate, more far-reaching projects. If it is my purpose, my will that others be able to count on me in the pursuit of their endeavor, it is essential that I be able to deliver myself into their hands more firmly than where they simply predict my future course. Thus the possibility of commitment permits an act of generosity on my part, permits me to pursue a project whose content is that *you* be permitted to pursue *your* project. But of course this purely altruistic motive is not the only motive worth facilitating. More central to our concern is the situation where we facilitate each other's projects, where the gain is reciprocal. Schematically the situation looks like this:

You want to accomplish purpose *A* and I want to accomplish purpose *B*. Neither of us can succeed without the cooperation of the other. Thus I want to be able to commit myself to help you achieve *A* so that you will commit yourself to help me achieve *B*.

Now if *A* and *B* are objects or actions that can be transferred simultaneously there is no need for commitment. As I hand over *A* you hand over *B,* and we are both satisfied. But very few things are like that. We need a device to permit a trade over time: to allow me to do *A* for you when you need it, in the confident belief that you will do *B* for me when I need it. Your commitment puts your future performance into my hands in the present just as my commitment puts my future performance into your hands. A future exchange is transformed into a present exchange. And in order to accomplish this all we need is a conventional device which we both invoke, which you know I am invoking when I invoke it, which I know that you know I am invoking, and so on.

The only mystery about this is the mystery that surrounds increasing autonomy by providing means for restricting it. But really this is a pseudomystery. The restrictions involved in promising are restrictions undertaken just in order to increase one's options in the long run,

and thus are perfectly consistent with the principle of autonomy—consistent with a respect for one's own autonomy and the autonomy of others. To be sure, in getting something for myself now by promising to do something for you in the future, I am mortgaging the interest of my future self in favor of my present self. How can I be sure my future self will approve?* This is a deep and difficult problem about which I say more later in this chapter. Suffice it to say here that unless one assumes the continuity of the self and the possibility of maintaining complex projects over time, not only the morality of promising but also any coherent picture of the person becomes impossible.

THE MORAL OBLIGATION OF PROMISE

Once I have invoked the institution of promising, why exactly is it wrong for me then to break my promise?

My argument so far does not answer that question. The institution of promising is a way for me to bind myself to another so that the other may expect a future performance, and binding myself in this way is something that I may want to be able to do. But this by itself does not show that I am morally obligated to perform my promise at a later time if to do so proves inconvenient or costly. That there should be a system of currency also increases my options and is useful to me, but this does not show why I should not use counterfeit money if I can get away with it. In just the same way the usefulness of promising in general does not show why I should not take advantage of it in a particular case and yet fail to keep my promise. That the convention would cease to function in the long run, would cease to provide benefits if everyone felt free to violate it, is hardly an answer to the question of why I should keep a particular promise on a particular occasion.

David Lewis has shown[12] that a convention that it would be in each person's interest to observe if everyone else observed it will be established and maintained without any special mechanisms of commitment or enforcement. Starting with simple conventions (for example that if a telephone conversation is disconnected, the person who initiated the call is the one who calls back) Lewis extends his argument to the

*Note that this problem does not arise where I make a present sacrifice for a future benefit, since by hypothesis I am presently willing to make that sacrifice and in the future I only stand to gain.

case of language. Now promising is different, since (unlike language, where it is overwhelmingly in the interest of all that everyone comply with linguistic conventions, even when language is used to deceive) it will often be in the interest of the promisor *not* to conform to the convention when it comes time to render his performance. Therefore individual self-interest is not enough to sustain the convention, and some additional ground is needed to keep it from unraveling. There are two principal candidates: external sanctions and moral obligation.

David Hume sought to combine these two by proposing that the external sanction of public opprobrium, of loss of reputation for honesty, which society attaches to promise-breaking, is internalized, becomes instinctual, and accounts for the sense of the moral obligation of promise.[13] Though Hume offers a possible anthropological or psychological account of how people feel about promises, his is not a satisfactory *moral* argument. Assume that I can get away with breaking my promise (the promisee is dead), and I am now asking why I should keep it anyway in the face of some personal inconvenience. Hume's account of obligation is more like an argument *against* my keeping the promise, for it tells me how any feelings of obligation that I may harbor have come to lodge in my psyche and thus is the first step toward ridding me of such inconvenient prejudices.

Considerations of self-interest cannot supply the moral basis of my obligation to keep a promise. By an analogous argument neither can considerations of utility. For however sincerely and impartially I may apply the utilitarian injunction to consider at each step how I might increase the sum of happiness or utility in the world, it will allow me to break my promise whenever the balance of advantage (including, of course, my own advantage) tips in that direction. The possible damage to the institution of promising is only one factor in the calculation. Other factors are the alternative good I might do by breaking my promise, whether and by how many people the breach might be discovered, what the actual effect on confidence of such a breach would be. There is no *a priori* reason for believing that an individual's calculations will come out in favor of keeping the promise always, sometimes, or most of the time.

Rule-utilitarianism seeks to offer a way out of this conundrum. The individual's moral obligation is determined not by what the best action

at a particular moment would be, but by the rule it would be best for him to follow. It has, I believe, been demonstrated that this position is incoherent: Either rule-utilitarianism requires that rules be followed in a particular case even where the result would not be best all things considered, and so the utilitarian aspect of rule-utilitarianism is abandoned; or the obligation to follow the rule is so qualified as to collapse into act-utilitarianism after all.[14] There is, however, a version of rule-utilitarianism that makes a great deal of sense. In this version the utilitarian does not instruct us what our individual moral obligations are but rather instructs legislators what the best rules are.[15] If legislation is our focus, then the contradictions of rule-utilitarianism do not arise, since we are instructing those whose decisions can *only* take the form of issuing rules. From that perspective there is obvious utility to rules establishing and enforcing promissory obligations. Since I am concerned now with the question of individual obligation, that is, moral obligation, this legislative perspective on the argument is not available to me.

The obligation to keep a promise is grounded not in arguments of utility but in respect for individual autonomy and in trust. Autonomy and trust are grounds for the institution of promising as well, but the argument for *individual* obligation is not the same. Individual obligation is only a step away, but that step must be taken.[16] An individual is morally bound to keep his promises because he has intentionally invoked a convention whose function it is to give grounds—moral grounds—for another to expect the promised performance.[17] To renege is to abuse a confidence he was free to invite or not, and which he intentionally did invite. To abuse that confidence now is like (but only *like*) lying: the abuse of a shared social institution that is intended to invoke the bonds of trust. A liar and a promise-breaker each *use* another person. In both speech and promising there is an invitation to the other to trust, to make himself vulnerable; the liar and the promise-breaker then abuse that trust. The obligation to keep a promise is thus similar to but more constraining than the obligation to tell the truth. To avoid lying you need only believe in the truth of what you say when you say it, but a promise binds into the future, well past the moment when the promise is made. There will, of course, be great social utility to a general regime of trust and confidence in promise and truthfulness. But this just shows that a regime of mutual respect allows men and women to accomplish what in a jungle of unrestrained self-interest could not be accomplished. If this advantage is to be firmly established, there must exist a ground for mutual confidence deeper than and independent of the social utility it permits.

The utilitarian counting the advantages affirms the general importance of enforcing *contracts.* The moralist of duty, however, sees *promising* as a device that free, moral individuals have fashioned on the premise of mutual trust, and which gathers its moral force from that premise. The moralist of duty thus posits a general obligation to keep promises, of which the obligation of contract will be only a special case—that special case in which certain promises have attained legal as well as moral force. But since a contract is first of all a promise, the contract must be kept because a promise must be kept.

To summarize: There exists a convention that defines the practice of promising and its entailments. This convention provides a way that a person may create expectations in others. By virtue of the basic Kantian principles of trust and respect, it is wrong to invoke that convention in order to make a promise, and then to break it.

WHAT A PROMISE IS WORTH

If I make a promise to you, I should do as I promise; and if I fail to keep my promise, it is fair that I should be made to hand over the equivalent of the promised performance. In contract doctrine this proposition appears as the expectation measure of damages for breach. The expectation standard gives the victim of a breach no more or less than he would have had had there been no breach—in other words, he gets the benefit of his bargain.[18] Two alternative measures of damage, reliance and restitution, express the different notions that if a person has relied on a promise and been hurt, that hurt must be made good; and that if a contract-breaker has obtained goods or services, he must be made to pay a fair (just?) price for them.[19] Consider three cases:

II-A. I enter your antique shop on a quiet afternoon and agree in writing to buy an expensive chest I see there, the price being about three times what you paid for it a short time ago.

When I get home I repent of my decision, and within half an hour of my visit—before any other customer has come to your store—I telephone to say I no longer want the chest.

II-B. Same as above, except in the meantime you have waxed and polished the chest and had your delivery van bring it to my door.

II-C. Same as above, except I have the use of the chest for six months, while your shop is closed for renovations.

To require me to pay for the chest in case II-A (or, if you resell it, to pay any profit you lost, including lost business volume) is to give you your expectation, the benefit of your bargain. In II-B if all I must compensate is your effort I am reimbursing your reliance, and in II-C to force me to pay a fair price for the use I have had of the chest is to focus on making me pay for, restore, an actual benefit I have received.

The assault on the classical conception of contract, the concept I call contract as promise, has centered on the connection—taken as canonical for some hundred years—between contract law and expectation damages. To focus the attack on this connection is indeed strategic. As the critics recognize and as I have just stated, to the extent that contract is grounded in promise, it seems natural to measure relief by the expectation, that is, by the promise itself. If that link can be threatened, then contract itself may be grounded elsewhere than in promise, elsewhere than in the will of the parties. In his recent comprehensive treatise, *The Rise and Fall of Freedom of Contract,* Patrick Atiyah makes the connection between the recourse to expectation damages and the emerging enforceability of executory contracts—that is, contracts enforced, though no detriment has been suffered in reliance and no benefit has been conferred. (Case II-A is an example of an executory contract.) Before the nineteenth century, he argues, a contractual relation referred generally to one of a number of particular, community-sanctioned relations between persons who in the course of their dealings (as carriers, innkeepers, surgeons, merchants) relied on each other to their detriment or conferred benefits on each other. It was these detriments and benefits that had to be reimbursed, and an explicit promise—if there happened to be one—was important primarily to establish the reliance or to show that the benefit had been conferred in expectation of payment, not officiously or as a gift. All this,

Atiyah writes, turned inside out when the promise itself came to be seen as the basis of obligation, so that neither benefit nor reliance any longer seemed necessary and the proper measure of the obligation was the promise itself, that is, the expectation. The promise principle was embraced as an expression of the principle of liberty—the will binding itself, to use Kantian language, rather than being bound by the norms of the collectivity—and the award of expectation damages followed as a natural concomitant of the promise principle.

The insistence on reliance or benefit is related to disputes about the nature of promising. As I have argued, reliance on a promise cannot alone explain its force: There is reliance because a promise is binding, and not the other way around. But if a person is bound by his promise and not by the harm the promisee may have suffered in reliance on it, then what he is bound to is just its performance. Put simply, I am bound to do what I promised you I would do— or I am bound to put you in as good a position as if I had done so. To bind me to do no more than to reimburse your reliance is to excuse me to that extent from the obligation I undertook. If your reliance is less than your expectation (in case II-A there is no reliance), then to that extent a reliance standard excuses me from the very obligation I undertook and so weakens the force of an obligation I chose to assume. Since by hypothesis I chose to assume the obligation in its stronger form (that is, to render the performance promised), the reliance rule indeed precludes me from incurring the very obligation I chose to undertake at the time of promising. The most compelling of the arguments for resisting this conclusion and for urging that we settle for reliance is the sense that it is sometimes harsh and ungenerous to insist on the full measure of expectancy. (This is part of Atiyah's thrust when he designates the expectation standard as an aspect of the rigid Victorian promissory morality.) The harshness comes about because in the event the promisor finds the obligation he assumed too burdensome.

This distress may be analyzed into three forms: (1) The promisor regrets having to pay for what he has bought (which may only have been the satisfaction of promising a gift or the thrill of buying a lottery ticket or stock option), though he would readily do the same thing again. I take it that this kind of regret merits no sympathy at all. Indeed if we gave in to it we would frustrate the promisor's ability to engage in his own continuing projects and so the promisor's plea is, strictly speaking, self-contradictory. (2) The promisor regrets his promise because he was mistaken about the nature of the burdens he was assuming—the purchaser in case II-A thought he would find the money for the antique but in fact his savings are depleted, or perhaps the chest is not as old nor as valuable as he had imagined, or his house has burned down and he no longer needs it. All of these regrets are based on mistaken assumptions about the facts as they are or as they turn out to be. As we shall see . . . , the doctrines of mistake, frustration, and impossibility provide grounds for mitigating the effect of the promise principle without at all undermining it.

Finally there is the most troublesome ground of regret: (3) The promisor made no mistake about the facts or probabilities at all, but now that it has come time to perform he no longer values the promise as highly as when he made it. He regrets the promise because he regrets the value judgment that led him to make it. He concludes that the purchase of an expensive antique is an extravagance. Compassion may lead a promisee to release an obligation in such a case, but he releases as an act of generosity, not as a duty, an certainly not because the promisor's repentance destroys the force of the original obligation. The intuitive reason for holding fast is that such repentance should be the promisor's own responsibility, not one he can shift onto others. It seems too easy a way of getting out of one's obligations. Yet our intuition does not depend on suspicions of insincerity alone. Rather we feel that holding people to their obligations is a way of taking them seriously and thus of giving the concept of sincerity itself serious content. Taking this intuition to a more abstract level, I would say that respect for others as free and rational requires taking seriously their capacity to determine their own values. I invoke again the distinction between the right and the good. The right defines the concept of the self as choosing its own conception of the good. Others must respect our capacity as free and rational persons to choose our own good, and that respect means allowing persons to take responsibility for the good they choose. And, of course, that choosing self is not an instantaneous self but one extended in time, so that to respect those determinations of the self is to respect their persistence over time. If we decline to take seriously the assumption of an obligation because we do not take seriously the promisor's prior conception of the good that led him to assume it, to that extent we do not take him seriously as a person. We infantilize him, as we do quite properly when we release the very young from the consequences of their choices.[20]

Since contracts invoke and are invoked by promises, it is not surprising that the law came to impose on the promises it recognized the same incidents as morality demands. The connection between contract and the expectation principle is so palpable that there is reason to doubt that its legal recognition is a relatively recent invention. It is true that over the last two centuries citizens in the liberal democracies have become increasingly free to dispose of their talents, labor, and property as seems best to them. The freedom to bind oneself contractually to a future disposition is an important and striking example of this freedom (the freedom to make testamentary dispositions or to make whatever present use of one's effort or goods one desires are other examples), because in a promise one is taking responsibility not only for one's present self but for one's future self. But this does not argue that the promise principle itself is a novelty—surely Cicero's, Pufendorf's and Grotius's discussions of it[21] show that it is not—but only that its use has expanded greatly over the years.

REMEDIES IN AND AROUND THE PROMISE

Those who have an interest in assimilating contract to the more communitarian standards of tort law have been able to obscure the link between contract and promise because in certain cases the natural thing to do *is* to give damages for the harm that has been suffered, rather than to give the money value of the promised expectation. But it does not follow from these cases that expectation is not a normal and natural measure for contract damages. First, these are situations in which the harm suffered is the measure of damages because it is hard to find the monetary value of the expectation. A leading case, *Security Stove & Mfg. Co.* v. *American Railway Express Co.,*[22] illustrates the type. The plaintiff stove manufacturer had arranged to have a new kind of stove shipped by the defendant express company to a trade convention, at which the plaintiff hoped to interest prospective buyers in his improved product. The president and his workmen went to the convention, but the defendant failed to deliver a crucial part of

the exhibit in time, and they had nothing to show. Plaintiff brought suit to recover the cost of renting the booth, the freight charges, and the time and expenses lost as a result of the fruitless trip to the convention. The recovery of these items of damages, which (with the possible exception of the prepaid booth rental) seem typical examples of reliance losses, is generally agreed to have been appropriate. There was no way of knowing what results the plaintiff would have obtained had he succeeded in exhibiting his product at the convention. There was no way of knowing what his expectancy was, and so the court gave him his loss through reliance. But this illustrates only that where expectancy cannot be calculated, reliance may be a reasonable surrogate. It is reasonable to suppose that the plaintiff's expectation in *Security Stove* was at least as great as the monies he put out to exhibit his goods—after all, he was a businessman and is assumed to have been exhibiting his goods to make an eventual profit. If it could somehow be shown that the exhibit would have been a failure and the plaintiff would have suffered a net loss, the case for recovery would be undermined, and most authorities would then deny recovery.* [23]

Second are the cases in which the amount needed to undo the harm caused by reliance is itself the fairest measure of expectation.

III-A. Buyer approaches manufacturer with the specifications of a small, inexpensive part— say a bolt—for a machine buyer is building. Manufacturer selects the part and sells it to buyer. The bolt is badly made, shears, and damages the machine.

The value of the thing promised, a well-made bolt, is negligible, but to give buyer his money back and no more would be a grave injustice. Here it does seem more natural to say that the manufacturer induced buyer's reasonable reliance and should compensate the resulting harm. But it is equally the case that it is a fair implica-

*A case like this may be seen as involving no more than the allocation of the burden of proof as to the expectation. The plaintiff shows his reliance costs and says that *prima facie* his expectation was at least that great. The burden then shifts to the defendant to show that indeed this was a losing proposition and the expectation was less than the reliance. It seems only fair that since the defendant's breach prevented the exhibition from taking place and thus prevented the drama on which the expectation depended from being played out, the defendant should at least bear the risk of showing that the venture would have been a failure.

tion of the simple-seeming original transaction that manufacturer not only delivered and promised to transfer good title to the bolt, but promised at the same time that the bolt would do the job it was meant to do.* [24]

It is for the (perhaps wholly innocent) breach of this implied promise that we hold manufacturers liable. The soundness of this analysis is brought home if we vary the facts slightly:

III-B. Same as above, except buyer purchases the bolt over the counter in a local hardware store, saying nothing about its use.

To make the owner of the hardware store or the manufacturer of the bolt responsbile for large damages in this case seems unfair. One can say that this is because they could not *foresee* harm of this magnitude arising out of their conduct. (A tort locution: The man who negligently jostles a package containing a bomb could not *foresee* and is not responsible for harm of the ensuing magnitude when the package explodes.) But one can as well cast the matter again in contractual terms, saying that they did not undertake this measure of responsibility. After all, if in the first version of this example the buyer and manufacturer had agreed that manufacturer would be responsible only up to a certain amount, say ten times the cost of the bolt, such a limitation would generally be respected. So in certain cases tort and contract ideas converge on the same result.[25] In III-A we may say that buyer justifiably relied on manufacturer. He relied in part because of the (implied) promise or warranty, and of course it *is* a primary function of promises to induce reliance.

Consider finally this variation:

III-C. Manufacturer makes not bolts but tinned goods. Buyer buys a can of peas at a grocer's and serves them to a guest who chips a tooth on a stone negligently included in the can.

Manufacturer promised the guest nothing. (In legal terminology there is between them no privity of contract.) Yet manufacturer should be responsible for the guest's injuries, just as the driver of a car should be responsible for the injuries of a pedestrian whom he negligently hits, though there too privity of contract is lacking.[26] One may say that the guest reasonably relied on the purity of the peas he ate, just as a pedestrian must rely on the due care of motorists. But I never argued that promise is the *only* basis of reliance or that contract is the only basis of responsibility for harms to others.

Third, there are cases in which wrongs are committed and loss is suffered in and around the attempt to make an agreement. In these cases too reliance is the best measure of compensation. A striking example is *Hoffman* v. *Red Owl Stores:*[27] A prospective Red Owl supermarket franchisee sold his previously owned business and made other expenditures on the assumption that his negotiations to obtain a Red Owl franchise would shortly be concluded. The award of reliance damages was not a case of enforcement of a promise at all, since the parties had not reached the stage where clearly determined promises had been made. Reliance damages were awarded because Red Owl had not dealt fairly with Hoffman. It had allowed him to incur expenses based on hopes that Red Owl knew or should have known were imprudent and that Red Owl was not prepared to permit him to realize. Red Owl was held liable not in order to force it to perform a promise, which it had never made, but rather to compensate Hoffman for losses he had suffered through Red Owl's inconsiderate and temporizing assurances.[28] There is nothing at all in my conception of contract as promise that precludes persons who behave badly and cause unnecessary harm from being forced to make fair compensation. Promissory obligation is not the only basis for liability; principles of tort are sufficient to provide that people who give vague assurances that cause foreseeable harm to others should make compensation. Cases like *Hoffman* are seen to undermine the conception of contract as promise: If contract is really discrete and if it is really based in promise, then whenever there has been a promise in the picture (even only a potential promise) contractual principles must govern the whole relation. To state the argument is to reveal it as a non sequitur. It is a logical fallacy of which the classical exponents of contract as

---

*In law the latter promise is called a warranty—a promise not merely that the promisor will do something in the future, but a taking of responsibility over and above the responsibility of well-meaning honesty that something is the case. For instance, a dealer may warrant that a violin is a Stradivarius. This means more than that he in good faith believes it to be one: he is promising that if it is not, he will be responsible. Uniform Commercial Code (hereafter cited as UCC) § 2-714. Cf. Smith v. Zimbalist, 2 Cal. App.2d 324, 38 P.2d 170 (1934), hearing denied 17 Jan. 1935.

promise were themselves supremely guilty in their reluctance to grant relief for fraud or for mistakes that prevented a real agreement from coming into being. Modern critics of contractual freedom have taken the classics at their word. Justice often requires relief and adjustment in cases of accidents in and around the contracting process, and the critics have seen in this a refutation of the classics' major premise. . . . Here it is sufficient to introduce the notion that contract as promise has a distinct but neither exclusive nor necessarily dominant place among legal and moral principles. A major concern of this book is the articulation of the boundaries and connection between the promissory and other principles of justice.*

The tendency to merge promise into its adjacent concepts applies also to the relation between it and the principle of restitution, which holds that a person who has received a benefit at another's expense should compensate his benefactor, unless a gift was intended. This principle does indeed appeal to a primitive intuition of fairness. Even where a gift was intended, the appropriateness at least of gratitude if not of a vague duty to reciprocate is recognized in many cultures. Aristotle refers the principle to the imperative that some balance be retained among members of a society, but this seems to restate the proposition rather than to explain it.[29] Since restitution, like reliance, is a principle of fairness that operates independently of the will of the parties, the attempt to refer promissory obligation to this principle is another attempt to explain away the self-imposed character of promissory obligation. I have already argued that this cannot be done without begging the question. Certainly the restitution principle cannot explain the force of a promise for which no benefit has yet been or ever will be given in return. (The legal recognition of such gift promises is tangled in the con-

fusions of the doctrine of consideration. . . .) The reduction of promise to restitution (or to restitution plus reliance) must fail. There are nevertheless breaches of promise for which restitution is the correct principle of relief.[30]

IV. In a case like *Security Stove,* where the freight charges have been prepaid but the goods never picked up or delivered as agreed, let us suppose the express company could show that the contemplated exhibit would have been a disaster and that the stove company was much better off never having shown at the fair. Perhaps in such a case there should be no award of reliance damages, but should the express company be allowed to keep the prepayment? Should it be able to argue that the stove company is lucky there was a breach?

In terms of both expectation and harm the stove company should get nothing. Its expectation is shown to be negative, and it suffered no harm. And yet it is entirely clear that Railway Express should make restitution. They did nothing for the money and should not keep it. But is this enforcing the promise? Not at all.

V. I owe my plumber ten dollars, so I place a ten-dollar bill in an envelope, which I mistakenly address and send to you.

On what theory can I get my ten dollars back from you? You made no promise to me. You have *done* me no wrong, and so that is not the ground of my demand that you return the money—though you wrong me now if you do not accede to my demand. The principle is a general one: It is wrong to retain an advantage obtained without justification at another's expense. And what justification can you offer for keeping the ten dollars?* [31] What justification can Railway Express offer for keeping the freight charges in case IV? That it has done the stove company a favor by spoiling the exhibit? But this is no favor the stove company asked for and not one that Railway Express had a right to thrust on it. And surely Railway Express cannot say it received the money properly under a con-

---

*There is a category of cases that has become famous in the law under the rubric of promissory estoppel or detrimental reliance. In these cases there has indeed generally been a promise, but the basis for *legal* redress is said to be the plaintiff's detrimental reliance on the promise. Courts now tend to limit the amount of the redress in such cases to the detriment suffered through reliance. But these cases also do not show that reliance and harm are the general basis for contractual recovery. Rather these cases should be seen for what they are: a belated attempt to plug a gap in the general regime of enforcement of promises, a gap left by the artificial and unfortunate doctrine of consideration. See . . . Fuller and Eisenberg, supra note 25, at 159-161.

---

*That you thought it was a present, spent it, and would now have to dip into the grocery budget to pay me back? Well, that might be a justification if it were true.

tract, since it has utterly repudiated that contract. The contract drops out leaving Railway Express without a justification. In this state of affairs the stove company wins.

Promise and restitution are distinct principles. Neither derives from the other, and so the attempt to dig beneath promise in order to ground contract in restitution (or reliance, for that matter) is misconceived. Contract is based on promise, but when something goes wrong in the contract process—when people fail to reach agreement, or break their promises—there will usually be gains and losses to sort out. The *Red Owl* case is one illustration. Here is another:

I. Britton signs on to work for Turner for a period of one year at an agreed wage of $120 to be paid at the end of his service. After nine months of faithful service he quits without justification, and Turner without difficulty finds a replacement for him.

On one hand Britton has not kept his promise; on the other Turner has had a substantial benefit at his expense.[32] The promise and restitution principles appear to point in opposite directions in this situation. . . . For the present it is sufficient to note that it is the very distinctness of the principles that causes such questions to arise. Certainly nothing about the promise principle, the conception of contract as promise, entails that all disputes between people who have tried but failed to make a contract or who have broken a contract must be decided solely according to that principle.

NOTES

1. On the right and the good the critical discussion is John Rawls, *A Theory of Justice* §§ 68, 83–85 (Cambridge, 1971), which harks back to Immanuel Kant, *Groundwork of the Metaphysics of Morals* (Paton trans., Harper Torchbooks ed. New York, 1964) where the contrast is made between the right and happiness. See also W. D. Ross, *The Right and the Good* (Oxford, 1930); Ronald Dworkin, "Liberalism," in *Public and Private Morality* (S. Hampshire ed. Cambridge, England, 1978). On the relation between liberalism and responsibility, see Friedrich Hayek, *The Constitution of Liberty* ch. 5 (Chicago, 1960); Charles Fried, *Right and Wrong* 124–126 (Cambridge, 1978); Rawls, supra at 519. For a different view see C. B. Macpherson, *The Political Theory of Possessive Individualism—Hobbes to Locke* (Oxford, 1962).

2. Immanuel Kant, *The Metaphysical Elements of Justice* 54–55 (Ladd trans. Indianapolis, 1965).

3. See Charles Fried, *An Anatomy of Values* 81–86 (Cambridge, 1970); Henry Sidgwick, *Elements of Politics,* quoted in Friedrich Kessler and Grant Gilmore, *Contracts* 4 (2d ed. Boston, 1970).

4. Sissela Bok, *Lying: Moral Choice in Public Life* (New York, 1978); Fried, supra note 1, ch. 3.

5. This example is based on Adams v. Gillig, 199 N.Y. 314, 92 N.E. 670 (1930).

6. See generally Page Keeton, "Fraud: Statements of Intention," 15 *Texas L. Rev.* 185 (1937).

7. See generally Robert Goff and Gareth Jones, *The Law of Restitution* ch. 1 (2d. ed. London, 1978).

8. For a strong statement of the tort and benefit principles as foundations of contract law, see Patrick Atiyah, *The Rise and Fall of Freedom of Contract* 1–7 (Oxford, 1979). A remarkable article stating the several moral principles implicit in contract law is George Gardner, "An Inquiry into the Principles of the Law of Contracts," 46 *Harv. L. Rev.* 1 (1932).

9. For a review of Anglo-American writing on promise from Hobbes to modern times, see Atiyah, supra note 8, at 41–60, 649–659. There has been a lively debate on the bases for the moral obligation of promises in recent philosophical literature. Some philosophers have taken a line similar to that of Atiyah and Gilmore, deriving the obligation of promise from the element of reliance. The strongest statement is Neil MacCormick, "Voluntary Obligations and Normative Powers," *Proceedings of the Aristotelian Society,* supp. vol. 46, at 59 (1972). See also Pall Ardal, "And That's a Promise," 18 Phil. Q. 225 (1968); F. S. McNeilly, "Promises Demoralized," 81 *Phil. Rev.* 63 (1972). G. J. Warnock, *The Object of Morality* ch. 7 (London, 1971), offers an effective refutation along the lines in the text, but his affirmative case proposes that the obligation of a promise rests on the duty of veracity, the duty to make the facts correspond to the promise. For an excellent discussion of this last suggestion and a proposal that accords with my own, see Don Locke, "The Object of Morality and the Obligation to Keep a Promise," 2 *Canadian J. of Philosophy* 135 (1972). Locke's emphasis on trust seems a clearer and sounder version of H. A. Prichard's proposal that the obligation of a Promise rests on a more general "agreement to keep agreements." *Moral Obligation* ch. 7 (Oxford, 1957).

10. A number of the philosophers who disagree with the Atiyah-MacCormick argument emphasize the conventional aspect of the invocation of the promissory form, as well as the self-imposed nature of the obligation. E.g. Joseph Raz, "Voluntary Obligations," *Proceedings of the Aristotelian Society,* supp. vol. 46, at 79 (1972); Raz, "Promises and Obligations," in *Law, Morality and Society* (Hacker, Raz eds. Oxford, 1977); John Searle, *Speech Acts* 33–42, 175–188 (Cambridge, 1969); Searle, "What Is a Speech Act?" in *The Philosophy of Language* (John Searle ed. Oxford, 1971). The locus classicus of this view of promising is John Rawls, "Two Concepts of Rules," 64 *Phil. Rev.* 3 (1955). The general idea goes back, of course, to Ludwig Wittgenstein, *Philosophical Investigations* § 23. For Hume's account of the conventional nature of promissory obligation, see *A Treatise of Human Nature* 516–525 (Selby-Bigge ed. Oxford, 1888).

11. Stanley Cavell's contention in *The Claim of Reason* 293–303 (Oxford, 1979) that promising is not a practice or an institution, because unlike the case of a game one cannot imagine setting it up or reforming it and because promising is not an office, seems to me beside the point. Kant's discussion, supra note 2, shows that morality can mandate that there be a convention with certain general features, as does Hume's discussion supra note 10, though Hume's morality is a more utilitarian one.

12. David Lewis, *Convention* (Cambridge, 1969).

13. Supra note 10.

14. Here I side with David Lyons, *The Forms and Limits of Utilitarianism* (Oxford, 1965) in a continuing debate. For the most recent statement of the contrary position, see Richard Brandt, *A Theory of the Good and Right* (Oxford, 1979). For an excellent introduction, see J. J. C. Smart and Bernard Williams, *Utilitarianism: For and Against* (Cambridge, England, 1973). I argue that it is a mistake to treat Rawls's discussion of promising in "Two Concepts of Rules," supra note 10, as an instance of rule-utilitarianism in my review of Atiyah,

93 Harv. L. Rev. 1863n18 (1980). See also Charles Landesman, "Promises and Practices," 75 *Mind* (n.s.) 239 (1966).

15. This was in fact Bentham's general perspective. See also Brandt, supra note 14.

16. Compare Rawls, supra note 1, ch. 6, where it is argued that (*a*) the deduction of the principles of justice for institutions, and (*b*) a showing that a particular institution is just are not sufficient to generate an obligation to comply with that institution. Further principles of natural duty and obligation must be established.

17. See Locke, supra note 9; Prichard, supra note 9; Raz, supra note 10.

18. American Law Institute, *Restatement (1st) of the Law of Contracts* [hereafter cited as *Restatement* (1st) or (2d)], § 329, Comment a: "In awarding compensatory damages, the effort is made to put the injured party in as good a position as that in which he would have been put by full performance of the contract . . . "; E. Allan Farnsworth, "Legal Remedies for Breach of Contract," 70 *Colum. L. Rev.* 1145 (1970); Gardner, supra note 8; Charles Goetz and Robert Scott, "Enforcing Promises: An Examination of the Basis of Contract," 80 *Yale L. J.* 1261 (1980).

19. See Fuller and Perdue, "The Reliance Interest in Contract Damages," 46 Yale L. J. 52, 373 (1936, 1937); Gardner, supra note 8.

20. For discussions of these issues see Fried, supra note 3, at 169–177; Rawls, supra note 1, § 85; and the essays in *The Identities of Persons* (Amelie Rorty ed. Berkeley, 1976) and *Personal Identity* (John Perry ed. Berkeley, 1975).

21. See Atiyah, supra note 8, at 140–141 for a discussion of these early sources. See my review of Atiyah, 93 *Harv. L. Rev.* 1858, 1864–1865 (1980) for a further discussion of these and other early sources.

22. 227 Mo. App. 175, 51 S.W.2d 572 (1932).

23. *Restatement* (1st) § 333(d).

24. Gardner, supra note 8, at 15, 22–23.

25. This is the problem that is standardly dealt with in contract texts under the rubric of consequential damages, or the principle in Hadley v. Baxendale 9 Exch. 341 (1854). See Gardner, supra note 8, at 28–30. Holmes, in Globe Refining Co. v. Landa Cotton Oil Co., 190 U.S. 540 (1903) explained the limitation of liability for consequential damages in terms of the agreement itself: The defendant is liable only for those risks he explicitly or tacitly agreed to assume. This conception has been generally rejected in favor of a vaguer standard by which defendant is liable for any risks of which he had "reason to know" at the time of the agreement. UCC § 2–715 comment 2. Holmes's test seems more consonant with the thesis of this work. See Pothier, *The Law of Obligations,* quoted in Lon Fuller and Melvin Eisenberg, *Basic Contract Law* 27 (3rd ed. St. Paul, 1972). The difference between the two positions is not great: first, because it is always within the power of the parties to limit or expand liability for consequential damages by the agreement itself, UCC § 2–719(3); second, because the "reason to know" standard means that the defendant at least has a fair opportunity to make such an explicit provision.

26. UCC § 2–318; William Prosser, *Torts* ch. 17 (4th ed. St. Paul, 1971).

27. 133 N.W.2d 267, 26 Wis.2d 683 (1965).

28. See Stanley Henderson, "Promissory Estoppel and Traditional Contract Doctrine," 78 *Yale L. J.* 343, 357–360 (1969); see generally Friedrich Kessler and Edith Fine, " *Culpa in Contrahendo,* Bargaining in Good Faith, and Freedom of Contract: A Comparative Study," 77 *Harv. L. Rev.* 401 (1964).

29. *Nicomachean Ethics,* bk. V, iv–v.

30. See John Dawson, "Restitution or Damages?," 20 *Ohio St. L. J.* 175 (1959); Gardner, supra note 8, at 18–27. For a fuller discussion of restitution and contracts see chapter 8 infra.

31. Goff and Jones, supra note 7, at 69; the problem raised in the footnote is treated at 88–89.

32. *Britton* v. *Turner,* 6 N.H. 281 (1834).

LOUIS KATZNER

Is the Favoring of Women and Blacks in Employment and Educational Opportunities Justified?*

There is presently a call to favor blacks and women in employment and educational opportunities because in the past many of them have been discriminated against in these areas. The basic concern of this paper is whether or not reverse discrimination in this sense is justified. Given that, as will be shown, all acts of reverse discrimination involve prejudgment, it is appropriate to scrutinize first the notion of discrimination itself. Next, the idea of reverse discrimination will be explicated by distinguishing among several different forms that it may take; and from this explication the set of conditions under which a bias of redress is justified will emerge. Finally, the situation of blacks and women in the United States will be examined to see what conclusions can be drawn concerning the justification of reverse discrimination for these two classes.

I. DISCRIMINATION

There are certain things that are relevant to the way people should be treated and certain things that are not. The size of one's chest is relevant to the size shirt he should have, but it has nothing to do with the size his shoes should be. The rate of one's metabolism is pertinent to the amount of food she should be served, but not to the color of the napkin she is given. People should be treated on the basis of their attributes and merits that are relevant to the circumstances. When they are, those who are similar are treated similarly and those who are dissimilar are treated differently. Although these distinctions do involve treating people differently (those with larger chests get larger shirts than those with smaller chests), it does not involve discrimination. For discrimination means treating people differently when they are similar in the relevant respects or treating them similarly when they are different in the relevant respects.

It follows that to determine what constitutes discrimination in vocational and educational op-

*This essay has not been published elsewhere.

portunities, we must first determine what qualities are relevant to a career and the capacity to learn. People today generally seem to accept the principle of meritocracy—that is, that an individual's potential for success, which is a combination of his native and/or developed ability and the amount of effort he can be expected to put forth, is the sole criterion that should be used in hiring and college admissions practices. It may be that until recently many people did not accept this view, and it may be that there are some even today who do not accept it. Nevertheless, this is one of the basic principles of the "American Dream"; it is the foundation of the civil service system; it is a principle to which even the most ardent racists and sexists at least give lipservice; and it is the principle that most people seem to have in mind when they speak of the problem of discrimination in hiring and college admissions practices. And because it is generally agreed that people with the same potential should be treated similarly in employment and college admissions, and that those with more potential should receive preference over those with less, the discussion begins with this assumption.

II. REVERSE DISCRIMINATION

With the notion of discrimination clarified, it is now possible to see what is involved in the idea of reverse discrimination. Reverse discrimination is much more than a call to eliminate bias; it is a call to offset the effects of past acts of bias by skewing opportunity in the opposite direction. This paper will consider only the claims that blacks, women, et cetera, have been discriminated against in the past (that is, they have been treated as if they have less potential than they actually do); and that the only way to offset their subsequent disadvantages is to discriminate now in their favor (that is, to treat them as if they have more potential than they actually do).

It follows that those who are currently calling for the revision of admission standards at our colleges because they do not accurately reflect a student's chances of success there are not calling for reverse discrimination. They are merely saying that we should find a way of determining precisely who is qualified (that is, who has the potential) to go to college, and then admit the most qualified. On the other hand, those who are calling for us to admit students whom they allow are less qualified than others who are denied admission, and to provide these less qualified students with special tutorial help, are calling for reverse discrimination.

This example clearly illustrates the basic problem that any justification of reverse discrimination must come to grips with—viz., that every act of reverse discrimination is itself discriminatory. For every less qualified person who is admitted to a college, or hired for a job, there is a more qualified person who is being discriminated against, and who has a right to complain. Hence the justification of reverse discrimination must involve not only a justification of *discriminating for* those who are benefiting from it, it must also involve a justification of discriminating *against* those at whose expense the reverse discrimination is being practiced.

III. JUSTIFICATION OF REVERSE DISCRIMINATION: DIRECT

There are at least two significantly different kinds of situations in which reverse discrimination can be called for. On the one hand, a person might argue that he should be favored because he was arbitrarily passed over at some time in the past. Thus, for example, a Chicano might maintain that since he was denied a job for which he was the most qualified candidate simply because of his race, he should now be given one for which he is not the most qualified candidate, simply because he was discriminated against in the past. On the other hand, one might argue that he should be given preference because his ancestors (parents, grandparents, great–grandparents, et cetera) were discriminated against. In this case, the Chicano would claim that he should be given a job for which he is not the most qualified applicant because his ancestors were denied jobs for which they were the most qualified.

In the former case, that of rectifying bias against an individual by unduly favoring him, there are several interesting points that can be made. First of all, the case for reverse discrimination of this type is strongest when the person to be passed over in the reverse discrimination is the same one who benefited from the initial discrimi-

natory act. Suppose, for example, that when it comes time to appoint the vice-president of a company, the best qualified applicant (that is, the one who has the most potential) is passed over because of his race, and a less qualified applicant is given the job. Suppose that the following year the job of president in the same firm becomes open. At this point, the vice-president, because of the training he had as second in command, is the most qualified applicant for the job. It could be argued, however, that the presidency should go to the person who was passed over for the vice-presidency. For he should have been the vice-president, and if he had been he would probably now be the best-equipped applicant for the top post; it is only because he was passed over that the current vice-president is now the most qualified candidate. In other words, since the current vice-president got ahead at his expense, it is warranted for him to move up at the vice-president's expense. In this way the wrong that was done him will be righted.

There are two main problems with this argument. First of all, certainly to be considered is how well the individual who benefited from the initial act of discrimination exploited his break. If he used this opportunity to work up to his capacity, this would seem to be a good reason for not passing him over for the presidency. If, on the other hand, although performing very adequately as vice-president, he was not working up to the limits of his capacity, then perhaps the job of president should be given to the man who was passed over in the first place—even though the vice-president's experience in his job leads one to think that he is the one most qualified to handle the difficult tasks of the presidency. In other words, how much a person has made of the benefit he has received from an act of discrimination seems to be relevant to the question of whether or not he should be discriminated against so that the victim of that discrimination may now be benefited.

Secondly, there are so few cases of this kind that even if reverse discrimination is justified in such cases, this would not show very much. In most instances of reverse discrimination, the redress is at the expense of someone who did not benefit from the initial act of discrimination rather than someone who did.

One species of this form of reverse discrimination is that in which the victim of the proposed act of reverse discrimination has not benefited from *any* acts of discrimination. In such a case, what is in effect happening is that the burden of discrimination is being transferred from one individual who does not deserve it to another individual who does not deserve it. There is no sense in which "the score is being evened," as in the case above. Because there is no reason for saying that one of the individuals deserves to be penalized by prejudice while the other one does not, it is difficult to see how this kind of reverse discrimination can be justified.

The only argument that comes to mind as a justification for this species of reverse discrimination is the following: The burdens of discrimination should be shared rather than placed on a few. It is better that the liabilities of discrimination be passed from person to person than that they remain the handicap only of those who have been disfavored. It follows that if we find someone who has been discriminated against, we are warranted in rectifying that injustice by an act of reverse discrimination, as long as the victim of the reverse discrimination has not himself been discriminated against in the past.

But this is not a very persuasive argument. For one thing, the claim that discrimination should be shared does not seem a very compelling reason for discriminating against a totally innocent bystander. Secondly, even if this is viewed as a forceful reason, the image of society that emerges is a horrifying one. The moment someone is discriminated against, he seeks out someone who has not been unfairly barred, and asks for reverse discrimination against this person to rectify the wrong he has suffered. Such a procedure would seem to entrench rather than eliminate discrimination, and would produce an incredibly unstable society.

Another species of this form of reverse discrimination is that in which the victim of the proposed reverse bias has benefited from a previous unfair decision, although it is not the particular act that is being rectified. In other words, he did not get ahead at the expense of the individual to whom we are trying to "make things up" by reverse discrimination, but he has benefited from bias against other individuals. In such a case, there is a sense, admittedly extended, in which a score is being evened.

Now it appears that such cases are more like those in which the victim of the proposed act of reverse discrimination benefited from the initial instance of discrimination than those in which he is a completely innocent bystander, and hence in such cases reverse discrimination can be justified. Of course it would be preferable if we could find the beneficiary of the original act of discrimina-

tion—but very often this just is not possible. And we must make sure that the reverse discrimination is proportionate to both the liability suffered by the proposed beneficiary and the advantage previously gained by the proposed victim—a very difficult task indeed. But there does not seem to be any reason for saying that reverse discrimination can only be visited upon those who benefited from the particular discriminatory act that is being rectified. It seems more reasonable to say that reverse discrimination can be visited upon those who benefited from either the particular instance of discrimination being rectified or from roughly similar acts.

Although the conclusions drawn from this discussion of the various species of one form of reverse discrimination do not seem conclusive, this discussion has brought to light three conditions which are necessary for the justification of reverse discrimination: First, there must have been an act of discrimination that is being rectified. Second, the initial act of discrimination must have in some way handicapped its victim, for if he has not been handicapped or set back in some way, then there is nothing to "make up to him" through reverse discrimination. And third, the victim of the proposed reverse discrimination must have benefited from an act of discrimination (either the one that is being rectified or a similar one); otherwise it is unacceptable to say that he should now be disfavored.

IV. JUSTIFICATION OF REVERSE DISCRIMINATION: INDIRECT

Not all of the claims that are made for reverse discrimination, however, assume that the individual involved has himself been the victim of bias. In many cases what is being claimed is that an individual is entitled to benefit from a rectifying bias because his ancestors (parents, grandparents, great grandparents, et cetera) were unfairly denied opportunity. Keeping in mind the three conditions necessary for reverse discrimination that we have just developed, this form of reverse discrimination will be examined.

In a society in which wealth could not be accumulated or, even if it could, it did not give one access to a better education and/or job, and a good education did not give one access to a better job and/or greater wealth, it would be hard to see how educational and/or economic discrimination against one's ancestors could be a handicap. That is, if education was not a key to economic success, then the educational discrimination one's ancestors suffered could not handicap one in the search for a job. If wealth did not buy better teachers and better schools, then the fact that one's ancestors have been handicapped economically could not be a reason for his being educationally disadvantaged. If wealth could not start a business, buy into a business, or give one direct access to a good job, then the economic shackling one's ancestors endured could in no way handicap her in the economic realm. But if wealth and education do these things, as in our society they clearly do, and if because of discrimination some people were not allowed to accumulate the wealth that their talents normally would bring, then it is quite clear that their offspring are handicapped by the discrimination they have suffered.

It is important to note that this point in no way turns on the controversy that is currently raging over the relationship between IQ and race. For it is not being claimed that unless there is complete equality there is discrimination. The members of a suppressed group may be above, below, or equal to the other members of society with regard to potential. All that is being claimed is that to the extent that the members of a group have been denied a fair chance to do work commensurate with their capacities, and to the extent that this has handicapped subsequent members of that group, reverse discrimination may be justified to offset this handicap.

But, as we have already seen, for reverse discrimination to be justified, not only must the victims of discrimination be handicapped by the discrimination, those who will suffer from its reversal must have benefited from the original injustice. In this particular case, it may be that they are the children of the beneficiaries of discrimination who have passed these advantages on to them. Or it may be that they benefit in facing reduced competition for schooling and jobs, and hence they are able to get into a better school and land a better job than they would if those suffering the effects of discrimination were not handicapped. Or they may have benefited from discrimination in some other way. But the proposed victims of reverse discrimination must be the beneficiaries of previous discrimination.

In addition to all of this, however, it seems that there is one more condition that must be met for reverse discrimination to be justified. Assuming that if we eliminated all discrimination immediately, the people who have suffered from it could compete on an equal basis with all other members of society, then reverse discrimination would not be justified. This of course is trivially true if it is only being claimed that if the elimination of all discrimination entails the eradication of all the handicaps it creates, then only the elimination of discrimination (and not reverse discrimination) is justified. But the claim involves much more than this. What is being argued is that even if the immediate elimination of all discrimination does not allow all suppressed people to compete equally with other members of society, as long as it allows equal opportunity to all children born subsequent to the end of discrimination, then reverse discrimination is not justified—*not even for those who have been handicapped by discrimination.* In other words, reverse discrimination will not prevent its debilitating effects from being passed on to generations yet unborn.

The justification of this claim is a straightforward utilitarian one (it cannot be a justification in terms of justice since what is being countenanced is blatant injustice). The social cost of implementing a policy of reverse discrimination is very high. The problems in determining who are the victims of discrimination and how great their handicaps, and who are the beneficiaries of discrimination and how great their benefits, as well as the problems in both developing and administering policies that will lead to a proper rectification of discrimination, are not merely enormously complex, they are enormously costly to solve. Moreover, the benefits of ending all discrimination are very great. Not only will many people be hired for jobs and admitted to colleges otherwise barred to them because of discrimination, but many people who have themselves been handicapped by discrimination will take great satisfaction in the knowledge that their offspring will not be held back as they have. This, of course, in no way eliminates the injustice involved in allowing acts of reverse discrimination to go unrectified. All it shows is that given the tremendous cost of implementing a comprehensive program of reverse discrimination, and given the tremendous benefits that would accrue simply from the elimination of all discrimination, it is reasonable to claim that reverse discrimination is justified only if the elimination of discrimination will not prevent its debilitating effects from being passed on to generations yet unborn.

Thus there is a fourth condition that must be added to the list of conditions that are necessary for the justification of reverse discrimination. Moreover, the addition of this condition renders the list jointly sufficient for the justification of reverse discrimination. Thus, reverse discrimination is justified if, and only if, the following conditions are met:

1. There must have been an initial act of discrimination that the reverse discrimination is going to rectify.
2. The beneficiary of the proposed act of reverse discrimination must have been handicapped by the initial act—either directly, if he was the victim of the initial discrimination, or indirectly, if he is the offspring of a victim (and inherited the handicap).
3. The victim of the proposed act of reverse discrimination must have benefited from an act of discrimination—the one that is being rectified or a similar one—and either directly, if he was the beneficiary of an initial act of discrimination or indirectly, if he is the offspring of a beneficiary (and inherited the benefit).
4. It must be the case that even if all discrimination were ended immediately, the debilitating effects of discrimination would be passed on to generations yet unborn.

V. REVERSE DISCRIMINATION FAVORING WOMEN AND BLACKS

A partial answer, at least, to the question of whether or not reverse discrimination is justified in the case of women and blacks is now possible. Let us begin with blacks.

It seems clear that the situation of many blacks in this country meets the four conditions shown to be individually necessary and jointly sufficient for the justification of reverse discrimination. First, there can be no doubt that many blacks have been the victims of educational and vocational discrimination. Second, given the relationships existing between wealth, education, and vocation, there can be no doubt that the discrimination that blacks have met with has handicapped both themselves and their offspring. Third, it also seems clear that within our economic framework, if blacks had not been discriminated against, there are many whites (those who got an education or a job at the expense of a more qualified black or in competition with the handicapped offspring of disadvantaged blacks) who would be in far less advantageous educational and vocational situations than they currently are —that is, there are people who have benefited from discrimination. And finally, again given the relationships existing among wealth, education, and vocation, even if all discrimination against

blacks were to cease immediately, many black children born subsequent to this time would not be able to compete for educational and vocational opportunities on the same basis that they would had there been no bias against their ancestors.

Of course this in no way shows that reverse discrimination for all blacks is justified. After all, there are some blacks who have not let themselves be handicapped by discrimination. There are also undoubtedly some whites who have not benefited from the discrimination against blacks. And finally, there are many whites who have endured discrimination in the same way blacks have. In other words, so far it has only been shown that all those who have been discriminated against in a way that meets the conditions established are entitled to reverse discrimination and that some blacks have been discriminated against in this way.

To move from this claim to the conclusion that blacks as a class are entitled to reverse discrimination, several additional things must be shown. First, it must be demonstrated that it is unfeasible to handle reverse discrimination on a case by case basis (for example, it might be argued that such a procedure would be far too costly). Second, it must be proven that the overwhelming percentage of blacks have been victimized by discrimination—that is, the number of blacks who would benefit from reverse discrimination, but who do not deserve to, must be very small. And finally, it must be shown that the overwhelming majority of the potential victims of bias of redress have benefited from the acts of discrimination (or similar acts) that are being rectified—that is, it must be that the number of whites who will suffer the effects of reverse discrimination, without deserving to, must also be very small. If these conditions are met, then although there will be some unwarranted discrimination resulting from the reverse discrimination in favor of blacks (that is, some blacks benefiting who were not victimized and some whites suffering who were not benefited), such cases will be kept to a bare minimum, and hence the basic result will be the offsetting of the handicaps with which blacks have unwarrantedly been saddled.

When it comes to the case of (white) women, however, the situation is quite different. There is little doubt that many women have been denied opportunity, and thus handicapped while many men have benefited from this discrimination (although I believe that discrimination has been far less pervasive in the case of women than it has been for blacks). But women generally do not constitute the kind of class in which the handicaps of discrimination are passed on to one's offspring. This is because, unlike blacks, they are not an isolated social group. Most women are reared in families in which the gains a father makes, even if the mother is limited by society's prejudice, work to the advantage of *all* offspring. (White) women have attended white schools and colleges and, even if they have been discriminated against, their children have attended these same schools and colleges. If all discrimination were ended tomorrow, there would be no external problem at all for most women in competing, commensurate with their potential, with the male population.

Two important things follow from this. First, it is illegitimate for most women to claim that they should be favored because their mothers were disfavored. Second, and most importantly, if all discrimination against women were ended immediately, in most cases none of its debilitating effects would be transmitted to the generations of women yet unborn; hence, for most women, the fourth condition necessary for the justification of reverse discrimination is not satisfied. Thus, reverse discrimination for women as a class cannot be justified, although there are undoubtedly some cases in which, for a particular woman, it can.

One must be careful, however, not to interpret this judgment too broadly. For one thing, the conclusion that reverse discrimination is not warranted for women as a class is contingent upon the immediate elimination of all discrimination. Hence it does not apply if discrimination against women continues. In other words, the conclusion does not show that reverse discrimination for women as a class is unjustified in the face of continuing bias against them. Under these circumstances, reverse discrimination may or may not be justified.

Secondly, as reverse discrimination has been described here, it involves offsetting the impact of a particular kind of discrimination (that is, in educational and job opportunities) by another instance of the same kind of discrimination (that is, preferential treatment in education and job opportunities). All our argument shows is that this is unwarranted for women as a class. One might, however, want to argue in favor of discriminating for women as a class in the area of education and jobs, not to offset previous discrimination in this area, but rather to counter the debilitating effects that institutionalized sexism has had on the female psyche. That is, one might argue that because our society has conditioned women to desire subservient roles (for example, that of a nurse rather than doctor, secretary rather than executive, housewife rather than breadwinner, and so on), even if all forms of discrimination were eliminated tomorrow, very few (or at least not enough) women would take advantage of the opportunities open to them. Hence we need (reverse) discrimination as a means of placing women in visible positions of success, so that other women will have models to emulate and will strive for success in these areas. Now although it is not clear whether or not such a program can legitimately be labelled "reverse discrimination," the important point is that this paper has not been addressed to this kind of problem, and hence has not shown that it is illegitimate to give preferential treatment to women (or blacks) for this reason.

LISA H. NEWTON

Reverse Discrimination As Unjustified*

I have heard it argued that "simple justice" requires that we favor women and blacks in employment and educational opportunities, since women and blacks were "unjustly" excluded from such opportunities for so many years in the not so distant past. It is a strange argument, an example of a possible implication of a true proposition advanced to dispute the proposition itself, like an octopus absent-mindedly slicing off his head with a stray tentacle. A fatal confusion underlies this argument, a confusion fundamentally relevant to our understanding of the notion of the rule of law.

Two senses of justice and equality are involved in this confusion. The root notion of justice, progenitor of the other, is the one that Aristotle (*Nichomachean Ethics 5. 6; Politics* 1. 2; 3. 1) assumes to be the foundation and proper virtue of the political association. It is the condition which free men establish among themselves when they "share a common life in order that their association bring them self-sufficiency"—the regulation of their relationship by law, and the establishment, by law, of equality before the law. Rule of law is the name and pattern of this justice; its equality stands against the inequalities—of wealth, talent, etc. —otherwise obtaining among its participants, who by virtue of that equality are called "citizens." It is an achievement—complete, or, more frequently, partial—of certain people in certain concrete situations. It is fragile and easily disrupted by powerful individuals who discover that the blind equality of rule of law is inconvenient for their interests. Despite its obvious instability, Aristotle assumed that the establishment of justice in this sense, the creation of citizenship, was a permanent possibility for men and that the resultant association of citizens was the natural home of the species. At levels below the political association, this rule-governed equality is easily found; it is exemplified by any group of children agreeing together

to play a game. At the level of the political association, the attainment of this justice is more difficult, simply because the stakes are so much higher for each participant. The equality of citizenship is not something that happens of its own accord, and without the expenditure of a fair amount of effort it will collapse into the rule of a powerful few over an apathetic many. But at least it has been achieved, at some times in some places; it is always worth trying to achieve, and eminently worth trying to maintain, wherever and to whatever degree it has been brought into being.

Aristotle's parochialism is notorious; he really did not imagine that persons other than Greeks could associate freely in justice, and the only form of association he had in mind was the Greek *polis*. With the decline of the *polis* and the shift in the center of political thought, his notion of justice underwent a sea change. To be exact, it ceased to represent a political type and became a moral ideal: the ideal of equality as we know it. This ideal demands that all men be included in citizenship—that one Law govern all equally, that all men regard all other men as fellow citizens, with the same guarantees, rights, and protections. Briefly, it demands that the circle of citizenship achieved by any group be extended to include the entire human race. Properly understood, its effect on our associations can be excellent: it congratulates us on our achievement of rule of law as a process of government but refuses to let us remain complacent until we have expanded the associations to include others within the ambit of the rules, as often and as far as possible. While one man is a slave, none of us may feel truly free. We are constantly prodded by this ideal to look for possible unjustifiable discrimination, for inequalities not absolutely required for the functioning of the society and advantageous to all. And after twenty centuries of pressure, not at all constant, from this ideal, it might be said that some progress has been made. To take the cases in point for this problem, we are now prepared to assert, as Aristotle would never have been, the equality of sexes and of persons of different colors. The ambit of American citizenship, once

* From *Ethics* 83, No. 4 (July, 1973): 308-12. © 1973 by the University of Chicago. Reprinted by permission of the author and the publisher, The University of Chicago Press.

restricted to white males of property, has been extended to include all adult free men, then all adult males including ex-slaves, then all women. The process of acquisition of full citizenship was for these groups a sporadic trail of half-measures, even now not complete; the steps on the road to full equality are marked by legislation and judicial decisions which are only recently concluded and still often not enforced. But the fact that we can now discuss the possibility of favoring such groups in hiring shows that over the area that concerns us, at least, full equality is presupposed as a basis for discussion. To that extent, they are full citizens, fully protected by the law of the land.

It is important for my argument that the moral ideal of equality be recognized as logically distinct from the condition (or virtue) of justice in the political sense. Justice in this sense exists *among* a citizenry, irrespective of the number of the populace included in that citizenry. Further, the moral ideal is parasitic upon the political virtue, for "equality" is unspecified—it means nothing until we are told in what respect that equality is to be realized. In a political context, "equality" is specified as "equal rights"—equal access to the public realm, public goods and offices, equal treatment under the law—in brief, the equality of citizenship. If citizenship is not a possibility, political equality is unintelligible. The ideal emerges as a generalization of the real condition and refers back to that condition for its content.

Now, if justice (Aristotle's justice in the political sense) is equal treatment under law for all citizens, what is injustice? Clearly, injustice is the violation of that equality, discriminating for or against a group of citizens, favoring them with special immunities and privileges or depriving them of those guaranteed to the others. When the southern employer refuses to hire blacks in white-collar jobs, when Wall Street will only hire women as secretaries with new titles, when Mississippi high schools routinely flunk all black boys above ninth grade, we have examples of injustice, and we work to restore the equality of the public realm by ensuring that equal opportunity will be provided in such cases in the future. But of course, when the employers and the schools *favor* women and blacks, the same injustice is done. Just as the previous discrimination did, this reverse discrimination violates the public equality which defines citizenship and destroys the rule of law for the areas in which these favors are granted. To the

extent that we adopt a program of discrimination, reverse or otherwise, justice in the political sense is destroyed, and none of us, specifically affected or not, is a citizen, a bearer of rights—we are all petitioners for favors. And to the same extent, the ideal of equality is undermined, for it has content only where justice obtains, and by destroying justice we render the ideal meaningless. It is, then, an ironic paradox, if not a contradiction in terms, to assert that the ideal of equality justifies the violation of justice; it is as if one should argue, with William Buckley, that an ideal of humanity can justify the destruction of the human race.

Logically, the conclusion is simple enough: all discrimination is wrong *prima facie* because it violates justice, and that goes for reverse discrimination too. No violation of justice among the citizens may be justified (may overcome the *prima facie* objection) by appeal to the ideal of equality, for that ideal is logically dependent upon the notion of justice. Reverse discrimination, then, which attempts no other justification than an appeal to equality, is wrong. But let us try to make the conclusion more plausible by suggesting some of the implications of the suggested practice of reverse discrimination in employment and education. My argument will be that the problems raised there are insoluble, not only in practice but in principle.

We may argue, if we like, about what "discrimination" consists of. Do I discriminate against blacks if I admit none to my school when none of the black applicants are qualified by the tests I always give? How far must I go to root out cultural bias from my application forms and tests before I can say that I have not discriminated against those of different cultures? Can I assume that women are not strong enough to be roughnecks on my oil rigs, or must I test them individually? But this controversy, the most popular and well-argued aspect of the issue, is not as fatal as two others which cannot be avoided: if we are regarding the blacks as a "minority" victimized by discrimination, what is a "minority"? And for any group—blacks, women, whatever—that has been discriminated against, what amount of reverse discrimination wipes out the initial discrimination? Let us grant as true that women and blacks were discriminated against, even where laws forbade such discrimination, and grant for the sake of argument that a history of discrimination must be wiped out by reverse discrimination. What follows?

First, are there other groups which have been discriminated against? For they should have the same right of restitution. What about American Indians, Chicanos, Appalachian Mountain whites, Puerto Ricans, Jews, Cajuns, and Orientals? And if these are to be included, the principle according to which we specify a "minority" is simply the criterion of "ethnic (sub) group," and we're stuck with every hyphenated American in the lower-middle class clamoring for special privileges for *his* group—and with equal justification. For be it noted, when we run down the Harvard roster, we find not only a scarcity of blacks (in comparison with the proportion in the population) but an even more striking scarcity of those second-, third-, and fourth-generation ethnics who make up the loudest voice of Middle America. Shouldn't they demand *their* share? And eventually, the WASPs will have to form their own lobby, for they too are a minority. The point is simply this: there is no "majority" in America who will not mind giving up just a bit of their rights to make room for a favored minority. There are only other minorities, each of which is discriminated against by the favoring. The initial injustice is then repeated dozens of times, and if each minority is granted the same right of restitution as the others, an entire area of rule governance is dissolved into a pushing and shoving match between self-interested groups. Each works to catch the public eye and political popularity by whatever means of advertising and power politics lend themselves to the effort, to capitalize as much as possible on temporary popularity until the restless mob picks another group to feel sorry for. Hardly an edifying spectacle, and in the long run no one can benefit: the pie is no larger—it's just that instead of setting up and enforcing rules for getting a piece, we've turned the contest into a free-for-all, requiring much more effort for no larger a reward. It would be in the interests of all the participants to reestablish an objective rule to govern the process, carefully enforced and the same for all.

Second, supposing that we do manage to agree in general that women and blacks (and all the others) have some right of restitution, some right to a privileged place in the structure of opportunities for a while, how will we know when that while is up? How much privilege is enough? When will the guilt be gone, the price paid, the balance restored? What recompense is right for centuries of exclusion? What criterion tells us when we are done? Our experience with the Civil Rights movement shows us that agreement on these terms cannot be presupposed: a process that appears to some to be going at a mad gallop into a black takeover appears to the rest of us to be at a standstill. Should a practice of reverse discrimination be adopted, we may safely predict that just as some of us begin to see "a satisfactory start toward righting the balance," others of us will see that we "have already gone too far in the other direction" and will suggest that the discrimination ought to be reversed again. And such disagreement is inevitable, for the point is that we could not *possibly* have any criteria for evaluating the kind of recompense we have in mind. The context presumed by any discussion of restitution is the context of rule of law: law sets the rights of men and simultaneously sets the method for remedying the violation of those rights. You may exact suffering from others and/or damage payments for yourself if and only if the others have violated your rights; the suffering you have endured is not sufficient reason for them to suffer. And remedial rights exist only where there is law: primary human rights are useful guides to legislation but cannot stand as reasons for awarding remedies for injuries sustained. But then, the context presupposed by any discussion of restitution is the context of preexistent full citizenship. No remedial rights could exist for the excluded; neither in law nor in logic does there exist a right to *sue* for a standing to sue.

From these two considerations, then, the difficulties with reverse discrimination become evident. Restitution for a disadvantaged group whose rights under the law have been violated is possible by legal means, but restitution for a disadvantaged group whose grievance is that there was no law to protect them simply is not. First, outside of the area of justice defined by the law, no sense can be made of "the group's rights," for no law recognizes that group or the individuals in it, qua members, as bearers of rights (hence *any* group can constitute itself as a disadvantaged minority in some sense and demand similar restitution). Second, outside of the area of protection of law, no sense can be made of the violation of rights (hence the amount of the recompense cannot be decided by any objective criterion). For both reasons, the practice of reverse discrimination undermines the foundation of the very ideal in whose name it is advocated; it destroys justice, law, equality, and citizenship itself, and replaces them with power struggles and popularity contests.

THOMAS NAGEL

Equal Treatment and Compensatory Discrimination*

It is currently easier, or widely thought to be easier, to get certain jobs or to gain admission to certain educational institutions if one is black or a woman than if one is a white man. Whether or not this is true, many people think it should be true, and many others think it should not. The question is: If a black person or a woman is admitted to a law school or medical school, or appointed to a certain academic or administrative post, in preference to a white man who is in other respects better qualified,[1] and if this is done in pursuit of a preferential policy or to fill a quota, is it unjust? Can the white man complain that he has been unjustly treated? It is important to investigate the justice of such practices, because if they are unjust, it is much more difficult to defend them on grounds of social utility. I shall argue that although preferential policies are not required by justice, they are not seriously unjust either—because the system from which they depart is already unjust for reasons having nothing to do with racial or sexual discrimination.

I

In the United States, the following steps seem to have led us to a situation in which these questions arise. First, and not very long ago, it came to be widely accepted that deliberate barriers against the admission of blacks and women to desirable positions should be abolished. Their abolition is by no means complete, and certain educational institutions, for example, may be able to maintain limiting quotas on the admission of women for some time. But deliberate discrimination is widely condemned.

Secondly, it was recognized that even without explicit barriers there could be discrimination, either consciously or unconsciously

motivated, and this gave support to self-conscious efforts at impartiality, careful consideration of candidates belonging to the class discriminated against, and attention to the proportions of blacks and women in desirable positions, as evidence that otherwise undetectable bias might be influencing the selections. (Another, related consideration is that criteria which were good predictors of performance for one group might turn out to be poor predictors of performance for another group, so that the continued employment of those criteria might introduce a concealed inequity.)

The third step came with the realization that a social system may continue to deny different races or sexes equal opportunity or equal access to desirable positions even after the discriminatory barriers to those positions have been lifted. Socially-caused inequality in the capacity to make use of available opportunities or to compete for available positions may persist, because the society systematically provides to one group more than to another certain educational, social, or economic advantages. Such advantages improve one's competitive position in seeking access to jobs or places in professional schools. Where there has recently been widespread deliberate discrimination in many areas, it will not be surprising if the formerly excluded group experiences relative difficulty in gaining access to newly opened positions, and it is plausible to explain the difficulty at least partly in terms of disadvantages produced by past discrimination. This leads to the adoption of compensatory measures, in the form of special training programs, or financial support, or day-care centers, or apprenticeships, or tutoring. Such measures are designed to qualify those whose reduced qualifications are due to racial or sexual discrimination, either because they have been the direct victims of such discrimination, or because they are deprived as a result of membership in a group or community many of whose other members have been discriminated against. The second of these types of influence covers a great deal, and the importance of the social contribution is not always

*Thomas Nagel, "Equal Treatment and Compensatory Discrimination," *Philosophy & Public Affairs,* Vol. 2, No. 4 (1973). Copyright ©1973 Princeton University Press. Reprinted with permission of Princeton University Press.

easy to establish. Nevertheless its effects typically include the loss of such goods as self-esteem, self-confidence, motivation, and ambition—all of which contribute to competitive success and none of which is easily restored by special training programs. Even if social injustice has produced such effects, it may be difficult for society to eradicate them.

This type of justification for compensatory programs raises another question. If it depends on the claim that the disadvantages being compensated for are the product of social injustice, then it becomes important how great the contribution of social injustice actually is, and to what extent the situation is due to social causes not involving injustice, or to causes that are not social, but biological. If one believes that society's responsibility for compensatory measures extends only to those disadvantages due to social injustice, one will assign political importance to the degree, if any, to which racial differences in average I.Q. are genetically influenced, or the innate contribution, if any, to the statistical differences, if any, in emotional or intellectual characteristics between men and women. Also, if one believes that among socially-produced inequalities, there is a crucial distinction for the requirement of compensation between those which are produced unjustly and those which are merely the incidental results of just social arrangements, then it will be very important to decide exactly where that line falls: whether, for example, certain intentions must be referred to in arguing that a disadvantage has been unjustly imposed. But let me put those issues aside for the moment.

The fourth stage comes when it is acknowledged that some unjustly caused disadvantages, which create difficulties of access to positions formally open to all, cannot be overcome by special programs of preparatory or remedial training. One is then faced with the alternative of either allowing the effects of social injustice to confer a disadvantage in the access to desirable positions that are filled simply on the basis of qualifications relevant to performance in those positions, or else instituting a system of compensatory discrimination in the selection process to increase access for those whose qualifications are lower at least partly as a result of unjust discrimination in other situations and at other times (and possibly against other persons). This is a difficult choice, and it would certainly be preferable to find a more direct method of rectification, than to balance inequality in one part of the social system by introducing a reverse inequality at a different point. If the society as a whole contains serious injustices with complex effects, there is probably, in any case, no way for a single institution within that society to adjust its criteria for competitive admission or employment so that the effects of injustice are nullified as far as that institution is concerned. There is consequently considerable appeal to the position that places should be filled solely by reference to the criteria relevant to performance, and if this tends to amplify or extend the effects of inequitable treatment elsewhere, the remedy must be found in a more direct attack on those differences in qualifications, rather than in the introduction of irrelevant criteria of appointment or admission which will also sacrifice efficiency, productivity, or effectiveness of the institution in its specific tasks.

At this fourth stage we therefore find a broad division of opinion. There are those who believe that nothing further can legitimately be done in the short run, once the *remediable* unjust inequalities of opportunity between individuals have been dealt with: the irremediable ones are unjust, but any further steps to counterbalance them by reverse discrimination would also be unjust, because they must employ irrelevant criteria. On the other hand, there are those who find it unacceptable in such circumstances to stay with the restricted criteria usually related to successful performance, and who believe that differential admission or hiring standards for worse-off groups are justified because they roughly, though only approximately, compensate for the inequalities of opportunity produced by past injustice.

But at this point there is some temptation to resolve the dilemma and strengthen the argument for preferential standards by proceeding to a fifth stage. One may reflect that if the criteria relevant to the prediction of performance are not inviolable it may not matter whether one violates them to compensate for disadvantages caused by injustice or disadvantages caused in other ways. The fundamental issue is what grounds to use in assigning or admitting people to desirable positions. To settle that issue, one does not have to settle the question of the degree to which racial or sexual discrepancies are socially produced, because the differentials in reward ordinarily correlated with differences in qualifications are not the result of natural justice, but simply the effect of a competitive system trying to fill positions and perform tasks efficiently. Certain abilities may be relevant to filling a job from the point of view of efficiency, but they are not relevant from the point of view of justice, because they provide no indication that one deserves the rewards that go with holding that job. The qualities, experience, and attainments that make success in a certain position likely do not in themselves merit the rewards that happen to attach to occupancy of that position in a competitive economy.

Consequently it might be concluded that if women or black people are less qualified, for *whatever* reason, in the respects that lead to success in the professions that our society rewards most highly, then it would be just to compensate for this disadvantage, within the limits permitted by efficiency, by having suitably different standards for these groups, and thus bringing their access to desirable positions more into line with that of others. Compensatory discrimination would not, on this view, have to be tailored to deal only with the effects of past injustice.

But it is clear that this is not a stable position. For if one abandons the condition that to qualify for compensation an inequity must be socially caused, then there is no reason to restrict the compensatory measures to well-defined racial or sexual groups. Compensatory selection procedures would have to be applied on an individual basis, within as well as between such groups—each person, regardless of race, sex, or qualifications, being granted equal access to the desirable positions, within limits set by efficiency. This might require randomization of law and medical school admissions, for example, from among all the candidates who were above some minimum standard enabling them to do the work. If we were to act on the principle that different abilities do not merit different rewards, it would result in much more equality than is demanded by proponents of compensatory discrimination.

There is no likelihood that such a radical course will be adopted in the United States, but the fact that it seems to follow naturally from a certain view about how to deal with racial or sexual injustice reveals something important. When we try to deal with the inequality in advantages that results from a disparity in qualifications (however produced) between races or sexes, we are up against a pervasive and fundmental feature of the system, which at every turn exacts costs and presents obstacles in response to attempts to reduce the inequalities. We must face the possibility that the primary injustice with which we have to contend lies in this feature itself, and that some of the worst aspects of what we now perceive as racial or sexual injustice are merely conspicuous manifestations of the great social injustice of differential reward.

II

If differences in the capacity to succeed in the tasks that any society rewards well are visibly correlated, for whatever reason, with other characteristics such as race or religion or social origin, then a system of liberal equality of opportunity will give the appearance of supporting racial or religious or class injustice. Where there is no such correlation, there can be the appearance of justice through equal opportunity. But in reality, there is similar injustice in both cases, and it lies in the schedule of rewards.

The liberal idea of equal treatment demands that people receive equal opportunities if they are equally qualified by talent or education to utilize those opportunities. In requiring the relativization of equal treatment to characteristics in which people are very unequal, it guarantees that the social order will reflect and probably magnify the initial distinctions produced by nature and the past. Liberalism has therefore come under increasing attack in recent years, on the ground that the familiar principle of equal treatment, with its meritocratic conception of relevant differences, seems too weak to combat the inequalities dispensed by nature and the ordinary workings of the social system.

This criticism of the view that people deserve the rewards that accrue to them as a result of their natural talents is not based on the idea that no one can be said to deserve anything.[2] For if no one deserves anything, then no inequalities are contrary to desert, and desert provides no argument for equality. Rather, I am suggesting that for many benefits and disadvantages, certain characteristics of the recipient *are* relevant to what he deserves. If people are equal in the relevant respects, that by itself constitutes a reason to distribute the benefit to them equally.[3]

The relevant features will vary with the benefit or disadvantage, and so will the weight of the resulting considerations of desert. Desert may sometimes, in fact, be a rather unimportant consideration in determining what ought to be done. But I do wish to claim, with reference to a central case, that differential abilities are not usually among the characteristics that determine whether people *deserve* economic and social benefits (though of course they determine whether people *get* such benefits). In fact, I believe that nearly all characteristics are irrelevant to what people deserve in this dimension, and that most people therefore deserve to be treated equally.[4] Perhaps voluntary differences in effort or moral differences in conduct have some bearing on economic and social desert. I do not have a precise view about what features are relevant. I contend only that they are features in which most people do not differ enough to justify very wide differences in reward.[5] (While I realize that these claims are controversial, I shall not try to defend them here, nor to defend the legitimacy of the notion of desert itself. If these things make no sense, neither does the rest of my argument.)

A decision that people are equally or unequally deserving in some respect is not the end of the story. First of all, desert can sometimes be overridden, for example by liberty or even by efficiency. In some cases the presumption of equality is rather weak, and not much is required to depart from it. This will be so if the interest in question is minor or temporally circumscribed, and does not represent an important value in the subject's life.

Secondly, it may be that although an inequality is contrary to desert, no one can benefit from its removal: all that can be done is to worsen the position of those who benefit undeservedly from its presence. Even if one believes that desert is a very important factor in determining just distributions, one need not object to inequalities that are to no one's disadvantage. In other words, it is possible to accept something like Rawls's Difference Principle from the standpoint of an egalitarian view of desert.[6] (I say it is possible. It may not be required. Some may reject the Difference Principle because they regard equality of treatment as a more stringent requirement.)

Thirdly (and most significantly for the present discussion), a determination of relative desert in the distribution of a particular advantage does not even settle the question of *desert* in every case, for there may be other advantages and disadvantages whose distribution is tied to

that of the first, and the characteristics relevant to the determination of desert are not necessarily the same from one advantage to another. This bears on the case under consideration in the following way. I have said that people with different talents do not thereby deserve different economic and social rewards. They may, however, deserve different opportunities to exercise and develop those talents.[7] Whenever the distribution of two different types of benefit is connected in this way, through social or economic mechanisms or through natural human reactions, it may be impossible to avoid a distribution contrary to the conditions of desert in respect of at least one of the benefits. Therefore it is likely that a dilemma will arise in which it appears that injustice cannot be entirely avoided. It may then be necessary to decide that justice in the distribution of one advantage has priority over justice in the distribution of another that automatically goes with it.

In the case under discussion, there appears to be a conflict between justice in the distribution of educational and professional opportunities and justice in the distribution of economic and social rewards. I do not deny that there is a presumption, based on something more than efficiency, in favor of giving equal opportunities to those equally likely to succeed. But if the presumption in favor of economic equality is considerably stronger, the justification for departing from it must be stronger too. If this is so, then when "educational" justice and economic justice come into conflict, it will sometimes be necessary to sacrifice the former to the latter.

III

In thinking about racial and sexual discrimination, the view that economic justice has priority may tempt one to proceed to what I have called the fifth stage. One may be inclined to adopt admission quotas, for example, proportional to the representation of a given group in the population, because one senses the injustice of differential rewards per se. Whatever explains the small number of women or blacks in the professions, it has the result that they have less of the financial and social benefits that accrue to members of the professions, and what accounts for those differences cannot justify them. So justice requires that more women and blacks be admitted to the professions.

The trouble with this solution is that it does not locate the injustice accurately, but merely tries to correct the racially or sexually skewed economic distribution which is one of its more conspicuous symptoms. We are enabled to perceive the situation as unjust because we see it, e.g., through its racial manifestations, and race is a subject by now associated in our minds with injustice. However, little is gained by merely transferring the same system of differential rewards, suitably adjusted to achieve comparable proportions, to the class of blacks or the class of women. If it is unjust to reward people differentially for what certain characteristics enable them to do, it is equally unjust whether the distinction is made between a white man and a black man or between two black men, or two white women, or two black women. There is no way of attacking the unjust reward schedules (if indeed they are unjust) of a meritocratic system by attacking their racial or sexual manifestations directly.

In most societies reward is a function of demand, and many of the human characteristics most in demand result largely from *gifts* or *talents*. The greatest injustice in this society, I believe, is neither racial nor sexual but intellectual. I do not mean that it is unjust that some people are more intelligent than others. Nor do I mean that society rewards people differentially simply on the basis of their intelligence: usually it does not. Nevertheless it provides on the average much larger rewards for tasks that require superior intelligence than for those that do not. This is simply the way things work out in a technologically advanced society with a market economy. It does not reflect a social judgment that smart people *deserve* the opportunity to make more moeny than dumb people. They may deserve richer educational opportunity, but they do not therefore deserve the material wealth that goes with it. Similar things could be said about society's differential reward of achievements facilitated by other talents or gifts, like beauty, athletic ability, musicality, etc. But intelligence and its development by education provide a particularly significant and pervasive example.

However, a general reform of the current schedule of rewards, even if they are unjust, is beyond the power of individual educational or business institutions, working through their admissions or appointments policies. A competitive economy is bound to reward those with certain training and abilities, and a refusal to do so will put any business enterprise in a poor competitive position. Similarly, those who succeed in medical school or law school will tend to earn more than those who do not—whatever criteria of admission the schools adopt. It is not the procedures of appointment or admission, based on criteria that predict success, that are unjust, but rather what happens as a result of success.

No doubt a completely just solution is not ready to hand. If, as I have claimed, different factors are relevant to what is deserved in the distribution of different benefits and disadvantages, and if the distribution of several distinct advantages is sometimes connected even though the relevant factors are not, then inevitably there will be injustice in some respect, and it may be practically impossible to substitute a principle of distribution which avoids it completely.

Justice may require that we try to reduce the automatic connections between material advantages, cultural opportunity, and institutional authority. But such changes can be brought about, if at all, only by large alterations in the social system, the system of taxation, and the salary structure. They will not be achieved by modifying the admissions or hiring policies of colleges and universities, or even banks, law firms, and businesses.

Compensatory measures in admissions or appointment can be defended on grounds of justice only to the extent that they compensate for specific disadvantages which have themselves been unjustly caused, by factors distinct from the general meritocratic character of the system of distribution of advantageous positions. Such contributions are difficult to verify or estimate; they probably vary among individuals in the oppressed group. Moreover, it is not obvious that where a justification for preferential treatment exists, it is strong enough to create an obligation, since it is doubtful that one element of a pluralistic society is obliged to adopt discriminatory measures to counteract injustice due to another element, or even to the society as a whole.

IV

These considerations suggest that an argument on grounds of justice for the imposition of racial or sexual quotas would be difficult to construct without the aid of premises about the source of unequal qualifications between members of different groups. The more speculative the premises, the weaker the argument. But the question with which I began was not whether compensatory discrimination is *required* by justice, but whether it is *compatible* with justice. To that question I think we can give a different answer. If the reflections about differential reward to which we have been led are correct, then compensatory discrimination need not be seriously unjust, and it may be warranted not by justice but by considerations of social utility. I say not *seriously* unjust, to acknowledge that a departure from the standards relevant to distribution of intellectual opportunities *per se* is itself a kind of injustice. But its seriousness is lessened because the factors relevant to the distribution of intellectual opportunity are irrelevant to the distribution of those material benefits that go with it. This weakens the claim of someone who argues that by virtue of those qualities that make him likely to succeed in a certain position, he deserves to be selected for that position in preference to someone whose qualifications make it likely that he will succeed less well. He cannot claim that justice requires the allocation of positions on the basis of ability, because the result of such allocation, in the present system, is serious injustice of a different kind.

My contention, then, is that where the allocation of one benefit on relevant grounds carries with it the allocation of other, more significant benefits to which those grounds are irrelevant, the departure from those grounds need not be a serious offense against justice. This may be so for two reasons. First, the presumption of equal treatment of relevantly equal persons in respect of the first benefit may not be very strong to begin with. Second, the fairness of abiding by the presumption may be overshadowed by the unfairness of the other distribution correlated with it. Consequently, it may be acceptable to depart from the "relevant" grounds for undramatic reasons of social utility, that would not justify more flagrant and undiluted examples of unfairness. Naturally a deviation from the usual method will appear unjust to those who are accustomed to regarding ability to succeed as the correct criterion, but this appearance may be an illusion. That depends on how much injustice is involved in the usual method, and whether the reasons for departing from it are good enough, even though they do not correct the injustice.

The problem, of course, is to say what a good reason is. I do not want to produce an argument that will justify not only compensatory discrimination on social grounds, but also ordinary racial or sexual discrimination designed to preserve internal harmony in a business, for instance. Even someone who thought that the system of differential economic rewards for different abilities was unjust would presumably regard it as an *additional* unjustice if standard racial, religious, or sexual discrimination were a factor in the assignment of individuals to highly rewarded positions.

I can offer only a partial account of what makes systematic racial or sexual discrimination so exceptionally unjust. It has no social advantages, and it attaches a sense of reduced worth to a feature with which people are born.[8] A psychological consequence of the systematic attachment of social disadvantages to a certain inborn feature is that both the possessors of the feature and others begin to regard it as an essential and important characteristic, and one which reduces the esteem in which its possessor can be held.[9] Concomitantly, those who do not possess the characteristic gain a certain amount of free esteem by comparison, and the arrangement thus constitutes a gross sacrifice of the most basic personal interests of some for the interests of others, with those sacrificed being on the bottom. (It is because similar things can be said about the social and economic disadvantages that attach to low intelligence that I am inclined to regard that, too, as a major injustice.)

Reverse discrimination need not have these consequences, and it can have social advantages. Suppose, for example, that there is need for a great increase in the number of black doctors, because the health needs of the black community are unlikely to be met otherwise. And suppose that at the present average level of premedical qualifications among black applicants, it would require a huge expansion of total medical school enrollment to supply the desirable absolute number of black doctors without adopting differential admission standards. Such an expansion may be unacceptable either because of its cost or because it would produce a total supply of doctors, black and white, much greater than the society requires. This is a strong argument for accepting reverse discrimination, not on grounds of justice but on grounds of social utility. (In addition, there is the salutary effect on the aspirations and expectations of other blacks, from the visibility of exemplars in formerly inaccessible positions.)

The argument in the other direction, from the point of view of the qualified white applicants who are turned away, is not nearly as strong as the argument against standard racial discrimination. The self-esteem of whites as a group is not endangered by such a practice, since the situation arises only because of their general social dominance, and the aim of the practice is only to benefit blacks, and not to exclude whites. Moreover, although the interests of some are being sacrificed to further the interests of others, it is the better placed who are being sacrificed and the worst placed who are being helped.[10] It is an important feature of the case that the discriminatory measure is designed to favor a group whose social position is exceptionally depressed, with destructive consequences both for the self-esteem of members of the group and for the health and cohesion of the society.[11]

If, therefore, a discriminatory admissions or appointments policy is adopted to mitigate a grave social evil, and it favors a group in a particularly unfortunate social position, and if for these reasons it diverges from a meritocratic system for the assignment of positions which is not itself required by justice, then the discriminatory practice is probably not unjust.[12]

It is not without its costs, however. Not only does it inevitably produce resentment in the better qualified who are passed over because of the policy, but it also allows those in the discriminated-against group who would in fact have failed to gain a desired position in any case on the basis of their qualifications to feel that they may have lost out to someone less qualified because of the discriminatory policy. Similarly, such a practice cannot do much for the self-esteem of those who know they have benefited from it, and it may threaten the self-esteem of those in the favored group who would in fact have gained their positions even in the absence of the discriminatory policy, but who cannot be sure that they are not among its beneficiaries. This is what leads institutions to lie about their policies in this regard, or to hide them behind clouds of obscurantist rhetoric about the discriminatory character of standard admissions criteria. Such concealment is possible and even justified up to a point, but the costs cannot be entirely evaded, and discriminatory practices of this sort will be tolerable only so long as they are clearly contributing to the eradication of great social evils.

V

When racial and sexual injustice have been reduced, we shall still be left with the great injustice of the smart and the dumb, who are so differently rewarded for comparable effort. This would be an injustice even if the system of differential economic and social rewards had no systematic sexual or racial reflection. On the other hand, if the social esteem and economic advantages attaching to different occupations and educational achievements were much more uniform, there would be little cause for concern about racial, ethnic, or sexual patterns in education or work. But of course we do not at present have a method of divorcing professional status from social esteem and economic reward, at least not without a gigantic increase in total social control, on the Chinese model. Perhaps someone will discover a way in which the socially produced inequalities (especially the economic ones) between the intelligent and the unintelligent, the talented and the untalented, or even the beautiful and the ugly, can be reduced without limiting the availability of opportunities, products and services, and without resort to increased coercion or decreased liberty in the choice of work or style of life. In the absence of such a utopian solution, however, the familiar task of balancing liberty against equality will remain with us.[13]

NOTES

1. By saying that the white man is "in other respects better qualified" I mean that if, e.g., a black candidate with similar qualifications had been available for the position, he would have been selected in preference to the black candidate who was in fact selected; or, if the choice had been between two white male candidates of corresponding qualifications, this one would have been selected. Ditto for two white or two black women. (I realize that it may not always be easy to determine similarity of qualifications, and that in some cases similarity of credentials may give evidence of a difference in qualifications—because, e.g., one person had to overcome more severe obstacles to acquire those credentials.)

2. Rawls appears to regard this as the basis of his own view. He believes it makes sense to speak of positive desert only in the context of distributions by a just system, and not as a pre-institutional conception that can be used to measure the justice of the system. John Rawls, *A Theory of Justice* (Cambridge, Mass., 1971), pp. 310-313.

3. Essentially this view is put forward by Bernard Williams in "The Idea of Equality," in *Philosophy, Politics, and Society*

(Second Series), ed. P. Laslett and W. G. Runciman (Oxford, 1964), pp. 110–131.

4. This is distinct from a case in which nothing is relevant because there *is* no desert in the matter. In that case the fact that people differed in no relevant characteristics would not create a presumption that they be treated equally. It would leave the determination of their treatment entirely to other considerations.

5. It is *not* my view that we cannot be said to deserve the *results* of anything which we do not deserve. It is true that a person does not deserve his intelligence, and I have maintained that he does not deserve the rewards that superior intelligence can provide. But neither does he deserve his bad moral character or his above-average willingness to work, yet I believe that he probably does deserve the punishments or rewards that flow from those qualities. For an illuminating discussion of these matters, see Robert Nozick, *Anarchy, State, and Utopia* (New York, Basic Books: forthcoming), chap. 7.

6. Rawls, *op. cit.*, pp. 75–80.

7. Either because differences of ability are relevant to degree of desert in these respects or because people are equally deserving of opportunities proportional to their talents. More likely the latter.

8. For a detailed and penetrating treatment of this and a number of other matters discussed here, see Owen M. Fiss, "A Theory of Fair Employment Laws," *University of Chicago Law Review* 38 (Winter 1971): 235–314.

9. This effect would not be produced by an idiosyncratic discriminatory practice limited to a few eccentrics. If some people decided they would have nothing to do with anyone left-handed, everyone else, including the left-handed, would regard it as a silly objection to an inessential feature. But if everyone shunned the left-handed, left-handedness would become a strong component of their self-image, and those discriminated against would feel they were being despised for their essence. What people regard as their essence is not independent of what they get admired and despised for.

10. This is a preferable direction of sacrifice if one accepts Rawls's egalitarian assumptions about distributive justice. Rawls, *op. cit.*, pp. 100–103.

11. It is therefore not, as some have feared, the first step toward an imposition of minimal or maximal quotas for all racial, religious, and ethnic subgroups of the society.

12. Adam Morton has suggested an interesting alternative, which I shall not try to develop: namely, that the practice is justified not by social utility, but because it will contribute to a more just situation in the future. The practice considered in itself may be unjust, but it is warranted by its greater contribution to justice over the long term, through eradication of a self-perpetuating pattern.

13. I have presented an earlier version of this paper to the New York Group of the Society for Philosophy and Public Affairs, the Princeton Undergraduate Philosophy Club, and the Society for Ethical and Legal Philosophy, and I thank those audiences for their suggestions.

PART 4

Responsibility

Critical judgments about what people do occupy a very large place in our daily life. Philosophers want to make sure that these judgments are valid, and so seek principles under which the judgments may themselves be criticized. There are urgent practical reasons for making sure that our criticism of conduct is sound. We spend our lives in a community of persons each of whom pursues his or her own interests, yet each is required to respect the interests of others in order to make possible the benefits of life in a civilized society. Since disinterested benevolence is not a regular feature of social life, people must be encouraged to avoid harming others as they seek their own ends. When harm is done, it is important that acceptable remedies be applied to undo the harm as much as possible. It is also important to take steps that will reduce the likelihood of harm being done in the future. This requires holding to account those (and only those) who properly are accountable when something untoward occurs. It is a matter of some importance also that those (and only those) who are entitled to recognition for good works receive it, so that encouragement of socially valuable activities is provided. What we need, then, are ways of criticizing conduct that are rational and fair. Theoretical work concerned with responsibility seeks to increase our understanding of our critical practices, and through better understanding to make our critical conclusions more reasonable and just.

Legal theory is nowhere more generously endowed with philosophical substance than in those parts that address questions of responsibility. It is also true that the law offers more promising material than any other human endeavor to the philosopher who seeks to develop a theory of responsibility. This happy coincidence makes the subjects sampled in this part of the volume preeminent among concerns of legal philosophy. It is the criminal law that presents the most philosophically important questions, for a just system of criminal liability requires as a foundation principles of responsibility that are just. Civil liability, especially the law of torts, also poses many similar questions under such textbook headings as fault, negligence, causation, and strict liability. Regarding criminal liability, we want to know when

485

punishment is warranted. Responsibility of the accused is always the first (and sometimes the only) consideration in deciding that. In considering civil liability, we want to know when a loss suffered by one person is to be made up by another; and that often (though not always) involves issues of responsibility, sometimes to the exclusion of all other questions.

THE IDEA OF RESPONSIBILITY

Even the little that has been said about responsibilty so far will likely have created an impression in the reader's mind that the very subject of the discussion is not entirely clear. With what exactly are those who speak of responsibility concerned? H. L. A. Hart distinguishes the separate though related ideas concerning responsibility that are marked by different forms of expression and different contexts. There are four major categories, and within them exist a considerable number of important distinctions. As this sorting of expressions makes clear, much in critical practice and in its theory depends upon recognizing differences among expressions that at face value appear alike. This reminds us of J. L. Austin's observation that "words are our tools, and, as a minimum, we should use clean tools: we should know what we mean and what we do not, and must forearm ourselves against the traps that language sets us." Even more important, through work like Professor Hart's we become clear about the word and as a result of that learn about responsibility itself. Again Austin put the point sharply. "When we examine what we should say when, what words we should use in what situations, we are looking again not *merely* at words (or 'meanings' whatever they may be) but also at the realities we use the words to talk about: we are using a sharpened awareness of words to sharpen our perception of, though not as final arbiter of, the phenomena." One may profitably consider here what the "final arbiter" is, with reference to responsibility as it is dealt with in Hart's analysis. If one wishes to understand what responsibility is, is there anything further that must be understood after one has exhaustively analyzed characteristic correct uses of the term? The value of Professor Hart's analysis is apparent to anyone who has experienced the confusion of responsibility and liability that permeates legal literature. Setting inappropriate requirements of responsibility for some legal liability, and imposing legal liability on some inappropriate occasions of responsibility, have both frequently resulted from just such confusion.

RESPONSIBILITY AND CAUSATION

In ordinary life or in legal proceedings, whenever we assert that a person is responsible for some harm, we may be challenged on grounds of causation. It often counts conclusively against responsibility that what was done by the accused did not cause the unhappy event for which we wish to hold him liable. Yet clear as that is, there is hardly a more difficult task for the theorist than that of spelling out principles which determine in any given case whether the act was or was not the cause of the harm. At the heart of the difficulty is understanding what we *mean* by a cause when the cause is an act. Formidable difficulties about causation arise when general accounts of the relations among events of the physical world are attempted, and these difficulties are often imported into the special cause accounting called for by issues of personal responsibility. But should they be? Causation in a theory of responsibility may be very different in important respects from causation in a theory of scientific explanation or in metaphysics. Many things which are singled out as counting for or against the causal status of one event in relation to another seem not really to matter, as it turns out, when we are talking about *acts* (as acts) and their consequences. Who can deny that in some sense an ancestor's act of reproduction was a cause of the death of the person that his descendent murdered, yet who would assert that the act of reproduction caused the death? Even more revealing, perhaps, is the fact that *doing* harm and *causing* harm are quite different notions, yet an act which is the *doing* surely is in some other more general sense a cause of the harm, every bit as much a cause as another act which is spoken of as *causing* it. This strongly suggests that there is indeed something special about conceiving acts as causes, quite unlike conceiving viruses or volcanoes as causes.

H. L. A. Hart and his Oxford colleague, A. M. Honoré, undertake to clarify causation as it bears on questions of responsibility in the law. In the first part of this selection from their book *Causation in the Law,* they consider the similarity in the concept of causation to be found in law and in morality. This can be accounted for by the common concern of both law and morality to ascertain responsibility. In this part they also point out certain differences, not in the very concept, but in the rules that are used by both law and morality to decide whether an act truly caused a harm. Considerations of legal policy require that the rules the law adopts be suited to the purposes the law must serve, and it is this that accounts for the difference. In the second and larger portion of this selection, the authors take up the master problem of when (ignoring such special restrictions) the consequences of an act can rightly be said to have been caused by it.

Three sorts of problematic cases are analyzed. All of them deal with intervening or supervening events but for which the harm would not have occurred. If what was done would not have resulted in the harm but for something subsequent which was quite usual, the subsequent event does not deprive the act of its causal status. If, however, there is an intervening voluntary act (subject to two major exceptions and certain qualifications), that deprives the earlier act of its causal status. Finally, in cases in which the harm is a result of mere coincidence of the consequence of the act and something else, the act is deprived of its causal status (though once again there is an important exception). After reading this selection, it seems appropriate to pose again and extend the question raised earlier. Is it the concept of causation one finds useful in explaining the physical world that is really germane to issues of responsibility? Have these authors been unduly influenced at any point by the problem of physical causation? And what, in any case, is it really that makes responsibility depend in part on whether one's act was the cause of the harm?

Robert E. Keeton shifts attention to risks in deciding whether or not an act caused harm. In "The Basic Rule of Legal Cause in Negligence Cases," Professor Keeton expounds a risk rule of causation which draws on the insight that causation issues in the law resolve themselves into issues about whether in acting one ought to have regard for some possible harm. The insight is not without its difficulties, however. One may wonder whether the modest claim that A is the cause of harm B has not been unduly enlarged in risk theory. It is not normally thought to be an objection to such a claim that act A was not negligent, for one who causes harm need not be at fault in doing so. Risk theory, however, seems to suggest the contrary. It suggests that when harm occurs and certain conduct caused it, the conduct is the cause of the harm because it created a risk of the harm and the harm was one that falls within the hazards of what was done. But creating a risk of the sort of harm that falls within the risks of what one is doing is (at the least) negligence. The challenge presented by risk analysis, then, is to separate its insight about risk from unwarranted implications concerning culpability.

The *New York Times* story reporting the tragedy of the Ault family presents a case in which the parents of the victim cannot be held liable for causing their daughter's death, even though they are the authors of the events that resulted in it. The story provides an opportunity for comparative testing of the voluntary intervention principle of Hart and Honoré, and the risk theory analysis of Keeton to see which provides the more illuminating account.

In the *Palsgraf* case, the Court's opinion by Judge Cardozo contains the following statement: "The law of causation, remote or proximate, is thus foreign to the case before us." Few on any court in the United States have been Cardozo's equal as a theorist of the law; yet in spite of his statement, this case has enjoyed the greatest popularity in American law schools as a case presenting the causation issue in torts. It therefore is incumbent on one who reads the case to ask first whether causation is indeed the issue. If the answer accords with the prevailing view, the next questions must be (1) what criteria are invoked in the opinions of the two judges to decide that issue (under whatever rubric they may place it); (2) what principle of causation, if any, can be extracted from the opinions; and (3) what could Judge Cardozo have meant?

CRIMINAL RESPONSIBILITY: SOME PROBLEMS

Some of the most interesting problems studied by legal philosophers fall in the area of criminal responsibility. The terms *excuse* and *justification* signal the fascinating issues that arise when the accused in a criminal case seeks to defend himself by saying that he couldn't help what he did (or what happened), that he didn't mean to do *that,* or that in the circumstances, what he did, however unfortunate it might be, wasn't really wrong. There are many issues of this sort. In this section, four particularly intriguing problems are presented as they emerged in cases real and imaginary.

Many cannibalism cases have come before the courts of civilized countries after the desperate survivors of some terrible disaster had decided to eat someone among their number in order to stay alive themselves. In "The Case of the Speluncean Explorers" Lon Fuller makes the fullest use of his inventive talents as he seeks to deploy a great variety of different sorts of arguments bearing on the question of criminal liability in such a case. It should be regarded as a case of justification rather than excuse. The opinions of the imaginary judges explore a number of different jurisprudential caverns. One is law in a state of nature. Another is the subterranean passages beneath legislation that only statutory interpretation can illuminate. Fuller's wide-ranging approach to this problem is not typical of actual cases. But it allows a full panoply of questions to be raised about liability under the criminal law in these very exceptional circumstances.

In *United States* v. *Holmes* there has been another disaster, this time at sea, which again created a situation in which the sacrifice of some victims seemed necessary to make possible the survival of others. The full report of the case is provided in this selection to illustrate the importance of the facts. It is useful to isolate the elements in the situation that really matter and to try to explain exactly what it is in the conduct of the accused and in the surrounding circumstances that tends to inculpate or to exculpate. Theorists of the law (and certainly philosophers of law) sometimes like to start with simple and quite general descriptions of the facts, and then go on to the ideas that emerge when relevant principles are examined. The report in this case offers a good opportunity to appreciate the importance of considering the facts in great detail in deciding morally sensitive questions.

An altogether different sort of problem in criminal responsibility confronts the court in *United States* v. *Oviedo*. One of the most controversial issues of criminal liability is to be found in an odd corner of the criminal law when there has not been a completed crime and it is said that clearly it was impossible that there ever could have been. If the attempt could not possibly have succeeded, why should there be any liability, and if there are good reasons for liability in such cases, do these hold for all cases of attempt, no matter how clearly impossible the accomplishment of the criminal purpose? The opinion of the court in this case analyzes the problem succinctly and supports a common-sense view of the matter that may still leave some moralists of the criminal law unsatisfied. In considering the issues that emerge one is forced to confront the most basic general questions surrounding criminal liability itself.

In *Oviedo* the accused apparently thought the substance he wished to sell was heroin, though it was not, and the prosecution's case rested ultimately on that mistaken belief. In *Director of Public Prosecutions* v. *Morgan* the alleged mistaken belief of the defendant is the foundation of the defense that was mounted in a rape case. When accused of aiding and abetting the rape of his wife by his drinking companions, the husband claimed he thought his wife was consenting to the violent sexual assault, and ultimately the highest court in England decided that such a defense, if believed, was a good one in law. In the essay entitled "Excusing Rape" E. M. Curley subjects the decision to careful critical analysis to make clear what is wrong with it. The mental element in crime is a constant source of difficulty for the theorist, and it is very important to understand what really should concern the law when such concepts as *intention* or *mens rea* are crucial to determing guilt or innocence. In *Morgan* there are also questions about the reasonableness and honesty of a belief. Examining these concepts and considering what should be required for a good defense is an exercise that will enlighten us about the foundations of criminal responsibility.

RESPONSIBILITY FOR NONINTERVENTION

Largely at the insistence of the medical profession, most American state legislatures in recent years have passed so-called "good samaritan statutes" to protect would-be rescuers and aid-givers (particularly physicians) from civil liability for negligence if they should accidentally make things worse for an imperiled party despite their good intentions. These statues, which create a rescuer's immunity from civil suit (except usually for gross negligence), should be distinguished from "bad samaritan statutes," which impose criminal liability on a party who fails to assist when he might do so with little danger or expense to himself. Bad samaritan statutes are much more controversial than good samaritan statutes, and no more than three American states have followed the lead of most European countries in passing them. The traditional reluctance of English-speaking countries to follow their European neighbors in this respect has been supported by numerous arguments. Some writers have maintained that a legal duty to rescue would require us not merely to refrain from harming others, but positively to benefit others as well. Such a requirement, they claim, amounts to an enforcement of generosity, which in turn would erase the distinctions between justice and charity, and between duty and supererogation. Other writers, following Thomas Macaulay, have argued that even if there is a *moral* duty to come to the assistance of imperiled strangers, it cannot be enforced by law. Their reasoning says there is no principled way of drawing the line between aid in unanticipated emergencies near at hand, and aid to starving paupers or the distant needy who cannot be saved without extreme inconvenience, unfair sacrifice, or unreasonable risk. Joel Feinberg, in his defense of what has been a minority position among Anglo-American writers, attempts to rebut both of these arguments.

MENTAL ABNORMALITY

When people who commit crimes are simply not right in the head it seems wrong to treat them as full-fledged criminals, or even to treat them as criminals at all. But it has proved exceeding difficult to draw the line that separates those who are mad from those who are bad and only incidentally mentally ill. Even if one accepts that such a crudely stated separation can be made, it seems not nearly comprehensive enough for the distinctions we need when dealing with mental abnormality in the criminal forum. Since we are still very much in the dark about matters of responsibility for normal people, we are especially perplexed when questions of responsibility are raised regarding the conduct of those who suffer some mental impairment. And beyond those questions we encounter no less difficult ones about how we ought to treat people who are more or less *capable* of behaving responsibly, but who behave in some untoward way because they are ill or handicapped. Considerations of humanity occupy us at that point, and we are forced to consider how much weight to give to considerations of criminal justice alone.

Four rather different positions are taken in the four selections that occupy most of the Mental Abnormality section. Little need be added here to these statements. It is useful to consider whether even as a fairly primitive medical science modern psychiatry cannot supply enough information about the psychopathology of most cases of prima facie abnormality to serve as the basis of dispositions that are satisfactory from a practical point of view even if not correct in principle according to more exacting standards of criminal responsibility. After all, looking at how we dispose of cases generally in the criminal justice system, isn't there a great deal more pragmatism than principle in the process and don't we accept this as a fact of public life so long as our moral intuitions are not disregarded? Isn't doing the best we can good enough even if it means letting some people with abnormal conditions get away with more than their abnormality really excuses?

In "Mental Abnormality as a Criminal Excuse," Hyman Gross endeavors to clarify the full range of exculpatory claims that look to mental abnormality and to discover what good reasons exist in principle for recognizing them as defenses in a criminal prosecution. He pays particular attention to the insanity defense in its various formulations, and he assesses each of these tests in the light of more general concerns about moral responsibility.

H. L. A. HART

Responsibility*

A wide range of different, though connected, ideas is covered by the expressions 'responsibility', 'responsible', and 'responsible for', as these are standardly used in and out of the law. Though connections exist among these different ideas, they are often very indirect, and it seems appropriate to speak of different *senses* of these expressions. The following simple story of a drunken sea captain who lost his ship at sea can be told in the terminology of responsibility to illustrate, with stylistically horrible clarity, these differences of sense.

'As a captain of the ship, X was responsible for the safety of his passengers and crew. But on his last voyage he got drunk every night and was responsible for the loss of the ship with all aboard. It was rumoured that he was insane, but the doctors considered that he was responsible for his actions. Throughout the voyage he behaved quite irresponsibly, and various incidents in his career showed that he was not a responsible person. He always maintained that the exceptional winter storms were responsible for the loss of the ship, but in the legal proceedings brought against him he was found criminally responsible for his negligent conduct, and in separate civil proceedings he was held legally responsible for the loss of life and property. He is still alive and he is morally responsible for the deaths of many women and children.'

This welter of distinguishable senses of the word 'responsibility' and its grammatical cognates can, I think, be profitably reduced by division and classification. I shall distinguish four heads of classification to which I shall assign the following names:
(a) Role-Responsibility
(b) Causal-Responsibility

*From the *Law Quarterly Review* (1967), Vol. 83. Reprinted by permission of the Editor. This selection was reprinted as the first part of an essay entitled "Postscript: Responsibility and Retribution" in H. L. A. Hart, *Punishment and Responsibility* (New York and Oxford: Oxford University Press, 1968), pp. 211–30.

(c) Liability-Responsibility
(d) Capacity-Responsibility.

I hope that in drawing these dividing lines, and in the exposition which follows, I have avoided the arbitrary pedantries of classificatory systematics, and that my divisions pick out and clarify the main, though not all, varieties of responsibility to which reference is constantly made, explicitly or implicitly, by moralists, lawyers, historians, and ordinary men. I relegate to the notes[1] discussion of what unifies these varieties and explains the extension of the terminology of responsibility.

ROLE-RESPONSIBILITY

A sea captain is responsible for the safety of his ship, and that is his responsibility, or one of his responsibilities. A husband is responsible for the maintenance of his wife; parents for the upbringing of their children; a sentry for alerting the guard at the enemy's approach; a clerk for keeping the accounts of his firm. These examples of a person's responsibilities suggest the generalization that, whenever a person occupies a distinctive place or office in a social organization, to which specific duties are attached to provide for the welfare of others or to advance in some specific way the aims or purposes of the organization, he is properly said to be responsible for the performance of these duties, or for doing what is necessary to fulfil them. Such duties are a person's responsibilities. As a guide to this sense of responsibility this generalization is, I think, adequate, but the idea of a distinct role or place or office is, of course, a vague one, and I cannot undertake to make it very precise. Doubts about its extension to marginal cases will always arise. If two friends, out on a mountaineering expedition, agree that the one shall look after the food and the other the maps, then the one is correctly said to be responsible for the food, and the other for the maps, and I would classify this as a case of role-responsibility. Yet such fugitive or temporary assignments with specific duties would not usually be considered by sociologists, who mainly use the word, as an example of a 'role'. So 'role' in my classification is extended to include a task assigned to any person by agreement or otherwise. But it is also important to notice that not all the duties which a man has in virtue of occupying what in a quite strict sense of role is a distinct role, are thought or spoken of as 'responsibilities'. A private soldier has a duty to obey his superior officer and, if commanded by him to form fours or present arms on a given occasion, has a duty to do so. But to form fours or present arms would scarcely be said to be the private's responsibility; nor would he be said to be responsible for doing it. If on the other hand a soldier was ordered to deliver a message to H.Q. or to conduct prisoners to a base camp, he might well be said to be responsible for doing these things, and these things to be his responsibility. I think, though I confess to not being sure, that what distinguishes those duties of a role which are singled out as responsibilities is that they are duties of a relatively complex or extensive kind, defining a 'sphere of responsibility' requiring care and attention over a protracted period of time, while short-lived duties of a very simple kind, to do or not do some specific act on a particular occasion, are not termed responsibilities. Thus a soldier detailed off to keep the camp clean and tidy for the general's visit of inspection has this as his sphere of responsibility and is responsible for it. But if merely told to remove a piece of paper from the approaching general's path, this would be at most his duty.

A 'responsible person', 'behaving responsibly' (not 'irresponsibly'), require for their elucidation a reference to role-responsibility. A responsible person is one who is disposed to take his duties seriously; to think about them, and to make serious efforts to fulfil them. To behave responsibly is to behave as a man would who took his duties in this serious way. Responsibilities in this sense may be either legal or moral, or fall outside this dichotomy. Thus a man may be morally as well as legally responsible for the maintenance of his wife and children, but a host's responsibility for the comfort of his guests, and a referee's responsibility for the control of the players is neither legal nor moral, unless the word 'moral' is unilluminatingly used simply to exclude legal responsibility.

CAUSAL RESPONSIBILITY

'The long drought was responsible for the famine in India'. In many contexts, as in this one, it is possible to substitute for the expression 'was responsible for' the words 'caused' or 'produced' or some other causal expression in referring to consequences, results, or outcomes. The converse, however, is not always true. Examples of this causal sense of responsibility are legion. 'His neglect was responsible for her distress.' 'The Prime Minister's speech was responsible for the panic.' 'Disraeli was responsible for the defeat of the Government.' 'The icy condition of the road was responsible for the accident.' The past tense of the verb used in this causal sense of the expression 'responsible for' should be noticed. If it is said of a living person, who has in fact caused some disaster, that he *is* responsible for it, this is not, or not merely, an example of causal responsibility, but of what I term 'liability-responsibility'; it asserts his liability on account of the disaster, even though it is also true that he is responsible in that sense *because* he caused the disaster, and that he caused the disaster may be expressed by saying that he was responsible for it. On the other hand, if it is said of a person no longer living that he was responsible for some disaster, this may be either a simple causal statement or a statement of liability-responsibility, or both.

From the above examples it is clear that in this causal sense not only human beings but also their actions or omissions, and things, conditions, and events, may be said to be responsible for outcomes. It is perhaps true that only where an outcome is thought unfortunate or felicitous is its cause commonly spoken of as responsible for it. But this may not reflect any aspect of the meaning of the expression 'responsible for'; it may only reflect the fact that, except in such cases, it may be pointless and hence rare to pick out the causes of events. It is sometimes suggested that, though we may speak of a human being's action as responsible for some outcome in a purely causal sense, we do not speak of a person, as distinct from his actions, as responsible for an outcome, unless he is felt to deserve censure or praise. This is, I think, a mistake. History books are full of examples to the contrary. 'Disraeli was responsible for the defeat of the Government' need not carry even an implication that he was deserving of censure or praise; it may be purely a statement concerned with the contribution made by one human being to an outcome of importance, and be entirely neutral as to its moral or other merits. The contrary view depends, I think, on the failure to appreciate sufficiently the ambiguity of statements of the form 'X *was* responsible for Y' as distinct from 'X *is* responsible for Y' to which I have drawn attention above. The former expression in the case of a person no longer living may be (though it *need* not be) a statement of liability-responsibility.

LEGAL LIABILITY-RESPONSIBILITY

Though it was noted that role-responsibility might take either legal or moral form, it was not found necessary to treat these separately. But in the case of the present topic of liability-responsibility, separate treatment seems advisable. For responsibility seems to have a wider extension in relation to the law than it does in relation to morals, and it is a question to be considered whether this is due merely to the general differences between law and morality, or to some differences in the sense of responsibility involved.

When legal rules require men to act or abstain from action, one who breaks the law is usually liable, according to other legal rules, to punishment for his misdeeds, or to make compensation to persons injured thereby, and very often he is liable to both punishment and enforced compensation. He is thus liable to be 'made to pay' for what he has done in either or both of the senses which the expression 'He'll pay for it' may bear in ordinary usage. But most legal systems go much further than this. A man may be legally punished on account of what his servant has done, even if he in no way caused or instigated or even knew of the servant's action, or knew of the likelihood of his servant so acting. Liability in such circumstances is rare in modern systems of criminal law; but it is common in all systems of civil law for men to be made to pay compensation for injuries caused by others, generally their servants or employees. The law of most countries goes further still. A man may be liable to pay compensation for harm suffered by others, though neither he nor his servants have caused it. This is so, for example, in Anglo-American law when the harm is caused by dangerous things which escape from a man's possession, even if their escape is not due to any act or omission of his or his servants, or if harm is caused to a man's employees by defective machinery whose defective condition he could not have discovered.

It will be observed that the facts referred to in the last paragraph are expressed in terms of 'liability' and not 'responsibility'. In the preceding essay in this volume I ventured the general statement that to say that someone is legally responsible for something often means that under legal rules he is liable to be made either to suffer or to pay compensation in certain eventualities. But I now think that this simple account of liability-responsibility is in need of some considerable modification. Undoubtedly, expressions of the form 'he is legally responsible for Y' (where Y is some action or harm) and 'he is legally liable to be punished or to be made to pay compensation for Y' are very closely connected, and sometimes they are used as if they were identical in meaning. Thus, where one legal writer speaks of 'strict responsibility' and 'vicarious responsibility', another speaks of 'strict liability' and 'vicarious liability'; and even in the work of a single writer the expressions 'vicarious responsibility' and 'vicarious liability' are to be found used without any apparent difference in meaning, implication, or emphasis. Hence, in arguing that it was for the law to determine the mental conditions of responsibility, Fitzjames Stephen claimed that this must be so because 'the meaning of responsibility is liability to punishment'.[2]

But though the abstract expressions 'responsibility' and 'liability' are virtually equivalent in many contexts, the statement that a man is responsible for his actions, or for some act or some harm, is usually not identical in meaning with the statement that he is liable to be punished or to be made to pay compensation for the act or the harm, but is directed to a narrower and more specific issue. It is in this respect that my previous account of liability-responsibility needs qualification.

The question whether a man is or is not legally liable to be punished for some action that he has done opens up the quite general issue whether all of the various requirements for criminal liability have been satisfied, and so will include the question whether the kind of action done, whatever mental element accompanied it, was ever punishable by law. But the question whether he is or is not legally responsible for some action or some harm is usually not concerned with this general issue, but with the narrower issue whether any of a certain range of conditions (mainly, but not exclusively, psychological) are satisfied, it being assumed that all other conditions are satisfied. Because of this difference in scope between questions of liability to punishment and questions of responsibility, it would be somewhat misleading, though not unintelligible, to say of a man who had refused to rescue a baby drowning in a foot of water, that he was not, according to English law, legally responsible for leaving the baby to drown or for the baby's death, if all that is meant is that he was not liable to punishment because refusing aid to those in danger is not generally a crime in English law. Similarly, a book or article entitled 'Criminal Responsibility' would not be expected to contain the whole of the substantive criminal law determining the conditions of liability, but only to be concerned with a specialized range of topics such as mental abnormality, immaturity, *mens rea,* strict and vicarious liability, proximate cause, or other general forms of connection between acts and harm sufficient for liability. These are the specialized topics which are, in general, thought and spoken of as 'criteria' of responsibility. They may be divided into three classes: (i) mental or psychological conditions; (ii) causal or other forms of connection between act and harm; (iii) personal relationships rendering one man liable to be punished or to pay for the acts of another. Each of these three classes requires some separate discussion.

(i) *Mental or psychological criteria of responsibility.* In the criminal law the most frequent issue raised by questions of responsibility, as distinct from the wider question of liability, is whether or not an accused person satisfied some mental or psychological conditions required for liability, or whether liability was strict or absolute, so that the usual mental or psychological condition were not required. It is, however, important to notice that these psychological conditions are of two sorts, of which the first is far more closely associated with the use of the word responsibility than the second. On the one hand, the law of most countries requires that the person liable to be punished should at the time of his crime have had the capacity to understand what he is required by law to do or not to do, to deliberate and to decide what to do, and to control his conduct in the light of such decisions. Normal adults are generally assumed to have these capacities, but they may be lacking where there is mental disorder or immaturity, and the possession of these normal capacities is very often signified by the expression 'responsible for his actions'. This is the fourth sense of responsibility which I discuss below under the heading of 'Capacity-Responsibility'. On the other hand, except where responsibility is strict, the law may excuse from punishment persons of normal capacity if, on particular occasions where their outward conduct fits the definition of the crime, some element of intention or knowledge, or some other of the familiar constituents of *mens rea,* was absent, so that the particular action done was defective, though the agent had the normal capacity of understanding and control. Continental codes usually make a firm distinction between these two main types of psychological conditions: Questions concerning

general capacity are described as matters of responsibility or 'imputability', whereas questions concerning the presence or absence of knowledge or intention on particular occasions are not described as matters of 'imputability', but are referred to the topic of 'fault' (*schuld, faute, dolo,* et cetera).

English law and English legal writers do not mark quite so firmly this contrast between general capacity and the knowledge or intention accompanying a particular action; for the expression *mens rea* is now often used to cover all the variety of psychological conditions required for liability by the law, so that both the person who is excused from punishment because of lack of intention or some ordinary accident or mistake on a particular occasion and the person held not to be criminally responsible on account of immaturity or insanity are said not to have the requisite *mens rea.* Yet the distinction thus blurred by the extensive use of the expression *mens rea* between a persistent incapacity and a particular defective action is indirectly marked in terms of responsibility in most Anglo-American legal writing, in the following way. When a person is said to be not responsible for a particular act or crime, or when (as in the formulation of the M'Naghten Rules and s. 2 of the Homicide Act, 1957) he is said not to be responsible for his 'acts and omissions in doing' some action on a particular occasion, the reason for saying this is usually some mental abnormality or disorder. I have not succeeded in finding cases where a normal person, merely lacking some ordinary element of knowledge or intention on a particular occasion, is said for that reason not to be responsible for that particular action, even though he is for that reason not liable to punishment. But though there is this tendency in statements of liability-responsibility to confine the use of the expression 'responsible' and 'not responsible' to questions of mental abnormality or general incapacity, yet all the psychological conditions of liability are to be found discussed by legal writers under such headings as 'Criminal Responsibility' or 'Principles of Criminal Responsibility'. Accordingly I classify them here as criteria of responsibility. I do so with a clear conscience, since little is to be gained in clarity by a rigid division which the contemporary use of the expression *mens rea* often ignores.

The situation is, however, complicated by a further feature of English legal and non-legal usage. The phrase 'responsible for his actions' is, as I have observed, frequently used to refer to the capacity-responsibility of the normal person, and, so used, refers to one of the major criteria of liability-responsibility. It is so used in s. 2 of the Homicide Act 1957, which speaks of a person's mental 'responsibility' for his actions being *impaired,* and in the rubric to the section, which speaks of persons 'suffering from diminished responsibility'. In this sense the expression is the name or description of a psychological condition. But the expression is also used to signify liability-responsibility itself, that is, liability to punishment so far as such liability depends on psychological conditions, and is so used when the law is said to 'relieve insane persons of responsibility for their actions'. It was probably also so used in the form of verdict returned in cases of successful pleas of insanity under English law until this was altered by the Insanity Act 1964: the verdict was 'guilty but insane so as not to be responsible according to law for his actions'.

(ii) *Causal or other forms of connection with harm.* Questions of legal liability-responsibility are not limited in their scope to psychological conditions of either of the two sorts distinguished above. Such questions are also (though more frequently in the law of tort than in the criminal law) concerned with the issue whether some form of connection between a person's act and some harmful outcome is sufficient according to law to make him liable; so if a person is accused of murder the question whether he was or was not legally responsible for the death may be intended to raise the issue whether the death was too remote a consequence of his acts for them to count as its cause. If the law, as frequently in tort, is not that the defendant's action should have caused the harm, but that there be some other form of connection or relationship between the defendant and the harm, for example, that it should have been caused by some dangerous thing escaping from the defendant's land, this connection or relationship is a condition of civil responsibility for harm, and, where it holds, the defendant is said to be legally responsible for the harm. No doubt such questions of connection with harm are also frequently phrased in terms of liability.

(iii) *Relationship with the agent.* Normally in criminal law the minimum condition required for liability for punishment is that the person to be punished should himself have done what the law forbids, at least so far as outward conduct is concerned; even if liability is 'strict'; it is not enough to render him liable for punishment that someone else should have done it. This is often expressed in the terminology of responsibility (though here, too, 'liability' is frequently used instead of 're-

sponsibility') by saying that, generally, vicarious responsibility is not known to the criminal law. But there are exceptional cases; an innkeeper is liable to punishment if his servants, without his knowledge and against his orders, sell liquor on his premises after hours. In this case he is vicariously responsible for the sale, and of course, in the civil law of tort there are many situations in which a master or employer is liable to pay compensation for the torts of his servant or employee, and is said to be vicariously responsible.

It appears, therefore, that there are diverse types of criteria of legal liability-responsibility: The most prominent consist of certain mental elements, but there are also causal or other connections between a person and harm, or the presence of some relationship, such as that of master and servant, between different persons. It is natural to ask why these very diverse conditions are singled out as criteria of responsibility, and so are within the scope of questions about responsibility, as distinct from the wider question concerning liability for punishment. I think that the following somewhat Cartesian figure may explain this fact. If we conceive of a person as an embodied mind and will, we may draw a distinction between two questions concerning the conditions of liability and punishment. The first question is what general types of outer conduct *(actus reus)* or what sorts of harm are required for liability? The second question is how closely connected with such conduct or such harm must the embodied mind or will of an individual person be to render him liable to punishment? Or, as some would put it, to what extent must the embodied mind or will be the author of the conduct or the harm in order to render him liable? Is it enough that the person made the appropriate bodily movements? Or is it required that he did so when possessed of a certain capacity of control and with a certain knowledge or intention? Or that he caused the harm or stood in some other relationship to it, or to the actual doer of the deed? The legal rules, or parts of legal rules, that answer these various questions define the various forms of connection which are adequate for liability, and these constitute conditions of legal responsibility which form only a part of the total conditions of liability for punishment, which also include the definitions of the *actus reus* of the various crimes.

We may therefore summarize this long discussion of legal liability-responsibility by saying that, though in certain general contexts legal responsibility and legal liability have the same meaning, to say that a man is legally responsible for some act or harm is to state that his connection with the act or harm is sufficient according to law for liability. Because responsibility and liability are distinguishable in this way, it will make sense to say that because a person is legally responsible for some action he is liable to be punished for it.

LEGAL LIABILITY-RESPONSIBILITY AND MORAL BLAME

My previous account of legal liability-responsibility, in which I claimed that in one important sense to say that a person is legally responsible meant that he was legally liable for punishment or could be made to pay compensation, has been criticized on two scores. Since these criticisms apply equally to the above amended version of my original account, in which I distinguish the general issue of liability from the narrower issue of responsibility, I shall consider these criticisms here. The first criticism, made by Mr. A. W. B. Simpson,[3] insists on the strong connection between statements of legal responsibility and moral judgment, and claims that even lawyers tend to confine statements that a person is legally responsible for something to cases where he is considered morally blameworthy, and, where this is not so, tend to use the expression 'liability' rather than 'responsibility'. But, though moral blame and legal responsibility may be connected in some ways, it is surely not in this simple way. Against any such view not only is there the frequent use already mentioned of the expressions 'strict responsibility' and 'vicarious responsibility', which are obviously independent of moral blameworthiness, but there is the more important fact that we can, and frequently do, intelligibly debate the question whether a mentally disordered or very young person who has been held legally responsible for a crime is morally blameworthy. The coincidence of legal responsibility with moral blameworthiness may be a laudable ideal, but it is not a necessary truth nor even an accomplished fact.

The suggestion that the statement that a man is responsible generally means that he is blameworthy and not that he is liable to punishment is said to be supported by the fact that it is possible to cite, without redundancy, the fact that a person is responsible as a ground or reason for saying that he is liable to punishment. But, if the various kinds or senses of responsibility are distinguished, it is plain that there are many explanations of this last mentioned fact, which are quite independent of any essential connection between legal responsibility and moral blameworthiness. Thus cases where the statement that the man is responsible constitutes a reason for saying that he is liable to punishment may be cases of role-responsibility (the master is legally responsible for the safety of his ship, therefore he is liable to punishment if he loses it) or capacity-responsibility (he was responsible for his actions therefore he is liable to punishment for his crimes); or they may even be statements of liability-responsibility, since such statements refer to part only of the conditions of liability and may therefore be given, without redundancy, as a reason for liability to punishment. In any case this criticism may be turned against the suggestion that responsibility is to be equated with moral blameworthiness; for plainly the statement that someone is responsible may be given as part of the reason for saying that he is morally blameworthy.

LIABILITY RESPONSIBILITY FOR PARTICULAR ACTIONS

An independent objection is the following, made by Mr. George Pitcher.[4] The wide extension I have claimed for the notion of liability-responsibility permits us to say not only that a man is legally responsible in this sense for the consequences of his action, but also for his action or actions. According to Mr. Pitcher 'this is an improper way of talking', though common amongst philosophers. Mr. Pitcher is concerned primarily with moral, not legal, responsibility, but even in a moral context it is plain that there is a very well established use of the expression 'responsible for his actions' to refer to capacity-responsibility for which Mr. Pitcher makes no allowance. As far as the law is concerned, many examples may be cited from both sides of the Atlantic where a person may be said to be responsible for his actions, or for his act, or for his crime, or for his conduct. Mr. Pitcher gives, as a reason for saying that it is improper to speak of a man being responsible for his own actions, the fact that a man does not produce or cause his own actions. But this argument would prove far too much. It would rule out as improper not only the expression 'responsible for his actions', but also our saying that a man was responsible vicariously or otherwise for harmful outcomes which he had not caused, which is a perfectly well established legal usage.

None the less, there are elements of truth in Mr. Pitcher's objection. First, it seems to be the case that even where a man is said to be legally responsible for what he has done, it is rare to find this expressed by a phrase conjoining the verb of action with the expression 'responsible for'. Hence, 'he is legally responsible for killing her' is not usually found, whereas 'he is legally responsible for her death' is common, as are the expressions 'legally responsible for his act (in killing her)'; 'legally responsible for his crime'; or, as in the official formulation of the M'Naghten Rules, 'responsible for his actions or omissions in doing or being a party to the killing'. These common expressions in which a noun, not a verb, follows the phrase 'responsible for' are grammatically similar to statements of causal responsibility, and the tendency to use the same form no doubt shows how strongly the overtones of causal responsibility influence the terminology ordinarily used to make statements of liability-responsibility. There is, however, also in support of Mr. Pitcher's view, the point already cited that, even in legal writing, where a person is said to be responsible for his act or his conduct, the relevant mental element is usually the question of insanity or immaturity, so that the ground in such cases for the assertion that the person is responsible or is not responsible for his act is the presence of absence of 'responsibility for actions' in the sense of capacity-responsibility, and not merely the presence or absence of knowledge or intention in relation to the particular act.

MORAL LIABILITY-RESPONSIBILITY

How far can the account given above of legal liability-responsibility be applied *mutatis mutandis* to moral responsibility? The *mutanda* seem to be the following: 'deserving blame' or 'blameworthy' will have to be substituted for 'liable to punishment', and 'morally bound to make amends or pay compensation' for 'liable to be made to pay compensation'. Then the moral counterpart to the account given of legal liability-responsibility would be the following: To say that a person is morally responsible for something he has done or for some harmful outcome of his own or others' conduct, is to say that he is morally blameworthy, or morally obliged to make amends for the harm, so far as this depends on certain conditions. These conditions relate to the character or extent of a man's control over his own conduct, or to the causal or other connection between his action and harmful occurrences, or to his relationship with the person who actually did the harm.

In general, such an account of the meaning of 'morally responsible' seems correct, and the striking differences between legal and moral responsibility are due to substantive differences between the content of legal and moral rules and principles rather than to any variation in meaning of responsibility when conjoined with the word 'moral' rather than 'legal'. Thus, both in the legal and the moral case, the criteria of responsibility seem to be restricted to the psychological elements involved in the control of conduct, to causal or other connections between acts and harm, and to the relationships with the actual doer of misdeeds. The interesting differences between legal and moral responsibility arise from the differences in the particular criteria falling under these general heads. Thus a system of criminal law may make responsibility strict, or even absolute, not even exempting very young children or the grossly insane from punishment; or it may vicariously punish one man for what another has done, even though the former had no control of the latter; or it may punish an individual or make him compensate another for harm which he neither intended nor could have foreseen as likely to arise from his conduct. We may condemn such a legal system which extends strict or vicarious responsibility in these ways as barbarous or unjust, but there are no conceptual barriers to be overcome in speaking of such a system as a legal system, though it is certainly arguable that we should not speak of 'punishment' where liability is vicarious or strict. In the moral case, however, greater conceptual barriers exist: The hypothesis that we might hold individuals morally blameworthy for doing things which they could not have avoided doing, or for things done by others over whom they had no control, conflicts with too many of the central features of the idea of morality to be treated merely as speculation about a rare or inferior kind of moral system. It may be an exaggeration to say that there could not logically be such a morality or that blame administered according to principles of strict or vicarious responsibility, even in a minority of cases, could not logically be moral blame; none the less, admission of such a system as a morality would require a profound modification in our present concept of morality, and there is no similar requirement in the case of law.

Some of the most familiar contexts in which the expression 'responsibility' appears confirm these general parallels between legal and moral liability-responsibility. Thus in the famous question 'Is moral responsibility compatible with determinism?' the expression 'moral responsibility' is apt just because the bogey raised by determinism specifically relates to the usual criteria of responsibility; for it opens the question whether, if 'determinism' were true, the capacities of human beings to control their conduct would still exist or could be regarded as adequate to justify moral blame.

In less abstract or philosophical contexts, where there is a present question of blaming someone for some particular act, the assertion or denial that a person is morally responsible for his actions is common. But this expression is as ambiguous in the moral as in the legal case: It is most frequently used to refer to what I have termed 'capacity-responsibility', which is the most important criterion of moral liability-responsibility; but in some contexts it may also refer to moral liability-responsibility itself. Perhaps the most frequent use in moral contexts of the expression 'responsible for' is in cases where persons are said to be morally responsible for the outcomes or results of morally wrong conduct, although Mr. Pitcher's claim that men are never said in ordinary usage to be responsible for their actions is, as I have attempted to demonstrate above with counter-examples, an exaggerated claim.

CAPACITY-RESPONSIBILITY

In most contexts, as I have already stressed, the expression 'he is responsible for his actions' is used to assert that a person has certain normal capacities. These constitute the most important criteria of moral liability-responsibility, though it is characteristic of most legal systems that they have given only a partial or tardy recognition to all these capacities as general criteria of legal responsibility. The capacities in question are those of understanding, reasoning, and control of conduct: the ability to understand what conduct legal rules or morality require, to deliberate and reach decisions concerning these requirements, and to conform to decisions when made. Because 'responsible for his actions' in this sense refers not to a legal status but to certain complex psychological characteristics of persons, a person's responsibility for his actions may intelligibly be said to be 'diminished' or 'impaired' as well as altogether absent, and persons may be said to be 'suffering from diminished responsibility' much as a wounded man may be said to be suffering from a diminished capacity to control the movements of his limbs.

No doubt the most frequent occasions for asserting or denying that a person is 'responsible for his actions' are cases where questions of blame or punishment for particular actions are in issue. But, as with other expressions used to denote

criteria of responsibility, this one also may be used where no particular question of blame or punishment is in issue, and it is then used simply to describe a person's psychological condition. Hence it may be said purely by way of description of some harmless inmate of a mental institution, even though there is no present question of his misconduct, that he is a person who is not responsible for his actions. No doubt if there were no social practice of blaming and punishing people for their misdeeds, and excusing them from punishment because they lack the normal capacities of understanding and control, we should lack this shorthand description for describing their condition which we now derive from these social practices. In that case we should have to describe the condition of the inmate directly, by saying that he could not understand what people told him to do, or could not reason about it, or come to, or adhere to any decisions about his conduct.

Legal systems left to themselves may be very niggardly in their admission of the relevance of liability to legal punishment of the several capacities, possession of which are necessary to render a man morally responsible for his actions. So much is evident from the history sketched in the preceding chapter of the painfully slow emancipation of English criminal law from the narrow, cognitive criteria of responsibility formulated in the M'Naghten Rules. Though some Continental legal systems have been willing to confront squarely the question whether the accused 'lacked the ability to recognize the wrongness of his conduct and to act in accordance with that recognition.'[5] such an issue, if taken seriously, raises formidable difficulties of proof, especially before juries. For this reason I think that, instead of a close determination of such questions of capacity, the apparently coarser-grained technique of exempting persons from liability to punishment if they fall into certain recognized categories of mental disorder is likely to be increasingly used. Such exemption by general category is a technique long known to English law; for in the case of very young children it has made no attempt to determine, as a condition of liability, the question whether on account of their immaturity they could have understood what the law required and could have conformed to its requirements, or whether their responsibility on account of their immaturity was 'substantially impaired', but exempts them from liability for punishment if under a specified age. It seems likely that exemption by medical category rather than by individualized findings of absent or diminished capacity will be found more likely to lead in practice to satisfactory results, in spite of the difficulties pointed out in the last essay in the discussion of s. 60 of the Mental Health Act, 1959.

Though a legal system may fail to incorporate in its rules any psychological criteria of responsibility, and so may apply its sanction to those who are not morally blameworthy, it is none the less dependent for its efficacy on the possession by a sufficient number of those whose conduct it seeks to control of the capacities of understanding and control of conduct which constitute capacity-responsibility. For if a large proportion of those concerned could not understand what the law required them to do or could not form and keep a decision to obey, no legal system could come into existence or continue to exist. The general possession of such capacities is therefore a condition of the *efficacy* of law, even though it is not made a condition of liability to legal sanctions. The same condition of efficacy attaches to all attempts to regulate or control human conduct by forms of *communication:* such as orders, commands, the invocation of moral or other rules or principles, arguments, and advice.

'The notion of prevention through the medium of the mind assumes mental ability adequate to restraint'. This was clearly seen by Bentham and by Austin, who perhaps influenced the seventh report of the Criminal Law Commissioners of 1833 containing this sentence. But they overstressed the point; for they wrongly assumed that this condition of efficacy must also be incorporated in legal rules as a condition of liability. This mistaken assumption is to be found not only in the explanation of the doctrine of *mens rea* given in Bentham's and Austin's works, but is explicit in the Commissioners' statement preceding the sentence quoted above that 'the object of penal law being the prevention of wrong, the principle does not extend to mere involuntary acts or even to harmful consequences the result of inevitable accident'. The case of morality is however different in precisely this respect: the possession by those to whom its injunctions are addressed of 'mental ability adequate to restraint' (capacity-responsibility) has there a double status and importance. It is not only a condition of the efficacy of morality; but a system or practice which did not regard the possession of these capacities as a necessary condition of liability, and so treated blame as appropriate even in the case of those who lacked them, would not, as morality is at present understood, be a morality.

NOTES

1. The author's discussion of this appears at pp. 264–65 of *Punishment and Responsibility* [editors].

2. *A History of The Criminal Law,* Vol. II, p. 183.

3. In a review of 'Changing Conceptions & Responsibility', in *Crim. L. R.* (1966) 124.

4. In 'Hart on Action and Responsibility', *The Philosophical Review* (1960), p. 266.

5. German Criminal Code, Art. 51.

H. L. A. HART
and A. M. HONORÉ
Causation and Responsibility*

I. RESPONSIBILITY IN LAW AND MORALS

We have so far traced the outline of a variety of causal concepts the diversity of which is to be seen in such familiar examples of the use of causal language as the following: "The explosion of gas caused the building to collapse," "He made him hand over his money by threatening to shoot," "The consequence of leaving the car unlocked was that it was stolen," "The strike was the cause of the drop in profits."

The main structure of these different forms of causal connection is plain enough, and there are many situations constantly recurring in ordinary life to which they have a clear application; yet it is also true that like many other fundamental notions these have aspects which are vague or indeterminate; they involve the weighing of matters of degree, or the plausibility of hypothetical speculations, for which no exact criteria can be laid down. Hence their application, outside the safe area of simple examples, calls for judgment and is something over which judgments often differ. Even the type of case which is most familiar, and most nearly approximates to Mill's model for "cause and effect," where causal connection between a physical event and some earlier initiating event or human action is traced through a series of physical events, involves an implicit judgment on such imprecise issues as the *normal* condition of the thing concerned and the *abnormality* of what is identified as the cause. Very often, in particular where an omission to take common precautions is asserted to be the cause of some disaster, a speculation as to what *would have* happened had the precaution been taken is involved. Though arguments one way or another over such hypothetical issues may certainly be rational and have more or less "weight," there is a sense in which they cannot be conclusive. When such areas of dispute are reached, the decision whether to describe the facts of a case in the terms of some given form of causal connection will be influenced very much by factors connected with the context and purpose of making the causal statement.

Hitherto we have discussed only one principal purpose for which causal language is used: i.e. when an explanation is sought or provided of some puzzling or unusual occurrence. But as well as this explanatory context, in which we are concerned with what *has* happened, there are many others. Our deliberations about our own conduct often take the form of an inquiry as to the future consequences of alternative actions; here causal connections are *ex hypothesi* bounded by the horizon of the foreseeable. But even if we confine ourselves to causal statements about the past there are still different contexts and purposes to be discriminated. Thus it would be wrong to think of the historian as using causal notions only when he is explaining. The movement of his thought is not always from the later problematic event to something earlier which explains it and in using causal language he is not always engaged in diagnosis. His thought very often takes the contrary direction; for in addition to providing explanations (answers to the question "why?") he is also concerned to trace the outcome, the results, or the consequences of the human actions and omissions which are his usual starting-points, though he may also work out the "effects" of natural events. So he will discuss the consequences of a king's policy or the effects of the Black Death. This is so because the narrative of history is scarcely ever a narrative of brute sequence, but is an account of the roles played by certain factors and especially by human agents. History is written to satisfy not only the need for explanation, but also the desire to identify and assess contributions made by historical figures to changes of importance; to triumphs and disasters, and to human happiness or suffering. This assessment involves tracing "consequences," "effects," or "results," and these are more frequently referred to than "causes" which has a primarily diagnostic or explanatory ring. In one sense of "responsibility" the historian determines the responsibility of human beings for certain types of change; and sometimes he does this with an eye to praising or blaming or passing other forms of moral judgment. But this need not be so; the historian, though concerned to trace the consequences of human action, need not be a moralist.

In the moral judgments of ordinary life, we have occasion to blame people because they have caused harm to others, and also, if less frequently, to insist that morally they are bound to compensate those to whom they have caused harm. These are the moral analogues of more precise legal conceptions; for, in all legal systems, liability to be punished or to make compensation frequently depends on whether actions (or omissions) have caused harm. Moral blame is not of course confined to such cases of causing harm. We blame a man who cheats or lies or breaks promises, even if no one has suffered in the particular case: this has its legal counterpart in the punishment of abortive attempts to commit crimes, and of offences constituted by the unlawful possession of certain kinds of weapons, drugs, or materials, for example, for counterfeiting currency. When the occurrence of harm is an essential part of the ground for blame the connection of the person blamed with the harm may take any of the forms of causal connection we have examined. His action may have initiated a series of physical events dependent on each other and culminating in injury to persons or property, as in wounding and killing. These simple forms are the paradigms for the lawyer's talk of harm "directly" caused. But we blame people also for harm which arises from or is the consequence of their neglect of common precautions; we do this even if harm would not have come about without the intervention of another human being deliberately exploiting the opportunities provided by neglect. The main legal analogue here is liability for "negligence." The wish of many lawyers to talk in this branch of the law of harm being "within the risk of" rather than "caused by" the negligent conduct manifests appreciation of the fact that a different form of relationship is involved in saying that harm is the consequence, on the one hand, of an explosion and, on the other, of a failure to lock the door by which a thief has entered. Again, we blame people for the harm which we say is the consequence of their influence over others, either exerted by non-rational means or in one of the ways we have designated "interpersonal transactions." To such grounds for responsibility there correspond many important legal conceptions: the instigation of crimes ("commanding" or "procuring") constitutes an important ground of criminal responsibility and the concepts of enticement and of inducement (by threats or misrepresentation) are an element in many civil wrongs as well as in criminal offences.

The law, however, especially in matters of compensation, goes far beyond these causal grounds for responsibility in such doctrines as the vicarious responsibility of a master for his servant's civil wrongs and that of the responsibility of an occupier of property for injuries suffered by passers-by from defects of which the occupier had no knowledge and which he had no opportunity to repair. There is a recognition, perhaps diminishing, of this non-causal ground of responsibility outside the law; responsibility is sometimes admitted by one person or group of persons, even if no precaution has been neglected by them, for harm done by persons related to them in a special way, either by family ties or as members of the same social or political association. Responsibility may be simply "placed" by moral opinion on one person for what others do. The simplest case of such vicarious moral responsibility is that of a parent for damage done by a child; its more complex (and more debatable) form is the moral responsibility of one generation of a nation to make compensation for their predecessors' wrong, such as the Germans admitted in payment of compensation to Israel.

At this point it is necessary to issue a caveat about the meaning of the expression "responsible" if only to avoid prejudicing a question about the character of *legal* determinations of causal connection. . . . Usually in discussion of the law and occasionally in morals, to say that someone is responsible for some harm means that in accordance with legal rules or moral principles it is at least permissible, if not mandatory, to blame or punish or exact compensation from him. In this use[1] the expression "responsible for" does not refer to a factual connection between the person held responsible and the harm but simply to his liability under the rules to be blamed, punished, or made to pay. The expressions "answerable for" or "liable for" are practically synonymous with "responsible for" in *this* use, in which there is no implication that the person held responsible actually *did* or *caused* the harm. In this sense a master is (in English law) responsible for the damage done by his servants acting within the scope of their authority and a parent (in French and German law) for that done by his children; it is in this sense that a guarantor or surety is responsible for the debts or the good behaviour of other persons and an insurer for losses sustained by the insured. Very often, however, especially in discussion of morals, to say that someone is responsible for some harm is to assert (*inter alia*) that he *did* the harm or *caused* it, though such a statement is perhaps rarely confined to this for it usually also carries with it the implication that it is at least permissible to blame or punish him. This double use of the expression no doubt arises from the important fact that doing or causing harm constitutes not only the most usual but the primary type of ground for holding persons responsible in the first sense. We still speak of inanimate or natural causes such as storms, floods, germs, or the failure of electricity supply as "responsible for" disasters; this mode of expression, now taken only to mean that they caused the disasters, no doubt orginated in the belief that all that happens is the work of spirits when it is not that of men. Its survival in the modern world is perhaps some testimony to the primacy of causal connection as an element in responsibility and to the intimate connection between the two notions.

We shall consider later an apparent paradox which interprets in a different way the relationship between cause and responsibility. Much modern thought on causation in the law rests on the contention that the statement that someone has caused harm either means no more than that the harm would not have happened without ("but for") his action or where (as in normal legal usage and in all ordinary speech), it apparently means more than this, it is a disguised way of asserting the "normative" judgment that he is responsible in the first sense, i.e. that it is proper

or just to blame or punish him or make him pay. On this view to say that a person caused harm is not really, though ostensibly it is, to give a *ground* or *reason* for holding him responsible in the first sense; for we are only in a position to say that he has caused harm when we have decided that he is responsible. Pending consideration of the theories of legal causation which exploit this point of view we shall use the expression "responsible for" only in the first of the two ways explained, i.e. without any implication as to the type of factual connection between the person held responsible and the harm; and we shall provisionally, though without prejudicing the issue, treat statements that a person caused harm as one sort of non-tautologous ground or reason for saying that he is responsible in this sense.

If we may provisionally take what in ordinary life we say and do at its face value, it seems that there coexist in ordinary thought, apart from the law though mirrored in it, several different types of connection between a person's action and eventual harm which render him responsible for it; and in both law and morals the various forms of causal connection between act or omission and harm are the most obvious and least disputable reasons for holding anyone responsible. Yet, in order to understand the extent to which the causal notions of ordinary thought are used in the law, we must bear in mind the many factors which must differentiate moral from legal responsibility in spite of their partial correspondence. The law is not only not bound to follow the moral patterns of attribution of responsibility but, even when it does, it must take into account, in a way which the private moral judgment need not and does not, the general social consequences which are attached to its judgments of responsibility; for they are of a gravity quite different from those attached to moral censure. The use of the legal sanctions of imprisonment, or enforced monetary compensation against individuals, has such formidable repercussions on the general life of society that the fact that individuals have a type of connection with harm which is adequate for moral censure or claims for compensation is only *one* of the factors which the law must consider, in defining the kinds of connection between actions and harm for which it will hold individuals legally responsible. Always to follow the private moral judgment here would be far too expensive for the law: not only in the crude sense that it would entail a vast machinery of courts and officials, but in the more important sense that it would inhibit or discourage too many other valuable activities of society. To limit the *types* of harm which the law will recognize is not enough; even if the types of harm are limited it would still be too much for any society to punish or exact compensation from individuals whenever their connection with harm of such types would justify moral censure. Conversely, social needs may require that compensation should be paid and even (though less obviously) that punishment be inflicted where no such connection between the person held responsible and the harm exists.

So causing harm of a legally recognized sort or being connected with such harm in any of the ways that justify moral blame, though vitally important and perhaps basic in a legal system, is not and should not be either always necessary or always sufficient for legal responsibility. All legal systems in response either to tradition or to social needs both extend responsibility and cut it off in ways which diverge from the simpler principles of moral blame. In England a man is not guilty of murder if the victim of his attack does not die within a year and day. In New York a person who negligently starts a fire is liable to pay only for the first of several houses which it destroys.[2] These limitations imposed by legal policy are *prima facie* distinguishable from limitations due to the frequent requirement of legal rules that responsibility be limited to harm caused by wrongdoing. Yet a whole school of thought maintains that this distinction does not exist or is not worth drawing.

Apart from this, morality can properly leave certain things vague into which a legal system must attempt to import some degree of precision. Outside the law nothing requires us, when we find the case too complex or too strange, to say whether any and, if so, which of the morally significant types of connection between a person's action and harm exists; we can simply say the case is too difficult for us to pass judgment, at least where moral condemnation of others is concerned. No doubt we evade less easily our questions about our own connection with harm, and the great novelists have often described, sometimes in language very like the lawyers, how the conscience may be still tortured by uncertainties as to the *character* of a part in the production of harm, even when all the facts are known.[3] The fact that there is no precise system of punishments or rewards for common sense to administer, and so there are no "forms of ac-

tion" or "pleadings" to define precise heads of responsibility for harm, means that the principles which guide common-sense attributions of responsibility give precise answers only in relatively simple types of case.

II. TRACING CONSEQUENCES

"To consequences no limit can be set": "Every event which would not have happened if an earlier event had not happened is the consequence of that earlier event." These two propositions are not equivalent in meaning and are not equally or in the same way at variance with ordinary thought. They have, however, both been urged sometimes in the same breath by the legal theorist[4] and the philosopher: they are indeed sometimes said by lawyers to be "the philosophical doctrine" of causation. It is perhaps not difficult even for the layman to accept the first proposition as a truth about certain physical events; an explosion may cause a flash of light which will be propagated as far as the outer nebulae; its effects or consequences continue indefinitely. It is, however, a different matter to accept the view that whenever a man is murdered with a gun his death was the consequence of (still less an "effect" of or "caused by") the manufacture of the bullet. The first tells a perhaps unfamiliar tale about unfamiliar events; the second introduces an unfamiliar, though, of course, a possible way of speaking about familiar events. It is not that this unrestricted use of "consequence" is unintelligible or never found; it is indeed used to refer to bizarre or fortuitous connections or coincidences: but the point is that the various causal notions employed for the purposes of explanation, attribution of responsibility, or the assessment of contributions to the course of history carry with them implicit limits which are similar in these different employments.

It is, then, the second proposition, defining consequence in terms of "necessary condition," with which theorists are really concerned. This proposition is the corollary of the view that, if we look into the past of any given event, there is an infinite number of events, each of which is a necessary condition of the given event and so, as much as any other, is its cause. This is the "cone"[5] of causation, so called because, since any event has a number of simultaneous conditions, the series fans out as we go back in time. The justification, indeed only partial, for calling this "the philosophical doctrine" of causation is that it resembles Mill's doctrine that "we have no right to give the name of cause to one of the conditions exclusive of the others of them." It differs from Mill's view in taking the essence of causation to be "necessary condition" and not "the sum total"[6] of the sufficient conditions of an event.

Legal theorists have developed this account of cause and consequence to show what is "factual," "objective," or "scientific" in these notions: this they call "cause in fact" and it is usually stressed as a preliminary to the doctrine that any more restricted application of these terms in the law represents nothing in the facts or in the meaning of causation, but expresses fluctuating legal policy or sentiments of what is just or convenient. Moral philosophers have insisted in somewhat similar terms that the consequences of human action are "infinite": this they have urged as an objection against the Utilitarian doctrine that the rightness of a morally right action depends on whether its consequences are better than those of any alternative action in the circumstances. "We should have to trace as far as possible the consequences not only for the persons affected directly but also for those indirectly affected and to these no limit can be set."[7] Hence, so the argument runs, we cannot either inductively establish the Utilitarian doctrine that right acts are "optimific" or use it in particular cases to discover what is right. Yet, however vulnerable at other points Utilitarianism may be as an account of moral judgment, this objection seems to rest on a mistake as to the sense of "consequence." The Utilitarian assertion that the rightness of an action depends on its consequences is not the same as the assertion that it depends on all those later occurrences which would not have happened had the action not been done, to which indeed "no limit can be set." It is important to see that the issue here is not the linguistic one whether the word "consequence" would be understood if used in this way. The point is that, though we could, we do not think in this way in tracing connections between human actions and events. Instead, whenever we are concerned with such connections, whether for the purpose of explaining a puzzling occurrence, assessing responsibility, or giving an intelligible historical narrative, we employ a set of concepts restricting in various ways what counts as a consequence. These restrictions colour *all* our thinking in causal terms; when we find them in the law we are not finding something invented

by or peculiar to the law, though of course it is for the law to say when and how far it will use them and, where they are vague, to supplement them.

No short account can be given of the limits thus placed on "consequences" because these limits vary, intelligibly, with the variety of causal connection asserted. Thus we may be tempted by the generalization that consequences must always be something intended or forseen or at least foreseeable with ordinary care: but counterexamples spring up from many types of context where causal statements are made. If smoking is shown to cause lung cancer this discovery will permit us to describe past as well as future cases of cancer as the effect or consequence of smoking even though no one foresaw or had reasonable grounds to suspect this in the past. What is common and commonly appreciated and hence foreseeable certainly controls the scope of consequences in certain varieties of causal statement but not in all. Again the voluntary intervention of a second person very often constitutes the limit. If a guest sits down at a table laid with knife and fork and plunges the knife into his hostess's breast, her death is not in any context other than a contrived one[8] thought of as caused by, or the effect or result of the waiter's action in laying the table; nor would it be linked with this action as its consequence for any of the purposes, explanatory or attributive, for which we employ causal notions. Yet as we have seen there are many other types of case where a voluntary action or the harm it does are naturally treated to the consequence of to some prior neglect of precaution. Finally, we may think that a simple answer is already supplied by Hume and Mill's doctrine that causal connection rests on general laws asserting regular connection; yet, even in the type of case to which this important doctrine applies, reference to it alone will not solve our problem. For we often trace a causal connection between an antecedent and a consequent which themselves very rarely go together: we do this when the case can be broken down into intermediate stages, which themselves exemplify different generalizations, as when we find that the fall of a tile was the cause of someone's death, rare though this be. Here our problem reappears in the form of the question: When can generalizations be combined in this way?

We shall examine first the central type of case where the problem is of this last-mentioned form. Here the gist of the causal connection lies in the general connection with each other of the successive stages; and is not dependent on the special notions of one person providing another with reasons or exceptional opportunities for actions. This form of causal connection may exist between actions and events, and between purely physical events, and it is in such cases that the words "cause" and "causing" used of the antecedent action or event have their most obvious application. It is convenient to refer to cases of the first type where the consequence is harm as cases of "causing harm," and to refer to cases where harm is the consequence of one person providing another with reasons or opportunities for doing harm as cases of "inducing" or "occasioning" harmful acts.[9] In cases of the first type a voluntary act, or a conjunction of events amounting to a coincidence, operates as a limit in the sense that events subsequent to these are not attributed to the antecedent action or event as its consequence even though they would not have happened without it. Often such a limiting action or coincidence is thought of and described as "intervening": and lawyers speak of them as "superseding" or "extraneous" causes "breaking the chain of causation." To see what these metaphors rest on (and in part obscure) and how such factors operate as a limit we shall consider the detail of three simple cases.

(i) A forest fire breaks out, and later investigation shows that shortly before the outbreak A had flung away a lighted cigarette into the bracken at the edge of the forest, the bracken caught fire, a light breeze got up, and fanned the flames in the direction of the forest. If, on discovering these facts, we hesitate before saying that A's action caused the forest fire this would be to consider the alternative hypothesis that in spite of appearances the fire only succeeded A's action in point of time, that the bracken flickered out harmlessly and the forest fire was caused by something else. To dispose of this it may be necessary to examine in further detail the process of events between the ignition of the bracken and the outbreak of fire in the forest and to show that these exemplified certain types of continuous change. If this is shown, there is no longer any room for doubt: A's action *was* the cause of the fire, whether he intended it or not. This seems and is the simplest of cases. Yet it is important to notice that even in applying our general knowledge to a case as simple as this, indeed in regarding it as simple, we make an implicit use of a distinction between types of factor which constitute a limit in tracing consequences and those which we regard as mere circumstances "through" which we trace them. For the breeze which sprang up after A dropped the cigarette, and without which the fire would not have spread to the forest, was not only subsequent to his action but entirely independent of it: it was, however, a common recurrent feature of the environment, and, as such, it is thought of not as an "intervening" force but as merely part of the circumstances in which the cause "operates." The decision so to regard it is implicitly taken when we combine our knowledge of the successive stages of the process and assert the connection.

It is easy here to be misled by the natural metaphor of a causal "chain," which may lead us to think that the causal process consists of a series of single events each of which is dependent upon (would not have occurred without) its predecessor in the "chain" and so is dependent upon the initiating action or event. In truth in any causal process we have at each phase not single events but complex sets of conditions, and among these conditions are some which are not only subsequent to, but independent of the initiating action or event. Some of these independent conditions, such as the evening breeze in the example chosen, we classify as mere conditions in or on which the cause operates; others we speak of as "interventions" or "causes." To decide how such independent elements shall be classified is also to decide how we shall combine our knowledge of the different general connections which the successive stages exemplify, and it is important to see that nothing *in* this knowledge itself can resolve this point. We may have to go to science for the relevant general knowledge before we can assert with proper confidence that A's action did cause the fire, but science, though it tells us that an air current was required, is silent on the difference between a current in the form of an evening breeze and one produced by someone who deliberately fanned the flames as they were flickering out in the bracken. Yet an air current in this deliberately induced form is not a "condition" or "mere circumstance" through which we can trace the consequence; its presence would force us to revise the assertion that A caused the fire. Conversely if science helped us to identify as a necessary factor in producing the fire some condition or element of which we had previously been totally ignorant, e.g. the persistence of oxygen, this would leave our original judgment undisturbed if this factor were a common or pervasive feature of the environment or of the thing in question. There is thus indeed an important sense in which it is true that the distinction between cause and conditions is not a "scientific" one. It is not determined by laws or generalizations concerning connections between events.

When we have assembled all our knowledge of the factors involved in the fire, the residual question which we then confront (the attributive question) may be typified as follows: Here is *A*'s action, here is the fire: can the fire be attributed to *A*'s action as its consequence given that there is also this third factor (the breeze or *B*'s intervention) without which the fire would not have happened? It is plain that, both in raising questions of this kind and in answering them, ordinary thought is powerfully influenced by the analogy between the straightforward cases of causal attribution (where the elements required for the production of harm in addition to the initiating action are all "normal" conditions) and even simpler cases of responsibility which we do not ordinarily describe in causal language at all but by the simple transitive verbs of action. These are the cases of the direct manipulation of objects involving changes in them or their position: cases where we say "He pushed it," "He broke it," "He bent it." The cases which we do confidently describe in causal language ("The fire was caused by his carelessness," "He caused a fire") are cases where no other human action or abnormal occurrence is required for the production of the effect, but only normal conditions. Such cases appear as mere long-range or less direct versions or extensions of the most obvious and fundamental case of all for the attribution of responsibility: the case where we can simply say "He did it." Conversely in attaching importance to thus causing harm as a distinct ground of responsibility and in taking certain kinds of factor (whether human interventions or abnormal occurrences), without which the initiating action would not have led to harm, to preclude the description of the case in simple causal terms, common sense is affected by the fact that here, because of the manner in which the harm eventuates, the outcome cannot be represented as a mere extension of the initiating action; the analogy with the fundamental case for responsibility ("He did it") has broken down.

When we understand the power exerted over our ordinary thought by the conception that causing harm is a mere extension of the primary case of doing harm, the interrelated metaphors which seem natural to lawyers and laymen, in describing various aspects of causal connection, fall into place and we can discuss their factual basis. The persistent notion that some kinds of event required in addition to the initiating action for the production of harm "break the chain of causation" is intelligible, if we remember that though such events actually *complete* the *explanation* of the harm (and so *make* rather than *break* the causal explanation) they do, unlike mere normal conditions, break the *analogy* with cases of simple actions. The same analogy accounts for the description of these factors as "new actions" (*novus actus*) or "new causes," "superseding," "extraneous," "intervening forces": and for the description of the initiating action when "the chain of causation" is broken as "no longer operative," "having worn out," *functus officio.*[10] So too when the "chain" is held not to be "broken" the initiating action is said to be still "potent,"[11] "continuing," "contributing," "operative," and the mere conditions held insufficient to break the chain are "part of the background,"[12] "circumstances in which the cause operates,"[13] "the stage set," "part of the history."

(ii) *A* throws a lighted cigarette into the bracken which catches fire. Just as the flames are about to flicker out, *B,* who is not acting in concert with *A,* deliberately pours petrol on them. The fire spreads and burns down the forest. *A*'s action, whether or not he intended the forest fire, was not the cause of the fire: *B*'s was.

The voluntary intervention of a second human agent, as in this case, is a paradigm among those factors which preclude the assimilation in causal judgments of the first agent's connection with the eventual harm to the case of simple direct manipulation. Such an intervention displaces the prior action's title to be called the cause and, in the persistent metaphors found in the law, it "reduces" the earlier action and its immediate effects to the level of "mere circumstances" or "part of the history." *B* in this case was not an "instrument" through which *A* worked or a victim of the circumstances *A* has created. He has, on the contrary, freely exploited the circumstances and brought about the fire without the co-operation of any further agent or any chance coincidence. Compared with this the claim of *A*'s action to be ranked the cause of the fire fails. That this and not the moral appraisal of the two actions is the point of comparison seems clear. If *A* and *B* both intended to set the forest on fire, and this destruction is accepted as something wrong or wicked, their moral wickedness, judged by the criterion of intention, is the same. Yet the causal judgment differentiates between them. If their moral guilt is judged by the outcome, this judgment though it would differentiate between them cannot be the source of the causal judgment; for it presupposes it. The difference just is that *B* has caused the harm and *A* has not. Again, if we appraise these actions as good or bad from different points of view, this leaves the causal judgments unchanged. *A* may be a soldier of one side anxious to burn down the enemy's hideout: *B* may be an enemy soldier who has decided that his side is too iniquitous to defend. Whatever is the moral judgment passed on these actions by different speakers it would remain true that *A* had not caused the fire and *B* had.

There are, as we have said, situations in which a voluntary action would not be thought of as an intervention precluding causal connection in this way. These are the cases discussed further below where an opportunity commonly exploited for harmful actions is negligently provided, or one person intentionally provides another with the means, the opportunity, or a certain type of reason for wrongdoing. Except in such cases a voluntary intervention is a limit past which consequences are not traced. By contrast, actions which in any of a variety of different ways are less than fully voluntary are assimilated to the means by which or the circumstances in which the earlier action brings about the consequences. Such actions are not the outcome of an informed choice made without pressure from others, and the different ways in which human action may fall short in this respect range from defective muscular control, through lack of consciousness or knowledge, to the vaguer notions of duress and of predicaments, created by the first agent for the second, in which there is no "fair" choice.

In considering examples of such actions and their bearing on causal judgments there are three dangers to avoid. It would be folly to think that in tracing connections through such actions instead of regarding them, like voluntary interventions, as a limit, ordinary thought has clearly separated out their non-voluntary aspect from others by which they are often accompanied. Thus even in the crude case where *A* lets off a gun (intentionally or not) and startles *B,* so that he makes an involuntary movement of his arm which breaks a glass, the commonness of such a reaction as much as its compulsive character may influence the judgment that *A*'s action was the cause of the damage.

Secondly we must not impute to ordinary thought all the fine discriminations that could be made and in fact are to be found in a legal system, or an equal willingness to supply answers to complex questions in causal terms. Where there is no precise system of punishment, compensation or reward to administer, ordinary men will not often have faced such questions as whether the injuries suffered by a motorist who collides with another in swerving to avoid a child are consequences attributable to the neglect of the child's parents in allowing it to wander on to the road. Such questions courts have to answer and in such cases common judgments provide only a general, though still an important indication of what are the relevant factors.

Thirdly, though very frequently non-voluntary actions are assimilated to mere conditions or means by which the first agent brings about the consequences, the assimilation is never quite complete. This is manifested by the general avoidance of many causal locutions which are appropriate when the consequences are traced (as in the first case) through purely physical events. Thus even in the case in which the second agent's role is hardly an "action" at all, e.g. where *A* hits *B,* who staggers against a glass window and breaks it, we should say that *A*'s blow made *B* stagger and break the glass, rather than that *A*'s blow caused the glass to break, though in any explanatory or attributive context the case would be *summarized* by saying that *A*'s action was the cause of the *damage.*

In the last two cases where *B*'s movements are involuntary in the sense that they are not part of any action which he chose or intended to do, their connection with *A*'s action would be described by saying that *A*'s blow *made B* stagger or *caused* him to stagger or that the noise of *A*'s shot *made* him jump. This would be true, whether *A* intended or expected *B* to react in this way or not, and the naturalness of treating *A*'s action as the cause of the ultimate damage is due to the causal character of this part of the process involving *B*'s action. The same is, however, true where *B*'s actions are not involuntary movements but *A* is considered to have made or caused *B* to do them by less crude means. This is the case if, for example, *A* uses threats or exploits his authority over *B* to make *B* do something, e.g. knock down a door. At least where

A's threats are serious harm, or *B*'s act was un-questionably within *A*'s authority to order, he too has made or forced or (in formal quasi-legal parlance) "caused" *B* to act.

Outside the area of such cases, where *B*'s will would be said either not to be involved at all, or to be overborne by *A*, are cases where *A*'s act creates a predicament for *B* *narrowing* the area of choice so that he has either to inflict some harm on himself or others, or sacrifice some important interest or duty. Such cases resemble coercion in that *A* narrows the area of *B*'s choice but differ from it in that this predicament need not be intentionally created. *A* sets a house on fire (intentionally or unintentionally): *B* to save himself has to jump from a height involving certain injury, or to save a child rushes in and is seriously burned. Here, of course, *B*'s movements are not involuntary; the "necessity" of his action is here of a different order. His action is the outcome of a choice between two evils forced on him by *A*'s action. In such cases, when *B*'s injuries are thought of as the consequence of the fire, the implicit judgment is made that his action was the lesser of two evils and in this sense a "reasonable" one which he was obliged to make to avoid the greater evil. This is often paradoxically, though understandably, described by saying that here the agent "had no choice" but to do what he did. Such judgments involve a comparison of the importance of the respective interests sacrificed and preserved, and the final assertion that *A*'s action was the cause of the injuries rests on evaluations about which men may differ.

Finally, the ground for treating some harm which would not have occurred without *B*'s action as the consequence of *A*'s action may be that *B* acted in ignorance of or under a mistake as to some feature of the situation created by *A*. Poisoning offers perhaps the simplest example of the bearing on causal judgments of actions which are less than voluntary in this Aristotelian sense. If *A* intending *B*'s death deliberately poisons *B*'s food and *B*, knowing this, deliberately takes the poison and dies, *A* has not, unless he coerced *B* into eating the poisoned food, caused *B*'s death: if, however, *B* does not know the food to be poisoned, eats it, and dies, *A* has caused his death, even if he put the poison in unwittingly. Of course only the roughest judgments are passed in causal terms in such cases outside law courts, where fine degrees of "appreciation" or "reckless shutting of the eyes" may have to be discriminated from "full knowl-edge." Yet, rough as these are, they indicate clearly enough the controlling principles.

Though in the foregoing cases *A*'s initiating action might often be described as "the cause" of the ultimate harm, this linguistic fact is of subordinate importance to the fact that, for whatever purpose, explanatory, descriptive, or evaluative, consequences of an action are traced, discriminations are made (except in the cases discussed later) between free voluntary interventions and less than voluntary reactions to the first action or the circumstances created by it.

(iii) The analogy with single simple actions which guides the tracing of consequences may be broken by certain kinds of conjunctions of physical events. *A* hits *B* who falls to the ground stunned and bruised by the blow; at that moment a tree crashes to the ground and kills *B*. *A* has certainly caused *B*'s bruises but not his death: for though the fall of the tree was, like the evening breeze in our earlier example, independent of and subsequent to the initiating action, it would be differentiated from the breeze in any description in causal terms of the connection of *B*'s death with *A*'s action. It is to be noticed that this is not a matter which turns on the intention with which *A* struck *B*. Even if *A* hit *B* inadvertently or accidentally his blow would still be the cause of *B*'s bruises: he would have caused them, though unintentionally. Conversely even if *A* had intended his blow to kill, this would have been an attempt to kill but still not the cause of *B*'s death, unless *A* knew that the tree was about to fall just at that moment. On this legal and ordinary judgments would be found to agree; and most legal systems would distinguish for the purposes of punishment[14] an attempt with a fatal upshot, issuing by such chance or anomalous events, from "causing death"—the terms in which the offenses of murder and manslaughter are usually defined.

Similarly the causal description of the case does not turn on the moral appraisal of *A*'s action or the wish to punish it. *A* may be a robber and a murderer and *B* a saint guarding the place *A* hoped to plunder. Or *B* may be a murderer and *A* a hero who has forced his way into *B*'s retreat. In both cases the causal judgment is the same. *A* had caused the minor injuries but not *B*'s death, though he tried to kill him. *A* may indeed be praised or blamed but not for causing *B*'s death. However intimate the connection between responsibility and causation, it does not determine causal judgments in this simple way.

Nor does the causal judgment turn on a refusal to attribute grave consequences to actions which normally have less serious results. Had A's blow killed B outright and the tree, falling on his body, merely smashed his watch we should still treat the coincidental character of the fall of the tree as determining the form of causal statement. We should then recognize A's blow as the cause of B's death but not the breaking of the watch.

The connection between A's action and B's death in the first case would naturally be described in the language of *coincidence*. "It was a coincidence: it just happened that, at the very moment when A knocked B down, a tree crashed at the very place where he fell and killed him." The common legal metaphor would describe the fall of the tree as an "extraneous" cause. This, however, is dangerously misleading, as an analysis of the notion of coincidence will show. It suggests merely an event which is subsequent to and independent of some other contingency, and of course the fall of the tree has both these features in relation to A's blow. Yet in these respects the fall of the tree does not differ from the evening breeze in the earlier case where we found no difficulty in tracing causal connection. The full elucidation of the notion of a coincidence is a complex matter for, though it is very important as a limit in tracing consequences, causal questions are not the only ones to which the notion is relevant. The following are its most general characteristics. We speak of a coincidence whenever the conjunction of two or more events in certain spatial or temporal relations (1) is very unlikely by ordinary standards and (2) is for some reason significant or important, provided (3) that they occur without human contrivance and (4) are independent of each other. It is therefore a coincidence if two persons known to each other in London meet without design in Paris on their way to separate independently chosen destinations; or if two persons living in different places independently decide to write a book on the same subject. The first is a coincidence of time and place ("It just happened that we were at the same place at the same time"), and the second a coincidence of time only ("It just happened that they both decided to write on the subject at the same time").

Use of this general notion is made in the special case when the conjunction of two or more events occurs in temporal and/or spatial relationships which are significant, because, as our general knowledge of causal processes shows, this conjunction is required for the production of some given further event. In the language of Mill's idealized model, they form a necessary part of a complex set of jointly sufficient conditions. In the present case the fall of the tree just as B was struck down within its range satisfies the four criteria for a coincidence which we have enumerated. First, though neither event was of a very rare or exceptional kind, their conjunction would be rated very unlikely judged by the standards of ordinary experience. Secondly, this conjunction was causally significant for it was a necessary part of the process terminating in B's death. Thirdly, this conjunction was not consciously designed by A; had he known of the impending fall of the tree and hit B with the intention that he should fall within its range B's death would not have been the result of any coincidence. A would certainly have caused it. The common-sense principle that a contrived conjunction cannot be a coincidence is the element of truth in the legal maxim (too broadly stated even for legal purposes) that an intended consequence cannot be too "remote." Fourthly, each member of the conjunction in this case was independent of the other; whereas if B had fallen against the tree with an impact sufficient to bring it down on him, this sequence of physical events, though freakish in its way, would not be a coincidence and in most contexts of ordinary life, as in the law, the course of events would be summarized by saying that in this case, unlike that of the coincidence, A's act was the cause of B's death, since each stage is the effect of the preceding stage. Thus, the blow forced the victim against the tree, the effect of this was to make the tree fall and the fall of the tree killed the victim.

One further criterion in addition to these four must be satisfied if a conjunction of events is to rank as a coincidence and as a limit when the consequences of the action are traced. This further criterion again shows the strength of the influence which the analogy with the case of the simple manipulation of things exerts over thought in causal terms. An abnormal *condition* existing at the time of a human intervention is distinguished both by ordinary thought and, with a striking consistency, by most legal systems from an abnormal event or conjunction of events subsequent to that intervention; the former, unlike the latter, are not ranked as coincidences or "extraneous" causes when the consequences of the intervention come to be traced. Thus A innocently gives B a tap over the head of a normally quite harmless character, but because B is then suffering from some rare disease the tap has, as we say, "fatal results." In this case A has caused B's death though unintentionally. The scope of the principle which thus distinguishes contemporaneous abnormal conditions from subsequent events is unclear; but at least where a human being initiates some physical change in a thing, animal, or person, abnormal physical states of the object affected, existing at the time, are ranked as part of the circumstances in which the cause "operates." In the familiar controlling imagery these are part of "the stage already set" before the "intervention."

Judgments about coincidences, though we often agree in making them, depend in two related ways on issues incapable of precise formulation. One of these is patent, the other latent but equally important. Just how unlikely must a conjunction be to rank as a coincidence, and in the light of what knowledge is likelihood to be assessed? The only answer is: "very unlikely in the light of the knowledge available to ordinary men." It is, of course, the indeterminacies of such standards, implicit in causal judgments, that make them inveterately disputable, and call for the exercise of discretion or choice by courts. The second and latent indeterminacy of these judgments depends on the fact that the things or events to which they relate do not have pinned to them some uniquely correct description always to be used in assessing likelihood. It is an important pervasive feature of all our empirical judgments that there is a constant possibility of more or less specific description of any event or thing with which they are concerned. The tree might be described not simply as a "tree" but as a "rotten tree" or as a "fir tree" or a "tree sixty feet tall." So too its fall might be described not as a "fall" but as a fall of a specified distance at a specified velocity. The likelihood of conjunctions framed in these different terms would be differently assessed. The criteria of appropriate description like the standard of likelihood are supplied by consideration of common knowledge. Even if the scientist knew the tree to be rotten and could have predicted its fall with accuracy, this would not change the judgment that its fall at the time when B was struck down within its range was a coincidence; nor would it make the description "rotten tree" appropriate for the assessment of the chances involved in this judgment. There are other controls over the choice of description derived from the degree of specificity of our interests in the final outcome of the causal process. We are concerned with the fall of an object sufficient to cause "death" by impact and the precise force or direction which may account for the detail of the wounds is irrelevant here.

OPPORTUNITIES AND REASONS

OPPORTUNITIES. The discrimination of voluntary interventions as a limit is no longer made when the case, owing to the commonness or appreciable risk of such harmful intervention, can be brought within the scope of the notion of providing an opportunity, known to be commonly exploited for doing harm. Here the limiting principles are different. When A leaves the house unlocked the range of consequences to be attributed to this neglect, as in any other case where precautions are omitted, depends primarily on the way in which such opportunities are commonly exploited. An alternative formulation of this idea is that a subsequent intervention would fall within the scope of consequences if the likelihood of its occurring is one of the reasons for holding A's omission to be negligent.

It is on these lines that we would distinguish between the entry of a thief and of a murderer; the opportunity provided is believed to be sufficiently commonly exploited by thieves to make it usual and often morally or legally obligatory not to provide it. Here, in attributing consequences to prior actions, causal judgments are directly controlled by the notion of the risk created by them. Neglect of such precautions is both unusual and reprehensible. For these reasons it would be hard to separate the two ways in which such neglect deviates from the "norm." Despite this, no simple identification can be made of the notion of responsibility with the causal connection which is a ground for it. This is so because the provision of an opportunity commonly taken by others is ranked as the cause of the outcome independently of the wish to praise or blame. The causal judgment may be made simply to assess a contribution to some outcome. Thus, whether we think well or ill of the use made of railways, we would still claim that the greater mobility of the population in the nineteenth century was a consequence of their introduction.

It is obvious that the question whether any given intervention is a sufficiently common exploitation of the opportunity provided to come within the risk is again a matter on which judgments may differ, though they often agree. The courts, and perhaps ordinary thought also, often describe those that are sufficiently common as "natural" consequences of the neglect. They have in these terms discriminated the entry of a thief from the entry of a man who burnt the house down, and refused to treat the destruction of the house as a "natural" consequence of the neglect.[15]

We discuss later . . . the argument that this easily intelligible concept of "harm within the risk," overriding as it does the distinctions between voluntary interventions and others, should be used as the general test for determining what subsequent harm should be attributed for legal purposes to prior action. The merits of this proposal to refashion the law along these simple lines are perhaps considerable, yet consequences of actions are in fact often traced both in the law and apart from it in other ways which depend on the discrimination of voluntary interventions from others. We distinguish, after all, as differing though related grounds of responsibility, causing harm by one's own action and providing opportunities for others to do harm, where the guiding analogy with the simple manipulation of things, which underlies causal thought, is less close. When, as in the examples discussed above, we trace consequences through the non-voluntary interventions of others our concern is to show that certain stages of the process have a certain type of connection with the preceding stages, and not, as when the notion of risk is applied, to show that the ultimate outcome is connected in some general way with the initiating action. Thus, when A's shot makes B start and break a glass it is the causal relationship described by the expression "made B start" that we have in mind and not the likelihood that on hearing a shot someone may break a glass. Causal connection may be traced in such cases though the initiating action and the final outcome are not contingencies that commonly go together.

Apart from these conceptual reasons for distinguishing these related grounds for responsibility, it is clear that both in the law . . . and apart from it we constantly treat harm as caused by a person's action though it does not fall "within the risk." If, when B broke the glass in the example given above, a splinter flew into C's eye, blinding him, A's action is indeed the cause of C's injury though we may not always blame him for so unusual a consequence.

REASONS. In certain varieties of interpersonal transactions, unlike the case of coercion, the second action is quite voluntary. A may not threaten B but may bribe or advise or persuade him to do something. Here, A does not "cause" or "make" B do anything: the strongest words we should use are perhaps that he "induced" or "procured" B's act. Yet the law and moral principles alike may treat one person as responsible for the harm which another free agent has done "in consequence" of the advice or the inducements which the first has offered. In such cases the limits concern the range of those actions done by B which are to rank as the consequence of A's words or deeds. In general this question depends on A's intentions or on the "plan of action" he puts before B. If A advises or bribes B to break in and steal from an empty house and B does so, he acts in consequence of A's advice or bribe. If he deliberately burns down the house this would not be treated as the consequence of A's bribe or advice, legally or otherwise, though it may in some sense be true that the burning would not have taken place without the advice or bribe. Nice questions may arise, which the courts have to settle, where B diverges from the detail of the plan of action put before him by A.

NOTES

1. Cf. *OED sub tit.* Responsible: Answerable, accountable (*to* another *for* something); liable to be called to account: 'being responsible to the King for what might happen to us', 1662; Hart, 'Varieties of Responsibility' (1967) 83 *LQR* 346, reprinted with additions as 'Responsibility and Retribution' in Hart, *Punishment and Responsibility* (Oxford, 1968), chap. IX.

2. The rule is defended on the ground that, most houseowners being insured, it promotes efficient loss distribution: Harper and James, *Torts*, s. 20.6 n. 1.

3. See the following passage from *The Golden Bowl* by Henry James. (Mrs Assingham, whose uncertain self-accusation is described here, had, on the eve of the Prince's marriage, encouraged him to resume an old friendship with Charlotte Stant. The relationship which developed came to threaten the marriage with disaster.) 'She had stood for the previous hour in a merciless glare, beaten upon, stared out of countenance, it fairly seemed to her, by intimations of her mistake. For what she was most immediately feeling was that she had in the past been active for these people to ends that were now bearing fruit and that might yet bear a greater crop. She but brooded at first in her corner of the carriage: it was like burying her exposed face, a face too helplessly exposed in the cool lap of the common indifference . . . a world mercifully unconscious and unreproachful. It wouldn't like the world she had just left know sooner or later what she had done or would know it only if the final consequence should be some quite overwhelming publicity. . . . The sense of seeing was strong in her, but she clutched at the comfort of not being sure of what she saw. Not to know what it would represent on a longer view was a help in turn to not making out that her hands

were embrued; since if she had stood in the position of a producing cause she should surely be less vague about what she had produced. This, further, in its way, was a step toward reflecting that when one's connection with any matter was too indirect to be traced, it might be described also as too slight to be deplored' (*The Golden Bowl,* Book 3, chap. 3). We are much indebted to Dame Mary Warnock for this quotation.

4.   Lawson, *Negligence in the Civil Law,* p. 53.

5.   Glanville Williams, *Joint Torts and Contributory Negligence,* p. 239.

6.   Mill, Book III, chap. v, s. 2.

7.   Ross, *The Right and the Good,* p. 36.

8.   E.g. if the guest was suspected of being a compulsive stabber and the waiter had therefore been told to lay only a plastic knife in his place.

9.   In Chaps. VI, VII, XII, XIII of *Causation and the Law* we distinguish these different relationships in the law.

10.   Davies v. Swan Motor Co. [1947] 2 KB 291, 318.

11.   Minister of Pensions v. Chennell [1947] KB 250, 256. Lord Wright (1950), 13 *MLR* 3.

12.   Norris v. William Moss & Son Ltd. [1954] 1 WLR 46, 351.

13.   Minister of Pensions v. Chennel [1947] KB 250, 256.

14.   For the bearing of the principles of punishment on such problems see Chap. XIV of our book, *Causation in the Law.*

15.   Bellows v. Worcester Storage Co. (1937) 297 Mass. 188, 7 NE 2d 588.

ROBERT E. KEETON

The Basic Rule of Legal Cause in Negligence Cases*

DIVERSE FORMULATIONS OF THE RISK RULE

STATEMENT AND ILLUSTRATION OF THREE FORMULATIONS

The defendant, proprietor of a restaurant, placed a large, unlabeled can of rat poison beside cans of flour on a shelf near a stove in a restaurant kitchen. The victim, while in the kitchen making a delivery to the restaurant, was killed by an explosion of the poison. Assume that the defendant's handling of the rat poison was negligent because of the risk that someone would be poisoned but that defendant had no reason to know of the risk that the poison would explode if left in a hot place. Is the defendant liable for the death of the victim?[1]

This question illustrates the central problem of scope of liability for negligence. The problem is commonly subdivided into issues associated with, first, the foreseeability of any kind of harm to the victim who, in fact, was harmed and, second, the foreseeability of the particular harm or kind of harm that occurred.

The predominant theme in judicial utterances on the scope of liability in negligence cases is expressed in a proposition that, for convenience, will be referred to as *the Risk Rule*. This rule, quite commonly expressed in substance both in charges to the jury and in appellate opinions, is as follows:

A negligent actor is legally responsible for that harm, and only that harm, of which *negligence* is a cause in fact.

Some explanatory comments are in order. First, this rule is addressed not only to matters uniformly classified as problems of legal cause but also to other matters sometimes classified as problems of duty. Comments directed specifically to this choice of terminology are reserved for the second and third chapters.[2]

Other explanatory comments that seem necessary at the outset are concerned with the meaning of the words "actor" and "negligence." "Actor" is used here to signify the person whose "conduct" is being judged, whether plaintiff or defendant, and whether charged with acting negligently or with negligently failing to act. "Conduct" is used in a sense that includes both "acting" and "failing to act." "Negligence," in the context of this rule, must be understood in a more precise sense than merely "the negligent actor's conduct." This statement of the Risk Rule makes no sense unless interpreted as meaning that the actor's *conduct* during the period of his negligence may be a cause of harm of which his *negligence* is not a cause. For example, in the case of the explosive rat poison, it is not enough to ask whether the defendant's conduct in placing the poison where he did was a cause of the death of the victim. We should, as well, ask whether the defendant's negligence was a cause of the death. As a means of arriving at a satisfactory answer to that question, it will be useful to consider another.

What was that aspect of the conduct of the defendant that caused it to be characterized as negligence? Placing rat poison on a shelf may or may not be negligence. The negligence here consisted of placing the poison where it was likely to be mistaken for something intended for human consumption. This description says nothing about the proximity of the shelf to heat. That circumstance is omitted because of the assumption that the defendant had no reason to know of the explosive character of the poison; in such a situation it would not have been negligent to put the poison in a place that happened to be near heat, provided it was not a place where the poison was likely to be mistaken as something intended for human consumption. Thus, the defendant's *negligence* (his placing the poison where it was

*Reprinted from *Legal Cause in the Law of Torts* by Robert E. Keeton, Copyright © 1963 by the Ohio State University Press, by permission of the author and the publisher.

likely to be mistaken for something intended for human consumption) was not a *sine qua non* of the harm. For present purposes I draw no distinction between the several expressions "but-for cause," "necessary antecedent," and "*sine qua non.*"[3] That is, I am speaking simply of the concept that it cannot be said that the harm of death from explosion would not have occurred but for defendant's placing the poison where it was likely to be mistaken for something intended for human consumption. Defendant's negligence was not in this sense a but-for cause, or a necessary antecedent, or a *sine qua non* of the death. But his conduct (placing the poison near heat) was, at least in a qualified sense, a *sine qua non.*

The qualification is concerned with the hypothetical character of the assertion. That is, the assertion that the harm would not have occurred but for the defendant's conduct is a hypothetical assertion the accuracy of which is not subject to demonstration. For example, how are we to know that, had the poison been placed elsewhere than near a hot stove, it would not have been exploded by some other source of heat that might have happened to be applied to the poison while the victim was present? Also, imbedded in the hypothetical assertion of what would not have happened are ambiguities in the meaning of "conduct" and "harm." Does "conduct" refer to placing the poison in the exact spot where it was placed? If so, might it not be said that the conduct was not a *sine qua non* since death at the same time and place might have occurred if the poison had been placed near a hot radiator rather than the stove? Does "the harm" refer merely to death of the victim, or to the time, place, and manner of death in all their detail, or to something between these extremes? In some instances, the ambiguity and hypothetical character of the assertion will present serious difficulty.[4] But, in the case of the explosive rat poison, we can readily understand and accept, in at least a rough sense, the assertion that the defendant's conduct was a *sine qua non* of the harm because there appears to have been no substantial possibility either that the harm in all its details would have occurred or that something generally resembling it would have occurred in the absence of defendant's conduct of placing the rat poison near heat. Also, no doubt, we can agree that if defendant's negligence is defined in the limited sense of that quality of his conduct consisting of his placing the poison where it was likely to be mistaken for something intended for human consumption, his negligence was not a *sine qua non.*

There is yet another difficulty, however, in the assertion that one aspect of his conduct was a cause of harm and another aspect of the same conduct, the same single action of putting down a can of poison, was not a cause of the harm. It is more normal, perhaps, to think of the conduct as indivisible and to reject the suggestion that the negligent aspect can be separated from other aspects for an inquiry into causal relation. Perhaps it will be helpful in this respect to think of negligence as the creation of unreasonable risks[5] and, rather than thinking of harm itself as the focus of the concept of risk, to think of a risk as a set of forces and conditions and circumstances that might foreseeably bring about harm.[6] No special point is made here regarding the choice among the terms "force," "condition," and "circumstance" to convey the intended idea, though the word "circumstance" seems the most congenial to the separation of aspects of a single state of affairs. Negligence, then, consists of creating a set of unduly risky forces or conditions or circumstances, and the negligence is a *sine qua non* of subsequent harm only if some force or condition or circumstance within this set is a *sine qua non.* In the case of the rat poison, the negligence consisted of creating a force or condition or circumstance of having a poisonous substance where it might be mistaken as something intended for human consumption. That circumstance was not a cause of the harm, though the coexisting circumstance of having an explosive substance near heat was a cause.

This focus upon the negligent aspect of conduct as the meaning of the unqualified word "negligence" in the statement of the Risk Rule presented above suggests a second, perhaps less ambiguous, formulation of exactly the same meaning:

A negligent actor is legally responsible for that harm, and only that harm, of which the *negligent aspect of his conduct* is a cause in fact.

In many cases it is less easy than in the case of the explosive rat poison to extract the negligent aspect from the total conduct. To meet this difficulty, still another formulation of the Risk Rule is helpful. A moment ago, we were thinking of risk with a focus upon the forces or conditions or circumstances that might produce harm. Shift the focus now to the harm that might be produced. With this focus, in order to find that the negligence (that is, the negligent aspect of the conduct) bears a causal relation to the harm, we must find that the harm that came about was one of the things that was risked. Another way of expressing the same idea is to say that the harm must be a result within the scope of at least one of the risks on the basis of which the actor is found to be negligent. Thus the Risk Rule of legal cause as stated in the first and second formulations above may be restated in a third formulation without change of meaning:

A negligent actor is legally responsible for the harm, and only the harm, that not only (1) is caused in fact by his conduct but also (2) is a result within the scope of the risks by reason of which the actor is found to be negligent.

In the case of the explosive rat poison, injury by explosion was not a result within the scope of the risks by reason of which the defendant was found to be negligent, though injury by poisoning would have been.

The third formulation of the rule is often expressed in the statement that the actor is responsible only for "results within the risk." Among those who remain constantly alert to its meaning, there is no objection to use of such a shorthand expression. But this cryptic phrase is apt to be misleading to the unsophisticated because it does not designate the point of view from which the composite of risks is defined. The concept of "risk" and the cognate concept of "probability" are founded on prediction from some selected point of view. But they do not necessarily imply any particular point of view, such as that of a reasonable man in the position of the actor. Thus, results that in the wisdom of hindsight are said to have been "probable" may yet have been beyond the scope of those risks by reason of which the actor's conduct is found to have been negligence. Also, such concepts as "risk," "probability," and "foreseeability" imply a point of view involving a degree of ignorance about the factors at work in a situation. To one who knows all, a future event is not "probable" or merely "foreseeable" but either certain to occur or certain not to occur. When we say a result was "probable" as a matter of hindsight, we are using a point of view that is neither that of a reasonable person in the actor's position nor that of an omniscient observer after the fact. It is a point of view based on foresight in the face of incomplete knowledge, but with greater knowledge or greater mental capacity than that of the actor or that of the standard man in the actor's circumstances. As used in the Risk Rule, on the other hand, "risk" implies a standard based on foresight from the point of view of the standard man in the actor's circumstances at the time of the conduct that is being judged.

As we examine the policy foundation of the Risk Rule, reasons will appear for using, in relation to problems of legal cause, this standard of foresight that is also used in determining whether the actor was negligent. But, first, we digress for further explanation of the use of three formulations of the Risk Rule.

WHY THREE FORMULATIONS?

The first formulation of the Risk Rule tracks language found in many jury charges today, as well as in appellate opinions, though supplemented usually by elaborations upon the theme and occasionally by qualifications. The third formulation tracks the rationale of exponents of what has come to be known as the risk theory of legal cause, and of Professor Seavey in particular.[7] Professors Harper and James also recommended an inquiry in terms generally consistent with the rationale expressed in the third formulation,[8] though they appear less happy than Professor Seavey with adherence to the limitation on scope of liability implicit in accepting this as the basic rule of legal cause. They also observed that in essence this is the same inquiry as the question whether there is causal relation "between *that aspect of the defendant's conduct which is wrongful* and the injury."[9] Thus, the second formulation offered here is supported by their analysis. This formulation is offered as a transitional bond between the first and the third, in the belief that the intended substance of these different expressions is the same. Candor requires disclosure that Professor Seavey dislikes both the first and the second formulations because of a concern, as I understand him, that they are more likely to mislead than to clarify. His disfavor is firm, though expressed in the warmhearted spirit that has characterized his rigorous intellectual assaults upon the ideas of generations of students, colleagues, and judges. At the risk of suffering an intermeddler's unhappy fate, I persist in offering the second formulation and in marshaling the three together in the hope of improving relations between adherents of two ways of thought that I believe to be compatibly directed toward the same goal.

THE RISK RULE AS A RULE OF CAUSATION

Perhaps a secondary benefit of this focus on three formulations of one rule is to expose rather persuasive evidence that the Risk Rule is indeed a rule of causation in a cause-in-fact sense. There are various deviations from the Risk Rule—some toward greater liability, some toward less—that are founded in notions beyond causation. But the predominant theme represented by the Risk Rule is a theme of causation. It concerns cause-in-fact relation between the negligent aspect of the conduct and the harm.

This conclusion is supported by only a few of the multitude of authors on legal cause—among them Professor Carpenter,[10] and, more recently, Professors Harper and James.[11] Even these three appear not willing to carry the separation of aspects of the conduct as far as is suggested here. The following passage from Harper and James is relevant:

But there are cases where causal relation exists between defendant's fault and the injury, yet where liability will not be imposed. Thus in Gorris v. Scott, L.R. 9 Ex. 125 (1874), defendants' wrongful failure to have pens for cattle on shipboard was the cause in fact of their being washed overboard in a heavy sea. There was no liability, however, since the statutory requirement was designed to protect the cattle only from perils from contagious disease, a hazard which was not encountered and from which their loss did not result. See Carpenter, Workable Rules for Determining Proximate Cause, 20 Calif. L. Rev. 396, 408 (1932).[12]

The claim of negligence in Gorris v. Scott was violation of orders issued pursuant to the Contagious Diseases (Animals) Act of 1869, the violation being failure to provide battens or foot-holds for the animals and failure to provide pens not larger than 9 by 15 feet each. Under the analysis suggested in this chapter, the negligent aspect of the conduct was not the circumstance that absence of such pens and foot-holds placed the cattle in position to be washed overboard. No doubt, reluctance to declare that there is no causal connection between the negligent aspect of the conduct and the result in these circumstances arises from the difficulty of imagining facts in which compliance with the required safeguards against disease would not also protect the cattle against being washed overboard. The case is thus unlike that of the speeding automobile that strikes a child who could not have been avoided by a driver proceeding at a reasonable speed; in that situation, speed causes the automobile to be at the scene at the critical time, but we can imagine the defendant's starting sooner and arriving in time to strike the child though he drives at a reasonable speed throughout the journey. Perhaps the converse point of view is also relevant, however. That is, perhaps we should consider not only whether situations can be imagined in which the required safeguard would have been ineffectual to prevent the particular kind of harm of which plaintiff is complaining but also whether situations can be imagined in which despite absence of the required safeguards the plaintiff would have been fully protected against this kind of harm. This is not to say that a required safeguard is intended to be an exclusive safeguard against the dangers to which it is directed. But this point of view does suggest that, when we treat one circumstance (that absence of pens placed the cattle in position to be washed overboard) as an aspect of the conduct separate from another circumstance (that absence of pens placed the cattle in position to be subject to an increased risk of contagious disease), we are no more attempting to separate inseparable aspects of a single faulty course of conduct than in the converse situation illustrated by the case of excessive speed. Pursuing this line of thought, we may observe that it would have been possible in Gorris v. Scott to have larger pens and no footholds and yet have the cattle protected against the risk of being washed overboard. In any event, the negligence was concerned with the circumstance that absence of the required safeguards increased the risks of disease, including the risk that affected cattle would communicate the disease widely among animals not separated into small groups by use of small enclosures. It was not concerned with the circumstance that the cattle were in position to be washed overboard. Thus, there was no causal relation between the negligent aspect of the conduct and the harm.

Possibly some passages in the recent broad study of causation by a distinguished pair of English scholars, Hart and Honoré, can also be fairly interpreted as supporting the assertion that the Risk Rule is concerned with causal relation between the negligent aspect of conduct and the harm of which plaintiff complains.[13] Yet, elsewhere they may be thought to be saying that foreseeability is a policy factor, that causal principles are policy neutral, and that use of foreseeability as a test for scope of liability is a departure from use of causal criteria.[14] They argue that the foreseeability test breaks down, especially in cases of what they call "ulterior" harm (e.g., harm following a foreseeable impact on an unforeseeably thin skull), and that causal criteria must be used instead.[15] Perhaps these several passages can be reconciled on the basis that Hart and Honoré mean not to declare that the foreseeability test is unconcerned with causal relation between the negligent aspect of the conduct and the harm but only that in some situations, especially those of "ulterior" harm, the scope of liability is fixed by a test of causal relation between conduct and harm rather than between negligent aspect of conduct and harm. If this reading of their book is proper, then the views of Hart and Honoré tend to support the assertion that the three separate formulations of the Risk Rule are in essence expressions of one idea and that this idea is concerned with cause-in-fact relation between the negligent aspect of the conduct and the harm.

To the contrary, other writers, probably a majority, have insisted that doctrines of legal cause generally, and the result-within-the-risk formulation in particular, are based on policy considerations having nothing to do with cause in fact.[16] The insight produced by a focus upon the relation between the negligent aspect of conduct and the ensuing harm is nevertheless persuasive. The persistence of courts in dealing with this problem under the rubric of causation is perhaps more than evidence of a judicial instinct for right results; perhaps it is also evidence that on occasion judicial perception surpasses that of the majority of reflective critics. This accolade to the courts is not intended to imply a preference for the first or the second formulation of the Risk Rule over the third. It does, however, express a conviction that the first and second formulations offer added illumination on the problem though the third is generally the more manageable in difficult applications. Inevitably, different formulations are likely to produce different nuances and connotations. Since all three formulations are expressions of a single theme, it will often be an aid to deliberate and rational choice to examine the implications of the Risk Rule from the several points of view of all three formulations.

THE POLICY FOUNDATION OF THE RISK RULE

SCOPE OF LIABILITY COMMENSURATE WITH THE BASIS OF LIABILITY

The policy foundation of the Risk Rule can be summarized in this way: The factors determining that the actor is liable for unintended harm caused by his conduct should also determine the scope of his liability. There is surely an interest of public policy in formulating rules that do not impose crushing liability.[17] Since the unintended consequences of one's conduct go on indefinitely, some limit of responsibility is a practical necessity. The theory of the Risk Rule is that the scope of liability should be commensurate with the basis of liability. "Prima facie at least, the reasons for creating liability should limit it."[18]

Opponents of the Risk Rule have argued that in applying the risk concept first to the issue of liability and again to the issue of scope of liability a court gives the defendant an unwarranted advantage by applying twice a restrictive test of foreseeability of harm.[19] The argument is not persuasive. In the first place, the test is expansive rather than restrictive if we start with the assumption that the burden is on the plaintiff to prove some good reason for entering a loss-shifting judgment. That is, when the test for negligence is found to have been fulfilled, liability is expanded in the sense of establishment of an obligation not previously acknowledged. Only if we make a comparison with an assumed state of broader liability, or if we start with the assumption that there is a burden on the defendant to prove nonliability, can we think of an application of the test of foreseeability of harm as restrictive rather than expansive. This is true whether it be applied to the liability issue alone, to the scope of liability issue as well, or to the combination as a unit. In the second place, separating the issues of liability and scope of liability is simply a means of organizing thought. There is no more reason for characterizing the process as a double application of a standard, either restrictive or expansive, when the issues are separated than when they are merged into one issue of liability for how much —none, all, or something between. This double-advantage argument is a conclusion derived from the premise that the scope of liability *should be* governed by a separate test. The opposing premise on which the Risk Rule is founded—the premise that the scope of liability should be limited by the factors accounting for liability—has been described as the view that there is only one question in negligence cases, not two.[20]

RELATION TO THE PRINCIPLE THAT LIABILITY IS BASED ON FAULT

The policy argument underlying use of the Risk Rule in negligence cases is a corollary of the foundation of tort law on fault. Generally one is not liable for an unintended harm caused by his nonnegligent conduct. If negligence in one respect were to make the actor liable for all unintended harms to follow, the legal consequences would be disproportionate to the fault. For example, suppose the defendant's negligence consisted of his transporting dynamite in an unmarked truck, otherwise carefully operated, and the only harm caused was injury to one who, without negligence, fainted, fell into the path of the truck, and was run down. Defendant was negligent with respect to risks of explosion but not with respect to risks of an injury of the kind that occurred. The policy judgment underlying the Risk Rule is that with respect to the kind of injury that occurred, the defendant was not at fault.

It may be argued that, as between a negligent defendant and a nonnegligent plaintiff, a loss of which defendant's conduct was a cause in fact ought to be imposed upon the defendant irrespective of whether it was a kind of loss within the risks by reason of which his conduct is characterized as negligence. But if it is relevant to take into account defendant's fault with respect to a risk different from any that would include the harm plaintiff has suffered, then would it not also be relevant to take into account his other faults as well? And would it not seem equally relevant to consider plaintiff's shortcomings? Shall we fix legal responsibility by deciding who is the better and who the worse person? An affirmative answer might involve us, and quickly too, in the morality of run-of-the-ranch TV drama, where the good guys always win.

If we reject this standard of judgment, then so long as liability is to be based on fault, should we not limit the scope of legal responsibility to those consequences with respect to which the actor was negligent—to those consequences of which the negligent aspect of his conduct was a cause? An affirmative answer implies, in relation to the hypothetical case of the transportation of explosives, that legal responsibility should be limited to damages caused by explosion or by conduct responsive to the explosion risk, rather than being extended to injuries that would have occurred even if the driver had used warning signs or had transported no explosives, while acting in other respects exactly as he did.

The policy foundation for the Risk Rule, though applicable more broadly to all problems of results outside the risk, is seen in its most persuasive context in relation to *persons outside the risk*. In this context Judge Learned Hand expressed the philosophy of the rule in an opinion that is especially illuminating on matters of legal cause. After noting that there are in tort law some instances of strict liability, he said:

But so long as it is an element of imposed liability that the wrongdoer shall in some degree disregard the sufferer's interests, it can only be an anomaly, and indeed vindictive, to make him responsible to those whose interests he has not disregarded.[21]

Perhaps this is as forcefully as one can fairly state the policy justification for the Risk Rule. Indeed, it is easy to exaggerate the weight of this argument as brought to bear upon one of those close cases about which dispute is likely. In the first place, this policy argument is essentially one of blameworthiness, resting distinctly on moral judgment. The twilight zones of disputed legal judgment are also zones of disputed moral judgment, not alone in the minds of judges, but as well in the views of the community at large.[22] Uncertainty is increased by the multiplicity of influences that bear on judgments of blameworthiness. Moreover, even aside from this element of uncertainty about which way underlying moral justifications point for a particular case in the twilight zone, the very fact that the policy is one based on a moral judgment exerts a restraint upon its influence, because we are less content today with moral justifications for our legal rules than with political, economic, and social justifications. It is characteristic of our time to be discomfited about the imposition of our moral judgments on others, especially judgments concerning individual rather than group morality.

One may disagree with the policy argument underlying the Risk Rule, or he may believe that it has been too widely influential, or he may believe that we should now move beyond the Risk Rule in sympathetic conformity with a trend away from liability based on fault and toward strict liability. But to believe that the Risk Rule is without rational policy foundation is to misunderstand, and to deny the existence of that foundation because of aversion to its moralizing quality is to misrepresent. Its force may be doubtful in a range of close cases; and, like most policy arguments, it falls short of providing a firm guide to decision in close cases. But demonstration of these uncertainties on the fringe leaves the hard core of the policy argument intact. This hard core continues to serve as the basic theme of decisions on legal cause.

NOTES

1. Cf. Larrimore v. American Nat'l Ins. Co., 184 Okla. 614, 89 P.2d 340 (1939). This hypothetical variation upon the facts of that case is chosen for the purpose of eliminating possible grounds of decision other than those to which attention is directed here.

2. The author's reference is to his discussion of the *Palgraf* case—Eds.

3. Challenges to some of the common assumptions about these expressions appear in Hart & Honoré, *Causation in the Law* 19 n.1, 84 n.2, 103–22 (1959); and in Becht & Miller, The Test of Factual Causation in Negligence and Strict Liability Cases 13–21 (1961). See also Williams, *Causation in the Law,* 1961 Camb. L. J. 62, 63–79, for comments evoked by the Hart & Honoré book.

4. See, *e.g.,* Hart & Honoré, *Causation in the Law* 95–96 (1959); 2 Harper & James, Torts 1138 (1956). Compare Becht & Miller, The Test of Factual Causation in Negligence and Strict Liability Cases 21–25 (1961), discussing the hypothetical character of any assertion that an omission was a cause of a subsequent occurrence. Their discussion is addressed to what might be thought of as the converse of the problem referred to here. Here the issue is, Would the same thing have happened if the actor had not engaged in the conduct (whether described as an act, an omission, or a combination) alleged to be negligent? The issue they discuss is, Would the same thing have happened if the actor had done a particular thing he omitted doing? Both inquiries are hypothetical.

5. In the context of this discussion of legal cause, the plural, "risks," is chosen in preference to the more commonly used singular form as a means of avoiding the confusion that the risk within which the result falls must be such that, standing alone, it would make the conduct unreasonable. A composite of substantial, foreseeable risks is weighed against utility in judging whether the conduct is unreasonable.

6. Cf. P. Keeton, *Negligence, Duty, and Causation in Texas,* 16 Texas L. Rev. 1, 11–12 (1937). Though the idea expressed in the text above was suggested to me by the cited passage, the subsequent development in that article of the meaning of "force" (*id.* at 12–14) indicates that its author might not regard the present idea as one of the legitimate progeny of his teaching.

7. E.g., see Seavey, Cogitations on Torts 31–36 (1954); Seavey *Principles of Torts,* 56 Harv. L. Rev. 72, 90–93 (1942); Seavey, *Mr. Justice Cardozo and the Law of Torts,* 39 Colum. L. Rev. 20, 29–39; 52 Harv. L. Rev. 372, 381–91; 48 Yale L.J. 390, 399–409 (1939). For expressions of generally compatible points of view from the other side of the Atlantic, see Goodhart, *Liability and Compensation,* 76 L.O. Rev. 567 (1960) and Williams, *The Risk Principle,* 77 L.Q. Rev. 179 (1961).

8. 2 Harper & James, Torts 1138 (1956).

9. Ibid. (emphasis in original).

10. Carpenter, *Workable Rules for Determining Proximate Cause,* 20 Calif. L. Rev. 229, 231, 408–19 (1932).

11. 2 Harper & James, Torts 1138 (1956). Perhaps some degree of support for this thesis can be found in the analysis of Becht and Miller, which, for the purpose of inquiries into "factual causation," distinguishes between conduct and the "negligent segment" of it. See Becht & Miller, The Test of Causation in Negligence and Strict Liability Cases 25–28 (1961). But both the explanation of their distinction and the applications of it in their book indicate that it is a physical, rather than a qualitative, distinction. That is, a segment of conduct is an act or an omission among the many acts and omissions that make up the conduct, rather than an unreasonably risky quality of either the total conduct or some part of it. Thus, their distinction is not directed to the question whether the Risk Rule concerns cause-in-fact relation between the harm and the negligent *aspect* of conduct, as that concept is developed here. Moreover, in some situations where their thesis produces a finding of causal relation between the negligent *segment* of the conduct and the harm (and either supports liability or else explains nonliability on

the "policy" ground that the harm is not within the type against which the rule of conduct is directed), the present thesis produces a finding of no causal relation between the negligent *aspect* of the conduct and the harm. *E.g.,* they find that the negligent segment of a plaintiff's conduct in sitting on an unsafe wall was a cause of the injury he suffered when the wall was knocked down by a careless motorist whose conduct would have caused the same injuries if the wall had been safe. See *id.* at 182–84, where they criticize the view of Hart and Honore that the plaintiff's negligence in this situation was causally irrelevant. Under the thesis presented here, as under the thesis of Hart and Honore apparently, the plaintiff's negligence consisted of placing himself where he was likely to be injured by the collapse of the wall, either without an external impact or under an external impact insufficient to cause the collapse of a safe wall. This aspect of his conduct was not a *sine qua non* of the injury he suffered.

12. 2 Harper & James, Torts 1138 n. 15 (1956).

13. Hart & Honoré, *Causation in the Law* 110–12, 192–93 (1959).

14. See, *e.g., id.* at 231–38, 259, and 266.

15. See *id.* at 259.

16. E.g., Green, *The Causal Relation Issue in Negligence Law,* 60 Mich. L. Rev. 543, 576 (1962) ("the *only cause issue* is the connection between the defendant's conduct and the victim's injury"; the issue of causal relation should be unloaded of other considerations [emphasis in the original]); Prosser, Torts 252, 258, 266 (2d ed. 1955), (proximate cause "is nearly always a matter of various considerations of policy which have nothing to do with the fact of causation"; the problem of scope of liability for unforeseeable consequences "is in no way one of causation, and it does not arise until causation has been established"; the problem of intervening causes is one of policy, not causation); Restatement, Torts § 433, Reason for Changes (1948 Supp.), (Legal cause consists of two elements: 'the substantial factor' element deals with causation in fact"; the second element is concerned with whether there is a rule of law restricting "liability for harm occurring in the particular manner" at issue, and "deals with a legal policy relieving the actor of liability for harm he has, as a matter of fact, caused"; "[i]t is completely faulty analysis" to confuse "the question of policy with the question of fact"). Insistence that the result-within-the-risk problem is not one of causation is found even among advocates of the principle expressed in the several formulations of the Risk Rule. For example, Professor Goodhart declares: "But consequences cannot 'flow' from negligence. Consequences 'flow' from an act or an omission." Goodhart, *Liability for the Consequences of a "Negligent Act,"* in Cambridge Legal Essays 101, 105–6 (1926), reprinted in Goodhart, Essays in Jurisprudence and the Common Law 110, 114 (1931). See also Foster, Grant & Green, *The Risk Theory and Proximate Cause—A Comparative Study,* 32 Neb. L. Rev. 72, 79–80 (1952) (advocating the risk theory and the "relational" quality of negligence, but declaring that "proximate cause often has little if anything to do with causation in fact, except that no issue of proximate cause arises unless actual causation is present," and observing of a typical case that if defendant is held not liable "it is not because its fault was not a cause of the disaster").

17. Cf. 2 Harper & James, Torts 1132–33 (1956).

18. Seavey, *Mr. Justice Cardozo and the Law of Torts,* 39 Colum. L. Rev. 20, 34; 52 Harv. L. Rev. 372, 386; 48 Yale L. J. 390, 404 (1939).

19. E. g., Smith, *Legal Cause in Actions of Tort,* 25 Harv. L. Rev. 103, 223, 245 (1912). Cf. Green, *Foreseeability in Negligence Law,* 61 Colum. L. Rev. 1401, 1408 (1961), noting

that there are numerous devices for controlling decisions of both liability and damages, and asserting that "the foreseeability formula" need not "reach beyond the negligence issue" into the area of other limitations on scope of liability.

20. See Pound, *Causation,* 67 Yale L. J. 1, 10 (1957), referring to Pollock's view. Pollock stated the question as one "whether the accepted test of liability for negligence in the first instance is or not also the proper measure of liability for the consequences of proved or admitted default." Pollock, *Liability for Consequences,* 38 L.Q. Rev. 165 (1922).

21. Sinram v. Pennsylvania R.R., 61 F.2d 767, 770 (2d Cir. 1932).

22. Cf. Morris, *Proximate Cause in Minnesota,* 34 Minn L. Rev. 185, 207 (1950).

THE AMBIGUOUS SUICIDE CASE

N.Y. Times, February 7, 1968: "Phoenix, Ariz., Feb. 6 (AP)—Linda Marie Ault killed herself, policemen said today, rather than make her dog Beauty pay for her night with a married man.

"I killed her. I killed her. It's just like I killed her myself," a detective quoted her grief-stricken father as saying.

"I handed her the gun. I didn't think she would do anything like that."

"The 21-year-old Arizona State University coed died in a hospital yesterday of a gunshot wound in the head.

"The police quoted her parents, Mr. and Mrs. Joseph Ault, as giving this account:

"Linda failed to return home from a dance in Tempe Friday night. On Saturday she admitted she had spent the night with an Air Force lieutenant.

"The Aults decided on a punishment that would 'wake Linda up.' They ordered her to shoot the dog she had owned about two years.

"On Sunday, the Aults and Linda took the dog into the desert near their home. They had the girl dig a shallow grave. Then Mrs. Ault grasped the dog between her hands, and Mr. Ault gave his daughter a .22-caliber pistol and told her to shoot the dog.

"Instead, the girl put the pistol to her right temple and shot herself.

"The police said there were no charges that could be filed against the parents except possibly cruelty to animals."

PALSGRAF v. THE LONG ISLAND RAILROAD CO.

New York Court of Appeals, 1928*

CARDOZO, Ch. J. Plaintiff was standing on a platform of defendant's railroad after buying a ticket to go to Rockaway Beach. A train stopped at the station, bound for another place. Two men ran forward to catch it. One of the men reached the platform of the car without mishap, though the train was already moving. The other man, carrying a package, jumped aboard the car, but seemed unsteady as if about to fall. A guard on the car, who had held the door open, reached forward to help him in, and another guard on the platform pushed him from behind. In this act, the package was dislodged, and fell upon the rails. It was a package of small size, about fifteen inches long, and was covered by a newspaper. In fact it contained fireworks, but there was nothing in its appearance to give notice of its contents. The fireworks when they fell exploded. The shock of the explosion threw down some scales at the other end of the platform, many feet away. The scales struck the plaintiff, causing injuries for which she sues.

The conduct of the defendant's guard, if a wrong in its relation to the holder of the package, was not a wrong in its relation to the plaintiff, standing far away. Relatively to her it was not negligence at all. Nothing in the situation gave notice that the falling package had in it the potency of peril to persons thus removed. Negligence is not actionable unless it involves in the invasion of a legally protected interest, the violation of a right. "Proof of negligence in the air, so to speak, will not do."* "Negligence is the absence of care, according to the circumstances."† The plaintiff as she stood upon the platform of the station might claim to be protected against intentional invasion of her bodily security. Such invasion is not charged. She might claim to be protected against unintentional invasion by conduct involving in the thought of reasonable men an unreasonable hazard that such invasion would ensue. These,

from the point of view of the law, were the bounds of her immunity, with perhaps some rare exceptions, survivals for the most part of ancient forms of liability, where conduct is held to be at the peril of the actor (*Sullivan* v. *Dunham,* 161 N.Y. 290). If no hazard was apparent to the eye of ordinary vigilance, an act innocent and harmless, at least to outward seeming, with reference to her, did not take to itself the quality of a tort because it happened to be a wrong, though apparently not one involving the risk of bodily insecurity, with reference to some one else. "In every instance, before negligence can be predicated of a given act, back of the act must be sought and found a duty to the individual complaining, the observance of which would have averted or avoided the injury."* "The ideas of negligence and duty are strictly correlative."* (BOWEN, L. J., in *Thomas* v. *Quartermaine,* 18 Q. B. D. 685, 694.) The plaintiff sues in her own right for a wrong personal to her, and not as the vicarious beneficiary of a breach of duty to another.

A different conclusion will involve us, and swiftly too, in a maze of contradictions. A guard stumbles over a package which has been left upon a platform. It seems to be a bundle of newspapers. It turns out to be a can of dynamite. To the eye of ordinary vigilance, the bundle is abandoned waste, which may be kicked or trod on with impunity. Is a passenger at the other end of the platform protected by the law against the unsuspected hazard concealed beneath the waste? If not, is the result to be any different, so far as the distant passenger is concerned, when the guard stumbles over a valise which a truckman or a porter has left upon the walk? The passenger far away, if the victim of a wrong at all, has a cause of action, not derivative, but original and primary. His claim to be protected against invasion of his bodily security is neither greater nor less because the act resulting in the invasion is a wrong to another far

*248 N.Y. 339 (1928).
†Citations omitted [Eds.]

*Citations omitted [Eds.]

removed. In this case, the rights that are said to have been violated, the interests said to have been invaded, are not even of the same order. The man was not injured in his person nor even put in danger. The purpose of the act, as well as its effect, was to make his person safe. If there was a wrong to him at all, which may very well be doubted, it was a wrong to a property interest only, the safety of his package. Out of this wrong to property, which threatened injury to nothing else, there has passed, we are told, to the plaintiff by derivation or succession a right of action for the invasion of an interest of another order, the right to bodily security. The diversity of interests emphasizes the futility of the effort to build the plaintiff's right upon the basis of a wrong to some one else. The gain is one of emphasis, for a like result would follow if the interests were the same. Even then, the orbit of the danger as disclosed to the eye of reasonable vigilance would be the orbit of the duty. One who jostles one's neighbor in a crowd does not invade the rights of others standing at the outer fringe when the unintended contact casts a bomb upon the ground. The wrongdoer, as to them is the man who carries the bomb, not the one who explodes it without suspicion of the danger. Life will have to be made over, and human nature transformed, before prevision so extravagant can be accepted as the norm of conduct, the customary standard to which behavior must conform.

The argument for the plaintiff is built upon the shifting meanings of such words as "wrong" and "wrongful," and shares their instability. What the plaintiff must show is "a wrong" to herself, *i. e.*, a violation of her own right, and not merely a wrong to some one else, nor conduct "wrongful" because unsocial, but not "a wrong" to any one. We are told that one who drives at reckless speed through a crowded city street is guilty of a negligent act and, therefore, of a wrongful one irrespective of the consequences. Negligent the act is, and wrongful in the sense that it is unsocial, but wrongful and unsocial in relation to other travelers, only because the eye of vigilance perceives the risk of damage. If the same act were to be committed on a speedway or a race course, it would lose its wrongful quality. The risk reasonably to be perceived defines the duty to be obeyed, and risk imports relation; it is risk to another or to others within the range of apprehension (Seavey, Negligence, Subjective or Objective, 41 H. L.

Rv. 6; *Boronkay* v. *Robinson & Carpenter,* 247 N.Y. 365). This does not mean, of course, that one who launches a destructive force is always relieved of liability if the force, though known to be destructive, pursues an unexpected path. It was not necessary that the defendant should have had notice of the particular method in which an accident would occur, if the possibility of an accident was clear to the ordinarily prudent eye (*Munsey* v. *Webb,* 231 U.S. 150, 156; *Condran* v. *Park & Tilford,* 213 N.Y. 341, 345; *Robert* v. *U.S.E.F. Corp.,* 240 N.Y. 474, 477). Some acts, such as shooting, are so imminently dangerous to any one who may come within reach of the missile, however unexpectedly, as to impose a duty of prevision not far from that of an insurer. Even today, and much oftener in earlier stages of the law, one acts sometimes at one's peril.* Under this head, it may be, fall certain cases of what is known as transferred intent, an act willfully dangerous to A resulting by misadventure in injury to B.* These cases aside, wrong is defined in terms of the natural or probable, at least when unintentional.* The range of reasonable apprehension is at times a question for the court, and at times, if varying inferences are possible, a question for the jury. Here, by concession, there was nothing in the situation to suggest to the most cautious mind that the parcel wrapped in newspaper would spread wreckage through the station. If the guard had thrown it down knowingly and willfully, he would not have threatened the plaintiff's safety, so far as appearances could warn him. His conduct would not have involved, even then, an unreasonable probability of invasion of her bodily security. Liability can be no greater where the act is inadvertent.

Negligence, like risk, is thus a term of relation. Negligence in the abstract, apart from things related, is surely not a tort, if indeed it is understandable at all.* Negligence is not a tort unless it results in the commission of a wrong, and the commission of a wrong imports the violation of a right, in this case, we are told, the right to be protected against interference with one's bodily security. But bodily security is protected, not against all forms of interference or aggression, but only against some. One who seeks redress at law does not make out a cause of action by showing without more that there

*Citations omitted [Eds.]

has been damage to his person. If the harm was not willful, he must show that the act as to him had possibilities of danger so many and apparent as to entitle him to be protected against the doing of it though the harm was unintended. Affront to personality is still the keynote of the wrong. Confirmation of this view will be found in the history and development of the action on the case. Negligence as a basis of civil liability was unknown to mediaeval law.* For damage to the person, the sole remedy was trespass, and trespass did not lie in the absence of aggression, and that direct and personal.* Liability for other damage, as where a servant without orders from the master does or omits something to the damage of another, is a plant of later growth.* When it emerged out of the legal soil, it was thought of as a variant of trepass, an offshoot of the parent stock. This appears in the form of action, which was known as trespass on the case.* The victim does not sue derivatively, or by right of subrogation, to vindicate an interest invaded in the person of another. Thus to view his cause of action is to ignore the fundamental difference between tort and crime.* He sues for breach of a duty owing to himself.

The law of causation, remote or proximate, is thus foreign to the case before us. The question of liability is always anterior to the question of the measure of the consequences that go with liability. If there is no tort to be redressed, there is no occasion to consider what damage might be recovered if there were a finding of a tort. We may assume, without deciding, that negligence, not at large or in the abstract, but in relation to the plaintiff, would entail liability for any and all consequences, however novel or extraordinary.* There is room for argument that a distinction is to be drawn according to the diversity of interests invaded by the act, as where conduct negligent in that it threatens an insignificant invasion of an interest in property results in an unforeseeable invasion of an interest of another order, as *e.g.,* one of bodily security. Perhaps other distinctions may be necessary. We do not go into the question now. The consequences to be followed must first be rooted in a wrong.

The judgment of the Appellate Division and that of the Trial Term should be reversed, and the complaint dismissed, with costs in all courts.

ANDREWS, J. (dissenting). Assisting a passenger to board a train, the defendant's servant negligently knocked a package from his arms. It fell between the platform and the cars. Of its contents the servant knew and could know nothing. A violent explosion followed. The concussion broke some scales standing a considerable distance away. In falling they injured the plaintiff, an intending passenger.

Upon these facts may she recover the damages she has suffered in an action brought against the master? The result we shall reach depends upon our theory as to the nature of negligence. Is it a relative concept—the breach of some duty owing to a particular person or to particular persons? Or where there is an act which unreasonably threatens the safety of others, is the doer liable for all its proximate consequences, even where they result in injury to one who would generally be thought to be outside the radius of danger? This is not a mere dispute as to words. We might not believe that to the average mind the dropping of the bundle would seem to involve the probability of harm to the plantiff standing many feet away whatever might be the case as to the owner or to one so near as to be likely to be struck by its fall. If, however, we adopt the second hypothesis we have to inquire only as the relation between cause and effect. We deal in terms of proximate cause, not of negligence.

Negligence may be defined roughly as an act or omission which unreasonably does or may affect the rights of others, or which unreasonably fails to protect oneself from the dangers resulting from such acts. Here I confine mysfelf to the first branch of the definition. Nor do I comment on the word "unreasonable." For present purposes it sufficiently describes that average of conduct that society requires of its members.

There must be both the act or the omission, and the right. It is the act itself, not the intent of the actor, that is important.* In criminal law both the intent and the result are to be considered. Intent again is material in tort actions, where punitive damages are sought, dependent on actual malice—not on merely reckless conduct. But here neither insanity nor infancy lessens responsibility.

As has been said, except in cases of contributory negligence, there must be rights which are or may be affected. Often though injury has occurred, no rights of him who suffers have been touched. A licensee or trespasser upon my land has no claim to affirmative care on my part that the land be made safe.* Where a railroad is required to fence its tracks against cattle, no man's rights are injured should he wander upon the road because such fence is absent.* An unborn child may not demand immunity from personal harm.*

But we are told that "there is no negligence unless there is in the particular case a legal duty to take care, and this duty must be one which is owed to the plaintiff himself and not merely to others."* This, I think too narrow a conception. Where there is the unreasonable act, and some right that may be affected there is negligence whether damage does or does not result. That is immaterial. Should we drive down Broadway at a reckless speed, we are negligent whether we strike an approaching car or miss it by an inch. The act itself is wrongful. It is a wrong not only to those who happen to be within the radius of danger but to all who might have been there—a wrong to the public at large. Such is the language of the street. Such the language of the courts when speaking of contributory negligence. Such again and again their language in speaking of the duty of some defendant and discussing proximate cause in cases where such a discussion is wholly irrelevant on any other theory.* As was said by Mr. Justice HOLMES many years ago, "the measure of the defendant's duty in determining whether a wrong has been committed is one thing, the measure of liability when a wrong has been committed is another."* Due care is a duty imposed on each one of us to protect society from unnecessary danger not to protect A, B or C alone.

It may well be that there is no such thing as negligence in the abstract. "Proof of negligence in the air, so to speak, will not do." In an empty world negligence would not exist. It does involve a relationship between man and his fellows. But not merely a relationship between man and those whom he might reasonably expect his act would injure. Rather, a relationship between him and those whom he does in fact injure. If his act has a tendency to harm some one, it harms him a mile away as surely as it does those on the scene. We now permit children to recover for the negligent killing of the father. It was never prevented on the theory that no duty was owing to them. A husband may be compensated for the loss of his wife's services. To say that the wrongdoer was negligent as to the husband as well as to the wife is merely an attempt to fit facts to theory. An insurance company paying a fire loss recovers its payment of the negligent incendiary. We speak of subrogation—of suing in the right of the insured. Behind the cloud of words is the fact they hide, that the act, wrongful as to the insured, has also injured the company. Even if it be true that the fault of father, wife or insured will prevent recovery, it is because we consider the original negligence not the proximate cause of the injury.*

In the well-known *Polemis Case* (1921, 3 K.B. 560), SCRUTTON, L.J., said that the dropping of a plank was negligent for it might injure "workman or cargo or ship." Because of either possibility the owner of the vessel was to be made good for his loss. The act being wrongful the doer was liable for its proximate results. Criticized and explained as this statement may have been, I think it states the law as it should be and as it is.*

The proposition is this. Every one owes to the world at large the duty of refraining from those acts that may unreasonably threaten the safety of others. Such an act occurs. Not only is he wronged to whom harm might reasonably be expected to result, but he also who is in fact injured, even if he be outside what would generally be thought the danger zone. There needs be duty due the one complaining but this is not a duty to a particular individual because as to him harm might be expected. Harm to some one being the natural result of the act, not only that one alone, but all those in fact injured may complain. We have never, I think, held otherwise. Indeed in the *Di Caprio* case we said that a breach of a general ordinance defining the degree of care to be exercised in one's calling is evidence of negligence as to every one. We did not limit this statement to those who might be expected to be exposed to danger. Unreasonable risk being taken, its consequences are not confined to those who might probably be hurt.

If this be so, we do not have a plaintiff suing

---

*Citations omitted [Eds.]

*Citations omitted [Eds.]

by "derivation or succession." Her action is original and primary. Her claim is for a breach of duty to herself—not that she is subrogated to any right of action of the owner of the parcel or of a passenger standing at the scene of the explosion.

The right to recover damages rests on additional considerations. The plantiff's rights must be injured, and this injury must be caused by the negligence. We build a dam, but are negligent as to its foundations. Breaking, it injures property down stream. We are not liable if all this happened because of some reason other than the insecure foundation. But when injuires do result from our unlawful act we are liable for the consequences. It does not matter that they are unusual, unexpected, unforeseen and unforeseeable. But there is one limitation. The damages must be so connected with the negligence that the latter may be said to be the proximate cause of the former.

These two words have never been given an inclusive definition. What is a cause in a legal sense, still more what is a proximate cause, depend in each case upon many considerations, as does the existence of negligence itself. Any philosophical doctrine of causation does not help us. A boy throws a stone into a pond. The ripples spread. The water level rises. The history of that pond is altered to all eternity. It will be altered by other causes also. Yet it will be forever the resultant of all causes combined. Each one will have an influence. How great only omniscience can say. You may speak of a chain, or if you please, a net. An analogy is of little aid. Each cause brings about future events. Without each the future would not be the same. Each is proximate in the sense it is essential. But that is not what we mean by the word. Nor on the other hand do we mean sole cause. There is no such thing.

Should analogy be thought helpful, however, I prefer that of a stream. The spring, starting on its journey, is joined by tributary after tributary. The river, reaching the ocean, comes from a hundred sources. No man may say whence any drop of water is derived. Yet for a time distinction may be possible. Into the clear creek, brown swamp water flows from the left. Later, from the right comes water stained by its clay bed. The three may remain for a space, sharply divided. But at last, inevitably no trace of separation remains. They are so commingled that all distinction is lost.

As we have said, we cannot trace the effect of an act to the end, if end there is. Again, however, we may trace it part of the way. A murder at Sarajevo may be the necessary antecedent to an assassination in London twenty years hence. An overturned lantern may burn all Chicago. We may follow the fire from the shed to the last building. We rightly say the fire started by the lantern caused its destruction.

A cause, but not the proximate cause. What we do mean by the word "proximate" is, that because of convenience, of public policy, of a rough sense of justice, the law arbitrarily declines to trace a series of events beyond a certain point. This is not logic, it is practical politics. Take our rule as to fires. Sparks from my burning haystack set on fire my house and my neighbor's. I may recover from a negligent railroad. He may not. Yet the wrongful act as directly harmed the one as the other. We may regret that the line was drawn just where it was, but drawn somewhere it had to be. We said the act of the railroad was not the proximate cause of our neighbor's fire. Cause it surely was. The words we used were simply indicative of our notions of public policy. Other courts think differently. But somewhere they reach the point where they cannot say the stream comes from any one source.

Take the illustration given in an unpublished manuscript by a distinguished and helpful writer on the law of torts. A chauffeur negligently collides with another car which is filled with dynamite, although he could not know it. An explosion follows. A, walking on the sidewalk nearby, is killed. B, sitting in a window of a building opposite, is cut by flying glass. C, likewise sitting in a window a block away, is similarly injured. And a further illustration. A nursemaid, ten blocks away, startled by the noise, involuntarily drops a baby from her arms to the walk. We are told that C may not recover while A may. As to B it is a question for court or jury. We will all agree that the baby might not. Because, we are again told, the chauffeur had no reason to believe his conduct involved any risk of injuring either C or the baby. As to them he was not negligent.

But the chauffeur, being negligent in risking the collision, his belief that the scope of the harm he might do would be limited is immaterial. His act unreasonably jeopardized the safety of any one who might be affected by it. C's injury and that of the baby were directly traceable to the collision. Without that, the injury would not have happened. *C* had the right to sit in his office, secure from such dangers. The baby was entitled to use the sidewalk with reasonable safety.

The true theory is, it seems to me, that the injury to *C,* if in truth he is to be denied recovery, and the injury to the baby is that their several injuries were not the proximate result of the negligence. And here not what the chauffeur had reason to believe would be the result of his conduct, but what the prudent would foresee, may have a bearing. May have some bearing, for the problem of proximate cause is not to be solved by any one consideration.

It is all a question of expediency. There are no fixed rules to govern our judgment. There are simply matters of which we may take account. We have in somewhat different connection spoken of "the stream of events." We have asked whether that stream was deflected—whether it was forced into new and unexpected channels.* This is rather rhetoric than law. There is in truth little to guide us other than common sense.

There are some hints that may help us. The proximate cause, involved as it may be with many other causes, must be, at the least, something without which the event would not happen. The court must ask itself whether there was a natural and continuous sequence between cause and effect. Was the one a substantial factor in producing the other? Was there a direct connection between them, without too many intervening causes? Is the effect of cause on result not too attentuated? Is the cause likely, in the usual judgment of mankind, to produce the result? Or by the exercise of prudent foresight could the result be foreseen? Is the result too remote from the cause, and here we consider remoteness in time and space,* where we passed upon the construction of a contract— but something was also said on this subject. Clearly we must so consider, for the greater the distance either in time or space, the more surely do other causes intervene to affect the result. When a lantern is overturned the firing of a shed is a fairly direct consequence. Many things contribute to the spread of the conflagration— the force of the wind, the direction and width of street, the character of intervening structures, other factors. We draw an uncertain and wavering line, but draw it we must as best we can.

Once again, it is all a question of fair judgment, always keeping in mind the fact that we endeavor to make a rule in each case that will be practical and in keeping with the general understanding of mankind.

Here another question must be answered. In the case supposed it is said, and said correctly, that the chauffeur is liable for the direct effect of the explosion although he had no reason to suppose it would follow a collision. "The fact that the injury occurred in a different manner than that which might have been expected does not prevent the chauffeur's negligence from being in law the cause of the injury." But the natural results of a negligent act—the results which a prudent man would or should foresee—do have a bearing upon the decision as to proximate cause. We have said so repeatedly. What should be foreseen? No human foresight would suggest that a collision itself might injure one a block away. On the contrary, given an explosion, such a possibility might be reasonably expected. I think the direct connection, the foresight of which the courts speak, assumes prevision of the explosion, for the immediate results of which, at least, the chauffeur is responsible.

It may be said this is unjust. Why? In fairness he should make good every injury flowing from his negligence. Not because of tenderness toward him we say he need not answer for all that follows his wrong. We look back to the catastrophe, the fire kindled by the spark, or the explosion. We trace the consequences—not indefinitely, but to a certain point. And to aid us in fixing that point we ask what might ordinarily be expected to follow the fire or the explosion.

This last suggestion is the factor which must determine the case before us. The act upon which defendant's liability rests is knocking an apparently harmless package onto the platform. The act was negligent. For its proximate consequences the defendant is liable. If its contents were broken, to the owner; if it fell upon and crushed a passenger's foot, then to him. If it exploded and injured one in the immediate vicinity, to him also as to *A* in the illustration. Mrs. Palsgraf was standing some distance away. How far cannot be told from the record—apparently twenty-five or thirty feet. Perhaps less. Except for the explosion, she would not have been injured. We are told by the appellant in his brief "it cannot be denied that the explosion was the direct cause of the plaintiff's injuries." So it was a substantial factor in producing the result—there was here a natural and continuous sequence—direct connection. The only intervening cause was that instead of blowing her to the ground the concussion smashed the weighing machine which in turn fell upon her. There was no remoteness in time, little in space. And surely, given such an explosion as here it needed no great foresight to predict that the natural result would be to injure one on the platform at no greater distance from its scene than was the plaintiff. Just how no one might be able to predict. Whether by flying fragments, by broken glass, by wreckage of machines or structures no one could say. But injury in some form was most probable.

Under these circumstances I cannot say as a matter of law that the plaintiff's injuries were not the proximate result of the negligence. That is all we have before us. The court refused to so charge. No request was made to submit the matter to the jury as a question of fact, even would that have been proper upon the record before us.

The judgment appealed from should be affirmed, with costs.

POUND, LEHMAN and KELLOGG, JJ., concur with CARDOZO, CH. J.; ANDREWS, J., dissents in opinion in which CRANE and O'BRIEN, JJ., concur.

Judgment reversed, etc.

LON L. FULLER

The Case of the Speluncean Explorers*

The defendants, having been indicted for the crime of murder, were convicted and sentenced to be hanged by the Court of General Instances of the County of Stowfield. They bring a petition of error before this Court. The facts sufficiently appear in the opinion of the Chief Justice.

TRUEPENNY, C. J. The four defendants are members of the Speluncean Society, an organization of amateurs interested in the exploration of caves. Early in May of 4299 they, in the company of Roger Whetmore, then also a member of the Society, penetrated into the interior of a limestone cavern of the type found in the Central Plateau of this Commonwealth. While they were in a position remote from the entrance to the cave, a landslide occurred. Heavy boulders fell in such a manner as to block completely the only known opening to the cave. When the men discovered their predicament they settled themselves near the obstructed entrance to wait until a rescue party should remove the detritus that prevented them from leaving their underground prison. On the failure of Whetmore and the defendants to return to their homes, the Secretary of the Society was notified by their families. It appears that the explorers had left indications at the headquarters of the Society concerning the location of the cave they proposed to visit. A rescue party was promptly dispatched to the spot.

The task of rescue proved one of overwhelming difficulty. It was necessary to supplement the forces of the original party by repeated increments of men and machines, which had to be conveyed at great expense to the remote and isolated region in which the cave was located. A huge temporary camp of workmen, engi-

neers, geologists, and other experts was established. The work of removing the obstruction was several times frustrated by fresh landslides. In one of these, ten of the workmen engaged in clearing the entrance were killed. The treasury of the Speluncean Society was soon exhausted in the rescue effort, and the sum of eight hundred thousand frelars, raised partly by popular subscription and partly by legislative grant, was expended before the imprisoned men were rescued. Success was finally achieved on the thirty-second day after the men entered the cave.

Since it was known that the explorers had carried with them only scant provisions, and since it was also known that there was no animal or vegetable matter within the cave on which they might subsist, anxiety was early felt that they might meet death by starvation before access to them could be obtained. On the twentieth day of their imprisonment it was learned for the first time that they had taken with them into the cave a portable wireless machine capable of both sending and receiving messages. A similar machine was promptly installed in the rescue camp and oral communication established with the unfortunate men within the mountain. They asked to be informed how long a time would be required to release them. The engineers in charge of the project answered that at least ten days would be required even if no new landslides occurred. The explorers then asked if any physicians were present, and were placed in communication with a committee of medical experts. The imprisoned men described their condition and the rations they had taken with them, and asked for a medical opinion whether they would be likely to live without food for ten days longer. The chairman of the committee of physicians told them that there was little possibility of this. The wireless machine within the cave then remained silent for eight hours. When communication was re-

*Lon L. Fuller, "The Case of the Speluncean Explorers," *Harvard Law Review,* Vol. 62 (1949), pp. 616–645. Reprinted by permission of the *Harvard Law Review* and Mr. John N. Roche.

established the men asked to speak again with the physicians. The chairman of the physicians' committee was placed before the apparatus, and Whetmore, speaking on behalf of himself and the defendants, asked whether they would be able to survive for ten days longer if they consumed the flesh of one of their number. The physicians' chairman reluctantly answered this question in the affirmative. Whetmore asked whether it would be advisable for them to cast lots to determine which of them should be eaten. None of the physicians present was willing to answer the question. Whetmore then asked if there were among the party a judge or other official of the government who would answer this question. None of these attached to the rescue camp was willing to assume the role of advisor in this matter. He then asked if any minister or priest would answer their question, and none was found who would do so. Thereafter no further messages were received from within the cave, and it was assumed (erroneously, it later appeared) that the electric batteries of the explorers' wireless machine had become exhausted. When the imprisoned men were finally released it was learned that on the twenty-third day after their entrance into the cave Whetmore had been killed and eaten by his companions.

From the testimony of the defendants, which was accepted by the jury, it appears that it was Whetmore who first proposed that they might find the nutriment without which survival was impossible in the flesh of one of their own number. It was also Whetmore who first proposed the use of some method of casting lots, calling the attention of the defendants to a pair of dice he happened to have with him. The defendants were at first reluctant to adopt so desperate a procedure, but after the conversations by wireless related above, they finally agreed on the plan proposed by Whetmore. After much discussion of the mathematical problems involved, agreement was finally reached on a method of determining the issue by the use of the dice.

Before the dice were cast, however, Whetmore declared that he withdrew from the arrangement, as he had decided on reflection to wait for another week before embracing an expedient so frightful and odious. The others charged him with a breach of faith and proceeded to cast the dice. When it came Whetmore's turn, the dice were cast for him by one of the defendants, and he was asked to declare any objections he might have to the fairness of the throw. He stated that he had no such objections. The throw went against him, and he was then put to death and eaten by his companions.

After the rescue of the defendants, and after they had completed a stay in a hospital where they underwent a course of treatment for malnutrition and shock, they were indicted for the murder of Roger Whetmore. At the trial, after the testimony had been concluded, the foreman of the jury (a lawyer by profession) inquired of the court whether the jury might not find a special verdict, leaving it to the court to say whether on the facts as found the defendants were guilty. After some discussion, both the Prosecutor and counsel for the defendants indicated their acceptance of this procedure, and it was adopted by the court. In a lengthy special verdict the jury found the facts as I have related them above, and found further that if on these facts the defendants were guilty of the crime charged against them, then they found the defendants guilty. On the basis of this verdict, the trial judge ruled that the defendants were guilty of murdering Roger Whetmore. The judge then sentenced them to be hanged, the law of our Commonwealth permitting him no discretion with respect to the penalty to be imposed. After the release of the jury, its members joined in a communication to the Chief Executive asking that the sentence be commuted to an imprisonment of six months. The trial judge addressed a similar communication to the Chief Executive. As yet no action with respect to these pleas has been taken, as the Chief Executive is apparently awaiting our disposition of this petition of error.

It seems to me that in dealing with this extraordinary case the jury and the trial judge followed a course that was not only fair and wise, but the only course that was open to them under the law. The language of our statute is well known: "Whoever shall willfully take the life of another shall be punished by death." N. C. S. A. (N. s.) § 12-A. This statute permits of no exception applicable to this case, however our sympathies may incline us to make allowance for the tragic situation in which these men found themselves.

In a case like this the principle of executive clemency seems admirably suited to mitigate the rigors of the law, and I propose to my colleagues that we follow the example of the jury and the trial judge by joining in the communications they have addressed to the Chief Executive. There is every reason to believe that these requests for clemency will be heeded, coming as they do from those who have studied the case and had an opportunity to become thoroughly acquainted with all its circumstances. It is highly improbable that the Chief Executive would deny these requests unless he were himself to hold hearings at least as extensive as those involved in the trial below, which lasted for three months. The holding of such hearings (which would virtually amount to a retrial of the case) would scarcely be compatible with the function of the Executive as it is usually conceived. I think we may therefore assume that some form of clemency will be extended to these defendants. If this is done, then justice will be accomplished without impairing either the letter or spirit of our statutes and without offering any encouragement for the disregard of law.

FOSTER, J. I am shocked that the Chief Justice, in an effort to escape the embarrassments of this tragic case, should have adopted, and should have proposed to his colleagues, an expedient at once so sordid and so obvious. I believe something more is on trial in this case than the fate of these unfortunate explorers; that is the law of our Commonwealth. If this Court declares that under our law these men have committed a crime, then our law is itself convicted in the tribunal of common sense, no matter what happens to the individuals involved in this petition of error. For us to assert that the law we uphold and expound compels us to a conclusion we are ashamed of, and from which we can only escape by appealing to a dispensation resting within the personal whim of the Executive, seems to me to amount to an admission that the law of this Commonwealth no longer pretends to incorporate justice.

For myself, I do not believe that our law compels the monstrous conclusion that these men are murderers. I believe, on the contrary, that it declares them to be innocent of any crime. I rest this conclusion on two independent grounds, either of which is of itself sufficient to justify the acquittal of these defendants.

The first of these grounds rests on a premise that may arouse opposition until it has been examined candidly. I take the view that the enacted or positive law of this Commonwealth, including all of its statutes and precedents, is inapplicable to this case, and that the case is governed instead by what ancient writers in Europe and America called "the law of nature."

This conclusion rests on the proposition that our positive law is predicated on the possibility of men's coexistence in society. When a situation arises in which the coexistence of men becomes impossible, then a condition that underlies all of our precedents and statutes has ceased to exist. When that condition disappears, then it is my opinion that the force of our positive law disappears with it. We are not accustomed to applying the maxim *cessante ratione legis, cessat et ipsa lex* to the whole of our enacted law, but I believe that this is a case where the maxim should be so applied.

The proposition that all positive law is based on the possibility of men's coexistence has a strange sound, not because the truth it contains is strange, but simply because it is a truth so obvious and pervasive that we seldom have occasion to give words to it. Like the air we breathe, it so pervades our environment that we forget that it exists until we are suddenly deprived of it. Whatever particular objects may be sought by the various branches of our law, it is apparent on reflection that all of them are directed toward facilitating and improving men's coexistence and regulating with fairness and equity the relations of their life in common. When the assumption that men may live together loses its truth, as it obviously did in this extraordinary situation where life only became possible by the taking of life, then the basic premises underlying our whole legal order have lost their meaning and force.

Had the tragic events of this case taken place a mile beyond the territorial limits of our Commonwealth, no one would pretend that our law was applicable to them. We recognize that jurisdiction rests on a territorial basis. The grounds of this principle are by no means obvious and are seldom examined. I take it that this principle is supported by an assumption that it is feasible to impose a single legal order upon a group of men only if they live together within the confines of a given area of the earth's surface. The premise that men shall coexist in a group underlies, then, the territorial principle, as it does all of law. Now I contend that a case may be removed morally from the force of a legal order, as well as geographically. If we look to the purposes of law and government, and to the premises underlying our positive law, these men when they made their fateful decision were as remote from our legal order as if they had been a thousand miles beyond our boundaries. Even in a physical sense, their underground prison was separated from our courts and writ-servers by a solid curtain of rock that could be removed only after the most extraordinary expenditures of time and effort.

I conclude, therefore, that at the time Roger Whetmore's life was ended by these defendants, they were, to use the quaint language of the nineteenth-century writers, not in a "state of civil society" but in a "state of nature." This has the consequence that the law applicable to them is not the enacted and established law of this Commonwealth, but the law derived from those principles that were appropriate to their condition. I have no hesitancy in saying that under those principles they were guiltless of any crime.

What these men did was done in pursuance of an agreement accepted by all of them and first proposed by Whetmore himself. Since it was apparent that their extraordinary predicament made inapplicable the usual principles that regulate men's relations with one another, it was necessary for them to draw, as it were, a new charter of government appropriate to the situation in which they found themselves.

It has from antiquity been recognized that the most basic principle of law or government is to be found in the notion of contract or agreement. Ancient thinkers, especially during the period from 1600 to 1900, used to base government itself on a supposed original social compact. Skeptics pointed out that this theory contradicted the known facts of history, and that there was no scientific evidence to support the notion that any government was ever founded in the manner supposed by the theory. Moralists replied that, if the compact was a fiction from a historical point of view, the notion of compact or agreement furnished the only ethical justification on which the powers of government, which include that of taking life, could be rested. The powers of government can only be justified morally on the ground that these are powers that reasonable men would agree upon and accept if they were faced with the necessity of constructing anew some order to make their life in common possible.

Fortunately, our Commonwealth is not bothered by the perplexities that beset the ancients. We know as a matter of historical truth that our government was founded upon a contract or free accord of men. The archeological proof is conclusive that in the first period following the Great Spiral the survivors of that holocaust voluntarily came together and drew up a charter of government. Sophistical writers have raised questions as to the power of those remote contractors to bind future generations, but the fact remains that our government traces itself back in an unbroken line to that original charter.

If, therefore, our hangmen have the power to end men's lives, if our sheriffs have the power to put delinquent tenants in the street, if our police have the power to incarcerate the inebriated reveler, these powers find their moral justification in that original compact of our forefathers. If we can find no higher source for our legal order, what higher source should we expect these starving unfortunates to find for the order they adopted for themselves?

I believe that the line of argument I have just expounded permits of no rational answer. I realize that it will probably be received with a certain discomfort by many who read this opinion, who will be inclined to suspect that some hidden sophistry must underlie a demonstration that leads to so many unfamiliar conclusions. The source of this discomfort is, however, easy to identify. The usual conditions of human existence incline us to think of human life as an absolute value, not to be sacrificed under any circumstances. There is much that is fictitious about this conception even when it is applied to the ordinary relations of society. We have an illustration of this truth in the very case before us. Ten workmen were killed in the process of removing the rocks from the opening to the cave. Did not the engineers and government officials who directed the rescue effort know that the operations they were undertaking were dangerous and involved a serious risk to the lives of the workmen executing them? If it was proper that these ten lives should be sacrificed to save the lives of five imprisoned explorers, why then are we told it was wrong for these explorers to carry out an arrangement which would save four lives at the cost of one?

Every highway, every tunnel, every building we project involves a risk to human life. Taking these projects in the aggregate, we can calculate with some precision how many deaths the construction of them will require; statisticians can tell you the average cost in human lives of a thousand miles of a four-lane concrete highway. Yet we deliberately and knowingly incur and pay this cost on the assumption that the values obtained for those who survive outweigh the loss. If these things can be said of a society functioning above ground in a normal and ordinary manner, what shall we say of the supposed absolute value of a human life in the desperate situation in which these defendants and their companion Whetmore found themselves?

This concludes the exposition of the first ground of my decision. My second ground proceeds by rejecting hypothetically all the premises on which I have so far proceeded. I concede for purposes of argument that I am wrong in saying that the situation of these men removed them from the effect of our positive law, and I assume that the Consolidated Statutes have the power to penetrate five hundred feet of rock and to impose themselves upon these starving men huddled in their underground prison.

Now it is, of course, perfectly clear that these men did an act that violates the literal wording of the statute which declares that he who "shall willfully take the life of another" is a murderer. But one of the most ancient bits of legal wisdom is the saying that a man may break the letter of the law without breaking the law itself. Every proposition of positive law, whether contained in a statute or a judicial precedent, is to be interpreted reasonably, in the light of its evident purpose. This is a truth so elementary that it is hardly necessary to expatiate on it. Illustrations of its application are numberless and are to be found in every branch of the law. In *Commonwealth* v. *Staymore* the defendant was convicted under a statute making it a crime to leave one's car parked in certain areas for a period longer than two hours. The defendant had attempted to remove his car, but was prevented from doing so because the streets were obstructed by a political demonstration in which he took no part and which he had no reason to anticipate. His conviction was set aside by this Court, although his case fell squarely within the wording of the statute. Again, in *Fehler* v. *Neegas* there was before this Court for construction a statute in which the word "not" had plainly been transposed from its intended position in the final and most crucial section of the act. This transposition was contained in all the successive drafts of the act, where it was apparently overlooked by the draftsmen and sponsors of the legislation. No one was able to prove how the error came about, yet it was apparent that, taking account of the contents of the statute as a whole, an error had been made, since a literal reading of the final clause rendered it inconsistent with everything that had gone before and with the object of the enactment as stated in its preamble. This Court refused to accept a literal interpretation of the statute, and in effect rectified its language by reading the word "not" into the place where it was evidently intended to go.

The statute before us for interpretation has never been applied literally. Centuries ago it was established that a killing in self-defense is excused. There is nothing in the wording of the statute that suggests this exception. Various attempts have been made to reconcile the legal treatment of self-defense with the words of the statute, but in my opinion these are all merely ingenious sophistries. The truth is that the exception in favor of self-defense cannot be reconciled with the *words* of the statute, but only with its *purpose*.

The true reconciliation of the excuse of self-defense with the statute making it a crime to kill another is to be found in the following line of reasoning. One of the principal objects underlying any criminal legislation is that of deterring men from crime. Now it is apparent that if it were declared to be the law that a killing in self-defense is murder such a rule could not operate in a deterrent manner. A man whose life is threatened will repel his aggressor, whatever the law may say. Looking therefore to the broad purposes of criminal legislation, we may safely declare that this statute was not intended to apply to cases of self-defense.

When the rationale of the excuse of self-defense is thus explained, it becomes apparent that precisely the same reasoning is applicable to the case at bar. If in the future any group of men ever find themselves in the tragic predicament of these defendants, we may be sure that their decision whether to live or die will not be controlled by the contents of our criminal code. Accordingly, if we read this statute intelligently it is apparent that it does not apply to this case. The withdrawal of this situation from the effect of the statute is justified by precisely the same considerations that were applied by our predecessors in office centuries ago to the case of self-defense.

There are those who raise the cry of judicial usurpation whenever a court, after analyzing the purpose of a statute, gives to its words a meaning that is not at once apparent to the casual reader who has not studied the statute closely or examined the objectives it seeks to attain. Let me say emphatically that I accept without reservation the proposition that this

Court is bound by the statutes of our Commonweath and that it exercises its powers in subservience to the duly expressed will of the Chamber of Representatives. The line of reasoning I have applied above raises no question of fidelity to enacted law, though it may possibly raise a question of the distinction between intelligent and unintelligent fidelity. No superior wants a servant who lacks the capacity to read between the lines. The stupidest housemaid knows that when she is told "to peel the soup and skim the potatoes" her mistress does not mean what she says. She also knows that when her master tells her to "drop everything and come running" he has overlooked the possibility that she is at the moment in the act of rescuing the baby from the rain barrel. Surely we have a right to expect the same modicum of intelligence from the judiciary. The correction of obvious legislative errors or oversights is not to supplant the legislative will, but to make that will effective.

I therefore conclude that on any aspect under which this case may be viewed these defendants are innocent of the crime of murdering Roger Whetmore, and that the conviction should be set aside.

TATTING, J. In the discharge of my duties as a justice of this Court, I am usually able to dissociate the emotional and intellectual sides of my reactions, and to decide the case before me entirely on the basis of the latter. In passing on this tragic case I find that my usual resources fail me. On the emotional side I find myself torn between sympathy for these men and a feeling of abhorrence and disgust at the monstrous act they committed. I had hoped that I would be able to put these contradictory emotions to one side as irrelevant, and to decide the case on the basis of a convincing and logical demonstration of the result demanded by our law. Unfortunately, this deliverance has not been vouchsafed for me.

As I analyze the opinion just rendered by my brother Foster, I find that it is shot through with contradictions and fallacies. Let us begin with his first proposition: these men were not subject to our law because they were not in a "state of civil society" but in a "state of nature." I am not clear why this is so, whether it is because of the thickness of the rock that imprisoned them, or because they were hungry, or because they had set up a "new charter of government" by which the usual rules of law were to be supplanted by a throw of the dice. Other difficulties intrude themselves. If these men passed from the jurisdiction of our law to that of "the law of nature," at what moment did this occur? Was it when the entrance to the cave was blocked, or when the threat of starvation reached a certain undefined degree of intensity, or when the agreement for the throwing of the dice was made? These uncertainties in the doctrine proposed by my brother are capable of producing real difficulties. Suppose, for example, one of these men had had his twenty-first birthday while he was imprisoned within the mountain. On what date would we have to consider that he had attained his majority—when he reached the age of twenty-one, at which time he was, by hypothesis, removed from the effects of our law, or only when he was released from the cave and became again subject to what my brother calls our "positive law"? These difficulties may seem fanciful, yet they only serve to reveal the fanciful nature of the doctrine that is capable of giving rise to them.

But it is not necessary to explore these niceties further to demonstrate the absurdity of my brother's position. Mr. Justice Foster and I are the appointed judges of a court of the Commonwealth of Newgarth, sworn and empowered to administer the laws of that Commonwealth. By what authority do we resolve ourselves into a Court of Nature? If these men were indeed under the law of nature, whence comes our authority to expound and apply that law. Certainly *we* are not in a state of nature.

Let us look at the contents of this code of nature that my brother proposes we adopt as our own and apply to this case. What a topsy-turvy and odious code it is! It is a code in which the law of contracts is more fundamental than the law of murder. It is a code under which a man may make a valid agreement empowering his fellows to eat his own body. Under the provisions of this code, furthermore, such an agreement once made is irrevocable, and if one of the parties attempts to withdraw, the others may take the law into their own hands and enforce the contract by violence—for though my brother passes over in convenient silence the effect of Whetmore's withdrawal, this is the necessary implication of his argument.

The principles my brother expounds contain other implications that cannot be tolerated. He argues that when the defendants set upon Whetmore and killed him (we know not how, perhaps by pounding him with stones) they were only exercising the rights conferred upon them by their bargain. Suppose, however, that Whetmore had had concealed upon his person a revolver, and that when he saw the defendants about to slaughter him he had shot them to death in order to save his own life. My brother's reasoning applied to these facts would make Whetmore out to be a murderer, since the excuse of self-defense would have to be denied to him. If his assailants were acting rightfully in seeking to bring about his death, then of course he could no more plead the excuse that he was defending his own life than could a condemned prisoner who struck down the executioner lawfully attempting to place the noose about his neck.

All of these considerations make it impossible for me to accept the first part of my brother's argument. I can neither accept his notion that these men were under a code of nature which this Court was bound to apply to them, nor can I accept the odious and perverted rules that he would read into that code. I come now to the second part of my brother's opinion, in which he seeks to show that the defendants did not violate the provisions of N. C. S. A. (N. S.) § 12-A. Here the way, instead of being clear, becomes for me misty and ambiguous, though my brother seems unaware of the difficulties that inhere in his demonstrations.

The gist of my brother's argument may be stated in the following terms: No statute, whatever its language, should be applied in a way that contradicts its purpose. One of the purposes of any criminal statute is to deter. The application of the statute making it a crime to kill another to the peculiar facts of this case would contradict this purpose, for it is impossible to believe that the contents of the criminal code could operate in a deterrent manner on men faced with the alternative of life or death. The reasoning by which this exception is read into the statute is, my brother observes, the same as that which is applied in order to provide the excuse of self-defense.

On the face of things this demonstration seems very convincing indeed. My brother's interpretation of the rationale of the excuse of self-defense is in fact supported by a decision of this court, *Commonwealth* v. *Parry*, a precedent I happened to encounter in my research on this case. Though *Commonwealth* v. *Parry* seems generally to have been overlooked in the texts and subsequent decisions, it supports unambiguously the interpretation my brother has put upon the excuse of self-defense.

Now let me outline briefly, however, the perplexities that assail me when I examine my brother's demonstration more closely. It is true that a statute should be applied in the light of its purpose and that *one* of the purposes of criminal legislation is recognized to be deterrence. The difficulty is that other purposes are also ascribed to the law of crimes. It has been said that one of its objects is to provide an orderly outlet for the instinctive human demand for retribution. *Commonwealth* v. *Scape*. It has also been said that its object is the rehabilitation of the wrongdoer. *Commonwealth* v. *Makeover*. Other theories have been propounded. Assuming that we must interpret a statute in the light of its purpose, what are we to do when it has many purposes or when its purposes are disputed?

A similar difficulty is presented by the fact that although there is authority for my brother's interpretation of the excuse of self-defense, there is other authority which assigns to that excuse a different rationale. Indeed, until I happened on *Commonwealth* v. *Parry* I had never heard of the explanation given by my brother. The taught doctrine of our law schools, memorized by generations of law students, runs in the following terms: The statute concerning murder requires a "willful" act. The man who acts to repel an aggressive threat to his own life does not act "willfully," but in response to an impulse deeply ingrained in human nature. I suspect that there is hardly a lawyer in this Commonwealth who is not familiar with this line of reasoning, especially since the point is a great favorite of the bar examiners.

Now the familiar explanation for the excuse of self-defense just expounded obviously cannot be applied by analogy to the facts of this case. These men acted not only "willfully" but with great deliberation and after hours of discussing what they should do. Again we encounter a forked path, with one line of reasoning leading us in one direction and another in a direction that is exactly the opposite. This perplexity is in this case compounded, as it were, for we have to set off one explanation, incorporated in a virtually unknown precedent of this Court, against another explanation, which forms a part of the taught legal tradition of our law schools, but which, so far as I know, has never been adopted in any judicial decision.

I recognize the relevance of the precedents cited by my brother concerning the displaced "not" and the defendant who parked overtime. But what are we do with one of the landmarks of our jurisprudence, which again my brother passes over in silence? This is *Commonwealth* v. *Valjean*. Though the case is somewhat obscurely reported, it appears that the defendant was indicted for the larceny of a loaf of bread, and offered as a defense that he was in a condition approaching starvation. The court refused to accept this defense. If hunger cannot justify the theft of wholesome and natural food, how can it justify the killing and eating of a man? Again, if we look at the thing in terms of deterrence, is it likely that a man will starve to death to avoid a jail sentence for the theft of a loaf of bread? My brother's demonstrations would compel us to overrule *Commonwealth* v. *Valjean,* and many other precedents that have been built on that case.

Again, I have difficulty in saying that no deterrent effect whatever could be attributed to a decision that these men were guilty of murder. The stigma of the word "murderer" is such that it is quite likely, I believe, that if these men had known that their act was deemed by the law to be murder they would have waited for a few days at least before carrying out their plan. During that time some unexpected relief might have come. I realize that this observation only reduces the distinction to a matter of degree, and does not destroy it altogether. It is certainly true that the element of deterrence would be less in this case than is normally involved in the application of the criminal law.

There is still a further difficulty in my brother Foster's proposal to read an exception into the statute to favor this case, though again a difficulty not even intimated in his opinion. What shall be the scope of this exception? Here the men cast lots and the victim was himself originally a party to the agreement. What would we have to decide if Whetmore had refused from the beginning to participate in the plan? Would a majority be permitted to overrule him? Or, suppose that no plan were adopted at all and the others simply conspired to bring about Whetmore's death, justifying their act by saying that he was in the weakest condition. Or again, that a plan of selection was followed but one based on a different justification than the one adopted here, as if the others were atheists and insisted that Whetmore should die because he was the only one who believed in an afterlife. These illustrations could be multiplied, but enough have been suggested to reveal what a quagmire of hidden difficulties my brother's reasoning contains.

Of course I realize on reflection that I may be concerning myself with a problem that will never arise, since it is unlikely that any group of men will ever again be brought to commit the dread act that was involved here. Yet, on still further reflection, even if we are certain that no similar case will arise again, do not the illustrations I have given show the lack of any coherent and rational principle in the rule my brother proposes? Should not the soundness of a principle be tested by the conclusions it entails, without reference to the accidents of later litigational history? Still, if this is so, why is it that we of this Court so often discuss the question whether we are likely to have later occasion to apply a principle urged for the solution of the case before us? Is this a situation where a line of reasoning not originally proper has become sanctioned by precedent, so that we are permitted to apply it and may even be under an obligation to do so?

The more I examine this case and think about it, the more deeply I become involved. My mind becomes entangled in the meshes of the very nets I throw out for my own rescue. I find that almost every consideration that bears on the decision of the case is counterbalanced by an opposing consideration leading in the opposite direction. My brother Foster has not furnished to me, nor can I discover for myself, any formula capable of resolving the equivocations that beset me on all sides.

I have given this case the best thought of which I am capable. I have scarcely slept since it was argued before us. When I feel myself inclined to accept the view of my brother Foster, I am repelled by a feeling that his arguments are intellectually unsound and approach mere rationalization. On the other hand, when I incline toward upholding the conviction, I am struck by the absurdity of directing that these men be put to death when their lives have been saved at the cost of the lives of ten heroic workmen. It is to me a matter of regret that the Prosecutor saw fit to ask for an indictment for murder. If we had a provision in our statutes making it a crime to eat human flesh, that would have been a more appropriate charge. If no other charge suited to the facts of this case could be brought against the defendants, it would have been wiser, I think, not to have indicted them at all. Unfortunately, however, the men have been indicted and tried, and we have therefore been drawn into this unfortunate affair.

Since I have been wholly unable to resolve the doubts that beset me about the law of this case, I am with regret announcing a step that is, I believe, unprecedented in the history of this tribunal. I declare my withdrawal from the decision of this case.

KEEN, J. I should like to begin by setting to one side two questions which are not before this Court.

The first of these is whether executive clemency should be extended to these defendants if the conviction is affirmed. Under our system of government, that is a question for the Chief Executive, not for us. I therefore disapprove of that passage in the opinion of the Chief Justice in which he in effect gives instructions to the Chief Executive as to what he should do in this case and suggests that some impropriety will attach if these instructions are not heeded. This is a confusion of governmental functions—a confusion of which the judiciary should be the last to be guilty. I wish to state that if I were the Chief Executive I would go farther in the direction of clemency than the pleas addressed to him propose. I would pardon these men altogether, since I believe that they have already suffered enough to pay for any offense they may have committed. I want it to be understood that this remark is made in my capacity as a private citizen who by the accident of his office happens to have acquired an intimate acquaintance with the facts of this case. In the discharge of my duties as judge, it is neither my function to address directions to the Chief Executive, nor to take into account what he may or may not do, in reaching my own decision, which must be controlled entirely by the law of this Commonwealth.

The second question that I wish to put to one side is that of deciding whether what these men did was "right" or "wrong," "wicked" or "good." That is also a question that is irrelevant to the discharge of my office as a judge sworn to apply, not my conceptions of morality, but the law of the land. In putting this question to one side I think I can also safely dismiss without comment the first and more poetic portion of my brother Foster's opinion. The element of fantasy contained in the arguments developed there has been sufficiently revealed in my brother Tatting's somewhat solemn attempt to take those arguments seriously.

The sole question before us for decision is whether these defendants did, within the meaning of N. C. S. A. (N. S.) § 12-A, willfully take the life of Roger Whetmore. The exact language of the statute is as follows: "Whoever shall willfully take the life of another shall be punished by death." Now I should suppose that any candid observer, content to extract from these words their natural meaning, would concede at once that these defendants did "willfully take the life" of Roger Whetmore.

Whence arise all the difficulties of the case, then, and the necessity for so many pages of discussion about what ought to be so obvious? The difficulties, in whatever tortured form they may present themselves, all trace back to a single source, and that is a failure to distinguish the legal from the moral aspects of this case. To put it bluntly, my brothers do not like the fact that the written law requires the conviction of these defendants. Neither do I, but unlike my brothers I respect the obligations of an office that requires me to put my personal predilections out of my mind when I come to interpret and apply the law of this Commonwealth.

Now, of course, my brother Foster does not admit that he is actuated by a personal dislike of the written law. Instead he develops a familiar line of argument according to which the court may disregard the express language of a statute when something not contained in the statute itself, called its "purpose," can be employed to justify the result the court considers proper. Because this is an old issue between myself and my colleague, I should like, before discussing his particular application of the argument to the facts of this case, to say something about the historical background of this issue and its implications for law and government generally.

There was a time in this Commonwealth when judges did in fact legislate very freely, and all of us know that during that period some of our statutes were rather thoroughly made over by the judiciary. That was a time when the accepted principles of political science did not designate with any certainty the rank and function of the various arms of the state. We all know the tragic issue of that uncertainty in the brief civil war that arose out of the conflict between the judiciary, on the one hand, and the executive and the legislature, on the other. There is no need to recount here the factors that contributed to that unseemly struggle for power, though they included the unrepresentative character of the Chamber, resulting from a division of the country into election districts that no longer accorded with the actual distribution of the population, and the forceful personality and wide popular following of the then Chief Justice. It is enough to observe that those days are behind us, and that in place of the uncertainty that then reigned we now have a clear-cut principle, which is the supremacy of the legislative branch of our government. From that principle flows the obligation of the judiciary to enforce faithfully the written law, and to interpret that law in accordance with its plain meaning without reference to our personal desires or our individual conceptions of justice. I am not copncerned with the question whether the principle that forbids the judicial revision of statutes is right or wrong, desirable or undesirable; I observe merely that this principle has become a tacit premise underlying the whole of the legal and governmental order I am sworn to administer.

Yet though the principle of the supremacy of the legislature has been accepted in theory for centuries, such is the tenacity of professional tradition and the force of fixed habits of thought that many of the judiciary have still not accommodated themselves to the restricted role which the new order imposes on them. My brother Foster is one of that group; his way of dealing with statutes is exactly that of a judge living in the 3900's.

We are all familiar with the process by which the judicial reform of disfavored legislative enactments is accomplished. Anyone who has followed the written opinions of Mr. Justice Foster will have had an opportunity to see it at work in every branch of the law. I am personally so familiar with the process that in the event of my brother's incapacity I am sure I could write a satisfactory opinion for him without any prompting whatever, beyond being informed whether he liked the effect of the terms of the statute as applied to the case before him.

The process of judicial reform requires three steps. The first of these is to divine some single "purpose" which the statute serves. This is done although not one statute in a hundred has any such single purpose, and although the objectives of nearly every statute are differently interpreted by the different classes of its sponsors. The second step is to discover that a mythical being called "the legislator," in the pursuit of this imagined "purpose," overlooked something or left some gap or imperfection in his

work. Then comes the final and most refreshing part of the task, which is, of course, to fill in the blank thus created. . . .

My brother Foster's penchant for finding holes in statutes reminds one of the story told by an ancient author abut the man who ate a pair of shoes. Asked how he liked them, he replied that the part he liked best was the holes. That is the way my brother feels about statutes; the more holes they have in them the better he likes them. In short, he doesn't like statutes.

One could not wish for a better case to illustrate the specious nature of this gap-filling process than the one before us. My brother thinks he knows exactly what was sought when men made murder a crime, and that was something he calls "deterrence." My brother Tatting has already shown how much is passed over in that interpretation. But I think the trouble goes deeper. I doubt very much whether our statute making murder a crime really has a "purpose" in any ordinary sense of the term. Primarily, such a statute reflects a deeply-felt human conviction that murder is wrong and that something should be done to the man who commits it. If we were forced to be more articulate about the matter, we would probably take refuge in the more sophisticated theories of the criminologists, which, of course, were certainly not in the minds of those who drafted our statute. We might also observe that men will do their own work more effectively and live happier lives if they are protected against the threat of violent assault. Bearing in mind that the victims of murders are often unpleasant people, we might add some suggestion that the matter of disposing of undesirables is not a function suited to private enterprise, but should be a state monopoly. All of which reminds me of the attorney who once argued before us that a statute licensing physicians was a good thing because it would lead to lower life insurance rates by lifting the level of general health. There is such a thing as overexplaining the obvious.

If we do not know the purpose of § 12-A, how can we possibly say there is a "gap" in it? How can we know what its draftsmen thought about the question of killing men in order to eat them? My brother Tatting has revealed an understandable, though perhaps slightly exaggerated revulsion to cannibalism. How do we know that his remote ancestors did not feel the same revulsion to an even higher degree? Anthropologists say that the dread felt for a forbidden act may be increased by the fact that the conditions of a tribe's life create special temptations toward it, as incest is most severely condemned among those whose village relations make it most likely to occur. Certainly the period following the Great Spiral was one that had implicit in it temptations to anthropophagy. Perhaps it was for that very reason that our ancestors expressed their prohibition in so broad and unqualified a form. All of this is conjecture, of course, but it remains abundantly clear that neither I nor my brother Foster knows what the "purpose" of § 12-A is.

Considerations similar to those I have just outlined are also applicable to the exception in favor of self-defense, which plays so large a role in the reasoning of my brothers Foster and Tatting. It is of course true that in *Commonwealth* v. *Parry* an obiter dictum justified this exception on the assumption that the purpose of criminal legislation is to deter. It may well also be true that generations of law students have been taught that the true explanation of the exception lies in the fact that a man who acts in self-defense does not act "willfully," and that the same students have passed their bar examinations by repeating what their professors told them. These last observations I could dismiss, of course, as irrelevant for the simple reason that professors and bar examiners have not as yet any commission to make our laws for us. But again the real trouble lies deeper. As in dealing with the statute, so in dealing with the exception, the question is not the conjectural *purpose* of the rule, but its *scope*. Now the scope of the exception in favor of self-defense as it has been applied by this Court is plain: it applies to cases of resisting an aggressive threat to the party's own life. It is therefore too clear for argument that this case does not fall within the scope of the exception, since it is plain that Whetmore made no threat against the lives of these defendants.

The essential shabbiness of my brother Foster's attempt to cloak his remaking of the written law with an air of legitimacy comes tragically to the surface in my brother Tatting's opinion. In that opinion Justice Tatting struggles manfully to combine his colleague's loose moralisms with his own sense of fidelity to the written law. The issue of this struggle could only be that which occurred, a complete default in the discharge of the judicial function. You simply cannot apply a statute as it is written and remake it to meet your own wishes at the same time.

Now I know that the line of reasoning I have developed in this opinion will not be acceptable to those who look only to the immediate effects of a decision and ignore the long-run implications of an assumption by the judiciary of a power of dispensation. A hard decision is never a popular decision. Judges have been celebrated in literature for their sly prowess in devising some quibble by which a litigant could be deprived of his rights where the public thought it was wrong for him to assert those rights. But I believe that judicial dispensation does more harm in the long run than hard decisions. Hard cases may even have a certain moral value by bringing home to the people their own responsibilities toward the law that is ultimately their creation, and by reminding them that there is no principle of personal grace that can relieve the mistakes of their representatives.

Indeed, I will go farther and say that not only are the principles I have been expounding those which are soundest for our present conditions, but that we would have inherited a better legal system from our forefathers if those principles had been observed from the beginning. For example, with respect to the excuse of self-defense, if our courts had stood steadfast on the language of the statute the result would undoubtedly have been a legislative revision of it. Such a revision would have drawn on the assistance of natural philosophers and psychologists, and the resulting regulation of the matter would have had an understandable and rational basis, instead of the hodgepodge of verbalisms and metaphysical distinctions that have emerged from the judicial and professorial treatment.

These concluding remarks are, of course, beyond any duties that I have to discharage with relation to this case, but I include them here because I feel deeply that my colleagues are insufficiently aware of the dangers implicit in the conceptions of the judicial office advocated by my brother Foster.

I conclude that the conviction should be affirmed.

HANDY, J. I have listened with amazement to the tortured ratiocinations to which this simple case has given rise. I never cease to wonder at my colleagues' ability to throw an obscuring curtain of legalisms about every issue presented to them for decision. We have heard this afternoon learned disquisitions on the distinction between positive law and the law of nature, the language of the statute and the purpose of the statute, judicial functions and executive functions, judicial legislation and legislative legislation. My only disappointment was that someone did not raise the question of the legal nature of the bargain struck in the cave—whether it was unilateral or bilateral, and whether Whetmore could not be considered as having revoked an offer prior to action taken thereunder.

What have all these things to do with the case? The problem before us is what we, as officers of the government, ought to do with these defendants. That is a question of practical wisdom, to be exercised in a context, not of abstract theory, but of human realities. When the case is approached in this light, it becomes, I think, one of the easiest to decide that has ever been argued before this Court.

Before stating my own conclusions about the merits of the case, I should like to discuss briefly some of the more fundamental issues involved—issues on which my colleagues and I have been divided ever since I have been on the bench.

I have never been able to make my brothers see that government is a human affair, and that men are ruled, not by words on paper or by abstract theories, but by other men. They are ruled well when their rulers understand the feelings and conceptions of the masses. They are ruled badly when that understanding is lacking.

Of all branches of the government, the judiciary is the most likely to lose its contact with the common man. The reasons for this are, of course, fairly obvious. Where the masses react to a situation in terms of a few salient features, we pick into little pieces every situation presented to us. Lawyers are hired by both sides to analyze and dissect. Judges and attorneys vie with one another to see who can discover the greatest number of difficulties and distinctions in a single set of facts. Each side tries to find cases, real or imagined, that will embarrass the demonstrations of the other side. To escape this embarrassment, still further distinctions are invented and imported into the situation. When a set of facts has been subjected to this kind of treatment for a sufficient time, all the life and juice have gone out of it and we have left a handful of dust.

Now I realize that wherever you have rules and abstract pirnciples lawyers are going to be able to make distinctions. To some extent the sort of thing I have been describing is a necessary evil attaching to any formal regulation of human affairs. But I think that the area which really stands in need of such regulation is greatly overestimated. There are, of course, a few fundamental rules of the game that must be accepted if the game is to go on at all. I would include among these the rules relating to the conduct of elections, the appointment of public officials, and the term during which an office is held. Here some restraint on discretion and dispensation, some adherence to form, some scruple for what does and what does not fall within the rule, is, I concede, essential. Perhaps the area of basic principle should be expanded to incude certain other rules, such as those designed to preserve the free civilmoign system.

But outside of these fields I believe that all government officials, including judges, will do their jobs best if they treat forms and abstract concepts as instruments. We should take as our model, I think, the good administrator, who accommodates procedures and principles to the case at hand, selecting from among the available forms those most suited to reach the proper result.

The most obvious advantage of this method of government is that it permits us to go about our daily tasks with efficiency and common sense. My adherence to this philosophy has, however, deeper roots. I believe that it is only with the insight this philosophy gives that we can preserve the flexibility essential if we are to keep our actions in reasonable accord with the sentiments of those subject to our rule. More governments have been wrecked, and more human misery caused, by the lack of this accord between ruler and ruled than by any other factor that can be discerned in history. Once we drive a sufficient wedge between the mass of people and those who direct their legal, political, and economic life, our society is ruined. Then neither Foster's law of nature nor Keen's fidelity to written law will avail us anything.

Now when these conceptions are applied to the case before us, its decision becomes, as I have said, perfectly easy. In order to demonstrate this I shall have to introduce certain realities that my brothers in their coy decorum have seen fit to pass over in silence, although they are just as acutely aware of them as I am.

The first of these is that this case has aroused an enormous public interest, both here and abroad. Almost every newspaper and magazine has carried articles about it; columnists have shared with their readers confidential information as to the next governmental move; hundreds of letters-to-the-editor have been printed. One of the great newspaper chains made a poll of public opinion on the question, "What do you think the Supreme Court should do with the Speluncean explorers?" About ninety per cent expressed a belief that the defendants should be pardoned or let off with a kind of token punishment. It is perfectly clear, then, how the public feels about the case. We could have known this without the poll, of course, on the basis of common sense, or even by observing that on this Court there are apparently four-and-a-half men, or ninety percent, who share the common opinion.

This makes it obvious, not only what we should do, but what we must do if we are to preserve between ourselves and public opinion a reasonable and decent accord. Declaring these men innocent need not involve us in any undignified quibble or trick. No principle of statutory construction is required that is not consistent with the past practices of this Court. Certainly no layman would think that in letting these men off we had stretched the statute any more than our ancestors did when they created the excuse of self-defense. If a more detailed demonstration of the method of reconciling our decision with the statute is required, I should be content to rest on the arguments developed in the second and less visionary part of my brother Foster's opinion.

Now I know that my brothers will be horrified by my suggestion that this Court should take account of public opinion. They will tell you that public opinion is emotional and capricious, that it is based on half-truths and listens to witnesses who are not subject to cross-examination. They will tell you that the law surrounds the trial of a case like this with elaborate safeguards, designed to insure that the truth will be known and that every rational consideration bearing on the issues of the case has been taken into account. They will warn you that all of these safeguards go for naught if a mass opinion formed outside this framework is allowed to have any influence on our decision.

But let us look candidly at some of the realities of the administration of our criminal law. When a man is accused of crime, there are, speaking generally, four ways in which he may escape punishment. One of these is a determination by a judge that under the applicable law he has committed no crime. This is, of course, a determination that takes place in a rather formal and abstract atmosphere. But look at the other three ways in which he may escape punishment. These are: (1) a decision by the Prosecutor not to ask for an indictment; (2) an acquittal by the jury; (3) a pardon or commutation of sentence by the executive. Can anyone pretend that these decisions are held within a rigid and formal framework of rules that prevents factual error, excludes emotional and personal factors, and guarantees that all the forms of the law will be observed?

In the case of the jury we do, to be sure, attempt to cabin their deliberations within the area of the legally relevant, but there is no need to deceive ourselves into believing that this attempt is really successful. In the normal course of events the case now before us would have gone on all of its issues directly to the jury. Had this occurred we can be confident that there would have been an acquittal or at least a division that would have prevented a conviction. If the jury had been instructed that the men's hunger and their agreement were no defense to the charge of murder, their verdict would in all likelihood have ignored this instruction and would have involved a good deal more twisting of the letter of the law than any that is likely to tempt us. Of course the only reason that didn't occur in this case was the fortuitous circumstance that the foreman of the jury happened to be a lawyer. His learning enabled him to devise a form of words that would allow the jury to dodge its usual responsibilities.

My brother Tatting expresses annoyance that the Prosecutor did not, in effect, decide the case for him by not asking for an indictment. Strict as he is himself in complying with the demands of legal theory, he is quite content to have the fate of these men decided out of court by the Prosecutor on the basis of common sense. The Chief Justice, on the other hand, wants the application of common sense postponed to the very end, though like Tatting, he wants no personal part in it.

This brings me to the concluding portion of my remarks, which has to do with executive clemency. Before discussing that topic directly, I want to make a related observation about the poll of public opinion. As I have said, ninety per cent of the people wanted the Supreme Court to let the men off entirely or with a more or less nominal punishment. The ten per cent constituted a very oddly assorted group, with the most curious and divergent opinions. One of our university experts has made a study of this group and has found that its members fall into certain patterns. A substantial portion of them are subscribers to "crank" newspapers of limited circulation that gave their readers a distorted version of the facts of the case. Some thought that "Speluncean" means "cannibal" and that anthropophagy is a tenet of the Society. But the point I want to make, however, is this: although almost every conceivable variety and shade of opinion was represented in this group, there was, so far as I know, not one of them, nor a single member of the majority of ninety per cent, who said, "I think it would be a fine thing to have the courts sentence these men to be hanged, and then to have another branch of the government come along and pardon them." Yet this is a solution that has more or less dominated our discussions and which our Chief Justice proposes as a way by which we can avoid doing an injustice and at the same time preserve respect for law. He can be assured that if he is preserving anybody's morale, it is his own, and not the public's, which knows nothing of his distinctions. I mention this matter because I wish to emphasize once more the danger that we may get lost in the patterns of our own thought and forget that these patterns often cast not the slightest shadow on the outside world.

I come now to the most crucial fact in this case, a fact known to all of us on this Court, though one that my brothers have seen fit to keep under the cover of their judicial robes. This is the frightening likelihood that if the issue is left to him, the Chief Executive will refuse to pardon these men or commute their sentence. As we all know, our Chief Executive is a man now well advanced in years, of very stiff notions. Public clamor usually operates on him with the reverse of the effect intended. As I have told my brothers, it happens that my wife's niece is an intimate friend of his secretary. I have learned in this indirect, but, I think, wholly reliable way, that he is firmly determined not to commute the sentence if these men are found to have violated the law.

No one regrets more than I the necessity for relying in so important a matter on information that could be characterized as gossip. If I had my way this would not happen, for I would adopt the sensible course of sitting down with the Executive, going over the case with him, finding out what his views are, and perhaps working out with him a common program for handling the situation. But of course my brothers would never hear of such a thing.

Their scruple about acquiring accurate information directly does not prevent them from being very perturbed about what they have learned indirectly. Their acquaintance with the facts I have just related explains why the Chief Justice, ordinarily a model of decorum, saw fit in his opinion to flap his judicial robes in the face of the Executive and threaten him with excommunication if he failed to commute the sentence. It explains, I suspect, my brother Foster's feat of levitation by which a whole library of law books was lifted from the shoulders of these defendants. It explains also why even my legalistic brother Keen emulated Pooh-Bah in the ancient comedy by stepping to the other side of the stage to address a few remarks to the Executive "in my capacity as a private citizen." (I may remark, incidentally, that the advice of Private Citizen Keen will appear in the reports of this court printed at taxpayer's expense.)

I must confess that as I grow older I become more and more perplexed at men's refusal to apply their common sense to problems of law and government, and this truly tragic case has deepened my sense of discouragement and dismay. I only wish that I could convince my brothers of the wisdom of the principles I have applied to the judicial office since I first assumed it. As a matter of fact, by a kind of sad rounding of the circle, I encountered issues like those involved here in the very first case I tried as Judge of the Court of General Instances in Fanleigh County.

A religious sect had unfrocked a minister who, they said, had gone over to the views and practices of a rival sect. The minister circulated a handbill making charges against the authorities who had expelled him. Certain lay members of the church announced a public meeting at which they proposed to explain the position of the church. The minister attended this meeting. Some said he slipped in unobserved in a disguise; his own testimony was that he had walked in openly as a member of the public. At any rate, when the speeches began he interrupted with certain questions about the affairs of the church and made some statements in defense of his own views. He was set upon by members of the audience and given a pretty thorough pommeling, receiving among other injuries a broken jaw. He brought a suit for damages against the association that sponsored the meeting and against ten named individuals who he alleged were his assailants.

When we came to the trial, the case at first seemed very complicated to me. The attorneys raised a host of legal issues. There were nice questions on the admissibility of evidence, and, in connection with the suit against the association, some difficult problems turning on the question whether the minister was a trespasser or a licensee. As a novice on the bench I was eager to apply my law school learning and I began studying these questions closely, reading all the authorities and preparing well-documented rulings. As I studied the case I became more and more involved in its legal intricacies and I began to get into a state approaching that of my brother Tatting in this case. Suddenly, however, it dawned on me that all these perplexing issues really had nothing to do with the case, and I began examining it in the light of common sense. The case at once gained a new perspective, and I saw that the only thing for me to do was to direct a verdict for the defendants for lack of evidence.

I was led to this conclusion by the following considerations. The melee in which the plaintiff was injured had been a very confused affair, with some people trying to get to the center of the disturbance, while others were trying to get away from it; some striking at the plaintiff, while others were apparently trying to protect him. It would have taken weeks to find out the truth of the matter. I decided that nobody's broken jaw was worth that much to the Commonwealth. (The minister's injuries, incidentally, had meanwhile healed without disfigurement and without any impairment of normal faculties.) Furthermore, I felt very strongly that the plaintiff had to a large extent brought the thing on himself. He knew how inflamed passions were about the affair, and could easily have found another forum for the expression of his views. My decision was widely approved by the press and public opinion, neither of which could tolerate the views and practices that the expelled minister was attempting to defend.

Now, thirty years later, thanks to an ambitious Prosecutor and a legalistic jury foreman, I am faced with a case that raises issues which are at bottom much like those involved in that case. The world does not seem to change much, except that this time it is not a question of a judgment for five or six hundred frelars, but of the life or death of four men who have already suffered more torment and humiliation than most of us would endure in a thousand years. I conclude that the defendants are innocent of the crime charged, and that the conviction and sentence should be set aside.

TATTING, J. I have been asked by the Chief Justice whether, after listening to the two opinions just rendered, I desire to re-examine the position previously taken by me. I wish to state that after hearing these opinions I am greatly strengthened in my conviction that I ought not to participate in the decision of this case.

The Supreme Court being evenly divided, the conviction and sentence of the Court of General Instances is *affirmed*. It is ordered that the execution of the sentence shall occur at 6 A.M., Friday, April 2, 4300, at which time the Public Executioner is directed to proceed with all convenient dispatch to hang each of the defendants by the neck until he is dead.

POSTSCRIPT

Now that the court has spoken, the reader puzzled by the choice of date may wish to be reminded that the centuries which separate us from the year 4300 are roughly equal to those that have passed since the Age of Pericles. There is probably no need to observe that the *Speluncean Case* itself is intended neither as a work of satire nor as a prediction in any ordinary sense of the term. As for the judges who make up Chief Justice Truepenny's court, they are, of course, as mythical as the facts and precedents with which they deal. The reader who refuses to accept this view, and who seeks to trace out contemporary resemblances where none is intended or contemplated, should be warned that he is engaged in a folic of his own, which may possibly lead him to miss whatever modest truths are contained in the opinions delivered by the Supreme Court of Newgarth. The case was constructed for the sole purpose of bringing into a common focus certain divergent philosophies of law and government. These philosophies presented men with live questions of choice in the days of Plato and

Aristotle. Perhaps they will continue to do so when our era has had its say about them. If there is any element of prediction in the case, it does not go beyond a suggestion that the questions involved are among the permanent problems of the human race.

UNITED STATES v. HOLMES

United States Circuit Court, 1842*

[1 Wall. Jr. 1.]¹

Circuit Court, E. D. Pennsylvania. April 22, 1842.

CONDUCT OF TRIAL—ADMISSION OF PERSONS WITHIN BAR—HOMICIDE BY SEAMAN—SHIPWRECK—ABANDONMENT OF PASSENGERS.

1. Although this court is deprived, by the act of March 2, 1831, of the power to punish, as for a contempt of court, the publication during trial, of testimony in a case, yet, having power to regulate the admission of persons, and the character of proceedings within its own bar, the court can exclude from within the bar any person coming there to report testimony during the trial. [Cited in U.S. v. Anon., 21 Fed. 768.]

2. Seamen have no right, even in cases of extreme peril to their own lives, to sacrifice the lives of passengers, for the sake of preserving their own. On the contrary, being common carriers, and so paid to protect and carry the passengers, the seamen, beyond the number necessary to navigate the boat, in no circumstances can claim exemption from the common lot of the passengers.

3. In the case here reported, the relative obligations of seamen and passengers, in the event of shipwreck or maritime disaster, are examined and stated.

4. The indictment charged that the prisoner did commit manslaughter on the high seas (1) by casting F. A. from a vessel belonging, etc., whose name was unknown; (2) by casting him from the long-boat of the ship W. B., belonging, etc. The indictment is sufficiently certain.

The American ship William Brown, left Liverpool on the 13th of March, 1841, bound for Philadelphia, in the United States. She had on board (besides a heavy cargo) 17 of a crew, and 65 passengers, Scotch and Irish emigrants. About 10 o'clock on the night of the 19th of April, when distant 250 miles southeast of Cape Race, Newfoundland, the vessel struck an iceberg, and began to fill so rapidly that it was evi-

*1 Wall Jr. 1 (C.C.E.D. Pa, 1842).

dent she must soon go down. The long-boat and jolly-boat were cleared away and lowered. The captain, the second mate, 7 of the crew, and 1 passenger got into the jolly-boat. The first mate, 8 seamen, of whom the prisoner was one (these 9 being the entire remainder of the crew), and 32 passengers, in all 41 persons, got indiscriminately into the long-boat.² The remainder of the passengers, 31 persons, were obliged to remain on board the ship. In an hour and a half from the time when the ship struck, she went down, carrying with her every person who had not escaped to one or the other of the small boats. Thirty-one passengers thus perished.³ On the following morning (Tuesday) the captain, being about to part company with the long-boat, gave its crew several directions, and, among other counsel, advised them to obey all the orders of the mate, as they would obey his, the captain's. This the crew promised that they would do. The long-boat was believed to be in general good condition; but she had not been in the water since leaving Liverpool, now thirty-five days; and as soon as she was launched, began to leak. She continued to leak the whole time; but the passengers had buckets, and tins, and, by bailing were able to reduce the water, so as to make her hold her own. The plug was about an inch and a half in diameter. It came out more than once, and finally, got lost; but its place was supplied by different expedients.

It appeared by the depositions of the captain, and of the second mate,⁴ (the latter of whom had followed the sea twenty-one years; the former being, likewise, well-experienced), that on Tuesday morning when the two boats parted company, the long-boat and all on board were in great jeopardy. The gunwale was within from 5 to 12 inches of the water. "From the experience" which they had had, they thought "the long-boat was too unmanageable to be saved." If she had been what, in marine phrase, is called a "leaky boat," she must have gone down. Even without a leak she would not have supported one-half her company, had there been "a moderate blow." "She would have swamped very quickly." The people were half naked, and were "all crowded up together like sheep in a pen." "A very little irregularity in the stowage would have capsized the long-boat." "If she had struck any piece of ice she would inevitably have gone down. There was great peril of ice for any boat." (Captain's and second mate's depositions.) Without going into more detail, the evidence of both these officers went to show that, loaded as the long-boat was on Tuesday morning, the chances of living were much against her. But the captain thought, that even if lightened to the extent to which she afterwards was, "it would have been impossible to row her to land; and that the chances of her being picked up, were ninty-nine to one against her." It appeared, further, that on Monday night, when the passengers on the ship (then settling towards her head and clearly going down) were shrieking, and calling on the captain to take them off on his boat, the mate on the long-boat said to them: "Poor souls! you're only going down a short time before we do." And, further, that on the following morning, before the boats parted company, the mate, in the long-boat, told the captain, in the jolly-boat, that the long-boat was unmanageable, and, that unless the captain would take some of the long-boat's passengers, it would be necessary to cast lots and throw some overboard. "I know what you mean," or, as stated by one witness, "I know what you'll have to do," said the captain. "Don't speak of that now. Let it be the last resort." There was little or no wind at this time, but pieces of ice were floating about.

Notwithstanding all this, the long-boat, loaded as she is above described to have been, did survive throughout the night of Monday, the day of Tuesday, and until 10 o'clock of Tuesday night,—full twenty-four hours after the ship struck the iceberg. The crew rowed, turn about, at intervals, and the passengers bailed. On Tuesday morning, after the long-boat and jolly-boat parted, it began to rain, and continued to rain throughout the day and night of Tuesday. At night the wind began to freshen, the sea grew heavier, and once, or oftener, the waves splashed over the boat's bow so as to wet, all over, the passengers who were seated there. Pieces of ice were still floating around, and, during the day, icebergs had been seen. About 10 o'clock of Tuesday night, the prisoner and the rest of the crew began to throw over some of the passengers, and did not cease until they had thrown over 14 male passengers. These, with the exception of two married men and a small boy, constituted all the male passengers aboard. Not one of the crew was cast over. One of them, the cook, was a negro.

It was among the facts of this case that, during these solemn and distressful hours, scarce a remark appeared to have been made in regard to what was going to be done, nor, while it was being done, as to the necessity for doing it. None of the crew of the long-boat were present at the trial, to testify, and, with the exception of one small boy, all the witnesses from the long-boat were women,—mostly quite young. It is probable that, by Tuesday night (the weather being cold, the persons on the boat partially naked, and the rain falling heavily), the witnesses had become considerably overpowered by exhaustion and cold, having been 24 hours in the boat. None of them spoke in a manner entirely explicit and satisfactory in regard to the most important point, viz. the degree and imminence of the jeopardy at 10 o'clock on Tuesday night, when the throwing over began. As has been stated, few words were spoken. It appeared, only, that, about 10 o'clock of Tuesday night, it being then dark, the rain falling rather heavily, the sea somewhat freshening, and the boat having considerable water in it, the mate, who had been bailing for some time, gave it up, exclaiming: "This work won't do. Help me, God. Men, go to work." Some of the passengers cried out, about the same time: "The boat is sinking. The plug's out. God have mercy on our poor souls." Holmes and the crew did not proceed upon this order; and after a little while, the mate exclaimed again: "Men, you must go to work, or we shall all perish." They then went to work; and, as has been already stated, threw out, before they ended, 14 male passengers, and also 2 women.[5] The mate directed the crew "not to part man and wife, and not to throw over any women." There was no other principle of selection. There was no evidence of combination among the crew. No lots were cast, nor had the passengers, at any time, been either informed or consulted as to what was now done. Holmes was one of the persons who assisted in throwing the passengers over. The first man thrown over was one Riley, whom Holmes and the others told to stand up, which he did. They then threw him over, and afterwards Duffy, who, in vain, besought them to spare him, for the sake of his wife and children, who were on shore. They then seized a third man, but, his wife being aboard, he was spared. Coming to Charles Conlin, the man exclaimed: "Holmes, dear, sure you won't put me out?" "Yes, Charley," said Holmes, "you must go, too." And so he was thrown over. Next was Francis Askin, for the manslaughter of whom the prisoner was indicted. When laid hold of, he offered Holmes five sovereigns to spare his life till morning, "when," said he, "if God don't send us some help, we'll draw lots, and it the lot falls on me, I'll go over like a man." Holmes said, "I don't want your money, Frank," and put him overboard. When one McAvoy was seized, he asked for five minutes to say his prayers, and, at the interposition of a negro, the cook, was allowed time to say them before he was cast overboard. It appeared, also, that when Askin was put out, he had struggled violently, yet the boat had not sunk. Two men, very stiff with cold, who had hidden themselves, were thrown over after daylight on Wednesday morning, when, clearly, there was no necessity for it.[6] On Wednesday morning, while yet in the boat, some of the witnesses had told the crew that they (i.e., the crew) should be made to die the death they had given to the others. The boat had provisions for six or seven days, close allowance; that is to say, 75 pounds of bread, 6 gallons of water, 8 or 10 pounds of meat, and a small bag of oatmeal. The mate had a chart, quadrant and compass. The weather was cold, and the passengers, being half clothed, much benumbed. On Wednesday morning the weather cleared, and early in the morning the long-boat was picked up by the ship "Crescent." All the persons who had not been thrown overboard were thus saved.

On the other hand the character of the prisoner stood forth, in many points, in manly and interesting relief. A Finn by birth, he had followed the sea from youth, and his frame and countenance would have made an artist's model for decision and strength. He had been the last man of the crew to leave the sinking ship. His efforts to save the passengers, at the time the ship struck, had been conspicuous, and, but that they were in discharge of duty, would have been called self-forgetful and most generous.[7] As a sailor, his captain and the second mate testified that he had ever been obedient to orders, faithful to his duty, and efficient in the performance of it,—"remarkably so," said the second mate. "He was kind and obliging in every respect," said the captain, "to the passengers, to his shipmates, and to everybody. Never heard one speak against him. He was always obedient to officers. I never had a better man on board ship. He was a first-rate man." (Captain's deposition.) While on the long-boat, in order to protect the women, he had parted with all his clothes, except his shirt and pantaloons; and his conduct and language to the women were kind. After Askin had been thrown out, some one asked if any more were to be thrown over. "No," said Holmes, "no more shall be thrown over. If any more are lost, we will all be lost together." Of both passengers and crew, he finally became the only one whose energies and whose hopes did not sink into prostration. He was the first to descry the vessel which took them up, and by his exertions the ship was made to see, and, finally, to save, them.[8]

The prisoner was indicted under the act of April 30, 1790, "for the punishment of certain crimes against the United States" (1 Story's Laws, 83 [1 Stat. 115], an act which ordains (section 12) that if any seaman, &c., shall commit manslaughter upon the high seas, &c., on conviction, he shall be imprisoned not exceeding three years, and fined not exceeding one thousand dollars. The indictment charged that Holmes—First, with force, &c., "unlawfully and feloniously" did make an assault, &c., and cast

and throw Askin from a vessel, belonging, &c., whose name was unknown, into the high seas, by means of which, &c., Askin, in and with the waters thereof then and there was suffocated and drowned; second, in the same way, on board the long-boat of the ship William Brown, belonging, &c., did make an assault, &c., and cast, &c. The trial of the prisoner came on upon the 13th of April, 1842, a few days before the anniversary of the calamitous events referred to. The case was replete with incidents of deep romance, and of pathetic interest. These, not being connected with the law of the case, of course do not appear in this report; but they had become known, in a general way, to the public, before the trial; and on the day assigned for the trial, at the opening of the court, several stenographers connected with the newspaper press appeared within the bar, ready to report the evidence for their expectant readers.

BALDWIN, Circuit Justice, on taking his seat, now said: "By an act of congress, passed some years since,[9] the court has no longer the power to punish, as for contempt, the publication of testimony pending a trial before us. We have, however, the power to regulate the admissions of persons and the character of proceedings within our own bar; and, as the court perceives several persons apparently connected with the daily press, whose object, we persume, is to report the proceedings and evidence in this case, as it advances, the court takes occasion to state that no person will be allowed to come within the bar of the court for the purpose of reporting, except on condition of suspending all publication till after the trial is concluded. On compliance with this condition, and not otherwise, the court will direct that a convenient place be afforded to the reporters of the press."

The reporters expressed their acquiescence in this order of the court, and the most respectful silence, on the part of the press, prevailed during the whole trial.

The prosecution was conducted by Mr. Wm. M. Meredith, U.S. Dist. Atty., Mr. Dallas, and O. Hopkinson; the defence by David Paul Brown, Mr. Hazelhurst, and Mr. Armstrong.

Mr. Dallas. The prisoner is charged with "unlawful homicide," as distinguished from that sort which is malicious. His defence is that the homicide was necessary to self-preservation. First, then, we ask: Was the homicide thus necessary? That is to say, was the danger instant, overwhelming, leaving no choice of means, no moment for deliberation? For, unless the danger were of this sort, the prisoner, under any admission, had no right, without notice or consultation, or lot, to sacrifice the lives of 16 fellow beings. Peril, even extreme peril, is not enough to justify a sacrifice such as this was. Nor would even the certainty of death be enough, if death were yet prospective. It must be instant. The law regards every man's life as of equal value. It regards it, likewise, as of sacred value. Nor may any man take away his brother's life, but where the sacrifice is indispensable to save his own. (Mr. Dallas then examined the evidence, and contended that the danger was not so extreme as is requisite to justify homicide.) But it will be answered, that death being certain, there was no obligation to wait until the moment of death had arrived. Admitting, then, the fact that death was certain, and that the safety of some persons was to be promoted by an early sacrifice of the others, what law, we ask, gives a crew, in such a case, to be the arbiters of life and death, settling, for themselves, both the time and the extent of the necessity? No. We protest against giving to seamen the power thus to make jettison of human beings, as of so much cargo; of allowing sailors, for their own safety, to throw overboard, whenever they may like, whomsoever they may choose. If the mate and seamen believed that the ultimate safety of a portion was to be advanced by the sacrifice of another portion, it was the clear duty of that officer, and of the seamen, to give full notice to all on board. Common settlement would, then, have fixed the principle of sacrifice, and, the mode of selection involving all, a sacrifice of any would have been resorted to only in dire extremity. Thus far, the argument admits that, at sea, sailor and passenger stand upon the same base, and in equal relations. But we take, third, stronger ground. The seaman, we hold, is bound, beyond the passenger, to encounter the perils of the sea. To the last extremity, to death itself, must he protect the passenger. It is his duty. It is on account of these risks that he is paid. It is because the sailor is expected to expose himself to every danger, that, beyond all mankind, by every law, his wages are secured to him. It is for this exposure that the seamen's claims are a "sacred lien," and "that if only a single nail of the ship is left, they are entitled to it." 3 Kent, Comm. 197, and in note. Exposure, risk, hardship, death, are the sailor's vocation,—the seaman's daily bread. He must perform whatever belongs to his duty. To this effect speaks Lord Bacon, when he says "that the law imposeth it upon every subject that he prefer the urgent service of his prince and country before the safety of his life." His lordship goes on to say that, "if a man be commanded to bring ordnance or munition to relieve any of the king's towns that are distressed, then he cannot, for any danger of tempest, justify the throwing of them overboard; for there it holdeth which was spoken by the Roman when he alleged the same necessity of weather to hold him from embarking: 'Necesse est et ut eam; non ut vivam.' " 13 Bacon's Works, by Montagu (Lond. 1831) p. 161.[10] No other doctrine than this one can be adopted. Promulgate as law that the prisoner is guiltless, and our marine will be disgraced in the eyes of civilized nations. The thousand ships which now traverse the ocean in safety will be consigned to the absolute power of their crews, and, worse than the dangers of the sea, will be added such as come from the violence of men more reckless than any upon earth.

Mr. Armstrong opened the defence, and was followed by Mr. Brown.

We protest against the prisoner being made a victim to the reputation of the marine law of the country. It cannot be, God forbid that it should ever be, that the sacrifice of innocence shall be the price at which the name and honour of American jurisprudence is to be preserved in this country, or in foreign lands. The malediction of an unrighteous sentence will rest more heavily on the law, than on the prisoner. This court (it would be indecent to think otherwise) will administer the law, "uncaring consequences." But this case should be tried in a long-boat, sunk down to its very gunwale with 41 half naked, starved, and shivering wretches,—the boat leaking from below, filling from above, a hundred leagues from land, at midnight, surrounded by ice, unmanageable from its load, and subject to certain destruction from the change of the most changeful of the elements, the winds and the waves. To these superadd the horrours of famine and the recklessness of despair, madness, and all the prospects, past utterance, of this unutterable condition. Fairly to sit in judgment on the prisoner, we should, then, be actually translated to his situation. It was a conjuncture which no fancy can image. Terrour had assumed the throne of reason, and passion had become judgment. Are the United States to come here, now, a year after the events, when it is impossible to estimate the elements which combined to make the risk, or to say to what extent the jeopardy was imminent? Are they, with square, rule and compass, deliberately to measure this boat, in this room, to weigh these passengers, call in philosophers, discuss specific gravities, calculate by the tables of a life insurance company the chances of life, and because they, these judges find that, by their calculation, this unfortunate boat's crew might have had the thousandth part of one poor chance of escape, to condemn this prisoner to chains and a dungeon, for what he did in the terror and darkness of that dark and terrible night. Such a mode of testing men's acts and motives is monstrous. We contend, therefore, that what is honestly and reasonably believed to be certain death will justify self-defence to the degree requisite for excuse. According to Dr. Rutherford (Inst. Nat. Law, bk. 1, c. 16, § 5): "This law,"—i.e. the law of nature,—"cannot be supposed to oblige a man to expose his life to such dangers as may be guarded against, and to wait till the danger is just coming upon him, before it allows him to secure himself." In other words, he need not wait till the certainty of the danger has been proved, past doubt, by its result. Yet this is the doctrine of the prosecution. They ask us to wait until the boat has sunk. We may, then, make an effort to prevent her from sinking. They tell us to wait till all are drowned. We may then, make endeavours to save a part. They command us to stand still till we are all lost past possibility of redemption, and then we may rescue as many as can be saved. Where the danger is instantaneous, the mind is too much disturbed, says Rutherford, in a passage hereafter cited, to deliberate upon the method of providing for one's own safety, with the least hurt to an aggressor. The same author then proceeds: "I see not, therefore, any want of benevolence which can be reasonably charged upon a man in these circumstances, if he takes the most obvious way of preserving himself, though perhaps some other method might have been found out, which would have preserved him as effectually, and have produced less hurt to the aggressor, if he had been calm enough, and had been allowed time enough to deliberate about it." Rutherf. Inst. Nat. Law, bk. 1, c. 16, § 5. Nor is this the language of approved text writers alone. The doctrine has the solemnity of judicial establishment. In Grainger v. State, 5 Yerg. 459, the supreme court of Tennessee deliberately adjudge, that "if a man, though in no great danger of serious bodily harm, through fear, alarm, or cowardice, kill another under the impression that great bodily injury is about to be inflicted on him, it is neither manslaughter nor murder, but self-defence." "It is a different thing," say the supreme court of the United States, in The Mariana Flora, 11 Wheat. [24 U.S.] 51, "to sit in judgment upon this case, after full legal investigations, aided by the regular evidence of all parties, and to draw conclusions at sea, with very imperfect means of ascertaining facts and principles which ought to direct the judgment." The decision in the case just cited, carried out this principle into practice, as the case of The Louis, 2 Dod. 264, decided by Sir William Scott, had done before. The counsel cited Lord Bacon, likewise (Works, by Montagu, vol. 13, Lond. 1831, p. 160), and 4 Bl. Comm. p. 186. But the prospect of sinking was not imaginary. It was well founded. It is not to be supposed that Holmes, who, from infancy, had been a child of the ocean, was causelessly alarmed; and, there being no pretence of animosity, but the contrary, we must infer that the peril was extreme. As regards the two men cast over on Wednesday, the presumption is that they were either frozen, or freezing to death. There being, at this time, no prospect of relief, the act is deprived of its barbarity. The evidence is that the two men were "very stiff with cold." Besides, this indictment is in regard to Askin alone. There is no evidence of inhumanity on Tuesday night, when this throwing over began; though it is possible enough, that, having proceeded so far in the work of horrour, the feelings of the crew became, at last, so disordered as to become unnatural. (The learned counsel then examined the evidence, in order to shew the extremity of the danger.)

Counsel say that lots are the law of the ocean. Lots, in cases of famine, where means of subsistence are wanting for all the crew, is what the history of maritime disaster records; but who has ever told of casting lots at midnight, in a sinking boat, in the midst of darkness, of rain, of terrour, and of confusion? To cast lots when all are going down, but to decide who shall be spared, to cast lots when the question is, whether any can be saved, is a plan easy to suggest, rather difficult to put in practice. The danger was instantaneous, a case, . . . "when the peace of mind is much too disturbed to deliberate, and where if it were 'more calm,' there would be no time for deliberation." The sailors adopted the only principle of selection which was possible in an emergency like theirs,—a principle more humane than lots. Man and wife were not torn asunder, and the women were all preserved. Lots would have rendered impossible this clear dictate of humanity. But again: the crew either were in their ordinary and original state of subordination to their officers, or they were in a state of nature. If in the former state, they are excusable in law, for having obeyed the order of the mate,—an order twice imperatively given. Independent of the mate's general authority in the captain's absence, the captain had pointedly directed the crew to obey all the mate's orders as they would his, the captain's; and the crew had promised to do so. It imports not to declare that a crew is not bound to obey an unlawful order, for to say that this order was unlawful is to postulate what remains to be proved. Who is to judge of the unlawfulness? The circumstances were peculiar. The occasion was emergent, without precedent, or parallel. The lawfulness of the order is the very question which we are disputing; a question about which this whole community has been agitated, and is still divided; the discussion of which crowds this room with auditors past former example; a question which this court, with all its resources, is now engaged in considering, as such a question demands to be considered, most deliberately, most anxiously, most cautiously. It is no part of a sailor's duty to moralize and to speculate, in such a moment as this was, upon the orders of his superior officers. The commander of a ship, like the commander of an army, "gives desperate commands. He requires instantaneous obedience." The sailor, like the soldier, obeys by instinct. In the memorable, immortal words of Carnot, when he surrendered Antwerp in obedience to a command which his pride, his patriotism, and his views of policy all combined to oppose: "The armed force is essentially obedient. It acts, but never deliberates." This greatest man of the French Revolution did here but define, with the precision of the algebraist, what he conceived with the comprehension of a statesman; and his answer was justification with every soldier in Europe. How far the principle was felt by this crew, let witness the case of this very mate, and of some of these very sailors, who, by the captain's order, left the jolly-boat, which had but 10 persons, for the long-boat, with more than four times that number. See ante, p. 360, note 2. They all regarded this as going into the jaws of death. Yet not a murmur. It is a well-known fact that in no marine on the ocean is obedience to orders so habitual and so implicit as in our own. The prisoner had been always distinguished by obedience. Whether the mate, if on trial here, would be found innocent, is a question which we need not decide. That question is a different one from the guilt or innocence of the prisoner, and one more difficult. But if the whole company were reduced to a state of nature, then the sailors were bound to no duty, not mutual, to the passengers. The contract of the shipping articles had become dissolved by an unforeseen and overwhelming necessity. The sailor was no longer a sailor, but a drowning man. Having fairly done his duty to the last extremity, he was not to lose the rights of a human being, because he wore a roundabout instead of a frock coat. We do not seek authorities for such doctrine. The instinct of these men's hearts is our authority,—the best authority. Whoever opposes it must be wrong, for he opposes human nature. All the contemplated conditions, all the contemplated possibilities of the voyage, were ended. The parties, sailor and passenger, were in a new state. All persons on board the vessel became equal. All became their own lawgivers; for artificial distinctions cease to prevail when men are reduced to the equality of nature. Every man on board had a right to make law with his own right hand, and the law which did prevail on that awful night having been the law of necessity, and the law of nature too, it is the law which will be upheld by this court, to the liberation of the prisoner.

On the 22d of April, the same day, Mr. Meredith, district attorney, replied, speaking principally to the evidence.

BALDWIN, Circuit Justice, charging jury, alluded to the touching character of the case; and, after stating to the jury what was the offence laid in the indictment, his honour explained, with particularity, the distinction between murder and manslaughter. He said that malice was of the essence of murder, while want of criminal intention was consistent with the nature of manslaughter. He impressed strongly upon the jury, that the mere absence of malice did not render homicide excusable; that the act might be unlawful, as well as the union of the act and intention, in which union consisted the crime of murder. After giving several familiar instances of manslaughter, to explain that, although homicide was committed, there was yet an absence of bad motive, his honour proceeded with his charge nearly as follows:

In such cases the law neither excuses the act nor permits it to be justified as innocent; but, although inflicting some punishment, she yet looks with a benignant eye, through the thing done, to the mind and to the heart; and when, on a view of all the circumstances connected with the act, no evil spirit is discerned, her humanity forbids the exaction of life for life. But though, said the court, cases of this kind are viewed with tenderness, and punished in mercy, we must yet bear in mind that man, in taking away the life of a fellow being, assumes an awful responsibility to God, and to society; and that the administrators of public justice do themselves assume that responsibility if, when called on to pass judicially upon the act, they yield to the indulgence of misapplied humanity. It is one thing to give a favourable interpretation to evidence in order to mitigate an offence. It is a different thing, when we are asked, not to extenuate, but to justify, the act. In the former case, as I have said, our decision may in some degree be swayed by feelings of humanity; while in the latter, it is the law of necessity alone which can disarm the vindicatory justice of the country. Where, indeed, a case does arise, embraced by this "law of necessity," the penal laws pass over such case in silence; for law is made to meet but the ordinary exigencies of life. But the case does not become "a case of necessity," unless all ordinary means of self preservation have been exhausted. The peril must be instant, overwhelming, leaving no alternative but to lose our own life, or to take the life of another person. An illustration of this principle occurs in the ordinary case of self-defense against lawless violence, aiming at the destruction of life, or designing to inflict grievous injury to the person; and within this range may fall the taking of life under other circumstances where the act is indispensably requisite to self-existence. For example, suppose that two persons who owe no duty to one another that is not mutual, should, by accident, not attributable to either, be placed in a situation where both cannot survive. Neither is bound to save the other's life by sacrificing his own, nor would either commit a crime in saving his own life in a struggle for the only means of safety. Of this description of cases are those which have been cited to you by counsel, from writers on natural law,—cases which we rather leave to your imagination than attempt minutely to describe. And I again state that when this great "law of necessity" does apply, and is not improperly exercised, the taking of life is devested of unlawfulness.

But in applying this law, we must look, not only to the jeopardy in which the parties are, but also to the relations in which they stand. The slayer must be under no obligation to make his own safety secondary to the safety of others. A familiar application of this principle presents itself in the obligations which rest upon the owners of stages, steamboats, and other vehicles of transportation. In consideration of the payment of fare, the owners of the vehicle are bound to transport the passengers to the place of contemplated destination. Having, in all emergencies, the conduct of the journey, and the control of the passengers, the owners rest under every obligation for care, skill, and general capacity; and if, from defect of any of these requisites, grievous injury is done to the passenger, the persons employed are liable. The passenger owes no duty but submission. He is under no obligation to protect and keep the conductor in safety, nor is the passenger bound to labour, except in cases of emergency, where his services are required by unanticipated and uncommon danger. Such, said the court, is the relation which exists on shipboard. The passenger stands in a position different from that of the officers and seamen. It is the sailor who must encounter the hardships and perils of the voyage. Nor can this relation be changed when the ship is lost by tempest or other danger of the sea, and all on board have betaken themselves, for safety, to the small boats; for imminence of danger can not absolve from duty. The sailor is bound, as before, to undergo whatever hazard is necessary to preserve the boat and the passengers. Should the emergency become so extreme as to call for the sacrifice of life, there can be no reason why the law does not still remain the same. The passenger, not being bound either to labour or to incur the risk of life, cannot be bound to sacrifice his existence to preserve the sailor's. The captain, indeed, and a sufficient number of seamen to navigate the boat, must be preserved; for, except these abide in the ship, all will perish. But if there be more seamen than are necessary to manage the boat, the supernumerary sailors have no right, for their safety, to sacrifice the passengers. The sailors and passengers, in fact, cannot be regarded as in equal positions. The sailor (to use the language of a distinguished writer) owes more benevolence to another than to himself. He is bound to set a greater value on the life of others than on his own. And while we admit that sailor and sailor may lawfully struggle with each other for the plank which can save but one, we think that, if the passenger is on the plank, even "the law of necessity" justifies not the sailor who takes it from him. This rule may be deemed a harsh one towards the sailor, who may have thus far done his duty, but when the danger is so extreme, that the only hope is in sacrificing either a sailor or a passenger, any alternative is hard; and would it not be the hardest of any to sacrifice a passenger in order to save a supernumerary sailor?

But, in addition, if the source of the danger have been obvious, and destruction ascertained to be certainly about to arrive, though at a future time, there should be consultation, and some mode of selection fixed, by which those in equal relations may have equal chance for their life. By what mode, then, should selection be made? The question is not without difficulty; nor do we know of any rule prescribed, either by statute or by common law, or even by speculative writers on the law of nature. In fact, no rule of general application can be prescribed for contingencies which are wholly unforeseen. There is, however, one condition of extremity for which all writers have prescribed the same rule. When the ship is in no danger of sinking, but all sustenance is exhausted, and a sacrifice of one person is necessary to appease the hunger of others, the selection is by lot. This mode is resorted to as the fairest mode, and, in some sort, as an appeal to God, for selection of the victim. This manner, obviously, was regarded by the mate, in parting with the captain, as the one which it was proper to adopt, in case the long-boat could not live with all who were on board on Tuesday morning. The same manner, as would appear from the response given to the mate, had already suggested itself to the captain. For ourselves, we can conceive of no mode so consonant both to humanity and to justice; and the occasion, we think, must be peculiar which will dispense with its exercise. If, indeed, the peril be instant and overwhelming, leaving no chance of means, and no moment for deliberation, then, of course, there is no power to consult, to cast lots, or in any such way to decide; but even where the final disaster is thus sudden, if it have been foreseen as certainly about to arrive, if no new cause of danger have arisen to bring on the closing catastrophe, if time have existed to cast lots, and to select the victims, then, as we have said, sortition should be adopted. In no other than this or some like way are those having equal rights put upon an equal footing, and in no other way is it possible to guard against partiality and oppression, violence and conflict. What scene, indeed, more horrible, can imagination draw than a struggle between sailor and sailor, passenger and passenger, or, it may be, a mixed affray, in which promiscuously, all destroy one another? This, too, in circumstances which have allowed time to decide, with justice, whose life should be calmly surrendered.

When the selection has been made by lots, the victim yields of course to his fate, or, if he resist, force may be employed to coerce submission. Whether or not "a case of necessity" has arisen, or whether the law under which death has been inflicted have been so exercised as to hold the executioner harmless, cannot depend on his own opinion; for no man may pass upon his own conduct when it concerns the rights, and especially, when it affects the lives, of others. We have already stated to you that, by the law of the land, homicide is sometimes justifiable; and the law defines the occasions in which it is so. The transaction must, therefore, be justified to the law; and the person accused rests under obligation to satisfy those who judicially scrutinize his case that it really transcended ordinary rules. In fact, any other principle would be followed by pernicious results, and, moreover, would not be practicable in application. Opinion or belief may be assumed, whether it exist or not; and if this mere opinion of the sailors will justify them in making a sacrifice of the passengers, of course, the mere opinion of the passengers would, in turn, justify these in making a sacrifice of the sailors. The passengers may have confidence in their own capacity to manage and preserve the boat, or the effort of either sailors or passengers to save the boat, may be clearly unavailing; and what, then, in a struggle against force and numbers, becomes of the safety of the seamen? Hard as is a seaman's life, would it not become yet more perilous if the passengers, who may outnumber them tenfold, should be allowed to judge when the dangers of the sea will justify a sacrifice of life? We are, therefore, satisfied, that, in requiring proof, which shall be satisfactory to you, of the existence of the necessity, we are fixing the rule which is, not merely the only one which is practicable, but, moreover, the only one which will secure the safety of the sailors themselves.

The court said, briefly, that the principles which had been laid down by them, as applicable to the crew, applied to the mate likewise, and that his order

(on which much stress had been laid), if an unlawful order, would be no justification to the seamen, for that even seamen are not justified, in law, by obedience to commands which are unlawful. The court added that the case was one which involved questions of gravest consideration, and, as the facts, in some sort, were without precedent, that the court preferred to state the law, in the shape of such general principles as would comprehend the case, under any view which the jury might take of the evidence.

After a few remarks upon the evidence, the case was given to the jury, who, about 16 hours afterwards, and after having once returned to the bar, unable to agree, with some difficulty, found a verdict of guilty. The prisoner was, however, recommended to the mercy of the court. On the same day a rule was obtained to show cause why judgment should not be arrested and a new trial granted. The following ground was relied on for a new trial: Because the court, instead of telling the jury that, in a state of imminent and deadly peril, all men are reduced to a state of nature, and that there is, then, no distinction between the rights of sailor and passenger, adopted a contrary doctrine, and charged the jury accordingly.

Mr. Brown subsequently showed cause. He insisted largely upon the existence of the state of nature, as distinguished from the social state, and contended that to this state of nature the persons in the long-boat had become reduced on Tuesday night, at 10 o'clock, when Askin was thrown overboard. He iterated, illustrated, and enforced the argument contained in the closing part of the defence. For the arrest of judgment he argued that the indictment was defective in not stating the name of the boat on which the homicide was alleged to have been committed; that the counts in this respect wanted certainty. The United States did not reply.

THE COURT held the application for some days under advisement, and, at a subsequent day, discharged the rule. They said that, during the trial (aware that no similar case was recorded in juridical annals), they had given to the subject studious and deliberate consideration, and they had paid like regard to what was now urged, but that, notwithstanding all that had been said (and the arguments, it was admitted, were powerful), no error had been perceived by the court in its instructions to the jury. It is true, said the court, as is known by every one, that we do find in the text writers, and sometimes in judicial opinions, the phrases, "the law of nature," "the principles of natural right," and other expressions of a like signification; but, as applied to civilized men, nothing more can be meant by those expressions than that there are certain great and fundamental principles of justice which, in the constitution of nature, lie at the foundation and make part of all civil law, independently of express adoption or enactment. And to give to the expressions any other signification, to claim them as shewing an independent code, and one contrariant to those settled principles, which, however modified, make a part of civil law in all Christian nations, would be to make the writers who use the expressions law down as rules of action, principles which, in their nature, admit of no practical ascertainment or application. The law of nature forms part of the municipal law; and, in a proper case (as of self-defence), homicide is justifiable, not because the municipal law is subverted by the law of nature, but because no rule of the municipal law makes homicide, in such cases, criminal. It is, said the court, the municipal or civil law, as thus comprehensive, as founded in moral and social justice,—the law of the land, in short, as existing and administered amongst us and all enlightened nations,—that regulates the social duties of men, the duties of man towards his neighbour, everywhere. Everywhere are civilized men under its protection; everywhere, subject to its authority. It is part of the universal law. We cannot escape it in a case where it is applicable; and if, for the decision of any question, the proper rule is to be found in the municipal law, no code can be referred to as annulling its authority. Varying however, or however modified, the laws of all civilized nations, and, indeed, the very nature of the social constitution, place sailors and passengers in different relations. And, without stopping to speculate upon overnice questions not before us, or to involve ourselves in the labyrinth of ethical subtleties, we may safely say that the sailor's duty is the protection of the persons intrusted to his care, not their sacrifice,—a duty we must again declare our opinion, that rests on him in every emergency of his calling, and from which it would be senseless, indeed, to absolve him exactly at those times when the obligation is most needed.

Respecting the form of the counts, the court said that the locality of the offence was sufficiently expressed, and that, in a case so peculiar, it was impossible to express the place with more precision.

When the prisoner was brought up for sentence, the learned judge said to him, that many circumstances in the affair were of a character to commend him to regard, yet, that the case was one in which some punishment was demanded; that it was in the power of the court to inflict the penalty of an imprisonment for a term of three years, and fine of $1,000, but, in view of all the circumstances, and especially as the prisoner had been already confined in gaol several months, that the court would make the punishment more lenient. The convict was then sentenced to undergo an imprisonment in the Eastern Penitentiary of Pennsylvania, (solitary confinement) at hard labour, for the term of six months, and to pay a fine of $20.

NOTE. Considerable sympathy having been excited in favour of Holmes, by the popular press, an effort was made by several persons, and particularly by the Seamen's Friend Society, to obtain a pardon from the executive. President Tyler refused, however, to grant any pardon, in consequence of the court's not uniting in the application. The penalty was subsequently remitted.

NOTES

1. [Reported by John William Wallace, Esq.]

2. The first mate and some of the crew of the long-boat were originally in the jolly-boat with the captain; but the mate, understanding navigation, was transferred, with a chart, quadrant, and compass, to the long-boat; and some of the crew were exchanged. The long-boat was 22 1/2 feet long, 6 feet in the beam, and from 2 1/2 to 3 feet deep.

3. One passenger had died after leaving Liverpool, and before the catastrophe of the 19th.

4. The captain and second mate, with the other persons in the jolly-boat, after having been out at sea six days, were picked up by a French fishing lugger. They afterwards came to Philadelphia, where, by consent of the United States, the depositions of the captain and mate were taken, and the testimony was now read in evidence.

5. It was a matter of doubt whether these women (two sisters of Frank Askin, an Irish youth, spoken of further on) had been thrown over, or whether their sacrifice was an act of self-devotion and affection to their brother. When Holmes seized him, his sisters entreated for his life, and said that if he was thrown over they wished to be thrown over too; that "they wished to die the death of their brother." "Give me only a dress to put around me," said one of the sisters, after her brother had been thrown out, "and I care not now to live longer."

6. The exact condition of these two men did not appear. Some of the witnesses thought that they were too much frozen to recover. Others swore differently.

7. On board the long-boat, a widowed mother, a Scotswoman, and her three daughters had escaped; but, just as the boat was about veering astern, and when there was great danger of being drawn into the vortex of the sinking ship, it was discovered that one of the family, a sick sister, had been left behind in the ship. Her mother was calling, "Isabel, Isabel, come, come!" But the girl was too sick to hear or to mind. Holmes, hearing the mother's cry, climbed up the ship's side (at great peril of his life, as was testified), ran astern, and, hoisting the sick girl upon his shoulders, swung himself and her over, by the tackle, by one arm, into the long-boat below. "O, mother, I am coming, I am coming!" responded the girl, as Holmes was lowering himself and her along the ship's side. On the trial, Holmes' counsel, after describing, with effect, the earlier circumstances of the catastrophe, thus opened his defence: "But hark, gentlemen! On that dreadful night, the crew and half the passengers having taken to the boats, the agonized voice of a mother is heard, even beyond the tumult and the outcry, calling

for the preservation of her daughter, who, in the consternation of the moment, had been forgotten, and remained on board the fated ship. In an instant you see an athletic sailor passing hand over hand, by means of a slender rope, until he regains the vessel. Behold him now on the quarter-deck, with one arm entwined around the sickly and half naked girl, in the depth of the night, surrounded by icebergs and the ocean, while, with the other, he swings himself and his almost lifeless burthen from the stern of the sinking ship into the boat below, and restores the child at once to the open arms and yearning heart of her mother. Yet, today, gentlemen, there, before you, sits that selfsame heroic sailor, arraigned upon the charge of having voluntarily and feloniously deprived a fellow creature of his life: and that, gentlemen, is the charge which you are summoned here to determine."

8. "The passengers, on Wednesday morning," said one of the witnesses, "looked very distressed; ;and Holmes told them to keep their hearts up." "The mate," said another witness, "asked the men what he should do. Holmes said we ought not to steer for Newfoundland, as we would never reach it, but to go south, as it would be warmer, and we might meet a vessel. The mate said he would do as Holmes wanted. He would give up all to Holmes. * * * I saw Holmes with a quilt. He tried to raise it to make a sail, but the wind was too strong. He then stood up and said that he saw the mast of a vessel, and afterwards got to work to raise a shawl on the end of an oar." In fact, as appeared by other parts of the testimony, Holmes' long-trained, labouring eye descried the Crescent's main-mast, in the distance, several minutes before it was at all visible to anybody on board: and, while most of the boat's assemblage lay yet exhausted or despairing, he had raised the signal of distress. His coolness and deep knowledge of sea life were not less manifested now, than his physical superiority had been before. The great distance of the Crescent rendered it almost impossible that Holmes' signal should be seen. The second mate of the vessel happened, however, to be aloft, watching for ice; and as soon as the ship, responding to the signal, put about, the voice of exultant joy and gratitude burst forth from the wretched assemblage on the long-boat. Some were crawling up the side of the boat to see the approaching vessel, and others, who had seemed congealed, now stood erect; "Lie down," said Holmes, "every soul of you, and be still." "If they make so many of us on board, they will steer off another way, and pretend they have not seen us."

9. Act March 2, 1831 (4 Story's Laws U.S. 2256), by which it is enacted "that the power of the several courts of the United States to issue attachments and inflict summary punishments for contempt of court, shall not be construed to extend to any cases except the misbehavior of any person or persons in the presence of the said courts, or so near thereto as to obstruct the administration of justice, the misbehaviour of any of the officers of the said courts, in their official transactions, and the disobedience or resistance by any officer of the said courts, party, juror, witness, or any other person or persons, to any lawful writ, process, order, rule, decree or command of the said courts."

10. The navy and army chronicles of England record many examples of Bacon's noble thought: "The duties of life are more than life." And certainly, in whatever circumstances witnessed, such testimonials will prove a vindication of all that counsel here asserted. But most of these heroic examples (some of which were cited in the argument) have been on the part of officers, in England especially, men of high association, and often highly educated. And we are ready to resolve much into the instinct of discipline, and much, perhaps, into the incentive of ambition, seeking the bubble reputation. An example more impressive than any of these, as it was that of a common sailor, occurred in our country, on Lake Erie, in the destruction of the steamboat Erie by fire, on the afternoon of the 9th of August, 1841. As soon as it was discovered that the flames could not be controlled, the captain ordered the helmsman to make for land, then within sight. The man accordingly turned the vessel. The fire having taken near midships, quickly reached the binnacle. Yet the man kept his post, and his hand was on the wheel. The wreathing flames ere long enclosed him, and when every soul had left the ship, his form was still to be seen amidst the flames, his clothes dropping from him, standing like a man of steel, and in performance of his duty, steering the flaming vessel to a headland.

UNITED STATES v. OVIEDO

(United States Court of Appeals, 5th Circuit, 1976)*

DYER, CIRCUIT JUDGE.

Oviedo appeals from a judgement of conviction for the attempted distribution of heroin.

Oviedo was contacted by an undercover agent, who desired to purchase narcotics. Arrangements were made for the sale of one pound of heroin. The agent met Oviedo at the appointed time and place. Oviedo transferred the substance to the agent, and asked for his money in return. However, the agent informed Oviedo that he would first have to test the substance. A field test was performed with a positive result. Oviedo was placed under arrest.

Subsequent to the arrest, a search warrant was issued for Oviedo's residence. When the search was executed, two pounds of a similar substance was found hidden in a television set. Up to this point, the case appeared unexceptional.

A chemical analysis was performed upon the substances seized, revealing that the substances were not in fact heroin, but rather procaine hyrdochloride, an uncontrolled substance. Since any attempt to prosecute for distribution of heroin would have been futile, the defendant was charged with an attempt to distribute heroin.

At trial, Oviedo took the stand and stated that he knew the substance was not heroin, and that he, upon suggestion of his cohorts, was merely attempting to "rip off" the agent. It was, in his view, an easy way to pocket a few thousand dollars.

The court instructed the jury that they could find Oviedo guilty of attempted distribution if he delivered the substance thinking it to be heroin. The jury rejected Oviedo's claimed knowledge of the true nature of the substance, and returned a verdict of guilty. Although Oviedo argues on appeal that there was insufficient evidence to establish that he thought the substance was heroin, this contention is without merit. We thus take as fact Oviedo's belief that the substance was heroin.

The facts before us are therefore simple—Oviedo sold a substance he thought to be heroin, which in reality was an uncontrolled substance. The legal question before us is likewise simple—are these combined acts and intent cognizable as a criminal attempt. The answer, however, is not so simple.

Oviedo and the government both agree the resolution of this case rests in an analysis of the doctrines of legal and factual impossibility as defenses to a criminal attempt. Legal impossibility occurs when the actions which the defendant performs or sets in motion, even if fully carried out as he desires, would not constitute a crime. Factual impossibility occurs when the objective of the defendant is proscribed by the criminal law but a circumstance unknown to the actor prevents him from bringing about that objective. The traditional analysis recognizes legal impossibility as a valid defense, but refuses to so recognize factual impossibility.

These definitions are not particularly helpful here, for they do nothing more than provide a different focus for the analysis. In one sense, the impossibility involved here might be deemed legal, for those *acts* which Oviedo set in motion, the transfer of the substance in his possession, were not a crime. In another sense, the impossibility is factual, for the *objective* of Oviedo, the sale of heroin, was proscribed by law, and failed only because of a circumstance unknown to Oviedo.

Although this issue has been the subject of numerous legal commentaries, federal cases reaching this question are few, and no consensus can be found.

In *Roman,* the defendants were transporting a suitcase containing heroin. Through the aid of an informer and unknown to the defendants, the contents of the suitcase were replaced with soap powder. The defendants were arrested when they attempted to sell the contents of the suitcase, and were subsequently charged with *attempted* possession with intent to distribute. The court rejected defendant's contention that they could not be charged with attempted possession, since it was impossible for them to possess heroin. Recognizing the difficulty in distinguishing between legal and factual impossibility, the court never so categorized the case. Nevertheless, the court concluded that since the objective of the defendants was criminal, impossibility would not be recognized as a defense.

The defendants in *Berrigan* were charged with attempting to violate 18 U.S.C.A. § 1791, prohibiting the smuggling of objects into or out of a federal

* 525 F.2d 881 (1976). Opinion compressed, and footnotes deleted.

correctional institution. Since the evidence established that the warden had knowledge of the smuggling plan, and since lack of knowledge was a necessary element of the offense, the defendants could not be found guilty of violating the statute. The court held that such knowledge by the warden would also preclude conviction for the attempt, since "attempting to do that which is not a crime is not attempting to commit a crime."

The *Berrigan* court rested its determination on a strict view of legal impossibility. According to the court, such impossibility exists when there is an intention to perform a physical act, the intended physical act is performed, but the consequence resulting from the intended act does not amount to a crime. In this analysis, the intent to perform a physical act is to be distinguished from the motive, desire or expectation to violate the law.

The application of the principles underlying these cases leads to no clearer result than the application of our previous definitions of legal and factual impossibility. Applying *Roman,* we would not concern ourselves with any theoretical distinction between legal and factual impossibility, but would affirm the conviction, since the objective of Oviedo was criminal. Applying *Berrigan,* we would look solely to the physical act which Oviedo "intended," the transfer of the procaine in his possession, and we would conclude that since the transfer of procaine is not criminal, no offense is stated. The choice is between punishing criminal intent without regard to objective acts, and punishing objective acts, regarding intent as immaterial.

In our view, both *Roman* and *Berrigan* miss the mark, but in opposite directions. A strict application of the *Berrigan* approach would eliminate any distinction between factual and legal impossibility, and such impossibility would *always* be a valid defense, since the "intended" physical acts are never criminal. The *Roman* approach turns the attempt statute into a new substantive criminal statute where the critical element to be proved is *mens rea simpliciter*. It would allow us to punish one's thoughts, desires, or motives, through indirect evidence, without reference to any objective fact. The danger is evident.

We reject the notion of *Roman,* adopted by the district court, that the conviction in the present case can be sustained since there is sufficient proof of intent, not because of any doubt as to the sufficiency of the evidence in that regard, but because of the inherent dangers such a precedent would pose in the future.

When the question before the court is whether certain conduct constitutes mere preparation which is not punishable, or an attempt which is, the possi-

bility of error is mitigated by the requirement that the objective acts of the defendant evidence commitment to the criminal venture and corroborate the *mens rea*. To the extent that this requirement is preserved it prevents the conviction of persons engaged in innocent acts on the basis of a *mens rea* proved through speculative inferences, unreliable forms of testimony, and past criminal conduct.

Courts could have approached the preparation–attempt determination in another fashion, eliminating any notion of particular objective facts, and simply could have asked whether the evidence at hand was sufficient to prove the necessary intent. But this approach has been rejected for precisely the reasons set out above, for conviction upon proof of mere intent provides too great a possibility of speculation and abuse.

In urging us to follow *Roman,* which found determinative the criminal intent of the defendants, the government at least implicitly argues that we should reject any requirement demanding the same objective evidentiary facts required in the preparation–attempt determination. We refuse to follow that suggestion.

When the defendant sells a substance which is actually heroin, it is reasonable to infer that he knew the physical nature of the substance, and to place on him the burden of dispelling the inference. However, if we convict the defendant of attempting to sell heroin for the sale of a nonnarcotic substance, we eliminate an objective element that has major evidentiary significance and we increase the risk of mistaken conclusions that the defendant believed the goods were narcotics.

Thus, we demand that in order for a defendant to be guilty of a criminal attempt, the objective acts performed, without any reliance on the accompanying *mens rea*, mark the defendant's conduct as criminal in nature. The acts should be unique rather than so commonplace that they are engaged in by persons not in violation of the law.

Here we have only two objective facts. First, Oviedo told the agent that the substance he was selling was heroin, and second, portions of the substance were concealed in a television set. If another objective fact were present, if the substance were heroin, we would have a strong objective basis for the determination of criminal intent and conduct consistent and supportive of that intent. The test set out above would be met, and, absent a delivery, the criminal attempt would be established. But when this objective basis for the detemination of intent is removed, when the substance is not heroin, the conduct becomes ambivalent, and we are left with a sufficiency-of-the-evidence determination of intent rejected in the preparation–attempt dichotomy. We cannot conclude that the objective acts of Oviedo apart from any direct evidence of intent mark his conduct as criminal in nature. Rather, those acts are consistent with a noncriminal enterprise. Therefore, we will not allow the jury's determination of Oviedo's intent to form the sole basis of a criminal offense.

The government also argues that *United States* v. *Mandujano,* although involving a preparation–attempt determination, compels a contrary result. In *Mandujano,* the defendant negotiated a sale of heroin with an undercover agent. After taking the agent's money, the defendant set about to find his source. He was unsuccessful, and returned a few hours later with the money and without the heroin. We found the evidence sufficient to take the case beyond preparation, and to support his conviction for attempted distribution.

In making that determination, we recognized that in order to be guilty of an attempt, the objective conduct of the defendant must strongly corroborate the firmness of the defendant's criminal intent. The objective acts must not be equivocal in nature. In that case, we had as objective facts defendant's act of taking money and his personal statements that he would purchase heroin with that money. Importantly, there were no objective facts which made these acts equivocal.

The situation in *Mandujano* is distinguishable from that now before us. Just as it is reasonable to infer a person's knowledge and criminal intent from the possession of a substance which is in fact narcotics, it is also reasonable to infer that same knowledge and intent from an individual's statement of future intention. However, just as it is impossible to infer that intent when the substance possessed is not in fact narcotics, it is also impossible to infer that intent when objective facts indicate that the person did not carry out his self-proclaimed intention.

Thus, when Mandujano stated that he would purchase heroin, we could infer that he intended to purchase heroin since there were no objective facts to the contrary. But here, Oviedo stated he would sell heroin and then sold procaine. Based on these objective facts, we cannot infer that he intended to do that which he said he was going to do, because he in fact did something else.

Reversed.

E. M. CURLEY

Excusing Rape*

In April 1975 the House of Lords, the highest court of criminal appeal in England, decided that if an accused in fact believed that the woman was consenting, whether or not that belief was based on reasonable grounds, he could not be found guilty of rape.[1] This ruling, which I shall refer to as "the *Morgan* rule," created a furor; it was widely referred to in the press as a "rapists' charter." A private member's bill, seeking to have the law changed, was immediately introduced in Parliament. And the Home Secretary promised government action by the end of the year.

Reaction was similar in Australia, where decisions of the House of Lords, though no longer binding, are still generally treated with great respect. The Women's Electoral Lobby demonstrated outside of Parliament. Dire predictions were made in the press—sometimes by lawyers—about the difficulty or impossibility of securing convictions under the *Morgan* rule. And the Attorney General promised action.

There was no comparable reaction in the United States, partly, perhaps, because the fall of Vietnam crowded other foreign news off the pages of the press. More important, probably, is the fact that British decisions have not been binding in the United States for some time. But as we shall see, the decision was based on legal principles which might well have found favor in an American court.[2]

My primary purpose here is to argue that the *Morgan* rule is unsound. Although many readers are likely to accept that conclusion without argument, I hope to provide the convinced with good reasons for their faith. Seeing clearly that the *Morgan* rule is unsound is more difficult than non-lawyers are apt to realize. The House of Lords' decision was based in part on claims about what is required in general for criminal responsibility, and their view of criminal responsibility is one which has deep roots in

traditional notions about the morality of punishment. So we must acknowledge that the case which can be made for the *Morgan* rule *looks* surprisingly strong.

Further, I hope to construct an argument capable of persuading those people—mainly lawyers—who are not yet converted. This perhaps quixotic ambition makes it necessary to pay attention to those considerations which weigh heavily with lawyers, and to the complex detail of legal argument.

I

Let us begin by considering the bizarre human behavior which provided the Lords with an occasion for deciding this point of law. Morgan, a senior noncommissioned officer in the R.A.F., in the course of an evening out with three junior colleagues, invited them to come to his house and have intercourse with his wife. According to the colleagues, Morgan told them that his wife, who was "kinky," would probably simulate reluctance but that she would really welcome intercourse. They claimed to have been incredulous at first, but to have been persuaded eventually that the invitation was serious. Morgan denied having said that his wife would feign resistance, but claimed his wife had suggested that he bring colleagues home for the purpose of intercourse, and that she had said afterwards that she enjoyed it.

In any case, on arrival at the Morgan household, the four men dragged Mrs. Morgan forcibly from a room in which she was sleeping to another room where there was a double bed. Each man had intercourse with her in turn, while the others restrained her. According to her evidence she protested and resisted as best she could in the circumstances. Immediately afterwards, she drove to a nearby hospital and complained that she had been raped, a complaint which hospital evidence supported. As her husband, Morgan could not be charged with rape. But he was charged with aiding and abetting. The other three men were charged both with rape and with aiding and abetting.

*Edwin M. Curley, "Excusing Rape," *Philosophy & Public Affairs*, Vol. 5, no. 4 (1976). Copyright © 1976 Princeton University Press. Reprinted by permission of Princeton University Press.

In summing up, the trial judge instructed the jury that, in addition to proving that the three colleagues had had intercourse with Mrs. Morgan without her consent, the prosecution was required to prove that each of them had *intended* to have intercourse with her without her consent, so that if any of them believed she did consent, he would not be guilty of rape. *But,* the judge added, a belief in consent would not be of any assistance to a defendant unless it was a reasonable belief, that is, "such a belief as a reasonable man would entertain if he applied his mind and thought about the matter." On those instructions the jury convicted all four defendants. We may note in passing that, though Morgan was not charged as a principal, he did receive a substantially longer sentence than did the other three.

The defendants appealed, urging that the trial judge's requirement that the belief be reasonable was incorrect in law, that a belief in consent, even if unreasonable, would be incompatible with an intention to commit rape, and that the unreasonableness of the belief was relevant only insofar as it might be very persuasive, though not necessarily conclusive, evidence that the belief was not genuinely held. This argument was rejected by the Court of Appeal, but was accepted by the House of Lords, with two of the five Lords dissenting.[3]

In view of some of the claims made in the press after the Lords' decision, it is only fair to note that, although the Lords held in favor of the appellants on the point of law, they nonetheless upheld the conviction. They found that, although the jury had been misdirected, there had been no miscarriage of justice in respect of any of the appellants. "In the light of all the evidence . . . no reasonable jury could have failed to convict the appellants" even if the jury had been properly directed, that is, directed in terms of the *Morgan* rule.[4]

However, before we take too much comfort from the fact that justice appears to have been done to Morgan and his associates, we should also note that the defendants contributed very substantially to their own undoing. In their statements to the police they corroborated Mrs. Morgan's version of what had happened. At the trial they chose—"most unwisely," as Lord Cross remarked—to repudiate their statements to the police, "to challenge the truth of Mrs. Morgan's evidence, and to assert that although to start with she manifested some unwillingness, when it came to the point she cooperated

in the proceedings with evident relish." This change in their story obviously created a bad impression.

Moreover, as the trial judge pointed out, before the jury could appropriately consider the defense of mistaken belief in consent, they must first have been satisfied beyond a reasonable doubt that Mrs. Morgan did *not* consent. If they were not so satisfied, then the defendants would be entitled to an acquittal on the ground of her consent. Hence the jury would have to be satisfied, beyond reasonable doubt, of the truth of Mrs. Morgan's testimony and the falsity of much of the defendants' testimony, before they could consider the question of intent. The judge added:

> You may consider—it is entirely a matter for you—it is a desperate defence to put forward, that even although you have rejected so much of their evidence . . . nevertheless you should have some doubt as to whether they honestly and reasonably believed she was consenting. There it is. The Defence invite you to consider the matter and you must give it such consideration as you think it right.

The judge here comes very close to directing the jury not to consider the evidence of lack of intent at all. And clearly, in trying to have it both ways, the Defense made matters very difficult for itself. In many cases, the double defense—"she consented, or at least I thought she did"—is a perfectly natural one. But if deploying it requires the defendant to contradict testimony previously given, it is probably quite imprudent.

So the Lords' confidence about the verdict that any reasonable jury would have come to was inspired by a combination of damaging admissions to the police and damaging changes in testimony. Conceivably, if the Defense had not raised the issue of consent at all, and had relied exclusively on the beliefs of the accused about consent, they would have had a better chance of success. Indeed, within two months of the decision in *Morgan,* in *another* case which involved a husband as aiding and abetting, the defense of belief in consent not based on reasonable grounds *was* successful.[5]

II

What is the rationale for the *Morgan* rule? It is a fundamental maxim of Ango-American-Australian criminal law that generally the performance of an act prohibited by the law does not render the agent liable to punishment unless he either intended to do an act of the kind the law prohibits, or was reckless as to whether he did an act of that kind.[6] This is not merely a parochial requirement of legal systems derived from the British model. According to Professor Hart:

All civilized penal systems make liability to punishment for at any rate serious crime dependent not merely on the fact that the person to be punished has done the outward act of a crime, but on his having done it in a certain state or frame of mind or will. These mental or intellectual elements are many and various and are collected together in the terminology of English jurists under the simple sounding description of *mens rea*, a guilty mind. But the most prominent of these mental elements, and in many ways the most important, is a man's intention; and . . . in English law and in most other legal systems, intention, *or something like it,* is relevant . . . when the question is "Can this man be convicted of this crime?"[7]

Arguably, on any theory of punishment some kind of *mens rea* will be required to make punishment justifiable.[8] A retributive theorist, emphasizing moral guilt as a necessary condition of punishment, will tend to feel that, where *mens rea* is lacking, the necessary element of personal fault is lacking. The utilitarian is apt to contend that the punishment of those whom the law typically excuses would not be efficacious. The madman, the infant child, the man who acts on a mistaken belief about the relevant circumstances—none of these is likely to be deterred by the threat of punishment. If we do punish them, we inflict suffering to no purpose.

This line of argument may not be ultimately satisfactory. Hart, for example, has argued that the recognition in Anglo-American-Australian law of various offenses of strict or absolute liability shows that there may well be utilitarian grounds for excluding excuses.[9] Generally speaking, offenses for which the prosecution need show no fault—no intention to commit an offense, or even negligence—are relatively minor ones (the sale of adulterated milk or tobacco, driving while disqualified, and so on). Commonly it is argued that if, in these cases, there were a requirement of proving intention or negligence, undue burdens would be placed on the prosecution, bogus defenses would be encouraged, and the ability of the law to deter offenders would suffer. So the interests of people who may have offended quite innocently are sacrificed to those of the public at large.

Now the point is that many people find the notion of strict liability for criminal offenses quite repugnant from a moral point of view; there is serious question about the propriety of having strict liability even for minor offenses, and there would be very strong resistance to introducing it for major ones. Nevertheless it is not clear that this resistance to strict liability can be justified in utilitarian terms—even if we were to take into account the insecurity and feelings of resentment which a general application of strict liability would certainly produce.

Whether or not we accept this criticism of utilitarian attempts to justify excuses, surely we must find it significant that those who so argue see this as a criticism of utilitarianism, not as a criticism of our practice of allowing certain conditions to excuse people from punishment. The possibility of revising the practice to bring it into line with theory is not considered. The requirement of *mens rea* stems from deeply held convictions about the conditions under which punishment is justifiable.

This is well illustrated by an earlier decision of the House of Lords, which took a very different direction from that taken in *Morgan,* but which generated a similar controversy. I refer to the case of *D.P.P.* v. *Smith.*[10] Smith and an accomplice were driving in a car, the rear of which was loaded with stolen goods. They were stopped by a police officer on point duty in the normal course of traffic control. Another officer, who had been on friendly terms with Smith for some time, came round to the driver's side of the car to speak to Smith. Noticing the goods in the back of the car, the officer told Smith to pull over to the side of the road as soon as the traffic was released. Smith started to do so, but then accelerated in an attempt to escape. The officer, who was at first walking, then running alongside the car, got his arm inside the open window on the driver's side and clung to the car. He managed to hang on as the car picked up speed. Traffic was heavy and Smith's car took an erratic course down the road, close to the traffic on the other side. They met four other cars coming from the opposite direction. The officer's body struck against the first three cars, but apparently without serious injury. Then he was shaken off, and fell in front of the fourth car, sustaining fatal injuries.

Smith continued on down the road, took a turn, stopped, unloaded the stolen goods and his companion, and returned alone to the place where the officer had been shaken off. On being told that the officer was dead, he said, "I am the driver of the car he was hanging on to. I knew the man. I wouldn't do that for the world. I only wanted to shake him off." Later he stated that he had been frightened by the officer's actions.

The fundamental question before the jury was whether Smith should be convicted of murder or manslaughter. An intention to kill is not necessary for murder, and no such intention was alleged against Smith. It is sufficient to sustain a charge of murder if there was an intention to cause grievous bodily harm. The trial judge instructed the jury in the following terms: "The intention with which a man did something can usually be determined by a jury only by inference from the surrounding circumstances, including the presumption of law that a man intends the natural and probable consequences of his acts." But the judge did not instruct the jury that this presumption could be rebutted by other evidence, and the jury convicted Smith of murder.

In the Court of Criminal Appeal, the main emphasis was on the character of this presumption. The court held that the trial judge was wrong not to point out to the jury that the presumption could be rebutted, citing with approval the judgment of Lord Goddard in *Steane:*

If the prosecution prove an act the natural and probable consequence of which would be a certain result, and no evidence or explanation is given, then a jury may, on a proper direction, find that the prisoner is guilty of doing the act with the intent alleged; but if, on the totality of the evidence, there is room for more than one view as to the intent of the prisoner, the jury should be directed that it is for the prosecution to prove the intent to the jury's satisfaction, and if, on a review of the whole evidence, they either think the intent did not exist, or they are left in doubt as to the intent, the prisoner is entitled to be acquitted.

One of the reasons why the *Smith* case is so interesting is that it fits these specifications very well. If you focus exclusively on the objective danger of serious harm which Smith's action involved, and if you think that in establishing intent the only question that need be asked is whether a reasonable man would have appreciated that danger, then it is difficult to avoid reaching the same conclusion the jury did—that Smith intended grievous bodily harm at least. But Smith's *subsequent* behavior affords very persuasive evidence that he did not in fact have that intention. The Court of Criminal Appeal accordingly substituted a verdict of manslaughter for the verdict of murder.

On appeal to the House of Lords this decision was reversed, and the verdict of murder was restored. Viscount Kilmuir, the Lord Chancellor, speaking for the Law Lords, argued that the jury need not have been told that the presumption was rebuttable, since the only thing which could have rebutted it was "proof of incapacity to form an intent, insanity or diminished responsibility" and there was no evidence in this case to support any of these defenses.

Although Viscount Kilmuir held that the jury had not been misdirected, he was nevertheless not happy with the use of the notions of a "presumption of law" and a "rebuttable presumption." These were apt to confuse the jury. The test of the reasonable man was simpler, more easily understood, and equally correct. In support of this he cited the authority of Mr. Justice Holmes, who argued, in his classic work, *The Common Law,* that

If the known present state of things is such that the act done will very certainly cause death, and the probability is a matter of common knowledge, one who does the act, knowing the present state of things, is guilty of murder, and the law will not inquire whether he did actually foresee the consequences or not. The test of foresight is not what *this very criminal foresaw,* but what *a man of reasonable prudence* would have foreseen.[11]

In adopting this test, Viscount Kilmuir incorporated into the English law of homicide Holmes' theory of objective liability. Objective liability may be seen as a compromise between strict liability, which would take *no* account of intention, knowledge, or foresight, and a subjective approach, which would require inquiry into the actual state of mind of the particular person accused of crime.

What are possible grounds for adopting a theory of objective liability? Viscount Kilmuir appears to have accepted Holmes' theory for reasons quite different from those Holmes himself invoked. In criticizing the decision of the Court of Criminal Appeal, the Lord Chancellor said that their "purely subjective approach" involved:

This, that if an accused *said* that he did not in fact think of the consequences, and the jury considered that that might well be true, he would be entitled to be acquitted of murder. [My emphasis]

Here the concern seems to be that a jury might be persuaded to entertain a doubt about an accused person's actual state of mind merely because of some subsequent assertion he makes about that state of mind. This concern springs, perhaps, from fears of jury gullibility and skepticism about the possibility of knowing other minds. A bit further on, the Lord Chancellor refers to the test of the reasonable man as "the only test available." One imagines he means that, apart from the assertions of the accused about his state of mind, the only possible evidence we could have of his intentions would be evidence of what a reasonable man would intend in the circumstances. But the *Smith* case shows that this is false. The facts that Smith returned to the scene of the crime, that he voluntarily identified himself as the offender, and that he voluntarily surrendered himself up to the police, all strongly support his assertions about his intentions. Perhaps juries are gullible; but if so, they could be directed to disregard uncorroborated denials of intention.

Holmes' reasons for adopting a theory of objective liability are more interesting. He is not a skeptic about the possibility of proving the existence of mental states. Dealing with the principle that ignorance of the law does not excuse, he argues that this cannot be defended on the ground of difficulty of proof:

If justice requires the fact to be ascertained, the difficulty of doing so is no ground for refusing to try . . . now that parties can testify, it may be doubted whether a man's knowledge of the law is any harder to investigate than many questions which are gone into. [*The Common Law*, p. 48]

And he thinks that the difficulty, "such as it is," could be met by making adjustments in the burden of proof.

The true explanation of the rule that ignorance of the law does not excuse is the same as that which accounts for the law's indifference to a man's particular temperament, faculties, and so forth. Public policy sacrifices the individual to the general good. It is desirable that the burden of all should be equal, but it is still more desirable to put an end to robbery and murder. [*The Common Law*, p. 48]

Holmes' view is that the overriding purpose of the criminal law is to insure that people act in external conformity with the law. If the law can achieve that purpose without injustice to the individual, well and good. But if doing justice to the individual interferes seriously with the law's attempt to secure obedience, then justice to the individual must be sacrificed. A system of strict liability, which punished all disobedience to the law, regardless of the difficulty of compliance, would be too severe; it would be contrary to the interests of society as a whole. A purely subjective approach to liability, which allowed as an excuse any fact that might relieve a man of moral culpability, would be equally contrary to the interests of society, by being too lenient. But a system of law which required everyone to come up to the level of rationality of the average member of society, though it might be very hard on the weakest members of society, would have a social utility sufficient to compensate for its injustices.

Whatever we may think of this kind of rationale for objective liability, the decision of the House of Lords in *Smith* generated a tremendous public uproar. The pages of *The Times* were filled with irate letters to the editor, the flavor of which is well captured by Professor Hart's contribution:

The House of Lords has shown that it is true, even if in mid-twentieth century it is almost unbelievable, that English law recognizes no distinction between a man who intends to kill and one who, without intending to either kill or seriously harm, does something to another which a reasonable man would realise would probably cause serious harm . . . this failure to distinguish between intentional and unintentional killing is just one among many indefensible barbarities which still disfigure English criminal law. The House of Lords did not misstate the law, but it is open to the serious criticism that in the Lord Chancellor's speech there was no expression of dissatisfaction with the failure of the law to recognize so vital a moral distinction.[12]

The *Smith* case is of considerable importance in Australian law, because it was the House of Lords' decision in *Smith* which prompted the High Court of Australia to declare its independence of British decisions. Chief Justice Dixon wrote that:

Hitherto I have thought that we ought to follow decisions of the House of Lords, at the expense of our own opinions and cases decided here; but having carefully studied *D.P.P.* v. *Smith* . . . I think that we cannot adhere to that . . . policy. There are propositions laid down in the judgment which I believe to be misconceived and wrong. They are fundamental and they are propositions which I could never bring myself to accept . . . *Smith's Case* . . . should not be used in Australia as authority at all.[13]

The decision in *Smith* no longer states the law in England either. Dissatisfaction with it was such that the courts avoided its application wherever possible.[14] And eventually it was overturned by the legislature in the Criminal Justice Act of 1967.

III

What has all of this to do with the *Morgan* rule? The *Smith* case was not discussed in the House of Lords' decision on *Morgan,* and would not have been to the point. For it concerned lack of foresight of consequences, not a mistaken belief about material circumstances. Even if someone were to adopt a theory of objective liability regarding foresight of consequences, he might not feel required to embrace such a theory regarding knowledge of fact. Holmes himself, in a passage cited by Viscount Kilmuir, made a distinction between them, holding that:

Ignorance of fact and inability to foresee a consequence have the same effect on blameworthiness. If a consequence cannot be foreseen, it cannot be avoided. But there is the practical difference, that whereas, in most cases, the question of knowledge is a question of the actual condition of the defendant's consciousness, the question of what he might have foreseen is determined by the standard of the prudent man. [*The Common Law,* p. 56]

So even if the decision of the House of Lords in *Smith* had still represented the law in England, it was not a case which the majority in *Morgan* had to discuss in justifying their decision.

Still, the *Smith* case, and the reaction against objective liability which it provoked, were very much in the minds of the majority in *Morgan.* Lord Hailsham was led to remark that:

To insist that a belief [in consent] must be reasonable to excuse [someone accused of rape] . . . is to insist on an objective element in the definition of intent, and this is a course which I am extremely reluctant to adopt, especially after the unhappy experience of the House after the decision in *D.P.P.* v. *Smith,* a case which is full of warnings for us all. . . .

The decision in *Morgan* is a part of the retreat from the objective liability embraced in *Smith.* The fundamental points which the majority wished to make were that (a) you could not justly convict a man of a serious crime unless he *actually* had the *mens rea* requisite for the offense, and (b) a man could not have the *mens rea* required for rape if he believed the woman was consenting.

Now it seems to me that this is a plausible, though erroneous, position. But before I attempt to argue against it, let us look at a case which the Lords *were* obliged to discuss. There had been no previous English rape cases of high authority where the defense of unreasonable belief in consent had been tried. There were Australian cases, which the Lords took note of, but these had not followed any consistent pattern, and so were not very helpful. The most important case cited in support of the requirement of reasonable belief was *Tolson,*[15] a bigamy case decided in 1889. Mrs. Tolson, deserted by her husband, remarried some five years and two months later. She believed her first husband to be dead, having made inquiries about him, and having been told by his elder brother and by others that he had been lost at sea, on a ship which went down with all hands on board. Within a year after her second marriage, Tolson turned up, and Mrs. Tolson was charged with bigamy.

Similar situations have provided plots for many a light comedy, but Mrs. Tolson's was potentially serious. Bigamy was not a crime at common law. Before it was made a statutory felony in the seventeenth century, it had been dealt with by the ecclesiastical courts; upon becoming a statutory offense, it was made punishable by death. Even in the nineteenth century it involved a punishment of up to seven years imprisonment or two years at hard labor.

There was no doubt that Mrs. Tolson's actions fell within the terms of the statute, which provided that anyone marrying a second time during the life of a former spouse would be guilty of a felony, except where the former spouse had been continually absent for at least seven years, and had not been known by the accused to have been alive during that time. The majority opinion in the Court of Crown Cases Reserved was that Mrs. Tolson's reasonable belief in her first husband's death entitled her to an acquittal. As Mr. Justice Wills put it, "at common law an honest and reasonable belief in the existence of circumstances, which, if true, would make the act for which the prisoner is indicted an innocent act has always been held to be a good defence." The minority view was that because the statute made an explicit exception for cases where the spouse had been missing for seven years, and made no other exceptions, the principle of literal construction of statutes required the offense to be treated as one of strict liability apart from the statutory exception.

Clearly, the decision in *Tolson* is not a very good precedent for requiring a reasonable belief in consent in rape cases. The question before the court in *Tolson* was whether even a reasonable mistake about material fact is sufficient to excuse an otherwise criminal act. The question to be decided in *Morgan* was whether *any* mistake about material fact, no matter how unreasonable, would be a sufficient excuse. Perhaps the majority in *Tolson,* because of their concern not to read too much into the statute, gave grounds for their decision which were narrower than the grounds they might properly have given. Mrs. Tolson's belief in her first husband's death had been found by a jury to be reasonable. Doing justice to her did not require them to consider the position of people whose beliefs were not reasonable.

Many writers on criminal law have felt that the *Tolson* rule does not go far enough and that even an unreasonable mistake should be a defense to bigamy and to criminal charges generally. For example, Professor Glanville Williams has written that:

Even if, as a result of decisions like this, it must now be conceded that unreasonable mistake is no defence in bigamy, this only means that bigamy can be committed negligently. It does not prove that other crimes can be committed negligently.

It is hard to justify the punishment of negligent bigamy on any rational ground.[16]

These words of Professor Williams were cited with approval by Lord Edmund-Davies,[17] as were the similar views of a leading American writer on criminal law, Professor Jerome Hall. And I agree that, in the case of bigamy at least, the test of liability might well be a subjective one. The House might have reconsidered *Tolson,* and held that in that case a correct result

was reached on incorrect, excessively narrow grounds.

Nevertheless, the majority in *Morgan* chose not to reconsider *Tolson,* but to distinguish it. The most substantial argument for the distinction was offered by Lord Cross. He could see no objection to the inclusion of the element of reasonableness in the *Tolson* case:

If the words defining an offence provide either expressly or impliedly that a man is not to be guilty of it if he believes something to be true, then he cannot be found guilty if the jury thinks that he may have believed it to be true, however inadequate were his reasons for doing so. But, if the definition of the offence is on the face of it "absolute" and the defendant is seeking to escape his prima facie liability by a defence of mistaken belief, I can see no hardship to him in requiring the mistake—if it is to afford him a defence—to be based on reasonable grounds . . . it can be argued with force that it is only fair to the woman and not in the least unfair to the man that he should be under a duty to take reasonable care to ascertain that she is consenting to the intercourse and be at the risk of a prosecution if he fails to take such care. . . .

Now here Lord Cross has embarked on a train of reasoning which, you might suppose, would lead him inexorably to apply the *Tolson* rule to rape. But at this point there is an extraordinary reversal:

. . . *if* the Sexual Offences Act 1956 had made it an offence to have intercourse with a woman who was not consenting to it, so that the defendant could only escape liability by application of the "Tolson" principle, I would not have thought the law unjust. [My emphasis]

But the Act does not say that. It says that a man who "rapes" a woman commits an offense. So the Act does not prohibit intercourse without consent unless the phrase "rape a woman" is equivalent to "have intercourse with a woman without her consent." And Lord Cross denies this equivalence. "Rape"

. . . is not a word in the use of which lawyers have a monopoly, and the question to be answered . . . is whether according to the ordinary use of the English language a man can be said to have committed rape if he believed that the woman was consenting to the intercourse and would not have attempted to have it but for his belief, whatever his grounds for so believing. I do not think he can. Rape, to my mind, imports at least indifference as the woman's consent.

And indifference as to consent is incompatible with a belief in consent such that the man would not have acted but for his belief.

Now it is not *preposterous* to claim that the correct use of the term "rape" ordinarily implies something about the mental state of the agent. Certainly there is a significant class of English verbs for which this is true, as most dictionaries will testify.[18] Lying, for example, is making a false statement with the knowledge that it is false and with intent to deceive. And the definitions of such other verbs as "murder," "steal," and "cheat" also usually incorporate a mental element. But if dictionaries are any guide to ordinary usage, "rape" does not in fact fall into this class of verbs. It is customarily defined simply in terms of intercourse without consent (with a reference, often, to force).

Perhaps even the best of dictionaries is not a good guide to ordinary usage on so subtle a point. Lord Cross supports his intuitions about usage by resorting to that favorite device of the philosopher in extremis, the thought experiment:

... in this connection the ordinary man would distinguish between rape and bigamy. To the question whether a man who goes through a ceremony of marriage with a woman [at a time when he believes, falsely, and on inadequate grounds, that his first wife is dead] commits bigamy, I think he would reply, "Yes—but I suppose the law contains an escape clause for bigamists who are not really to blame." On the other hand, to the question whether a man who has intercourse with a woman [at a time when he believes, falsely, and on inadequate grounds, that she is consenting to it], commits rape, I think that he would reply, "No, If he was grossly careless then he may deserve to be punished but not for rape."

Well, it is refreshing to find that philosophers are not the only ones to engage in a priori lexicography. But this seems a most unlikely thing for the ordinary man to say. Carelessness—even *gross* carelessness—hardly seems the appropriate fault to find.[19] But however that may be, why should the ordinary man not say, "Yes, he did commit rape, though he *may* not deserve to be punished for it."

To one thought experiment, we may oppose another. Consider the following case. Cogan and Leak arrive at Leak's house after a night of drinking. Leak tells Mrs. Leak that Cogan wants intercourse with her and that he, Leak, will see that she complies. He wishes to punish her for past misconduct, and intends that she be raped. Mrs. Leak, in terror, submits to intercourse with Cogan, who believes her to be consenting. He has been told by her husband that she would consent, and is too drunk to appreciate her distress. Under the *Morgan* rule, Cogan is acquitted. Let us suppose, for the sake of argument, that Cogan's belief in Mrs. Leak's consent *should* excuse him from punishment. The question still remains as to whether he did an act of the kind prohibited by the law.

Lord Cross' view, on the face of it, requires us to say that no act of rape occurred. But it seems a perverse construction of ordinary language which would hold that Leak's intention that his wife be raped was frustrated by Cogan's false belief in her consent. As Lord Justice Lawton remarked when the case came to the Court of Appeal, no one outside a court of law would say that Mrs. Leak had not been raped: "one fact is clear—the wife had been raped. Cogan had had sexual intercourse with her without her consent."[20]

Perhaps it makes little practical difference whether we say, "Yes, Cogan raped Mrs. Leak, though justice requires that he not be punished for it," or, "No, he did not rape her because he lacked the necessary intent." But it does make *some* difference to the form of proceeding which is taken against the man who, on anyone's view of the matter, deserves punishment, viz. Leak. If Cogan did not rape Mrs. Leak, it seems illogical to convict Leak of aiding and abetting a rape, as the Court of Appeal conceded. Leak did not escape punishment. His conviction for aiding and abetting was upheld on the ground that he would certainly have been convicted had he been properly charged as a principal acting through an innocent agent.[21] But this rationale is open to the criticism that the doctrine of innocent agency is intended to apply to situations where one person brings about a prohibited act "through a person who lacks the *mens rea* necessary to constitute the crime, in such circumstances that [the first person] can fairly be said to have committed the crime himself."[22] In fact the court arrived at its decision by finding that Leak had *procured Cogan to rape* Mrs. Leak. And that does seem the most natural way of describing what happened.

Literal construction of the Sexual Offences Act requires us to regard rape as an offense which, *on the face of it,* is absolute; justice, of course, requires that a defense of reasonable mistake be available.

IV

What can we say against the *Morgan* rule? First, consider the following utilitarian argument.

Rape is a serious crime, for which the prosecution finds it more than usually difficult to get a conviction. There is good evidence to indicate that increasing the penalties for rape does not deter offenders.[23] But more prospective rapists might be deterred if the chances of conviction were increased, particularly since there is evidence that a high percentage of rapes are at least partially planned, not "explosive," events.[24]

Moreover, there are other considerations of public welfare which motivate a stricter policy toward rape defendants. An affront to the person of the magnitude of rape can generate strong desires for vengeance. It is important to society as a whole that those who have such desires be made to feel that they have a fair chance of receiving satisfaction through the legal system. It is not in anyone's interest that the passion for revenge be forced to find its satisfaction outside the law. And a woman who has been raped by a man acquitted under the *Morgan* rule is not likely to feel that she has been treated fairly.

There are many ways in which the task of prosecution might be made easier. One popular suggestion is that we drop the requirement that the complainant's testimony be corroborated,[25] a requirement usually justified on the ground that complaints of sexual offenses

. . . are particularly subject to the danger of deliberately false charges, resulting from sexual neurosis, phantasy, jealousy, spite, or simply a girl's refusal to admit that she consented to an act of which she is now ashamed.[26]

It must be admitted that there are powerful motives which operate in some people to encourage false complaints, and that the nature of those motives may particularly encourage false complaints of sexual offenses.

But sexually based malice may find expression in other types of false complaint, as may neuroses with little or no sexual component. Moreover, some of the motives which tend to discourage true complaints of sexual offenses[27]—fear of the ordeal of police investigation and appearance in court, fear of loss of reputation even if the charge is proved to the satisfaction of a jury, fear of retaliation by the accused—would also tend to discourage false complaints. Without evidence more convincing than anecdotal reports of false prosecutions, we cannot claim to know that sexual offenses attract a higher rate of false complaint than other offenses do.

Still, abandoning the corroboration rule would, to some uncertain degree, increase the risk of convicting the innocent. One attraction of abandoning the *Morgan* rule is that there is a sense in which it does not have that disadvantage. The question of criminal responsibility can arise only when there is evidence capable of persuading a jury, beyond reasonable doubt, (a) that the defendant *did* have intercourse with the complainant, and (b) that the complainant *did not* consent. So in any case in which the *Morgan* rule is critical, we must have evidence satisfying stringent standards that the defendant has, at least, done what the law forbids. If he is to be found "innocent," it will be because of a moral judgment incorporated in our legal standard of responsibility, a judgment we might well wish to reconsider; his "innocence" will be of a very different kind from that of someone who is, say, mistakenly identified as the offender, or someone who had intercourse with a woman who consented.

It may be objected that threatening to punish men who engage in intercourse, genuinely but falsely believing in the woman's consent, will not deter anyone from rape. If the man believes, however unreasonably, that she is consenting, he will not be deterred by a law forbidding intercourse without consent. This is parallel to Glanville Williams' argument to show that there is no rational ground for punishing negligent bigamy. But the objection is unsound. Men may well be encouraged by such a law to take more care in forming their beliefs, or in acting on them.

A more cogent ground of objection to the utilitarian argument is that abandoning the *Morgan* rule is not likely to have much effect on conviction rates for rape. The *Morgan* rule can only give a different result from that which the *Tolson* rule would give where there is *both* evidence capable of persuading a jury beyond reasonable doubt that any belief in consent the defendant may have had would have been unreasonable *and* evidence capable of raising a reasonable doubt as to his actual belief. If the first condition is not satisfied, the defendant will be entitled to acquittal even under the *Tolson* rule; if the second is not satisfied, then the jury will be entitled to infer, from the fact that a belief in consent would not have been reasonable, that such a belief was not held. Such situations must be infrequent. So against the utilitarian argument we may say this—if there is an important principle of justice at stake, the gain in social utility we may expect from abandoning the *Morgan* rule is not likely to be sufficient to warrant any sacrifice of justice to the individual.

Nevertheless, I cannot see that there is an important principle of justice at stake. It has been urged, against objective theories of liability, that we ought not to punish people "for the good of others, unless they have broken the law when they had the capacity and a fair opportunity to conform to its requirements."[28] But we are dealing here with people who are in a situation in which acting on a false belief involves immediate, serious, and irremediable harm to someone else, while refraining from acting on a true belief would involve a small loss to anyone. Moreover, the character of the mistake is such that the man who makes it must believe in consent, not merely without evidence, but in spite of quite definite evidence to the contrary, evidence capable of persuading a jury beyond reasonable doubt not merely that the woman did not consent at the relevant time but that any belief in consent which the defendant may have had at that time would have been unreasonable. It has been said that the criminal law is designed to punish the vicious, not the stupid or the credulous.[20] What I argue is that, in these circumstances, the disposition to act on an unreasonable belief is a vice.

We might take a different line, holding that while (a) the criminal law is designed to punish the vicious (in the sense that, apart from exceptional offenses such as manslaughter, for which negligence suffices, the types of serious misconduct the law proscribes are ones whose instances typically manifest some vice), nevertheless (b) the criminal law does sometimes justifiably punish nonvicious individuals for committing such offenses. It is difficult to see how (b) could be denied, so long as we inquire only into the defendant's intention and not into his motives. To that extent Holmes was right to insist on the relevance of the law's disregard of motives in attempting to justify his doctrine of objective liability.

But it is not necessary to concede so much with respect to defendants for whom the *Morgan* rule is critical. The suggestion that a *Mor-*

gan defendant is merely careless, or stupid, or credulous, but not vicious, is a strange one. Certainly many moral philosophers have taken a strict view about belief on insufficient evidence. Clifford, for example, contended forcefully that "it is wrong always, everywhere, and for anyone, to believe anything on insufficient evidence." On his view, credulity is, in itself, a vice.

Elsewhere I have argued that Clifford goes too far, that the examples on which he asks us to bring our moral intuitions to bear support only a more modest thesis—that, in certain circumstances, the disposition to act on an unreasonable belief is a vice.[30] What I wish to show here is that the circumstances which would make that disposition a vice obtain in cases where the *Morgan* rule is critical. The best way to bring this out will be to consider what kind of legal fault we ought to find in a *Morgan* defendant.

Lawyers tend to equate the imposition of objective liability with making negligence a basis of criminal responsibility. To say that negligence is a fault sufficient to warrant conviction for a serious crime such as rape would be a radical departure from tradition. But it was conceded by the majority in *Morgan* that recklessness as to the woman's consent would show a mind sufficiently guilty to sustain a charge of rape. What their Lordships do not seem to have considered adequately is the possibility of regarding *Morgan* defendants as reckless. The assumption appears to be that a belief in consent, no matter how unreasonable, is incompatible with recklessness.[31] But, intuitively, recklessness seems a highly appropriate fault to find here, and on an adequate analysis of the concept, it should be possible to show that the criteria for recklessness must be satisfied by *Morgan* defendants.

A widely accepted definition of recklessness is that adopted by the American Law Institute in its Model Penal Code:

A person acts recklessly with respect to a material element of an offense when he consciously disregards a substantial and unjustifiable risk that the material element exists or will result from his conduct.[32]

It will be convenient to consider this in two parts.

Conscious Disregard of a Risk. This is the key element for the distinction between recklessness and negligence. Negligence implies inadvertence to a risk which should have been adverted to, whereas recklessness implies advertent disregard of risk. Now how could it plausibly be maintained, in any case where the *Morgan* rule is critical, that the defendant did not advert to the risk that the woman was not consenting? If it is alleged on his behalf that he believed her to be consenting, and if we are invited to excuse him on the grounds of that belief, then we must assume that he considered the possibility that she was not consenting and rejected it. Moreover, it is inconceivable that a properly instructed and sensible jury would unanimously agree in finding his belief to be, beyond reasonable doubt, unreasonable, without also finding that the complainant had given the defendant good evidence of her lack of consent. This is what makes it so inappropriate to speak of negligence here.

Substantial and Unjustifiable Risk. A substantial risk is one where there is a significant probability of the outcome risked. But it is not possible to specify how high the probability must be to be significant, without also considering the question of justification. If the harm to be anticipated in acting on a false belief is very great, and the good which may be lost in failing to act on a true belief is slight, then it will not take a very high probability to make the risk a substantial one. Perhaps we do lose something if we insist that men take a woman's resistance seriously. But one of the things we would be saying, in favoring the *Tolson* rule over the *Morgan* rule, is that those benefits do not count for much when weighed against the harm that can come from being wrong. People who have acted on an unreasonable mistake in committing bigamy may well be merely negligent. But given this account of recklessness, it is difficult to see why it should be thought that in rape any belief in consent, no matter how unreasonable, excludes recklessness as to consent. Indeed, the law already recognizes, under the heading of willful blindness,[33] the possibility that mistake about a material element may coincide with recklessness regarding that element.

In this connection it is interesting that the House had great difficulty knowing what to make of the reference to "honest" belief in the *Tolson* rule. Lord Simon remarked that it was "tautologous, but useful"; Lord Edmund-Davies, that it was "superfluous, but conve-

nient." Lord Fraser said, "Strictly speaking, I do not think that a belief, if held at all, can be held otherwise than honestly, but I read that last phrase as a warning to the jury to consider carefully whether the evidence of the defendant's belief was honest." I suppose this means that the belief was honest if subsequent testimony as to its existence is honest.

But just as a woman might come to believe, falsely, that she had not consented, so a man might come to believe, falsely, that he had believed the woman was consenting. No one seems to have considered the possibility that the term "honest" might refer to the process by which the belief was acquired—for example, whether there was any stifling of doubts. Yet even if we assume that Morgan's three colleagues did believe Mrs. Morgan was consenting, it is difficult to resist concluding that they could not have cared much whether that belief was correct, if they persisted in it in the face of her behavior. Cogan may seem a more sympathetic defendant, since we can attribute his mistake partly to his drunkenness. But the law does not normally regard drunkenness as an excuse, and I see no reason why it should make an exception for drunken rapists.

V

Abandoning the Morgan rule would be a small step in the direction of a more equitable rape law, but it is a step which no legitimate concern for the rights of the accused forbids us to take. What other steps might be taken?

I have already mentioned abandonment of the corroboration rule. Another step, involving similar issues, would be the exclusion of information regarding the complainant's sexual history. Quite apart from the effect of these inquiries on the complainant, there is persuasive evidence that juries attach too much weight to that kind of information; there is also evidence to suggest that some victims may be chosen precisely because it is known that their bad reputation will make it difficult for them to have their complaints listened to.[34] On the other hand, I cannot see how there could justifiably be a blanket exclusion of all such evidence. For example, if there is a history of past consenting relationships between the complainant and the accused, then I should think that this must be relevant to the question of what the accused may reasonably have believed. I do not say that it should settle that question, only that it might properly be considered to have some bearing on reasonable belief.

These issues of evidence are very difficult, but they are now getting some discussion in the feminist critique of the law. I should like to conclude by considering one issue that I think is not receiving proper attention.

We do not get much insight into the workings of our system of criminal justice by focusing exclusively on anecdotal evidence about how this defendant was wrongly acquitted, or that one wrongly convicted. Nor are the official criminal statistics much help. If conviction rates for one type of crime were very high, we might merely suspect that police and prosecutorial discretion was permitting only the very strongest cases to come to court. But recently there has been a fascinating and very instructive study of the workings of the jury system in the United States.

A team of lawyers and sociologists secured the cooperation of over 500 trial judges throughout that country, and acquired from them information on over 3,500 trials. Forcible rape was well represented in the sample. The judges were asked to fill out detailed questionnaires on a wide variety of aspects of each case—kinds of evidence presented, circumstances of the crime, the conduct of the prosecution and defense cases, characteristics of the defendant and the victim (if any), and court procedure. The judge was asked to say (before the jury returned its verdict) how he would have decided the case. If there was disagreement between judge and jury, the judge was to say why he thought the jury had taken a different view of the case. The primary focus of the study was on the explanation of judge/jury disagreements.

This study produced a number of important findings relevant to our present concerns. For example, it appears that facts known only to the judge play a very small role in accounting for disagreements. One reason for this is that the extra information which the judge most frequently has—information about the defendant's previous criminal record—quite often does get before the jury. Indeed, in 59 percent of the cases where the defendant had a criminal record, the jury learned of that record. So it is not surprising that facts known only to the judge accounted for judge/jury disagreements in only about 2 percent of those disagreements where the jury was more lenient than the judge.[35]

This suggests that the habitual rapist who gains an acquittal because his record is kept from the jury is relatively rare, a conclusion which is also supported by the fact that, though men charged with rape often have a previous record of some sort, they do not often have a previous record for rape.[36] Indeed, the danger of an unwarranted acquittal is probably much greater in the case of the defendant who has no previous record. For one of the most striking findings of the Jury Project was that where defendants without a previous record are charged with a serious crime and take the stand in their own defense, juries are much more prone to give credence to their denials than judges are. And many persons charged with rape do not conform to popular stereotypes of what a rapist is like.

But the most important finding of the Jury Project for our purposes is that very frequently judge/jury disagreements result from jury dissatisfaction with the law. Sometimes this works to the advantage of the prosecution. For example, it is suggested that juries are often less rule-bound than judges in dealing with uncorroborated complaints in sexual cases.[37] But more commonly, jury sentiments about the law work to the advantage of the defendant. One of the most important ways in which this happens is through the jury's introduction into the criminal law of concepts prominent in the law of tort—the concepts of contributory negligence and assumption of risk.

It should be stressed that the jury's disposition to inquire into the behavior of the victim, and to be lenient where that behavior is thought to have contributed significantly to the occurrence of the offense, is prominent in all crimes that have a victim. Sometimes in homicide cases, the victim's behavior is "almost insanely reckless." But the jury's response to the victim's behavior is not limited to such clear-cut cases. A fairly typical situation in rape cases is that where the complainant and the defendant meet for the first time in a bar or at a dance, have a number of drinks together, and she agrees to let him take her home. This would more naturally be called a case of assumption of risk. An example of contributory fault would be a situation where the victim consents to a limited degree of love-making, but draws the line at intercourse, or consents to intercourse, but changes her mind prior to penetration.

Now the law very properly says that the woman does not consent unless she consents at the time of penetration, no matter what her previous behavior may have been, whether she has unintentionally aroused expectations she has no wish to satisfy, or given the man considerable encouragement. But juries are often reluctant to give the law full force:

> The jury's stance is not so much that involuntary intercourse under these circumstances is no crime at all, but rather that it does not have the gravity of rape. If given the option of finding a lesser offense, the jury will avail itself of it. However, if this option is not available, the jury appears to prefer to acquit the defendant rather than to find him guilty of rape.[38]

The jury is frequently forced to choose the lesser of two evils, and it frequently exercises that option in favor of the defendant, sometimes very unfairly to the complainant.

What this suggests is that there is a need for the law to recognize a lesser offense of nonconsensual intercourse. Not that there are not already in the law lesser offenses with which offenders may be charged. But these offenses—attempted rape and indecent assault—are aimed at situations where there is no intercourse, not at situations where the victim may have been partly responsible, without actually consenting. The cases we are considering are ones where, as the law now stands, the facts will support a charge of rape or nothing. To convict of one of the existing lesser offenses would be an illogical compromise.

The proposal that a lesser offense be introduced needs to be distinguished from another which has been very popular lately, viz. that the crime of rape

> . . . be removed from the law, and replaced by a crime of aggravated assault, so that the argument over the degree of encouragement which a woman is alleged to have given becomes less important and instead attention is concentrated on the question: did the man in the whole situation behave brutally?[39]

There seem to me to be serious problems in trying to make assault do the work of rape. First, any rape is already at least a simple assault according to the usual definition of that offense.[40] Insofar as the proposal makes a difference to existing law, it is by treating rape situations as ones where the assault is aggravated. Now the question is, What is to be the aggravating factor? Professor Sawer seems to be suggesting that we should emphasize the use of brutal physical force. But of course rape very often does not involve the actual use of

physical brutality,[41] and surely we do not wish to say that offenders can be prosecuted on the more serious charge only if they have used brutality. What really distinguishes this kind of assault is that it involves an infringement of the victim's right of sexual self-determination. But if that is made the aggravating factor, then the offense of rape is really retained in the law under a different name.

Again, where an assault does not involve a serious degree of bodily harm, the consent of the victim is normally a good defense.[42] So it is difficult to see how the issue of consent can be avoided. Moreover, even where the rape is accompanied by considerable violence, juries frequently acquit where they can see assumption of risk or contributory fault on the part of the victim.[43]

Of course even the mere relabeling of rape might have some good effects; and if an appropriate lesser offense were introduced, then although it would still *be* rape (i.e., intercourse without consent), it should probably not be called "rape," but should be given some label which does not have the same associations.

The importance of this can be illustrated by reference again to the case of *Smith*. The only question in that instance was whether Smith should be found guilty of murder or of manslaughter. Technically murder was a capital offense, but it was known that the death penalty would not be imposed. In practical terms, the choice was between a possible life sentence for murder or a sentence of 10 years for manslaughter. Defendant's counsel acknowledged that

> . . . in some circumstances life imprisonment for murder would be a sentence preferable to one of 10 years, since it might be reviewed after five years, but it is important to [Smith] personally not to be classed as a murderer.

If an offender convicted of homicide is prepared to risk a possibly longer sentence to avoid the stigma attached to murder, juries will no doubt also be influenced by that consideration. A more neutral label might produce fewer unwarranted acquittals.

Smith's conviction for murder, when there was a more appropriate lesser offense available, was repugnant because it demonstrated an insensitivity the law sometimes shows to important moral distinctions. There are many ways this may happen. It happens when the law, by not providing an appropriate lesser offense, fails to take account of the wide variety of circumstances in which intercourse may be imposed on an unwilling woman. It happens also when the law excuses both the man who acts on a reasonable belief in consent and the man who acts on an unreasonable belief in consent. The imposition of objective standards of liability does not always represent the triumph of utility over justice.

APPENDIX ON TWO EMPIRICAL ISSUES

The argument of this paper does not depend heavily on the assumption that it is substantially more difficult to obtain convictions for rape than for other serious offenses, but our attitude towards it will inevitably affect our attitude towards the law regarding rape. Let us take at least a brief look at the evidence for it.

Texts on criminal law still frequently quote, or paraphrase, the dictum of a distinguished seventeenth-century judge, Lord Hale:

It is true rape is a most detestable crime, and therefore ought severely and impartially to be punished with death; but it must be remembered, that it is an accusation easily to be made and hard to be proved, and harder to be defended by the party accused, tho never so innocent. . . .[44]

In some jurisdictions in the United States, similar sentiments are expressed in the cautionary instructions customarily given to juries, departure from which can constitute a reversible error. For example, in California juries are normally told that rape is a charge which, "generally speaking is easily made, and once made, difficult to disprove," as if there were a burden of disproof on the defendant. And this is given as a reason for examining the complainant's testimony with special care.

Not surprisingly, this kind of claim has been under sharp attack recently. For example, Le Grand writes that "very few apprehended rapists are ever charged with and convicted of rape," and supports her claim by appeal to the *Uniform Crime Reports:*

National figures show that in 1970, 56% of all rape complaints ended in arrests. 62% of those arrested were prosecuted. 36% of those prosecuted were convicted of rape; 18% were convicted of lesser offences: 46% ended in acquittals or dismissals due to prosecutorial problems (as compared to 29% acquittal or dismissal rate for all crimes). . . . Assuming that those rape complaints are valid (F.B.I. figures exclude "unfounded" rapes) a man who rapes a woman who reports the rape to police has roughly seven chances out of eight of walking away without any conviction. Assuming only one woman in five reports the rape, his chances increase to 39 out of 40. . . . Forcible rape has a lower conviction rate than any other crime listed in the *Uniform Crime Report.* . . . Jury attitudes no doubt contribute to these astonishing figures.[45]

No doubt they do. But the figures are not so astonishing when looked at more closely. And the matter is too important to be treated lightly.

The main point is that Le Grand is relying on F.B.I. data and interpretations. For years the Bureau's presentation of its criminal statistics, with its "crime clocks," has been under attack from serious criminologists.[46] To be quite frank, the *Uniform Crime Reports* are used by the F.B.I. as a propaganda device for arousing public concern about crime, and influencing legislative and judicial decisions. Anyone who wishes to use them to learn how our system of criminal justice really works, needs to exercise extreme caution. The data *may* be accurate, but the F.B.I.'s interpretations of those data are highly suspect.

Support for Le Grand's claim can certainly be found on the pages of the *U.C.R.*, she refers to, but if you continue reading until you reach the statistical table on which the F.B.I. summary is based, it tells a somewhat less dramatic story. First, in relation to "offenses known to the police," the percentage of adults convicted (either as charged or of a lesser offense) varies considerably from one crime category to another, from a high of 34.9 percent (murder and non-negligent manslaughter) to a low of 2.8 percent (auto theft). But the percentages for all crimes are low enough to encourage doubts about the capacity of the criminal law to deter anyone bent on calculating the expected utilities and well informed about the likelihood of his being convicted of an offense.[47] The percentage for rape (15.7 percent) does not differ markedly from that for the offense with which it is most naturally compared, aggravated assault (17.4 percent).

Second, Le Grand compares the acquittal or dismissal rate for rape (46 percent) with that for "all crimes" (29 percent), by which she means all crimes on the F.B.I.'s "Crime Index." The Index offenses are seven offenses selected for special attention by the F.B.I. because of their seriousness, frequency and likelihood of being reported. But in fact the *only* Index crime which has an acquittal or dismissal rate lower than the average for all Index offenses is larceny. Because larcenies account for 57 percent of all Index offenses known to the police,[48] their very low acquittal or dismissal rate (23 percent) has a considerable effect on the average. The percentage for rape is higher than that for any other Index offense, but does not look so much higher when compared with those for other serious offenses against the person, e.g., murder and non-negligent manslaughter (41 percent) and aggravated assault (40 percent).

Still, there is a substantial difference in the official acquittal rates, even when the appropriate comparisons are made, and this does lend support to the contention that prosecution for rape is more difficult than prosecution for other serious offenses. Against this it might be argued that prosecution for rape will always be difficult, given the kind of evidence usually available in such cases. Typically, much depends on which of two stories is believed and, perhaps, so long as we remain committed to the presumption of innocence, some difference in acquittal rates is inevitable. Perhaps the statistics do not constitute an indictment of existing law.[49] Certainly it is difficult to know how significant the statistics are without knowing more than we do about what accounts for the differences in acquittal rates.

My own conjecture is that the official statistics conceal more than they reveal, and that if we had more reliable evidence it would confirm feminist criticisms of the law. The most persuasive evidence for this arises in connection with the figures for unfounded complaints. F.B.I. figures for "offenses known to the police" are supposed to exclude complaints where the police conclude, as a result of their investigations, that the crime did not happen or was not attempted. For 1970, the F.B.I. reported that about 18 percent of rape complaints were classified by local police as "unfounded," as compared with 4 percent for Crime Index offenses in general. If we disregard the fact that larceny once again has the lowest rate (3 percent), these figures might be used to support claims that false complaints of rape are much more frequent than false complaints of other crimes.

The difficulty with this argument, however, is that the police do not classify complaints as unfounded only when the F.B.I. thinks they should, that is, only when "the investigation proves that the crime did not happen or was not attempted." Local police are anxious to protect their departments' records for efficiency and their communities' reputations for order. This concern frequently leads them to classify as "unfounded" many complaints which they know will be difficult to prove in court, but do not believe to be false. Considerations which ought only to influence the decision to prosecute regularly influence the decision that a crime has been committed.

Moreover, a great many rape complaints which police classify as unfounded do not appear in police records as unfounded *rape* complaints. They are more likely to be dismissed under other, catch-all headings, such as "investigation of persons" or "suspicious circumstances." One recent study of this process in Philadelphia estimated, conservatively, that *at least* 50 percent of all rape complaints were treated as unfounded under one heading or another.[50] So it seems likely that a large number of valid rape complaints never reach court, or even show up in the police records as rape complaints.

In the body of the paper, I suggest that the evidence commonly offered for there being an unusually high frequency of false complaints of sexual offenses is largely anecdotal and hence unsatisfactory. Brandon and Davies' study of wrongful imprisonment in England offers a statistical argument purporting to show that three types of charge are particularly liable to result in wrongful imprisonment: robbery, malicious or willful damage, and sexual offenses.[51] Their criterion of wrongful imprisonment was the receipt of a free pardon or the reversal of a conviction (on grounds other than technical legal ones). They then compared the frequencies of wrongful imprisonment for the various types of offense with the frequencies of persons convicted for those offenses in the prison population. They found that people were unjustly convicted for these three offenses more often than one would expect, given the frequency with which people are convicted for them. The expected and observed frequencies, respectively were: robbery (2.6 percent/12 percent), malicious or willful damage (2.3 percent/8 percent), and sexual offenses (3.4 percent/6 percent).

The crucial question is whether these differences between the expected and observed frequencies are significant, that is, whether they can be ascribed to chance or to some systematic factor. The hypothesis is that the nature of the evidence in these types of offenses predisposes the courts to convict erroneously.

The authors calculate the probabilities of the differences occurring by chance for the first two types of offense: .0018 for robbery, and .0279 for malicious damage. The first of these probabilities is clearly low enough to satisfy normal criteria for statistical significance. The second is more questionable. Sometimes sociologists treat any probability of less than .05 as indicating statistical significance; sometimes they employ a more stringent criterion of .01 or less. In this instance there are good reasons for being more stringent, since the figures for both observed and expected frequencies involve a projection. The authors assume that those actually pardoned are representative of those deserving a pardon, even though they believe the former group to be a small sample of the latter group. Whereas their figures for pardons are taken over a twenty-year period (1950–1970), the figures for imprisonments are taken from one year (1968), and it is assumed that the frequencies of imprisonment for the various offenses during that year are representative of the frequencies over the twenty-year period. The scope for error is thus considerable.

In any case, the authors do not present any calculation of the probability of the difference arising by chance for the sexual offenses. And in fact that probability (.15) is far too high for the difference to be statistically significant even on a fairly liberal criterion of significance. So although Brandon and Davies claim that all three types of charge are more than usually liable to result in erroneous convictions, their statistics support their claims for robbery and (perhaps) malicious damage, but not for sexual offenses.

NOTES

A version of this paper was originally presented to the annual conference of the Australasian Association of Philosophy, meeting at Macquarie University in Sydney, August 1975. For help with this paper, I am indebted to David Dumaresq and my wife Ruth, who assisted in the initial research; to Stephen White, Geoffrey Sawer, Judith Jarvis Thomson, John Kleinig, and Jerome Hall, who made useful comments on the first draft; and to Pat McDonnell, who checked the probabilities referred to at the end of the appendix.

1. *Director of Public Prosecutions* v. *Morgan* [1975] 2 All ER 347. For the decision of the Court of Appeal, see [1975] 1 All ER 8.

2. See, for example Gary V. Dubin, "*Mens Rea* Reconsidered: A Plea for a Due Process Concept of Criminal Responsibility," *Stanford Law Review* 18 (1966): 322–395; or Gerhard

Mueller, "On Common Law *Mens Rea*," *Minnesota Law Review* 42: 1043–1104.

3. Note for American readers. In connection with criminal appeals, the House of Lords is not the same body as the one which forms a part of the legislature. When the House is sitting to hear appeals, only the Law Lords vote.

4. The provision of British (and Australian) criminal appeal procedure which permits such a result is rarely invoked, since judges are reluctant to encroach on the jury's role as the trier of fact. Nevertheless it seems sensible that a defendant should not go free because of a misdirection which did not materially affect the outcome of the trial.

A similar result was reached in a case decided in January 1975 in South Australia (*R.* v. *Brown*, Law Society Judgment Scheme, 403). The trial judge's direction in terms of reasonable belief was ruled incorrect by the Court of Criminal Appeal, but the proviso was invoked. Chief Justice Bray remarked that if the jury "had swallowed the camel of honest belief, I cannot think there is a real possibility that they would have strained at the gnat of reasonableness."

5. *R.* v. *Cogan and Leak, The Times*, 10 June 1975.

6. See, for example, Glanville Williams, *Criminal Law, The General Part* (London, 1961), pp. 30–31; Jerome Hall, *General Principles of Criminal Law* (Indianapolis, 1947), pp. 138–168; Colin Howard, *Australian Criminal Law* (Melbourne, 1970), pp. 10–13.

7. H.L.A. Hart, *Punishment and Responsibility* (Oxford, 1968), p. 114. First emphasis mine, second emphasis Hart's.

8. For an argument of this sort, see, e.g. Glanville Williams, *Criminal Law*, pp. 30–31.

9. Hart, *Punishment and Responsibility*, pp. 18–21.

10. [1961] A.C. 290.

11. *The Common Law*, by Oliver Wendell Holmes, Jr. (Boston, 1949), pp. 53–54 (my emphasis). It is open to question whether the citation of this passage by Viscount Kilmuir was appropriate to the Smith case. Certainly it would be hard to argue that the circumstances known to Smith were such that his act would "very certainly cause death."

12. *The Times*, 12 November 1960.

13. *Parker* v. *the Queen*, [1963], 111 C.L.R. 611.

14. See Buston, "The Retreat from Smith," *Criminal Law Review*, 1966; and Glanville Williams, *The Mental Element in Crime* (Jerusalem, 1965).

15. *R.* v. *Tolson*, [1889], 23 QBD 168.

16. *Criminal Law*, pp. 204–205. Cf. Hall, *Principles of Criminal Law*, pp. 329–343.

17. However, although Lord Edmund-Davies agreed that the defense of mistake *should* not be restricted to reasonable mistakes, he felt constrained by precedent to dissent from the majority opinion in *Morgan*, leaving it to the legislature to reform this part of the law "just as it did in relation to the former presumption of intending the reasonable consequence of one's actions" (another reference to *Smith*).

18. For example, the "condemnatory" verbs of Pitcher's "Hart on Action and Responsibility," *Philosophical Review* 69 (1960): 226–235. Hart appears to have been persuaded, in part by Pitcher's criticism, that the main contentions of his classic article, "The Ascription of Responsibility and Rights," are no longer defensible. See the Preface to Hart, *Punishment and Responsibility*.

19. Surely Austin was correct to think that finding the right fault is sometime a matter of great importance. See his "A Plea for Excuses," *Proceedings of the Aristotelian Society,* 1956, pp. 1–30.

20. *R.* v. *Cogan, R.* v. *Leak,* [1975], 2 All ER 1059.

21. It is interesting that Leak's status as a husband did not protect him: "The reason a man cannot by his own physical act rape his wife during cohabitation is because the law presumes consent from the marriage ceremony. . . . There is no such presumption when a man procures a drunken friend to do the physical act for him." [1975] 2 All ER 1062. Seventeenth-century precedent is cited. For a similar result in an American case involving a husband coercing another man to rape his wife, see *Blackwell,* [1965], 407 P.2d 618.

22. *Criminal Law Review,* 1975, p. 585.

23. See "The Effect in Philadelphia of Pennsylvania's Increased Penalties for Rape and Attempted Rape," *Journal for Criminal Law, Criminology and Police Science* 59 (1968): 509–515.

24. A startling 82 percent, according to Menachem Amir's *Patterns in Forcible Rape* (Chicago, 1971), pp. 140–141. Amir, however, cites another study which showed a lower frequency of planning, and this may reflect either a difference in the criteria for planning or a difference in their interpretation.

25. See, for example, Camille Le Grand, "Rape and Rape Laws: Sexism in Society and Law," *California Law Review* 61 (1973): 919–941.

26. Glanville Williams, *The Proof of Guilt* (London, 1963), p. 159.

27. See Amir, *Patterns of Forcible Rape,* p. 29, for a list of factors favoring nonreporting. Amir emphasizes that his list is incomplete. One factor he omits is that victims not sufficiently sophisticated about the legal aspects of rape may not realize that they have been raped. They may not be aware, for example, that *any* penetration is sufficient for the physical act, or that a woman who submits (because she recognizes that further resistance is futile and dangerous) does not thereby consent, though it may be more difficult for her to establish lack of consent.

28. Hart, *Punishment and Responsibility,* p. 244.

29. By Chief Justice Bray in *R.* v. *Brown,* cited above in fn. 4.

30. "Descartes, Spinoza and the Ethics of Belief," in *Spinoza, Essays in Interpretation,* ed. M. Mandelbaum and E. Freeman, Open Court, 1975.

31. This assumption appears quite explicitly in some legal texts, e.g. Howard, *Australian Criminal Law,* p. 160.

32. Proposed Official Draft, S. 2.02 (2) (c). For discussion see Herbert Packer, "The Model Penal Code and Beyond," *Columbia Law Review* 63 (1963): 594–607; or Howard, *Australian Criminal Law,* pp. 355–362. Cf. Hart, *Punishment and Responsibility,* pp. 136–137.

33. Cf. Glanville Williams, *Criminal Law,* pp. 157–159, or Howard, *Australian Criminal Law,* pp. 58–59.

34. See, for example, Ross Barber, "Judge and Jury Attitudes to Rape," *Australian and New Zealand Journal of Criminology* 7 (1974): 157–172; Menachem Amir, *Patterns in Forcible Rape* (Chicago, 1971), p. 257.

35. See Kalven and Zeisel, *The American Jury* (Boston, 1966), pp. 121–148.

36. See Amir, *Patterns in Forcible Rape,* pp. 109–125; Don Gibbons, *Society, Crime and Criminal Careers* (New York, 1968), pp. 384–385.

37. Kalven and Zeisel, *The American Jury,* pp. 514–515. Forcible rape, like most crimes against the person, showed a higher rate of judge/jury disagreement than most crimes against property. But it had a relatively low rate of "net jury leniency," indicating that juries are stricter than the judge would have been more frequently in forcible rape than in other crimes.

38. Kalven and Zeisel, *The American Jury,* pp. 250–251. Amir's study found "victim-precipitation" in about 19 percent of the cases studied. His concept of victim-precipitation seems designed to cover both the types of situation discussed in the text, though the term "victim-precipitation" is a most unfortunate one. It is becoming well-entrenched in the criminological literature on offenses against the person in general, but in discussions of rape it is apt to suggest a denial of the offender's ultimate responsibility. I don't think Amir intends this, and I certainly don't. But Medea and Thompson (*Against Rape,* p. 152) find Amir's book "sexist in the extreme," principally, it seems, because he refers to victims as well as rapists as "participants in the crime."

39. Professor Geoffrey Sawer, *Canberra Times,* 7 May 1975.

40. See, e.g. Howard, *Australian Criminal Law,* pp. 129–132.

41. See Amir, *Patterns in Forcible Rape,* pp. 150–158.

42. Howard, *Australian Criminal Law,* pp. 137–141.

43. Kalven and Zeisel, *The American Jury,* p. 251.

44. Quoted in Brett and Waller, *Cases and Materials in Criminal Law* (Melbourne, 1962), p. 209a; paraphrased in Howard, *Australian Criminal Law,* p. 157.

45. "Rape and Rape Laws: Sexism in Society and Law," p. 927, fn. 42.

46. See, for example, Sophia Robinson, "A Critical View of the *Uniform Crime Reports,*" *Michigan Law Review* 64 (1966): 1031–1054; and Marvin Wolfgang, "*Uniform Crime Reports:* A Critical Appraisal," *University of Pennsylvania Law Review* 111 (1963): 708–738.

47. It is worth noting that a very thorough study of unreported crimes conducted by the National Opinion Research Center showed that a great deal of crime in nearly all categories goes unreported and that the most common reason for not reporting offenses was a belief that the police were incapable of dealing with them. (See Gibbon, *Society, Crime and Criminal Careers,* p. 112.) To judge from the *U.C.R.* figures that belief is quite a reasonable one. The only consolation I can see is that the crimes least likely to lead to a conviction are property offenses which are the ones most apt to provide the basis for a "career in crime," so that as the criminal repeats his offense, he raises the probability of his eventually being convicted for some offense.

48. One reason why the larceny figures are so high in Table 17 of the *U.C.R.* is that they include both grand and petit larcenies (as may be inferred from the ratio of grand larcenies to burglaries in other tables, e.g., 6 and 9). Petit larcenies would account for at least half of the larceny offenses known. The Bureau's pretensions to provide us with an index of serious crime are grossly exaggerated.

49. This seems to be the view taken in a leading British study, *Sexual Offences, a Report of the Cambridge Department*

of Criminal Science, Preface by L. Radzinowicz (London, 1957), pp. 50–51. Their figures indicated an acquittal rate of 47 percent for rape, as compared with 19 percent for heterosexual offenses in general. They give no figures for nonsexual offenses. The Home Office's *Criminal Statistics, England and Wales, 1972,* gives acquittal rates for murder (21 percent), rape (31 percent), assault (2 percent), wounding or other act endangering life (31 percent), and other wounding (24 percent). But comparison with figures for the United States is difficult since the categories are not uniformly defined. For example, the wounding offenses, which in some respects correspond most closely to aggravated assault, also include various offenses involving the possession of firearms.

50. See "Police Discretion and the Judgment that a Crime Has Been Committed—Rape in Philadelphia," *University of Pennsylvania Law Review* 117 (1968): 277ff.; Jerome Skolnick, *Justice Without Trial* (New York, 1966). Though he is not concerned specifically with rape, Skolnick provides a great deal of material which may help to explain why rape victims frequently feel that the police are unsympathetic. A suspicious temperament is both a prerequisite for success in police work and one of its occupational hazards.

51. Ruth Brandon and Christie Davies, *Wrongful Imprisonment* (London, 1973). See particularly pp. 264–265.

THOMAS BABINGTON MACAULAY

Notes on the Indian Penal Code*

Early in the progress of the Code it became necessary for us to consider the following question: When acts are made punishable on the ground that those acts produce, or are intended to produce, or are known to be likely to produce, certain evil effects, to what extent ought omissions which produce, which are intended to produce, or which are known to be likely to produce, the same evil effects to be made punishable?

Two things we take to be evident; first, that some of these omissions ought to be punished in exactly the same manner in which acts are punished; secondly, that not all these omissions ought to be punished. It will hardly be disputed that a jailer who voluntarily causes the death of a prisoner by omitting to supply that prisoner with food, or a nurse who voluntarily causes the death of an infant entrusted to her care by omitting to take it out of a tub of water into which it has fallen, ought to be treated as guilty of murder. On the other hand, it will hardly be maintained that a man should be punished as a murderer because he omitted to relieve a beggar, even though there might be the clearest proof that the death of the beggar was the effect of this omission, and that the man who omitted to give the alms knew that the death of the beggar was likely to be the effect of the omission. It will hardly be maintained that a surgeon ought to be treated as a murderer for refusing to go from Calcutta to Meerut to perform an operation, although it should be absolutely certain that this surgeon was the only person in India who could perform it, and that if it were not performed, the person who required it would die. It is difficult to say whether a penal code which should put no omissions on the same footing with acts, or a penal code which should put all omissions on the same footing with acts, would produce consequences more absurd and revolting. There

is no country in which either of these principles is adopted. Indeed, it is hard to conceive how, if either were adopted, society could be held together.

It is plain, therefore, that a middle course must be taken; but it is not easy to determine what that middle course ought to be. The absurdity of the two extremes is obvious. But there are innumerable intermediate points; and wherever the line of demarcation may be drawn it will, we fear, include some cases which we might wish to exempt, and will exempt some which we might wish to include. . . .

What we propose is this, that where acts are made punishable on the ground that they have caused, or have been intended to cause, or have been known to be likely to cause, a certain evil effect, omissions which have caused, which have been intended to cause, or which have been known to be likely to cause the same effect, shall be punishable in the same manner, provided that such omissions were, on other grounds, illegal. An omission is illegal . . . if it be an offense, if it be a breach of some direction of law, or if it be such a wrong as would be a good ground for a civil action.

We cannot defend this rule better than by giving a few illustrations of the way in which it will operate. *A* omits to give *Z* food, and by that omission voluntarily causes *Z*'s death. Is this murder? Under our rule it is murder if *A* was *Z*'s gaoler, directed by the law to furnish *Z* with food. It is murder if *Z* was the infant child of *A,* and had, therefore, a legal right to sustenance, which right a Civil Court would enforce against *A*. It is murder if *Z* was a bedridden invalid, and *A* a nurse hired to feed *Z*. It is murder if *A* was detaining *Z* in unlawful confinement, and had thus contracted . . . a legal obligation to furnish *Z*, during the continuance of the confinement, with necessaries. It is not murder if *Z* is a beggar, who has no other claim on *A* than that of humanity.

A omits to tell *Z* that a river is swollen so

---

*From *Works of Lord Macaulay,* Trevelyan, ed., Vol. 7 (1866), pp. 493–97.

high that Z cannot safely attempt to ford it, and by this omission voluntarily causes Z's death. This is murder, if A is a peon stationed by authority to warn travellers from attempting to ford the river. It is a murder if A is a guide who had contracted to conduct Z. It is not murder if A is a person on whom Z has no other claim than that of humanity.

A savage dog fastens on Z. A omits to call off the dog, knowing that if the dog not be called off, it is likely that Z will be killed. Z is killed. This is murder in A, if the dog belonged to A, inasmuch as his omission to take proper order with the dog is illegal. But if A be a mere passer-by, it is not murder.

We are sensible that in some of the cases which we have put, our rule may appear too lenient; but we do not think that it can be made more severe without disturbing the whole order of society. It is true that the man who, having abundance of wealth, suffers a fellow creature to die of hunger at his feet, is a bad man, a worse man, probably, than many of those for whom we have provided very severe punishment. But we are unable to see where, if we make such a man legally punishable, we can draw the line. If the rich man who refuses to save a beggar's life at the cost of a little copper is a murderer, is the poor man just one degree above beggary also to be a murderer if he omits to invite the beggar to partake his hard-earned rice? Again, if the rich man is a murderer for refusing to save the beggar's life at the cost of a little copper, is he also to be a murderer if he refuses to save the beggar's life at the cost of a thousand rupees? Suppose A to be fully convinced that nothing can save Z's life unless Z leave Bengal and reside a year at the Cape; is A, however wealthy he may be, to be punished as a murderer because he will not, at his own expense, send Z to the Cape? Surely not. Yet it will be difficult to say on what principle we can punish A for not spending an anna to save Z's life, and leave him unpunished for not spending a thousand rupees to save Z's life. The distinction between a legal and an illegal omission is perfectly plain and intelligible; but the distinction between a large and a small sum of money is very far from being so, not to say that a sum which is small to one man is large to another.

The same argument holds good in the case of the ford. It is true that none but a very depraved man would suffer another to be drowned when he might prevent it by a word. But if we punish such a man, where are we to stop? How much exertion are we to require? Is a person to be a murderer if he does not go fifty yards through the sun of Bengal at noon in May in order to caution a traveller against a swollen river? Is he to be a murderer if he does not go a hundred yards?—if he does not go a mile?—if he does not go ten? What is the precise amount of trouble and inconvenience which he is to endure? The distinction between the guide who is bound to conduct the traveller as safely as he can, and a mere stranger is a clear distinction. But the distinction between a stranger who will not give a halloo to save a man's life, and a stranger who will not run a mile to save a man's life, is very far from being equally clear.

It is, indeed, most highly desirable that men should not merely abstain from doing harm to their neighbours, but should render active services to their neighbours. In general, however, the penal law must content itself with keeping men from doing positive harm, and must leave to public opinion, and to the teachers of morality and religion, the office of furnishing men with motives for doing positive good. It is evident that to attempt to punish men by law for not rendering to others all the service which it is their duty to render to others would be preposterous. We must grant impunity to the vast majority of those omissions which a benevolent morality would pronounce reprehensible, and must content ourselves with punishing such omissions only when they are distinguished from the rest by some circumstance which marks them out as peculiarly fit objects of penal legislation. Now, no circumstance appears to us so well fitted to be the mark as the circumstance which we have selected. It will generally be found in the most atrocious cases of omission; it will scarcely ever be found in a venial case of omission; and it is more clear and certain than any other mark that has occurred to us. That there are objections to the line which we propose to draw, we have admitted. But there are objections to every line which can be drawn, and some lines must be drawn. . . .

JOEL FEINBERG

The Moral and Legal Responsibility of the Bad Samaritan*

In the biblical parable,[1] the good Samaritan was a person who came upon the victim of a violent crime, a total stranger to him, lying "half dead" on the side of the road. Instead of passing him by on the other side, as a priest and a Levite had done earlier, and thus staying "uninvolved," he bound up the stranger's wounds, transported him to an inn, prepaid the bill, and otherwise offered him aid and succor. We can speak, in contrast, of the "bad samaritan," referring to any person who is a stranger to a given endangered person and who, like the priest and the Levite in the biblical story, fails to come to that person's aid. More exactly, the bad samaritan is

(a) a stranger standing in no "special relationship" to the endangered party,

(b) who omits to do something—warn of unperceived peril, undertake rescue, seek aid, notify police, protect against further injury, etc—for the endangered party,

(c) which he could have done without unreasonable cost or risk to himself or others,

(d) as a result of which the other party suffers harm, or an increased degree of harm,

(e) and for these reasons the omitter is "bad" (morally blameworthy).

Among the many questions for legal policy raised by the bad samaritan, the central one for our purposes is whether statutes may legitimately be enacted threatening him with criminal liability for his failure to prevent harm to others.

Among European nations, Portugal was the first to enact a bad samaritan criminal statute in the mid-nineteenth century. One hundred years later, a legal duty to undertake "easy rescue" had been recognized by the criminal codes of fifteen European nations.[2] In striking contrast, the English-speaking countries have remained apart from the European consensus. Their common law has never imposed liability either in tort or in criminal law for failures to rescue (except where there exist *special* duties to rescue, as, for example, those of a paid lifeguard toward the specific persons who bathe on his stretch of beach), and with few exceptions, the statutory law of Great Britain, the United States, Canada, and Australia has also treated the bad samaritan with grudging tolerance. By and large, it has left unpunished even harmful omissions of an immoral kind—malicious failures to warn a blind person of an open sewer hole, to lift the head of a sleeping drunk out of a puddle of water, to throw a rope from a bridge to a drowning swimmer, to rescue or even report the discovery of a small child wandering lost in a wood, and so on.

No doubt many legislatures in common law countries have declined to pass bad samaritan statutes for entirely practical reasons, including fear of administrative complications. With them I have no quarrel. I do find grave flaws, however, in various standard arguments presented by writers in the common law tradition that purport to show not simply that bad samaritan laws would be costly or inconvenient to administer, but that they are somehow morally illegitimate in principle. There are several such arguments, or classes of arguments, but I shall limit my discussion here to three: the "enforced benevolence argument," the closely related "line-drawing argument," and the argument from the superior strength of negative to positive duties. I shall devote most of my attention to the enforced benevolence argument because it charges, in effect, that bad samaritan statutes can be justified *only* as an enforcement of morality or "coercion to virtue," not as a way of protecting prospective victims from violations of their rights.

THE ENFORCED BENEVOLENCE ARGUMENT

The first class of arguments identifies active aid as such with gratuitous benefit, a mistake (as it

* From Joel Feinberg, "The Moral and Legal Responsibility of the Bad Samaritan," *Criminal Justice Ethics,* Vol. 3, No. 1 (Winter/Spring, 1984), pp. 56–66. Reprinted by permission of the author and publisher.

seems to me) which is made with remarkable frequency. It matters not to the writers who argue in this fashion that a given instance of active aid required hardly any effort by or danger to the actor, or that it was necessary to the very survival of the imperiled party. Insofar as it is active, these writers insist, it confers a mere gratuitous benefit, and therefore cannot have been required by duty, not even by *moral* duty. Thus, Jeffrie G. Murphy (to select one of many possible examples) writes:

I can be highly morally lacking even in cases where I violate no one's rights. For example, I am sitting in a lounge chair next to a swimming pool. A child (not mine) is drowning in the pool a few inches from where I am sitting. I notice him and realize that all I would have to do to save him is put down my drink, reach down, grab him by the trunks, and pull him out (he is so light I could do it with one hand without even getting out of my seat). *If I do not save him I violate no rights* (*strangers do not have a right to be saved by me*) but would still reveal myself as a piece of moral slime properly to be shunned by all decent people.[3]

These remarks are very puzzling to me, for the more natural view, I would think, is that the child in Murphy's example has a moral claim against the lounger, that in ignoring it the lounger violates the child's right to be saved, that the child's parents therefore not only have justification for reviling the lounger, for assigning him low moral grades, and for shunning him; they also have a legitimate personal *grievance* against him, both on their child's behalf and on their own.

In the passage quoted, Murphy gives no arguments for his surprising interpretation of the drowning child example. But insofar as he fits into the tradition of writers with his view, his unstated assumptions are that apart from special moral relationships, our moral claim against others is only to be let alone—that is, not actively harmed; that any active help we get from others is a positive "benefit," and benefits, as opposed to nonharms, cannot be claimed against strangers as a matter of right. In Murphy's example, that which would have to be classified as "a mere benefit" is the child's very life!

Perhaps Murphy and others are misled by the fact that persons in desperate straits characteristically *implore* others for their help rather than claim or demand it, and, after rescue, express their gratitude and even offer rewards. These facts have independent explanations, however, that are quite compatible with a right to be assisted. A person is in no mood to be morally high and mighty and make righteous demands when he is drowning. Pleading for help is the natural animal response to imminent peril, as are warm appreciation and the impulse to reciprocate after the rescue. Rights are rarely in the forefront of attention through the typical salvation episode; they become more visible when they are infringed.

Another American philosopher, Lance K. Stell, proposes an analysis of the omissions in the biblical parable similar to that offered by Murphy of his own example of the drowning child. According to Stell, defenders of a right to be rescued have confused the moral requirements of justice with those of benevolence:

In the parable of the Good Samaritan: the injustice (violation of right) done to the man on the road to Jericho occurred at the hands of the thieves who beat, robbed, and left him for dead. The priest and the Levite who passed him by definitely did something immoral, but their immorality did not constitute a violation of the wounded man's *rights*. Their moral defect was to fail in kindness or benevolence. . . . Similarly, the wounded man did not have a right to the Good Samaritan's aid. That aid reflected the true spirit of brotherly love—the disposition to respond with compassion to human need even though justice does not require it. . . .[4]

In my defense of what I take to be the more natural account of the matter, I could concede to Stell that the moral defect that led the priest and the Levite to pass the victim by may well have been a failure in kindness, benevolence, compassion, and good will. But whatever character flaw *explains* their omission, it may yet be true that it was their *duty* that they failed to do and the victim's *rights* that were violated. If the recovered victim, months later, were to encounter the priest or Levite (having learned of their conduct toward him), he could indignantly voice a grievance against them, accusing them of having done him wrong. When wrongdoers knowingly violate the rights of others, their conduct, whether active or omissive, normally manifests the character flaw of injustice, but frequently such conduct is morally overdetermined, manifesting also a failure of sensitivity, sympathy, or benevolence. When the latter virtues are conspicuously missing, we may well choose to emphasize their absence in our subsequent account of the actor's wrongdoing. But it can remain true nonetheless that a victim's rights were violated, that a blamably cold-hearted person, precisely because of his lack of benevolence, has committed an *injustice*.

The biblical Samaritan, of course, was more than merely neighborly. He did his duty and then some. The victim would have had no complaint against him if he had done a good deal less. Rights tend to be rather minimal claims. But to have done nothing at all, in the manner of the priest and the Levite, would have been to fall well below the required minimum. As Judith Thomson has pointed out, there are minimally decent samaritans, good samaritans, very good samaritans, and splendid samaritans.[5] The biblical Samaritan was a splendid samaritan indeed. Justice required only that he be minimally decent. A surplus of benevolence prompted him to be more.

MISTAKEN VIEWS OF SAMARITAN INTERVENTIONS

Holding before our minds such examples of minimally decent samaritanism as that of Murphy's pool lounger had he pulled in the child, and the biblical Samaritan had he merely comforted the victim and reported his injuries to the authorities (or called an ambulance as would be required in our time), let us, in summary fashion, consider the overlapping descriptions that have been given of these actions by various writers (not always the same writers) in the common law tradition, namely: (1) as "mere" conferrals of benefits; (2) as gratuitous favors; (3) as fulfillments of the general imperfect duty to be charitable; (4) as performances of a specific duty toward *this* person, but one without a correlative right in the beneficiary; (5) as acts of supererogation. I think that all of these descriptions are mistaken accounts of minimally decent samaritan interventions, but perhaps the root mistake is the first one, in the application of the concept of benefitting.

1 Conferrals of Benefit Speaking of an example similar to Murphy's pool lounger, James Barr Ames (writing in 1908) reports the orthodox Anglo-American view:

however revolting the conduct of a man who declined to interfere, he was in no way responsible for the perilous situation; he did not increase the jeopardy; *he simply failed to confer a benefit upon a stranger*. As the law stands today, there would be no legal liability, either civilly or criminally, in . . . these cases. *The law does not compel active benevolence* between man and man. It is left to one's conscience whether [one] . . . shall be the good Samaritan or not. (Italics added)[6]

Whether or not *A,* the samaritan, intervenes to save *B,* the endangered party, in these cases, determines whether *B's* interest remains as it was in the *status quo ante* (before the onset of his peril) or is disastrously set back. Yet Ames contends that the intervention positively benefits *B,* implying that it advances his interests to a condition superior to that of the *status quo ante,* so that *B* receives a kind of net windfall profit, all because of *A's* munificent generosity. It is in this respect much as if *A* had walked up to a stranger on the street and handed him a $100 bill!

Something has gone wrong here, and the cause must be the concept of benefitting someone, which evidently has more than one sense. The legal writers who have defended the common law seem often to use the term in a generic sense to refer to any and all ways of affecting another party's interest for the better: advancing it beyond its present condition, advancing it beyond its normal condition, preventing it from getting worse than it is at the moment, preventing it from remaining worse than it normally is, and so on. These conceptions naturally invite use of the metaphors of the computational ledger and the business profit-loss curve plotted on graph paper, with various indicated starting points or "baselines" for comparison. To save a drowning person is indeed to "benefit" him in this generic sense, for it is to affect his interest in a favorable as opposed to an adverse or neutral way. It is to prevent his interest-curve from taking a sharp decline from the baseline of its normal condition as well as from the alternative measuring point of its immediately present condition.

The trouble with this generic usage is that it creates an especially tempting danger of equivocation. When it is so very obvious that the generic notion of "benefit" is applicable, it is easy to slide into one of the specific senses of "benefit" whose applicability is by no means evident. It does not follow from the fact that a rescuer affects the endangered party's interests favorably that he "benefits" him in the sense of elevating his interest-curve to a point on the graph *above* the baseline of his condition before he fell into the water. It is only the latter sense of "benefitting" that would support further description of the rescue as benevolent generosity, "active service," "positive good," and so on, or the effect on the rescued party as "profit," "gain," or "advantage." Benefitting another, in this latter sense, is often to go beyond duty in a manner approved by our moral ideals but not required by moral rules. The liberal advocate of a bad samaritan statute can agree that in this precise sense of "benefit," governmental coercion can never be used to force one person to benefit another. But he should insist that easy rescue of a drowning child is not a "mere benefitting" in this sense. It is a benefit only in the generic sense of affecting the child's interest favorably and specifically preventing a drastic decline in his fortunes from a normal baseline. That is quite another thing than conferring a windfall profit on him.

2 Gratuitous Favors We have no duties to do favors or confer gifts on those to whom we stand in no special moral relationship. On the other hand, we are morally required to perform beneficial services for those to whom we have made promises, or to whom we are parents, children, spouses, immediate neighbors, nurses, guides, or protectors. On the view I am defending, a good swimmer on a bridge who watches a stranger drown in the water below has inflicted a harm, and a grievous one, by his omission, and this is so not only because death is the sort of thing we regard as a harm whatever its cause, but also because the victim has a right to the assistance of the stranger, and the stranger has a correlative duty to save him. Merely being a fellow human being is enough of a "relationship," on this view, to ground a duty to rescue when the threatened harm is that severe. On the contrary view, two mere stangers are not closely enough related for one party to have a duty to "benefit" the other (though it would be commendable to do so anyway), for in the absence of a special duty derived from job, role, or prior commitment, a successful rescue would be like a favor or a gift, and failing to help cannot be considered to be a way of harming.

How good a model is the gratuitous favor for the easy rescue situation? Consider a clear example of a failure to make a genuinely gratuitous rescue, the example of a condemned murderer whose last minute appeal for clemency is denied by the governor. Here it is plausible to say that the governor merely "withheld a bene-

fit" by his omission. The cause of the "harm" to the prisoner was his own crime and subsequent conviction, not any action or omission of the governor. At least part of the reason why this is so is that the governor had no duty to save the prisoner and the prisoner had no right to demand clemency. Clemency is something given freely, something "beyond duty," like a favor or a gift. This clear example provides us with a third specific sense of "benefit." One person benefits another (1) by restoring his interest to or maintaining it at a normal condition, or (2) by advancing his interests beyond a properly selected baseline (in this sense benefit is gain or profit), or (3) by any favorable effect on his interests (any generic benefit) that is *gratuitous* (like an act of grace or clemency).

Bestowing executive clemency *is* a good example of benefitting a person by preventing his interest-curve from sinking even lower. Withholding clemency in the same circumstances would not be to harm (further) the prisoner. These are precisely the two contentions held by my opponents about the easy rescues of drowning swimmers. The withholding of executive clemency can hardly be a model, however, for interpreting the bad samaritan's failure to make an easy rescue of another party from imminent and severe peril, though as we gradually change the examples to weaken the severity or probability of the threatened harm, or to increase the difficulty or danger of a rescue attempt, the model of the gratuity becomes more plausible.

When there is no duty to aid, for whatever reason, we use a different baseline for measuring benefits and harms in the first two senses. If the governor commutes the prisoner's death sentence, then since he had no duty to do so, we measure the prisoner's improved interest-condition from its state at the moment the governor's rescue is effected. By preventing the convict's condition from deteriorating from that point, *when he had no duty to do so,* the governor conferred on him a benefit in the second sense—a gain, profit, or advantage. If he had had a duty to commute the sentence, on the other hand, then the beneficial effect on the prisoner's interest-curve would be measured from some earlier "normal" point before death impended, and the governor's action would merely have restored the prisoner to his normal condition without any further profit or advantage. Similarly, the bystander's easy rescue of the drowning swimmer, given his prior duty to do so, does not advance the rescued party's condition beyond the normal baseline. Instead it simply restores the swimmer to his condition at that baseline. It is therefore not a "sheer gain"—not a net profit—for the imperiled party. When measured from the appropriate (duty-assigned) baseline, it is simply the prevention of a harm without a further gain.

3 Imperfect Duties Some opponents of bad samaritan laws admit that there is a duty to aid those in peril, but interpret that duty as a mere "imperfect duty" in J. S. Mill's sense. Mill, obviously taking charitable contributions as his model, defined "duties of imperfect obligation" as "those in which, though the act is obligatory, the particular occasions of performing it are left to our choice, as in the case of charity or beneficence, which we are indeed bound to practice, but not toward any definite person, nor at any prescribed time."[7] If there are more deserving needy people than I can help, and more worthy causes than I have funds to support, then a duty to be charitable can only require me to contribute a reasonable net amount, allocated as I see fit, among the eligible recipients. In the very nature of the case, some must do without help from me, deserving though they may be. It follows from their equal worthiness and my inadequate capacity to serve them all, that *none* of them has a right to my help, even though I have a duty to help as many of them as I can. In short, the reason why my duty is "imperfect," lacking determinate recipients with correlative claims against me, is entirely a logistic one, a problem of coordination that could be solved, if at all, by a cooperative scheme among similarly situated donors, defined by set rules. Nothing like this is involved in either Murphy's drowning child example or the parable of the good Samaritan, where the emergency is clear and present, and the aid can be given to one victim without being withheld from any other. There is no reason to think of the rescuer's duty as merely to select from among the equally needy those he can afford to help, for there is no other need so near and pressing as that which commands his attention and demands his help right now.

We encounter a more serious problem, however, when we modify Murphy's example by adding more imperiled parties. Suppose that there are *two* drowning babies in the pool, one twenty meters to the lounger's right and the other twenty meters to his left, and that the circumstances make it clear that the lounger, by taking a few steps in either direction, can easily scoop up one baby, but that there is insufficient time to rescue both. (We can suppose that the lounger is unable himself to swim or stay afloat in the water.) Now the lounger's duty begins to resemble the "imperfect duty" to contribute to charitable agencies. Since the lounger can save one but not both babies, neither baby, it will be said, can claim as a matter of right that *he* be the one who is saved. If the lounger is the same scoundrel as in Murphy's original example, he will be no more inclined to rescue one of two imperiled babies than he was to rescue the solitary baby, and he will let them *both* die. If he is philosophically clever, he will say in his own defense afterward, that while, of course, he deserves low moral grades for his heartlessness and for his failure to discharge a duty of imperfect obligation, nevertheless he violated no one's rights; no one was wronged; no one has a legitimate grievance against him. And for that reason (he will add) he cannot rightly be punished in the earlier example where he neglected only a single drowning child. To compound the paradox, the greater the number of hypothetical imperiled babies we throw into the fictitious pool, the more plausible will the lounger's case seem to become, that none of them had a right to his assistance!

These results are intolerably paradoxical in their own terms, but they are particularly unsettling to the liberal, for they seem to force him to embrace an inconsistent triad of propositions:

1 Criminal prohibitions are legitimate only when they protect individual rights, that is, there should be no victimless crimes;
2 Murphy's lounger in the two-or-more-drowning-baby cases should be criminally liable;
3 but Murphy's lounger in those cases violated no one's rights.

I cannot escape this trap by giving up proposition (1), for that would be utterly to abandon either the liberalism that I have tried to defend in a number of publications, or else the analysis of harm as right-violating setback to interest. Proposition (2) is hardly any easier to abandon. Since I would argue that the lounger should be criminally liable in the case where there is only one party in peril, I cannot, in all consistency, argue for his immunity when there are two or more in peril and it is easy for him to rescue one. The statute imposing that liability could have some legitimacy, I suppose, on the ground that it functions to diminish setbacks to interest, in this case to prevent the loss of salvageable human life, but that legitimacy would tend to be undermined by the bad samaritan's claim that his crime lacked a determinate victim since neither drowned child had a moral right against him to be saved (proposition 3). The reply to this claim must be that in fact at least one of the babies did have rights that were violated by the lounger's deliberate omission to act. Now the problem becomes that of giving a plausible account of those rights.

One possibility is to say that each child had a right against the lounger that he save as many of them as he could without unreasonable risk to himself. In this case that would be a right that each baby has that the lounger save one or another of them. It would follow that by failing to act at all, the lounger violated the rights of both babies, even though by hypothesis it would have been impossible to save one of them. A somewhat odd consequence of this view of the matter is that if the lounger had rescued one of the babies then he would have entirely fulfilled the moral right of the other, and his duty to the one baby would be entirely discharged by his rescue of the other.

Another interpretation is that each baby had a right, not to a rescue attempt from the lounger, but rather to equal consideration, and that by rescuing neither he violated that right. There are some difficulties with this view too. In giving neither imperiled party *any* consideration, the lounger treated them with perfect equality. Moreover, if one baby had been a boy and the other a girl, or one a black and the other a white, a different hypothetical lounger, able to save only one but not both, chose on the basis of his bigoted racial or sexual preferences, it is not clear that the neglected party's rights would thereby be violated, especially if we add to the example that *this* pool lounger would have saved both had he been able to do so. It is part of the conception of a duty of imperfect obligation that the obligated party must save as many as he reasonably can, but that it be left up to his own free choice which ones are selected for rescue. In any case, the moral charge against our original lounger is not that he gave the babies unequal chances, but that he gave neither of them any chance at all. And for that reason, it might be thought that each of them has, equally, a grievance against him.

A final interpretation of the babies' violated rights does not conceive of them as rights that each held equally against the lounger. Rather, on this view we would say that only one of the babies was wronged by the lounger's omission, but that it is impossible to say which one. This view avoids the odd consequence of the joint-right theories that the lounger, had he rescued one baby, would thereby have fulfilled his obligation toward the other. Now we can say instead that had he rescued one baby he would have satisfied that baby's right against him without violating *or* fulfilling any right of the other baby, since the other baby is the one (we now know) who had no right against the lounger, and to whom the lounger had no duty. This third interpretation of the rights and duties of the parties in the two-baby case has some advantages, but like the others, it raises some daunting difficulties. One obvious drawback is that we cannot say who the bad samaritan's wronged victim is when the number who perished is greater than he could have saved, even though we can say that at least one of those who died was indeed his victim.

In some ways, however, this "drawback" has the advantage of congruing with the way we think of the grievances of the unrescued when the numbers of those imperiled are vastly greater than the resources for rescuing them. When 1,000 overboard passengers are imperiled, and only one can be saved (there is room for only one more in a tiny rescue craft), but the boatman chooses to rescue no one, the grievances of the 1,000 (or their surviving loved ones) are greatly diluted. On the theory considered here, only one of the 1,000 had a right against the boatman to be rescued, namely the one the boatman would have selected had he been willing to rescue anyone at all, and, of course, we cannot know who that one is. But the odds are 1,000 to 1 against its being any given one of those left to die. Mourning relatives can therefore believe only that there is one chance in a thousand that the boatman violated their relative's right to be saved, and modulate their resentment accordingly. The two sets of parents of the drowning babies, on the other hand, have a much stronger grievance. The chances that the lounger violated their child's right are 50-50. In either case the law could consistently charge the bad samaritan with something like "homicide by omission" on the grounds that the probability that the defendant violated the right to life of *someone or other,* on the facts given, is one hundred percent, even though that person, in the formulation of the charge, would have to remain nameless.

The more serious flaw in this third account of the rights of the unrescued is that it appears to imply, in the two baby cases, that only one child (we know not which) has a right to be saved by the lounger, even though there are no morally relevant factual differences between the drowning children or their circumstances. This result would appear to violate the rationality of right-ascriptions, in particular what is sometimes called the condition of "supervenience" that all ethical terms, properly employed, must satisfy.[8] Rights and other ethical predicates are said to be supervenient in the sense that their existence in a given case derives from other characteristics: we have the right *in virtue of the fact* that we have the other characteristics. It follows from supervenience that if we lacked the right-generating characteristic we should lack the right, and if we have exactly the same characteristics as some other person then we cannot differ from that person in respect to right-ownership. Without supervenience in this sense, the language of rights would be infected with arbitrariness.

My preference then is for some variant of the first kind of account, that which recognizes a claim against the undermanned rescuer in all the imperiled parties. Corresponding to these claims, Murphy's lounger has only a duty of an "imperfect" kind—imperfect in still another way—that is to say that he is morally required only to do his best to save as many as he can. If he saves one, and the other drowns despite his best efforts, then he has not violated the other's right, for the drowning baby's only claim against him was that he save as many as he could, and that claim was honored. If he let them both die, he violated the rights of both babies by giving neither any chance at all.

Which one then was his victim? The answer, I should think, is that both babies had rights against him which he violated by his omission, but that his victim was the wronged party who would have survived but for that omission. Again, we cannot know who that party was, but it does not follow that this was a "victimless crime," because we *do* know that that victim was either baby *A* or baby *B*. There was definitely a victim then, even though he cannot be more definitely named. The victim, it should be emphasized, had no rights that the other drowning baby lacked. This solution does not violate supervenience. The two babies were equally wronged, but the victim was the one whose death was *the consequence* of the lounger's wrongful omission. The lounger committed homicide against one or another of the children by equally neglecting their rights against him. But given the unhappy circumstances and the lounger's limited opportunity, only one of the children died as a result of his wrongdoing. That one should be quite sufficient, however, to convict him of homicide.

The lack of a determinate victim, however, makes tort liability (say for wrongful death) problematic. If it is impossible to say which baby is the victim, then there is no plaintiff with clear standing to bring civil suit. All who perished were wronged, but only the wronged party who was *harmed* as a result can collect damages. Perhaps I should advocate some innovative tort policy that would permit a court to estimate the civil damages due the unknown victim(s) in cases where there were many more imperiled than could be saved, and permit claimants who can prove their rights were violated to divide that amount equally.

Whatever difficulties may remain for this sketchy account of the rights violated in a total default of a duty of imperfect obligation, they are likely to be slight when compared to the moral paradoxes in the view of Professors Murphy and Stell, that neither drowning baby has any right that is violated by the samaritan who omits to aid either of them when he could have rescued one safely and easily. I conclude, then, that when a person in a situation of scarce resources discharges his duty of imperfect obligation by saving some rather than others from among those equally eligible for his aid, he violates no one's rights, no matter how arbitrary his selection procedures. But when he violates his duty in that situation by giving aid to no one at all, then he violates the rights of at least some, and on the view I prefer, *all* of the eligible recipients who suffer subsequent harm.

4 Determinate Duties Without Correlative Rights It is not entirely clear which of the two typical characteristics of imperfect duties Mill meant to be the defining one: the lack of a determinate beneficiary or the lack of a correlated right-to-be-assisted in the beneficiary, or both. If the defining feature of imperfect duties is the lack of a particular assignable person at whom the duty can be said to be directed, then there can be perfect duties (with perfectly determinate recipients) which nevertheless cannot be claimed by the person at whom they are directed as his right. Some (but not all) duties toward the third party beneficiaries of promises may fall into this category. There are also examples of saintly or heroic persons who think of themselves as having special duties derived from their personal ideals, or from their self-assigned vocation in life, or from God, that require them to do services for others much in excess of what they believe the others can demand as their right. We may dismiss such people as moralistic egotists, but we cannot convict them of a conceptual error. It is no contradiction to speak of a duty to help others that is not logically correlated with any right in the recipients to be assisted. Finally, I might mention as an example in this category the duties of *noblesse oblige* that were thought to be owed by nobles even to their unworthy underlings, simply because the duties attached to the station occupied by the nobles. Lords had duties to their servants, under the feudal system, that the servants could not rightly claim as their due.

It is possible, I suppose, for a philosopher to claim any or all of these duties as models for understanding the pool lounger's duty to rescue the drowning child, or the samaritan's duty to assist the battered victim of crime. It is possible for philosophers to claim anything at all. There is no conclusive way of refuting the claim that the drowning child and the battered victim have no moral right to be rescued correlative to the moral duty that others have to rescue them. However, there is a simple phenomenological test that all these models fail when applied to the child and the victim. When we agree that the bystanders ought to offer assistance in these cases, indeed that they *must* offer assistance, do we also think that *moral indignation* on behalf of the recipient of the duty would be fitting if the bystander failed to do his duty, or would we just give the bystander low moral grades, adding that his flaws are no business of the person he declined to aid, nothing that person has a right to complain about? If *A* is pompous, vain, silly, dull-witted, or unimaginative, what is that to *B*, who is a mere stranger, a passive observer? *B* can make these adverse judgments about *A* and avoid his company, but can he claim as a personal grievance against *A* that *A* has these failings? Clearly not; and that is a sign that he has no right that *A* be a better person in these respects. That is *A*'s business, not his. But the parents of the drowned child will feel understandably and plausibly aggrieved, and we can share

their indignation vicariously with them. We would not acknowledge that their child's right was infringed if we thought of the bad samaritan's neglected duty as something like a duty of *noblesse oblige*. But clearly we cannot think of it that way; the persisting sense of grievance will not permit it.

5 Acts of Supererogation The fifth version of the view I am attacking is the least plausible of all, and we need not spend much time on it, despite its surprising popularity.[9] That is the view that the lounger and the samaritan, having no duty whatever to give assistance, perform "acts of supererogation," if they do. There are two common ways to interpret the concept of a supererogatory act, one quite specific, the other generic. In the specific sense, supererogatory acts tend to be *harder* than most acts required by duty. They are "above and beyond duty." Like the acts of saints and heroes, they are "meritorious, abnormally risky nonduties."[10] Minimally decent acts of easy rescue, *by definition,* are not supererogatory in this sense. There is nothing risky about calling an ambulance or yanking a small child out of the water. In the generic sense, a supererogatory act is an act "whose performance we praise but whose nonperformance we do not condemn."[11] But in that sense, easy rescues like that open to Murphy's pool lounger, fail to be supererogatory since even Murphy condemns their nonperformance.

MACAULAY'S OBJECTIONS TO BAD SAMARITAN STATUTES

There is no plausibility then in the view that a positive act of assistance *as such* is a "mere conferral of benefit" (either in the sense of profit or the sense of favor) or an act of generosity, charity, or supererogation. A more plausible argument concedes that the minimally decent samaritan acts required by the European statutes are moral duties correlated with the moral rights of endangered persons to be assisted, but insists that it is impossible in principle for the law to be formulated in such a way that these moral duties are enforced without at the same time requiring persons in other contexts to perform acts that *are* above and beyond their actual moral duties. There is, according to this argument, no nonarbitrary way of drawing and holding the line.

The classic statement of the line-drawing objection to bad samaritan statutes is that of Lord

Thomas Macaulay who discussed the question in the introductory notes he wrote in 1837 for the commission to revise the Indian penal code, of which he was a member.[12] Macaulay begins by asking to what extent omissions should be punishable when they produce the same consequences as positive acts that are punishable because of their harmfulness. His problem is to draw the line that separates the harmful omissions that *are* punishable from those that are not. He concludes by drawing the line where the Anglo-American law has always drawn it, in effect to immunize "samaritans," those persons in a position to help others in distress to whom they stand in no "special relations." The following is one of Macaulay's examples:

A omits to tell *Z* that a river is swollen so high that *Z* cannot safely attempt to ford it, and by this omission voluntarily causes *Z's* death. This is murder if *A* is a person stationed by authority to warn travellers from attempting to ford the river. It is murder if *A* is a guide who had contracted to conduct *Z*. It is not murder if *A* is a person on whom *Z* has no other claim than that of humanity.[13]

Macaulay uses this example to illustrate his central contention that precise line-drawing, once we allowed criminal liability for samaritan omissions, would be impossible:

It is true that none but a very depraved man would suffer another to be drowned when he might prevent it by a word. But if we punish such a man where are we to stop? How much exertion are we to require? Is a person to be a murderer if he does not go fifty yards through the sun of Bengal at noon in May in order to caution a traveller against a swollen river? Is he to be a murderer if he does not go a hundred yards? —if he does not go a mile? —if he does not go ten? What is the precise amount of trouble and inconvenience which he is to endure? The distinction between the guide who is bound to conduct the traveller as safely as he can, and a mere stranger, is a clear distinction. But the distinction between a stranger who will not give a halloo to save a man's life, and a stranger who will not run a mile to save a man's life, is very far from being equally clear.[14]

This example puts the advocate of bad samaritan statutes in a familiar kind of quandary. If it is reasonable to impose a duty to walk one step to warn the traveler, then surely it is reasonable to require two steps. The difference between two steps and one is so insignificant mor-

ally that it would be inconsistent to charge a bad samaritan with murder for failing to take one step, while letting another off for failing to take two. But the difference between two steps and three is equally insignificant, so it would be unreasonable to draw the line of duty at two steps. Similarly insignificant is the difference between three steps and four, or between 29 and 30, or between 999 and 1,000. So there will be no place to draw the line, the argument goes, that will not mark an arbitrary difference between those made liable and those exempted.

It is clear at this point that something has gone wrong with the argument. There may be no morally relevant difference between any two adjacent places on the spectrum, but there is a very clear difference between widely separated ones. It would be inconsistent to exempt one bad samaritan for failing to take two steps while convicting another for failure to take one, but there would be no inconsistency in convicting one for failure to take half a dozen steps while exempting another for failure to run two kilometers. So the distinction between clearly good and clearly bad samaritans is not undermined.

One way of coping with Macaulay's quandary is to divide up the spectrum of hypothetical cases into three segments: (1) clear cases of opportunity to rescue with no unreasonable risk, cost, or inconvenience to the rescuer or others (including cases of no risk, cost, or inconvenience whatever); (2) clear cases of opportunity to rescue but only at unreasonable risk, cost, or inconvenience to the rescuer or others; and (3) everything in the vast no-man's land of uncertain and controversial cases in between the extremes. To err only on the side of caution, we would hold no one in the middle (uncertain) category liable. Then we could hold everyone liable who *clearly* deserves to be liable, while exempting all those who do not clearly deserve to be liable, both those who clearly deserve *not* to be liable, as well as those whose deserts are uncertain. Careful draftsmanship of statutes could leave it up to juries to decide where reasonable doubts begin. After all, the English tradition restricts jury findings of guilt to the stage before *any* reasonable doubts appear anyway, so there is no lack of precedent for using juries to determine such points. This solution to Macaulay's quandary has two very attractive merits. First, it allows for the ascription of criminal responsibility to some very bad samaritans who would escape altogether if Macaulay's test were used; and second, it avoids the absurdity of holding that there is no moral difference between widely separated points on the scale just because there is none between any two nearly adjacent ones. Murphy's lounger and others only slightly farther from the swimming pool deserve to be punished for not rescuing the child, whereas observers 100 and 200 meters away do not.

My proposed solution to Macaulay's problem then is to formulate bad samaritan statutes in relatively vague terms that allow juries the discretion to apply standards of reasonable danger, cost, and inconvenience. Elsewhere in the criminal law, juries have traditionally been assigned such responsibilities, for example when they are charged with deciding whether an admitted killer pleading self-defense retreated as far as he reasonably could (ten steps? fifty meters? two kilometers?), and used deadly force only because it was reasonable in the circumstances to believe that lesser force would not protect him. Are not these judgments of reasonableness as much a matter of degree as judgments of "how far one should have to walk in the midday heat to save the life of another"?[15]

As for the danger of uncontrolled prosecutorial discretion and its malicious use against decent but unheroic samaritans, I think the interpretation I have suggested of the unreasonable risk standard should be an adequate guard against the danger. Prosecutors have no motive for bringing charges against nonrescuers whom they know juries will not convict, and juries in nonrescue cases would be instructed to acquit defendants if they judge that the personal risks of rescue had reached the threshhold—not of actual unreasonableness—but of the first germs of doubt about unreasonableness. Prosecutors could hope for convictions only in those cases where the reasonableness of the required effort's costs was uninfected by the slightest trace of uncertainty.[16]

Before leaving Macaulay, we should consider one of his favorite types of examples of nonpunishable omissions: failure to give money to starving beggars.[17] He was writing, of course, about India in 1835, and these examples were by no means as quaint as they may seem to us in a twentieth-century welfare state. In the India of Macaulay's time, a resident Englishman would encounter hordes of beggars on every street corner, and thousands of these would die every year of malnutrition or starvation. It was manifestly absurd to hold that each time a wealthy man encountered a beggar, he had a duty to rescue him by making a small contribution. Such rescues were not at all analogous to pulling drowning children out of the water and thus eliminating their peril once and for all; rather, the inevitable harm could only be forestalled. One way of looking at the contributions when they did occur was as beneficent gifts or favors beyond the call both of the donor's duty and the recipient's right. Perhaps a more plausible interpretation of them was as acts of charity discharging an imperfect obligation to give help to some, when help to all was impossible. In theory, it might be possible to require everyone, to a degree proportionate to his ability to pay, to contribute a fixed percentage of his income to some beggars or other, or to some charitable agencies or other, on pain of punishment, but the complexities of administration would be staggering. The problems would be too many even to mention here, but the most striking of them would be the coordination problem. Many beggars would still starve, since no one of them would have an enforcible right against any particular benefactor, and many might simply be overlooked in the confusion. Other recipients might collect from numerous sources, if only by lucky accident, while the most guileful of the mendicants might acquire fortunes. Any practical fair-minded person would be opposed to such a system, but if such a person were also humane, he would desire instead some sort of scheme of coordination that would allow the starving as a class to be rescued by the wealthy as a class without unjust enrichments of the unworthy or unfair disproportions in the contributions exacted from the donors. A modern state's welfare system, with its maintenance of an income floor for indigents paid out of taxes from those able to pay, is just such a system. Now no one can plausibly be charged with failure to prevent a beggar's death by not making him a direct contribution, since agencies of the state will not permit the pauper to die in any case, and one can always plead in one's own defense that the state's money for this purpose comes from tax funds to which one has already contributed one's fair share. It may have seemed obvious to Macaulay that no unrelated samaritan has a duty to save a starving person's life by giving him money, but now we all have a general duty, enforced in a coordinated way, to support welfare with taxes, and the reasonableness of that duty is no longer seriously questioned.[18]

On the other hand, the random and unpredictable emergencies of life that require time and effort, rather than money, from chance passersby, are not obviated by state welfare systems. "Often an imminent peril cannot wait assistance from the appropriate social institutions. . . . Moreover, there are no unfairness problems in singling out a particular person to receive the aid [thus the rescuer's duty is "perfect" and determinate], and *easy* rescues do not unfairly burden the chance rescuer."[19] It is consistent, therefore, to defend a bad samaritan statute for the latter cases, while preferring a state system of income maintenance to handle the hungry mendicant cases.

NEGATIVE VS. POSITIVE DUTIES

A final argument against bad samaritan statutes rests on an alleged morally significant distinction between active doing and passive omitting reflected in many commonsense moral rules that impose much stricter "negative duties" *not* to inflict harm than corresponding "positive duties" to prevent harm, even when the degree of harm resulting, and the intentions and motivations of the actor, are the same in the two cases. Admittedly, where minimal effort is required to prevent harm, the moral duty to prevent it seems every bit as stringent as the negative duty not to inflict that same harm directly. Grey gives a typical example where the parity of positive and negative duties seems to hold: "*B* has a heart attack and reaches for the bottle of medicine that will save him. What difference does it make . . . if *A* pushes the bottle out of his reach or it is just out of his reach and *A* could easily give it to him, but does not?"[20] (assuming that motive, intention, and capacity are the same in the two cases). When more than minimal effort is required, however, then negative duties appear much stronger than corresponding positive ones, and indeed there may be no corresponding positive duties at all. There seems no doubt that in some cases, although not in all the cases bad samaritan statutes would cover, "we are under greater obligation to avoid taking a life than to save a life even though effort and motivation are constants,"[21] and that "we feel obligated to go to almost any length to avoid killing someone, but not under equally great obligation to save someone."[22] But if it is the *certainty* of an endangered party's death that is to be weighed against only a *risk* of harm to ourselves, and his gravely serious harm that is to be weighed against our mere effort, or inconvenience, or expense, however great, why should we not be ob-

ligated to go to "almost any length" to save him? After all, everything else being the same, we are obligated to endure almost any sacrifice in preference to killing him. Even though minimalist bad samaritan statutes can be justified independently of these questions, the questions cry out for our attention, if only because of the possibility they raise that juries should employ a much stricter test than I have suggested of the "unreasonableness" of the risk, cost, or inconvenience required by a rescue effort.

Tracing the superiority of negative over positive duties to the deeper distinctions on which that superiority is based is a complex matter, and only a light sketch is possible here. The underlying reason for the general superiority of the negative duties is that positive duties, if framed in the same unconditional terms ("Thou must save all of those in need that thou can"), would lead to unsolvable coordination problems. Moral duties, whether positive or negative, are derived from "moral rules" which, like all regulatory rules, are inherently social in scope and in function. Rules allocate *shares* of social responsibility to individuals. Their imposed requirements are the dues we pay for our membership in the collective community. They also assign persons to special jobs, roles, and offices defined by special duties or delegated tasks. Public morality is not simply a general name for the sum of all the autonomous private moralities; rather, it is essentially a way of coordinating private efforts for common goals. In some matters it makes no sense to determine what an individual's duty is in isolation from the public system of assigned shares and responsibilities. One does not determine each person's fair share without regard to similar assignments to all the others, and then hope that the results balance out. Rather each person's duty is determined in part by the nature and scope of the duties assigned to the others.

Assigning certain important negative duties can normally be made in a simple and unqualified way to each citizen without raising difficult coordination and motivational problems. A negative duty (e.g., the duty not to kill others) can be discharged completely, and the duty rarely costs us great effort or sacrifice. "It is a rare case when we must really exert ourselves to keep from killing a person."[23] Thus each of us is capable of assigning to himself the unqualified moral duty—"Thou shalt not kill." On the other hand, we must in principle consult with our fellow citizens to determine a suitable rule, even a *moral* rule, governing our positive duty to rescue, because an individual duty to aid everyone who needs aid cannot be discharged completely. It would be unfair to those who attempt to do so on their own if others do not make similar efforts, and utterly chaotic if everyone tried, on his own, to discharge such a duty, independently of any known assignments of "shares" and special responsibilities.

It is true, therefore, that each has a duty to go to almost any length to avoid killing another, but not a parallel duty to go to almost any length to save others. But this moral truism can be very misleading. Part of the reason why I don't have a duty to maximize the harm-preventing I can achieve on my own, is that society collectively has preempted that duty and reassigned it in fair shares to private individuals. *Collectively* there *is* hardly any limit to how far we are prepared to go to prevent serious harms to individuals. Suppose a small child falls into a well. I am a mere bystander unrelated to the child's family, merely one of a crowd of frightened and concerned citizens drawn to the scene. There is very little that can be required of me, beyond passive cooperation and noninterference. The actual rescue attempt will be made by individuals who have been assigned that responsibility by political authorities or specially related parties. They are the instruments of our combined social effort, and we all contribute (in theory) our own fair share of the costs. Collectively, we regard one child's life as a precious thing, almost beyond price, and no effort is spared to save it. But if each of us were charged simply and vaguely with the duty of doing the maximal amount of harm-preventing we possibly can, then there would be an uncoordinated mess. A system of such duties would be socially self-defeating, and full of inequities in the sharing of burdens as well as the receiving of needed assistance. Moreover, it would encourage officious intermeddling by the overzealous, among other forms of harmful blundering.

Each of us has a duty to call the fire department whenever we discover a fire. Beyond that we have no positive duty to fight the flames. That is the special responsibility of the skilled professionals we support with our funds. The reason why we have the duty to report the fire but not the duty to fight it is not just that there is minimal effort required in the one case and not in the other. It is rather that the very strict social duty of putting out fires is most effectively and equitably discharged if it is split up in advance through the sharing of burdens and the assigning of special tasks. Positive duties to rescue *are* every bit as serious and weighty as negative duties not to harm. Unlike the latter, however, they must be divided into parts, allocated in shares, and (often) executed by appropriate specialists. That way their full crushing weight does not fall equally on all shoulders in all cases, but is more efficiently and equitably borne by the community as a whole.

When all is said and done, however, there remains one class of positive duties to give assistance that cannot be discharged by institutional mechanisms and special assignments, namely those cases of sudden and unanticipated peril to others that require immediate attention, and are such that a bystander can either make an "easy rescue" himself or else sound the alarm to notify those whose job it is to make difficult rescues. These positive duties, like corresponding negative ones, can be discharged completely and without exertion or risk. A sound system of social coordination would assign them to everyone. A citizen's duty to call the fire department, after all, is a vital part of our coordinated system of fire-fighting. Even samaritans can be required to do these social duties, for their cost is not burdensome, and the consequences of their omission can be disastrous.

NOTES

This paper is a revised version of my contribution to the Eleventh World Congress on Philosophy of Law and Social Philosophy, August 17, 1983, in Helsinki, Finland. It is reprinted here by special permission of the editors of the Congress proceedings who own the copyright. A version of this paper was also presented to the Chapel Hill Colloquium on October 15th, 1983. A modified version of the paper here appeared in Professor Feinberg's HARM TO OTHERS, published by Oxford University Press in 1984. The essay is reprinted with permission of the publisher.

1. *Luke* 10:25–27.

2. Rudzinski, *The Duty to Rescue: A Comparative Analysis*, in THE GOOD SAMARITAN AND THE LAW 92 (J. Ratcliff ed. 1966). The countries listed are Portugal (1967), the Netherlands (1881), Italy (1889 and 1930), Norway (1902), Russia (1903–17), Turkey (1926), Denmark (1930), Poland (1932), Germany (1935 and 1953), Roumania (1938), France (1941 and 1945), Hungary (1948 and 1961), Czechoslovakia (1950), Belgium (1961), and Switzerland (various cantons at various dates). Finland (1969) has now joined the list.

3. Murphy, *Blackmail: A Preliminary Inquiry*, 63 THE MONIST, 168 n.6 (1980).

4. Stell, *Dueling and The Right to Life*, 90 ETHICS 12 (1979).

5. Thomson, *A Defense of Abortion*, 1 PHIL. & PUBLIC AFFAIRS 62–64 (1971).

6. Ames, *Law and Morals*, 22 HARV. L. REV. (1980), reprinted in THE GOOD SAMARITAN AND THE LAW 19 (J. Ratcliff ed. 1966). Ames here advocates changes of the traditional rule. A major source of the argument Ames criticizes is Lord Macaulay who wrote in

1837: "It is indeed most highly desirable that men should not merely abstain from doing harm to their neighbors, but should render active service to their neighbors. In general, however, the penal law must content itself with keeping men from doing positive harm, and must leave to public opinion, and to the teachers of morality and religion, the office of furnishing men with motives for doing positive good."— T. B. MACAULAY, *Notes on the Indian Penal Code,* 7 WORKS 497 (1897).

7. J. S. MILL, UTILITARIANISM 61 (1957).

8. The term was first introduced for this purpose by R. M. HARE in his THE LANGUAGE OF MORALS 80 (1952).

9. *See e.g.,* Epstein, *A Theory of Strict Liability* 2 J. LEGAL STUD. 200 (1973).

10. *See* my essay *Supererogation and Rules* in DOING AND DESERVING 13 (1970).

11. H. SIDGWICK, METHODS OF ETHICS 219 (7th ed. 1907). *Cf.* Chisholm, *Supererogation and Offense: A Conceptual Scheme for Ethics,* 5 RATIO 1 (1963).

12. Macaulay, *supra* note 6, at 497.

13. *Id.* at 495.

14. *Id.* at 496-97.

15. T. GREY, THE LEGAL ENFORCEMENT OF MORALITY 159-60 (1983).

16. In litigious twentieth century America one of the risks incurred by good samaritans (particularly physicians) is civil liability for negligence if they should somehow accidently make things worse despite their good intentions. For that reason a criminal bad samaritan statute should create not only a duty to rescue but also a rescuer's immunity from civil suit except perhaps for *gross* negligence.

Many states already exempt physicians in this way when they provide voluntary emergency care. The immunity is good policy when there is no legal duty to offer assistance; it is required by justice when there is such a duty.

17. Macaulay's treatment of these cases is precisely parallel to his treatment of the river-fording case. "We are unable to see where . . . we can draw the line. If the rich man who refuses to save a beggar's life at the cost of a little copper is a murderer, is the poor man just one degree above beggary also to be a murderer if he omits to invite the beggar to partake of his hard-earned rice? Again, if the rich man is a murderer for refusing to save the beggar's life at the cost of a little copper, is he also to be a murderer if he refuses to save the beggar's life at the cost of a thousand rupees? . . . The distinction between a legal and an illegal omission is perhaps plain and intelligible; but the distinction between a large and a small sum of money is very far from being so, not to say that a sum which is small to one man is large to another." *Supra* note 6, at 496. With the addition of the appropriate moral premise, Macaulay's argument can be converted into an argument for the modern welfare state financed by the graduated income tax.

18. The points in this paragraph are suggested by Grey, *supra* note 15, and developed in a convincing way by Weinrib, *The Case for a Duty to Rescue,* 90 YALE L. J. 291-92 (1980).

19. *Id.* at 292.

20. Grey, *supra* note 15 at 158.

21. Trammel, *Saving Life and Taking Life,* in KILLING AND LETTING DIE 167 (B. Steinbock ed. 1980).

22. *Id.*

23. *Id.* at 168.

THE M'NAGHTEN RULES
House of Lords, 1843*

(Q.I.) "What is the law respecting alleged crimes committed by persons afflicted with insane delusion in respect of one or more particular subjects or persons: as for instance, where, at the time of the commission of the alleged crime, the accused knew he was acting contrary to law, but did the act complained of with a view, under the influence of insane delusion, of redressing or revenging some supposed grievance or injury, or of producing some supposed public benefit?"

(A.I.) "Assuming that your lordships' inquiries are confined to those persons who labor under such partial delusions only, and are not in other respects insane, we are of opinion that notwithstanding the accused did the act complained of with a view, under the influence of insane delusion, of redressing or avenging some supposed grievance or injury, or of producing some public benefit, he is nevertheless punishable, according to the nature of the crime committed, if he knew at the time of committing such crime that he was acting contrary to law, by which expression we understand your lordships to mean the law of the land."

(Q.II.) "What are the proper questions to be submitted to the jury where a person alleged to be afflicted with insane delusion respecting one or more particular subjects or persons is charged with the commission of a crime (murder, for example), and insanity is set up as a defence?"

(Q.III.) "In what terms ought the question to be left to the jury as to the prisoner's state of mind at the time when the act was committed?"

(A.II and A.III.) "As these two questions appear to us to be more conveniently answered together, we submit our opinion to be that the jury ought to be told in all cases that every man is presumed to be sane, and to possess a sufficient degree of reason to be responsible for his crimes, until the contrary be proved to their satisfaction; and that to establish a defence on the ground of insanity it must be clearly proved that, at the time of committing the act, the

*10 Cl. 2nd F. 200 at p. 209.

accused was labouring under such a defect of reason, from disease of the mind, as not to know the nature and quality of the act he was doing, or, if he did know it, that he did not know he was doing what was wrong. The mode of putting the latter part of the question to the jury on these occasions has generally been whether the accused at the time of doing the act knew the difference between right and wrong: which mode, though rarely, if ever, leading to any mistake with the jury, is not, as we conceive, so accurate when put generally and in the abstract as when put with reference to the party's knowledge of right and wrong, in respect to the very act with which he is charged. If the question were to be put as to the knowledge of the accused solely and exclusively with reference to the law of the land, it might tend to confound the jury, by inducing them to believe that an actual knowledge of the law of the land was essential in order to lead to conviction: whereas, the law is administered upon the principle that everyone must be taken conclusively to know it, without proof that he does know it. If the accused was conscious that the act was one that he ought not to do, and if that act was at the same time contrary to the law of the land, he is punishable; and the usual course, therefore, has been to leave the question to the jury, whether the accused had a sufficient degree of reason to know that he was doing an act that was wrong; and this course we think is correct, accompanied with such observations and explanations as the circumstances of each particular case may require."

(Q.IV.) "If a person under an insane delusion as to existing facts commits an offence in consequence thereof, is he thereby excused?"

(A.IV.) "The answer must, of course, depend on the nature of the delusion; but making the same assumption as we did before, namely, that he labors under such partial delusion only, and is not in other respects insane, we think he must be considered in the same situation as to responsibility as if the facts with respect to which the delusion exists were real. For example, if under the influence of his delusion he supposes another man to be in the act of attempting to take away his life, and he kills that man, as he supposes in self-defence, he would be exempt from punishment. If his delusion was that the deceased had inflicted a serious injury to his character and fortune, and he killed him in revenge for such supposed injury, he would be liable to punishment."

THE ROYAL COMMISSION ON CAPITAL PUNISHMENT (1953)*

Legal Insanity

(III) CONCLUSIONS
PRELIMINARY

278. We make one fundamental assumption, which we should hardly have thought it necessary to state explicitly if it had not lately been questioned in some quarters. It has for centuries been recognized that if a person was, at the time of his unlawful act, mentally so disordered that it would be unreasonable to impute guilt to him, he ought not to be held liable to conviction and punishment under the criminal law. Views have changed and opinions have differed, as they differ now, about the standards to be applied in deciding whether an individual should be exempted from criminal responsibility for this reason; but the principle has been accepted without question. Recently, however, the suggestion has sometimes been made that the insane murderer should be punished equally with the sane, or that, although he ought not to be executed as a punishment, he should be painlessly exterminated as a measure of social hygiene. The argument is in each case the same—that his continued existence will be of no benefit to himself, and that he will be not only a useless burden, but also a potential danger to the community, since there is always a risk that he may escape and commit another crime. Such doctrines have been preached and practiced in National-Socialist Germany, but they are repugnant to the moral traditions of Western civilization and we are confident that they would be unhesitatingly rejected by the great majority of the population of this country. We assume the continuance of the ancient and humane principle that has long formed part of our common law.

*Reprinted from *Royal Commission on Capital Punishment 1949–53 Report* (London: Her Majesty's Stationery Office, 1953), pp. 98–105, 107–16, by permission of the Controller of Her Britannic Majesty's Stationery Office.

279. For us, therefore, there are two essential questions—Do the M'Naghten Rules provide a just and reasonable standard by which to assess whether the mental state of an accused person was at the time of the crime so abnormal that he ought to be held irresponsible and exempted from punishment? And, if not, what change in the law, whether by amendment or by abrogation of the Rules, would be practicable and desirable? We shall approach these questions in a practical and empirical spirit, and we shall try to answer them without losing ourselves in the labyrinthine legal and philosophical arguments which have led to much barren controversy in the past.

The Nature of Criminal Responsibility

280. It has often been said that the question of criminal responsibility, although it is closely bound up with medical and ethical issues, is primarily a legal question. There is an important sense in which this is true. There is no *a priori* reason why every person suffering from any form of mental abnormality or disease, or from any particular kind of mental disease, should be treated by the law as not answerable for any criminal offense which he may commit, and be exempted from conviction and punishment. Mental abnormalities vary infinitely in their nature and intensity and in their effects on the character and conduct of those who suffer from them. Where a person suffering from a mental abnormality commits a crime, there must always be some likelihood that the abnormality has played some part in the causation of the crime; and, generally speaking, the graver the abnormality and the more serious the crime, the more probable it must be that there is a causal connection between them. But the closeness of this connection will be shown by the facts brought in evidence in individual cases and cannot be decided on the basis of any general medical principle. On the other hand, few persons, if any, would go so far as to suggest

that anyone suffering from any mental abnormality, however slight, ought on that ground to be wholly exempted from responsibility under the criminal law. It therefore becomes necessary for the law to provide a method of determining what kind and degree of mental abnormality shall entitle offenders to be so exempted; and also to decide what account shall be taken of lesser degrees of mental abnormality, whether by way of mitigation of sentence or otherwise.

281. Yet, although in this sense the question of criminal responsibility may rightly be described as a question of law, there is another, and more important, sense in which this is at best a misleading half-truth. Discussion of this subject is often befogged through failure to distinguish clearly between the two questions "what is the law?" and "what ought the law to be?" The first is obviously a purely legal question; the second is obviously not. A just and adequate doctrine of criminal responsibility cannot be founded on legal principles alone. Responsibility is a moral question; and there is no issue on which it is more important that the criminal law should be in close accord with the moral standards of the community. There can be no pre-established harmony between the criteria of moral and of criminal responsibility, but they ought to be made to approximate as nearly as possible. The views of ordinary men and women about the moral accountability of the insane have been gradually modified by the development of medical science, and, if the law cannot be said to have always kept pace with them, it has followed them at a distance and has slowly adjusted itself to their changes. It is therefore proper and necessary to enquire from time to time whether the doctrine of criminal responsibility, as laid down by the common law and applied by the courts, takes due account of contemporary moral standards and of modern advances in medical knowledge about the effects of mental abnormality on personality and behavior.

282. This principle is no doubt easier to enunciate than to apply. The last hundred years have seen striking advances in scientific knowledge of insanity and mental abnormality; yet psychological medicine remains one of the youngest branches of science and it is often difficult to define the limits of recognized knowledge. There are many important questions on which psychiatrists of different schools are not agreed: there is no clear, precise, or universally accepted terminology; and there is not infrequently a marked conflict of views on individual cases. When we leave the domain of medicine and enter that of ethics or law, we find that there is no greater unanimity, and that psychiatrists express differing views about the kind and degree of mental abnormality which should entitle an offender to be absolved from responsibility for a criminal act.

283. These difficulties would be very grave, and perhaps insuperable, if responsibility were primarily a medical question. Even if it were on other grounds desirable to do so, it would, in the present state of medical knowledge, be out of the question to remove the issue of criminal responsibility from the courts and entrust its determination to a panel of medical experts, as has sometimes been suggested. In our view the question of responsibility is not primarily a question of medicine, any more than it is a question of law. It is essentially a moral question, with which the law is intimately concerned and to whose solution medicine can bring valuable aid, and it is one which is most appropriately decided by a jury of ordinary men and women, not by medical or legal experts.

284. Neither the law nor ethics can reasonably be expected to base itself on extreme and untried medical theories or to go beyond what appears to be the general consensus of moderate medical opinion. If the problem of criminal responsibility is approached from this point of view, it should not prove impossible to find a solution which will satisfactorily reconcile the requirements of justice with the moral feelings of the community at large.

285. As we have previously observed, mental abnormality varies widely in its intensity and in the extent to which it affects the behavior of the patient and his capacity to conduct himself like a normal person. It follows that the extent to which a mentally abnormal person should be considered less responsible for his actions than a normal person varies equally widely: there is an almost infinite range of degrees of responsibility. For practical purposes, however, the law must divide mentally abnormal offenders into a limited number of groups for the purpose of assessing criminal responsibility. In effect, the existing law of England takes cognizance of three such groups—those who are to be regarded as wholly irresponsible; those who are not regarded as wholly irresponsible and entirely exempted from conviction and punishment, but

are nevertheless considered so much less responsible than a normal person as to justify some mitigation of punishment (by the exercise of the Prerogative of Mercy in capital cases, by the courts in others); and, lastly, those whose responsibility for their actions is so little affected that they can properly be dealt with in the same way as a normal person. But it must be recognized that the boundary between the first and the second group is not a clear-cut line of demarcation, and that the question whether an accused person should be regarded as wholly irresponsible is essentially a question of degree, which can be decided only by the exercise of a subjective, and to some extent arbitrary, judgment. There are not two all-inclusive classes—the black and the white, the responsible and the irresponsible—into one or other of which every offender must fall; the question is rather whether the offender, as a result of insanity or mental abnormality, is so much less responsible than a normal person that it is just and right to treat him as wholly irresponsible. And if it appears that the crime was wholly or very largely caused by insanity, he ought to be treated as irresponsible; for to punish a person for a crime caused by insanity would in effect be to punish him for his insanity; and this would not be in harmony with the moral feelings of the community.

286. The views expressed by medical witnesses differed in emphasis rather than in substance. The general conclusions we draw from their evidence are these. The question of criminal responsibility must be considered by the jury in each individual case on the basis of all the relevant evidence given by medical and other witnesses. It is not possible to define in medical terms any category of mental disease which should always, and without exception, exempt an offender from responsibility; and there must always be doubtful and borderline cases, where it will be difficult to decide whether the accused ought to be held wholly irresponsible, either because it is difficult to diagnose his mental condition at the time of the offense or because it is difficult to judge how his mental condition affected his responsibility for his actions. Nevertheless, where a grave crime is committed by a person who is suffering from a psychosis and is so grossly disordered mentally that, in the opinion of experienced medical men, he could properly be certified as insane, the presumption that the crime was wholly or largely caused by the insanity is, in ordinary circumstances, overwhelmingly strong. It cannot indeed be maintained that if a person is certified, or certifiable, as insane, he should necessarily be held irresponsible in all cases, mainly because . . . certification is sometimes determined by pragmatic considerations; it may be necessary to certify a patient whose mental disorder is comparatively slight in order to ensure that he should receive proper care and treatment. But cases will be extremely rare in which an accused person ought to be held criminally responsible when he is certifiable as insane and there is no reason to think that his condition was materially different at the time of the crime.

287. An equally strong presumption arises in relation to the grosser forms of mental deficiency (idiocy and imbecility) and to certain epileptic conditions. . . . It does not, we think, arise in relation to any forms of minor mental disorder. Where the accused is suffering from some lesser degree of abnormality, the evidence may sometimes be sufficient to show that he ought to be treated as irresponsible; usually, however, it will not justify such a conclusion, although his moral responsibility may often be diminished to such an extent as to justify mitigation of the extreme penalty.

288. Under the existing law, as we have seen, if a person charged with murder is alleged to be insane, three different tests of insanity are applied at different stages in the proceedings. The test applied by the jury to determine whether the accused should be found insane on arraignment is whether he is fit to plead, to understand the proceedings, and to instruct counsel. . . . The test applied by the jury in determining whether at the time of the offense he was insane so as not to be responsible for his actions and should therefore be found guilty but insane is that laid down by the M'Naghten Rules—whether he was laboring under such a defect of reason, from disease of the mind, that he did not know the nature and quality of his act or did not know that it was wrong. . . . The test applied by the Home Secretary in deciding whether he is precluded from allowing the prisoner to go to execution if convicted and sentenced to death is whether he is certifiable as insane. . . . Although there are reasons, as we have pointed out in paragraph 286, for which it would not be appropriate to assimilate the test applied by the jury to that later applied by the Home Secretary, and make criminal irresponsibility coextensive with certifiable insanity, we

have no doubt that it would be desirable to approximate the two tests more closely than at present, and it seems clear that, if this were done, it would obviate the passing of the death sentence in some of the cases in which it will not be carried out.

The Inadequacy of the M'Naghten Rules

289. It remains for us to consider whether amendment of the law is necessary in order to achieve this object. It may be suggested that, owing to the broadening interpretation of the M'Naghten Rules, few insane persons are in fact convicted of murder and sentenced to death, and that this tendency may be expected to continue and to develop still further. It may also be pointed out that . . . by no means all of the 48 persons who in the years 1900–1949 were convicted of murder and subsequently certified insane after a statutory medical inquiry had been convicted as a result of the operation of the M'Naghten Rules. It may therefore be argued that in practice few persons who ought to be found irresponsible are convicted of murder, and even fewer are so convicted owing to the application of the M'Naghten Rules, and that the mischief to be remedied is therefore too small to justify amendment of the law, which would certainly be difficult and controversial and which might make it too easy for offenders to escape just punishment.

290. We think that this argument is misconceived. The objections to retaining the M'Naghten Rules in their present form on the ground that in practice they rarely produce injustice were cogently stated by an American witness, Mr. Justice Frankfurter, in his evidence:

. . . The M'Naghten Rules were rules which the Judges, in response to questions by the House of Lords, formulated in the light of the then existing psychological knowledge. . . . I do not see why the rules of law should be arrested at the state of psychological knowledge of the time when they were formulated. . . . If you find rules that are, broadly speaking, discredited by those who have to administer them, which is, I think, the real situation, certainly with us—they are honored in the breach and not in the observance—then I think the law serves its best interests by trying to be more honest about it . . . I think that to have rules which cannot rationally be justified except by a process of interpretation which distorts and often practically nullifies them, and to say the corrective process comes by having the Governor of a State charged with the responsibility of deciding when the consequences of the rule should not be enforced, is not a desirable system . . . I am a great believer in being as candid as possible about my institutions. They are in large measure abandoned in practice, and therefore I think the M'Naghten Rules are in large measure shams. That is a strong word, but I think the M'Naghten Rules are very difficult for conscientious people and not difficult enough for people who say "We'll just juggle them" . . . I dare to believe that we ought not to rest content with the difficulty of finding an improvement in the M'Naghten Rules . . .

291. In our view the test of criminal responsibility contained in the M'Naghten Rules cannot be defended in the light of modern medical knowledge and modern penal views. It is well established that there are offenders who know what they are doing and know that it is wrong (whether "wrong" is taken to mean legally or morally wrong), but are nevertheless so gravely affected by mental disease that they ought not to be held responsible for their actions. It would be impossible to apply modern methods of care and treatment in mental hospitals, and at the same time to maintain order and discipline, if the great majority of the patients, even among the grossly insane, did not know what is forbidden by the rules and that, if they break them, they are liable to forfeit some privilege. Examination of a number of individual cases in which a verdict of guilty but insane was returned, and rightly returned, has convinced us that there are few indeed where the accused can truly be said not to have known that his act was wrong. We have been struck, for example, by the large number of cases where the offender was undoubtedly insane both at the time of the crime and afterward, but clearly showed, by his subsequent actions or by a remark made immediately after the crime (such as "I have killed her; shall I be hanged?"), that he knew what he was doing and that it was punishable by law.

292. This narrow scope of the Rules was long ago recognized by Lord Bramwell (although he regarded it as a merit) when he observed, in a famous phrase: "I think that, although the present law lays down such a definition of madness, that nobody is hardly ever really mad enough to be within it, yet it is a logical and good definition."[1] Lord Bramwell's view was that many insane persons may be influenced by the

same motives and considerations as the sane and that if a lunatic knew what he was doing and knew that it was wrong, and if he was so far amenable to threats that he would not have "yielded to his insanity if a policeman had been at his elbow," then, not only was there no reason why he should not be punished, but it was eminently desirable that he should be punished, so that persons whose power of self-control was weakened by mental disease might at any rate be restrained by the sanctions of the criminal law.

293. This view has long been abandoned, and, in most cases where the strict application of the M'Naghten Rules will require a verdict of "guilty" to be given against an insane person, this consequence is obviated by the common sense of juries and the readiness of judges to recognize that, when common sense says the verdict should be "guilty but insane" and the M'Naghten Rules say it should be "guilty," common sense must prevail. But the fact that usually a way is found of obviating the evil consequences liable to flow from the Rules is not a sufficient reason for retaining them. The evil consequences are not always obviated. Occasionally the Rules lead to a verdict of "guilty" and a sentence of death which might otherwise be avoided. Nor can we disregard the deplorable impression which the Rules make on the minds of persons interested in penal matters. The Rules bring the criminal law into disrepute and the doubts and anxieties they create in the minds of many critics are not removed by the consideration that the actual harm they do is much less than they are capable of doing.

294. Moreover the burden of "stretching" the M'Naghten Rules, so as to avoid the unfortunate results of their strict application, falls largely and unfairly on medical witnesses. If a doctor is prepared to infer from his diagnosis of the nature and degree of the prisoner's insanity that at the moment when he committed his act of violence he was probably unconscious that it was wrong, the court will often be ready to accept that inference, although there may be no other evidence to support it, and even when the prisoner's acts or words seem to belie it. It is unfair to the medical witness to place him in a position where he is aware that his evidence as to the nature and degree of the prisoner's mental disease and its effect on his responsibility may be treated as irrelevant unless he is prepared to hazard the opinion that at the crucial moment the prisoner was probably unaware of the wrongfulness of his act. We are aware that medical evidence is sometimes unsatisfactory and open to justified criticism, but we have little doubt that its defects are often in large measure due to the impossible position in which medical witnesses are placed by what is to them the manifest absurdity of the M'Naghten test, and that amendment of the law, by relieving them of this embarrassment, would do much to improve the quality of psychiatric evidence.

295. Finally, even if by a liberal and generous interpretation the M'Naghten Rules were in practice so applied as to exempt from criminal responsibility all those offenders who ought to be so exempted, they would still be open to the most serious objection. It is nearly fifty years since a medical man who had devoted much sober and careful study to this question wrote that, although judges, in trying a case that did not come within the original scope of the M'Naghten Rules, might sometimes direct juries in other terms, "the much more usual course is for the judge to adhere strictly to the terms of the answers, and then to stretch the plain meaning of the language of those answers, until the ordinary nonlegal user of the English language is aghast at the distortions and deformations and tortures to which the unfortunate words are subjected, and wonders whether it is worth while to have a language which can apparently be taken to mean anything the user pleases."[2] When the gap between the natural meaning of the law and the sense in which it is commonly applied has for so long been so wide, it is impossible to escape the conclusion that an amendment of the law, to bring it into closer conformity with the current practice, is long overdue.

296. For these reasons we are agreed that the time has come when the law ought to be amended. We have already described the two alternative remedies proposed by our witnesses. One is that the M'Naghten Rules should be extended, on the lines of the formula proposed by the British Medical Association, to cover cases where the accused "was laboring, as a result of disease of the mind, under . . . a disorder of emotion such that, while appreciating the nature and quality of the act, and that it was wrong, he did not possess sufficient power to prevent himself from committing it." The other is that the Rules should be entirely abrogated and the jury be given express

discretion to determine, on all the medical and other evidence, untrammeled by any rule of law, whether the accused was so insane (or mentally defective) as not, in the opinion of the jury, to be responsible for his actions.

297. Before examining these alternatives we must deal with the often repeated suggestion that if the present criterion of responsibility were enlarged, this would have dangerous repercussions in relation to other crimes, especially sexual crimes and crimes of violence against the person. In our view the probable effect of any such change on the general administration of the criminal law can easily be exaggerated. It is only in trials for murder that a defense of insanity is raised in a considerable proportion of cases and a verdict of guilty but insane frequently returned. In trials for other offenses the plea of insanity is seldom put forward. The explanation is no doubt the one usually given—that indefinite detention as a Broadmoor patient appears a preferable alternative only where the sentence on conviction is death, and that in other cases the accused prefers to run the risk of a fixed sentence of imprisonment, however long. We see no reason to suppose that this natural reluctance to court detention for an indeterminate period would be weakened by any change in the test of criminal responsibility or that, if the present test were relaxed, this would be likely to lead to an undesirable or unjustified increase in pleas of insanity or verdicts of guilty but insane in relation to offenses other than murder.

* * *

Should the M'Naghten Rules Be Revised?

308. The proposal to extend the M'Naghten Rules to cover those cases where a crime is committed as a result of insanity affecting not the reason or the intellect but the will or the emotions has much to commend it, and clearly merits the most careful consideration. This was the course proposed by the Atkin Committee, when they recommended that the Rules should be extended so as to include cases where the act was "committed under an impulse which the prisoner was by mental disease in substance deprived of any power to resist." To add such a limb to the formula which has been used in the courts for more than a hundred years would be a less radical change than to abrogate the Rules and leave the jury to decide the issue at large; and, other things being equal, a limited

change is to be preferred to a more far-reaching one.

309. There can, moreover, be no doubt that if an adequate criterion of criminal responsibility could be devised, expressed in clear and simple nontechnical language, it would be a helpful guide to the jury. In many cases it may be very difficult to decide whether the accused was so gravely disordered mentally that he ought not to be held responsible for his actions. In capital cases a plea of insanity is often advanced on weak and inadequate grounds. Some medical evidence is obscure and may be imperfectly understood by the jury. There may be conflicting medical testimony, and the jury may have no standard by which to assess the relative value of the evidence given on either side. In such cases, if the test of responsibility is defined by law and the Judge is able to tell the jury that they may only return a verdict of guilty but insane if they find that the accused was, as a result of insanity, subject to certain specified incapacities of reason or will, the application of this yardstick may save them from being led astray and help them to arrive at a just conclusion.

310. The first question we have to consider is whether the M'Naghten Rules, as they stand, cover adequately those cases where insanity does result in a "defect of reason," or call for amendment in relation to cases of this kind as well as those where it results in disorder of the emotions or the will. It is beyond dispute that if, as a result of mental disease, a person does not know the nature and quality of the act—if, for example, he thinks that he is squeezing an orange when he is in fact strangling a human being—or if he does not know that the act is forbidden by law, he ought not to be held criminally responsible. The criterion is therefore sound so far as it goes. But it has for long been objected that it is too narrow. It has been pointed out, for example, that it does not cover the case of the lunatic who commits a crime, knowing that it is contrary to the laws of man, but believing that it is commanded by God. It has therefore been suggested that "wrong" should be interpreted to mean "morally wrong," as opposed to "punishable by law." This proposal does not however resolve the difficulty. If "morally wrong" is interpreted objectively to mean "wrong according to commonly accepted moral standards," it will not materially enlarge the present criterion; for a person who knows that a serious crime is for-

bidden by law will almost certainly also know that it is generally regarded as morally wrong. The alternative is to interpret "morally wrong" subjectively. The British Medical Association, for example, suggested that the existing test should be amended to provide that "wrong" should mean "not 'punishable by law' but morally wrong in the accused person's own opinion." We cannot regard this suggestion as satisfactory. The test would then become "whether the accused was laboring under a defect of reason such that he did not know that he was doing what was morally wrong in his own opinion." This somewhat confused formula would in effect substitute "did not think that it was wrong" for "did not know that it was wrong"; but if "defect of reason" is retained as a test of responsibility, it must be related to an objective standard. The substitution for "know" of a more subjective word, such as "appreciate," is open to similar objections. Our conclusion is that it is not practicable to enlarge the scope of the M'Naghten Rules by rewording the existing limbs, and that some other test must be added to those contained in the present formula if the Rules are to cover satisfactorily cases where a person knows what he is doing and that it is unlawful, but, as a result of insanity, does not regard it as morally wrong or falls so far short of understanding or appreciating how wrong it is that he ought to be regarded as irresponsible.

311. We recognize the difficulties of framing a precise formula which will not be open to objections, and we shall discuss them later in detail, but we must first consider the objections of a more general character that have been brought against any proposal to extend the M'Naghten Rules to cover cases where the accused knew what he was doing and that it was wrong, but, as a result of insanity, to borrow a phrase from common language, "he could not help doing it."

312. It is often suggested, and was suggested by some of our witnesses, that any such change in the law would lead to unjustified acquittals on the ground of insanity. We believe that these apprehensions are largely without foundation. We should expect that the new formula would make it easier for medical witnesses to give a full and straightforward opinion on the mental condition of the accused, and that it would be reasonably interpreted by juries under wise guidance from the judges, who would emphasize that the jury must be satisfied not merely that the accused was unable to control himself (or to resist an impulse, or to prevent himself from committing the act) but that this inability was due to "insanity" or "disease of the mind." We see little reason to fear that it would be found too wide or would exempt persons suffering from lesser degrees of mental abnormality insufficient to excuse them. No doubt the question whether it was impossible, or only difficult, for the accused to control himself, or to prevent himself from committing the offense, would not always be easy for the medical witness to answer or for the jury to determine. But we agree with the British Medical Association that it would not in essence be more difficult than the question they have now to decide under the M'Naghten Rules. It is never possible, as the Association point out, "to provide scientific and conclusive proof of a complete lack of power to control conduct at the time when a crime was committed"; but the jury would have only to decide whether on a balance of probability the accused was unable to control himself, and we think that they should be capable of coming to a reasonable conclusion on this issue in the light of all the evidence.

313. Discussion of the merits of such proposals for enlarging the scope of the M'Naghten Rules to take account of the consensus of modern medical knowledge and opinion has been obscured by the long-standing controversy about the "irresistible impulse," and much of the evidence which we heard was colored by it. This is regrettable, not only because the concept of the "irresistible impulse" has been largely discredited as a result of past controversy, but because it is inherently inadequate and unsatisfactory. This is not because, as has often been suggested, it would be impossible for a jury to distinguish between an irresistible and a merely unresisted impulse. We do not think it would be impossible, though no doubt it might often be very difficult. Nor do we believe that recognition of the irresistible impulse would be likely to lead to unjustifiable verdicts of insanity in cases of crimes prompted by anger or by normal or perverted sexual passion, provided that it was always made clear to the jury that they must be satisfied not only that there was an irresistible impulse but that the impulse was due to disease of the mind; and it must be remembered that no responsible person has ever proposed the recognition of irresistible impulse except in conjunction with insanity or mental disease. The general consensus of psy-

chiatric opinion does not regard an aggressive psychopath or a sadist—and still less a person who is merely hot-tempered or sexually unrestrained—as suffering from insanity or mental disease; and though it might sometimes be possible to find medical witnesses prepared to express such views, their evidence would not be likely to find favor with a jury.

314. The real objection to the term "irresistible impulse" is that it is too narrow, and carries an unfortunate and misleading implication that, where a crime is committed as a result of emotional disorder due to insanity, it must have been suddenly and impulsively committed after a sharp internal conflict. In many cases, such as those of melancholia, this is not true at all. The sufferer from this disease experiences a change of mood which alters the whole of his existence. He may believe, for instance, that a future of such degradation and misery awaits both him and his family that death for all is a less dreadful alternative. Even the thought that the acts he contemplates are murder and suicide pales into insignificance in contrast with what he otherwise expects. The criminal act, in such circumstances, may be the reverse of impulsive. It may be coolly and carefully prepared; yet it is still the act of a madman. This is merely an illustration; similar states of mind are likely to lie behind the criminal act when murders are committed by persons suffering from schizophrenia or paranoid psychoses due to disease of the brain.

315. If, therefore, the M'Naghten Rules are to be extended by the addition of a third limb to meet the case of insanity affecting not the reason but the will, it is important that this should be formulated not merely in terms of inability to resist an impulse, but in wider terms, which will allow the court to take account of those cases where an insane person commits a crime after a long period of brooding and reflection or is gradually carried toward it without any real attempt to resist this tendency.

316. In considering how this might best be done, we were attracted by the provisions of some of the Continental Penal Codes, and notably by the words of the Swiss Code, "incapable of appreciating the unlawful nature of his act or of acting in accordance with such appreciation." We think that this provision, reasonably interpreted, should enable the court to deal appropriately with any accused person who ought, as a result of any form of mental abnormality, whether permanent or transitory, to be

regarded as not criminally responsible. But we have reluctantly been forced to the conclusion that, whatever the merits of such a definition, the concepts which it employs and the language in which it is expressed are rooted in a different system of law and could not satisfactorily be grafted on to rules whose purpose is to furnish an objective test for juries in this country.

317. The proposal of the British Medical Association . . . is that the M'Naghten Rules should be enlarged by adding to the existing tests the test whether the accused was laboring, as a result of disease of the mind, under "a disorder of emotion such that, while appreciating the nature and quality of the act, and that it was wrong, he did not possess sufficient power to prevent himself from committing it." No formula will be perfect or immune from criticism; but we think that some such words as these (though we should prefer to say more simply "was incapable of preventing himself") are as good as could be devised for enlarging the Rules so as to cover defect of will as well as of reason; and we therefore think it unnecessary to examine in detail the language of the numerous formulae which have been at different times propounded with the same object. We feel, however, that in the formula suggested by the Association the distinction drawn between "defect of reason" and "disorder of emotion," though it may have its place in the evidence of a medical witness or in a Judge's summing-up, is not suitable for inclusion in the formula itself. We think that the purport of the Association's formula would be adequately expressed more shortly in the following terms:

The jury must be satisfied that, at the time of committing the act, the accused, as a result of disease of the mind (or mental deficiency) (a) did not know the nature and quality of the act of (b) did not know that it was wrong or (c) was incapable of preventing himself from committing it.

318. Such an extension of the M'Naghten Rules would remove the most glaring defect of the present law, namely, that they enjoin a verdict of guilty unless certain conditions are fulfilled, and those conditions ignore one of the commonest causes of irresponsibility due to insanity. But would it remove this defect in a way that would prove in practice adequate? To examine this question it will be instructive to test the formula on the facts of a recent case of some notoriety—that of Ley ("the Chalkpit murder"), who coolly conceived and carried

out an elaborate criminal plan over a period of time. There seems no doubt that he could not rightly be held responsible for his crime. The Lord Chief Justice, before whom he was tried, said in evidence before us, "I had no doubt the prisoner was insane; his whole conduct showed a typical case of paranoia." It is no less certain that he knew the nature and quality of his act and that it was wrong. If therefore he had pleaded insanity (which he refused to do), the jury would have been bound to find him guilty by the test of the M'Naghten Rules. Would decisions of this sort be avoided by adding the third question "was he incapable of preventing himself from committing it?"

319. The answer depends on the interpretation put on the words "incapable of preventing himself." Ley, because of his insanity, lived in a twilight world of distorted values which resulted not so much in his being "incapable of preventing himself" from committing his crime, in the strict sense of those words, as in his being incapable of appreciating, as a sane man would, why he should try to prevent himself from committing it. It seems to us reasonable to argue that the words "incapable of preventing himself" should be construed so as to cover such states of mind; that they should be interpreted as meaning not merely that the accused was incapable of preventing himself if he had tried to do so, but that he was incapable of wishing or of trying to prevent himself, or incapable of realizing or attending to considerations which might have prevented him if he had been capable of realizing or attending to them. If each of Ley's acts is considered separately, it would be difficult to maintain that he could not have prevented himself from committing them. Yet if his course of conduct is looked at as a whole, it might well be argued that, as a result of his insanity, he was incapable of preventing himself from conceiving the murderous scheme, incapable of judging it by other than an insane scale of ethical values, and, in that sense, incapable of preventing himself from carrying it out. If the addition to the M'Naghten Rules were construed in this way, it would serve its purpose well, and the Rules thus amended should cover most of the cases where a defense of insanity ought to be admitted. But they would fall very far short of the needs of the case if the courts felt bound to interpret the new rule narrowly, and it were held that a defense of insanity on the ground that the accused was incapable of preventing

himself from committing the crime was bound to fail unless the jury were satisfied that he would not have refrained from committing it even if a policeman had been standing beside him. Such a construction would cover only acts committed in a state of semiconsciousness, automatism, or frenzy. In view of the rigidity with which the existing Rules are now sometimes construed, it is impossible to be sure that the broader interpretation would prevail, especially since, if the change were made by statute—as it would presumably have to be—judges might feel less free to apply them otherwise than strictly.

320. The question may well be asked whether, if the words we have suggested admit of so wide a difference of interpretation, it would not be better to remove doubt by wording the third limb in such a way as to make it clear that the wider interpretation is intended. We do not see how this could be done without destroying what is claimed to be the essential justification for the formulation of rules for the jury's guidance. That is that the jury must have simple, objective, factual questions to answer. "Did he know the nature and quality of his act?" and "Did he know that it was wrong?" are such questions. So is "Was he incapable of preventing himself?", however difficult it may be to answer. "Was he incapable of wishing or trying to prevent himself, or of realizing or attending to considerations which might have prevented him?" is not. For the Rules to formulate the question expressly in these wider terms would be tantamount to asking the jury to decide whether, on a balance of probabilities, the insanity of the accused was the effective cause of his unlawful act. That would be no different from asking them whether he was so insane that he ought not to be regarded as responsible and abandoning the attempt to formulate rules for their guidance.

Should the M'Naghten Rules Be Abrogated?

321. This brings us to the alternative solution of dispensing with a legal formula altogether. The assumption which underlies the M'Naghten Rules, and would underlie any new criterion of criminal responsibility, is that, since insanity and irresponsibility cannot be taken as coextensive, some formula must be provided defining the relations between them. It is argued that, in the absence of some such formula, the jury have no objective standard by

which to decide whether the degree of mental abnormality from which the accused suffers (whether it is insanity, mental deficiency, or some other mental disease) is such that he ought not to be held criminally responsible, and that this question cannot properly be left to their decision without some such guidance. It is therefore the function of the law to define the state or states of mind resulting from insanity which justify exemption from responsibility; and the function of the jury is limited to deciding a question of fact, namely, whether at the time of the offense the accused was in such a state of mind.

322. It seems clear from our evidence that this theory has largely broken down in practice. If the M'Naghten Rules were consistently applied, juries would be obliged to convict many persons who at the time of the offense were so insane that it would be wrong to hold them responsible. Sometimes they do, but usually such verdicts are not returned, because, unless the Judge charges them strictly in accordance with the M'Naghten Rules (and occasionally even when he does), juries exercise the discretion which the law in theory withholds from them. As stated in paragraph 293, when common sense says the verdict should be "guilty but insane" and the M'Naghten Rules say it should be "guilty," judges and juries usually recognize that common sense must prevail. And it is not only in cases where the M'Naghten criterion conflicts with common sense that it is apt to be disregarded. In many cases where a medical witness hazards the opinion that the accused at the time of his act was not conscious that it was wrong, it is difficult to suppose that the ordinary juryman regards this point as crucial; there can be little doubt that he often addresses his mind to the essential question whether the accused was so insane that it would be unreasonable to hold him responsible for his actions. We have already referred . . . to the reply given by Lord Cooper, when he was asked whether it was not desirable to have some yardstick to guide the jury:

> I do not think so, for this reason. . . . However much you charge a jury as to the M'Naghten Rules or any other test, the question they would put to themselves when they retire is—"Is this man mad or is he not?"

We have little doubt that English juries often do the same.

323. The advantage of a new rule of law, widening the criterion laid down in the M'Naghten Rules, is that conflicts between the rule and common sense should be less frequent. But they could hardly be eliminated. Whatever the rule of law may say, and however broadly it may be interpreted, it can never be all-embracing and it must be expected that members of the jury will sometimes find that their common sense drives them to look behind the rule and to address their minds directly to the essential question of responsibility. For we are bound to recognize that it is not possible to define with any precision the state of mind which should exempt an insane person from responsibility. This opinion was emphatically expressed by Lord Blackburn as long ago as 1874.[3] He said:

> To that I can only say that on the question what amounts to insanity, that would prevent a person being punishable or not, I have read every definition which I ever could meet with, and never was satisfied with one of them, and have endeavoured in vain to make one satisfactory to myself; I verily believe that it is not in human power to do it. You must take it that in every individual case you must look at the circumstances and do the best you can to say whether it was the disease of the mind which was the cause of the crime, or the party's criminal will.

324. The gravamen of the charge against the M'Naghten Rules is that they are not in harmony with modern medical science, which, as we have seen, is reluctant to divide the mind into separate compartments—the intellect, the emotions, and the will—but looks at it as a whole and considers that insanity distorts and impairs the action of the mind as a whole. The existing Rules, which so patently divorce the reason from other mental functions, are peculiarly open to this objection, and it would manifestly be lessened by the addition we have suggested. But the same argument applies, in varying degree, to any attempt to define responsibility in terms of impairment of any particular mental function whose sound operation is conceived to be a necessary element in criminal intent (*mens rea*). It is of course true that in an insane person the power to distinguish right from wrong, or the power of self-control, may be significantly impaired or even wholly lost, and in such a case it is right to hold a person not responsible. Yet these are abstractions from a single undivided reality—the disease of the mind as a whole. Such abstractions

may often be harmless, and may sometimes serve a useful purpose, but they are all too likely to confuse the issue and to mislead those who seek to apply them. The symptoms of the disease can be classified; their effect on conduct can be described; but the state of mind itself remains indefinable. It is that state of mind to which Hamlet refers when he says "Hamlet does it not. . . . Who does it then? His madness." This indefinable state of mind has in different individuals different effects. To abstract particular mental faculties, and to lay it down that unless these particular faculties are destroyed or gravely impaired, an accused person, whatever the nature of his mental disease, must be held to be criminally responsible, is dangerous. Any rule based on such abstractions is liable to be fallible. It may be satisfactory when applied to some, perhaps to the majority, of the criminal cases which come before the courts, but it is likely that in others its application will lead to unjustifiable verdicts of "guilty."

325. On the other hand it may be said with truth that a criterion of criminal responsibility is not necessarily to be rejected because it is imperfect and cannot be guaranteed to cover every case which it ought to cover. All legal definitions necessarily involve an element of abstraction and approximation, which may make their application difficult in marginal cases and may reasonably exclude cases which ought to be included; this is inevitable, since it is precisely the function of the law to draw clear lines for general guidance where there is no clear line in nature, and to deal with the difficulties and anomalies inherent in borderline cases by preserving a reasonable flexibility of interpretation. The rejoinder made to this argument is that, though it is valid generally, there are two reasons that make it inapplicable to the question of criminal responsibility. The first is that a criterion of criminal responsibility in relation to mental disease differs in this important respect from other legal definitions, that, if it is too narrow, it will result in the pronouncing of unjustifiable death sentences. The second is that (for reasons we shall consider more fully in the following paragraphs) a definition of the conditions of responsibility is unnecessary, and in practice only makes the issue more, rather than less, complicated and difficult for the jury.

326. In another sphere the law has already recognized that medical science can have no general definition which, when applied to all the varied types and manifestations of insanity, will enable a doctor to say "if as a result of mental disease the patient is in such or such a state of mind, he is so insane as to be irresponsible, and if he is not in such or such a state of mind, it can safely be inferred that, whatever his mental malady may be, he is not so insane as to be irresponsible for his actions." The lunacy law does not contain any definition of lunacy for the purpose of certification, or require that the magistrate, before making an order placing a lunatic under control, must find that he is in some specified state of mind. It is recognized that to lay down such a rule would be more likely to hinder than to help right decisions. The magistrate, after scrutinizing the medical certificates and making such enquiries as he may think advisable, is called on to exercise his discretion on each individual case, and to decide whether "the alleged lunatic is a lunatic and a proper person to be taken charge of and detained under care and treatment," or, where a petition is presented, whether a reception order "may properly be made."

327. To abrogate the Rules would mean abandoning the assumption that it is necessary to have a rule of law defining the relation of insanity to criminal responsibility; the jury would be left free to decide, in the light of all the evidence given in each particular case, whether the accused was by reason of mental disease (or mental deficiency) not responsible for his actions at the time of the act or omission charged. The objection most strongly urged to this course is that it would lay on the jury a difficult, indeed an impossible, task. It was said that it would require them to decide a purely medical issue beyond their capacity, and that they could not be expected to come to a sound conclusion on technical matters, of which they had no expert knowledge, and which they could not fully understand unless they were able to apply a simple test and the problem was presented to them in terms which they could appreciate and assess as ordinary men and women. We think that this objection is put too high: that it rests on a misapprehension about the nature of the issue and on too low an estimate of the capacity and common sense of juries, which in other contexts were highly praised by many witnesses. The issue, as we have pointed out, is not a purely medical one, but is essentially an ethical question, in which both medicine and the law are closely involved.

Juries have shown themselves capable of deciding extremely complicated, and technical issues without the aid of definitions or formulae, for example in some civil actions in respect of technical or professional negligence, and should not be incapable of deciding the issue of responsibility in cases of insanity or mental abnormality.

328. Indeed, such an addition to the existing Rules as "Was the accused at the time of the act incapable by reason of disease of the mind of preventing himself from committing it?", if interpreted in the broad way in which alone it would be useful (see paragraph 319), might not convey to members of a jury any better or clearer conception of the question they have to decide than the words "Was the accused at the time of his unlawful act insane to such a degree that he was not responsible for his actions?" It may sometimes be very difficult to decide whether the accused was insane to such a degree as not to be responsible for his actions, but in such cases it will usually be equally difficult to decide whether by reason of insanity he was "incapable of preventing himself from committing the act." The difficulties are due to the obscurity of the problem of insanity and to the limitations of present-day knowledge; and these inherent difficulties cannot be mitigated by any definition.

329. The most convincing answer to the objection that this would be too difficult a task for juries seems to us to be that they so often perform it already in cases where the application of the M'Naghten Rules would lead to a clearly wrong verdict. As Mr. Justice Frankfurter said:

I know the danger and the arguments against leaving too much discretion, but I submit with all due respect that at present the discretion is being exercised but not candidly. . . . I think probably the safest thing to do would be to do what they do in Scotland, because it is what it gets down to in the end anyhow.

If this were done, it would not be the first time in the history of English criminal law that juries, with the encouragement of judges, have found their own means of mitigating the harshness of a law that is no longer in accord with common sense or common humanity, and the law has been obliged to follow them at a distance.

330. We recognize that in capital cases pleas of insanity are often advanced on insufficient grounds; and it is important that proper measures should be taken to help the jury to come to right decisions in such cases. Witnesses have told us of the value of the M'Naghten Rules for this purpose. Because the M'Naghten definition is so narrow that it would exclude many good pleas of insanity if it were applied to them, it provides an easy and effective method of ensuring the failure of bad pleas; and it is suggested that some definition will always be essential for this purpose. This seems to us to be a highly questionable argument. If the Rules were abolished, there would of course be some risk of the jury's using their discretion wrongly in either direction, though we do not think it likely that they would send to Broadmoor scoundrels who ought to be convicted and punished. But the risk of human error is an inevitable risk which it is justifiable to take. It is a very different matter to guard against misguided leniency, by enshrining in the law a fallible definition, knowing that its fallibility may conduce to unwarranted sentences of death.

331. The strongest protection against pleas advanced on insufficient grounds is the common sense of juries; and one of the advantages claimed for dispensing with a definition, and placing on the jury express responsibility for deciding whether the accused can properly be held irresponsible, is that it would lessen any risk of jurors thinking that they have not to use their own judgment on this question, but must decide it in accordance with some legal definition.

332. It has been suggested that if there were no legal definition of criminal responsibility, the judges would find it necessary to devise one, or in particular cases to give directions to the jury as to the mental conditions which may exempt a person alleged to be insane from responsibility. But if the duty of deciding this question in the light of the facts of each case were placed squarely on the jury, the Judge, in summing up, would be free—as he was before 1843—to bring to their attention all such evidence as might tell for and against a decision that the accused was so insane as not to be responsible for his actions, and he might be helped rather than hindered by not being required to direct them that they must concentrate their attention on such points as are specified in a legal definition, to the exclusion or subordination of other points which may be of equal or greater importance for the right determination of the particular case before the court.

CONCLUSIONS

333. Our conclusions on this part of our Terms of Reference are as follows:

  (i) (Mr. Fox-Andrews dissenting) that the test of responsibility laid down by the M'Naghten Rules is so defective that the law on the subject ought to be changed.
 (ii) That an addition to the Rules on the lines suggested in paragraph 317 is the best that can be devised, consistently with their primary object, for improving them; and (Mr. Fox-Andrews dissenting) that it would be better to amend them in that way than to leave them as they are.
(iii) (Dame Florence Hancock, Mr. Macdonald and Mr. Radzinowicz dissenting) that a preferable amendment of the law would be to abrogate the Rules and to leave the jury to determine whether at the time of the act the accused was suffering from disease of the mind (or mental deficiency) to such a degree that he ought not to be held responsible.

(We shall also recommend . . . that, whether the M'Naghten Rules are retained, or amended, or abrogated, it should be made clear that mental deficiency no less than disease of the mind is a possible cause of irresponsibility.)

NOTES

1. Minutes of Evidence of Select Committee on the Homicide Law Amendment Bill, 1874, Q. 186.

2. C. Mercier, *Criminal Responsibility* (New York, 1905), p. 169.

3. Minutes of Evidence of the Select Committee on the Homicide Law Amendment Bill, 1874, Q. 274.

DURHAM v. UNITED STATES

U.S. Court of Appeals, D.C. Cir., 1954*

BAZELON, Circuit Judge.

Monte Durham was convicted of housebreaking,[1] by the District Court sitting without a jury. The only defense asserted at the trial was that Durham was of unsound mind at the time of the offense. We are now urged to reverse the conviction (1) because the trial court did not correctly apply existing rules governing the burden of proof on the defense of insanity, and (2) because existing tests of criminal responsibility are obsolete and should be superseded.[2]

I.

Durham has a long history of imprisonment and hospitalization. In 1945, at the age of 17, he was discharged from the Navy after a psychiatric examination had shown that he suffered "from a profound personality disorder which renders him unfit for Naval service." In 1947 he pleaded guilty to violating the National Motor Theft Act[3] and was placed on probation for one to three years. He attempted suicide, was taken to Gallinger Hospital for observation, and was transferred to St. Elizabeths Hospital, from which he was discharged after two months. In January of 1948, as a result of a conviction in the District of Columbia Municipal Court for passing bad checks, the District Court revoked his probation and he commenced service of his Motor Theft sentence. His conduct within the first few days in jail led to a lunacy inquiry in the Municipal Court where a jury found him to be of unsound mind. Upon commitment to St. Elizabeths, he was diagnosed as suffering from "psychosis with psychopathic personality." After 15 months of treatment, he was discharged in July 1949 as "recovered" and was returned to jail to serve the balance of his sentence. In June 1950 he was conditionally released. He violated the conditions by leaving the District. When he learned of a warrant for his arrest as a parole violator, he fled to the "South and Midwest obtaining money by passing a number of bad checks." After he was found and returned to the District, the Parole Board referred him to the District Court for a lunacy inquisition, wherein a jury again found him to be of unsound mind. He was readmitted to St. Elizabeths in February 1951. This time the diagnosis was "without mental disorder, psychopathic personality." He was discharged for the third time in May 1951. The housebreaking which is the subject of the present appeal took place two months later, on July 13, 1951.

According to his mother and the psychiatrist who examined him in September 1951, he suffered from hallucinations immediately after his May 1951 discharge from St. Elizabeths. Following the present indictment, in October 1951, he was adjudged of unsound mind in proceedings under §4244 of Title 18 U.S.C., upon the affidavits of two psychiatrists that he suffered from "psychosis with psychopathic personality." He was committed to St. Elizabeths for the fourth time and given subshock insulin therapy. This commitment lasted 16 months—until February 1953—when he was released to the custody of the District Jail on the certificate of Dr. Silk, Acting Superintendent of St. Elizabeths, that he was "mentally competent to stand trial and . . . able to consult with counsel to properly assist in his own defense."

He was thereupon brought before the court on the charge involved here. The prosecutor told the court:

> So I take this attitude, in view of the fact that he has been over there [St. Elizabeths] a couple of times and these cases that were charged against him were dropped, I don't think I should take the responsibility of dropping these cases against him; then Saint Elizabeths would let him out on the street, and if that man committed a murder next week then it is my responsibility. So we decided to go to trial on one case, that is the case where we found him right in the house, and let him bring in the defense, if he wants to, of unsound mind at the time the crime was committed, and then Your Honor will find him on that, and in your decision send him back to Saint Elizabeths Hospital, and then if they let him out on the street it is their responsibility.

Shortly thereafter, when the question arose whether Durham could be considered competent to stand trial merely on the basis of Dr. Silk's ex parte statement, the court said to defense counsel:

> I am going to ask you this, Mr. Ahern: I have taken the position that if once a person has been found of unsound mind after a lunacy hearing, an ex parte certificate of the superintendent of Saint Elizabeths is not sufficient to set aside that finding and I have held another lunacy hearing. That has been my custom. However, if you want to waive that you may do it, if you admit that he is now of sound mind.

The court accepted counsel's waiver on behalf of Durham, although it had been informed by the pros-

*214 F. 2d 862 (1954). Excerpts only. The footnotes are numbered here as in the original.

ecutor that a letter from Durham claimed need of further hospitalization, and by defense counsel that ". . . the defendant does say that even today he thinks he does need hospitalization; he told me that this morning."[4] Upon being so informed, the court said, "Of course, if I hold he is not mentally competent to stand trial I send him back to Saint Elizabeths Hospital and they will send him back again in two or three months."[5] In this atmosphere Durham's trial commenced.

II.

. . . It has been ably argued by counsel for Durham that the existing tests in the District of Columbia for determining criminal responsibility, that is, the so-called right-wrong test supplemented by the irresistible impulse test, are not satisfactory criteria for determining criminal responsibility. We are urged to adopt a different test to be applied on the retrial of this case. This contention has behind it nearly a century of agitation for reform.

A. The right-wrong test, approved in this jurisdiction in 1882,[13] was the exclusive test of criminal responsibility in the District of Columbia until 1929 when we approved the irresistible impulse test as a supplementary test in Smith v. United States.[14] The right-wrong test has its roots in England. There, by the first quarter of the eighteenth century, an accused escaped punishment if he could not distinguish "good and evil," that is, if he "doth not know what he is doing, no more than . . . a wild beast."[15] Later in the same century, the "wild beast" test was abandoned and "right and wrong" was substituted for "good and evil."[16] And toward the middle of the nineteenth century, the House of Lords in the famous M'Naghten case[17] restated what had become the accepted "right-wrong" test[18] in a form which has since been followed, not only in England[19] but in most American jurisdictions,[20] as an exclusive test of criminal responsibility:

. . . the jurors ought to be told in all cases that every man is to be presumed to be sane, and to possess a sufficient degree of reason to be responsible for his crimes, until the contrary be proved to their satisfaction; and that, to establish a defence on the ground of insanity, it must be clearly proved that, at the time of the committing of the act, the party accused was labouring under such a defect of reason, from disease of the mind, as not to know the nature and quality of the act he was doing, or, if he did know it, that he did not know he was doing what was wrong.[21]

As early as 1838, Isaac Ray, one of the founders of the American Psychiatric Association, in his now classic Medical Jurisprudence of Insanity, called knowledge of right and wrong a "fallacious" test of criminal responsibility.[22] This view has long since been substantiated by enormous developments in knowledge of mental life.[23] In 1928 Mr. Justice Cardozo said to the New York Academy of Medicine: "Everyone concedes that the present [legal] definition of insanity has little relation to the truths of mental life."[24]

Medico-legal writers in large numbers,[25] The Report of the Royal Commission on Capital Punishment 1949–1953,[26] and The Preliminary Report by the Committee on Forensic Psychiatry of the Group for the Advancement of Psychiatry[27] present convincing evidence that the right-and-wrong test is "based on an entirely obsolete and misleading conception of the nature of insanity."[28] The science of psychiatry now recognizes that a man is an integrated personality and that reason, which is only one element in that personality, is not the sole determinant of his conduct. The right-wrong test, which considers knowledge or reason alone, is therefore an inadequate guide to mental responsibility for criminal behavior. As Professor Sheldon Glueck of the Harvard Law School points out in discussing the right-wrong tests, which he calls the knowledge tests:

It is evident that the knowledge tests unscientifically abstract out of the mental make-up but one phase or element of mental life, the cognitive, which, in this era of dynamic psychology, is beginning to be regarded as not the most important factor in conduct and its disorders. In brief, these tests proceed upon the following questionable assumptions of an outworn era in psychiatry: (1) that lack of knowledge of the 'nature or quality' of an act (assuming the meaning of such terms to be clear), or incapacity to know right from wrong, is the sole or even the most important symptom of mental disorder; (2) that such knowledge is the sole instigator and guide of conduct, or at least the most important element therein, and consequently should be the sole criterion of responsibility when insanity is involved; and (3) that the capacity of knowing right from wrong can be completely intact and functioning perfectly even though a defendant is otherwise demonstrably of disordered mind.[29]

Nine years ago we said:

The modern science of psychology . . . does not conceive that there is a separate little man in the top of one's head called reason whose function it is to guide another unruly little man called instinct, emotion, or impulse in the way he should go.[30]

By its misleading emphasis on the cognitive, the right-wrong test requires court and jury to rely upon what is, scientifically speaking, inadequate, and most often, invalid[31] and irrelevant testimony in determining criminal responsibility.[32]

The fundamental objection to the right-wrong test, however, is not that criminal responsibility is made to rest upon an inadequate, invalid or indeterminable symptom or manifestation, but that it is made to rest upon *any* particular symptom.[33] In attempting to define insanity in terms of a symptom, the courts have assumed an impossible role,[34] not merely one for which they have no special competence.[35] As the Royal Commission emphasizes, it is dangerous "to abstract particular mental faculties, and to lay it down that unless these particular faculties are destroyed or gravely impaired, an accused person, whatever the nature of his mental disease, must be held to be criminally responsible. . . ."[36] In this field of law as in others, the fact finder should be free to consider all information advanced by relevant scientific disciplines.[37]

Despite demands in the name of scientific advances, this court refused to alter the right-wrong test at the turn of the century.[38] But in 1929, we considered in response to "the cry of scientific experts" and added the irresistible impulse test as a supplementary test for determining criminal responsibility. Without "hesitation" we declared, in *Smith* v. *United States,* "it to be the law of this District that, in cases where insanity is interposed as a defense, and the facts are sufficient to call for the application of the rule of irresistible impulse, the jury should be so charged."[39] We said:

> . . . The modern doctrine is that the degree of insanity which will relieve the accused of the consequences of a criminal act must be such as to create in his mind an uncontrollable impulse to commit the offense charged. This impulse must be such as to override the reason and judgment and obliterate the sense of right and wrong to the extent that the accused is deprived of the power to choose between right and wrong. The mere ability to distinguish right from wrong is no longer the correct test either in civil or criminal cases, where the defense of insanity is interposed. The accepted rule in this day and age, with the great advancement in medical science as an enlightening influence on this subject, is that the accused must be capable, not only of distinguishing between right and wrong, but that he was not impelled to do the act by an irresistible impulse, which means before it will justify a verdict of acquittal that his reasoning powers were so far dethroned by his diseased mental condition as to deprive him of the will power to resist the insane impulse to perpetrate the deed, though knowing it to be wrong.[40]

As we have already indicated, this has since been the test in the District.

Although the Smith case did not abandon the right-wrong test, it did liberate the fact finder from exclusive reliance upon that discredited criterion by allowing the jury to inquire also whether the accused suffered from an undefined "diseased mental condition [which] deprive[d] him of the will power to resist the insane impulse. . . ."[41] The term "irresistible impulse," however, carries the misleading implication that "diseased mental condition[s]" produce only sudden, momentary or spontaneous inclinations to commit unlawful acts.[42] As the Royal Commission found:

> . . . In many cases . . . this is not true at all. The sufferer from [melancholia, for example] experiences a change of mood which alters the whole of his existence. He may believe, for instance, that a future of such degradation and misery awaits both him and his family that death for all is a less dreadful alternative. Even the thought that the acts he contemplates are murder and suicide pales into insignificance in contrast with what he otherwise expects. The criminal act, in such circumstances, may be the reverse of impulsive. It may be coolly and carefully prepared; yet it is still the act of a madman. This is merely an illustration; similar states of mind are likely to lie behind the criminal act when murders are committed by persons suffering from schizophrenia or paranoid psychoses due to disease of the brain.[43]

We find that as an exclusive criterion the right-wrong test is inadequate in that (a) it does not take sufficient account of psychic realities and scientific knowledge, and (b) it is based upon one symptom and so cannot validly be applied in all circumstances. We find that the "irresistible impulse" test is also inadequate in that it gives no recognition to mental illness characterized by brooding and reflection and so relegates acts caused by such illness to the application of the inadequate right-wrong test. We conclude that a broader test should be adopted.[44]

In the District of Columbia, the formulation of tests of criminal responsibility is entrusted to the courts[45] and, in adopting a new test, we invoke our inherent power to make the change prospectively.[46]

The rule we now hold must be applied on the retrial of this case and in future cases is not unlike that followed by the New Hampshire court since 1870.[47] It is simply that an accused is not criminally responsible if his unlawful act was the product of mental disease or mental defect.[48]

We use "disease" in the sense of a condition which is considered capable of either improving or deteriorating. We use "defect" in the sense of a condition which is not considered capable of either improving or deteriorating and which may be either congenital, or the result of injury, or the residual effect of a physical or mental disease.

Whenever there is "some evidence" that the accused suffered from a diseased or defective mental condition at the time the unlawful act was committed, the trial court must provide the jury with guides for determining whether the accused can be held criminally responsible. We do not, and indeed could not, formulate an instruction which would be either appropriate or binding in all cases. But under the rule now announced, any instruction should in some way convey to the jury the sense and substance of the following: If you the jury believe beyond a reasonable doubt that the accused was not suffering from a diseased or defective mental condition at the time he committed the criminal act charged, you may find him guilty. If you believe he was suffering from a diseased or defective mental condition when he committed the act, but believe beyond a reasonable doubt that the act was not the product of such mental abnormality, you may find him guilty. Unless you believe beyond a reasonable doubt either that he was not suffering from a diseased or defective mental condition, or that the act was not the product of such abnormality, you must find the accused not guilty by reason of insanity. Thus your task would not be completed upon finding, if you did find, that the accused suffered from a mental disease or defect. He would still be responsible for his unlawful act if there was no causal connection between such mental abnormality and the act.[49] These questions must be determined by you from the facts which you find to be fairly deducible from the testimony and the evidence in this case.[50]

The questions of fact under the test we now lay down are as capable of determination by the jury as, for example, the questions juries must determine upon a claim of total disability under a policy of insurance where the state of medical knowledge concerning the disease involved, and its effects, is obscure or in conflict. In such cases, the jury is not required to depend on arbitrarily selected "symptoms, phases or manifestations"[51] of the disease as criteria for determining the ultimate questions of fact upon which the claim depends. Similarly, upon a claim of criminal irresponsibility, the jury will not be required to rely on such symptoms as criteria for determining the ultimate question of fact upon which such claim depends. Testimony as to such "symptoms, phases or manifestations," along with other relevant evidence, will go to the jury upon the ultimate questions of fact which it alone can finally determine. Whatever the state of psychiatry, the psychiatrist will be permitted to carry out his principal court function which, as we noted in Holloway v. U.S., "is to inform the jury of the character of [the accused's] mental disease [or defect]."[52] The jury's range of inquiry will not be limited to, but may include, for example, whether an accused, who suffered from a mental disease or defect did not know the difference between right and wrong, acted under the compulsion of an irresistible impulse, or had "been deprived of or lost the power of his will. . . ."[53]

Finally, in leaving the determination of the ultimate question of fact to the jury, we permit it to perform its traditional function which, as we said in Holloway, is to apply "our inherited ideas of moral responsibility to individuals prosecuted for crime. . . ."[54] Juries will continue to make moral judgments, still operating under the fundamental precept that "Our collective conscience does not allow punishment where it cannot impose blame."[55] But in making such judgments, they will be guided by wider horizons of knowledge concerning mental life. The question will be simply whether the accused acted because of a mental disorder, and not whether he displayed particular symptoms which medical science has long recognized do not necessarily, or even typically, accompany even the most serious mental disorder.[56]

The legal and moral traditions of the western world require that those who, of their own free will and with evil intent (sometimes called *mens rea*), commit acts which violate the law, shall be criminally responsible for those acts. Our traditions also require that where such acts stem from and are the product of a mental disease or defect as those terms are used herein, moral blame shall not attach, and hence there will not be criminal responsibility.[57] The rule we state in this opinion is designed to meet these requirements.

Reversed and remanded for a new trial.

NOTES

1. D.C. Code §§ 22–1801, 22–2201, and 22–2202 (1951).

2. Because the questions raised are of general and crucial importance, we called upon the Government and counsel whom we appointed for the indigent appellant to brief and argue this case a second time. Their able presentations have been of great assistance to us. On the question of the adequacy of prevailing tests of criminal responsibility, we received further assistance from the able brief and argument of Abram Chayes, *amicus curiae* by appointment of this Court, in Stewart v. United States, 94 U.S.App. D.C.—, 214 F.2d 879.

3. 18 U.S.C. § 408 (1946). 1948 Revision, 18 U.S.C. §§ 10, 2311–2313.

4. Durham showed confusion when he testified. These are but two examples:
"Q. Do you remember writing it? A. No. Don't you forget? People get all mixed up in machines.
"Q. What kind of a machine? A. I don't know, they just get mixed up.
"Q. Are you cured now? A. No, sir.
"Q. In your opinion? A. No, sir.
"Q. What is the matter with you? A. You hear people bother you.
"Q. What? You say you hear people bothering you? A. Yes.
"Q. What kind of people? What do they bother you about? A. (No response.)"
Although we think the court erred in accepting counsel's admission that Durham was of sound mind, the matter does not require discussion since we reverse on other grounds and the principles governing this issue are fully discussed in our decision today in Gunther v. United States, 94 U.S.App.D.C.—, 215 F.2d 493.

5. The court also accepted a waiver of trial by jury when Durham indicated, in response to the court's question, that he preferred to be tried without a jury and that he waived his right to a trial by jury.

13. 1882, 12 D.C. 498, 550, 1 Mackey 498, 550. The right-wrong test was reaffirmed in United States v. Lee, 1886, 15 D.C. 489, 496, 4 Mackey 489, 496.

14. 1929, 59 App.D.C. 144, 36 F.2d 548, 70 A.L.R. 654.

15. Glueck, Mental Disorder and the Criminal Law 138–39 (1925), citing Rex v. Arnold, 16 How.St.Tr. 695, 764 (1724).

16. Id. at 142–52, citing Earl Ferrer's case, 19 How.St.Tr. 886 (1760). One writer has stated that these tests originated in England in the 13th or 14th century, when the law began to define insanity in terms of intellect for purposes of determining capacity to manage feudal estates. Comment, *Lunacy and Idiocy—The Old Law and Its Incubus.* 18 U. of Chi.L. Rev. 361 (1951).

17. 8 Eng.Rep. 718 (1843).

18. Hall, Principles of Criminal Law 480, n. 6 (1947).

19. Royal Commission on Capital Punishment 1949–1953 Report (Cmd. 8932) 79 (1953) (hereinafter cited as Royal Commission Report).

20. Weihofen, *The M'Naghten Rule in Its Present Day Setting,* Federal Probation 8 (Sept. 1953); Weihofen, Insanity as a Defense in Criminal Law 15, 64–68, 109–147 (1933); Leland v. State of Oregon, 1952, 343 U.S. 790, 800, 72 S.Ct. 1002, 96 L.Ed. 1302.
"In five States the M'Naghten Rules have been in substance re-enacted by statute." Royal Commission Report 409; see, for example, "Sec. 1120 of the [New York State] Penal Law [McK.Consol. Laws, c. 40] [which] provides that a person is not excused from liability on the grounds of insanity, idiocy or imbecility, except upon proof that at the time of the commission of the criminal act he was laboring under such a defect or reason as (1) not to know the nature and quality of the act he was doing or (2) not to know that the act was wrong." Ploscowe, *Suggested Changes in the New York Laws and Procedures Relating to the Criminally Insane and Mentally Defective Offenders,* 43. J.Crim.L., Criminology & Police Sci. 312, 314 (1952).

21. 8 Eng.Rep. 718, 722 (1843). "Today, Oregon is the only state that requires the accused, on a plea of insanity, to establish that defense beyond a reasonable doubt. Some twenty states, however, place the burden on the accused to establish his insanity by a preponderance of the evidence or some similar measure of persuasion." Leland v. State of Oregon, supra, note 20, 343 U.S. at page 798, 72 S.Ct. 1002. Since Davis v. United States, 1895, 160 U.S. 469, 484, 16 S.Ct. 353, 40 L.Ed. 499, a contrary rule of procedure has been followed in the Federal courts. For example, in compliance with Davis, we held in Tatum v. United States, supra, note 8, 88 U.S.App.D.C. 386, 389, 190 F.2d 612, 615, and text, "as soon as 'some evidence of mental disorder is introduced, . . . sanity, like any other fact, most be provided as part of the prosecution's case beyond a reasonable doubt.' "

22. Ray, Medical Jurisprudence of Insanity 47 and 34 et seq. (1st ed. 1838). "That the insane mind is not entirely deprived of this power of moral discernment, but in many subjects is perfectly rational, and displays the exercise of a sound and well balanced mind is one of those facts now so well established, that to question it would only betray the height of ignorance and presumption." Id. at 32.

23. See Zilboorg, *Legal Aspects of Psychiatry* in One Hundred Years of American Psychiatry 1844–1944, 507, 552 (1944).

24. Cardozo, What Medicine Can Do For the Law 32 (1930).

25. For a detailed bibliography on Insanity as a Defense to Crime, see 7 The Record of the Association of the Bar of the City of New York 158–62 (1952). And see, *for example,* Alexander, the Criminal, the Judge and the Public 70 et seq. (1931); Cardozo, What Medicine Can Do For the Law 28 et seq. (1930); Cleckley, the Mask of Sanity 491 et seq. (2d ed. 1950); Deutsch, The Mentally Ill In America 389–417 (2d ed. 1949); Glueck, Mental Disorder and the Criminal Law (1925). Crime and Justice 96 et seq. (1936); Guttmacher & Weihofen, Psychiatry and the Law 218, 403–23 (1952); Hall, Principles of Criminal Law 477–538 (1947); Menninger, The Human Mind 450 (1937); Hall & Menninger, *"Psychiatry and the Law"—A Dual Review,* 38 Iowa L.Rev. 687 (1953); Overholser, The Psychiatrist and the Law 41–43 (1953); Overholser & Richmond, Handbook of Psychiatry 208–15 (1947); Ploscowe, *Suggested Changes in the New York Laws and Procedures Relating to the Criminally Insane and Mentally Defective Offenders,* 43. J.Crim.L., Criminology & Police Sci. 312, 314 (1952); Ray, Medical Jurisprudence of Insanity (1st ed. 1838) (4th ed. 1860); Reik, *The Doc-Ray Correspondence: A Pioneer Collaboration in the Jurisprudence of Mental Disease,* 63 Yale L.J. 183 (1953); Weihofen, Insanity as a Defense in Criminal Law (1933), *The M'Naghten Rule in Its Present Day Setting,* Federal Probation 8 (Sept. 1953); Zilboorg, Mind, Medicine and Man 246–97 (1943), *Legal Aspects of Psychiatry,* American Psychiatry 1844–1944, 507 (1944).

26. Royal Commission Report 73–129.

27. The Committee on Forensic Psychiatry (whose report is hereinafter cited as Gap Report) was composed of Drs. Philip Q. Roche, Frank S. Curran, Lawrence Z. Freedman and Manfred S. Guttmacher. They were assisted in their deliberations by leading psychiatrists, jurists, law professors, and legal practitioners.

28. Royal Commission Report 80.

29. Glueck, *Psychiatry and the Criminal Law,* 12 Mental Hygiene 575, 580 (1928), as quoted in Deutsch, The Mentally Ill in America 396 (2d ed. 1949); and see, *for example,* Menninger, The Human Mind 450 (1937); Guttmacher & Weihofen, Psychiatry and the Law 403–08 (1952).

30. Holloway v. United States, 1945, 80 U.S.App.D.C. 3, 5, 148 F.2d 665, 667, certiorari denied, 1948, 334 U.S. 852, 68 S.Ct. 1507, 92 L.Ed. 1774.
More recently, the Royal Commission, after an exhaustive survey of legal, medical and lay opinion in many Western countries, including England and the United States made a similar finding. It reported: "The gravamen of the charge against the M'Naghten Rules is that they are not in harmony with modern medical science, which, as we have seen, is reluctant to divide the mind into separate compartments—the intellect, the emotions and the will—but looks at it as a whole and considers that insanity distorts and impairs the action of the mind as a whole." Royal Commission Report 113. The Commission lends vivid support to this conclusion by pointing out that "It would be impossible to apply modern methods of care and treatment in mental hospitals, and at the same time to maintain order and discipline, if the great majority of the patients, even among the grossly insane, did not know what is forbidden by the rules and that, if they break them, they are liable to forfeit some privilege. Examination of a number of guilty but insane [the nearest English equivalent of our acquittal by reason of insanity] was returned, and rightly returned, has convinced us that there are few indeed where the accused can truly be said not to have known that his act was wrong." Id. at 103.

31. See Guttmacher & Weihofen, Psychiatry and the Law 421, 422 (1952). The M'Naghten rules "constitute not only an arbitrary restriction on vital medical data, but also impose an improper onus of decision upon the expert witness. The Rules are unanswerable in that they have no consensus with established psychiatric criteria of symptomatic description save for the case of disturbed consciousness or of idiocy, . . ." From statement by Dr. Philip Q. Roche, quoted id. at 407. See also United States ex rel. Smith v. Baldi, 3 Cir., 1951, 192 F.2d 540, 567 (dissenting opinion).

32. In a very recent case, the Supreme Court of New Mexico recognized the inadequacy of the right-wrong test, and adopted what it called an "extension of the M'Naghten Rules." Under this extension, lack of knowledge of right and wrong is not essential for acquittal "if, by reason of disease of the mind, defendant has been deprived of or lost the power of his will. . . ." State v. White, N.M., 270 P.2d 727, 730.

33. Deutsch, The Mentally Ill in America 400 (2d ed. 1949); Keedy, *Irresistible Impulses as a Defense in Criminal Law,* 100 U. of Pa. Law Rev. 956, 992 (1952).

34. John Whitehorn of the Johns-Hopkins Medical School, in an informal memorandum on this subject for a Commission on Legal Psychiatry appointed by the Governor of Maryland, has said: "Psychiatrists are challenged to set forth a crystal-clear statement of what constitutes insanity. It is impossible to express this adequately in words, alone, since such diagnostic judgments involve clinical skill and experience which cannot wholly be verbalized. . . . The medical profession would be baffled if asked to write into the legal code universally valid criteria for the diagnosis of the many types of psychotic illness which may seriously disturb a person's responsibility, and even if this were attempted, the diagnostic criteria would have to be rewritten from time to time, with the progress of psychiatric knowledge." Quoted in Guttmacher & Weihofen, Psychiatry and the Law 419–20 (1952).

35. ". . . the legal profession were invading the province of medicine, and attempting to install old exploded medical theories in the place of facts established in the progress of scientific knowledge." State v. Pike, 1870, 49 N.H. 399, 438.

36. Royal Commission Report 114. And see State v. Jones, 1871, 50 N.H. 369, 392–393.

37. Keedy, *Irresistible Impulse as a Defense in Criminal Law,* 100 U. of Pa.L. Rev. 956, 992–93 (1952).

38. See, for example, Taylor v. United States, 1895, 7 App.D.C. 27, 41–44, where we rejected "emotional insanity" as a defense, citing with approval the following from the trial court's instruction to the jury: "Whatever may be the cry of scientific experts, the law does not recognize, but condemns the doctrine of emotional insanity—that a man may be sane up until a moment before he commits a crime, insane while he does it, and sane again soon afterwards. Such a doctrine would be dangerous in the extreme. The law does not recognize it; and a jury cannot without violating their oaths." This position was emphatically reaffirmed in Snell v. United States, 1900, 16 App.D.C. 501, 524.

39. 1929, 59 App.D.C. 144, 146, 36 F.2d 548, 550, 70 A.L.R. 654.

40. 59 App.D.C. at page 145, 36 F.2d at page 549.

41. 59 App.D.C. at page 145, 36 F.2d at page 549.

42. Impulse, as defined by Webster's New International Dictionary (2d ed. 1950), is:
"1. Act of impelling, or driving onward with *sudden* force;

impulsion, esp., force so communicated as to produce motion *suddenly,* or *immediately*. . . .
"2. An incitement of the mind or spirit, esp. in the form of an *abrupt* and vivid suggestion, prompting some *unpremeditated* action or leading to unforeseen knowledge or insight; a *spontaneous* inclination. . . .
"3. . . . motion produced by a *sudden* or *momentary* force. . . ." [Emphasis supplied.]

43. Royal Commission Report 110; for additional comment on the irresistible impulse test, see Glueck, Crime and Justice 101–03 (1936); Guttmacher & Weihofen, Psychiatry and the Law 410–12 (1952); Hall, General Principles of Criminal Law 505–26 (1947); Keedy, *Irresistible Impulse as a Defense in Criminal Law,* 100 U. of Pa.L.Rev. 956 (1952); Wertham, The Show of Violence 14 (1949).
The New Mexico Supreme Court in recently adopting a broader criminal insanity rule, note 32, supra, observed: ". . . insanity takes the form of the personality of the individual and, if his tendency is toward depression, his wrongful act may come at the conclusion of a period of complete lethargy, thoroughly devoid of excitement."

44. As we recently said, ". . . former common law should not be followed where changes in conditions have made it obsolete. We have never hesitated to exercise the usual judicial function of revising and enlarging the common law." Linkins v. Protestant Episcopal Cathedral Foundation, 1950, 87 U.S.App.D.C. 351, 355, 187 F.2d 357, 361, 28 A.L.R. 2d 521, Cf. Funk v. United States, 1933, 290 U.S. 371, 381–382, 43 S.Ct. 212, 78 L.Ed. 369.

45. Congress, like most state legislatures, has never undertaken to define insanity in this connection, although it recognizes the fact that an accused may be acquitted by reason of insanity. See D.C. Code § 24–301 (1951). And as this court made clear in Hill v. United States, Congress has left no doubt that "common-law procedure, in all matters relating to crime . . . still continues in force here in all cases except where special provision is made by statute to the exclusion of the common-law procedure." 22 App.D.C. 395, 401 (1903), and statutes cited therein; Linkins v. Protestant Episcopal Cathedral Foundation, 87 U.S. App.D.C. at pages 354–55, 187 F.2d at pages 360–361; and see Fisher v. United States, 1946, 328 U.S. 463, 66 S.Ct. 1318, 90 L.Ed. 1382.

46. See Great Northern R. v. Sunburst Oil & Refining Co., 1932, 287 U.S. 358, 53 S.Ct. 145, 77 L.Ed. 360; National Labor Relations Board v. Guy F. Atkinson Co., 9 Cir., 1952, 195 F.2d 141, 148; Concurring opinion of Judge Frank in Aero Spark Plug Co. v. B. G. Corporation, 2 Cir., 1942, 130 F.2d 290, 298, and note 24; Warring v. Colpoys, 1941, 74 App.D.C. 303, 122 F.2d 642, 645, 136 A.L.R. 1025; Moore & Oglebay, *The Supreme Court, Stare Decisis and Law of the Case,* 21 Texas L.Rev. 514, 535 (1943); Carpenter, *Court Decisions and the Common Law,* 17 Col.L.Rev. 593, 606–07 (1917). But see von Moschzisker, *Stare Decisis in Courts of Last Resort.* 37 Harv.L.Rev. 409, 426 (1924). Our approach is similar to that of the Supreme Court of California in People v. Maughs, 1906, 149 Cal. 253, 86 P. 187, 191, where the court prospectively invalidated a previously accepted instruction, saying:
". . . we think the time has come to say that in all future cases which shall arise, and where, after this warning, this instruction shall be given, this court will hold the giving of it to be so prejudicial to the rights of a defendant, secured to him by our Constitution and laws, as to call for the reversal of any judgment which may be rendered against him."

47. State v. Pike, 1870, 49 N.H. 399.

48. Cf. State v. Jones, 1871, 50 N.H. 369, 398.

49. "There is no *a priori* reason why every person suffering from any form of mental abnormality or disease, or from any particular kind of mental disease, should be treated by the law as not answerable for any criminal offence which he may commit, and be exempted from conviction and punishment. Mental abnormalities vary infinitely in their nature and intensity and in their effects on the character and conduct of those who suffer from them. Where a person suffering from a mental abnormality commits a crime, there must always be some likelihood that the abnormality has played some part in the causation of the crime; and, generally speaking, the graver the abnormality, . . . the more probable it must be that there is a causal connection between them. But the closeness of this connection will be shown by the facts brought in evidence in individual cases and cannot be decided on the basis of any general medical principle." Royal Commission Report 99.

50. The court may always, of course, if it deems it advisable for the assistance of the jury, point out particular areas of agreement and conflict in the expert testimony in each case, just as it ordinarily does in summing up any other testimony.

51. State v. Jones, 1871, 50 N.H. 369, 398.

52. 1945, 80 U.S.App.D.C. 3, 5, 148 F.2d 665, 667.

53. State v. White, see n. 32, supra.

54. 80 U.S.App.D.C. at page 5, 148 F.2d at page 667.

55. 80 U.S.App.D.C. at pages 4–5, 148 F.2d at pages 666–667.

56. See text, supra, 214 F.2d 870–872.

57. An accused person who is acquitted by reason of insanity is presumed to be insane, Orencia v. Overholser, 1947, 82 U.S.App.D.C. 285, 163 F.2d 763; Barry v. White, 1933, 62 App.D.C. 69, 64 F.2d 707, and may be committed for an indefinite period to a "hospital for the insane." D.C.Code § 24–301 (1951).

We think that even where there has been a specific finding that the accused was competent to stand trial and to assist in his own defense, the court would be well advised to invoke this Code provision so that the accused may be confined as long as "the public safety and . . . [his] welfare" require. Barry v. White, 62 App.D.C. at page 71, 64 F.2d at page 709.

THE AMERICAN LAW INSTITUTE

From the Model Penal Code*

ARTICLE 4, RESPONSIBILITY

SECTION 4.01. MENTAL DISEASE OR DEFECT EXCLUDING RESPONSIBILITY

(1) A person is not responsible for criminal conduct if at the time of such conduct as a result of mental disease or defect he lacks substantial capacity either to appreciate the criminality of his conduct or to conform his conduct to the requirements of law.

(2) The terms "mental disease or defect" do not include an abnormality manifested only by repeated criminal or otherwise antisocial conduct.

Alternative formulations of paragraph (1)

(a) A person is not responsible for criminal conduct if at the time of such conduct as a result of mental disease or defect his capacity either to appreciate the criminality of his conduct or to conform his conduct to the requirements of law is so substantially impaired that he cannot justly be held responsible.

(b) A person is not responsible for criminal conduct if at the time of such conduct as a result of mental disease or defect he lacks substantial capacity to appreciate the criminality of his conduct or is in such state that the prospect of conviction and punishment cannot constitute a significant restraining influence upon him.

* * *

COMMENTS § 4.01. ARTICLE 4. RESPONSIBILITY

SECTION 4.01. MENTAL DISEASE OR DEFECT EXCLUDING RESPONSIBILITY

THE PROBLEM OF DEFINING THE CRITERIA OF IRRESPONSIBILITY

1. No problem in the drafting of a penal code presents larger intrinsic difficulty than that of determining when individuals whose conduct would otherwise be criminal ought to be exculpated on the ground that they were suffering from mental disease or defect when they acted as they did. What is involved specifically is the drawing of a line between the use of public agencies and public force to condemn the offender by conviction, with resultant sanctions in which there is inescapably a punitive ingredient (however constructive we may attempt to make the process of correction) and modes of disposition in which that ingredient is absent, even though restraint may be involved. To put the matter differently, the problem is to discriminate between the cases where a punitive-correctional disposition is appropriate and those in which a medical-custodial disposition is the only kind the law should allow.

2. The traditional M'Naghten rule resolves the problem solely in regard to the capacity of the individual to know what he was doing and to know that it was wrong. Absent these minimal elements of rationality, condemnation and punishment are obviously both unjust and futile. They are unjust because the individual could not, by hypothesis, have employed reason to restrain the act; he did not and he could not know the facts essential to bring reason into play. On the same ground, they are futile. A madman who believes that he is squeezing lemons when he chokes his wife or thinks that homicide is the command of God is plainly beyond reach of the restraining influence of

law; he needs restraint but condemnation is entirely meaningless and ineffective. Thus the attacks on the M'Naghten rule as an inept definition of insanity or as an arbitrary definition in terms of special symptoms are entirely misconceived. The *rationale* of the position is that these are cases in which reason can not operate and in which it is totally impossible for individuals to be deterred. Moreover, the category defined by the rule is so extreme that to the ordinary man the exculpation of the persons it encompasses bespeaks no weakness in the law. He does not identify such persons and himself; they are a world apart.

Jurisdictions in which the M'Naghten test has been expanded to include the case where mental disease produces an "irresistible impulse" proceed on the same *rationale*. They recognize, however, that cognitive factors are not the only ones that preclude inhibition; that even though cognition still obtains, mental disorder may produce a total incapacity for self-control. The same result is sometimes reached under M'Naghten proper, in the view, strongly put forth by Stephen, that "knowledge" requires more than the capacity to verbalize right answers to a question, it implies capacity to function in the light of knowledge. Stephen, *History of English Criminal Law*, Vol. 2, p. 171. . . . In modern psychiatric terms, the "fundamental difference between verbal or purely intellectual knowledge and the mysterious other kind of knowledge is familiar to every clinical psychiatrist; it is the difference between knowledge divorced from affect and knowledge so fused with affect that it becomes a human reality." Zilboorg, "Misconceptions of Legal Insanity," 9 *Am. J. Orthopsychiatry*, pp. 540, 552. . . .

3. The draft accepts the view that any effort to exclude the nondeterrables from strictly penal sanctions must take account of the impairment of volitional capacity no less than of impairment of cognition; and that this result should be achieved directly in the formulation of the test, rather than left to mitigation in the application of M'Naghten. It also accepts the criticism of the "irresistible impulse" formulation as inept in so far as it may be impliedly restricted to sudden, spontaneous acts as distinguished from insane propulsions that are accompanied by brooding or reflection. . . .

Both the main formulation recommended and alternative (a) deem the proper question on this branch of the inquiry to be whether the defendant is without capacity to conform his conduct to the requirements of law. . . .

Alternative (b) states the issue differently. Instead of asking whether the defendant had capacity to conform his conduct to the requirements of law, it asks whether, in consequence of mental disease or defect, the threat of punishment could not exercise a significant restraining influence upon him. To some extent, of course, these are the same inquiries. To the extent that they diverge, the latter asks a narrower and harder question, involving the assessment of capacity to respond to a single influence, the threat of punishment. Both Dr. Guttmacher and Dr. Overholser considered the assessment of responsiveness to this one influence too difficult for psychiatric judgment. Hence, though the issue framed by the alternative may well be thought to state the question that is most precisely relevant for legal purposes, the Reporter and the Council deemed the inquiry impolitic upon this ground. In so far as nondeterrability is the determination that is sought, it must be reached by probing general capacity to conform to the requirements of law. The validity of this conclusion is submitted, however, to the judgment of the Institute.

4. One further problem must be faced. In addressing itself to impairment of the cognitive capacity, M'Naghten demands that impairment be complete: the actor must *not* know. So, too, the irresistible impulse criterion presupposes a complete impairment of capacity for self-control. The extremity of these conceptions is, we think, the point that poses largest difficulty to psychiatrists when called upon to aid in their administration. The schizophrenic, for example, is disoriented from reality; the disorientation is extreme; but it is rarely total. Most psychotics will respond to a command of someone in authority within the mental hospital; they thus have some capacity to conform to a norm. But this is very different from the question whether they have the capacity to conform to requirements that are not thus immediately symbolized by an attendant or policeman at the elbow. Nothing makes the inquiry into responsibility more unreal for the psychiatrist than limitation of the issue to some ultimate extreme of total incapacity, when clinical experience reveals only a graded scale with marks along the way. . . .

We think this difficulty can and must be met. The law must recognize that when there is no black and white it must content itself with different shades of gray. The draft, accordingly, does not demand *complete* impairment of capacity. It asks instead for *substantial* impairment. This is all, we think, that candid witnesses, called on to infer the nature of the situation at a time that they did not observe, can ever confidently say, even when they know that a disorder was extreme.

If substantial impairment of capacity is to suffice, there remains the question whether this alone should be the test or whether the criterion should state the principle that measures how substantial it must be. To identify the degree of impairment with precision is, of course, impossible both verbally and logically. The recommended formulation is content to rest upon the term "substantial" to support the weight of judgment; if capacity is greatly impaired, that presumably should be sufficient. Alternative (a) proposes to submit the issue squarely to the jury's sense of justice, asking expressly whether the capacity of the defendant "was so substantially impaired that he cannot justly be held responsible." Some members of the Council deemed it unwise to present questions of justice to the jury, preferring a submission that in form, at least, confines the inquiry to fact. The proponents of the alternative contend that since the jury normally will feel that it is only just to exculpate if the disorder was extreme, that otherwise conviction is demanded, it is safer to invoke the jury's sense of justice than to rest entirely on the single word "substantial," imputing no specific measure of degree. The issue is an important one and it is submitted for consideration by the Institute.

5. The draft rejects the formulation warmly supported by psychiatrists and recently adopted by the Court of Appeals for the District of Columbia in *Durham* v. *United States*, 214, F. 2d 862 (1954), namely, "that an accused is not criminally responsible if his unlawful act was the product of mental disease or defect." . . .

The difficulty with this formulation inheres in the ambiguity of "product." If interpreted to lead to irresponsibility unless the defendant would have engaged in the criminal conduct even if he had not suffered from the disease or defect, it is too broad: an answer that he would have done so can be given very rarely; this is intrinsic to the concept of the singleness of personality and unity of mental processes that psychiatry regards as fundamental. If interpreted to call for a standard of causality less relaxed than but-for cause, there are but two alternatives to be considered: (1) a mode of causality involving total incapacity or (2) a mode of causality which involves substantial incapacity. See Wechsler, "The Criteria of Criminal Responsibility," 22 *U. of Chi. L. Rev.* (1955), p. 367. But if either of these causal concepts is intended, the formulation ought to set it forth.

The draft also rejects the proposal of the majority of the recent Royal Commission on Capital Punishment, namely, "to leave to the jury to determine whether at the time of the act the accused was suffering from disease of the mind (or mental deficiency) to such a degree that he ought not to be held responsible." *Report* (1953), par. 333, p. 116. While we agree, as we have indicated, that mental disease or defect involves gradations of degree that should be recognized, we think the legal standard ought to focus on the *consequences* of disease or defect that have a bearing on the justice of conviction and of punishment. The Royal Commission proposal fails in this respect.

6. Paragraph (2) of section 4.01 is designed to exclude from the concept of "mental disease or defect" the case of so-called "psychopathic personality." The reason for the exclusion is that, as the Royal Commission put it, psychopathy "is a statistical abnormality; that is to say, the psychopath differs from a normal person only quantitatively or in degree, not qualitatively; and the diagnosis of psychopathic personality does not carry with it any explanation of the causes of the abnormality." While it may not be feasible to formulate a definition of "disease," there is much to be said for excluding a condition that is manifested only by the behavior phonomena that must, by hypothesis, be the result of disease for irresponsibility to be established. Although British psychiatrists have agreed, on the whole, that psychopathy should not be called "disease," there is considerable difference of opinion on the point in the United States. Yet it does not seem useful to contemplate the litigation of what is essentially a matter of terminology; nor is it right to have the legal result rest upon the resolution of a dispute of this kind.

HYMAN GROSS

Mental Abnormality As a Criminal Excuse*

A person's mental condition at the time he engages in criminal conduct may relieve him from criminal liability. When this is the case, we say that he is not criminally liable because he was not a responsible person at the time of the offense. To say that one was not responsible in this sense is to assert the most personal of all excuses. What interests us is not something about the performance but something about the actor. The actor is said not to have had available those personal resources that are necessary to qualify him as accountable for his conduct. Since he is not accountable he cannot be faulted for his conduct and so enjoys exemption from judgments of culpability.

Mental abnormality of a sort relevant to excusing exists, then, when mental resources necessary for accountability are lacking. There are four varieties of relevant abnormality: One is mental illness that, formerly in medical literature and still in legal literature, would be characterized as a *disease* of the mind, by virtue of a sufficiently definite pathology and sufficiently pronounced morbidity. Intoxication, whatever its source, is another variety. Mental defectiveness is a third sort of relevant abnormality, encompassing cases of serious deficiency mainly in intelligence but including deficiency of any mental capacity necessary to control behavior. Finally, there is a variety of abnormality that may be conveniently referred to as automatism, which includes behavioral phenomena diverse in origin but which all are instances of a gross separation of consciousness and action such as exists during hypnosis, somnambulism, and epileptic seizures.

Relevant impairments of mental capacity may have an origin which is extrapsychic or intrapsychic. Drugs, alcohol, hypnotic suggestion, a blow on the head, emotional shock, an extra chromo-some, or a brain tumor are all ways in which incapacitation may be produced by external interventions upon normal mental functioning. It is clear that a person may himself be responsible for some of these interventions by doing something to himself or allowing others to. When this is the case, he is deemed responsible for the resulting condition he is in, though not otherwise. Still, one's being responsible for his condition does not always entail being criminally liable for what he does while in that condition. If he suffers mental incapacitation sufficient for him not to be responsible, he is then treated as one who is not, regardless of his having been a responsible person with reference to putting himself in that condition. A person may ultimately cause himself to suffer sieges of delirium tremens by the gradual effects of his own alcoholic indulgence. Yet he is entitled to be treated as not responsible regarding acts done during those sieges no less than a person whose delusions have an origin utterly beyond his control. But if a person while responsible does things to put himself in a state of incapacitation in which harmful conduct is expectable—he intoxicates himself to a dangerous degree—he may be liable for that when the harm occurs or, even without it occurring, when he engages in conduct that threatens the harm. The reason is that incapacitating himself while still a responsible person is itself a dangerous act, and so may be regarded as culpable. Other examples would be persons who willingly submit to drugs or hypnosis under circumstances portending harm, or who place themselves in dangerous situations knowing they are epileptics or sleepwalkers prone to violence. Culpability in such cases properly extends only to conduct that produces the loss of capacity and not the further conduct that is engaged in while the person is not responsible. One person may kill another quite deliberately under delusions produced by drugs taken quite deliberately, yet culpability is not for deliberate killing because the accused is not responsible at all for his homicidal conduct but only for the act of taking the drugs.

*This essay appears in a slightly altered version at pages 293–316 of *A Theory of Criminal Justice,* by Hyman Gross (Oxford University Press, 1979).

Not without some awkwardness in principle, the lesser culpability is usually reflected in the criminal law by liability for homicide of a lesser degree.

When mental impairment is intrapsychic in origin, the excuse based on it is received more charily. The same debilitation which would easily pass muster for an excuse if externally induced is regarded with skepticism when its origin is not palpably outside the mind of the actor. Initial suspicion is indeed warranted because of increased opportunity for deception. But even after genuineness of the psychopathology is established, there is often lingering skepticism regarding its significance for judgments of responsibility. This skepticism is justified to the extent that it reflects sound opinion that the actor was quite capable of doing otherwise in spite of his illness. But it is not justified when it reflects the belief that a person is in some measure responsible for his mental illness since its origins are within him and, unlike the case of mental abnormalities having identifiable physical causes, it pertains to him in an especially intimate way because of its purely psychic character. Holding a person responsible for his mental illness is in general even more unjust than holding him responsible for his physical illness. Such medical knowledge as we have bearing on the etiology of serious mental illness makes it quite clear that in most cases the sick person could not reasonably be expected to do such things as would probably have prevented the onset of his illness, while in the case of physical illness effective precautions often might quite easily have been taken.

II

It is not any mental abnormality that excuses. Even when the abnormality is of a kind that is relevant to responsibility, certain conditions of incapacitation must be met if there is to be an excuse. In the criminal law these conditions have been formulated as rules which govern the insanity defense. These rules look mainly to mental illness and defectiveness, but the conditions for excusing under them have a rationale which extends to mental abnormality of whatever variety. Four basic versions of this defense have developed in the criminal law and, as shall be shown, the conditions required by each are less dissimilar from those required by the others than would appear from the terms used in formulating each. The first version, which dominates among Anglo-American jurisdictions, turns out to be too meager. The second of these versions (which in some form is now the law in a third of the American

jurisdictions and under the Model Penal Code) represents the most satisfactory statement. The third and fourth versions, though lending themselves to suitably restrictive interpretation, as they stand offer too great opportunity for unwarranted excuses and in fact are the versions most often preferred by those advocating unsound excuses. First, each version will be briefly scanned and then good reasons will be distinguished from bad among excuses of this sort. The concern here is only with why a person is not responsible, and so the very difficult medical questions having to do with exactly what states of abnormality leave a person in a condition in which he is not responsible will remain unexplored. Only the more basic question of what it means not to be responsible is taken up here. But without answers to that, one does not know what exculpatory significance, if any, to attach ultimately to the medical facts.

The first version of the insanity defense is represented by the M'Naghten rules. Stated in their original terms, these rules provide that a person has a defense of insanity if he did not know the nature and quality of the act he was doing, or did not know that it was wrong, because laboring under a defect of reason from disease of the mind. There was in the original M'Naghten rules a further proviso that, even if not so afflicted, a person would have a defense if at the time of his act he was suffering from an insane delusion about something such that if—but only if—it were in fact the case, it would furnish a defense. This part of the M'Naghten rules has been generally disregarded because of the limitation it places on delusions which may excuse, though as we shall see the right reason for ignoring the rule on these grounds has not been generally apprehended. There has been a continuing need for a rule extending the defense generally to all those who have insane delusions about the circumstances under which they act, and this requirement has encouraged strained applications of the remainder of the M'Naghten doctrine to cover such cases.

Despite variations in language and differences in fine points of interpretation, the gist of the M'Naghten formula has remained unchanged in the many jurisdictions that have adopted it since its introduction in England well over a century ago. Serious incapacitation may make it impossible for the actor to be sufficiently aware of what he is doing so that he could choose to do otherwise. It may deprive him of appreciation of the harmfulness of his conduct, or of appreciation of the harm itself, so that a normal disposition to restrain harmful conduct is not aroused. It may deprive him of the ability to comprehend the circumstances in which he acts and so make it impossible for him to choose not to do what under the circumstances is not justifiable. It may make him incapable of knowing that the law prohibits what he does, when only the fact of legal prohibition is a reason for not doing it. In any of these cases, because of a failure of personal resources he cannot help what he does.

The second version of the insanity defense consists of some form of M'Naghten to which is added an excuse based on grossly deficient inhibitory capacity. This additional part is usually referred to as the irresistible impulse rule, though any suggestion that the act need be impulsive to qualify would be seriously misleading. Under this provision, if the accused was incapable of restraining himself from doing what he knew he was doing and knew he ought not to be doing, he may invoke as an excuse his inability to exercise self-control.

The gravamen of this excuse is again the actor's helplessness in being unable to avoid doing or causing harm. The excuse is even stronger than the claim of compulsion that is asserted when one has been forced to do something harmful. Instead of succumbing to pressures which one is nevertheless able to resist, the person without significant capacity for inhibition is simply unable to resist. The excuse is sometimes misconceived, however, so that it is the untoward urge rather than the inhibitory failure which receives primary attention. This distorts the rationale of the excuse. We do not excuse because the actor wanted very desperately to do what he did. By itself powerful determination to do harm is not grounds for exemption from judgments of culpability. On the contrary, it is grounds for a judgment of greater culpability.

The third version of the insanity defense makes mental disease or defect, *when it produces criminal conduct,* the basis of an excuse for that conduct. This version has been adopted in four American jurisdictions (though recently discarded in the one that gave it the name by which it is best known), enjoys considerable psychiatric advocacy, and is generally referred to as the Durham rule. It relies heavily in practice on the same rationale of excuse as the previous version, but offers opportunities for the troublesome departures that will be discussed shortly.

A final version is constituted by those criminal insanity provisions in which mental derangement or deficiency at the time of the act is itself an excuse. The actor need only be seriously defective or not in possession of his faculties in order for his conduct in such a state to be excusable. Unlike the previous version, the relation between the abnormality and the criminal conduct is not of concern here so long as the two are contemporaneous. This version has in somewhat primitive forms preceded M'Naghten in the commom law and now appears in the criminal law of some civil law jurisdictions. It enjoys strong support among those of the medical profession who are interested in these forensic matters and is probably even more congenial to psychiatric views of the insanity defense than is the Durham version. As with Durham there is heavy reliance in practice on the same rationale of excuse that support M'Naghten and irresistible impulse; but again, as with Durham, opportunities for excusing on other grounds are made possible, and these call for careful investigation.

III

The preceding discussion has shown what grounds the law has recognized for an excuse of mental abnormality when the excuse is presented in its most dramatic form as the insanity defense. Many of those who favor the third or fourth version of the insanity defense think it a good defense simply that a person was mentally ill at the time of his criminal act, or that his criminal conduct was a result of the mental illness he suffered at the time. There are three important arguments here, one grounded in moral considerations regarding avoidance of cruelty, and the other two in exculpatory considerations thought to apply to sick persons.

The first contention is that it is wrong to punish a person *when he is sick.* It is generally regarded as inhumane to neglect the suffering of those who are in a debilitated condition and even more inhumane to inflict further suffering on them. It would therefore be barbarous if the criminal law not only withheld comfort and cure from the sick who are subject to its processes but imposed upon such persons a penal regime. Directed to present concerns, this principle of humane treatment clearly requires that a person mentally abnormal at the time of his crime not be subjected to punitive treatment while he continues to be in such a state, but that instead he receive medical treatment.

The principle of humane treatment is unquestionably sound and must be given full effect at all times. It does not, however, confer a cloak of immunity on persons who are sick when committing a crime. Conduct may be culpable even though the actor had chicken pox, pneumonia or multiple sclerosis. It may be culpable when the disorder is mental rather than physical. When a sick person's conduct is culpable, he is to be treated for his illness so long as it lasts by those in whose hands he is placed by virtue of liability for such culpable conduct. But liability for culpable conduct is not avoided by the mere fact of sickness. It is also true that even determination of liability to punishment must be postponed if the continuing illness of the accused makes impossible the proceedings necessary for a just determination of liability, and that those having custody of him must during this time abide by the imperatives of humane treatment. But again there is nothing in this to entitle the accused to exemption from liability.

A second argument derives from general requirements for culpability. It is wrong to punish someone *for being sick*. The reason is that in being sick a person has not done anything blameworthy. Since merely falling ill does not constitute culpable conduct, it may not be punished. (A person might indeed be rightly blamed for making himself sick, or allowing himself to become or to be made sick, and we might well decide that such conduct then deserves punishment when it was understood that the well-being of others depended upon the fitness of the one who became sick. In such a case there is culpability because the accused could have acted to prevent his illness.)

But insofar as a person is being punished for his conduct and not for his disorder, the requirement of culpability is not transgressed. Nevertheless, it is sometimes claimed that when a mentally disordered person is punished for his conduct, he is being punished for his disorder since the conduct is a symptom of it. Such claims are especially prominent in arguments advocating extension of a mental abnormality defense to those persons, often characterized as psychopaths or sociopaths, whose dedication to wrongdoing is especially strong and free of internal conflicts. This claim rests on a misunderstanding of what it means to be punished for something. A person may be punished for a criminal act and that act may in various other perspectives be viewed quite accurately as a symptom of his illness, or indeed of society's illness, as an act of dedicated self-sacrifice, or as an act to advance a socially worthwhile cause. Still in all these cases we are punishing him only for his culpable conduct. We may punish in spite of causes, motives, or intentions, so long as they

do not furnish an excuse or other reason for not punishing.

The third argument is that it is wrong to punish someone for what he does *as a result of being mentally sick*. Unlike the previous argument, the position here is not that it is wrong to punish someone for the illness evidenced by criminal conduct, but rather that it is wrong to punish someone for his conduct when it is *produced* by the disorder. The criminal conduct is not viewed as part of a pattern of behavior such that if one so behaves one must by that very fact be judged to be abnormal. Rather the conduct is viewed as determined by the abnormality in the sense that but for the abnormality there would have been no warrant for expecting such conduct.

Treating the fact that conduct resulted from mental abnormality as a reason to excuse the conduct leaves us with no principle on which to rest the excuse. Exculpation by way of justification would indeed be warranted by a principle that what is morbidly determined is not wrong, but there are no good reasons for recognizing as a justifying principle the proposition that condemnation ought to be restricted to healthy determinations to act harmfully. It is true that a person's mental abnormality, if it is to excuse his criminal conduct, must in some significant way be related to that conduct as its cause. This may be put in an even stronger form by saying that we ought to excuse when, but only when, conduct is the "product" of abnormality in the sense that the abnormality is a sufficient condition for the conduct. In that case, but only in that case, the accused was unable to do otherwise because of the abnormality and so is entitled to be excused. It is not true that we ought to excuse simply because the wrong thing that was done would likely not have been done but for the abnormality. Otherwise we should have to excuse anyone who acted from some untoward tendency attributable to a mental abnormality whenever it is unlikely that he would have done the act if he were normal, even in cases where he was quite as capable of acting otherwise as is a normal person subject to the same tendency. This would mean that a bank employee ought to be excused when he embezzles money only because of powerful unconscious wishes to be caught which he could effectively have chosen not to succumb to, although another employee who embezzles only because tempted by healthy fantasies of a life of leisure ought not to be excused.

There is a fourth argument for not punishing wrongdoers who suffered from mental abnormality that in effect requires for an excuse too much rather than too little. It has eminent philosophical credentials and is to be found in the best legal circles as well. The argument derives from general considerations bearing on justification of punishment.

It is pointed out that prescribing punishment for what the insane do is futile since the threat of punishment can have no deterrent effect on such persons. Anyone, therefore, who considers the practice of punishment to be justified by its deterrent effect must hold punishment of the insane to be unjustified and, in fact, a purposeless infliction of suffering. It has been argued in reply that punishment of the insane may still have a deterrent effect on sane persons since it deprives them of hope of escaping punishment by successfully advancing fraudulent claims of having been insane at the time of their offense. That answer is good only to the extent that crimes are committed after decisions to commit them which include deliberation on possible legal tactics to avoid conviction. But since most crimes are committed without decisions of this sort, the deterrent effect of a threat of punishment that makes no allowance for insanity is in any event largely otiose.

There are, however, other answers to the "no deterrence" objection to punishing the insane that do not require belief in such fictitious deliberations by would-be criminals.

If it is being suggested that nondeterrability has been the rationale for the insanity defense in the law as it has developed, we may ask why the law does not refuse by the same rationale to punish those who were genuinely and blamelessly ignorant of the law they broke. Such persons were in a position indistinguishable from the insane with respect to the futility of prospective punishment, and so to punish them is equally a purposeless infliction of suffering. Yet, as we know, in the law as it stands such innocent ignorance does not excuse, and this inconsistency must raise doubts about this rationale for the insanity defense.

But there is a more cogent objection than one based on inconsistency. It is not the case that all, or perhaps even most, insane persons are incapable of being deterred by threat of punishment. Under the prevailing Anglo-American insanity defense, the M'Naghten rules, there is an excuse if the accused by virtue of a defect of reason from disease of the mind did not know he was doing what was wrong. The Model Penal Code similarly establishes as a defense a person's lack of substantial capacity to appreciate the criminality of his conduct (which means more than mere knowledge that it is criminally prohibited) as a result of mental disease or defect. There are many persons who fit these specifications in being unable to appreciate that what they do is wrong and in fact think it for some reason justified, yet are aware and in awe of the threat of punishment quite as much as normal persons. In some of the most notable cases of the insanity defense, the defendant committed murder under the delusion that he was carrying out a divine command, or was giving his due to a man believed to be very wicked, or was killing someone who was bent on harming him. Less dramatic but far more frequent are the family and sex intrigue homicides where the killing was done in a suitably extreme abnormal mental state—usually spoken of as temporary insanity—in which the accused was likewise at the time convinced that he was justified. There is no reason to believe that in general their abnormality rendered the accused in these insanity cases incapable of being deterred by the threat of punishment, though of course like many normal defendants they were not in fact deterred by it. There is, further, every reason to believe that certain abnormal persons who would be entitled to exoneration on grounds of insanity were in fact deterred, just as normal persons would be because the law has made the conduct they contemplated punishable. If these things were not so, the insanity defense could consist simply in establishing the one point that by reason of mental abnormality the accused could not at the time of his crime be deterred by the threat of punishment. In fact what distinguishes the sane from the insane under criminal law standards is the inability of the insane to appreciate the *culpability*, not the punishability, of their conduct. Because of their abnormality the insane cannot at the time apprehend what justifies condemnation of their conduct. Even though amenable to threats of punishment, they lack a resource of appreciation that is necessary if one is to have a reason apart from avoidance of punishment for not doing what the law prohibits. Punishing such persons is indeed a useless infliction of suffering, for it can not serve to uphold the standards that the criminal law exists to preserve.

There is one other argument against mental abnormality defenses that should be noted here. Again it is an argument that by implication requires too much rather than too little for excuse. Many persons who are mentally ill and have committed crimes are dangerous, yet the very abnormality that is evidence of his being dangerous serves to shield the accused from liability. Those who see confinement of dangerous persons as a principal purpose of the criminal law are particularly distressed by this, for in effect just those who are thought to be most properly the concern of the criminal law are allowed to escape its restraints.

The answer to this argument is that not all restraint by the state need be based on criminal liability. If a person is dangerous because of mental abnormality, he may be prevented from doing harm by noncriminal commitment regardless of whether his conduct provided a basis for criminal liability. It is true that persons usually' are not found to be a menace for purposes of commitment unless they have done something which would at least provide the substance of a criminal charge. But it is still dangerousness of the person and not criminality of his conduct that warrants deprivation of liberty. Since determinations of dangerousness and determinations of criminal liability are independent matters, a defense of insanity to a criminal charge does not weigh against the accused's subsequent liability to commitment because he is dangerous. Conversely, elimination or postponement of the question of insanity when determining liability would result in branding as criminals persons, whether dangerous or not, who are not to blame for what they did.

IV

The rationale of excusing for mental abnormality may be summarized in this way. Certain forms of mental incapacity deprive a person of ability to act other than the way he does because resources for an effective choice are lacking. When a person lacks capacity to tell what he is doing, whether it is offensive, or what is likely to happen; or lacks capacity to appreciate its harmful significance, or to restrain himself, he is in such a condition. It is apparent that a person incapacitated in any of these ways lacks a resource necessary for control and so necessary for culpable conduct. It is for this reason that an excuse of mental abnormality preempts the field of excuse and makes excuses going directly to culpability inappropriate. There is no point in being concerned about whether something was intentional, when whether it is intentional or not the actor was not a responsible agent. And conversely, when there is a complement of those personal resources that are necessary for responsible conduct, there is a duty to draw upon such resources to avoid harmful conduct. It follows that when a normal person claims he did not at the time appreciate the significance of sticking a knife into another person—his mind

was elsewhere—he offers a different kind of excuse than the mentally abnormal man who makes the same claim. The normal man can only expect by showing less culpability to blunt an accusation of conduct of a higher degree of culpability—he didn't harm the victim knowingly, but only negligently through absent–mindedness in failing to pay attention to the dangers of what he was occupied in doing. But the man who establishes that his failure of appreciation was due to a lack of necessary mental resources exempts himself from any judgment of culpability.

The distinction and connections between lack of responsibility and mere lack of culpability are important with regard to several difficulties surrounding the insanity defense.

We have already mentioned the usually discarded third part of the original M'Naghten rule. It provided that even if the accused person who suffered a defect of reason from disease of the mind could know the nature and quality of his act, and even if he could know that what he was doing was wrong, he still might have a defense if at the time of his act he suffered from a delusion such that had it been a correct belief it would have afforded a defense. This part of the rule has been dropped, but not in order to exclude insanity defenses based on delusion; in fact, delusion cases have always been recognized as paradigms of criminal insanity and are allowed in all M'Naghten rule jurisdictions by strained interpretations of the other parts. It is the limitation upon the kinds of delusion which are acceptable that has been found objectionable. The usual argument is that the limitation leads to absurd results. For example, in accordance with conventional legal rules that preclude criminal jurisdiction for crimes of foreign nationals committed in foreign countries, a homicide defendant in England who in a delusion at the time of his crime believed himself to be Bluebeard reenacting one of his murders in France would have a good defense. But a homicide defendant also in England who in his similar delusion believed himself to be Jack the Ripper would not. Even when the rule has been confined to delusions which bear on exculpatory claims (typically provocation and self-defense), as undoubtedly it was intended to be by its original proponents, criticism has not abated though the reason for rejecting the rule is less clear.

It seems, in fact, that the original rule was a sound one based on the premises concerning the facts of mental abnormality which the M'Naghten judges accepted, but that these premises are incorrect. The mistake from which the rule proceeded has been characterized as the doctrine of partial insanity. It holds that a person whose insanity consists merely in delusions is still capable of choosing to act in conformity with the law that governed the situation as he perceived it. He therefore is to be held accountable for not acting in conformity with law as it would apply to the situation he perceived, though by virtue of his inability to perceive the situation correctly he could not be held accountable for breaking the law with respect to the situation as it actually was. However, according to better medical knowledge, the fact of the matter is that such persons in the grip of their delusions are normally so severely incapacitated that they cannot even choose to act otherwise. We therefore cannot hold them responsible when they act as their delusion dictates and so must consider them ineligible for blame. Questions about matters of culpability (usually matters of justification) which the original rule raises are for this reason superfluous.

A second problem concerns what is meant by "wrong" under the terms of the M'Naghten rule. If the accused, because of a defect of reason from disease of the mind, did not know that what he was doing was wrong he has a defense on grounds of insanity. The question which has persistently troubled courts both in England and the United States is whether the failure of knowledge required is of legal or of moral wrong. Does a psychotic person who knows murder is a crime but believes he may nevertheless commit it because divinely commanded have a defense? What about a mental defective who knows he is not supposed to hurt other people but cannot even comprehend what a criminal law is? The Model Penal Code speaks of the accused's lack of capacity to appreciate the criminality of his conduct, but the difficulty remains, for appreciating the criminality of conduct is not the equivalent of knowing that it has been made a crime. Indeed the final draft of the Code provision offers "wrongfulness" as an optional substitute for "criminality".

The difficulty is removed by recognizing that what is crucial is capacity to know, rather than knowledge; and that it is a capacity to know something that is necessary for culpability. In a just legal system conduct ought not to be treated as legally culpable unless reasonable opportunity exists to become aware of its legal interdiction. Such opportunity for awareness has significance only if there also is ability to take advantage of it.

That in turn depends on ability to appreciate the untowardness of conduct, ability to be aware of the range of normal concerns of the law, as well as the ability to become acquainted with the law itself. If there is disabling incapacity with respect to any of these necessary conditions the person incapacitated is not responsible, for to that degree he lacks ability to take advantage of the opportunity to become aware of criminal liabilities and so his conduct cannot be deemed culpable. It turns out, then, that it is misleading to ask whether legal or moral wrong is meant. The question to be answered is whether the accused was deprived of any abilities that are necessary to take advantage of the opportunity of becoming aware of criminal liability.

Another difficulty concerns the irresistible impulse defense. There has been great hesitation in legal circles in admitting as an excuse an inability to exercise self-restraint. It challenges common sense appreciation of behavior to assert that a person possessed of all the abilities necessary to control what he is doing, nevertheless does not have the self-control to choose effectively not to do it. The excuse is therefore often construed as a direct denial of culpability analogous to external compulsion—he didn't mean to do that, he was forced to—rather than as a denial of responsibility by virtue of incapacity. The excuse so construed is then rejected as being too easy a way out for persons who either have not chosen to resist with sufficient determination powerful untoward urges or have failed to take precaution against succumbing to the urge and are therefore no less culpable than persons who lose their temper and, while in the grip of their rage, commit crimes.

But this excuse of no responsibility becomes plausible as understanding of human pathology advances, and it becomes increasingly clear that there are serious mental abnormalities which consist in inability either by repression or precaution to inhibit acting on certain urges. The claim of irresistible impulse is then no longer construed as one simply of not having effectively chosen to do otherwise, but rather more, as not having the personal resources that are necessary to choose effectively.

V

A stark separation according to mental abnormality of those who are responsible from those who are not seems at times unsatisfactory. We are bound to recognize that sometimes there is not sheer incapacity with regard to elements of control, yet there is deviation from normal capacities great enough to make desirable a limitation on accountability. Accordingly, there has developed in the law a doctrine of diminished (or partial) responsibility which, though still only little and narrowly accepted, offers a path for receiving into the law continuing insights respecting varieties of limited impairment bearing on control of conduct. The most notable legal recognition so far has been in the English Homicide Act of 1957, which reduces what otherwise would be murder to culpable homicide when the accused suffered from such abnormality of mind as "substantially impaired his mental responsibility" for his acts. The rationale for diminished responsibility is simple. If a person who is incapacitated is ineligible for blame, a person who is seriously impaired though not incapacitated is eligible to be blamed only within limits. While not utterly bereft of resources required for accountability, his resources of control are dimished to a point where full faulting according to the tenor of the conduct is inappropriate. But for reasons previously given, it would be a serious mistake to construe the defense of diminished responsibility as a declaration that the somewhat sick, simply because they are sick, ought not to be held to a liability as great as that of the healthy person. Indeed, perfectly healthy persons who have perfectly natural reactions that put them in an abnormal emotional state may rightly claim diminished responsibility. Typically, this is the case when a person acts under the influence of extreme anger or fear because provoked or threatened.

Mental abnormality may affect culpability in a more direct way, however, and some confusion about this has arisen in discussions of diminished responsibility. By virtue of his abnormality, a person may be unable to act in a way that is criminally culpable, or at least not as culpable as the conduct charged. Or, though capable of such conduct, he may simply not have been acting in the way charged but rather was acting in some other way dictated by his abnormal processes. In either case he may lodge an exculpatory claim that his conduct is different than alleged with respect to elements bearing on culpability, and he would rely on the evidence of his mental abnormality to establish this. Such an exculpatory claim in essence is no different from the sort that is appropriate when a normal person has not acted culpably, but the kind of argument which supports the claim is different. Instead of evidence indicating simply that the accused was engaged in a somewhat different enterprise than alleged, the evidence indicates that by virtue of

his abnormal mental condition at the time, the accused could not or simply did not engage in the enterprise alleged. Two exculpatory claims are made in this way. Both of them have as their point what in the language of traditional criminal law theory would be called a lack of *mens rea*.

Suppose a prisoner attacks a guard with a knife and inflicts serious wounds. The prisoner is charged with first degree assault, an element of which is intent to cause serious physical injury. It is claimed on his behalf that he was at the time suffering severe paranoid anxieties which led him to misinterpret a routine warning as a sign that he was about to be attacked by the guard, and that he slashed at the guard only to fend off what he believed to be imminent blows. Evidence of his abnormal state would tend to show that he did not have the specific intent to cause serious physical injury. This would mean that while admittedly he exercised control in conducting an assault, he did not exercise control with regard to those features of it that produced the serious injury. The act done, therefore, was something less culpable than the act charged. The same would hold true for a person accused of burglary, which requires an intent to commit a felony, and who at the time of breaking and entering a home was in such a mental condition as to be incapable of having any definite further purpose.

The other challenge to culpability by way of abnormality does not concern the purpose which informs the act, but rather the earlier stages of planning the accomplishment of objectives and attending to the course of conduct while it is in progress. Such operational design and supervision as is referred to by "malice aforethought," "premeditation," "deliberation," "willfully," and "knowingly" may be beyond the accused's capacities or may simply be nonexistent by virtue of his abnormality. Powerful effects of intoxication or of lingering mental illness may render a person unable or unconcerned to form the plan or to remain in control of its execution, and so one is required to conclude that his homicidal attack was not designed with reference to the death of his victim. The Model Penal Code extends this variety of abnormality defense to all cases where evidence of mental disease or defect is relevant to the question of whether the accused had a required state of mind at the time of the crime, so that even recklessness or negligence may be disproved by evidence of appropriate abnormality.

In both of these "criminal intent" challenges based on mental abnormality, it is not responsibility that properly is said to be diminished. Culpability is what is really claimed to be diminished, and diminished to a point where the conduct is less culpable than is required for the offense charged.

VI

The excuse of insanity has presented far greater difficulties than any other for the criminal process. The main reason is that the point of the proceedings is lost sight of and confusion arises in deciding who may appropriately answer the very different kinds of questions involved, and also in deciding what the consequences of accepting or rejecting the excuse ought to be.

Much of the controversy in which medical and legal views of the insanity defense appear to be at odds results from a failure to appreciate that the law must ultimately be concerned not with who is sick but with whose conduct is excusable. Deciding that issue requires several subsidiary decisions that fall peculiarly within either medical or legal competence. There must, in the first place, be standards which set forth generally the nature of the incapacities that render a person not responsible. It is these standards that constitute the rules of the insanity defense, and deciding upon them is the responsibility of those with legislative and judicial authority who must make the law. It bears emphasis that what is called for here is not some general description of relevant clinical abnormalities in language lawyers are used to. What is required is a statement of the kinds of mental failures (due to mental illness or defectiveness) that entitle us to conclude for purposes of criminal liability that the accused could not help doing what he did. Once there are such standards of mental abnormality, proceedings to judge the abnormalities of a particular defendant with reference to such standards are possible. Then it is the opinion of medical experts which must first be looked to in order to determine the nature of the defendant's debilitation and the extent to which it affects capacities necessary for responsible conduct. Such expert opinion may be critically examined by lawyers, as indeed any expert opinion may be in a legal proceeding to determine a disputed issue. But that is not a means of substituting an inexpert for an expert opinion, but only a way of ensuring that its acceptance is ultimately based on reason rather than authority. There is finally a decision of vast discretion that is normally made by the jury. It is a conclusion about whether, according to the expert account of the mental condition that is finally accepted, there is debilitation sufficient to excuse according to the legal standards. Asking psychiatrists for expert opinions about whether such standards of incapacity are met is asking them to perform a role which is not within their special professional competence. But the job to be done in making the ultimate determination does require specialized skill in sifting among psychiatric opinions to arrive at a sound appreciation of the defendant's mental condition with reference to those features that are significant for judgments of responsibility. The paramount procedural problem of the insanity defense is to combine this specialist's appreciation with the layman's considered views about when choices to act are no longer meaningful or even possible. There is for this reason a great deal to recommend in principle suggestions, such as H. L. A. Hart's, that we adopt an "apparently coarser grained technique of exempting persons from liability to punishment if they fall into certain recognized categories of mental disorder", on the model of exemption from liability for persons under a specified age. But the establishment of a comprehensive scheme of clear categories seems at the present state of medical art a remote prospect.

Another sort of misapprehension deflects concern from responsibility to other matters, at the cost of both justice and humaneness in the administration of the criminal law. It is assumed that determining the accused to be responsible and so liable to have his conduct judged culpable is a warrant for treating him punitively rather than therapeutically. But in fact, it is said, many persons who meet legal standards for responsible conduct are nevertheless quite sick and sending them to a prison rather than a hospital is uncivilized. It is urged that the mentally ill ought therefore not to be treated as criminally responsible.

The mistake here is in giving priority to existing institutional arrangements and then attempting to have rules of liability which are humane in their effect under those arrangements. A rational and morally concerned society designs its institutions to treat in a humane way those who are liable according to just principles of liability. When a person who is liable according to proper standards of responsibility and culpability is also sick, principles of humane treatment, which are in no way inferior moral considerations, require that he be treated as sick. To the extent that inappropriate treatment may at present be expected under existing institutional arrangements and regimes, that is cause for reform of institutional arrangements and regimes, not of the rules of criminal liability.

PART 5

Punishment

Philosophical theories of punishment have always taken punishment for crime as the paradigm instance of punishment. More often than not, such theories tend to discuss criminal punishment as a problem within the general sphere of moral affairs, identifying morally blameworthy conduct as the subject at hand. Some philosophers, as well as some theorists with a different sort of intellectual base, have approached the problems of criminal punishment differently, stressing the practical purposes to be served by this important social institution rather than pursuing immediately the implications of morally wrong conduct. Whichever way these problems are considered, the first order of business is to clarify precisely what sorts of measures count as criminal punishment.

WHAT IS PUNISHMENT?

No one has difficulty in identifying punishment when the law responds to crime by imposing it. Knowing what it is and what gives it its distinctive character is not as easy. In "The Expressive Function of Punishment" Joel Feinberg makes it clear that disapproval, reprobation, and condemnation are at the heart of the matter. Certain conceptual difficulties emerge when full-fledged punishment seems inappropriate or when a certain sort of harsh measure is said not to be punishment at all. Feinberg both explains and resolves these difficulties by reference to the central role that condemnation plays on occasions of true punishment. It is useful to consider to what extent the hard treatment that represents reprobation might be reduced, and why its total elimination seems unsatisfactory even if the most dramatic rituals of public condemnation were to be substituted. From another point of view, it is worth considering whether modern sentences are always reprobative. How about sentences that manifestly aim at providing compensation to the victim in the form of reparation, or to the community in the form of community service? How about sentences like involuntary medical treatment that are designed only to benefit the perpetrator? If these sentences are not reprobative, are they a substitute for punishment, or are they an argument against the comprehensiveness of Feinberg's view of criminal punishment?

THE JUSTIFICATION OF PUNISHMENT

If the first question to be asked about legal punishment is what it is, the second must be how it is to be justified. The practice of punishment directly inflicts pain, suffering, and loss of liberty on those subjected to it, violating what would otherwise be their natural rights to life, liberty, and the pursuit of happiness. A minority of writers, including such diverse figures as the dramatist George Bernard Shaw and the behaviorist psychologist B.F. Skinner, argue that legal punishment, at least as it is generally practiced, in fact cannot be justified, but that seems to be too extreme a position to have much immediate appeal. Among those who do state justifying conditions for legal punishment two rival positions have prevailed. Those who defend what is called the *utilitarian theory of punishment* argue that punishment is justified only when, and only because, it seems likely to achieve certain social benefits or to avert certain social harms. Considered only in itself apart from the consequences, it is an evil. If it is to be justified at all, then, it must be in terms of such beneficial consequences as prevention of other crimes by the person punished, and deterrence of other would-be offenders. If a projected punishment of a law-breaker cannot be justified by its consequences then it is, in the words of Thomas Hobbes, "a triumph or glorying in the hurt of another tending to no end" (*Leviathan*, Part One, Chapter 15). Those who defend what it called the *retributive theory of punishment,* in contrast, argue that the primary and essential justification of legal punishment is not to be provided by a social cost/benefit analysis, but rather by the simple fact, located in the past, that the criminal did a forbidden and/or wicked act. We justify punishment retributively by showing that in virtue of a criminal's blame-worthy conduct he has it coming as his due. Giving a criminal his just deserts is a requirement of justice, not mere social utility, and it implies that retribution is a moral end in itself.

In his essay that introduces the subsection on justification, Joel Feinberg describes some of the standard dialectical moves made by disputants in the great debate between utilitarians and retributivists. The reader should be aware that Feinberg's method for classifying theories is not accepted by all writers. Feinberg defines the utilitarian theory rather precisely and then stipulates that any nonutilitarian theory is a retributive one, whereas most writers, perhaps, take the opposite tack, defining retributivism very precisely in such moralistic terms as "guilt," "desert," "justice," and "due," and then stipulating that any nonretributive theory is by definition a utilitarian one. Most writers would agree, however, that whichever principle of classification we accept is a matter of convenience only, not a question of substance. Another interesting feature of Feinberg's discussion is that he distinguishes between defenders of the utilitarian theory of punishment who simply derive their theory of justified punishment from their more general utilitarian theory of justified conduct, and those who do not argue from the more general moral theory to their particular conclusions about punishment. He also classifies those who justify legal punishment as *vengeance* with the utilitarians, not the retributivists, a classification that may strike the beginner as surprising until he thinks about it.

The great impasse between the utilitarian and retributive theories was largely undisturbed by a century and a half of disputation, until a rash of rather original articles in the 1950s and 1960s appeared—to many these views made a genuine breakthrough. The article by Rawls, included here, was one of the more important pieces. A common tactic in these works was to make more and better distinctions, for example, between definition and justification, moral and legal guilt, necessary and sufficient conditions, single acts and general practices, and to hold to these distinctions rigorously, thus permitting the formulation of new and sharper questions about punishment. Retributivism and utilitarianism could then be put forward as complementary answers to different questions, rather than conflicting answers to the same question.

H. L. A. Hart's "Prolegomenon to the Principles of Punishment" is a classic survey of the problems that criminal punishment presents for philosophers. Almost every issue in the great justification debate is raised, and though Hart's position may seem a swift and summary treatment of rather complex matters, the absolute clarity with which the issues are framed make this essay a most excellant prolegomenon.

In "Culpability and Desert," Hyman Gross presents a view of desert that is free of the traditional elements of retribution, and considers the role in sentencing that desert ought to play. The persistent moral core of retribution (which Mackie discusses in the following paper) shows itself here in a demand that must always be respected: not allowing people to get away with their crimes.

In this analysis, distributing punishment simply according to what the crime (or criminal) deserves is not morally justifiable. This view distinguishes the author's position from more conventional "desert" theories currently much in evidence in debates about sentencing policy. An important point for critical attention concerns the question of possible guidelines to give a judge who wished to incorporate these views in his or her sentencing practice, particularly with reference to a concern for avoidance arbitrariness in the assessment of culpability and mitigation.

In "Retributivism: A Test Case for Ethical Objectivity," J. L. Mackie analyzes with extraordinary clarity and precision the concept of retribution and the standard arguments of principle that are invoked to support retribution. This is done as a long and illuminating prelude to Mackie's solution to what he has elsewhere called the paradox of retribution: "that on the one hand, a retributive principle of punishment cannot be explained or developed within a reasonable system of moral thought, while, on the other hand, such a principle cannot be eliminated from our moral thinking." In this previously unpublished paper of the distinguished Oxford philosopher, there is as powerful a challenge as may be found in the literature to the widespread and comfortable assumption that there must be good reasons in objective moral theory for following our instincts when crime seems, as a matter of moral certainty, to call for punishment as its desert.

It has for some time been unfashionable to advocate retribution as a positively good thing. In a purely moral light, understanding, forgiving, and forgetting seem very much superior. In terms of the sophistication of the political culture that surrounds a criminal justice system, retribution seems a kind of collective vengeance administered in a suitably dispassionate way under an elaborate system of rules. It seems an unenlightened and purely backward-looking response when in fact we have an occasion that offers opportunities for improving things. Much of the literature countenancing retributive attitudes in enforcing the law takes retribution to be a fact of social and personal life that cannot be left out of account as long as people have the emotional makeup they now do. Michael Moore's "The Moral Worth of Retribution" argues with great force that retributive justice is a morally worthy program which, far from needing to be justified, is required if we are not to be judged morally deficient in the face of crime. There are many points at which this admirable exposition of the retributivist position might be challenged. Perhaps a good way to start is to consider Moore's imagining of the victim's experience, which he invites us to share and react to emotionally. Is our reaction a reliable guide to moral judgment? And, in any event, is the sort of case he treats as a paradigm sufficiently representative of crime in general for the purposes at hand?

Can criminal punishment be viewed as moral education? Jean Hampton argues that it can in "The Moral Education Theory of Punishment." A number of points need examination. Educators usually offer theories of education that suggest how various aims of education might be advanced. In the absence of any such theory here it might be useful to consider just what moral education might consist of in the context of criminal punishment. Are we sure that people who commit crimes are in need of moral education? Are we even sure that most crimes, seen in the full context in which they are committed, are *morally* wrong acts? Closer and fuller investigations, by writers who give us book-length accounts and by those who just prepare presentencing reports, put the matter vey much in doubt. Even the concept of laws as moral standards seems doubtful. Rummaging through the hundreds and thousands of laws whose violation may entail criminal punishment in a modern jurisdiction, one sees huge numbers that are on the statute books only because some policy requires certain conduct to be discouraged, though nothing is at stake morally. Finally, if moral education is really what punishing crime is all about, it would be hard to imagine a more unsuitable institution than prison for carrying on that program of education, whatever it might turn out to be.

In his essay "Mercy and Legal Justice" Jeffrie Murphy doubts that in sentencing offenders mercy is an autonomous virtue. He argues that in the context of legal justice mercy is an autonomous moral virtue only when a claim is not pressed by a private litigant because of the harsh consequences its enforcement would have. But is it entirely clear exactly what an "autonomous virtue" is, or why a virtue that is heteronomous might not be of equal or even greater importance? Justice in enforcing the law, for example, may not be an autonomous virtue but may depend upon whether the law itself is just. Would justice then be a less important virtue? And would it be right to rebuke a judge as having acted unjustly if he allowed sentiment to influence him toward leniency in sentencing because he pitied the defendant? Is there a requirement in criminal justice that everyone gets what he deserves for his crime regardless of how the consequences of the sentence may appear in the light of moral considerations other than justice? If there is no such requirement, how *are* the requirements of just desert to be dealt with when compassionate concerns are advanced?

EXACTLY WHAT IS BEING PUNISHED?

Crimes seem at first glance to be simple events. They are occasions of wrongdoing for which the law has created a liability to punishment. But a closer look dispels the illusion of simplicity and we become aware that there are several basic ingredients in a crime. What (if anything) was intended, is one important question. What (exactly) was done, is another. And what happened as a result, is the third important query.

In measuring criminal liability the law in general aims to impose greater liability for more serious crimes. The question that must then be answered is which of these ingredients matter in deciding about seriousness, and why. Should what is intended or what is done matter more when the two are not the same? Should it matter that the outcome of what was done was just a matter of chance and not at all the sort of thing that would normally be expected? Suppose what was intended does occur, but only by accident. What should the law say then about liability for what happened?

These problems are brought into sharp focus by the dilemma of criminal attempts. If the harm required for a completed crime does not occur on a particular occasion, even though everything normally necessary to bring it about has been done, what reason, if any, is there for punishing the crime less severely, as the law normally does? Conversely, why should there be punishment for acts that never could have succeeded in their purpose even though the purpose was clearly criminal? The three selections in this section investigate these problems and reach rather different conclusions.

In "Blame, Punishment, and the Role of Result" Richard Parker argues that there is no reason why attempts and completed crimes should be treated as punishable in different degrees when the crime turns out to be an attempt only as a matter of luck. Starting with the premise that like cases should be treated alike, he sees no difference between such attempts and the completed versions of the same crime since the conduct in both cases is the same. The culpability of criminal conduct is what matters on this account, and culpability is measured by the harm it puts in prospect rather than the harm it actually produces. Since it is the harm actually produced that makes us punish completed crimes more severely, we punish such crimes unjustly to the extent that we are punishing for the harm and not the conduct. The prevailing view in most legal systems is therefore an encouragement to unjust sentences.

Quite a different conclusion is argued by Michael Davis in "Why Attempts Deserve Less Punishment than Complete Crimes." He recognizes that most theorists think there is no difference in principle between the completed crime and the attempt when only matters unrelated to the perpetrator's conduct makes the difference, but thinks that the law reflects a sounder view in punishing the two differently. Davis rejects an analysis based on the harm threatened by conduct serving as a general principle of culpability that ought to guide decisions about sentences. Instead he adopts a view that has punishment redressing a balance of benefits and burdens that is upset when a crime is committed. People who commit crimes are seen as gaining an unfair advantage over those who don't in a society that imposes restraints on everyone in order to promote everyone's safety. It is not entirely clear whether a fear of crime is in this view a fear of the unfair advantage it represents, or whether it is a more straightforward fear of the harm that is threatened by criminal conduct. In any case, it is suggested that the relative seriousness of crimes may be gauged by imagining an auction in which licenses to commit various crimes are on offer, and a protective association is in a position to make preemptive bids that are calculated according to how much particular crimes are feared. Attempts, it is argued, will fetch a lower price than completed crimes, are therefore less serious, and so deserve less punishment.

In taking up the same problem, David Lewis employs the imaginary device of a penal lottery in "The Punishment That Leaves Something to Chance." Considering several models for such a lottery, Lewis concludes that our practice may best be viewed as a kind of lottery in which the law treats the outcome of each person's crime as a matter of chance with different stakes prescribed depending on the outcome. The question of justice is left open, with a strong suggestion that such a procedure might well turn out to be unjust if only we knew how to argue for its injustice.

Together, these three essays make clear the philosophical importance of the law of attempts as a cornerstone of criminal jurisprudence. It is interesting to note that none of the authors considers the possibility that an attempt might represent a welcome opportunity to dispense with some measure of the punishment prescribed for the completed crime, which is the crime in its normal form. All of these authors share as a premise the proposition that punishment should be only for conduct and not for occurrences that are merely fortuitous. When there is only conduct without harm the suffering and outrage that only harm can produce is lacking, and the demands for retribution are therefore not as great. Why should advantage not be taken then of the more moderate emotional climate to sentence more moderately? A somewhat complex answer to the title of this section is suggested by such an approach, and the reasons for punishing crime appear in a new perspective.

THE DEATH PENALTY

Among all the issues that criminal punishment raises, none has been the subject of greater public controversy than capital punishment. Only utopian views conceive a society without the need for some form of meaningful condemnation of persons who wrongfully do harm of serious public concern. The most dramatic form that such public response may take still causes great debate in the United States and elsewhere, as it has for several centuries throughout the civilized world. In the United States, Supreme Court cases questioning the constitutionality of the death penalty have produced the full range of arguments for and against capital punishment. With this in mind, selections from the opinions in two of these cases are presented here.

In 1972, the Supreme Court of the United States held that the imposition and carrying out of the death penalty in one case of murder and two of rape was unconstitutional because violative of the "cruel and unusual punishment" restriction of the Eighth Amendment. There was nothing special about the sentence, the proceedings, or the law under which the defendants were sentenced in these cases, and the Supreme Court's decision was based on general considerations regarding the death penalty. The selections from four of the nine separate opinions in *Furman* v. *Georgia* that are included here present all of the important arguments that were advanced. Two themes are sounded with special prominence, and they have appeared earlier in this volume in other contexts. One is the issue of arbitrary and even discriminatory application of the capital provisions of the law by judges and (even more) by juries. It is the unprincipled (though perhaps well-meaning) exercise of discretionary power that is objected to, and the objection is especially weighty because of the awful consequences that attend such abuse. The other recurring theme addresses the moral sentiments of the community. If there is general disinclination in the community to invoke the death penalty, then that should count conclusively against its continued existence. There is disagreement among members of the Court only concerning the true sentiment of the community.

The state of the law following *Furman* was unclear. If only arbitrariness is a fatal objection, as some state legislatures and proponents of congressional bills assumed, it would seem that in principle, at least, suitable remedies could be found. There are ways of specifying the extreme culpability that would set the capital crime apart, and of framing specific questions bearing on culpability for jurors to answer in determining whether the death penalty is warranted. If it were mandatory whenever warranted, that would seem to preclude arbitrariness. One suspects, however, that such a consequence would ordinarily cause jurors to shrink from following their instructions, with the result that unconstitutional arbitrariness would again exist for the occasional death sentence; of the death penalty would in effect become a dead letter on the books. Some of those wishing to preserve the death penalty have advocated a Draconian resort to simple-minded mandatory death penalties, which do not provide opportunity for the consideration of all matters bearing on culpability. The preclusion of exculpatory considerations by such stark provisions would seem to introduce a new arbitrariness far worse than the old. It would indeed avoid the evil of discriminatory imposition of the death penalty of which Justice Douglas speaks, but would institute a regime of equal *injustice* by requiring its infliction on all members of a class regardless of culpability—all those who intentionally and with out justification kill a police officer, for example, regardless of what reason there might have been which the law does not recognize as a defense.

The community sentiment argument seems not to have been fully appreciated in the *Furman* opinions. Certainly it is wrong to require jurors to condemn to death those they find guilty if something more than the natural distaste and regret that would ordinarily accompany the performance of such a duty is generally experienced. If revulsion normally overcomes those citizens who are asked as jurors to do their duty under the law, we may expect that only when there is a passionate hatred of the convicted person will capital punishment be imposed, and that would surely result in many irrational decisions that constitute precisely the injustice of discriminatory sentences which are objectionable on separate grounds. But an even more basic consideration is whether, according to principles of right and wrong that are universally invoked in the community, the death penalty is wrong. The answer is by no means plain on the face of things, and only extended moral argument can make it plain. Strong popular feeling of revulsion by itself counts only as evidence that the practice of killing a person for the crime he committed *may be* morally unacceptable. In spite of such feeling, it may not be morally unacceptable. Slaughter of animals for food may evoke such feelings, yet it may turn out not to be morally wrong, in which case the public revulsion is reason to carry on the activity discreetly, but not to prohibit it. Superficial evidence of possible general moral objection to capital punishment, such as polls that elicit unfavorable attitudes toward it, are only the first word and certainly not the last. What justification exists for such attitudes is the question whose answer will tell us whether the death penalty is morally wrong.

In *Gregg* v. *Georgia,* a measure of uncertainty about the death penalty was removed when the United States Supreme Court upheld the procedures prescribed by carefully drafted Georgia legislation. The case was one of homicide committed in the course of armed robbery. The Court found that the dangers of arbitrary senctence of death no longer existed under the new bifurcated system. This system provided for reaching a verdict first; then, under separate instruction, deciding on a recommendation for sentence with reference to specific findings of fact; and, with judicial review by the State Supreme Court, comparing death sentences to ensure against disproportionality. Ample portions of the opinions in the case are presented here in order to allow careful critical assessment of all the arguments on both sides, those fully developed as well as those merely hinted at.

In "The Right to Like and the Right to Kill" Hugo Bedau surveys the moral arguments for and against the death penalty, and concludes that from a moral point of view there is no principle upon which the controversy can be resolved. In the larger context of a legal practice in operation in the real world there are, however, very strong reasons for not treating the matter as inconclusive. Those on either side of this great public debate will find the important quesitons to be answered clearly presented in Bedau's comprehensive discussion of the issues.

JOEL FEINBERG

The Expressive Function of Punishment*

It might well appear to a moral philosopher absorbed in the classical literature of his discipline, or to a moralist sensitive to injustice and suffering, that recent philosophical discussions of the problem of punishment have somehow missed the point of his interest. Recent influential articles[1] have quite sensibly distinguished between questions of definition and justification, between justifying general rules and particular decisions, between moral and legal guilt. So much is all to the good. When these articles go on to *define* 'punishment,' however, it seems to many that they leave out of their ken altogether the very element that makes punishment theoretically puzzling and morally disquieting. Punishment is defined, in effect, as the infliction of hard treatment by an authority on a person for his prior failing in some respect (usually an infraction of a rule or command).[2] There may be a very general sense of the word 'punishment' which is well expressed by this definition; but even if that is so, we can distinguish a narrower, more emphatic sense that slips through its meshes. Imprisonment at hard labor for committing a felony is a clear case of punishment in the emphatic sense; but I think we would be less willing to apply that term to parking tickets, offside penalties, sackings, flunkings, and disqualifications. Examples of the latter sort I propose to call *penalties* (merely), so that I may inquire further what distinguishes punishment, in the strict and narrow sense that interests the moralist, from other kinds of penalties.[3]

One method of answering this question is to focus one's attention on the class of nonpunitive penalties in an effort to discover some clearly identifiable characteristic common to them all, and absent from all punishments, on which the distinction between the two might be

grounded. The hypotheses yielded by this approach, however, are not likely to survive close scrutiny. One might conclude, for example, that mere penalties are less severe than punishments, but although this is generally true, it is not necessarily and universally so. Again we might be tempted to interpret penalties as mere 'price-tags' attached to certain types of behavior that are generally undesirable, so that only those with especially strong motivation will be willing to pay the price.[4] So, for example, deliberate efforts on the part of some western states to keep roads from urban centers to wilderness areas few in number and poor in quality are essentially no different from various parking fines and football penalties. In each case a certain kind of conduct is discouraged without being absolutely prohibited: Anyone who desires strongly enough to get to the wilderness (or park overtime, or interfere with a pass) may do so provided he is willing to pay the penalty (price). On this view penalties are, in effect, licensing fees, different from other purchased permits in that the price is often paid afterward rather than in advance. Since a similar interpretation of punishments seems implausible, it might be alleged that this is the basis of the distinction between penalties and punishments. However, while a great number of penalties can, no doubt, plausibly be treated as retroactive license fees, this is hardly true of all of them. It is certainly not true, for example, of most demotions, firings, and flunkings, that they are 'prices' paid for some already consumed benefit; and even parking fines are sanctions for rules "meant to be taken seriously as . . . standard[s] of behavior,"[5] and thus are more than mere public parking fees.

Rather than look for a characteristic common and peculiar to the penalties on which to ground the distinction between penalties and punishments, we would be better advised, I think, to cast our attention to the examples of punish-

*Joel Feinberg, *Doing and Deserving* (Princeton, N.J.: Princeton University Press, 1970), pp. 95–118.

ments. Both penalties and punishments are authoritative deprivations for failures; but apart from these common features, penalties have a miscellaneous character, whereas punishments have an important additional characteristic in common. That characteristic, or specific difference, I shall argue, is a certain expressive function: Punishment is a conventional device for the expression of attitudes of resentment and indignation, and of judgments of disapproval and reprobation, either on the part of the punishing authority himself or of those "in whose name" the punishment is inflicted. Punishment, in short, has a *symbolic significance* largely missing from other kinds of penalties.

The reprobative symbolism of punishment and its character as 'hard treatment,' while never separate in reality, must be carefully distinguished for purposes of analysis. Reprobation is itself painful, whether or not it is accompanied by further 'hard treatment'; and hard treatment, such as fine of imprisonment, because of its conventional symbolism, can itself be reprobatory; but still we can conceive of ritualistic condemnation unaccompanied by any *further* hard treatment, and of inflictions and deprivations which, because of different symbolic conventions, have no reprobative force. It will be my thesis in this essay that (1) both the hard treatment aspect of punishment and its reprobative function must be part of the *definition* of legal punishment; and (2) each of these aspects raises its own kind of question about the *justification* of legal punishment as a general practice. I shall argue that some of the jobs punishment does, and some of the conceptual problems it raises, cannot be intelligibly described unless (1) is true; and that the incoherence of a familiar form of the retributive theory results from failure to appreciate the force of (2).

I. PUNISHMENT AS CONDEMNATION

That the expression of the community's condemnation is an essential ingredient in legal punishment is widely acknowledged by legal writers. Henry M. Hart, for example, gives eloquent emphasis to the point:

What distinguishes a criminal from a civil sanction and all that distinguishes it, it is ventured, is the judgment of community condemnation which accompanies . . . its imposition. As Professor Gard-

ner wrote not long ago, in a distinct but cognate connection:

"The essence of punishment for moral delinquency lies in the criminal conviction itself. One may lose more money on the stock market than in a courtroom; a prisoner of war camp may well provide a harsher environment than a state prison; death on the field of battle has the same physical characteristics as death by sentence of law. It is the expression of the community's hatred, fear, or contempt for the convict which alone characterizes physical hardship as punishment."

If this is what a 'criminal' penalty is, then we can say readily enough what a 'crime' is. . . . It is conduct which, if duly shown to have taken place, will incur a formal and solemn pronouncement of the moral condemnation of the community. . . . Indeed the condemnation plus the added [unpleasant physical] consequences may well be considered, compendiously, as constituting the punishment.[6]

Professor Hart's compendious definition needs qualification in one respect. The moral condemnation and the 'unpleasant consequences' that he rightly identifies as essential elements of punishment are not as distinct and separate as he suggests. It is not always the case that the convicted prisoner is first solemnly condemned and then subjected to unpleasant physical treatment. It would be more accurate in many cases to say that the unpleasant treatment itself expresses the condemnation, and that this expressive aspect of his incarceration is precisely the element by reason of which it is properly characterized as punishment and not mere penalty. The administrator who regretfully suspends the license of a conscientious but accident-prone driver can inflict a deprivation without any scolding, express or implied; but the reckless motorist who is sent to prison for six months is thereby inevitably subject to shame and ignominy—the very walls of his cell condemn him and his record becomes a stigma.

To say that the very physical treatment itself expresses condemnation is to say simply that certain forms of hard treatment have become the conventional symbols of public reprobation. This is neither more nor less paradoxical than to say that certain words have become conventional vehicles in our language for the expression of certain attitudes, or that champagne is the alcoholic beverage traditionally used in celebration of great events, or that black is the color of mourning. Moreover, particular kinds of punishment are often used to express quite specific attitudes (loosely speaking, this is part of their 'meaning'); note the differences, for example, between beheading a nobleman and hanging a yeoman, burning a heretic and hanging a traitor, hanging an enemy soldier and executing him by firing squad.

It is much easier to show that punishment has a symbolic significance than to say exactly what it is that punishment expresses. At its best, in civilized and democratic countries, punishment surely expresses the community's strong *disapproval* of what the criminal did. Indeed it can be said that punishment expresses the *judgment* (as distinct from any emotion) of the community that what the criminal did was wrong. I think it is fair to say of our community, however, that punishment generally expresses more than judgments of disapproval; it is also a symbolic way of getting back at the criminal, of expressing a kind of vindictive resentment. To any reader who has in fact spent time in a prison, I venture to say, even Professor Gardner's strong terms—'hatred, fear, or contempt for the convict'—will not seem too strong an account of what imprisonment is universally taken to express. Not only does the criminal feel the naked hostility of his guards and the outside world—that would be fierce enough—but that hostility is self-righteous as well. His punishment bears the aspect of legitimized vengefulness; hence there is much truth in J. F. Stephen's celebrated remark that "The criminal law stands to the passion of revenge in much the same relation as marriage to the sexual appetite."[7]

If we reserve the less dramatic term 'resentment' for the various vengeful attitudes, and the term 'reprobation' for the stern judgment of disapproval, then perhaps we can characterize *condemnation* (or denunciation) as a kind of fusing of resentment and reprobation. That these two elements are generally to be found in legal punishment was well understood by the authors of the Report of the Royal Commission on Capital Punishment:

Discussion of the principle of *retribution* is apt to be confused because the word is not always used in the same sense. Sometimes it is intended to mean vengeance, sometimes reprobation. In the first sense the idea is that of satisfaction by the State of a wronged individual's desire to be avenged; in the second it is that of the State's *marking its disapproval* of the breaking of its laws by a punishment proportionate to the gravity of the offense [my italics].[8]

II. SOME DERIVATIVE SYMBOLIC FUNCTIONS OF PUNISHMENT

The relation of the expressive function of punishment to its various central purposes is not always easy to trace. Symbolic public condemnation added to deprivation may help or hinder deterrence, reform, and rehabilitation—the evidence is not clear. On the other hand, there are other functions of punishment, often lost sight of in the preoccupation with deterrence and reform, that presuppose the expressive function and would be impossible without it.

1. *Authoritative Disavowal.* Consider the standard international practice of demanding that a nation whose agent has unlawfully violated the complaining nation's rights should punish the offending agent. For example, suppose that an airplane of nation *A* fires on an airplane nation *B* while the latter is flying over international waters. Very likely high authorities in nation *B* will send a note of protest to their counterparts in nation *A* demanding, among other things, that the transgressive pilot be punished. Punishing the pilot is an emphatic, dramatic, and well understood way of *condemning* and thereby *disavowing* his act. It tells the world that the pilot had no right to do what he did, that he was on his own in doing it, that his government does not condone that sort of thing. It testifies thereby to government *A*'s recognition of the violated rights of government *B* in the affected area, and therefore to the wrongfulness of the pilot's act. Failure to punish the pilot tells the world that government *A* does not consider him to have been personally at fault. That in turn is to claim responsibility for the act, which in effect labels that act as an 'instrument of deliberate national policy,' and therefore an act of war. In that case either formal hostilities or humiliating loss of face by one side or the other almost certainly follows. None of this makes any sense without the well understood reprobative symbolism of punishment. In quite parallel ways punishment enables employers to disavow the acts of their employees (though not civil liability for those acts), and fathers the destructive acts of their sons.

2. *Symbolic Nonacquiescence: 'Speaking in the Name of the People.'* The symbolic func-

tion of punishment also explains why even those sophisticated persons who abjure resentment of criminals and look with small favor generally on the penal law are likely to demand that certain kinds of conduct be punished when or if the law lets them go by. In the state of Texas, so-called 'paramour killings' are regarded by the law as not merely mitigated, but completely justifiable.[9] Many humanitarians, I believe, will feel quite spontaneously that a great injustice is done when such killings are left unpunished. The sense of violated justice, moreover, might be distinct and unaccompanied by any frustrated *schaden-freude* toward the killer, lust for blood or vengeance, or metaphysical concern lest the universe stay 'out of joint.' The demand for punishment in cases of this sort may instead represent the feeling that paramour killings deserve to be *condemned*, that the law in condoning, even approving of them, speaks for all citizens in expressing a wholly inappropriate attitude toward them. For, in effect, the law expresses the judgment of the 'people of Texas,' in whose name it speaks, that the vindictive satisfaction in the mind of the cuckolded husband is a thing of greater value than the very life of his wife's lover. The demand that paramour killings be punished may simply be the demand that this lopsided value judgment be withdrawn and that the state *go on record* against paramour killings, and the law *testify to the recognition* that such killings are wrongful. Punishment no doubt would also help deter killers. This too is a desideratum and a closely related one, but it is not to be identified with reprobation; for deterrence might be achieved by a dozen other techniques, from simple penalties and forfeitures to exhortation and propaganda; but effective public denunciation and, through it, symbolic nonacquiescence in the crime, seem virtually to require punishment.

This symbolic function of punishment was given great emphasis by Kant, who, characteristically, proceeded to exaggerate its importance. Even if a desert island community were to disband, Kant argued, its members should first execute the last murderer left in its jails, "for otherwise they might all be regarded as participators in the [unpunished] murder. . . ."[10] This Kantian idea that in failing to punish wicked acts society endorses them and thus becomes *particeps criminis* does seem to reflect, however dimly, something embedded in common sense. A similar notion underlies whatever is intelligible in the widespread notion that all citizens share the responsibility for political atrocities. Insofar as there is a coherent argument behind the extravagant distributions of guilt made by existentialists and other literary figures, it can be reconstructed in some such way as this: To whatever extent a political act is done 'in one's name,' to that extent one is responsible for it. A citizen can avoid responsibility in advance by explicitly disowning the government as his spokesman, or after the fact through open protest, resistance, and so on. Otherwise, by 'acquiescing' in what is done in one's name, one incurs the responsibility for it. The root notion here is a kind of 'power of attorney' a government has for its citizens.

3. *Vindication of the Law.* Sometimes the state goes on record through its statutes, in a way that might well please a conscientious citizen in whose name it speaks, but then through official evasion and unreliable enforcement, gives rise to doubts that the law really means what it says. It is murder in Mississippi, as elsewhere, for a white man intentionally to kill a Negro; but if grand juries refuse to issue indictments or if trial juries refuse to convict, and this is well understood by most citizens, then it is in a purely formal and empty sense indeed that killings of Negroes by whites are illegal in Mississippi. Yet the law stays on the books, to give ever-less-convincing lip service to a noble moral judgment. A statute honored mainly in the breach begins to lose its character as law, unless, as we say, it is *vindicated* (emphatically reaffirmed); and clearly the way to do this (indeed the only way) is to punish those who violate it.

Similarly, *punitive damages*, so-called, are sometimes awarded the plaintiff in a civil action, as a supplement to compensation for his injuries. What more dramatic way of vindicating his violated right can be imagined than to have a court thus forcibly condemn its violation through the symbolic machinery of punishment?

4. *Absolution of Others.* When something scandalous has occurred and it is clear that the wrongdoer must be one of a small number of suspects, then the state, by punishing one of these parties, thereby relieves the others of suspicion, and informally absolves them of blame. Moreover, quite often the absolution of an accuser hangs as much in the balance at a criminal trial as the inculpation of the accused. A good example of this can be found in James

Gould Cozzen's novel, *By Love Possessed*. A young girl, after an evening of illicit sexual activity with her boy friend, is found out by her bullying mother, who then insists that she clear her name by bringing criminal charges against the boy. He used physical force, the girl charges; she freely consented, he replies. If the jury finds him guilty of rape, it will by the same token absolve her from (moral) guilt; and her reputation as well as his rides on the outcome. Could not the state do this job without punishment? Perhaps, but when it speaks by punishing, its message is loud, and sure of getting across.

III. THE CONSTITUTIONAL PROBLEM OF DEFINING LEGAL PUNISHMENT

A philosophical theory of punishment that, through inadequate definition, leaves out the condemnatory function, not only will disappoint the moralist and the traditional moral philosopher; it will seem offensively irrelevant as well to the constitutional lawyer, whose vital concern with punishment is both conceptual, and therefore genuinely philosophical, and practically urgent. The distinction between punishment and mere penalties is a familiar one in the criminal law, where theorists have long engaged in what Jerome Hall calls "dubious dogmatics distinguishing 'civil penalties' from punitive sanctions, and 'public wrongs' from crimes."[11] Our courts now regard it as true (by definition) that all criminal statutes are punitive (merely labeling an act a crime does not make it one unless sanctions are specified); but to the converse question whether all statutes specifying sanctions are *criminal* statutes, the courts are reluctant to give an affirmative reply. There are now a great number of statutes that permit 'unpleasant consequences' to be inflicted on persons and yet are surely not criminal statutes—tax bills, for example, are aimed at regulating, not forbidding, certain types of activity. How to classify boderline cases as either 'regulative' or 'punitive' is not merely an idle conceptual riddle; it very quickly draws the courts into questions of great constitutional import. There are elaborate constitutional safeguards for persons faced with the prospect of punishment; but these do not, or need not, apply when the threatened hard treatment merely 'regulates an activity.'

The 1960 Supreme Court case of Flemming v. Nestor[12] is a dramatic (and shocking) exam-

ple of how a man's fate can depend on whether a government-inflicted deprivation is interpreted as a "regulative" or 'punitive' sanction. Nestor had immigrated to the United States from Bulgaria in 1913, and in 1955 became eligible for old-age benefits under the Social Security Act. In 1956, however, he was deported in accordance with the Immigration and Nationality Act, for having been a member of the Communist Party from 1933 to 1939. This was a hard fate for a man who had been in America for forty-three years and who was no longer a Communist; but at least he would have his social security benefits to support him in his exiled old age. Or so he thought. Section 202 of the amended Social Security Act, however,

provides for the termination of old-age, survivor, and disability insurance benefits payable to . . . an alien individual who, after September 1, 1954 (the date of enactment of the section) is deported under the Immigration and Nationality Act on any one of certain specified grounds, including past membership in the Communist Party.[13]

Accordingly, Nestor was informed that his benefits would cease.

Nestor then brought suit in a District Court for a reversal of the administrative decision. The court found in his favor and held §202 of the Social Security Act unconstitutional, on the grounds that

termination of [Nestor's] benefits amounts to punishing him without a judicial trial, that [it] constitutes the imposition of punishment by legislative act rendering §202 a bill of attainder; and that the punishment exacted is imposed for past conduct not unlawful when engaged in, thereby violating the constitutional prohibition on *ex post facto* laws.[14]

The Secretary of Health, Education, and Welfare, Mr. Flemming, then appealed this decision to the Supreme Court.

It was essential to the argument of the District Court that the termination of old-age benefits under §202 was in fact punishment, for if it were properly classified as nonpunitive deprivation, then none of the cited constitutional guarantees was relevant. The constitution, for example, does not forbid all retroactive laws, but only those providing punishment. (Retroactive tax laws may also be hard and unfair, but they are not unconstitutional.) The question before the Supreme Court then was whether the hardship imposed by §202 was punishment. Did this not bring the Court face to face with the properly philosophical question 'What is punishment?' and is it not clear that under the usual definition that fails to distinguish punishment from mere penalties, this particular judicial problem could not even arise?

The fate of the appellee Nestor can be recounted briefly. The five man majority of the court held that he had not been punished—this despite Mr. Justice Brennan's eloquent characterization of him in a dissenting opinion as "an aging man deprived of the means with which to live after being separated from his family and exiled to live among strangers in a land he quit forty-seven years ago."[15] Mr. Justice Harlan, writing for the majority, argued that the termination of benefits, like the deportation itself, was the exercise of the plenary power of Congress incident to the regulation of an activity.

Similarly, the setting by a State of qualifications for the practice of medicine, and their modification from time to time, is an incident of the State's power to protect the health and safety of its citizens, and its decision to bar from practice persons who commit or have committed a felony is taken as evidencing an intent to exercise that regulatory power, and not a purpose to add to the punishment of ex-felons.[16]

Mr. Justice Brennan, on the other hand, argued that it is impossible to think of any purpose the provision in question could possibly serve except to "strike" at "aliens deported for conduct displeasing to the lawmakers."[17]

Surely Justice Brennan seems right in finding in the sanction the expression of Congressional reprobation, and therefore 'punitive intent'; but the sanction itself (in Justice Harlan's words, "the mere denial of a noncontractual governmental benefit"[18]) was not a conventional vehicle for the expression of censure, being wholly outside the apparatus of the criminal law. It therefore lacked the reprobative symbolism essential to punishment generally, and was thus, in its hybrid character, able to generate confusion and judicial disagreement. It was as if Congress had 'condemned' a certain class of persons privately in stage whispers, rather than by pinning the infamous label of criminal on them and letting that symbol do the condemning in an open and public way. Congress without question "intended" to punish a certain class of aliens and did indeed select sanctions of appropriate severity for that use; but the deprivation they selected was not

of an appropriate kind to perform the function of public condemnation. A father who 'punishes' his son for a displeasing act the father had not thought to forbid in advance, by sneaking up on him from behind and then throwing him bodily across the room against the wall, would be in much the same position as the legislators of the amended Social Security Act, especially if he then denied to the son that his physical assault on him had had any 'punitive intent,' asserting that it was a mere exercise of his parental prerogative to rearrange the household furnishings and other objects in his own living room. This would be to tarnish the paternal authority and infect all later genuine punishments with hollow hypocrisy. This also happens when legislators go outside the criminal law to do the criminal law's job.

In 1961 the New York State Legislature passed the so-called "Subversive Drivers Act" requiring "suspension and revocation of the driver's license of anyone who has been convicted, under the Smith Act, of advocating the overthrow of the Federal government." *The Reporter* magazine[19] quoted the sponsor of the bill as admitting that it was aimed primarily at one person, Communist Benjamin Davis, who had only recently won a court fight to regain his driver's license after his five year term in prison. *The Reporter* estimated that at most a "few dozen" people would be kept from driving by the new legislation. Was this punishment? Not at all, said the bill's sponsor, Assemblyman Paul Taylor. The legislature was simply exercising its right to regulate automobile traffic in the interest of public safety:

Driving licenses, Assemblyman Taylor explained . . . are not a "right" but a "valuable privilege." The Smith Act Communists, after all, were convicted of advocating the overthrow of the government by force, violence, or assassination. ("They always leave out the assassination," he remarked. "I like to put it in.") Anyone who was convicted under such an act had to be "a person pretty well dedicated to a certain point of view," the assemblyman continued, and anyone with that particular point of view "can't be concerned about the rights of others." Being concerned about the rights of others, he concluded, "is a prerequisite of being a good driver."[20]

This shows how transparent can be the effort to mask punitive intent. The Smith Act ex-convicts were treated with such severity and in such circumstances that no nonpunitive legislative purpose could *plausibly* be maintained; yet that *kind* of treatment (quite apart from its severity) lacks the reprobative symbolism essential to clear public denunciation. After all, aged, crippled, and blind persons are also deprived of their licenses, so it is not *necessarily* the case that reprobation attaches to that kind of sanction. And so victims of a cruel law understandably claim that they have been punished, and retroactively at that. Yet strictly speaking they have not been *punished*; they have been treated much worse.

IV. THE PROBLEM OF STRICT CRIMINAL LIABILITY

The distinction between punishments and mere penalties, and the essentially reprobative function of the former, can also help clarify the controversy among writers on the criminal law about the propriety of so-called 'strict liability offenses'—offenses for the conviction of which there need be no showing of 'fault' or 'culpability' on the part of the accused. If it can be shown that he committed an act proscribed by statute then he is guilty irrespective of whether he had justification or excuse for what he did. Perhaps the most familiar examples come from the traffic laws: Leaving a car parked beyond the permitted time in a restricted zone is automatically to violate the law, and penalties will be imposed however good the excuse. Many strict liability statutes do not even require an overt act; these proscribe not certain conduct but certain *results*. Some make mere unconscious possession of contraband, firearms, or narcotics a crime, others the sale of misbranded articles or impure foods. The liability for so-called 'public welfare offenses' may seem especially severe:

> . . . with rare exceptions, it became definitely established that *mens rea* is not essential in the public welfare offenses, indeed that even a very high degree of care is irrelevant. Thus a seller of cattle feed was convicted of violating a statute forbidding misrepresentation of the percentage of oil in the product, despite the fact that he had employed a reputable chemist to make the analysis and had even understated the chemist's findings.[21]

The rationale of strict liability in public welfare statutes is that violation of the public interest is more likely to be prevented by unconditional liability than by liability that can be defeated by some kind of excuse; that even though liability without 'fault' is severe, it is one of the known risks incurred by businessmen; and that besides, the sanctions are *only fines*, hence not really 'punitive' in character. On the other hand, strict liability to *imprisonment* (or 'punishment proper') "has been held by many to be incompatible with the basic requirements of our Anglo-American, and indeed, any civilized jurisprudence."[22] Why should this be? In both kinds of case, defendants may have sanctions inflicted upon them even though they are acknowledged to be without fault; and the difference cannot be simply that imprisonment is always and necessarily a greater hurt than fine, for this is not always so. Rather, the reason why strict liability to imprisonment (punishment) is so much more repugnant to our sense of justice than is strict liability to fine (penalty) is simply that imprisonment in modern times has taken on the symbolism of public reprobation. In the words of Justice Brandeis, "It is . . . imprisonment in a penitentiary, which now renders a crime infamous."[23] We are familiar with the practice of penalizing persons for 'offenses' they could not help. It happens every day in football games, business firms, traffic courts, and the like. But there is something very odd and offensive in *punishing* people for admittedly faultless conduct; for not only is it arbitrary and cruel to *condemn* someone for something he did (admittedly) without fault, it is also self-defeating and irrational.

Though their abundant proliferation[24] is a relatively recent phenomenon, statutory offenses with nonpunitive sanctions have long been familiar to legal commentators, and long a source of uneasiness to them. This is "indicated by the persistent search for an appropriate label, such as 'public torts,' 'public welfare offenses,' 'prohibitory laws,' 'prohibited acts,' 'regulatory offenses,' 'police regulations,' 'administrative misdemeanors,' 'quasi-crimes,' or 'civil offences.' "[25] These represent alternatives to the unacceptable categorization of traffic infractions, inadvertent violations of commercial regulations, and the like, as *crimes*, their perpetrators as *criminals*, and their penalties as *punishments*. The drafters of the new Model Penal Code have defined a class of infractions of penal law forming no part of the substantive criminal law. These they call 'violations,' and their sanctions 'civil penalties.'

Section 1.04. Classes of Crimes: Violations

(1) An offense defined by this code or by any other statute of this State, for which a sentence of [death or of] imprisonment is authorized, constitutes a crime. Crimes are classified as felonies, misdemeanors, or petty misdemeanors.

[(2), (3), (4) define felonies, misdemeanors, and petty misdemeanors.]

(5) An offense defined by this Code or by any other statute of this State constitutes a violation if it is so designated in this Code or in the law defining the offense or if no other sentence than a fine, or fine and forfeiture or other civil penalty is authorized upon conviction or if it is defined by a statute other than this Code which now provides that the offense shall not constitute a crime. A violation does not constitute a crime and conviction of a violation shall not give rise to any disability or legal disadvantage based on conviction of a criminal offense.[26]

Since violations, unlike crimes, carry no social stigma, it is often argued that there is no serious injustice if, in the interest of quick and effective law enforcement, violators are held unconditionally liable. This line of argument is persuasive when we consider only parking and minor traffic violations, illegal sales of various kinds, and violations of health and safety codes, where the penalties serve as warnings and the fines are light. But the argument loses all cogency when the 'civil penalties' are severe—heavy fines, forfeitures of property, removal from office, suspension of a license, withholding of an important 'benefit,' and the like. The condemnation of the faultless may be the most flagrant injustice, but the good natured, noncondemnatory infliction of severe hardship on the innocent is little better. It is useful to distinguish violations and civil penalties from crimes and punishments; but it does not follow that the safeguards of culpability requirements and due process which justice demands for the latter are always irrelevant encumbrances to the former. Two things are morally wrong: (1) to condemn a faultless man while inflicting pain or deprivation on him however slight (unjust punishment); and (2) to inflict unnecessary and severe suffering on a faultless man even in the absence of condemnation (unjust civil penalty). To exact a two dollar fine from a hapless violator for overtime parking, however, even though he could not possibly have helped it, is to do neither of these things.

V. JUSTIFYING LEGAL PUNISHMENT; LETTING THE PUNISHMENT FIT THE CRIME

Public condemnation, whether avowed through the stigmatizing symbolism of punishment or unavowed but clearly discernible (mere 'punitive intent'), can greatly magnify the suffering caused by its attendant mode of hard treatment. Samuel Butler keenly appreciated the difference between reprobative hard treatment (punishment) and the same treatment sans reprobation:

. . . we should hate a single flogging given in the way of mere punishment more than the amputation of a limb, if it were kindly and courteously performed from a wish to help us out of our difficulty, and with the full consciousness on the part of the doctor that it was only by an accident of constitution that he was not in the like plight himself. So the Erewhonians take a flogging once a week, and a diet of bread and water for two or three months together, whenever their straightener recommends it.[27]

Even floggings and imposed fastings do not constitute punishments, then, where social conventions are such that they do not express public censure (what Butler called 'scouting'); and as therapeutic treatments simply, rather than punishments, they are easier to take.

Yet floggings and fastings do hurt, and far more than is justified by their Erewhonian (therapeutic) objectives. The same is true of our own State Mental Hospitals where criminal psychopaths are often sent for 'rehabilitation': Solitary confinement may not hurt *quite* so much when called 'the quiet room,' or the forced support of heavy fire extinguishers when called 'hydrotherapy';[28] but their infliction on patients can be so cruel (whether or not their quasi-medical names mask punitive intent) as to demand justification.

Hard treatment and symbolic condemnation, then, are not only both necessary to an adequate definition of 'punishment'; each also poses a special problem for the justification of punishment. The reprobative symbolism of punishment is subject to attack not only as an independent source of suffering but as the vehicle of undeserved responsive attitudes and unfair judgments of blame. One kind of skeptic, granting that penalties are needed if legal rules are to be enforced, and also that society would be impossible without general and predictable obedience to such rules, might nevertheless question the need to add condemnation to the penalizing of violators. Hard treatment of violators, he might grant, is an unhappy necessity, but reprobation of the offender is offensively self-righteous and cruel; adding gratuitous insult to necessary injury can serve no useful purpose. A partial answer to this kind of skeptic has already been given. The condemnatory aspect of punishment does serve a socially useful purpose: It is precisely the element in punishment that makes possible the performance of such symbolic functions as disavowal, nonacquiescence, vindication, and absolution.

Another kind of skeptic might readily grant that the reprobative symbolism of punishment is necessary to and justified by these various derivative functions. Indeed, he may even add deterrence to the list, for condemnation is likely to make it clear where it would not otherwise be so that a penalty is not a mere price-tag. Granting that point, however, this kind of skeptic would have us consider whether the ends that justify public condemnation of criminal conduct might not be achieved equally well by means of less painful symbolic machinery. There was a time, after all, when the gallows and the rack were the leading clear symbols of shame and ignominy. Now we condemn felons to penal servitude as the way of rendering their crimes infamous. Could not the job be done still more economically? Isn't there a way to stigmatize without inflicting any further (pointless) pain to the body, to family, to creative capacity?

One can imagine an elaborate public ritual, exploiting the trustiest devices of religion and mystery, music and drama, to express in the most solemn way the community's condemnation of a criminal for his dastardly deed. Such a ritual might condemn so very emphatically that there could be no doubt of its genuineness, thus rendering symbolically superfluous any further hard physical treatment. Such a device would preserve the condemnatory function of punishment while dispensing with its usual physical forms—incarceration and corporal mistreatment. Perhaps this is only idle fantasy; perhaps there is more to it. The question is surely open. The only point I wish to make here is one about the nature of the question. The problem of justifying punishment, when it

takes this form, may really be that of justifying our particular symbols of infamy.

Whatever the form of skeptical challenge to the institution of punishment, however, there is one traditional answer to it that seems to me to be incoherent. I refer to that form of the Retributive Theory which mentions neither condemnation nor vengeance, but insists instead that the ultimate justifying purpose of punishment is to match off moral gravity and pain, to give each offender exactly that amount of pain the evil of his offense calls for, on the alleged principle of justice that the wicked should suffer pain in exact proportion to their turpitude.

I will only mention in passing the familiar and potent objections to this view.[29] The innocent presumably deserve *not* to suffer just as the guilty are supposed to deserve to suffer; yet it is impossible to hurt an evil man without imposing suffering on those who love or depend on him. Deciding the right amount of suffering to inflict in a given case would require an assessment of the character of the offender as manifested through his whole life, and also his total lifelong balance of pleasure and pain, an obvious impossibility. Moreover, justice would probably demand the abandonment of general rules in the interests of individuation of punishment since there will inevitably be inequalities of moral guilt in the commission of the same crime, and inequalities of suffering from the same punishment. If not dispensed with, however, general rules must list all crimes in the order of their moral gravity, all punishments in the order of their severity, and the matchings between the two scales. But the moral gravity scale would have to list motives and purposes, not simply types of overt acts, for a given crime can be committed from any kind of 'mental state,' and its 'moral gravity' in a given case surely must depend in part on its accompanying motive. Condign punishment then would have to match suffering to motive (desire, belief, etc.), not to dangerousness or to amount of harm done. Hence some petty larcenies would be punished more severely than some murders. It is not likely we should wish to give power to judges and juries to make such difficult moral judgments. Worse than this, the judgments required are not merely 'difficult,' they are in principle impossible. It may seem 'self-evident' to some moralists that the passionate impulsive killer, for example, deserves less suffering for his wickedness than the scheming deliberate killer; but if the question of comparative *dangerousness* is left out of mind, reasonable men not only can but will disagree in their appraisals of comparative blameworthiness, and there appears no rational way of resolving the issue.[30] Certainly, there is no rational way of demonstrating that one deserves exactly twice or three-eighths or twelve-ninths as much suffering as the other; yet on some forms, at least, of this theory, the amount of suffering inflicted for any two crimes should stand in exact proportion to the 'amounts' of wickedness in the criminals.

For all that, however, the pain-fitting-wickedness version of the retributive theory does erect its edifice of moral superstition on a foundation in moral common sense, for justice *does* require that in some (other) sense "the punishment fit the crime." What justice requires is that the *condemnatory aspect* of the punishment suit the crime, that the crime be of a kind that is truly worthy of reprobation. Further, the degree of disapproval expressed by the punishment should 'fit' the crime only in the unproblematic sense that the more serious crimes should receive stronger disapproval than the less serious ones, the seriousness of the crime being determined by the amount of harm it generally causes and the degree to which people are disposed to commit it. That is quite another thing than requiring that the hard treatment component, considered apart from its symbolic function, should 'fit' the moral quality of a specific criminal act, assessed quite independently of its relation to social harm. Given our conventions, of course, condemnation is expressed by hard treatment, and the degree of harshness of the latter expresses the degree of reprobation of the former; still this should not blind us to the fact that it is social disapproval and its appropriate expression that should fit the crime, and not hard treatment (pain) as such. Pain should match guilt only insofar as its infliction is the symbolic vehicle of public condemnation.

NOTES

1. See especially the following: A. Flew, "The Justification of Punishment," *Philosophy*, 29 (1954), 291–307; S. I. Benn, "An Approach to the Problems of Punishment," *Philosophy*, 33 (1958), 325–341; and H. L. A. Hart, "Prolegomenon to the Principles of Punishment," *Proceedings of the Aristotelian Society*, 60 (1959–60), 1–26.

2. Hart and Benn both borrow Flew's definition. In Hart's paraphrase, punishment "(i) . . . must involve pain or other consequences normally considered unpleasant. (ii) It must be for an offense against legal rules. (iii) It must be of an actual or supposed offender for his offense. (iv) It must be intentionally administered by human beings other than the offender. (v) It must be imposed and administered by an authority constituted by a legal system against which the offense is committed." (*op. cit.*, p. 4.)

3. The distinction between punishments and penalties was first called to my attention by Dr. Anita Fritz of the University of Connecticut. Similar distinctions in different terminologies have been made by many. Pollock and Maitland speak of 'true afflictive punishments' as opposed to outlawry, private vengeance, fine, and emendation. (*History of English Law*, 2d ed., II, pp. 451 ff.) The phrase 'afflictive punishment' was invented by Bentham (*Rationale of Punishment*, London, 1830): "These [corporal] punishments are almost always attended with a portion of ignominy, and this does not always increase with the organic pain, but principally depends upon the condition [social class] of the offender." (p. 83). James Stephen says of legal punishment that it "should always connote . . . moral infamy." (*History of the Criminal Law*, II, p. 171.) Lasswell and Donnelly distinguish 'condemnation sanctions' and 'other deprivations.' ("The Continuing Debate over Responsibility: An Introduction to Isolating the Condemnation Sanction," *Yale Law Journal*, 68, 1959.) The traditional common law distinction is between 'infamous' and 'noninfamous' crimes and punishments. Conviction of an 'infamous crime' rendered a person liable to such postpunitive civil disabilities as incompetence to be a witness.

4. That even punishments proper are to be interpreted as taxes on certain kinds of conduct is a view often associated with O. W. Holmes, Jr. For an excellent discussion of Holmes's fluctuations on this question see Mark De Wolfe Howe, *Justice Holmes, The Proving Years* (Cambridge, Mass., 1963), pp. 74–80. See also Lon Fuller, *The Morality of Law* (New Haven, 1964), Chap. II, part 7, and H. L. A. Hart, *The Concept of Law* (Oxford, 1961), p. 39, for illuminating comparisons and contrasts of punishment and taxation.

5. H. L. A. Hart, *loc. cit.*

6. Henry M. Hart, "The Aims of the Criminal Law," *Law and Contemporary Problems*, 23 (1958), II, A, 4.

7. *General View of the Criminal Law of England*, First ed. (London, 1863), p. 99.

8. (London, 1953), pp. 17–18.

9. The Texas Penal Code (Art. 1220) states: "Homicide is justifiable when committed by the husband upon one taken in the act of adultery with the wife, provided the killing takes place before the parties to the act have separated. Such circumstances cannot justify a homicide when it appears that there has been on the part of the husband, any connivance in or assent to the adulterous connection." New Mexico and Utah have similar statutes. For some striking descriptions of perfectly legal paramour killings in Texas, see John Bainbridge, *The Super-Americans* (Garden City, 1961), pp. 238 ff.

10. *The Philosophy of Law*, trans. W. Hastie (Edinburgh, 1887), p. 198.

11. *General Principles of Criminal Law*, 2d ed. (Indianapolis, 1960), p. 328, hereafter cited as GPCL.

12. Flemming *v.* Nestor 80 S. Ct. 1367 (1960).

13. *Ibid.*, p. 1370.

14. *Ibid.*, p. 1374 (Interspersed citations omitted).

15. *Ibid.*, p. 1385.

16. *Ibid.*, pp. 1375–6.

17. *Ibid.*, p. 1387.

18. *Ibid.*, p. 1376.

19. *The Reporter* (May 11, 1961), p. 14.

20. *Loc. cit.*

21. Jerome Hall, GPCL, p. 329.

22. Richard A. Wasserstrom, "Strict Liability in the Criminal Law," *Stanford Law Review*, 12 (1960), p. 730.

23. United States *v.* Moreland, 258 U.S. 433, 447–48. Quoted in Hall, GPCL, p. 327.

24. "A depth study of Wisconsin statutes in 1956 revealed that of 1113 statutes creating criminal offenses [punishable by fine, imprisonment, or both] which were in force in 1953, no less than 660 used language in the definitions of the offenses which omitted all reference to a mental element, and which therefore, under the canons of construction which have come to govern these matters, left it open to the courts to impose strict liability if they saw fit." Colin Howard, "Not Proven," *Adelaide Law Review*, 1 (1962), 274. The study cited is: Remington, Robinson and Zick, "Liability Without Fault Criminal Statutes," *Wisconsin Law Review* (1956), 625, 636.

25. Rollin M. Perkins, *Criminal Law* (Brooklyn, 1957), pp. 701–2.

26. American Law Institute, *Model Penal Code, Proposed Official Draft* (Philadelphia, 1962).

27. *Erewhon* (London, 1901), Chapter 10.

28. These two examples are cited by Francis A. Allen in "Criminal Justice, Legal Values and the Rehabilitative Ideal," *Journal of Criminal Law, Criminology and Police Science*, 50 (1959), 229.

29. For more convincing statements of these arguments, see *iter alia:* W. D. Ross, *The Right and the Good* (Oxford, 1930), pp. 56–65; J. D. Mabbott, "Punishment," *Mind*, 49 (1939); A. C. Ewing, *The Morality of Punishment* (London, 1929), Chap. 1; and F. Dostoevsky, *The House of the Dead.*

30. Cf. Jerome Michael and Herbert Wechsler, *Criminal Law and Its Administration* (Chicago, 1940), "Note on Deliberation and Character," pp. 170–2.

JOEL FEINBERG
The Classic Debate*

The traditional debate among philosophers over the justification of legal punishment has been between partisans of the "retributive" and "utilitarian" theories. Neither the term "retributive" nor the term "utilitarian" has been used with perfect uniformity and precision, but, by and large, those who have been called utilitarians have insisted that punishment of the guilty is at best a necessary evil justified only as a means to the prevention of evils even greater than itself. "Retributivism," on the other hand, has labeled a large miscellany of theories united only in their opposition to the utilitarian theory. It may best serve clarity, therefore, to define the utilitarian theory with relative precision (as above) and then define retributivism as its logical contradictory, so that the two theories are not only mutually exclusive but also jointly exhaustive. Discusssion of the various varieties of retributivism can then proceed.

Perhaps the leading form of the retributive theory includes major elements identifiable in the following formulations:

It is an end in itself that the guilty should suffer pain...The primary justification of punishment is always to be found in the fact that an offense has been committed which deserves the punishment, not in any future advantage to be gained by its infliction.[1]

Punishment is justified only on the ground that wrongdoing merits punishment. It is morally fitting that a person who does wrong should suffer in proportion to his wrongdoing. That a criminal should be punished follows from his guilt, and the severity of the appropriate punishment depends on the depravity of the act. The state of affairs where a wrongdoer suffers punishment is morally better than one where he does not, and is so irrespective of consequences.[2]

Justification, according to these accounts, must look backward in time to guilt rather than forward to "advantages"; the formulations are rich in moral terminology ("merits," "morally fitting," "wrongdoing," "morally better"); there is great emphasis on *desert*. For those reasons, we might well refer to this as a "moralistic" version of the retributive theory. As such it can be contrasted with a "legalistic" version, according to which punishment is for lawbreaking, not (necessarily) for wrongdoing. Legalistic retributivism holds that the justification of punishment is always to be found in the fact that a rule has been broken for the violation of which a certain penalty is specified, whether or not the offender incurs any moral guilt. The offender, properly apprised in advance of the penalty, voluntarily assumes the risk of punishment, and when he or she receives comeuppance, he or she can have no complaint. As one recent legalistic retributivist put it,

Punishment is a corollary not of law but of lawbreaking. Legislators do not choose to punish. They hope no punishment will be needed. Their laws would succeed even if no punishment occurred. The criminal makes the essential choice: he "brings it on himself."[3]

Both moralistic and legalistic retributivism have "pure" and "impure" variants. In their pure formulations, they are totally free of utilitarian admixture. Moral or legal guilt (as the case may be) is not only a necessary condition for justified punishment, it is quite sufficient "irrespective of consequences." In the impure formulation, both guilt (moral or legal) and conducibility to good consequences are necessary for justified punishment, but neither is sufficient without the other. This mixed theory could with some propriety be called "impure utilitarianism" as well as "impure retributivism." Since we have stipulated, however, that

---

*Published in previous editions as part of the Introduction to this section.

a retributive theory is one which is not wholly utilitarian, we are committed to the latter usage.

A complete theory of punishment will not only specify the conditions under which punishment should and should not be administered, it will also provide a general criterion for determining the amount or degree of punishment. It is not only unjust to be punished undeservedly and to be let off although meriting punishment, it is also unfair to be punished severely for a minor offense or lightly for a heinous one. What is the right amount of punishment? There is one kind of answer especially distinctive of retributivism in all of its forms: an answer in terms of fittingness or proportion. The punishment must *fit* the crime; its degree must be *proportionate* to the seriousness or moral gravity of the offense. Retributivists are often understandably vague about the practical interpretations of the key notions of fittingness, proportion, and moral gravity. Sometimes aesthetic analogies are employed (such as matching and clashing colors, or harmonious and dissonant chords). Some retributivists, including Immanuel Kant, attempt to apply the ancient principle of *lex talionis* (the law of retaliation): The punishment should match the crime not only in the degree of harm inflicted on its victim, but also in the mode and manner of the infliction: fines for larceny, physical beatings for battery, capital punishment for murder. Other retributivists, however, explicitly reject the doctrine of retaliation in kind; hence, that doctrine is better treated as a logically independent thesis commonly associated with retributivism rather than as an essential component of the theory.

Defined as the exhaustive class of alternatives to the utilitarian theory, retributivism of course is subject to no simple summary. It will be useful to subsequent discussions, however, to summarize that popular variant of the theory which can be called *pure moralistic retributivism* as consistent (at least) of the following propositions:

1. Moral guilt is a necessary condition for justified punishment.
2. Moral guilt is a sufficient condition ("irrespective of consequences") for justified punishment.
3. The proper amount of punishment to be inflicted upon the morally guilty offender is that amount which fits, matches, or is proportionate to the moral gravity of the offense.

That it is never justified to punish a morally blameless person for his or her "offense" (thesis 1) may not be quite self-evident, but it does find strong support in moral common sense. Thesis 2, however, is likely to prove an embarrassment for the pure retributivist, for it would have him or her approve the infliction of suffering on a person (albeit a *guilty* person) even when no good to the offender, the victim, or society at large is likely to result. "How can two wrongs make a right, or two evils a good?" he or she will be asked by the utilitarian, and in this case it is the utilitarian who will claim to speak for "moral common sense." In reply, the pure retributivist is likely to concede that inflicting suffering on an offender is not "good in itself," but will also point out that single acts cannot be judged simply "in themselves" with no concern for the context in which they fit and the events preceding them which are their occasion. Personal sadness is not a "good in itself" either, and yet when it is a response to the perceived sufferings of another it has a unique appropriateness. Glee, considered "in itself," looks much more like an intrinsically good mental state, but glee does not morally fit the perception of another's pain any more than an orange shirt aesthetically fits shocking pink trousers. Similarly, it may be true (the analogy is admittedly imperfect) that "while the moral evil in the offender and the pain of the punishment are each considered separately evils, it is intrinsically good that a certain relation exist or be established between them."[4] In this way the pure retributivist, relying on moral intuitions, can deny that a deliberate imposition of suffering on a human being is either good in itself or good as a means, and yet find it justified, nevertheless, as an essential component of an intrinsically good relation. Perhaps that is to put the point too strongly. All the retributivist needs to establish is that the complex situation preceding the infliction of punishment can be made better than it otherwise would be by the addition to it of the offender's suffering.

The utilitarian is not only unconvinced by arguments of this kind, he or she is also likely to find a "suspicious connection" between philosophical retributivism and the primitive lust for vengeance. The moralistic retributivist protests that he or she eschews anger or any other passion and seeks not revenge, but justice and the satisfaction of desert. Punishment, after all, is not the only kind of treatment we bestow upon persons simply because we think they deserve it. Teachers give students the grades they have earned with no thought of "future advantage," and with eyes firmly fixed on past performance. There is no necessary jubilation at good performance or vindictive pleasure in assigning low grades. And much the same is true of the assignments of rewards, prizes, grants, compensation, civil liability, and so on. Justice requires assignment on the basis of desert alone. To be sure, there is

a great danger of revengeful and sadistic tendencies finding vent under the unconscious disguise of a righteous indignation calling for just punishment, since the evil desire for revenge, if not identical with the latter, bears a resemblance to it sufficiently close to deceive those who want an excuse.[5]

Indeed, it is commonly thought that our modern notions of retributive justice have grown out of earlier practices, like the vendetta and the law of deodand, that were through and through expressions of the urge to vengeance.[6] Still, the retributivist replies, it is unfair to *identify* a belief with one of its corruptions, or a modern practice with its historical antecedents. The latter mistake is an instance of the "genetic fallacy" which is committed whenever one confuses an account of how something came to be the way it is with an analysis of what it has become.

The third thesis of the pure moralistic retributivist has also been subject to heavy attack. Can it really be the business of the state to ensure that happiness and unhappiness are distributed among citizens in proportion to their moral deserts? Think of the practical difficulties involved in the attempt simply to apportion pain to moral guilt in a given case, with no help from utilitarian considerations. First of all, it is usually impossible to punish an offender without inflicting suffering on those who love or depend upon him and may themselves be entirely innocent, morally speaking. In that way, punishing the guilty is self-defeating from the moralistic retributive point of view. It will do more to increase than to diminish the disproportion between unhappiness and desert throughout society. Secondly, the aim of apportioning pain to guilt would in some cases require punishing "trivial" moral offenses, like rudeness, as heavily as more socially harmful crimes, since there can be as much genuine

wickedness in the former as the latter. Thirdly, there is the problem of accumulation. Deciding the right amount of suffering to inflict in a given case would entail an assessment of the character of the offender as manifested throughout his or her whole life (and not simply at one weak moment) and also an assessment of his or her total lifelong balance of pleasure and pain. Moreover, there are inevitably inequalities of moral guilt in the commission of the same crime by different offenders, as well as inequalities of suffering from the same punishment. Application of the pure retributive theory then would require the abandonment of fixed penalties for various crimes and the substitution of individuated penalties selected in each case by an authority to fit the offender's uniquely personal guilt and vulnerability.

The utilitarian theory of punishment holds that punishment is never good in itself, but is (like bad-tasting medicine) justified when, and only when, it is a means to such future goods as *correction* (reform) of the offender, *protection* of society against other offenses from the same offender, and *deterrence* of other would-be offenders. (The list is not exhaustive.) Giving the offender the pain he deserves because of his wickedness is either not a coherent notion, on this theory, or else not a morally respectable independent reason for punishing. In fact, the utilitarian theory arose in the eighteenth century as part of a conscious reaction to cruel and uneconomical social institutions (including prisons) that were normally defended, if at all, in righteously moralistic terms.

For purposes of clarity, the utilitarian theory of punishment should be distinguished from utilitarianism as a general moral theory. The standard of right conduct generally, according to the latter, is conducibility to good consequences. Any act at all, whether that of a private citizen, a legislator, or a judge, is morally right if and only if it is likely, on the best evidence, to do more good or less harm all around than any alternative conduct open to the actor. (The standard for judging the goodness of consequences, in turn, for Jeremy Bentham and the early utilitarians was the amount of human happiness they contained, but many later utilitarians had more complicated conceptions of intrinsic value.) All proponents of general utilitarianism, of course, are also supporters of the utilitarian theory of punishment, but there is no logical necessity that in respect to punishment a utilitarian be a general utilitarian across the board.

The utilitarian theory of punishment can be summarized in three propositions parallel to those used above to summarize pure moralistic retributivism. According to this theory:

1. Social utility (correction, prevention, deterrence, et cetera) is a necessary condition for justified punishment.
2. Social utility is a sufficient condition for justified punishment.
3. The proper amount of punishment to be inflicted upon the offender is that amount which will do the most good or the least harm to all those who will be affected by it.

The first thesis enjoys the strongest support from common sense, though not so strong as to preclude controversy. For the retributivist, as has been seen, punishing the guilty is an end in itself quite apart from any gain in social utility. The utilitarian is apt to reply that if reform of the criminal could be secured with no loss of deterrence by simply giving him or her a pill that would have the same effect, then nothing would be lost by not punishing him or her, and the substitute treatment would be "sheer gain."

Thesis 2, however, is the utilitarian's greatest embarrassment. The retributivist opponent argues forcefully against it that in certain easily imaginable circumstances it would justify punishment of the (legally) innocent, a consequence which all would regard as a moral abomination. Some utilitarians deny that punishment of the innocent could *ever* be the alternative that has the best consequences in social utility, but this reply seems arbitrary and dogmatic. Other utilitarians claim that "punishment of the innocent" is a self-contradiction. The concept of punishment, they argue,[7] itself implies hard treatment imposed upon the guilty as a conscious and deliberate response to their guilt. That guilt is part of the very definition of punishment, these writers claim, is shown by the absurdity of saying "I am punishing you for something you have not done," which sounds very much like "I am curing you even though you are not sick." Since all punishment is understood to be for guilt, they conclude, they can hardly be interpreted as advocating punishing without guilt. H. L. A. Hart[8] calls this move a "definitional stop," and charges that it is an "abuse of definition," and indeed it is, if put forward by a proponent of the general utilitarian theory. If the right act in all contexts is the one which is likely to have the best consequences, then conceivably the act of framing an innocent man could sometimes be right; and the question of whether such mistreatment of the innocent party could properly be called "punishment" is a mere question of words having no bearing on the utilitarian's embarrassment. If, on the other hand, the definitional stop is employed by a defender of the utilitarian theory of the justification of punishment who is not a utilitarian across the board, then it seems to be a legitimate argumentative move. Such a utilitarian is defending official infliction of hard treatment (deprivation of liberty, suffering, et cetera) on *those who are legally guilty,* a practice to which he or she refers by using the word "punishment," as justified when and only when there is probably social utility in it.

No kind of utilitarian, however, will have plausible recourse to the definitional stop in defending thesis 3 from the retributivist charge that it would, in certain easily imaginable circumstances, justify excessive and/or insufficient penalties. The appeal again is to moral common sense: It would be manifestly unfair to inflict a mere two dollar fine on a convicted murderer or life imprisonment, under a balance of terror policy, for parking offenses. In either case, the punishment imposed would violate the retributivist's thesis 3, that the punishment be proportional to the moral gravity of the offense. And yet, if these were the penalties likely to have the best effects generally, the utilitarian in the theory of punishment would be committed to their support. He or she could not argue that excessive or deficient penalties are not "really" punishments, Instead he would have to argue, as does Jeremy Bentham, that the proper employment of the utilitarian method simply could not lead to penalties so far out of line with our moral intuitions as the retributivist charges.

So far vengeance has not been mentioned except in the context of charge and countercharge between theorists who have no use for it. There are writers, however, who have kind words for vengeance and give it a central role in their theories of the justification of punishment. We can call these approaches the Vindictive Theory of Punishment (to distinguish them from legalistic and moralistic forms of retributivism) and then subsume its leading varieties under either the utilitarian or the retributive rubrics. Vindictive theories are of three different kinds: (1) The *escape-valve version,* commonly associated with the names of James Fitzjames Stephen and Oliver Wendell Holmes, Jr., and currently in favor with some psychoanalytic writers, holds that legal punishment is an orderly outlet for aggressive feelings, which would otherwise demand satisfaction in socially disruptive ways. The prevention of private vendettas through a state monopoly on vengeance is one of the chief ways in which legal punishment has social utility. The escape-valve theory is thus easily assimilated by the utilitarian theory of punishment. (2) The *hedonistic version* of the vindictive theory finds the justification of punishment in the pleasure it gives people (particularly the victim of the crime and his or her loved ones) to see the criminal suffer for the crime. For most utilitarians, and certainly for Bentham, any kind of pleasure—even spiteful, sadistic, or vindictive pleasure, just insofar as it *is* pleasure—counts as a good in the computation of social utility, just as pain—any kind of pain—counts as an evil. (This is sufficient to discredit hedonistic utilitarianism thoroughly, according to its retributivist critics.) The hedonistic version of the vindictive theory, then, is also subsumable under the utilitarian rubric. Finally, (3) the *romantic version* of the vindictive theory, very popular among the uneducated, holds that the justification of punishment is to be found in the emotions of hate and anger it expresses, these emotions being those allegedly felt by all normal or right-thinking people. I call this theory "romantic," despite certain misleading associations of that word, because, like any philosophical theory so labeled, it holds that certain emotions and the actions they inspire are self-certifying, needing no further justification. It is therefore not a kind of utilitarian theory and must be classified as a variety of retributivism, although in its emphasis on feeling it is in marked contrast to more typical retributive theories that eschew emotion and emphasize proportion and desert.

Many anthropologists have traced vindictive feelings and judgments to an origin in the "tribal morality" which universally prevails in primitive cultures, and which presumably governed the tribal life of our own prehistoric ancestors. If an anthropologist turned his attention to our modern criminal codes, he would discover evidence that tribalism has never entirely vacated its position in the criminal law. There are some provisions for which the vindictive theory (in any of its forms) would provide a ready rationale, but for which the utilitarian and moralistic retributivist theories are hard put to discover a plausible defense. Completed crimes, for example, are punished more severely than attempted crimes that fail for accidental reasons. This should not be surprising since the more harm caused the victim, his or her loved ones, and those of the public who can identify imaginatively with them, the more anger there will be at the criminal. If the purpose of punishment is to satisfy that anger, then we should expect that those who succeed in harming will be punished more than the bunglers who fail, even if the motives and intentions of the bunglers were every bit as wicked.

NOTES

1. A. C. Ewing, *The Morality of Punishment* (London: Kegan Paul, 1929), p. 13.

2. John Rawls, "Concepts of Rules," *The Philosophical Review,* LXIV (1955), pp. 4, 5.

3. J. D. Mabbott, "Punishment," *Mind,* LXVIII (1939), p. 161.

4. A. C. Ewing, *Ethics* (New York: Macmillan, 1953), pp. 169–70.

5. Ewing, *Morality of Punishment,* p. 27.

6. See O. W. Holmes, Jr., *The Common Law* (Boston: Little, Brown, 1881) and Henry Maine, *Ancient Law.* 1861 Reprint. (Boston: Beacon Press, 1963).

7. See, for example, Anthony Quinton, "On Punishment," *Analysis,* XIV (1954), pp. 1933–42.

8. H. L. A. Hart, *Punishment and Responsibility* (New York and Oxford: Oxford University Press, 1968), pp. 5, 6.

JOHN RAWLS
Punishment*

TWO CONCEPTS OF RULES

In this paper I want to show the importance of the distinction between justifying a practice[1] and justifying a particular action falling under it, and I want to explain the logical basis of this distinction and how it is possible to miss its significance. While the distinction has frequently been made,[2] and is now becoming commonplace, there remains the task of explaining the tendency either to overlook it altogether, or to fail to appreciate its importance.

To show the importance of the distinction I am going to defend utilitarianism against those objections which have traditionally been made against it in connection with punishment and the obligation to keep promises. I hope to show that if one uses the distinction in question then one can state utilitarianism in a way which makes it a much better explication of our considered moral judgments than these traditional objections would seem to admit.[3] Thus the importance of the distinction is shown by the way it strengthens the utilitarian view regardless of whether that view is completely defensible or not.

To explain how the significance of the distinction may be overlooked, I am going to discuss two conceptions of rules. One of these conceptions conceals the importance of distinguishing between the justification of a rule or practice and the justification of a particular action falling under it. The other conception makes it clear why this distinction must be made and what is its logical basis.

The subject of punishment, in the sense of attaching legal penalties to the violation of legal rules, has always been a troubling moral question.[4] The trouble about it has not been that people disagree as to whether or not punishment is justifiable. Most people have held that, freed from certain abuses, it is an acceptable institution.

*From "Two Concepts of Rules" by John Rawls, *The Philosophical Review,* Vol. 64 (1955), pp. 3–13. Reprinted by permission of the author and the publisher.

Only a few have rejected punishment entirely, which is rather surprising when one considers all that can be said against it. The difficulty is with the justification of punishment: various arguments for it have been given by moral philosophers, but so far none of them has won any sort of general acceptance; no justification is without those who detest it. I hope to show that the use of the aforementioned distinction enables one to state the utilitarian view in a way which allows for the sound points of its critics.

For our purposes we may say that there are two justifications of punishment. What we may call the retributive view is that punishment is justified on the grounds that wrongdoing merits punishment. It is morally fitting that a person who does wrong should suffer in proportion to his wrongdoing. That a criminal should be punished follows from his guilt, and the severity of the appropriate punishment depends on the depravity of his act. The state of affairs where a wrongdoer suffers punishment is morally better than the state of affairs where he does not; and it is better irrespective of any of the consequences of punishing him.

What we may call the utilitarian view holds that on the principle that bygones are bygones and that only future consequences are material to present decisions, punishment is justifiable only by reference to the probable consequences of maintaining it as one of the devices of the social order. Wrongs committed in the past are, as such, not relevant considerations for deciding what to do. If punishment can be shown to promote effectively the interest of society it is justifiable, otherwise it is not.

I have stated these two competing views very roughly to make one feel the conflict between them: one feels the force of *both* arguments and one wonders how they can be reconciled. From my introductory remarks it is obvious that the resolution which I am going to propose is that in this case one must distinguish between justifying a practice as a system of rules to be applied and enforced, and justifying a particular action which falls under these rules; utilitarian arguments are appropriate with regard to questions about practices, while retributive arguments fit the application of particular rules to particular cases.

We might try to get clear about this distinction by imagining how a father might answer the question of his son. Suppose the son asks, "Why was *J* put in jail yesterday?" The father answers, "Because he robbed the bank at *B*. He was duly tried and found guilty. That's why he was put in jail yesterday." But suppose the son had asked a different question, namely, "Why do people put other people in jail?" Then the father might answer, "To protect good people from bad people" or "To stop people from doing things that would make it uneasy for all of us; for otherwise we wouldn't be able to go to bed at night and sleep in peace." There are two very different questions here. One question emphasizes the proper name: It asks why *J* was punished rather than someone else, or it asks what he was punished for. The other question asks why we have the institution of punishment: Why do people punish one another rather than, say, always forgiving one another?

Thus the father says in effect that a particular man is punished, rather than some other man, because he is guilty, and he is guilty because he broke the law (past tense). In his case the law looks back, the judge looks back, the jury looks back, and a penalty is visited upon him for something he did. That a man is to be punished, and what his punishment is to be, is settled by its being shown that he broke the law and that the law assigns that penalty for the violation of it.

On the other hand we have the institution of punishment itself, and recommend and accept various changes in it, because it is thought by the (ideal) legislator and by those to whom the law applies that, as a part of a system of law impartially applied from case to case arising under it, it will have the consequence, in the long run, of furthering the interests of society.

One can say, then, that the judge and the legislator stand in different positions and look in different directions: one to the past, the other to the future. The justification of what the judge does, *qua* judge, sounds like the retributive view; the justification of what the (ideal) legislator does, *qua* legislator, sounds like the utilitarian view. Thus both views have a point (this is as it should be since intelligent and sensitive persons have been on both sides of the argument); and one's initial confusion disappears once one sees that these views apply to persons holding different offices with different duties, and situated differently with respect to the system of rules that make up the criminal law.[5]

One might say, however, that the utilitarian view is more fundamental since it applies to a more fundamental office, for the judge carries out the legislator's will so far as he can determine it. Once the legislator decides to have laws and to assign penalties for their violation (as things are there must be both the law and the penalty) an institution is set up which involves a retributive conception of particular cases. It is part of the concept of the criminal law as a system of rules that the application and enforcement of these rules in particular cases should be justifiable by arguments of a retributive character. The decision whether or not to use law rather than some other mechanism of social control, and the decision as to what laws to have and what penalties to assign, may be settled by utilitarian arguments; but if one decides to have laws then one has decided on something whose working in particular cases is retributive in form.[6]

The answer, then, to the confusion engendered by the two views of punishment is quite simple: One distinguishes two offices, that of the judge and that of the legislator, and one distinguishes their different stations with respect to the system of rules which make up the law; and then one notes that the different sorts of considerations which would usually be offered as reasons for what is done under the cover of these offices can be paired off with the competing justifications of punishment. One reconciles the two views by the time-honored device of making them apply to different situations.

But can it really be this simple? Well, this answer allows for the apparent intent of each side. Does a person who advocates the retributive view necessarily advocate, as an *institution,* legal machinery whose essential purpose is to set up and preserve a correspondence between moral turpitude and suffering? Surely not.[7] What retributionists have rightly insisted upon is that no man can be punished unless he is guilty, that is, unless he has broken the law. Their fundamental criticism of the utilitarian account is that, as they interpret it, it sanctions an innocent person's being punished (if one may call it that) for the benefit of society.

On the other hand, utilitarians agree that punishment is to be inflicted only for the violation of law. They regard this much as understood from the concept of punishment itself.[8] The point of the utilitarian account concerns the institution as a system of rules: utilitarianism seeks to limit its use by declaring it justifiable only if it can be shown to foster effectively the good of society. Historically it is a protest against the indiscriminate and ineffective use of the criminal law.[9] It seeks to dissuade us from assigning to penal institutions the improper, if not sacrilegious, task of matching suffering with moral turpitude. Like others, utilitarians want penal institutions designed so that, as far as humanly possible, only those who break the law run afoul of it. They hold that no official should have discretionary power to inflict penalties whenever he thinks it for the benefit of society; for on utilitarian grounds an institution granting such power could not be justified.[10]

The suggested way of reconciling the retributive and the utilitarian justifications of punishment seems to account for what both sides have wanted to say. There are, however, two further questions which arise, and I shall devote the remainder of this section to them.

First, will not a difference of opinion as to the proper criterion of just law make the proposed reconciliation unacceptable to retributionists? Will they not question whether, if the utilitarian principle is used as the criterion, it follows that those who have broken the law are guilty in a way which satisfies their demand that those punished deserve to be punished? To answer this difficulty, suppose that the rules of the criminal law are justified on utilitarian grounds (it is only for laws that meet his criterion that the utilitarian can be held responsible). Then it follows that the actions which the criminal law specifies as offenses are such that, if they were tolerated, terror and alarm would spread in society. Consequently, retributionists can only deny that those who are punished deserve to be punished if they deny that such actions are wrong. This they will not want to do.

The second question is whether utilitarianism doesn't justify too much. One pictures it as an engine of justification which, if consistently adopted, could be used to justify cruel and arbitrary institutions. Retributionists may be supposed to concede that utilitarians *intend* to reform the law and to make it more humane; that utilitarians do not *wish* to justify any such thing as punishment of the innocent; and that utilitarians may appeal to the fact that punishment presupposes guilt in the sense that by punishment one understands an institution attaching penalties to the infraction of legal rules, and therefore

that it is logically absurd to suppose that utilitarians in justifying *punishment* might also have justified punishment (if we may call it that) of the innocent. The real question, however, is whether the utilitarian, in justifying punishment, hasn't used arguments which commit him to accepting the infliction of suffering on innocent persons if it is for the good of society (whether or not one calls this punishment). More generally, isn't the utilitarian committed in principle to accepting many practices which he, as a morally sensitive person, wouldn't want to accept? Retributionists are inclined to hold that there is no way to stop the utilitarian principle from justifying too much except by adding to it a principle which distributes certain rights to individuals. Then the amended criterion is not the greatest benefit of society *simpliciter* [simply], but the greatest benefit of society subject to the constraint that no one's rights may be violated. Now while I think that the classical utilitarians proposed a criterion of this more complicated sort, I do not want to argue that point here.[11] What I want to show is that there is *another* way of preventing the utilitarian principle from justifying too much, or at least of making it much less likely to do so: namely, by stating utilitarianism in a way which accounts for the distinction between the justification of an institution and the justification of a particular action falling under it.

I begin by defining the institution of punishment as follows: a person is said to suffer punishment whenever he is legally deprived of some of the normal rights of a citizen on the ground that he has violated a rule of law, the violation having been established by trial according to the due process of law, provided that the deprivation is carried out by the recognized legal authorities of the state, that the rule of law clearly specifies both the offense and the attached penalty, that the courts construe statutes strictly, and that the statute was on the books prior to the time of the offense.[12] This definition specifies what I shall understand by punishment. The question is whether utilitarian arguments may be found to justify institutions widely different from this and such as one would find cruel and arbitrary.

This question is best answered, I think, by taking up a particular accusation. Consider the following from Carritt:

... the utilitarian must hold that we are justified in inflicting pain always and only to prevent worse pain or bring about greater happiness. This, then, is all we need to consider in so-called punishment, which must be purely preventive. But if some kind of very cruel crime becomes common, and none of the criminals can be caught, it might be highly expedient, as an example, to hang an innocent man, if a charge against him could be so framed that he were universally thought guilty; indeed this would only fail to be an ideal instance of utilitarian 'punishment' because the victim himself would not have been so likely as a real felon to commit such a crime in the future; in all other respects it would be perfectly deterrent and therefore felicific.[13]

Carritt is trying to show that there are occasions when a utilitarian argument would justify taking an action which would be generally condemned; and thus that utilitarianism justifies too much. But the failure of Carritt's argument lies in the fact that he makes no distinction between the justification of the general system of rules which constitutes penal institutions and the justification of particular applications of these rules to particular cases by the various officials whose job it is to administer them. This becomes perfectly clear when one asks who the "we" are of whom Carritt speaks. Who is this who has a sort of absolute authority on particular occasions to decide that an innocent man shall be "punished" if everyone can be convinced that he is guilty? Is this person the legislator, or the judge, or the body of private citizens, or what? It is utterly crucial to know who is to decide such matters, and by what authority, for all of this must be written into the rules of the institution. Until one knows these things one doesn't know what the institution is whose justification is being challenged; and as the utilitarian principle applies to the institution one doesn't know whether it is justifiable on utilitarian grounds or not.

Once this is understood it is clear what the countermove to Carritt's argument is. One must describe more carefully what the *institution* is which his example suggests, and then ask oneself whether or not it is likely that having this institution would be for the benefit of society in the long run. One must not content oneself with the vague thought that, when it's a question of *this* case, it would be a good thing if *somebody* did something even if an innocent person were to suffer.

Try to imagine, then, an institution (which we may call "telishment") which is such that the officials set up by it have authority to arrange a trial for the condemnation of an innocent man whenever they are of the opinion that doing so would be in the best interests of society. The discretion of officials is limited, however, by the rule that they may not condemn an innocent man to

undergo such an ordeal unless there is, at the time, a wave of offenses similar to that with which they charge him and telish him for. We may imagine that the officials having the discretionary authority are the judges of the higher courts in consultation with the chief of police, the minister of justice, and a committee of the legislature.

Once one realizes that one is involved in setting up an *institution,* one sees that the hazards are very great. For example, what check is there on the officials? How is one to tell whether or not their actions are authorized? How is one to limit the risks involved in allowing such systematic deception? How is one to avoid giving anything short of complete discretion to the authorities to telish anyone they like? In addition to these considerations, it is obvious that people will come to have a very different attitude towards their penal system when telishment is adjoined to it. They will be uncertain as to whether a convicted man has been punished or telished. They will wonder whether or not they should feel sorry for him. They will wonder whether the same fate won't at any time fall on them. If one pictures how such an institution would actually work, and the enormous risks involved in it, it seems clear that it would serve no useful purpose. A utilitarian justification for this institution is most unlikely.

It happens in general that as one drops off the defining features of punishment one ends up with an institution whose utilitarian justification is highly doubtful. One reason for this is that punishment works like a kind of price system: By altering the prices one has to pay for the performance of actions, it supplies a motive for avoiding some actions and doing others. The defining features are essential if punishment is to work in this way; so that an institution which lacks these features, for example, an institution which is set up to "punish" the innocent, is likely to have about as much point as a price system (if one may call it that) where the prices of things change at random from day to day and one learns the price of something after one has agreed to buy it.[14]

If one is careful to apply the utilitarian principle to the institution which is to authorize particular actions, then there is *less* danger of its justifying too much. Carritt's example gains plausibility by its indefiniteness and by its concentration on the particular case. His argument will only hold if it can be shown that there are utilitarian arguments which justify an institution whose publicly ascertainable offices and powers are such as to permit officials to exercise that kind of discretion in particular cases. But the requirement of having to build the arbitrary features of the particular decision into the institutional practice makes the justification much less likely to go through.

NOTES

1. I use the word "practice" throughout as a sort of technical term meaning any form of activity specified by a system of rules which defines offices, roles, moves, penalties, defenses, and so on, and which gives the activity its structure. As examples one may think of games and rituals, trials and parliaments.

2. The distinction is central to Hume's discussion of justice in *A Treatise of Human Nature,* bk. III, pt. ii, esp. secs. 2–4. It is clearly stated by John Austin in the second lecture of *Lectures on Jurisprudence* (4th ed.; London, 1873), I, 116ff. (1st ed., 1832). Also it may be argued that J. S. Mill took it for granted in *Utilitarianism;* on this point cf. J. O. Urmson, "The Interpretation of the Moral Philosophy of J. S. Mill," *Philosophical Quarterly,* vol. III (1953). In addition to the arguments given by Urmson there are several clear statements of the distinction in *A System of Logic* (8th ed.; London, 1872), bk. VI, ch. xii pars. 2, 3, 7. The distinction is fundamental to J. D. Mabbott's important paper, "Punishment," *Mind,* n.s., vol. XLVIII (April, 1939). More recently the distinction has been stated with particular emphasis by S. E. Toulmin in *The Place of Reason in Ethics* (Cambridge, 1950), see esp. ch. xi, where it plays a major part in his account of moral reasoning. Toulmin doesn't explain the basis of the distinction, nor how one might overlook its importance, as I try to in this paper, and in my review of this book (*Philosophical Review,* vol. LX [October, 1951]), as some of my criticisms show, I failed to understand the force of it. See also H. D. Aiken, "The Levels of Moral Discourse," *Ethics,* vol. LXII (1952), A. M. Quinton, "Punishment," *Analysis,* vol. XIV (June, 1954), and P. H. Nowell-Smith, *Ethics* (London, 1954), pp. 236–239, 271–273.

3. On the concept of explication see the author's paper *Philosophical Review,* vol. LX (April, 1951).

4. While this paper was being revised, Quinton's appeared; footnote 2 supra. There are several respects in which my remarks are similar to his. Yet as I consider some further questions and rely on somewhat different arguments, I have retained the discussion of punishment and promises together as two test cases for utilitarianism.

5. Note the fact that different sorts of arguments are suited to different offices. One way of taking the differences between ethical theories is to regard them as accounts of the reasons expected in different offices.

6. In this connection see Mabbott, *op. cit.,* pp. 163–164.

7. On this point see Sir David Ross, *The Right and the Good* (Oxford, 1930), pp. 57–60.

8. See Hobbes's definition of punishment in *Leviathan,* ch. xxviii; and Bentham's definition in *The Principle of Morals and Legislation,* ch. xii, par. 36, ch. xv, par. 28, and in *The Rationale of Punishment,* (London, 1830), bk. I, ch. i. They could agree with Bradley that: "Punishment is punishment only when it is deserved. We pay the penalty, because we owe it, and for no other reason; and if punishment is inflicted for any other reason whatever than because it is merited by wrong, it is a gross immorality, a crying injustice, an abominable crime, and not what it pretends to be." *Ethical Studies* (2nd ed.; Oxford, 1927), pp. 26–27. Certainly by definition it isn't what it pretends to be. The innocent can only be punished by mistake; deliberate "punishment" of the innocent necessarily involves fraud.

9. Cf. Leon Radzinowicz, *A History of English Criminal Law: The Movement for Reform 1750–1833* (London, 1948), esp. ch. xi on Bentham.

10. Bentham discusses how corresponding to a punitory provision of a criminal law there is another provision which stands to it as an antagonist and which needs a name as much as the punitory. He calls it, as one might expect, the *anaeti-osostic,* and of it he says: "The punishment of guilt is the object of the former one: the preservation of innocence that of the latter." In the same connection he asserts that it is never thought fit to give the judge the option of deciding whether a thief (that is, a person whom he believes to be a thief, for the judge's belief is what the 300 tion must always turn upon) should hang or not, and so the law writes the provision: "The judge shall not cause a thief to be hanged unless he have been duly convicted and sentenced in course of law" (*The Limits of Jurisprudence Defined,* ed. C. W. Everett [New York, 1945], pp. 238–239).

11. By the classical utilitarians I understand Hobbes, Hume, Bentham, J. S. Mill, and Sidgwick.

12. All these features of punishment are mentioned by Hobbes; cf. *Leviathan,* ch. xxviii.

13. *Ethical and Political Thinking* (Oxford, 1947), p. 65.

14. The analogy with the price system suggests an answer to the question how utilitarian considerations insure that punishment is proportional to the offense. It is interesting to note that Sir David Ross, after making the distinction between justifying a penal law and justifying a particular application of it, and after stating that utilitarian considerations have a large place in determining the former, still holds back from accepting the utilitarian justification of punishment on the grounds that justice requires that punishment be proportional to the offense, and that utilitarianism is unable to account for this. Cf. *The Right and the Good,* pp. 61–62. I do not claim that utilitarianism can account for this requirement as Sir David might wish, but it happens, nevertheless, that if utilitarian considerations are followed penalties will be proportional to offenses in this sense: the order of offenses according to seriousness can be paired off with the order of penalties according to severity. Also the absolute level of penalties will be as low as possible. This follows from the assumption that people are rational (i.e., that they are able to take into account the "prices" the state puts on actions), the utilitarian rule that a penal system should provide a motive for preferring the less serious offense, and the principle that punishment as such is an evil. All this was carefully worked out by Bentham in *The Principles of Morals and Legislation,* chs. xiii–xv.

H. L. A. HART

Prolegomenon to the Principles of Punishment*

I. INTRODUCTORY

The main object of this paper is to provide a framework for the discussion of the mounting perplexities which now surround the institution of criminal punishment, and to show that any morally tolerable account of this institution must exhibit it as a compromise between distinct and partly conflicting principles.

General interest in the topic of punishment has never been greater than it is at present and I doubt if the public discussion of it has ever been more confused. The interest and the confusion are both in part due to relatively modern skepticism about two elements which have figured as essential parts of the traditionally opposed 'theories' of punishment. On the one hand, the old Benthamite confidence in fear of the penalties threatened by the law as a powerful deterrent, has waned with the growing realization that the part played by calculation of any sort in anti-social behaviour has been exaggerated. On the other hand a cloud of doubt has settled over the keystone of 'retributive' theory. Its advocates can no longer speak with the old confidence that statements of the form 'This man who has broken the law could have kept it' had a univocal or agreed meaning; or where scepticism does not attach to the *meaning* of this form of statement, it has shaken the confidence that we are generally able to distinguish the cases where a statement of this form is true from those where it is not.[1]

Yet quite apart from the uncertainty engendered by these fundamental doubts, which seem to call in question the accounts given of the efficacy, and the morality of punishment by all the old competing theories, the public utterances of those who conceive themselves to be expounding, as plain men for other plain men, orthodox or common-sense principles (un-

*H.L.A. Hart, "Prolegomenon to the Principles of Punishment," *Proceedings of the Aristotelian Society,* Suppl. 1960. Reprinted in H.L.A. Hart, *Punishment and Responsibility* (New York and Oxford: Oxford University Press, 1968). Reprinted by permission of the Editor of the Aristotelian Society.

touched by modern psychological doubts) are uneasy. Their words often sound as if the authors had not fully grasped their meaning or did not intend the words to be taken quite literally. A glance at the parliamentary debates or the *Report of the Royal Commission on Capital Punishment*[2] shows that many are not troubled by the suspicion that the view that there is just one supreme value or objective (e.g., Deterrence, Retribution or Reform) in terms of which *all* questions about the justification of punishment are to be answered, is somehow wrong; yet, from what is said on such occasions no clear account of what the different values or objectives are, or how they fit together in the justification of punishment, can be extracted.[3]

No one expects judges or statesmen occupied in the business of sending people to the gallows or prison, or in making (or unmaking) laws which enable this to be done, to have much time for philosophical discussion of the principles which make it morally tolerable to do these things. A judicial bench is not and should not be a professorial chair. Yet what is said in public debates about punishment by those specially concerned with it as judges or legislators is important. Few are likely to be more circumspect, and if what they say seems, as it often does, unclear, one-sided and easily refutable by pointing to some aspect of things which they have overlooked, it is likely that in our inherited ways of talking or thinking about punishment there is some persistent drive towards an over-simplification of multiple issues which require separate consideration. To counter this drive what is most needed is *not* the simple admission that instead of a single value or aim (Deterrence, Retribution, Reform or any other) a plurality of different values and aims should be given as a conjunctive answer to some *single* question concerning the justification of punishment. What is needed is the realization that different principles (each of which may in a sense be called a 'justification') are relevant at different points in any morally acceptable account of punishment. What we should look for are answers to a number of different questions such as: What justifies the general practice of punishment? To whom may punishment be applied? How severely may we punish? In dealing with these and other questions concerning punishment we should bear in mind that in this, as in most other social institutions, the pursuit of one aim may be qualified by or provide an opportunity, not to be missed, for the pursuit of others. Till we have developed this sense of the complexity of punishment (and this prolegomenon aims only to do this) we shall be in no fit state to assess the extent to which the whole institution has been eroded by, our needs to be adapted to, new beliefs about the human mind.

2. JUSTIFYING AIMS AND PRINCIPLES OF DISTRIBUTION

There is, I think, an analogy worth considering between the concept of punishment and that of property. In both cases we have to do with a social institution of which the centrally important form is a structure of *legal* rules, even if it would be dogmatic to deny the names of punishment or property to the similar though more rudimentary rule-regulated practices within groups such as a family, or a school, or in customary societies whose customs may lack some of the standard or salient features of law (e.g., legislation, organized sanctions, courts). In both cases we are confronted by a complex institution presenting different inter-related features calling for separate explanation; or, if the morality of the institution is challenged, for separate justification. In both cases failure to distinguish separate questions or attempting to answer them all by reference to a single principle ends in confusion. Thus in the case of property we should distinguish between the question of the *definition* of property, the question why and in what circumstance it is a *good* institution to maintain, and the questions in what ways individuals may become *entitled* to acquire property and *how much* they should be allowed to acquire. These we may call questions of *Definition, General Justifying Aim,* and *Distribution* with the last subdivided into questions of *Title* and *Amount*. It is salutary to take some classical exposition of the idea of property, say Locke's chapter 'Of Property' in the *Second Treatise,*[4] and to observe how much darkness is spread by the use of a single notion (in this case 'the labour of (a man's) body and the work of his hands') to answer all these different questions which press upon us when

we reflect on the institution of property. In the case of punishment the beginning of wisdom (though by no means its end) is to distinguish similar questions and confront them separately.

(A) DEFINITION

Here I shall simply draw upon the recent admirable work scattered through English philosophical[5] journals and add to it only an admonition of my own against the abuse of definition in the philosophical discussion of punishment. So with Mr. Benn and Professor Flew I shall define the standard or central case of 'punishment' in terms of five elements:

(i)   It must involve pain or other consequences normally considered unpleasant.

(ii) It must be for an offence against legal rules.

(iii) It must be of an actual or supposed offender for his offence.

(iv) It must be intentionally administered by human beings other than the offender.

(v)   It must be imposed and administered by an authority constituted by a legal system against which the offence is committed.

In calling this the standard or central case of punishment I shall relegate to the position of sub-standard or secondary cases the following among many other possibilities:

(a)   Punishments for breaches of legal rules imposed or administered otherwise than by officials (decentralised sanctions).

(b)   Punishments for breaches of non-legal rules or orders (punishments in a family or school).

(c)   Vicarious or collective punishment of some member of a social group for actions done by others without the former's authorization, encouragement, control or permission.

(d)   Punishment of persons (otherwise than under (*c*)) who neither are in fact nor supposed to be offenders.

The chief importance of listing these sub-standard cases is to prevent the use of what I shall call the 'definitional stop' in discussions of punishment. This is an abuse of definition especially tempting when use is made of conditions (ii) and (iii) of the standard case in arguing against the utilitarian claim that the practice of punishment is justified by the beneficial consequences resulting from the observance of the laws which it secures. Here the stock 'retributive' argument[6] is: If *this* is the justification of punishment, why not apply it, when it pays to do so, to those innocent of any crime, chosen at random, or to the wife and children of the offender? And here the wrong reply is: *That,* by definition, would not be 'punishment' and it is the justification of punishment which is in issue.[7] Not only will this definitional stop fail to satisfy the advocate of 'Retribution,' it would prevent us from investigating the very thing which modern scepticism most calls in question: namely the rational and moral status of our preference for a system of punishment under which measures painful to individuals are to be taken against them only when they have committed an offence. Why do we prefer this to other forms of social hygiene which we might employ to prevent anti-social behaviour and which we do employ in special circumstances, sometimes with reluctance? No account of punishment can afford to dismiss this question with a definition.

(B) THE NATURE OF AN OFFENCE

Before we reach any question of justification we must identify a preliminary question to which the answer is so simple that the question may not appear worth asking; yet it is clear that some curious 'theories' of punishment gain their only plausibility from ignoring it, and others from confusing it with other questions. This question is: Why are certain kinds of action forbidden by law and so made crimes or offences? The answer is: To announce to society that these actions are not to be done and to secure that fewer of them are done. These are the common immediate aims of making any conduct a criminal offence and until we have laws made with these primary aims we shall lack the notion of a 'crime' and so of a 'criminal.' Without recourse to the simple idea that the criminal law sets up, in its rules, standards of behaviour to encourage certain types of conduct and discourage others we cannot distinguish a punishment in the form of a fine from a tax on a course of conduct.[8] This indeed is one grave objection to those theories of law which

in the interests of simplicity or uniformity obscure the distinction between primary laws setting standards for behaviour and secondary laws specifying what officials must or may do when they are broken. Such theories insist that all legal rules are 'really' directions to officials to exact 'sanctions' under certain conditions, e.g., if people kill.[9] Yet only if we keep alive the distinction (which such theories thus obscure) between the primary objective of the law in encouraging or discouraging certain kinds of behaviour, and its merely ancillary sanction or remedial steps, can we give sense to the notion of a crime or offence.

It is important however to stress the fact that in thus identifying the immediate aims of the criminal law we have not reached the stage of justification. There are indeed many forms of undesirable behaviour which it would be foolish (because ineffective or too costly) to attempt to inhibit by use of the law and some of these may be better left to educators, trades unions, churches, marriage guidance councils or other non-legal agencies. Conversely there are some forms of conduct which we believe cannot be effectively inhibited without use of the law. But it is only too plain that in fact the law may make activities criminal which it is morally important to promote and the suppression of these may be quite unjustifiable. Yet confusion between the simple immediate aim of any criminal legislation and the justification of punishment seems to be the most charitable explanation of the claim that punishment is *justified* as an 'emphatic denunciation by the community of a crime.' Lord Denning's dictum that this is the ultimate justification of punishment[10] can be saved from Mr. Benn's criticism, noted above, only if it is treated as a blurred statement of the truth that the aim not of punishment, but of criminal legislation is indeed to denounce certain types of conduct as something not to be practiced. Conversely the immediate aim of criminal legislation cannot be any of the things which are usually mentioned as justifying punishment: for until it is settled what conduct is to be legally denounced and discouraged we have not settled from what we are to *deter* people, or who are to be considered *criminals* from whom we are to exact *retribution,* or on whom we are to wreak *vengeance,* or whom we are to *reform.*

Even those who look upon human law as a mere instrument for enforcing 'morality as such' (itself conceived as the law of God or

Nature) and who at the stage of justifying punishment wish to appeal not to socially beneficial consequences but simply to the intrinsic value of inflicting suffering on wrong-doers who have disturbed by their offence the moral order, would not deny that the aim of criminal legislation is to set up types of behaviour (in this case conformity with a pre-existing moral law) as legal standards of behaviour and to secure conformity with them. No doubt in all communities certain moral offences, e.g., killing, will always be selected for suppression as crimes and it is conceivable that this may be done not to protect human beings from being killed but to save the potential murderer from sin; but it would be paradoxical to look upon the law as designed not to discourage murder at all (even conceived as sin rather than harm) but simply to extract the penalty from the murderer.

(C) GENERAL JUSTIFYING AIM

I shall not here criticize the intelligibility or consistency or adequacy of those theories that are united in denying that the practice of a system of punishment is justified by its beneficial consequences and claim instead that the main justification of the practice lies in the fact that when breach of the law involves moral guilt the application to the offender of the pain of punishment is itself a thing of value. A great variety of claims of this character, designating 'Retribution' or 'Expiation' or 'Reprobation' as the justifying aim, fall in spite of differences under this rough general description. Though in fact I agree with Mr. Benn[11] in thinking that these all either avoid the question of justification altogether or are in spite of their protestations disguised forms of Utilitarianism, I shall assume that Retribution, defined simply as the application of the pains of punishment to an offender who is morally guilty, may figure among the conceivable justifying aims of a system of punishment. Here I shall merely insist that it is one thing to use the word Retribution *at this point* in an account of the principle of punishment in order to designate the General Justifying Aim of the system, and quite another to use it to secure that to the question 'To whom may punishment be applied?' (the question of Distribution), the answer given is 'Only to an offender for an offence.' Failure to distinguish Retribution as a General Justifying Aim from retribution as the simple insistence that only those who have broken the law—and voluntarily broken it—may be punished, may be traced in many writers: even perhaps in Mr. J. D. Mabbott's[12] otherwise most illuminating essay. We shall distinguish the latter from Retribution in General Aim as 'retribution in Distribution.' Much confusing shadow-fighting between utilitarians and their opponents may be avoided if it is recognized that it is perfectly consistent to assert *both* that the General Justifying Aim of the practice of punishment is its beneficial consequences *and* that the pursuit of this General Aim should be qualified or restricted out of deference to principles of Distribution which require that punishment should be only of an offender for an offence. Conversely it does not in the least follow from the admission of the latter principle of retribution in Distribution that the General Justifying Aim of punishment is Retribution though of course Retribution in General Aim entails retribution in Distribution.

We shall consider later the principles of justice lying at the root of retribution in Distribution. Meanwhile it is worth observing that both the old fashioned Retributionist (in General Aim) and the most modern sceptic often make the same (and, I think, wholly mistaken) assumption that sense can only be made of the restrictive principle that punishment be applied only to an offender for an offence if the General Justifying Aim of the practice of punishment is Retribution. The sceptic consequently imputes to all systems of punishment (when they are restricted by the principle of retribution in Distribution) all the irrationality he finds in the idea of Retribution as a General Justfying Aim; conversely the advocates of the latter think the admission of retribution in Distribution is a refutation of the utilitarian claim that the social consequences of punishment are its Justifying Aim.

The most general lesson to be learnt from this extends beyond the topic of punishment. It is, that in relation to any social institution, after stating what general aim or value its maintenance fosters we should enquire whether there are any and if so what principles limiting the unqualified pursuit of that aim or value. Just because the pursuit of any single social aim always has its restrictive qualifier, our main social institutions always possess a plurality of features which can only be understood as a compromise between partly discrepant principles. This is true even of relatively minor legal institutions like that of a contract. In general this is designed to enable individuals to give effect to their wishes to create structures of legal rights and duties, and so to change, in certain ways, their legal position. Yet at the same time there is need to protect those who, in good faith, understand a verbal offer made to them to mean what it would ordinarily mean, accept it, and then act on the footing that a valid contract has been concluded. As against them, it would be unfair to allow the other party to say that the words he used in his verbal offer or the interpretation put on them did not express his real wishes or intention. Hence principles of 'estoppel' or doctrines of the 'objective sense' of a contract are introduced to prevent this and to qualify the principle that the law enforces contracts in order to give effect to the joint wishes of the contracting parties.

(D) DISTRIBUTION

This as in the case of property has two aspects (i) Liability (Who may be punished?) and (ii) Amount. In this section I shall chiefly be concerned with the first of these.[13]

From the foregoing discussion two things emerge. First, though we may be clear as to what value the practice of punishment is to promote, we have still to answer as a question of Distribution 'Who may be punished?' Secondly, if in answer to this question we say 'only an offender for an offence' this admission of retribution in Distribution is not a principle from which anything follows as to the severity or amount of punishment; in particular it neither licenses nor requires, as Retribution in General Aim does, more severe punishments than deterrence or other utilitarian criteria would require.

The root question to be considered is, however, why we attach the moral importance which we do to retribution in Distribution. Here I shall consider the efforts made to show that restriction of punishment to offenders is a simple consequence of whatever principles (Retributive or Utilitarian) constitute the Justifying Aim of punishment.

The standard example used by philosophers to bring out the importance of retribution in Distribution is that of a wholly innocent person who has not even unintentionally done anything which the law punishes if done intentionally. It is supposed that in order to avert some social catastrophe officials of the system fabricate evidence on which he is charged, tried, convicted and sent to prison or death. Or it is supposed that without resort to any fraud more persons may be deterred from crime if wives and children of offenders were punished vicariously for their crimes. In some forms this kind of thing may be ruled out by a consistent sufficiently comprehensive utilitarianism.[14] Certainly expedients involving fraud or faked charges might be very difficult to justify on utilitarian grounds. We can of course imagine that a negro might be sent to prison or executed on a false charge of rape in order to avoid wide-spread lynching of many others; but a *system* which openly empowered authorities to do this kind of thing, even if it succeeded in averting specific evils like lynching, would awaken such apprehension and insecurity that any gain from the exercise of these powers would be any utilitarian calculation be offset by the misery caused by their existence. But official resort to this kind of fraud on a particular occasion in breach of the rules and the subsequent indemnification of the officials responsible might save many lives and so be thought to yield a clear surplus of value. Certainly vicarious punishment of an offender's family might do so and legal systems have occasionally though exceptionally resorted to this. An example of it is the Roman *Lex Quisquis* providing for the punishment of the children of those guilty of *majestas*.[15] In extreme cases many might still think it right to resort to these expedients but we should do so with the sense of sacrificing an important principle. We should be conscious of choosing the lesser of two evils, and this would be inexplicable if the principle sacrificed to utility were itself only a requirement of utility.

Similarly the moral importance of the restriction of punishment to the offender cannot be explained as merely a consequence of the principle that the General Justifying Aim is Retribution for immorality involved in breaking the law. Retribution in the Distribution of punishment has a value quite independent of Retribution as Justifying Aim. This is shown by the fact that we attach importance to the restrictive principle that only offenders may be punished, even where breach of this law might not be thought immoral. Indeed even where the laws themselves are hideously immoral as in Nazi Germany, e.g., forbidding activities (helping the sick or destitute of some racial group) which might be thought morally obligatory, the absence of the principle restricting punishment to the offender would be a further *special* iniquity; whereas admission of this principle would represent some residual respect for justice shown in the administration of morally bad laws.

3. JUSTIFICATION, EXCUSE AND MITIGATION

What is morally at stake in the restrictive principle of Distribution cannot, however, be made clear by these isolated examples of its violation by faked charges or vicarious punishment. To make it clear we must allot to their place the appeals to matters of Justification, Excuse and Mitigation made in answer to the claim that someone should be punished. The first of these depends on the General Justifying Aim; the last two are different aspects of the principles of Distribution of punishment.

(A) JUSTIFICATION AND EXCUSE

English lawyers once distinguished between 'excusable' homicide (e.g., accidental non-negligent killing) and 'justifiable' homicide (e.g., killing in self-defence or in the arrest of a felon) and different legal consequences once attached to these two forms of homicide. To the modern lawyer this distinction has no longer any legal importance: he would simply consider both kinds of homicide to be cases where some element, negative or positive, required in the full definition of criminal homicide (murder or manslaughter) was lacking. But the distinction between these two different ways in which actions may fail to constitute a criminal offence is still of great moral importance. Killing in self-defence is an exception to a general rule making killing punishable; it is admitted because the policy or aims which in general justify the punishment of killing (e.g., protection of human life) do not include cases such as this. In the case of 'justification' what is done is regarded as something which the law does not condemn, or even welcomes.[16] But where killing (e.g., accidental) is excused, criminal responsibility is excluded on a different footing. What has been done is something which is deplored, but the psychological state of the agent when he did it exemplified one or more of a variety of conditions which are held to rule out the public condemnation and punishment of individuals. This is a requirement of fairness or of justice to individuals independent of whatever the General Aim of punishment is, and remains a value whether the laws are good, morally indifferent or iniquitous.

The most prominent of these excusing conditions are those forms of lack of knowledge which make action unintentional: lack of muscular control which makes it involuntary, subjection to gross forms of coercion by threats, and types of mental abnormality, which are believed to render the agent incapable of choice or of carrying out what he has chosen to do. Not all these excusing conditions are admitted by all legal systems for all offenders. Nearly all penal systems, as we shall see, make some compromise at this point with other principles; but most of them are admitted to some considerable extent in the case of the most serious crimes. Actions done under these excusing conditions are in the misleading terminology of Anglo-American law done without *mens rea*,[17] and most people would say of them that they were not 'voluntary' or 'not wholly voluntary.'

(B) MITIGATION

Justification and Excuse though different from each other are alike in that if either is made out then conviction and punishment are excluded. In this they differ from the idea of Mitigation which presupposes that someone is convicted and liable to be punished and the question of the severity of his punishment is to be decided. It is therefore relevant to that aspect of Distribution which we have termed amount. Certainly the severity of punishment is in part determined by the General Justifying Aim. A utilitarian will for example exclude in principle punishments the infliction of which is held to cause more suffering than the offence unchecked, and will hold that if one kind of crime causes greater suffering than another then a greater penalty may be used, if necessary, to repress it. He will also exclude degrees of severity which are useless in the sense that they do no more to secure or maintain a higher level of law-observance or any other valued result than less severe penalties. But in addition to restrictions on the severity of punishment which follow from the aim of punishing, special limitations are imported by the idea of Mitigation. These, like the principle of Distribution restricting liability to punishment to offenders, have a status which is independent of the general Aim. The special features of Mitigation are that a good reason for administering a less severe penalty is made out if the situation or mental state of the convicted criminal is such that he was exposed to an unusual or specially great temptation, or his ability to control his actions is thought to have been impaired or weakened otherwise than by his own action, so that conformity to the law which he has broken was a matter of special difficulty for him as compared with normal persons normally placed.

The special features of the idea of Mitigation are however often concealed by the various legal techniques which make it necessary to distinguish between what may be termed 'informal' and 'formal' Mitigation. In the first case the law fixes a maximum penalty and leaves it to the judge to give such weight as he thinks proper, in selecting the punishment to be applied to a particular offender, to (among other considerations) mitigating factors. It is here that the barrister makes his 'plea in mitigation.' Sometimes however legal rules provide that the presence of a mitigating factor shall always remove the offence into a separate category carrying a lower maximum penalty. This is 'formal' mitigation and the most prominent example of it is Provocation which in English law is operative only in relation to homicide. Provocation is not a matter of Justification or Excuse for it does not exclude conviction or punishment; but 'reduces' the charges from murder to manslaughter and the possible maximum penalty from death to life imprisonment. It is worth stressing that not every provision reducing the maximum penalty can be thought of as 'Mitigation': the very peculiar provisions of s. 5 of the Homicide Act 1957 which (inter alia) restricted the death penalty to types of murder not including, for example, murder by poisoning, did not in doing this recognize the use of poison as a 'mitigating circumstance.' Only a reduction of penalty made in view of the individual criminal's special difficulties in keeping the law which he has broken is so conceived.

Though the central cases are distinct enough the border lines between Justification, Excuse and Mitigation are not. There are many features of conduct which can be and are thought of in more than one of these ways. Thus, though little is heard of it, duress (coercion by threat of serious harm) is in English law in relation to some crimes an Excuse excluding responsibility. Where it is so treated the conception is that

since B has committed a crime only because A has threatened him with gross violence or other harm, B's action is not the outcome of a 'free' or independent choice; B is merely an instrument of A who has 'made him do it.' Nonetheless B is not an instrument in the same sense that he would have been had he been pushed by A against a window and broken it: unless he is literally paralysed by fear of the threat, we may believe that B could have refused to comply. If he complies we may say 'coactus voluit' and treat the situation not as one making it intolerable to punish at all, but as one calling for mitigation of the penalty as gross provocation does. On the other hand if the crime which A requires B to commit is a petty one compared with the serious harm threatened (e.g., death) by A there would be no absurdity in treating A's threat as a justification for B's conduct though few legal systems overtly do this. If this line is taken coercion merges into the idea of 'necessity'[18] which appears on the margin of most systems of criminal law as an exculpating factor.

In view of the character of modern sceptical doubts about criminal punishment it is worth observing that, even in English law, the relevance of mental disease to criminal punishment is not always as a matter of Excuse though exclusive concentration on the M'Naghten rules relating to the criminal responsibility of the mentally diseased encourages the belief that it is. Even before the Homicide Act 1957 a statute[19] provided that if a mother murdered her child under the age of twelve months while 'the balance of her mind was disturbed' by the processes of birth or lactation she should be guilty only of the felony of infanticide carrying a maximum penalty of life imprisonment. This is to treat mental abnormality as a matter of (formal) Mitigation. Similarly in other cases of homicide the M'Naghten rules relating to certain types of insanity as an Excuse no longer stand alone; now such abnormality of mind as 'substantially impaired [the] mental responsibility'[20] of the accused is a matter of formal mitigation, which like provocation reduces the homicide to the category of manslaughter.

4. THE RATIONALE OF EXCUSES

The admission of excusing conditions is a feature of the Distribution of punishment and it is required by distinct principles of Justice which restrict the extent to which general social aims may be pursued at the cost of individuals. The moral importance attached to these in punishment distinguishes it from other measures which pursue similar aims (e.g., the protection of life, wealth or property) by methods which like punishment are also often unpleasant to the individuals to whom they are applied, e.g., the detention of persons of hostile origin or association in war time, or of the insane, or the compulsory quarantine of persons suffering from infectious disease. To these we resort to avoid damage of a catastrophic character.

Every penal system in the name of some other social value compromises over the admission of excusing conditions and no system goes as far (particularly in cases of mental disease) as many would wish. But it is important (if we are to avoid a superficial but tempting answer to modern scepticism about the meaning or truth of the statement that a criminal could have kept the law which he has broken) to see that our moral preference for a system which does recognize such excuses cannot, any more than our reluctance to engage in the cruder business of false charges or vicarious punishment, be explained by reference to the General Aim which we take to justify the practice of punishment. Here, too, even where the laws appear to us morally iniquitous or where we are uncertain as to their moral character so that breach of law does not entail moral guilt, punishment of those who break the law unintentionally would be an added wrong and refusal to do this some sign of grace.

Retributionists (in General Aim) have not paid much attention to the rationale of this aspect of punishment; they have usually (wrongly) assumed that it has no status except as a corollary of Retribution in General Aim. But Utilitarians have made strenuous, detailed efforts to show that restriction of the use of punishment to those who have voluntarily broken the law is explicable on purely utilitarian lines. Bentham's efforts are the most complete and their failure is an instructive warning to contemporaries.

Bentham's argument was a reply to Blackstone who, in expounding the main excusing conditions recognized in the criminal law of his day,[21] claimed that 'all the several pleas and excuses which protect the committer of a forbidden act from punishment which is otherwise annexed thereto may be reduced to this single consideration: the want or defect of *will*'. . .

[and to the principle] 'that to constitute a crime . . . there must be first, a vitious will.' In his Introduction to the Principles of Morals and Legislation[22] under the heading 'Cases unmeet for punishment' Bentham sets out a list of the main excusing conditions similar to Blackstone's; he then undertakes to show that the infliction of punishment on those who have done, while in any of these conditions, what the law forbids 'must be inefficacious: it cannot act so as to prevent the mischief.' All the common talk about the want or defect of will or lack of a 'vitious' will is, he says, 'nothing to the purpose,' except so far as it implies the reason (inefficacy of punishment) which he himself gives for recognising these excuses.

Bentham's argument is in fact a spectacular *non sequitur*. He sets out to prove that to *punish* the mad, the infant child or those who break the law unintentionally or under duress or even under 'necessity' must be inefficacious; but all that he proves (at the most) is the quite different proposition that the *threat* of punishment will be ineffective so far as the class of persons who suffer from these conditions is concerned. Plainly it is possible that though (as Bentham says) the *threat* of punishment could not have operated on them, the actual *infliction* of punishment on those persons, may secure a higher measure of conformity to law on the part of normal persons than is secured by the admission of excusing conditions. If this is so and if Utilitarian principles only were at stake, we should, without any sense that we were sacrificing any principle or value or were choosing the lesser of two evils, drop from the law the restriction on punishment entailed by the admission of excuses: unless, of course, we believed that the terror or insecurity or misery produced by the operation of laws so Draconic was worse than the lower measure of obedience to law secured by the law which admits excuses.

This objection to Bentham's rationale of excuses is not merely a fanciful one. Any increase in the number of conditions required to establish criminal liability increases the opportunity for deceiving courts or juries by the pretence that some condition is not satisfied. When the condition is a psychological factor the chances of such pretence succeeding are considerable. Quite apart from the provision made for mental disease, the cases where an accused person pleads that he killed in his sleep or accidentally or in some temporary abnormal state of unconsciousness show that deception is certainly feasible. From the Utilitarian point of view this may lead to two sorts of "losses." The belief that such deception is feasible may embolden persons who would not otherwise risk punishment to take their chance of deceiving a jury in this way. Secondly, a criminal who actually succeeds in this deception will be left at large, though belonging to the class which the law is concerned to incapacitate. Developments in Anglo-American law since Bentham's day have given more concrete form to this objection to his argument. There are now offences (known as offences of 'strict liability') where it is not necessary for conviction to show that the accused either intentionally did what the law forbids or could have avoided doing it by use of care; selling liquor to an intoxicated person, possessing an altered passport, selling adulterated milk[23] are examples out of a range of 'strict liability' offences where it is no defence that the accused did not offend intentionally, or through negligence, e.g., that he was under some mistake against which he had no opportunity to guard. Two things should be noted about them. First, the common justification of this form of criminal liability is that if proof of intention or lack of care were required guilty persons would escape. Secondly, 'strict liability' is generally viewed with great odium and admitted as an exception to the general rule, with the sense that an important principle has been sacrificed to secure a higher measure of conformity and conviction of offenders. Thus Bentham's argument curiously ignores both the two possibilities which have been realized. First, actual punishment of these who act unintentionally or in some other normally excusing manner may have a utilitarian value in its effects on others; and secondly, when because of this probability, strict liability is admitted and the normal excuses are excluded, this may be done with the sense that some other principle has been overridden.

On this issue modern extended forms of Utilitarianism fare no better than Bentham's whose main criterion here of 'effective' punishment was deterrence of the offender or of others by example. Sometimes the principle that punishment should be restricted to those who have voluntarily broken the law is defended not as a principle which is rational or morally important in itself but as something so engrained in popular conceptions of justice[24] in certain societies, including our own, that not to recognize it would lead to disturbances, or to the nullification of the criminal law since officials or juries might refuse to co-operate in such a system. Hence to punish in these circumstances would either be impracticable or would create more harm than could possibly be offset by any superior deterrent force gained by such a system. On this footing, a system should admit excuses much as, in order to prevent disorder or lynching, concessions might be made to popular demands for more savage punishment than could be defended on other grounds. Two objections confront this wider pragmatic form of Utilitarianism. The first is the factual observation that even if a system of strict liability for all or very serious crime would be unworkable, a system which admits it on its periphery for relatively minor offences is not only workable but an actuality which we have, though many object to it or admit it with reluctance. The second objection is simply that we do not dissociate ourselves from the principle that it is wrong to punish the hopelessly insane or those who act unintentionally, etc., by treating it as something merely embodied in popular *mores* to which concessions must be made sometimes. We condemn legal systems where they disregard this principle; whereas we try to educate people out of their preference for savage penalties even if we might in extreme cases of threatened disorder concede them.

It is therefore impossible to exhibit the principle by which punishment is excluded for those who act under the excusing conditions merely as a corollary of the general Aim—Retributive or Utilitarian—justifying the practice of punishment. Can anything positive be said about this principle except that it is one to which we attach moral importance as a restriction on the pursuit of any aim we have in punishing?

It is clear that like all principles of Justice it is concerned with the adjustment of claims between a multiplicity of persons. It incorporates the idea that each individual person is to be protected against the claim of the rest for the highest possible measure of security, happiness or welfare which could be got at his expense by condemning him for a breach of the rules and punishing him. For this a moral licence is required in the form of proof that the person punished broke the law by an action which was the outcome of his free choice, and then recognition of excuses is the most we can do to ensure that the terms of the licence are observed. Here perhaps, the elucidation of this restrictive principle should stop. Perhaps we (or I) ought simply to say that it is a requirement of Justice, and Justice simply consists of principles to be observed in adjusting the competing claims of human beings which (i) treat all alike as persons by attaching special significance to human voluntary action and (ii) forbid the use of one human being for the benefit of others except in return for his voluntary actions against them. I confess however to an itch to go further; though what I have to say may not add to these principles of Justice. There are, however, three points which even if they are restatements from different points of view of the principles already stated, may help us to identify what we now think of as values in the practice of punishment and what we may have to reconsider in the light of modern scepticism.

(a) We may look upon the principle that punishment must be reserved for voluntary offences from two different points of view. The first is that of the rest of society considered as *harmed* by the offence (either because one of its members has been injured or because the authority of the law essential to its existence has been challenged or both). The principle then appears as one securing that the suffering involved in punishment falls upon those who have voluntarily harmed others: this is valued, not as the Aim of punishment, but as the only fair terms on which the General Aim (protection of society, maintenance of respect for law, etc.) may be pursued.

(b) The second point of view is that of society concerned not as harmed by the crime but as *offering* individuals including the criminal the protection of the laws on terms which are fair, because they not only consist of a framework of reciprocal rights and duties, but because within this framework each individual is given a *fair* opportunity to choose between keeping the law required for society's protection or paying the penalty. From the first point of view the actual punishment of a criminal appears not merely as something useful to society (General Aim) but as justly extracted from the criminal who has voluntarily done harm; from the second it appears as a price justly extraced because the criminal had a fair opportunity beforehand to avoid liability to pay.

(c) Criminal punishment as an attempt to secure desired behaviour differs from the manipulative techniques of the Brave New World (conditioning, propaganda, etc.) or the simple incapacitation of those with anti-social tendencies, by taking a risk. It defers action till harm has been done; its primary operation consists simply in announcing certain standards of behaviour and attaching penalites for deviation, making it less eligible, and then leaving individuals to choose. This is a method of social control which maximizes individual freedom within the coercive framework of law in a number of different ways, or perhaps, different sense. First, the individual has an option between obeying or paying. The worse the laws are, the more valuable the possiblity of exercising this choice becomes in enabling an individual to decide how he shall live. Secondly, this system not only enables individuals to exercise this choice but increases the power of individuals to identify beforehand periods when the law's punishments will not interfere with them and to plan their lives accordingly. This very obvious point is often overshadowed by the other merits of restricting punishment to offences voluntarily committed, but is worth separate attention. Where punishment is not so restricted individuals will be liable to have their plans frustrated by punishments for what they do unintentionally, in ignorance, by accident or mistake. Such a system of strict liability for all offences, if logically possible,[25] would not only vastly increase the number of punishments, but would diminish the individual's power to identify beforehand particular periods during which he will be free from them. This is so because we can have very little ground for confidence that during a particular period we will not do something unintentionally, accidentally, etc.; whereas from their own knowledge of themselves many can say with justified confidence that for some period ahead they are not likely to engage intentionally in crime and can plan their lives from point to point in confidence that they will be left free during that period. Of course the confidence thus justified, though drawn from knowledge of ourselves, does not amount to certainty. My confidence that I will not during the next twelve months intentionally engage in any crime and will be free from punishment, may turn out to be misplaced; but it is both greater and better justified than my belief that I will not do unintentionally any of the things which our system punishes if done intentionally.

5. REFORM AND THE INDIVIDUALIZATION OF PUNISHMENT

The idea of Mitigation incorporates the conviction that though the amount or severity of punishment is primarily to be determined by reference to the General Aim, yet Justice requires that those who have special difficulties to face in keeping the law which they have broken should be punished less. Principles of Justice however are also widely taken to bear on the amount of punishment in at least two further ways. The first is the somewhat hazy requirement that 'like cases be treated alike.' This is certainly felt to be infringed at least when the ground for different punishment for those guilty of the same crime is neither some personal characteristic of the offender connected with the commission of the crime nor the effect of punishment on him. If a certain offence is specially prevalent at a given time and a judge passes heavier sentences than on previous offenders ('as a warning') some sacrifice of justice to the safety of society is involved though it is often acceptable to many as the lesser of two evils.

The further principle that different kinds of offence of different gravity (however that is assessed) should not be punished with equal severity is one which like other principles of Distribution may qualify the pursuit of our General Aim and is not deducible from it. Long sentences of imprisonment might effectually stamp out car parking offences, yet we think it wrong to employ them; *not* because there is for each crime a penalty 'naturally' fitted to its degree of iniquity (as some Retributionists in General Aim might think); not because we are convinced that the misery caused by such sentences (which might indeed be slight because they would rarely need to be applied) would be greater than that caused by the offences unchecked (as a Utilitarian might argue). The guiding principle is that of a proportion within a system of penalties between those imposed for different offences where these have a distinct place in a commonsense scale of gravity. This scale itself no doubt consists of very broad judgments both of relative moral iniquity and harmfulness of different types of offence: it draws rough distinctions like that between parking offences and homicide, or between

'mercy killing' and murder for gain, but cannot cope with any precise assessment of an individual's wickedness in committing a crime. (Who can?) Yet maintenance of proportion of this kind may be important: for where the legal gradation of crimes expressed in the relative severity of penalties diverges sharply from this rough scale, there is a risk of either confusing common morality or flouting it and bringing the law into contempt.

The ideals of Reform and Individualization of punishment (e.g., corrective training, preventive detention) which have been increasingly accepted in English penal practices since 1900 plainly run counter to the second if not to both of these principles of Justice or proportion. Some fear, and others hope, that the further intrusion of these ideals will end with the substitution of 'treatment' by experts for judicial punishment. It is, however, important to see precisely what the relation of Reform to punishment is because its advocates too often misstate it. 'Reform' as an objective is no doubt very vague; it now embraces any strengthening of the offender's disposition and capacity to keep within the law, which is intentionally brought about by human effort otherwise than through fear of punishment. Reforming methods include the inducement of states of repentance, or recognition of moral guilt, or greater awareness of the character and demands of society, the provision of education in a broad sense, vocational training and psychological treatment. Many seeing the futility and indeed harmful character of much traditional punishment speak as if Reform could and should be the General Aim of the whole practice of punishment or the dominant objective of the criminal law:

The *corrective theory* based upon a conception of multiple causation and curative-rehabilitative treatment, should clearly predominate in legislation and in judicial and administrative practices.[26]

Of course this is a possible ideal but is not an ideal for punishment. Reform can only have a place within a system of punishment as an exploitation of the opportunities presented by the conviction or compulsory detention of offenders. It is not an alternative General Justifying Aim of the practice of punishment but something the pursuit of which within a system of punishment qualifies or displaces altogether recourse to principles of justice or proportion in determining the amount of punishment. This is where both Reform and individualized punishment have run counter to the customary morality of punishment.

There is indeed a paradox in asserting that Reform should 'predominate' in a system of Criminal Law, as if the main purpose of providing punishment for murder was to reform the murderer not to prevent murder; and the paradox is greater where the legal offence is not a serious moral one: e.g. infringing a state monopoly of transport. The objection to assigning to Reform this place in punishment is not merely that punishment entails suffering and Reform does not; but that Reform is essentially a remedial step for which *ex hypothesi* there is an opportunity only at the point where the criminal law has failed in its primary task of securing society from the evil which breach of the law involves. Society is divisible at any moment into two classes (i) those who have actually broken a given law and (ii) those who have not yet broken it but may. To take Reform as the dominant objective would be to forego the hope of influencing the second and—in relation to the more serious offences—numerically much greater class. We should thus subordinate the prevention of first offences to the prevention of recidivism.

Consideration of what conditions or beliefs would make this appear a reasonable policy brings us to the topic to which this paper is a mere prolegomenon: modern sceptical doubt about the whole institution of punishment. If we believed that nothing was achieved by announcing penalties or by the example of their infliction, either because those who do not commit crimes would not commit them in any event or because the penalties announced or inflicted on others are not among the factors which influence them in keeping the law, then some dramatic change concentrating wholly on actual offenders, would be necessary. Just because at present we do not entirely believe this, we have a dilemma and an uneasy compromise. Penalties which we believe are required as a threat to maintain conformity to law at its maximum may convert the offender to whom they are applied into a hardened enemy of society; while the use of measures of Reform may lower the efficacy and example of punishment on others. At present we compromise on this relatively new aspect of punishment as we do over its main elements. What makes this compromise seem tolerable is the belief that the influence which the threat and example of

punishment extracts is often independent of the severity of the punishment, and is due more to the disgrace attached to conviction for crime or to the deprivation of freedom which many reforming measures at present used in any case involve.

NOTES

1. See Barbara Wootton, *Social Science and Social Pathology* (1959) for a comprehensive modern statement of these doubts.

2. (1953) Cmd. 8932.

3. In the Lords' debate in July 1956 the Lord Chancellor agreed with Lord Denning that 'the ultimate justification of any punishment is not that it is a deterrent but that it is the emphatic denunciation by the community of a crime' yet also said that 'the real crux' of the question at issue is whether capital punishment is a uniquely effective deterrent. See 198 *H. L. Deb* (5th July) 576, 577, 596 (1956). In his article, 'An Approach to the Problems of Punishment,' *Philosophy* (1958), Mr. S. I. Benn rightly observes of Lord Denning's view that denunciation does not imply the deliberate imposition of suffering which is the feature needing justification (p. 328, n. 1).

4. Chapter V.

5. K. Baier, 'Is Punishment Retributive?,' *Analysis* (1955), p. 25. A. Flew, 'The Justification of Punishment,' *Philosophy* (1954), p. 291. S. I. Benn, op. cit., pp. 325–6.

6. A. C. Ewing, *The Morality of Punishment,* D. J. B. Hawkins, *Punishment and Moral Responsibility* (The King's Good Servant, p. 92), J. D. Mabbott, 'Punishment,' *Mind* (1939), p. 152.

7. Mr. Benn seemed to succumb at times to the temptation to give 'The short answer to the critics of utilitarian theories of punishment—that they are theories of *punishment* not of any sort of technique involving suffering' (op. cit., p. 332). He has since told me that he does not now rely on the definitional stop.

8. This generally clear distinction may be blurred. Taxes may be imposed to discourage the activities taxed though the law does not announce this as it does when it makes them criminal. Conversely fines payable for some criminal offences because of a depreciation of currency become so small that they are cheerfully paid and offences are frequent. They are then felt to be mere taxes because the sense is lost that the rule is meant to be taken seriously as a standard of behaviour.

9. cf. Kelsen, *General Theory of Law and State* (1945), pp. 30–33, 33–34, 143–4. 'Law is the primary norm, which stipulates the sanction. . . .' (ibid. 61).

10. In evidence to the Royal Commission on Capital Punishment, Cmd. 8932. para. 53 (1953). *Supra*, p. 2, n. 3.

11. Op. cit., pp. 326–35.

12. Op. cit. *supra* p. 5, n. 6. It is not always quite clear what he considers a 'retributive' theory to be.

13. Amount is considered below in Section III (in connexion with Mitigation) and Section V.

14. See J. Rawls, 'Two Concepts of Rules,' *Philosophical Review* (1955), pp. 4–13.

15. Constitution of emperors Arcadius and Honorius (A.D. 397).

16. In 1811 Mr. Purcell of Co. Cork, a septuagenarian, was knighted for killing four burglars with a carving knife. Kenny, *Outlines of Criminal Law*, 5th ed., p. 103, n. 3.

17. Misleading because it suggests moral guilt is a necessary condition of criminal responsibility.

18. I.e., when breaking the law is held justified as the lesser of two evils.

19. Infanticide Act, 1938.

20. Homicide Act, 1957, s. 2.

21. *Commentaries*, Book IV, Chap. II.

22. Chap. XIII esp. para. 9, n. 1.

23. See Glanville Williams, *Criminal Law*, 2nd ed., Chap. VI, for a discussion of the protest against 'strict responsibility.'

24. Michael and Wechsler, 'A Rationale of the Law of Homicide' (1937), 37 *C. L. R.*, 701, esp. pp. 752–7, and Rawls, op. cit.

25. Some crimes, e.g., demanding money by menaces, cannot (logically) be committed unintentionally.

26. Hall and Glueck, *Cases on Criminal Law and Its Enforcement* (1951) p. 14.

HYMAN GROSS

Culpability and Desert*

My purpose in this paper is to explain the idea of just deserts in criminal punishment, and to explain why it is a good thing when deciding on a sentence to decide first what punishment is deserved, even though the right sentence may well turn out to be less punishment than the crime deserves. It seems that attitudes toward criminal punishment have changed and that liberal opinion no longer need be ashamed to associate itself with concern about just deserts. Vengeance has long been shunned as an embarrassment to the idea of desert, and now even retribution is unwelcome to those who wish to exclude vindictive and self-righteous motives from criminal punishment. A certain modesty survives the disappearance of shame, however, and in the absence of suitable theory it still is difficult to know how best to make punishment fit the crime, or even why it is worth bothering about at all.

I

Before parting company, all theorists of criminal punishment will almost certainly agree that punishment must be deserved. This maxim gives voice to a double warning. Any punishment at all, no matter what its measure, must be deserved. And beyond this, the particular measure of punishment in each case must not be undeserved. Some obvious points in connection with the first principle are not always noticed, and I mention these now before going on to the more obscure points that are associated with the second one.

Guilt or innocence is what we must know about first of all, and this means finding out if the person we may wish to punish really did commit the crime. We must also be sure he committed the sort of crime we wish to punish him for and not (as it turns out) another sort of crime, or no crime at all, which indeed is just

what we may find once we look into *his* true circumstances, or into the full circumstances surrounding what we at first supposed was a crime, or perhaps even if we just take a harder and better look at the law. These questions of innocence which are normally pursued through legal proceedings must be distinguished from another sort of question that is usually pursued outside the law. This is the question that asks if the sort of conduct under consideration ever really presents a fit occasion for punishment. Is it right ever to punish when there is only negligence, or when there is simply no opportunity to avoid or to prevent harm? Is it right ever to punish for slander, or for blasphemy, or for attempting suicide? If such conduct can never merit criminal punishment, punishment for it could not be deserved.

These problems of who are deserving and who are not have their share of difficulties, but they seem by contrast quite manageable when compared with the problem of deciding just what is deserved by those who are deserving. Proportion between crime and punishment is most often taken to be the key to just deserts, but there are good reasons why the achievement of proportion seems a hopelessly elusive affair.

A scale of crimes according to their seriousness is the first of a number of difficult requirements to be met. It is easy enough to recognise that some sorts of crime are more serious than others, but it is not at all easy to decide the relative seriousness of all crimes. Murder and burglary leave no room for doubt. But rape, kidnapping, armed robbery, and espionage, for example, can produce long and inconclusive argument about the relative seriousness of each. The difficulties are compounded when one considers the great range of cases that fall within the ambit of each kind of crime. Murder may be more serious than burglary, but it is easy enough to imagine two cases in which a murder to end the victim's hopeless torment seems rather pale when contrasted with a particularly malicious burglary. Quite clearly, then, we must expect a great deal of overlapping among crimes that are arranged on a scale of seriousness; and it will not always be clear how extensively they

* Hyman Gross, "Culpability and Desert" from ARSP, *Archiv Für Rechts Und Sozialphilosophie,* 19 (1983), Wiesbaden, Franz Steiner Verlag. Reprinted by permission of the publisher.

overlap one another, or just which case of each represents a case of average seriousness.

This leads naturally to a second requirement. Within the scale of seriousness for each sort of crime we must be able to tell the proper interval (at least for the average case) between one sort of crime and another. Most of us would agree that rape is more serious than burglary, and murder more serious than rape. But is the more serious in each case equally more serious? A scale of crimes which in the end offers only an order of relative seriousness without an arrangement that indicates how much more serious is useless as a basis for proportionality.

A third requirement is one of pitch. Even if all crimes were ordered according to relative seriousness, and how much more serious could be determined as well, there would still remain the question of a general level of seriousness at which to locate the entire scale. The problem can be seen in historical perspective or by a comparison of the general level of sentences in different countries at any time, and to a great extent the differences in general levels of severity must reflect differences in the perceived seriousness of crimes in general.

This last difficulty suggests another. Severity of punishment is itself not the easy question it seems at first glance, for punishment and crime both are without settled principles of order, interval, or pitch. That this is so for punishment as well as crime may not be apparent immediately, since it seems plain enough that a five-year prison sentence is more severe than a one-year sentence, that it is five times as severe, and that the severity of either sentence might be similarly appreciated wherever and whenever imposed. In fact the variety of kinds of sentence and penal regimes available in any modern sentencing system make it impossible to rely generally on such simple calculations. Even straightforward time sentences within the same regime of incarceration defy comparative measurement. The person to be sentenced may be twenty or he may be sixty, and this surely will make a difference to what punishment a sentence represents, as will a great many other things about the prisoner that have nothing to do with his crime. Just how severe any particular sentence is thought to be will no doubt be a matter of prevailing levels at the time, but there is no fixed reference point for determining how high or how low the levels themselves are.

It is time now for a new start, and I shall first look into the matter of culpability of criminal

conduct, for it is precisely this culpability that determines how serious any crime is.

II

Murder is punished more severely than burglary. It is also punished more severely than manslaughter. A full-fledged murder that is completed and leaves someone dead is punished more severely than acts well on the way to doing that but thwarted while still only an attempt. Kill someone quite deliberately under circumstances in which it is your life or his, and the homicide may not be punishable at all. It is differences in culpability that make the difference in all these cases. Four features of conduct determine culpability.

First, it is important to know that the conduct of the accused was in fact a full-fledged example of the right type of criminal conduct. The question can be looked at in two ways. Was the act really under, or within, the control of the actor in all respects bearing on its dangerousness? After all, mistakes can be made in believing or in doing. Any mind has its lapses, and some may even lack capacity to manage affairs in a normal way. Mishaps occur in carrying on and carrying out, and they are due not only to the imperfections of physical activity but even more (far more) to the way the rest of the world impinges on us in ways we cannot anticipate or cannot counteract. We want to attribute to those we accuse only the harms and dangers they have brought about or have allowed within those parts of the world that are (or should be) under their control, but not the misfortunes that occur beyond their sphere of management. The other perspective leads us to ask if what was done is really the sort of conduct for which we now seek to impose liability. Murder and manslaughter are in essence two different varieties of conduct that produce death. The greater threat of death that is presented by the conduct in cases of murder accounts for its greater culpability. In murder the events and states of affairs within the control of the actor present a more immediate threat of death; typically the conduct is directed to bringing it about. In the case of manslaughter, certain events and states of affairs that were under the control of the actor also endangered the life that was lost, but not nearly so immediately, for much more than with murder the outcome depended on matters not under the control of the actor. Those kinds of conduct whose differences turn on characterisations such as recklessly, negligently, knowingly, purposely, and the like are all different in culpability for the same reason.

The second element of criminal culpability is harm. Losing one's life seems an altogether more serious business than losing one's property, and because it is taken to be more serious the conduct that poses a danger of it is thought more culpable, other things being equal. Intuitions about harm tell us that some kinds of harm are more serious than others, but the matter need not rest there. Harms are greater or less because our interests are not all of the same importance, and the acts which violate those interests are more or less serious according to the importance we attach to the interest invaded.

A third feature of culpability is its dangerousness. This is not a matter of the actor's control over events, but of nearness or farness of the harm in prospect. Dangerous conduct brings harm closer as it progresses. In its early stages it can hardly represent the threat that is so clear in later stages, and especially in the final stage when everything is done that would normally be sufficient to accomplish the harmful purpose. Earlier there might be a change of mind or heart, intervention by others, or just a fortuitous turn of events that frustrates the harmful outcome of what is under way. Because this is so, the harm cannot be assumed to be immanent in the conduct that well might bring it about, and conduct is accounted less dangerous when there is more opportunity for the harm in prospect to be frustrated. Similarly, the conduct may seem more or less dangerous depending upon what the circumstances portend—a thrust less ominous when with a butter knife and not a butcher knife.

There is finally the matter of a right to engage in dangerous conduct. Endangering and even harming others can often be justified as the only reasonable alternative to some very likely harm to ourselves or to other innocent victims. Normally we are expected to abide by the rules and to rely on the law to protect us. But sometimes this would entail so great a sacrifice that only very heroic (or very cowardly) people could be expected to forbear from self-help, and we then have a right to harm those who would cause us harm if that is necessary for our own protection. Such a right makes our conduct less culpable, or not culpable at all.

If any of these four elements fail completely the conduct is without criminal culpability. An analogy might be a table without height, or without width, or without length. It makes no more sense to assert that certain conduct is criminally culpable while conceding that it is simply not fraught with any harm, or so remote from the occurrence of harm as not to be dangerous, or not under (or within) the actor's control, or quite justifiable. And just as a table's size depends upon its height, width, and length, so culpability depends on how great or how small culpability turns out to be in each of its four dimensions. Greater culpability may derive from any of the elements, and so may the greater size of the table, though in both cases it is useful to know just what the judgment rests on.

No doubt some may feel that this account of criminal culpability is incomplete and find themselves wondering what might have happened to the guilty mind. I do not propose to lay the ghost of *mens rea* here, and will say only that I have no need of any such hypothesis. I hope even those who may think my account incomplete will agree that it does regard as more serious those crimes that are in fact more serious, and in general assesses blame for what was done with a decent respect for all those things that we ordinarily think should matter.

There remains the question of why those who commit crime deserve to be punished according to the culpability of their conduct. I shall make no attempt to put my finger on the answer straightaway, but turn now to consider the alternatives.

III

There are three other views of desert. The first of these takes the proper measure of punishment to be the harm or suffering that has befallen the victim rather than the conduct that produced it. The second looks to the person rather than his conduct to determine culpability as the basis of punishment. And finally, there is a third way of attempting to make the punishment fit the crime that dispenses with proportionality and instead adopts a scheme in which broad uniformity is the goal.

It is frequently suggested that punishment is unsatisfactory if it does not mete out to the criminal an equivalence of the harm his crime represents. Both historically and psychologically this harm principle of desert has roots in ideas of negative compensation, and it has found its purest expression as the law of the talion. Making the perpetrator a victim who suffers in the same way as his victim and is similarly reduced is not without its difficulties. Even a life for a life is not the easy proposition it seems at first, for in a civilised society there are the prolonged agonies of persons awaiting execution that surely must increase their suffering beyond what any ordinary murder victim would experience. And of course such a crime as rape could begin a long list of offences in which any attempt to reproduce the harm would be ludicrous as well as barbarous.

The quest for harm in kind is carried on now only in the imagination. Parity of suffering is a far more acceptable principle of desert. Prison sentences are presumed to inflict suffering that can be increased according to the length of the sentence and the kind of penal regime, and in the popular imagination as well as in judicial decisions a prison sentence is often meant to requite suffering with suffering.

We may pass the question of how a tolerably accurate equivalence of suffering might be achieved, and look at an even more serious problem. On this view of desert it is still necessary to associate the harm which the crime represents with the person who is said to be responsible for it. If the harm principle is relied on exclusively, only responsibility in a causal sense need be shown to establish the association. Questions of fault are irrelevant, for harm caused deliberately and harm caused accidentally are then on an equal footing. If fault is once admitted as a relevant consideration, it is conduct and not harm that must immediately occupy the center of the stage. And of course considerations of fault must be admitted if we are to protect the control a person has over his own destiny through his choosing what he does.

It is important to note, however, that admitting conduct just in order to determine fault does not allow full scope for consideration of culpability. There is no need to consider just how dangerous the conduct was in view of remaining opportunities for the harm to be frustrated. Nor need the legitimacy of conduct enter into judgments of desert. Only the question of whether relevant matters were under or within the control of the actor bear on fault, and only that question need be looked into to distinguish accidental from deliberate harms, or to make other similar discriminations. Even this fault-enriched harm principle, then, is unable to comprehend all those exculpatory claims that seem so clearly to bear on the question of how much punishment is deserved.

Desert based on harm is inadequate in another and even more obvious way. Much criminal conduct does not result in harm but only threatens harm. Inchoate crimes (attempts, conspiracies, solicitations, and the like) are all crimes of this sort. So are the many crimes in which the completed crime is simply dangerous conduct, like reckless driving or illegal possession of explosives. So too are crimes in which certain conduct is prohibited as part of a larger scheme of regulation, like smuggling or drug trafficking. In all these cases conduct alone is used to measure punishment, and there is nothing in our criminal jurisprudence to suggest that in cases where harm occurs the punishment deserved ought to rest on other grounds.

It is quite natural to speak of a person as being culpable, and this suggests a second alternative view of desert. Indeed it seems that really conduct can be said to be culpable only with reference to some person who engages in it, for it is he who is blamed, and his conduct simply the reason for blaming him. It seems reasonable then to put the person in the spotlight when he has done something wrong, and to punish him according to what *he* deserves. Sometimes the state of mind associated with the criminal episode is regarded as the essence of culpability. Sometimes more general characterological features are thought to be revealed by the criminal conduct, and these are taken to be the measure of the perpetrator's culpability. In either case the crime becomes a moment of revelation, and what it reveals about the offender is taken to be the proper basis of his punishment.

Sentencing judges frequently indulge in talk about states of mind and types of persons when it is time to pass sentence, though nowhere in legal proceedings is there greater uncertainty and arbitrariness than here. The reason is that no one is very clear about what (in any relevant sense) a state of mind is, and it is therefore not surprising that no evidence of it is ever introduced or even thought appropriate. Similarly, traits of character that are supposed to be revealed by criminal conduct turn out to be no more than judgments of conduct over an extended period expressed in the language of dispositions. Dangerous characters (in this sense) there may be, for example, and under certain conditions they may be kept out of circulation because of the harm they do, but their detention is then for some other reason and not to give them the punishment they deserve.

Culpability of a person apart from the culpability of his conduct turns out, then, to be an illusion and an encouragement to injustice through reliance on prejudice disguised as common sense.

Even if punishment is deserved only for culpable conduct, it is still possible to abandon the attempt to make punishment proportionate to culpability and settle instead for a simpler principle. Suppose that uniformity were substituted for proportionality, and that all sentences (or most) were disproportionately large or disproportionately small when measured against culpability. All felonies might be punished by hanging (a proposal by no means fanciful in the light of our legal history), so that once a major threshold of culpability has been crossed and the crime is great rather than small, no further assessment need be made. Similarly, overcrowded prisons and overburdened resources for prosecution may lead to arbitrarily (though uniformly) short sentences as a matter of judicial policy or as a result of bargains contrived to induce guilty pleas. Beyond expediency in administration, there is considerable temptation to turn toward uniformity and away from proportion to avoid having to confront the difficulties of getting the proportion right, as well as to avoid the complaints of inequitable disparity in sentencing that are inevitable when cases that are superficially alike are not treated alike.

If all serious crimes were to be treated with a severity appropriate to only the most serious, there would be strong encouragement to regard all serious crimes as equally serious and an inducement to commit whichever seem most convenient in carrying out a criminal purpose—a mandate to kill in order to steal, if that seems an easier and safer way under the circumstances. The result may be less dramatic when the divisions are less stark, but any lumping in the interest of uniformity is bound to have similar undesirable consequences.

It is hard to imagine as the normal state of affairs a year in prison for ordinary cold-blooded murder. It is not hard to imagine what the consequences would be if such sentences were part of a general policy of gross leniency. There are often good reasons for punishing less than the crime itself deserves, and I shall soon have more to say about this. But good reasons aside, if those who commit crimes are allowed to get away with a slap on the wrist, general reliance on the protective power of the law and adherence to its strictures may be expected to disappear. How great an encouragement this would be to criminal self-help and to other illegal activities depends upon the character of the community, but there is little doubt that slowly or swiftly there would be a change in the law-abiding attitudes that now dominate and that are necessary for peaceful coexistence in civil society. When legal proceedings are seen to confer virtual impunity no one need bother himself very much about the law, and we can expect a state of affairs in which the strong prevail over the weak unless the weak have the wealth or influence required to buy the protection they need.

Uniformity which disregards culpability may come in a mixed bag, some parts disproportionately great and some disproportionately small. Indeed judicial fiat that gives free range to those uncritical notions of right and wrong that have a broad popular appeal seems now to be the preferred way of achieving uniformity in sentencing and it is uniformity in such a mixed bag that appears now most often as the test of justice in sentencing. It avoids the inconvenient difficulties of culpability, and allows the judge to give voice to a full range of popular sentiment without laying himself open to accusations of personal prejudice in the case.

Having raised the alarm by pointing to the undesirable consequences of disproportionate punishment, I must now confess the failure of these arguments to establish a requirement in justice for proportionality between crime and punishment. In the end these arguments point only to the utility of punishment according to desert. Something more is required to explain the offence to our sense of justice.

To the extent that punishment is undeserved there is punishment no different than punishment of the innocent. The point is regularly obscured by a powerfully seductive fallacy. It is easy to suppose that conviction of a crime entails a loss of innocence, and that the guilty person (as we call him) deserves to be punished according to how great his guilt is. In the first place we must decide the question of guilt or innocence. But once innocence is lost it is thought to be lost altogether. The trouble is that persons convicted of crimes are really not like fallen angels, and like the rest of us are entitled to be free of all liability to punishment except for the particular criminal conduct for which they stand convicted. Since their innocence apart from that is no different than anyone else's, the same offence against justice that occurs whenever the innocent are punished occurs whenever they receive punishment that is not deserved.

The offence to justice in unjustifiably lenient sentences has mainly to do with the blessings of innocence conferred on those who are not entitled to enjoy them. Those who conform their conduct to the law and remain genuinely innocent rightly resent what in effect is the spurious innocence of those who commit crimes with impunity, whether total or measured. Getting away with one's crime is an instance of justice not being done. Being allowed to get away with it, even if only to a limited extent, is a case of injustice, for quite inequitably it confers a benefit that is not deserved.

IV

Briefly stated, the position is this. Innocence is lack of culpability, perhaps utter and complete, or perhaps only insufficient to satisfy fully the particular culpability requirements set by the law for the criminal liability in question. A person deserves to be punished according to the culpability of his criminal conduct because that measures exactly the extent to which his innocence has been lost. To the extent his innocence is lost, he deserves punishment. To the extent his innocence remains intact, he deserves impunity.

Matters of extent seem crucially important, and it is time to look again now at those troublesome questions of proportion which I raised earlier as questions of order, interval, and pitch.

Particular crimes (of the same sort or of different sorts) may be compared and judged more or less serious by references to those four elements of culpability that are immanent in our criminal jurisprudence. Judgments about how much more serious are likewise made by references to the constituents of culpability. Complex argument is often required to settle these matters, but we know quite well how to argue and how to judge which is the better argument. Harm, danger, risks, rights and issues about just what was done intentionally are all matters of common controversy about which we may finally find ourselves in temporary disagreement, though never nonplussed; for new facts and new ideas can always be advanced to carry the argument further. When there is a sufficient opportunity to argue these matters, in court or in the course of reaching legislative decisions, there is no reason why matters of order and interval can not be dealt with properly.

How seriously crime in general ought to be regarded and how severely it ought to be punished is another matter. There is little agreement about the kind of arguments that are appropriate to decide the question. There are of course very different levels of punishment at different times and different places, and whenever there is movement afoot to increase or decrease the general level the cause is almost always argued on grounds of some expediency, rather than desert. I have already suggested that the avoidance of undeserved impunity is the demand made by justice when it requires that those who are guilty not be allowed to get away with their crimes. The minimum punishment necessary to satisfy that requirement for each crime is punishment at the right level for that crime. Crimes with their corresponding minimum punishments necessary to prevent any impunity, when viewed in the aggregate, will compose a scale of crimes and punishments at the right pitch. Another demand of justice was noted previously, and this requires that punishment be measured by loss of innocence, so that nothing in excess of culpability is acceptable. But once we determine the minimum that is necessary to avoid impunity, we have established the correspondence we seek with culpability. It appears, therefore, that punishment in excess of the minimum required to avoid any impunity is punishment beyond the bounds of lost innocence, and so undeserved. From the point of view of just deserts, then, the right punishment is the least that is necessary to prevent impunity when criminal culpability (and only that) is fully considered. It is arrived at by making a finely tuned judgment of culpability that takes into account all and only those elements of culpability that bear on liability.[1]

Whether a sentence is justifiable is not the same question as whether it represents just deserts for the crime. Since punishment is justified only by a need to prevent impunity anything beyond that is needless suffering and morally wrong not as an injustice but for those reasons that make the infliction of needless suffering wrong. Punishment to fit the crime is therefore best viewed as a *prima facie* sentence and a ceiling for punishment.[2] It is subject to reduction in three possible ways to achieve a justifiable sentence.[3]

In the first place there are exculpatory considerations other than those that the law admits to affect criminal liability. In arriving at a sentence we put justice in peril if we fail to give due weight to arguments resting on such claims, though they have no bearing on criminal culpability and the verdict which depends on it. In general, there are thought to be good reasons in policy for not allowing the motive from which a crime was committed to serve as a defence. After all, it is conduct and not what prompted it that matters, even when the reason for criminal conduct is quite benign. When the reason for doing something is thought to matter in a way that ought to render what was done an innocent act, the crime is defined differently to take account of that. For the rest, innocent and even worthy motives are left a part to play only at the sentencing stage. In a similar vein, the law often refuses to recognise the cause of criminal conduct as a defence, though the exculpatory force of the facts seems plain enough. Drunkenness, a volatile temper, deprived circumstances, all seem to suggest themselves as good excuses on many occasions, at least to mitigate the severity of the law. But clearly it would make a shambles of the law if it were generally a defence that at the time of the crime the offender happened to be quite drunk, or sadly impecunious, or a man whose very short temper was showing itself. These claims the law cannot allow as a defence even though the influences they point to were very important, but it can allow such claims in mitigation of punishment. Indeed it is bound to allow these considerations to weigh when the claims represent good reasons for a lesser sentence and so are a good answer to anyone who might say the lesser sentence means impunity.

The second set of considerations are not exculpatory at all, but argue for a lesser sentence on moral grounds other than those that affect justice. It is cruel, not unjust, to treat someone who is very old or very ill in the same way as someone who is not. Compassion has its moral standing, and at the time of sentencing makes its moral claims as an ally and not an antagonist of justice. It is less clear how a morally worthy life or how morally meritorious acts in the past ought to count in reducing punishment, though there is little question that such matters are widely accepted to counter the suggestion that the offender is being allowed to get away with his crime when his sentence is less than it would otherwise be. The danger in those moral claims that have a hollow ring is the inequitable disparity they introduce into sentencing, for it is only those claims that survive critical argument unimpaired that will provide the sort of reasons

that are good and can be made to seem so to anyone who takes a disinterested view of them.

The third set of reasons for reducing sentences rests on assorted considerations of public policy. If they lead to inequitable disparities or in any other way are morally unacceptable the reasons offered are not good reasons. I confess some doubt about the common practice of favouring witnesses for the prosecution and those offenders who provide information to the police, and think it is a serious corruption of criminal justice when, as is frequently done, lesser sentences are given to those who are induced to plead guilty and so spare the state the trouble and expense of proving its case. In general, it is not enough that most people are satisfied that there are good reasons for reducing the *prima facie* sentence and will not think that someone has got away with his crime. Unless reasons stand up in critical argument as good ones, they produce unacceptable differences in sentence among convicted persons, as well as the undeserved benefit of a measure of innocence.

If this is right, the punishment deserved *prima facie* and the sentence finally to be passed both turn out to be the minimum necessary to prevent the offender from getting away with his crime.[4] The formulation may seem incomplete since it does not indicate who must be satisfied on this point. It would be a mistake to suppose that current public opinion is the arbiter, even though the point of the exercise is to maintain a healthy respect for the law in the community at large. The prevailing angry mood that will often support inhumanity in the name of justice is not to be appeased but rather met with arguments that appeal to conscience. Weighing in a suitably sensitive way all those things that are ingredients of such argument and that ought to be admitted when arriving at a sentence is a difficult business, though no more difficult and time consuming than other matters that present challenges to judges and call for the exercise of sophisticated discretion in other sorts of legal proceedings where the stakes are considerably less.[5]

NOTES

1. Everyone enjoys a right that is coextensive with his innocence to remain free from punishment, and punishment is limited by culpability because there is such a right. Punishment is also limited to what is necessary to prevent impunity, for otherwise in some measure punishment would represent needless suffering. The limiting principle of culpability is therefore a principle of justice, while the limiting principle of prevention of impunity is a principle of humane

concern. But is it possible that the two principles may be in conflict? Is it possible that in some cases it is necessary to punish more severely than culpability warrants in order to prevent impunity? Is it possible that in other cases the punishment warranted by culpability would be greater than what is required to prevent impunity? I think not. If ever it appears that someone is getting away with his crime when punished according to its culpability, there is something wrong with the appearance. A belief in such an appearance commits one to the nonsensical view that someone has received what he deserves but is nevertheless getting away with his crime. With reference to the second possibility, it is quite true that what is deserved is sometimes more than is necessary to prevent someone from getting away with his crime. But that is just to say that in the end, when *all* things are considered that ought to be considered, what is justifiable may well be less than what is deserved. This point is developed in what follows in the text.

The relationship of the culpability principle and the principle of prevention of impunity may be seen by an analogy to economics to be complementary and not conflicting. Various articles may be valued in relation to one another according to such things as the cost of their production and the market demand for them. They can then be arranged in an order of more or less expensive, and with judgments of how much more or less expensive not difficult to make. But valuation in the abstract is not enough. To assign prices it is necessary to make reference to the purchasing power of money in an economic community. In the first instance we are able to value a Rolls and a Mini and conclude that one should be about fourteen times as expensive as the other, yet only when we go on to consider the second

matter can we decide whether the right price for each is £100 and £1,400; £100,000 and £1,400,000; or something in between.

I am indebted both to Peter Lipton and to Marc Owen for raising these questions.

2. There is of course the question of what considerations might justify a sentence greater than what is deserved. I do not take up that question here since it is the question of whether offenders may be treated in a way that benefits others or themselves, quite apart from matters of desert.

3. What the offender deserves, in contrast to what is deserved for the crime, suggests itself as another way of describing what I call a justifiable sentence. I find myself in the end unhappy with this suggestion since at least some of the considerations that may require a reduction in the sentence seem to have no bearing on the justice of the sentence.

4. Each, of course, has a different set of determinants. The reason for first making a determination of what is deserved is to ensure that the starting point in finally arriving at a sentence is not in excess of what justice will allow. Including matters bearing on culpability with other considerations from the start would only encourage disorderly deliberations in which motley elements obscure the exact extent to which innocence has been lost.

5. In particular one thinks of determination of fair market value, or of assessments of loss (such as loss of amenities) where there are no fixed pecuniary indices, since in reaching these decisions there is similarly complex consideration of disparate elements. Yet no one would deny that there are in these matters procedures for reaching conclusions that can be defended against charges of unfairness.

J. L. MACKIE

Retributivism: A Test Case for Ethical Objectivity*

I

In my *Ethics: Inventing Right and Wrong* I have argued that there is a real issue about the objectivity or subjectivity of moral principles and values, and I have tried to clarify this issue, which is often treated in a confused way, and to say what I take the central problem to be. I have also argued that neither objectivism nor subjectivism can be dismissed as incoherent, and neither view can be established merely by conceptual or linguistic analysis, or indeed by any other sort of *a priori* argument. To decide whether moral principles and values are objective or subjective in the important sense, we have to consider which view can be developed so as to provide the best overall explanation of all the relevant phenomena or data, all the moral (or related) "appearances" with which we are confronted. I would relate this question to what Hume, for example, says in Book III of the *Treatise*. I do not think that he has *shown* in any conclusive way by the end of Book III Part i that moral distinctions are not derived from "reason" and that they are derived from a "moral sense" or from "sentiment." Hume's case for these theses is still incomplete at this point. It is completed only when he has shown, by the end of Book III Part iii, how on a "sentimentalist" foundation he can develop a sociological and psychological explanation of both the "artificial" and the "natural" virtues, that is, can explain why these various dispositions occur and why they are cultivated and approved of in human society, fairly uniformly though with some variations.

An examination of retributivism will, I suggest, contribute usefully to this discussion. Many people seem to have moral intuitions of a retributivist sort. But are these genuine intuitions which reveal objectively valid moral principles or requirements, or are they rather expressions of sentiments for which we should

seek, and can find, psychological or sociological or even biological explanations? I shall argue that purportedly objective retributivist *principles* cannot be defended, but that retributivist *sentiments*—deeply ingrained, highly developed and organized—can be readily understood.

It is becoming more common for philosophers to declare their adherence to the retributive theory of punishment. This may be understood as an offshoot of the widespread tendency to reject utilitarianism in favour of some view which takes as central such concepts as those of justice and rights. However, this adherence may go along with a very broad or loose account of what the retributive theory is. Thus Jeffrie G. Murphy says that "A retributive theory of punishment is one which characterizes punishment primarily in terms of the concepts of justice, rights, and desert—i.e. is concerned with the just punishment, the punishment the criminal deserves, the punishment society has the right to inflict (and the criminal has the right to expect)."[1] J. G. Cottingham, in an admirable recent article, finds among views which have been called retributivist at least nine distinct approaches, and almost as many distinct strategies for justifying punishment, not all of which would fall under Murphy's description, broad though it is.[2]

Cottingham's headings are as follows: Repayment Theory (that by being punished the criminal repays a debt to society); Desert Theory (which seems to reduce to the bald assertion that crime deserves punishment, that it simply is just that the offender should be punished); Penalty Theory and Minimalism (I shall say more about these two later); Satisfaction Theory (that punishment is justified by the satisfaction that it gives to the victim of the crime or to others who have been injured or outraged by it); Fair Play Theory (that failure to punish would be unfair to those who, unlike the criminal, have obeyed the rules, and so have forgone satisfactions or advantages that the criminal has gained by breaking them); Placation Theory (that a god who has been angered by, say, a murder must be placated by the execution of the murderer, or

*From "Retributivism: A Test Case for Ethical Objectivity" by J. L. Mackie. Published by permission of Mrs. Joan Mackie. All rights to further publication reserved.

else he will go on being angry with the whole nation); Annulment Theory (that the punishment somehow cancels or annuls the crime); and Denunciation Theory (that punishment is justified as an emphatic denunciation of a crime).

These are certainly a mixed bag. Cottingham takes the notion of repayment of a debt as what is central in retributivism, and rightly complains that several of the approaches he has listed have little to do with this. But let me suggest a way of bringing some sort of order into this mass of ideas.

It is true that *retribuo* in Latin means "I pay back." But surely the central notion is not that the criminal repays a debt, pays something back to society, but that someone else pays the criminal back for what he has done. Punitive retribution is the repaying of harm with harm, as reward is the repaying of benefit with benefit. We can class as an essentially retributivist approach any that sees at least some *prima facie* rightness in the repaying of evil with evil, especially a proportionate evil, but returning no evil where no evil has been done. This entails that justifications of punishment are retributive in so far as they are retrospective. On the other hand, suggestions (which Cottingham mentions under Penalty Theory and Minimalism) that a previous wrong act is a merely logical or definitional requirement for something to count as punishment, not in any way a moral justification, would be better not counted as retributivist.

Approaches that count as retributivist in this sense of involving retrospective justification must, however, be further subdivided. One important division is between what I would call *positive* and *negative* retributivism. Positive retributivism sees the previous wrong act as in itself a reason for inflicting a penalty. The crime at least tends positively to justify a penalty; but it may or may not be held that the wrong act is in itself morally *sufficient* for the penalty, or that it absolutely requires the penalty, irrespective of all other considerations. Negative retributivism (for which "minimalism" may be another name) holds that those who are not guilty must not (that is, morally must not, not *logically cannot*) be punished, that the absence of a crime morally requires the non-infliction of a penalty. There is also a quantitative variant of negative retributivism, that even if someone is guilty of a crime it is wrong to punish him more severely than is proportional to the crime. And of course

there is an analogous quantitative variant of positive retributivism, that a crime of a certain degree of wrongness positively calls for a proportionate penalty.

This distinction is important for at least two reasons. One is that once they are distinguished negative retributivism will be found to have a greater measure of general acceptance than positive retributivism. Many thinking people who hold firmly that it is morally wrong in itself to punish the innocent—not merely definitionally impossible—and also wrong in itself to punish the guilty beyond the degree of their guilt, are far less confident that a previous wrong act in itself, if considerations of deterrence and the like are clearly set aside, even tends to provide a positive justification of a penalty. People are often negative but not positive retributivists. The other reason is that if we try to develop and explain these various retributivist theses, the positive and negative ones seem to call for or to fit in with quite different lines of thought. For example, very general and obviously attractive principles about the rights of individuals or human rights provide immediate backing for the thesis that it is wrong to punish the innocent; but these take us no distance at all towards a positive reason for punishing the guilty just because they are guilty.

Even negative retributivism, however, is not without its problems, particularly if it is taken to include permissive clauses: you must not punish the innocent, but *you may punish the guilty;* you must not punish excessively, but *you may punish up to a proportionate degree.* These permissive clauses still do not assert positive retributivism, they do not say that wrong acts are positively a reason *for* imposing penalties; but they do say that wrong acts somehow cancel the basic reason for not imposing penalties; the guilty person loses his immunity in proportion to his guilt. Strictly, then, we should recognize permissive retributivism as a third variety, intermediate between negative and positive. The three principles can be stated briefly as follows:

Negative retributivism: One who is not guilty must not be punished.

Permissive retributivism: One who is guilty may be punished.

Positive retributivism: One who is guilty ought to be punished. (This "ought" may vary in strength between indicating only a weak *prima facie* reason and asserting an absolute requirement.)

The "must not," "may," and "ought" in each of these is moral. Also, these are to be considered as principles, morally valid in their own right. Obviously, the same statements could occur as derived rules in, for example, a utilitarian theory, where they would be explained and justified by their beneficial consequences, but they would not then constitute any sort of retributivism. For completeness, we should add quantitative variants of each of these three principles. Once these complications have been introduced, some further explanation is certainly needed both for the quantitative version of negative retributivism and for both versions of the permissive view. However, I leave these problems aside; they are as nothing compared with the difficulties in positive retributivism.

So far I have been drawing mainly formal distinctions, and have thus isolated the general form of a positive retributivist thesis, that a wrong act in itself positively calls for the imposition of a (proportionate) penalty. But this is a very dark saying. *Why* should it be so? Is there any way in which we can make sense of this curious principle, at least by relating it to some network of other moral ideas?

It is here, as developments or explanations or further justifications of the positive retributivist thesis, that several of the approaches listed by Cottingham come in: repayment, satisfaction, fair play, placation, annulment, denunciation. "Desert" is not such a further explanation, but is just the general, as yet unexplained, notion of positive retributivism itself. But these (and one or two more that have been suggested, which Cottingham does not list) are a remarkably unimpressive collection. They are, indeed, the philosophical analogues of the sort of opponents that a chessplayer would like to have if he were going to play, blindfold, a dozen or so opponents at once. Each of them can be despatched, with ease, in a very few moves.

Satisfaction: What this might justify, if it justified anything, would seldom be proportional to the wrongness of the crime. It would entail severer penalties where the surviving victims of the crime were of a vindictive nature, but lighter ones where the victims were forgiving or "Christian" in spirit. It would entail the punishment of any behaviour in proportion to its unpopularity, whether it was criminal or not. In any case, this is obviously a consequentialist justification: the penalty is being justified by the satisfaction it is likely to produce. Its connection with retributivism is merely that widespread satisfaction, felt by others besides the surviving victims of the crime, will be produced by the punishment of criminals only if many members of the society are already retributivists. But that does not make this itself a retributivist justification, and it has no power to explain any strictly retributivist principle.

Placation: This, too, is obviously consequentialist. The reason it offers for punishing rests upon the supposed bad consequences of failing to punish—the god will still be angry. But these consequences themselves depend upon the supposed retributivist opinions of the god in question. Far from explaining retributivism, this account requires that there should be some *other* morally adequate explanation of retributivism, if it is to be ascribed to a morally respectable god.

Denunciation: This also seems to be consequentialist. It has sometimes been called the "educative" theory of punishment. It tries to justify punishment by way of its tendency to produce in the public an attitude of greater hostility to the crime. This also, therefore, has no tendency to explain the retributivist principle, though, like satisfaction and placation, it may presuppose retributivist views. A public which already sees punishment as being deserved by the wrongness of the previous act is more likely to interpret a punishment as a dramatic assertion that the act punished was wrong.

These three approaches, then, are not really retributivist, though in one way or another they ride on the back of retributivism. Three others of the approaches listed, repayment, annulment, and fair play, do a little better in that they are genuinely retributivist in our sense. They are retrospective, non-consequentialist, because in each case the alleged justification is complete once the penalty has been inflicted; no further results of this are relied upon. But otherwise these approaches are equally unsatisfactory.

Repayment: How does the criminal's suffering or deprivation pay anything to society? No doubt repaying a debt often hurts the person who pays it, but it does not follow that anything that hurts someone amounts to his repaying a debt. If Jones owes Smith $10, it will hurt Jones just as much if he has to throw $10 away as if he has to give it to Smith, but throwing it away will not repay the debt. If the criminal's suffering or deprivation or incarceration doesn't do any good to society, it cannot be the payment of a debt to society. So this account is simply incoherent unless it is transformed into a theory of reparations, which are not punishment, or into the satisfaction theory which, as we saw, is consequentialist and will not explain retributivism.

Annulment: This notion, as Cottingham says, goes back at least to Hegel. But the remark he quotes (" . . . das Aufheben des Verbrechens, das sonst gelten würde, und die Wiederherstellung des Rechts") would be better translated as referring to "the annulment of the crime, which would otherwise *remain in force,* and the restoration of right." Hegel's idea seems to be that as long as a criminal goes scot-free, the crime itself still exists, still flourishes, but when the criminal is adequately punished the crime itself is somehow wiped out. It is not, therefore, by any sort of repayment or restitution that "right is restored," but just by trampling on the previously flourishing crime. But this notion is simply incoherent: there is no comprehensible way in which a penalty wipes out an otherwise still-existing crime. What makes this suggestion plausible is a confusion with deterrence and prevention. A penalty may help, by deterrence, to wipe out, not the past crime, but other similar crimes which, but for the deterrence, would be committed either by this same criminal or by others; that is, it may help to wipe out a criminal tradition or practice. Similarly, the locking up or killing of a criminal will put a temporary or a permanent stop to his criminal career. But in neither case is it the past crime that is annulled or wiped out, and deterrence and prevention are plainly consequentialist justifications, not retributivist ones.

Kant's remark that if the "last murderer" is not executed blood-guilt will adhere to the people, which Cottingham takes as an appeal to the placation theory, might be better understood as something like an anticipation of Hegel's notion of annulment. The guilt, the badness, of the crime is still floating around as long as the criminal is unpunished, and by letting him go free the people would share in this guilt as accessories after the act. But to suppose that this guilt is extinguished by the carrying out of the penalty requires the incomprehensible Hegelian notion of annulment, and to say that the people would be accessories if they did not punish the criminal presupposes, and therefore cannot explain, the principle that the crime in itself morally requires the penalty.

Fair play: Here the suggestion is that the various members of society are all in competition with one another, a competition governed by rules. The criminal has gained an unfair advantage by breaking the rules; to restore fairness this advantage must be taken away from him. Unlike our last two approaches, this one is not incoherent; it makes perfectly good sense in certain contexts. It has its clearest exemplification in the award of a penalty in football (soccer) when there has been a foul in the penalty area, that is, when a player or his shot has been illegally stopped in the neighbourhood of the other side's goal. It is also retributivist in our basic sense of being retrospective; the justification is complete when the penalty has been imposed; fairness has then (roughly at least) been restored, irrespective of whether there are or are not any further desirable consequences. The trouble with this approach, however, is that it has little relation to most cases of punishment. Any serious attempt to apply it would lead to bizarre results, not at all well correlated with what is thought of as desert or degree of wrongness or guilt. It implies that penalties should as far as possible be proportional to the advantage that the criminal has gained, in the social competition, by breaking the rules, just as a foul near the opponents' goal is penalized much more than one elsewhere. Thus if a businessman has secured a contract worth $100,000, but has exceeded the speed limit in order to get to the relevant appointment on time, he should presumably be fined $100,000, whereas a fine of $1 would be enough for someone who murders a blind cripple to rob him of $1. And so on. Unsuccessful attempts at murder (or anything else) should not be punished at all. There should be an advantage rule, as there is in football, where the referee will not penalize an infringement if the innocent side still has the advantage anyway. So while there are things that this fair play principle can plausibly be used to justify, it has little bearing on most legal penalties and will not serve as an expansion or explanation of the basic priciple of retribution or desert, of the idea that a wrong act in itself calls for a penalty proportionate to its degree of wrongness.

But perhaps it will be said that what matters is not the loot but the self-indulgence. Someone who commits a crime, even if he gets very little out of it, has still let himself go in a way that law-abiding people do not, and his punishment only brings him back into balance with their self-restraint. But when we switch to this topic of self-indulgence the analogy of a competitive game becomes even less apt. The ideal of equality in self-indulgence is so remote that we hardly even think of it. If it were unusual self-indulgence that we objected to and wanted to counterbalance, it would be the rich, the owners of yachts and racehorses, and businessmen with elastic expense accounts, that we should be getting after, not thieves and murderers. Again many murders arise out of domestic conflicts, and most of these only from long-standing problems. When people eventually kill their husbands or wives or lovers, they have probably already shown far more self-restraint, in not having so earlier, than those who are more happily or more placidly situated, and on the score of equality in restraint and indulgence would be entitled to let their hair down and kill someone once in a while.

What is basically wrong with the fair play approach, as these rather fantastic examples bring out, is that it focuses on the advantage that may have been gained by the criminal in some sort of social competition, whereas the point of punishment surely lies not in this but in wrongness of his act and the harm that he has done or tried to do. We can agree that he has acted unfairly, and that this implies that he cannot say that it is unfair if he suffers some proportionate penalty, if someone acts against him in a way that would otherwise have been similarly wrong. But this takes us only to a defence of permissive retributivism. It is still quite unclear how fairness *to the law abiding* is secured by the punishing of the law-breaker in itself, that is, unless this punishment secures some benefit for the law-abiding. So the fair play theory still fails to yield any defence of the principle of positive retributivism.

A suggestion not on Cottingham's list, which is often used to support retributivism, is that it peculiarly respects the dignity of persons on whom penalties may or may not be imposed. We can see the force of this as a support for negative retributivism, though it is an understatement to say only that someone's dignity has been invaded if, while innocent, he is made to suffer for the sake of some benefit to others. Again, it may help to explain permissive retributivism: someone's dignity is perhaps being respected if it is his own choice that cancels his immunity. Penalties which accord with negative and permissive retributivism do not invade anyone's basic area of freedom. But these consider-

ations give no support whatever to positive retributivism once it has been clearly distinguished from the other two views. It is quite incomprehensible how punishing a person because he has done wrong respects or enhances his dignity. Even as an argument against retributivism's traditional rivals as positive justifications of punishment, deterrence and utilitarianism generally, this has force. At most it shows that there should be restrictions on the deterrent (etc.) use of punishment, and this is commonly agreed by utilitarians although they hold that deterrence and the like are the only positive reasons for punishing. The utilitarian view can be and usually is developed in a way that introduces the negative and permissive theses as derived rules. Positive retributivism cannot gain even a comparative advantage by this appeal to dignity.

An even stranger suggestion on the retributivist side is that the criminal has a right to be punished. In general a right is something that the right-holder can either exercise or waive as he chooses, and most criminals would gladly waive this alleged right. If one of them would not, it could only be either because he actually wanted the penalty for itself, and then it would not be a punishment, or because he was himself a very keen retributivist—but then this, as a moral explanation of retributivism, would be circular, like the theories of satisfaction and placation we considered earlier. An associated view is that the criminal wills his own punishment. This may be just the point already noted, that it is by his own choice that he has lost his immunity; but this supports only the negative and permissive theses, not the positive one. Alternatively, what is invoked here may be Rousseau's general will: the criminal, *qua* citizen, subscribes to and helps to make the universal law by an application of which he is punished. Where this is true, it will help to justify punishment, and may indeed justify positive retributivist theses as derived rules about the imposition of penalties. Once the validity of the universal law attaching a penalty to a crime is established, the only further justification needed to provide *some* positive reason for imposing the penalty in a particular case is the retrospective one that a crime of the relevant sort has been committed. But this—which is, perhaps, the core of what Cottingham calls the penalty theory—explains positive retributivism only as a working rule, not as a justifying principle in its own right. Everything depends on the prior validity of the universal law, and this, on the present approach, depends on the two questions, whether the general will has actually made the universal law that is being applied and whether it was reasonable for it to do so. Since all the arguments for the positive retributivist *principle* are so weak, an affirmative answer to the second of these questions would have either to invoke non-retributivist considerations, or to move to some non-objectivist point of view, or both.

II

And that, it seems, is that. Every one of these approaches fails completely to supply any coherent expansion or explanation of the retributivist principle, and, as far as I know, there are no others on offer. On the other hand it is plain that a considerable number of people have what would be called an intuition that a wrong action in itself calls for the infliction of suffering or deprivation on the agent. In fact we might go further than this. Many people, perhaps most people, find unsatisfactory what I might call the standard compromise position about punishment.

What I mean by the compromise position is this. Negative retributivism is explained as a consequence of the rights of innocent persons, and permissive retributivism on the ground that a non-innocent person has to some extent lost those rights: rights make sense within a system of reciprocal rights, so that someone who has violated the rights of others cannot fairly claim the corresponding rights for himself. This system of reciprocal rights may in turn be explained within, say, some kind of utilitarian theory, or again it may be put forward on its own. In either case, this line of thought brings us to the point that someone who has done wrong *may* be punished, though someone who has done no wrong must not. But—the compromise runs—the positive decision to punish is justified, if at all, by the benefits that are likely to result from so doing, for example, by way of the deterrence of crime. So we combine negative and permissive retributivism (themselves explained immediately in terms of rights, though *perhaps* also, more indirectly, in terms of utility) with a positive justification of penalties that appeals directly to utility.

This compromise looks neat, and has therefore commended itself to some philosophers. But I think that most people will, on reflection, find it unsatisfactory. They will not feel happy about imposing a penalty on someone for the sake of benefits to others, even if he has lost his right to immunity, unless they can say further that he positively deserves this penalty. Strange though this may be, we want to be able to appeal to a positive retributivist principle as well as to whatever utilitarian or in general consequentialist justifications there may be. Also, positive retributivism is not a completely isolated moral principle: it has a counterpart in the view that gratitude and reward are morally appropriate. We feel that someone who has helped another person deserves gratitude, and that someone who has done good generally, especially something outstanding good, deserves some reward. And he deserves a reward simply because of what he has done, not because rewarding him will bring about this or that good further consequence.

Indeed, we could go further still: our basic moral concepts themselves of good and bad, right and wrong, cannot be adequately analysed unless we include a retributive element, the notion of returning benefit for benefit and harm for harm. What is bad or wrong, for example, is not simply what is harmful or what is forbidden: it is thought of also as what deserves condemnation, where condemnation is some kind of hostile and unpleasant reaction. Equally, what is good or right is not simply what is beneficial or what is recommended: it is thought of also as what deserves praise and commendation, what calls for a friendly and pleasant response.

Have we, then, been engaged in a vain and unnecessary task of trying to explain and justify positive retributivism? It is rather true merely by definition that what is wrong or bad deserves punishment and that what is right or good deserves reward? Is is part of the very concepts of wrong, bad, right, and good that they carry such deserts with them?

It would be a mistake thus to dismiss the problem. For even if it is part of these concepts that good and bad deserve reward and punishment, there is still the question whether and how those concepts themselves are to be justified or explained. For example, if the concept of something's being bad combines the notions of its being *harmful* and *forbidden* and *deserving a hostile response*, we still have the question why these three notions should go together, in particular why what is harmful and forbidden deserves a hostile response. That these elements go together is a synthetic judgment, even though the combination of them emerges from the analysis of *bad.*

Now as allegedly objective moral principles, this combination, and the corresponding combination of being *beneficial, recommended,* and *deserving of a favorable response,* are still quite obscure, though they are undoubtedly deeply entrenched in our thought. But as soon as we make the Humean move of saying that moral distinctions are founded on sentiment, not on reason, the obscurity disappears. If we ask, not, "Why do wrong actions deserve penalties and good actions deserve reward?" but rather "Why do we have an ingrained tendency to see wrong actions as calling for penalties and good actions as calling for reward?" then it is not difficult to outline an answer.

First let us consider the tendency to feel and show gratitude for benefits, and its hostile counterpart, the tendency to feel and express resentment of injuries. There is no doubt that these are very widespread human dispositions, and what look like the same or similar tendencies are not difficult to detect in some non-human animals. Nor is there the slightest difficulty in understanding how such instinctive patterns of behaviour, and feelings that harmonize with that behaviour, could have developed by an evolutionary process of biological natural selection. Since gratitude will reward the benefactor, and since tendencies that are rewarded are thereby psychologically reinforced, gratitude will tend to encourage further similar benefactions, and so will benefit the creature that feels and displays gratitude. We are not, of course, saying (as Hobbes did) that what looks like gratitude is really egoistically calculated behaviour aimed at encouraging future benefits. The feeling of gratitude may be and normally is straightforward, sincere, and non-calculating; it is, so to speak, the natural selection process that does the calculating, not the grateful agent himself. Thus uncalculating gratitude will be produced *because* of the benefits it is likely to bring, but the agent himself does not act gratefully *for the sake of* or *in anticipation of* those benefits. Similarly resentment of injuries is likely to discourage similar injuries, and so again will benefit the creature that feels and displays resentment, and thus there will be natural selection in favour of resentment, though again the resent-

ment in the agent himself will normally be spontaneous, not calculated.

Gratitude, however, is a favourable reaction by a particular agent to actions that have benefited *him,* and resentment similarly is a hostile reaction by a particular agent to actions that have harmed *him.* Reward and punishment are more generalized forms of retribution: they are responses to actions that are seen as good or bad in general, not as good or bad to some particular agent, and the retributive attitudes which we have to explain are those of seeing the good or bad actions as calling for reward or punishment as such, not as calling for favourable or hostile reactions *from* particular agents. The attitudes to be explained, therefore, are generalizations of gratitude and resentment in these two respects: specific reference to those to whom good or harm has been done is eliminated, and the attitudes arise in persons generally who know about the good or harm, not only in those who are themselves benefited or harmed.

However, once we have explained gratitude and resentment, it is easy to understand these generalizations of them. Hume would say that such generalization arises from sympathy; but a sociological explanation would be better than this purely psychological one. Within a social group, people tend to feel and show gratitude and resentment on behalf of one another, in some respects at least, because they are reciprocally benefited by doing so. Cooperation in resentment and gratitude grows up for the same reason that gratitude itself does, that it tends to be beneficial to each of the cooperators. This may be either an instinctive tendency, to be explained by biological natural selection, or a cultural trait or "meme," to be explained by a process of social evolution that is an analogue of biological selection. In saying this, we must guard against three errors. First, we are not saying that this cooperation is calculating from the point of view of the cooperators themselves: they feel genuine sympathy, righteous indignation, and the like. But they have come to feel in these ways as a result of some biological or social selective process in which the benefits of such cooperation has played a key role. But, secondly, we are not saying that this cooperation in gratitude and resentment has arisen because of its general utility, because the social group as a whole has been benefited by it. No doubt the group is benefited, but that would not in itself be a good explanation. A practice which *would* be socially useful may fail to arise; it is unlikely to arise unless it produces results which favour its own spreading and surviving, unless it works so as to propagate the genes or "memes" on which it depends; and in general this requires that it should benefit the individuals who engage in that practice. But cooperation in gratitude and resentment meets this requirement: it can grow up as a convention which in fact benefits all parties, even without being deliberately adopted for that purpose. However, thirdly, it is just not the case that all sorts of gratitude and resentment are generalized equally. Only some kinds of harm are socially, cooperatively, resented, and cooperation in gratitude is even more restricted. Again we must seek and can find sociological reasons for these differences: only with particular kinds of harm are the conditions favourable for the growth of a convention of cooperative hostility to them, so only some kinds of harm are seen as wrong and as calling for general resentment and punishment. For example, theft is cooperatively resented, but commercial competition is not.

In conclusion, therefore, I maintain that it is easy to understand why we have a deeply ingrained tendency to see wrong actions as calling for penalties and some sorts of good actions as calling for reward. Though retributive principles cannot be defended, with any plausibility, as allegedly objective moral truths, retributive attitudes can be readily understood and explained as sentiments that have grown up and are sustained partly through biological processes, and partly through analogous sociological ones.

That is why I have, in the title of this paper, called retributivism a test case for ethical objectivity. On objectivist assumptions, its force and its persistence are incomprehensible, but on a subjectivist or (in Hume's sense) sentimentalist approach they are easily understood.

NOTES

1. Jeffrie G. Murphy, in "Cruel and Unusual Punishments," to appear in the proceedings of the 1979 Conference of the Royal Institute of Philosophy on Law and Morality.
2. J. G. Cottingham, "Varieties of Retribution," *Philosophical Quarterly,* July 1979.

MICHAEL S. MOORE
The Moral Worth of Retribution*

RETRIBUTIVISM AND THE POSSIBLE MODES OF ITS JUSTIFICATION

Since I will in this chapter seek to justify the retributive theory of punishment, I will first say what such a theory is. *Retributivism* is the view that punishment is justified by the moral culpability of those who receive it. A retributivist punishes because, and only because, the offender deserves it. Retributivism thus stands in stark contrast to utilitarian views that justify punishment of past offenses by the greater good of preventing future offenses. It also contrasts sharply with rehabilitative views, according to which punishment is justified by the reforming good it does the criminal.

Less clearly, retributivism also differs from a variety of views that are often paraded as retributivist, but that in fact are not. Such views are typically put forward by people who cannot understand how anyone could think that moral desert by itself could justify punishment. Such persons scramble about for other goods that punishment achieves and label these, quite misleadingly, "retributivism." The leading confusions seem to me to be seven in number.

1. First, retributivism is sometimes identified with a particular measure of punishment such as *lex talionis,* an eye for an eye (e.g., Wilson and Herrnstein, 1985, p. 496), or with a kind of punishment such as the death penalty. Yet retributivism answers a question prior to the questions to which these could be answers. True enough, retributivists at some point have to answer the "how much" and "what type" questions for specific offenses, and they are committed to the principle that punishment should be graded in proportion to desert; but they are not committed to any particular penalty scheme nor to any particular penalty as being deserved. Separate argument is needed to answer these "how much" and "what type"

questions, *after* one has described why one is punishing at all. It is quite possible to be a retributivist and to be against both the death penalty and *lex talionis,* the idea that crimes should be punished by like acts being done to the criminal.

2. Contrary to Anthony Quinton (1954) and others (see Hart, 1968), retributivism is *not* "the view that only the guilty are to be punished." A retributivist will subscribe to such a view, but that is not what is distinctive about retributivism. The distinctive aspect of retributivism is that the moral desert of an offender is a *sufficient* reason to punish him or her; the principle Quinton advocates make such moral desert only a *necessary* condition of punishment. Other reasons—typically, crime prevention reasons—must be added to moral desert, in this view, for punishment to be justified. Retributivism has no room for such additional reasons. That future crime might also be prevented by punishment is a happy surplus for a retributivist, but no part of the justification for punishing.

3. Retributivism is not the view that punishment of offenders satisfies the desires for vengeance of their victims. The harm that is punishment can be justified by the good it does psychologically to the victims of crime, whose suffering is thought to have a special claim on the structuring of the criminal justice system (see Honderich, 1969, p. 30). To me, this is not retributivism. A retributivist can justify punishment as deserved even if the criminal's victims are indifferent (or even opposed) to punishing the one who hurt them. Indeed, a retributivist should urge punishment on all offenders who deserve it, even if *no* victims wanted it.

4. Relatedly, retributivism is not the view that the preferences of all citizens (not just crime victims) should be satisfied. A preference utilitarian might well believe, as did Sir James Fitzjames Stephen (1967 at p. 152), that punishment should be exacted "for the sake of gratifying the feeling of hatred—call it revenge, resentment, or what you will—which

*Michael S. Moore, "The Moral Worth of Retribution," in Ferdinand Schoeman (ed.), *Responsibility, Character, and the Emotions* (Cambridge and New York: Cambridge University Press, 1987), pp. 179–219. Reprinted by permission of the author and Cambridge University Press.

the contemplation of such [criminal] conduct excites in healthily constituted minds . . . ," or that "the feeling of hatred and the desire of vengeance . . . are important elements of human nature which ought . . . to be satisfied in a regular public and legal manner." Yet a retributivist need not believe such things, but only that morally culpable persons should be punished, irrespective of what other citizens feel, desire, or prefer.

5. Relatedly, retributivism is not the view that punishment is justified because without it vengeful citizens would take the law into their own hands. Usually it is those who are hostile to retributivism, such as Justice Marshall (1976), who link it to this indefensible idea. Punishment for a retributivist is not justified by the need to prevent private violence, which is an essentially utilitarian justification. Even in the most well-mannered state, those criminals who deserve punishment should get it, according to retributivism.

6. Nor is retributivism to be confused with denunciatory theories of punishment (Feinberg, 1971). In this latter view punishment is justified because punishment is the vehicle through which society can express its condemnation of the criminal's behavior. This is a utilitarian theory, not a retributive one, for punishment is in this view to be justified by the good consequences it achieves—either the psychological satisfactions denunciation achieves, or the prevention of private violence, or the prevention of future crimes through the education benefits of such denunciation. A retributivist justifies punishment by none of these supposed good consequences of punishing.

7. Finally, retributivism should not be confused with a theory of formal justice (the treating of like cases alike). Retributivism is not, as McCloskey (1965) has urged, "a particular application of a general principle of justice, namely, that equals should be treated equally and unequals unequally." True, a retributivist who also subscribes to the principle of formal justice is committed to punishing equally those persons who are equally deserving. However, the principle of formal justice says nothing about punishing anybody for anything; such a principle only dictates that, *if* we punish anyone, we must do so equally. Why we should punish anyone is the question retributivism purports to answer, a question not answered by the distinct principle of formal justice.

Retributivism is a very straightforward theory of punishment: We are justified in punishing because and only because offenders deserve it. Moral culpability ("desert")[1] is in such a view both a sufficient as well as a necessary condition of liability to punitive sanctions. Such justification gives society more than merely a right to punish culpable offenders. It does this, making it not unfair to punish them, but retributivism justifies more than this. For a retributivist, the moral culpability of an offender also gives society the *duty* to punish. Retributivism, in other words, is truly a theory of justice such that, if it is true, we have an obligation to set up institutions so that retribution is achieved.

Retributivism, so construed, joins corrective justice theories of torts, natural right theories of property, and promissory theories of contract as deontological alternatives to utilitarian justifications; in each case, the institutions of punishment, tort compensation, property, and contract are justified by the rightness or fairness of the institution in question, not by the good consequences such institution may generate. Further, for each of these theories, moral desert plays the crucial justificatory role: Tort sanctions are justified whenever the plaintiff does not deserve to suffer the harm uncompensated and the defendant by his or her conduct has created an unjust situation that permits corrective action; property rights are justified whenever one party, by his or her labor, first possession, or intrinsic ownership of his or her own body, has come by such actions or status morally to deserve such entitlements; and contractual liability is justified by the fairness of imposing it on one who deserves it (because of his or her voluntary undertaking, but subsequent and unexcused breach).

Once the deontological nature of retributivism is fully appreciated, it is often concluded that such a view cannot be justified. You either believe punishment to be inherently right, or you do not, and that is all there is to be said about it. As Hugo Bedau (1978) once put it:

Either he [the retributivist] appeals to something else—some good end—that is accomplished by the practice of punishment, in which case he is open to the criticism that he has a nonretributivist, consequentialist justification for the practice of punishment. Or his justification does not appeal to something else, in which case it is open to the criticism that it is circular and futile.

Such a restricted view of the justifications open to a retributivist leads theorists in one of two directions: Either they hang on to retributivism, urging that it is to be justified "logically" (i.e., non-morally), as inherent in the ideas of punishment (Quinton, 1954) or of law (Fingarette, 1977); or they give up retributivism as an inherently unjustifiable view (Benn and Peters, 1959). In either case, retributivism is unfairly treated, since the first alternative trivializes it and the second eliminates it.

Bedau's dilemma is surely overstated. Retributivism is no worse off in the modes of its possible justification than any other deontological theory. In the first place, one might become (like Bedau himself, apparently) a kind of "reluctant retributivist." A reluctant retributivist is someone who is somewhat repelled by retributivism but who nonetheless believes: (1) that there should be punishment; (2) that the only theories of punishment possible are utilitarian, rehabilitative, retributive, or some mixture of these; and (3) that there are decisive objections to utilitarian and rehabilitative theories of punishment, as well as to any mixed theory that uses either of these views in any combination. Such a person, as I have argued elsewhere (Moore, 1982b; also Moore, 1984, chap. 6), becomes, however reluctantly, a retributivist by default.

In the second place, positive arguments can be given for retributivism that do not appeal to some good consequences of punishing. It simply is not true that "appeals to authority apart, we can justify rules and institutions only by showing that they yield advantages" or that "to justify is to provide reasons in terms of something else accepted as valuable" (Benn and Peters, 1959, pp. 175–6). Coherence theories of justification in ethics allow two non-consequentialist possibilities here:

1. We might justify a principle such as retributivism by showing how it follows from some yet more general principle of justice that we think to be true.
2. Alternatively, we can justify a moral principle by showing that it best accounts for those of our more particular judgments that we also believe to be true.

In a perfectly coherent moral system, the retributive principle would be justified in both these ways, by being part of the best theory of our moral sentiments, considered as a whole.

The first of these deontological argument strategies is made familiar to us by arguments such as that of Herbert Morris (1976), who urges that retributivism follows from some general ideas about reciprocal advantage in social relations. Without assessing the merits of these proposals one way or another, I wish to pursue the other strategy. I examine the more particular judgments that seem to be best accounted for in terms of a principle of punishment for just deserts.

These more particular judgments are quite familiar. I suspect that almost everyone at least has a tendency—one that he may correct as soon as he detects it himself, but at least a tendency—to judge culpable wrongdoers as deserving of punishment. Consider some examples Mike Royko has used to get the blood to the eyes of readers of his newspaper column:

The small crowd that gathered outside the prison to protest the execution of Steven Judy softly sang "We Shall Overcome". . . .

But it didn't seem quite the same hearing it sung out of concern for someone who, on finding a woman with a flat tire, raped and murdered her and drowned her three small children, then said that he hadn't been "losing any sleep" over his crimes. . . .

I remember the grocer's wife. She was a plump, happy woman who enjoyed the long workday she shared with her husband in their ma-and-pa store. One evening, two young men came in and showed guns, and the grocer gave them everything in the cash register.

For no reason, almost as an afterthought, one of the men shot the grocer in the face. The woman stood only a few feet from her husband when he was turned into a dead, bloody mess.

She was about 50 when it happened. In a few years her mind was almost gone, and she looked 80. They might as well have killed her too.

Then there was the woman I got to know after her daughter was killed by a wolfpack gang during a motoring trip. The mother called me occasionally, but nothing that I said could ease her torment. It ended when she took her own life.

A couple of years ago I spent a long evening with the husband, sister and parents of a fine young woman who had been forced into the trunk of a car in a hospital parking lot. The degenerate who kidnapped her kept her in the trunk, like an ant in a jar, until he got tired of the game. Then he killed her.

[Reprinted by permission: Tribune Media Services]

Most people react to such atrocities with an intuitive judgment that punishment (at least of some kind and to some degree) is warranted. Many will quickly add, however, that what accounts for their intuitive judgment is the need for deterrence, or the need to incapacitate such a dangerous person, or the need to reform the person. My own view is that these addenda are just "bad reasons for what we believe on instinct anyway," to paraphrase Bradley's general view of justification in ethics.

To see whether this is so, construct a thought experiment of the kind Kant (1965, p. 102) originated. Imagine that these same crimes are being done, but that there is no utilitarian or rehabilitative reason to punish. The murderer has truly found Christ, for example, so that he or she does not need to be reformed; he or she is not dangerous for the same reason; and the crime can go undetected so that general deterrence does not demand punishment (alternatively, we can pretend to punish and pay the person the money the punishment would have cost us to keep his or her mouth shut, which will also serve the ends of general deterrence). In such a situation, should the criminal still be punished? My hypothesis is that most of us still feel some inclination, no matter how tentative, to punish. That is the particular judgment I wish to examine. (For those persons—saints or moral lepers, we shall see which—who do not have even a tentative inclination to punish, I argue that the reason for affirming such inclinations are also reasons to feel such inclinations.)

THE CASE AGAINST RETRIBUTIVE JUDGMENTS

The puzzle I put about particular retributive judgments is this: Why are these particular judgments so suspect—"primitive," "barbarous," "a throwback"—when other judgments in terms of moral desert are accorded places of honor in widely accepted moral arguments? Very generally, there seem to me to be five explanations (and supposed justifications) for this discriminatory treatment of retributive judgments about deserved punishment.

1. First and foremost there is the popularly accepted belief that punishment for its own sake does no good. "By punishing the offender you cannot undo the crime," might be the slogan for this point of view. I mention this view only to put it aside, for it is but a reiteration of the consequentialist idea that only further good consequences achieved by punishment could possibly justify the practice. Unnoticed by those who hold this position is that they abandon such consequentialism when it comes to other areas of morals. It is a sufficient justification not to scapegoat innocent individuals, that they do not deserve to be punished; the injustice of punishing those who do not deserve it seems to stand perfectly well by itself as a justification of our practices, without need for further good consequences we might achieve. Why do not we similarly say that the injustice of the guilty going unpunished can equally stand by itself as a justification for punishment, without need of a showing of further good consequences? It simply is not the case that justification always requires the showing of further good consequences.

Those who oppose retributivism often protest at this point that punishment is a clear harm to the one punished, and the intentional causing of this harm requires some good thereby achieved to justify it; whereas *not* punishing the innocent is not a harm and thus does not stand in need of justification by good consequences. Yet this response simply begs the question against retributivism. Retributivism purports to be a theory of justice, and as such claims that punishing the guilty achieves something good—namely, justice—and that therefore reference to any other good consequences is simply beside the point. One cannot defeat the central retributivist claim—that justice is achieved by punishing the guilty—simply by assuming that it is false.

The question-begging character of this response can be seen by imagining a like response in areas of tort, property, or contract law. Forcing another to pay tort or contract damages, or to forgo use and possession of some thing, is a clear harm that corrective justice theories of tort, promissory theories of contract, or natural right theories of property are willing to impose on defendants. Suppose no one gains anything of economic significance by certain classes of such impositions—as, for example, in cases where the plaintiff has died without heirs after his cause of action accrued. "It does no good to force the defendant to pay," interposed as an objection to corrective justice theories of tort, promissory theories of contract, or natural right theories of property simply denies what these theories assert: that something good *is* achieved by imposing liability in such cases—namely, that justice is done.

This "harm requires justification" objection thus leaves untouched the question of whether the rendering of justice cannot in all such cases be the good that justifies the harm all such theories impose on defendants. I accordingly put aside this initial objection to retributivism, relying as it does either on an unjustifiable discrimination between retributivism and other deontological theories, or upon a blunderbuss assault on deontological theories as such.

2. A second and very popular suspicion about retributive judgments is that they presuppose an indefensible objectivism about morals. Sometimes this objection is put metaphysically: There is no such thing as desert or culpability (J. Mackie, 1982). More often the point is put as a more cautious epistemological modesty: "Even if there is such a thing as desert, we can never know who is deserving." For religious people, this last variation usually contrasts us to God, who alone can know what people truly deserve. As Beccaria (1964, pp. 17–18) put it centuries ago:

[W]hat insect will dare take the place of divine justice . . . ? The gravity of sin depends upon the inscrutable wickedness of the heart. No finite being can know it without revelation. How then can it furnish a standard for the punishment of crimes?

We might call this the "don't play God" objection.

One way to deal with this objection is to show that moral judgments generally (and judgments about culpability particularly) are both objectively true and knowable by persons. Showing both is a complicated business, and since I have attempted such a showing elsewhere (Moore, 1982a), let me try a different tack. A striking feature of the "don't play God" objection is how inconsistently it is applied. Let us revert to our use of desert as a limiting condition on punishment: We certainly seem confident both that it is true and that we can know that it is true, that we should not punish the morally innocent because they do not deserve it. Neither metaphysical skepticism nor epistemological modesty gets in our way when we use lack of moral desert as a reason not to punish. Why should it be different when we use presence of desert as a reason to punish? If we can know when someone does *not* deserve pun-

ishment, mustn't we know when someone *does* deserve punishment? Consider the illogic in the following passages from Karl Menninger (1968):

The very word *justice* irritates scientists. No surgeon expects to be asked if an operation for cancer is just or not. No doctor will be reproached on the grounds that the dose of penicillin he has prescribed is less or more than *justice* would stipulate. (p. 17)

It does not advance a solution to use the word *justice*. It is a subjective emotional word. . . . The concept is so vague, so distorted in its applications, so hypocritical, and usually so irrelevant that it offers no help in the solution of the crime problem which it exists to combat but results in its exact opposite—injustice, injustice to everybody. (pp. 10–11)

Apparently Dr. Karl knows injustice when he sees it, even if justice is a useless concept.

Analogously, consider our reliance on moral desert when we allocate initial property entitlements. We think that the person who works hard to produce a novel deserves the right to determine when and under what conditions the novel will be copied for others to read. The novelist's labor gives him or her the moral right. How can we know this—how can it be true—if desert can be judged only by those with Godlike omniscience, or worse, does not even exist? Such skepticism about just deserts would throw out a great deal that we will not throw out. To me, this shows that no one really believes that moral desert does not exist or that we could not know it if it did. Something else makes us suspect our retributive judgments than supposed moral skepticism or epistemological modesty.

3. One particular form of moral skepticism merits separate attention in this context: This is the skepticism that asserts that no one is really responsible for anything because everything we do is caused by factors over which we have no control, and therefore none of us is really guilty or deserving of punishment. "Tout comprendre c'est tout pardonner," as the folk wisdom has it.

The main problem with this bit of folk wisdom is that it is false. To understand all (the causes of behavior) is not to forgive all. To match proverb for proverb: "Everybody has a story," as many convicts well know, realizing that such stories hardly excuse (Morse, 1984, p. 1499).

To do more than match proverbs against this objection to retributivism requires an extended excursion into compatibilist moral psychology. Having done that recently (Moore, 1985a), I will not recapitulate the argument defending the view that most people are responsible for what they do irrespective of the truth of determinism. In any case, if retributivism is to be rejected on hard determinist grounds, all justice theories in property, contract, and torts would have to be rejected as well, since no one could act in a way (viz., freely) so as to deserve anything.

4. A fourth popular suspicion about using moral desert as a justification to punish takes the opposite tack from the last objection. Here the thought is not that *none* of us are guilty, but rather that *all* of us are guilty—so that if we each got what we truly deserved, we would all be punished. How, then, can such a ubiquitous human condition be used to single out some but not all for punishment? Christ, of course, is the most famous purveyor of this argument when he dissuades the Pharisees from stoning an adulteress with an explicit appeal to their own guilt: "He that is without sin among you, let him first cast a stone at her" (John 8:3–11).

If we take this literally (I will give it a more charitable interpretation later), this is pretty clumsy moral philosophy. It is true that all of us are guilty of some immoralities, probably on a daily basis. Yet for most people reading this essay, the immoralities in question are things like manipulating others unfairly; not caring deeply enough about another's suffering; not being charitable for the limitations of others; convenient lies; and so forth (Shklar, 1984). Few of us have raped and murdered a woman, drowned her three small children, and felt no remorse about it afterward, to revert to one of Royko's examples. It is simply false—and obviously so—to equate guilt at the subtle immoralities of personal relationships with the gross violations of persons that violent crime represents. We do not all deserve the punishment of a murderer for the simple and sufficient reason that we are not all murderers, or anything like murderers in culpability.

One can of course quote more scripture here—"He that lusts after a woman has already committed adultery with her"—but that also is to miss some obvious and basic moral distinctions. Freud is surely to be preferred to scripture here, when he urged that we must give credit where credit is due: If our conscience is such that we do not allow ourselves to act on our admittedly wicked fantasies, that makes us a better person than one who not only dreams of such atrocities, but brings them about (see Moore, 1980, p. 1629, n. 198; compare Fingarette, 1955; Morris, 1976, p. 124).

The short of it is that desert is not such an ubiquitous feature of human personality that it cannot be a marker of punishment. To think otherwise is to gloss over obvious moral distinctions, a glossing that to me is so obviously wrong that it can only be a cover for a judgment made on other grounds.

5. It is often said that retributive judgments are "irrational." They are irrational, it is said, because they are based on "emotion rather than reason." Such irrational emotion cannot be the basis for justifying a legal institution such as punishment. Legal institutions can be justified only by reason, not by yielding to irrational emotions, whether ours or others'. Henry Weihofen (1956, pp. 130–1) once stated this objection forthrightly:

> It is not only criminals who are motivated by irrational and emotional impulses. The same is true also of lawyers and judges, butchers and bakers. And it is especially true on such a subject as punishment of criminals. This is a matter on which we are all inclined to have deep feelings. When a reprehensible crime is committed, strong emotional reactions take place in all of us. Some people will be impelled to go out at once and work off their tensions in a lynching orgy. Even the calmest, most law-abiding of us is likely to be deeply stirred. . . . It is one of the marks of a civilized culture that it has devised legal procedures that minimize the impact of emotional reactions and strive for calm and rational disposition. But lawyers, judges and jurors are still human, and objective, rational inquiry is made difficult by the very irrationality of the human mind itself. . . . Consciously we want to be rational. We prefer to think of ourselves as governed by reason rather than as creatures swept by irrational emotions. . . .

[Excerpt from *The Urge to Punish* by Henry Weihofen. Copyright © 1956 by Henry Weihofen. Reprinted by permission of Farrar, Straus and Giroux, Inc.]

This objection, as stated, proves far too much for its own good. Think for a moment about the intimate connection between our emotions and morality, a matter we explore later in this chapter. Although Kantian beings who could know morality without relying upon their emotions are perhaps conceivable—just barely—that surely is not us. We need our emotions to know about the injustice of racial discrimination, the unfairness of depriving another of a favorite possession, the immorality of punishing the innocent. Our emotions are our main heuristic guide to finding out what is morally right.

We do both of them and morality a strong disservice when we accept the old shibboleth that emotions are opposed to rationality. There is, as I have argued elsewhere (Moore, 1982a, 1984; see also de Sousa, 1980; Scruton, 1980), a rationality of emotions that can make them trustworthy guides to moral insight. Emotions are rational when they are intelligibly proportionate in their intensity to their objects, when they are not inherently conflicted, when they are coherently orderable, and instantiate over time an intelligible character. We also judge when emotions are appropriate to their objects; that is, when they are *correct*.

The upshot is that unless one severs any connection of our legal institutions to morals, one cannot condemn an institution because it is based on "emotion." Some emotions generate moral insights our legal system could hardly do without, such as the insight that it is outrageously unfair to punish an innocent person. Imagine condemning the legal ban on punishing the innocent because it is based on emotion and not on reason.

To be sure, there is also a sense of rationality opposed to emotionality (Moore, 1984, pp. 107–8). This is the sense in which we view rationality as reason and will and see these faculties as "unhinged" by powerful emotional storms. It is this sense of emotionality we use when we partially excuse a killer because the act was the product of extreme passion, not cool rationality. It is also this sense of rationality versus emotionality that is sometimes played upon by those making this objection to retributivism. The picture is one in which the retributivist emotions unhinge our reason by their power.

Karen Horney's assumption that vindictiveness is always neurotic (and thus always undesirable) is based upon this kind of characterization:

Often there is no more holding back a person driven toward revenge than an alcoholic determined to go on a binge. Any reasoning meets with cold disdain. Logic no longer prevails. Whether or not the situation is appropriate does not matter. It overrides prudence. Consequences for himself and others are brushed aside. He is as inaccessible as anybody who is in the grip of a blind passion. (Horney, 1948, p. 5)

There is more than a little truth to this conception of the emotional base of retributivism. Literature is rich in faithful depictions of otherwise rational and moral people being unhinged by an urge to punish another for a wrong. Susan Jacoby (1984) recounts the tale of Michael Kohlhaas, written into a novel in 1806 by Heinrich von Kleist. Kohlhaas is depicted as a benevolent man, a horse dealer, friendly, kind, loyal to those around him, but one whose life is altered by the dominating passion of revenge. Kohlhaas's animals are maltreated by his neighbor—a man of higher social position— and Kohlhaas, in his unbending quest to make the offending squire pay, "eventually destroys his business and his marriage (his wife is killed by the enemies he has made); burns down the squire's house; murders innocent inhabitants of the castle; and incites a revolt that lays waste to much of the surrounding countryside" (pp. 51–2).

This is pathological and is fairly described as reason being overcome by a domineering, obsessive emotion. Yet it is surely not the case that the retributive urge always operates like this. Pathological cases can be found for any emotions, including benevolent ones. We should not judge the moral worth of an emotion by cases where it dominates reason, unless we are willing to say that such an emotion typically leads to such pathology; and the retributive intuition described here does not. One can have the intuition that the guilty deserve punishment, and one can have emotional outrage when they do not get it, without having one's reason dominated by an emotional storm. We may feel morally outraged at some guilty criminal going unpunished, but that need be no more unhinging of our reason than our outrage at the innocent being punished. In both cases, intense emotions may generate firm moral convictions; in each case, the emotions can get out of hand and dominate reason—but that is not reason to discount the moral judgments such emotions support when they do *not* get out of hand.

Despite the foregoing, I think that the most serious objection to retributivism as a theory of punishment lies in the emotional base of retributive judgments. As thus far construed, the objection is, as we have seen, ill-fated. If stated as an objection to there being an emotional base at all to judgments about deserved punishment, the objection is far too broad to be acceptable. All moral judgments would lose to such a charge if it were well founded. If stated as an objection to the unhinging quality of retributive emotions, the objection is psychologically implausible. Any emotion in pathological cases can unhinge reason, and there is nothing about retributive emotions that make it at all plausible that they always unhinge our reason when we experience them. The objection thus needs a third construction, which is this: The emotions that give rise to retributive judgments are always pathological—not in their intensity or their ability to unhinge our reason, but in their very nature. Some emotions, such as racial prejudice, have no moral worth even if typically experienced in a not very intense way. The true objection here is that the retributive urge is one such emotion.

In discussing this version of the objection to the emotional base of retributivism, I shall by and large rely on Nietzsche, who to my mind remains one of the most penetrating psychologists of the unsavory side of our emotional life. He is also one of the few thinkers to have delved deeply into the psychology of revenge. There is surprisingly little written on revenge in modern psychiatry, in large part because psychiatrists regard revenge "like sex before Freud . . . ,condemned as immature and undesirable and thus unworthy of serious scientific investigation" (Harvey Lomas, quoted in Jacoby, 1984, p. 169).

"Mistrust," Nietzsche's Zarathustra advises us, "all in whom the impulse to punish is powerful" (*Zarathustra,* p. 212). Nietzsche clearly believes that the retributive emotions can get in the way of that celebration of life that makes us better—I would say virtuous—human beings. As he said in *The Gay Science*: "I do not want to wage war against what is ugly. I do not want to accuse; I do not even want to accuse those who accuse. *Looking away* shall be my only negation" (p. 223). And as he repeated later: "Let us not become darker ourselves on their [criminals'] account, like all those who punish others and feel dissatisfied. Let us sooner step aside. Let us look away" (p. 254).

What is the awful vision from which we should avert our gaze? If Nietzsche is right, truly a witch's brew: resentment, fear, anger, cowardice, hostility, aggression, cruelty, sadism, envy, jealousy, guilt, self-loathing, hypocrisy and self-deception—those "reactive affects" that Nietzsche sometimes lumped under the French term *ressentiment* (*Genealogy,* p. 74). All this, Nietzsche believed, lies behind our judgments of retributive justice.

Consider first resentment. One of Nietzsche's deepest insights into moral genealogy (Danto, 1965) is how much the retributive urge is based on resentment. As Max Scheler (1961, p. 46), once explained Nietzsche's insight here: "Revenge . . . , based as it is upon an experience of impotence, is always primarily a matter of those who are 'weak' in some respect." If we feel physically, psychologically, or politically weak, we will feel threatened by those we perceive to be stronger, such as those willing and able to use physical violence. Moreover, if we are actually or vicariously injured by such stronger persons, our weakness may prevent us from venting in the most direct way the anger such violation generates. Rather than either venting such anger directly through our own action (of retaliation), or at least feeling able to do so but choosing to refrain, our real or perceived helplessness transforms the anger into the brooding resentment of those who lack power. Such resentment, Nietzsche rightly thinks, can poison the soul, with its unstable equilibrium of repressed anger and repressing fear. A resentful person is burdened with an emotional conflict that is both ugly and harmful. It is better for us, because of this, to "look away" rather than to brood about revenge.

Our weakness and its accompanying emotions of fear and resentment can also make our retributive inclination seem cowardly, herdlike, and weak. As Nietzsche observed at one point: "'Punishment' . . . is simply a copy . . . of the normal attitude toward a hated, disarmed, prostrated enemy, who has lost not only every right and protection, but all hope of quarter as well . . ." (*Genealogy,* pp. 72–3). Yet unlike the victor in a fight who has won and who can afford to be merciful to a vanquished foe, those who wish to punish may feel that this is their first opportunity to get back, an opportunity they cannot afford to pass up. When Christ talks about throwing stones, it is not because we are all equally guilty that we should not throw the stones; rather, there is something cowardly in a group of persons throwing stones at one who is now helpless. Such cowardice can be exhibited by the need of such persons for group reinforcement (which is why avengers may refuse to throw the *first* stone—it would set one apart from the group). It is no accident that the retributive urge calls up images of mobs, groups who together finally find the strength to strike back at an only now helpless foe. Our fear and our resentment of criminals can make us look small and cowardly in our retaliation in a way that immediate retaliation by one without fear or resentment does not.

Our fear of criminals need not always be due to our sense of their power to hurt; sometimes we may feel such fears just because they are different. For some people, there is a link between fear of strangers and fear of criminals, a link partly reflected by the extraordinary group reinforcement they receive when their retributive urges are shared. Such a link is also reflected in the we–they attitude many adopt about criminals, an attitude suggesting that criminals are fundamentally different and outside the group about whom we need be concerned. This is the criminal as outlaw, an attitude that, although neither causing nor caused by prejudice and bigotries of various kinds, nonetheless invites such other fears of differences to get expressed in retributive judgments.

Even when we do not feel weak and threatened by criminals, we may find other emotions underlying our retributive judgments that are not very pretty. Surely one of the uglier spectacles of our times are the parties by fraternity boys outside the gates of prisons when an execution is taking place. What makes such spectacles so ugly is the cruelty and sadistic pleasure at the suffering of others that they express. Such people feel entitled to let go of the normal constraints on expressing such unsavory emotions because the legitimacy of retribution licenses it. It is all right to enjoy the suffering of criminals, because it is deserved suffering. Deserved punishment, as Nietzsche perceived, can be "a warrant for and title to cruelty" (*Genealogy*, p. 65). It can give us "the pleasure of being allowed to vent [our] power freely upon one who is powerless, the voluptuous pleasure of doing evil for the pleasure of doing it, the enjoyment of violation" (p. 65). Our retributive judgments, in such a case, look like a rationalization of, and excuse for, venting emotions we would be better off without.

There are admittedly other avenues in this society for people to vent sadistic enjoyment of another's suffering. One that comes to mind are

such films as *The Texas Chainsaw Massacre*. Reported audience reaction to a scene depicting a helpless female about to be dismembered by a chainsaw included cries of "Cut the bitch." The unrestrained sadism in such reactions is a deep sickness of the soul. To the extent that our inclinations to punish are based on a like emotion, it too, as Menninger says (1968, p. 201), lines us "up with the Marquis de Sade, who believed in pleasure, especially the pleasure derived from making someone else feel displeasure."

There is also envy and jealousy sometimes to be found lying at the emotional base of our retributive inclinations (*Zarathustra*, p. 213). We seem to have some admiration for criminals, an admiration reflected in the attention we give them in the media and the arts. We may admire their strength and courage; criminals, as Herbert Morris (1976, p. 132) aptly describes it, may manifest "what we too often do not, power and daring, a willingness to risk oneself for the satisfaction of strong desires." Thackeray had the same insight, writing *Vanity Fair* in large part to show us how much more we admire strength (Becky) than we do more conventional moral virtues (Amelia). Moreover, within the breasts of most of us beat some criminal desires. Not only may we admire the strength of will criminals may exhibit, but we may also be excited by the desires they allow themselves to satisfy. We thus may suffer a double dose of envy, both of the desires acted on and the strength that is exhibited in acting on them. Such envy and jealousy fuels the retributive urge, because punishment will tear down the object of such feelings.

Guilt has an interesting relationship to envy here. If criminals sometimes do what we might like to do but restrain ourselves from doing by our guilt, crime may excite a particularly virulent kind of envy. We may be envious not only of the power and the satisfaction of desires represented by criminal behavior, but even more of the freedom from guilt we may attribute to the criminal. Our own guilt in such a case may be challenged by apparent examples of such guiltless freedom to act on forbidden desires; if so, our defense is to transform the envy into the desire to destroy that which so challenges our own precarious balance between good and evil.

Guilt can give rise to our retributive judgments about others without the "good offices" of the emotions of envy and jealousy. Such retributivist judgments may simply project our own guilt onto the criminal and by doing so, lessen our guilt feelings because we are better than he. Henry Weihofen (1956, p. 138) aptly describes this Freudian insight about retribution:

No one is more ferocious in demanding that the murderer or the rapist "pay" for his crime than the man who has felt strong impulses in the same direction. No one is more bitter in condemning the "loose" woman that the "good" women who have on occasion guiltily enjoyed some purple dreams themselves. It is never he who is without sin who casts the first stone.

Along with the stone, we cast our own sins onto the criminal. In this way we relieve our own sense of guilt without actually having to suffer the punishment—a convenient and even pleasant device for it not only relieves us of sin, but makes us feel actually virtuous.

The retributive urge often seems to be accompanied by the additional nonvirtues of self-deception and hypocrisy. Few people like to think of themselves as weak and resentful, fearful, cowardly, cruel and sadistic, envious, jealous, and guilt-ridden. Accordingly, if they possess such emotions and traits when they make retributive judgments, they have every reason to deceive themselves about it. Such self-deception Nietzsche thought to be "the masterpiece of these black magicians, who make whiteness, milk, and innocence of every blackness . . ." (*Genealogy*, p. 47; see also Horney, 1948, p. 4). "These cellar rodents full of vengefulness and hatred" have reconceived their black emotions into an abstract virtue:

"We good men—*we are the just*"—what they desire they call, not retaliation, but "the triumph of *justice*"; what they hate is not their enemy, no! They hate "injustice," they hate "godlessness"; what they believe in and hope for is not the hope of revenge . . . but the victory of God, of the *just* God, over the godless. . . . (*Genealogy*, p. 48)

Self-deception and hypocrisy themselves are vices, and to the extent that our retributive judgments encourage them—because we cannot affirm the emotional base of such judgments—we would be better without them.

To this basically Nietzschean indictment of the emotions on which retributive judgments seem to be based, we may add the insight of some feminists that the urge to retaliate is an instance of a male and macho stereotype that is itself no virtue. As Susan Jacoby (1984, chap. 6) points out, there are actually two not entirely consistent stereotypes that operate here. One is that revenge is a male prerogative because it is the manly thing to do. The other is that women are the greatest avengers because (harking back to Nietzsche) their physical and political weakness demands subtler, more repressed, and thus more intense modes of retaliation. Such views are compliments neither to men nor to women. Such stereotypes, like racial prejudice and other differences mentioned earlier, do not cause our retributive judgments so much as they find in such judgments a vehicle for their expression.

Finally, consider the kind of "scoring mentality" that accompanies retributive judgments. As Scheler (1961, p. 46) noted: "It is of the essence of revenge that it always contains the *consciousness* of 'tit for tat,' so that it is never a mere emotional reaction." Nietzsche too scorned the "shopkeeper's scales and the desire to balance guilt and punishment" (*Dawn*, p. 86) as a part of the retributive urge. Retributivism requires a kind of keeping track of another's moral ledger that seems distasteful. Retributive judgments seem legalistic, a standing on one's rights or a satisfaction with "doing one's duty" that psychologically crowds out more virtuous modes of relating to others. "Bother justice," E. M. Forster has his protagonist exclaim in *Howard's End*. Margaret later goes on to say that she will have "none of this absurd screaming about justice. . . . Nor am I concerned with duty. I'm concerned with the character of various people whom we know, and how, things being as they are, things may be made a little better" (p. 228). Aristotle (Book VII) understood the same point in his familiar thought that "between friends there is no need of justice." Relate to others in a way that does not concern itself with giving them their just deserts, positive or negative. Those who keep track of favors owed, debts due, or punishments deserved cut themselves off from modes of relating to others that can be both more virtuous (because supererogatory) and also more rewarding than demanding rights or acting on duties.

There is no question, I think, that insofar as the retributive urge is based on such emotions as these, or causes us to instantiate traits such as self-deception, the urge is bad for us. It makes us less well formed, less virtuous human beings to experience such emotions—or, more accurately, to be the sort of person who has such emotions. This insight about what are and what are not virtuous emotions to have persuades many people that they ought not to make retributive judgments. For it is natural to feel that such judgments are contaminated by their black emotional sources. Defense lawyers have long recognized our tendency to withdraw or soften our retributive demands once we see the emotional base for them. Consider Clarence Darrow's appeals to Judge Caverly's virtue in Darrow's famous closing argument in the Loeb and Leopold sentencing hearing:

I have heard in the last six weeks nothing but the cry for blood. I have heard from the office of the State's Attorney only ugly hate. I have heard precedents quoted which would be a disgrace to a savage race.

. . .

[Y]our Honor stands between the future and past. I know the future is with me. . . . I am pleading for life, understanding, charity, kindness, and the infinite mercy that considers all. I am pleading that we overcome cruelty with kindness and hatred with love. . . . I am pleading for a time when hatred and cruelty will not control the hearts of men. When we can learn by reason and judgment and understanding and faith that . . . mercy is the highest attribute of man. . . . If I can succeed . . . I have done something to help human understanding, to temper justice with mercy, to overcome hate with love. I was reading last night of the aspiration of the old Persian poet, Omar Khayyam. It appealed to me as the highest that I can vision. I wish it was in my heart, and I wish it was in the hearts of all. "So I be written in the Book of Love, I do not care that Book above, erase my name or write it as you will, so I be written in the Book of Love." (Hicks, 1925, pp. 995, 1084)

Persuasive words. For who does not want to be written in the Book of Love? Who wants to be written in the books of hate, cruelty, cowardice, envy, resentment, and the like? Judge Caverly certainly did not, and decided against a death sentence for Loeb or Leopold.

Yet the more one looks at this argument, the more questionable it becomes. What does the virtue of the holder of a judgment have to do with the truth (or lack of it) of that judgment? Why should we think that Judge Caverly's damaging his virtue by deciding against Loeb and Leopold—increasing his virtue if he decides the other way—has anything to do with the truth of the judgment "Loeb and Leopold deserve to die"? How can a judge expect to

reach sound moral conclusions about Loeb and Leopold by focusing on which decision will most enhance *his* (the judge's) virtue? This seems to be a form of ad hominem argument, and a rather selfish version to boot, given its narcissistic preoccupation with one's own virtue.

The most persuasive case against retributivism is thus in danger of complete collapse. The charge is this: Even if it makes us morally worse to make retributive judgments—because of the emotions that give rise to such judgments—that lack of virtue on our part is simply irrelevant to the assessment of whether retributive judgments are true. To assess this issue requires that we look in greater detail at the connections between our emotions and our moral judgments, which I propose to do next.

MORALITY AND THE EMOTIONS

The charge laid at the end of the last section is a form of the "genetic fallacy" objection. Such an objection urges that it is fallacious to infer the falsity of a proposition from some truths (no matter how unsavory) about the genesis of people's belief in that proposition. A common example is to infer the falsity of our moral beliefs from the fact that they are caused by an education that could easily have been otherwise (see Moore, 1982a, pp. 1097–101). The ad hominem argument presented in the last section is like this, because it infers the falsity of retributivism from the unnice emotional origins of people's belief in retributivism.

To respond adequately to this genetic fallacy objection, the antiretributivist must establish that the emotional base of a moral judgment is relevant to that judgment's truth. If we leave ethics for a moment, one can see that sometimes it is no fallacy to infer the falsity of a judgment from the truth of some explanation of why people come to such judgment. Suppose the proposition in question was: "Sticks become bent when immersed in water, straight again when removed." Suppose the common explanation for why people believe this proposition to be true is in terms of their perceptual experience with sticks partly immersed in water—namely, they look bent to them. If we have grounds to believe that these perceptual experiences as a class are unreliable—an "illusion"—then it is no fallacy to infer the falsity of the proposition from an explanation of people's beliefs showing such beliefs to be the product of an illusion. Knowing what we do about the unreliability of perceptual experience when light is refracted in mediums of different density, we are entitled to disbelieve those who rely on such experiences in coming to their beliefs about sticks in liquid.

The antiretributivist would make a similar construction of the Nietzschean case against retributivism, likening Nietzsche's explanation of people's beliefs in retributivism (as due to the emotions of *ressentiment*) to an explanation of a perceptual belief in terms of a known illusion or hallucination. Whether there can be such a thing as a moral hallucination or illusion, and if so, whether the emotions of *ressentiment* should be seen as such hallucinating experiences, depends upon an affirmative answer to two questions:

1. Are any emotions epistemically relevant to the truth of moral judgments?
2. If so, is it the virtuous nature of an emotion that tells us whether it has epistemic import?

I shall consider these questions in order.

With respect to the first question, we should distinguish four different views on how the emotions are relevant either to the discovery or to the justification of moral judgments.

1. One is suggested by Kant's famous remarks in the *Groundwork* (1964, pp. 65–7) to the effect that moral worth is found in actions motivated only by reverance for the moral law, not in actions motivated by the inclinations, no matter how benevolent or virtuous. Such a view would make the emotions that generate a moral belief irrelevant to the truth of that belief. Good emotions could as easily generate false beliefs as true ones, and bad emotions could as easily generate true beliefs as false ones. The truth of a moral proposition would be governed solely by reasoning from the categorical imperative or other supreme principle of morality itself discoverable by reason alone, not from any emotional experience.

In this view there is no analogy between the relation of the emotions and moral truth, on the one hand, and the relation of perceptual experiences and scientific truth, on the other. Accordingly, a Kantian about this should find the genetic fallacy objection conclusive when applied to Nietzsche; the lack of virtue of the emotions that generate retributivism has nothing to do with the truth of retributivism because the emotions generally have no epistemic import for the truth of moral judgments. In this view the emotions are relevant neither to justifying a moral judgment as true nor to discovering it to be true.

2. An opposite conclusion about the force of the genetic fallacy objection in this context should be drawn by those who think that the emotions have everything to do with moral truth. This second view about the connection of the emotions to moral truth is the view of the conventionalist (or relativist) about morals. Lord Devlin's writings (1971) on the morality of homosexual behavior provide a convenient example. According to Devlin, homosexual behavior is immoral (and may be legally prohibited) whenever enough people feel deeply enough that it is bad. "It is not nearly enough," Devlin reminds us, "to say that a majority dislike a practice, there must be a real feeling of reprobation. . . . No society can do without intolerance, indignation, and disgust; they are the forces behind the moral law . . ." (p. 40).

In this view, the emotions of a people constitute moral truth. If most people feel deeply enough that a practice is immoral, then it is immoral, in this conventionalist view. This means that if the emotional base for some moral belief is undermined, then necessarily the belief cannot be true. If Nietzsche, for example, can show that the emotions that generate retributivist beliefs are contaminated, then necessarily retributivism is not morally right.

How could Devlin admit the possibility of this kind of undermining of the emotional base of retributivism, given the total absence of reason checking emotion in his conventionalist view of morals? For someone like Devlin, after all, morals just *are* feelings shared by a majority. Yet such majority feelings can be changed if that majority can be emotionally repelled by a subset of its own emotions. And if enough people are repelled enough by the Nietzschean case against *ressentiment,* then the retributive urge must be excluded from those conventions of shared feelings that constitute morality.

This conventionalist view about morality results in there being no genetic fallacy objection to be interposed against Nietzsche. To attack the emotional base of retributivism would be to attack retributivism itself.

Yet such a strong epistemic connection of the emotions to moral truth cannot be sustained. That a large percentage of Americans, perhaps a majority, have feelings of disgust, fear, and hatred of gays does not end a moral inquiry into the truth or falsity of the proposition that gays may be discriminated against, in housing, employment, or elsewhere. A person seeking to arrive at the truth about just treatment for minorities cannot accept his or her own emotional reactions as settling the issue (nor, more obviously, can the person accept the emotional reactions of others). Each must judge for himself or herself whether those emotions are harbingers of moral insight or whether they are the "hallucinations" of the emotional life that must be discarded in our search for the truth. The same, of course, is true for our sense perceptions vis-à-vis scientific truths. Sticks may look bent when partly immersed in water, but that does not mean that they really are bent. Our sense perception is not veridical, and there is no reason to suppose that our emotions are any better guarantors of knowledge.

3. This analogy of the emotions to sensory perception suggests a third way of thinking of the epistemic connection of the emotions to morality, a conception that is also, unfortunately, misleading. This is the route of intuitionism. An intuitionist, as I am here using the word, believes that the emotions stand to moral judgment in a relation exactly analogous to the relation between perceptual experience and scientific judgment. For an intuitionist, the analogy is only an analogy, however, for such a person sees morals and science as distinct realms of knowledge, each with their own distinct experiential base. Such an intuitionist will usually be a metaphysical dualist, believing that such distinct modes of knowing must imply that there are distinct modes of being. (An example of this is how introspectionism goes hand in hand with dualism in the philosophy of mind.)

In any case, the intuitionist will regard emotions as crucial to morals, for they are the data from which moral theory is constructed. Without the emotions generating intuitions, there could be no moral insight, for this kind of intuitionist. An intuitionist is not committed to the emotions being veridical; indeed, to maintain the parallel to sensory perception, the intuitionist should say that the felt justice of punishing for its own sake is *good evidence* that it is just to punish for its own sake, but allow that the inference could be mistaken.

4. I must confess there is much in the intuitionist's account that I find tempting. Still, the dead ends of dualistic metaphysics and the lumpy epistemology of discrete cognitive realms is sufficient reason to avoid intuitionism and nonnaturalism in ethics, as it is to avoid introspectionism and dualism in psychology (Moore, 1985, 1987). We can avoid this metaphysical and epistemological lumpiness by thinking of the emotions as heuristic guides to moral insight, but not as the experience out of which moral theory is constructed. In this view, moral knowledge does not rest on its own unique experiential base, the emotions. Such a view could even concede the empiricist idea that all knowledge (moral knowledge included) rests on sensory experience and the inferences drawable from it.

Consider a judgment that another is morally culpable for some harm. An intuitionist would view culpability as a special kind of property not observable by the senses (a "nonnatural" property), and known only by that special faculty of intuition provided by our emotional life. I think, on the contrary, that culpability is not a property in some special realm. True, we cannot see it but must infer its existence from other properties, such as voluntariness of action, accountability, intention, causation, lack of excuse or justification. But then we cannot see those properties either. We infer the existence of an intention in another from behavioral clues; we do not see causal relations, but infer their existence as well. Culpability is no less a natural property of persons than is intentionality, voluntariness, and so on; none are visible properties, all must be inferred from other evidence. Yet these facts do not demand a special mode of existence, and a special mode of knowing, for any of such properties (see my response to Mackie's well-known "queerness" objection in Moore, 1982a).

If we think of (moral) properties such as culpability in this way, then the emotions are not strictly necessary for there to be moral knowledge. We can imagine a being who could make correct inferences about culpability, as about other things such as intentionality, even if he or she were devoid of any relevant emotional life. True, the being would not *feel* about, for example, justice as we feel about it; yet he or she could know injustice, in the sense of being able to pick it out, as well as we.

The emotions are thus heuristic guides for us, an extra source of insight into moral truths beyond the knowledge we can gain from sensory and inferential capacities alone. One might think of them as I would think of conscious experience vis-à-vis knowledge of mind:

My conscious experience of deciding to get a haircut is one way I can come to know that I intend to get a haircut; yet I or others can come to know that I intend to get a haircut in a variety of other ways, including perhaps someday by physiological measurements. My introspective, "privileged access" is only a heuristic guide to learning about my sensations, intentions, and so on that others do not possess. It is not essential to an intention that I be conscious of it, any more than it is essential to the injustice of an institution that I or others feel negatively toward it. The usual judgments I make about my intentions may be judgments reached by reflection on my conscious deliberative processes, just as my usual judgments about justice may be reached via some strong feelings; but the usual route to knowledge—of minds or morals—is not to be confused with what mental states or moral qualities *are*.

The upshot of this is that our emotions are important but not essential in our reaching moral truths. Contra Kant, there is an epistemic connection between our emotions and morality, but it is neither of the strong connections that conventionalism or intuitionism would posit. In the present context, the payoff of seeing this latter point lies in seeing when we may find some emotions wanting as epistemic indicators of moral truth. It is possible, in this last view, for there to be emotions that are "moral hallucinations," and it is therefore open to a Nietzschean to claim that our retributive inclinations are of this kind.

We come, then, to the second question—is the virtue of possessing an emotion relevant to that emotion's epistemic import? We should begin by being clear about the two different ways in which the emotions may be connected to morality before we inquire into the relation between them. We have hitherto been discussing what I would call the epistemic connection of the emotions to morality, distinguishing strong views of this connection (like Devlin's) from weaker views, such as my own or Kant's. Yet there is another possible way in which morality is related to our emotional life. This is where the emotions are themselves the objects of moral judgment. I call this the substantive connection of morality to the emotions.

The substantive connection can be grasped by reflecting on the judgments we make when we are not concerned with ascribing legal liability. The part of morality that is incorporated into our criminal law is by and large the moral-

ity of will and reason, by virtue of which we make the crudest of responsibility ascriptions. Voluntariness of action, accountability, intentionality, causation, justification, and excuse are the primary categories in terms of which we judge someone as morally culpable and thus legally punishable (Moore, 1984, chap. 2). Compare the less legalistic moral judgments we make in daily life: We often think of ourselves or others as more or less virtuous, depending on what emotions we feel on what occasions (Lyons, 1980; Dent, 1984). We make judgments, in other words, not just about the wrong actions a bad person wills, but also about the evil emotions a bad person feels. As Bernard Williams (1973, p. 207) has noted, there is a morality

. . . about what a man ought or ought not to feel in certain circumstances, or, more broadly, about the ways in which various emotions may be considered as distinctive, mean or hateful, while others appear as creative, generous, admirable, or—merely—such as one would hope for from a decent human being. Considerations like these certainly play a large part in moral thought, except perhaps in that of the most restricted and legalistic kind. . . .

Consider a person who feels little or no compassion for others less fortunate. This person's behavior need not be that of a scrooge—he may do all the morally acceptable things, such as donate to charities, help blind persons across the street, not inflict needless suffering, and so on. Yet he does such things out of a priggish concern for propriety, including the propriety he attains by having a good opinion of himself. He does not feel any compassion for the objects of his charity; indeed, he regards them as inferior beings who exist for him mainly to be the objects of his virtue. Such a person is morally inferior to—less virtuous than—another whose actions may be no better but whose emotional life includes compassion (Blum, 1980).

Contrast this collection of the emotions and morality with the epistemic connection. Staying with the example of compassion: We may take our feelings of compassion for some disadvantaged persons to be the harbingers of a moral insight about what that group deserves. Suppose you travel to India and find the poverty of many Indians to be distressing. You might take that feeling of compassion to be the originator of a moral insight about the nature of distributive justice—namely, that the geographic limits you had previously observed in applying some ideal of distributive justice seem arbitrary, a matter of political expediency at best. In such a case, the emotional experience of compassion may generate a firm moral conviction that distributive justice knows no political boundaries or geographical limits, but extends to all persons.

The epistemic connection of the emotions to morality is quite different from the substantive connection. With the latter, we judge the emotions as virtuous or not; the emotions in such a case are the object of moral evaluation. With the former, we are not seeking to judge the moral worth of an emotion as a virtue; rather, we seek to learn from such emotions the correct moral judgments to make about some other institution, practice, act, or agent.

Having distinguished the two connections of morality to the emotions, it remains to inquire whether there is not some relation between them. One wishing to use Nietzsche's kind of insights to attack retributivism, and yet escape the genetic fallacy objection, must assert that there is some such relation. The idea is that we use our own virtue in possessing an emotion as the touchstone of whether that emotion is "hallucinatory" or not: If the possession of an emotion makes us more virtuous, then that emotion is a good heuristic for coming to moral judgments that are true; if the possession of an emotion makes us less virtuous, then that emotion is a good heuristic for coming to moral judgments that are false. This possibility, of course, would complete the antiretributivist's answer to the genetic fallacy charge. For then the vice of possessing the emotions of *ressentiment* gives us good reason to suppose that the moral judgments to which those emotions give rise—namely, retributive judgments—are false.

This is possible, but what reason do we have to think that such a connection—between the judge's virtue, and the truth of the judgment he or she is making—holds? Counterexamples certainly spring to mind; consider two of them.

1. As Herbert Morris has examined . . . there is such a thing as nonmoral guilt. Think, for example, of the guilt one might feel at having made a tragic choice: There were only two options, neither happy ones, and one chose to do the lesser evil. Using Philippa Foot's much-discussed example: A railroad switchman can only turn a moving trolley car onto one line or another, but he cannot stop it; he chooses to turn the car onto the line where only one trapped workman will be killed; on the other line, five workmen were trapped and would have been killed had the trolley car gone their way. The switchman is not morally culpable in directing the trolley on the line where only one workman would be killed. The alternative being even worse, the switchman was justified in doing what he did. Still the switchman should feel regret, remorse, and even guilt at killing the one workman. The switchman who experiences such emotions is a more virtuous person than one who has a "don't cry over what can't be helped" attitude toward the whole affair.

If both moral judgments are right—the switchman is not culpable (guilty), but his feeling guilty is virtuous—then we cannot say that the emotions that make us virtuous are necessarily the emotions that are good heuristic guides to moral truth. For if the latter were true, this switchman's (virtuous) feeling guilty should mean that the associated judgment, "I am guilty," is true; but it is not.

2. Just as some emotions are virtuous even though their associated judgments are not true, so some emotions that are not virtuous to possess may nonetheless spawn judgments that are true. Think of the institution of private property and its Lockean justifications in terms of the exercised liberty of one who mixes her labor with a thing. I think that the Lockean judgment, "she deserves the property right because she created the thing in the first place," to be true when applied to a novelist seeking copyright protections for a novel. Yet I also think that the emotions that are my heuristic guide to that judgment are suspect, at the least, in their enhancement of my virtue.

For are not the emotions that call to mind Lockean intuitions about deserved property entitlements essentially selfish emotions that make us worse for possessing them? (See E. M. Forster, 1936, pp. 22–6; Becker, 1977, p. 96). We are entitled, from what we have done, to exclude others from the enjoyment of the products of our labor. My intuition is that this is true, but I am not proud of the selfish emotions that generate this intuition. They seem to consist too much of pride and self-congratulation to be virtues. To me at least, the nonvirtuous nature of the emotional base of Lockean property theories does not make me doubt their truth; it would be unfair to deprive another of the products of his or her labor, however much it would be better if we (and the other) did not beat our chests so much about our own accomplishments.

These examples are perhaps controversial, but I doubt that the point they illustrate is. The virtue (or lack of it) in the possession of our emotion is not an infallible guide to the epistemic import such as emotion may possess.

Is the first even a *fallible* guide to the second? A defender of retributivism might well think not. Such a person might compare the situation in science: What is the relevance, he or she might ask, of the virtue of a perceptual experience (say one induced by drugs) to the epistemic import of such an experience? What possible reason is there to think that the moral worth of a visual experience will correlate with its epistemic import? Tripping on LSD and looking at pornography may be equally lacking in virtue, but only one of them is likely to produce untrue beliefs about, for example, anatomical features of human beings.

Yet what if we substituted an example where the virtue in question is not so obviously removed from the truth of any scientific judgments? Suppose we focused on what might be called the "virtues of a scientist," traits such as analytical capacity, creativity, curiosity, being careful, and ambition. It is not nearly so implausible to think that beliefs produced through the exercise of these traits are more likely true, and that those produced by the analytically dull, the plodding, the mechanical, the careless or the lazy are more likely false.

Similarly, in ethics we should recognize that the virtue of (or vice) of an emotion may often, but not always, be taken as an indication of the truth (or falsity) of the judgment to which it leads. Indeed, would it not be remarkable to think that one could arrive at the judgments about science or morals only through emotions or traits that made one morally odious? Although not contradictory, it would surely be an oddly cohering morality that valued, say, equal treatment and also extolled the virtue of those prejudiced attitudes that typically produce discriminating judgments. We value moral and scientific truth too highly to think that there could be any virtues so counterproductive to the attainment of truth.

In any case, what other criterion could there be for the epistemic reliability of the emotions? If such reliability had nothing to do with the virtue of such emotions, what would be our test? Rawls (1971, p. 48) suggests that we look to those "conditions favorable for deliberation and judgment in general" when we seek to isolate those "considered judgments" that in reflective equilibrium justify his two principles of justice. Which conditions are these?

[We] can discard those judgments made with hesitation, or in which we have little confidence. Similarly, those given when we are upset or frightened, or when we stand to gain one way or the other can be left aside. All these judgments are likely to be erroneous or to be influenced by an excessive attention to our own interests. (p. 47; see also Copp, 1984)

Yet this test is too dispassionate, too judicial. Rawls's test for *judgments* that have epistemic import cannot be turned into a test for *emotions* because Rawls, like Kant, pretty much ignores the emotional base of moral judgment.

If we look in this way for a purely cognitive test for when emotions are epistemically reliable, my suspicion is that we will always end up slighting the role of the emotions in generating moral insight. We will do this because a purely cognitive test will inevitably seek to derive a criterion of epistemic warrant that is independent of any theory generated from the emotions themselves. It is like attempting to set up a criterion of epistemic warrant for perceptual experiences without using any theory derived from such experiences. Yet surely in science we do not expect to have to come up with some prescientific test for the epistemic import of sensory experience *before* we meld those experiences into a scientific theory. Rather, we rely on the body of scientific theory itself to justify exclusions of experience from the data. It is because we know what we do about optics that leads us to discount the illusion that a stick partly immersed in water looks bent; it is because we know what we do about drugs, mental disease, sensory deprivation, and the like, that we discount hallucinatory perceptual experiences. In science we quite literally explain such experiences away by using the very theories of which such experiences are part of the data. We are entitled to make the parallel move in ethics, so that our substantive moral theories—not some pale, preliminary, judicial, nonmoral litmus test—give us the criteria for weeding out emotions with misleading epistemic import. Those substantive theories of what justice is, for example, make it very unlikely that prejudice could be a virtue, or that compassion could not.

The upshot of all of this is that the genetic fallacy objection with which we began this section is inconclusive when interposed by the retributivist against the Nietzschean analysis of the retributive urge. If Nietzsche is right in asserting that our retributive beliefs are always motivated by the emotions of *ressentiment,* and right that the possession of those emotions makes us less virtuous, then we have grounds to reject retributivism as a philosophy of punishment. True, such a Nietzschean argument could not be a knockdown winner—from what has been said, it is possible that the nonvirtuous emotions of *ressentiment* nonetheless generate true moral judgments about what wrongdoers deserve. Yet this would have to be established by justifying the retributive principle in some way other than by showing it to be the best expression of our more particular judgments about criminals. Without such independent justification of retributivism, Nietzsche gives us reason to believe the retributive principle to be false when he shows us how lacking in virtue are the emotions that generate retributive judgments. For without such an independent justification, here as elsewhere we are entitled to rely on the connection that generally (but not inevitably) holds between the virtue in possessing an emotion and the truth of the judgment that that emotion generates.

THE CORRECTNESS OF RETRIBUTIVE JUDGMENTS

As previewed in the first part of this chapter, there are two justificatory routes a coherentist might use in justifying retributivism. First, because of the Nietzschean attack on the retributive urge, a retributivist might abandon the justificatory route that begins with our particular judgments about punishment in individual cases, and instead focus on how retributivism is justified because of its coherence with other, more general moral beliefs we are prepared to accept. He or she might show how there is an odd lacunae in our moral judgments about desert if the retributive principle is not accepted. That is, when passing out rewards, the desert of those whose labor produced them is (for Lockeans) both a necessary and a sufficient condition for allocating a property entitlement in them. The presence of such desert justifies giving the reward to them; the absence of such desert justifies withholding it from them. Similarly, when passing out legal duties to pay for harms caused, the culpability of he or she who caused the harm and the lack of culpability of

he or she who suffers the harm, is (in standard corrective justice theories) both necessary and sufficient to justify tort liability. It is only with punishment that we have an asymmetry; namely (as even most nonretributivists will assert), that desert is a necessary condition of punishment, but not sufficient by itself to justify punishment.

Such an asymmetry does not by itself render a deontologist's social theory incoherent if he or she rejects retributivism (although it might if one isolated a general principle of just deserts common to corrective justice, property allocations, and retributive justice). My only point here is that if there were such incoherence without retributivism, the latter would be justified even if the retributive urge is unworthy of us. Nothing in the Nietzschean case against retributivism could prevent this. Still, since my approach is to justify retributivism by using our more particular judgments about punishment, I need to take seriously the Nietzschean case against those judgments.

The problem with the Nietzschean case against retributivism does not lie, as we have seen, in its presupposition that generally there is a strong connection between virtuous emotions and true moral judgments, vices and false moral judgments. The real problem for the Nietzschean critic is to show that retributive judgments are *inevitably* motivated by the black emotions of *ressentiment.* For if the critic cannot show this, then much of the contamination of those particular judgments is lifted. It is lifted because the retributive judgment would then not arise out of the kind of moral hallucination nonvirtuous emotions typically represent; rather, the retributive judgment would be only the vehicle for the expression of the emotions of *ressentiment*—dangerous for that reason, but not lacking in epistemic import for that reason.

Consider an analogy in meta ethics. The position I have defended elsewhere (Moore, 1982a), moral realism, is an admittedly dangerous view about which to proselytize. It is dangerous because many people use moral realism as a vehicle to express intolerance and contempt for autonomy. Many people may even accept moral realism because it seems to them to have this potential for intolerant imperialism against the differing moral beliefs of others. Yet these psychological facts, to my mind, constitute no argument against the truth of moral realism. They do not because I am able to separate moral realism from intolerance: logically I see that a moral realist can defend tolerance, pluralism, and autonomy as much (more?) as anyone, and psychologically I do not see any inevitability in my moral realist views being motivated by intolerance. Making these separations, the fact that many people use moral realism to express their intolerance—or even are motivated to moral realist beliefs by their intolerance—loses any epistemic sting. It makes me cautious about holding forth about moral realism with intolerant audiences, but it does not give me reason to be cautious about the truth of moral realism.

As much seems to me to be true about retributivism. I shall make the argument in three steps: First, that the inevitability of linking *ressentiment* emotions to retributive judgments is weakened when one notes, as Nietzsche himself did, that *anti*retributive judgments are also often motivated by some of those same nonvirtuous emotions; second, that in our own individual cases we can imagine being motivated to make retributive judgments by the virtuous emotions of guilt and fellow feeling; and third, that because punishment is a social institution, unlike private vengeance, it can help us to control the emotions retributive punishment expresses by controlling the aspects of punishment that all too easily allow it to express *ressentiment*.

1. A paraphrase of Zarathustra, of which Nietzsche no doubt would have approved, would be that we should beware all those in whom the urge to punish is either actually, or claimed to be, nonexistent. As Nietzsche does tell us:

> if you are cursed, I do not like it that you want to bless. Rather, join a little in the cursing. And if you have been done a great wrong, then quickly add five little ones: a gruesome sight is a person single-mindedly obsessed by a wrong. . . . A wrong shared is half right. . . . A little revenge is more human than no revenge. (*Zarathustra*, p. 180)

Everyone gets angry when their bodily integrity or other important interests are violated by another. If they care about other human beings, they are vicariously injured when someone close to them—or distant, depending on the reach of their empathy—is wronged. It is human to feel such anger at wrongful violation, and Nietzsche's thought is that not to express the anger in some retaliation is a recipe for *ressentiment* itself.

One might of course think that retaliation is a second best solution; better not to feel the anger at all so that the choice of expressing it in action, or of repressing it into the subtle revenge of pity, is not necessary (see Horney, 1948, p. 3). Leaving aside whether such willing away of anger is possible, is it desirable? While it has a saintly ring to it to turn the other cheek so long as it is one's own cheek that has just been slapped, is it virtuous to feel nothing stronger than sympathy for the suffering of others at the hands of wrongdoers? Where is that compassionate concern for others that is outraged because another person could have so unnecessarily caused such suffering?

Karen Horney concluded that "[t]he vindictive person thus is egocentric . . . because he has more or less severed his emotional relations to other human beings" (1948, p. 12). Yet isn't this even more often true of one who feels anger only when he himself suffers at the hands of a wrongdoer, not when others suffer? An egocentric lack of compassion for others may explain the antiretributivist, forgiving attitude as easily as it may explain the desire for vengeance.

Sometimes the compassion for victims is not absent, but gets transferred to the person who is now about to suffer; namely, the wrongdoer. Such a transfer of compassion is not justified by the relative merits of the two classes of persons, unless we are to think that there is some reason to prefer wrongdoers to victims as the appropriate objects of compassion. "Out of sight, out of mind" is the reason that suggests itself, but this psychological tendency can hardly justify forgetting those who have suffered at the hands of others. My own view is that such a transfer of concern from victim to criminal occurs in large part because of our unwillingness to face our own revulsion at what was done (Gaylin, 1983, p. 123). It allows us to look away from the horror that another person was willing to cause.

We almost cannot bear the sight. We invent for the wrongdoers a set of excusing conditions that we would not tolerate for a moment in ourselves. When they transgress, virtuous people know how ill it lies to "excuse" themselves by pointing to their own childhood or past, their lack of parental love, their need for esteem, and other causes (Moore, 1985a). Virtuous people do not use the childish "something made me do it" because they know that that denies their essential freedom in bringing about some harm. They know that they did it, chose to do it, caused though that choice surely was by factors themselves unchosen. Yet we cannot stand to apply to criminals the same standard of responsibility that we apply to ourselves because we cannot stand to acknowledge that there is such a thing as evil in the world—and, worst of all, that it is not "inhuman" but a part of creatures not so different from ourselves. Lack of anger at criminals, if it does not represent simple indifference to the sufferings of others, may represent our self-deception about the potential for evil in humanity.

Such lack of anger may also represent the same fear of criminals that can motivate retributive judgments. Nietzsche:

There is a point in the history of society when it becomes so pathologically soft and tender that among other things it sides even with those who harm it, criminals, and does this quite seriously and honestly. Punishing somehow seems unfair to it, and it is certain that imagining "punishment" and "being supposed to punish" hurts it, arouses fear in it. "It is not enough to render him *undangerous?* Why still punish? Punishing itself is terrible." With this question, herd morality, the morality of timidity, draws its ultimate consequence. . . . The imperative of herd timidity: "We want that some day there should be *nothing anymore to be afraid of!*" (*Beyond Good and Evil,* p. 114)

By repressing anger at wrongful violation, we may be attempting to deny that we live in a society in which there really are fearful and awful people.

Yet again, our transfer of fellow-feeling from victim to criminal, and its accompanying elimination of anger, may represent something other than indifference or inability to face evil or our own fears. It may represent a narcissism that is itself no virtue. A criminal, after all, represents an opportunity to exercise (and display, a separate point) one's virtue. The virtue in question is compassion for someone now threatened with harm. Yet such egoistic compassion becomes something other than compassion. It becomes just what Nietzsche said it becomes, the elevation of self by pity. Remarkably, one can lose compassionate concern for another by the self-conscious egoistic caricature of compassion we distinguish as pity. In pity we do not care about the other any more for his own sake, but only insofar as he allows *us* to become, in our own and others' eyes, better. We should beware, to adopt yet another paraphrase of Nietzsche, this one by Philippa

Foot (1973, p. 168), all those who find others best when they find them most in need. We should beware of them because such people lack precisely the ability to feel that compassion whose outward form they ape.

2. Resentment, indifference to others, self-deception, fear, cowardice, and pity are not virtues. They do not perhaps add up to the witches' brew of a full batch of the *ressentiment* emotions, but to the extent they motivate antiretributive judgments, they make such judgments suspect. If one accepts, as Nietzsche did, that both retributive and antiretributive judgments are often motivated by, or at least expressions of, nonvirtuous emotions, where does that leave us? It should leave us asking whether we cannot make our judgments about punishment in such a way that they are not motivated by either set of unworthy emotions.

When we make a retributive judgment—such as that Stephen Judy deserved the death penalty for his rape-murder of a young mother and his murder of her three children—we need not be motivated by the *ressentiment* emotions. Nor is the alternative some abstract, Kantian concern for justice, derived by reason alone and unsullied by any strong emotional origin. Our concern for retributive justice might be motivated by very deep emotions that are nonetheless of a wholly virtuous nature. These are the feelings of guilt we would have if we did the kinds of acts that fill the criminal appellate reports of any state.

The psychiatrist Willard Gaylin interviewed a number of people closely connected to the brutal hammering death of Bonnie Garland by her jilted boyfriend, Richard Herrin. He asked a number of those in a Christian order that had been particularly forgiving of Richard whether they could imagine themselves performing such an act under any set of circumstances. Their answer was uniformly "Yes." All of us can at least find it conceivable that there might be circumstances under which we could perform an act like Herrin's—not exactly the same, perhaps, but something pretty horrible. All of us do share this much of our common nature with the worst of criminals. (For those with a greater we–they attitude toward criminals, the thought experiment that follows must be run with a somewhat less horrible act than Richard's.)

Then ask yourself: What would you feel like if it was you who had intentionally smashed open the skull of a 23-year-old woman with a claw hammer while she was asleep, a woman whose fatal defect was a desire to free herself from your too clinging embrace? My own response, I hope, would be that I would feel guilty unto death. I couldn't imagine any suffering that could be imposed upon me that would be unfair because it exceeded what I deserved.

Is that virtuous? Such deep feelings of guilt seem to me to be the only tolerable response of a moral being. "Virtue" is perhaps an odd word in the context of extreme culpability, but such guilt seems, at the least, very appropriate. One ought to feel so guilty one wants to die. Such sickness unto death is to my mind more virtuous than the nonguilty state to which Richard Herrin brought himself, with some help from Christian counseling about the need for self-forgiveness. After three years of prison on an eight- to twenty-five-year sentence for "heat of passion" manslaughter, Richard thought he had suffered quite enough for the killing of Bonnie:

HERRIN: I feel the sentence was excessive.

GAYLIN: Let's talk about that a little.

HERRIN: Well, I feel that way now and after the first years. The judge had gone overboard. . . .

Considering all the factors that I feel the judge should have considered: prior history of arrest, my personality background, my capacity for a productive life in society—you know, those kinds of things—I don't think he took those into consideration. He looked at the crime itself and responded to a lot of public pressure or maybe his own personal feelings, I don't know. I'm not going to accuse him of anything, but I was given the maximum sentence. This being my first arrest and considering the circumstances, I don't think I should have been given eight to twenty-five years.

GAYLIN: What do you think would have been a fair sentence?

HERRIN: Well, after a year or two in prison, I felt that was enough. . . .

GAYLIN: How would you answer the kind of person who says, for Bonnie, it's her whole life; for you it's eight years. What's eight years compared to the more years she might have had?

HERRIN: I can't deny that it's grossly unfair to Bonnie but there's nothing I can do about it. . . . She's gone—I can't bring her back. I would rather that she had survived as a complete person, but she didn't. I'm not, again . . . I'm not saying that I

shouldn't have been punished, but the punishment I feel is excessive. I feel I have five more years to go, and I feel that's just too much. There's no . . . I don't see any purpose in it. It's sad what happened, but it's even sadder to waste another life. I feel I'm being wasted in here.

GAYLIN: But what about the people who say, Look, if you got two years, then someone who robs should get only two days. You know, the idea of commensurate punishment. If it is a very serious crime it has to be a very serious punishment. Are you saying two years of prison is a very serious punishment considering what you did?

HERRIN: For me, yes.

[From W. Gaylin, *The Killing of Bonnie Garland*, pp. 325–7. Copyright © 1982 by Pip Enterprises, Inc. Reprinted by permission of Simon & Schuster, Inc.]

Compared to such shallow, easily obtained self-absolution for a horrible violation of another, a deep sense of guilt looks very virtuous indeed.

To be sure, there is an entire tradition that regards guilt as a useless passion (see Kaufmann, 1973). For one thing, it is always backward-looking rather than allowing one to get on with life. For another, it betrays an indecision that Nietzsche among others found unattractive: "The bite of conscience is indecent," Nietzsche thought (*Twilight*, p. 467), because it betrays the earlier decision about which one feels guilty. Yet Nietzsche and his followers are simply wrong here. Guilt feelings are often a virtue precisely because they do look to the past. As Herbert Morris (1976, p. 108) has argued, morality itself—including the morality of good character—has to take the past seriously. The alternative, of not crying over spilt milk (or blood), is truly indecent. A moral being *feels* guilty when he or she *is* guilty of past wrongs.

The virtue of feeling guilty is not raised so that punishment can be justified by its capacity to induce guilt. That is a possible retributive theory of punishment—a kind of moral rehabilitative theory—but it is not mine (see Morris, 1981). Rather, the virtue of our own imagined guilt is relevant because of the general connection between the virtue of an emotion and its epistemic import. We should trust what our imagined guilt feelings tell us; for acts like those of Richard Herrin, that if we did them we would be so guilty that some extraordinarily severe punishment would be deserved. We should trust the judgments such imagined guilt feelings spawn because nonneurotic guilt, unlike *ressentiment,* comes with good epistemic credentials.

Next, we need to be clear just what judgments it is that our guilt feelings validate in this way. First and foremost, to *feel* guilty causes the judgment that we *are* guilty, in the sense that we are morally culpable. Second, such guilt feelings typically engender the judgment that we deserve punishment. I mean this not only in the weak sense of desert—that it would not be unfair to be punished—but also and more important in the strong sense that we *ought* to be punished.

One might think that this second judgment of desert (in either its weak or its strong sense) is uncalled for by our feelings of guilt, that the judgment to which our guilt feelings lead is the judgment that we ought to repair as best we can the damage we have done. Such a view would justify corrective justice theories of punishment, but not retributive theories. Yet I think that this puts too nice a face on our guilt feelings. They do not generate only a judgment that we ought to make amends in this compensatory way. Rather—and this is what troubles many critics of guilt as an emotion—to feel guilty is to judge that we must suffer. We can see this plainly if we imagine ourselves having made provisions for Bonnie's family, comforting them in any way possible, and then feeling that our debt for killing her has been paid. It is so clear that such corrective actions do *not* satisfy guilt that to feel that they do is not to have felt guilty to begin with.

Our feelings of guilt thus generate a judgment that we deserve the suffering that is punishment. If the feelings of guilt are virtuous to possess, we have reason to believe that this last judgment is correct, generated as it is by emotions whose epistemic import is not in question.

Last, we should ask whether there is any reason not to make the same judgment about Richard Herrin's actual deserts as we are willing to make about our own hypothetical deserts. If we experience any reluctance to transfer the guilt and desert *we* would possess, had we done what Richard Herrin did, to Herrin himself, we should examine that reluctance carefully. Doesn't it come from feeling more of a person than Richard? We are probably not persons who grew up in the barrio of East Los Angeles, or who found Yale an alien and dis-

orienting culture. In any case, we certainly have never been subject to the exact same stresses and motivations as Richard Herrin. Therefore, it may be tempting to withhold from Richard the benefit each of us gives himself or herself: the benefit of being the subjective seat of a will that, although caused, is nonetheless capable of both choice and responsibility (Moore, 1985a).

Such discrimination is a temptation to be resisted, because it is no virtue. It is elitist and condescending toward others not to grant them the same responsibility and desert you grant to yourself. Admittedly, there are excuses the benefit of which others as well as yourself may avail themselves. Yet that is not the distinction invoked here. Herrin had no excuse the rest of us could not come up with in terms of various causes for our choices. To refuse to grant him the same responsibility and desert as you would grant yourself is thus an instance of what Sartre called bad faith, the treating of a free, subjective will as an object (see also Strawson, 1968). It is a refusal to admit that the rest of humanity shares with us that which makes us most distinctively human, our capacity to will and reason—and thus to be and do evil. Far from evincing fellow feeling and the allowing of others to participate in our moral life, it excludes them as less than persons.

Rather than succumbing to this elitism masquerading as egalitarianism, we should ask ourselves what Herrin deserves by asking what *we* would deserve had we done such an act. In answering this question we should listen to our guilt feelings, feelings whose epistemic import is not in question in the same way as are those of *ressentiment.* Such guilt feelings should tell us that to do an act like Herrin's is to forfeit forever any lighthearted idea of going on as before. One should feel so awful that the idea of again leading a life unchanged from before, with the same goals and hopes and happiness, should appear revoltingly incomprehensible.[2]

3. It is admittedly not an easy task to separate the emotions one feels, and then in addition, discriminate which of them is the cause of one's retributive judgments. We can no more choose which emotion it will be that causes our judgments or actions than we can choose the reason for which we act. We can choose whether to act or not and whether to judge one way or another, but we cannot make it be true that some particular reason or emotion caused our action or our judgment. We must look in-

ward as best we can to detect, but not to will, which emotions bring about our judgments; and here there is plenty of room for error and self-deception.

When we move from our judgments about the justice of retribution in the abstract, however, to the justice of a social institution that exists to exact retribution, perhaps we can gain some greater clarity. For if we recognize the dangers retributive punishment presents for the expression of resentment, sadism, and so on, we have every reason to design our punishment institutions to minimize the opportunity for such feelings to be expressed. There is no contradiction in attempting to make a retributive punishment system humane; doing so allows penitentiaries to be faithful to their names—places for penance, not excuses for sadism, prejudice, hatred, and the like.

Even the old biblical injunction—"Vengeance is mine, saith the Lord"—has something of this insight behind it. Retributive punishment is dangerous for individual persons to carry out, dangerous to their virtue and, because of that, unclear in its justification. But implicit in the biblical injunction is a promise that retribution will be exacted. For those like myself who are not theists, that cleansing function must be performed by the state, not God. If the state can perform such a function, it removes from retributive punishment, not the guilt, as Nietzsche (*Genealogy,* p. 95) and Sartre (1955) have it, but the ressentiment.

NOTES

1. "Moral culpability" as I am here using the phrase does not presuppose that the act done is morally bad, only that it is legally prohibited. An actor is culpable in this conception when, in doing an action violating some criminal prohibition, he or she satisfies those conditions of fair fault ascription. On this, see Moore (1985b), pp. 14–15. Usually, of course, most serious crimes are also serious moral breaches.

2. One may have noticed that the thought experiment just concluded has six steps to it. It is perhaps helpful to separate them explicitly: (1) The psychological presupposition that it is possible to engage in the thought experiment at all—that we can imagine we could do an act like Richard Herrin's. (2) The psychological question of what we would feel if we did such an action—guilty and deserving of punishment. (3) The moral question of the virtue of that feeling—that guilt is a virtuous emotion to feel when we have done such a wrongful act. (4) The psychological question of what judgments are typically caused by the emotions of guilt—the judgments that we are guilty (culpable) and that we deserve to be punished. (5) The moral question of the correctness of the first person judgment that we deserve to be punished—as an inference drawn from the virtue of the emotion of guilt that spawns such a judgment. (6)

The moral question of the correctness of the third person judgment that Richard Herrin deserves to be punished—as an inference drawn from the fact that we would deserve to be punished if we had done the act that Herrin did. One might believe that the thought experiment requires a seventh step—namely, that the state ought to punish those who deserve it. And in terms of a complete justification of a retributive theory of punishment, this last step is a necessary one. My aim throughout this paper has been more limited: to validate particular judgments, such as that Stephen Judy deserved the death penalty. The thought experiment is designed to get us only this far, leaving for further argument (hinted at in the text that closes this section) that the state has the right and the duty to set up institutions which give persons their just deserts.

REFERENCES

Beccaria, *On Crimes and Punishments* (J. Grigson, trans.), in A. Manzoni (ed.), *The Column of Infamy* (Oxford: Oxford University Press, 1964).

L. Becker, *Property Rights* (London: Routledge and Kegan Paul, 1977).

H. Bedau, "Retribution and the Theory of Punishment," *Journal of Philosophy,* Vol. 75 (1978): 601–20.

S. I. Benn and R. S. Peters, *Social Principles and the Democratic State* (London: Allen and Unwin, 1959).

L. Blum, "Compassion," in A. Rorty (ed.), *Explaining Emotions* (Berkeley and Los Angeles: University of California Press, 1980).

C. Calhoun, "Cognitive Emotions?" in C. Calhoun and R. Soloman (eds.), *What Is an Emotion?* (Oxford: Oxford University Press, 1984).

D. Copp, "Considered Judgments and Moral Justification: Conservatism in Moral Theory," in D. Copp and D. Zimmerman (eds.), *Morality, Reason and Truth* (Totowa, NJ: Rowman and Allenheld, 1984).

A. Danto, *Nietzsche as Philosopher* (New York: Macmillan, 1965).

M. Dent, *The Moral Psychology of the Virtues* (Cambridge: Cambridge University Press, 1984).

P. Devlin, "Morals and the Criminal Law," in R. Wasserstrom (ed.), *Morality and the Law* (Belmont, CA: Wadsworth, 1971).

J. Feinberg, "The Expressive Function of Punishment," in his *Doing and Deserving* (Princeton, NJ: Princeton University Press, 1971).

H. Fingarette, "Punishment and Suffering," *Proc. Amer. Phil. Assoc.,* Vol. 50 (1977): 499–525.

"Psychoanalytic Perspectives on Moral Guilt and Responsibility: A Re-evaluation," *Philos. and Phenomenological Research,* Vol. 16 (1955): 18–36.

P. Foot, "Nietzsche: The Revaluation of Values," in R. Solomon (ed.), *Nietzsche: A Collection of Critical Essays* (Garden City, NY: Doubleday Anchor Books, 1973).

E. M. Forster, *Howard's End* (New York: Knopf, 1921).

"My Woods," in his *Abinger Harvest* (New York: Harcourt, Brace and World, 1936).

W. Gaylin, *The Killing of Bonnie Garland* (New York: Penguin Books, 1983).

H. L. A. Hart, *Punishment and Responsibility* (Oxford: Oxford University Press, 1968).

C. E. Hicks (ed.), *Famous American Jury Speeches* (St. Paul, MN: West Publishing, 1925).

T. Honderich, *Punishment: The Supposed Justifications* (London: Hutchinson, 1969).

K. Horney, "The Value of Vindictiveness," *Amer. Journal of Psychoanalysis*, Vol. 8 (1948): 3–12.

S. Jacoby, *Wild Justice: The Evolution of Revenge* (New York: Harper and Row, 1984).

I. Kant, *Groundwork of the Metaphysics of Morals* (Paton trans.) (New York: Harper, 1964).

The Metaphysical Elements of Justice (J. Ladd trans.) (Indianapolis: Bobbs-Merrill, 1965).

W. Kaufmann, *Without Guilt and Justice* (New York: Dell, 1973).

W. Lyons, *Emotion* (Cambridge: Cambridge University Press, 1980).

H. J. McCloskey, "A Non-Utilitarian Approach to Punishment," *Inquiry*, Vol. 8 (1965): 249–63.

J. Mackie, "Morality and the Retributive Emotions," *Criminal Justice Ethics*, Vol. 1 (1982): 3–10.

T. Marshall, concurring in *Gregg* v. *Georgia*, 428 U.S. 153 (1976).

K. Menninger, *The Crime of Punishment* (New York: Viking Press, 1968).

M. Moore, "Responsibility and the Unconscious," *Southern California Law Review*, Vol. 53 (1980): 1563–675.

"Moral Reality," *Wisconsin Law Review*, Vol. [1982]: 1061–1156 (1982a).

"Closet Retributivism," *USC Cites*, Vol. [Spring–Summer 1982]: 9–16 (1982b).

Law and Psychiatry: Rethinking the Relationship (Cambridge: Cambridge University Press, 1984).

"Causation and the Excuses," *California Law Review*, Vol. 73 (1985a): 201–59.

"The Moral and Metaphysical Sources of the Criminal Law," in J. R. Pennock and J. Chapman (eds.), *Nomos XXVII: Criminal Justice* (New York: New York University Press, 1985b).

"Mind, Brain, and Unconscious," in C. Wright and P. Clark (eds.), *Mind, Psychoanalysis, and Science* (Oxford: Blackwell, 1987).

H. Morris, *On Guilt and Innocence* (Berkeley and Los Angeles: University of California Press, 1976).

"Nonmoral Guilt," this volume, Chapter 9.

"A Paternalistic Theory of Punishment," *Amer. Phil. Quarterly*, Vol. 18 (1981): 263–71.

S. Morse, "Justice, Mercy, and Craziness," *Stanford Law Review*, Vol. 36 (1984): 1485–1515.

F. Nietzsche, *Beyond Good and Evil* (Kaufmann, trans.) (New York: Vintage, 1966).

Thus Spoke Zarathustra, in W. Kaufmann (ed.), *The Portable Nietzsche* (New York: Viking, 1954).

The Dawn, in W. Kaufmann (ed.), *The Portable Nietzsche* (New York: Viking, 1954).

The Gay Science (Kaufmann, trans.) (New York: Vintage, 1974).

On the Genealogy of Morals (Kaufmann, trans.) (New York: Vintage, 1969).

Twilight of the Idols, in W. Kaufmann (ed.), *The Portable Nietzsche* (New York: Viking, 1954).

A. Quinton, "On Punishment," *Analysis*, Vol. 14 (1954): 1933–42.

J. Rawls, *A Theory of Justice* (Cambridge, MA: Harvard University Press, 1971).

Mike Royko, "Nothing Gained by Killing a Killer? Oh Yes, There Is," *Los Angeles Times*, March 13, 1981, Sec. II, p. 7.

J.-P. Sartre, *The Flies*, in *No Exit and Three Other Plays* (New York: Vintage, 1955).

M. Scheler, *Ressentiment* (Holdheim trans.) (New York: Free Press, 1961).

R. Scruton, "Emotion, Practical Knowledge, and Common Culture," in A. Rorty (ed.), *Explaining Emotions* (Berkeley and Los Angeles: University of California Press, 1980).

J. Shklar, *Ordinary Vices* (Cambridge, MA: Harvard University Press, 1984).

R. de Sousa, "The Rationality of the Emotions," in A. Rorty (ed.), *Explaining Emotions* (Berkeley and Los Angeles: University of California Press, 1980).

Sir James Stephen, *Liberty, Equality, Fraternity* (Cambridge: Cambridge University Press, 1967).

P. F. Strawson, "Freedom and Resentment," in his *Studies in the Philosophy of Thought and Action* (Oxford: Oxford University Press, 1968).

H. Weihofen, *The Urge to Punish* (New York: Farrar, Straus and Cudahy, 1956).

B. Williams, "Morality and the Emotions," in his *Problems of Self* (Cambridge: Cambridge University Press, 1973).

J. Wilson and R. Herrnstein, *Crime and Human Nature* (New York: Simon and Schuster, 1985).

JEAN HAMPTON

The Moral Education Theory of Punishment*

*We ought not to repay injustice with injustice
or to do harm to any man, no matter what we
may have suffered from him.*

Plato, *Crito*, X, 49

There are few social practices more time-honored or more widely accepted throughout the world than the practice of punishing wrongdoers. Yet if one were to listen to philosophers discussing this practice, one would think punishment impossible to justify and difficult even to understand. However, I do not believe that one should conclude that punishment as a practice is morally unjustifiable or fundamentally irrational. Instead I want to explore the promise of another theory of punishment which incorporates certain elements of the deterrence, retributivist, and rehabilitation views, but whose justification for punishment and whose formula for determining what punishment a wrongdoer deserves are distinctive and importantly different from the reasons and formulas characterizing the traditional rival theories.

This view, which I call the moral education theory of punishment, is not new. There is good reason to believe Plato and Hegel accepted something like it,[1] and more recently, Herbert Morris and Robert Nozick have maintained that the moral education which punishment effects is at least part of punishment's justification.[2] I want to go further, however, and suggest that by reflecting on the educative character of punishment we can provide a full and complete justification for it. Hence my discussion of the moral education theory in this paper is meant to develop it as a complete justification of punishment and to distinguish it from its traditional rivals. Most of my discussion will focus on the theory's application to the state's punishment of criminal offenders, but I will also be looking at the theory's implications for punishment

within other societal institutions, most notably the family.

I will not, however, be able to give an adequate development of the theory in this paper. It is too complex, and too closely connected to many difficult issues, including the nature of law, the foundation of ethical reasoning, and the way human beings develop ethical concepts. Hence what I shall do is simply to *introduce* the theory, sketching its outlines in the first half, and suggesting what seem to be certain advantages and drawbacks of the view in the second half. Much more work needs to be done before anyone is in a position to embrace the view wholeheartedly, hence I won't even attempt to argue in any detailed way here that it is superior to the three traditional views. But I hope my discussion will show that this theory is promising, and merits considerably more discussion and study by the larger intellectual community.

I. THE JUSTIFICATION

Philosophers who write about punishment spend most of their time worrying about whether the *state's* punishment of criminals is justifiable, so let us begin with that particular issue.

When does punishment by the state take place? The answer to this question seems simple: the state carries out punishment upon a person when he or she has broken a *law*. Yet the fact that the state's punishment always follows the transgression of a law is surely neither coincidental nor irrelevant to the understanding and justification of this practice. What is the nature of law? This is a thorny problem which has vexed philosophers for hundreds of years. For the purposes of this article, however, let us agree with Hart that there are (at least) two kinds of law, those which are power-conferring rules, for example, rules which specify how to make a contract or a will, and those which are "rules of obligation."[3] We are concerned with the latter kind of rule, and philosophers and legal theorists have generally analyzed the

*Jean Hampton, "The Moral Education Theory of Punishment," *Philosophy & Public Affairs*, Vol. 13, No. 3 (1984), pp. 208–238. Copyright © 1984 Princeton University Press. Reprinted by permission of Princeton University Press.

structure of this sort of law as "orders backed by threats" made by the state.

What is the subject matter of these orders? I will contend (consistent with a positivist account of law) that the subject matter *ought* to be (although it might not always be) drawn either from ethical imperatives, of the form "don't steal," or "don't murder," or else from imperatives made necessary for moral reasons, for example, "drive on the right"—so that the safety of others on the road is insured, or "advertise your university job in the professional journals"—so that blacks and women will not be denied an opportunity to secure the job.[4] The state makes these two kinds of commands not only to define a minimal set of duties which a human being in that community must follow in his or her dealings with others, but also to designate actions which, when followed by all members of the society, will solve various problems of conflict and coordination.[5]

And the threat? What role does it play? In the end, this is the central question for which we must have an adequate answer if we are to construct a viable theory of punishment.

The threat, which specifies the infliction of pain if the imperative is not obeyed, gives people a nonmoral incentive, that is, the avoidance of pain, to refrain from the prohibited action. The state hopes this incentive will block a person's performance of the immoral action whenever the ethical incentive fails to do so. But insofar as the threat given in the law is designed to play this kind of "deterring" role, carrying out the threat, that is, punishing someone when he or she has broken the law, is, at least in part, a way of "making good" on the threat. The threat will only deter the disobedience of the state's orders if people believe there is a good chance the pain will be inflicted upon them after they commit the crime. But if the state punishes in order to make good on its threats, then the deterrence of future crime cannot be wholly irrelevant to the justification of punishment. And anyone, including Kant, who analyzes laws as orders backed by threats must recognize that fact.[6]

Moreover, I believe we must accept the deterrence theorist's contention that the justification of punishment is connected with the fact that it is a necessary tool for preventing future crime and promoting the public's well-being. Consider standard justifications of the state: philosophers from Plato to Kant to Hart have argued that because a community of people cannot tolerate violent and destructive behavior in its midst, it is justified in establishing a state which will coercively interfere in people's lives for publicly announced and agreed-upon reasons so that an unacceptable level of violence and harm can be prevented. Whereas we normally think the state has to respect its citizens' choices about how to live, certain choices, for example, choices to rape, to murder, or to steal, cannot be respected by a community which is committed to preserving and pursuing the well-being of its members. So when the state annexes punishment to these damaging activities, it says that such activities are not a viable option for anyone in that community.

But to say that the state's punishment is needed to prevent crime is not to commit oneself to the deterrence justification of punishment—it all depends on what one takes prevention to entail. And, as Hegel says, if we aimed to prevent wrongdoing only by deterring its commission, we would be treating human beings in the same way that we treat dogs.[7] Consider the kind of lesson an animal learns when, in an effort to leave a pasture, it runs up against an electrified fence. It experiences pain and is conditioned, after a series of encounters with the fence, to stay away from it and thus remain in the pasture. A human being in the same pasture will get the same message and learn the same lesson—"if you want to avoid pain, don't try to transgress the boundary marked by this fence." But, unlike the animal in the pasture, a human being will also be able to reflect on the reasons for that fence's being there, to theorize about *why* there is this barrier to his freedom.

Punishments are like electrified fences. At the very least they teach a person, via pain, that there is a "barrier" to the action she wants to do, and so, at the very least, they aim to deter. But because punishment "fences" are marking *moral* boundaries, the pain which these "fences" administer (or threaten to administer) conveys a larger message to beings who are able to reflect on the reasons for these barriers' existence: they convey that there is a barrier to these actions *because* they are morally wrong. Thus, according to the moral education theory, punishment is not intended as a way of conditioning a human being to do what society wants her to do (in the way that an animal is conditioned by an electrified fence to stay within a pasture); rather, the theory maintains that punishment is intended as a way of teaching the wrongdoer that the action she did (or wants to do) is forbidden because it is morally wrong and should not be done for that reason. The theory also regards that lesson as public, and thus as directed to the rest of society. When the state makes its criminal law and its enforcement practices known, it conveys an educative message not only to the convicted criminal but also to anyone else in the society who might be tempted to do what she did.

Comparing punishments to electrical fences helps to make clear how a certain kind of deterrent message is built into the larger moral point which punishment aims to convey. If one wants someone to understand that an offense is immoral, at the very least one has to convey to him or her that it is prohibited—that it ought not to occur. Pain is the way to convey that message. The pain says "Don't!" and gives the wrongdoer a reason for not performing the action again; an animal shocked by a fence gets the same kind of message and the same kind of incentive. But the state also wants to use the pain of punishment to get the human wrongdoer to reflect on the moral reasons for that barrier's existence, so that he will make the decision to reject the prohibited action for *moral* reasons, rather than for the self-interested reason of avoiding pain.

If those who are punished (or who watch the punishment take place) reject the moral message implicit in the punishment, at least they will learn from it that there is a barrier to the actions they committed (or are tempted to commit). Insofar as they choose to respond to their punishment (or the punishment of others) merely as a threat, it can keep them within moral boundaries in the same way that fences keep animals in a pasture. This deterrent effect of punishment is certainly welcome by the state whose role is to protect its citizens, and which has erected a "punishment barrier" to certain kinds of actions precisely because those actions will seriously harm its citizens. But on the moral education view, it is incorrect to regard simple deterrence as the aim of punishment; rather, to state it succinctly, the view maintains that punishment is justified as a way to prevent wrongdoing insofar as it can teach both wrongdoers and the public at large the moral reasons for *choosing* not to perform an offense.

I said at the outset that one of the reasons any punishment theory is complicated is that it involves one in taking stands on many difficult ethical and legal issues. And it should be quite clear already that particular positions on the nature of morality and human freedom are presupposed by the moral education view which distinguish the theory from its traditional rivals. Given that the goal of punishment, whether carried out by the state on criminals or by parents on children, is the offender's (as well as other potential offenders') realization of an action's wrongness, the moral education view naturally assumes that there is a fact of the matter about what is right and what is wrong. That is, it naturally rests on ethical objectivism. Perhaps certain sophisticated subjectivists could adapt the theory to accommodate their ontological commitments (punishment, they might say, teaches what society defines as right and wrong). But such an accommodation, in my view, does real damage to the theory, which purports to explain punishment as a way of conveying when an action *is* wrong. Given that the theory holds that punishment is a way of teaching ethical *knowledge,* if there is no such thing, the practice seems highly suspect.

The theory also takes a strong stand on human freedom. It rests on the idea that we can act freely in a way that animals cannot. If we were only like animals, attempts at punishment would affect us in the way that electrical fences affect animals—they would deter us, nothing more. But this theory assumes that we are autonomous, that we can choose and be held accountable for our actions. Thus it holds that punishments must attempt to do more than simply deter us from performing certain offenses; they must also, on this view, attempt to provide us with moral reasons for our *choosing* not to perform these actions. Only creatures who are free to determine their lives according to their moral values can choose not to do an action because it is wrong. Insofar as the moral education view justifies punishment as a way of promoting that moral choice, it assumes that punishment is (and ought only to be) inflicted on beings who are free in this sense.[8] It might be that human beings who have lost their autonomy and who have broken a law can be justifiably treated in a painful way so as to deter them (even as we would deter dangerous animals) from behaving similarly in the future, but this theory would not call such treatment punishment.

Thus one distinction between the moral education view and the deterrence justification of punishment is that on the moral education view, the state is not concerned to use pain coercively so as to progressively eliminate certain types of behavior; rather, it is concerned to educate its citizens morally so that they choose not to engage in this behavior. Moreover, there is another important difference between the two views. On the deterrence view, the infliction of pain on certain individuals is justified as a way of promoting a larger social end. But critics of the deterrence view have pointed out that this is just to say that it is all right to *use* certain individuals to achieve a desirable social goal. The moral education theory, however, does not sanction the use of a criminal for social purposes; on the contrary, it attempts to justify punishment as a way to benefit the person who will experience it, a way of helping him to gain moral knowledge if he chooses to listen. Of course other desirable social goals will be achieved through his punishment, goals which include the education of the larger community about the immorality of the offense, but none of these ends is to be achieved at the expense of the criminal. Instead the moral good which punishment attempts to accomplish within the wrongdoer makes it something which is done *for* him, not *to* him.

There are also sharp differences between the moral education view and various rehabilitative theories of criminal "treatment." An advocate of the moral education view does not perceive punishment as a way of treating a "sick" person for a mental disease, but rather as a way of sending a moral message to a person who has acted immorally and who is to be held responsible for her actions.[9] And whereas both theorists are concerned with the good which punishment can do for the wrongdoer, they disagree about what that good is, one defining it as moral growth, the other as the wrongdoer's acceptance of society's mores and her successful operation in the community. In addition, as we shall discuss in Section II, they disagree about what methods to use to achieve these different ends.

Some readers might wonder how close the moral education view is to the old retribution theory. Indeed references in the literature to a view of this type frequently characterize it as a variant of retribution.[10] Nonetheless, there are sharp and important differences between the two views, which we will explore in more detail in Section II. Suffice to say now that whereas retributivism understands punishment as performing the rather metaphysical task of "negating the wrong" and "reasserting the right," the moral education theorist argues that there is a concrete moral *goal* which punishment should be designed to accomplish, and that goal includes the benefiting of the criminal himself. The state, as it punishes the lawbreaker, is trying to promote his moral personality; it realizes that "[h]is soul is in jeopardy as his victim's is not."[11] Thus, it punishes him as a way of communicating a moral message to him, which he can accept or not, as he chooses.

Certain retributivists have also been very attracted to the idea that punishment is a kind of speech act. For example, Robert Nozick in his book *Philosophical Explanations* has provided a nice nine-point analysis of punishment which presents it as a kind of communication and which fits the account of meaning put forward by H. P. Grice.[12] Yet if punishment is a way of (morally) speaking with a wrongdoer, then why doesn't this show that it is fundamentally justified *as a communication*, in virtue of what it is trying to communicate, rather than, in Nozick's view, as some kind of symbolic "linkage" of the criminal with "correct values"?[13]

Indeed, I would maintain that regarding punishment as a kind of moral communication is intuitively very natural and attractive. Consider, for example, what we say when we punish others: a father who punishes his child explains that he does so in order that the child "learn his lesson"; someone who has been physically harmed by another demands punishment "so that she will understand what she did to me"; a judge recently told a well-known user of cocaine that he was receiving a stiff sentence because his "matter-of-fact dabbling in cocaine . . . tells the whole world it is all right to use it."[14] These kinds of remarks accompanying our punishment efforts suggest that our principal concern as we punish is to get the wrongdoer to stop doing the immoral action by communicating to her that her offense was immoral. And the last remark by the judge to the cocaine user shows that when the state punishes it is important that these communications be public, so that other members of society will hear the same moral message. Even people who seem to be seeking revenge on wrongdoers behave in ways which show that they too want to make a moral point not only to the wrongdoer, but to anyone else who will listen. The hero seeking revenge in a Western movie, for example, never simply shoots the bad guy in the back when he finds him—he always confronts the bad guy first (usually in the presence of other people) and tells him *why* he is about to die. Indeed, the movie would be unsatisfying if he didn't make that communication. And surely, the hero's desire to explain his actions is linked with his desire to convey to the bad guy and to others in society that the bad guy had "done him wrong."[15]

Moreover, if one understands punishment as a moral message aimed at educating both the wrongdoer and the rest of society about the immorality of the offense, one has a powerful explanation (at least as powerful as the one offered by retributivism) of why victims so badly want their assailants punished. If the point of punishment is to convey to the criminal (and others) that the criminal *wronged* the victim, then punishment is implicitly recognizing the victim's plight, and honoring the moral claims of that individual. Punishment affirms as a *fact* that the victim has been wronged, and as a *fact* that he is owed a certain kind of treatment from others. Hence, on this view, it is natural for the victim to demand punishment because it is a way for the community to restore his moral status after it has been damaged by his assailant.

Thus far, I have concentrated on how the state's punishment of criminals can be justified as an attempt at moral education. But I want to contend that punishment efforts by *any* institution or individual should be perceived as efforts at moral education, although the nature and extensiveness of the legitimate educative roles of these institutions and individuals might differ sharply. For example, I believe it is quite clear that parents want to make such a moral communication through their punishments.[16] Suppose for example, that a mother sees her daughter hitting another child. After stepping in to stop this violent behavior, the mother will reflect on what she can do to prevent its reoccurrence. If the mother chooses to try to do this by punishing her daughter, one of the things she "says" through the punishment is, "if you do this again, you will experience the same unpleasantness," and this message is directed at any other children in the family, as well as at this daughter. Hence, one of the things the mother is doing is introducing the incentive of avoiding pain into the children's "calculations" about how to act if and when they are tempted in the future to hurt each other. If a genuine concern for each other's well-being is absent from the children's minds, at least this incentive (as well as fear of losing her approval)

might be strong enough to prevent them from hurting each other in the future.[17] But clearly the mother is also trying to get her children to appreciate that there is a *moral* reason for prohibiting this action. The punishment is supposed to convey the message, "don't do this action again because it is *wrong*; love and not hatred or unwarranted violence is what one should display towards one another." The ultimate goal of the punishment is not merely to deter the child from performing the bad action in the future, but to deter her *by convincing her* (as well as the other children) to renounce the action because it is wrong. And the older and more ethically mature the child becomes, the less the parent will need to resort to punishment to make her moral point, and the more other techniques, like moral suasion, discussion, or debate, will be appropriate.

However, although both state and parental punishment should, according to this theory, be understood as efforts at moral communication and education, the theory does not regard the two kinds of punishment as exactly the same. While punishment should always be regarded as moral education, the "character" of that education can vary enormously, depending in particular on the nature of the institution or individual charged with inflicting the punishment. For example, a parent who is responsible for the full maturation and moral development of her child is naturally thought to be entitled to punish her children for many more offenses and in very different ways, than the children's schoolteacher, or the neighbor down the street. We also think of a university as having punishment rights over its students, but we certainly reject the idea that this sort of institution acts *in loco parentis* towards its students generally. Hence, the theory would not have us understand the punishment role of all institutions, and particularly governments, as the *same* as punishment by parents.[18] None of us, I believe, thinks that the state's role is to teach its citizens the entire content of morality—a role we might characterize as "moral paternalism." A variety of considerations are important in limiting the mode and extent of the state's punishment.

Nonetheless, some readers still might think the moral education theory implies a paternalistic theory of the state—after all, doesn't it maintain that the state can interfere in people's lives for their own good? But when such philosophers as John Stuart Mill have rejected paternalism, what they have rejected is a certain position on what should be law; specifically, they have rejected the state's passing any law which would restrict what an individual can do to *himself* (as opposed to what he can do to another). They have not objected to the idea that when the state justifiably interferes in someone's life *after* he has broken a law (which prohibited harm to another), it should intend good rather than evil towards the criminal. Now it is possible they might call this theory paternalistic anyway, not because it takes any stand on what should be law, but because it views the state's punishment as interference in his life plans without his consent for his own good. But why should paternalism in this sense be offensive? It would be strange indeed if philosophers insisted that the state should only try to prevent further harm to the community by actively intending to harm, or use, or at least be indifferent to, the people it punishes!

But, Mill might complain, if you are willing to allow the state to morally educate those who harm others, why not allow it to morally educate those who harm themselves? This is a good question, but one the moral education theory cannot answer. Indeed, answering it is the same as answering the question: What ought to be made law? Or, alternatively, what is the appropriate area for legislation? Though central to political theory, these questions are ones to which the moral education theory can give no answer, for while the theory maintains that punishment of a certain sort should follow the transgression of a law, it is no part of the theory to say *what* ethical reasons warrant the imposition of a law. Indeed, one of the advantages of the theory is that one can adopt it no matter what position one occupies on the political spectrum.

But, critics might insist, isn't this theory arguing that the state should be in the business of deciding and enforcing morality, overriding the autonomous moral decisions of its citizens? Yes, that is exactly the theory's point, the state *is* in that business in a very limited way. Imagine a murderer saying: "You, the state, have no right to tell me that my murder of this man is wrong," or a rapist protesting: "Who is the state to tell me that my rape of this woman is immoral?" These statements sound absurd, because we believe not merely that such actions are wrong, but that they are also heinous and morally appalling. The state is justified in punishing rapists and murderers because their choices about what to do betray a serious in-ability to make decisions about immoral and moral actions, which has resulted in substantial harm to some members of that community. And while some readers might find it offensive to contemplate the state presuming to morally educate anyone but serious felons, is this not exactly the kind of sentiment behind the libertarians' call for extensive constraints on the state's role and power?

Moreover, I wonder whether, by calling this theory paternalistic, one might not be irritated more by the thought of being governed than by the thought of what this particular theory says being governed involves. Yet, unless one is prepared to be an anarchist, one must admit that being governed is necessary as long as we, as human beings, are prone to immoral acts. We do not outgrow cruelty, or meanness, or the egoistic disregard for others when we reach the age of majority. On this view, the state exists because even adults need to be governed, although not in the way that children require governing by their parents. (Indeed, these ideas suggested by the theory form a germ of an argument against anarchism, which I can only pursue in another place.)

But, critics might insist, it is this theory's view of what governing involves that is objectionable. Who and what is the state, that it can presume to teach us a moral lesson? Yet I regard this question not as posing a challenge to the moral education view itself, but rather as posing a challenge *by* that theory to any existing state. Not only does the theory offer a partial explanation of the state's role, but it also proposes a view of what the state *ought* to be like if its punishment activities have any legitimacy. For example, insofar as the state should be morally educating when it punishes, this theory implies that the state's laws should be arrived at by reflection on what is right or wrong, and not on what is in the best interest of a particular class, or race, or sex. That this is not always true of the laws of our society is an indictment of our state, and punishments inflicted as a way of enforcing these biased laws cannot be justified. Moreover, if we accept the idea that the state is supposed to morally educate its citizens, it is natural to argue that all of its citizens should participate either directly or through representatives in the legislative branch of that institution in order to control and supervise its moral enforcement so that the resulting laws reflect the moral consensus of the community rather than the views of one class. Hence the moral education view can underlie an argument for the democratic structure of a state.

Finally, I would contend that the moral education theory illuminates better than any of its theoretical rivals the strategy of those who are civilly disobedient. Martin Luther King, Jr. wrote that it is critical for anyone who wants to be civilly disobedient to accept the penalty for his or her lawbreaking, not only to express "the very highest respect for law" but also "to arouse the conscience of the community over its injustice."[19] The moral education theory explains how both these objectives are achieved. The civilly disobedient person, when she accepts the penalty for lawbreaking, is respecting the state's right to punish transgressors of its laws, but she is also forcing the state to commit itself, in full view of the rest of society, to the idea that her actions show she needs moral education. And when that person is protesting, as Gandhi or King did, offensive and unjust laws, she knows the state's punishment will appear morally outrageous and will arouse the conscience of anyone sensitive to the claims of justice. Therefore, the civilly disobedient person is, on this view, using the idea of what the state and its laws ought to be like if its punishment activities have legitimacy in order to effect moral improvement in the legal system.

II. QUESTIONS AND CRITICISMS

Although I will not fully develop and defend the moral education view in this article, I now want to put some flesh on the skeletal presentation of the view just given by considering some questions which spring naturally to mind as one reflects on the theory.

1. *What is this theory's punishment formula?* Punishment formulas always follow directly from punishment justifications. If punishment is justified as a deterrent, then it follows from that justification that particular punishments should be structured so as to deter. But if punishment is justified as a way of morally educating the wrongdoer and the rest of society about the immorality of the act, then it follows that one should punish in ways that promote this two-part goal. But how do we go about structuring punishments that morally educate? And would this way of determining punishments yield intuitively more just punishments than those yielded by the formulas of the traditional theories?

One reason these formulas of all the traditional theories have been attacked as unjust is that all of them fail to incorporate an acceptable upper bound on what punishments can be legitimately inflicted on an offender. Consider that, once the deterrence theorist has defined his deterrence goal, any punishment that will achieve this goal is justified, including the most brutalizing. Similarly, the retributivist's *lex talionis* punishment formula (dictating that punishments are to be somehow equal to the crime) would seem to recommend, for example, torturing the torturer, murdering *all* murderers, and such recommendations cast serious doubt on the formula's moral adequacy.[20] Even the rehabilitation theory does not place strict limits on the kinds of "treatments" which can legitimately be given to offenders. If the psychiatric "experts" decide that powerful drugs, shock treatments, lobotomies or other similar medical procedures are legitimate and necessary treatments of certain criminals, why shouldn't they be used? The only upper bound on the treatments inherent in this theory derives from the consciences of psychiatrists and their consensus about what constitutes "reasonable" treatment, and many contend that history has shown such an upper bound to be far too high.[21]

The moral education theory, however, does seem to have the resources to generate a reasonable upper limit on how much punishment the state can legitimately administer. Because part of the goal of punishment is to educate the criminal, this theory insists that as he is educated, his autonomy must be respected. The moral education theorist does not want "education" confused with "conditioning." Shock treatments or lobotomies that would damage or destroy the criminal's freedom to choose are not appropriate educative techniques. On this view the goal of punishment is not to destroy the criminal's freedom of choice, but to persuade him to use his freedom in a way consistent with the freedom of others. Thus, any punishment that would damage the autonomy of the criminal is ruled out by this theory.

In addition, it is important to remember that, on this view, punishments should be designed to convey to the criminal and to the rest of society the idea that the criminal's act was wrong. And it seems difficult if not impossible for the state to convey this message if it is carrying out cruel and disfiguring punishments such as torture or maiming. When the state climbs into the moral gutter with the criminal in this way it cannot credibly convey either to the criminal or to the public its moral message that human life must always be respected and preserved, and such actions can even undercut its justification for existing. Note that both of these considerations indicate this theory rules out execution as punishment.[22] (Of course, the moral education theory says nothing about whether the execution of criminals might be justified not as punishment but as a method of "legitimate elimination" of criminals who are judged to have lost all of their essential humanity, making them wild beasts of prey on a community that must, to survive, destroy them. Whether such a justification of criminal execution can be morally tolerable is something I do not want to explore here.)

But, the reader might wonder, how can inflicting *any* pain upon a criminal be morally educational? And why isn't the infliction of mild sorts of pains and deprivations also climbing into the moral gutter with the criminal? The moral education theorists must provide an explanation of why certain sorts of painful experiences (whose infliction on others we would normally condemn) may legitimately be inflicted in order to facilitate moral growth. But is such an explanation possible? And even if it is, would the infliction of pain always be the right way to send a moral message? If a criminal's psychological make-up is such that pain would not reform him, whereas "inflicting" a pleasurable experience would produce this reform, are we therefore justified only in giving him that pleasurable experience? Retributivists like Robert Nozick think the answer to this last question is yes, and thus reject the view as an adequate justification of punishment by itself.[23]

All three of these worries would be allayed if the moral education theorist could show that only the infliction of pain of a certain sort following a wrongdoing is *necessarily* connected with the promotion of the goal of moral education. In order to establish this necessary connection between certain sorts of painful experiences and moral growth, the moral education theorist needs an account of what moral concepts are, and an account of how human beings come to acquire them (that is, what moral education is). I cannot even attempt to propose, much less develop, answers to these central ethical issues here. But I will try to offer

reasons for thinking that painful experiences of a particular sort would seem to be necessary for the communication of a certain kind of moral message.

It is useful to start our discussion by getting a good understanding of what actions count as punishment. First, if we see punishment from the offender's standpoint, we appreciate that it involves the loss of her freedom. This is obviously true when one is locked up in a penitentiary, but it is also true when, for example, parents stop their child's allowance (money that had previously been defined as hers is withheld—whether she likes it or not) or when they force her to experience a spanking or a lecture. I would argue that this loss of freedom is why (autonomous) human beings so dislike punishment. Second, whereas it is very natural to characterize punishment as involving pain or other unpleasant consequences, the infliction of what we intuitively want to call punishment might involve the wrongdoer in performing actions which one would not normally describe as painful or unpleasant. For example, a doctor who cheated the Medicare system and who is sentenced to compulsory week-end service in a state-supported clinic would not be undergoing what one would normally describe as a painful or unpleasant experience (he isn't being incarcerated, whipped, fined). Nonetheless, insofar as some of his free time is being taken away from him, the state is depriving him of his freedom to carry out his own plans and to pursue the satisfaction of his own interests. In this case, the state is clearly punishing an offender, but it sounds distorted to say that it is inflicting pain on him. Thus we need a phrase to describe punishment which will capture better than "infliction of pain" all of the treatments which we intuitively want to call punishment. For this purpose I propose the phrase "disruption of the freedom to pursue the satisfaction of one's desires," a phrase which is suitably general and which fits a wide variety of experiences that we want to call experiences of *punishment*. (It may well be *too* general, but I do not want to pursue that issue here.)[24]

Thus I understand punishment as an experience which a wrongdoer is forced by an authority to undergo in virtue of the fact that he has transgressed (what ought to be) a morally derived rule laid down by that authority, and which disrupts (in either a major or a minor way) the wrongdoer's freedom to pursue the satisfaction of his desires. Given that punishment is understood in this way, how do coercion and the disruption of one's self-interested pursuits convey a *moral* message?

Before answering this question, it is important to make clear that punishment is only *one* method of moral education. Upon reflection, it is clear, I think, that we choose to employ this method only when we're trying to teach someone that an action is *wrong*, rather than when we are trying to teach someone what (imperfect) moral duties he or she ought to recognize. (We punish a child when he kicks his brother; we don't punish him in order to get him to give Dad a present on Father's Day.)

What is one trying to get across when one wants to communicate an action's wrongness? The first thing one wants to convey is that the action is forbidden, prohibited, "fenced off." Consider a mother who sees her child cheating at solitaire. She might say to the child, "You mustn't do that." Or if she saw her child putting his left shoe on his right foot, she would likely say, "No, you mustn't dress that way." In both cases it would be highly inappropriate for her to follow these words with punishment. She is communicating to her child that what he is doing in these circumstances is inadvisable, imprudent, not playing by the rules, but she is not communicating (and not trying to communicate) the idea that such actions violate one's moral duty to others (or, for that matter, one's moral duty to oneself). Now consider this mother seeing her son kick the neighbor's young daughter. Once again she might say, "You mustn't do that," to the child, but the "mustn't" in the mother's words here is unique. It is more than "you shouldn't" or "it isn't advisable" or "it's against the rules of the game." Rather, it attempts to convey the idea that the action is forbidden, prohibited, intolerable.

But merely telling the child that he "mustn't do that" will not effectively convey to the child that there is this profound moral boundary. Without punishment why shouldn't the child regard the "mustn't" in the parent's statement just as he did the "mustn't" in "You mustn't cheat at solitaire"? The mother needs to get across to the child the very special nature of the prohibition against this immoral act. How can she do this? Consider the fact that someone who (for no moral reason) violates a positive duty to others is not acting out of any interest in the other's well-being. A teenager who steals from a passer-by because she needs the money, a

man who rapes a woman so that he can experience a sense of power and mastery—such people are performing immoral acts in order to satisfy their own needs and interests, insensitive to the needs and interests of the people they hurt. The way to communicate to such people that there is a barrier of a very special sort against these kinds of actions would seem to be to link performance of the actions with what such people care about most—the pursuit of their own pleasure. Only when disruption of that pursuit takes place will a wrongdoer appreciate the special force of the "mustn't" in the punisher's communication. So the only effective way to "talk to" such people is through the disruption of their own interests, that is, through punishment (which has been defined as just such a disruption).

What conclusions will a person draw from this disruption of his pleasure? At the very least he will conclude that his society (in the guise of the family, the state, the university, etc.) has erected a barrier to that kind of action, and that if he wants to pursue the satisfaction of his own desires, he won't perform that action again. So at the very least, he will understand his punishment as society's attempt to deter him from committing the action in the future. Such a conclusion does not have moral content. The person views his punishment only as a sign of society's condemnation of the act, not as a sign of the act's *wrongness*. But it is a start, and a *necessary first start*. If a wrongdoer has little or no conception of an action's wrongness, then the first thing one must do is to communicate to him that the action is prohibited. We must put up the electrical fence in an attempt to keep him out of a forbidden realm.

But given that we want the offender to understand the moral reasons for the action's condemnation, how can punishment communicate those reasons? The punisher wants the wrongdoer to move from the first stage of the educative process initiated by punishment—the realization that society prohibits the action—to a second stage, where the moral reasons for the condemnation of the action are understood and accepted. Can punishment, involving the disruption of a person's self-interested pursuits, help an offender to arrive at this final moral conclusion, to understand, in other words, why this fence has been erected?

What is it that one wants the wrongdoer to see? As we noted before, someone who (for no moral reason) violates her (perfect) moral duty to others is not thinking about the others' needs and interests, and most likely has little conception of, or is indifferent to, the pain her actions caused another to suffer. Hence, what the punisher needs to do is to communicate to the wrongdoer *that* her victims suffered and how much they suffered, so that the wrongdoer can appreciate the harmfulness of her action. How does one get this message across to a person insensitive to others? Should not such a person be made to endure an unpleasant experience designed, in some sense, to "represent" the pain suffered by her victim(s)? This is surely the intuition behind the *lex talionis* but it best supports the concept of punishment as moral education. As Nozick admits,[25] it is very natural to regard the pain or unpleasantness inflicted by the wrongdoer as the punisher's way of saying: "This is what you did to another. You hate it; so consider how your victim felt." By giving a wrongdoer something like what she gave to others, you are trying to drive home to her just how painful and damaging her action was for her victims, and this experience will, one hopes, help the wrongdoer to understand the immorality of her action.

Of course, the moral education formula does not recommend that punishments be specifically *equal* to the crime—in many instances this doesn't even make sense. But what does the "representation" of the wrongful act involve, if not actual equality? This is a terribly difficult question, and I find I can only offer tentative, hesitant answers. One way the moral education theorist can set punishments for crimes is to think about "fit." Irrespective of how severe a particular crime is, there will sometimes be a punishment that seems naturally suited to it; for example, giving a certain youth charged with burglarizing and stealing money from a neighbor's house the punishment of supervised compulsory service to this neighbor for a period of time, or giving a doctor charged with cheating a government medical insurance program the punishment of compulsory unremunerated service in a state medical institution. And probably such punishments seem to fit these crimes because they force the offender to compensate the victim, and thus help to heal more effectively the "moral wound" which the offense has caused. Another way the moral education theorist can make specific punishment recommendations is to construct an ordinal scale of crimes, going from most offensive to least offensive, and then to link determinate

sentences to each crime, respecting this ordinal comparison, and insuring proportionality between crime and punishment. But it is not easy to use either method to fashion a tidy punishment table because it is not easy to determine which painful experiences will be educative but not cruel, both proportional to the offense committed and somehow relevant to that offense. Indeed, our society has been notoriously unsuccessful in coming up with punishments that are in any way morally educative. And I would argue that it speaks in favor of this theory that it rejects many forms of incarceration used today as legitimate punishments, insofar as they tend to make criminals morally worse rather than better.

But even if this theory can tell us how to represent wrongdoing in a punishment, it must still handle other questions which I do not have time to pursue properly in this article. For example, how does that representation help the wrongdoer to understand and *accept* the fact that she did wrong and should do otherwise in the future? And if we want to send the most effective message possible in order to bring about this acceptance, should we try to tailor punishments to the particular psychological and moral deficiencies of the wrongdoer, or must considerations of equal treatment and fairness override this? Finally, does the view justify the state's punishing people who are innocent of any illegal act but who seem to need moral education?

The theory has a very interesting and complicated response to this last question. We have said that punishment is not the appropriate method to teach every sort of moral lesson, but only the lesson that a certain action is wrong. But on whom is the state justified in imposing such a lesson?—clearly, a person who has shown she needs the lesson by committing a wrong which the state had declared illegal, and clearly *not* a person who has shown she already understands this lesson (at least in some sense) by conscientiously obeying that law. We also believe that the state is justified in imposing this lesson on a person who has not broken that law but who has *tried* to do so. She might, for example, be punished for "attempted murder" or "attempted kidnapping." (And do we make the punishments for such attempts at wrongdoing less than for successful wrongdoings because we're not sure the attempts provide conclusive evidence that such people would have carried through?) But what about a person who has not broken a law or even attempted to do so but who has, say, talked about doing so publicly? Is that enough evidence that she needs moral education? Probably—by *some* person or institution, but not by the state. The point is that we believe the state should refrain from punishing immoral people who have nonetheless committed no illegal act, not because they don't need moral education but because the state is not the appropriate institution to effect that education. Indeed, one of the reasons we insist that the state operate by enacting laws is that doing so defines when it may coercively interfere in the lives of its citizens and when it may not; its legislation, in other words, defines the extent of its educative role (and there might exist constitutional rules guiding this legislation). So if the state were to interfere with its citizens' lives when they had not broken its laws, it would exceed its own legitimate role. In the end, the state may not punish immoral people who are innocent of any crime not because they don't need moral education, but because the state is not justified in giving it to them.

However, there is another question relevant to the issue of punishing the innocent. Given that I have represented the moral education theory as having a two-part goal—the moral education of the criminal and the moral education of the rest of society—it might be that a punishment which would achieve one part of this goal would not be an effective way of realizing the other part. Must we choose between these two objectives, or is it possible to show that they are inextricably linked? And if they are not, could it be that in order to pursue the goal of morally educating *society,* it would be necessary to punish an innocent person? More generally, could it be justifiable on this view to punish a wrongdoer much more (or much less) severely than her offense (if any) would seem to warrant if doing so would further society's moral education? If this were true, the theory would not preserve proportionality between crime and punishments. However, there are reasons for thinking that educating the criminal and educating the community are inextricably linked. For example, if the state aims to convey a moral lesson to the community about how other human beings should be treated, it will completely fail to do so if it inflicts pain on someone innocent of any wrongdoing—indeed, it would send a message exactly contrary to the one it had intended. But even if we suppose, for the sake of argument, that these educational objectives could become disengaged, we can preserve proportionality between a person's crime and her punishment by making the moral education of the criminal lexically prior to the moral education of the community (after all, we *know* she needs the lesson, we're less sure about the community).[26]

However, giving adequate arguments for solutions to any of the problems I have posed in this section requires a much more fully developed account of what moral education is and of how punishment would help to effect it. Some readers might think that developing such an account is simply an empirical rather than a philosophical task. But before we can know how to morally educate, we need a better theoretical understanding of what moral knowledge is, and why human beings do wrong. (Is it because, as Kant insists, we choose to defy the power of the moral law or because, as Socrates argues, we are morally ignorant?) Moreover, we need a better appreciation of the source and extent of the state's authority if we are to understand its legitimate role as moral educator. Further work on this theory has to come to grips with these issues in moral and political philosophy before we can know whether to embrace it. But I have tried to suggest in my remarks in this section that certain kinds of approaches to these issues are at least promising.

2. *Is the moral education of most criminals just a pipe dream?* How can we really expect hard-core criminals convicted of serious offenses to be able to change and morally improve? In answer to this last question, the moral education theorist will admit that the state can predict that many of the criminals it punishes will refuse to accept the moral message it delivers. As I have stressed, the moral education theory rests on the assumption of individual autonomy, and thus an advocate of this theory must not only admit but insist that the choice of whether to listen to the moral message contained in the punishment belongs to the criminal. Thus it is very unlikely that society will be 100 percent successful in its moral education efforts, no matter how well it uses the theory to structure punishments.

But at least the punishment the state delivers can have a deterrent effect; even if the criminal refuses to understand the state's communication about why there is a barrier to his action, at least he will understand *that* the barrier exists. Hegel once wrote that if a criminal is coerced by a punishment, it is because he *chooses* to be so coerced; such a person rejects the moral message and accepts instead the avoidance of pain as his sole reason for avoiding the action.[27] In the end, punishments might only have deterrent effects because that is all wrongdoers will let them have.

However, neither the state nor anyone else can determine who the "losers" are. None of us can read another's mind, none of us knows the pressures, beliefs, and concerns motivating another's actions and decisions. The state cannot, even with the help of a thousand psychiatrists, *know for sure* who is a hopeless case and who isn't. Nor is this just a simple epistemological problem. Insofar as the state, on this view, should regard each person it punishes as autonomous, it is committed to the view that the choice of whether to reform or not is a free one, and hence one the state cannot hope to predict. Finally, the state's assumption that the people it is entitled to punish are free means it must never regard any one it punishes as hopeless, insofar as it is assuming that each of these persons still has the ability to choose to be moral. Thus, as Hegel puts it,[28] punishment is the criminal's "right" as a free person—to refuse to punish him on the grounds that he has been diagnosed as hopeless is to regard him as something other than a rational human being.

But even if it seems likely that punishing some criminals will not effect their moral growth, and may not even deter them, the moral education of the community about the nature of their crimes can still be promoted by their punishment. Indeed any victim of crime is going to be very sensitive to this fact, insofar as he has been the one against whom the wrong has been committed, and is the one who is most interested in having the community acknowledge that what happened to him *shouldn't* have happened. And as long as the person whom we punish is admitted to be an autonomous human being, we cannot be convicted of using her as we educate the community about the wrongness of her offense, because we are doing something to her which is *for* her, which can achieve a great deal of good for her, if she will but let it.

3. *Shouldn't the moral education theory imply an indeterminate sentencing policy?* Throughout your discussion, rehabilitationists might complain, you have been assuming that punishment by the state should proceed from determinate sentences for specific crimes. But isn't indeterminate sentencing fairer? Why keep a criminal who has learned his moral lesson in jail just because his sentence has not run out, and why release a criminal who is unrepentant and who will probably harm the public again, just because his sentence has run out?

However, the moral education theorist has very good reasons, provided by the foundations of the theory itself, for rejecting the concepts of indeterminate sentencing and parole boards. First, this theorist would strongly disagree with the idea that a criminal should continue to receive "treatment" until his reform has been effected. Recall that it is an important tenet of the view that the criminals we punish are free beings, responsible for their actions. And you can't *make* a free human being believe something. In particular, you can't coerce people to be just for justice's sake. Punishment is the state's attempt to teach a moral lesson, but whether or not the criminal will listen and accept it is up to the criminal himself.

The moral education theorist takes this stand not simply because she believes one ought to respect the criminal's autonomy, but also because she believes one has no choice but to respect it. The fact that parole boards in this country have tried to coerce repentance is, from the standpoint of this theorist, a grave and lamentable mistake. (Consider James McConnell's claim, in an article in *Psychology Today*, that "Somehow we've got to *force* people to love one another, to force them to want to behave properly.")[29] Indeed, critics of present parole systems in the United States maintain that these systems only open the way for manipulation.[30] The parole board uses the threat of the refusal of parole to get the kind of behavior it wants from the criminal, and the criminal manipulates back—playing the game, acting reformed, just to get out. In the process, no moral message is conveyed to the criminal, and probably no real reformation takes place. The high recidivism rate in the United States tells the tale of how successful parole boards have been in evaluating the rehabilitation of prisoners. As one prisoner put it: "If they ask if this yellow wall is blue, I'll say, of course it's blue. I'll say anything they want me to say if they're getting ready to let me go."[31]

The moral education theorist doesn't want the state to play this game. A sentence for a crime is set, and when the criminal breaks a law, the sentence is inflicted on him as a way of teaching him that what he did was wrong. When the sentence is up, the criminal is released. The state hopes its message was effective, but whether it was or not is largely up to the criminal himself.

There is another important reason why the moral education theorist does not want to insist on repentance before release. Even a good state can make mistakes when it enacts law. It is not just possible but probable that the state at one time or another will declare a certain action immoral which some of its citizens will regard as highly moral. These citizens will often decide to disobey this "immoral" law, and while being punished, will steadfastly refuse to repent for an action they believe was right. Martin Luther King, Jr., never repented for breaking various segregation laws in the South while he was in jail; few draft resisters repented for refusing to go to Vietnam when they were in prison. By not insisting on the repentance of its criminals, the state is, once again, respecting the freedom of its citizens—particularly each citizen's freedom of conscience, and their right, as free beings, to disagree with its rulings. Hence, the moral educational theorist doesn't want the state to insist on repentance because it doesn't want Solzhenitsyns rotting in jail until they have "reformed."[32]

How can the moral education theorist justify the punishment of a criminal who is already repentant prior to his sentencing, or who repents before his sentence is completely served? The theorist's response to this question is complicated. Because it is difficult to be sure that a seemingly repentant criminal is *truly* repentant, and thus because a policy of suspending or shortening sentences for those who seem repentant to the authorities could easily lead the criminal to fake repentance before a court or a parole board, the moral education theorist would be very reluctant to endorse such a policy.

Moreover, it might well be the case that, prior to or during sentencing, a criminal's experience of repentance is produced in large part by the expectation of receiving the full punishment, so that the state's subsequent failure to inflict it could lead to a weakening of the criminal's renunciation of the action. Like a bad but repentant child who will conclude, if he is not punished by his parents, that his action must not have been so bad, the repentant criminal might well need to experience his complete sentence in order to "learn his lesson" effectively.

Finally, the lesson learning effected by punishment can also involve a purification process for a wrongdoer, a process of healing. As Herbert Morris has written, experiencing the pain of punishment can be a kind of catharsis for the criminal, a way of "burning out" the evil in his soul.[33] Novelists like Dostoevsky have explored the criminal's need, born of guilt and shame, to experience pain at the hands of the society he has wronged in order to be reconciled with them. Thus the rehabilitationist who would deny the criminal the experience of pain at the hands of the state would deny him what he may want and need to be forgiven—both by society and by himself. And punishment understood as moral education would explain how it could be perceived as a purification process. For how is it that one overcomes shame? Is it not by becoming a person *different* from the one who did the immoral action? The subsiding of shame in us seems to go along with the idea, "Given who I was, I did the action then, but I'm different now—I'm *better* now—and I wouldn't do the same act again." But how do we become different, how do we change, improve? Insofar as punishment is seen as a way of educating oneself about the offense, undergoing that experience is a way of changing for the better. It might well be the yearning for that change which drives a person like Raskolnikov towards his punishment.

Nonetheless, if there were clear evidence that a criminal was very remorseful for his action and had already experienced great pain because of his crime (had "suffered enough"), this theory would endorse a suspension of his sentence or else a pardon (*not* just a parole). His moral education would have already been accomplished, and the example of his repentance would be lesson enough for the general public. (Indeed, punishment under these circumstances would make the state appear vindictive.) In addition, because the state conceives itself to be punishing a wrong, it is appropriate for it to allow certain sorts of excuses and mitigating circumstances to lessen the penalty normally inflicted for the crime in question.

4. *Does the moral education theory actually presuppose the truth of retribution?* Retributivists have a very interesting criticism of the moral education theory available to them. Granted, they might maintain, that punishment is connected with moral education, still this only provides an additional reason for

punishing someone—it does not provide the fundamental justification of punishment. That fundamental justification, they would argue, is retributive: wrongdoers simply *deserve* to experience pain for the sake of the wrong they have committed. As Kant has argued, however much good one intends one's punishment to effect,

> yet it must first be justified in itself as punishment, i.e., as mere harm, so that if it stopped there, and the person punished could get no glimpse of kindness hidden behind this harshness, he must yet admit that justice was done him, and that his reward was perfectly suitable to his conduct.[34]

Moreover, such modern retributivists as Walter Moberly have argued that it is only when the wrongdoer can assent to his punishment as already justified in virtue of his offense that the punishment can do him any good.[35]

In a certain sense, Moberly's point is simply that a criminal will perceive his punishment as vindictive and vengeful unless he understands or accepts the fact that it is justified. But should the justification of punishment be cashed out in terms of the retributive concept of desert, given that it has been difficult for retributivists to say what they mean by the criminal's "deserving" punishment simply in virtue of his offense? Robert Nozick tries to cash out the retributive link between crime and "deserved" punishment by saying that the punishment represents a kind of "linkage" between the criminal and "right values."[36] But why is inflicting pain on someone a way of effecting this linkage? Why isn't the infliction of a pleasurable experience for the sake of the crime just as good a way of linking the wrongdoer with these right values? And if Nozick explains the linkage of pain with crime by saying that the pain is necessary in order to communicate to the criminal that his action was wrong, he has answered the question but lost his retributive theory. Other philosophers, like Hegel,[37] speak of punishment as a way of "annulling" or "canceling" the crime and hence "deserved" for that reason. But although Hegel's words have a nice metaphorical ring to them, it is hard to see how they can be given a literal force that will explain the retributivist concept of desert. As J. L. Mackie has written, insofar as punishment occurs after the crime, it certainly cannot cancel it—past events are not eliminated by later ones.[38]

It is partly because retributivists have been at a loss to explain the notion of desert implicit in their theory of punishment that I have sought to propose and explore a completely non-retributivist justification of punishment. But my reasons for rejecting retributivism are deeper. The retributive position is that it is somehow morally appropriate to inflict pain for pain, to take an eye for an eye, a tooth for a tooth. But how is it ever morally appropriate to inflict one evil for the sake of another? How is the society that inflicts the second evil any different from the wrongdoer who has inflicted the first? He strikes first, they strike back; why is the second strike acceptable but the first not? Plato, in a passage quoted at the start of this article, insists that both harms are wrong; and Jesus attacks retributivism[39] for similar reasons:

> You have learned that they were told, 'Eye for eye, tooth for tooth.' But what I tell you is this: Do not set yourself against the man who wrongs you. . . . You have heard that they were told 'Love your neighbor, hate your enemy.' But what I tell you is this: Love your enemy and pray for your persecutors; only so can you be children of your heavenly father, who makes the sun rise on good and bad alike, and sends the rain on the honest and dishonest. [Matt. 5:38–9, 43–6]

In other words, both reject retributivism because they insist that the only thing human beings "deserve" in this life is *good,* that no matter what evil a person has committed, no one is justified in doing further evil to her.

But if one accepts the idea that no one can ever deserve ill, can we hope to justify punishment? Yes, if punishment can be shown to be a good for the wrongdoer. The moral education theory makes just such an attempt to explain punishment as a good for those who experience it, as something done *for* them, not to them, something designed to achieve a goal that includes their own moral well-being. This is the justification of punishment the criminal needs to hear so that he can accept it as legitimate rather than dismiss it as vindictive. Therefore, my interest in the moral education theory is connected with my desire to justify punishment *as a good* for those who experience it, and to avoid any theoretical justification of punishment that would regard it as a deserved evil.[40] Reflection on the punishment activities of those who truly love the people they punish, for example, the infliction of pain by a parent on a beloved but naughty child, suggests to me that punishment should not be justified as a deserved evil, but rather as an attempt, by someone who cares, to improve a wayward person.

Still, the moral education theory can incorporate a particular notion of desert which might be attractive to retributivists. Anyone who is punished according to this theory would know that his punishment is "deserved," that is, morally required, insofar as the community cannot morally tolerate the immoral lesson that his act conveys to others (for example, the message that raping a woman is all right if it gives one a feeling of self-mastery) and cannot morally allow that he receive no education about the evil of his act.

So the theory's point is this: Wrong occasions punishment not because pain deserves pain, but because evil deserves correction.

NOTES

I have many people to thank for their help in developing the ideas in this paper; among them: Warren Quinn, Thomas Hill, Judith De Cew, Marilyn Adams, Robert Adams, Richard Healey, Christopher Morris, Norman Dahl, Julie Heath, George Fletcher, Robert Gerstein, David Dolinko, and especially Herbert Morris. I also want to thank the Editors of *Philosophy & Public Affairs* for their incisive comments, and members of my seminar on punishment at UCLA in the Spring of 1983 for their lively and helpful discussions of the theory. Portions of the article were also read, among other places, at the 1982 Pacific Division APA Meeting, at C.S.U. Northridge, and at the University of Rajasthan, Jaipur, India.

1. See Hegel, *Philosophy of Right*, trans. T. Knox (Oxford: Clarendon Press, 1952), sections 90–104 (pp. 66–74); and see Plato, in particular the dialogues: *The Laws* (bks. 5 and 9), *Gorgias* (esp. pp. 474ff.), *Protagoras* (esp. pp. 323ff.) and Socrates's discussion of his own punishment in the *Apology*, and the *Crito*. I am not convinced that this characterization of either Hegel's or Plato's views is correct, but I do not have time to pursue those issues here. J. E. McTaggart has analyzed Hegel's position in a way that suggests it is a moral education view. See his "Hegel's Theory of Punishment," *International Journal of Ethics* 6 (1896), pp. 482–99; portions reprinted in *Philosophical Perspectives On Punishment*, ed. Gertrude Ezorsky (Albany, NY: State University of New York Press, 1972). In her *Plato on Punishment*, M. M. Mackenzie's presentation of Plato's position suggests it is not a strict moral education view.

2. Recently Morris has been explicitly advocating this view in "A Paternalistic Theory of Punishment," *American Philosophical Quarterly* 18, no. 4 (October 1981), but only as *one aspect* of the justification of punishment. Morris argues that punishment is sufficiently complicated to require a justification incorporating all of the justificatory reasons offered by the traditional theories of punishment as well as by the moral education view. I do not think this sort of patchwork approach to punishment will work and, in this article, I explore the idea that the moral education view can, by itself, give an adequate justification of punishment.

See also Nozick's recent book *Philosophical Explanations* (Cambridge: Harvard University Press, 1981), pp. 363–97.

3. See Hart, *The Concept of Law* (Oxford, Clarendon Press, 1961), chaps. 5 and 6.

4. As stated, this is a positivist definition of law. However, with John Chipman Gray I am maintaining that morality, although not the same as law, should be the source of law. (See Gray's *The Nature and Source of Law* [New York: Macmillan, 1921], p. 84.)

5. See Edna Ullman-Margalit, *The Emergence of Norms* (Oxford: Clarendon Press, 1977) for a discussion of how law can solve coordination and conflict problems.

6. Although Kant's position on punishment is officially retributive (see his *Metaphysical Elements of Justice*, trans. J. Ladd [Indianapolis: Bobbs-Merrill, 1965], p. 100, Academy edition, p. 331), his definition of law conflicts with his retributivist position. Note, for example, the deterrent flavor of his justification of law:

if a certain use of freedom is itself a hindrance to freedom according to universal laws (that is, unjust), then the use of coercion to counteract it, inasmuch as it is the prevention of a hindrance to freedom according to universal laws, is consistent with freedom according to universal laws; in other words, this use of coercion is just (p. 36, Academy edition, p. 231; see also *Metaphysical Elements of Justice*, pp. 18–9, 33–45; Academy edition, pp. 218–21, 229–39).

7. Hegel, *Philosophy of Right*, addition to par. 99, p. 246.

8. Kantians who see a close connection between autonomy and moral knowledge will note that this connection is suggested in these remarks.

9. Rehabilitationists disagree about exactly what disease criminals suffer from. See for example the various psychiatric diagnoses of Benjamin Karpman in "Criminal Psychodynamics: A Platform," reprinted in *Punishment and Rehabilitation*, ed. J. Murphy (Belmont, CA: Wadsworth, 1973) as opposed to the behaviorist analysis of criminal behavior offered by B. F. Skinner in *Science and Human Behavior* (New York: Macmillan, 1953), pp. 182–93 and 446–49.

10. See for example Nozick's characterization of the view as "teleological retributivism," pp. 370–74 and Gertrude Ezorsky's use of that term in *Philosophical Perspectives on Punishment*.

11. Morris, "The Paternalistic Theory of Punishment," p. 268.

12. Nozick, pp. 369–80.

13. Ibid., pp. 374ff. The point is that if one is going to accept the idea that punishment is a communication, one is connecting it with human purposive activity, and hence the *purpose* of speaking to the criminal (as well as to the rest of society) becomes central to the justification of the communication itself. To deny this is simply to regard punishment as something fundamentally different from a species of communication (for example, to regard it as some kind of "value-linkage device") which Nozick seems reluctant to do.

14. *Los Angeles Times*, 30 July 1981, part. 4, p. 1.

15. Nozick has also found the "communication" element in comic book stories about revenge; see *Philosophical Explanations*, pp. 368–69.

16. Parental punishment can take many forms; although spanking and various kinds of corporal punishment are usually what spring to mind when one thinks of parental punishment, many parents punish through the expression of anger or disap-

proval, which can be interpreted by the child as a withdrawal of love or as the (at least temporary) loss of the parent's friendship. Such deprivations are in many ways far more serious than the momentary experience of bodily pain or the temporary loss of certain privileges, and hence, although they seem to be mild forms of punishment, they can in actuality be very severe. I am indebted to Herbert Morris for suggesting this point.

17. Because children are not completely responsible, rational beings, punishing them can also be justified as a way of encouraging in them certain kinds of morally desirable habits, insofar as it has "conditioning like" effects. Aristotle seems to regard punishment of children as, at least in part, playing this role. See for example *Nicomachean Ethics*, bk. I, chap. 4. I would not want to deny that aspect of parental punishment.

18. It is because I believe there are sharp and important differences between parental and state punishment that I eschew Herbert Morris's title for this type of punishment theory (that is, his title "the paternalistic theory of punishment").

19. Martin Luther King, Jr., "Letter from a Birmingham Jail," from *Civil Disobedience*, ed. H. A. Bedau (New York: Pegasus, 1969), pp. 78–9.

20. Some retributivists have tried to argue that the *lex talionis* needn't be regarded as a formula whose upper bound *must* be respected; see, for example, K. C. Armstrong, "The Retributivist Hits Back," *Philosophy of Punishment*, ed. H. B. Acton (London: Macmillan, 1969). However, critics can object that Armstrong's weaker retributivist position still does not *rule out* barbaric punishments (like torture) as permissible, nor does it explain why and when punishments which are less in severity than the criminal act can be legitimately inflicted.

21. Consider the START program used in a Connecticut prison to "rehabilitate" child molesters: electrodes were connected to the prisoner's skin, and then pictures of naked boys and girls were flashed on a screen while electric shocks were applied. The Federal Bureau of Prisons canceled this program just before they were about to lose a court challenge to the program's constitutionality (see David J. Rothman's discussion of this in "Behavior Modification in Total Institutions," *Hastings Center Report 5*, no. 1 [1975]: 22).

22. Apart from the fact that killing someone is hardly an appropriate technique for educating him, it is likely that this action sends a poor message to the rest of society about the value of human life. Indeed, in one of their national meetings, the Catholic bishops of the United States argued that repeal of capital punishment would send "a message that we can break the cycle of violence, that we need not take life for life, that we can envisage more human and more hopeful and effective responses to the growth of violent crime." ("Statement on Capital Punishment," *Origins* 10, no. 24 [27 November 1980]: 374.)

23. Nozick, pp. 373–74.

24. George Fletcher, in *Rethinking Criminal Law* (Boston: Little, Brown, 1978), p. 410, worries about defining punishment so that it doesn't include too much (for example, it should not include the impeachment of President Nixon, despite the fact that it would be a case of unpleasant consequences inflicted on Nixon by an authority in virtue of a wrongdoing). I do not have time here to consider how to hone my definition such that it will not encompass impeachments, deportation, tort damages, and so forth. Indeed, perhaps the only way one can do this is to bring into the definition of punishment its justification as moral education.

25. Compare Nozick's discussion of the content of the Gricean message of punishment, pp. 370–74.

26. I have profited from discussions with Katherine Shamey on this point.

27. See Hegel, *Philosophy of Right*, sec. 91.

28. Ibid., sec. 100, p. 70.

29. From "Criminals Can be Brainwashed—Now," *Psychology Today*, April 1970, p. 14; also quoted in Rick Carlson's *The Dilemma of Corrections* (Lexington, MA: Lexington Books, 1976), p. 35.

30. See "The Crime of Treatment," American Friends Service Committee from *The Struggle for Justice*, chap. 6 (New York: Hill and Wang, 1971) reprinted in *Punishment: Selected Readings*, eds., Feinberg and Gross.

31. Quoted by Carlson, p. 161; from David Fogel, *We Are the Living Proof* (Cincinnati: W. H. Anderson, n.d.).

32. Jeffrie Murphy has argued that instituting a rehabilitationist penal system would deny prisoners many of their present due process rights. See "Criminal Punishment and Psychiatric Fallacies," especially pp. 207–209, in *Punishment and Rehabilitation*, ed. J. Murphy. The American Friends Service Committee has also charged that the California penal system, which was heavily influenced by the rehabilitation theory, has in fact done this. See "The Crime of Treatment," pp. 91–93, in Feinberg et al.

33. See Morris's discussion of certain wrongdoers' need to experience punishment in "The Paternalistic Theory of Punishment," p. 267.

34. Kant, *Critique of Practical Reason*, "The Analytic of Pure Practical Reason," Remark II. (Abbott trans. in *Kant's Theory of Ethics* [London: Longman, 1959], p. 127; Academy edition, p. 38.)

35. Walter Moberly, *The Ethics of Punishment* (London: Faber & Faber, 1968), p. 141.

36. Nozick, pp. 374ff.

37. For example, see Hegel, *The Philosophy of Right*, sec. 101–103.

38. J. L. Mackie, "Morality and the Retributive Emotions," in *Criminal Justice Ethics* 1, no. 1 (Winter/Spring 1982): 3–10. In the face of the retributivists' failure to explain why punishment is deserved, Mackie wants to argue that our retributive intuitions spring from fundamental retributive emotions, which are part of a human being's fundamental moral make-up (and he gives a sketch of how our evolution as a species could have generated such emotions). But many retributivists, particularly the Kantian sort, would eschew such an explanation which, in any case, is hardly a *justification* of the retributive impulse itself.

39. Jesus rejected not only "negative retributivism," that is, the idea that we deserve bad for doing bad, but also "positive retributivism," that is, the idea that we deserve good for doing good, but I cannot go into that here.

40. Indeed, I believe that it is because retribution would justify punishment as a deserved evil that it strikes many as much too close to revenge.

JEFFRIE G. MURPHY
Mercy and Legal Justice*

I looked at him. Alive. His lap a puddle of blood. With the restoration of the normal order of matter and sensation, I felt I was seeing him for the first time as a person. The old human muddles and quirks were set flowing again. Compassion, remorse, mercy.

Don DeLillo
White Noise

Internal and External Questions. The most profound questions in ethics, social philosophy, and the philosophy of law are foundational; i.e., they are questions that call the entire framework of our ordinary evaluations into doubt in order to determine to what degree, if at all, that framework can be rationally defended. Such questions, called "external" by Rudolf Carnap, are currently dominating my own philosophical reflections and are forcing me to rethink a variety of positions I have in the past defended.[1]

Because my current thinking about external foundational questions is in such a state of flux, it is with some anxiety that I turn to the "internal" questions that motivate the present essay, i.e., questions that accept "our" ordinary framework of evaluation as a given and seek to explore certain tensions and puzzles within that framework in order to see to what degree that framework is internally coherent. The goal is to attain, if possible, that nirvana of moral epistemology that John Rawls calls "reflective equilibrium."[2] In spite of my increasing skepticism about the value of reflective equilibrium in foundational moral theory,[3] I am still inclined to believe (a) that internal coherence is relevant to external evaluation and (b) that questions of an internal nature, if properly explored with an appreciation of their limits, can be interesting and important in their own right.[4] Thus, I shall temporarily suppress my initial anxiety and plow ahead on the matter at hand.

*Jeffrie G. Murphy, ''Mercy and Legal Justice,'' *Social Philosophy and Policy*, Vol. 4, No. 1 (1986), pp. 1–14. Reprinted by permission of Basil Blackwell Ltd.

Mercy and Justice. We are ordinarily inclined to believe—or at least pay lip service to—the claim that justice and mercy are both moral virtues. We are also inclined to maintain that both of these virtues are characteristic of such lofty objects as God (as conceived in the Judeo-Christian tradition[5]) and of such all too human objects as legal systems—where in literature and folklore we celebrate (perhaps without fully understanding what we are saying) those judges who can "temper their justice with mercy." As we expect God as cosmic judge to manifest both justice and mercy, so too do we expect this of secular judges. Or so we often say. Shakespeare's two important "comedies of mercy," for example, contain some of the most often quoted sentiments on mercy and justice in our civilization—so often quoted, indeed, that they have attained the status of clichés and may any day find their way onto Hallmark cards or table napkins:

The quality of mercy is not strain'd;
It droppeth as the gentle rain from heaven
Upon the place beneath: it is twice blessed;
It blesseth him that gives and him that takes:
'Tis mightiest in the mightiest; it becomes
The throned monarch better than his crown;
His sceptre shows the force of temporal power,
The attribute to awe and majesty,
Wherein doth sit the dread and fear of kings;
But mercy is above this scepter'd sway,—
It is enthroned in the heart of kings,
It is an attribute to God himself;
And earthly power doth then show likest God's
When mercy seasons justice.
(*Merchant of Venice*, IV, I; Portia speaks)

No ceremony that to great ones 'longs,
Not the king's crown, nor the deputed sword,
The marshall's truncheon, nor the judge's robe,
Become them with one half so good a grace
As mercy does.
(*Measure for Measure*, II, II; Isabella speaks)

These passages express some fairly widely held—and closely related—views about mercy:

(1) It is an *autonomous* moral virtue (i.e., it is not reducible to some other virtue—especially justice). (2) It is a virtue that tempers or "seasons" justice, something that one adds to justice (the primary virtue) in order to dilute it and perhaps—if one takes the metallurgical metaphor of tempering seriously—to make it stronger. (3) It is never owed to anyone as a right or a matter of desert or justice. It always, therefore, transcends the realm of strict moral obligation and is best viewed as a free gift—an act of grace, love, or compassion that is beyond the claims of right, duty, and obligation. ("The quality of mercy is not [con]strained.") (4) As a moral virtue, it derives its value at least in part from the fact that it flows from a certain kind of *character*—a character disposed to perform merciful acts from love or compassion while not losing sight of the importance of justice. (5) It requires a generally retributive outlook on punishment and responsibility. Mercy is often regarded as found where a judge, out of compassion for the plight of a particular offender, imposes upon that offender a hardship less than his just deserts. This way of conceptualizing mercy requires, of course, that we be operating with a rich concept of "just desert"—something that is not easy to come by on a utilitarian/deterrence analysis.[6]

The foregoing suggests that there are certain other virtues or, at least, *desiderata* of moral and legal systems with which mercy often is but should not be confused: excuse, justification, and forgiveness. If a person has actually done the right thing (i.e., his conduct was justified), or if he was not responsible for what he did (i.e., he had a valid excuse), then it would simply be *unjust* to punish him, and no question of mercy need arise—for there is no responsible wrongdoing, and responsible wrongdoing is (it is commonly thought) the proper object of mercy.

Forgiveness is trickier. As I have argued elsewhere,[7] forgiveness is primarily a matter of changing how one *feels* with respect to a person who has done *oneself* an injury. It is particularly a matter of overcoming, on moral grounds, the *resentment* that a self-respecting person quite properly feels as a result of such an injury. Mercy, though related to forgiveness, is clearly different in at least these two respects. To be merciful to a person requires not merely that one change how one feels about that person but, also, requires a specific kind

of action (or omission)—namely, treating that person less harshly than, in the absence of the mercy, one would have treated him. This explains how we can forgive in our heart of hearts but cannot show mercy in our heart of hearts, why we can forgive the dead but cannot show mercy to the dead, and so forth. Also, it is not a requirement of my showing mercy that I be an injured party. All that is required is that I stand in a certain relation to the potential beneficiary of mercy. This relation—typically established by legal or other institutional rules—makes it *fitting* (I purposely speak vaguely here for reasons that will later become clear) that I impose some hardship upon the potential beneficiary of mercy.

The Paradoxes of Mercy. All is not well with the above rosy picture. For the following pattern of argument seems tempting: If mercy requires a tempering of justice, than there is a sense in which mercy may require a departure from justice. (Temperings are tamperings.) Thus, to be merciful is, perhaps, to be *unjust*. But it is a vice, not a virtue, to manifest injustice. Thus, mercy must be not a virtue, but a vice—a product of morally dangerous sentimentality. This is particularly obvious in the case of a sentencing judge. We (society) hire this individual to enforce the rule of law under which we live. We think of this as "doing justice," and the doing of this is surely his sworn obligation. What business does he have, then, ignoring his obligations to justice while he pursues some private, idiosyncratic, and not publicly accountable virtue of love or compassion?[8] Shakespeare, always sensitive to both sides of complex moral issues, captures this thought well even in the midst of his dramatic sermons on mercy:

I show [pity] most of all when I show justice,
For then I pity those I do not know,
Which a dismissed offense would after gall;
And do him right that, answering one foul wrong,
Lives not to act another.
(*Measure for Measure*, II, II; Angelo speaks[9])

Perhaps the clearest statements of the paradoxes I want to develop on mercy come from St. Anselm. His worry is about the divine nature—how God can be both just and merciful—but the paradoxes he formulates can easily be adapted to secular and legal concerns. He writes:

What justice is it that gives him who merits eternal death everlasting life? How, then, gracious Lord, good to the wicked, canst thou save the wicked if this is not just, and thou dost not aught that is not just? (*Proslogium* IX)

But if it can be comprehended in any way why thou canst will to save the wicked, yet by no consideration can we comprehend why, of those who are alike wicked, thou savest some rather than others, through supreme goodness, and why thou dost condemn the latter, rather than the former, through supreme justice. (*Proslogium* XI)

Though Anselm's specific worry is about the divine nature (Are the divine attributes of perfect justice and perfect compassion coherently ascribable to the same being?), he raises a general worry about the concepts of justice and mercy themselves—namely, to what degree (if at all) are they consistent? More specifically: If we simply use the term "mercy" to refer to certain of the demands of justice (e.g., the demand for individuation), then mercy ceases to be an autonomous virtue and instead becomes a part of (is reducible to a part of) justice. It thus beomes obligatory, and all the talk about gifts, acts of grace, supererogation, and compassion becomes quite beside the point. If, on the other hand, mercy is totally different from justice and actually requires (or permits) that justice sometimes be set aside, it then counsels injustice.[10] In short: mercy is either a vice (injustice) or redundant (a part of justice). (This is a gloss on Anselm's first paradox—from IX. The second paradox—from XI—will be explored in a later section.)

Some Specific Cases and Some Good Journal Articles. Two of the most interesting articles on mercy are those by Alwynne Smart and Claudia Card.[11] Both seek to establish that there is indeed a place for mercy in a world that takes the value of justice seriously, and both (Smart especially) develop a discussion of this general issue in terms of specific cases—cases that are supposed to test and hone our intuitions so that we can be in "reflective equilibrium" about the issues of justice and mercy.

Smart asks that we consider the following pairs of cases—cases that might face a sentencing judge who, we may suppose, has some discretion and is not bound by mandatory sentencing rules:

A	B
(1) The defendant, convicted of vehicular homicide, had his own child—whom he loved deeply—as his victim.	The defendant has been convicted of killing another person in cold blood.
(2) The defendant is a young and inexperienced criminal.	The defendant is a hardened career criminal.

According to Smart, "we" would all agree that the judge should impose a lighter sentence on those persons under *A* than on those under *B* and that it would be proper, in a perfectly ordinary sense of the word "mercy," to express "our" conviction about what he should do by saying that he should show mercy in those cases.

Let us suppose that Smart is correct here. It is proper for the judge to go easy here, and such easing up would be called by many people (prior to reading this essay) an act of mercy. This still strikes me as philosophically confused and as an obstacle to philosophical clarity on the concept of mercy. If we feel that the judge should go easy in cases under *A*, this is surely because we believe that there is some morally relevant feature that distinguishes these cases from those under *B*. What might this feature be? In (1) it is no doubt our conviction that the criminal has already suffered a great deal—perhaps even that he has suffered enough—and that the infliction of any additional misery by the state would be gratuitous and cruel.[12] In (2) we are no doubt influenced by the idea that the character of a younger person is less mature and thus less responsible than that of a hardened criminal.[13] But, if this is our thinking, then why talk of mercy here and confuse what we are doing with some moral virtue that requires the tempering of justice? For to avoid inflicting upon persons more suffering than they deserve, or to avoid punishing the less responsible as much as the fully responsible, is a simple—indeed, obvious—demand of *justice*. A basic demand of justice is that like cases be treated alike, and that morally relevant differences between persons be noticed and our treatment of those persons be affected by those differences. This demand for individuation—a tailoring of our retributive reponse to the individual natures of the persons with whom we are dealing—is a part of what we mean by taking persons seriously as persons and is thus a basic demand of justice. One could introduce a sense of "mercy" that means "seeking to tailor our response to morally relevant individual differences." But this would be confusing and dangerous: confusing because it would make us think that the rich literature noted above (Shakespeare, Anselm) was somehow relevant to this; dangerous because it might lead us to suppose that individuation was not owed to persons as a right and was thus somehow optional as a free gift or act of grace. But this would be deeply wrong. The legal rules, if they are just, will base required penal treatment on morally relevant differences *or* they will give judges the discretion to so do; and criminal defendants surely have a *right* that it be this way.[14] One could talk of mercy here, but why? (One might as well protest strict criminal liability offenses by saying that they are unmerciful.) Judges or lawmakers who are unmindful of the importance of individuated response are not lacking in mercy; they lack a sense of justice.[15] Recall our earlier dilemma: mercy is either a vice or is redundant. The above cases illustrate redundancy.

Smart is sensitive to the fact that not everyone will find her initial cases representative of mercy in any deep or interesting sense, and she thus introduces some additional cases in an attempt to capture a different and more important kind of mercy. These are cases where (unlike the earlier cases) we agree that some punishment *P* is, *all* relevant things about Jones considered, the just punishment for what Jones had done. Still, on moral grounds, we argue that a punishment less than *P* should be inflicted. We now have a virtue that is not redundant—is not merely reducible to justice. These are the cases:

(1) Jones's family, who need his support very much, would be harmed to an unacceptable degree if *P* is inflicted on Jones. Thus, we ought to show mercy to Jones and inflict less than *P*.

(2) Adverse social consequences will result if **P** is inflicted on Jones. (Perhaps he is a popular leader of the political opposition, and his followers will riot or commit acts of terrorism if **P** is inflicted on Jones.) Thus, we should show mercy to Jones.

(3) Jones has been in jail for a long time and has so reformed that he is, in a very real sense, a

"new person." Thus, we should show him mercy and grant him an early release.

These cases strike me as unpersuasive. It strikes me as analytic that mercy is based on a concern for the *defendant's* plight, and this feature is absent in (1) and (2). If we are showing mercy to anyone in (1) it is to Jones's family, and he is simply the indirect beneficiary of the mercy. But even this seems a confusing way to talk. In (1) and (2) one is basically choosing to bring about a net gain in utility. This may be reasonable if a utilitarian moral outlook is reasonable. But these cases would not be interestingly unique given that outlook; and, for reasons sketched above, it is not an outlook in which a concern with mercy as a special virtue would arise.

Case (3) is, of course, very different. But it, like Smart's earlier cases, seems simply a matter of justice. I am suspicious of "new person" talk. However, if there really are cases where we should take it literally, then it is obviously a matter of justice that one not punish one person for the crime of another. Why talk of mercy here?

In summary: We have yet to find one case of genuine mercy as an autonomous virtue. The cases we have explored represent either virtuous behavior that is simply a matter of justice *or* they represent cases of unjustified sentimentality *or* they represent cases where the demands of justice are thought to be overridden by the demands of utility. Thus some skepticism about mercy seems in order. Judges in criminal cases are obligated to do justice.[16] So too, I would argue, are prosecutors and parole boards in their exercise of discretion.[17] There is thus simply no room for mercy as an autonomous virtue with which their justice should be tempered. Let them keep their sentimentality to themselves for use in their private lives with their families and pets.

A New Paradigm for Mercy.[18] But could all the rich and moving literature of mercy be totally worthless—nothing but propaganda for mindless sentimentality? I think not; and I shall spend the remainder of this essay attempting to think about mercy in a new way—one which may allow us to give it some meaningful life as an autonomous moral virtue.

Thus far we have been operating with what might be called the Criminal Law Paradigm of mercy—thinking of mercy as a virtue that most typically would be manifested by a sentencing judge in a criminal case. This is the paradigm represented in *Measure for Measure,* where Isabella begs that Angelo, a judge in a criminal case involving her brother, will show her brother mercy. It is this paradigm, I have suggested, that is probably a failure.

But there is another paradigm—that represented in *Merchant of Venice*—a paradigm that I will call the Private Law Paradigm. In that play, you will recall, the central focus is on a *civil* case—a contract dispute. Antonio has made a bad bargain with Shylock and, having defaulted, is contractually obligated to pay Shylock a pound of his flesh. Portia, acting as judge, asks that Shylock show mercy to Antonio by not demanding the harsh payment.[19]

Note how radically this case differs from the criminal law case. A judge in a criminal case has an *obligation* to do justice—which means, at a minimum, an obligation to uphold the rule of law. Thus, if he is moved, even by love or compassion, to act contrary to the rule of law— to the rules of justice—he acts wrongly (because he violates an obligation) and manifests a vice rather than a virtue. A criminal judge, in short, has an obligation to impose the just punishment; and all of his discretion within the rules is to be used to secure greater justice (e.g., more careful individuation). No rational society would write any other "job description" for such an important institutional role.

But a litigant in a civil suit is not the occupier—in anything like the same sense—of an institutional role. He occupies a private role. He does not have an antecedent obligation, required by the rules of justice, to impose harsh treatment. He rather has, in a case like Shylock's, a *right* to impose harsh treatment. Thus, if he chooses to show mercy, he is simply *waiving a right* that he could in justice claim— not violating an obligation demanded by justice.[20] (Consider here the analogy with the rules of chivalric combat. The fallen knight begs for mercy. He is not asking that the victor violate an obligation to kill him but is, rather, asking that the victor waive a right to kill him.) And there is no contradiction, paradox, or even tension here. I do not necessarily show a lack of respect for justice by waiving my justice-based rights as I would by ignoring my justice-derived obligations.[21] Thus, in the Private Law Paradigm, the virtue of mercy is revealed when a person, out of compassion for the hard position of the person who owes him an obligation,

waives the right that generates the obligation and frees the individual of the burden of that obligation. People who are always standing on their rights, indifferent to the impact that this may have on others, are simply intolerable. Such persons cannot be faulted on grounds of justice, but they can certainly be faulted. And the disposition to mercy helps to check these narrow and self-involved tendencies present in each of us.[22] There is thus room for mercy as an important moral virtue with impact upon the law, but it is a virtue to be manifested by private persons using the law—*not* by officials enforcing the law.[23]

Note also that this Private Law Paradigm might help, by analogy, with Anselm's theological puzzle about mercy. Anselm sees a paradox in attributing both justice and mercy to God because he seems to see God as analogous to a judge in a criminal case—as someone with an obligation to enforce certain rules. But surely this is not the only model of God. God (at least on one fairly common view) is not bound by independent rules of obligation with respect to his creatures; for the rules of morality are, on this view, simply His commands. He does, however, have many *rights* with respect to His creatures. Thus, His mercy may be viewed as His deciding, out of love or compassion, to waive certain rights that He has—*not* to violate certain obligations that He has. Anselm's first paradox disappears.

Rationality and the Equal Protection Paradox. Is everything now coherent in the land of mercy? Is its status as an autonomous virtue, different from and tempering justice, intact, ready to be dispensed from our compassionate natures as a free gift or act of grace? Not quite. For Anselm's second paradox now appears to haunt us:

> But if it can be comprehended in any way why thou canst will to save the wicked, yet by no consideration can we comprehend why, of those who are alike wicked, thou savest some rather than others, through supreme goodness, and why thou dost condemn the latter, rather than the former, through supreme justice. (*Proslogium* XI)

Anselm here seems to be raising a kind of "equal protection" paradox: If God (or any other rational being) shows mercy, then the mercy must not be arbitrary or capricious, but must rather rest upon some good reason—some morally relevant feature of the situation that made the mercy seem appropriate. Compassion and love are, after all, cognitively loaded emotions; they are not sensations like headaches or tickles. Thus, they are the sorts of reactions for which reasons may be given; and where reasons are given, it is possible to distinguish good from bad reasons, relevant from irrelevant ones. ("I showed him mercy because he was so sick" has a kind of sense lacking in "I showed him mercy because he was so handsome.") But once a reason, always a reason. And does not the Principle of Sufficient Reason require that if I, as a rational being, showed mercy to Jones because of characteristic C, then it is presumably required of me (rationally required, not morally required) that I show comparable mercy to C-bearing Smith?[24] But if so, then what becomes of all this grace/free gift talk when applied to mercy? (Of course, there can even be reasons for gifts: "It is your birthday.") Is it nothing more than this: I am not ever required to show mercy, but if I show it even once then I am rationally required to show it to all relevantly similar persons? But if I show mercy for a reason (which must be the case, if mercy is not simply capricious) does not that reason then *require* that I show mercy whenever I recognize the presence of that reason? The showing of mercy may not be an obligation in the strong sense (based on rights), but it may be something I *ought-for-a-reason* to do. In that case it cannot *totally* be a free act of grace. Some of Anselm's second paradox thus remains.

Internal and External Again.[25] Let me briefly return to the worry about foundations. It seems to be the case that "we" (all well brought up, educated, middle-class intellectuals?) see justice to be the primary value with respect to law, but that we also want to find some place for mercy as a secondary virtue to temper or otherwise have some effect on justice. It is interesting to inquire into why we think this and into whether our common pattern of thought is rationally justified.

Suppose that Gilbert Harman is right about ethics: our moral views are simply conventions that result from tacit bargains struck between the weak and poor and the rich and powerful—bargains where each attempts to maximize his self-interest while still securing the vital benefits of social cooperation.[26] This might be a start toward explaining some of our ordinary views about justice and mercy. Justice—the

regular enforcement of the rules that make social stability (and thus social life) possible—will be a strong priority of all parties to the bargain—whether rich or poor, strong or weak. Not all will have the same stake in these rules, but all (or almost all) will have a high stake. Thus, it is not difficult to see why conventions of justice should have a very high priority. Mercy, however, is a different matter. It is more likely to be needed by the poor and weak than by the rich and powerful, and thus it is easy to see why it is present (some level of it is perhaps required to secure the cooperation and compliance of the disadvantaged) but also easy to see why it does not have the dominant role that justice has—why it only tempers justice but never replaces or supersedes it.

The bargaining model of moral conventions might also provide a start toward dealing with Anselm's second paradox—namely, if I show mercy to C-bearing Jones, how can I consistently (morally?) fail to show mercy to equally C-bearing Smith? If moral conventions are viewed as agreements based on rational self-interest, then the impact *on me* of my continued showings of mercy would become relevant. Thus, what relevantly distinguishes the Jones case from the Smith case will not be some feature that distinguishes Jones from Smith but, rather, some feature that distinguishes the impact on me of mercy to Jones from the impact on me of mercy to Smith. The mere fact that Jones got there first (or I noticed him first) might then make a great deal of difference. I show mercy to Jones, who is pitiful to degree P, and thus forgive his debt to me of five dollars. Smith, who is also pitiful to degree P, also owes me five dollars. I do not show him mercy, however, because, though I can afford the loss of five dollars, I cannot afford the loss of ten. Also, I may begin to fear—quite legitimately—that if I start to make a practice of showing mercy instead of simply showing it every now and then when the spirit moves me, I will be taken for an easy mark in future dealings with those who might attempt to exploit my perceived good will. Thus, if rational persons thought that once having shown mercy they would be stuck with making a regular practice of it, they might be inclined never to show it at all. But since, as I argued above, there are reasons why rational agents would agree to conventions establishing some level of mercy, they would not want to adopt a principle of mercy that would give rational persons incentives never to show it. And thus they would probably agree with the adoption of mercy as what Kant called an imperfect duty—a duty that admits of wide latitude in the time and manner of its fulfilment.[27]

And what does all this have to do with rational justification? I am not sure. But I suppose that, with respect to any bargain or convention, if it is the case that it represents, for each party, the best deal he could have struck for himself under the circumstances, then it may be called rational in some minimal sense. This may not be much (not what Kant, for example, would like the connection between morality and rationality to be), but it strikes me as a more impressive argument for a moral view than the argument that the view would put Mr. and Mrs. Front Porch in a state of reflective equilibrium with respect to their moral intuitions. But this is a very complex issue and should be—and will be—left to be pursued in another context.

NOTES

Several persons were kind enough to comment on earlier drafts of this paper, and I wish to thank them here: Lewis Beck, Ray Elugardo, Herbert Granger, Joshua Halberstam, Sterling Harwood, Margaret Holmgren, Lisa Isaacson, David Lyons, and Gareth Matthews. I learned a great deal from each of their comments—far more than the few changes I was able to make in the paper will indicate.

1. See Jeffrie G. Murphy and Jules L. Coleman, *The Philosophy of Law* (Totowa: Rowman and Allenheld, 1984) and Jeffrie G. Murphy, "Retributivism, Moral Education, and the Liberal State," *Criminal Justice Ethics*, vol. 4 (Winter/Spring 1985).

2. John Rawls, *A Theory of Justice* (Cambridge: Harvard University Press, 1971) pp. 48–51.

3. See my "Rationality and Constraints on Democratic Rule," J. Roland Pennock and John W. Chapman, eds., *Nomos XXVIII: Justification* (New York: New York University Press, 1986), pp. 141–164.

4. See, for example, Joel Feinberg, *Harm to Others* (Oxford: Oxford University Press, 1984). Feinberg explicitly refuses to address foundational issues (taking a kind of "liberalism" as a given) and still manages to enrich our thinking about morality and the criminal law to a profound degree.

5. "Even God prays. What is His prayer? 'May it be My will that My love of compassion overwhelm My demand for strict justice.' " Mahzhor for Yom Kippur, The Rabbinical Assembly of New York, 439 (from Berakhot 7a).

6. Note that this is a list of commonly held views about mercy and its relation to justice. I shall later argue that some of these views—(5) in particular—are distorted or mistaken.

7. "Forgiveness and Resentment," Peter A. French, *et al.*, eds. *Midwest Studies in Philosophy, VII: Social and Political Philosophy* (Minneapolis: University of Minnesota Press, 1982) pp. 503–516.

8. Note that I describe the judge's job to be that of upholding the *rule of law*. I mean by this the upholding of legal rules that meet certain standards of justice, not the mechanical upholding of any legal rules at all no matter how unjust they may be. Of course, I do not believe that judges should enforce legal rules in the absence of any reflection on the merits of those rules from the point of view of justice. If the rules are unjust, then if the judge has discretion, he should use that discretion to seek to do justice. (If the judge has no discretion and if the rules are terribly unjust, then such drastic acts as resignation or civil disobedience may be in order.) These complexities, however, do not show a need for a special virtue of mercy; and only a highly impoverished view of justice (i.e., that it is simply mechanical rule following) would make one think that these complexities could not be dealt with in terms of a sophisticated theory of justice.

9. The point here, I take it, is that the judge who is influenced by the plight of the offender before him may lose sight of the fact that his job is to uphold an entire system of justice that protects the rights and security of all citizens.

10. A critic has suggested that I am here confusing the unjust with the *non*-just—that I fail to notice that some acts (perhaps some acts of mercy) are non-just (neutral from the point of view of justice) in that they are neither unjust nor required by justice. What bearing might this observation have, even if correct, on the issue of mercy in a criminal law context? None that I can see. To be morally acceptable, a non-just act would at least have to be *permitted* by the rules of justice; but, on standard versions of retributive justice (e.g., Kant's), it is *not* permitted from the moral point of view that persons receive less punishment than, in justice, they deserve. To give them less punishment would be to do an injustice.

11. Alwynne Smart, "Mercy," H. B. Acton, ed., *The Philosophy of Punishment* (New York: St. Martin's Press, 1969), pp. 212–227. (Smart's article originally appeared in *Philosophy*, October 1968). Claudia Card, "Mercy," *Philosophical Review*, vol. XLIII (April 1972), pp. 182–207. Since Smart's essay provides me with a useful starting point from which to develop what I want to say about mercy, I will focus my discussion primarily around her piece and will thus not give Card's rich essay the detailed discussion it deserves. I will comment on it only in passing. Card, like Smart, operates within what I will later call the Criminal Law Paradigm for mercy (a paradigm I will reject) and, also like Smart, she seems to offer a view of mercy that makes it a part of justice (on a sophisticated theory of justice) and not an autonomous moral virtue.

12. The idea that natural suffering can serve as a substitute for legally imposed suffering is complex and perhaps incoherent; see my "Forgiveness and Resentment," p. 509 and note 17.

13. Perhaps we also think that prison will be harder on them and thus that they may suffer more than they deserve. Perhaps we might also think that young people are more likely to be influenced by the bad environment that prison represents.

The idea that it is immoral to impose a level of suffering out of proper proportion to a person's character is also central to Card's view of mercy. She writes: "Mercy ought to be shown to an offender when it is evident that otherwise (1) he would be made to suffer unusually more on the whole, owing to his peculiar misfortunes, than he deserves in view of his basic character and (2) he would be worse off in this respect than those who stand to benefit from the exercise of their right to punish him (or to have him punished). When the conditions of this principle are met, the offender deserves mercy." ("Mercy," p. 184) Card thus seems explicitly to classify merciful acts as a subcategory of just acts, and not as acts autonomous from justice. But then I fail to understand how she can say (also on p. 184) that "desert of mercy does not give rise to an obligation."

14. In commenting on an earlier draft of this paper, Lewis Beck raised the question of how the demand for individuation (which I suggest is a demand of justice) can be squared with the common and intuitively compelling metaphor that "justice is blind." The short answer, I think, is this: justice is not to be totally blind but is, rather, to be blind to all aspects of an individual that do not have a bearing on the question of what his just treatment or just deserts really are, e.g., race, sexual attractiveness and willingness, ability to bribe, etc.

15. Those who desire to talk about mercy in this context probably do so because they have an overly restricted and simplistic conception of justice and thus fail to appreciate all that would be involved in a sophisiticated theory of retributive justice and the role of the judiciary in implementing such a theory. It might be worth noting, in this regard, that in our particular legal system most visible law-reforming judicial activism in the cause of greater individuation will take place at the level of a court of appeals. Trial judges (in giving instructions, for example) and trial juries (in refusing to convict, for example) may move toward greater justice in particular cases, but what they do does not become a public and permanent part of the law in the obvious way provided by written opinions of a court of appeals (particularly the Supreme Court).

16. Recall that by this claim I do not mean that judges are always obligated to enforce any rule no matter how unjust that rule may be. My point is rather this: the focus of a judge, either in enforcing a rule *or* in seeking a way to modify or get around it, is to be on the question of what is required by justice—not on what he may be prompted out of compassion to do.

17. Special problems may arise for a chief executive or head of state in his exercise of the power of pardon. The "job description" for such an office may, to borrow some language from Aquinas, involve a concern for the common good or common welfare of the community in the executive's care. This might mean that, in deciding whether or not to pardon an individual, the chief executive (unlike a judge) might legitimately draw upon values other than the requirements of justice and thus might legitimately ignore the just deserts of an individual and pardon that individual if the good of the community requires it. This whole account, of course, presupposes a political theory of the various offices and roles required by society and a theory of the proper values and decision-making criteria proper to (and perhaps unique to) each of the offices and roles. Space does not allow the articulation, must less the defense, of such a theory here.

18. This section draws heavily on P. Twambley's important article "Mercy and Forgiveness," *Analysis,* vol. 36 (January 1976), pp. 84–90.

19. Portia serves a complex role in the play. She does not simply represent the virtue of mercy but also stands as a representative of hypocrisy, unjust manipulation, and anti-Semitism.

20. There may be special problems in cases (defamation?) where tort suits aid in upholding certain socially important rules and protections. In this sense they are not purely private legal matters even though they are handled in the private law rather than in the criminal law. Thus, there may be cases where an individual might feel a public responsibility to proceed with a private lawsuit.

21. I say "not necessarily" because there are cases where a refusal to stand on one's rights and demand just treatment would reveal a lack of self-respect and a lack of respect for oneself as a morally relevant object (and thus a lack of respect for the rules of morality themselves). Of course, not every case of standing on one's rights (no matter how trivial) is of this nature.

22. Sterling Harwood has suggested to me in correspondence that the tempering metaphor might illuminate if applied to persons and their dispositions rather than to the rules of justice themselves. A person, on this view, should temper his just personality (a dominant disposition to see that justice is done) by developing (if possible) a disposition to be merciful (an openness to being moved by the plight of others to the degree that one will not always demand one's just rights from them). This suggestion seems correct to me. Bishop Butler, in his classic sermons "Upon Resentment" and "Upon the Forgiveness of Injuries" is, of course, brilliant on such topics.

23. Should judges in civil cases folow Portia's lead and encourage litigants in some cases to show mercy? Perhaps; but there are problems here. The desire to settle cases and avoid the human and financial costs of litigation is certainly a reasonable one; but, as Jules Coleman and Charles Silver have argued elsewhere in this volume, there are serious social costs involved in settlement as well, e.g., the cost of not having the law clarified in the way that actual litigation makes possible.

24. For a discussion of the Principle of Sufficient Reason (a rational being will not prefer one thing over another without basing that preference upon some relevant difference between the things) and equal protection, see my "Justifying Departures from Equal Treatment," *Journal of Philosophy* (October 1984), pp. 587–593.

25. This section of the paper was greatly improved by some comments and suggestions of Ray Elugardo.

26. Gilbert Harman, "Justice and Moral Bargaining," *Social Philosophy and Policy,* vol. 1 (Autumn 1983), pp. 114–131. Similar views may also be found in such otherwise diverse thinkers as Hume, Marx, and Nietzsche.

27. For a stimulating argument that Kantian conclusions can be generated from egoistic premises and that central Kantian doctrines can be rationally reconstructed on the basis of models that initially seem anti-Kantian, see David Gauthier, "The Unity of Reason: A Subversive Reinterpretation of Kant," *Ethics,* vol. 96 (October 1985), pp. 74–88. As Lisa Isaacson has pointed out to me, the analysis presented in this final section of the paper will probably not help with the paradoxes of divine mercy, for it is probably not reasonable to view God's morality as a result of a bargain He strikes with humanity in order to advance His interests.

EXACTLY WHAT IS BEING PUNISHED?

RICHARD PARKER
Blame, Punishment, and the Role of Result*

Rasputin, the story goes, was poisoned with cyanide, shot with pistols, bludgeoned, stabbed, emasculated, then tied with cords, wrapped in cloth and dumped through a hole in the ice in the Neva River. When the body was found, it was discovered that he had worked part way out of his bonds before he succumbed; the cause of death was drowning. Let us suppose for a moment that the object of these horrors had proved, incredibly, to be an even more recalcitrant victim than he was and that he had actually survived his ordeal. Clearly, this supposition has no effect at all with respect to the intentions of Prince Yusupov and his cohorts, the perpetrators of the crime, nor does it affect their conduct in any substantial way—they did everything they could to ensure Rasputin's death, employing means well beyond those ordinarily required. Had he survived, due to his own incredible efforts and constitution, would that diminish the seriousness of the crime committed against him? However we decide to answer this question, it is clear that Rasputin's survival would substantially change the culpability and statutory punishability of Yusupov and company in practically every jurisdiction within the scope of Anglo-American law. It is true, of course, that the parties guilty of such a crime could be punished very severely under existing statutes, but, compared to the penalty for murder, the sanctions attached to aggravated assault, attempted murder, battery, and mayhem—the offenses for which Yusupov is most likely indictable on our supposition—are clearly less forbidding.

I bring up this rather exotic example from the history of homicide to introduce what seems to me to be a serious difficulty in our system of criminal justice. The difficulty, in its most general form, can be put in terms of a question: on what rational grounds can we proportion punishment to the results of an actor's conduct when those results are largely or entirely beyond the actor's control? The distinction between attempts and completed crimes is only the most visible of many which call up this question. Felony-murder, misdemeanor-manslaughter, and reckless or negligent conduct of many kinds involve the same or an analogous problem. In what follows I'll concentrate on a few rather more mundane examples than the Rasputin incident, with particular attention to certain moral aspects of the issues.

I

It is often said that one who engages in criminal wrongdoing thereby incurs a debt to society; the wrongdoer's punishment is conceived as the coin in which the debt is payable. That he owes the debt to *society* rather than to some private individual or collective (who may have suffered a loss at his hands) is often said to be the key to the distinction between criminal law and tort law, or, perhaps better, between criminal harm and tortious harm. Lawrence Becker has discussed this matter[1] with helpful results especially with respect to the analysis of criminal or "social" harm and the role this notion should rightly play in the law of attempts. The position he takes is that it is the *attempt* to accomplish harm, whether the attempt succeed or fail, which is properly the concern of the society and hence the business of criminal law. Attempts, Becker argues, produce as much justifiable social volatility—his phrase for upset, anxiety, fear, and generally unfavorable reaction—as do successful crimes.[2] Hence the

*Richard Parker, "Blame, Punishment, and the Role of Result," a revision of a paper in *American Philosophical Quarterly*, Vol. 21, no. 3 (1984), pp. 1–11. Reprinted by permission of the author and *American Philosophical Quarterly*.

criminal law should make no distinction as regards punishability between a full-fledged attempt and a success, other things being equal.

In a few moments, I shall argue for Becker's conclusion on other, but related, grounds. First, though, I should point out how strongly this conclusion runs counter to both current practice and popular opinion.

In the history of criminal law, the punishment of unsuccessful attempts and other conduct which fails to produce harm is a relatively recent development.[3] Indeed, among the "basic premises which underlie the whole of Anglo-American criminal law" is the statement that, "since the criminal law aims to prevent harm to the public, there can be no crime without harm."[4] Clearly, we do not follow this dictum to the letter, as the law defines many criminal offenses which merely *tend* to have harmful consequences (such as forgery) or which merely produce dangerous situations (such as reckless driving). Still, the emphasis put on actual harm caused is a principal ingredient of the method we use to grade the seriousness of crimes and to determine the severity of punishments.[5] It can also make the difference between criminal and noncriminal conduct.[6]

As is usually the case with the substantive criminal law, there seems to be a connection between the law's emphasis on harm and certain moral intuitions which many people apparently share. It may strike us as gratuitous, for example, to punish a person for an action which in fact caused nobody any harm. What are we punishing him for? one might ask. On the other hand, there is a clear answer to this question if a harmful result is actually produced: he is punished for causing that result. Furthermore, since the criminal law is connected to moral blameworthiness (at least in a way that tort law is not),[7] it is not surprising that most people seem to find it easier to blame one who causes harm more than one who does not. I believe that blameworthiness and punishability should where possible run parallel in the law, but I think it is false that results are generally relevant either to one's blameworthiness or to his punishability.

Consider the following story: you and I attend a party and get roaring drunk. In our host's den we discover a pair of loaded rifles and decide to find out which of us is the better shot by firing out a window at a lamp across the street. Each of us takes several shots, with no ill effect on the lamp. One of your shots, how-

ever, ricochets off the lamppost or by some similar means finds its way into a citizen who, unknown to us, happened to be nearby. The citizen dies as a result of his wound. Now, given the similarity of our conduct, it seems perfectly appropriate to claim equal blameworthiness on our parts. This can be made quite clear, I think, by varying the case a bit. Suppose first that it is not immediately known which of our bullets, yours or mine, that caused the fatal result. It seems strange that we should have to wait to apportion blame until this determination is made, for most people would surely agree that what is necessary to make this apportionment is present in this case before we know whose bullet caused the death. If we *never* discover whose bullet did the fatal damage, is there some hesitancy, some cloudiness of our intuition with respect to how much comparative blame the two of us deserve? I think not. I think most people would be satisfied with equal blame between us, and, importantly, nobody would worry much about a mistake having been made—the mistake of one of us being blamed for something he didn't do or the other for not being blamed for something he did do. If unequal blame is due us, the pain of inconsistency can be avoided only by showing a relevant difference between us. And, if it can be shown that the only difference is that made by the fact that one fired the fatal bullet and one did not, and if it can further be determined that this difference is due to chance (which would be the case if, e.g., only a ballistics test could show whose bullet it was), then there clearly is no *morally* relevant difference between us at all. Hence we are equally blameworthy despite the unequal results of our conduct.

A possible argument on the other side goes this way: one of us is *more blameable* because he is blameable *for more*.[8] I believe that either this argument is question begging, in which case it is valid but has a premise that is false, or else it is a non sequitur. The second alternative is simpler to explain. "Blameable for" is connected in obvious ways to "caused." If you, in our story of a while ago, are said to be blameable for more merely in the sense that you caused more harm, then I have no objection beyond the remark that this way of putting it is misleading. But in this case it simply doesn't follow that you are more blameable in the sense of *morally* blameable. The alternative view of the argument has an individual being blameworthy, in the straightforward moral sense, for the *result* of the action as well as the action itself. The blameworthiness for these *two* items is apparently supposed to "add up" to more blame. Now, there is an obvious distinction between an actor's conduct on one hand and, on the other, that chain of events that begins where his conduct stops and which continues on indefinitely. The view I am urging here is that, properly speaking, only an actor's conduct can be blameworthy. I do not believe that it makes good sense to blame a person for the consequences that in fact flow from his conduct even if they are within the risk of that conduct.[9] I hasten to add that I do not mean that he cannot be held responsible for harm caused that is within the risk of his conduct. I maintain only that such harm is tortious rather than criminal and should be actionable only as such. A burden may rightfully be placed on a person for the harm he causes, but this is conceptually distinct from punishment and does not entail blameworthiness. The individual is blameworthy and punishable, on my view, only for the conduct itself, where conduct is construed as a combination of overt action, state of mind (including intention, knowledge, etc.) and circumstances. Common sense will have to serve here as a guide, and there is good reason to believe that it can.

Consider another example. Imagine that A takes a rifle to a place overlooking a stadium where he knows an event is underway and recklessly fires the weapon in the direction of the grandstands. Let us suppose the fortunate consequence of the bullet's striking the bleachers harmlessly after narrowly missing members of the crowd. Compare this with the situation of B, who takes his rifle to the same spot on a day when he knows there is no event scheduled and in fact believes the grandstands to be entirely empty. He too fires toward the seats but with unfortunate results: a lone custodian is present policing the stands and he is struck and killed by B's bullet. It takes either a considerable stretch of the imagination or adherence to a bad theory, or both, to want to hold B more blameworthy than A. Truly, the harm caused by B's conduct far outweighs that cause by A's, the latter being negligible. But it is A, on the view I am defending, who is the more blameworthy and whose desert is the greater punishment.

The last example makes it clear what I want to use as a substitute for harm as the device for determining blameworthiness and punishment: the *risk* of harm that the conduct creates.

In the example as described there is another relevant factor: A's *knowingly* creating the risk—he knew there was a crowd in the stands—and B's ignorance of the custodian's presence. In the usual terminology, these circumstances are captured by saying that A's conduct was reckless while B's was negligent. And it is true that we generally find more fault in the former than in the latter. There are at least two things to be said about that. First, I would hold the same view of A's and B's blameworthiness and punishability if B's behavior were reckless instead of merely negligent; if, that is, he had known about the presence of the custodian. In such case, both A and B knowingly create risks, but A creates the greater risk and hence is more punishable. Second, it seems very plausible to believe that one reason why we judge reckless behavior more culpable than negligent behavior is that the former is riskier. A person who will perform an action *knowing* it is likely to cause harm is more apt to actually cause harm than one who would act only if he were ignorant of the likely harm, and this is the case even if the latter *should* have been aware of the harmful prospects (i.e., he is negligent by the standard of the reasonable man).

In cases of recklessness and negligence, it is fair and accurate to speak of the person who causes harm and, on current practice, is punished for it beyond what he would have been had no harm resulted, as being punished for his bad luck. (And it is his bad luck that he is being punished!) Seen this way, I think it is plain that the "extra" punishment is impossible to justify morally. In fact, if there is *something* wrong with punishing for harm caused in cases like these, then there is *everything* wrong with it. Let me borrow a statement of the relevant principle from Hyman Gross—the principle that liability ought to match culpability, a "general principle of proportion between crime and punishment,"

is a principle of just desert that serves as the foundation of every criminal sentence that is justifiable. . . . Indeed, the requirement that punishment not be disproportionately great, which is a corollary of just desert, is dictated by the same principle that does not allow punishment of the innocent, for any punishment in excess of what is deserved for the criminal conduct is punishment without guilt.[10]

I need to add only that nobody is ever guilty of having bad luck, at least not in any relevant sense of "guilty."

In the recent examples, the person causing the harm in each case might indeed be said to be guilty by misfortune. The other side of this coin are those who are innocent by good fortune. Attempters, among others, fall into this category, and the position I advocate in such cases is in principle the same as that regarding negligently and recklessly caused harm. Whether we are talking about intentional or unintentional creation of risk, that is to say, has nothing to do with the point at issue: a person who performs a last step attempt—that is, one who does everything within his power that he believes necessary to complete a crime—and whose failure is due to a chance event not within his control, is no less blameworthy and ought to be no less punishable than one who is successful in bringing his intended result about. The reason is exactly analogous to those in the earlier cases: there are no grounds for punishing the attempter and the successful offender differently aside from the already criticized grounds of punishing for whatever good or bad luck attends one's activities. Punishment on these grounds is no less immoral than unequal punishment for unequal results in cases of negligence. For, if a given punishment is the just desert for a completed crime, then no less a punishment is the just desert of at least some attempts to commit that crime.[11] On the other hand, if we punish the attempter less than the successful offender, we punish the latter "in excess of what is deserved for the criminal conduct." Indeed, the punishment we visit on the successful criminal beyond that which we visit on the attempter is nothing less than "punishment without guilt."

II

The conclusion just reached may seem strange at first. If it does it is probably because of an underlying conceptual shift entailed by the present view. The shift is as follows. I've said that it is the risk-creating aspect of conduct that makes it punishable and not the results of that conduct. Implicit in that claim is a change in the very notion of a crime. For anything that counts as a *result* of conduct rather than a *part of* that conduct ought not strictly speaking be a part of a crime; only conduct can be criminal. This produces some admittedly strange results. For example, on the view I present, there can be no such crime as murder, at least as it is currently conceived, because on the current

view the production of a corpse is, in a crucial sense, an irrelevant feature. (The sense in which it *is* relevant will be noted in a moment.) What is crucially relevant is the *likelihood* of a death resulting from the conduct in question. Consider the case of A, who produces a water pistol and begins squirting water at B, confident in his belief that he can kill B by eroding him to death.[12] We are not quick to find A guilty of a serious crime because, despite his intention and his action, he has done little that is likely to produce serious harm to B. Possibly more serious is the case of C, who puts a harmless drug in D's drink, thinking it is strychnine. The kind of conduct of which C is guilty may be dangerous indeed; exactly how dangerous it is depends largely upon what measures he took to ensure that the drug was strychnine. If it was incompetence that produced the mistake—he was suffering from the delusion that strychnine was contained in the sugar bowl on D's dinner table, for example—then the seriousness, and the likelihood of his harming D, is minimal. If it was chance—e.g., he happened to pick up an unlabeled bottle of saccharin that was next to his unlabeled strychnine bottle—then the seriousness and the dangerousness of the conduct escalate dramatically.

Gross provides a notion of harmful conduct that helps clarify matters. Harmful conduct is conduct that may or may not cause actual harm, but, if it does not, this fortunate consequence is due merely to chance.[13] This notion allows a concise statement of the primary claim I seek to defend: conduct is blameworthy and may create liability for punishment because and to the extent that it is harmful. There is also the corollary that an act may be deemed a crime to the extent that it is harmful.[14]

This principle (or these principles) may, with luck, capture the intuitions of those who were persuaded by the earlier claim that we ought not to punish those whose actions produce harm as the result of chance any more than those whose similar actions produce no harm. But it is important to notice that an action performed with evil intent is as well included under this principle as one performed negligently; we are talking about the entire array of criminal activity because we are talking about the very notion of a crime.

I indicated that the harm actually produced by conduct is not always irrelevant to an evaluation of the culpability attributable to that conduct, even on the theory proposed here. The relevance of a harmful result is in the form of evidence that the conduct in question was indeed harmful. In the case of the drunken shooting match that you and I held a few pages back, there is a claim that I can make that you cannot, i.e., that I *knew* that my bullets would not strike anybody. Under the circumstances described I would hardly be able to give any grounds for it, but it might, with corroborating evidence, provide a defense under circumstances where my conduct was not *ex hypothesi* as risky as that which actually produced the fatal harm. In general, the production of a harmful result is *prima facie* evidence that the conduct that produced it was likely to produce it. Such a result, or lack of one, would ordinarily help to locate properly a burden of proof on the defense or the prosecution, respectively. This, it seems to me, is the proper function of result. If it actually played this role, the conceptual scheme in many criminal cases would be substantially different from what it is currently. For example, the crime of involuntary manslaughter—a felony in most states—would be stricken from the books. A person who, on current practice, is indictable for such a crime would stand trial, on my view, for an offense of negligence or recklessness, and the death he caused would be offered as evidence of the negligence or recklessness of his conduct.

III

Let's next take a brief look at what seems to be behind most of the opposition to the view I have presented. There are two items that bear scrutiny in the accepted opinion. First, there is the view that, when an individual does something that might cause harm, he is taking a gamble of a sort, and when one gambles there are times when he wins and times when he loses. If one wins, so much the better; there is no harm done and nothing to pay for. If he loses, then he should be prepared to pay for it. After all, one hears, life itself is a gamble. This view has very little to recommend it. While it is true that we all take risks whether we get out of bed in the morning or not, surely we do not want to increase the amount of risk to which we are subject by building them into our system of criminal justice. We ought not to gear punishment to actual harm caused for exactly the same reason that we ought not to determine whether a person should be punished by flipping a coin or casting dice. Fortune may make us healthy,

wealthy, or wise, but it ought not determine whether we go to prison.

A second point has to do with an explanation of why, in the common view, we fixate so readily on result when we consider the enormity or triviality of a crime. The result, when it is produced, provides a focus for our attention—it provides something tangible for us to get upset about. We do take the business of punishment seriously, and, given the kind of creatures we are, we are hesitant about punishing a person when we do not *feel* an actual loss of some sort. Take the person who drunkenly drives his automobile at a high rate of speed, jumps a curb, and careens down a sidewalk. We may think of the harm he *might* have caused, but that brings only a kind of "abstract" loss to mind. If he actually strikes and kills a child, however, there is a particular harm caused, and this gives our attention—our fears, our sense of outrage—a focal point: it was *this* child's life that was lost. And this is something that operates more powerfully in us, something that sets off our "retributive urge."[15] The point is confirmed, I think, by what we ordinarily do in the case of a near miss. Should the drunkenly driven automobile narrowly miss a child walking down the sidewalk, we are apt to be more outraged by the driver's conduct than if no child had been present. In such a case we have something more than an abstraction (an imagined child that might have been on the sidewalk when in fact none was nearby) on which to focus—the details of what might have happened are more clear. "You might have killed *that* child," we want to say, whereas we have nobody to refer to if there is no near miss. But, if we carefully consider what is operating here, I think we will conclude that what the presence of the child who is narrowly missed really furnishes us is *evidence* that the driver was in no position to avoid hitting whomever might have been in the way. The evidence is simply greater when a death or injury actually occurs. If ample evidence can be given that the driver would have killed a person on the sidewalk, had there been one there, then we have as much *right* to be upset—and to punish—as if there actually had been a victim, even if in fact we are less inclined to be upset—and to punish—in such a case. But the proper conclusion is stronger than this; we are bound by the principle of justice that like cases be treated alike to punish the same whether there is a child struck, a child narrowly missed, or nobody on the sidewalk at all, provided the evidence is sufficient to show that the driver would have done what he did regardless of anyone's presence in his path. So the difference in emotional response is understandable but not really relevant to the culpability of the offender.

The fact that we respond emotionally to results of offenses has sometimes been offered as a reason for grading and creating offenses on the basis of their results. J. F. Stephen criticized (and managed to get amended) the Indian Penal Code for the omission of the crime of negligent manslaughter. The omission failed to recognize "the effect which an offense produces on the feelings and imagination of mankind."[16] Stephen admitted that result might be due purely to fortune and that it had nothing to do with the punishment one might deserve. But still, in a case where two negligent actors produce different results, "it gratifies a natural public feeling to choose out for punishment that one who actually has caused great harm, and the effect in the way of preventing a repetition of the offense is much the same as if both were punished."[17] Stephen's first point hardly requires rebuttal; it might gratify a public feeling to stage gladiatorial contests on television but it is not therefore the business of the government to produce them. True, public sentiment must be taken into some account in the structure of the system, but it is as much the business of that system to lead and to mold public opinion as it is to gratify public feelings.

Deterrence does not help the other side either. Let's distinguish between special deterrence (deterring *this* offender from repeating his offense) and general deterrence (deterring other members of the society). With respect to the first, unequal punishment appears to accomplish nothing; a lighter penalty for an attempt or nonharmful result could hardly discourage an offender from repeating his conduct, and, other things being equal, it is not at all clear that he is less apt to commit the offense again than one who actually causes harm—my suspicion is that quite the contrary is true. Other factors than result are almost certainly more relevant to determining the likelihood of repetition: the offender's personality, background, etc. In the case of general deterrence a number of problems arise, many of them speculative or empirical in nature and too complex to be dealt with here.[18] From a moral point of view, however, we might note that a general deterrence justification of unequal treatment

has the criminal justice system *using* an individual to accomplish a general social end not directly connected with his own culpability.[19] The situation is no different from unusually harsh "exemplary" sentences and no less unjust.

To close, let me sum up. I take the principle that like cases should be treated alike to be a main part of the notion of justice that operates in our treatment of criminal offenders as well as in society at large. It is a person's conduct, I contend, for which we may properly blame him and hold him liable for punishment. Harm that results from a person's conduct is not strictly speaking a part of that conduct and does not provide grounds for distinguishing between culpability and nonculpability, nor does it form a basis for grading offensive conduct with respect to liability for punishment. This becomes especially clear when we notice how much the results of conduct are susceptible to the intervention of chance—factors not a part of the actor's conduct and not within his direct control. The extent to which a given offense, consequences aside, is culpable and merits punishment depends, among other factors, upon the likelihood that harm will result from it. Whatever harm is actually produced should serve only as the basis for a rebuttable claim about the likelihood of such harm.

When result is allowed to form the basis for unequal punishment in otherwise similar cases, I have argued, the effect is to punish one whose action produces harm beyond what is that person's just desert. And this provides a moral ground for ruling out result as a factor in determining the severity of punishment.

Implicit in this view is a conceptual change in the notion of a crime. In principle, this notion should not include reference to harm actually caused but be restricted solely to conduct. The problem of determining more or less exactly what the scope and limits of conduct are looms large, but it is present already in many regions of the criminal law and common sense, properly directed, will serve sufficiently as a reliable guide.

The principle of liability for risk-creating or harmful conduct (in the sense of "harmful" described above) should serve as a guiding principle in the definitions of crimes and in the determination of appropriate sentences. At a bare minimum, it requires the elimination of certain current statutory provisions that mandate unequal punishment for offenses that are otherwise distinguished only by fortune. Otherwise we must simply face the rude fact that one of the most crucial elements of our system—indeed, our *notion*—of criminal justice is blind luck.

NOTES

A slightly different version of this paper appeared in the *American Philosophical Quarterly*, Volume 21, Number 3, July 1984. The first draft was written with support from a grant from the National Endowment for the Humanities.

1. In "Criminal Attempt and the Theory of the Law of Crimes," *Philosophy and Public Affairs*, vol. 3 (1974), pp. 262–94.

2. *Ibid.*, pp. 271–75.

3. See W. LaFave and A. Scott, *Criminal Law* (St. Paul, 1972), p. 423.

4. *Ibid.*, p. 7.

5. Attempt is punishable in California by a maximum of one-half the maximum term for the completed crime. The Model Penal Code of the American Law Institute makes a misdemeanor of reckless conduct which creates a risk of injury if no harm or even bodily injury occurs; but if death occurs, the offense is manslaughter, a second degree felony. §§ 211.1 (1)(a), 211.2, 210.3 (Official Draft, 1962).

6. "Negligent conduct, not criminal in the absence of harm, becomes a misdemeanor if bodily injury occurs under some limited circumstances, and a felony of the third degree if death results." J. Schulhofer, discussing the Model Penal Code in "Harm and Punishment," *University of Pennsylvania Law Review*, vol. 122 (1974), p. 1499.

7. LaFave and Scott, *op. cit.*, pp. 9ff. Hart argues that the criminal law must not be permitted to create crimes out of conduct that lacks the blameworthiness deserving of moral condemnation. See H. M. Hart, Jr., "The Aims of the Criminal Law," in *Law and Contemporary Problems*, vol. 23 (1958), pp. 401, 404–6.

8. This argument was once suggested to me, not very enthusiastically, by the late F. A. Siegler.

9. A harm is "within the risk" of an action if, under the circumstances, it is a reasonably expectable or foreseeable (some say "natural") consequence of that action.

10. *A Theory of Criminal Justice* (Oxford, 1978), p. 436.

11. For some attempts it would *not* be the just desert, or we could not know that it was, because of an evidentiary point that is discussed later.

12. The example is cribbed from Richard Wasserstrom, whom I thank for discussions on this topic.

13. Gross, *op. cit.*, pp. 428ff.

14. It may not *be* a crime simply because it may not be against the law.

15. The phrase is due to John Junker, who is also responsible for stimulating my initial interest in this topic.

16. *History of the Criminal Law*, vol. III (London, 1883), pp. 311ff.

17. *Ibid.*

18. A treatment of several aspects of the problem is available in Schulhofer, *op. cit.*, pp. 1572–77.

19. See Gross, *op. cit.*, pp. 390ff.

MICHAEL DAVIS

Why Attempts Deserve Less Punishment than Complete Crimes*

Rifle ready, an assassin lies in wait. He aims carefully as the intended victim comes in view but holds fire until only a few yards separate them. Then he pulls the trigger. The "victim" walks on, unaware that only a faulty cartridge has saved him from death.

A would-be robber enters a bank, goes to a teller window, hands in a threatening note, and displays a toy pistol. An alert guard, seeing the "weapon," immediately intervenes. The robbery has aborted.

These are both attempts to commit a serious crime. Should they be punished as severely as the corresponding complete crime? The answer of most legal theorists today is: Yes. That is surprising for two reasons.

One reason for surprise is that the answer clearly goes against common practice. Most legal systems statutorily provide for penalties for attempts substantially less severe than for the corresponding complete crimes. And some jurisdictions (for example, Illinois) which for a time yielded to the theorists (especially the American Law Institute's highly influential *Model Penal Code*) have gone back to providing lesser penalties for most attempts. Legal theory is seldom so out of step with practice.

The other reason the theorists' answer is surprising is that it is (virtually) *the* theorists' answer. That a few theorist should set themselves against practice is hardly worth notice. We expect theory to be (to some degree) a criticism of practice. But that so many theorists, retributivists and deterrentists, rehabilitationists and incapacitationists, could all agree in the face of opposed practice certainly is worth notice. When, as here, the agreement arises not from each appealing to some common principle external to their several theories,

but from distinct principles, each internal to the theory in question, we have a state of things inviting one to conclude; "Well, there must be something to it."

Perhaps there is. And perhaps too it would be worthwhile to find out what "it" is. Nevertheless, I shall not do that here. Instead, I shall try something more risky and so more interesting. I shall try to show that the theorists, though nearly unanimous, are mistaken. I shall argue that, if we accept a certain relatively defensible version of retributivism, we must recognize the injustice of punishing attempts as severely as we punish complete crimes because attempts *deserve* less punishment. Most retributivists will, I hope, find the argument decisive. Deterrentists, rehabilitationists, and incapacitationists will, I suppose, not find it even relevant except insofar as they recognize justice as an external constraint on what may be derived from their respective theories. But, because most non-retributivists today recognize justice as at least a factor to be considered along with deterrence, rehabilitation, or incapacitation, the conclusion drawn here should be of interest even to them.

There is also a more practical reason for interest in the conclusion drawn here—at least for Americans. The United States Supreme Court has recently revived the doctrine that punishment must be proportioned to the seriousness of the offense. At first, the doctrine was applied only in capital cases. But it has now been extended to cover cases involving a life sentence for repeated conviction of minor felonies.[1] There is no principled reason not to extend it further (though there may well be reasons of policy preventing such an extension soon). The conclusion drawn here suggests one way in which it might be extended. If punishing a criminal more than he deserves for his crime is unjust, and if attempts deserve less punishment than the corresponding complete crime, it seems to follow that any state which in fact punished an attempt as severely as the corre-

*Michael Davis, "Why Attempts Deserve Less Punishment than Complete Crimes," *Law and Philosophy*, Vol. 5 (1986), pp. 1–32. Copyright © 1986 D. Reidel Publishing Co. Reprinted by permission of Kluwer Academic Publishers.

sponding complete crime would risk having the sentence overturned as unconstitutional because the punishment for the attempt was out of proportion to the crime.

I. TWO PROBLEMS OF ATTEMPT

Legal theorists have until recently attended so little to attempts that it would not be much of an exaggeration to say that "the problem of attempts" is a discovery (or invention) of this century.[2] There are really two problems. One is what we might call a "problem of demarcation"; the other, a "problem of proportion."

The problem of demarcation is to set limits to what can justifiably be punished as attempt. The problem has one aspect for virtually all deterrentists, rehabilitationists, incapacitationists, and even traditional retributivists, but another aspect for certain contemporary retributivists. For deterrentists, rehabilitationists, and incapacitationists, there is no difficulty about explaining why attempts should be punished. If the purpose of the criminal law is to prevent certain acts and if punishing criminals is (in one way or another) the means by which the criminal law achieves that purpose, then the only question is how early is too early to begin preventing. For traditional retributivists, there is also no difficulty about justifying the punishment of attempts. If the purpose of punishment is, say, to "annul" the evil intention embodied in an act, then whether the act failed or was completed is irrelevant to whether the act should be punished. The problem for such retributivists, as for non-retributivists, is not so much to *justify* punishing attempts as to justify *not* punishing "mere preparation."

The problem of demarcation has a different aspect only for those retributivists who conceive punishment as proportioned to a certain sort of (nonlegal) *harm*. Each complete crime has (they say) its characteristic harm (which, indeed, is what justifies making it a crime). But attempts, because they are incomplete or failed crimes, cannot involve the same harm that the complete crime does. Attempts must (it seems to these retributivists) either do some other harm or be an exception to the principle that punishment should be proportioned to wrongdoing (since there would be nothing of a retributive sort to proportion punishment to). Because proportion between punishment and crime is the foundation of retributivism, such

theorists have had to look for some harm characteristic of attempts. The results remain controversial at best.[3]

I shall say little more about this first problem here. I have identified it only to distinguish it from the one that concerns me. If we think of this first problem as one of *demarking* the punishable from the non-punishable, then we may think of the second problem as one of *apportioning* punishment among punishable acts. We need not suppose that the principles that settle demarcation will settle proportion as well. Indeed, one lemma of the argument I shall make here is that the problems of demarcation and proportion are largely independent of one another.

Legal theorists have had less to say about the problem of proportion than about the problem of demarcation. They have generally supposed that the reason for making some act a crime should determine as well how much the crime should be punished. That supposition has generally led them to conclude that the lenient treatment of attempts is either utterly wrongheaded or at best justified by rather speculative considerations (for example, that failure to complete a crime shows lack of resolve or that the lesser penalty for attempts is an implicit recognition of the difficulties of proving intent in the absence of the complete crime). Let me briefly review those theories before examining the alternative.

Rehabilitationists have argued against leniency for attempts in this way: The purpose of punishment is to prevent socially dangerous acts by changing the dangerous person so that he is no longer a danger (and by holding him in a safe place until he is changed). One who attempts a crime is in general as dangerous as one who succeeds (unless the crime is broken off because of a change of heart). So, in general, punishment for attempt should be the same as punishment for complete crime. Since incapacitationists differ from rehabilitationists only in having given up hope of reform, their argument against leniency for attempts would differ only in that way.[4]

Deterrent theorists have reasoned only somewhat differently. We might put their argument this way: The purpose of punishment is to prevent socially dangerous acts by making them uninviting in prospect. A crime is just any act recognized as sufficiently dangerous to be worth discouraging by the threat of punishment. Hardly anyone plans a mere attempt. In prospect virtually all crimes are conceived as complete (and highly successful!). But, insofar as criminals do consider the possibility that their crime might fail or abort, they should consider the lower penalty for mere attempt as making the attempt less uninviting than it would be were the penalty for attempt the same as that for the complete crime. "If we fail," they might say, "all we risk is 4–15 years. Only if we succeed need we worry about 6–30 years." The distinction between attempt and complete crime is therefore not only pointless but positively inconsistent with the purpose of punishment. So (the deterrentist would conclude), punishment for attempt should be the same as for the complete crime.[5]

Retributivists want to proportion punishment to wrongdoing rather than to some social good such as prevention of dangerous acts. Their reasoning about attempts should then be quite different from the three forward-looking sorts of theory already described. It has not been. Traditionally, the wrong in question was understood as moral wrong (law or no law), an evil intention realized in an act. What seemed important was the intention's having been realized in some act or other, not the particular way in which it was in fact realized. I am (it would be said) morally just as blameworthy for attempting to rob a bank and failing as I would be if I succeeded. I meant to succeed, and only, say, the bank guard's alertness prevented me from "making a haul." If punishment should be proportioned to moral blameworthiness, what I deserve for my attempts is just what I would deserve had I succeeded. So, attempts should (such retributivists held) generally be punished as severely as complete crimes.

More recently, retributivists have shifted their concern somewhat from the intention (or other state of mind) to the act itself. Wrongdoing, it is now often said, is a matter of what is done as well as of what is intended. For example, reckless driving is bad, but (it is said) killing someone as a result is morally worse. There are, I think, at least two forms of this "loss-based" approach. One kind would emphasize the harm done to individuals; the other, the loss of social discipline or security.[6] Both approaches would allow for treating some attempts as deserving less punishment than some complete crimes. But neither is altogether satisfactory. There appears, for example, little reason to conclude that I would do significantly more individual or social harm by completing

a bank robbery (and being arrested as I left the bank) than I would if arrested *before* the teller gave me anything or *once* he gave me a bag of worthless paper. Yet, the loss-based approach seems to require us either to equate the attempt with the complete crime or to produce some reason to believe the complete crime would do significantly more harm than the attempt.

Hyman Gross provides an especially interesting example of this sort of retributivism. Gross does *not* argue that every attempt should be punished as severely as the corresponding complete crime. Instead, he proposes "a middle way," distinguishing between various kinds of attempts based on their "dangerousness." Some crimes become mere attempts because of (what Gross calls) "manifest impossibility" (for example, the use of what one knows to be a toy gun in an—"irrational"—attempt to kill a public official). Other crimes fail because of (what Gross calls) "overt impossibility" (for example, the use of a rifle everyone but the actor knows to be inadequate for the crime attempted). But most crimes that fail to do so because of "covert impossibility" (for example, use of ammunition that, though ordinarily reliable, happens to be from a bad batch). According to Gross, a crime that fails because of covert impossibility should be punished as severely as the complete crime because the act was "as dangerous as it could be" and so, "harmful conduct" (even though "by chance" no harm occurred). Crimes that fail because of *overt* impossibility are, however, less culpable because they are less dangerous. And crimes that fail because of manifest impossibility are even less culpable because they are not dangerous at all.

There is something appealing in this, especially in Gross' handling of "manifest impossibility" (which seems to invite a straightjacket rather than a prison term). But there is trouble too. Gross' guiding principle is that the same conduct should receive the same punishment. To those who might object that attempts and complete crimes cannot be the same conduct because one is merely dangerous while the other is actually harmful, Gross responds that the harmfulness of conduct is a matter not of the harm done but of the harm risked. (He expressly rules out of the equation feelings to be assuaged, injuries to be compensated, and any other "differences that the occurrence of harm might make.") He defends that response by claiming that an attempt defeated by covert impossibility is as *blameworthy* as the complete crime would be. The assassin of our initial example is, it seems, "morally speaking" a murderer whether he succeeds in his attempt or not. Gross thus falls back on something like the traditional retributivist view that the criminal law punishes morally blameworthy acts (in proportion to their moral blameworthiness) because they deserve punishment law or no law. But he cannot fairly do that until he shows blameworthiness to be independent of actual outcome. And it is hard to see how he can do that since, for example, we ordinarily blame the reckless driver who kills someone much more severely than the reckless driver who just happens to do no harm. Even Gross' subtlety seems unable to make the loss-based approach work.[7]

There is, however, a third form of retributivism, one which proposes to measure wrongdoing by the *unfair advantage* the criminal takes by breaking the law rather than by the harm done or risked. This form of retributivism, though increasingly popular among legal theorists, has not, so far as I know, been systematically applied to the second problem of attempts. I shall attempt such an application here.

II. UNFAIR ADVANTAGE AND THE PROBLEM OF PROPORTION

Most retributivists today would, I think, accept the following propositions:

(a) that the criminal law of a relatively just legal system is a means of maintaining a fair balance between the benefits and burdens of those subject to it;

(b) that providing for punishment if someone disobeys the law (in such a legal system) is justified, in part at least because provision for such punishment helps to assure that the law will be obeyed; and

(c) that punishing someone for a particular act of disobedience (in such a legal system) is justified only insofar as the punishment reestablishes the balance the act of disobedience itself disturbed.

Retribution is a theory of *just* punishment. The theory presupposes something approximating a just legal system because it is hard to make

sense of the idea of "just punishment" outside of such a system. (If this claim seems exaggerated, consider what punishment—if any—would be deserved if, say, an inmate of Auschwitz steals food from a guard.) Keeping in mind this connection between just punishment and just legal system, we can, I think, easily see why the three propositions retributivists accept together set surprisingly strict limits to the penalties that may be provided for violation of particular statutes. I believe that what I shall now say follows from the three propositions above (together with a number of even less controversial assumptions). But much of it is not, like those propositions, uncontroversial even among retributivists. Space does not allow me to make anything like a full defense of what I shall say in this section. Nor is it necessary that I should. I have already defended the general theory upon which I now propose to rely.[8] The purpose of this section is simply to say enough to make plausible the method used in Section III.

The criminal law protects a society from what its legislators fear would happen were there no law forbidding certain acts. That much we may take for granted. Whether the object of legislative fear is (or should be) harm to individuals only, social harm of some sort, the moral integrity of society, or some combination of these or other concerns does not matter here. The object of legislative fear is relevant only to demark the boundaries of the criminal law. What *does* matter here is that in a relatively just legal system, the criminal law protects each person subject to it from most of what he or she fears others would do otherwise (whatever that is). The criminal law can do that for each person only insofar as everyone else refrains from doing (or at least does not do) what the law forbids (and does what the law requires).

How does the criminal law get people to refrain from doing what they would otherwise do? While each person may want to forbid this or that act because he or she fears that he or she (or someone or something for which he or she cares) will suffer it (by someone else's act), people cannot refrain from such acts themselves for that reason. Insofar as they are of good character, they may refrain simply because doing otherwise is unthinkable. Insofar as they are morally self-conscious agents, they may refrain because doing otherwise (in a relatively just legal system) would be taking unfair advantage of those who refrained while they did not. And so on. Only insofar as someone is a potential criminal will he refrain, if he does refrain, because he fears detection and punishment. Punishment (of others) is one means, but only one means, of assuring each person that he may reasonably do as the law says.

Whatever the reasons people have for refraining from what the criminal law forbids (and for doing what the criminal law requires), this much seems plain: Generally, if the criminal law forbids an act, some people would find the act attractive enough to do—were there no law against it. Legislators may, of course, sometimes be moved by analogy, false fears, or inertia to forbid what no one would do anyway. But such legislation is so rare that we may, I think, safely ignore it here. What no one will do will (except by error or conspiracy) never be punished.

We may then assume that any act the criminal law forbids is one some people would otherwise do. To assume that is, however, not to assume that the act is attractive to everyone or equally attractive to those who find the crime somewhat so. The criminal law should be viewed as a single system benefiting each by restraining the rest. Each may *not* be restrained from exactly the same acts, by the same reasons, or to the same degree, or be benefited equally or in the same way. The *overall* balance of protection and restraint is what is important. The criminal law will help to maintain a just legal system so long as it does not create or aggravate unjustified inequalities. The criminal law will be justified insofar as it helps to maintain a just legal system.

Doing what the criminal law forbids will generally be advantageous to the person doing it (provided, of course, doing the act does not much bother his conscience, lead to punishment, or otherwise turn out badly). But the advantage of lawbreaking is *not* something existing prior to the criminal law. It exists only because the criminal law is itself a living system of cooperation. The advantage of lawbreaking is the advantage one gets by a certain sort of cheating, whatever the cheating itself ultimately accomplishes. One takes some of the fruits of social cooperation one is not entitled to while depending on others not to do the same. Similarly, refraining from what the law forbids while others do not, will generally be disadvantageous. The disadvantage is the disadvantage of not cheating while others do. One is exposed to harm one would not otherwise be exposed to because others are doing what they are not entitled to do while one does not.

Considerations relevant to demarcation are, then, not likely to be relevant to proportion too (or, at least, not relevant in the same way). The problem of demarcation concerns what the criminal law should be. The unfair advantage one takes by breaking the law is an advantage one gets by "cheating" (that is, by taking unfair advantage of those who abide by the criminal law). It is at least possible that there are several equally just (and otherwise justifiable) ways to draw the line between criminal and noncriminal conduct. Such solutions might be mutually inconsistent. Under one, for example, sex between consenting adults in private might be beyond the criminal sanction while, under another, it would not be. Even so, the problem of proportion would be the same. The unfair advantage one takes by lawbreaking is (within a relatively just legal system) not so much a matter of the reasons for the particular law as it is one of general distribution of burdens and benefits existing because there is such a law guiding the action of others.

Doing what the law forbids while others abide by the law will, then, generally be taking unfair advantage (provided the law is part of a relatively just legal system). The unfair advantage may, I believe, not unreasonably be thought of as a "license" others do not have because they did not "take" it. We can gauge the unfair advantage of a particular crime by determining the value of the corresponding "license." While any fair procedure for setting prices should serve to gauge the value, there is one at least that seems especially appropriate given much of the language of retribution. It is an auction in which everyone subject to the criminal law of a particular society may bid on a small number of "licenses" to do the act in question. These may be thought of as "pardons-in-advance" (or as a currency by which one may "pay one's debt to society"). The number of licenses is determined in much the way the number of licenses to hunt a certain animal in a certain season is determined, that is, by considering how much "hunting" can be done without leaving less to "hunt" in years to come. (The analogy here is not as farfetched as it may at first seem. The criminal law must maintain a certain level of "order," "security," or the like for it to be worth having and it is this level of social well-being that corresponds to the animal population of concern to game wardens.)

The price of "pardons-in-advance" should be an index of the advantage taken unfairly by doing the forbidden act without a license. (That is so, of course, because the auction is itself a fair means of setting the price of such entities.) But the actual "price" of a particular license has no significance apart from the actual "price" of other licenses (just as the price of a particular commodity has no significance except relative to the price of other commodities within the same monetary system). So, the outcome of this procedure should produce only a fair *ranking* of crimes, not anything we could reasonably treat as the appropriate table of "prices" in our society.[9]

If such an auction included all crimes prohibited by a particular legal system, the auction would yield a complete ranking of crimes according to the unfair advantage taken. That ranking could be set beside a similar ranking of (humane) penalties to determine what each crime deserves in punishment. The extremes would be settled automatically. The crime ranked highest in unfair advantage would be assigned the highest penalty unless there is some pressing reason to start lower in the scale. The crime ranked lowest in unfair advantage would be assigned the lowest penalty. The procedure would allow some free play only between the extremes. Not all penalties need be assigned. Crimes differing in unfair advantage might be assigned the same penalty. But the free play would be limited. The *relative* ranking of crimes (and penalties) would have to be respected (to preserve fairness). A crime taking more advantage than another could be assigned no less a penalty than the other. A crime taking less advantage than another could be assigned no greater penalty than the other. Prudence would suggest not assigning the same penalty to too many crimes of differing rank and would, as well, suggest trying to spread the crimes more or less evenly between the extremes. (The finer the grading of crimes, the more likely it is that the penalties will discourage more those crimes people would like to discourage more.)

The scale of crimes thus produced should also be a scale of seriousness in the sense necessary to proportion punishment to the seriousness of the crime (as all retributivists agree it should be). The more serious the crime, the more (all else equal) we fear its occurrence; the less serious, the more (all else equal) we would be willing to have some other crime occur instead. Society will then, be willing to issue fewer licenses for the more serious crimes than for the less serious. Those fearing a certain crime may wish to bid on the appropriate licenses to keep them from those who would actually use them. They might well form associations to buy up and hold licenses. There is, I think, no reason to disallow such "protective associations." Allowing such associations helps to ensure that licenses for crimes feared more will in general go for more than licenses for crimes feared less (since, presumably, the associations would bid up a price until allowing the crime seemed more desirable than paying to prevent it). In a relatively just legal system, money should be distributed evenly enough to assure that such an auction would not substantially overrate or underrate the fears of any particular group. So, the scale of unfair advantage should be (more or less) homologous with our intuitive notion of seriousness (or, at least, with that notion of seriousness relevant to deciding what punishment a crime deserves).[10]

If we accept this analysis of how to make the punishment fit the crime, the problem of lesser penalties for attempts becomes (a) to distinguish the special unfair advantage one takes by committing a complete crime from that one takes by committing a mere attempt and (b) to gauge the relative value of these advantages as reflected in the price the appropriate licenses would fetch in an auction of the sort just described.

III. WHAT TO LICENSE

If an attempt deserves less punishment than the corresponding complete crime, the license for the attempt must, I suggested, be worth less than a license to do the complete crime. But, what is it we would license if we licensed a mere attempt? How should we formulate a license to attempt? And how would that license differ from a license to commit the complete crime?

A complete crime ordinarily consists of: (a) a state of affairs the law is supposed to prevent, the "*actus reus*" (for example, the unlawful taking of another's property or an involuntary death at the hands of another); (b) some state of mind, the so-called "*mens rea*" (for example, the intent to do great bodily harm or a failure to exercise reasonable care); and (c) a certain connection between *mens rea* and *actus reus* (for example, a theft being the result of acting with the intent to deprive another of his property or a death that is a natural and probable outcome of what the actor knew himself to be doing). What constitutes the *actus reus* or *mens rea* of a "complete crime" (or the appropriate connection between them) will, of course, be determined by the statute creating that crime (or by the common law when the statutes are silent). A license for the complete crime would mirror the statute, pardoning in advance commission of the *actus reus* done with a certain *mens rea*. Would a license for attempt have the same structure? Let us begin with *actus reus*.

What makes an act a mere attempt is that the *actus reus* of the complete crime never occurs. The actor fails in his attempt. For example, the would-be bank robber is arrested before the teller hands him the money. Nothing of value is taken. The harm characteristic of robbery, forced deprivation of one's valued property, does not occur, even for an instant. The presence or absence of such characteristic harm seems to be crucial to the distinction between attempt and complete crime. The actor's plans can miscarry in all sorts of ways without reducing his crime to a mere attempt, provided he does the characteristic harm (or something like it). For example, if by mistake a bank robber robs the bank next door to the one he intended to rob, he is still guilty of robbery, not merely of *attempting* to rob the bank he intended. He did not do all he intended, but he did do the harm characteristic of robbery, intending to do just that, and that is all that he needs to do to commit robbery.

Since what makes an act an attempt is that the harm characteristic of the complete crime is not done, either an attempt will have a characteristic harm of its own or it will not be possible to identify the special *actus reus* of attempt without deriving it from the *mens rea*. It is plain, I think, that we cannot in general specify a harm characteristic of attempt. For example, suppose that two men enter a bank, each waving a gun, and that one intends to kill a certain teller while the other only intends to rob the bank. And suppose too that each is arrested just before he can complete what he set out to do. The one who intends to kill the teller will be guilty of attempted murder while the other will only be guilty of attempted robbery. They will be guilty of different attempts even though each has performed exactly the same ("outward") act in making his attempt.

There are, of course, some crimes even the attempt of which ordinarily includes harm characteristic of *lesser* offenses. For example, attempted bank robbery ordinarily includes one or more assaults. The robber must put the teller in "reasonable apprehension of battery" to get him to hand over the money. That harm characteristic of assault will, however, hardly explain the penalty for attempted robbery. We punish even attempted robbery much more severely than assault, however aggravated. For example, in Illinois, aggravated assault is a class-A misdemeanor (maximum of one year imprisonment) while attempted armed robbery is a class-1 felony (4–15 years imprisonment).[11] The second problem of attempts becomes interesting only if we assume that talking about attempts is more than a roundabout way of talking about lesser complete crimes (and their characteristic harms).

There are also certain "attempts" that do have their own characteristic harm. For example, assault is often thought of as an attempt to commit battery. The "assaulter" intends "an unlawful touching" but fails and that is why he is guilty of assault rather than battery. Thought of in that way, assault is a true attempt. But assault can also be thought of in a way giving it a characteristic harm of its own. An "assault" ordinarily puts someone in fear of battery. Many statutes define "assault" in terms of that *fear*. Thus, Illinois defines "assault" as placing another "in reasonable apprehension of receiving a battery."[12] Under such statutes, there would be assault even if the "assaulter" intended no more than to place his victim in reasonable apprehension of receiving a beating (*rather than* to beat his victim or otherwise "touch" him). "Assault" so defined would not be a crime of attempted battery but itself a complete crime (though one making express reference to another). The person who intended battery but only achieved assault would be very much like the person who intended to kill his victim but achieved only bodily harm. The intended harm would be enough like the harm he did to count as within the intention (or within what he risked by what he did). We must, then, be careful to exclude from the class of attempts all those "attempts" that have a characteristic harm. For our purposes, attempts are, as such, harmless.

Because (as we shall assume hereafter) attempts do not characteristically do harm in the way complete crimes do, attempt must be a crime primarily of *mens rea*. But not any *mens rea* will do. Attempts seem to require a certain *mens rea*. For example, a reckless driver does not "attempt" negligent homicide just because his driving is grossly negligent but "fails" to result in death. Certain crimes like reckless driving cannot be attempted even though they can easily be committed. An attempt requires an intent, an intent to bring about the *actus reus* of a complete crime (or something like it). Attempts are distinguished according to the complete crime intended. Entering a bank waving a gun is attempted bank robbery if the actor intends to rob the bank but attempted murder if he intends to kill a teller.[13]

A license to attempt would, then, have to identify a certain act, the *actus reus* of the *complete* crime (for example, robbery), and pardon the license holder for intending to do such an act and beginning to do it, but *not* pardon him for doing the harm characteristic of the complete crime. A license to attempt is, by definition, silent concerning the actuality of the *actus reus* of the corresponding complete crime.

Perhaps the notion of "beginning a crime" deserves a word or two. Some may want to define "beginning" so that the interference with liberty from cutting off "mere preparation" is less than the interference with liberty from crimes allowed to get beyond that stage. Others may insist that the line between mere preparation and actual attempt be drawn so that the attempt itself seems too close for comfort (for example, because it inspires insecurity once reported). And others may want to think of "beginning" in other more or less restrictive ways. We need not concern ourselves with that here. That is a matter of demarcation. Whatever the demarcation, our problem would be the same, that is, to determine whether licenses to attempt would be worth less than "licenses to succeed."

Each license for attempt will have to be written as if the corresponding complete crime were possible. (The license must be written to cover an act a would-be criminal can do and no one can even begin to attempt what he believes impossible.) That does not rule out punishing those who attempt the "legally impossible," that is, those trying to do what, if successful, would in fact be no crime at all. Possibility as represented in a license to attempt is possibility as the actor sees it, not as it is in fact. So, there could be a law making punishable as an attempt

doing something in the belief that what was done was a crime. For example, we could punish as attempted theft taking one's own umbrella believing it to be another's or as attempted smuggling the covert importation of nondutiable lace in the belief that it was dutiable. We could even have a law to punish as "generic attempt" those acts the actor intends to be unlawful even though there is no traditional category of crime into which to put what the success would be, for example, marrying someone in the belief that all marriage is illegal, and intending in that way to begin a life of crime. Whether prohibition of such attempts would be wise is, of course, a matter of demarcation that need not concern us here. Our concern is simply to point out that, while what constitutes an attempt will depend on what the complete crime would be, it will not necessarily depend on whether the intended crime is possible in fact or in law.[14]

IV. WHAT PRICE ATTEMPTS?

Now that we have distinguished mere licenses to attempt from licenses to commit the complete crime, we are ready to gauge the relative value of these two kinds of license. I should like to do that by considering three potentially serious objections to the conclusion I want to draw. Each rests on an incomplete understanding of our auction. That, anyway, is what I shall try to show. In the course of showing that, I will, I believe, show as well that (in general) a license to attempt a certain crime will be worth substantially less than a license to commit the complete crime but still substantially more than no license at all.

The first objection we must consider purports to show that mere licenses to attempt would not be bought at the auction we are using to model considerations of fairness. Given the function of the auction, this would amount to showing that, according to the retributive approach taken here, attempts deserve no punishment whatever. If this objection could be made out, it certainly would discredit our approach. It would reveal the retributivism assumed here to be more at odds with common practice than the other theories of punishment seem to be.

We might put the first objection this way: It seems that a mere license to attempt would be worth nothing at all. Hardly anyone undertaking a crime plans to fail. But, a mere license to attempt is no more than a "license to fail." So (it seems), no one would want such a license. What no one wants, no one would bid for and what no one would bid for will be worth nothing at our auction. So (the objection concludes), licenses merely to attempt would be worth nothing because no one wants them.

This objection seems to rest on the assumption that, for every person intent upon some crime, there will be a license to commit that (complete) crime at a price he can afford. Only on that assumption is it possible to show that there would be no demand for mere licenses to attempt. Otherwise, it seems that such a license would certainly be worth something. Most would-be criminals would, we may suppose, recognize the possibility of failure even if failing is not in their plan. If there were too few "licenses to succeed" to go around, might not would-be criminals reason that a "license to fail" is better than no license at all? "Well," we might imagine them to explain, "with a license to attempt this crime, at least we're covered if we fail."

So, the objection assumes that the number of licenses to commit complete crimes will always be large enough to satisfy the demand. The objection fails because that assumption is quite unreasonable. For almost any crime, society cannot afford (or, at least, will not tolerate) as many instances of it as people would commit were there no law prohibiting it. That is the most common reason for making an act illegal. So, licenses to succeed would, for most crimes, be (far) too few to meet the demand. Some people who intend to succeed will not be able to get a license to succeed and will either have to make do with a "license to fail" or go without a license—which, for our purposes, means either not committing any crime or instead engaging in "poaching."

The objection cannot be saved by pointing out that it is possible to "poach" rather than buy a license. "Poaching" must itself be a crime. (Were it not, there could be little reason to buy any license). And, for our purposes, "poaching" must be a crime of a special sort, that is, one which carries penalties of a different order or kind from those we are equating with the penalties an ordinary legal system imposes. "Poaching," as we understand it here, is a crime against the market we are imagining, a crime against the way we are modeling the problem, a "meta-crime" having no counterpart in the domain we are using the model to understand.

"Poaching" has, then, a small but special role in our model. We need not suppose our criminals to be completely "law abiding" within the model (that is, to commit crimes only when they have a pardon in advance). We need only suppose that they would like to keep their (punishable) lawbreaking to a minimum (because they do not want to be punished) and that buying licenses permits them to avoid punishment (without making the crime itself too expensive to be worth committing). The society will, of course, do its best to discourage "poaching" by making the punishment for that crime severe. But, we may suppose, it is either unwilling or unable to punish "poaching" severely enough to assure that no one would dare to "poach." No large society has been able to rid itself of crime, however horrible the punishments imposed.

How then shall we imagine these licenses to work? Licensing can keep punishable lawbreaking to a minimum whether we imagine a license to attempt to work by pardoning the entire crime provided it fails (or aborts) or instead by forgiving part of the punishment the criminal would otherwise receive. But because our concern here is whether a lower penalty for attempt is what justice requires, though what justice requires of us who have no auction to set penalties, not what justice requires of the society in our model where penalties are set by the fair procedure of an auction, our conclusion will probably be less open to suspicion if we imagine the license as pardoning the entire crime *provided it fails* (or aborts) rather than as forgiving part of the penalty for the complete crime.

This way of imagining a license to attempt also fits nicely with our analysis of the distinction between licenses to attempt and licenses to commit a complete crime. We are supposing that licenses merely to attempt license only *mens rea* with the resulting act (provided it is not the *actus reus* of the complete crime). So, a license merely to attempt cannot pardon a complete crime (or pardon such a crime completely) because a mere license to attempts cannot pardon the *actus reus* of the complete crime. A license to commit the complete crime must, on the other hand, pardon failure too because every success includes the *mens rea* of failure (with the resulting act) as well as the harm characteristic of success.

This suggests another reason for potential criminals to buy a license to attempt, but one operating even if they already have the corresponding license to succeed (provided a license to attempt is less expensive). *If* a mere license to attempt were less expensive than a license to succeed at the same crime, potential criminals might buy the appropriate license to attempt as a backup. "Why waste a license to succeed," they might reason, "to pardon a failure if we can get pardoned by turning in a cheaper 'license to attempt'?"

So, there should be some demand for mere licenses to attempt, especially if they cost less than licenses to succeed. But, would licenses to attempt *cost less*? That brings us to the second objection. This objection purports to show just the opposite of the first, that is, that a license to attempt would be worth just as much at our auction as a license to commit the complete crime. Showing that would, of course, amount to showing that, according to the approach taken here, attempts deserve the same punishment as the corresponding complete crime. The objection would, if proved, be less serious than the first. The "different" retributivism championed here would have led to roughly the same conclusion as its competitors did. We would not have shown it to be better (or worse) than its competitors in the handling of attempts. This second objection is, then, while not quite as serious as the first, still serious enough.

The objection assumes a special role for the "protective associations." We might put the objection this way: Whatever the criminals may think about the relative value of licenses to attempt and licenses to succeed, the protective associations would fear attempted crimes just as much as complete crimes. They would not want people "out there" seeing whether they would succeed or fail at this or that crime. They would want potential criminals to be faced with the choice of "poaching" or obeying the law. They would (the objection runs) bid up the price of licenses to attempt just as they would the price of licenses to succeed. So, licenses to fail should cost about the same as licenses to succeed.

This objection rests in part on the assumption that protective associations can determine the price of any license to attempt. That assumption is correct. The society we are imagining—like our own—must choose to tolerate a certain level of disorder because it is unwilling or unable to do what is necessary to reduce that disorder further. The protective associations

exist to reduce that disorder further by buying up (and not using) licenses that would otherwise be bought up (and used) by potential criminals. The protective associations would, we may suppose, have substantial assets, far more than most criminals would have. So, for any particular license offered at auction, some protective association should be able to outbid any individual criminal (and so, be able as well legitimately to bid up the license to the highest price criminals are willing to pay). But, like the assets of any criminal, the assets of the protective associations must be finite. While there may be no practical limit to the price they can pay for any particular license, there will be a limit to the total number they can buy. And because of that, they cannot control the price of licenses in general.

The objection seems to need the further assumption that our auction is a one-time affair in which all the licenses are auctioned from a fixed supply the protective associations do not affect by what they do. That is not what should be assumed. Such an assumption would make our model less realistic (and so, less useful) than need be. What should be assumed is that those running the auction will calculate from time to time the amount of social disorder (or whatever) the previous selling of licenses produced. If the social disorder produced last time was too great, they would want to lower the number of licenses offered for sale this time. If the social disorder produced last time was tolerable, the auctioneers would be able to offer the same number of licenses this time. And if the social disorder produced last time was lower than expected, they would be able to offer even more licenses without exceeding the limit of disorder the society was willing to tolerate. We must, of course, suppose our auctioneers to want to offer as many licenses as possible consistent with tolerable social disorder so as to produce the maximum revenue permitted—the equivalent in our society of keeping the costs of law enforcement as low as possible consistent with maintaining a certain level of "law and order."

The continuing nature of the auction together with the limited resources of the protective associations make the associations far less important than required for the objection. The protective associations buy licenses to prevent their use. Any license a protective association buys will, then, *not* be a claim on the fund of public order. Such licenses will instead produce almost pure profit (much as the sale of postage stamps to collectors does for the post office). So, of course, the auctioneers will want to offer substantially more licenses than the protective associations can buy. The *use* of those "surplus" licenses (even when combined with unavoidable "poaching") will not produce disorder beyond the limit society has set. So, it is certain that, in the long run, the criminals will get a good share of the licenses. Because the protective associations must budget their resources and because the number of licenses offered at auction will depend upon the effect on social order of the last offering, the number of licenses offered for auction must in general exceed by a substantial amount the number the protective associations can buy.

It may seem, then, that protective associations are engaged in a foolish undertaking, that they would be able to accomplish just as much did they do nothing at all. That is not so. They guarantee that the price of this or that license will not fall too low (that is, so low that it no longer reflects how much people in general fear that crime being committed). If the would-be criminals stop bidding too soon, a protective association could buy the bargain and at least assure that that crime will not be committed this time (or, at least, not at such a low price). Of course, part of the price of that purchase may be more licenses put on the market next time. But that is a problem for next time. The protective associations might reasonably be formed with the short-range goal of preventing certain licenses from being used. Once formed, they might continue operating because, should they leave the auction, there would be a sudden glut of licenses. Their exit would trigger a "crime wave." Such a crime wave might, of course, be prevented if the associations notified the auctioneers of the planned withdrawal far enough in advance. Let us suppose they could. They would still have good reason not to withdraw. Withdrawing would leave the criminals free to pick up bargains or even to form conspiracies to keep prices low.

So, it seems, whether they are protective associations or not, there will be some licenses would-be criminals will be able to buy. It also seems that licenses merely to attempt would be useful to would-be criminals, though not as useful as licenses to commit the corresponding complete crimes (since a license to attempt would pardon only a failure, while a license to commit the complete crime would pardon the attempt even if it succeeds). So, any rational would-be criminal should be willing to bid significantly more for a license to succeed than for a mere license to attempt. Since the actual price of licenses will in general be determined by what the would-be criminals would bid, not by what the protective associations would bid, licenses merely to attempt should in general be worth less than the corresponding licenses to succeed.

That brings us to the third objection. This one, while tacitly rejecting the second, still threatens to discredit our approach. The objection is that all mere licenses to attempt should be of equal worth, since all license approximately the same thing, failure. This objection purports to show that, according to our version of retributivism, attempted murder deserves no more punishment than, say, attempted theft.

We might state the objection in this way: It seems that the number of licenses to commit various complete crimes will in general be proportioned to the seriousness of the characteristic harm that sort of crime does. For example, we would expect a society to issue fewer licenses to murder than licenses to steal because societies find it easier to tolerate theft than murder. But (the objection continues), attempts do no harm (though they may risk it). Attempts differ from one another (primarily) in *mens rea*. Depending on the intention of the actor, the same (harmless) act could be attempted murder or only attempted robbery. So, society has no more reason to limit licenses for one sort of attempt than licenses for another. And so (the objection concludes), it seems that (insofar as quantity is the determinant of price), all licenses to attempt should sell for the same price.

This third objection makes an important point. Society might justifiably be said to have no reason to limit the number of licenses to attempt (that is, no reason to punish attempts) except insofar as there is some connection between attempts and the harm society seeks to prevent by prohibiting the corresponding complete crimes. Where there is no such connection, a license for one sort of attempt is likely to sell for no more than a license for another—because the selling price of both should be *nothing*. Consider, for example, two licenses to attempt what Gross called the "manifestly impossible." One license would, let us suppose, pardon an attempt to kill using means everyone including the actor knows to be insufficient (for example, killing someone by "shooting" him with what is obviously a toy pistol). The other license, let us also suppose, would pardon stealing from those even the thief knows to have nothing to steal (for example, picking pockets even the thief knows to be empty). A society might issue an infinite number of such licenses without fear of suffering any significant loss of order. If the society we are imagining issued all licenses of that kind it could issue, the price such licenses would fetch at the auction would be nominal (supposing anyone to be moved to bid on them at all). So, whether or not it is wise to outlaw attempting the manifestly impossible, it is certainly unjust to punish those who commit such attempts.

The fallacy of the third objection is that it generalizes this insight to cover all attempts. While Gross may have made too much of risk, this objection makes too little of it. Most attempts do risk the harm of the corresponding complete crime. There failure cannot be known in advance by the would-be criminal (as in the case of manifest impossibility) or even by the society generally (as in the case of what Gross called "overt impossibility"). Society therefore has good reason to limit the number of licenses to attempt (even though, as we are supposing, attempts as such never do harm). Each license to attempt held by someone without the corresponding license to succeed is an invitation to "poach." "If I fail, I'm safe," the would-be criminal might reason, "and I'm willing to take my chances if I succeed." It seems that generally the greater the number of "real" attempts (that is, attempts that fail, if they fail, only because of "covert impossibility"), the larger the number of crimes that will succeed. Whatever reason there is to fear the complete crime is, then, also a reason to fear the attempt (though it is not as much of a reason). Whatever reason there is to limit the number of licenses to commit a certain crime will also be a reason to limit proportionately the number of licenses to attempt it. So, insofar as quantity of licenses determines the price, there should be some proportion between the price of a license for the complete crime and the price of a license for the corresponding attempt.[15]

V. CONCLUDING REMARKS

The auction is, of course, only a way to help us see better the unfair advantage criminals take in *our* society when they attempt or succeed at this or that crime. So, it is now time to summarize the foregoing argument in the language of unfair advantage with which we began: Someone who attempts a crime but fails to do the harm characteristic of success still (ordinarily) risks doing that harm. He deserves punishment for risking that harm because even risking such harm is an advantage the law abiding do not take. He deserves less punishment for the attempt than he would for the complete crime because being able to risk doing harm is not as great an advantage as being able to do it. To attempt murder is, for example, not worth as much as to succeed. The successful murderer has the advantage of having done what he set out to do. The would-be murderer whose attempt failed has only had the *chance* to do what he set out to do. The difference is substantial. Because even the criminal guilty only of attempting a serious crime takes a substantial advantage the law abiding do not, he deserves substantial punishment for what he did. But because merely attempting a serious crime is substantially less of an advantage than actually succeeding at it, such a criminal deserves substantially less in punishment for the attempt than he would for the complete crime.

There is an important difference between this argument and that Gross made to show that attempting the "covertly impossible" deserves the same punishment as committing the complete crime while attempting the "overtly impossible" deserves less punishment. Because Gross seems to me to have presented the best systematic defense of retributivism to date, it will, I think, be worth our time to contrast briefly his treatment of attempts with ours. Gross' argument turned on degree of "culpability"; the argument made here turns instead on degree of "unfair advantage." Though most retributivists seem to take these two notions to be equivalent, the punishment of attempts is one place where they prove to be strikingly different.

Let us begin with attempting the *covertly* impossible. Gross observes that a person whose attempt turns out to be covertly impossible is just as culpable (that is, blameable) as the person who actually succeeds. Such a criminal fails to do the characteristic harm not because he is incapable of doing it or because he failed to do everything in his power to do it. He fails only "by chance" and chance does not reduce culpability.

We may agree with most of this. All we must deny is that punishment should be proportioned to "culpability" as such. *Our* position is that punishment should be proportioned only to a certain sort of culpability, the culpability specifically connected with "cheating," that is, with the unfair advantage one takes by breaking the law in question. While our criminal may be just as bad a person, just as culpable generally, whether or not he succeeds or fails at this or that crime, he is not therefore equally well off. To cheat successfully is to take a greater advantage than one takes by cheating unsuccessfully. That is why a license to commit a complete crime is worth more (in our model) than a mere license to attempt the same crime (and it is that additional advantage which the additional punishment is supposed to "annul").

There is, of course, some connection between the advantage one takes by risking a certain harm and the advantage one takes by achieving it. The proportion may even vary from one category of crime to another with the proportion between attempts and successes. Attempts to commit crimes that are rarely successfully committed may deserve relatively little punishment while attempts to commit crimes that are almost always committed successfully may deserve a punishment much like that the complete crime deserves. But an attempt, no matter how close to being a "sure thing," could never take the same advantage as the corresponding complete crime. There is always a significant difference between any probability of an outcome, even if the probability is one, and the occurrence of the outcome itself. For example, I can (all else equal) rationally exchange my dollar for yours. But I cannot (all else equal) rationally exchange my dollar for a ticket in a lottery even if I believe it to be a fair lottery in which only one ticket will be sold and the pot of which will consist of all money paid in for tickets. Rational agents are in general "risk-adversive." So, if the punishment the criminal deserves for what he did should be proportional to the unfair advantage he took, the criminal guilty of an attempt always deserves less in punishment for what he did than the criminal who succeeded at the very same crime.

The distinction between "general culpability" and that "special culpability" corresponding to unfair advantage taken comes out nowhere more clearly than in the case of attempting the "*overtly* impossible." According to

Gross, the person attempting the overtly impossible deserves more punishment than the person guilty of attempting the manifestly impossible because what he did was more dangerous than attempting the manifestly impossible, but deserves less punishment than the person guilty of attempting the covertly impossible because what he did was less dangerous than that. Our conclusion must be the same. But our explanation is, I think, better.

Gross explains the lesser culpability of those who attempt the overtly impossible by appealing to the lesser danger such attempts pose. Certainly he is right to claim that overtly impossible attempts are less dangerous than covertly impossible attempts. But the trouble is that he must also claim that overtly impossible attempts are *more* dangerous than manifestly impossible attempts. The only difference between these two kinds of attempt is that, in a manifestly impossible attempt, even the criminal himself knows (in some sense) that what he is doing is harmless while in an overtly impossible attempt everyone but the criminal knows that. How does the criminal's knowledge in one case or ignorance in the other change the dangerousness of the act itself? I am at a loss to answer. Of course, the difference in knowledge may correspond to a difference in character. The person who would undertake an overtly impossible crime today seems likely to improve his technique in prison and succeed next time he tries, while the person guilty of a manifestly impossible attempt seems much more likely to go on failing harmlessly. But neither Gross nor I believe such facts about the person are relevant to determining what he deserves for his *crime* (though both of us are willing to allow such personal factors to count in mitigation of sentence). So, Gross' explanation of why it is just to impose some punishment for overtly impossible attempts seems to be no explanation at all.

What have we to put in its place? For us, the question must be whether the advantage one takes by attempting the overtly impossible is worth more than the advantage one takes by attempting the manifestly impossible. The question is not hard to answer. For a rational person, a license to attempt the manifestly impossible would be worth nothing. After all, why would a rational person attempt the manifestly impossible when he can do exactly the same physical acts legally (provided he does not intend to do what he knows he cannot do anyway)? He has it within his power to make sure at no cost that he will never need such a license. In contrast, a license to attempt the overtly impossible would have some use. Even a rational person now and then does something stupid. A license to attempt the overtly impossible is, in effect, insurance against one's own stupidity. The license pardons an attempt that fails because the would-be criminal did not think to "ask around," "case out," or otherwise exercise what even he would ordinarily recognize as reasonable care. Such a license would, however, not be worth much. Because its use is more specialized than a general license to attempt, it would have to sell for less than a general license to attempt. So, it seems clear that the unfair advantage taken by attempting the overtly impossible must be less than that taken by any covertly impossible attempt but significantly more than that taken by any manifestly impossible attempt.

This, of course, is all very rough—but not, I hope, so rough that the advantage of our approach over the alternatives is not now plain.

NOTES

Work on this paper was begun under an Organized Research Grant from Illinois State University (June 1984) and completed under National Endowment for the Humanities Fellowship Grant FB-22388-84. I am grateful to both institutions for their support.

1. *Herman Solem, Warden, Petitioner v. Jerry Buckley Helm,*____U.S.____ , 51 LW 5019 (1983).

2. There are at least two notable exceptions. See Plato, *Laws,* IX: 877 (an interesting paragraph arguing for a lesser penalty for attempted murder than for successful murder); and Cesare Beccaria, *On Crimes and Punishments,* Ch. XIV (two sentences) and perhaps Ch. XXVII (one sentence). Bentham is notable for his absence.

3. See, for example, Charles R. Carr, 'Punishing Attempts,' *Pacific Philosophical Quarterly* 62 (January 1981): 61–68; and H. L. A. Hart, *Punishment and Responsibility* (New York: Oxford University Press, 1968), pp. 130–131. The retributive approach is now often represented by the formula $H \times R = P$ (where H represents the harm the criminal did; R, the degree of his responsibility; and P, the deserved punishment). Given that representation, the problem attempts poses for retributivism is obvious. If H is zero (that is, if attempts do no harm), then deserved punishment must be zero too.

4. See, for example, Barbara Wootton, *Crime and the Criminal Law* (London: Stevens, 1963), especially pp. 32–57.

5. See, for example, Lawrence C. Becker, 'Criminal Attempts and the Theory of the Law of Crimes,' *Philosophy and Public Affairs* 3 (Spring 1974): 262–294; and Hart: 128–129.

6. For an extremely useful discussion of these (and other possibilities, see George Fletcher, *Rethinking Criminal Law* (Boston: Little, Brown, and Co., Inc., 1978), pp. 472–483.

Recent concern with victims and restitution seems to correspond to the individual-harm emphasis. See, for example, Randy E. Barnett, 'Restitution: A New Paradigm of Criminal Justice,' *Ethics* 87 (July 1977): 279–301. The second emphasis is, of course, much more common.

7. Hyman Gross, *A Theory of Criminal Justice* (New York: Oxford University Press, 1979), pp. 430–434. For similar criticism of Gross, see Michael Bayles, 'Punishment for Attempts,' *Social Theory and Practice* 8 (Spring 1982); 19–29.

8. Michael Davis, 'How to Make the Punishment Fit the Crime,' *Ethics* 93 (July 1983): 726–752 (reprinted in slightly revised form in *Nomos* XXVII (1985): 119–155) and 'Harm and Retribution,' *Philosophy and Public Affairs,* forthcoming. For application of this analysis to other pressing problems in the theory of punishment, see 'Death, Deterrence, and the Method of Common Sense,' *Social Theory and Practice* 7 (Summer 1981): 145–177; 'Sentencing: Must Justice Be Even-Handed?,' *Law and Philosophy* 1 (Summer 1982): 139–152; 'Guilty But Insane?,' *Social Theory and Practice* 10 (Spring 1984): 1–23; 'Setting Penalties: What Does Rape Deserve?,' *Law and Philosophy* 3 (April 1984): 62–111; 'Just Deserts for Recidivists,' *Criminal Justice Ethics* 4 (Summer/Fall 1985), pp. 29–50.

9. Gross, it should be noted, accepts the idea of a "fair market value" for particular crimes but makes no attempt to work it out (p. 439).

10. The distinction seems to be worth keeping in mind. Sociologists have done a number of empirical studies of "seriousness" in which people were asked to grade crimes according to their seriousness without any guidance concerning what seriousness might be. The results were sometimes shocking. For example, most people interviewed for one study seemed to think "assassinating a public official" *less serious* than "assaulting a policeman with a gun." Peter Rossi *et al.*, 'The Seriousness of Crimes: Normative Structure and Individual Differences,' *American Sociological Review* 39 (1974): 224–237.

11. *Illinois Annotated Statutes* (St. Paul, MN: West Publishing Company, 1983), ch. 38, secs. 8–4, 12–2, 18–2, 1005-8-1 (2), and 1005-8-3. Note too the special provision for enhancement of the penalty for armed robbery, ch. 38, sec. 1005-8-2.

12. Ibid., sec. 12-1.

13. Compare Glanville Williams, 'Problem of Reckless Attempts,' *Criminal Law Review* (June 1983): 365–375. This is, however, not as clear to some people as it seems to Williams and me. See Note, '*State v. Grant*: Is Intent an Essential Element of Criminal Attempt in Maine,' *Main Law Review* 34 (1982): 479–494.

14. For a recent practical discussion of forbidding attempts to do the legally impossible, see Ian Dennis, 'The Criminal Attempts Act 1981,' *Criminal Law Review* (1982): 5–16.

15. One reviewer for this journal objected to the use of the auction as a model that "I would pay more to get a license for theft than for a license for manslaughter, because the latter is an unplanned crime . . . [even though] I would pay more to prevent manslaughter than theft being committed against me." I do not, of course, have space here to provide a full response to this objection. But because it is one that may occur to many readers, let me at least suggest how I might answer it in full: The auction does not, I think, require that manslaughter be punished more, less, or the same as theft. These crimes do not belong to the same "type" (that is, they are not crimes a potential

criminal would normally choose between). (See 'How to Make the Punishment Fit the Crime': 739–740.) Because manslaughter and theft are not of the same type, their relative seriousness is not directly a matter of justice (if it is a matter of justice at all). The same would be true of the relative seriousness of theft and attempted theft, or of murder and (say) negligent homicide, *were there not other considerations making the one less serious than the other*. I have tried in this paper to explain the relation between theft and attempted theft. I take up the relation between crimes differing only in *mens rea* in another paper. See my 'Strict Liability: Deserved Punishment for Faultless Conduct,' forthcoming.

DAVID LEWIS

The Punishment that Leaves Something to Chance*

I

We are accustomed to punish criminal attempts much more severely if they succeed than if they fail. We are also accustomed to wonder why. It is hard to find any rationale for our leniency toward the unsucccessful. Leniency toward aborted attempts, or mere preparation, might be easier to understand. (And whether easy or hard, it is not my present topic.) But what sense can we make of leniency toward a completed attempt—one that puts a victim at risk of harm, and fails only by luck to do actual harm?

Dee takes a shot at his enemy, and so does Dum. They both want to kill; they both try, and we may suppose they try equally hard. Both act out of malice, without any shred of justification or excuse. Both give us reason to fear that they might be ready to kill in the future. The only difference is that Dee hits and Dum misses. So Dee has killed, he is guilty of murder, and we put him to death.[1] Dum has not killed, he is guilty only of attempted murder, and he gets a short prison sentence.

Why? Dee and Dum were equally wicked in their desires. They were equally uninhibited in pursuing their wicked desires. Insofar as the wicked deserve to be punished, they deserve it equally. Their conduct was equally dangerous: they inflicted equal risks of death on the respective victims. Insofar as those who act dangerously deserve to be punished, again they deserve it equally. Maybe Dee's act was worse than Dum's act, just because of Dee's success; but it is not the act that suffers punishment, it is the agent. Likewise, if we want to express our abhorrence of wickedness or of dangerous conduct, either exemplar of what we abhor is fit to star in the drama of crime and punishment. Further, Dee and Dum have equally engaged in conduct we want to prevent by deterrence. For we prevent succcessful attempts by preventing attempts generally. We cannot deter success separately from deterring attempts, since attempters make no separate choice about whether to succeed. Further, Dee and Dum have equally shown us that we might all be safer if we defended ourselves against them; and one function of punishment (at any rate if it is death, imprisonment, or transportation) is to get dangerous criminals off the streets before they do more harm. So how does their different luck in hitting or missing make any difference to considerations of desert, expression, deterrence, or defense? How can it be just, on any credible theory of just punishment, to punish them differently?

Here is one rationale for our peculiar practice. If the gods see innocent blood shed, they will be angry; if they are angry, none of us will be safe until they are propitiated; and to propitiate the gods, we must shed guilty blood. Whereas if by luck no innocent blood is shed, the gods will not be angered just by the sight of unsuccessful wickedness, so there will be no need of propitiation.—This rationale would make sense, if its premises were true. And if we put "the public" or "the victim's kin" for "the gods" throughout it still makes sense; and that way, maybe the premises are true, at least sometimes and to some extent. But this rationale does nothing at all to defend our practice *as just*. If our practice is unjust, then the ways of the gods (or the public, or the kin) are unjust, although if the powers that be want to see injustice done, it might be prudent to ignore justice and do their bidding.

A purely conservative rationale is open to the same complaint. Maybe it is a good idea to stay with the practice we have learned how to operate, lest a reform cause unexpected problems. Maybe it is good for people to see the law go on working as they are accustomed to expect it to. Maybe a reform would convey unintended and disruptive messages: as it might be, that we have decided to take murder less seriously than we used to. These considerations may be excellent reasons why it is prudent to leave well

*David Lewis, "The Punishment that Leaves Something to Chance," *Philosophy and Public Affairs*, Vol. 18, No. 1 (1989), pp. 53–67. Copyright ©1989 Princeton University Press. Reprinted by permission of Princeton University Press.

enough alone, and condone whatever injustice there may be in our present practice. They do nothing at all to defend our practice as just.

Another rationale concerns the deterrence of second attempts. If at first you don't succeed, and if success would bring no extra punishment, then you have nothing left to lose if you try, try again. "If exactly the same penalty is prescribed for successes as for attempts, there will be every reason to make sure that one is successful."[2] It cannot hurt to have some deterrence left after deterrence has failed. Maybe the experience of having tried once will make the criminal more deterrable than he was at first.—But why is this any reason for punishing successful attempts more severely? It might as well just be a reason for punishing two attempts more severely than one, which we could do regardless of success. If each separate attempt is punished, and if one share of punishment is not so bad that a second share would be no worse, then we have some deterrence against second attempts.

Another rationale sees punishment purely as a deterrent, and assumes that we will have deterrence enough if we make sure that crime never pays. If so, there is no justification for any more penal harm than it takes to offset the gains from a crime. Then a failed attempt needs no punishment: there are no gains to be offset, so even if unpunished it still doesn't pay.—I reply that in the first place, this system of minimum deterrence seems likely to dissuade only the most calculating of criminals. In the second place, punishment is not just a deterrent. I myself might not insist on retribution per se, but certainly the expressive and defensive functions of punishment are not to be lightly forsaken.

Another rationale invokes the idea of "moral luck."[3] Strange to say, it can happen by luck alone that one person ends up more wicked than another. Perhaps that is why the successful attempter, by luck alone, ends up deserving more severe punishment?—I rely, first, that to some extent this suggestion merely names our problem. We ask how Dee can deserve more severe punishment just because his shot hits the mark. Call that "moral luck" if you will; then we have been asking all along how this sort of moral luck is possible. But, second, it may be misleading to speak of the moral luck of the attempter, since it may tend to conflate this case with something quite different. The most intelligible cases of moral luck are those in which the lucky and the unlucky alike are disposed to become wicked if tempted, and only the unlucky are tempted. But then, however alike they may have been originally, the lucky and the unlucky do end up different in how they are and in how they act. Not so for the luck of hitting or missing. It makes no difference to how the lucky and the unlucky are, and no difference to how they act.[4]

Finally, another rationale invokes the difference between wholehearted and halfhearted attempts.[5] Both are bad, but wholehearted attempts are worse. A wholehearted attempt involves more careful planning, more precautions aginst failure, more effort, more persistence, and perhaps repeated tries. *Ceteris paribus,* a wholehearted attempt evinces more wickedness—stronger wicked desires, or less inhibition about pursuing them. *Ceteris paribus,* a wholehearted attempt is more dangerous. It is more likely to succeed; it subjects the victim, knowingly and wrongfully, to a greater risk. Therefore it is more urgently in need of prevention by deterrence. *Ceteris paribus,* the perpetrator of a wholehearted attempt is more of a proven danger to us all, so it is more urgent to get him off the streets. So from every standpoint—desert, expression, deterrence, defense—it makes good sense to punish attempts more severely when they are wholehearted. Now, since wholehearted attempts are more likely to succeed, success is some evidence that the attempt was wholehearted. Punishing success, then, is a rough and ready way of punishing wholeheartedness.

I grant that it is just to punish wholehearted attempts more severely—or better, since "heartedness" admits of degrees, to proportion the punishment to the heartedness of the attempt. And I grant that in so doing we may take the probability of success—in other words, the risk inflicted on the victim—as our measure of heartedness. That means not proportioning the punishment simply to the offender's wickedness, because two equally wicked attempters may not be equally likely to succeed. One may be more dangerous than the other because he has the advantage in skill or resources or information or opportunity. Then if we proportion punishment to heartedness measured by risk, we may punish one attempter more severely not because he was more wicked, but because his conduct was more dangerous. From a purely retributive standpoint, wickedness might seem the more appropriate measure; but from the expressive standpoint, we may prefer to dramatize our abhorrence not of wickedness per se but of dangerous wickedness; and from the standpoint of deterrence or defense, clearly it is dangerous conduct that matters.

So far, so good; but I protest that it is unjust to punish success as a rough and ready way of punishing wholeheartedness. It's just too rough and ready. Success is some eveidence of wholeheartedness, sure enough. But it is very unreliable evidence: the wholehearted attempt may very well be thwarted, the half- or quarterhearted attempt may succeed. And we can have other evidence that bears as much or more on whether the attempt was wholehearted. If what we really want is to punish wholeheartedness, we have no business heeding only one unreliabe fragment of the total evidence, and then treating that fragment as if it were conclusive. Suppose we had reason— *good* reason—to think that on average the old tend to be more wholehearted than the young in their criminal attempts. Suppose even that we could infer wholeheartedness from age somewhat more reliably than we can infer it from success. Then if we punished attempters more severely in proportion to their age, that would be another rough and ready way of punishing wholeheartedness. *Ex hypothesi,* it would be less rough and ready than what we do in punishing success. It would still fall far short of our standards of justice.

II

In what follows, I shall propose a new rationale. *I do not say that it works.* I do say that the new rationale works better than the old ones. It makes at least a prima facie case that our peculiar practice is just, and I do not see any decisive rebuttal. All the same, I think that the prima facie case is probably not good enough, and probably there is no adequate justification for punishing attempts more severely when they succeed.

Our present practice amounts to a disguised form of *penal lottery*—a punishment that leaves something to chance. Seen thus, it *does* in some sense punish all attempts alike, regardless of success. It is no less just, and no more just, than an undisguised penal lottery would be. Probably any penal lottery is seriously unjust, but it is none too easy to explain why.

By a penal lottery, I mean a system of punishment in which the convicted criminal is subjected to a risk of punitive harm. If he wins the lottery, he escapes the harm. If he loses, he does not. A pure penal lottery is one in which the winners suffer no harm at all; an impure penal loettery is one in which winners and losers alike suffer some harm, but the losers suffer more harm. It is a mixture: part of the punishment is certain harm, part is the penal lottery.

An overt penal lottery is one in which the punishment is announced explicitly as a risk— there might be ways of dramatizing the fact, such as a drawing of straws on the steps of the gallows. A covert penal lottery is one in which the punishment is not announced as a risk, but it is common knowledge that it brings risk with it. (A covert lottery must presumably be impure.)

A historical example of an overt penal lottery is the decimation of a regiment as punishment for mutiny. Each soldier is punished for his part in the mutiny by a one-in-ten risk of being put to death. It is a fairly pure penal lottery, but not entirely pure: the terror of waiting to see who must die is part of the punishment, and this part falls with certainty on all the mutineers alike.

Covert and impure penal lotteries are commonplace in our own time. If one drawback of prison is that it is a place where one is exposed to capricious violence, or to a serious risk of catching AIDS,[6] then a prison sentence is in part a penal lottery. If the gulag is noted for its abysmal standards of occupational health and safety, then a sentence of forced labor is in part a penal lottery.

III

What do we think, and what should we think, of penal lotteries? Specifically, what should we think of a penal lottery, with death for the losers, as the punishment for all attempts at murder, regardless of success? Successful or not, the essence of the crime is to subject the victim, knowingly and wrongfully, to a serious risk of death. The proposed punishment is to be subjected to a like risk of death.

We need a standard of comparison. Our present system of leniency toward the unsuccessful is too problematic to make a good standard, so let us instead compare the penal lottery with a hypothetical reformed system. How does the lottery compare with a system that punishes all attempts regardless of success, by the certain harm of a moderate prison term? A moderate term, because if we punished successful and unsuccessful attempts alike, we would presumably set the punishment somewhere between our present severe punishment of the one and our lenient punishment of the other. (Let the prison be a safe one, so that in the comparison case we have no trace of a penal lottery.) Both for the lottery and for the comparison case, I shall assume that we punish regardless of success. In the one case, success per se makes no difference to the odds; in the other case, no difference to the time in prison. This is not to say that every convicted criminal gets the very same sentence. Other factors might still make a difference. In particular, heartedness (measured by the risk inflicted) could make a difference, and success could make a difference to the extent that it is part of our evidence about heartedness.

Now, how do the two alternatives compare?

The penal lottery may have some practical advantages. It gets the case over and done with quickly. It is not a crime school. A prison costs a lot more than a gallows plus a supply of long and short straws.[7]

(Likewise a prison with adequate protection against random brutality by guards and fellow inmates costs more than a prison without. So it seems that we have already been attracted by the economy of a system that has at least some covert admixture of lottery.)

Like a prison term (or fines, or flogging) and unlike the death penalty *simpliciter,* the penal lottery can be graduated as finely as we like. When we take the crime to be worse, we provide fewer long straws to go with the fatal short straws. In particular, that is how we can provide a more severe punishment for the more wholehearted attempt that subjected the victim to a greater risk.

From the standpoint of dramatizing our abhorrence of wicked and dangerous conduct, a penal lottery seems at least as good as a prison sentence. Making the punishment fit the crime, Mikado-fashion, is *poetic* justice. The point we want to dramatize, both to the criminal and to the public, is that what we think of the crime is just like what the criminal thinks of his punishment. If it's a risk for a risk, how can anybody miss the point?

From the standpoint of deterrence, there is no doubt that we are sometimes well deterred by the prospect of risk.[8] It happens every time we wait to cross the street. It is an empirical question how effective a deterrent the penal lottery might be. Compared with the alternative

punishment of a certain harm, such as a moderate prison term, the lottery might give us more deterrence for a given amount of penal harm, or it might give us less. Whether it gives us more or less might depend a lot on the details of how the two systems operate. If the lottery gave us more, that would make it preferable from the standpoint of deterrence.

(We often hear about evidence that certainty is more deterring than severity. But to the extent that this evidence pertains only to the uncertainty of getting caught, getting convicted, and serving the full sentence, it is scarcely relevant. The criminal might think of escaping punishment as a game of skill—his skill, or perhaps his lawyer's. For all we know, a risk of losing a game of chance might be much more deterring than an equal risk of losing a game of skill.)

From the standpoint of defense, the penal lottery gets some dangerous criminals off the streets forever, while others go free at once. Moderate prison terms would let all go free after a longer time, some of them perhaps reformed and some of them hardened and embittered. It is another empirical question which alternative is the more effective system of defense. Again, the answer may depend greatly on the details of the two systems, and on much else that we cannot easily find out.[9]

IV

So far we have abundant uncertainties, but no clear-cut case against the penal lottery. If anything, the balance may be tipping in its favor. So let us turn finally to the standpoint of desert. Here it is a bit hard to know what to make of the penal lottery. If the court has done its job correctly, then all who are sentenced to face the same lottery, with the same odds, are equally guilty of equally grave crimes. They deserve equal treatment. Do they get it?—Yes and no.

Yes. We treat them alike because we subject them all to the very same penal lottery, with the very same odds. And when the lots are drawn, we treat them alike again, because we follow the same predetermined contingency plan— death for losers, freedom for winners—for all of them alike.

No. Some of them are put to death, some are set free, and what could be more unequal than that?

Yes. Their fates are unequal, of course. But that is not our doing. They are treated unequally by Fortune, not by us.

No. But it is we who hand them over to the inequity of Fortune. We are Fortune's accomplices.

Yes. Everyone is exposed to the inequity of Fortune, in ever so many ways. However nice it may be to undo some of these inequities, we do not ordinarily think of this as part of what is required for equal treatment.

No. It's one thing not to go out of our way to undo the inequities of Fortune; it's another thing to go out of our way to increase them.

Yes. We do that too, and think it not at all contrary to equal treatment. When we hire astronauts, or soldiers or sailors or firemen or police, we knowingly subject these people to more of the inequities of Fortune than are found in ordinary life.

No. But the astronauts are volunteers . . .

Yes. . . . and so are the criminals, when they commit the crimes for which they know they must face the lottery. The soldiers, however, sometimes are not.

No. Start over. We agreed that the winners and losers deserve equal punishment. That is because they are equally guilty. Then they deserve to suffer equally. But they do not.

Yes. They do not suffer equally; but if they deserve to, that is not our affair. We seldom think that equal punishment means making sure of equal suffering. Does the cheerful man get a longer prison sentence than the equally guilty morose man, to make sure of equal suffering? If one convict gets lung cancer in prison, do we see to it that the rest who are equally guilty suffer equally? When we punish equally, what we equalize is not the suffering itself. What we equalize is our contribution to expected suffering.

No. This all seems like grim sophistry. Surely, equal treatment has to mean more than just treating people so that *some* common description of what we are doing will apply to them all alike.

Yes. True. But we have made up our minds already, in other connections, that lotteries

count as equal treatment, or near enough. When we have an indivisible benefit or burden to hand out (or even one that is divisible at a significant cost) we are very well content to resort to a lottery. We are satisfied that all who have equal chances are getting equal treatment—and not in some queer philosophers' sense, but in the sense that matters to justice.

It seems to me that "Yes" is winning this argument, but that truth and justice are still somehow on the side of "No." The next move, dear reader, is up to you. I shall leave it unsettled whether a penal lottery would be just. I shall move on to my second task, which is to show that our present practice amounts to a covert penal lottery. If the penal lottery is just, so is our present practice. If not, not.

V

To show that they do not matter, I shall introduce the differences between an overt penal lottery and our present practice one at a time, by running through a sequence of cases. I claim that at no step is there any significant difference of justice between one case and the next. Such differences as there are will be practical advantages only, and will come out much in favor of our present practice.

Case 1 is the overt penal lottery as we have imagined it already, with one added stipulation, as follows. We will proportion the punishment to the heartedness of the attempt, as measured by the risk of death[10] the criminal knowingly and wrongfully inflicted on the victim. We will do this by sentencing the criminal to a risk equal to the one he inflicted on the victim. If the criminal subjected his victim to an 80 percent risk of death, he shall draw his straw from a bundle of eight short and two long; whereas if he halfheartedly subjected the victim to a mere 40 percent risk, he shall draw from four short and six long; and in this way his punishment shall fit his crime. Therefore the court's task is not limited to ascertaining whether the defendant did knowingly and wrongfully subject the victim to a risk of death; also the court must ascertain how much of a risk it was.

Case 2 is like Case 1, except that we skip the dramatic ceremony on the steps of the gallows and draw straws ahead of time. In fact, we have the drawing even before the trial. It is not the defendant himself who draws, but the Public

Drawer. The Drawer is sworn to secrecy; he reveals the outcome only when and if the defendant has been found guilty and sentenced to the lottery. If the defendant is acquitted and the drawing turns out to have been idle, no harm done. Since it is not known ahead of time whether the sentence will be eight and two, four and six, or what, the Drawer must make not one but many drawings ahead of time. He reveals the one, if any, that turns out to be called for.

Case 3 is like Case 2, except without the secrecy. The Drawer announces at once whether the defendant will win or lose in case he is found guilty and sentenced. (Or rather, whether he will win or lose if he is sentenced to eight and two, whether he will win or lose if he is sentenced to four and six, and so on.) This means that the suspense in the courtroom is higher on some occasions than others. But that need not matter, provided that the court can stick conscientiously to the task of ascertaining whether the defendant did knowingly and wrongfully subject the victim to risk, and if so how much risk. It is by declaring that a criminal deserves the lottery that the court expresses society's abhorrence of the crime. So the court's task is still worth doing, even when it is a foregone conclusion that the defendant will win the lottery if sentenced (as might happen if he had won all the alternative draws). But the trial may seem idle, and the expression of abhorrence may fall flat, when it is known all along that, come what may, the defendant will never face the lottery and lose.

Case 4 is like Case 3, except that we make the penal lottery less pure. Losers of the penal lottery get death, as before; winners get a short prison sentence. Therefore it is certain that every criminal who is sentenced to the lottery will suffer at least some penal harm. Thus we make sure that the trial and the sentence will be taken seriously even when it is a foregone conclusion that the defendant, if sentenced, will win the lottery.

Case 1 also was significantly impure. If the draw is held at the last minute, on the very steps of the gallows, then every criminal who is sentenced to face the lottery must spend a period of time—days? weeks? years?—in fear and trembling, and imprisoned, waiting to learn whether he will win or lose. This period of terror is a certain harm that falls on winners and losers alike. Case 2 very nearly eliminates the impurity, since there is no reason why the

Drawer should not reveal the outcome very soon after the criminal is sentenced. Case 3 eliminates it entirely. (In every case, a defendant must spend a period in fear as he waits to learn whether he will be convicted. But this harm cannot count as penal, because it falls equally on the guilty and the innocent, on those who will be convicted and those who will be acquitted.) Case 4 restores impurity, to whatever extent we see fit, but in a different form.

Case 5 is like Case 4, except that the straws are replaced by a different chance device for determining the outcome of the lottery. The Public Drawer conducts an exact reenactment of the crime. If the victim in the reenactment dies, then the criminal loses the lottery. If it is a good reenactment, the risk to the original victim equals the risk to the new victim in the reenactment, which in turn equals the risk that the criminal will lose the lottery; and so, as desired, we punish a risk by an equal risk.

If the outcome of the lottery is to be settled before the trial, as in Cases 2, 3, and 4, then it will be necessary for the Drawer to conduct not just one but several reenactments. He will entertain all reasonable alternative hypotheses about exactly how the crime might have happened—exactly what the defendant might have done by way of knowingly and wrongfully inflicting risk on the victim. He will conduct one reenactment for each hypothesis. The court's task changes. If the court finds the defendant guilty of knowingly and wrongfully inflicting a risk of death, it is no longer required also to measure the amount of risk. Nobody need ever figure out whether it was 80 percent, 40 percent, or what. Instead, the court is required to ascertain which hypothesis about exactly how the crime happened is correct. Thereby the court chooses which of all the hypothetical reenactment is the one that determines whether the criminal wins or loses his lottery. If the court finds that the criminal took careful aim, then the chosen reenactment will be one in which the criminal's stand-in also took careful aim, whereas if the court finds that the criminal halfheartedly fired in the victim's general direction, the chosen reenactment will be one in which the stand-in did likewise. So the criminal will be more likely to lose his lottery in the first case than in the second.

The drawbacks of a lottery by reenactment are plain to see. Soon we shall find the remedy. But first, let us look at the advantages of a lottery by reenactment over a lottery by drawing straws. We have already noted that with straws, the court had to measure how much risk the criminal inflicted, whereas with reenactments, the court has only to ascertain exactly how the crime happened. Both tasks look well-nigh impossible. But the second must be easier, because the first task consists of the second plus more besides. The only way for the court to measure the risk would be to ascertain just what happened, and then find out just how much risk results from such happenings.

Another advantage of reenactments over straws appears when we try to be more careful about what we mean by "amount of risk." Is it (1) an "objective chance"? Or is it (2) a reasonable degree of belief for a hypothetical observer who knows the situation in as much minute detail as feasible instruments could permit? Or is it (3) a reasonable degree of belief for someone who knows just as much about the details of the situation as the criminal did? Or is it (4) the criminal's actual degree of belief, however unreasonable that might have been? It would be nice not to have to decide. But if we want to match the criminal's risk in a lottery by straws to the victim's risk, then we must decide. Not so for a lottery by reenactment. If the reenactment is perfect, we automatically match the amount of risk in all four senses. Even if the reenactment is imperfect, at least we can assure ourselves of match in senses (3) and (4). It may or may not be feasible to get assured match in senses (1) and (2), depending on the details of what happened. (If it turns out that the criminal left a bomb hooked up to a quantum randomizer, it will be comparatively easy. If he committed his crime in a more commonplace way, it will be much harder.) But whenever it is hard to get assured match in senses (1) and (2), it will be harder still to measure the risk and get assured match in a lottery by straws. So however the crime happened, and whatever sense of match we want, we do at least as well by reenactment as by straws, and sometimes we do better.

Case 6 is like Case 5, except that enactment replaces *re*enactment. We use the original crime, so to speak, as its own perfect reenactment. If the criminal is sentenced to face the lottery, then if his victim dies, he loses his lottery and he dies too, whereas if the victim lives, the criminal wins, and he gets only the short prison sentence. It does not matter when the lottery takes place, provided only that is not settled so soon that the criminal may know its outcome before he decides whether to commit his crime.

The advantages are many: we need no Drawer to do the work; we need not find volunteers to be the stand-in victims in all the hypothetical reenactments; the "reenactment" is automatically perfect, matching the risk in all four senses; we spare the court the difficult task of ascertaining exactly how the crime happened. If we want to give a risk for a risk, and if we want to match risks in any but a very approximate and uncertain fashion, the lottery by enactment is not only the easy way, it is the only remotely feasible way.

The drawback is confusion. When a criminal is sentenced to face the lottery by straws, nobody will think him more guilty or more wicked just because his straw is short. And when a criminal is sentenced to face the lottery by reenactment, nobody will think him more guilty just because the stand-in victim dies.[11] But if he is sentenced to the lottery by enactment, then one and the same event plays a double role: if his victim dies, that death is at once the main harm done by his crime and also the way of losing his lottery. If we are not careful, we are apt to misunderstand. We may think that the successful attempter suffers a worse fate because he is more guilty when he does a worse harm, rather than because he loses his lottery. But it is not so: his success is irrelevant to his guilt, his wickedness, his desert, and his sentence to face the lottery—exactly as the shortness of his straw would have been, had he been sentenced to the lottery by straws.

VI

I submit that our present practice is exactly Case 6: punishment for attempts regardless of success, a penal lottery by enactment, impurity to help us take the affair seriously even when the lottery is won, and the inevitable confusion. We may not understand our practice as a penal lottery—confused as we are, we have trouble understanding it at all—but, so understood, it does make a good deal of sense. It is another question whether it is really just. Most likely it isn't, but I don't understand why not.

NOTES

This article arose out of discussion of a lecture by Judith Thomson about the guilt of successful and unsuccessful attempters. I am grateful for comments by John Broome, Stephanie Lewis, T. M. Scanlon, Thomas Schelling, and Jonathan

Suzman; by the Editors of *Philosophy & Public Affairs*; and by audiences at Monash University, the Australian National University, and the Russellian Society (Sydney).

1. I do not wish to enter the debate about whether the traditional death penalty is ever justified. If you think not, substitute throughout whatever you think is the correct maximum penalty; my argument will go through almost without change.

2. John Kleinig, *Punishment and Desert* (The Hague: Martinus Nijhoff, 1973), p. 132. Kleinig does not take this to afford an adequate justification.

3. See Thomas Nagel, "Moral Luck," *Proceedings of the Aristotelian Society*, supp. vol. 50 (1976): 141, repr. in Nagel, *Mortal Questions* (Cambridge: Cambridge University Press, 1979), p. 29. Nagel distinguishes, as he should, between the "moral luck" of the attempter and the different sort of moral luck that makes some genuine difference to how one is and how one acts.

4. The luck of hitting and missing does make a difference to how their actions of shooting may be described: Dee's is a killing. Dum's is not. Dee's causes harm and thereby invades the victim's rights in a way that Dum's does not. (Dee invades the victim's right not to be harmed, as well as his right not to be endangered; Dum invades only the latter right.) But this is no difference in how they act, since the description of an action in terms of what it causes is an extrinsic description. The actions themselves, events that are finished when the agent has done his part, do not differ in any intrinsic way.

You might protest that a killing is not over when the killer has done his part; it is a more prolonged event that ends with the death of the victim; so there is, after all, an intrinsic difference between Dee's action of killing and Dum's action of shooting and missing.—No; an action of killing is different from the prolonged event of someone's getting killed, even though "the killing" can denote either one.

5. See Lawrence C. Becker, "Criminal Attempt and the Theory of the Law of Crimes," *Philosophy & Public Affairs* 3, no. 3 (Spring 1974): 288. Becker does not take this to afford an adequate justification.

6. See A. Hough and D. M. Schwartz, "AIDS and Prisons," in *Meeting the Challenge: Papers of the First National Conference on AIDS*, ed. Adam Carr (Canberra: Australian Government Publishing Service, 1986), pp. 171–80.

7. This point would disappear if something less cheap and quick than death were the penalty for losers of the lottery.

8. See Thomas C. Schelling, "The Threat That Leaves Something to Chance," in his book *The Strategy of Conflict* (Cambridge: Harvard University Press, 1960). Schelling does not discuss penal lotteries as such, but much of his discussion carries over. What does not carry over, or not much, is his discussion of chancy threats as a way to gain credibility when one has strong reason not to fulfill one's threat.

9. This question would have to be reconsidered if something other than death were the maximum penalty, and so the penalty for losers of the lottery. It would remain an empirical question, and probably a difficult one, which is the more effective system of defense.

10. I note a complication once and for all, but I shall ignore it in what follows. The relevant risk is not really the victim's risk of death, but rather the risk of being killed—that is, of dying a death which is caused, perhaps probabilistically, and in the appropriate insensitive fashion, by the criminal's act. Likewise for the criminal's risk in the penal lottery. (On probabilistic and insensitive causation, see my *Philosophical Papers*, vol. II [New York: Oxford University Press, 1986], pp. 175–88.)

11. If it were known that the victim's risk was fifty-fifty, or if we did not care about matching risks, we could just as well reverse the lottery by enactment: the criminal loses if the victim lives, wins if the victim dies. Certainly nobody will think the criminal is more guilty if the victim *lives*.

FURMAN v. GEORGIA

United States Supreme Court, 1972*

Mr. Justice Douglas, concurring.

In these three cases the death penalty was imposed, one of them for murder, and two for rape. In each the determination of whether the penalty should be death or a lighter punishment was left by the State to the discretion of the judge or of the jury. In each of the three cases the trial was to a jury. They are here on petitions for certiorari which we granted limited to the question whether the imposition and execution of the death penalty constitutes "cruel and unusual punishment" within the meaning of the Eighth Amendment as applied to the States by the Fourteenth. I vote to vacate each judgment, believing that the exaction of the death penalty does violate the Eighth and Fourteenth Amendments.

. . . We cannot say from facts disclosed in these records that these defendants were sentenced to death because they were black. Yet our task is not restricted to an effort to divine what motives impelled these death penalties. Rather, we deal with a system of law and of justice that leaves to the uncontrolled discretion of judges or juries the determination whether defendants committing these crimes should die or be imprisoned. Under these laws no standards govern the selection of the penalty. People live or die, dependent on the whim of one man or of 12.

. . . In a Nation committed to equal protection of the laws there is no permissible "caste" aspect[18] of law enforcement. Yet we know that the discretion of judges and juries in imposing the death penalty enables the penalty to be selectively applied, feeding prejudices against the accused if he is poor and despised, and lacking political clout, or if he is a member of a suspect or unpopular minority, and saving those who by social position may be in a more protected position. In ancient Hindu law a Brahman was exempt from capital punishment,[19] and in those days, "[g]enerally, in the law books, punishment increased in severity as social status diminished."[20] We have, I fear, taken in practice the same position, partially as a result of making the death penalty discretionary and partially as a result of the ability of the rich to purchase the services of the most respected and most resourceful legal talent in the Nation.

The high service rendered by the "cruel and unusual" punishment clause of the Eighth Amendment is to require legislatures to write penal laws that are evenhanded, nonselective, and nonarbitrary, and to require judges to see to it that general laws are not applied sparsely, selectively, and spottily to unpopular groups.

A law that stated that anyone making more than $50,000 would be exempt from the death penalty would plainly fall, as would a law that in terms said that blacks, those who never went beyond the fifth grade in school, those who made less than $3,000 a year, or those who were unpopular or unstable should be the only people executed. A law which in the overall view reaches that result in practice[21] has no more sanctity than a law which in terms provides the same.

Thus, these discretionary statutes are unconstitutional in their operation. They are pregnant with discrimination and discrimination is an ingredient not compatible with the idea of equal protection of the laws that is implicit in the ban on "cruel and unusual" punishments.

Any law which is nondiscriminatory on its face may be applied in such a way as to violate the Equal Protection Clause of the Fourteenth Amendment. *Yick Wo* v. *Hopkins,* 118 U.S. 356. Such conceivably might be the fate of a mandatory death penalty, where equal or lesser sentences were imposed on the elite, a harsher one or the minorities or members of the lower castes. Whether a mandatory death penalty would otherwise be constitutional is a question I do not reach.

I concur in the judgments of the Court.

Mr. Justice Brennan, concurring.

. . . There are, then, four principles by which we may determine whether a particular punishment is "cruel and unusual." The primary principle, which I believe supplies the essential predicate for the application of the others, is that a punishment must not by its severity be degrading to human dignity. The paradigm violation of this principle would be the infliction of a tortur-

*408 U.S. 238 (1972). Excerpts only. Footnotes numbered as in the original. Two cases from Georgia and one from Texas were considered and decided together by the Supreme Court.

ous punishment of the type that the Clause has always prohibited. Yet "[i]t is unlikely that any State at this moment in history," *Robinson* v. *California,* 370 U.S., at 666, would pass a law providing for the infliction of such a punishment. Indeed, no such punishment has ever been before this Court. The same may be said of the other principles. It is unlikely that this Court will confront a severe punishment that is obviously inflicted in wholly arbitrary fashion; no State would engage in a reign of blind terror. Nor is it likely that this Court will be called upon to review a severe punishment that is clearly and totally rejected throughout society; no legislature would be able even to authorize the infliction of such a punishment. Nor, finally, is it likely that this Court will have to consider a severe punishment that is patently unnecessary; no State today would inflict a severe punishment knowing that there was no reason whatever for doing so. In short, we are unlikely to have occasion to determine that a punishment is fatally offensive under any one principle.

Since the Bill of Rights was adopted, this Court has adjudged only three punishments to be within the prohibition of the Clause. See *Weems* v. *United States,* 217 U.S. 349 (1910) (12 years in chains at hard and painful labor); *Trop* v. *Dulles,* 356 U.S. 86 (1958) (expatriation); *Robinson* v. *California,* 370 U.S. 660 (1962) (imprisonment for narcotics addiction). Each punishment, of course, was degrading to human dignity, but of none could it be said conclusively that it was fatally offensive under one or the other of the principles. Rather, these "cruel and unusual punishments" seriously implicated several of the principles, and it was the application of the principles in combination that supported the judgment. That, indeed, is not surprising. The function of these principles, after all, is simply to provide means by which a court can determine whether a challenged punishment comports with human dignity. They are, therefore, interrelated, and in most cases it will be their convergence that will justify the conclusion that a punishment is "cruel and unusual." The test, then, will ordinarily be a cumulative one: If a punishment is unusually severe, if there is a strong probability that it is inflicted arbitrarily, if it is substantially rejected by contemporary society, and if there is no reason to believe that it serves any penal purpose more effectively than some less severe punishment, then the continued infliction of that punishment violates the command of the Clause that the State may not inflict inhuman and uncivilized punishments upon those convicted of crimes.

. . . The question, then, is whether the deliberate infliction of death is today consistent with the command of the Clause that the State may not inflict punishments that do not comport with human dignity. I will analyze the punishment of death in terms of the principles set out above and the cumulative test to which they lead: It is a denial of human dignity for the State arbitrarily to subject a person to an unusually severe punishment that society has indicated it does not regard as acceptable, and that cannot be shown to serve any penal purpose more effectively than a significantly less drastic punishment. Under these principles and this test, death is today a "cruel and unusual" punishment.

Death is a unique punishment in the United States. In a society that so strongly affirms the sanctity of life, not surprisingly the common view is that death is the ultimate sanction. This natural human feeling appears all about us. There has been no national debate about punishment, in general or by imprisonment, comparable to the debate about the punishment of death. No other punishment has been so continuously restricted, see *infra,* at 296–298, nor has any State yet abolished prisons, as some have abolished this punishment. And those States that still inflict death reserve it for the most heinous crimes. Juries, of course, have always treated death cases differently, as have governors exercising their communication powers. Criminal defendants are of the same view. "As all practicing lawyers know, who have defended persons charged with capital offenses, often the only goal possible is to avoid the death penalty." *Griffin* v. *Illinois,* 351 U.S. 12, 28 (1956) (Burton and Minton, JJ., dissenting). Some legislatures have required particular procedures, such as two-stage trials and automatic appeals, applicable only in death cases. "It is the universal experience in the administration of criminal justice that those charged with capital offenses are granted special considerations." *Ibid.* See *Williams* v. *Florida,* 399 U.S. 78, 103 (1970) (all States require juries of 12 in death cases). This Court, too, almost always treats death cases as a class apart.[34] And the unfortunate effect of this punishment upon the functioning of the judicial process is well known; no other punishment has a similar effect.

The only explanation for the uniqueness of death is its extreme severity. Death is today an unusually severe punishment, unusual in its pain, in its finality, and in its enormity. No other existing punishment is comparable to death in terms of physical and mental suffering. Although our information is not conclusive, it appears that there is no method available that guarantees an immediate and painless death.[35] Since the discontinuance of flogging as a constitutionally permissible punishment, *Jackson* v. *Bishop,* 404 F. 2d 571 (CA8 1968), death remains as the only punishment that may involve the conscious infliction of physical pain. In addition, we know that mental pain is an inseparable part of our practice of punishing criminals by death for the prospect of pending execution exacts a frightful toll during the inevitable long wait between the imposition of sentence and the actual infliction of death. Cf *Ex parte Medley,* 134 U.S. 160, 172 (1890). As the California Supreme Court pointed out, "the process of carrying out a verdict of death is often so degrading and brutalizing to the human spirit as to constitute psychological torture." *People* v. *Anderson,* 6 Cal. 3d 628, 649, 493 P. 2d 880, 894 (1972).[36] Indeed, as Mr. Justice Frankfurter noted, "the onset of insanity while awaiting execution of a death sentence is not a rare phenomenon." *Solesbee* v. *Balkcom,* 339 U.S. 9, 14 (1950) (dissenting opinion). The "fate of ever-increasing fear and distress" to which the expatriate is subjected, *Trop* v. *Dulles,* 356 U.S., at 102, can only exist to a greater degree for a person confined in prison awaiting death.[37]

The unusual severity of death is manifested most clearly in its finality and enormity. Death, in these respects, is in a class by itself. Expatriation, for example, is a punishment that "destroys for the individual the political existence that was centuries in the development," that "strips the citizen of his status in the national and international political community," and that puts "[h]is very existence" in jeopardy. Expatriation thus inherently entails "the total destruction of the individual's status in organized society." *Id.,* at 101. "In short, the expatriate has lost the right to have rights." *Id.,* at 102. Yet, demonstrably, expatriation is not "a fate worse than death." *Id.,* at 125 (Frankfurther, J., dissenting).[38] Although death, like expatriation, destroys the individual's "political existence" and his "status in organized society," it does more, for, unlike expatriation, death also destroys "[h]is very existence." There is, too at least the possibility that the expatriate will in the future regain "the right to have rights." Death forecloses even that possibility.

Death is truly an awesome punishment. The calculated killing of a human being by the State involves, by its very nature, a denial of the executed person's humanity. The contrast with the plight of a person punished by imprisonment is evident. An individual in prison does not lose "the right to have rights." A prisoner retains, for example, the constitutional rights to the free exercise of religion, to be free of cruel and unusual punishments, and to treatment as a "person" for purposes of due process of law and the equal protection of the laws. A prisoner remains a member of the human family. Moreover, he retains the right of access to the courts. His punishment is not irrevocable. Apart from the common charge, grounded upon the recognition of human fallibility, that the punishment of death must inevitably be inflicted upon innocent men, we know that death has been the lot of men whose convictions were unconstitutionally secured in view of later, retroactively applied, holdings of this Court. The pun-

ishment itself may have been unconstitutionally inflicted, see *Witherspoon* v. *Illinois,* 391 U.S. 510 (1968), yet the finality of death precludes relief. An executed person has indeed 'lost the right to have rights." As one 19th century proponent of punishing criminals by death declared, "When a man is hung, there is an end of our relations with him. His execution is a way of saying, 'You are not fit for this world, take your chance elsewhere.' "[39]

In comparison to all other punishments today, then, the deliberate extinguishment of human life by the State is uniquely degrading to human dignity. I would not hesitate to hold, on that ground alone, that death is today a "cruel and unusual" punishment, were it not that death is a punishment of longstanding usage and acceptance in this country. I therefore turn to the second principle—that the State may not arbitrarily inflict an unusually severe punishment.

. . . When the punishment of death is inflicted in a trivial number of the cases in which it is legally available, the conclusion is virtually inescapable that it is being inflicted arbitrarily. Indeed, it smacks of little more than a lottery system. The States claim, however, that this rarity is evidence not of arbitrariness, but of informed selectivity: Death is inflicted, they say, only in "extreme" cases.

Informed selectivity, of course, is a value not to be denigrated. Yet presumably the States could make precisely the same claim if there were 10 executions per year, or five, or even if there were but one. That there may be as many as 50 per year does not strengthen the claim. When the rate of infliction is at this low level, it is highly implausible that only the worst criminals or the criminals who commit the worst crimes are selected for this punishment. No one has yet suggested a rational basis that could differentiate in those terms the few who die from the many who go to prison. Crimes and criminals simply do not admit of a distinction that can be drawn so finely as to explain, on that ground, the execution of such a tiny sample of those eligible. Certainly the laws that provide for this punishment do not attempt to draw that distinction; all cases to which the laws apply are necessarily "extreme." Nor is the distinction credible in fact. If, for example, petitioner Furman or his crime illustrates the "extreme," then nearly all murderers and their murders are also "extreme."[48] Furthermore, our procedures in death cases, rather than resulting in the selection of "extreme" cases for this punishment, actually sanction an arbitrary selection. For this Court has held that juries may, as they do, make the decision whether to impose a death sentence wholly unguided by standards governing that decision. *McGautha* v. *California,* 402 U.S. 183, 196–208 (1971). In other words, our procedures are not constructed to guard against the totally capricious selection of criminals for the punishment of death.

Although it is difficult to imagine what further facts would be necessary in order to prove that death is, as my Brother Stewart puts it, "wantonly and . . . freakishly" inflicted, I need not conclude that arbitrary infliction is patently obvious. I am not considering this punishment by the isolated light of one principle. The probability of arbitrariness is sufficiently substantial that it can be relied upon, in combination with the other principles, in reaching a judgment on the constitutionality of this punishment.

When there is a strong probability that an unusually severe and degrading punishment is being inflicted arbitrarily, we may well expect that society will disapprove of its infliction. I turn, therefore, to the third principle. An examination of the history and present operation of the American practice of punishing criminals by death reveals that this punishment has been almost totally rejected by contemporary society.

. . . The progressive decline in, and the current rarity of, the infliction of death demonstrate that our society seriously questions the appropriateness of this punishment today. The States point out that many legislatures authorize death as the punishment for certain crimes and that substantial segments of the public, as reflected in opinion polls and referendum votes, continue to support it. Yet the availability of this punishment through statutory authorization, as well as the polls and referenda, which amount simply to approval of that authorization, simply underscores the extent to which our society has in fact rejected this punishment. When an unusually severe punishment is authorized for wide-scale application but not, because of society's refusal, inflicted save in a few instances, the inference is compelling that there is a deep-seated reluctance to inflict it. Indeed, the likelihood is great that the punishment is tolerated only because of its disuse. The objective indicator of society's view of an unusually severe punishment is what society does with it, and today society will inflict death upon only a small sample of the eligible criminals. Rejection could hardly be more complete without becoming absolute. At the very least, I must conclude that contemporary society views this punishment with substantial doubt.

The final principle to be considered is that an unusually severe and degrading punishment may not be excessive in view of the purposes for which it is inflicted. This principle, too, is related to the others. When there is a strong probability that the State is arbitrarily inflicting an unusually severe punishment that is subject to grave societal doubts, it is likely also that the punishment cannot be shown to be serving any penal purpose that could not be served equally well by some less severe punishment.

The States' primary claim is that death is a necessary punishment because it prevents the commission of capital crimes more effectively than any less severe punishment. The first part of this claim is that the infliction of death is necessary to stop the individuals executed from committing further crimes. The sufficient answer to this is that if a criminal convicted of a capital crime poses a danger to society, effective administration of the State's pardon and parole laws can delay or deny his release from prison, and techniques of isolation can eliminate or minimize the danger while he remains confined.

The more significant argument is that the threat of death prevents the commission of capital crimes because it deters potential criminals who would not be deterred by the threat of imprisonment. The argument is not based upon evidence that the threat of death is a superior deterrent. Indeed, as my Brother Marshall establishes, the available evidence uniformly indicates, although it does not conclusively prove, that the threat of death has no greater deterrent effect than the threat of imprisonment. The States argue, however, that they are entitled to rely upon common human experience, and that experience, they say, supports the conclusion that death must be a more effective deterrent than any less severe punishment. Because people fear death the most, the argument runs, the threat of death must be the greatest deterrent.

It is important to focus upon the precise import of this argument. It is not denied that many, and probably most, capital crimes cannot be deterred by the threat of punishment. Thus the argument can apply only to those who think rationally about the commission of capital crimes. Particularly is that true when the potential criminal, under this argument, must not only consider the risk of punishment, but also distinguish between two possible punishments. The concern, then, is with a particular type of potential criminal, the rational person who will commit a capital crime knowing that the punishment is long-term imprisonment, which may well be for the rest of his life, but will not commit the crime knowing that the punishment is death. On the face of it, the assumption that such persons exist is implausible.

In any event, this argument cannot be appraised in the abstract. We are not presented with the theoretical question whether under any imaginable circumstances the threat of death might be a greater deterrent to the commission of capital crimes than the threat of imprisonment. We are concerned with the practice of punishing criminals by death as it exists in the United States today. Proponents of this argument necessarily admit that its validity depends upon the existence of a system in which the punishment of death is invariably and swiftly imposed. Our system, of course, satisfies neither condition. A rational person contemplating a murder or rape is confronted, not with the certainty of a speedy death, but with the slightest possibility that he will be executed in the distant future. The risk of death is remote and improbable; in contrast, the risk of long-term imprisonment is near and great. In short, whatever the speculative validity of the assumption that the threat of death is a superior deterrent, there is no reason to believe that as currently administered the punishment of death is necessary to deter the commission of capital crimes. Whatever might be the case were all or substantially all eligible criminals quickly put to death, unverifiable possibilities are an insufficient basis upon which to conclude that the threat of death today has any greater deterrent efficacy than the threat of imprisonment.[54]

There is, however, another aspect to the argument that the punishment of death is necessary for the protection of society. The infliction of death, the States urge, serves to manifest the community's outrage at the commission of the crime. It is, they say, a concrete public expression of moral indignation that inculcates respect for the law and helps assure a more peaceful community. Moreover, we are told, not only does the punishment of death exert this widespread moralizing influence upon community values, it also satisfies the popular demand for grievous condemnation of abhorrent crimes and thus prevents disorder, lynching, and attempts by private citizens to take the law into their own hands.

The question, however, is not whether death serves these supposed purposes of punishment, but whether death serves them more effectively than imprisonment. There is no evidence whatever that utilization of imprisonment rather than death encourages private blood feuds and other disorders. Surely if there were such a danger, the execution of a handful of criminals each year would not prevent it. The assertion that death alone is a sufficiently emphatic denunciation for capital crimes suffers from the same defect. If capital crimes require the punishment of death in order to provide moral reinforcement for the basic values of the community, those values can only be undermined when death is so rarely inflicted upon the criminals who commit the crimes. Furthermore, it is certainly doubtful that the infliction of death by the State does in fact strengthen the community's moral code; if the deliberate extinguishment of human life has any effect at all, it more likely tends to lower our respect for life and brutalize our values. That, after all, is why we no longer carry out public executions. In any event, this claim simply means that one purpose of punishment is to indicate social disapproval of crime. To serve that purpose our laws distribute punishments according to the gravity of crimes and punish more severely the crimes society regards as more serious. That purpose cannot justify any particular punishment as the upper limit of severity.

Mr. Justice White, concurring.

. . . Most important, a major goal of the criminal law —to deter others by punishing the convicted criminal —would not be substantially served where the penalty is so seldom invoked that it ceases to be the credible threat essential to influence the conduct of others. For present purposes I accept the morality and utility of punishing one person to influence another. I accept also the effectiveness of punishment generally and need not reject the death penalty as a more effective deterrent than a lesser punishment. But common sense and experience tell us that seldom-enforced laws become ineffective measures for controlling human conduct and that the death penalty, unless imposed with sufficient frequency, will make little contribution to deterring those crimes for which it may be exacted.

The imposition and execution of the death penalty are obviously cruel in the dictionary sense. But the penalty has not been considered cruel and unusual punishment in the constitutional sense because it was thought justified by the social ends it was deemed to serve. At the moment that it ceases realistically to further these purposes, however, the emerging question is whether its imposition in such circumstances would violate the Eighth Amendment. It is my view that it would, for its imposition would then be the pointless and needless extinction of life with only marginal contributions to any discernible social or public purposes. A penalty with such negligible returns to the State would be patently excessive and cruel and unusual punishment violative of the Eighth Amendment.

It is also my judgment that this point has been reached with respect to capital punishment as it is presently administered under the statutes involved in these cases. Concededly, it is difficult to prove as a general proposition that capital punishment, however administered, more effectively serves the ends of the criminal law than does imprisonment. But however that may be, I cannot avoid the conclusion that as the statutes before us are now administered, the penalty is so infrequently imposed that the threat of execution is too attenuated to be of substantial service to criminal justice.

I need not restate the facts and figures that appear in the opinions of my Brethren Nor can I "prove" my conclusion from these data. But, like my Brethren, I must arrive at judgment; and I can do no more than state a conclusion based on 10 years of almost daily exposure to the facts and circumstances of hundreds and hundreds of federal and state criminal cases involving crimes for which death is the authorized penalty. That conclusion, as I have said, is that the death penalty is exacted with great infrequency even for the most atrocious crimes and that there is no meaningful basis for distinguishing the few cases in which it is imposed from the many cases in which it is not. The short of it is that the policy of vesting sentencing authority primarily in juries—a decision largely motivated by the desire to mitigate the harshness of the law and to bring community judgment to bear on the sentence as well as guilt or innocence—has so effectively achieved its aims that capital punishment within the confines of the statutes now before us has for all practical purposes run its course.

Mr. Chief Justice Burger, with whom Mr. Justice Blackmun, Mr. Justice Powell, and Mr. Justice Rehnquist join, dissenting.

. . . There are no obvious indications that capital punishment offends the conscience of society to such a degree that our traditional deference to the legislative judgment must be abandoned. It is not a punishment such as burning at the stake that everyone would ineffably find to be repugnant to all civilized standards. Nor is it a punishment so roundly condemned that only a few aberrant legislatures have retained it on the statute books. Capital punishment is authorized by statute in 40 States, the District of Columbia, and in the federal courts for the commission of certain crimes.[7] On four occasions in the last 11 years Congress has added to the list of federal crimes punishable by death.[8] In looking for reliable indicia of contemporary attitude, none more trustworthy has been advanced.

One conceivable source of evidence that legislatures have abdicated their essentially barometric role with respect to community values would be public opinion polls, of which there have been many in the past decade addressed to the question of capital punishment. Without assessing the reliability of such polls, or intimating that any judicial reliance could ever be placed on them, it need only be noted that the reported results have shown nothing approximating the universal condemnation of capital punishment that might lead us to suspect that the legislatures in general have lost touch with current social values.[9]

Counsel for petitioners rely on a different body of empirical evidence. They argue, in effect, that the number of cases in which the death penalty is imposed, as compared with the number of cases in which it is statutorily available, reflects a general revulsion toward the penalty that would lead to its repeal if only it were more generally and widely enforced. It cannot be gainsaid that by the choice of juries—and sometimes judges[10]—the death penalty is imposed in far fewer than half the cases in which it is available.[11] To go further and characterize the rate of imposition as "freakishly rare," as petitioners insist, is unwarranted hyperbole. And regardless of its characterization, the rate of imposition does not impel the conclusion that capital punishment is now regarded as intolerably cruel or uncivilized.

It is argued that in those capital cases where juries have recommended mercy, they have given expression to civilized values and effectively renounced the legislative authorization for capital punishment. At the same time it is argued that where juries have made the awesome decision to send men to their deaths, they have acted arbitrarily and without sensitivity to prevailing standards of decency. This explanation for the infrequency of imposition of capital punishment is unsupported by known facts, and is inconsistent in principle with everything this Court has ever said about the functioning of juries in capital cases.

In *McGautha* v. *California,* decided only one year ago, the Court held that there was no mandate in the Due Process Clause of the Fourteenth Amendment that juries be given instructions as to when the death penalty should be imposed. After reviewing the autonomy that juries have traditionally exercised in capital cases and noting the practical difficulties of framing manageable instructions, this Court concluded that judicially articulated standards were not needed to insure a responsible decision as to penalty. Nothing in *McGautha* licenses capital juries to act arbitrarily or assumes that they have so acted in the past. On the contrary, the assumption underlying the *McGautha* ruling is that juries "will act with due regard for the consequences of their decision." 402 U.S., at 208.

The responsibility of juries deciding capital cases in our system of justice was nowhere better described than in *Witherspoon* v. *Illinois, supra:*

"[A] jury that must choose between life imprisonment and capital punishment can do little more—and must do nothing less—than express *the conscience of the community* on the ultimate question of life or death."

"And one of the most important functions any jury can perform in making such a selection is to maintain a link between contemporary community values and the penal system—a link without which the determination of punishment could hardly reflect 'the evolving standards of decency that mark the progress of a maturing society'" 391 U.S., at 519 and n. 15 (emphasis added).

The selectivity of juries in imposing the punishment of death is properly viewed as a refinement on rather than a repudiation of, the statutory authorization for that penalty. Legislatures prescribe the categories of crimes for which the death penalty should be available, and, acting as "the conscience of the community," juries are entrusted to determine in individual cases that the ultimate punishment is warranted. Juries are undoubtedly influenced in this judgment by myriad factors. The motive or lack of motive of the perpetrator, the degree of injury or suffering of the victim or victims, and the degree of brutality in the commission of the crime would seem to be prominent among these factors. Given the general awareness that death is no longer a routine punishment for the crimes for which it is made available, it is hardly surprising that juries have been increasingly meticulous in their imposition of the penalty. But to assume from the mere fact of relative infrequency that only a random assortment of pariahs are sentenced to death, is to cast grave doubt on the basic integrity of our jury system.

It would, of course, be unrealistic to assume that juries have been perfectly consistent in choosing the cases where the death penalty is to be imposed, for no human institution performs with perfect consistency. There are doubtless prisoners on death row who would not be there had they been tried before a different jury or in a different State. In this sense their fate has been controlled by a fortuitous circumstance. However, this element of fortuity does not stand as an indictment either of the general functioning of juries in capital cases or of the integrity of jury decisions in individual cases. There is no empirical basis for concluding that juries have generally failed to discharge in good faith the responsibility described in *Witherspoon*—that of choosing between life and death in individual cases according to the dictates of community values.[12]

. . . It seems remarkable to me that with our basic trust in lay jurors as the keystone in our system of criminal justice, it should now be suggested that we take the most sensitive and important of all decisions away from them. I could more easily be persuaded that mandatory sentences of death, without the intervening and ameliorating impact of lay jurors, are so arbitrary and doctrinaire that they violate the Constitution. The very infrequency of death penalties imposed by jurors attests their cautious and discriminating reservation of that penalty for the most extreme cases. I had thought that nothing was clearer in history, as we noted in *McGautha* one year ago, than the American abhorrence of "the common-law rule imposing a mandatory death sentence on all convicted murderers." 402 U.S., at 198. As the concurring opinion of Mr. Justice Marshall shows, *ante,* at 339, the 19th century movement away from mandatory death sentences marked an enlightened introduction of flexibility into the sentencing process. It recognized that individual culpability is not always measured by the category of the crime committed. This change in sentencing practice was greeted by the Court as a humanizing development. See *Winston* v. *United States,* 172 U.S. 303 (1899); cf. *Calton* v. *Utah,* 130 U.S. 83 (1889). See also *Andres* v. *United States,* 333 U.S. 740, 753 (1948) (Frankfurter, J., concurring). I do not see how this history can be ignored and how it can be suggested that the Eighth Amendment demands the elimination of the most sensitive feature of the sentencing system.

As a general matter, the evolution of penal concepts in this country has not been marked by great progress, nor have the results up to now been crowned with significant success. If anywhere in the whole spectrum of criminal justice fresh ideas deserve sober analysis, the sentencing and correctional area ranks high on the list. But it has been widely accepted that mandatory sentences for crimes do not best serve the ends of the criminal justice system. Now, after the long process of drawing away from the blind imposition of uniform sentences for every person convicted of a particular offense, we are confronted with an argument perhaps implying that only the legislatures may determine that a sentence of death is appropriate, without the intervening evaluation of jurors or judges. This approach threatens to turn back the progress of penal reform, which has moved until recently at too slow a rate to absorb significant setbacks.

NOTES

1. The opinion of the Supreme Court of Georgia affirming Furman's conviction of murder and sentence of death is reported in 225 Ga. 253, 167 S. E. 2d 628, and its opinion affirming Jackson's conviction of rape and sentence of death is reported in 225 Ga. 790, 171 S. E. 2d 501. The conviction of Branch of rape and the sentence of death were affirmed by the Court of Criminal Appeals of Texas and reported in 447 S. W. 2d 932.

18. See Johnson, The Negro and Crime, 217 Annals Amer. Acad. Pol. & Soc. Sci. 93 (1941).

19. See J. Spellman, Political Theory of Ancient India 112 (1964).

20. C. Drekmeier, Kingship and Community in Early India 233 (1962).

21. Cf. B. Prettyman, Jr., Death and The Supreme Court 296–297 (1961). "The disparity of representation in capital cases raises doubt about capital punishment itself, which has been abolished in only nine states. If a James Avery [345 U.S. 559] can be saved from electrocution because his attorney made timely objection to the selection of a jury by the use of yellow and white tickets, while an Aubry Williams [349 U.S. 375] can be sent to his death by a jury selected in precisely the same manner, we are imposing our most extreme penalty in an uneven fashion.

"The problem of proper representation is not a problem of money, as some have claimed, but of a lawyer's ability, and it is not true that only the rich have able lawyers. Both the rich and the poor usually are well represented—the poor because more often than not the best attorneys are appointed to defend them. It is the middle-class defendant, who can afford to hire an attorney but not a very good one, who is at a disadvantage. Certainly William Fikes [352 U.S. 191], despite the anomalous position in which he finds himself today, received as effective and intelligent a defense from his court-appointed attorneys as he would have received from an attorney his family had scraped together enough money to hire.

"And it is not only a matter of ability. An attorney must be found who is prepared to spend precious hours—the basic commodity he has to sell—on a case that seldom fully compensates him and often brings him no fee at all. The public has no conception of the time and effort devoted by attorneys to indigent cases. And in a first-degree case, the added responsibility of having a man's life depend upon the outcome exacts a heavy toll."

34. "That life is at stake is of course another important factor in creating the extraordinary situation. The difference between capital and non-capital offenses is the basis of differentiation in law in diverse ways in which the distinction becomes relevant." *Williams* v. *Georiga,* 349 U.S. 375, 391 (1955) (Frankfurter, J.). "When the penalty is death, we, like state court judges, are tempted to strain the evidence and even, in close cases, the law in order to give a doubtfully condemned man another change." *Stein* v. *New York,* 346 U.S. 156, (1953) (Jackson, J.). "In death cases doubts such as those presented here should be resolved in favor of the accused." *Andres* v. *United States,* 333 U.S. 740, 752 (1948) (Reed, J.). Mr. Justice Harlan expressed the point strongly: "I do not concede that whatever process is 'due' an offender faced with a fine or a prison sentence necessarily satisfies the requirements of the Constitution in a capital case. The distinction is by no means novel, . . . nor is it negligible, being literally that between life and death." *Reid* v. *Covert,* 354 U.S. 1, 77 (1957) (concurring in result). And, of course, for many years this Court distinguished death cases from all others for purposes of the constitutional right to counsel. See *Powell* v. *Alabama,* 287 U.S. 45 (1932); *Betts* v. *Brady,* 316 U.S. 455 (1942); *Bute* v. *Illinois,* 333 U.S. 640 (1948).

35. See Report of Royal Commission on Capital Punishment 1949–1953, ¶¶ 700–789, pp. 246–273 (1953); Hearings on S. 1760 before the Subcommittee on Criminal Laws and Procedures of the Senate Committee on the Judiciary, 90th Cong., 2d Sess., 19–21 (1968) (testimony of Clinton Duffy); H. Barnes & N. Teeters, New Horizons in Criminology 306–309 (3d ed. 1959); C. Chessman, Trial by Ordeal 195–202 (1955); M. DiSalle, The Power of Life and Death 84–85 (1965); C. Duffy, 88 Men and 2 Women 13–14 (1962); B. Eshelman, Death Row Chaplain 26–29, 101–104, 159–164 (1962); R. Hammer, Between Life and Death 208–212 (1969); K. Lamott, Chronicles of San Quentin 228–231 (1961); L. Lawes, Life and Death in Sing Sing 170–171 (1928); Rubin, The Supreme Court, Cruel and Unusual Punishment, and the Death Penalty, 15 Crime & Delin. 121, 128–129 (1969); Comment, The Death Penalty Cases, 56 Calif. L. Rev. 1268, 1338–1341 (1968); Brief *amici curiae* filed by James V. Bennett, Clinton T. Duffy, Robert G. Sarver, Harry C. Tinsley, and Lawrence E. Wilson 12–14.

36. See H. Barnes & N. Teeters, New Horizons in Criminology 309–311 (2d ed. 1959); Camus, Reflections on the Guillotine, in A. Camus, Resistance, Rebellion, and Death 131, 151–156 (1960); C. Duffy, 88 Men and 2 Women 68–70, 254 (1962); R. Hammer, Between Life and Death 222–235, 244–250, 269–272 (1969); S. Rubin, The Law of Criminal Correction 340 (1963); Bluestone & McGahee, Reaction to Extreme Stress: Impending Death by Execution, 119 Amer. J. Psychiatry 393 (1962; Gottlieb, Capital Punishment, 15 Crime & Delin. 1, 8–10 (1969); West, Medicine and Capital Punishment, in Hearings on S. 1760 before the Subcommittee on Criminal Laws and Procedures of the Senate Committee on the Judiciary, 90th Cong., 2d Sess., 124 (1968); Ziferstein, Crime and Punishment, The Center Magazine 84 (Jan. 1968); Comment, The Death Penalty Cases, 56 Calif. L. Rev. 1268, 1342 (1968); Note, Mental Suffering under Sentence of Death: A Cruel and Unusual Punishment, 57 Iowa L. Rev. 814 (1972).

37. The State, of course, does not purposely impose the lengthy waiting period in order to inflict further suffering. The impact upon the individual is not the less severe on that account. It is no answer to assert that long delays exist only because condemned criminals avail themselves of their full panoply of legal rights. The right not to be subjected to inhuman treatment cannot, of course, be played off against the right to pursue due process of law, but, apart from that, the plain truth is that it is society that demands, even against the wishes of the criminal, that all legal avenues be explored before the execution is finally carried out.

38. It was recognized in *Trop* itself that expatriation is a "punishment short of death." 356 U.S., at 99. Death, however, was distinguished on the ground that it was "still widely accepted." *Ibid.*

39. Stephen, Capital Punishments, 69 Fraser's Magazine 753 763 (1864).

48. The victim surprised Furman in the act of burglarizing the victim's home in the middle of the night. While escaping, Furman killed the victim with one pistol shot fired through the closed kitchen door from the outside. At the trial, Furman gave his version of the killing:

"They got me charged with murder and I admit, I admit going to these folks' home and they did caught me in there and I was coming back out, backing up and there was a wire down there on the floor. I was coming out backwards and fell back and I didn't intend to kill nobody. I didn't know they was behind the door. The gun went off and I didn't know nothing about no murder until they arrested me, and when the gun went off I was down on the floor and I got up and ran. That's all to it." App. 54–55.

The Georgia Supreme Court accepted that version:
"The admission in open court by the accused . . . that during the period in which he was involved in the commission of a criminal act at the home of the deceased, he accidentally tripped over a wire in leaving the premises causing the gun to go off, together with other facts and circumstances surrounding the death of the deceased by violent means, was sufficient to support the verdict of guilty of murder. . . ." *Furman* v. *State,* 225 Ga. 253, 254, 167 S. E. 2d 628, 629 (1969).

About Furman himself, the jury knew only that he was black and that, according to his statement at trial, he was 26 years old and worked at "Superior Upholstery." App. 54. It took the jury one hour and 35 minutes to return a verdict of guilt and a sentence of death. *Id.,* at 64–65.

54. There is also the more limited argument that death is a necessary punishment when criminals are already serving or subject to a sentence of life imprisonment. If the only punishment available is further imprisonment, it is said, those criminals will have nothing to lose by committing further crimes, and accordingly the threat of death is the sole deterrent. But "life" imprisonment is a misnomer today. Rarely, if ever, do crimes carry a mandatory life sentence without possibility of parole. That possibility ensures that criminals do not reach the point where further crimes are free of consequences. Moreover, if this argument is simply an assertion that the threat, of death is a more effective deterrent than the threat of increased imprisonment by denial of release on parole, then, as noted above, there is simply no evidence to support it.

7. See Department of Justice, National Prisoner Statistics No. 46, Capital Punishment 1930–1970, p. 50 (Aug. 1971). Since the publication of the Department of Justice report, capital punishment has been judicially abolished in California, *People* v. *Anderson,* 6 Cal. 3d 628, 493 P. 2d 880, cert. denied, 406 U.S. 813 (1972). The States where capital punish-

ment is no longer authorized are Alaska, California, Hawaii, Iowa, Maine, Michigan, Minnesota, Oregon, West Virginia, and Wisconsin.

8.   See Act of Jan. 2, 1971, Pub. L. 91–644, Tit. IV, § 15, 84 Stat. 1891, 18 U.S.C. § 351; see Act of Oct. 15, 1970, Pub. L. 91–452, Tit. XI, § 1102 (a), 84 Stat. 956, 18 U.S.C. § 844 (f) (i); Act of Aug. 28, 1965, 79 Stat. 580, 18 U.S.C. § 1751; Act of Sept. 5, 1961, § 1, 75 Stat. 466, 49 U.S.C. § 1472 (i). See also opinion of Mr. Justice Blackmun, *post,* at 412–413.

9.   A 1966 poll indicated that 42% of those polled favored capital punishment while 47% opposed it, and 11% had no opinion. A 1969 poll found 51% in favor, 40% opposed, and 9% with no opinion. See Erskine, The Polls: Capital Punishment, 34 Public Opinion Quarterly 290 (1970).

10.   The jury plays the predominant role in sentencing in capital cases in this country. Available evidence indicates that where the judge determines the sentence, the death penalty is imposed with a slightly greater frequency than where the jury makes the determination. H. Kalven & H. Zeisel, The American Jury 436 (1966).

11.   In the decade from 1961–1970, an average of 106 persons per year received the death sentence in the United States, ranging from a low of 85 in 1967 to a high of 140 in 1961; 127 persons received the death sentence in 1970. Department of Justice, National Prisoner Statistics No. 46, Capital Punishment 1930–1970, p. 9. See also Bedau, The Death Penalty in America, 35 Fed. Prob., No. 2, p. 32 (1971). Although accurate figures are difficult to obtain, it is thought that from 15% to 20% of those convicted of murder are sentenced to death in States where it is authorized. See, for example, McGee, Capital Punishment as Seen by a Correc-

tional Administrator, 28 Fed. Prob., No. 2, pp. 11, 12 (1964); Bedau, Death Sentences in New Jersey 1907–1960, 19 Rutgers L. Rev. 1, 30 (1964); Florida Division of Corrections, Seventh Biennial Report (July 1 1968, to June 30, 1970) 82 and the few other crimes made punishable by death in certain States is considerably lower. See, for example, Florida Division of Corrections, Seventh Biennial Report, *supra,* at 83; Partington, The Incidence of the Death Penalty for Rape in Virginia, 22 Wash. & Lee L. Rev. 43–44, 71–73 (1965).

12.   Counsel for petitioners make the conclusory statement that "[t]hose who are selected to die are the poor and powerless, personally ugly and socially unacceptable." Brief for Petitioner in No. 68–5027, p. 51. However, the sources cited contain no empirical findings to undermine the general premise that juries impose the death penalty in the most extreme cases. One study has discerned a statistically noticeable difference between the rate of imposition on blue collar and white collar defendants; the study otherwise concludes that juries do follow rational patterns in imposing the sentence of death. Note, A Study of the California Penalty Jury in First-Degree-Murder Cases, 21 Stan. L. Rev. 1297 (1969). See also H. Kalven & H. Zeisel, The American Jury 434–449 (1966).

Statistics are also cited to show that the death penalty has been imposed in a racially discriminatory manner. Such statistics suggest, at least as a historical matter, that Negroes have been sentenced to death with greater frequency than whites in several States, particularly for the crime of interracial rape. See, for example, Koeninger, Capital Punishment in Texas, 1924–1968, 15 Crime & Delin. 132 (1969).

GREGG v. GEORGIA
United States Supreme Court (1976)*

Judgment of the Court, and opinion of MR. JUSTICE STEWART, MR. JUSTICE POWELL, and MR. JUSTICE STEVENS, announced by MR. JUSTICE STEWART.

The issue in this case is whether the imposition of the sentence of death for the crime of murder under the law of Georgia violates the Eighth and Fourteenth Amendments.

I

The petitioner, Troy Gregg, was charged with committing armed robbery and murder. In accordance with Georgia procedure in capital cases, the trial was in two stages, a guilt stage and a sentencing stage. The evidence at the guilt trial established that on November 21, 1973, the petitioner and a traveling companion, Floyd Allen, while hitchhiking north in Florida were picked up by Fred Simmons and Bob Moore. Their car broke down, but they continued north after Simmons purchased another vehicle with some of the cash he was carrying. While still in Florida, they picked up another hitchhiker, Dennis Weaver, who rode with them to Atlanta, where he was let out about 11 p. m. A short time later the four men interrupted their journey for a rest stop along the highway. The next morning the bodies of Simmons and Moore were discovered in a ditch nearby.

On November 23, after reading about the shootings in an Atlanta newspaper, Weaver communicated with the Gwinnet County police and related information concerning the journey with the victims, including a description of the car. The next afternoon, the petitioner and Allen, while in Simmons' car, were arrested in Asheville, N.C. In the search incident to the arrest a .25-caliber pistol, later shown to be that used to kill Simmons and Moore, was found in the petitioner's pocket. After receiving the warnings required by *Miranda* v. *Arizona,* 384 U. S. 436 (1966), and signing a written waiver of his rights, the petitioner signed a statement in which he admitted shooting, then robbing Simmons and Moore. He justified the slayings

on grounds of self-defense. The next day, while being transferred to Lawrenceville, Ga., the petitioner and Allen were taken to the scene of the shootings. Upon arriving there, Allen recounted the events leading to the slayings. His version of these events was as follows: After Simmons and Moore left the car, the petitioner stated that he intended to rob them. The petitioner then took his pistol in hand and positioned himself on the car to improve his aim. As Simmons and Moore came up an embankment toward the car, the petitioner fired three shots and the two men fell near a ditch. The petitioner, at close range, then fired a shot into the head of each. He robbed them of valuables and drove away with Allen.

A medical examiner testified that Simmons died from a bullet wound in the eye and that Moore died from bullet wounds in the cheek and in the back of the head. He further testified that both men had several bruises and abrasions about the face and head which probably were sustained either from the fall into the ditch or from being dragged or pushed along the embankment. Although Allen did not testify, a police detective recounted the substance of Allen's statments about the slayings and indicated that directly after Allen had made these statements the petitioner had admitted that Allen's account was accurate. The petitioner testified in his own defense. He confirmed that Allen had made the statements described by the detective, but denied their truth or ever having admitted to their accuracy. He indicated that he had shot Simmons and Moore because of fear and in self-defense, testifying they had attacked Allen and him, one wielding a pipe and the other a knife.[1]

The trial judge submitted the murder charges to the jury on both felony-murder and nonfelony-murder theories. He also instructed on the issue of self-defense but declined to instruct on manslaughter. He submitted the robbery case to the jury on both an armed-robbery theory and on the lesser included offense of robbery by intimidation. The jury found the petitioner guilty of two counts of armed robbery and two counts of murder.

At the penalty stage, which took place before the same jury, neither the prosecutor nor the petitioner's

*428 U.S. 153. Excerpts only. Footnotes have been renumbered.

lawyer offered any additional evidence. Both counsel, however, made lengthy arguments dealing generally with the propriety of capital punishment under the circumstances and with the weight of the evidence of guilt. The trial judge instructed the jury that it could recommend either a death sentence or a life prison sentence on each count. The judge further charged the jury that in determining what sentence was appropriate the jury was free to consider the facts and circumstances, if any, presented by the parties in mitigation or aggravation.

Finally, the judge instructed the jury that it "would not be authorized to consider [imposing] the penalty of death" unless it first found beyond a reasonable doubt one of these aggravating circumstances:

"One—That the offense of murder was committed while the offender was engaged in the commission of two other capital felonies, to-wit the armed robbery of [Simmons and Moore].
"Two—That the offender committed the offense of murder for the purpose of receiving money and the automobile described in the indictment.
"Three—The offense of murder was outrageously and wantonly vile, horrible and inhuman, in that they *[sic]* involved the depravity of [the] mind of the defendant." Tr. 476–477.

Finding the first and second of these circumstances, the jury returned verdicts of death on each count.

The Supreme Court of Georgia affirmed the convictions and the imposition of the death sentences for murder. 233 Ga. 177, 210 S. E. 2d 659 (1974). After reviewing the trial transcript and the record, including the evidence, and comparing the evidence and sentence in similar cases in accordance with the requirements of Georgia law, the court concluded that, considering the nature of the crime and the defendant, the sentences of death had not resulted from prejudice or any other arbitrary factor and were not excessive or disproportionate to the penalty applied in similar cases.[2] The death sentences imposed for armed robbery, however, were vacated on the grounds that the death penalty had rarely been imposed in Georgia for that offense and that the jury improperly considered the murders as aggravating circumstances for the robberies after having considered the armed robberies as aggravating circumstances for the murders. *Id.,* at 127, 210 S. E. 2d, at 667.

We granted the petitioner's application for a writ of certiorari limited to his challenge to the imposition of the death sentences in this case as "cruel and unusual" punishment in violation of the Eighth and the Fourteenth Amendments. . .

Four years ago, the petitioners in *Furman* and its companion cases predicated their argument primarily upon the asserted proposition that standards of decency had evolved to the point where capital punishment no longer could be tolerated. The petitioners in those cases said, in effect, that the evolutionary process had come to an end, and that standards of decency required that the Eighth Amendment be construed finally as prohibiting capital punishment for any crime regardless of its depravity and impact on society. This view was accepted by two Justices. Three other Justices were unwilling to go so far; focusing on the procedures by which convicted defendants were selected for the death penalty rather than on the actual punishment inflicted, they joined in the conclusion that the statutes before the Court were constitutionally invalid.

The petitioners in the capital cases before the Court today renew the "standards of decency" argument, but developments during the four years since *Furman* have undercut substantially the assumptions upon which their argument rested. Despite the continuing debate, dating back to the 19th century, over the morality and utility of capital punishment, it is now evident that a large proportion of American society continues to regard it as an appropriate and necessary criminal sanction.

The most marked indication of society's endorsement of the death penalty for murder is the legislative response to *Furman.* The legislatures of at least 35 States have enacted new statutes that provide for the death penalty for at least some crimes that result in the death of another person. And the Congress of the United States, in 1974, enacted a statute providing the death penalty for aircraft piracy that results in death. These recently adopted statutes have attempted to address the concerns expressed by the Court in *Furman* primarily (i) by specifying the factors to be weighed and the procedures to be followed in deciding when to impose a capital sentence, or (ii) by making the death penalty mandatory for specified crimes. But all of the post-*Furman* statutes make clear that capital punishment itself has not been rejected by the elected representatives of the people.

In the only statewide referendum occurring since *Furman* and brought to our attention, the people of California adopted a constitutional amendment that authorized capital punishment, in effect negating a prior ruling by the Supreme Court of California in *People* v. *Anderson,* 6 Cal. 3d 628, 493 P. 2d 880, cert. denied, 406 U.S. 958 (1972), that the death penalty violated the California Constitution.

The jury also is a significant and reliable objective index of contemporary values because it is so directly involved. See *Furman* v. *Georgia,* 408 U.S., at 439–440 (POWELL, J., dissenting). See generally Powell, Jury Trial of Crimes, 23 Wash. & Lee L. Rev. 1 (1966). The Court has said that "one of the most important functions any jury can perform in making . . . a selection [between life imprisonment and death for a defendant convicted in a capital case] is to maintain a link between contemporary community values and the penal system." *Witherspoon* v. *Illinois,* 391 U.S. 510, 519 n. 15 (1968). It may be true that evolving standards have influenced juries in recent decades to be more discriminating in imposing the sentence of death. But the relative infrequency of jury verdicts imposing the death sentence does not indicate rejection of capital punishment *per se.* Rather, the reluctance of juries in many cases to impose the sentence may well reflect the humane feeling that this most irrevocable of sanctions should be reserved for a small number of extreme cases. See *Furman* v. *Georgia, supra,* at 388 (BURGER, C. J., dissenting). Indeed, the actions of juries in many States since *Furman* are fully compatible with the legislative judgments, reflected in the new statutes, as to the continued utility and necessity of capital punishment in appropriate cases. At the close of 1974 at least 254 persons had been sentenced to death since *Furman,* and by the end of March 1976, more than 460 persons were subject to death sentences.

As we have seen, however, the Eighth Amendment demands more than that a challenged punishment be acceptable to contemporary society. The Court also must ask whether it comports with the basic concept of human dignity at the core of the Amendment. *Trop* v. *Dulles,* 356 U. S., at 100 (plurality opinion). Although we cannot "invalidate a category of penalties because we deem less severe penalties adequate to serve the ends of penology," *Furman* v. *Georgia, supra,* at 451 (POWELL, J., dissenting), the sanction imposed cannot be so totally without penological justification that it results in the gratuitous infliction of suffering. *Cf. Wilkerson* v. *Utah,* 99 U.S., at 135–136; *In re Kemmler,* 136 U.S., at 447.

The death penalty is said to serve two principal social purposes: retribution and deterrence of capital crimes by prospective offenders.

In part, capital punishment is an expression of society's moral outrage at particularly offensive conduct. This function may be unappealing to many, but it is essential in an ordered society that asks its citizens to rely on legal processes rather than self-help to vindicate their wrongs.

"The instinct for retribution is part of the nature of man, and channeling that instinct in the administration of criminal justice serves an important purpose in promoting the stability of a society governed by law. When people begin to believe that organized society is unwilling or unable to impose upon criminal offenders the punishment they 'deserve' then there are sown the seeds of anarchy—of self-help, vigilante justice, and lynch law." *Furman* v. *Georgia, supra,* at 308 (STEWART, J., concurring).

"Retribution is no longer the dominant objective of the criminal law," *Williams* v. *New York,* 337 U.S. 241, 248 (1949), but neither is it a forbidden objective nor one inconsistent with our respect for the dignity of men. *Furman* v. *Georgia,* 408 U. S., at 394–395 (Burger, C. J., dissenting); id., at 452–454 (Powell, J., dissenting); *Powell* v. *Texas,* 392 U. S., at 531 535–536 (plurality opinion). Indeed, the decision that capital punishment may be the appropriate sanction in extreme cases is an expression of the community's belief that certain crimes are themselves so grievous an affront to humanity that the only adequate response may be the penalty of death: . . .

We now turn to consideration of the constitutionality of Georgia's capital-sentencing procedures. In the wake of *Furman,* Georgia amended its capital punishment statute, but chose not to narrow the scope of its murder provisions. See Part II, *supra.* Thus, now as before *Furman,* in Georgia "[a] person commits murder when he unlawfully and with malice aforethought, either express or implied, causes the death of another human being." Ga. Code Ann., § 26-1101 (a) (1972). All persons convicted of murder "shall be punished by death or by imprisonment for life." § 26-1101 (c) (1972).

Georgia did act, however, to narrow the class of murderers subject to capital punishment by specifying 10 statutory aggravating circumstances, one of which must be found by the jury to exist beyond a reasonable doubt before a death sentence can ever be imposed. In addition, the jury is authorized to consider any other appropriate aggravating or mitigating circumstances. § 27-2534.1 (b) (Supp. 1975). The jury is not required to find any mitigating circumstance in order to make a recommendation of mercy that is binding on the trial court, see §27-2302 (Supp. 1975), but it must find a *statutory* aggravating circumstance before recommending a sentence of death.

These procedures require the jury to consider the circumstances of the crime and the criminal before it recommends sentence. No longer can a Georgia jury do as Furman's jury did: reach a finding of the defendant's guilt and then, without guidance or direction, decide whether he should live or die. Instead, the jury's attention is directed to the specific circumstances of the crime: Was it committed in the course of another capital felony? Was it committed for money? Was it committed upon a peace officer or judicial officer? Was it committed in a particularly heinous way or in a manner that endangered the lives of many persons? In addition, the jury's attention is focused on the characteristics of the person who committed the crime: Does he have a record of prior convictions for capital offenses? Are there any special facts about this defendant that mitigate against imposing capital punishment (*e. g.,* his youth, the extent of his cooperation with the police, his emotional state at the time of the crime)? As a result, while some jury discretion still exists, "the discretion to be exercised is controlled by clear and objective standards so as to produce non-discriminatory application." *Coley* v. *State,* 231 Ga. 829, 834, 204 S. E. 2d 612, 615 (1974).

As an important additional safeguard against arbitrariness and caprice, the Georgia statutory scheme provides for automatic appeal of all death sentences to the State's Supreme Court. That court is required by statute to review each sentence of death and determine whether it was imposed under the influence of passion or prejudice, whether the evidence supports the jury's finding of a statutory aggravating circumstance, and whether the sentence is disproportionate compared to those sentences imposed in similar cases. § 27-2537 (c) (Supp. 1975).

In short, Georgia's new sentencing procedures require as a prerequisite to the imposition of the death penalty, specific jury findings as to the circumstances of the crime or the character of the defendant. Moreover, to guard further against a situation comparable to that presented in *Furman,* the Supreme Court of Georgia compares each death sentence with the sentences imposed on similarly situated defendants to ensure that the sentence of death in a particular case is not disproportionate. On their face these procedures seem to satisfy the concerns of *Furman.* No longer should there be "no meaningful basis for distinguishing the few cases in which [the death penalty] is imposed from the many cases in which it is not." 408 U. S., at 313 (White, J., concurring).

The petitioner contends, however, that the changes in the Georgia sentencing procedures are only cosmetic, that the arbitrariness and capriciousness condemned by *Furman* continue to exist in Georgia— both in traditional practices that still remain and in the new sentencing procedures adopted in response to *Furman.*

1

First, the petitioner focuses on the opportunities for discretionary action that are inherent in the processing of any murder case under Georgia law. He notes that the state prosecutor has unfettered authority to select those persons whom he wishes to prosecute for a capital offense and to plea bargain with them. Further, at the trial the jury may choose to convict a defendant of a lesser included offense rather than find him guilty of a crime punishable by death, even if the evidence would support a capital verdict. And finally, a defendant who is convicted and sentenced to die may have

his sentence commuted by the Governor of the State and the Georgia Board of Pardons and Paroles.

The existence of these discretionary stages is not determinative of the issues before us. At each of these stages an actor in the criminal justice system makes a decision which may remove a defendant from consideration as a candidate for the death penalty. *Furman,* in contrast, dealt with the decision to impose the death sentence on a specific individual who had been convicted of a capital offense. Nothing in any of our cases suggests that the decision to afford an individual defendant mercy violates the Constitution. *Furman* held only that, in order to minimize the risk that the death penalty would be imposed on a capriciously selected group of offenders, the decision to impose it had to be guided by standards so that the sentencing authority would focus on the particularized circumstances of the crime and the defendant.[3]

2

The petitioner further contends that the capital-sentencing procedures adopted by Georgia in response to *Furman* do not eliminate the dangers of arbitrariness and caprice in jury sentencing that were held in *Furman* to be violative of the Eighth and Fourteenth Amendments. He claims that the statute is so broad and vague as to leave juries free to act as arbitrarily and capriciously as they wish in deciding whether to impose the death penalty. While there is no claim that the jury in this case relied upon a vague or overbroad provision to establish the existence of a statutory aggravating circumstance, the petitioner looks to the sentencing system as a whole (as the Court did in *Furman* and we do today) and argues that it fails to reduce sufficiently the risk of arbitrary infliction of death sentences. Specifically, Gregg urges that the statutory aggravating circumstances are too broad and too vague, that the sentencing procedure allows for arbitrary grants of mercy, and that the scope of the evidence and argument that can be considered at the presentence hearing is too wide.

The petitioner attacks the seventh statutory aggravating circumstance, which authorizes imposition of the death penalty if the murder was "outrageously or wantonly vile, horrible or inhuman in that it involved torture, depravity of mind, or an aggravated battery to the victim," contending that it is so broad that capital punishment could be imposed in any murder case. It is, of course, arguable that any murder involves depravity of mind or an aggravated battery. But this language need not be construed in this way, and there is no reason to assume that the Supreme Court of Georgia will adopt such an open-ended construction. In only one case has it upheld a jury's decision to sentence a defendant to death when the only statutory aggravating circumstance found was that of the seventh, see McCorquodale v. State, 233 Ga. 369, 211 S. E. 2d 577 (1974), and that homicide was a horrifying torture-murder.

The petitioner also argues that two of the statutory aggravating circumstances are vague and therefore susceptible of widely differing interpretations, thus creating a substantial risk that the death penalty will be arbitrarily inflicted by Georgia juries. In light of the decisions of the Supreme Court of Georgia we must disagree. First, the petitioner attacks that part of § 27-2534.1 (b)(1) that authorizes a jury to consider whether a defendant has a "substantial history of serious assaultive criminal convictions." The Supreme Court of Georgia, however, has demonstrated a concern that the new sentencing procedures provide guidance to juries. It held this provision to be impermissibly vague in *Arnold v. State,* 236 Ga. 534, 540, 224 S. E. 2d 386, 391 (1976), because it did not provide the jury with "sufficiently 'clear and objective standards.' " Second, the petitioner points to §27-2534.1 (b)(3) which speaks of creating a "great risk of death to more than one person." While such a phrase might be susceptible of an overly broad interpretation, the Supreme Court of Georgia has not so construed it. The only case in which the court upheld a conviction in reliance on this aggravating circumstance involved a man who stood up in a church and fired a gun indiscriminately into the audience. See *Chenault v. State,* 234 Ga. 216, 215 S. E. 2d 223 (1975). On the other hand, the court expressly reversed a finding of great risk when the victim was simply kidnaped in a parking lot. See *Jarrell* v. *State,* 234 Ga. 410, 424, 216 S. E. 2d 258, 269 (1975).

The petitioner next argues that the requirements of *Furman* are not met here because the jury has the power to decline to impose the death penalty even if it finds that one or more statutory aggravating circumstances are present in the case. This contention misinterprets *Furman.* See *supra,* at 198-199. Moreover, it ignores the role of the Supreme Court of Georgia which reviews each death sentence to determine whether it is proportional to other sentences imposed for similar crimes. Since the proportionality requirement on review is intended to prevent caprice in the decision to inflict the penalty, the isolated decision of a jury to afford mercy does not render unconstitutional death sentences imposed on defendants who were sentenced under a system that does not create a substantial risk of arbitrariness or caprice.

The petitioner objects, finally, to the wide scope of evidence and argument allowed at presentence hearings. We think that the Georgia court wisely has chosen not to impose unnecessary restrictions on the evidence that can be offered at such a hearing and to approve open and far-ranging argument. See, *e. g., Brown* v. *State,* 235 Ga. 644, 220 S. E. 2d 922 (1975). So long as the evidence introduced and the arguments made at the presentence hearing do not prejudice a defendant, it is preferable not to impose restrictions. We think it desirable for the jury to have as much information before it as possible when it makes the sentencing decision. See *supra, at* 189-190.

3

Finally, the Georgia statute has an additional provision designed to assure that the death penalty will not be imposed on a capriciously selected group of convicted defendants. The new sentencing procedures require that the State Supreme Court review every death sentence to determine whether it was imposed under the influence of passion, prejudice, or any other arbitrary factor, whether the evidence supports the findings of a statutory aggravating circumstance, and "[w]hether the sentence of death is excessive or disproportionate to the penalty imposed in similar cases, considering both the crime and the defendant." § 27-2537 (c)(3) (Supp. 1975). In performing its sentence-review function, the Georgia court has held that "if the death penalty is only rarely imposed for an act or it is substantially out of line with sentences imposed for other acts it will be set aside as excessive." *Coley* v. *State,* 231 Ga., at 834, 204 S. E. 2d, at 616. The court on another occasion stated that "we view it to be our duty under the similarity standard to assure that no death sentence is affirmed unless in similar cases throughout the state the death penalty has been imposed generally...." *Moore* v. *State,* 233 Ga. 861, 864, 213 S. E. 2d 829, 832 (1975). See also *Jarrell* v. *State, supra,* at 425, 216 S. E. 2d, at 270 (standard is whether "juries generally throughout the state have imposed the death penalty"); *Smith* v. *State,* 236 Ga. 12, 24, 222 S. E. 2d 308, 318 (1976) (found "a clear pattern" of jury behavior).

It is apparent that the Supreme Court of Georgia has taken its review responsibilities seriously. In *Coley,* it held that "[t]he prior cases indicate that the past practice among juries faced with similar factual situations and like aggravating circumstances has been to impose only the sentence of life imprisonment for the offense of rape, rather than death." 231 Ga., at 835, 204 S. E. 2d, at 617. It thereupon reduced Coley's sentence from death to life imprisonment. Similarly, although armed robbery is a capital offense under Georgia law, § 26-1902 (1972), the Georgia court concluded that the death sentences imposed in this case for that crime were "unusual in that they are rarely imposed for [armed robbery]. Thus, under the test provided by statute, ... they must be considered to be excessive or disproportionate to the penalties imposed in similar cases." 233 Ga., at 127, 210 S. E. 2d, at 667. The court therefore vacated Gregg's death sentences for armed robbery and has followed a similar course in every other armed robbery death penalty case to come before it. See *Floyd v. State,* 233 Ga. 280, 285, 210 S. E. 2d 810, 814 (1974); *Jarrell v. State,* 234 Ga., at 424-425, 216 S. E. 2d, at 270. See *Dorsey v. State,* 236 Ga. 591, 225 S. E. 2d 418 (1976).

The provision for appellate review in the Georgia capital-sentencing system serves as a check against the random or arbitrary imposition of the death penalty. In particular, the proportionality review substantially eliminates the possibility that a person will be sentenced to die by the action of an aberrant jury. If a time comes when juries generally do not impose the death sentence in a certain kind of murder case, the appellate review procedures assure that no defendant convicted under such circumstances will suffer a sentence of death.

V

The basic concern of *Furman* centered on those defendants who were being condemned to death capriciously and arbitrarily. Under the procedures before the Court in that case, sentencing authorities were not directed to give attention to the nature or circumstances of the crime committed or to the character or record of the defendant. Left unguided, juries imposed the death sentence in a way that could only be called freakish. The new Georgia sentencing procedures, by contrast, focus the jury's attention on the particularized nature of the crime and the particularized characteristics of the individual defendant. While the jury is permitted to consider any aggravating or mitigating circumstances, it must find and identify at least one statutory aggravating factor before it may impose a penalty of death. In this way the jury's discretion is channeled. No longer can a jury wantonly and freakishly impose the death sentence; it is always circumscribed by the legislative guidelines. In addition, the review function of the Supreme Court of Georgia affords additional assurance that the concerns that prompted our decision in *Furman* are not present to any significant degree in the Georgia procedure applied here.

For the reasons expressed in this opinion, we hold that the statutory system under which Gregg was sentenced to death does not violate the Constitution. Accordingly, the judgment of the Georgia Supreme Court is affirmed.

Mr. JUSTICE BRENNAN, dissenting.

. . . This Court inescapably has the duty, as the ultimate arbiter of the meaning of our Constitution, to say whether, when individuals condemned to death stand before our Bar, "moral concepts" require us to hold that the law has progressed to the point where we should declare that the punishment of death, like punishments on the rack, the screw, and the wheel, is no longer morally tolerable in our civilized society.[4] My opinion in *Furman v. Georgia* concluded that our civilization and the law had progressed to this point and that therefore the punishment of death, for whatever crime and under all circumstances, is "cruel and unusual" in violation of the Eighth and Fourteenth Amendments of the Constitution. I shall not again canvass the reasons that led to that conclusion. I emphasize only that foremost among the "moral concepts" recognized in our cases and inherent in the Clause is the primary moral principle that the State, even as it punishes, must treat its citizens in a manner consistent with their intrinsic worth as human beings —a punishment must not be so severe as to be degrading to human dignity. A judicial determination whether the punishment of death comports with human dignity is therefore not only permitted but compelled by the Clause. 408 U. S., at 270.

I do not understand that the Court disagrees that "[i]n comparison to all other punishments today . . . the deliberate extinguishment of human life by the State is uniquely degrading to humna dignity." Id., at 291. For three of my Brethren hold today mandatory infliction of the death penalty constitutes the penalty cruel and unusual punishment. I perceive no principled basis for this limitation. Death for whatever crime and under all circumstances "is truly an awesome punishment. The calculated killing of a human being by the State involves, by its very nature, a denial of the executed person's humanity. . . . An executed person has indeed 'lost the right to have rights.'" Id., at 290. Death is not only an unusually severe punishment, unusual in its pain, in its finality, and in its enormity, but it serves no penal purpose more effectively than a less severe punishment; therefore the principle inherent in the Clause that prohibits infliction of excessive punishment when less severe punishment can adequately achieve the same purposes invalidates the punishment. Id., at 279.

The fatal constitutional infirmity in the punishment of death is that it treats "members of the human race as nonhumans, as objects to be toyed with and discarded. [It is] thus inconsistent with the fundamental premise of the Clause that even the vilest criminal remains a human being possessed of common human dignity." Id. at 273. As such it is a penalty that "subjects the individual to a fate forbidden by the principle of civilized treatment guaranteed by the [Clause]." I therefore would hold, on that ground alone, that death is today a cruel and unusual punishment prohibited by the Clause. "Justice of this kind is obviously no less shocking than the crime itself, and the new 'official' murder, far from offering redress for the offense committed against society, adds instead a second defilement to the first."

NOTES

1.   On cross-examination the State introduced a letter written by the petitioner to Allen entitled, "[a] statement for you," with the instructions that Allen memorize and then burn it. The statement was consistent with the petitioner's testimony at trial.

2.   The court further held, in part, that the trial court did not err in refusing to instruct the jury with respect to voluntary manslaughter since there was no evidence to support that verdict.

3.   The petitioner's argument is nothing more than a veiled contention that *Furman* indirectly outlawed capital punishment by placing totally unrealistic conditions on its use. In order to repair the alleged defects pointed to by the petitioner, it would be necessary to require that prosecuting authorities charge a capital offense whenever arguably there had been a capital murder and that they refuse to plea bargain with the defendant. If a jury refused to convict even though the evidence supported the charge, its verdict would have to be reversed and a verdict of guilty entered or a new trial ordered, since the discretionary act of jury nullification would not be permitted. Finally, acts of executive clemency would have to be prohibited. Such a system, of course, would be totally alien to our notions of criminal justice.

Moreover, it would be unconstitutional. Such a system in many respects would have the vices of the mandatory death penalty statutes we hold unconstitutional today in *Woodson* v. *North Carolina, post,* p. 280, and *Roberts* v. *Louisiana, post,* p. 325. The suggestion that a jury's verdict of acquittal could be overturned and a defendant retried would run afoul of the Sixth Amendment jury trial guarantee and the Double Jeopardy Clause of the Fifth Amendment. In the federal system it also would be unconstitutional to prohibit a President from deciding, as an act of executive clemency, to reprieve one sentenced to death. U. S. Cons., Art. II § 2.

HUGO ADAM BEDAU

The Right to Life and the Right to Kill*

In evaluating the death penalty from the moral point of view, we can proceed in several different ways. For those whose moral thinking is inspired primarily by religious tradition, reflection may well begin with acknowledging the sacred quality of human life, affirmed in Genesis and elsewhere in the Bible. Secular moralists who prefer a utilitarian (or some other cost/benefit) orientation would begin with an attempt to calculate whether the death penalty for murder, or for any crime, is more likely to increase a community's overall well-being (taking into account the well-being of the criminal, too) than any of the alternatives, such as long-term imprisonment. I looked at this approach briefly in the previous chapter and will do so in much greater detail in the next. A third line of analysis concentrates on the *rights* involved—those of society and of the individual. Such an approach might naturally begin with the assumption that the state has the right to defend itself against domestic or internal enemies, and then inquire whether this implies the right to kill them under certain conditions. Aspects of this approach were raised in the previous chapter; the purpose here is to explore them more thoroughly.

I

A sense of "the state has the right" exists, of course, in which all we mean is that some presumptively valid law gives the government the legal right to do something. Let us call this the *legal* sense of "has the right." Whenever a legislature enacts a statute authorizing the death penalty for murder, it can be asserted in this sense that the state now has the right to kill convicts as their punishment. As soon as such a law is repealed by a subsequent legislature or nulllified on constitutional grounds by an ap-

pellate court, however, the state no longer has such a right. Legal rights in this sense can be cancelled or revoked as easily as they can be created in the first place. Similarly, in this purely legal sense of "has the right," it will turn out that at one and the same time some jurisdictions do and others do not have the right to use death as a punishment. Likewise, a given jurisdiction will have this right at some times and not at other times, and it will have this right regarding the punishment of some crimes but not of others.

Whether the state has the right to use death as a punishment in this legal sense of "has the right" is not a matter for debate, because the answer rests on fairly straightforward questions of fact. In the United States today, most jurisdictions have at least one death penalty statute that has sustained constitutional challenges, a few have a death penalty statute whose constitutionality is unsettled, and a few other jurisdictions have no such statutes. Consequently, anyone who wants to argue over whether the state has the right to use death as a punishment must be thinking of some sense of the phrase "has the right" other than the legal sense. We can call this other sense the *moral* sense of "has the right." Only if we recognize that the phrase has a meaning of this sort can we make sense of such sensible claims as these: Although a state has a constitutionally valid death penalty statute, it still has no right to use death as a punishment; or even if a state has no death penalty laws, it has the right to enact and enforce them. Let us, then, put aside the idea of the state's legal right to kill and begin at the beginning in an attempt to understand the moral sense of "has the right." That is what really underlies the controversy.

We cannot get very far in thinking about rights and their normative force without distinguishing clearly the claim that (1) *the state has the right to use death as a punishment* from the very different claim to the effect that (2) *the state is right to use death as a punishment*. The difference between the two propositions can most readily be seen if we consider their contradictories. The negation of (1) is that *the state does not have the right to use death as a punishment*. The negation of (2) is quite different; we deny (2) when we assert that *it is not right* (i.e., *it is wrong*) *for the state to use death as a punishment*. Clearly there is an important difference between the right to kill (or to be a killer), as in (1), and what might be called the moral rectitude of killing (or doing the right thing when one kills), as in (2).

We can also see the difference between the two when we consider what arguments would establish these two propositions. Roughly, we establish that some agent—a person, a group, or the state—*has a right* when we establish one or more of three different things. One is that the agent is under no duty or obligation not to act in a certain way, in which case the agent has a right in the sense of being free or at liberty to do as he wishes. Another is that others are under a duty or obligation not to interfere with (or are even under a duty or obligation to facilitate) the action of the agent if the agent chooses to act in the way in question. A third is that the agent has been authorized to act in a certain manner by others who have the authority (i.e., the right) so to empower the agent. How we establish, in their turn, one or more of these conditions is a further problem that need not concern us for the moment.

But if the question is whether *it is right* for a person or a group to act in a certain way, this can be answered in the affirmative only by much more comprehensive and diffuse considerations. Everything now turns on the content of our entire moral theory—or, if we don't have a moral theory, then on the set of moral principles we hold and their logical consequences, in particular cases, which justify the action in question from our moral pont of view. Merely knowing who has the right to what does not always settle the morality of anyone's conduct. Important as our rights are, they are not always the last word in the moral evaluation of how to act. We can always ask, for example, whether persons or groups who act on their rights are really doing the best thing, all things considered. We can often give moral reasons for doing something even though someone's rights are thereby violated.

To put the distinction between (1) and (2) in yet a third way, the question of whether the state is right when it kills as punishment can be answered (in the affirmative or the negative) without any reference to a theory or doctrine of rights. In fact, a theory of morally right action might not recognize or acknowledge any fundamental rights at all—as was true of most moral and political theories prior to the seventeenth century. But when we ask whether the state has a right to use death as a punishment (and are not using the phrase "has a right" in the purely legal sense), we obviously cannot answer in the affirmative without such a theory. Indeed, any affirmative answer will require us to explain the scope and origin of the right, as well as how the right is related to other moral and empirical (political, social, economic) conditions. These reasons make manifest the gap—both conceptual and moral—between *having a right* to do a thing and *doing the right* thing.

Given the distinction between the state's right to use death as a punishment and the overall moral propriety of state-authorized killing as punishment, closer investigation might support any of four possible positions on the death penalty itself. At one extreme the state could have the right, and the state could be right when it exercises the right (consistent with due process of law). Presumably, this is what most contemporary defenders of the death penalty believe. At the other extreme is the possibility that the state does not have the right to use death as a punishment, and the state never does the right thing when it kills even a duly convicted offender. Many contemporary opponents of the death penalty believe this to be true. Advocates and opponents of the death penalty rarely take up positions openly defending the one extreme and attacking the other, however. If they did, then witnesses to debates on the issue would at least know exactly what is being asserted and what denied.

The other two possibilities lie in between. One is that the state has no moral right to kill, but that it is not always wrong when it does kill—a position that may initially sound somewhat bizarre, though it is not incoherent. The remaining possibility is that the state has the right to kill, although rarely if ever does the state do the right thing when it acts on this right.

Of these four possibilities, the one that most nearly accords with my views is the last one. Like most professing constitutional democratic liberals, I am neither a pacifist nor an anarchist. Consequently, I can conceive of conditions under which it is within the state's authority or power—and in that sense, within its rights—to decide whether to kill a person.

Yet I do oppose the death penalty in all cases in our society, so I think whenever our government decides to kill someone as his punishment, the state on whose behalf it acts does the wrong thing. Let us defer for the moment the large question of whether it is ever right for the state to use death as a punishment, however, in order to elaborate further on the idea of the state's right to do so.

First, the right to kill persons as a punishment is unlike many rights in that *only* the state can have it. You and I can kill, and a person may even have the right (legal as well as moral) to kill another person in certain cases. But many rights (such as the right to declare war, the right to tax, the right to make a treaty) are such that no individual person has them, except as a function of some office he or she holds. The right to punish crimes is one of these rights; only the agents of a state—government officials suitably empowered and authorized to act on behalf of a society—have the right to impose the death penalty and carry it out. To think otherwise is to confuse the lethal acts of private individuals, such as murder, lynching, and killing in self-defense, with the lethal act of carrying out the death penalty. Nothing is gained by such confusion.

Second, the state's right to kill persons as a punishment (if there is such a right) is neither a "natural" nor a fundamental right. Rather, it is an artificial or highly contingent and derivative right, because states and their moral authority are derivative and to that extent artificial; they are the products of human social and political contrivance and their powers are justified solely by the extent to which they serve humane purposes, social and individual. When (as I point out in Chapter 4) John Locke defined political power as "a right of making laws with penalties of death," he viewed this right as derivative from the natural rights of individual persons in a "state of nature." In the spirit if not the letter of Locke's thinking, we might say that the right to use death as a punishment is indeed not fundamental but derivative. It is derived from the state's fundamental duty to enact and enforce just laws (i.e., laws that protect and permit the exercise of individual rights in a manner fair to all persons) and its right to use the means necessary and appropriate to secure this end. If, as in Locke's theory, the state is the repository of all and only such rights of individuals as are transferred to it, so that the government is always the fidu-

ciary and trustee of individual rights, then we must be able to point to some such individual rights that are (or are reasonably believed to be) protected by every exercise of governmental power.

Finally, the state's right to use death as a punishment might turn out to conflict with other rights or with certain duties. The possibility of conflicts arises because the right to use death as a punishment is not an *absolute* right and it is not the *only* right of the state. Any appeal to a right, whether an individual's, a group's, or a state's, always invites challenge by reference to other rights and duties. In the event of a conflict, a choice must be made between exercising one of these rights and either violating some other right(s) or failing to perform (or frustrating the performance of) certain duties. Resolving conflicts (if they occur) in favor of the state's right to kill can be done only if it can be shown that this right is paramount, that it works like trumps in the games of Bridge and Hearts, because it always prevails over conflicting rights and duties. Whether the state's right to use death as a punishment can be exercised without infringement of other rights and without violation of any duties remains to be seen.

II

We get a clearer picture of the state's right to use death as a punishment if we look at two other rights, one that is in opposition to this one and another that is analogous to it. The former is the individual's *right to life* and the latter is the individual's *right of self-defense*. We will look at the latter first.

Except for pacifist anarchists, most people generally agree that in morals and in law each individual has the right of self-defense (and third parties the right to intervene to assist) in warding off unprovoked and undeserved harm at the hands of an intending felon. Does this right include the right to use lethal force? It does, but only under certain provisos—that retreat or escape is not possible, and that the would-be victim (or intervener) reasonably believes that no lesser degree of force will suffice to ward off the felonious harm. Legal niceties apart, that is the essence of the traditional idea of the right of self-defense and the use of lethal force in exercise of that right.

What kind of state's right is there, if any, parallel to the individual's right of self-defense? A few paragraphs earlier, I noted that the state has the duty to defend its laws insofar as they are just or fair (the duty to protect just institutions), and that in exercise of this duty the state may threaten punishment for those who are found guilty of intentionally violating just laws to the harm of individuals, groups, or the state itself. Thus I accept a kind of analogy between the individual's right of self-protection against undeserved and unprovoked invasions of personal liberties, and the state's duty to defend just institutions; the analogy is not perfect, because it holds between an individual's *right* and the state's *duty*. To the extent that a right is unlike a duty, there is no parallel at all. To put this another way, whereas an individual may choose *not* to defend himself (that is the nature of an individual's right—one violates no duty if one does not choose to act or stand on one's rights), the state *must* defend its laws and just institutions. The reason is that the state has a duty to defend the rights of its members, and this cannot be done unless on some occasions the state uses not only persuasion and threats but force to protect just laws and institutions against those who would violate or refuse to support them.[1]

Lethal force may be used by the individual in self-defense with considerably more freedom than by the state. I am, perforce, the judge of whether, in the course of self-defense, I should shoot to kill the intruder. I do not have days or hours to decide, much less months and years. (Of course, I must eventually answer to others for my use of lethal force; unlike the fictional James Bond, no ordinary private citizen has a "license to kill.") Consequently, moral judgment and legal tribunals tend to err in the direction of generous excuse of those who use excessive or lethal force in self-defense.

The state's use of the death penalty as an exercise of a right to kill (in contrast, say, to a policeman's use of lethal force against an escaping felon), however, can be employed only well after the crimes it punishes and before any crimes its use might be intended to prevent. Consequently, the circumstances of the use of lethal force in the course of exercising the two rights are completely different. Typically, the individual must act without due deliberation and may shoot to wound and disable, rather than to kill; the state, however, acts *only* after due deliberation and its officials *always* shoot, electrocute, gas, hang, or inject with the intention of causing death. Wrongful exercise of the

right to kill as punishment is thus impossible to excuse in any ordinary sense. One does not properly *excuse* the deliberate and the intentional, but only the accidental, inadvertent, involuntary, and the like. Rather, one *justifies* the deliberate and the intentional actions of individuals and of governments acting on behalf of the state—or one justifies them if one can.

This exploration of the analogy between the individual's right of self-defense and the state's right to kill as punishment shows the analogy is far from perfect. The analogy is closest at the point where it suggests that when one person kills another, it must be as a last resort, because there is no feasible alternative. Constitutional lawyers will recognize this as the moral imperative parallel to the "least restrictive means to enforce a compelling state interest" test, a familiar principle of constitutional law but not one usually used to review legislatively authorized punishments. . . .

We see now more clearly why the state's right to use death as a punishment is a derivative and contingent matter, rather than anything fundmental. Locke and others who think that it is fundamental are simply wrong. Not even the state's right to punish, much less the right to punish *in this or that particular manner,* is fundamental. The state's right to punish is properly derived from its duty to protect just laws, which in turn is a means to protect the rights of individual persons. Punishment is justified in part by its necessity as a means to this end; insofar as it is not necessary to that end, it is unjustified and other responses to crime and the threat of crime are appropriate.[2] But the right to impose the punishment of death, rather than some lesser punishment, depends upon whether such a severe punishment is necessary to achieve public protection. No doubt the government is rightfully empowered to pursue whatever means are necessary to its proper ends, as long as doing so does not violate any important moral principle. The right to kill as punishment cannot be derived from this consideration alone, however. It depends also on the empirical claim that such an extreme penalty is a necessary means to a just end. This imposes a weighty burden of empirical proof upon any state that would choose a severe punishment over a less severe punishment in order to achieve a good end. The state—at least, a state that deserves our respect and allegiance—is not free to choose whatever means to its ends it may desire. Put less abstractly, a government is not justified in defending its preference for the death penalty by appealing to the state's right to punish violations of just laws. The government must also show that no lesser punishment suffices to reach this end. That a severe punishment *suffices* to reach this end is not enough; it must be *necessary* as well. And the government, as the duly authorized agent of the society, must provide some evidence of this necessity when challenged.

III

We turn now to examine the individual's "natural" right to life and the conflict, such as there is, between that right and the state's alleged right to use death as a punishment. In the previous chapter something of the history of the idea of individual rights as natural, fundamental, and inalienable was reviewed. Over the three centuries between Locke's day and ours, the right to life has yet to be articulated in a manner adequate for its reliable use in all the contexts in which it plays a role in our moral and political thinking. As I have noted elsewhere,[3] talk about the right to life shows that its advocates treat it as a portmanteau concept; protections concerning the termination and prevention of human life are found in it along with guarantees concerning the preservation and fulfillment of human ambitions and potentialities. The right to life has been applied to such different and disconnected questions as the morality of abortion, the duties of famine relief, and even the plight of third-world peoples seeking to develop the natural resources of their countries for their own (rather than the first-world's) benefit.[4] The scope of this right appears to be quite broad, or would be if one were to accept all that has been asserted by those who would invoke it. Unfortunately, such a broad use has not been accompanied by any increased understanding of the nature and status of the right.

No less problematic is the weight, or stringency, of the right. Opponents of abortion and the death penalty often speak and write in a manner that implies they accord *absolute* moral weight to the right to life. Yet it is difficult to see how this can be correct. If the right to (human) life is absolute, then it must always be morally wrong to kill another, whether by acting on one's own authority or under the orders of another, whether or not one is acting intentionally, whether the person killed is oneself or someone else, whether or not the victim-to-be has consented, and whether or not there is any less drastic alternative to protect the innocent. The result is that *all* of killing—suicide, euthanasia, murder, legal executions, killing in wartime, self-defense, and abortion (if that involves the killing of a human person)—violate this right and are therefore morally wrong. But this is not all. If the moral status of the distinction between *killing* and *letting die* is collapsed (as many contemporary philosophers have argued that it should be), deliberately failing to intervene to prevent death would also violate this absolute right. Surely, these extreme consequences serve only to discredit the very idea of the right to life as an absolute right in the first place.

A more defensible position would hold that the right to life expresses the presumption of wrongness in causing anyone's death, and thus this right would provide the weightiest of moral reasons—but not an absolute prohibition—against, above all, the deliberate killing of any person by anyone else capable of forming and acting on that intention. The right to life conceived in this more modest fashion not only underlies the law against criminal homicide but also provides the justification for the use of lethal force in self-defense and by the police. This account, of course, does not tell the whole story about the right to life; but whatever the rest of the story involves, it would be folly to undermine or override this fundamental part.

Even if the right to life is understood not to be absolute, that does not suffice to avoid the possibility of a conflict of rights with the state, once it is granted that the state has a right to use death as a punishment. I think it is important for both sides in the death penalty controversy to grant that, as soon as one holds the view that individuals have a natural (albeit not absolute and perhaps not inalienable)[5] right to life and that the state has the right to use death as a punishment, then there is a conflict whenever the state undertakes to exercise its right. The conflict can be avoided in practice only by the state not exercising that right. It can be avoided in theory either by denying that one (or both) of these rights is genuine, or by establishing a fixed ranking in the relative weight of these two rights (so that one always prevails over the other), or by some other tactic.

I will put aside without further examination the first alternative (the outright denial that one or both of these rights is genuine), since it undermines the whole point of the present investigation. The second alternative (a fixed ranking in the moral weight of otherwise conflicting rights) is interesting, but it may also be ignored here because there is no settled version of this doctrine at our disposal. The third alternative is the only one in need of scrutiny.

IV

The classic version of this alternative is the one sketched by Locke three hundred years ago, popularized a century later by Blackstone, and widely adopted since: the doctrine of the *forfeiture* of natural rights (discussed at the beginning of the previous chapter). According to this doctrine, a person forfeits one or more of his rights by any act in which he violates the rights of another. Some such maneuver seems necessary, for at least two reasons. The first is that the usual things done by the state to punish a person, such as killing or incarcerating him, or imposing a fine, would be obvious violations of that person's rights if done without his consent by any agent other than the state. Capital punishment would be murder and thus a deprivation of life, imprisonment a deprivation of liberty, a fine a deprivation of property—in each case of violation of the individual's rights. Since these acts of punishment by the state are usually not regarded in principle as a violation of anyone's rights, the rights of individual offenders must somehow be put aside; this is precisely what their forfeiture accomplishes. The second reason for subscribing to the doctrine of forfeiture is that, on any plausible theory, the offender has by virtue of his criminal act put himself in the wrong both with respect to the state (whose laws he violated) and to whichever person(s) he victimized (whose rights he violated). In saying this, I assume, of course, that moral reflection would sustain the judgment that the criminal act in question really is a violation of the rights of the innocent, as murder surely is. Once this is granted, it seems morally unacceptable that the offender's rights should nevertheless remain intact, since if they did that would bar any response to his deed that takes the form of restricting his liberty or property or person without his consent.

The doctrine of the forfeiture of natural rights as a devise to permit the state to kill as a punishment has its problems, however. First,

exactly what right does a person supposedly forfeit where some crime other than murder has been committed? Our society currently imprisons many different kinds of offenders, including over 95 percent of all convicted murderers and many offenders convicted of property crimes. Apparently, so far as current law is concerned, either the offender can forfeit a given right of his without having violated that particular right of some victim; or the government's choice among modes of punishment does not rest on the idea of the forfeiture by the offender of some *particular* right.

Locke, as it happens, seems to have preferred the first alternative. He argued that a person forfeits his life by virtue of any criminal act that "deserves death," but he supplied no criterion to enable us to distinguish between those criminal acts that deserve death and those that do not. Like others of his day, he indicated no reservations about the death penalty for crimes against the state or for crimes against property and his notion of criminal acts deserving death went far beyond what a criterion such as *lex talionis* ("a life for a life") would yield. The obvious way to improve on Locke's silence is to adapt this very criterion to provide that a person forfeits, not his very life itself, but his *right* to life, always and only by the crime of murder.

If we adopt Locke's position as modified in the manner suggested, then we have established a basis for asserting that the state is authorized—and in this sense, has the right—to put a convicted murderer to death. Even so, we can still ask whether the state *must* put him to death, and whether it *ought* to do so. How should we answer these questions? Since (as we have seen earlier) acting on one's rights is not the same as doing the right thing, and since having the right to do something is not the same as having a duty to do it, even if the state has the right to take a convicted offender's life, it is still an open question whether that is what it *must* or even *ought* to do. Suppose—as does happen—the surviving friends and family of the murdered victim very much want the convicted offender put to death; or suppose the rest of society does; or suppose the offender himself wants to be put to death for his crime. Are these good reasons for the state to do what it has a right to do? Or, in the absence of such demands for the death of a murderer, should mercy prevail and the murderer, despite his forfeited right to life, nonetheless be allowed to live?

Fortunately, our society has long abandoned such populist decision-making policies, and no good reasons counsel a return to them either in general or solely where the punishment of murder is concerned. Nevertheless, the criminal justice system does provide for choosing to execute only some among those who (by hypothesis) have forfeited their lives. The system allows this choice to be made openly and deliberately at exactly two points: when the trial court (judge or jury), in the absence of any mandatory death penalty statute, decides how to sentence someone convicted of a capital crime; and when the chief executive (governor, president, or whoever it is that exercises the clemency power) decides whether to commute a death sentence rather than sign the death warrant. On what grounds are these decisions made? Are they rational, predictable, morally acceptable, or are they arbitrary, whimsical, or—worse than that—governed by discernible prejudices? Since executive clemency in recent years has become so rare,[6] and no empirical research has been conducted on its exercise, we cannot answer these questions. Trial court decisions over the past decade, however, have resulted in some two hundred or so death sentences per year,[7] and large numbers of these decisions have been studied with scrupulous care. I shall say more below about what these studies show.

Yet the doctrince that the murderer forfeits his right to live surely suggests that there is no room for such decisions as these. The doctrine entails that these decisions are the result not of justice but of mercy, or of some other moral consideration that is allowed to outweigh the requirements of justice in particular cases. What the doctrine of forfeiture seems to require is nothing less than a policy of mandatory death penalties, with an execution guaranteed once the accused has been convicted of murder. The practice of mandatory capital punishment, however, is complex and, it has proved, historically, virtually impossible to achieve. Understood in the strictest manner—no choice by the prosecutor whether to indict for capital murder or some lesser degree of homicide, no choice by the trial court in sentencing once the offender is convicted of murder, no choice by the chief executive to commute the sentence from death to life—mandatory capital punishment has never existed in our history.[8] Few really want it today, if we can trust public opinion polls and the policies implied by those who

have defended the death penalty in recent years in the public forum.[9] The fact that such statutes would also certainly be unconstitutional . . . as the punishment for most kinds of murder is not without interest, though it hardly settles what morality requires.

I can conclude only that those who insist on the dictum that a murderer forfeits his right to life either do not mean what they seem to be saying, or that our society has never been able to muster the courage to do what justice requires where the punishment of murder and other grave crimes is concerned. The only death penalty system that our society knows is one in which convicted murderers (and other capital offenders) are executed only after others acting in their official capacities have made further decisions—and the outcome of these decisions is that very few are actually executed. There is, of course, a third possibility: The doctrine of forfeiture is simply too crude—too primitive and too muddled—to enable us to understand what justice and the recognition of our rights requires.

The standard response of those who defend the doctrine of forfeiture is that, since all those convicted of a capital crime deserve death (because by their own acts they forfeited the right to live), it cannot be unfair to execute only some rather than all. Whom would it be unfair to? Not those we choose to kill, since by hypothesis they deserve to die. Surely it is not unfair to those we don't kill; very few complain of being unfairly treated when spared the death penalty despite a conviction for murder. Left in this neat form, the rejoinder may look convincing. But what it omits, or attempts to conceal, is crucial: The fact that all the members of a class (viz., the class of persons convicted of a capital crime) have forfeited their rights, according to the argument, fails to explain *why only some* are executed, rather than all, and why *these some* and not some others are the ones who get what all deserve. Forfeiture, as we have seen, at most explains how the state gets the *right to execute* them all. Something else has to explain why the agents of the state in any given case do the right thing when they decide not to act on this right in the vast majority of the cases that come before them.[10]

The defender of the death penalty at this point must take one of two lines of reply. One reply concedes that the decision is not in fact based on justice, but insists that it is still based on considerations no less legitimate. (The analogy to selective law enforcement by overworked police forces is a favorite.) The other reply defends each of the decisions for death on grounds of justice—but not the justice of forfeited rights and desert. Neither reply is convincing. We can see this clearly, but only if we are willing to examine in detail exactly how those with the power of decision in particular cases actually make these decisions in our society. To tell this story in the detail needed to convince the skeptic would require a book twice the size of this one. Fortunately, a detailed account continues to unfold in the writings of other researchers. . . . Suffice it to say here that I believe my rejection of the argument made by the defender of the death penalty is amply supported by the available eveidence.

The attempt to nullify the relevance of an individual's right to life by claiming that a murderer forfeits this right is not, I conclude, successful. The idea of forfeiture simply does not fit either the right-to-life doctrine or our actual practice, historic or current.

V

With the doctrine of the forfeiture of rights behind us, we can now return to the most fundamental question. Assuming, then, that the state has the right to punish by death and that the individual's right to life raises no more than a strong presumption against such killing, on what ground if any should the state proceed to enact capital statutes in the first place? Earlier in this chapter I claimed that the state is right to enact such laws and then enforce them only if it has at its disposal no other alternative, no less severe or less final mode of punishment as the necessary means to reach the end or goal of public safety and respect for the equal rights of others. Although, as we have seen, the individual may very well not have, or reasonably not think he has, any less drastic method to protect himself short of killing, or trying to kill, the intending felon against whom he is defending himself or some innocent third party, the state is never reduced to such desperation.

Certainly a modern state such as ours, with its wealth of resources, has plenty of alternatives sufficient to protect just institutions and respond to the violation of its criminal laws without resorting to the use of death as a punishment. This is simply a statement of fact, even though its truth seems to be doubted in many quarters. What seems to put it in doubt is the fact that convicted murderers who are not executed sometimes live to murder again. I say "sometimes" because the records show that recidivist murders do occur about two times for every thousand murderers paroled or otherwise released.[11] Not a perfect record, to be sure, but certainly good enough to exempt release authorities from a criticism of gross incompetence.

Since prison authorities would not turn a convicted murderer loose inside prison, much less back on the streets, if they *knew* he would kill again, the only cure for the problem seems to be one of the following: (a) Execute all convicted murderers, not because they have forfeited their rights, but because an unknown few of them will otherwise kill again; or (b) release no convicted murderers, but keep each of them under lock and key in solitary confinement until their natural death; or (c) improve the information available to prison authorities regarding the postconviction behavior of every convicted murderer so that the few who are truly dangerous can be without exception segregated from the rest; or (d) content ourselves with current practice. Alternative (a) has never been and cannot now or in the future be put into practice. The same is true of alternative (b), as any study of the theory and practice of incarceration will confirm. Alternative (c) has much to be said for it, but it is not clear that it can be carried out; it may be no more than a utopian aspiration. This apart, it is really only a muchimproved version of current policy, alternative (d). Since this alternative is obviously feasible, it is clear that society does have a less severe and final mode of punishment available. Thus it would be wrong for the state to kill in exercise of its right to punish.

The only way around this conclusion is to argue that there is at least one "compelling state purpose" that only the death penalty can accomplish. What might such a purpose be? Perhaps the best candidate is the purpose of retribution. (It is little short of remarkable the way that retribution, over the past decade or so, has emerged from the darkness as the least defensible doctrine of penal theory into the light as the most defensible among penologists, philosophers, and members of the Supreme Court.[12]) I do not dispute that retribution is a valid purpose of punishment. But much turns on what one means by the term. For me, it is not a euphemism for "revenge"; it is simply another term for "deserved punishment" or for "justice in punishment." I will not even discuss whether the state is right in seeking to achieve retributive purposes; I readily grant that it is. Having granted this, the only way to avoid granting as well that it is right for the state to kill as a punishment is to show either that (a) retribution, contrary to the moral intuitions of many, does not require death for murder, or that (b) some other equally or perhaps more compelling state purpose is incompatible with retribution and should prevail over it. I think that both (a) and (b) can be defended.

Retribution, in so far as we think of it as a rational goal that the theory of punishment can defend, does not require the death penalty for murder. (This point is made more than once elsewhere in this book, and it suffices here to repeat the conclusions on the topic reached in the previous chapter.) What a responsible theory of punitive or retributive justice requires, insofar as reason and theory can defend it, is only this: (1) Punishments must impose a deprivation on offenders, just as crimes do on their victims; (2) only convicted offenders—those whose guilt is established as reliably as human institutions permit—are eligible for punishment; and (3) the severity of the punishment must be graded according to the gravity of the crime. From these principles it obviously follows that murder, the gravest (or one of the gravest) of crimes, must be punished with the utmost permissible severity; and that society should bend considerable effort to arrest, try, convict, and sentence murderers. These principles, however, tell us nothing about *which* modes of punishment should be used. In particular, they are silent on the upper bound of permissible severity.

In this connection, it is worth noting that death penalty advocates who are unwilling to compromise with their own professed retributive intuitions face an uncomfortable dilemma. If justice in punishment requires punishments that imitate the crime ("a life for a life"), then retributivists should openly favor decapitation, say, for murderers who dismember the body of the victim, and other equally savage modes of inflicting the death penalty where the murder itself was unusually savage. If they are not willing to go this far, then it must be because they tacitly recognize some upper bound to the necessary brutality even of retributive punishments. In fixing this upper bound, either they rely on some moral principle or they do not. If

they do not, then they obviously beg the question in their own favor—they simply want to punish murder (and other crimes?) with death, no matter what moral principles or a consistent theory of punishment requires. But admitting to this discredits their views from any further serious consideration. If they take the other alternative and rely on some principle limiting the degree of savagery and brutality permitted in lawful punishment, then they must defend their principle against competing principles that would draw the line of permissible severity elsewhere.

Are there any principles according to which the death penalty is too severe? My earlier discussion shows, I believe, that the right to life itself can be seen as the source of such principles. . . . One important and relevant principle is this: As the severity of punishments goes up (severity being measured not primarily by the infliction of physical pain but by the extent and quality of the deprivation imposed and the degree to which it is not reversible or compensable), so does the burden on society to be consistent and fair, rather than arbitrary or inequitable.

The Supreme Court tacitly acknowledged this principle more than a decade ago in the important case of *Furman v. Georgia* (1972). Evidence then and subsequently showed that the principle was most flagrantly violated where the death penalty was used in the punishment of rape. The *only* way to explain the relatively high frequency with which black males were sentenced to death for the rape of white females was the racial factor—the racial *prejudice* that permitted all-white juries to bring in death sentences as if a black man's life were less valuable than a white man's and a white woman's violated virtue more deserving of punitive vindication than a black woman's.[13] With the death penalty for rape now a thing of the past . . . attention properly focuses solely on the extent to which racist sentiments and institutional practices, both conscious and unconscious, as well as other arbitrary and irrelevant factors, play a role in determining how the death penalty for murder is actually imposed by the criminal justice system. Social scientists are currently in disagreement[14] over some aspects of this large topic, but as I read the cumulative results of two decades of empirical research into this complex matter, I see no way to deny the arbitrariness and discrimination in the system.

As I see it, defenders of the death penalty who would argue that the state has the right to use the death penalty and that the state ought to act on this right must show one of two things. They must demonstrate either that (a) there are no principles other than retributive ones governing the upper bound of the severity of punishment, and retributive principles require the death penalty, or that (b) although there are such non-retributive principles (for example, the one I advocated above concerning the requirement of fairness in the administration of very severe penalties), the evidence shows the death penalty is and will probably continue to be administered with the requisite degree of fairness. Retributivists would like to defend (a), but, as I have tried to show, they cannot do so with consistency; their own retributivism requires them to acknowledge the proper function of precisely such non-retributive principles. (We can safely ignore the question-begging appeal to "a life for a life" for reasons explained [earlier.]) The defense of (b) requires us to look carefully at all of the evidence and propose punitive policies in its light. Without all that empirical evidence before the reader, I cannot convincingly argue the point here. Experience living in our society nonetheless tells me that we cannot count on our sense of fairness to dominate the workings of the criminal justice system in the future, any more than it has in the past, in such a way that factors like socio-economic status, lack of firm roots in the community, gender, and especially race and color—which ought to be irrelevant to why some are punished more severely than others—have little or no effect on whether an accused killer is indicted, tried, convicted, sentenced to death, and executed. Defenders of the death penalty, whether in scholarly treatises or in letters to the newspaper, have yet to carry the burden of persuasion on this important point.

VI

I hazard the view that an awareness of the undeniably superior incapacitative effects of the death penalty, yoked to the illusion that retribution requires death for murder ("murderers forfeit their lives"), results in what passes for rational belief that society at present needs the death penalty. Add to this the further illusion that the more severe the threatened punishment the better a deterrent it is, and the nagging and annoying conviction that it costs the public treasury thousands of dollars each year to keep a convicted murderer in prison when that same money could be put to better social use, and you have the mind-set of the modern believer in capital punishment.

The state's alleged right to use death as a punishment, and all that this idea entails, is rarely considered very seriously or thoughtfully. Perhaps it would be a good thing if it were. If my argument is correct, then we have to conclude either that the state has no such right, or that it is right for the state to punish by death only under conditions that do not in fact prevail today in our society, that have not at any time in the past, and that almost certainly will not in the foreseeable future.

NOTES

1. Viewing the duty of the state and the justification of punishment this way goes, I believe, very naturally with a general theory of social justice such as that advanced by John Rawls, *A Theory of Justice* (1971).

2. I have discussed this point at greater length in another paper, a preliminary version of which was published as "Punishment in a Just Society: Could It Be Eliminated?" in Robert E. Cleary, ed., *The Role of Government in the United States: Practice and Theory* (1985), pp. 168–79.

3. See Bedau, "The Right to Life," *The Monist* 52 (1968): 550–72. For a more general discussion of this and related problems, see my essay "International Human Rights" in Tom Regan and Donald VanDeVeer, eds., *And Justice For All* (1982), pp. 287–308.

4. All these examples and more can be found in B. G. Ramcharan, ed., *The Right to Life in International Law* (1985).

5. Whether the right to life really is inalienable, as Locke and others have insisted, may be doubted. If it is inalienable, then no one could have the right to take his or her own life, no one could have the right to enlist others to that end, and no one could have the right to agree to provide such assistance.

6. According to the bulletin *Capital Punishment*, published annually by the Bureau of Justice Statistics, United States Department of Justice, only forty-three commutations of death sentences were granted in the United States between 1973 and 1985.

7. According to *Capital Punishment* (supra), during the years 1973–1983, state prisons received from the courts 2,266 persons under death sentence.

8. A thorough history of capital punishment in the United States, showing the details state by state, crime by crime, of efforts to impose and to repeal mandatory death penalties, has yet to be written. See, however, Philip English Mackey, "The Inutility of Mandatory Capital Punishment: An Historical Note," reprinted in Bedau and Pierce, eds., *Capital Punishment in the United States* (1976), pp.49–53; and the sketch of the nation's experience with mandatory death penalties in the plurality opinion for the Supreme Court, by Justice Stewart, in Woodson v. North Carolina (1976).

9. In 1983, a Harris Survey reported that "no more than 27 percent of the people nationwide feel that all who are found guilty [of the crime of first-degree murder] should be put to death." When the crime is killing a policeman or prison guard, still only 31 percent favor a mandatory death penalty. Louis Harris, "Sizable Majorities Against Mandatory Death Penalty," *Harris Survey,* 10 February 1983, p. 1. Earlier data are reported in Bedau, ed., *The Death Penalty in America,* 3d ed. (1982), p. 89. Supporters of the death penalty looking for guidance on this point from serious scholarly treatises written in its defense—Ernest van den Haag's *Punishing Criminals* (1975), Walter Berns's *For Capital Punishment* (1979), and Raoul Berger's *Death Penalties* (1982)—will find neither a defense of mandatory death penalties nor an explanation of why nonmandatory death penalties are to be preferred.

10. I am indebted to Stephen Nathanson's excellent discussion of this point in his essay, "Does It Matter if the Death Penalty is Arbitrarily Administered?" *Philosophy & Public Affairs* 14 (1985): 149–64.

11. Based on national data for the years 971–75, concerning parole outcome during the first (but not any subsequent) year after release from conviction of willful homicide;

see Bedau, ed., *The Death Penalty in America,* 3d ed. (1982), pp. 173–80.

12. I have discussed the "new" retributivism more fully in "Retribution and the Theory of Punishment," *Journal of Philosophy* 75 (1978): 601–20. For different views, see Roger Wertheimer, "Understanding Retribution," *Criminal Justice Ethics* 2 (Summer/Fall 1983): 19–38; and Jeffrie G. Murphy, "Retributivism, Moral Education, and the Liberal State," *Criminal Justice Ethics* 4 (Winter/Spring 1985): 3–11. An interesting popular discussion may be found in Susan Jacoby, *Wild Justice: The Evolution of Revenge* (1983).

13. The now-classic research on this point is by Marvin E. Wolfgang and Marc Riedel, "Race, Judicial Discretion, and the Death Penalty," *The Annals* 407 (May 1973): 119–33.

14. On the racial aspects of the death penalty, the most recent data are discussed in the articles by Samuel R. Gross, by Arnold Barnett, and by David C. Baldus, George Woodworth, and Charles A. Pulaski, Jr., in *U.C. Davis Law Review* 18 (1985). On the arbitrariness of the decisions by trial courts to impose the death sentence, see Michael L. Radelet's article in the same volume; also Radelet and Glenn L. Pierce, "Race and Prosecutorial Discretion in Homicide Cases," *Law & Society Review* 19 (1985): 587–621.